Aim High!
Concentrate

R v Kennedy

Trustee → Beneficiary

Stack v Dowden

Donoghue ...evenson

Actus reus + Mens... + No defence

Concentrate Revision & Study Guides
Concentrate Questions & Answers
Both series available in your campus bookstore
or buy online at **www.oup.com/lawrevision**

Family Law

EDITED BY

RUTH LAMONT

University of Manchester

OXFORD

UNIVERSITY PRESS

OXFORD
UNIVERSITY PRESS

Great Clarendon Street, Oxford, OX2 6DP,
United Kingdom

Oxford University Press is a department of the University of Oxford.
It furthers the University's objective of excellence in research, scholarship,
and education by publishing worldwide. Oxford is a registered trade mark of
Oxford University Press in the UK and in certain other countries

Published in the United States of America by Oxford University Press
198 Madison Avenue, New York, NY 10016, United States of America

British Library Cataloguing in Publication Data
Data available

Library of Congress Control Number: 2017954632

ISBN 978–0–19–874965–3

Printed in Great Britain by
Bell & Bain Ltd., Glasgow

This book is for my parents, for all their assistance and support

Preface

The law regulating the family is a fast changing field of study and practice, covering a broad range of issues and concerns arising from personal relationships. The aim of this text in explaining and exploring the field of family law in England and Wales is to guide the reader through the legal principles, but also through the social context that gives rise to family problems where law is part of the solution. The social and personal nature of family life and relationships means that there is often more than one solution to the problem presented, and more than one perspective on the policies or values associated with family life underpinning the law. One of the key purposes of this book is to help the reader understand these debates and develop their own reasoned opinion on the issues raised in each chapter's 'Debates'. These are designed to address the wider perspectives on the law, beyond the legal rules themselves. Drawing on each individual contributors' expertise and understanding of their field, these 'Debates' will aid the reader's critical insight into family law and the factors affecting decision-making.

Each chapter of this book has been written by an academic contributor who is a specialist in the field of law they are writing about. Each chapter has a similar approach but adopts an individualistic style, and gains from the insights and specialism of the author. This has encouraged an engaging and thorough explanation of the law and the surrounding debates that are a focus of this text. It has been a fascinating process and, as the editor, I am very grateful to each contributor for their enthusiasm and involvement with the project, and for their positive engagement with the approach of the book.

I am indebted to each of the contributors for their knowledge and expertise. Andy Hayward researches the historical and modern regulation of adult relationships, including marriage and civil partnerships and contributes a chapter on this topic. Edwina Higgins and Kathryn Newton have extensive experience in family law and contribute a fascinating chapter on the law of divorce. Polly Morgan has practised and founded a family law solicitors firm, and brings this experience to her explanation of the division of assets on divorce. Warren Barr is a trusts law expert who was enthusiastic about the challenge of reflecting on the family law perspective on trusts of the family home, and to whom I am particularly grateful for encouraging me to pursue this project. Lara Walker is an expert on international maintenance obligations and contributes a chapter on domestic family rules on child maintenance in England and Wales. Anna Carline and Roxanna Dehaghani draw on their extensive expertise researching the incidence of family violence to explain and critique the law relating to domestic violence and forced marriage. Kirsty Horsey is an expert in the law relating to human reproduction and genetic technologies and uses this knowledge in her chapter on the attribution of parenthood and parental responsibility. Annika Newnham draws on her research into the decision-making in the family courts and disputes between parents of children in her chapter on private child law disputes. Dianne Scullion has researched in the field of protection of vulnerable children and mediation, and contributes a chapter on the medical treatment of children. Penelope Russell is a former solicitor and member of Sheffield City Council's Safeguarding Children Executive Board, and contributes her insights on public law child protection. Julie Doughty explains the law of adoption, drawing on her current work as a member of an interdisciplinary team researching the impact of adoption on a cohort of children in Wales. Helen Stalford is a world leading expert on children's rights and with Seamus Byrne, a former practitioner, contributes a chapter on the changes made by, and potential impact of, children's rights in family law disputes. Patrick Nicholls is a practising solicitor and founder of the family law firm Nicholls Solicitors, and draws on his current knowledge of family law practice to a chapter on reforms and practice in family law. It has been a pleasure to work on this project with my colleagues and to read their contributions and insights into family law in England and Wales.

The idea behind this textbook originated with Tom Young at OUP. The book would not have been conceived or completed without his skills and enthusiasm and I am very grateful for his commitment to the project throughout the process. The drafting process has been maintained by the excellent editorial assistance of Hetty Marx who has been a fantastic support in coordinating and feeding back on individual contributions, and in managing the development of the text. The book would not have been delivered without either the assistance of Hetty or Tom and I would like to express my thanks to them both.

From a personal perspective, I would like to take this opportunity to express my thanks to my best friend Di, and my sister, Alison, for their kindness in encouraging me in developing this book. Thank you to John and Amelia for inspiring the idea behind the front cover.

Dr Ruth Lamont,
December 2017

Guide to the book

Family Law has been carefully structured to be the best possible source of support for you as you embark on your study of the subject. The book includes a range of different features that are designed to focus in on the issues, context and information that you really need to know.

LEARNING OBJECTIVES

After reading this chapter you will be able to:

- Identify the common law rules and presumptions that determine legal
- Understand how legal parenthood is awarded following the use of diffe assisted conception, and the differing rules that apply to each of these;
- Critically analyse different concepts and understandings of parenthood inform and underpin legal rules;
- Appreciate who may obtain parental responsibility for a child, and its i

Learning objectives

At the start of each chapter these frame your study of each key topic that will be covered on your course. If you reach the end of a chapter and don't feel that you have achieved all of these objectives, then revisit the relevant section to reinforce your knowledge.

DEBATE 1: IS THE COURT THE BEST PLACE FOR PRIVA DISPUTES?

In both news and fiction, we see stories about bitter parents who use th their own battles or punish each other, while their lawyers use aggressive everything out and make more money. It is not surprising that many peop policy-makers, think this is the reality of most cases.[31] The campaign grou for example, claim that legal professionals deliberately stoke conflict to m and increase their income.[32] Their factsheet ends with an unattributed quo a father: 'If divorce is like a burning house then going into the family cour plane-load of napalm onto the situation.'[33] There are a small number of lon

Debates

These are the central feature of this book. Family law can have immense influence over our lives, and consequently many aspects of it are highly contentious. At the start of each chapter you will find a list of the key debates relevant to the topic you are about to study. They are there in order to place them front and centre in your mind, and you should hold them there as you read through the chapter. At the relevant point in the text, a Debate box will pick up the issue and explore all sides of the argument—thus equipping you to identify the different perspectives on the law and reach your own informed conclusions. The key points of each debate are recapped at the end of the chapter.

CONTEXT 2: DIVORCE NUMBERS AND DIVORCE RATES

There are a number of different ways of measuring divorces. We can simp ber of divorces, and, provided the population is (fairly) stable, this is a trends over a number of years. However, it does not help us to compare ju it does not account for population differences (e.g. the number of divor Wales being double that of another country is no cause for surprise or co tion is also double).

The crude divorce rate is the number of divorces per 1000 people compare levels of divorce across differing populations. The UK's was

Context

Family law is continually developing over time in response to changes to the makeup of society, and to our values and opinions. These boxes explore and explain such changes—making use of government statistics, academic research, and case studies.

Key Case 7: *Re J (Children) (Care Proceedings: Threshold* ⟨...⟩
UKSC 9

This case concerned three children living with a woman who had been in ⟨...⟩
perpetrators. The woman's first child had died seven years previously of n⟨...⟩
ries. At that time, the woman was living with a former partner and it was no⟨...⟩
evidence who had caused the fatal injuries to her first child. Subsequently t⟨...⟩
to live with a new partner and have a child with him. He had two children ⟨...⟩
tionship who also lived with them.

The issue for the Supreme Court was whether the woman's inclusion i⟨...⟩
perpetrators in earlier proceedings involving a different child and a⟨...⟩

Key cases

Much of family law is shaped by judicial precedent, so a thorough knowledge of the key cases is essential. These boxes highlight the most crucial cases: setting out the facts giving rise to the litigation; explaining the decision that the court reached; and discussing the significance of the precedent set.

Key Legislation 5: Article 3 Hague Abduction Convention

A *removal* or *retention* of a child is viewed to be wrongful where it is in ⟨...⟩
custody attributed to a person, an institution or any other body, either⟨...⟩
under the law of the State in which *the child was habitually resident* im⟨...⟩
the removal or retention and at the time of the removal or retention t⟨...⟩
actually exercised ...

The child must have been wrongfully *removed* or *retained* from their ha⟨...⟩
moval and retention are alternative concepts: a child is either removed or ⟨...⟩
occurs where the child is moved across an international border. A retenti⟨...⟩

Key legislation

Extracts from the most important statutes are provided in boxes, in order to highlight the central statutory provisions for you to read these key sources of family law for yourself.

SUMMARY

The changing nature of special guardianship as a more common perm⟨...⟩
been recognised by new regulations and guidance in England in 2016, in⟨...⟩
the benefits of the adoption support fund to guardians.[116]

SUMMARY

1. How should legal obligations to provide continued support to the child b⟨...⟩
   with the privacy and autonomy of family life?

Summaries

Each chapter concludes with a short summary that draws together the central points from the chapter, set in the context of the key debates. Use the summaries, together with the learning objectives, to check that you have fully understood what you have read.

Further Reading

BETTINSON, V. 'Criminalising Coercive Control in Domestic Violence ⟨...⟩
follow the path of England and Wales?' (2016) 3 *Criminal Law Review*⟨...⟩
  • Provides a critical analysis of the development of the offence⟨...⟩
    England and Wales and considers the extent to which a sim⟨...⟩
    introduced in Scotland.
BURTON, M. 'Emergency Barring Orders in Domestic Violence Cases: ⟨...⟩
Wales Learn From Other European Countries?' (2015) 27 *Child and F*⟨...⟩
  • Provides a critical evaluation of the introduction of the dome⟨...⟩

Further reading

Select from these lists the source of further information that is most relevant to you, and use them to deepen and grow your expertise as a family lawyer.

Online resources

Family Law is accompanied by a range of free online resources designed to support you throughout your family law module.

www.oup.com/uk/lamont/

Research each topic…

A resource bank of links to crucial sources of further information is the ideal starting point when you need to research a particular aspect of family law. The bank contains links to a range of resources including:

- Relevant government reports
- Journal articles and other research literature
- Video clips
- The key statutes and case reports that are the main sources of family law

Be inspired…

Short video pieces from the expert contributors to this book expand on key issues raised in the relevant chapters. Focusing either on a crucial debate or case, these pieces are designed to pique your curiosity and help you get to grips with the contentious nature of family law.

Test your knowledge…

Multiple-choice questions, linked to the content of the book, help you to check your understanding of each topic and identify where you need to focus your revision.

Acknowledgements

The editor and publisher would like to sincerely thank the expert teachers of family law who gave their time to review draft chapters throughout the writing process. Your help was invaluable.

Anjana Bahl, London Metropolitan University
Philip Bremner, University of Sussex
Eugenia Caracciolo di Torella, University of Leicester
Brigitte Clark, Oxford Brookes University
Aoife Daly, University of Liverpool
Ian Doerfler, Leeds Beckett University
Sara Fovargue, Lancaster University
Robert Jago, Royal Holloway, University of London
Kelvin Johnstone, Keele University
Laura Milner, University of Hull

Outline contents

Detailed contents

Notes on contributors

Editor

Ruth Lamont is a Senior Lecturer in Family and Child Law at the School of Law, University of Manchester. She teaches Family Law, and her research has focused on the regulation of children and their relationships across international borders in a modern and a historical context.

Contributors

Warren Barr, PFHEA is Head of Department and Professor of Law at Liverpool Law School, University of Liverpool. He is a member of the Charity Law and Policy Unit, School of Law & Social Justice, University of Liverpool. His research interests include charity law, social housing, and property law, on which he has published extensively. He is the author and co-author of textbooks on the areas of Equity & Trusts law (with Robert Pearce) and Land law (forthcoming).

Seamus Byrne is a Graduate Teaching Assistant and PhD Candidate at the School of Law and Social Justice, University of Liverpool. His research interests lie in children's socio-economic rights and specifically their 'progressive realization'. He uses participatory methodological approaches in furthering his research interests.

Anna Carline is an Associate Professor in Law at the University of Leicester. Dr Carline currently teaches family law, criminal law, and law and gender. She has conducted extensive research into the legal system's response to violence against women.

Roxanna Dehaghani is a Lecturer in Law at Cardiff School of Law and Politics. She has previously taught Family Law and her research focuses on vulnerability in police custody. She is interested in the law's response to domestic violence.

Julie Doughty is a Lecturer in Family Law and Media Law at Cardiff University School of Law and Politics. She has also worked as a solicitor, for local authorities and for Cafcass. She is a member of the Wales Adoption Study research team.

Andy Hayward is an Assistant Professor at Durham Law School. Alongside teaching family law, he researches the legal regulation of formalised and non-formalised adult relationships and, in particular, the property consequences generated by their breakdown.

Edwina Higgins is a Senior Learning and Teaching Fellow at Manchester Law School. She teaches Family Law and English Legal Systems. Her research interests include private child law and divorce, as well as learning and teaching and the development of academic legal skills.

Kirsty Horsey is a Reader in Law at the University of Kent, teaching contract and tort law. Her research interests lie in the overlap of medical, family and tort law. She is editor of a number of edited collections on the regulation of assisted reproduction including, most recently, *Revisiting the Regulation of Human Fertilisation and Embryology* (Routledge, 2015) and is a regular contributor to *BioNews* (bionews.org). She is co- author (with Erika Rackley) of *Tort Law* (5th edn, OUP, 2017) and *Kidner's Casebook on Torts* (14th edn, OUP, 2017).

Polly Morgan lectures in family law at the University of East Anglia. A qualified solicitor, she practised as a partner at a specialist family law firm that she co-founded, spending most of her time on financial remedies. She wishes to thank her students, who read the draft chapter.

Annika Newnham is a Lecturer at the University of Reading. She teaches Family Law as well as Property Law. Her research has focused on private child law, looking at the way disputes are resolved in our English and Welsh courts, and comparing shared parenting in Sweden and in this jurisdiction.

Kathryn Newton is a Principal Lecturer in Law and Director of the Legal Practice Course at Manchester Law School. She teaches Family Law and used to practise as a Family solicitor. Her research interests include private child law and divorce.

George Patrick Nicholls has been a practicing solicitor for 32 years and a part-time teacher at the University of Manchester for the last 20 years. He has successfully represented a diverse range of clients in many courts and tribunals including in the Court of Appeal and Privy Council. He is grateful to his father (a former Chairman of the Stockport Magistrates Family Court Bench) and his Co-Director in Nicholls Solicitors, Sarah Louise Amatiello (President of the Trafford Law Society and also an Alumini of the 1824 University of Manchester) for proof reading his chapter.

Penelope Russell is a Lecturer in Law at the University of Sheffield. After working as a Family Law solicitor in leading law firms for nine years, Penelope joined the School of Law at the University of Sheffield in 2003. As well as convening and teaching family law, Penelope carries out historical and empirical research into family law and practice. Linked with her expertise and interest in family law, Penelope sits on the Safeguarding Children's Executive Board at Sheffield City Council.

Dianne Scullion is a Senior Lecturer in Law at Lancashire Law School, University of Central Lancashire. She teaches Tort Law and Child Law and her research has focused on child trafficking, mediation, and children's rights.

Helen Stalford is Professor of Law at the University of Liverpool and founding director of the European Children's Rights Unit. Her research focuses on children's rights in the context of European Law, Migration and the Legal Process.

Lara Walker is a Senior Lecturer in Law at the School of Law, Politics and Sociology, University of Sussex. She teaches Family Law and International Family Law. Her research has focussed on the cross-border regulation of family law in areas such as child abduction and child support.

Table of cases

Table of legislation

International treaties and conventions

European legislation

1

Family Life and the Law

Ruth Lamont

LEARNING OBJECTIVES

After reading this chapter you will be able to:

- Identify the role of family law in regulating family life;
- Discuss different conceptions of the family and the way in which the law interacts with the family to regulate aspects of family life;
- Identify the role and importance of the use of discretion in family law to accommodate different family practices.

DEBATES

After reading this chapter you should be equipped to discuss your opinion on the following central debates:

1. Who are our 'family' and how should the law identify family relationships?
2. What role should the law play in regulating our family life?
3. How should the law respond to social changes in family life?

1. Introduction

This textbook examines the field of family law, considering the formation and dissolution of adult relationships, and the regulation of relationships with children. Each chapter is written by a different author, who is an expert in their field of law, but with common approaches adopted throughout. The book examines different types of family relationship regulated by English law, and the impact of the rights and obligations arising from those relationships. The aim is to provide a thorough and detailed insight from the research into each field covered by the book.

In this introductory chapter, the nature of family life and the role of the law in family relationships will be explored to identify the particular challenges facing family lawyers. In particular, it will consider how the law interacts with family life, how family relationships are identified in law, and what role the law plays in regulating family behaviour. The nature of the discipline of family law is considered, and the approach taken in the later chapters of this book is discussed. The incidence and nature of these family relationships is closely informed by our social practice of family life. This brings issues to bear in family law that are not present in other areas of law, and deserve reflection before the specific forms of relationships, and the rights and obligations arising from them, are examined in more detail.

2. The discipline of family law

Most people will be able to point to the experience of being part of a family in some form during their lifetime. The family is often regarded as the basic unit of society, to be enjoyed, promoted, and protected. Family life can bring great joy at the centre of our lives, a focus of love, comfort, and affection. Family ties can form an important source of identity and belonging developed through mutual support and understanding. The ties of love and affection generated by family are not replicated in any other social context and can be the defining experience of our lives. Yet, whilst 'family life' may be promoted as a supportive positive source of care and love,[1] despite our aspirations, personal relationships and family ties are, in reality, normally much more complex. Family often generates happiness, but can also be a place of pain and suffering. Inherent to family life is the emotion of being attached to, and affected by, other family members. Whilst those emotions can be a source of joy, they are more commonly mixed positive and negative feelings, and when relationships break down may become damaging and dangerous in expression. Whilst the practice of family life is a common human experience, it is at the same time a highly personal and subjective experience.

Whether these experiences are positive or negative, how we practise and carry out family life, who we count as our 'family', is informed by our social, cultural, and religious understanding of family life. Within that social and cultural context, how families choose to organise themselves and practice family life will vary greatly, and will also change over time. Our own individual experience of family relationships will suggest the broad variety of family arrangements and day-to-day routines. The ties labelled 'family relationships' can be created in different ways, but may bring strong emotional attachments and responses, or none at all.

Given this diversity and personalised experience of 'family', the role of the law in these processes is complex. There are two central issues for family lawyers. First, the identification of a relationship as being one of 'family' for the purposes of the law is an important label, and may give rise to specific rights and obligations, even if the particular relationship bears no significance for the individual. By contrast, where the law fails to recognise a relationship as being one of 'family' the significance of the relationship for individuals committed to it may be undermined in wider society. Secondly, identifying the nature of the rights and obligations arising from a family relationship is central to determining the significance of the relationship. Once the law accepts a relationship as one of 'family', regulating the rights and obligations arising from this acceptance can be complicated. Individuals will practise family life in their own way, whilst the law seeks to operate on a general basis with limited scope for the personal and subjective experience. The emotional aspect of the relationship can affect the response individuals have to the law; it can be difficult to act rationally when strong emotions are engaged, yet the law often demands rational reasoned responses. These aspects of family life pose particular challenges for family lawyers in responding to the issues raised in regulating family life.

---

[1] Eekelaar, J. 'Family Law and Love' (2016) 28 *Child and Family Law Quarterly* 289.

2.1 Nature of family law

2.1.1 Regulating family life

The family plays an important role in society and social expectations surround the conduct and understandings of what is meant by 'family' life, as opposed to other aspects of our lives.[2] Whilst these expectations are not required or expected as such by law, they are an important part of family life. These expectations influence all aspects of family life, from practical issues such as parenting practices, to small social traditions. For example, when a marriage is celebrated, there may be lots of traditions and expectations surrounding the conduct of the wedding, from the idea that the bride should wear 'something old, something new, something borrowed and something blue' for luck, to the speech by the groom's best man. These expectations will be influenced by family culture and social and religious practices.

Social expectation regarding the conduct of family life affects our own behaviour in forming relationships and maintaining them. These social norms and expectations can be a powerful influence on our choices and may effectively regulate our family life depending on the social acceptability of our behaviour, and our response to those expectations. Expectations of family life evolve over time and in any particular society can be negotiated by individuals, accepted and rejected as they choose. The social consequences of the rejection of particular expectations regarding family life may also change over time and the scope for acceptance of difference in family practices varies.[3] In addition, whilst expectations of family life may change in society generally, individual opinions on the social acceptability of relationships and traditions may remain traditional, or be more radical.

Not all aspects of family life can, or should, be made subject to legal regulation. For example, whilst the traditions for the celebration of a wedding are a matter of social practice, to contract a valid marriage the conduct and form of the marriage ceremony are regulated by the Marriage Act 1949. If these legal formalities are not complied with, irrespective of the other aspects of the celebration, there will not be a valid marriage.[4] For example, there is no legal obligation on the parties to exchange rings as part of the ceremony, although this is a normal social aspect of the celebration of a marriage. By contrast, the requirement of two witnesses to the ceremony is obligated by Marriage Act 1949.[5]

However, social rules and expectations may be strongly influenced by the law, and may in turn influence the development of the law as social practices change. This interaction is in evidence in the law relating to same-sex relationships. Sexual acts in private between homosexuals could result in criminal prosecution until s. 1 of the Sexual Offences Act 1967 decriminalised the offence for persons over 21 years of age. After that date, whilst homosexual acts were not illegal, they were often regarded as socially unacceptable and there were few family and social rights for homosexual couples.[6] By the early twenty-first century there was a shift in social attitudes in the UK, encouraging legal change, with the development of the registered partnership status, allowing homosexual couples to contract a legal relationship under the Civil Partnership Act 2004. Subsequently, the adoption of the Marriage (Same-Sex) Couples Act 2013 opened the status of marriage up to homosexual couples (see Chapter 2) indicating the broad social acceptance of homosexual relationships (see further 1.2).

The law makes a powerful statement of social acceptability of family forms and practices. Yet, individuals are still influenced by social opinions and this acts as a form of

---

[2] Jamieson, J. *Intimacy: Personal Relationships in Modern Societies* (1998, Polity Press).

[3] Cohen, D. *Family Secrets: Living With Shame From the Victorians to the Present Day* (OUP, 2013).

[4] Matrimonial Causes Act 1973, s. 11(a)(iii).

[5] Registration of the marriage must be signed by the person celebrating the marriage, the parties to the marriage, and two witnesses, see s. 55(2) of the Marriage Act 1949.

[6] Hale, B. 'Homosexual Rights' (2004) 16 *Child and Family Law Quarterly* 125.

regulation of social behaviour beyond the law.[7] The extent to which the law can engage with the complexities of social behaviours raises important questions of whether abstract legal rules can respond effectively to family life. Smart and Neale have argued that the family law and the Family Court should not work towards abstract legal principles, but instead work from the complexities of real family relationships to reach decisions that respond to the circumstances of the individual.[8] Family lawyers have to be aware of this complex interrelationship between the law, the social norms of family behaviour, and the perception of what is acceptable in the conduct family life. Within the social expectations and norms, the law has to accommodate a broad range of acceptable family practices and account for the circumstances and context of different families.

2.1.2 Discretionary decision-making

The individualised and contextual process of creating our own personal family relationships and carrying them out means that the question of who is a family member and what rights and interests they obtain through that relationship may be difficult to capture in a legal framework. What will work for one family may be inappropriate for another. To manage this inherent difference in the performance of family life, the law relating to the family is frequently characterised by the use of discretion. Within a legal framework identifying factors relevant to reaching a decision, a range of possible outcomes is available depending on the particular factual circumstances of the parties.

The exercise of discretion is central to important aspects of family law.

 Key legislation 1: Children Act 1989, s. 1, welfare principle

In relation to decisions affecting children s. 1(1) of the Children Act 1989 states that:

> When the court determines any question with respect to the upbringing of a child or the administration of a child's property or the application of any income arising from it, the child's welfare should be the paramount consideration.

This is a general statement that the child's welfare should be the paramount consideration for the court taking a decision. A decision that secures the welfare of one child in their personal circumstances, will not secure the welfare of another. To help the court determine what is in the individual child's welfare s. 1(3) of the Children Act 1989 lists a series of factors that should be taken into account to enable the court to determine the child's welfare. This includes the wishes and feelings of the child; the child's physical, emotional, and educational needs; the likely effect of any change of circumstances; the child's characteristics; any harm the child has suffered or may be at risk of suffering; and the capacity of the persons caring for the child. These factors will be assessed individually for each child to help determine what is in their welfare. The circumstances of the child are central to the legal assessment and this fact-based approach encourages the law to be responsive to context, but promotes individualised decision-making.

Discretion is also important for assessing the division of assets between former spouses following divorce. Whilst s. 25 of the Matrimonial Causes Act 1973 contains a list of factors relevant to the division of assets such as their needs and income, the point of considering those factors is to account for personal circumstances and relative financial resources of the spouses which will be key to establishing the financial independence of each party

---

[7] Barrett, M. and McIntosh, M. *The Anti-Social Family*. (Verso, 1982).
[8] Smart, C. and Neale, B. *Family Fragments* (Polity Press, 1999) 190.

from the other after the divorce. The statute however gives no guidance on the overall aim to be achieved in dividing the assets and what will be a 'fair' settlement (see Chapter 4). In *McFarlane v McFarlane*; *Miller v Miller*[9] the House of Lords gave guidance on the approach to be taken for the fair division of assets, based on meeting the needs of the parties, compensation, and equal division of the assets. However, within this framework there remains a broad range of potential decisions that may be deemed 'fair'.

Whilst granting discretion permits flexibility and enables the law and the presiding judge to respond to the family circumstances, it can give rise to great uncertainty over decision-making. This can cause practical problems. Uncertainty makes it difficult for lawyers to advise clients of their risk and potential outcomes, encouraging litigation between the parties because there is scope for argument. This can make family law more expensive and inconsistent. Drawing a balance between responsive discretionary decision-making and certainty in the law is a tension running throughout family law decision-making. In some areas of law, such as parental payments for child maintenance, this perceived inconsistency and uncertainty has provoked reform to remove any discretion from decision-making (see Chapter 6).[10]

2.1.3 Family decision-making and personal autonomy

Rather than relying on the discretion of the courts to take decisions on behalf of families, it has been suggested that the ability of the parties to organise their own personal family arrangements is a way to give the parties certainty that responds to their own circumstances. Recently, the emphasis has been on giving the parties to a relationship the autonomy to negotiate and determine between them their own family arrangements. The emphasis on personal autonomy is based on the idea that individuals negotiate and are free to reach their own agreement, delivering certainty to the parties in the context of their own personal circumstances.

Herring states that autonomy is resonant of individual choice, liberty, and self-sufficiency and holds a 'sacred status' in the modern law.[11] Adult relationships are regarded as equal partnerships where each partner can exercise their autonomy.[12] Respecting such autonomy is an expression of formal equality in that each party has identical rights and powers over their own decisions affecting the relationship. There have been increasing shifts to encourage parties to exercise their autonomy and to negotiate arrangements for their family, for example relating to finances and children after divorce, away from the court. Changes to legal aid remove the financial support from parties wishing to litigate a settlement in private family law matters, such as divorce (see Chapter 3) encouraging them to agree between themselves on their arrangements. The system of child maintenance has been changed to promote private ordering of financial maintenance arrangements (see Chapter 6). The parties to a family dispute may themselves regard this as desirable because they can determine their own arrangements, rather than having someone else make decisions on their behalf.

This approach can be desirable in allowing family members control over their circumstances, but it is premised on a concept of the family consisting of autonomous individuals making rational decisions.[13] The emotional impact of the breakdown of a marriage, for example, may affect the response of one former spouse to the other and

---

[9] [2006] UKHL 24.   [10] Child Support Act 1991.

[11] Herring, J. 'Relational Autonomy and Family Law' in J. Wallbank, S. Choudhry, and J. Herring (eds), *Rights, Gender and Family Law* (Routledge, 2010) 267–8, 267.

[12] Barlow, A. 'Solidarity, Autonomy and Equality: Mixed Messages for the Family?' (2015) 27 *Child and Family Law Quarterly* 223, 223.

[13] Diduck, A. 'Autonomy and Family Justice' (2016) 28 *Child and Family Law Quarterly* 133, 133.

their abilities to negotiate 'rationally'. The influence of emotion on family relationships may affect any negotiation. For negotiation to be effective, the parties must also have an understanding of what outcomes are possible under the relevant legal principles so that they understand what they could potentially be entitled to under the existing legal provisions, even if they choose to vary it themselves. It is also important to remember the protective function of the law. Where individuals are in a weaker bargaining position, for example because they do not have the money to pay for legal advice, or there has been violence or abuse in a relationship, allowing unlimited autonomy potentially gives scope for exploitation.[14] The risk is that individuals do not reach an agreement securing their entitlement or equivalent under the relevant legal principles, undermining the law and affecting the circumstances of the family. For these reasons, allowing parties to exercise their autonomy cannot be unchecked by the law and external processes for protection of the individuals, and there is normally a process of oversight by the court to ensure that the potential for exploitation is to some extent limited.

2.2 Skills for family law

The emphasis on discretion and fact sensitive decision-making in family law means that family lawyers have to be sensitive to context and have a strong grasp of the scope of the legal and policy framework underpinning a decision.

The fact sensitive nature of decision-making in family law means that there will often be several cases considering the interpretation and application of one particular legislative provision. Seemingly minor differences in the particular facts at the basis of a dispute can give rise to questions over how the discretion of the court should be exercised, and whether the application of the law should be entirely consistent with previous decisions in the same context. The emphasis on the factual context and the influence this has on the courts' decision-making in family law means that there can be a large number of case law decisions over the interpretation of the same legislative provision on a similar point. For example, in the context of the welfare principle under s. 1(1) of the Children Act 1989, decisions over whether a child should be permitted to leave the country with one parent to relocate abroad are normally argued on the basis of the principles outlined in a Court of Appeal decision, *Payne v Payne*.[15] The decision in this case outlines the approach courts should take to assessing an application to relocate abroad, which affects the child's relationship and contact with a parent remaining behind in England, and how to approach determining whether relocation will secure the child's welfare. However, there are many subsequent cases[16] on relocation of children that present different arguments on the facts to test when giving permission to relocate secures the child's welfare (see Chapter 9). In some fields, such as the property rights of cohabitants when the relationship breaks down, the law has been developed entirely through the case law decided by the courts (see Chapter 5).[17]

The importance of fact-based, contextual decision-making in family law means that there can be a large volume of case law to understand and analyse in one particular field. Managing and analysing a number of case law authorities from different courts over time is key to several aspects of family law. Making sense of a line of cases, being able to effectively distinguish cases from one another, and identify themes in the analysis in the relevant judgments are central skills in family law. The basis upon which the court made

---

[14] Hale, B. 'Equality and Autonomy in Family Law' (2011) 33 *Journal of Social Welfare and Family Law* 3.

[15] [2001] EWCA Civ 166.

[16] See, e.g., *Re F (A Child) (Permission to Relocate)* [2012] EWCA Civ 1364; *Re AR (A Child) (Relocation)* [2010] EWHC 1346 (Fam); *Re A (Leave to Remove: Cultural and Religious Considerations)* [2006] EWHC 421 (Fam).   [17] *Lloyds Bank v Rossett* [1991] 1 AC 107.

its decision and how it turns on its facts plays an important role in the refinement of legal principles in a particular field. This requires paying close attention to the development of case law authority, and being able to identify the key decisions in a particular field that shape the subsequent reasoning of the courts. To help this process, this book will identify the key cases in each chapter for consideration.

Interpretation of legislation is also a key aspect of family law. Legislation provides the basis for decisions in many areas of family law including marriage and divorce (Chapters 2 and 3),[18] children (Chapters 8 and 9),[19] family violence (Chapter 7),[20] and child maintenance (Chapter 6).[21] In each chapter of this book, the key legislative provisions in the particular field will be identified. Arguments over the interpretation of legislation are often underpinned by policy concerns regarding how the family should be regulated. Lawyers have to be aware of the underpinning moral and social debates around the family to comprehend the impact of the law on the parties, and on wider society. In some fields, courts may engage in a purposive interpretation of legislation, identifying the underlying policy behind a legislative provision and interpreting it in accordance with this policy. Engagement with these policy and political aims may be subject to criticism and, in some cases, the emphasis the court has placed on protecting particular rights may be regarded as problematic. For example, in relation to orders aimed at restricting violence within the family home, conflicts between different rights of housing and property may prevent an order being granted to oust an abuser from the family home.[22]

The role of rights in family law plays an increasingly important role in the development of the law and reasoning in case law. In particular, family lawyers have to be aware of the impact of the Human Rights Act 1998 and the rights relevant to family disputes under the European Convention on Human Rights and Fundamental Freedoms 1950 (ECHR). The Human Rights Act 1998 incorporated the ECHR into English law. Under s. 3 of the Human Rights Act 1998, the English courts must read and give effect to English law in a way that is compatible with Convention rights. If this is not possible, then the court may make a declaration of incompatibility under s. 4 of the Human Rights Act 1998 which means the particular provision or rule cannot be interpreted as compliant with the Convention and should be amended. Under Article 8 of the Convention:

 Key legislation 2: Article 8 ECHR, the right to respect for private and family life

Everyone has the right to respect for his private and family life, his home and his correspondence. There shall be no interference by a public authority with the exercise of this right except as is in accordance with the law and is necessary in a democratic society in the interests of national security, public safety or the economic well-being of the country, for the prevention of disorder or crime, for the protection of health or morals, or for the protection of the rights and freedoms of others.

The right to respect for private and family life is not unlimited; it may be infringed by the state if it can demonstrate that infringement was in accordance with the law and necessary and proportionate in a democratic society. All family members will hold an Article 8 right

---

18 Matrimonial Causes Act 1973.   19 e.g. Children Act 1989.   20 e.g. Family Law Act 1996.
21 e.g. Child Support Act 1991.
22 Family Law Act 1997, s. 33(7); *Re Y (Children) (Occupation Order)* [2000] 2 FCR 470.

to respect for their private and family life, but these rights may conflict with one another.[23] For example, when a child is identified as being at risk of harm from a parent, that parent has the right to respect for their family relationship with the child, but this right can be infringed and a child removed from the parents' care because the child is at risk. This infringement must be in accordance with the law provided in Children Act 1989.[24]

Article 8 does not specifically account for the rights and interests of children as a family member, or suggest that children deserve particular rights and protection. Case law on the interpretation of Article 8 by the European Court of Human Rights, however, has indicated that the welfare of a child, where it conflicts with the exercise of Article 8 rights by a family member, may be the primary consideration under Article 8. A child's Article 8 right may potentially take precedence over the exercise of Article 8 by another family member in the child's interests.[25]

Whilst the ECHR does not account specifically for the rights and interests of children, being concluded before children's rights were widely acknowledged,[26] the UN Convention on the Rights of the Child 1990 (UNCRC) is designed specifically to protect and promote the rights of children. The UK has ratified this Convention, but has not incorporated it into English law. It is not therefore binding on the English courts when adjudicating cases, but the UK Supreme Court has indicated that where possible English law should be interpreted consistently with international human rights standards, including the UNCRC.[27] The position in Wales is slightly different following the adoption by the Welsh Assembly of the Rights of Children and Young Persons (Wales) Measure 2011. This Measure imposes an obligation on Welsh Ministers to have due regard to the UNCRC when adopting legislation in the scope of its devolved legislative powers.

The UNCRC and the additional Protocols establish extensive political, economic, social, and cultural rights for all children. Four Articles in the Convention form the general principles of the UNCRC: Article 2 covers non-discrimination; Article 3 states that the child's welfare is the primary consideration in decisions affecting them; Article 6 is the right to survival and development; and Article 12 establishes the right of the child to be heard and have their opinion taken into account in accordance with their age and maturity. The UN Committee on the Rights of the Child monitors compliance of signatory states to the terms of the UNCRC and states are required to report periodically to the Committee.[28] The principles expressed in the UNCRC are reflected to some extent in English law, even though the treaty has not been incorporated into English law. Under s. 1(1) of the Children Act 1989, the child's welfare is the court's paramount consideration when taking decisions.[29] Under s. 1(3), a child of appropriate age and maturity will be heard in family law proceedings, usually through an officer from Children and Families Court Advisory and Support Service (Cafcaas) who interviews the child and reports to the court.[30] Whilst the UNCRC is not directly binding on the English courts, family lawyers have to be aware of its influence and the importance of the general principles underpinning the Convention.

The human rights obligations affect litigation in both public law and private family law disputes. Family law covers both civil law private disputes between family members,

---

[23] Choudhry, S. and Herring, J. *European Human Rights and Family Law* (Hart Publishing, 2010).

[24] Children Act 1989, s. 31(2).   [25] *Johansen v Norway* App. No. 17383/90 (1997) 23 EHRR 33.

[26] Kilkelly, U. *The Child and the European Convention on Human Rights* (Ashgate, 1999).

[27] *ZH (Tanzania) v Secretary of State for the Home Department* [2011] 2 AC 166.

[28] http://www.ohchr.org/EN/HRBodies/CRC/Pages/Membership.aspx, accessed 10 March 17.

[29] The child's welfare is paramount under s. 1(1) of the Children Act 1989, rather than the primary consideration under Article 3 UNCRC, see Bonner, D., Fenwick, H., and Harris-Short, S. 'Judicial Approaches to the Human Rights Act' (2003) 52 *International and Comparative Law Quarterly* 549.

[30] The judge rarely hears from a child directly in the English courts, see Raitt, F. 'Hearing Children in Family Law Proceedings: Can Judges make a difference?' (2007) 19 *Child and Family Law Quarterly* 204.

for example litigation over parental arrangements following a divorce, and public law where the state takes action to protect a child from harm by other family members. In the context of private law disputes between family members, family law has been affected by changes to the legal aid system brought about by the Legal Aid, Sentencing and Punishment of Offenders Act 2012 (LASPO). This Act restricted the availability of legal aid to private family law litigation, although it is still available for certain types of dispute if, for example, there has been domestic violence in the family.[31] The Act is designed to encourage private resolution of family disputes away from the courts and supports provision for mediation. The impact of LASPO 2012 is explored further in Chapter 15, but lawyers are still engaged in these processes and must be aware of the legal options in order to deliver effective advice. Negotiation of disputes between private parties should occur in the shadow of the law,[32] meaning that the parties must be aware of the likely outcome according to law, but exercise their autonomy to reach their own agreement.

Defining the material scope of family law can be difficult as family life interacts with several fields of law (see further section 3). The impact of family relationships in other fields of law may require the adaptation of legal principles to accommodate the family context. In the context of the breakdown of family relationships outside of marriage, the law on trusts has been adapted to provide for the protection of property rights in the family home through the development of the common intention constructive trust[33] (see Chapter 4). This concept developed the law on implied trusts, adapting specifically to the family context. Family lawyers have to be aware of the principles underpinning other fields of law and be sensitive to the family context, considering the extent to which it should affect decisions and the development of the law.

Some behaviour in a family context may also form the basis of a criminal prosecution, for example, forms of domestic violence[34] or child abuse.[35] The standard of proof in criminal law requires proof beyond reasonable doubt before an individual can be convicted. By contrast, in civil law, the standard of proof is on the balance of probabilities. This means that the evidence necessary to prove an incident took place in a civil court can be less than is necessary in a criminal court. This can cause confusion and controversy, as occurred in the case of Poppi Worthington. The evidence of parental abuse to Poppi causing her death was sufficient on the balance of probabilities for action to be taken by the state to protect Poppi's siblings in the civil law on child protection under the Children Act 1989, but was not sufficient to pursue a criminal prosecution, even though the father was identified as the perpetrator of Poppi's death in the civil proceedings.[36]

Family law has to be particularly responsive to social and political changes as our practice of family life changes and societal perceptions of family life shifts. This means that family lawyers have to be aware of insights and research on the family outside the context of the law, and open and critical of potential law reform. The Law Commission is an independent statutory body created to review and make recommendations for law reform, including reform of family law.[37] The Law Commission has conducted important reviews of various areas of law, such as the property rights of cohabitants, that can inform thinking on the weaknesses and development in the law.[38] In some contexts, there may

---

[31] LASPO 2012, Sch 1.

[32] Mnookin, R.N. and Kornhauser, L. 'Bargaining in the Shadow of the Law: The Case of Divorce' (1979) 88 *Yale Law Journal* 950.   [33] *Lloyds Bank v Rosset* [1991] 1 AC 107.

[34] Serious Crime Act 2015, s. 76.   [35] Children and Young Persons Act 1933, s. 1.

[36] *F v Cumbria CC and M (Fact Finding No. 2)* [2016] EWHC 14 (Fam).

[37] Law Commissions Act 1965: http://www.lawcom.gov.uk/, accessed 19 September 2017.

[38] Law Commission, *Cohabitation: The Financial Consequences of Relationship Breakdown* (Law Com No. 307, 2007).

be independent public enquiries forming the basis of law and practice reform, such as the Laming Inquiry into the failures of child protection following the death of Victoria Climbie.[39] The research by academics can also play an important role in the development of the law, both in commenting on and feeding into the development of legislation, and in forming the basis of recommendations for changes to the law.[40] The potential for social and political development, and research into the social behaviour of families and their use of the law is key to the practice of family law and its ability to respond effectively to family relationships.

To help exploration of these issues the chapters in this book include context boxes to explain the social and family context in which legal problems may arise. The fact that family law is underpinned by social and political changes means that there is great scope for different perceptions of the best way to address a particular social problem through law, and over the content and interpretation of the legal provisions. This will be explored in the debates in each chapter. Whilst there is no clear 'correct' answer to any of these debates, being able to identify and discuss the points underpinning the debate, and consider them critically is a valuable skill for family lawyers.

3. Identifying and regulating 'the family'

The practices associated with family life change over time. How the law identifies members of 'the family' and regulates family life may also change, but these changes often raise controversy over the acceptability of family forms, how the law should respond to social change, and the impact the law has on family practices.

 CONTEXT 1: CHANGING FAMILY PRACTICES

The evidence for changes in the conduct of family life can be considered from the statistics recording certain family status over time:

Marriage: In 2014 there were 247,372 marriages between opposite-sex couples in England and Wales. This was a 2.7% increase from 2013, but there were 6.2% more marriages celebrated in 2012.

In 2014, there were 1,683 civil partnerships concluded between same-sex couples, but 4,850 marriages were celebrated between same-sex couples.[41] This is a 70% reduction in the number of civil partnerships from 2013 when 5,646 civil partnerships were concluded,[42] before marriage between same-sex couples became legal.[43]

Cohabitation: In 2015, 12% of the population over 16 were cohabiting in England and Wales, compared to 48% of the population married or in a civil partnerships, and 39.6%

---

[39] Lord Laming, *Report on the Victoria Climbie Inquiry* (Cm 5730, 2003). Available at: https://www.gov.uk/government/publications/the-victoria-climbie-inquiry-report-of-an-inquiry-by-lord-laming, accessed 19 September 2017.

[40] Cretney, S. *Law, Law Reform and the Family* (Clarendon, 2008).

[41] ONS Statistical Bulletin 'Marriages in England and Wales 2014'. Available at: https://www.ons.gov.uk/peoplepopulationandcommunity/birthsdeathsandmarriages/marriagecohabitationandcivilpartnerships/bulletins/marriagesinenglandandwalesprovisional/2014, accessed 18 June 2017.

[42] ONS Statistical Bulletin 'Civil Partnerships in England and Wales 2014'. Available at: https://www.ons.gov.uk/peoplepopulationandcommunity/birthsdeathsandmarriages/marriagecohabitationandcivilpartnerships/bulletins/civilpartnershipsinenglandandwales/2015-10-20, accessed 18 June 2017.

[43] Marriage (Same-Sex Couples) Act 2013 came into force in March 2014.

who were single and not living as a couple.[44] Cohabitation is the fastest growing family form and is increasingly common in England and Wales, especially for younger people preceding marriage.[45]

Divorce: 111,169 divorces in England and Wales in 2014 down from 113,949 in 2009. In 1969, 20% of marriages had ended by the 15th wedding anniversary, compared to 33% of marriages in 1994.[46]

3.1 Debating the role and purpose of family law

Statistical changes can demonstrate that family form adopted by individuals change over time, as the significance and acceptability of particular family forms also shifts. The social acceptability of cohabitation means that it is now a commonly adopted family form, where it was much less so in the mid-twentieth century.[47] These processes can be inhibited, or encouraged by the law. The extent to which the law should be involved in regulating family life, and how it should respond to social change, are important political questions. The perception of 'family life' and what constitutes a family can be heavily informed by social and cultural background and, as suggested by the statistical changes shown earlier, family practices in England and Wales have become much more diverse over time. The role the law should play in responding to these changes and diversity in family practices is not always clear and can be highly politicised as a statement of the values attached to family life by the state. The political dimension can heavily influence the likelihood and content of any law reform.

The site of reform to the law to respond to social changes can also be important to the development of the law. In some fields of family law, the role of Parliament has been very important in promoting reform, for example in opening the status of marriage to same-sex couples by the Marriage (Same-Sex Couples) Act 2013.[48] In others, despite attempts at reform through Parliament, no legislative measures have been adopted, and the role of the courts in deciding cases has played a key role in developing the law. The reform of the law relating to cohabitation is a good example of the failure of Parliament to provide a legislative framework. Despite a report and recommendations from the Law Commission,[49] attempts to legislate through a Private Members Bill have failed to progress through the legislative process.[50]

---

[44] ONS Statistical Bulletin, 'Population Estimates by Marital Status and Living Arrangements: England and Wales 2002–2015'. Available at: https://www.ons.gov.uk/peoplepopulationandcommunity/populationandmigration/populationestimates/bulletins/populationestimatesbymaritalstatusandlivingarrangements/2002to2015#the-population-who-are-single-never-married-or-civil-partnered-are-increasingly-cohabiting, accessed 18 June 2017.

[45] ONS Statistical Bulletin 'Families and Households 2015'. Available at: https://www.ons.gov.uk/peoplepopulationandcommunity/birthsdeathsandmarriages/families/bulletins/familiesandhouseholds/2015-11-05, accessed 18 June 2017.

[46] ONS Statistical Bulletin 'Divorces in England and Wales'. Available at: http://webarchive.nationalarchives.gov.uk/20160105160709/http://www.ons.gov.uk/ons/rel/vsob1/divorces-in-england-and-wales/2009/divorces-in-england-and-wales.pdf, accessed 18 June 2017.

[47] Probert, R. *The Changing Legal Regulation of Cohabitation: From Fornicators to Family, 1600–2010'* (Cambridge University Press, 2012).

[48] Eekelaar, J. 'Perception of Equality: The Road to Same-Sex Marriage in England and Wales' (2014) 28 *International Journal of Law, Policy and the Family* 1.

[49] Law Commission, Cohabitation: The Financial Consequences of Relationship Breakdown' (Law Com No. 307, 2007).

[50] 'Cohabitation Rights Bill (HL)' 2015–16, 4 June 2015: Column 513. 'Relationships (Civil Registration) Bill and Civil Partnerships Bill' (HL) Bill 36 and Bill 41 of 2001–2002.

DEBATE 1: HOW SHOULD THE LAW RESPOND TO SOCIAL CHANGES IN FAMILY LIFE?

Family law seeks to regulate social practices. Such practices are not uniform, as they are to some extent malleable to personal choice, and evolve over time. The law is a powerful tool in defining the concept of family and the acceptability of certain relationships or behaviour.[51] This means that there may be some tension between the social conceptions of 'the family' and who society regards as a family member, and the legal conception of family and what behaviour should be regulated by law. This also raises the question of whether law should lead and encourage development of family practices. For example, by recognising new types of relationship such as the rights of same-sex parents to the status of parenthood, (see Chapter 8) the law makes an important statement about the validity and acceptability of these family forms and behaviours.[52] Or, alternatively, should law wait until it becomes clear that legal intervention is necessary to address a social problem and then intervene to remedy the situation, through case law arising in the courts, or by legislation. The relationship between law and family is symbiotic but not perfect; there will always be some mismatch between family life and family law.

Many family forms and practices we now regard as socially acceptable and 'normal', such as cohabitation without marriage, same-sex relationships, or divorce, were even a short time ago regarded as socially embarrassing or questionable. Social attitudes to these practices have changed, but there has not been a comprehensive approach taken to law reform to match, or address the consequences of these changes. In the context of same-sex relationships, the law has evolved dramatically to permit same-sex couples to contract valid marriages. The law on cohabitation has evolved in some respects, so the legal consequences for a child born outside marriage have been largely addressed,[53] but the property rights acquired during a cohabitation relationship have only evolved through the case law on trusts. Despite attempts at law reform in the Family Law Act 1996, the law on divorce has remained the same since 1969, despite significant social change in the numbers and social acceptability of seeking a divorce. The law on determining parenthood of a child has seen significant legislative intervention in the Human Fertilisation and Embryology Acts of 1990 and 2008.

In seeking reform of the law, the role of Parliament is of central importance as the democratically elected body, considering and scrutinising legislative proposals aimed at responding to social change. However, as will become clear in this book, Parliament has not always responded to attempts to reform law relating to the family. Even when the Law Commission has made recommendations for law reform, for example on the law relating to cohabitation and property rights, Parliament has not responded with legislation, leaving it to the courts to adapt and develop the law on trusts.[54] Yet, in other contexts, such as permitting same-sex marriage, legislation has been forthcoming.

How choices are made regarding what the law regulates and who develops the law is informed by political and cultural values. To some extent, the political acceptability of a particular family issue will affect whether it is addressed by Parliament, or not. This can leave politically difficult or controversial proposals unaddressed, or with dated legal frameworks. In the recent case of *Owens v Owens* regarding the refusal of a divorce petition, the President of the Family Division stated that: 'Parliament has decreed that it is not a ground for

---

[51] Douglas, G. *Introduction to Family Law* (OUP, 2001) 14.

[52] Human Fertilisation and Embryology Act 2008.

[53] Legitimacy Act 1976; Children Act 1989; Child Support Act 1991.

[54] Law Commission, *The Financial Consequences of Relationship Breakdown* (Law Com No. 307, 2007).

divorce that you find yourself in a wretchedly unhappy marriage, though some people may say it should be. Such is the law which it is our duty to apply.'[55] Even where there is evidence of a need for law reform, Parliament may not respond with legislation and it is important to question why reform has not been forthcoming, and whether there is a significant case for any proposed reform.

When Parliament does not engage in law reform, it may be the courts making decisions in individual cases leading to development of family law. This may result in judicial development of the law, or, in some cases application of law the court regards as problematic. The use of precedent to adapt or develop the law must be examined closely. Arguably, the courts are not an appropriate forum for law reform because of their limited scope for appreciating social change and the legal impact of a judgment, but if there is scope for adjustment of the law in accordance with legal principle, judicial decision-making can be an important aspect of achieving justice. For example, the interpretation of the Matrimonial Causes Act 1973 by the House of Lords in *White v White*[56] that division of assets between the parties on divorce should be based on equality represented an important development in the law and a significant shift away from previous precedent that favoured the financially stronger party in the marriage. The close examination of the judgments and underpinning concepts and values in such significant cases is important to understand and criticise the reasoning and the validity of the decision-making.

3.2 Identifying a family relationship in law

Most of us could point to individuals we regard as our family members. Our conception of 'normal' family life may not reflect the reality of how families actually live and may be quite exclusive. Often our conception of the family is dominated by what is known as a nuclear family, consisting of a married female mother and male father of the opposite sex, with children of the marriage. We can extend this conception to include relations such as grandparents and grandchildren. It is based around the core aspects of marriage between adult consenting parties, and children of the marriage identified on the basis of a genetic link. Meaning is attached to the status held and our understanding of these statuses, such as marriage or parenthood.

This conception of family life will not capture family relationships that we may wish to regard as important family relationships, such as step-parents and children, or adopted children. The concept of family is difficult to define and has to be flexible to adapt to new social circumstances.

3.2.1 Functionalist approaches to the family

If we can identify the functions of the family, by identifying the individuals who carry out those functions, we can identify family members. This approach requires us to think about what we regard as the core functions of family life and how we define the obligations and interaction of 'family' members. For example, we may look for relationships where there is evidence of mutual love and support, financial interdependence, sharing a household, or some degree of stability in the relationship. This approach permits an evolving conception of what 'family life' entails, not based purely around marriage or genetic relationships. This approach can capture new forms of 'family' relationship as it can adapt to the practice and circumstances of individuals.

---

[55] [2017] EWCA Civ 182, paras 84–5.   [56] [2000] UKHL 54.

Identifying 'family life' however, is often done through a process of analogy with marital or other recognised family relationships.[57] In *Burden v United Kingdom*,[58] the European Court of Human Rights examined a claim from two siblings that their relationship was analogous to a marital relationship in that they shared a household and provided mutual love and support to one another. On this basis they argued that differential treatment for siblings in relation to inheritance tax in UK law was a breach of Article 8 and Article 14 ECHR. Their claim was however rejected, because the nature of the relationship was qualitatively different, being based on consanguinity (blood relationship), rather than a mutually assumed marital tie. The role of sexual relations for procreation and the care of children are often central to functional definitions of the family, leaving those outside of those aspects of family life unrecognised.

Defining family members in this way requires us to address what functions we think family life should perform and then identify who fits within these functions. Whilst it reflects changing family practices, it may also capture relationships that we would not personally label as 'family', but do entail family-like functions, such as close friendship. It could mean that moral obligations of support and love become legal obligations[59] on individuals, requiring them to act in a particular way even if the individual accepts no tie or obligation to another. It also means that the underlying assumptions regarding the nature of family life, the behaviour we wish to encourage or discourage, are left unquestioned, instead focusing on how family life is being carried out. It does not challenge the social acceptability of forms of family behaviour.

3.2.2 Relationships of care

Instead of focusing on the functions of the family, it has been suggested that the key element of all family relationships is the aspect of care for one another.[60] Rather than emphasising the autonomy of individuals in making decisions, vulnerability can be regarded as a universal status inherently requiring care from others to survive and thrive.[61] Those caring relationships should be valued as the core of family relationships. Individuals feel an obligation to care for other family members and support them when they are in need.

In focusing on caring relationships, the concept of family may be extended beyond marital or genetic relationships. In these circumstances, for example, a child cared for by a person who is not their genetic parent could still be regarded as a family member and this may be very desirable. It acknowledges what many regard to be central to our experience as humans, and key to the practice of family life. The approach values the importance of care in the functioning of our society, moving away from an emphasis on individual behaviour. However, the concepts of 'care' and 'vulnerability' are themselves inherently undefined[62] and difficult to apply to legal processes. If two people contract an otherwise valid marriage, but never live together or support one another, they will still be regarded as married and we would still call them family members, even without the element of care being present in the relationship. Emphasising vulnerability may also mean that we regard certain individuals as powerless within the family. For example, children could be

---

[57] See, e.g., *Schalk v Austria* App. No. 30141/04 (2011) 53 EHRR 20; Douglas, G. *Introduction to Family Law* (OUP, 2001) 41.   [58] *Burden v United Kingdom* App. No. 13378/05 (2008) 47 EHRR 38.

[59] Eekelaar, J. 'Self-Restraint: Social Norms, Individualism and the Family' (2012) 13 *Theoretical Inquiries in Law* 75.

[60] Herring, J. *Caring and the Law* (Hart Publishing, 2013).

[61] Fineman, M. and Grear, A. (eds) *Vulnerability: Reflections on a New Ethical Foundation for Law and Politics* (Ashgate, 2013).

[62] Wallbank, J. and Herring, J. 'Vulnerabilities, Care and Family Law' in J. Wallbank, and J. Herring (eds) *Vulnerabilities, Care and Family Law* (Taylor and Francis, 2013) 16.

regarded as vulnerable and in need of care, but this perception may effectively undermine their right to be heard and have an opinion, risking the possibility that decisions are taken on their behalf.[63] We may also regard a parent as being obliged to provide financially for their child, even if they play no other role in caring for them (see Chapter 6).

3.2.3 Obligations and commitment

Family law regulates intimate relationships on the basis that there is an element of mutual responsibility between the parties to the family relationship. Gillian Douglas[64] has explored the basis of these responsibilities arising from family law and has suggested that the law has moved away from the concept of an obligation from one family member to another, towards identifying a commitment between the parties that gives rise to responsibility. She argues that any obligations arising from family law, such as the obligation to maintain a child, may only be regarded as a soft obligation, without defined scope and subject to change over time. The shift towards identifying a commitment between two parties that forms the basis of responsibility for another person is an aspect of increasing individualism in family law. A person will only be responsible if they have voluntarily assumed a commitment[65] to which they will then have to respond. This approach examines the consequences of a relationship and responds to the context of the particular relationship and the nature of the commitment expressed.

Normally, family relationships are identified by the law through consideration of a number of factors, including our perspective on a particular family status or relationship, the voluntary assumption of a relationship, genetic links, the presence of a family function, or a relationship of care.

 Debate 2: Who are our 'Family' and how should the Law Identify Family Relationships?

Acceptance by the law of a relationship as a 'family' relationship can entail access to certain benefits and rights. Some of these statuses are clearly defined as family statuses, such as marriage. Other family relationships are recognised over time, or may fall entirely outside the scope of legal recognition, with significant impact on individual rights. Who we regard as our family may be different to the legal definition, and the law may have to adapt to identify types of family relationship not previously recognised. The process of how the law identifies relationships as being 'family' can be incremental and the law has shown some flexibility in adapting to family forms.

In *Fitzpatrick v Sterling Housing Association Ltd*[66] Mr Fitzpatrick had, in 2001, lived in a stable cohabitation relationship with his same-sex partner, who had now died. Mr Fitzpatrick sought to succeed to the protected tenancy held by his partner, but entitlement was limited to the 'surviving spouse' or 'a member of the original tenant's family'.[67] The House of Lords stated that the concept of 'spouse' had been expressly limited to opposite-sex marital and cohabitant partners. The law had to account for changes of attitude and the concept of family member include same-sex partners, as the relationship was one of mutual interdependence, sharing lives with love, commitment and support, of sufficient longevity.[68] Mr Fitzpatrick qualified to succeed the tenancy as a 'family member' of his same-sex partner.

---

[63] Article 12 UNCRC.
[64] Douglas, G. 'The Basis of Obligation and Commitment in Family Law' (2016) 36 *Legal Studies* 1.
[65] Douglas, G. 'The Basis of Obligation and Commitment in Family Law' (2016) 36 *Legal Studies* 1, 19.
[66] [2001] 1 AC 27.   [67] Rent Act 1977, Sch 1, para 3.   [68] [2001] 1 AC 27, 37 per Lord Slynn.

Fitzpatrick was followed by *Ghaidan v Godin-Mendoza*[69] in 2004. By 2004, the Human Rights Act 1998 had entered into force and under s. 3 of the Act, the English courts must read and give effect to English law in a way that is compatible with Convention rights. Mr Ghaidan had been in a stable same-sex relationship since 1972 with a protected tenant and he sought to be recognised as a spouse to succeed to the tenancy on the death of his partner.[70] He argued that he should be recognised under the category of 'spouse' on the basis of his right to respect for his private and family life under Article 8 ECHR, combined with Article 14 ECHR, prohibiting discrimination on the ground of sexuality in protection of ECHR rights. Despite the conclusion in *Fitzpatrick* that the concept of 'spouse' precluded the inclusion of same-sex relationships, the definition of a same-sex partner as a 'family member' resulted in the survivor of a same-sex partnership being treated less favourably than the survivor of an opposite-sex partnership. In *Ghaidan,* the Court found that this discrimination could not be justified and was in breach of Articles 8 and 14 of the Convention.[71] To ensure equality of treatment, the concept of 'spouse' under the legislation should now be read and interpreted to include survivors of same-sex partners.[72] The obligations arising under the Human Rights Act 1998 meant that same-sex partners were not generic 'family members', but could be recognised as falling within the concept of spouse, where the relationship was marked by the same characteristics as a stable opposite-sex relationship, even though at the time, same-sex couples could not contract a valid marriage.

Before the adoption of the Civil Partnership Act 2004, there was no provision in English law for same-sex couples to contract a recognised status that was legally regulated, giving access to rights and entitlements. The Civil Partnership Act 2004 allowed same-sex couples to conclude a legally recognised relationship, embodying many of the rights and obligations associated with marital status (see Chapter 2). Subsequently, the status of marriage was also opened to same-sex couples following the Marriage (Same-Sex) Couples Act 2013.

The family relationships underpinning the changing legal status of same-sex couples did not change during this period; individual relationships would continue. Couples in same-sex relationships may have regarded themselves as being 'family' even if the law did not treat them as fulfilling either the status of 'family member' or 'spouse'. However, the legal acceptance of those relationships shifted quickly, in a short period of time. The social status of same-sex partners was also changed as a result. The Lord Chancellor, Lord Falconer argued:[73] 'For same sex couples [the Civil Partnership Act 2004] was about gaining recognition of their relationships in law, something they had previously been unable to do. Being invisible in the eyes of the law was a cause of many day-to-day injustices for same sex couples.'

To what extent does legal acceptance change our perceptions of family relationships? We may regard people as part of our family when the law does not, but the law has an important normative role in defining the wider acceptability of family forms and behaviour. The process of determining who the law defines as 'family' is important both in terms of the normative value attached to the status, and the rights that can be accessed as a result of holding the status. The cases of *Fitzpatrick* and *Ghaidan* demonstrate that, even though the parties regarded themselves as family members, entitled to the benefits of and entitlements that may bring, the law did not initially identify them as fulfilling this status, and even once recognised the change was incremental, from 'family member' to 'spouse', before legislative change

---

[69] [2004] UKHL 30.   [70] Rent Act 1977, Sch 1, para 2.   [71] [2004] UKHL 30, at [18].
[72] [2004] UKHL 30, at [35].
[73] Lord Falconer 'Church, State and Civil partners' (2007) 9 *Ecclesiastical Law Journal* 5, 7.

further solidified the status of same-sex couples. How the law develops in recognising and refusing family status is uneven and contested and carries with it political controversy and significance in terms of social acceptability. How the law identifies and regulates particular relationships is a central question for family lawyers.

3.3 Regulating family relationships through law

Once a family relationship has been identified, the extent to which the law can and should intervene to regulate family life is contested. We do not expect the law to determine the conduct of our day-to-day family relationships, and nor should it.

Traditionally, the family is regarded as the private sphere, protected from regulation by the state. This is in contrast to the public sphere of the market and public affairs. Theoretically, the law draws a boundary between the public and private by direct regulation of the public sphere.[74] Regulation of the family is left to other social mechanisms, leaving the family as a place of personal freedom to order its own affairs. This element of privacy means that intervention in family life should be avoided by the state. The types of relationship existing in the private sphere of the family will be different in nature to those in the public sphere of work and professional behaviour.[75]

It is not desirable to have an entirely strict division between public life and private behaviour, untouched by the law. A strict division places behaviour in private beyond the scope of legal regulation and this puts individuals at risk of harm. For example, if someone is experiencing violence at the hands of an intimate partner in the home, the law should be able to intervene to punish and restrain such behaviour.[76] Eekelaar suggests that the concept of public and private spheres has dissolved because law is a public instrument, but has to be used when the apparently private behaviour of the family impacts on the public interest.[77] He argues that the public interest is served by the proper functioning of the family, and so justifies the intervention of the law in regulating family life, but means that the family may no longer be described as entirely 'private' and beyond public regulation by the law.

The analysis of the family as being private and beyond the scope of the law does not capture the many ways in which the law may influence the conduct of family life, both directly and indirectly. Elliot highlights that welfare and legal provision can privilege certain family forms, for example by granting tax advantages to married couples in order to encourage adults to contract marriages. Although certain family forms may be privileged, this does not mean that families' lives are necessarily defined and organised in this way.[78] There still remains personal choice in the arrangement of family life. The public-private analysis also fails to capture the reality that both family and public behaviour such as work are inherently interlinked and the practices of each influence one another.

This approach to considering the role of law in affecting family practices identifies the role the law plays in constructing and defining 'appropriate' behaviour of family members holding particular status. Feminist scholars have regarded this insight as particularly important as a way in which the concepts of family relationships influence the perception

---

[74] O'Donovan, K. *Sexual Divisions in Law* (Weidenfield and Nicholson, 1985), 14.

[75] Eekelaar, J. 'What is "Critical" Family Law?' (1989) 105 *Law Quarterly Review* 244, 254.

[76] Dobash, R. and Dobash, R. 'Violence Against Women in the Family' in S. Katz *et al* (eds) *Cross Currents: Family Law and Policy in the US and England* (OUP, 2000).

[77] Eekelaar, J. 'What is "Critical' Family Law?' (1989) 105 *Law Quarterly Review* 244, 256.

[78] Elliot, F. 'The Family: Private Arena or Adjunct of the State?' (1989) 16 *Journal of Law and Society* 443, 450.

of gender roles and affect women's roles in the family and wider society.[79] The power of the law in defining the identity and role of individuals within the family can constrain choices and construct values around behaviour[80] of both men and women. These norms encourage certain forms of behaviour, often in accordance with gender norms. For example, although it is more common for women to maintain a form of paid employment after they have given birth, they are more likely than the father to be in part-time employment, partly because the mother is likely to be less well paid, and partly because of gendered expectations surrounding the care of children. However, these norms can change and develop over time and the law may change also. It used to be the case that only women obtained maternity leave on giving birth, but leave can now be split between the parents.[81] The interaction of employment law with the management and allocation of parental obligations demonstrates that it may not be family law directly that impacts on family life, but other areas of law as well.

 Debate 3: What Role should the Law Play in Regulating our Family Life?

Just because the law incentivises, requires, or prohibits a certain type of behaviour, it does not control it in reality and family law does not control all aspects of family life. Lots of decisions about family life are taken without any reference to the law and the reality of family life is so mixed and complex that it is not always clear what effect the law may have in affecting the behaviour of individuals, or of societal practices more broadly. Other aspects of the law, beyond family law, may significantly influence family behaviour, such as entitlement to leave on the birth of a child, effectively identifying the child's primary carer. Social expectations of 'family' may be more determinative of individual behaviour in forming and leaving relationships than any legal incentive or disincentive. Family law may incentivise certain types of behaviour or relationship, but it may not obligate that type of behaviour. There remains significant scope for individual choice in the practise of 'family'.

Often the law and legal options are considered at the point at which family relationships have broken down and the parties to a relationship no longer cooperate and call themselves 'family' as they once did. Whilst family life is functioning, the legal regulation of the rights and responsibilities between the parties is less pertinent because they are being carried out in whatever individualised fashion the parties have organised for themselves. This aspect of family life is one of the most difficult for family lawyers; that, because of the previous happy functioning of the family, often little thought or planning has gone into the worst case scenario. The law is often providing a solution, and potentially protection, where the usual family functioning has failed in some way.

John Dewar has suggested that this is part of the 'normal chaos' of family law.[82] The emotional nature of decision-making in relation to the family, that is, not based necessarily in rational choices, and the importance of discretion in responding to individual circumstances makes the law chaotic. He argues that this 'chaos' is a normal part of the discipline of family law because the law is seeking to regulate a social and unpredictable phenomenon that is inherently personal.

This raises the question of whether the law can effectively regulate family behaviour, or merely influence it? Is it acceptable for an area of law to be described as 'in chaos'?

---

[79] Diduck, A. *Law's Families* (Butterworths, 2003).
[80] Smart, C. 'The Woman of Legal Discourse' (1992) 1 *Social and Legal Studies* 29.
[81] Shared Parental Leave Regulations 2014 (SI 2014/3050).
[82] Dewar, J. 'The Normal Chaos of Family Law' (1998) 61 *Modern Law Review* 467.

SUMMARY

1. Who are our 'family' and how should the law identify family relationships?
   - Identifying family relationships is not necessarily easy and the law has to adapt to changing social and cultural circumstances to recognise and regulate new forms of family life to be effective.

2. What role should the law play in regulating our family life?
   - To some extent, the way we carry out our family life is our own business, untouched by the law and the state. However, the state has to intervene to regulate formalised relationships, identify the rights and obligations flowing from family relationships, and to protect those at risk of harm in the family.

3. How should the law respond to social and political changes in family life?
   - Families are individualised and subjective and the law has to respond to the emotional impact of relationships and provide answers to complex disputes. The use of discretion in decision-making provides flexibility to the law but may result in uncertainty. Increasingly there is an emphasis on personal autonomy to allow individuals to organise their own arrangements.

Further Reading

Barlow, A. 'Solidarity, Autonomy and Equality: Mixed Messages for the Family?' 27 *Child and Family Law Quarterly* 223
- Considers the role autonomy has in modern family law and the value and limits of the concept in this context.

Dewar, J. 'The Normal Chaos of Family Law' (1998) 61 *Modern Law Review* 467
- Analyses the nature of family law and reasons why it could be described as 'chaotic', including the role of discretion in family law.

Douglas, G. 'The Basis of Obligation and Commitment in Family Law' (2016) 36 *Legal Studies* 1
- Critically assesses the development of obligations in modern family law and the shift towards the concept of commitment in family relationships.

Eekelaar, J. *Family Life and Personal Life* (OUP, 2006)
- Provides a broad examination of the nature of family law and how the state should seek to regulate our private relationships.

Gilmore, S., Herring, J., and Probert, R. *Great Debates in Family Law* (Palgrave, 2015)
- Provokes a series of debates around different aspects of family law, and considers the legal issues and underlying policy concerns in each field.

2
Relationships between Adults: Marriage, Civil Partnerships, and Cohabitation

Andy Hayward

LEARNING OBJECTIVES

After reading this chapter you will be able to:

- Appreciate the historical development and significance of marriage in the creation of modern family law;
- Identify the formalities required for entry into both opposite-sex and same-sex marriages alongside the consequences for non-compliance;
- Understand the impetus behind the introduction of civil partnerships and their future in an era of same-sex marriage;
- Appreciate the relationship between the formalised statuses of marriage and civil partnership versus cohabitation;
- Assess the arguments for and against statutory cohabitation reform.

DEBATES

After reading this chapter you should be equipped to discuss your opinion on the following central debates:

1. Should we overhaul the formalities for entry into marriage?
2. Is there a continuing need for a law of nullity?
3. Do civil partnerships have a future in an era of same-sex marriage?
4. Should there be reform of the law relating to cohabitation?

1. Introduction

England and Wales recognises two formalised relationship statuses: marriage and civil partnership. Marriage between opposite-sex couples has been celebrated in this jurisdiction for centuries and, even in an era of diversity as to family forms, is widely viewed as the idealised adult relationship. Marriage was originally regulated exclusively through ecclesiastical law but, following the Marriage Act 1836, civil marriages could be created. Furthermore, after the Matrimonial Causes Act 1857, a secular civil court determined all issues relating to the validity and consequences of marriage.

Civil partnerships were introduced in December 2005 through the Civil Partnership Act 2004. As this chapter will demonstrate, civil partnerships confer nearly the same legal consequences and entitlements as marriage and therefore have been regarded as 'marriage in all but name'.[1] Same-sex marriage was introduced in March 2014 following the passage of the Marriage (Same Sex Couples) Act 2013 but, rather surprisingly, the law on civil partnerships remained unchanged. This legislative inertia has profound consequences for both same-sex and opposite-sex couples. For the former, it now can be questioned whether there remains a need for civil partnerships as same-sex relationships can be formalised through marriage that many believe represents the 'gold standard'.[2] For the latter, a key debate in this chapter focuses on whether the ban on opposite-sex couples forming a civil partnership should remain, particularly when it is appreciated that England and Wales (alongside Scotland) permits same-sex couples access to two relationship forms yet limits opposite-sex couples to one.

From the 1970s onwards there has also been a rise in couples cohabiting; indeed, statistics reveal that it is now the fastest growing relationship form.[3] Whilst marriage and civil partnerships entail extensive legal consequences, cohabitants benefit from piecemeal legal protections scattered across a range of disparate areas of law. This means that in some contexts cohabitants have the same entitlements as married couples or civil partners, whereas, in others, a marked disparity exists. Furthermore, England and Wales currently does not possess a comprehensive statutory regime granting cohabitants rights and remedies following relationship breakdown.

This chapter will explore the historical development and modern statutory framework applicable to adult formalised and non-formalised relationships. Its objective is to instil a thorough understanding of the key principles applicable to the formation and subsequent regulation of these relationships. Owing to rapid change in family forms and the growing legal recognition of same-sex relationships, the statutory framework has evolved. This chapter will assess how far these frameworks have successfully accommodated modern family forms and whether further reform is required.

2. The evolution of marriage

The systematic privileging of marriage by both the Church and state has significantly informed the development of family law in England and Wales. Lord Penzance provided the classic definition of marriage in *Hyde v Hyde & Woodmansee*:

---

[1] *Wilkinson v Kitzinger (No. 2)* [2006] EWHC 2022 (Fam), at [88] (Potter P). See also Baroness Hale of Richmond, 'Homosexual Rights' (2004) 16 *Child and Family Law Quarterly* 125, 132.

[2] See Golombok, S. *Modern Families: Parents and Children in New Family Forms* (Cambridge University Press, 2015) and Ball, C.A. *Same-Sex Marriage and Children: A Tale of History, Social Science and Law* (OUP, 2014).

[3] See ONS Statistical Bulletin, 'Families and Households in the UK: 2017'. Available at: https://www.ons.gov.uk/peoplepopulationandcommunity/birthsdeathsandmarriages/families/bulletins/familiesandhouseholds/2017 accessed 23 November 2017, noting cohabiting couples were the fastest growing family type between 1996 and 2017, more than doubling from 1.5 million families to 3.3 million families.

> Marriage, as understood in Christendom, may . . . be defined as the voluntary union for life of one man and one woman to the exclusion of all others.[4]

Often recited at wedding ceremonies, this formulation is generally used as a starting point for any discussion about marriage. Interestingly, Probert has argued that Lord Penzance actually never intended for this statement to become a 'definition' of marriage and, in light of the issues at stake in that case, it was, in fact, merely a contemporaneous defence of the concept of marriage in England and Wales.[5] The following section will explore in more detail the constituent elements of Lord Penzance's definition to illustrate the gradual evolution of society's understanding of marriage.

Lord Penzance's definition envisages that marriage is a public act and, as will be explored later in this chapter, this places marriage in stark contrast to the private nature of cohabitation. However, whilst marriage often involves a public expression of commitment through the use of a ceremony and the giving notice of the intent to marry, how far it is publicly acknowledged is largely up to the parties themselves. Marriages can range from large, lavish affairs to small, intimate ceremonies. This diversity reflects not only the desire of parties to sculpt their own marriages but also raises questions as to how far the parties themselves can modify the foundational elements of marriage.

Historically, marriage was exclusively a religious act and it was the ecclesiastical courts, not the secular courts, that determined questions as to its validity.[6] In the early case of *Manby v Scott*, marriage was conceptualised as:

> A holy state . . . ordained by Almighty God in Paradise before the fall of man, signifying that mystical union which is between Christ and His Church.[7]

Whilst many still value the religious origins of marriage and marry in accordance to those rites, secular or civil marriage has been permitted in England and Wales since 1837. Interestingly, civil marriages have become very popular owing to the greater flexibility as to marriage venue that is offered. For example, religious ceremonies accounted for 28% of marriages between opposite-sex couples and 0.5% of marriages between same-sex couples in 2014.[8] Civil marriages first started to exceed religious ceremonies in 1976 and have consistently outnumbered religious marriages every year since 1992.

Lord Penzance envisages that marriage is a voluntary act.[9] Marriage has always required the voluntary consent of the parties and, as will be explored later, duress in the form of pressure that destroys the reality of party consent constitutes a basis for a decree of nullity.[10] Similarly, reference to marriage being 'to the exclusion of all others' is another aspect of this definition that remains accurate today as a marriage will be deemed void if entered into by someone who is already married or in a civil partnership.[11]

One of the most controversial challenges to Lord Penzance's definition is same-sex marriage. For centuries only parties of the opposite sex could enter into marriage. Lord

---

[4] (1866) LR 1 P&D 130.

[5] Probert, R. '*Hyde v Hyde*: Defining or Defending Marriage?' (2007) 19 *Child and Family Law Quarterly* 322. See also Poulter, S. 'The Definition of Marriage in English Law' (1979) 42 *Modern Law Review* 409.

[6] On the early history of marriage, see Baker, J. *An Introduction to Legal History* (Butterworths, 2000).

[7] (1663) 1 Mod 124.

[8] See ONS Statistical Bulletin, 'Marriages in England and Wales: 2014'. Available at: https://www.ons.gov.uk/peoplepopulationandcommunity/birthsdeathsandmarriages/marriagecohabitationandcivilpartnerships/bulletins/marriagesinenglandandwalesprovisional/2014 accessed 23 November 2017.

[9] On the historical development of marriage formalities, see Probert, R. *Marriage Law and Practice in the Long Eighteenth Century: A Reassessment* (Cambridge University Press, 2009).

[10] See 5.3.3 on duress.   [11] See 5.2.4.

Nicholls acknowledged this aspect, more recently, in *Bellinger v Bellinger* when he observed that:

> Marriage is an institution, or relationship, deeply embedded in the religious and social culture of this country. It is deeply embedded as a relationship between two persons of the opposite sex.[12]

The rationales behind this requirement were the religious basis of marriage and the expectation that the union would involve procreation. However, whilst sexual relations featured heavily in the historical conception of marriage, the ability to procreate is no longer a determining feature of either marriage itself or its legal validity as Lord Nicholls acknowledged in *Bellinger*:

> There was a time when the reproductive functions of male and female were regarded as the primary raison d'être of marriage. The Church of England Book of Common Prayer of 1662 declared that the first cause for which matrimony was ordained was the 'procreation of children'. For centuries this was proclaimed at innumerable marriage services. For a long time now the emphasis has been different. Variously expressed, there is much more emphasis now on the mutual society, help and comfort that the one ought to have of the other.[13]

Following the Marriage (Same Sex Couples) Act 2013, marriage is no longer exclusively reserved for opposite-sex couples and now can be entered into by couples of the same sex.[14]

The final element of Lord Penzance's definition envisages marriage as an enduring act involving a union for life. Although romantics may wish marriage to be a lifelong commitment, there is neither prohibition on divorce nor any restriction on the amount of marriages one contracts in a lifetime, provided they are not subsisting at the same time, that is, bigamous. Indeed, as Thorpe LJ remarked, we now live 'in an age when marriage is not generally regarded as a sacrament and divorce is a statistical commonplace'.[15]

 CONTEXT 1: MARRIAGE STATISTICS

Marriage today has a multiplicity of meanings and understandings. Although some critics have argued that recent amendments to the traditional concept of marriage have fundamentally changed its inherent nature, marriage still remains a popular choice for many couples.

In 2014, there were 247,372 marriages between opposite-sex couples in England and Wales. This was an increase of 2.7% from the amount of marriages contracted in 2013 (240,854).[16] The average (mean) age for men marrying in 2014 was 37 years and for women it was 34.6 years. Furthermore, in comparison to 2013, civil ceremonies among opposite-sex couples increased by 4.1% in 2014 while religious ceremonies decreased by 0.8%.

Among same-sex couples, civil marriage is also proving very popular. In 2014, there were only 23 religious ceremonies accounting for 0.5% of all marriages of same sex-couples.

Before focusing on the formalities that need to be satisfied to create a valid marriage, same-sex marriage will be further analysed as a recent key development in this area.

---

[12] [2003] UKHL 21, at [46].   [13] [2003] UKHL 21, at [46].

[14] The old prohibition under s. 11(c) of the Matrimonial Causes Act 1973 (a marriage is void if the parties are not male and female) was repealed by the Marriage (Same Sex Couples) Act 2013, Sch 7, Part 2, s. 27.

[15] *Radmacher v Granatino* [2009] EWCA Civ 649, at [29].

[16] ONS Statistical Bulletin 'Marriages in England and Wales: 2014'. Available at: https://www.ons.gov.uk/peoplepopulationandcommunity/birthsdeathsandmarriages/marriagecohabitationandcivilpartnerships/bulletins/marriagesinenglandandwalesprovisional/2014, accessed 18 June 2017.

3. The formal recognition of same-sex relationships

It took some time before society was willing to accept same-sex marriage. Prior to its intro-duction in March 2014, some legal protections did exist for individuals in same-sex relation-ships.[17] For example, same-sex partners were able to obtain protection from domestic violence under Part IV of the Family Law Act 1996. After the House of Lords' decision in *Fitzpatrick v Sterling Housing Association*, same-sex partners were recognised as members of the other partner's family under the Rent Act 1977 for the purposes of succession to a tenancy.[18] The Human Rights Act 1998 enhanced the recognition of same-sex relationships even further by enabling the rights enshrined within the European Convention on Human Rights (ECHR), such as the right to respect to private and family life (Article 8) and freedom from discrimi-nation (Article 14), to be invoked by litigants in domestic courts. The introduction of the Human Rights Act 1998, in particular the use of s. 3 of that Act compelling domestic courts to read and give effect to domestic legislation in a manner compatible with the Convention, enabled the House of Lords in *Ghaidan v Godin-Mendoza* to allow a same-sex partner to suc-ceed to their deceased partner's tenancy, not merely as a member of the tenant's family, but as a spouse.[19] Crucially, these developments did not confer upon the survivor a formal status nor did they comprehensively address all areas of family law. They were largely evidence of the courts adopting a functional analysis of family relationships; that is, giving recognition based on whether the individuals functioned like a recognised relationship such as marriage.[20]

The key precursor to same-sex marriage was civil partnership which was introduced through the Civil Partnership Act 2004. At a general level, civil partnerships, or registered partnerships as they are more widely known in Europe, operate as a statutory registration process for couples that either do not wish to marry or for those that are unable to do so. Unlike the piecemeal recognition discussed earlier, civil partnerships confer a formal status on the parties without individuals needing to further demonstrate evidence of their relationship by, for example, showing cohabitation for a period of time.

Despite early proposals for civil partnerships available to both opposite-sex and same-sex couples,[21] the Women and Equality Unit of the Department for Trade and Industry produced a Report in June 2003 that advocated a registration process for only same-sex couples.[22] This scheme was largely modelled on civil marriage and later became the Civil Partnership Act 2004. This Act conferred rights and responsibilities upon civil partners largely akin to those received by married couples. The government rejected inclusion of opposite-sex couples within the scheme on the basis that they were in a position that was 'significantly different from that of same-sex couples who wish to formalise their relation-ships but currently are unable to do so'.[23]

Even after the introduction of civil partnerships in England and Wales, there were calls for the introduction of same-sex marriage by activists, LGBT organisations, and Members of Parliament. The Equal Civil Marriage consultation was conducted in 2012 and it

---

[17] See, generally, Cretney, S. *Same Sex Relationships: From 'Odious Crime' to 'Gay Marriage'* (OUP, 2006).
[18] [2001] 1 AC 27.   [19] [2004] UKHL 30.
[20] On the dangers of using functionality as a tool to recognise an interpersonal relationship, see Notes, 'Looking for a Family Resemblance: The Limits of the Functional Approach to the Legal Definition of Family' (1990–1) 104 *Harvard Law Review* 1640.
[21] See Jane Griffith MP's Relationships (Civil Registration) Bill introduced into the House of Commons in October 2001 and Lord Lester's Civil Partnerships Bill introduced into the House of Lords in January 2002.
[22] Department of Trade and Industry, Women and Equality Unit, *Civil Partnership: A Framework for the Legal Recognition of Same-Sex Couples*, London, 2003.
[23] Department of Trade and Industry, Women and Equality Unit, *Civil Partnership: A Framework for the Legal Recognition of Same-Sex Couples*, London, 2003, 13.

received the highest ever number of responses to a public consultation (approximately 228,000).[24] With the majority of respondents supporting the introduction of same-sex marriage, a proposal was put forward that later became the Marriage (Same Sex Couples) Act 2013, which received Royal Assent in July 2013.

Section 1(1) of the Act provides that '[m]arriage of same sex couples is lawful'. The Act enables same-sex couples to marry using a civil ceremony or a religious ceremony provided that the religious organisation has 'opted-in'.[25] Whilst some organisations have opted-in, owing to strong religious opposition to same-sex marriage, the Church of England is statutorily banned from performing same-sex weddings. Same-sex couples marrying under the new Act largely have the same rights on separation and divorce as heterosexual couples.[26] Controversially, the Act does not abolish civil partnerships and gives same-sex couples, exclusively, the choice either to marry or to register their relationship under the Civil Partnership Act 2004. Indeed, those currently in a civil partnership may 'convert' their civil partnership into a same-sex marriage, which has the effect of terminating the civil partnership but treats the parties as married from the date they were civil partnered.[27]

England and Wales has now reached a position where two formalised relationship statuses exist: marriage and civil partnership. As will be explored further later, this position has been criticised extensively, particularly when it is noted that England and Wales (alongside Scotland) now permits same-sex couples access to two relationship forms yet limits opposite-sex couples to one. The Court of Appeal recently acknowledged in *Steinfeld & Keidan v Secretary of State for Education* that this position was, at face value, discriminatory to opposite-sex couples.[28] The current framework has now generated renewed debate as to the value and significance of state recognition of a relationship and whether alternatives to marriage should exist.

4. Legal consequences and formalities for entry into marriage

Marriage is a formalised relationship status. Entry into marriage generates extensive legal consequences for the individuals concerned. Historically, these consequences were particularly profound as marriage had the effect of merging the legal personalities of husband and wife under the common law doctrine of unity. Blackstone remarked that the result of this doctrine was that:

> the very being or legal existence of the woman is suspended during the marriage, or at least is incorporated and consolidated into that of the husband; under whose wing, protection, and cover, she performs everything.[29]

Although thought to be a mechanism that protected wives, this doctrine had far-reaching and largely negative consequences on the ability of wives to own real and personal property, enter contracts, or sue in their own right. After a fierce campaign and calls for reform during the Victorian period, the effects of this doctrine were gradually removed and, ultimately, the wife's separate legal existence was recognised in law.[30] Similarly, marital

---

[24] Government Equalities Office, *Equal Civil Marriage: A Consultation*, London, 2012.

[25] See s. 2 of the Marriage (Same Sex Couples) Act 2013.

[26] One key exception, in relation to occupational pension schemes, was recently removed following a successful challenge in the Supreme Court in *Walker v Innospec Ltd and others* [2017] UKSC 47.

[27] See s. 9 of the Marriage (Same Sex Couples) Act 2013.   [28] [2017] EWCA Civ 81.

[29] Blackstone, W. *Commentaries* (1753), I and 442.

[30] See, e.g., the Married Women's Property Acts 1870 and 1882 and also the Law Reform (Married Women and Tortfeasors) Act 1935.

status had important consequences in relation to children. If a child was born to a married couple, the child would be regarded as legitimate, resulting in rights and duties imposed on the parents. Conversely illegitimate children were *filius nullius* and had no relationship status with their parents. These disabilities were removed in a piecemeal manner via the Family Law Reform Acts 1967 and 1987 and, as a result, illegitimacy currently has a very limited role to play in the law relating to children. Nowadays, whilst marriage no longer involves the same extensive consequences as before, it still is an important legal status; so much so that the right to marry is even protected as a human right under Article 12 ECHR, albeit for opposite-sex couples only.[31]

At a general level, marriage today will create kinship links between the married couple and their respective families. Between the couple themselves, the status of marriage will generate legal consequences in relation to the duty to support one another and the ability to apply for financial orders following judicial separation, nullity, or divorce. This shows that although marriage can be viewed as a contract into which the parties freely enter, it simultaneously is an institution that the state regulates through a 'package which the law of the land lays down'.[32]

In terms of formalities for entry into marriage, parties must satisfy publicly mandated rules before their union will be recognised. This point is accepted by the Law Commission when it noted that 'a wedding is a legal transition in which the state has a considerable interest'.[33] However, these rules have their origins in the ecclesiastical jurisdiction and are notoriously complex. Commenting in 1971, the Law Commission noted that the law was 'not understood by members of the public or even by all those who have to administer it'.[34] These issues were recently explored in a Law Commission Scoping Paper, *Getting Married*, but in September 2017 the Government announced that it did not support the undertaking of a full review of this area.[35]

The Marriage Act 1949 (as amended) consolidated the provisions for the creation of a marriage and the law stated here relates largely to opposite-sex marriage (with reference, where relevant, to same-sex marriage). Civil partnership formalities will be dealt with separately, at section 6.2. At a generalised level, formalities can be divided into three distinct categories:

- preliminaries;
- ceremony;
- registration.

It will soon be discovered that the simplicity stops here. Despite the Marriage Act 1949 attempting to clarify the legal framework for the solemnisation of marriages, these ensuing rules are complex and, at times, illogical. What is more, additional complexity arises as different sets of rules apply depending on whether the marriage is a civil marriage or one conducted in accordance with a particular religious denomination. The separate provision for same-sex marriage and restrictions placed on certain religious organisations officiating same-sex ceremonies complicates matters even further.

---

[31] See *R (Baiai and Others) v Secretary of State for the Home Department* [2008] UKHL 53. See also Probert, R. 'The Right to Marry and the Impact of the Human Rights Act 1998' (2003) *International Family Law* 29.

[32] *Radmacher v Granatino* [2010] UKSC 42, at [132] (Lady Hale).

[33] Law Commission, *Getting Married: A Scoping Paper* (2015) 1.

[34] Law Commission, *Report on the Solemnisation of Marriage in England and Wales* (Law Com No. 53, 1971) Annex para 6.

[35] Law Commission, *Getting Married: A Scoping Paper* (2015). See Barton, C. 'Weddings: The Law Commission's "Scoping Paper"' [2016] *Family Law* 719.

4.1 **Preliminaries**

The preliminary requirements for marriage largely concern the giving of notice of an intention to marry and, in certain contexts, the obtaining of third-party consent. The justification behind these rules is historic; forewarning of a pending wedding gives individuals an opportunity to object for a variety of reasons such as either party not having the capacity to marry or that the prospective marriage would be bigamous.

4.1.1 Parental (or institutional) consent if the parties to the marriage are under 18

The consent of third parties is sometimes needed. Parental consent is required for a marriage of individuals who have not yet reached the age of majority, that is, 18 but who are over the age of 16.[36] In this context, 'parental' encompasses any parent with parental responsibility (with both parents needing to consent), a legal guardian, or an institution such as a local authority in possession of parental responsibility. If the consent is refused, the court can override this refusal, if necessary. If the consent holder is absent, inaccessible, or disabled, the Superintendent Registrar can dispense with the consent requirement. Strangely, though, the absence of parental consent does not render the marriage void but may mean that the parties are liable for prosecution for making a false statement.[37]

4.1.2 Publication of the intent to marry (Church of England)

The rites of the Church of England envisage several ways in which an opposite-sex couple can publicise their intent to marry. A traditional route is use of the banns of marriage where the intent to marry is published on three successive Sundays during the church ceremony.[38] This process permits objection to a potential marriage based on any 'just cause or impediment'. The marriage may be permitted under the authority of a common licence, which is the religious equivalent to the Superintendent Registrar's Certificate used in civil ceremonies, discussed in 4.1.3.[39] In addition, there is the Special Licence, which is a very rare power exercised by the Archbishop of Canterbury, who can license a marriage at any time and in any place irrespective of whether the place is consecrated.

It should be noted that same-sex couples cannot publicise an intent to marry using these rules in light of the Church of England ban on the officiation of same-sex ceremonies.

4.1.3 Publication of the intent to marry (marriages other than the Church of England)

In light of the popularity of civil marriage, the majority of ceremonies will be conducted under the following principles that involve parties obtaining a Superintendent Registrar's Certificate and the procedure can be summarised as follows:

- both parties must inform the registrar of their intent to marry;
- both parties must have resided in the district where they intend to marry for seven days;
- both parties must supply requisite details, including name, marital status, occupation, place of residence, and nationality, which is then publicised in the marriage notice book;
- both parties must wait 28 days before the certification can take place;[40]
- if no objections are made then the Superintendent Registrar will issue a certificate that enables the solemnisation of the marriage.[41]

---

[36] Marriage Act 1949, s. 3.   [37] Marriage Act 1949, s. 48(1)(b).   [38] Marriage Act 1949, s. 6.
[39] See ss. 14–15 of the Marriage Act 1949.
[40] Marriage Act 1949, s. 31(1), as amended by the Immigration Act 2014.   [41] Marriage Act 1949, s. 33.

4.2 **Ceremony**

The rules governing ceremony are complex and vary depending on the type of marriage. For a religious marriage in accordance with the rites of the Church of England, the ceremony must take place in an Anglican church, which is often the church in which the banns of marriage are published. Generally, parties must show some connection to the church or the parish. In addition, the ceremony must be solemnised by a clerk in holy orders in the presence of two or more witnesses.[42]

Jews and Quakers have long benefited from extensive freedom when solemnising marriages.[43] Since 1754 Jewish and Quaker marriages have not been subject to legal regulation as to venue or content regarding their marriages, provided the civil preliminaries are complied with and that the marriage is subsequently registered. Other religions, in contrast, have to satisfy different sets rules than those imposed by the Church of England, mentioned earlier.[44] For a valid non-Anglican ceremony, the venue must be certified as a place of 'religious worship' and be a registered building.[45] In addition, an authorised person or registrar of marriages must be present to ensure compliance with the Marriage Act 1949 requirements. Same-sex marriages can be conducted on this basis provided that the religious organisation 'opts in'.[46]

Finally, civil marriages are regulated very differently and generally parties have much greater flexibility in terms of venue and the ceremony itself. Civil marriages can take place in a register office or an 'approved premise'.[47] There needs to be two witnesses, the Superintendent Registrar and the registrar of the district in which the premises are located. The main requirement is that the prescribed words are used. This means that parties must declare they can freely enter the marriage (known as 'declaratory words') and then must recite the requisite legal words expressing an intention to be bound (known as 'contracting words').[48] The required words are as follows:

> Declaratory Words
>
> I do solemnly declare that I know not of any lawful impediment why I...may not be joined in matrimony to . . .
>
> Contracting Words
>
> I call upon these persons here present to witness that I . . . do take thee . . . to be my lawfully wedded wife [or husband].

A key distinguishing feature of civil marriage is that it must be secular and involve no religious elements. Naturally, parties are free to have a religious ceremony or blessing after the register office ceremony but this, technically, has no legal effect.

4.3 **Registration**

The final stage for all marriages is registration and this requirement applies irrespective of religious denomination or whether the ceremony is opposite-sex or same-sex.[49] This

---

[42] Marriage Act 1949, s. 22.

[43] Marriage Act 1949, s. 47. Note that Jews and Quakers are still required to satisfy the civil marriage preliminaries.

[44] Same-sex marriages can be conducted by Jews and Quakers provided they opt into the statutory scheme (Marriage (Same Sex Couples) Act 2013, s. 5).   [45] Marriage Act 1949, ss. 41–2.

[46] Section 4 and Sch 1 of the Marriage (Same Sex Couples) Act 2013.   [47] Marriage Act 1949, s. 26.

[48] Marriage Act 1949, s. 45(1), as amended by the Marriage Ceremony (Prescribed Words) Act 1996.

[49] Marriage Act 1949, s. 53.

requirement underlines the fact that marriage is a public status. The Registrar General maintains an index of marriages and any person can search this for proof of a particular marriage.[50]

4.4 **Failure to comply with formalities**

The previous section has identified a significant amount of requirements that need to be satisfied before a marriage can be validly created. Unsurprisingly, a large body of case law has developed dealing with the consequences of individuals failing to meet these requirements. The following section will analyse the applicable legal principles.

It should be noted from the outset that a distinction is drawn between void and voidable marriages and this is further explored in 5.1. The grounds for void marriages are listed in s. 11 of the Matrimonial Causes Act 1973 and these invalidating factors affect marriages where there is a strong state interest in preventing their formation (e.g., marriages between a parent and child or marriages that are bigamous). As a result, such marriages can be challenged by any interested party and are void *ab intio*. In contrast, s. 12 of that Act also covers voidable marriages where there is a lesser state interest in their regulation and the defects are more personal to the parties themselves (e.g., an inability of either party to consummate the marriage). These marriages are treated as subsisting until one party seeks an annulment.

For present purposes, the following section will focus only on one statutory provision; namely s. 11(a)(iii) of the Matrimonial Causes Act 1973 that results in a void marriage 'where the parties have intermarried in disregard of certain requirements as to the formation of marriage'. The other void grounds, that are unrelated to marriage formalities, will be analysed separately in 5.2.

In addition to a void marriage for disregard of marriage formalities, two other options are available to the court that are not found in the statutory framework. These are a non-marriage (or non-existent marriage) and a presumed marriage. The judicial interpretation of these grounds, and also the relationship between them, lend support to the view that the area of marriage formalities is undoubtedly ripe for reform.

Thus, in summary, the three main outcomes for failure to comply with marriage formalities are:

- void marriage for disregard of marriage formalities under the Matrimonial Causes Act 1973, s. 11(a)(iii);
- non-Marriage/non-existent marriage;
- presumed marriage.

4.4.1 **Void marriage for disregard of marriage formalities under the Matrimonial Causes Act 1973, s. 11(a)(iii)**

One basis for a void marriage is when the parties 'knowingly and wilfully intermarry' in disregard of formal requirements.[51] This original terminology comes from the earlier Marriage Act 1823. That Act was passed in response to individuals marrying but, often inadvertently, failing to comply with some of the formalities laid down in the earlier Marriage Act 1753.[52] As a result of this terminology, only certain forms of non-compliance will now generate a void marriage for disregard of formalities and this has generated difficulties

---

[50] Marriage Act 1949, s. 65.

[51] The term 'intermarry' in this context has a meaning synonymous with 'marry'.

[52] Parker, S. 'The Marriage Act 1753: A Case Study in Family Law-Making' (1987) 1 *International Journal of Law Policy and the Family* 133.

for the courts in determining the validity of certain ceremonies. Added complexity arises when it is appreciated that s. 11(a)(iii) of the Matrimonial Causes Act 1973 needs to be read in conjunction with the Marriage Act 1949, as amended, as that statute governs the rules relating to the solemnisation and registration of marriages.

 Key Legislation 1: Marriage Act 1949, s. 49

Section 49 of the Marriage Act 1949 covers void civil marriages.[53]

> If any persons knowingly and wilfully intermarry under the provisions of this Part of this Act:
>
> (a) without having given due notice of marriage to the superintendent registrar;
> (b) without a certificate for marriage having been duly issued, in respect of each of the persons to be married, by the superintendent registrar to whom notice of marriage was given;
> (c)/(d) . . .
> (e) in any place other than the church, chapel, registered building, office or other place specified in the notices of marriage and certificates of the superintendent registrar;
>   . . .
> (f) in the case of a marriage in a registered building (not being a marriage in the presence of an authorised person), in the absence of a registrar of the registration district in which the registered building is situated;
> (g) in the case of a marriage in the office of a superintendent registrar, in the absence of the superintendent registrar or of a registrar of the registration district of that superintendent registrar;
>   the marriage shall be void.

Section 49 provides a list of defects that will render the marriage void provided the parties knowingly and wilfully intermarry. However, the crucial issue is how the courts determine the meaning of 'knowing and wilful' in this context.

 Key Case 1: *Gereis v Yagoub* [1997] 1 FLR 854

The petitioner and respondent married in a Coptic Christian Orthodox church. The ceremony was conducted by a priest that did not possess a licence to officiate marriages and took place in a church that was unlicensed. In addition, the parties failed to give notice of their intent to marry to the Superintendent Registrar. The priest advised the parties that they should undertake a civil marriage but no ceremony was ever carried out. Following the breakdown of the relationship, the petitioner sought a decree of nullity.

Judge Aglionby, sitting in the Family Division of the High Court, held that marriages would be void under s. 49 of Marriage Act 1949 where no notice was given to the Superintendent Registrar. As the ceremony 'bore the hallmarks of an ordinary Christian marriage', the only obstacle to validity was the parties' non-compliance with the Marriage Act 1949.[54] In light of the failure to give notice of an intent to marry, Judge Aglionby found that the parties had knowingly and wilfully intermarried in disregard of formal requirements.

---

[53] For similar provision but in relation to the rites of the Church of England, see s. 25 of the Marriage Act 1949.
[54] [1997] 1 FLR 854, 858.

4.4.2 Non-marriage

Operating alongside a void marriage for disregard of marriage formalities is the concept of non-marriage or non-existent marriage. Without possessing a precise definition, a non-marriage may arise when there has been manifold non-compliance with the Marriage Acts. This may occur where the non-compliance is so substantial that the ceremony in no way purports to comply with the Act. To illustrate this, take the example of the fictional marriage between Romeo and Juliet in Shakespeare's famous play.[55] When performed, it cannot be said that the actor and actress created a valid marriage as there clearly has been no compliance with legal formalities. Nevertheless, the actor and actress cannot technically obtain a void marriage as that is *only* permitted where there is 'knowing and wilful' failure to comply with marriage formalities. Thus, without an express statutory provision that can invalidate this theatrical ceremony, the only options would be either a valid marriage or non-marriage. As the former would be ridiculous, given the marriage took place within a play and the ceremony never purported to be a genuine marriage, the courts have adopted the more sensible, latter option.

Leaving aside the extreme example of marriage in a play, non-marriage has been deployed in instances where parties go through ceremonies that have some of the trappings or 'hallmarks' of a marriage ceremony but are, nevertheless, non-compliant with the law. In these scenarios, it can be asked whether the defects here should be overlooked or, alternatively, whether they are so fundamental that they render the ceremony a non-marriage. Problematically, following *Gereis v Yagoub*, the search for the hallmarks of marriage often involved judges drawing comparisons to Christian marriage. As Probert[56] has identified, this may explain why non-Christian ceremonies had a greater likelihood of being rendered non-marriages, as seen in *Chief Adjudication Officer v Bath* (concerning a ceremony in a Sikh temple),[57] *A-M v A-M* (an Islamic ceremony in a private flat),[58] and *Gandhi v Patel* (a Hindu marriage by a Brahmin priest in a London restaurant).[59]

The approach taken by the courts here is highly fact-specific. However, it should be noted that the consequences of a finding of non-marriage are particularly far-reaching, as it will mean that the parties cannot apply for financial orders under the Matrimonial Causes Act 1973 (unlike parties to a void marriage).

 Key Case 2: *Hudson v Leigh* [2009] EWHC 1306

A Christian ceremony took place in South Africa. The wife was a 'devout Christian' and the husband was an 'atheist Jew'.[60] It was decided by the parties that a religious ceremony would take place in South Africa but that it would not create a valid marriage as specific passages from the wedding service were omitted. The parties intended to return to the UK to undertake a civil marriage at a later date. Upon their return, the relationship broke down prior to the civil ceremony. The issue was the validity of the South African ceremony. It was contended by the wife that the ceremony had produced either a valid marriage or, in the alternative, a void marriage, both of which, would permit an application for financial orders under Part II of the Matrimonial Causes Act 1973. The husband argued that the ceremony produced a non-marriage, thereby barring the wife from her right to apply for such orders.

---

[55] See Probert, R. 'When are we married? Void, non-existent and presumed marriages' (2002) 22 *Legal Studies* 398 and Probert, R. 'The Evolving Concept of Non-Marriage' (2013) 25 *Child and Family Law Quarterly* 315.

[56] Probert, R. 'When are we married? Void, non-existent and presumed marriages' (2002) 22 *Legal Studies* 398, 403. See, further, Gaffney-Rhys, R. 'Hudson v Leigh—the Concept of Non-Marriage' (2010) 22 *Child and Family Law Quarterly* 351.   [57] [2000] 1 FLR 8.

[58] [2001] 2 FLR 6.   [59] [2001] 1 FLR 603.   [60] [2009] EWHC 1306, at [8] (Bodey J).

Bodey J in the High Court held that the South Africa ceremony was a non-marriage. Refusing to give a definition or test to apply when determining whether a ceremony was a non-marriage, Bodey J provided four factors that the court could take into account:

(a) whether the ceremony or event set out or purported to be a lawful marriage;
(b) whether it bore all or enough of the hallmarks of marriage;
(c) whether the three key participants (most especially the officiating official) believed, intended and understood the ceremony as giving rise to the status of lawful marriage; and
(d) the reasonable perceptions, understandings and beliefs of those in attendance.

It is important to note that Bodey J omitted reference to 'Christian' when discussing the hallmarks of marriage. Using these factors, he found that the ceremony had fundamentally failed to create a valid marriage and instead should be recognised as a non-marriage. In particular, he was influenced by the fact that the celebrant and both of the parties intended that the ceremony 'should positively not create the status of marriage and were purposely responsible for omissions and deficiencies to that end'.[61]

The principles of *Hudson v Leigh* have now been applied in subsequent cases yet there still remains uncertainty as to what defects necessitate a finding of non-marriage. What appears to be emerging is a preference for compliance with objective Marriage Act 1949 formalities and a downplaying of the subjective intentions of the parties, which was identified as a factor for consideration in *Hudson v Leigh*.[62] In *Dukali v Lamrani*[63] the parties married in the Moroccan Consulate, which was not an approved premise, and, in addition, the parties had also failed to give notice of their intent to marry. In light of the manifold non-compliance with English law, it was found that it was a non-marriage, irrespective of the wife's firm belief she had contracted 'a proper civil marriage in the fullest sense'.[64] Similarly, in *El Gamal v Al Maktoum* there was an Islamic wedding ceremony in a flat, which failed to comply with the Marriage Act 1949.[65] Despite the belief of the wife that she had entered into a marriage, this was not enough for the court to overlook the extensive non-compliance with marriage formalities.

Further complexity arises where intention has been used to render a marriage that, at face value, appears to be valid, a non-marriage. In *Galloway v Goldstein*,[66] the parties married in America. The parties returned to England and had a larger, second ceremony at a hotel for friends and family. After the first marriage in America was terminated by divorce, the High Court deemed the second marriage to be a non-marriage as it was as much a charade as the ceremony in South Africa was in *Hudson v Leigh*. Here it is arguable that party intention played a crucial role in rendering a marriage purportedly complying with marriage formalities a non-marriage, as the parties must have realised that the second ceremony had no legal validity because the parties were already married. These cases, again, highlight the lack of logic inherent in the Marriage Act 1949 and the need for a comprehensive overhaul of marriage formalities.

---

[61] [2009] EWHC 1306 [71] (Bodey J).

[62] See, generally, Bevan, C. 'The Role of Intention in Non-Marriage Cases post *Hudson v Leigh*' (2013) *Child and Family Law Quarterly* 80.   [63] [2012] EWHC 1748.

[64] [2012] EWHC 1748, at [15].   [65] [2011] EWHC B27 (Fam).

[66] [2012] EWHC 60. See also *Asaad v Kurter* [2013] EWHC 3852 (Fam) where intention played a slightly more prominent role than in the aforementioned cases.

4.4.3. Presumed marriage

A finding of non-marriage has far-reaching consequences. This fact has led the courts to occasionally save what would otherwise be a non-marriage by invoking the presumption of marriage.[67] There are two presumptions that apply yet both lack coherence as to when they operate. First, the parties may be presumed married, despite the absence of evidence of a ceremony, where they have lived together for a period of time and are reputed to be married. Second, where a ceremony has taken place and the parties then subsequently live together as husband and wife, this will raise a presumption that the ceremony complied with marriage formalities. As the following case will illustrate there have been some suspect applications of these principles in the case law.

Key Case 3: A-M v A-M [2001] 2 FLR 6

The couple underwent an Islamic ceremony in a flat in London. The husband was already married and the marriage was polygamous. A few years later, the husband sought to recognise the wife. He was told to obtain a divorce (a talaq) in a country that permitted polygamy and then to remarry the wife. The couple went to Sharjah but the judge refused to accept the talaq. The wife did not know this. The couple lived together as husband and wife for 20 years and had two children together. The relationship broke down and the wife petitioned for divorce. The issue was whether there was a valid marriage ceremony.

Hughes J, sitting in the High Court, found that the ceremony that had taken place in the London flat had not created a valid marriage under English law as 'it in no sense purported to be effected according to the Marriage Acts, which provide for the only way of marrying in England'.[68] Nevertheless, the wife was able to rely on the presumption of marriage in light of the parties' lengthy cohabitation and their reputation as husband and wife. This meant that a valid polygamous marriage was *presumed* to have been created in an Islamic country. Furthermore, as there was a possibility that the wife could not have been physically present at the ceremony, the court presumed that the wife may have contracted an Islamic marriage by proxy through giving her husband a power of attorney.

This case clearly illustrates the court wishing to protect the position of a vulnerable party. Another example of this tendency can be seen in *Chief Adjudication Officer v Bath* where a young couple married in 1956 in a Sikh temple and lived together as husband and wife for 37 years.[69] After the husband's death, Mrs Bath was refused a widow's pension on the basis that there was not a valid marriage as the Sikh temple was not registered at the time of the ceremony. Ultimately, the presumption of marriage was used to grant Mrs Bath pension entitlement in light of the parties' lengthy period of cohabitation.

Whilst protection of a vulnerable party is a laudable aim, Probert has challenged the reasoning of the court in *A-M v A-M* arguing that the presumption has been used in an unprincipled, incoherent manner and, whilst remaining part of the law, the presumption should have a 'limited role to play in a modern bureaucratic society'.[70]

Debate 1: Should we Overhaul the Formalities for Entry into Marriage?

Marriage has long been recognised and supported by the state as the preferred family form as many believe that it offers stability and enhances the development of dependent

---

[67] See, generally, Borkowski, A. 'The Presumption of Marriage' (2002) 14 *Child and Family Law Quarterly* 251.

[68] [2001] 2 FLR 6, 24.   [69] [2000] 1 FLR 8. See also *Pazpena de Vire v Pazpena de Vire* [2001] 1 FLR 460.

[70] Probert, R. 'When are we married? Void, non-existent and presumed marriages' (2002) 22 *Legal Studies* 398, 418.

children.[71] Whilst family law regulates, albeit to a lesser extent, a myriad of other family forms, marriage has an important heritage and status within society that other relationships simply do not possess.

Therefore it is clear that the state has a clear interest in regulating the formalities for entry into marriage. Poulter has argued that this interest involves ensuring that 'the basic requirements for a valid marriage are complied with in terms of capacity and consent, and preventing fraud and abuse'.[72] But how extensive should this regulation be? Should distinctions as to formalities be drawn, as is currently the case, between secular civil marriage and religious marriages? More importantly, are some formalities more essential than others?

As has been demonstrated, the formalities for marriage are complex, misunderstood, and prone to cause injustice. This has been the case for quite some time. In 1973, a Law Commission Working Party noted that marriage law lacked 'simplicity and intelligibility'.[73] Furthermore, there was 'a bewildering diversity in the consequences of a failure properly to comply with the rules'.[74] These criticisms were echoed in 2002 when the then government issued proposals to streamline and simplify the celebration and registration of marriages.[75] Ultimately, and owing to the complexities involved, no action was taken. This prompts important questions as to whether marriage formalities should be placed back on the reform agenda.

A radical approach, short of the even more controversial option of abolishing marriage, is to state that only civil marriages would be recognised in law.[76] This approach would avoid the complexity of the different rules applying to different religious groups. It would mean that religious ceremonies would have no legal effect and that individuals would have to follow-up a religious ceremony with a secular civil marriage or vice-versa. Channeling marriages through one standardised process would provide simplicity and uniform treatment across religions but is highly unlikely to occur owing to opposition from religious organisations that have long benefited from the ability to solemnise marriages.

A variant of recognising only civil marriage is advanced by Peter Edge, who argues that the state should no longer have any role in marriage and its only role should be in the administration of civil partnerships for all couples.[77] This proposal for universal civil partnerships would enable secular rules determined by the state to govern entry to a relationship. It would also mean that the problematic historical and religious connotations and expectations of marriage would no longer colour the formal expression of adult relationships.

Another radical approach advanced by John Eekelaar focuses on how the beliefs and intentions of the parties should have real significance if we accept that marriage is a major event in the lives of the parties.[78] On that basis 'it should not matter what type of ceremony accompanies the formation of marriage if it fulfills those requirements for the parties'.[79]

---

[71] See, generally, Shanley, M.L. *Just Marriage* (OUP, 2004).

[72] Poulter, S. *English Law and Ethnic Minority Customs* (Butterworths, 1986) 33.

[73] Law Commission, *Report on Solemnisation of Marriage in England and Wales* (Law Com No. 53, 1973) Annex Para 6.

[74] Law Commission, *Report on Solemnisation of Marriage in England and Wales* (Law Com No. 53, 1973) Annex Para 6.

[75] GRO, *Civil Registration: Vital Change—Birth, Marriage and Death Registration in the Twenty-First Century* (Cm 5355, 2002).

[76] And this idea has been mooted by academics, see Clive E. 'Marriage: An Unnecessary Legal Concept?' in J. Eekelaar and S. Katz, *Marriage and Cohabitation in Contemporary Societies* (Butterworths, 1981) and Fineman, M.A. 'Why Marriage?' (2001) 9 *Virginia Journal of Social Policy and the Law* 239.

[77] Edge, P.W. 'Let's Talk about a Divorce: Religious and Legal Weddings' in J. Miles, P. Mody, and R. Probert, *Marriage Rites and Rights* (Hart Publishing, 2015) 255.

[78] Eekelaar, J. 'Marriage: A Modest Proposal' [2013] *Family Law* 83.

[79] Eekelaar, J. 'Marriage: A Modest Proposal' [2013] *Family Law* 83, 84.

This would mean that provided the parties satisfy preliminaries such as the giving of notice, there would be extensive flexibility as to the form and venue of the ceremony. This echoes the sentiment of the 2002 proposals, noted earlier, that required all couples to give notice of their intention to marry but, once that was completed, gave them flexibility as to the location of the ceremony.[80]

With a radical overhaul of marriage formalities unlikely, a final approach would be for the existing principles to be modified and rationalised. Here, more modest change could happen. For example, one way of minimising the damaging impact of a finding of non-marriage for the parties would be to limit its application to certain factual scenarios. As Probert has argued, non-marriage should only apply where there is manifest non-compliance with the Marriage Act 1949. Where there is disregard of marriage formalities that falls short of being knowing and wilful, the marriage should be deemed valid provided the parties have given notice of intent to marry or married in the correct location. Sadly, following the production in 2015 of a detailed Scoping Paper on marriage law by the Law Commission, the Government responded in September 2017 stating that it did not support a full review of this area at this point in time.

5. Nullity

A failure to comply with marriage formalities under s. 11(a)(iii) of the Matrimonial Causes Act 1973 is not the only basis on which a marriage can be rendered void. As noted earlier at 4.4, other void grounds exist under s. 11 of that Act and these operate alongside the voidable grounds in s. 12. Cumulatively, both grounds constitute the law of nullity in England and Wales and illustrate the principle that a decree of nullity can be sought on the basis that a marriage is defective from its very inception.

Nullity has existed for centuries and was developed as a response to the fact that divorce was historically not permitted in England and Wales. As marriage was a Holy Estate that, according to the Bible, 'no man could put asunder', many marriages existed until one party died. Faced with unhappy or unsuitable marriages, ecclesiastical lawyers were called upon to devise ways of circumventing the prohibition on divorce. They developed the concept of *divorce a vinculo matrimonii* based on the marriage possessing one or more defects present at its inception thereby rendering it subject to challenge. It was not divorce in the modern sense of the word though. The courts, as Baker noted, 'could not break the chains, but they could declare that the chains were never there'.[81] The most famous historical example of nullity was Henry VIII's 'divorce' from Catherine of Aragon in order for him to marry his second wife, Anne Boleyn. Often mistakenly described as a divorce, the process used to enable the king to remarry was, in fact, nullity.

5.1 The legal consequences of nullity

The law distinguishes between two types of defective marriages; namely, void and voidable. In *De Reneville v De Reneville*, Lord Greene MR stated:

> a void marriage is one that will be regarded by every court in any case in which the existence
> of the marriage is in issue as never having taken place and can be so treated by both parties
> to it without the necessity of any decree annulling it: a voidable marriage is one that will be

---

[80] See Barton, C. 'White Paper Weddings—The Beginnings, Muddles and Ends of Wedlock' [2002] *Family Law* 431.   [81] Baker, J. *Introduction to Legal History* (4th edn, Butterworths, 2002) 491.

regarded by every court as a valid subsisting marriage until a decree annulling it has been pronounced by a court of competent jurisdiction.[82]

Whereas a void marriage is deemed to have never existed, a voidable marriage is considered a valid and subsisting marriage until an application is made by one of the parties to set it aside. This traditional distinction still remains today but, in effect, the legal consequences for both are relatively similar. For example, children from a void marriage are treated as their parents' legitimate issue if, at the time of conception or marriage, both or either of the parents had a reasonable belief that the marriage was valid.[83] One key point to note is that there is no prohibition on bringing a nullity petition within the first year of marriage as is the case for divorce stipulated in s. 3 of the Matrimonial Causes Act 1973.[84]

5.2 **Void marriages**

A void marriage possesses a fundamental defect and, as a result, is void *ab initio*. These marriages are governed by s. 11 of the Matrimonial Causes Act 1973. As will be shown below, the defects listed in s. 11 are serious and there is a much stronger state interest in policing these types of union than that present in relation to voidable marriages. In light of their severity, there is technically no need for a court order to declare that the marriage is void but, in reality, parties to such a marriage are advised to obtain one in order to seek financial orders and remarry without the fear of that subsequent union being deemed bigamous. Any interested party can challenge the validity of these marriages whether during the lifetime of the spouses or after their deaths. Unlike voidable marriages, there are also no procedural bars to bringing an application for annulment. The following section will explore the various void grounds under s. 11 of the Matrimonial Causes Act 1973.

 Key Legislation 2: Matrimonial Causes Act 1973, s. 11

Grounds on which a marriage is void.

A marriage celebrated after 31st July 1971 shall be void on the following grounds only, that is to say—

(a) that it is not a valid marriage under the provisions of the Marriage Acts 1949 to 1986 (that is to say where—
   (i) the parties are within the prohibited degrees of relationship;
   (ii) either party is under the age of sixteen; or
   (iii) the parties have intermarried in disregard of certain requirements as to the formation of marriage);
(b) that at the time of the marriage either party was already lawfully married or a civil partner;
(c) . . . [85]
(d) in the case of a polygamous marriage entered into outside England and Wales, that either party was at the time of the marriage domiciled in England and Wales.

For the purposes of paragraph (d) of this subsection a marriage is not polygamous if at its inception neither party has any spouse additional to the other.

---

[82] [1948] P. 100, 111.

[83] Legitimacy Act 1976, s. 1(1). Similarly, claims for reasonable provision from the estate of a deceased individual extend to persons subject to a void marriage entered into in good faith under s. 1(1)(a) of the Inheritance (Provision for Family and Dependants) Act 1975.   [84] See Chapter 3 on divorce.

[85] Section 11(c) which required that both parties must be respectively male and female was repealed following the passage of the Marriage (Same Sex Couples) Act 2013.

5.2.1 The parties are within the prohibited degrees—Matrimonial Causes Act 1973, s. 11(a)(i)

Marriage between certain categories of individual is prohibited. The prohibited degrees are a historic classification of relationships and can be divided into two categories, as stated in Schedule 1 of the Marriage Act 1949 and the Marriage (Prohibited Degrees of Relationship) Act 1986; namely, consanguinity (relationships linked through blood) or affinity (relationships created through marriage).

For relationships of consanguinity, a person is prohibited from marrying either of their parents, their sibling, child, grandchild, aunt, uncle, niece, or nephew.[86] The justifications behind prohibiting marriages between these individuals focus either on societal values or biological reasons. For the former, marriages between those who are related by blood are generally viewed as religiously and morally reprehensible. For the latter, these prohibitions prevent marriage, and potentially procreation, between parties that are genetically inter-linked. Interestingly, it should be noted that cousin marriage does not fall within these prohibitions.[87]

Marriages between in-laws, or relationships created via marriage, were historically extensively prohibited. The rationales behind prohibition centred on fears that boundaries within the family unit would become blurred and that any children of the marriage would find the relationship structures confusing. Now, following *B and L v UK*,[88] the only prohibition existing is that a parent and step-child cannot intermarry unless it can be shown that both are over 21 years old and that the step-child was never a 'child of the family' before reaching the age of 18.

5.2.2 Marriage where either party is under the age of 16—Matrimonial Causes Act 1973 s. 11(a)(ii)

Although marriages between children were historically valid, the modern position is that a void marriage will be created where either party is under the age of 16. The prohibition is based on the fact that child marriages are more likely to be unstable, especially those that produce children, and the parties may not necessarily understand the consequences stemming from marriage. A much stronger justification relates to sexual activity and the fact that criminal law prohibits sexual intercourse with a child under the age of 16. As noted earlier in 4.1.1, where one of the parties is over the age of 16 but under the age of 18, they will require the consent of specific individuals to marry.

5.2.3 Disregard of marriage formalities—Matrimonial Causes Act 1973 s. 11(a)(iii)

Here, the Matrimonial Causes Act 1973 links back to the Marriage Act 1949 and addresses the failure of parties to observe specific marriage formalities. These principles spanning non-marriage, presumed marriage, and void marriage on the basis of knowing and wilful failure to comply with formalities were covered earlier in 4.4.1–4.4.3.

5.2.4 Either party was already lawfully married or a civil partner—Matrimonial Causes Act 1973, s. 11(b)

An individual may not have more than one spouse or civil partner at any one time. If a party who is already married enters into a subsequent marriage, without the termination of the first marriage through death, annulment, or divorce, the subsequent marriage will be rendered void.[89] This will continue to be treated as void even if after the second

---

[86] These prohibitions also extend to certain relationships created through adoption.
[87] See Deech, R. 'Cousin Marriage' [2010] *Family Law* 619.   [88] [2006] 1 FLR 35.
[89] See Barton, C. 'Bigamy and Marriage—Horse and Carriage?' [2004] *Family Law* 517.

marriage ceremony, the spouse from the first marriage dies. The person entering the subsequent marriage may also have committed the criminal offence of bigamy.[90]

5.2.5 Polygamous whilst domiciled in England and Wales—Matrimonial Causes Act 1973, s. 11(d)

The final void ground invalidates marriages that are polygamous where certain conditions are met. This is a complex area engaging private international law as England and Wales recognises polygamous marriages celebrated in jurisdictions where that practice is permitted and the parties have the capacity to contract such a marriage (see 2.4.2, in Chapter 15). Validity depends on whether the marriage was *potentially* polygamous; that is, where the husband marries a first wife but is open to marry another and can do so under the law of his domicile, or *actually* polygamous, where the husband has, in fact, married more than one wife. A potentially polygamous marriage contracted outside of England and Wales but when either party is domiciled in England and Wales will be deemed valid. If a second marriage is then celebrated creating an actually polygamous marriage, the first marriage will remain valid whilst the second will be void. Conversely, if either party attempts to contract a polygamous marriage in England and Wales whilst domiciled here, the likely result would be either a void marriage or a non-marriage, discussed earlier at 4.4.2.

5.3 Voidable marriages

Some defects are not so fundamental that they render a marriage void. These grounds are stated in s. 12 of the Matrimonial Causes Act 1973. They generate a voidable marriage meaning that, until challenged by one of the parties, the marriage exists in law and is valid. As there is less state interest in the regulation of these types of marriages, only the parties to the marriage can challenge its validity. Furthermore, and unlike void marriages, there are procedural barriers to the bringing of applications for voidable marriages. In addition, it should be noted that some of these defects can be relied on both by the petitioner and respondent, whereas others can only be asserted by the petitioner against the respondent. The following section will explore the grounds for voidable marriages.

5.3.1 Incapacity of either party to consummate—s. 12(1)(a) of the Matrimonial Causes Act 1973

Before analysing the meaning of incapacity, the definition of consummation must be explored. Consummation is defined in *D v A* as 'ordinary and complete intercourse' between a male and a female.[91] It must involve penetration of the vagina by the penis for a reasonable length of time. Ejaculation or orgasm is not necessary.[92] Similarly, following *Baxter v Baxter*, the insistence on the use of contraceptives will not prevent the act of consummation.[93] If no intercourse has taken place but the wife gives birth to a child via artificial insemination that will not be proof of consummation.[94] Crucially, consummation must take place after the parties marry; the fact that the parties had sexual intercourse prior to marriage will not evidence consummation.[95] In relation to alleging incapacity, it is important to note that either party can petition for incapacity and must prove the incapacity alleged. This may involve the petitioner relying on his or her own incapacity, or alternatively an assertion of incapacity being made against the respondent.

In *S v S*, Karminski J stated that 'the true test of incapacity is the practical impossibility of consummation'.[96] In practice, this impossibility has been evidenced on the basis of

---

[90] See Perjury Act 1911, s. 3 and Offences Against the Person Act 1861, s. 57.   [91] (1845) 163 ER 1039.
[92] *R v R (otherwise F)* [1952] 1 All ER 1194.   [93] *Baxter v Baxter* [1948] AC 274.
[94] *Clarke v Clarke* [1943] 2 All ER 540.   [95] *Ford v Ford* [1987] Fam Law 232.   [96] [1956] P. 1, 11.

either a permanent, incurable physical condition or, alternatively, an 'invincible repugnance'. For the former, medical evidence will be used to assess whether the condition is incurable and it will be deemed as such if undergoing treatment would be dangerous. For the latter, incapacity can also be established if there was 'such a paralysis and distortion of will as to prevent the victim thereof from engaging in the act of consummation'.[97] This means that lack of attraction to the other spouse or mere unwillingness is not enough. As Karminski LJ stated in *Singh v Singh*, where a young Sikh girl had never seen her husband and, when she did, refused to engage in sexual activity, there must be 'a psychiatric or sexual aversion'.[98]

The position in relation to same-sex spouses is noteworthy. Consummation has been interpreted in a heterosexual manner and thus same-sex spouses and civil partners cannot petition for nullity on this basis.[99] It could be argued that these omissions stem from unwillingness, or perhaps inability, to define sexual intercourse between same-sex couples.[100]

5.3.2 Wilful refusal of the respondent to consummate—s. 12(1)(b) of the Matrimonial Causes Act 1973

A petitioner is unable to rely on his or her own wilful refusal to consummate. According to *Horton v Horton*, wilful refusal to consummate is comprised of two elements; namely, 'a settled and definite decision come to without just excuse'.[101]

A settled and definite decision not to consummate requires more than a loss of ardour.[102] It is a resolved decision and often involves severing contact with the other spouse. In addition, the petition will be refused if the respondent can point to a just excuse for not consummating the marriage. In *Ford v Ford*, the wife alleged wilful refusal on the part of her husband for him refusing to consummate whilst he was serving a prison sentence.[103] The fact that sexual activity constituted a violation of prison rules provided the husband a just excuse. However, after his release from prison, the husband's refusal to consummate was no longer covered by the former just excuse and was found to constitute wilful refusal.

A modified version of this test has been used for certain religious marriages. For example, in *Kaur v Singh*, a husband failed to organise a religious ceremony after a civil ceremony (as is common in Sikh marriages) and the wife petitioned for nullity.[104] The Court treated the husband's failure to do this as evidence tantamount to *his own* wilful refusal and, in addition, that he did not have a just excuse to act in that particular way.

5.3.3 Either party did not validly consent—s. 12(1)(c) of the Matrimonial Causes Act 1973

This ground is comprised of different strands all relating to whether there was genuine consent to marry.

Duress: Entry into marriage as a result of fear or threat may render such marriage voidable. Historically, threats to 'life, limb and liberty' readily amounted to duress. Thus, in *Scott v Sebright*, duress was clearly apparent after the bride was blackmailed, threatened with bankruptcy, told her name would be besmirched in London high society, and threatened with murder immediately before the ceremony.[105] Similarly, in *Szechter v Szechter*, duress was established when a man married a woman in order for her to escape squalid

---

[97] *G v G* [1924] AC 349, 367.   [98] [1971] P. 226.

[99] See *Clarkson v Clarkson* (1930) 143 LT 775 and *Dennis v Dennis* [1955] P. 153. See also the Matrimonial Causes Act 1973, s. 1(6).

[100] See Crompton, L. 'Where's the Sex in Same-Sex Marriage' [2013] 43 *Family Law* 564 and Herring, J. 'Why Marriage Needs to be Less Sexy' in J. Miles, P. Mody, and R. Probert, *Marriage Rites and Rights* (Hart Publishing, 2015).   [101] [1947] 2 All ER 871.

[102] *Potter v Potter* (1975) Fam. 161.   [103] [1987] Fam Law 232.   [104] [1972] 1 WLR 105.

[105] (1886) 12 PD 21.

prison conditions in Poland and threats of re-imprisonment after she was released.[106] Crucially, as illustrated in *Szechter*, there is no requirement that the duress must come only from the other spouse.

Following *Hirani v Hirani,* it was held that more subtle pressures that fell short of a threat to life, limb, or liberty could constitute duress.[107] Thus, in *Hirani*, a Hindu woman underwent a marriage after being told that failure to do so would result in her being ostracised by her community and thrown out of the family home. The Court determined that the test for duress was whether 'the threats, pressure, or whatever it is, is such as to destroy the reality of consent and overbears the will of the individual'.[108] This case showed a movement away from an objective analysis of the threat itself to instead a more subjective analysis of the impact such threat had on the ability to consent of the specific individual concerned.

It is important to note that parties who are forced into marriage in light of physical, sexual, or psychological pressure no longer have to exclusively rely on duress. The Forced Marriage (Civil Protection) Act 2007 now provides civil law protection to actual or potential victims of forced marriages.[109] Under that Act the court is given extensive powers, through the medium of a Forced Marriage Protection Order, to prohibit removal of a potential victim from the UK for the purpose of marrying them overseas (see Chapter 7). Similarly, it can be used to prevent individuals named in the order from contacting the potential victim. It should be noted that, unlike arranged marriages that are permissible in England and Wales, forced marriages are strongly prohibited as they constitute 'a form of domestic violence that dehumanises people by denying them their right to choose how to live their lives'.[110]

Mistake: Certain mistakes affect the consent to marry. Only two forms of mistake are permitted; namely, mistakes as to the identity of the other person or mistakes as to the ceremony.

For identity, it is important that the mistake relates to the individual's identity rather than his or her attributes. For example, in *C v C*, a woman married a man who held himself out as a famous and wealthy Australian boxer.[111] The wife later discovered this man was not who she thought he was but she was unable to petition on the basis of mistake as she was mistaken as to his attributes and not his true identity.

A mistake as to ceremony is also permissible and may involve being duped into attending an informal family gathering that, in fact, is a marriage ceremony.[112] For example, in *Mehta v Mehta*, mistake was established when a woman believed she was undergoing a ceremony of conversion to Hinduism but, in reality, it involved a marriage ceremony.[113]

Unsoundness of Mind (also known as Lack of Capacity) or Otherwise: Lack of consent can also be established if there is unsoundness of mind at the time of marriage. This must involve a failure to comprehend or understand the significance of marriage and its incumbent responsibilities.[114] For example, in *Sheffield City Council v E* the court had to determine whether an individual with severe disabilities should marry a man who possessed a history of sexual violence. Munby J stated that the individual must not simply understand the ceremony of marriage but must also comprehend the duties and responsibilities that attach to marriage. Nevertheless, he went on to note:

---

[106] [1971] 2 WLR 170. See McClean, D. and Hayes, M. 'Szechter v Szechter: But I Didn't Really Want to Get Married' in S Gilmore *et al Landmark Cases in Family Law* (Hart Publishing, 2011).

[107] [1983] 4 FLR 232.   [108] [1983] 4 FLR 232, 234.

[109] For an overview of the Act, see Vallance-Webb, G. 'Forced Marriage: A Yielding of the Lips Not the Mind [2008] *Family Law* 565 and Anitha, S. and Gill, A. 'Coercion, Consent and the Forced Marriage Debate in the UK (2009) 17 *Feminist Legal Studies* 165.

[110] *Re K; A Local Authority v N and others* [2005] EWHC 2956 (Fam), at [85] (Munby J).

[111] [1942] NZLR 356. See also *Militante v Ogunwomoju* [1993] 2 FCR 355.

[112] See *Valier v Valier* (1925) 133 LT 830.   [113] [1945] 2 All ER 690.   [114] [2004] EWHC 2808.

There are many people in society who may be of limited or borderline capacity but whose lives are immensely enriched by marriage. We must be careful not to set the test of capacity to marry too high, lest it operate as an unfair, unnecessary and indeed discriminatory bar against the mentally disabled.[115]

Interestingly, unsoundness of mind may cover intoxication provided that it is extreme in its nature and it undermines the ability for the individual to give consent. It was suggested, albeit obiter, in *Sullivan v Sullivan* that getting another person drunk and then 'marrying [them] in that perverted state of mind' could result in a voidable marriage.[116]

5.3.4 Mental disorder under the Mental Health Act 1983 rendering the person unfitted for marriage—s. 12(1)(d) of the Matrimonial Causes Act 1973

Either party can rely on their own continuous or intermittent mental disorder falling under the Mental Health Act 1983. It is important to note that, whereas the previous ground involved the individual lacking capacity to consent to marriage, this particular ground covers individuals that can validly consent yet are 'unfitted for marriage' at the time of the ceremony.[117] Determining what makes someone unfitted for marriage is a difficult question and generally involves an assessment of the party's ability to appreciate the ordinary duties, behaviour, and responsibilities of marriage. Thus, it could be argued that depression, for example, may not render someone unfitted for marriage, whereas severe, episodic schizophrenia might.

5.3.5 Respondent suffering from a communicable venereal disease—s. 12(1)(e) of the Matrimonial Causes Act 1973

A marriage may be annulled if at the time of ceremony the respondent was suffering from a venereal disease. This provision, which does not extend to civil partners, clearly has its origin in the ecclesiastical jurisdiction and appears somewhat strange to modern eyes. It is difficult to apply in practice as there is no definitive list of which venereal diseases are covered. For example, does it apply to those that are much harder to treat such as HIV or would it cover those curable through antibiotics? Note also that the petitioner may not rely on his or her own venereal disease and, instead, must argue that the respondent was suffering from one at the time of marriage.

5.3.6 Respondent was pregnant by person other than the petitioner—s. 12(1)(f) of the Matrimonial Causes Act 1973

This provision requires that a woman be pregnant at the time of the marriage by someone other than her husband. Interestingly, there is no correlating provision for a wife to petition on the basis that another woman is pregnant by her husband at the time of their marriage. This is another outdated ground for nullity that was first introduced in 1937 and is rarely used in practice.

5.3.7 Post-marriage an interim gender recognition certificate had been issued to either party to the marriage—s. 12(1)(g) of the Matrimonial Causes Act 1973

To understand this ground, it is important to note the development of the law in relation to the legal recognition of transsexual persons. Gender dysphoria is a recognised gender identity disorder whereby an individual's biological sex does not correspond with the gender with which they identify.[118] The development of the law

---

[115] [2004] EWHC 2808, at [144].   [116] (1818) 2 Hag Con 238, 246.
[117] See *Bennett v Bennett* [1969] 1 All ER 539.
[118] See, generally, Scherpe, J.M. *The Legal Status of Transsexual and Transgender Persons* (Intersentia, 2016).

in this area stems from *Corbett v Corbett (Otherwise Ashley)* where Ormrod J stated that an individual's biological sex was determined at birth and could not be altered through subsequent medical treatment (i.e. a sex-change operation).[119] This biological test meant that it was impossible for a transsexual person to have their acquired gender legally recognised for the purposes of marriage. Following a series of human rights cases,[120] and in particular the House of Lords decision in *Bellinger v Bellinger (Lord Chancellor Intervening)*,[121] pressure was exerted on the government to reform the law so as to enable the legal recognition of individuals in their acquired gender. This resulted in the Gender Recognition Act 2004 that came into force in April 2005 and created a legal framework applicable to those wishing to live permanently in their acquired genders.

Within the Act there is a distinction drawn between 'full' and 'interim' gender recognition certificates.[122] An individual can apply for a full gender recognition certificate under s. 2(1) of the Gender Recognition Act 2004 if:

- they have or have had gender dysphoria;
- they have lived in the acquired gender for a period of two years;
- they intend to live in the newly acquired gender until they die.

According to s. 3 of the Gender Recognition Act 2004, medical opinion is needed to attest to this. Once satisfied, the person's gender becomes the acquired gender under s. 9(1) and a new birth certificate is issued. In contrast, interim gender recognition certificates are issued where there are some impediments to the grant of the full certificate. For example, prior to the introduction of same-sex marriage, where an opposite-sex couple married and one party changed gender, the marriage was rendered voidable and the individual would not legally be recognised in their acquired gender (to do otherwise would be same-sex marriage through the backdoor). The only option was to end the marriage if the person wanted full legal recognition of their acquired gender.

Now that same-sex marriage is permitted, if an opposite-sex couple marry and one party subsequently changes gender, the following happens:

- If the other spouse consents, a full gender recognition certificate will be issued (thereby changing the marriage to a fully valid, same-sex marriage). The marriage will be classed as subsisting from the point it was first formed as an opposite-sex marriage.

- If the other spouse does not consent, an interim gender recognition certificate will be issued, thereby no legal change of gender will be recognised and the marriage remains voidable as per section 12(1)(g) of the Matrimonial Causes Act 1973.

5.3.8 At time of the marriage, respondent had acquired gender under the Gender Recognition Act 2004—s. 12(1)(h) of the Matrimonial Causes Act 1973

If one party marries without knowing that the other party has previously acquired legal recognition of their acquired gender then the marriage will be voidable. The petitioner will be able to seek a decree of nullity but must not know of the fact that an acquired gender had been obtained at the time of ceremony.

---

[119] [1970] 2 WLR 1306. For commentary on this decision, see Gilmore, S. '*Bellinger v Bellinger*—Not Quite Between the Ears and Between the Legs—Transsexualism and Marriage in the Lords' (2003) 15 *Child and Family Law Quarterly* 295.

[120] See *Rees v UK* [1987] 2 FLR 111; *Cossey v UK* [1991] 2 FLR 494; and *Goodwin v UK* [2002] 2 FLR 487.

[121] [2003] 1 FLR 1043.

[122] See Gilmore, S. 'The Gender Recognition Act 2004' [2004] *Family Law* 741.

5.4 **Bars to a decree**

Unlike the position with void marriages, there are several procedural bars to a decree applicable exclusively to voidable marriages. The bars to decree in relation to civil partnerships are found in s. 51 of Civil Partnership Act 2004.

5.4.1 **Statutory bar based on petitioner's conduct (formerly approbation)**

This bar in s. 13(1) of the Matrimonial Causes Act 1973 applies in the following scenario. Where the petitioner knew that there was a basis on which they could seek a decree of nullity and consequently led the respondent to 'reasonably believe' they would not avoid the marriage, the court may refuse to grant a decree if it would be unjust to the respondent. The rationale behind an earlier version of this bar was stated in *G v M* as follows:

> In a suit for nullity of marriage there may be facts and circumstances proved which so plainly imply, on the part of the complaining spouse, a recognition of the existence and validity of the marriage, as to render it most inequitable and contrary to public policy that he or she should be permitted to go on to challenge it with effect.[123]

In practice, this bar is rarely used, particularly as the court can make orders relating to finances in the context of nullity applications and can adequately respond to any injustice that may potentially occur.

5.4.2 **Time delay**

As stated in s. 13(2), the ability to petition for nullity can be time-limited depending on the ground used. For ss. 12(c)–(h), the petitioner has to bring a petition within three years of the date of marriage. For s. 12(g), proceedings must be initiated within six months of the receipt of an interim gender recognition certificate.

5.4.3 **Knowledge of defect**

If the petitioner knew at the time of marriage the presence of a particular defect, s. 13(3) will bar them from bringing a petition against the respondent. This bar applies only to applications based on the respondent suffering from a venereal disease (s.12(1)(e)), the respondent being pregnant by someone other than the husband (s.12(1)(f)), and the respondent having acquired a legal gender prior to marriage (s.12(1)(g)).

 Debate 2: Is there a Continuing Need for Nullity?

The law relating to nullity is clearly rooted in its ecclesiastical origins. Even after secular courts were granted the ability to issue decrees of nullity following the Matrimonial Causes Act 1857, these early foundations and influences remained in the legal framework. Now that secular courts are exploring personal defects in a marriage, many of which have religious or biblical connotations, it certainly becomes questionable whether nullity has a continuing role to play.

One factor that highlights the absence of a continuing role for nullity is the prevalence of applications as compared to the number of divorces granted in England and Wales. In 2011, there were 119,610 divorces finalised by way of decree absolute as opposed to 206 nullity decrees.[124] As Anthony Lincoln J observed in *A v J* '[n]ullity proceedings are nowadays rare, though not wholly extinct'.[125] Interestingly, whilst there has been a steady decrease in divorce

---

[123] (1885) 10 App Cas 171, 197–8.
[124] Ministry of Justice, *Judicial and Court Statistics (Annual) Family Matters* (28 June 2012).
[125] [1989] FLR 110, 111.

petitions, the number of nullity petitions, both submitted and ultimately made absolute by the court, has remained relatively static despite, overall, being relatively small in number.

Another factor that may suggest a limited role for nullity is the accessibility of divorce. The small proportion of nullity decrees could be attributable to the fact that England and Wales possesses a relatively swift process for obtaining a divorce (see Chapter 3 on divorce). A connection between access to divorce and nullity petitions can also be identified. For example, there was a marked decrease in nullity petitions following the Matrimonial and Family Proceedings Act 1984 that reduced the waiting period for divorce from three years to one. Furthermore, the administrative process for divorce could be viewed as preferable to applicants as it does not involve a rigorous interrogation of the cause of marital breakdown unlike a nullity petition that is arguably more personal and intrusive. Problematically, we must be mindful of the fact that nullity comprises both void and voidable marriages. Whilst many of the grounds forming the basis of voidable marriages could theoretically be subsumed within divorce, it is questionable whether void marriages such as those relating to the prohibited degrees or contracted with individuals under the age of 16, should be treated in the same manner. Likewise, it should be noted that using divorce instead of nullity may not always be advantageous as for the former there is a statutory prohibition on bringing an application within the first year of marriage.

Lastly, the courts have also equalised the legal consequences that stem from divorce and nullity. With the exception of non-marriage, discussed earlier, a void or voidable marriage dissolved through nullity generates virtually the same entitlement to seek orders relating to finance or children as one stemming from a divorce.

Whilst the ease and prevalence of divorce might suggest abolishing nullity in its entirety, it must be accepted that there are individuals who possess strong religious opposition to divorce. For these people, nullity generates less of a stigma and may not result in ostracism from their religious and cultural communities.[126] This aspect may explain why there is a small, albeit consistent, number of nullity petitions submitted and subsequently made absolute each year.

6. Civil partnerships

In addition to marriage, England and Wales also allows couples to enter civil partnerships.[127] Widely used in other jurisdictions, civil partnerships are created through the act of registration and confer upon the parties virtually the same rights and responsibilities as those received through marriage. A key feature of the regime in England and Wales, currently regulated by the Civil Partnership Act 2004, is that only same-sex couples can enter a civil partnership. The exclusion of opposite-sex couples is a particularly controversial aspect of this scheme alongside the issue of whether civil partnerships for same-sex couples possess a future now that same-sex marriage has been introduced.

6.1 The journey to the Civil Partnership Act 2004

In January 2002 the Women and Equality Section of the Department of Trade and Industry undertook an examination of the legal position of same-sex couples.[128] A

---

[126] This point was advanced in *P v R (Forced Marriage: Annulment: Procedure)* [2003] 1 FLR 661.

[127] See Cretney, S. *Same Sex Relationships: From 'Odious Crime' to 'Gay Marriage'* (OUP, 2006) and Hayward, A. 'Registered Partnerships in England and Wales' in J.M. Scherpe and A. Hayward, *The Future of Registered Partnerships* (Intersentia. 2017).

[128] Department of Trade and Industry, *Civil Partnership: A Framework for the Legal Recognition of Same-Sex Couples*, London 2003.

major source of guidance in this consultation exercise was an earlier Private Member's Bill presented by Lord Lester of Herne Hill that proposed a scheme of civil partnerships open to both same-sex and opposite-sex couples. Whilst this Bill proved influential, the consultation exercise proceeded on the basis that same-sex couples were not in an analogous position to opposite-sex couples as the former had no means of legal recognition of their relationship whereas the latter could marry. The Report, *Responses to Civil Partnerships*, published in November 2003, saw 83% of respondents supporting the introduction of civil partnerships.[129] With considerable cross-party support, the government put forward a Bill into the House of Lords in March 2004 and then the House of Commons in July 2004.

There was some opposition to the proposal and this came primarily from religious groups. The main arguments advanced against the introduction of civil partnerships were that they undermined the institution of marriage (even though, at that time, same-sex couples could not marry) and that they represented 'gay marriage' by another name. The government response to this opposition was clear in stating that there was no intention, at that time, to introduce same-sex marriage. Interestingly, there was also some opposition by LGBT activists who believed that civil partnerships were a form of second-class marriage and that same-sex couples should simply be allowed to marry.[130]

The Civil Partnership Act 2004 came into force on 5 December 2005 with the first ceremonies taking place on 21 December 2005. It is a long and complicated Act amounting to 429 pages in a statute book. Despite its complexities, it was heralded at the time as a major breakthrough for the formal recognition of same-sex relationships. The LGBT charity, Stonewall, welcomed the introduction of civil partnerships calling the move a 'historic step forward' and clear evidence that Britain was 'a tolerant twenty-first century nation'.[131] Indeed, studies have since shown that the Civil Partnership Act 2004 facilitated 'significant positive impacts around improving the sense of social inclusion and reducing perceived discrimination amongst members of same-sex couples'.[132]

 CONTEXT 2: CIVIL PARTNERSHIP STATISTICS

As the first civil partnerships were celebrated only in December 2005, it is hardly surprising that the number registered in that year was relatively low at 1,857. That said, there was clearly a demand for registration as 1,227 civil partnerships were concluded during the first three days of the Act coming into force. In 2006, there were 14,943 registrations with 9,003 between men and 5,940 between women. The level of registrations gradually decreased over time with around 6,000 civil partnerships being concluded per year.

More recently, the introduction of same-sex marriage has had a dramatic effect on civil partnership registrations. In 2013 there were 5,646 civil partnership registrations but after the introduction of same-sex marriage in March 2014 this number decreased to 1,683. December 2013 saw 314 civil partnership registrations whereas, one year later, only 58 were formed, which represents a drop of 82%.

---

129 Department of Trade and Industry, *Responses to Civil Partnership: A Framework for the Legal Recognition of Same-Sex Couples*, London 2003.

130 See Tatchell, P. 'Civil Partnerships are Divorced from Reality', *The Guardian*, 19 December 2005.

131 Stonewall Press Release, 17 November 2004.

132 Mitchell, M., Dickens, S., and O'Connor, W. *Same Sex Couples and the Impact of Legislative Changes*, National Centre for Social Research, 2009, xiv.

6.2 Civil partnership formalities

A civil partnership is defined in the Act as 'a relationship between two people of the same sex . . . which is formed when they register as civil partners of each other'.[133] Parties must be of the same sex to enter a civil partnership.[134] Both of the parties must be over the age of 16[135] and also not within the prohibited degrees of relationship.[136] Parties must not already be married or in a civil partnership.[137] The Act emphasises the fact that a civil partnership is a formalised adult relationship as s. 1(3) states that 'a civil partnership ends only on death, dissolution or annulment'.

The formalities for entry into a civil partnership are very similar to those used for a civil marriage. Under the standard procedure, the parties will give notice of their intention to form a civil partnership after residing in England or Wales for at least seven days. These notices record that the proposed civil partners know of no impediment to the civil partnership. Like the procedure used for marriage, discussed earlier, notice will also be publicised which offers any person the ability to object to a forthcoming civil partnership.[138] After a 'waiting period', either party can apply to the relevant district registrar who is then under a duty to issue a Civil Partnership Schedule, provided they are satisfied that there are no lawful impediments. The parties will sign the Schedule in the presence of each other and witnesses. Whereas marriages are documented using hard copy records, civil partnerships are recorded electronically and must be registered 'as soon as is practicable'.[139]

Despite being a lengthy statute, the Civil Partnership Act gives very little guidance on the inherent nature of the relationship. This stands in contrast to religious and civil marriages where some of the content and expectations imposed on the parties can be identified from the vows and the ceremony itself. Furthermore, it is the act of registration that is central to civil partnerships. This means that, unlike civil marriage in its insistence on declaratory and contracting words, civil partnerships can theoretically be entered into in complete silence. This fact is perhaps indicative of the desire by those that drafted the Act to ensure that civil partnerships were viewed as completely distinct from marriage.

Civil partnerships are conceptualised as a secular construct. When civil partnerships were originally introduced they were not permitted to take place on religious premises. However, following s. 202 of the Equality Act 2010 and the Marriage and Civil Partnerships (Approved Premises) (Amendment) Regulations 2011, civil partnerships can now be conducted on religious premises. Crucially, religious organisations are under no obligation to conduct a civil partnership and the final act of registration of the civil partnership must remain secular.

6.3 Failure to comply with civil partnerships formalities

Like marriage, discussed earlier, the presence of certain defects may render a civil partnership void or voidable. The void grounds for a civil partnership are found in s. 49 of the Civil Partnership Act 2004. The grounds, referencing s. 3 of that Act, can be summarised as follows:

- parties are already married or in a civil partnership;
- parties are underage;

---

[133] Civil Partnership Act 2004, s. 1(1). See Harper, M. *et al, Same Sex Marriage and Civil Partnerships: The New Law* (Jordan Publishing, 2014).   [134] Civil Partnership Act 2004, ss. 1(1) and 3(1)(a).
[135] Civil Partnership Act 2004, s. 3(1)(c). As per s. 4(1) parental consent to form a civil partnership is required if one of the parties is over 16 but under the age of 18.
[136] Civil Partnership Act 2004, s. 3(1)(d) and Sch 1, Part I.   [137] Civil Partnership Act 2004, s. 3(1)(b).
[138] Civil Partnership Act 2004, s. 13(1).   [139] Civil Partnership Act 2004, s. 2(4)(b).

- parties are not of the same sex;
- parties are within the prohibited degrees;
- parties have knowingly failed to comply with certain formalities.

It should be noted that the above grounds are similar to those used for marriage, discussed earlier at 5.2, except for entry into a polygamous marriage outside England and Wales whilst currently domiciled in England and Wales. The omission of polygamy rendering civil partnerships void is based on the fact that no country in the world recognises polygamous civil partnerships. Another key point to note is that civil partners, unlike married couples, cannot commit the crime of bigamy. Rather, where a civil partner forms another civil partnership or marriage when already in a pre-existing civil partnership or marriage, they commit the offence of 'making a false statement with reference to a civil partnership' carrying upon conviction either imprisonment for a term not exceeding seven years or a fine (or both).[140]

In contrast, the voidable grounds are found in s. 50(1) of the Civil Partnership Act 2004.

 Key Legislation 3: Civil Partnership Act 2004, s. 50

Grounds on which civil partnership is voidable:

(1) Where two people register as civil partners of each other in England and Wales, the civil partnership is voidable if:
   (a) either of them did not validly consent to its formation (whether as a result of duress, mistake, unsoundness of mind or otherwise);
   (b) at the time of its formation either of them, though capable of giving a valid consent, was suffering (whether continuously or intermittently) from mental disorder of such a kind or to such an extent as to be unfitted for civil partnership;
   (c) at the time of its formation, the respondent was pregnant by some person other than the applicant;
   (d) an interim gender recognition certificate under the Gender Recognition Act 2004 (c. 7) has, after the time of its formation, been issued to either civil partner;
   (e) the respondent is a person whose gender at the time of its formation had become the acquired gender under the 2004 Act.

Section 50 of the Civil Partnership Act 2004 has some noticeable omissions. Unlike the voidable grounds for marriage specified in s. 12 of the Matrimonial Causes Act 1973, a decree of nullity cannot be obtained for a civil partnership on the grounds of incapacity of either party to consummate, wilful refusal of the respondent to consummate, or that at the time of the ceremony the respondent had a communicable venereal disease. These omissions highlight a key issue for civil partnerships; namely, whether civil partnerships are to be conceptualised as encompassing a sexual relationship.[141] Various reasons could be proffered for these omissions such as the religious heritage of these grounds, which would be incompatible with predominantly secular nature of civil partnerships, or an unwillingness to define what would constitute consummation in the context of a same-sex relationship. Similarly, the omission for civil partners may indicate an implicit prioritisation of sexual activity that

---

[140] Civil Partnership Act 2004, s. 80, amending s. 3(1) of the Perjury Act 1911.
[141] Barker, N. 'Sex and the Civil Partnership Act: The Future of (Non) Conjugality? (2006) 14 *Feminist Legal Studies* 241.

results in procreation.[142] Baroness Scotland explained these omissions as the state simply not wishing to 'look at the nature of the sexual relationship' because the concept of civil partnership was 'totally different in nature' to marriage.[143] This approach of marginalising the sexual nature of civil partnership also applies to the inability for civil partners to petition on the basis of adultery when dissolving their civil partnership.[144]

It should be noted that the bars to relief when a civil partnership is voidable are set out in s. 51 of the Civil Partnership Act 2004 and mirror those for marriage (discussed in 5.4).

❓ DEBATE 3: DO CIVIL PARTNERSHIPS HAVE A FUTURE IN AN ERA OF SAME-SEX MARRIAGE?

The Marriage (Same Sex Couples) Act 2013 has produced a fundamental problem that is the continuing need, role, and future of civil partnerships. With same-sex couples now able to formalise their relationship through marriage, is there any need for an additional method to marriage for the formalisation of a relationship? This is particularly significant when it is appreciated that, with the exception of a few areas of law, the rights conferred by civil partnership are virtually identical to those received via marriage. Thus, is the civil partnership now a redundant family form seeing as, for some, it was originally conceived as a 'stepping stone' to same-sex marriage or can it play a meaningful future role in England and Wales?[145]

The types of questions currently being asked range from whether civil partnerships should be phased out entirely, continued in an unaltered form as an alternative formalised relationship structure exclusively for same-sex couples, or modified to enable opposite-sex couples access to this relationship form. This questioning commenced during the parliamentary debates for the Marriage (Same Sex Couples) Act 2013 but a comprehensive review was postponed to a later date. Section 15 of the Marriage (Same Sex Couples) Act 2013 compelled the Secretary of State to conduct a formal review of the operation and future of civil partnerships following a full public consultation. The consultation document was released in January 2014.[146] The government's initial position was that civil partnership was a 'well-understood legal institution' that 'plays an important role in the lives of many couples'.[147]

After a 12-week consultation period, the Department for Culture, Media and Sport released their Report in June 2014.[148] The consultation received around 11,500 responses but it should be noted that this was considerably lower than the responses received to the earlier Equal Civil Marriage consultation.[149] 30% of respondents supported the abolition of civil partnerships with 55% against.[150] For the proponents of retaining civil partnerships, it was

---

[142] See Cretney, S. 'Sex is Important' [2004] *Family Law* 777; Crompton, L. 'Where's the Sex in Same-Sex Marriage' [2013] 43 *Family Law* 564 and Herring, J. 'Why Marriage Needs to be Less Sexy' in J. Miles, P. Mody, and R. Probert, *Marriage Rites and Rights* (Hart Publishing, 2015).

[143] Hansard HL, col 1479 (17 November 2004).   [144] See Chapter 3 on divorce.

[145] Department for Culture, Media and Sport, *Civil Partnership Review (England and Wales): A Consultation*, London, 2014, 18.

[146] Department for Culture, Media and Sport, *Civil Partnership Review (England and Wales): A Consultation*, London, 2014.

[147] Department for Culture, Media and Sport, *Civil Partnership Review (England and Wales): A Consultation*, London, 2014, 9, para 1.4.

[148] Department for Culture, Media and Sport, *Civil Partnership Review (England and Wales): Report on Conclusions*, London, 2014.

[149] Department for Culture, Media and Sport, 'Equal Marriage Consultation'. London, 2012. Available at: https://www.gov.uk/government/consultations/equal-marriage-consultation, accessed 11 October 2017.

[150] Department for Culture, Media and Sport, *Civil Partnership Review (England and Wales): Report on Conclusions*, London, 2014, 8, para 2.3. Note that the remaining 15% of respondents held no view.

believed that abolition would indicate that civil partnerships were 'never truly recognised in the same light as marriage'.[151] Those in favour of abolition believed that civil partnerships were surplus to requirement following marriage equality and that with two options available it was highly probable that people would opt for marriage over civil partnership. In addition, it was viewed as cumbersome and complicated to run two parallel schemes for the formalisation and legal recognition of same-sex relationships.

In light of inconclusive findings and as same-sex marriage had only recently been introduced, it was decided that no action should be taken before more research had been conducted and statistical data was made available on the uptake of same-sex civil partnerships following the introduction of same-sex marriage.

Comparative family law is useful here when predicting the future direction for England and Wales as several jurisdictions have had to grapple with the issue of what to do with a civil partnership regime following the introduction of same-sex marriage.[152] Two models can be discerned:

- Where a jurisdiction has introduced civil or registered partnerships for same-sex couples *only* and then introduced same-sex marriage, the earlier partnership regime is normally abolished. Examples of this approach include Norway, Iceland, Sweden, Denmark, and, more recently, Ireland. The rationale is often that the partnership regimes were originally conceptualised, and operated, as functional equivalents to marriage for same-sex couples and that need has now gone.
- Where a jurisdiction has introduced partnerships for both opposite and same-sex couples, and then subsequently introduced same-sex marriage, the earlier partnership regime is often retained. Examples would be the Netherlands and New Zealand. Similar approaches can be seen in France and Belgium but the legal rights are not as far-reaching and extensive. The rationale for retention is that the partnership regimes operated as an alternative to marriage from their outset, which endures even after the introduction of same-sex marriage.

The future of civil partnerships for same-sex couples is unclear. It is certainly the case that by failing to abolish civil partnerships following the introduction of same-sex marriage, England and Wales (alongside Scotland) is now travelling in a new direction. What is clear though is that the future of same-sex civil partnerships is very much bound up with a consideration of whether the Civil Partnership Act 2004 should be extended to include opposite-sex couples.

6.4 Opposite-sex couples and the Civil Partnership Act 2004

The current civil partnership regime in England and Wales excludes opposite-sex couples. When the idea of civil partnerships was first mooted, the inclusion of opposite-sex couples was not viewed by many as a key priority, as unlike same-sex couples who had no means of formalising their relationship, opposite-sex couples had the option of marrying. An early challenge to this position was the Equal Love Campaign. In February 2011, an application was made to the European Court of Human Rights that sought the extension of marriage to same-sex couples alongside the opening up of civil partnership to opposite-sex couples.[153] It was argued that failure to extend civil partnerships violated Article 8 ECHR (the right to respect for private and family life) either read alone or in conjunction with Article

---

[151] Department for Culture, Media and Sport, *Civil Partnership Review (England and Wales): Report on Conclusions*, London, 2014, 9, para 2.5.

[152] For a comparative analysis of 15 jurisdictions, see Scherpe, J.M. and Hayward, A. *The Future of Registered Partnerships* (Intersentia, 2017). See also Scherpe, J.M. 'Quo Vadis, Civil Partnership?' (2015) 46 *Victoria University of Wellington Law Review* 755.

[153] *Ferguson et al v UK* App. No. 8254/11.

14 ECHR (freedom from discrimination). Furthermore, the availability of marriage and civil partnership for certain couples segregated individuals into different legal institutions that conferred the same rights and responsibilities and generally lacked objective and reasonable justification. The case, *Ferguson et al v UK*, was ultimately declared inadmissible in December 2013, arguably because half of the complaint had fallen away as the Marriage (Same Sex Couples) Act 2013 had received Royal Assent earlier that year.[154]

More recent decisions such as *Vallianatos v Greece*[155] and *Oliari v Italy*[156] reveal a greater willingness on the part of the European Court of Human Rights to police discrimination on the basis of sexual orientation.[157] Indeed, the court in *Oliari* went so far as to recognise under Article 8 of the Convention a right to a legal framework for the recognition of same-sex relationships when no such regime exists within a jurisdiction.[158] Nevertheless, those cases are not directly analogous to the position in England and Wales because they both concerned same-sex, not opposite-sex couples.

Momentum for change has materialised at a domestic level with the Equal Civil Partnerships campaign now pushing for a change in the law. This has resulted in judicial challenge to the ban on opposite-sex civil partnerships that was recently heard in the Court of Appeal.

 ### Key Case 4: *Steinfeld & Keidan v Secretary of State for Education* [2017] EWCA Civ 81

An unmarried, opposite-sex couple brought a legal challenge following refusal by registrars to accept notice of their proposed civil partnership. The refusal was because the parties were not of the same sex. The couple possessed strong ideological opposition to marriage viewing it to be a patriarchal institution. Furthermore, they wanted to express their relationship in what they believed to be a more egalitarian, secular manner. The applicants argued that the refusal to permit opposite-sex civil partnerships was a breach of Article 8 ECHR (right to respect to private and family life) read with Article 14 ECHR (freedom from discrimination).

In the High Court, Andrews J dismissed their claim as not falling within the ambit of Article 8 ECHR.[159] Largely adopting the approach of the House of Lords in *M v Secretary of State for Work and Pensions*,[160] Andrews J observed that, whilst a violation of a substantive Convention right is not required in order to invoke Article 14 ECHR, the applicants needed to show that 'a personal interest close to the core of such a right is infringed'.[161] Adopting an approach at clear variance with the European Court of Human Rights,[162] Andrews J was, in effect, requiring evidence of an

---

[154] Barker, N. 'Civil Partnerships: An Alternative to Marriage? An Analysis of the Application in Ferguson and Others v United Kingdom' [2012] 42 *Family Law* 499.

[155] (2014) 59 EHRR 12. See George, R. 'Civil Partnerships, Sexual Orientation and Family Life' (2014) 73 *Cambridge Law Journal* 260.   [156] (2015) ECHR 716.

[157] Both building upon the approach laid down in the earlier decision of that Court in *Schalk and Kopf v Austria* (2011) 53 EHRR 20. See generally, Fenwick, H. 'Same Sex Unions at the Strasbourg Court in a Divided Europe: Driving Forward Reform or Protecting the Court's Authority Via Consensus Analysis?' (2016) 3 *European Human Rights Law Review* 249.

[158] See Hayward, A. 'Same-sex Registered Partnerships—A Right to be Recognised?' (2016) 75 *Cambridge Law Journal* 27. See also *Ratzenböck and Seydl v Austria* App. No. 28475/12.

[159] [2016] EWHC 128 (Fam). For commentary, see Ferguson, L. 'The Curious Case of Civil Partnership: The Extension of Marriage to Same-Sex Couples and the Status-Altering Consequences of a Wait-and-See Approach' (2016) 28 *Child and Family Law Quarterly* 347 and Wintemute, R. 'Civil Partnership and Discrimination in *R (Steinfeld) v Secretary of State for Education*' (2016) *Child and Family Law Quarterly* 365.

[160] [2006] UKHL 11.   [161] [2016] EWHC 128 (Fam), at [25].

[162] See Scherpe, J. M. 'Family and Private Life, Ambits and Pieces—*M v Secretary of State for Work and Pensions*' (2007) 19 *Child and Family Law Quarterly* 32 and Fenton-Glynn, C. 'Opposite Sex Civil Partnerships and the Ambit of Article 8' [2016] 46 *Family Law* (Last Orders).

interference, which was absent in the present case. Indeed, as Andrews J observed, '[t]he only obstacle to the Claimants obtaining the equivalent legal recognition of their status and the same rights and benefits as a same-sex couple is their conscience'.[163] There was no obligation imposed on the State to offer a *further* means of formalisation. Furthermore, the applicants were not subjected to 'humiliation, derogatory treatment, or any other lack of respect for their private lives on grounds of their heterosexual orientation'.[164]

The Court of Appeal dismissed the couple's appeal by a 2:1 majority and focused on two substantive issues: ambit (engaging the right) and justification.[165] Giving the main opinion, Arden LJ noted that Article 8(1) ECHR encompasses a positive obligation to respect family life for both same-sex and opposite-sex couples. The legal mechanisms used to formally express relationships fell within that specific obligation. The fact that the couple concerned could marry did not mean they no longer possessed a personal interest close to the core of Article 8 ECHR nor did it mean that any discrimination ceased. Rejecting the approach taken in the High Court, the Court of Appeal recognised that the couple's inability to legally express their relationship as a civil partnership was linked to an 'individual's existence and identity'.[166] Thus, on the issue of whether the couple's claim fell within the ambit of Article 8 ECHR, the Court of Appeal was unanimous in believing that it did.

After engaging the right, the Court of Appeal was then divided as to whether any interference with it could be justified. All members of the Court believed that awaiting statistical data on the uptake of civil partnerships following same-sex marriage constituted a legitimate aim. That aim is clearly to avert a potentially disruptive and costly exercise of extending civil partnerships to opposite-sex couples only to find that there is no demand for them. However, whilst Beatson LJ and Briggs LJ both believed that the government's position was justifiable now (albeit not indefinitely), Arden LJ considered that the discrimination faced by the couple was unjustified, especially as it impacted upon 'one the closest relationships which one adult has with another'.[167]

The Court of Appeal decision in *Steinfeld* raises several issues. First, the case clearly establishes that the current framework of civil partnerships is discriminatory to opposite-sex couples and that the government must remove such discrimination. Whilst no timeframe was imposed on the government, change is required and must take place in the imminent future. Although it is conceivable that the government may follow the example recently set by the Isle of Man and extend the coverage of civil partnerships to opposite-sex couples,[168] the government may also choose to remove the discrimination by phasing out civil partnerships altogether. The latter approach would mean that marriage would be the only option for both opposite-sex and same-sex couples. This approach certainly offers simplicity but it also overlooks the value that many same-sex couples attach to civil partnerships and fails to meaningfully engage with the objections to the institution of marriage held by the litigants in *Steinfeld*.[169]

Secondly, it is certainly correct that the government's decision regarding the reform of civil partnerships must be informed by statistics and data. However, the approach advocated in *Steinfeld* of analysing the uptake of civil partnerships between same-sex couples following the introduction of same-sex marriage is erroneous, as it will not reveal any indication or evidence as to the desire among opposite-sex couples for civil partnerships. It would, therefore, be unfortunate if civil partnerships were abolished on the basis of an incomplete picture of the trends and motivations of couples wishing to formalise their relationships.

---

[163] [2016] EWHC 128 (Fam), at [39].   [164] [2016] EWHC 128 (Fam), at [38].

[165] See Hayward, A. 'Justifiable Discrimination—The Case of Opposite-Sex Civil Partnerships' (2017) 76 *Cambridge Law Journal* 243.   [166] [2017] EWCA Civ 81, at [62] (Arden LJ).

[167] [2017] EWCA Civ 81, at [110].

[168] See the Isle of Man's Marriage and Civil Partnership (Amendment) Act 2016.

[169] See Haskey, J. 'Civil Partnerships and Same-Sex Marriages in England and Wales: A Social and Demographic Perspective' [2016] *Family Law* 44.

Alongside the *Steinfeld* litigation, Tim Loughton, a Member of Parliament, introduced into the House of Commons in July 2017 the Civil Partnerships, Marriages and Deaths (Registration Etc.) Bill 2017–2019. He previously introduced identical Bills in September 2014, October 2015, and July 2016.[170] The Bill extends civil partnerships to opposite-sex couples by an amendment to s. 1 of the Civil Partnership Act 2004 redacting the requirement of the partners to be 'of the same sex'. All primary and secondary legislation would then be read accordingly. When introducing an early version of the Bill, he stated that his 'simple proposal' involved 'no complications'[171] and would respond to the 'unintended but glaring inequality' produced by failing to open up civil partnerships to opposite-sex couples when same-sex marriage was introduced.[172] He also believed that the ability for opposite-sex couples to register civil partnerships would assist cohabitants through providing greater stability to them and their children alongside offering important legal protections following relationship breakdown. A second reading of the Bill is scheduled for February 2018. The absence of reform in this area means that England and Wales (alongside Scotland) continues to operate an overly complex and, at face value, discriminatory system of civil partnerships that both the courts and government accept must be changed in the near future.

7. Cohabitation

When exploring what constitutes a family, marriage has always taken centre stage. Cretney is accurate when he acknowledges that 'for much of the 20th century, family law was able simply to ignore the family outside marriage'.[173] Indeed, the early leading treatises dealing with legal issues that we today would term family law rarely mention cohabitation.[174] Despite this fact, cohabitation has existed for centuries and there are several reasons why people cohabited in the past. One explanation for cohabitation was an inability to divorce. As discussed in Chapter 5, divorce was, historically, only available to a spouse that was the victim of the other spouse's matrimonial offence. If a party had committed a matrimonial offence such as adultery they could not rely on their own misconduct to obtain a divorce. Similarly, the other innocent spouse could not be divorced against their will. People in this scenario wishing to embark upon a new relationship were ultimately forced to cohabit (or, in more extreme cases, commit the crime of bigamy). Another explanation for cohabitation in the past was ideological. Progressive writers in the late Victorian period and early twentieth century such as George Eliot and George Bernard Shaw often criticised the idolisation of marriage by society and, as noted earlier at 4, the negative financial impediments that marriage imposed on spouses, especially women.

Despite cohabitation existing, the practice was largely ignored by the state and policymakers. One reason for this was to ensure that the institution of marriage remained prioritised. Marriage has always been viewed by the state as the preferred social unit and was the only union in which legitimate children could be born.[175] Relationships that did not conform to this image received limited and, in many instances, no legal recognition.

---

[170] For further details see: https://services.parliament.uk/bills/2017-19/civilpartnershipsmarriagesanddeaths registrationetc.html, accessed 23 November 2017.

[171] Hansard HC, col 962, 21 October 2015.   [172] Hansard HC, col 960, 21 October 2015.

[173] Cretney, S. *Family Law in the Twentieth Century* (OUP, 2005) 517.

[174] For a detailed account of the historical treatment of cohabitation, see Probert, R. *The Changing Legal Regulation of Cohabitation: From Fornicators to Family 1600–2010* (Cambridge University Press, 2012).

[175] See generally, Ball, C.A. *Same-Sex Marriage and Children: A Tale of History, Social Science and Law* (OUP, 2014) and Golombok, S. *Modern Families: Parents and Children in New Family Forms* (Cambridge University Press, 2015).

Moreover, cohabitation often received criticism by the courts. An example of this can be found in the Court of Appeal decision in *Gammans v Ekins*, decided in 1953, concerning succession to a tenancy.[176] The claimant in this case had lived with the deceased for over 20 years. They were viewed as a married couple, despite being cohabitants, but after the death of the tenant, the Court of Appeal refused to allow the claimant to take over the deceased's tenancy on the basis that it was 'anomalous that a person can acquire a "status of irremovability" by living or having lived in sin'.[177] As the couple had been 'masquerading' as husband and wife, the claimant was unable to establish that he was a member of the tenant's family.[178]

In the 1970s, more progressive attitudes towards cohabitation can be identified. In addition, surveys and statistics started to emerge revealing the growing prevalence of cohabitation as a family form.[179] The views expressed by the Court of Appeal in *Gammans* can be contrasted with those of Bridge LJ in the later decision in *Dyson Holdings Ltd v Fox* when he noted:

> Now, it is, I think, not putting it too high to say that between 1950 and 1975 there has been a complete revolution in society's attitude to unmarried partnerships of the kind under consideration. Such unions are far commoner than they used to be. The social stigma that once attached to them has almost, if not entirely, disappeared.[180]

Thus the latter half of the twentieth century witnessed an important revolution in society's perception of cohabitation. Judicial comments referencing the morality of the parties' conduct began to decline and there was a gradual shift in opinion in favour of recognising relationships that functioned in a similar manner to a marriage. In *Fitzpatrick v Sterling Housing Association*, this progressive outlook was acknowledged when Waite LJ noted the trend of 'terms like partner now being more generally used than the once-preferred references to "common-law spouse", "mistress" or even . . . living in sin'.[181]

As we will see later, even with considerable public support for cohabitation reform, this relationship is not fully legally recognised. Resultantly, England and Wales does not currently possess a comprehensive statutory regime applicable to cohabitants.

 CONTEXT 3: HOW PREVALENT IS COHABITATION?

Cohabitation is growing in popularity.[182] Married or civil partner couple families were the most common family form in the UK in 2017.[183] Nevertheless, cohabiting couple families were the fastest growing family type over the last 20 years, more than doubling from 1.5 million families in 1996 to 3.3 million families in 2017. This suggests that either cohabitation is being chosen as a precursor to marriage or civil partnership or it is being selected as an alterative. In 2017, there were 3.3 million opposite-sex cohabiting couple families and 101,000 same-sex cohabiting couple families in the UK.

---

[176] [1950] 2 KB 328. See also *Upfill v Wright* [1911] 1 KB 506 where Darling J analogises the position of a cohabitant with that of a prostitute.

[177] [1950] 2 KB 328, 331 (Asquith LJ).   [178] [1950] 2 KB 328, 331 (Asquith LJ).

[179] Haskey, J. 'Demographic Aspects of Cohabitation in Great Britain' (2001) 15 *International Journal of Law, Policy and the Family* 51.

[180] [1976] QB 503, 512.   [181] [1998] 1 Ch 304, 308.

[182] See Barlow, A. *et al Cohabitation and the Law: Myths, Money and the Media* in British Social Attitudes *24th Report* (Sage Publishing, 2008).

[183] See ONS Statistical Bulletin, 'Families and Households in the UK: 2017'. Available at: https://www.ons.gov.uk/peoplepopulationandcommunity/birthsdeathsandmarriages/families/bulletins/familiesandhouseholds/2017 accessed 23 November 2017.

7.1 Key legal differences between marriage and cohabitation

Unlike marriage and civil partnership that have consequences which are heavily regulated by the state, cohabitation is a private relationship with parties not needing to comply with any formalities for its creation. As a result of the increase in cohabitation and coupled with the need to protect individuals that may be potentially vulnerable, cohabitants have obtained some legal recognition of their relationship. However, these protections are piecemeal and context-specific. This means that in some instances cohabitants have similar benefits to married couples but in others they have little or no legal protection. The following section will illustrate the key areas where the legal treatment of married couples and cohabitants differ.[184]

7.1.1 Ownership of property

Unlike married couples, cohabitants have no mutual duty to maintain each other or provide financial support during the relationship or following relationship breakdown. Furthermore, there is a stark difference in the treatment of cohabitants versus married couples and civil partners in relation to ownership of the family home. Married couples retain separate property during their relationship but following divorce, nullity, or judicial separation can apply to the court for financial orders under the Matrimonial Causes Act 1973 (see Chapter 4).[185] This Act grants the court a wide, structured judicial discretion to determine property ownership between the spouses. Crucially, as Lord Denning MR noted, provision for spouses under this statutory scheme does not necessarily involve 'paying any too nice a regard to their legal or equitable rights' but instead is based on 'what is the fairest provision for the future'.[186]

Cohabitants cannot access this judicial discretion and when ownership is in dispute the courts must determine the issue using property law and trusts. The principles used to establish ownership were not developed with interpersonal relationships in mind and have long been criticised as capable of causing injustice. This injustice flows from the fact that trusts largely respond to the intention of the parties, which is often hard to identify in interpersonal relationships where conversations as to who owns what are rare and, in practice, difficult to prove (see Chapter 5). As Jacob LJ in the Court of Appeal decision in *Jones v Kernott* remarked:

> In the real world unmarried couples seldom enter into express agreements into what should happen to property should the relationship fail and often do not settle matters clearly when they do. Life is untidier than that. In reality human emotional relationships simply do not operate as if they were commercial contracts and it is idle to wish that they did.[187]

Intentions as to ownership can also be inferred through party conduct but only financial contributions to the acquisition of property are enough to generate entitlement.[188] Whereas the Matrimonial Causes Act 1973 enables the court to take into account homemaker contributions such as childcare and work in the home, these important activities cannot form the basis of a trust interest.[189] This illustrates what Bottomley termed the 'relationship blindness' of the law and the adverse effect of these principles are noticeable in numerous cases.[190]

---

[184] See Chapter 5 on cohabitation and the family home.   [185] A similar ability applies to civil partners.

[186] *Hanlon v The Law Society* [1981] AC 124, 147.

[187] [2010] EWCA Civ 578, at [90]. See also Glover, N. and Todd, P. 'The Myth of Common Intention' (1996) 16 *Legal Studies* 325.

[188] See *Lloyds Bank v Rosset* [1990] UKHL 14.

[189] See Oldham, M. 'Homemaker Services and the Law' in D. Pearl and R. Pickford, *Frontiers of Family Law* (2nd edn, Wiley, 1995).

[190] Bottomley, A. 'Women and Trust(s): Portraying the Family in the Gallery of Law' in S. Bright and J. Dewar, *Land Law: Themes and Perspectives* (OUP, 1998).

Key Case 5: *Burns v Burns* [1984] Ch 317

Mrs Burns cohabited with her partner Mr Burns for 17 years. Fully accepting that Mr Burns would not marry her, Mrs Burns changed her name to his and both parties held themselves out to be married. Mr Burns purchased his own property, which he financed by paying the deposit and subsequently discharging a mortgage using his own funds. Mrs Burns did not work for most of the long period of cohabitation and when she did work she used her earnings to pay for household expenses. The relationship ended and Mrs Burns claimed that she was entitled to a beneficial interest that had been acquired through a resulting trust and was in shares to be determined by the court.

   The Court of Appeal denied Mrs Burns a beneficial interest in the property on the basis that her claim did not evidence either an agreement to share beneficially or conduct through which the court could infer a common intention to share the property.[191] Using trust principles, there needed to be an express trust (that to be enforceable required writing), a resulting trust, or a constructive trust. Fox LJ ruled out an express trust owing to the absence of writing and stated that her non-financial contributions did not suffice to form the basis of a resulting trust. In relation to a constructive trust, Fox LJ dismissed her claim stating that:

> She provided no money for the purchase; she assumed no liability in respect of the mortgage; there was no understanding or arrangement that the plaintiff would go out to work to assist with the family finances; the defendant did nothing to lead her to change her position in the belief that she would have an interest in the house.[192]

Whilst accepting that Mrs Burns 'can justifiably say that fate has not been kind to her', May LJ believed that the 'remedy for any inequity' was a matter for Parliament and not the courts.[193]

   Burns v Burns was decided 1984 and it might be thought that the law would have developed since then in a more sympathetic manner to cohabitants. Unfortunately, as noted more recently in *Curran v Collins* in 2013, trust principles can still be viewed as 'unfair' and capable of acting harshly upon litigants, especially women.[194]

7.1.2 Occupation of the family home

For the purposes of property law, possession of a beneficial interest in the family home triggers a right to occupation of the property under s. 12(1) of the Trusts of Land and Appointment of Trustees Act 1996. For family law, the result is different depending on whether parties are married or cohabiting. Married couples have automatic statutory occupation rights to the matrimonial home under s. 30 of the Family Law Act 1996. This protects their right of occupation as against their spouse but is also capable of being protected in the system of land registration against a particular property so that it can bind any subsequent purchasers of that property. Cohabitants, on the other hand, do not possess such home rights. Nevertheless, in the context of domestic violence, cohabitants can apply for orders under Part IV of the Family Law Act 1996 and this may extend to their occupation of the family home.[195]

---

[191] See Mee, J. 'Burns v Burns: The Villain of the Piece' in S. Gilmore, J. Herring, and R. Probert, *Landmark Cases in Family Law* (Hart Publishing, 2010).

[192] [1984] 1 All ER 244, 251.   [193] [1984] 1 All ER 244, 265.

[194] *Curran v Collins (Permission to Appeal)* [2013] EWCA Civ 382, at [9].

[195] See Chapter 7 on domestic violence.

7.1.3 Testate and intestate succession

In terms of testate succession, that is, succession through a will, there are no significant differences between married couples and cohabitants. Testamentary freedom is key meaning that the deceased's will stipulates who is to benefit. However, where a spouse or civil partner dies intestate, the survivor has an automatic right to inherit. Furthermore, the surviving spouse or civil partner is exempt from paying inheritance tax. The converse applies to cohabitants with them having no automatic entitlement on intestacy and thus any property goes to the deceased's children or parents. Similarly, cohabitants are also required to pay inheritance tax on a willed gift to partner.[196]

In addition to the testate and intestate rules, the Inheritance (Provision for Family and Dependants) Act 1975 allows someone being maintained at the time of death of the deceased to claim for 'reasonable financial provision' against their estate where the deceased's will failed to adequately provide for them.[197] Equally it applies if the deceased dies intestate. This allows a cohabitant to claim provided they were economically dependent and had been living with the deceased for two years prior to their death.[198] In contrast, a widow or widower is automatically entitled to apply and does not need to show economic dependence.

The Law Reform (Succession) Act 1995 amended this position by permitting another basis on which an individual could apply; namely, as a cohabitant in their own right. This allows a person living with the deceased '*as* husband and wife' to claim against their estate, although they still must show that they have been living with the deceased for two years immediately before death.[199] It equalised the eligibility but limited awards to necessary maintenance unlike the more extensive provision available for widows or widowers. A similar provision is found in the Fatal Accidents Act 1982 that allows a cohabitant to recover compensation against a negligent defendant who has killed their partner. The same requirements of 'as husband and wife' and two years residency prior to death also exist.

7.1.4 Children

There are several distinctions in how the law treats cohabitants and married couples in relation to children. The obligation to pay child support and maintain children applies equally to both relationships. Similarly, provision can be made for a child under Schedule 1 of the Children Act 1989 (see Chapter 6). This Schedule enables the court to make an order transferring property or awarding a lump sum to an unmarried parent for the benefit of a dependent child up until the child reaches the age of majority. However, only married couples and unmarried mothers automatically acquire parental responsibility in relation to a child. The unmarried father does not automatically acquire parental responsibility.[200]

7.2 Common law marriage myth

Operating alongside the aforementioned disparity in legal treatment between cohabitants and spouses is also a widespread misunderstanding as to legal entitlements. The myth centres on the belief held by some cohabitants that living together for a certain period of time enables them to acquire property rights against the other party.[201]

---

[196] See *Burden v UK* (2008) 47 EHRR 857. See also Sloan, B. 'The Benefits of Conjugality and the Burdens of Consanguinity' (2008) 67 *Cambridge Law Journal* 484.

[197] See Sloan, B. *Borkowski's Law of Succession* (OUP, 2017) Chapter 9.

[198] Inheritance (Provision for Family and Dependants) Act 1975, s. 1(1)(e).

[199] Inheritance (Provision for Family and Dependants) Act 1975, s. 1(1)(ba).

[200] See ss. 2(1)–(2) of the Children Act 1989.

[201] On misunderstandings as to the myth, see *Churchill v Roach* [2004] 2 FLR 989. More recently, research conducted in 2013 by the charity One Plus One found that almost half (47%) of the British public believed in the myth.

In 2000, 56% of respondents in a British Social Attitudes Survey believed in the common law marriage myth[202] and, according to Hibbs, Barton, and Beswick, 69% of engaged couples believed in the myth in 2001.[203] Furthermore, Probert notes in her research that the number of references in newspapers reinforcing the myth outnumbered those rejecting the myth.[204] Ultimately, the myth produces dangerous misconceptions and the later realisation by a party that they possess little or, more often than not, no legal entitlement following relationship breakdown. In *Clibbery v Allen* the cohabitant, detrimentally affected by the myth, even wished to use their case to 'alert members of the general public to the lack of a concept of 'common law marriage' and that women should be aware of how little rights they have on the breakdown of such a relationship'.[205]

? DEBATE 4: SHOULD THERE BE REFORM OF THE LAW RELATING TO COHABITATION?

The question of whether the law should be reformed to grant cohabitants specific rights and remedies following relationship breakdown has troubled policy-makers for decades. A marked difference in legal treatment clearly exists, especially in relation to ownership of real property and the inability of a former cohabitant to receive maintenance following relationship breakdown. Whilst cohabitants are free to enter into contracts to regulate their affairs, these are relatively uncommon and are dependent on the parties knowing the deficiencies of the current law and the need for protection before they are drafted.[206] When it is accepted that among the public there is a dangerous level of misunderstanding as to entitlements owing to the common law marriage myth, it is perhaps understandable why many political parties and family law practitioners' organisations such as Resolution have called for comprehensive reform.[207]

The case against such reform is multifaceted. A traditional argument advanced is that reform would undermine the institution of marriage. Cohabitants should not have the benefits normally associated with married couples because they have deliberately chosen not to formalise their relationship. Thus, in *Supporting Families* published in 1998, the government stated that:

> marriage is still the surest foundation for raising children and remains the choice of the majority of people in Britain. We want to strengthen the institution of marriage to help more marriages succeed.[208]

Interestingly, the Law Society noted that encouraging greater awareness of the differences in legal treatment between cohabitants and married couples would be beneficial, as it would 'underline the importance and significance of marriage'.[209] Whilst marriage is unlikely to lose

---

[202] British Social Attitudes Survey (2000). Over half of the respondents to the later 2008 British Social Attitudes Survey believed that common law marriage exists.

[203] Hibbs, M., Barton, C., and Beswick, J. 'Why Marry? Perceptions of the Affianced' [2001] 31 *Family Law* 197.

[204] See, generally, Probert, R., 'Why Couples Still Believe in Common-Law Marriage' [2007] 37 *Family Law* 403 and Probert, R. 'Common-Law Marriage: Myths and Misunderstandings' (2008) 20 *Child and Family Law Quarterly* 1.

[205] [2002] 1 FLR 565.

[206] See *Sutton v Mischon de Reya* [2004] 1 FLR 837 and Probert, R. 'Cohabitation Contracts and Swedish Sex Slaves' (2004) 16 *Child and Family Law Quarterly* 453.

[207] See observations made by Baroness Butler-Sloss as to the vulnerability of cohabitants in the House of Lords debate on the Cohabitation Bill 2008 (Hansard HL cols 1429–30, 13 March 2009).

[208] Home Office, *Supporting Families* (Stationery Office, 1998).

[209] Law Society, *Cohabitation: The Case for Clear Law. Proposals for Reform* (2007).

its privileged status anytime soon, especially now that same-sex marriage is permitted, this argument is somewhat flawed. In 7.3 it will be demonstrated that all reform proposals in this area have decided not to simply extend the rights received by spouses to cohabitants. The extent of protection for cohabitants will be limited, and perhaps less attractive, than that generated by marriage. Furthermore, the fact of cohabitation is not always attributable to a deliberate ideological rejection of marriage; it can be attributable to a variety of different reasons.[210]

Similarly, another argument against reform is that it will be too difficult to implement in practice as cohabitation is a very dynamic and varied relationship. It is difficult, for example, to prove a start and end point. With such variation in cohabiting relationships, questions arise as to the basis on which legal protection should be provided. Should the law intervene to remedy economic disadvantage generated, however short the relationship, or should there be an assessment of the level of commitment between the parties? Furthermore, what rights and remedies should be available?[211] Tyrer J noted the definitional difficulties surrounding cohabitation in *Kimber v Kimber* but, nevertheless, went on to list a series of factors such as financial support, stability, and the presence of a sexual relationship, that could be used when determining whether a couple was cohabiting.[212] The difficulty of classifying the relationship is encapsulated by Mee who notes the existence of a spectrum with cohabitation, at the one end, being a union 'which has all the characteristics of a marital relationship save the blessing of the law' to, at the other end:

> a relationship which is no more than that of two persons . . . who, finding each other sexually attractive, decide, for the convenience of their primary interest in each other, to occupy the same dwelling, neither intending the relationship to have the quality of permanence.[213]

Another key issue is the structure of the reform proposal and, as will be explored later, a distinction is drawn between opt-in and opt-out regimes. For the former, couples register their relationship but this can arguably produce a form of second-class marriage and may not address the vulnerability of cohabitants in England and Wales in light of the aforementioned common law marriage myth.[214] Nevertheless, some jurisdictions use opt-in systems effectively with the French *pacte civil de solidarité* (PACS) being a key example that sits below marriage, whilst conferring some of the rights traditionally acquired through marriage. For the latter, unless the parties opt-out, a default regime of legal protections apply provided the parties satisfy eligibility criteria such as having a child together or cohabiting for a specific period of time.

Despite operating in several jurisdictions, opt-out schemes are controversial in that couples may become subject to a regime that they did not voluntarily choose. Deech, a vocal opponent of cohabitation reform, is fearful of this intrusion on the autonomy of the parties and has advocated that there needs to be a 'corner of freedom' for couples that is free from any intervention by the State.[215] Furthermore, Deech argues that cohabitation reform would

---

[210] See generally, Barlow A. and Smithson J. 'Legal Assumptions, Cohabitants' Talk and the Rocky Road to Reform' (2010) 22 *Child and Family Law Quarterly* 328.

[211] Fox, L. 'Reforming Family Property: Comparisons, Compromises and Common Dimensions' (2003) 15 *Child and Family Law Quarterly* 1.

[212] [2000] 1 FLR 383. See also Wong, S. 'Shared Commitment, Interdependency and Property Relations: A Socio-Legal Project for Cohabitation' (2012) 24 *Child and Family Law Quarterly* 60.

[213] Mee, J. *The Property Rights of Cohabitees* (Hart Publishing, 1999) 2.

[214] For a rejection of an opt-in regime in England and Wales, see Law Commission, *Cohabitation: The Financial Consequences of Relationship Breakdown* (Law Com No. 307, 2007) 9–10.

[215] Deech, R. 'The Case Against the Legal Recognition of Cohabitation' (1980) 29 *International and Comparative Law Quarterly* 480.

create economic dependency by women on men and detract from the inherent virtues of cohabitation such as privacy, autonomy, and non-intervention.[216] She notes:

> In sum, cohabitation law retards the progress of women, disrespects the relationship, is a recipe for instability, takes away choice, is too expensive and extends an already unsatisfactory maintenance law to another large category. It will certainly be a charter for the footballer's girlfriend but not for the ordinary working woman.[217]

7.3 Law reform proposals

Responding to the deficiencies of the current legal framework, a number of cohabitation reform proposals have been published.[218] As an early starting point, the *Supporting Families* Green Paper, published in 1998, acknowledged the need for public awareness of the difference in legal treatment between married couples and cohabitants. It stated:

> [c]ouples who co-habit . . . take on legal rights and responsibilities, though they are often unaware of them. It might therefore be worthwhile to produce a similar guide for co-habitees, perhaps made available through Citizens Advice Bureaux, libraries etc.[219]

Despite modern support for the introduction of rights and remedies by Resolution and attempts to raise awareness of the legal position among cohabitants, no comprehensive reform has materialised.[220] The following key reform proposals are noteworthy for highlighting the difficulty in securing reform and revealing the tension between protecting vulnerable individuals and preserving the autonomy of couples to be free from regulation of their relationship. However it should be noted that these proposals are context-specific and predominately focus on the property consequences generated by relationship breakdown.

7.3.1 Law Commission, *Sharing Homes—A Discussion Paper* (2002)

The *Sharing Homes* project began in 1993 and published a discussion paper in July 2002.[221] It is important to note that this was not a formal Law Commission Consultation Paper; it was a scoping document and no Draft Bill was attached. It explored the legal position of 'home sharers', very broadly defined, covering married couples, cohabitants in an intimate relationship, parties who could not formalise their relationship owing to the prohibited degrees (i.e. a brother and sister living together), and also platonic relationships of convenience. However, the scheme did not apply where the parties were in a commercial relationship such as landlord and tenant. The Law Commission was keen to stress that it was not focusing on the rights of cohabitants but rather on a broader myriad of relationships taking place within a home.

---

[216] See also Auchmuty R. 'The Limits of Marriage Protection in Property Allocation When a Relationship Ends' (2016) 28 *Child and Family Law Quarterly* 303.   [217] Hansard HL, col 1418, 13 March 2009.
[218] See Miles, J. 'Property Law v Family Law: Resolving the Problems of Family Property' (2003) 23 *Legal Studies* 624 and Mee, J. 'Property Rights and Personal Relationships: Reflections on Reform' (2004) 24 *Legal Studies* 414.   [219] Home Office, *Supporting Families* (Stationery Office 1998) 32.
[220] See, e.g., the Living Together Campaign, available at: http://www.advicenow.org.uk/living-together/, accessed 22 September 2017, discussed in Barlow, A. Burgoyne, C, and Smithson, J. 'The Living Together Campaign—the Impact on Cohabitants' [2007] *Family Law* 166.
[221] See Bridge, S. 'The Property Rights of Cohabitants—Where Do We Go From Here?' [2002] 32 *Family Law* 743.

The proposal adopted a 'property model' and looked at the way parties contributed to the acquisition of property. Where the home was occupied by two or more persons, each of whom occupied it as a home, and where at least one of the parties had an interest in the property, there was potential for the court to create a statutory trust that responded to the financial and non-financial contributions made by the parties to the shared home. The proposal only applied to the 'family home' so typical family law awards such as maintenance payments, lump sum awards, and pension sharing orders were outside its coverage.

The project ultimately failed to make any direct recommendations for reform. The Law Commission noted that they '[c]oncluded that it is not possible to devise a statutory scheme for the determination of shares in the shared home which can operate fairly and evenly across all the diverse circumstances which are now to be encountered'.[222] Perhaps surprisingly for an organisation tasked with law reform, the Law Commission advocated judicial development in the area of the implied trusts (in particular broadening the class of contributions capable of triggering an inferred common intention constructive trust (see Chapter 5)). Whilst the project was unsuccessful, it did recognise the rise of cohabitation and the need to respond to economic disadvantage that can be generated following the acquisition of property and the sharing of a home.

7.3.2 Law Commission, *Cohabitation: The Financial Consequences of Relationship Breakdown* (2007)

Published in 2007, the Law Commission *Cohabitation* Report focused exclusively on cohabitants. It was released after the significant House of Lords decision in *Stack v Dowden* that advocated a more family-sensitive, contextual approach to determining property ownership between former cohabitants.[223]

This Report is an important cohabitation reform proposal, which was produced after a lengthy and robust consultation exercise.[224] Its initial starting point was that a bespoke legal framework was needed as opposed to mere extension of the provisions used by spouses or civil partners for the division of assets found in the Matrimonial Causes Act 1973 and Civil Partnership Act 2004. Similarly, modification of Schedule 1 of the Children Act 1989 was also rejected. The rationale for these moves was to allay fears from critics that any reform proposal would undermine the institution of marriage.

The system for making a claim under these proposals is relatively complex but, in essence, centres on remedying financial disadvantage that may have arisen following the cohabiting relationship. The claim must be brought within two years following the end of the cohabiting relationship.

To apply under the scheme, the applicant must have cohabitant status. Cohabitants were defined as two people (either opposite or same sex) living together in the same household in a relationship. Only intimate relationships were covered. 'Carer' relationships, commercial relationships, or prohibited degrees relationships, that is, between siblings were also excluded. After falling within this definition, further eligibility criteria needed to be satisfied. The parties must have had a child together born before, during, or following the parties' cohabitation or, if no child was born, the parties must have cohabited for a minimum time duration. This was set at two to five years. Interestingly, step-children families had to rely on duration of cohabitation and not the presence of a child.[225]

---

[222] Law Commission, *Sharing Homes—A Discussion Paper* (2002) ix.

[223] [2007] UKHL 17. See Hayward, A. 'Finding a Home for 'Family Property': *Stack v Dowden* and *Jones v Kernott*' in N. Gravells, *Landmark Cases in Land Law* (Hart Publishing 2013).

[224] See Bridge, S. 'Cohabitation: Why Legislative Reform is Necessary' [2007] 37 *Family Law* 911 and Bridge, S. 'Financial Relief for Cohabitants: How the Law Commission's Scheme Would Work' [2007] 37 *Family Law* 998.

[225] See Hughes, D., Davis, M., and Jacklin, L. 'Come Live With Me and Be My Love—A Consideration of the 2007 Law Commission Proposals on Cohabitation Breakdown' [2008] *Conveyancer and Property Lawyer* 197.

In addition, the parties must not have formed a valid Opt-Out Agreement. Unlike marriage or a registered partnership scheme where couples enter into a formal status, the Law Commission selected an opt-out regime. Provided certain requirements were satisfied, this meant that all couples could fall within the scheme's ambit unless they chose to disapply the scheme. To opt-out, the agreement expressing that intention must be in writing and signed by both parties. Furthermore, the court may revoke such agreement if enforcement would cause 'manifest unfairness'.

After satisfying eligibility requirements, the applicant then needed to show that the respondent has a 'retained benefit' whether through an increase in capital, income, or earning capacity and that they suffered from an 'economic disadvantage' based on their qualifying contributions such as a present or future loss, that is, diminution in current savings as a result of expenditure. Crucially, and departing from the principles of property law routinely used by cohabitants, a qualifying contribution was any contribution arising from the cohabiting relationship which was made to the parties' shared lives or to the welfare of members of their families. Contributions were not limited to financial contributions, and included future contributions, in particular to the care of the parties' children following separation.

Once the applicant demonstrated an economic imbalance, the court could then make an order to adjust the retained benefit by reversing it in so far as that was reasonable and practicable having regard to the discretionary factors. The discretionary factors were:

- the welfare while a minor of any child of both parties who has not attained the age of eighteen;
- the financial needs and obligations of both parties;
- the extent and nature of the financial resources which each party has or is likely to have in the foreseeable future;
- the welfare of any children who live with, or might reasonably be expected to live with, either party; and
- the conduct of each party, defined restrictively but so as to include cases where a qualifying contribution can be shown to have been made despite the express disagreement of the other party.

If, after the reversal of any retained benefit, the applicant would still bear an economic disadvantage, the court may make an order sharing that loss equally between the parties, in so far as it was reasonable and practicable to do so, having regard to the discretionary factors. In making an order to share economic disadvantage, the court was not able to place the applicant, for the foreseeable future, in a stronger economic position than the respondent.

As to the relief available, the court would have a wide array of remedies at its disposal which included a property transfer, lump sum payments, pension-sharing but, interestingly, not periodic maintenance payments as the proposal strongly favoured a 'clean break' and the severing of financial ties between the parties.

Despite the formation of a comprehensive and detailed proposal, there were concerns expressed by some academics as to how the scheme would work in practice and whether economic imbalance was the most effective basis for intervention.[226] The government response was to wait for the research findings of a similar scheme implemented in Scotland

---

[226] For criticism of the proposal, see Hughes, D., Davis, M., and Jacklin, L. 'Come Live With Me and Be My Love—A Consideration of the 2007 Law Commission Proposals on Cohabitation Breakdown' [2008] *Conveyancer and Property Lawyer* 197.

via the Family Law (Scotland) Act 2006.[227] In March 2008 the then Parliamentary Under-Secretary of State for Justice, Bridget Prentice, stated:

> The government propose to await the outcome of this research and extrapolate from it the likely cost to this jurisdiction of bringing into effect the scheme proposed by the Law Commission and the likely benefits it will bring. For the time being, therefore, the government will take no further action.[228]

In September 2011, after the findings had been published in a comprehensive report,[229] the government decided to take no further action believing that the law in Scotland did not provide 'a sufficient basis for a change in the law' and that it would be imprudent to reform the law in light of on-going changes to the family justice system.[230] Nevertheless, in *Gow v Grant*, a Supreme Court decision concerning the Scottish provisions, Lady Hale responded with disappointment to the decision not to reform the law in England and Wales:

> The main lesson from this case, as also from the research so far, is that a remedy such as this is both practicable and fair. It does not impose upon unmarried couples the responsibilities of marriage but redresses the gains and losses flowing from their relationship. As the researchers comment, 'The Act has undoubtedly achieved a lot for Scottish cohabitants and their children'. English and Welsh cohabitants and their children deserve no less.[231]

7.3.3 Private Members Bills

Several Private Members Bills have been introduced into Parliament, many of which are responses to a failure by the government to implement the Law Commission's proposal in 2007. In December 2008, Liberal Democrat peer Lord Lester of Herne Hill introduced such a Bill into the House of Lords.[232] The motivation behind the Bill was similar to that of the Law Commission's proposal. When introducing the Bill he stated that '[i]t is a scandal in modern Britain that existing law does almost nothing to prevent such people from losing their home or sliding into poverty if their relationship breaks down or if their partner dies'.[233] Nevertheless, the scheme did possess several distinct features.

In order to claim under Lord Lester's proposal, the applicant needed to have lived together as a couple with their partner for either two years or have a child together. Unlike the economic imbalance concept that underpinned the Law Commission's *Cohabitation Report*, the court under this Bill could make awards 'when just and equitable to do so, having regard to all the circumstances'. This would be after recourse to a statutory checklist referencing reasonable needs of the parties, provision for children, and also an assessment of the level of commitment exhibited in the relationship. The relief available mirrored that available to divorcing couples and, unlike the Law Commission proposal, permitted maintenance payments. Parties could disapply the application of the scheme but could revoke any opt-out agreement if manifestly unfair.

---

[227] On the Scottish provisions, see Miles, J., Wasoff, F., and Mordaunt, E. 'Cohabitation: Lessons From Research North of the Border?' (2011) 23 *Child and Family Law Quarterly* 302, and McCarthy, F. 'Cohabitation: Lessons From North of the Border?' (2011) 23 *Child and Family Law Quarterly* 277.

[228] Col. 122WS, 6 March 2008.

[229] Nuffield Foundation Study, *Legal Practitioners' Perspectives on the Cohabitation Provisions of the Family Law (Scotland) Act 2006* (2010).

[230] Col. 16WS, 6 September 2011 (Jonathan Djanogly (The Parliamentary Under-Secretary of State for Justice)).

[231] *Gow v Grant* [2012] UKSC 29, at [56].

[232] See generally, Probert, R. 'The Cohabitation Bill' [2009] 39 *Family Law* 150 and Morris, G. 'The Cohabitation Bill' [2009] 39 *Family Law* 627. A similar Private Member's Bill by Mary Creagh MP was introduced into the House of Commons in 2009 but did not progress any further.

[233] Resolution, 'New Bill to Tackle Living Together Injustice' (10 July 2008).

Overall, Lord Lester's proposal received criticism for being a very discretionary scheme with many elements that were too similar to the Matrimonial Causes Act 1973. In particular, Deech expressed fears that such cohabitation reform would create economic dependency on the part of women:

> What message would such a Cohabitation Bill give to young girls contemplating further education when it opens the way to huge handouts to women who have been fortunate enough to live with a rich man for a while; while others, equally deserving, will get nothing at the end of a relationship because there are no assets available to be shared? The Lester Bill would be a windfall for lawyers but for no one else except the gold digger. It would be bad for Bridget Jones; bad for commitment, stability and children; and a breach of the right to private life and the freedom to marry or not.[234]

Whereas the Law Commission sought to clearly differentiate their proposal from how the court divides assets between spouses and civil partners, Lord Lester's proposal echoed much of the discretion and flexibility available in that system. Like the fate of many Private Member's Bills, no further progress was made.

The most recent development in this area is Lord Marks' Cohabitation Rights Bill. This Private Members Bill was introduced into the House of Lords in 2016 for a third time. It received its first reading in July 2017 with a second reading yet to be scheduled. This Bill largely mirrors the Law Commission proposal but with some minor modifications as to eligibility. Nevertheless, as Lord Marks does not have the backing of the government, it is unlikely that this Bill will proceed any further. This means that, despite multiple attempts at reform, cohabitation will remain a largely unregulated area of family law and any vulnerability generated by relationship breakdown will continue to be inadequately addressed by the courts.

SUMMARY

1. Should we overhaul the formalities for entry into marriage?
   - Marriage is a formalised family form and status. Certain rights and legal protections are imposed on spouses.
   - Despite continued support for marriage, particularly following the introduction of same-sex marriage in 2014, the legal framework applicable to formalities remains outdated, overly complex, and prone to cause injustice.
   - Failure to comply with marriage formalities can have profound consequences. Whilst a void marriage following knowing and wilful disregard of formalities generates the ability for a party to seek financial orders, a finding of non-marriage by the court does not.

2. Is there a continuing need for a law of nullity?
   - The ecclesiastical courts first developed the law of nullity at a time when divorce was not permitted. Religion heavily informed the grounds upon which parties could seek a decree of nullity.
   - Nullity plays a much lesser role in modern family law. Even though England and Wales possesses a fast, administrative divorce procedure, there are still litigants that seek to annul their marriages on the basis of nullity.

---

[234] See Deech, R. 'Cohabitation' [2010] *Family Law* 39. For an opposing view on the characterisation of women as 'gold-diggers', see Thompson, S. 'In Defence of the "Gold Digger" (2016) 6 *Oñati Socio-Legal Series* 1225.

- The legal framework for nullity has several features that to modern eyes look anachronistic and not appropriate for the twenty-first century. Nevertheless, for individuals who have faith-based opposition to divorce, nullity provides an important option for the termination of their relationship.

3. Do civil partnerships have a future in an era of same-sex marriage?
    - When introduced in 2005, civil partnerships were an important break-through for same-sex couples that hitherto were unable to have their relationships recognised formally. They offered same-sex couples virtually the same benefits as those received by married couples.
    - Civil partnerships were popular when first introduced. Part of this popularity must be attributed to the fact that at the time of introduction there was no prospect of same-sex marriage and therefore civil partnerships were the only formal means of obtaining legal protection.
    - A more pressing issue today is whether opposite-sex couples should be able to form a civil partnership. The availability of civil marriage has been cited as a reason against extending the Civil Partnership Act 2004 to opposite-sex couples. However, for those couples with strong opposition to marriage, it is understandable why a secular, administrative process could be viewed as attractive.

4. Should there be reform of the law relating to cohabitation?
    - Cohabitation has occurred for centuries but has received little attention by the state. Whereas entry into marriage and civil partnership triggers certain legal consequences, cohabitation is private, informal and, in many ways, outside the control of the state.
    - There are marked differences between how the law treats cohabitants and married couples or civil partners. Furthermore, the public is dangerously unaware of this difference in treatment.
    - Those opposing reform see the private and flexible nature of cohabitation as important virtues. Imposition of remedies onto a class of individuals that, arguably, do not want them nor have signed up for them, is viewed as a violation of private autonomy.

Further Reading

AUCHMUTY, R. 'The Limits of Marriage Protection in Property Allocation When a Relationship Ends' (2016) 28 *Child and Family Law Quarterly* 303
- Challenges the view that cohabitation generates party vulnerability and calls for public education as to the legal rights of cohabitants.

BARLOW, A. and SMITHSON, J. 'Legal Assumptions, Cohabitants' Talk and the Rocky Road to Reform' (2010) 22 *Child and Family Law Quarterly* 328
- Categorises cohabitants into four relationship types and analyses recent law reform attempts.

DEECH, R. 'The Case Against the Legal Recognition of Cohabitation' (1980) 29 *International and Comparative Law Quarterly* 480
- Argues against the introduction of a legal framework giving rights to cohabitants on the basis that it would intrude on the autonomy of the parties.

FENWICK, H. and HAYWARD, A. 'Rejecting asymmetry of access to formal relationship statuses for same and different-sex couples at Strasbourg and domestically' (2017) *European Human Rights Law Review* 544
  - Analyses the domestic and human rights implications stemming from the failure to open civil partnerships to opposite-sex couples in England and Wales.

GAFFNEY RHYS, R. 'Same Sex Marriage but not Mixed-Sex Partnerships: Should the Civil Partnership Act 2004 be extended to Opposite Sex Couples?' (2014) 24 *Child and Family Law Quarterly* 173
  - Calls for the extension of civil partnerships to opposite-sex couples on the basis of equality, privacy, dignity, and autonomy.

HAYWARD, A. 'Family Property' and the Process of Familialization of Property Law' (2012) 23 *Child and Family Law Quarterly* 284
  - Considers attempts by the courts to ameliorate the harshness of property law when applied to cohabiting relationships.

PROBERT, R. 'Hyde v Hyde: Defining or Defending Marriage?' (2007) 19 *Child and Family Law Quarterly* 322
  - Questions whether *Hyde v Hyde* provided a definition of marriage and argues that it offered a defence of marriage that should not be invoked in the future.

PROBERT, R. 'The Evolving Concept of Non-Marriage' (2013) 25 *Child and Family Law Quarterly* 314
  - Explores case law that has developed the concept of non-marriage and calls for a downplaying of party intention as a determining factor.

3

Seeking a Divorce

Edwina Higgins and Kathryn Newton

LEARNING OBJECTIVES

After reading this chapter you will be able to:

- Appreciate the historical and societal factors that have influenced current divorce law and practice;
- Identify the rules establishing and proving legal reasons for breakdown of marriage and civil partnerships, and the procedures to bring those relationships to a formal end;
- Critically assess the issues raised by fault-based divorce law and process and arguments for reform;
- Critique arguments about the relationship between the divorce law and divorce rates;
- Identify and discuss alternative models of divorce law.

DEBATES

After reading this chapter, you should be equipped to discuss your opinion on the following central debates:

- Should divorce law be reformed?
- Why is adultery between people of the same sex not recognised as adultery by the law?
- What does *Owens v Owens* add to interpretation of behaviour in divorce law?
- Does divorce law influence the divorce rate and does this matter?
- Should the state regulate the reasons for divorce?

---

1. Introduction

In this chapter, we consider the law and process for seeking a divorce in England and Wales. Divorce simply means the legal ending of a marriage. We will also—where relevant—consider the law and process required to end a civil partnership (the marriage-like status available for same-sex couples) (see Chapter 2), which is called dissolution rather than divorce.

Divorce is rather different from many topics on the family law syllabus. Unlike most other topic areas, there is a considerable gap between the law and the practice. In order to understand the topic properly, it is important to distinguish between the legal principles that govern divorce (see 3.1 and 3.2) and the procedure for divorce (see 3.3). The practical reality is that almost anyone who wants a divorce can get one (eventually)—as long as he or she follows the correct procedure. A few seconds on google throws up numerous websites offering quick divorces at a knockdown price. Unless the other spouse defends the divorce—and 98% of divorce petitions are undefended[1]—the legal principles are not meaningfully applied or tested in court. It is extremely rare for a divorce petition to be refused because of a failure to satisfy the legal test for divorce—so unusual, in fact, that it attracted headline news when a defended petition was refused by the Court of Appeal in March 2017 in the case of *Owens v Owens*.[2]

110,951 divorces were granted in England and Wales in 2014, well down from the peak of 164,556 in 1993 but still a significant number for the courts to process.[3] Recent reforms affecting divorce have tended to focus on matters of procedure—including, for example, creating divorce centres, and piloting of online divorce—to manage the high volume of applications efficiently. However, the problems with the substantive law have been highlighted by *Owens* and have revived calls for reform.[4]

 DEBATE 1: SHOULD DIVORCE LAW BE REFORMED?

The need for reform of the substantive law of divorce underpins this chapter and there is overwhelming evidence in favour of it. Criticisms of the current legal framework principally focus on the concept of the 'matrimonial fault'. By this, we mean proving your entitlement to a divorce by reference to the conduct of your spouse: showing that in some way he or she has 'breached' the standards required in marriage (e.g. by having an affair, or behaving badly). Fault-based divorce is a concept rooted in historical and patriarchal expectations of what marriage entails. Opponents of fault argue that it has no place in a modern divorce law, and many jurisdictions globally have moved away from it. The commonest objection is that allegations of fault worsen relations between the couple needlessly, and that this serves no useful purpose in determining whether the marriage should end. This leads to a further criticism: that the legal procedures give only lip service to the letter of the law in undefended cases. The procedure for undefended divorces means that fault-based petitions can be processed quickly (the so-called 'quickie' divorce, usually based on behaviour).

The debate over whether proving fault should play a part in a modern divorce law is part of a wider theoretical question: whether (and to what extent) the state should regulate the reasons behind a decision to divorce. To put it another way: is (or should) marital breakdown

[1] Ministry of Justice, *Family Justice: Guide to Family Law Courts* (15 December 2016). Available at: https://www.gov.uk/government/uploads/system/uploads/attachment_data/file/577009/guide-to-family-court-statistics.pdf, accessed 1 March 2017, 8.

[2] *Owens v Owens* [2017] EWCA Civ 182. See. e.g., BBC news, 'Wife of 39 years fails in divorce refusal appeal' (24 March 2017). Available at: http://www.bbc.co.uk/news/uk-england-hereford-worcester-39380779, accessed 24 March 2017; Owen Boycott, 'Woman "trapped in loveless marriage" after judges refuse divorce', *The Guardian*, 24 March 2017. Available at: https://www.theguardian.com/lifeandstyle/2017/mar/24/tini-owens-trapped-loveless-marriage-judges-refuse-divorce, accessed 24 March 2017.

[3] ONS Statistical Bulletin, 'Divorces in England and Wales: 2014'. Available at: https://www.ons.gov.uk/peoplepopulationandcommunity/birthsdeathsandmarriages/divorce/bulletins/divorcesinenglandandwales/2014#divorces-continue-to-decline-in-2014, accessed 1 March 2017.

[4] *Owens v Owens* [2017] EWCA Civ 182, at [98], per Munby P.

be a private decision, or should there be some form of accountability for, and scrutiny of, that decision before it can be translated into the legal end of a marriage (or civil partnership)? At the heart of this debate is whether the act of entering into the legal and public status of marriage justifies a restriction on an individual's—or a couple's—autonomy in respect of ending their personal relationships.

Calls for reform in the twenty-first century have come from divorce practitioners, judges, and academics with increasing frequency. One obvious question to ask is why this has not yet happened. The short answer is that it nearly did. Part II of the Family Law Act 1996 introduced 'no-fault' divorce, based on a neutral process, including a waiting period. However, these provisions were never brought into force.

The long answer is more complex. The history of divorce reform has been controversial. Supporters of retaining state scrutiny argue that reform, especially removal of fault-based grounds, makes divorce easier, which in turn causes a rise in the divorce rate and undermines the institution of marriage. Supporters of reform counter that marital breakdown is a private matter, and divorce law should reflect this. If divorce is difficult, this will (obviously) affect the number of divorces, but a lower number of divorces may mask an unknown number of marital breakdowns. In other words, the concept of 'marital breakdown' is not the same as divorce, and thus a rise in divorce is not necessarily caused by making divorce easier but may instead represent the formal ending of marriages that had broken down anyway. Supporters of reform also point to the example of the 'quickie' divorce as evidence that fault-based divorce is in practical terms easy in any case.

It seems likely that calls for reform will be strengthened in the light of *Owens v Owens* in which the Court of Appeal stated that reform of the substantive law was a matter for Parliament.[5]

In this chapter, we examine the current legal framework and the gap between the 'law in books' and the practical reality. We look at the current legal provisions (see section 3), the criticisms that have been made of them (section 4) and explore whether there are any strengths to the current law (section 5). We place this discussion in the context of divorce statistics, to discuss what link there is between the divorce law and the divorce rate, and discuss whether this matters (section 6). In doing so, we consider how much of a role the state should play in regulating divorce—with reference to autonomy—and the place of 'fault' in a modern divorce law. We also consider matters of process and procedure and whether reform of process rather than substantive law is the right focus (section 7). We start with a note on divorce terminology before turning to a brief history of divorce reform, to give context to the current position.

1.1 Terminology

Proceedings for divorce and dissolution of civil partnerships take place in the Family Court at a designated divorce centre.[6] The procedure and terminology for undefended divorce and dissolution proceedings (the vast majority) is shown in Figure 3.1.

Note that Step 3 represents the intersection between the law and procedure, since this is the point at which the legal principles are notionally applied.

---

[5] [2017] EWCA Civ 182.

[6] The Family Court was set up under the County Courts Act 1984, s. 31A, as inserted by the Crime and Courts Act 2013; the decision to designate certain locations as Divorce Centres was taken by HM Courts and Tribunals Service soon afterwards.

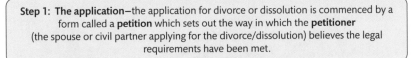

Step 1: The application—the application for divorce or dissolution is commenced by a form called a **petition** which sets out the way in which the **petitioner** (the spouse or civil partner applying for the divorce/dissolution) believes the legal requirements have been met.

Step 2: Acknowledgment of service—the petition is sent to the **respondent** (the other spouse or civil partner) who is required to complete a form called an **acknowledgement of service** in which s/he confirms receipt of the petition and indicates whether or not s/he wishes to oppose the application for divorce/dissolution. The respondent files the acknowledgment of service at court.

Step 3: Application for Decree Nisi or Conditional Order - when the respondent has returned the acknowledgment of service indicating that s/he does not wish to defend, the petitioner applies for:

Decree Nisi (the provisional order for divorce) OR

Conditional Order (the provisional order for dissolation of a CP)

A District Judge or Legal Adviser considers whether the petitioner has met the legal requirement. This is done on paper, by checking the documents that have been filed at court. If the requirements are satisfied, a certificate is issued to confirm that the petitioner is entitled to Decree Nisi and the date on which the Decree Nisi will be pronounced.

Step 4 (Marriage): Decree Absolute— the petitioner can apply for the final decree, Decree Absolute, which ends the marriage and finalises the divorce, six weeks after the date of the Decree Nisi.

Step 4 (Civil Partnership): Final Order— the petitioner can apply for the **final order** which ends the civil partnership and finalises the dissolution, six weeks after the date of the conditional order.

Figure 3.1 Procedure and terminology for undefended divorce and dissolution proceedings

2. Historical and social context

Current arguments around divorce reform and whether the concept of the 'matrimonial fault' has a place in modern divorce law are rooted in the historical origins of divorce law. Figure 3.2 outlines key steps in the development of the law and practice, and the arrows underneath show how the grounds for divorce have been extended from 1857 to the present.

2.1 Origins of court-administered divorce

Before 1858, there was no judicial procedure for divorce. Instead, the church courts could issue a separation decree and the secular courts could award damages for 'criminal conversation'.[7] A private Act of Parliament (Parliamentary divorce) was needed to end the marriage and permit remarriage. Parliamentary divorce was available on the grounds of adultery only, as the Church of England was prepared to sanction this because there was

---

[7] An extraordinary tort in which a husband could claim substantial damages against a man for having sex with his wife; the wife was not involved in the suit and no wife could claim any damages for the adultery of her husband.

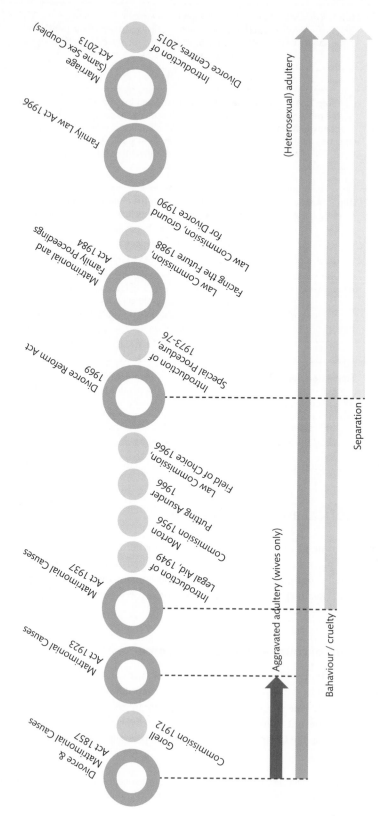

Figure 3.2 Timeline of key events in development of divorce law and extension of grounds

some justification for it in its religious doctrine.[8] The influence of the established Church on legislation relating to marriage and divorce remained an important factor in debates about reform during the twentieth century. Parliamentary divorce was generally also only accessible to men.[9]

The Divorce and Matrimonial Causes Act 1857 transferred divorce to the jurisdiction of the secular courts (a newly created divorce court in London). The ground for divorce for a husband was his wife's adultery; for a wife, her husband's incestuous adultery or adultery plus an 'aggravating factor'.[10] Divorce was available therefore solely to an 'innocent' spouse based on a matrimonial fault committed by their husband or wife. These were all the same principles that had existed before the Act (i.e. those for a Parliamentary divorce); the reform was one of procedure rather than of principle.

Not surprisingly, since divorce was complex and expensive divorce numbers were low before the Act (averaging two to five a year—almost all by husbands—between 1800 and 1850). Numbers rose after the Act; by 1900 there were nearly 600 divorces a year. The relationship between the divorce rate and both the nature of divorce law and the accessibility and expense of divorce procedure remain significant factors in current reform debates. See Figures 3.5–3.7 and 6 for further discussion of divorce statistics.

2.2 Early twentieth century

During the first half of the twentieth century, there were significant reforms, partly influenced by a Royal Commission that reported in 1912.[11] The Commission recommended removal of the discrimination between husbands and wives in respect of adultery, and allowing other matrimonial faults beyond adultery to constitute grounds for divorce. The third significant recommendation was to extend mechanisms for divorce adjudication outside London, so divorce became less dependent on the wealth of the petitioner.

It took some time to implement any of these recommendations. The Matrimonial Causes Act 1923 allowed wives to petition for simple adultery, though the reform was driven by pragmatism over legal anomalies as much as removal of discrimination.[12] The Church of England Bishops in the House of Lords opposed extension of the grounds beyond adultery. Supporters of widening the grounds pointed out that the adultery ground was being (mis) used in so-called 'hotel room' cases, where one spouse (usually the husband) agreed to be 'caught' in a hotel bed with a member of the opposite sex, hired for the purpose, to manufacture evidence of adultery that had not actually happened. The courts generally accepted this, despite the collusion involved, and these 'hotel cases' are an example of couples exercising mutual autonomy over the ending of their relationship despite the fault requirements not being met in reality. This is still a relevant issue today, where the respondent's admission of adultery is sufficient evidence for a petition to be granted, or where a couple agree to proceed on allegations of behaviour that they know to be manufactured or exaggerated.

The Matrimonial Causes Act 1937[13] finally widened the grounds beyond adultery to include cruelty, wilful desertion for three years and incurable insanity for five years.

---

[8] The 'Matthaean Exception', referring to the verses of Saint Matthew within the Bible from which the view that adultery was a valid reason for ending a marriage derived authority.

[9] Only four women successfully petitioned for divorce in this period (albeit not based on adultery alone but adultery plus some other factor).

[10] Wilful desertion for two years, bigamy or cruelty, or rape, sodomy or bestiality.

[11] The Gorell Commission, *Report of the Royal Commission on Divorce and Matrimonial Causes* (Cd 6478, 1912).

[12] Probert, R. 'The Controversy of Equality and the Matrimonial Causes Act 1923' (1999) 11 *Child and Family Law Quarterly* 33, para 2.

[13] Introduced as a Private Member's Bill by A.P. Herbert MP, a prominent supporter of divorce reform.

Arguably, this final ground was the first allowance of 'no-fault' divorce in the sense that allowing divorce where the respondent was incurably insane was allowing divorce without attaching moral blame to the respondent. But it was not really 'no-fault' in the sense it is used in contemporary debates, of being able to divorce without having to specify circumstances related to the conduct of the other spouse at all. The 1937 Act also introduced a bar on beginning divorce proceedings within three years of the marriage, though there was judicial discretion to allow proceedings to commence sooner to alleviate hardship (e.g. in cases of violence). The introduction of the bar was a compromise to allay the concerns of those worried that widening the grounds for divorce undermined the institution of marriage.

It is too narrow to look at divorce law reform without also considering developments in divorce procedure and the financing of divorce. Two such developments are worth noting at this point: the first was the implementation of recommendations from the Denning Committee[14] to expand divorce jurisdiction to some County Court judges. This was a measure to cope with the rising number of petitions after the Second World War, and is an example of a pragmatic procedural response to increased demand for divorce. The second was the provision of Legal Aid for divorce in 1950 following the Rushcliffe Report.[15] The Legal Aid and Advice Act 1949 aimed to 'provide legal advice for those of slender means and resources'.[16] Both of these provisions made divorce far more accessible in practical terms than it had been before.

2.3 The Divorce Reform Act 1969

In the 1950s, calls were made for further reform, and in particular for the removal of fault. However, a further Royal Commission, the Morton Commission,[17] made no recommendations for reform of the substantive grounds for divorce, emphasising the value to the state in having stable marriages. The impetus towards no-fault divorce was temporarily halted, but it remained a matter of debate during the 1960s, in the context of liberalising legislation on a number of other matters of private morality (e.g. decriminalisation of homosexual acts in private between consenting adults, and abortion).

Reformers argued that there were increasing numbers of couples in 'empty shell' marriages, that is, those in which there was *de facto* marital breakdown but no access to divorce. Some formed new relationships but could not marry, leading to a rise in children born outside marriage. A driver for reform was therefore to permit remarriage and legitimise the children of these unions.

Two reports in 1966 advocated reform. The first of these was *Putting Asunder*, published by a special group set up by the Archbishop of Canterbury.[18] Significantly, this marked the end of the established Church's opposition to the removal of the matrimonial fault, which had been a barrier to previous reform attempts. The second was *The Field of Choice*,[19] from

---

[14] *Final Report of the Committee on Procedure in Matrimonial Causes (the Denning Committee)* (Cmd 7024, 1946).

[15] Committee on Legal Aid and Legal Advice (chaired by Lord Rushcliffe), *Report of the Committee on Legal Aid and Legal Advice* (Cmd 6641, 1945).

[16] Cited in: Brooke, Sir H. 'The History of Legal Aid 1945 to 2010' (*Henry Brooke Musings, Memories and Miscellanea*, 16 July 2016). Available at: https://sirhenrybrooke.me/2016/07/16/the-history-of-legal-aid-1945-to-2010, accessed 15 February 2017.

[17] Lord Chancellor's Department, *Royal Commission on Marriage and Divorce* (Cmd 9678, 1956).

[18] Archbishop of Canterbury's Group on the Reform of Divorce, *Putting Asunder, A divorce law for contemporary society* (1966).

[19] Law Commission, *Reform of the Grounds for Divorce: The Field of Choice* (Cmnd 3123, Law Com No. 6, 1966).

the newly formed Law Commission. *Putting Asunder* recommended marital breakdown as the test, investigated by means of a judicial inquest. The Law Commission agreed but felt that an inquest into the full circumstances of the breakdown was impractical. A compromise—based on an inquiry into whether one of a range of reasons deemed to establish breakdown was proven—was enacted as the Divorce Reform Act 1969.[20]

The 1969 Act—which came into force on 1 January 1971, and was later consolidated into the Matrimonial Causes Act 1973—introduced the current substantive law, based on the concept of irretrievable breakdown of the marriage as the sole ground for divorce. It was heralded as no-fault divorce, though (as discussed in 3) irretrievable breakdown could only be established by proving one of five 'facts', three of which were based on the matrimonial fault grounds of the previous legislation (adultery, behaviour—instead of cruelty—and desertion). The other two facts were both based on 'living apart' (known as the 'separation' facts), either for two years, where the spouses agreed to divorce, or five years where they did not. The separation facts enabled divorce without citing any form of conduct by the other spouse for the first time. There was a protective mechanism, for a spouse 'innocent' of a matrimonial fault, to contest a five year separation divorce. This allayed fears that the five year separation fact constituted what was described as a 'Casanova's charter'.[21] The three-year bar on presentation of a petition was retained, and as a further measure towards 'marriage-saving', solicitors acting for petitioners were required to file a certificate confirming that they had discussed with the petitioner whether there was any prospect of reconciliation.

Therefore, sitting behind the no-fault concept of irretrievable breakdown, there was in reality a mixed system, partly based on fault and partly no-fault reasons for divorce. The general expectation was that most people would use one of the two living apart facts, thus reducing the reliance on alleging matrimonial fault. This did not prove to be the case. After an initial glut of petitions based upon five years' separation—in most cases, representing the 'empty shell' marriages that did not fit any of the previously available grounds—most divorces continued to be granted on the basis of adultery or behaviour, both quicker than waiting to establish separation. Use of the fault of desertion declined, as separation was easier to establish.

2.4 Procedural developments in the 1970s

Following the changes to the substantive law, there were changes to the divorce process with the introduction of the Matrimonial Causes Rules[22] (this was secondary legislation—a statutory instrument).

The judicial inquiry into irretrievable breakdown took place at a Decree Nisi hearing in open court at which the judge heard evidence, even if the divorce was undefended. At the end of the hearing, the judge, if satisfied, granted the Decree Nisi of divorce. In 1973 an exception to this procedure was introduced, a so-called 'special procedure',[23] solely for undefended divorces for childless couples divorcing by agreement after living apart for two years, under which there was no requirement to attend court for a hearing. Instead, the inquiry was a paper exercise, with the petitioner providing a sworn affidavit to provide the necessary evidence of irretrievable breakdown and the fact of separation.[24] Significant changes in the 1970s meant that the special procedure was extended to all undefended

---

[20] Divorce Reform Act 1969, s. 1(3) and Matrimonial Causes Act 1973, s. 1(3).
[21] See, e.g., the comments of Lord Stow-Hill, Hansard HL, vol 303, col 296 (30 June 1969).
[22] Matrimonial Causes Rules 1973 (SI 1973/2016).
[23] Matrimonial Causes Rules 1973 (SI 1973/2016), r. 33(3).
[24] Matrimonial Causes Rules 1973 (SI 1973/2016), r. 33(3).

divorces and therefore the old judicial inquiry in court became a paper exercise for the majority of divorce applications.

Why were these procedural changes made? In short, to cope with rising divorce numbers and spiralling legal aid costs. In 1974, the Finer Report,[25] which called for a unified system of family courts, had asked questions about the cost of divorce jurisdiction.[26] Even before the 1969 Divorce Reform Act, there was considerable concern about legal aid expenditure on divorce. A study in Birmingham in 1969 showed that 86% of legal aid certificates related to family cases.[27] Some contemporary commentators denied there was a simple causal link between the availability of legal aid and the number of divorces[28] but the cost of civil legal aid had trebled by the early 1970s and momentum was growing for a change to the legal aid system to stem its rising costs and target its resources (see Chapter 15).

The number of petitions rose to over 100,000 after the 1969 Act (see Figure 3.7) and by 1973 the proportion of undefended divorce had risen by more than 50%.[29] Attention turned to the amount of court time spent on judicial hearings for undefended petitions. Research in 1973 (by Elston and others) into undefended divorces[30] found Decree Nisi hearing inefficient and costly, commenting that the 'challenge facing the legal system is to provide a procedure which enables courts to perform more realistically the duties required by substantive law . . .'[31]

The special procedure was seized upon as a scheme that had the potential to meet the challenge Elston identified. In 1975,[32] the special procedure was extended to undefended divorces between childless couples relying on adultery, desertion, and five years' separation. From 1 April 1977,[33] it was extended to all undefended divorces, irrespective of whether there were children and whatever the fact relied on. By this point, it was no longer 'special', though the name stuck, and since then, it has been the respondent's decision whether or not to defend the divorce that determines whether the case follows the special procedure or is heard in open court.

These changes were contentious. The judiciary warned that scrutiny of irretrievable breakdown should not be a 'rubber stamp' even where the parties agreed the divorce.[34] Their concern was that in making divorce easier and quicker, the special procedure would dilute the judicial function. Freeman, in 1976, cited examples of scenarios of fault and no-fault facts to demonstrate that the evidence required by precedent would no longer be tested[35] and predicted that universal special procedure would result in a 'text-book account of the rules which will gradually lag further and further behind the law in action'.[36]

---

[25] Department of Health and Social Security, *Report of the Finer Committee on One-Parent Families* (Cmnd 5629, 1974).

[26] Department of Health and Social Security, *Report of the Finer Committee on One-Parent Families* (Cmnd 5629, 1974) 424.

[27] Lee Bridges, L. *et al*, *Legal Services in Birmingham* (1975), 146 cited by Freeman, M. 'Divorce without Legal Aid' (1976) 6 *Family Law* 255, 256.

[28] Freeman, M. 'Divorce without Legal Aid' (1976) 6 *Family Law* 255, 257.

[29] Elston, E., Fuller, J., and Murch, M. 'Judicial Hearings of Undefended Divorce Petitions' (1975) 38 *Modern Law Review* 609, 609.

[30] Elston, E., Fuller, F., and Murch, M. 'Judicial Hearings of Undefended Divorce Petitions' (1975) 38 *Modern Law Review* 609.

[31] Elston, E., Fuller, F., and Murch, M. 'Judicial Hearings of Undefended Divorce Petitions' (1975) 38 *Modern Law Review* 609, 640.

[32] Matrimonial Causes Rules 1975 (SI 1975/1359), r. 3.

[33] Matrimonial Causes Rules 1977 (SI 1977/344), r, 33(3).

[34] *Santos v Santos* [1972] Fam 247 CA.

[35] Freeman, M. 'Divorce without Legal Aid' (1976) 6 *Family Law* 255, 257, e.g., s. 1(2)(b) and s. 1(2)(d).

[36] Freeman, M. 'Divorce without Legal Aid' (1976) 6 *Family Law* 255, 258.

Early evidence of the effect of the procedural changes was identified by Westcott in 1978. [37] He was sceptical that the special procedure made divorce quicker, arguing that the time to get a decree depended more on the volume of work in individual courts, but he agreed with Freeman about the gap between the rules and the law in action. As we will see, the prediction turned out to be right.

The extension of the special procedure then coincided with and justified the withdrawal of legal aid for undefended divorce in the expectation that savings to the legal aid budget would be made. In fact those savings did not materialise, in part because a system of advice and assistance to petitioners acting in person was introduced (known as the Green Form Scheme[38]) and in larger part because legal aid continued to be available for related proceedings (meaning disputes over finances and children), 'the areas of real contest'.[39] Nonetheless, whilst it did not have the expected financial impact, the extension of the special procedure to all undefended divorces 'can in retrospect be seen to have transformed the whole basis of divorce law'[40] and process. Its effects underpin some of the present criticisms of the current law (see section 4) and are all the more remarkable since the original special procedure and its extensions were introduced without any debate at all, implemented as they were by statutory instruments. [41]

2.5 Towards the Family Law Act 1996

Throughout the 1970s and 1980s, divorce numbers continued to rise. In 1970, there were under 60,000 divorces, in 1985, nearly 160,000 (see Figure 3.7). The law was amended slightly by the Matrimonial and Family Proceedings Act 1984, to reduce the three-year bar (discussed in 2.2) on filing a petition after the marriage to a one year absolute bar.[42] The shortened length of time can be seen as part of the picture of modernising divorce, and the removal of judicial discretion to shorten the bar as another compromise to allay concerns that this would undermine marriage.

The Law Commission looked at divorce again in the late eighties, issuing two reports advocating reform, *Facing the Future* in 1988[43] and *The Ground for Divorce* in 1990.[44] These made comprehensive criticisms of the Matrimonial Causes Act 1973 framework (detailed in 4) and proposed no-fault divorce based on irretrievable breakdown, proved by a lapse of time following an initial statement of breakdown and intention to make arrangements for the future. No-fault divorce by process was eventually endorsed by the government.[45] The government proposal was similar to the Law Commission's: divorce based on irretrievable breakdown, but proved by going through a series of procedural steps including a lengthy waiting period, rather than by proving any particular facts or circumstances. The ethos of the reform promoted autonomy by allowing spouses to declare that their marriage was irretrievably broken down without saying why, but with a shift to ensuring the decision was

---

[37] Westcott, J.M. 'The Special Procedure—One Year Later—A Practitioner's View' [1978] 8 *Family Law* 209, 211.

[38] Introduced under the Legal Aid Act 1988.

[39] Hansard HL, vol 371, cols 1218–19.

[40] Cretney, S. *Family Law in the Twentieth Century* (OUP, 2005) 383.

[41] All of the procedural rules were introduced by statutory instrument pursuant to the Matrimonial Causes Act 1973, s. 50.

[42] Matrimonial and Family Proceedings Act 1984, s. 1, amending s. 3 of the Matrimonial Causes Act 1973.

[43] Law Commission, *Facing the Future: A Discussion Paper on the Ground for Divorce* (HC 479, Law Com No. 170, 1988).

[44] Law Commission, *Family Law: The Ground for Divorce* (HC 192, Law Com No. 192, 1990).

[45] In a Green Paper, Lord Chancellor's Department, *Looking to the Future—Mediation and the Ground for Divorce: a Discussion Paper* (Cm 2424, 1993), followed by a White Paper, Lord Chancellor's Department, *Looking to the Future—Mediation and the Ground for Divorce: the Government's Proposals* (Cm 2799, 1995).

well informed and considered. Personal responsibility for the decision was to be promoted (or even enforced) through compulsory information (at an information meeting not included in the Law Commission report[46]), potential referral to mediation, and a period of reflection. Therefore, although it liberalised divorce in terms of the removal of fault, it did so with a 'marriage-saving agenda'[47] with the information meeting 'as a means of influencing behaviour'.[48]

The Family Law Bill had a rocky passage through Parliament, reviving many familiar arguments about the role of the state, the institution of marriage, and the need to prevent 'easy' divorce that had occurred during debates on earlier Bills. In the same sort of compromise measure that characterised previous reforms, a statement of general principles was added, affirming that 'the institution of marriage is to be supported'[49] and detailing the balance to be struck between encouraging parties to save the marriage[50] and allowing broken down marriages to be ended with minimum hostility and cost.[51] The reference to cost illustrates continuing concern over public funding for divorce and consequential proceedings over financial matters and children.

The Bill was eventually passed as the Family Law Act 1996, but following unsuccessful piloting of the information sessions[52] the government put implementation of the new legislation on hold, as it did 'not meet Government objectives of saving marriages or helping divorcing couples to resolve problems with a minimum of acrimony'.[53] The problem was that very few couples had been diverted into mediation by the information sessions (7%) and instead there was a reported increase in the number who planned to see a solicitor.[54] Part II of the Family Law Act 1996 was eventually repealed in 2014.[55] However, the attempt to steer people to family mediation to resolve their disputes remained with a further amendment to legal aid provision requiring assessment/suitability for mediation as a prerequisite to applying for legal aid to bring financial or children proceedings[56] (see Chapter 15).

2.6 **Twenty-first century developments**

By the turn of the century, the number of divorces in England and Wales was at its lowest since 1979. Numbers rose slightly in the early 2000s but have since continued to fall (see Figure 3.7). This must be read in the context of a significant decrease in the number of marriages in the same period, since by definition only married couples can divorce. During this period, marriage was extended to same-sex couples, legal aid was withdrawn from divorce (and consequential finance and children proceedings),[57] and calls for reform of divorce law revived.

---

[46] Eekelaar, J. 'Family Law: Keeping us "on message"' (1999) 11 *Child and Family Law Quarterly* 387.

[47] Sclater, S.D. and Piper, C. 'Re-moralising the Family? Family Policy, Family law and Youth Justice' (2000) 12 *Child and Family Law Quarterly* 135.

[48] Eekelaar, J. 'Family Law: Keeping Us "On Message"' (1999) 11 *Child and Family Law Quarterly* 387.

[49] Family Law Act 1996, s. 1(a).   [50] Family Law Act 1996, s. 1(b).

[51] Family Law Act 1996, s. 1(c).

[52] Newcastle Centre for Family Studies, *Information Meetings & Associated Provisions within the Family Law Act 1996, Final Evaluation* (University of Newcastle upon Tyne, 2000).

[53] Lord Chancellor's Department, *Divorce Law Reform—Government proposes to repeal Part II of the Family Law Act 1996* (Press Release, 16 January 2001).

[54] Collier, R. 'The Dashing of a Liberal Dream? The Information Meeting, The "New Family" and the Limits of Law' (1999) 11 *Child and Family Law Quarterly* 257.

[55] Children and Families Act 2014, s. 18(1). The statement of general principles in Part I was retained, but confined to the operation of mediation by s. 18(4) of the same Act.   [56] Access to Justice Act 1999.

[57] Legal Aid, Sentencing and Punishment of Offenders Act 2013, although it remains available where certain conditions are met in cases involving violence.

2.6.1 Provision for same-sex couples

Until 2014, marriage—and therefore divorce—was confined to couples who were 'respectively male and female' under s. 11(c) of the Matrimonial Causes Act 1973 (see Chapter 2). The Civil Partnership Act 2004 created a status for same-sex couples to enter into a form of legal union, short of marriage, but with many of same legal rights and responsibilities. The Act also created a mechanism for dissolution similar to divorce. The Marriage (Same Sex Couples) Act 2013 removed the discriminatory restriction on marrying for same-sex couples. Same-sex marriages can be ended by divorce under the Matrimonial Causes Act 1973 in the same way as heterosexual marriages. The substantive law on these points will be discussed further in 3.

2.6.2 Further calls for reform

After the announcement in 2001 of the intention to repeal Part II of the Family Law Act 1996, interest in divorce reform appeared to wane for a while. It seems strange that after the Law Commission made such a compelling case for reform (detailed in section 4) the whole subject of no-fault divorce should have been dropped, and Shepherd points out that the 'failure' of the information meetings was no reason to abandon plans to reform the law at all.[58] However, calls have revived in recent years, in particular for the removal of fault from the process from, for example, senior members of the judiciary, including Baroness Hale,[59] Lord Wilson[60] and successive Presidents of the Family Division, including the current President James Munby,[61] and the late Nicholas Wall,[62] practitioners' organisations including Resolution[63] and the Law Society, and the government's Mediation Task Force.[64] The Family Justice Review (an extensive investigation into a wide range of family justice matters), specifically commenting that reform of the substantive law on divorce was outside its remit, made a number of proposals in relation to procedure and terminology.[65]

The Coalition government confirmed, in an answer to a written question in the House of Commons in 2012, that it did not intend to amend the substantive grounds for divorce, though it would introduce administrative reform.[66] There was discussion of no-fault divorce during the progress of the Children and Families Bill in 2013 (when the clause repealing Part II of the Family Law Act 1996 was considered). The (then) Justice Minister Tom McNally MP claimed the 'utmost respect' for those who supported the principle of no-fault divorce and said he understood 'why proponents of no-fault divorce believe that

---

[58] Shepherd, N. 'Ending the Blame Game: Getting No Fault Divorce Back on the Agenda' [2009] *Family Law* 122, 126.

[59] Bentham, M. 'Top judge calls for rules which force women to take off veils when giving evidence in court' *Evening Standard*, 12 December 2014. Available at: http://www.standard.co.uk/news/uk/top-judge-calls-for-rules-which-force-women-to-take-off-veils-when-giving-evidence-in-court-9920224.html, accessed 22 September 2017.

[60] Ames, J. 'No-fault divorce is long overdue, says top judge' *The Times*, 27 February 2017, 14.

[61] Munby, J. 'The Family Justice Reforms: remarks by Sir James Munby' (29 April 2014). Available at: https://www.judiciary.gov.uk/wp-content/uploads/2014/05/family-justice-reforms-29042014.pdf, accessed 1 March 2017 and *Owens v Owens* [2017] EWCA Civ 182, at [98].

[62] Wall, N. 'Speech to the Annual Resolution Conference' (24 March 2012). Available at: https://www.judiciary.gov.uk/wp-content/uploads/JCO/Documents/Speeches/pfd-speech-resolution-annual-conference-240312.pdf, accessed 1 March 2017.

[63] Edwards, J. 'MPs need to get behind no-fault divorce if they're serious about reducing family conflict' (Resolution Press Release, 3 December 2015). Available at: http://www.resolution.org.uk/news-list.asp?page_id=228&n_id=301, accessed 17 February 2017.

[64] Family Mediation Task Force, *Report of the Family Mediation Task Force* (2014).

[65] Norgrove, Sir D. *Family Justice Review Final Report* (2011), para 4.164.

[66] Grant, H. Hansard HC, col 390W (6 September 2012). Available at: https://www.publications.parliament.uk/pa/cm201213/cmhansrd/cm120906/text/120906w0001.htm#12090632000051.

the approach . . . would have helped to reduce conflict and acrimony'.[67] In 2015, a No Fault Divorce Bill was introduced as a Private Member's Bill. The title was somewhat misleading, since the Bill did not propose the removal of fault: instead it proposed that in addition to the existing provisions, divorce—and civil partnership dissolution—could take place after 12 months by mutual consent. The Bill failed to progress to second reading. This was the last time that Parliament considered legislation to amend the divorce law. We will return to the current prospects for reform at the end of the chapter.

3. Current law and process

As we have seen, the divorce provisions in Part II of the Family Law Act 1996 were never implemented, so by the 'current law' we mean the Matrimonial Causes Act 1973. This was a consolidating statute, combining the divorce elements of the Divorce Reform Act 1969 with provisions on financial remedies from the Matrimonial Proceedings and Property Act 1970. It has since been amended by the Matrimonial and Family Proceedings Act 1984, the Marriage (Same Sex Couples) Act 2013, and by the Children and Families Act 2014. The current law on civil partnerships is found in the Civil Partnership Act 2004.

3.1 One-year bar on proceedings

Under s. 3(1) there is absolute bar (discussed in 2.5) on filing a divorce petition within one year of the marriage, although circumstances from the first year may be used as evidence.[68] There is an identical provision for applications for dissolution of a civil partnership.[69]

3.2 Ground for divorce and dissolution of a civil partnership

There is one ground for divorce: that the marriage has 'irretrievably broken down'.[70] This is also the sole ground for dissolution of a civil partnership.[71]

 Key Legislation 1: Matrimonial Causes Act 1973, s. 1(1) and Civil Partnership Act 2004, s. 45(1)

Subject to the one-year bar:
The ground for divorce under s. 1(1) of the Matrimonial Causes Act 1973:

> a petition for divorce may be presented to the court by either party to a marriage on the ground that the marriage has broken down irretrievably.

The ground for dissolution under s. 45(1) of the Civil Partnership Act 2004:

> an application for a dissolution order may be made to the court by either civil partner on the ground that the civil partnership has broken down irretrievably.

---

[67] Hansard HL, col GC365 (23 October 2013). Available at: https://www.publications.parliament.uk/pa/ld201314/ldhansrd/text/131023-gc0001.htm#13102369000129, accessed 22 September 2017.

[68] Matrimonial Causes Act 1973, s. 3(1), as amended by the Matrimonial and Family Proceedings Act 1984.

[69] Civil Partnership Act 2004, s. 41.   [70] Matrimonial Causes Act 1973, s. 1(1).

[71] Civil Partnership Act 2004, s. 45(1).

Irretrievable breakdown can *only* be established by proving one of a number of 'facts' (which are therefore *de facto* grounds for divorce and dissolution).

 Key Legislation 2: The divorce facts under Matrimonial Causes Act 1973, s. 1(2)

The court hearing a petition for divorce shall not hold the marriage to have broken down irretrievably unless the petitioner satisfies the court of one or more of the following facts, that is to say:

(a) that the respondent has committed adultery and the petitioner finds it intolerable to live with the respondent;

(b) that the respondent has behaved in such a way that the petitioner cannot reasonably be expected to live with the respondent;

(c) that the respondent has deserted the petitioner for a continuous period of at least two years immediately preceding the presentation of the petition;

(d) that the parties to the marriage have lived apart for a continuous period of at least two years immediately preceding the presentation of the petition (hereafter in this Act referred to as 'two years' separation') and the respondent consents to a decree being granted;

(e) that the parties to the marriage have lived apart for a continuous period of at least five years immediately preceding the presentation of the petition (hereafter in this Act referred to as 'five years' separation').

Dissolution of a civil partnership is also based solely on the ground of irretrievable breakdown, and irretrievable breakdown can only be proved by a fact. The facts mirror four of those for divorce but irretrievable breakdown of a civil partnership cannot be proved by adultery.[72] Both divorce and dissolution are therefore available under a mixed system of fault and no-fault circumstances.

The court is under a duty to 'inquire, so far as it reasonably can, into the facts alleged by the petitioner/applicant and into any facts alleged by the respondent'.[73] Proving a fact raises a rebuttable presumption of irretrievable breakdown.[74] This means it is not possible to prove irretrievable breakdown without proving a fact, but it *is* possible to prove a fact without this constituting irretrievable breakdown, if the respondent produces evidence to rebut the presumption.

It is not necessary to prove that the irretrievable breakdown was *caused* by the occurrence of the s. 1(2) fact: 'the requirements in s. 1(1) and (2) of the 1973 Act are to be read disjunctively . . . they are separate requirements'.[75] This is a little odd, since there is clearly a link—the legal requirement of irretrievable breakdown *cannot* be proved without proving a fact—but the point is that the link need not be causal. As long as a s. 1(2) fact can be proved, the marriage may, in reality, have broken down for any reason.

---

[72] Civil Partnership Act 2004, s. 45(5).

[73] Matrimonial Causes Act 1973, s. 1(3); Civil Partnership Act 2004, s. 44(2).

[74] Matrimonial Causes Act 1973, s. 1(4); Civil Partnership Act 2004, s. 44(4).

[75] *Buffery v Buffery* [1988] 2 FLR 365, per May LJ at 366. See also *Stevens v Stevens* [1979] 1 WLR 885, per Sheldon J at 887: 'It is not necessary . . . that husband's behaviour, of which she now complains, was in any way responsible for the breakdown of the marriage.'

3.2.1 Adultery and 'intolerability'

The adultery fact is relevant only to discussion of divorce, not dissolution of a civil partnership.

Adultery

In *Dennis v Dennis*,[76] the court quoted the definition from *Rayden on Divorce*: 'Adultery may be defined as consensual sexual intercourse between a married person and a person of the opposite sex during the subsistence of the marriage.'[77] The Marriage (Same Sex Couples) Act 2013 inserted a new s. 1(6) into the Matrimonial Causes Act 1973 stating that 'only conduct between the respondent and a person of the opposite sex' can constitute adultery for the purpose of proving the fact for divorce. This confirmed the previous case law position.

As we have seen, adultery was historically the sole matrimonial 'offence' giving access to divorce, arising principally from Christian religious doctrines as to the functions of marriage, and the notion of sexual fidelity as cornerstone of the institution. Now that other reasons for granting a divorce are available, adultery has become less significant—around 13% of divorces in 2014 were granted on the basis of adultery petitions, a steady decline from around a quarter of divorces in the 1970s.[78]

The adultery element of the fact is objective, and must be evidenced, through an admission by the respondent or by some other evidence from which the court can presume that adultery has taken place. In practice, the respondent will usually admit the adultery so the question of proving it does not arise. If the respondent denies adultery, it may be presumed from evidence such as a couple spending the night together. In an adultery petition, the petitioner has the opportunity to name the (or a) co-respondent, which means the person with whom the extra-marital relationship took place (from whom costs may be claimed). Changes to the practice of naming co-respondents were consulted on in 2006, but not implemented.[79]

Whether or not the marriage is a same-sex one, therefore, a spouse having sex with someone of the same sex cannot form the basis of an adultery petition. Instead, it could form the basis of a behaviour petition. This discrepancy has been criticised.

DEBATE 2: WHY IS ADULTERY BETWEEN PEOPLE OF THE SAME SEX NOT LEGALLY RECOGNISED AS ADULTERY?

Adultery is specifically confined in law to sex between heterosexuals for the purposes of marriage, and it is not a recognised factor in the dissolution of a civil partnership. While marriage itself was confined to heterosexual couples, there was at least *some* logic in limiting adultery to heterosexual sex only, but now that the discrimination in marriage has been removed, it is an anomaly that an affair with someone else of the same sex does not constitute adultery. In effect, since it is much more likely that an extra-marital affair by someone in a same-sex marriage will also be with someone of the same sex, same-sex couples do not have access to divorce on realistically equivalent terms to heterosexual couples, including not being able to

---

[76] [1955] All ER 51.   [77] [1955] All ER 51, 55.

[78] ONS Dataset, 'Divorces in England and Wales: dataset 2014'. Available at: https://www.ons.gov.uk/peoplepopulationandcommunity/birthsdeathsandmarriages/divorce/datasets/divorcesinenglandandwales, accessed 17 February 2017.

[79] HMCS, *Family Procedure Rules: a new procedural code for Family Proceedings* (CP 19/06, 2006). Available at: http://217.35.77.12/CB/england/papers/pdfs/2006/cp1906.pdf, accessed 17 February 2017; HMCS and Ministry of Justice, *Family Procedure Rules: a new procedural code for Family Proceedings, Response to Consultation* (CP(R) 19/06, 2008). Available at: http://217.35.77.12/archive/England/papers/justice/pdfs/cp1307resp.pdf, accessed 17 February 2017.

name (and potentially claims costs against) a co-respondent. It also means that where the respondent is bisexual, the petitioner would have to cite a different divorce fact in the event of an extra-marital relationship by their spouse, depending on whether or not the infidelity was heterosexual.

Why is this? The problem was presented during the Parliamentary debates as a practical one: that extending the legal concept of adultery beyond heterosexual sex would have presented problems of definition. In the debates on the Bill, Hugh Robertson suggested this 'would not give couples adequate clarity'. He explained:

> The current definition of adultery has been developed in case law, and is detailed and explicit about the nature of sexual relations between members of the opposite sex that constitute adultery. The definition of adultery does not cover sexual relations between members of the same sex, or the precise acts which would constitute adultery between a man and another man, or a woman and another woman. That would of course need to be determined over time by the courts.[80]

This is not really a valid argument for a number of reasons: first, that something is problematic to define is not a reason for the law to refuse to acknowledge that it is exists. Secondly, (as Robertson acknowledged), heterosexual sex is not defined in the Act either; the nature of heterosexual sex is defined by a series of cases on consummation of marriage (see 5.3.1, in Chapter 2). Perhaps there was a reluctance to see the courts delving into the same matters in relation to homosexual sex, but in reality it is unlikely that this would be necessary: the vast majority of adultery allegations are admitted by the respondent. Even if they are not admitted, going to bed with someone of the opposite sex is sufficient to raise a presumption of sex having taken place, and this approach would work equally well for same-sex allegations. Thirdly, sexual acts between men, at least, were sufficiently capable of legal definition to constitute a criminal offence until 1967.

The debate smacks of reluctance by Parliament to admit that sex is not the sole province of heterosexual couples. The underlying message is that sexual fidelity is less important in a same-sex marriage than it is in a heterosexual marriage. Since the adultery fact is strongly rooted in perceptions of morality in marriage, this appears to pander to prejudices that same-sex relationships are less 'moral' than heterosexual ones.

Strangely, in the debates at the Committee stage on the Bill, the only support for same-sex adultery provisions came from opponents of same-sex marriage. They argued that it created a double standard; that effectively heterosexual couples are expected to treat their marriage as a faithful union, but same-sex couples are not. The Bill's opponents argued this proved their wider point; that marriage was intrinsically not equal and should be reserved for heterosexual couples. They used the government's omission to acknowledge same-sex adultery as evidence for their cause: that unions between couples of the same sex should continue to be recognised as civil partnerships rather than marriage.

How else could this have been tackled? Parliament could simply, of course, have omitted to put the case law confining adultery to heterosexual sex into the statute. It is difficult to see that any real problems would have been caused by this, other than potential opposition in the form of squeamishness from opponents of homosexuality generally. If there were really any problems in determining the nature of sexual intercourse, it could have been redefined, perhaps as 'sexual intimacy'.[81]

---

[80] PBC (Bill 126) 2012–13, col 439, 7 March 2013. Available at: https://www.publications.parliament.uk/pa/cm201213/cmpublic/marriage/130307/pm/130307s01.pdf, accessed 22 September 2017.

[81] Crompton, L. 'Where's the Sex in Same Sex Marriage?' [2013] *Family Law* 564, 572.

An alternative solution would have been to remove adultery as a fact altogether for all divorces,[82] so that extra-marital sex of any kind would constitute behaviour rather than adultery regardless of gender. It is clear from the discussions during the Marriage (Same Sex Couples) Bill that such a move would have faced opposition from the self-styled upholders of marriage as an institution requiring adherence to fidelity and vows.

Opposition to the removal of the adultery fact has also been voiced from the opposite perspective: it has been argued that removing adultery as a divorce fact—thus giving the appearance of 'demoting' the importance of sexual fidelity in marriage—at the same time as opening marriage to same-sex couples, could have sent a message that gay people were not capable of having the same type of committed relationship as heterosexuals.[83]

Implementation of a completely no-fault scheme of divorce would also of course address this problem.

Intolerability

The requirement that the petitioner finds it intolerable to live with the respondent is subjective, but must be evidenced in some way (in other words, the court is not supposed to simply accept the petitioner's word for it without reasons). The 'intolerablity' does not have to have been caused by adultery.

 Key Case 1: *Cleary v Cleary* [1974] 1 All ER 498

The wife had an affair and left the husband to live with her boyfriend. She then left him and returned to the husband. They 'tried again' for a few weeks before she left altogether—not to return to the boyfriend, but to her mother's. The husband eventually petitioned for divorce based on her adultery, even though he had forgiven her for that. It was her final departure that made him realise that the marriage was over and he could never live with her again.

The Court therefore had to decide whether there needed to be a causal link between the two requirements of s. 1(2)(a): the adultery, and the husband's assertion that it was intolerable to live with his wife. Lord Denning in the Court of Appeal decided there did not, though the court should inquire into the reasons for the intolerability alleged by the petitioner.

Under s. 2(2), Matrimonial Causes Act 1973 there is a supplementary provision under which a couple can continue to live together for up to six months in total after the discovery of the adultery without it affecting whether the petitioner finds it intolerable to live with the respondent. This is to allow the spouses to test, by continued cohabitation, whether their marriage can survive the knowledge that one has committed adultery. More than six months' continued cohabitation after the last act of known adultery is an absolute bar[84]: a spouse cannot cite adultery that occurred more than six months before the date of the petition, if he or she knew about it and has continued to cohabit, unless the affair is continuing. This provision is not easily reconciled with the interpretation in *Cleary* since if the adultery need not be the cause of the intolerability, why does it need to be recent?

---

[82] Naughton, C. 'Equal Civil Marriage for All Genders' [2013] *Family Law* 426, 429.

[83] Crompton, L. 'Where's the Sex in Same Sex Marriage?' [2013] *Family Law* 564, 573.

[84] Matrimonial Causes Act 1973, s. 2(1).

3.2.2 Behaviour

Behaviour under s. 1(2)(b) of the Matrimonial Causes Act 1973 is the easiest fact to prove and the commonest fact used in divorce proceedings. The proportion of behaviour petitions has gradually risen from around 30% in 1979 to almost 50% in the twenty-first century (see Figure 3.4). The gap between law and reality highlighted in the introduction is particularly applicable to the behaviour fact, as was pointed out in the case of *Owens*[85] recently. In practice, unless it is undefended, it is extremely unusual for a behaviour petition to fail: *Owens* itself is a rare example of a defended case where the divorce was refused and we consider it further later in this section.

This fact is often abbreviated to 'unreasonable behaviour' but this is not strictly accurate; the statutory wording makes it clear that the 'unreasonable' element is in relation to the respondent's continued cohabitation with the petitioner rather than the behaviour itself. To some extent this is semantics, as there will inevitably be a link between the two; the worse a respondent's behaviour, the less reasonable it can be to expect a petitioner to put up with it. However, the wording of the section does make it clear that there is an element of subjectivity required.

There are mixed messages from the case law as to what constitutes behaviour. The test is usually taken from *Livingstone-Stallard v Livingstone-Stallard*,[86] a High Court authority but expressly approved by the Court of Appeal in *O'Neill v O'Neill*[87] and endorsed in *Buffery v Buffery*[88] and *Butterworth v Butterworth*.[89]

 Key Case 2: *Livingstone-Stallard v Livingstone-Stallard* [1974] Fam 47

The wife petitioned for divorce based on the husband's behaviour. The husband denied both the behaviour and that the marriage had irretrievably broken down. The husband was 32 years older than the wife. Her evidence in the petition was that he was very critical of her, domineering, and treated her 'like a stupid child'. The judge made findings of fact that this had been the case, and that the husband had spat at her, tried to kick her out of bed, and called her names when angry. The husband admitted that he criticised her but claimed that this was because she had the potential to take the criticism and therefore improve herself. Further findings of fact were made that the husband had thrown the wife out of the house one night and locked the door; when she broke a window to try to get in he threw water on her. There was medical evidence that soon after this incident, she went to her doctor with injuries consistent with a violent assault, although the case report does not make it clear whether the husband perpetrated this assault.

The issue was whether this constituted behaviour such that it would not be reasonable to expect the wife to continue cohabiting with the husband. The judge decided to approach the issue by making a direction to himself and then considering whether on the evidence the divorce should be granted according to that direction. His direction was:

> Would any right-thinking person come to the conclusion that this husband has behaved in such a way that this wife cannot reasonably be expected to live him, taking into account the whole of the circumstances and the characters and personalities of the parties?[90]

In applying his own test, the circumstances amounted to a 'constant atmosphere of criticism, disapproval and boorish behaviour on the part of the husband' which no right thinking person would expect the wife to put up with and therefore the petition was granted.

---

85 *Owens v Owens* [2017] EWCA Civ 182.   86 [1974] Fam 47.   87 [1975] 3 All ER 289.
88 [1988] 2 FLR 365, 367–8.   89 [1997] 2 FLR 336, 340.   90 [1974] Fam 47, 54.

The behaviour test proposed in *Livingstone-Stallard* is part objective and part subjective. The subjective element is that the couple must be judged on their own behaviour and characteristics, rather than against how a reasonable person might act or feel. The objective element is whether a reasonable person would consider that, in the context of this particular couple, the test is satisfied; it is not simply a matter of the petitioner certifying that they themselves do not find it reasonable to continue living with the respondent.

Although it is comforting to have a test or standard to apply to given circumstances when interpreting the law, Dunn J's direction is not as useful as it might appear. It requires examination into the parties' characteristics, which is difficult to assess, and when dissected, does nothing more than give an instruction to grant the divorce if the judge thinks the particular petitioner cannot be expected to put up with the respondent's behaviour—which adds little to the wording of the statute.

Whether the test is satisfied will be determined as a question of fact, viewed in the context of the marriage (and, generally, layered with subjectivity on the part of the judge). Ormrod LJ in *Pheasant v Pheasant* admitted that determining whether the behaviour fact is made out 'requires the court to make a value judgment about the behaviour of the respondent and its effect on the petitioner'.[91]

A wholly subjective test for behaviour—in other words simply relying on whether or not the petitioner says they can continue living with the respondent—would amount to 'divorce on demand' for behaviour. The objective element prevents this but presents the following difficulties:

1. Is there a minimum threshold required for the behaviour?

2. Can a course of conduct—by this, we mean an accumulation of (perhaps minor) incidents over time, rather than specific major incidents—satisfy the test?

3. What if the behaviour of the respondent is not their fault, for example because of a medical condition?

4. Can a failure to act in a particular way (omission), rather than positive acts, satisfy the test?

These are all questions that the courts have had to determine in defended behaviour cases. Before proceeding, it would be wise to recognise that the principles that emerge do not form a coherent answer to these questions; there are discrepancies that cannot be completely reconciled, particularly in respect of whether a certain threshold of behaviour is required.

Is a minimum 'threshold' of behaviour required?

This is not an issue where the behaviour is serious. Clearly, incidents of violence constitute behaviour (provided they are proved[92]). Lesser incidents have proved more problematic. The case of *O'Neill*[93] is sometimes cited as evidence that trivialities can amount to behaviour since the husband in this case was a DIY enthusiast and the wife was tired of living in a constant state of renovation. However, closer examination of the facts demonstrates that the Court was as much influenced by the husband's act of copying in his 17-year-old daughter on a letter doubting that he was her father, an incident that could hardly be characterised as trivial.

The case of *Buffery v Buffery*[94] is more helpful. Although the petition failed, and his comments were therefore obiter, May LJ rejected the principle of a threshold, stating that

---

[91] *Pheasant v Pheasant* [1972] 1 All ER 587, 590.   [92] *Butterworth v Butterworth* [1997] 2 FLR 336.
[93] [1975] 3 All ER 289.   [94] [1988] 2 FLR 365, 367.

'. . . the gravity or otherwise of the conduct complained of is of itself immaterial'. His approach is consistent with *Livingstone-Stallard*: if the effect on the petitioner must be judged subjectively, then it is logical that no objective level of behaviour is required. However, May LJ drew a distinction between trivial behaviour (not necessarily a cause to reject a petition) and a situation where a couple have merely 'drifted apart'. The behaviour fact was not met in *Buffery* because there was no behaviour at all; they had simply lost interest in each other.

However, and problematically, the threshold approach was endorsed in *Pheasant v Pheasant*. The husband's petition was based on the wife's failure to give him the 'spontaneous demonstrative affection' he felt his nature demanded. Ormrod J, refusing to grant the divorce, stated that a threshold of behaviour is required because otherwise a 'respondent whose behaviour is beyond reproach by any standards other than the petitioner's would be liable to be divorced without any possibility of resistance'. [95]

The fault in this reasoning is that a minimum threshold of behaviour is not necessary to 'save' a respondent in such a case. The outcome could have been achieved by the objective assessment of whether continued cohabitation is reasonable (which takes into account both the behaviour *and* the petitioner's reaction to it, as required by the statute). In other words, that rather than the husband failing to prove any particular threshold, the petition should have failed because it was not unreasonable to expect him to continue living with the wife, even taking into account his characteristics.

The approach in *Buffery*, albeit obiter, is preferable. However, arguments on this point must be reviewed in the light of *Owens*, which we consider later.

Can the test be met by a course of conduct?

According to the statute, the answer to this question should be yes in principle, provided that the course of conduct could lead to a conclusion that the petitioner cannot reasonably be expected to live with the respondent. This question was also considered in *Livingstone-Stallard*, where the husband was generally domineering and critical of the wife (though as we saw earlier, there were also several more serious incidents as well). Dunn J ruled that '. . . in a case which depends on a course of conduct and on the character of the other spouse rather than on a series of dramatic incidents, perhaps of violence, the effect of the conduct may be nonetheless serious in the long run'.[96]

Both of these questions, whether there is a minimum threshold, and whether a course of conduct could satisfy the behaviour test, came before the Court of Appeal in 2017.

 Key Case 3: *Owens v Owens* [2017] EWCA Civ 182

Tini and Hugh Owens were very wealthy, having built up a substantial business, and had been married for 37 years. The wife's petition cited a number of instances of behaviour on the part of her husband following an extra-marital relationship she had had in 2012. These included 'berating' her in front of their housekeeper and friends, arguing with her in public at an airport in a humiliating way, and refusing to speak to her during a meal out. She stated that she was desperately unhappy in the marriage. The husband argued that she had exaggerated the incidents in her petition, that they did not satisfy the behaviour test, and that the marriage had not irretrievably broken down. The Family Court judge dismissed the petition, finding the wife's allegations 'flimsy' and 'scraping the barrel'—the matters she alleged were 'minor' and 'to be expected' in married life. He criticised the wife for being over-sensitive; the husband's conduct

---

[95] *Pheasant v Pheasant* [1972] 1 All ER 587, 590f.   [96] [1974] Fam 47, 54.

was excused as 'old-school'. The case received extensive publicity when Mrs Owens appealed to the Court of Appeal.

The grounds of appeal included that the Family Court had failed to take into account the wife's subjective characteristics, the cumulative effect of the husband's behaviour, and had not applied the law properly. The Court of Appeal dismissed all these arguments. They disagreed with the husband that there was any future in the marriage, accepting that Mrs Owens was miserably unhappy. But she had not satisfied the requirements of the behaviour fact under s. 1(2)(b) of the Matrimonial Causes Act 1973. Sir James Munby P reviewed the key case law, and whilst stating that his interpretation 'did not add to the jurisprudence' (in other words, that he did not intend to change interpretation of existing case law), he summarised that the key principle is to evaluate what has been proved:

1) In *this* marriage;
2) Looking at *this* wife and *this* husband;
3) In the light of all the circumstances;
4) Having regard to the cumulative effect of all the respondent's conduct.[97]

Thus, the Court of Appeal clearly endorsed the possibility of a course of conduct being sufficient to satisfy the behaviour test. However, the finding that the cumulative effect had not been met in this case, despite the acknowledgement of the wife's unhappiness, appears to confirm a threshold for the behaviour itself, and not merely the expectation that the petitioner would put up with it (since it does not seem reasonable to expect any petitioner to put up with conduct that causes misery). A subsidiary ground of appeal that the first instance ruling breached Mrs Owen's right to marry under Article 12 ECHR, and her Article 8 ECHR right to respect for her private and family life, was also dismissed. The Court of Appeal applied the approach of the European Court of Human Rights that there is no right to divorce.[98]

The *Owens* case attracted considerable attention, not surprisingly since it was the first Court of Appeal ruling on a divorce petition for 20 years. The Court gave a strong call for divorce law reform, though it remains to be seen what effect this will have. At the time of writing, Mrs Owens has been granted leave to appeal the decision to the Supreme Court.[99]

 DEBATE 3: WHAT DOES *OWENS* ADD TO INTERPRETATION OF THE BEHAVIOUR FACT?

The case appears to endorse an objective threshold for the behaviour fact by finding that the Family Court judge could not be considered plainly wrong in considering that Mrs Owens had not met it. *Owens* tells us that where there is a trivial level of behaviour, no matter what its effect on the petitioner, the correct legal solution is to separate and use the separation with consent fact under s. 1(2)(d) of the Matrimonial Causes Act 1973.

The Court of Appeal determined that they were not changing the substantive law, yet unfortunately did not consider the discrepancy between *Buffery* and *Pheasant* on the question of a threshold. This should not be seen as criticism of the Court of Appeal. The advocates in the case did not draw the conflicting approaches to the Court's attention. However this

---

[97] [2017] EWCA Civ 182, at [37].

[98] *Johnston v Ireland* (1986) 9 EHRR 203; *Babiarz v Poland* App. No. 1955/10.

[99] Supreme Court, News, Permission to Appeal. Available at: https://www.supremecourt.uk/news/permission-to-appeal-decision-in-owens-v-owens.html, accessed 9 August 2017.

was a missed opportunity and has resulted in a decision that appears to undermine the very case law that the Court of Appeal explicitly endorsed in its judgment.

The strengthening of the threshold approach is surprising, given that the statute imposes the concept of reasonableness in respect of the expectation of continued cohabitation. Munby P expressly referred to the concept of the 'speaking statute', by which he meant that a statute may be interpreted according to the moral norms at the time of the hearing, rather than those that prevailed at the time the legislation was passed. So whatever a reasonable person in 1969 might have thought, the growing importance of the companionate function of marriage by 2017 (see 6.1) could have justified a finding that it was not reasonable to expect Mrs Owens to continue cohabiting with a husband whose 'old school' behaviour did not satisfy that function. This is especially so since the Court of Appeal acknowledged that what might be normal behaviour in a happy marriage would be 'salt in the wound' of an unhappy one.

Perhaps the most startling aspect of the decision in *Owens* was how strongly it highlighted the discrepancy between defended and undefended divorces, not only in terms of the procedure but also in terms of the application of the legal principles.

Mr Owens denied that the marriage had broken down irretrievably, placing the burden on Mrs Owens to prove that the behaviour fact was established. She did not prove that; if she had, he could not have rebutted the presumption that the marriage had irretrievably broken down since all the judges were agreed that, in real terms, it had. In most cases where a petition is refused, there is often judicial comment that the marriage has, to all intents and purposes, broken down.[100] However, what was unusual in *Owens* was the acknowledgement of the gap between law and practice, and that the law might be applied differently in a defended case than an undefended case. Sir James Munby pointed out: 'many petitions are anodyne in the extreme. The petition in the present case is a good example; I cannot help thinking that, if the husband had not sought to defend, the petition would have gone through under the special procedure without any thought of challenge from the court'.[101] The open admission that a petition may be granted where undefended but not granted where defended, on the same facts, produces the unjust position that not only the process but also the application of the legal principles differs between defended and undefended divorces.

The decision in *Owens* may make very little difference to the law on divorce, despite the media attention it attracted. However, the admission that the legal principles operate differently in a defended case than an undefended case may, perhaps, lead to more rigid scrutiny of petitions under the undefended procedure than is currently the case. There is some anecdotal evidence that behaviour petitions are becoming 'beefier', in terms of making stronger allegations against the respondent[102] though Resolution's guidance on drafting petitions (specifically, that 'courts will allow unreasonable behaviour petitions based on mild particulars to proceed') still stands.[103] It may also lead to more divorces being defended, though perhaps only for the few as this would be expensive since legal aid is not available (see Chapter 15). Perhaps, short of defending, respondents will refuse to accept stronger allegations and seek to delay the progress of a divorce by giving notice of intention to defend, perhaps as a bargaining tool to seek the petitioner's agreement to withdraw any claim for costs of the divorce.

---

[100] *Pheasant v Pheasant* [1972] 1 All ER 587 is one exception; the judge appeared to accept the wife's optimism that there was still hope for the marriage, though the divorce was still refused for non-satisfaction of the fact rather than under the s. 1(4) rebuttal.   [101] [2017] EWCA Civ 182, at [93].

[102] Rogers, M. 'Unreasonable behaviour petitions "far more acrimonious" since *Owens v Owens*', *Solicitors Journal*, 5 June 2017. Available at: https://www.solicitorsjournal.com/news/201706/unreasonable-behaviour-petitions-%E2%80%98far-more-acrimonious%E2%80%99-owens-v-owens, accessed 28 June 2017.

[103] Resolution, *Guide to Good Practice on Drafting Documents* (March 2017), 6. Available at: http://www.resolution.org.uk/site_content_files/files/25_drafting_documents.pdf, accessed 28 June 2017.

These possibilities risk increased hostility and bitterness between the couple, in the pursuit of an unrealistic expectation of impartial scrutiny of the private nature of relationship breakdown, and worsening the operation of a fact that is subject to considerable criticism already.

The Court of Appeal clearly intended to strengthen the case for legislative reform of divorce. Long term, this may be the result.

Must the behaviour be blameworthy?

The answer to this question provides another example of a pragmatic approach to the interpretation of behaviour. In *Katz v Katz*[104] the husband was mentally ill, and the wife cited his critical, suspicious, and obsessive behaviour. When she decided to leave him, his reaction was so bad that she attempted suicide. Clearly, he was not to blame for his behaviour, but its effect on her was such that she could not reasonably be expected to continue living with him and the divorce was granted. Whilst this might be the right approach in practical terms, in allowing a marriage that is to all intents and purposes over to be brought formally to an end, it is problematic that this is done by alleging fault for which the respondent is not responsible.

Must the behaviour constitute an act (or series of acts), or can an omission constitute behaviour?

This question arose in the case of *Thurlow*.

Key case 4: *Thurlow v Thurlow* [1976] Fam 32

The wife suffered from epilepsy and a gradually deteriorating illness that meant that she needed full-time institutional care, being unable to stand unaided, feed, or dress herself. The husband had made 'heroic attempts' to look after her before his own health gave way and his wife had to go into hospital. The wife's condition was never going to improve.

The issue was whether this state of affairs could constitute behaviour by the wife. The Official Solicitor, intervening on behalf of the wife, argued that it could not. The Court held that total passivity could be behaviour. The Court agreed with the principle from *Katz* that conduct under the behaviour fact did not need to be blameworthy, though where it resulted from illness, the obligations of marriage did create a duty to tolerate it to some extent. Rees J stated:

> If the behaviour stems from misfortune such as the onset of mental illness or from disease of the body, or from accidental physical injury, the court will take full account of the obligations of the married state. These will include the normal duty to accept and to share the burdens imposed on the family as a result of the mental or physical ill-health of one member. It will also consider the capacity of the petitioner to withstand the stresses imposed by the behaviour, the steps taken to cope with it, the length of time during which the petitioner has been called on to bear it and the actual or potential effect on his or her health.[105]

To test how far this principle might be stretched, the Court in *Thurlow* was asked to consider a hypothetical situation of a spouse with what we would now call unresponsive wakefulness syndrome or a permanent vegetative state (PSV), perhaps because of an accident. This is an

---

[104] [1976] Fam 32.   [105] [1976] Fam 32, 44F.

extreme example of extending the pragmatic approach to behaviour but Rees J felt there was a limit. He commented that a petitioner would face 'very considerable difficulties' in establishing behaviour in such a case. This seems at odds with the general approach to behaviour in cases of omission and illness. Perhaps the comment is indicative of the Court's distaste for the legal mechanism available being one that appears to consign blame to conduct which is not blameworthy.

A final point to note is that s. 2(3) of the Matrimonial Causes Act 1973 provides that continued cohabitation of up to six months in total after the date of the most recent incident of behaviour can be disregarded in determining whether the petitioner cannot reasonably be expected to live with the respondent. This allows the couple to attempt reconciliation. We saw a similar provision in relation to adultery but that more than six months total cohabitation is an absolute bar for the purposes of 'intolerability' under s. 1(2)(a). In contrast, continued cohabitation for more than six months does not prevent the court finding it unreasonable to expect the petitioner to continue living with the respondent under s. 1(2)(b).

3.2.3 Desertion

Desertion under s.1(2)(c) covers a situation where the respondent has, without reason, left the petitioner.

It is the last of the fault-based facts and the least cited fact by far, accounting for well under 1% of decrees granted in 2014 (see Figure 3.4). This is for two reasons: first, it is the most complicated to prove, and second, one of the requirements for desertion is two years' separation, and therefore a petition under s. 1(2)(d) can be used instead providing that the respondent consents to the decree. Since by the nature of the desertion the respondent is the one who has left, it is very likely that they would consent to a decree, thus sidestepping the need to use desertion at all. Desertion may be relevant where the respondent has not only left the petitioner but disappeared altogether, and cannot be traced in order to give consent. Normally a petition must be served on the respondent but this can be waived where the court is satisfied every possible attempt at service has been made.

Desertion requires four elements (which must have existed for two years before a petition can be presented):

- that the respondent has left the petitioner—in other words that the parties are physically separated;
- that the respondent who has left regards the marriage as being at end—that is, the separation is an intentional and permanent one;
- that the respondent left 'without just cause'—that is, that it was not because of bad behaviour on the part of the petitioner (if it was, the respondent could simply have issued their own petition for behaviour without waiting two years);
- the petitioner did not consent to the departure (if the separation is consensual, then s. 1(2)(d) should be used instead).

Of these, the first two are the most significant because they are also relevant to the final two facts, based on living apart.

3.2.4 Living apart

The facts in s. 1(2)(d) and s. 1 (2)(e) of the Matrimonial Causes Act 1973, based on living apart, or separation, represent the no-fault elements of the current divorce law. The s. 1(2)(d) fact represents mutual agreement to divorce because the respondent must consent to the decree being granted. The s. 1(2)(e) fact represents unilateral autonomy by the petitioner since the respondent's consent is not required. This is the rationale for the different length of separation required—two years in the case of s. 1(2)(d) and five years in the case of s. 1(2)(e).

The separation facts were initially popular when first introduced but by the late 1970s, the figures settled down to around a quarter of divorces for s. 1(2)(d) and approaching a tenth for s. 1(2)(e) petitions. Section 1(2)(d) petitions have fairly steadily accounted for around a quarter of divorces during the last 10 years. Petitions under s. 1(2)(e) have become slightly more popular as a proportion of overall divorces in the last few years— around 12% of divorces in 2014 were based on five years' separation (see Figure 3.4).

Demonstrating separation is usually straightforward—simply a matter of showing on what date one party moved out. In most cases, this satisfies the requirements of physical separation and mental separation, that is, regarding the marriage as being at an end.

Certain situations may pose some difficulty. The first is where the parties separate whilst still sharing the matrimonial home. Section 2(6) of the Matrimonial Causes Act 1973 says that living apart means 'not living together in the same household' which means that it is possible to be separated whilst under the same roof, as long as separate *households* are established. What counts as a separate household? Case law establishes that separate bedrooms is not enough—there must be a 'complete cessation of communal living'. For example, the couple must not share meals or do household tasks for each other. In *Mouncer v Mouncer*, the couple slept in separate rooms but ate meals together to be with their children and shared the cleaning. This was deemed insufficient separation.[106] One caveat is the case of *Fuller v Fuller*,[107] where the wife had moved in with her new partner but allowed her supposedly terminally-ill husband to move into their home where she cooked for him and did his washing. The husband paid a form of rent. Sympathetic to the wife's kindness, the Court was prepared to allow this as an exception to the 'complete cessation' rule, on the basis that they were not living as husband and wife; the husband was in the position of a 'paying guest'.[108]

The second situation that may pose difficulty is where there is an ostensible reason for the separation short of one party regarding the marriage as being over, for example where one spouse is working away from home, or has temporarily moved to care for elderly relatives, or is in prison. In these circumstances there is physical separation, but if the couple expect this to be temporary, that is, their marriage is intended to continue despite it, there is not the required level of mental separation. The couple are not living apart for the purposes of the separation facts unless and until one or both of them decides that the marriage is over, by deciding not to return—or allow the other back—once the reason for the temporary separation is at an end. There is no requirement to communicate this decision to the other spouse.[109] When the decision was formed can simply be stated in the petition and the separation period would then run from that date.

3.2.5 The s. 5 defence

There is an additional protection in respect of s. 1(2)(e) Matrimonial Causes Act 1973 petitions, known as the s. 5 defence. In relation to the other facts, the respondent may defend by disputing the circumstances alleged in the petition, or by arguing that they do not meet the test required by the particular fact alleged. This is also true of s. 1(2)(e),

---

[106] [1972] 1 WLR 321, drawing on the test in *Hopes v Hopes* [1948] 2 All ER 920 (which was a desertion case under the 1937 Act, but the test is the same).   [107] [1973] 2 All ER 650.

[108] The husband himself had not sought to defend the petition—he was 'only too willing' to accept the couple were living apart throughout; this was prior to the introduction of the special procedure.

[109] *Santos v Santos* [1972] Fam 247.

since a respondent may seek to establish that the parties have not been living apart for five years. However s. 5 is a mechanism for this fact only, for the respondent to ask, even where it is admitted that has been five years' separation, for the divorce not to be granted on the basis that:

(a) it would cause the respondent grave financial or other hardship;

(b) it would be wrong in all the circumstances to dissolve the marriage.

The defence is very little used. Originally, the 'grave financial hardship' limb was usually pleaded in relation to loss of pension rights,[110] although a petitioner with sufficient money to do so could make a financial offer to counter the effects of such hardship.[111] The courts now have greater powers to deal with pensions when dividing the assets on relationship breakdown, so the situation of grave financial hardship is less likely to occur. In any case, the courts have always tended to take a pragmatic approach to the s. 5 defence, by looking at whether any hardship would be caused by the divorce that had not already realistically been caused by the separation.[112] Since the defence can only be used in situations where the couple had already been separated for five years, the courts have been extremely cautious about perpetuating an 'empty shell marriage', particularly if the petitioner was young and/or wanted to remarry.[113]

3.3 Current procedure for divorce and dissolution of civil partnership

An application for divorce or dissolution of a civil partnership is now called an application for a matrimonial order and proceeds under Part 7 of the Family Procedure Rules 2010[114] and its associated Practice Directions, which also specifies the prescribed forms.

All applications follow the same initial steps. The application is commenced by petition, Form D8,[115] accompanied by a certificate of reconciliation (Form D6) where the petitioner is represented by a solicitor.[116]

Once proceedings are issued, the court serves the respondent (by post) and the respondent is required to return an acknowledgment of service (Form D10) within seven days of service indicating, amongst other things, whether the application is defended.[117] If it is not, the divorce follows the undefended route shown in Figure 3.3. Following this route the petitioner files an application for Decree Nisi/Conditional Order (Form D84)[118] with a Statement in Support of the petition (Form D80)[119] exhibiting the respondent's acknowledgment of service Form D10, to prove that the respondent agrees the marriage has irretrievably broken down and does not dispute the contents of the petition. The legal adviser[120] then checks the papers and, if satisfied from the petition and statement in support that the petitioner has proved the contents of the petition, issues a certificate of entitlement

---

[110] As, e.g., in *Johnson v Johnson* (1982) 12 Fam Law 116.

[111] This was the case in *Le Marchant v Le Marchant* [1977] 3 All ER 610.

[112] *Rukat v Rukat* [1975] 1 All ER 343; *Balraj v Balraj* (1981) 11 Fam Law 110.

[113] *Mathias v Mathias* [1972] 3 All ER 1; *Parker v Parker* [1972] 1 All ER 410.

[114] The Family Procedure Rules 2010 (FPR) were introduced by statutory instrument SI 2010/2955, effective from 6 April 2011, and replaced both the Matrimonial Causes Rules and the Family Proceedings Rules (which had governed family proceedings relating to children) to govern all family proceedings. SI 2014/524 amended the FPR following the enactment of the Marriage (Same Sex Couples) Act 2013.

[115] Family Procedure Rules 2010 (SI 2010/2955), r. 5 and PD5A Form D8.

[116] Family Procedure Rules 2010 (SI 2010/2955), r. 7.6 Form D6.

[117] Family Procedure Rules 2010 (SI 2010/2955), r. 7.12(3) Form D10.

[118] Family Procedure Rules 2010 (SI 2010/2955), r. 19(1).

[119] Family Procedure Rules 2010 (SI 2010/2955), r. 7.19(4) as amended by SI 2014/843.

[120] Following the enactment of the Crime and Courts Act 2013, s. 17.

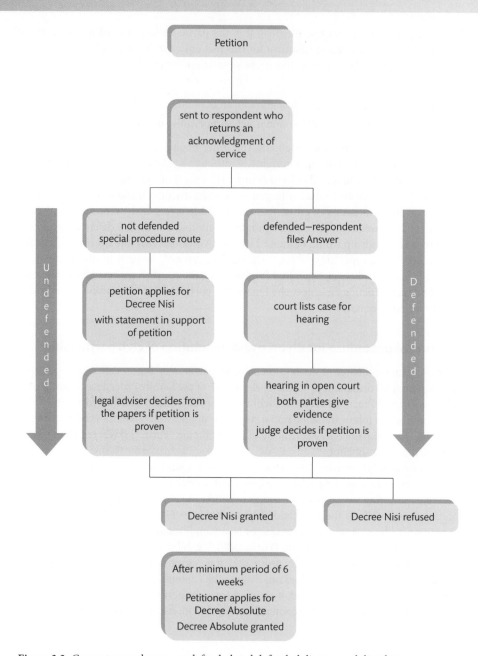

Figure 3.3 Current procedure on undefended and defended divorce and dissolution

to Decree Nisi (Form D84A)[121] or certificate of entitlement to an order (D584A).[122] Decree Nisi is then pronounced later, on the date specified on the certificate.

In the rare event that the acknowledgement of service shows an indication to defend, the respondent then has 21 days in which to file an answer to the petition.[123] The case then follows the defended route shown in Figure 3.3. Once an answer is filed, the court lists the case for hearing before a judge in open court and the parties attend court to give evidence.

---

[121] Family Procedure Rules 2010 (SI 2010/2955), r. 7.20(2).
[122] Family Procedure Rules 2010 (SI 2010/2955), r. 7.20(2).
[123] Family Procedure Rules 2010 (SI 2010/2955), r. 7.12(8).

The judge will determine whether the petition is proved or not; if it is, Decree Nisi is then pronounced at the hearing.

The final steps are common to all divorces. The petition can apply for a Decree Absolute to end the marriage six weeks after the Decree Nisi.[124] If the petitioner does not apply, the respondent can apply after a further three months, and the application must be on notice to the petitioner[125].

The Family Procedure Rules have been subject to a number of amendments since 2010 to reflect various recent changes to the family justice system. In early 2012, the then Coalition government promised administrative reform of the family justice system[126] following the Family Justice Review which had, amongst other things, recommended reforms to divorce procedure. Administrative reform has indeed happened. The 2013 Crimes and Courts Act created the Family Court and gave legal advisers, rather than district judges, the power to consider Decree Nisi applications.[127] Since 2015, divorce proceedings have taken place in one of 11 regional divorce centres, the idea being to improve efficiency. The Children and Families Act 2014 removed the requirement (under s. 41 of the Matrimonial Causes Act 1973 and s. 63 of the Civil Partnership Act 2004) for the court to consider whether it should exercise its powers under the Children Act 1989 and consequently the need to file a Statement of Arrangements for Children,[128] marking the abandonment of the judicial check that concerns about the children should be a barrier to divorce. Disputes over children now sit procedurally and substantively outside the divorce process, better reflecting the reality that it is, arguably, the breakdown of parents' relationships, rather than the status of that relationship, which impacts on children (see Chapter 9). In 2017 there has also been a move to online divorce, but this is not as radical as it might sound: it is simply that certain stages in the process can be undertaken electronically rather than by submitting paper copies of documents.[129]

The system can cope with high volume but the gap between the letter of the law and its application has widened. For undefended cases and the fault facts, concerns about rigour and scrutiny first identified by Freeman (see 2.4) continue to be exposed, ironically nowhere more so than in the defended case of *Owens*.[130]

 CONTEXT 1: THE REALITY OF DIVORCE UNDER THE MATRIMONIAL CAUSES ACT 1973

Number of divorces granted in England and Wales, 2015: 101,055 (down from a peak of 164,556 in 1993)[131]

Number of petitions filed in England and Wales in 2016: 113,996;

Number of Acknowledgements of service giving notice of intention to defend in 2016: 2,600 (2.28% of all petitions);[132]

---

[124] Family Procedure Rules 2010 (SI 2010/2955), r. 7.32.

[125] Family Procedure Rules 2010 (SI 2010/2955), r. 7.33.

[126] Ministry of Justice, 'Major overhaul to reform family justice system' (Press Release, 6 February 2012). Available at: https://www.gov.uk/government/news/major-overhaul-to-reform-family-justice-system--4, accessed 15 February 2017.   [127] Following the enactment of the Crime and Courts Act 2013, s. 17.

[128] Children and Families Act 2014, s. 17 and Sch 10.

[129] Family Procedure Rules 2010 (SI 2010/2955), r. 36.2 PD36D.

[130] *Owens v Owens* [2017] EWCA Civ 182, discussed further in 3.2.2.

[131] ONS Dataset, 'Divorces in England and Wales: dataset 2015'. Available at: https://www.ons.gov.uk/peoplepopulationandcommunity/birthsdeathsandmarriages/divorce/datasets/divorcesinenglandandwales, accessed 28 June 2017.

[132] Cited in *Owens v Owens* [2017] EWCA Civ 182, at [98] as figures to January 2017 (official figures not yet published).

Answers filed and divorces actually defended in 2016: 760 (0.67% of all petitions);[133]

Average time from petition to Decree Nisi in 2016: 24 weeks;[134]

Percentage of marriages expected to end in divorce by the 20th wedding anniversary: 34%.[135]

Percentage of petitions granted to wives in 2015: 62% (down from 72% in 1985)[136]

Six in ten divorces proceed on the basis of fault (down from three in four in 1989).[137] The breakdown of petitions by fact for 2014 is shown in Figure 3.4.[138]

4. Criticisms of the current law

To critique the current law and evaluate alternatives, we need an idea of what a 'good' divorce law should look like. The Law Commission considered this in their reports. In *The Field of Choice* (1966), they said:

A good divorce law should seek:

(a) to buttress, rather than to undermine, the stability of marriage; and

(b) when a marriage has irretrievably broken down to enable the empty legal shell to be destroyed with the maximum fairness, and the minimum bitterness, distress, and humiliation.[139]

In *Ground for Divorce* (1990), they identified that the divorce law should:

(i) try to support those marriages which are capable of being saved;

(ii) enable those which cannot be saved to be dissolved with the minimum of avoidable distress, bitterness and hostility;

(iii) encourage, so far as possible, the amicable resolution of practical issues relating to the couple's home, finances and children and the proper discharge of their responsibilities to one another and to their children;

(iv) seek to minimise the harm that the children of the family may suffer both at the time and in the future, and to promote so far as possible continued sharing of parental responsibility for them. [140]

---

[133] Cited in *Owens v Owens* [2017] EWCA Civ 182, at [98] as figures to January 2017 (official figures not yet published).

[134] Ministry of Justice, *Family court statistics quarterly: July to September 2016* (15 December 2016). Available at: https://www.gov.uk/government/statistics/family-court-statistics-quarterly-july-to-september-2016, accessed 1 February 2017.

[135] ONS, 'What percentage of marriages end in divorce?' (9 February 2013). Available at: http://webarchive.nationalarchives.gov.uk/20160105160709/http://www.ons.gov.uk/ons/rel/vsob1/divorces-in-england-and-wales/2011/sty-what-percentage-of-marriages-end-in-divorce.html, accessed 1 February 2017.

[136] ONS Dataset, 'Divorces in England and Wales: dataset 2015'. Available at: https://www.ons.gov.uk/peoplepopulationandcommunity/birthsdeathsandmarriages/divorce/datasets/divorcesinenglandandwales, accessed 28 June 2017.

[137] ONS Dataset, 'Divorces in England and Wales: dataset 2014'. Available at: https://www.ons.gov.uk/peoplepopulationandcommunity/birthsdeathsandmarriages/divorce/datasets/divorcesinenglandandwales, accessed 17 February 2017.

[138] ONS Dataset, 'Divorces in England and Wales: dataset 2014'. Available at: https://www.ons.gov.uk/peoplepopulationandcommunity/birthsdeathsandmarriages/divorce/datasets/divorcesinenglandandwales, accessed 17 February 2017.

[139] Law Commission, *Reform of the Grounds for Divorce: The Field of Choice* (Cmnd 3123, Law Com No. 6, 1966).   [140] Law Commission, *Family Law: The Ground for Divorce* (HC 192, Law Com No. 192, 1990).

All petitioners:

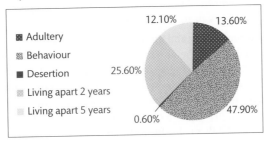

Wives:

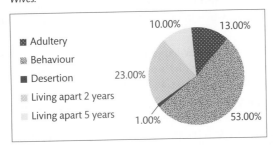

Husbands:

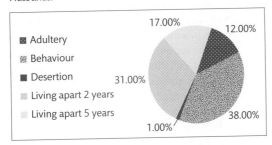

Figure 3.4 Petitions by fact (heterosexual marriages), England and Wales, 2014

Source: ONS Dataset, 'Divorces in England and Wales: dataset 2014'. Available at: https://www.ons.gov.uk/peoplepopulationandcommunity/birthsdeathsandmarriages/divorce/datasets/divorcesinenglandandwales, accessed 17 February 2017.

It is questionable the extent to which the law on divorce could ever be expected to support the institution of marriage, a difficulty Hassan describes as the 'basic duality' of divorce law.[141] Collier argues that the notion of 'marriage-saving' hampers discussion of an effective model of divorce by assuming that divorce is 'bad'.[142]

Even if marriage-saving is an unrealistic goal for the divorce law, it is difficult to quarrel with the other objectives. Measured against these goals, current divorce law falls short in almost all respects, as identified by the Law Commission:

1. **The law is confusing and misleading** because it is based on the 'false' definition of irretrievable breakdown, limited to five divorce facts. The Commission particularly

---

[141] Hassan, E. 'Setting a Standard or Reflecting Reality? The "Role" of Divorce Law, and the Case of the Family Law Act 1996' (2003) 17 *International Journal of Law Policy and the Family* 338, 340.

[142] Collier, R. 'The Dashing of a Liberal Dream? The Information Meeting, the "New Family" and the Limits of Law' (1999) 11 *Child and Family Law Quarterly* 257.

criticised the behaviour fact as problematic. There is a misapprehension that the 'truth' of the breakdown is investigated, when in reality it rarely is, and the divorce will usually proceed as an administrative process.

2. **The law is discriminatory and unjust** because of the difficulty lower income couples face in establishing the no-fault facts compared to better off couples. There are financial barriers to living apart—there is some evidence that the fault facts may be more heavily relied on by those in lower socio-economic groups—thus forcing couples to 'recriminate' rather than separate'. They also contended that there was a lack of justice for a respondent, particularly on a behaviour petition, as while defending a divorce is theoretically possible, in reality it is difficult (and in any case likely to be counterproductive). This denies the respondent a chance to refute allegations against them, which gives the impression they were responsible for the breakdown when in reality the causes might well have been much more complex.

3. **The law distorts the parties' bargaining positions** since a party who is keener for the divorce to take place may be in a weaker position in relation to agreeing matters in relation to children, property, and finances.

4. **The law provokes unnecessary hostility and bitterness**. Here, the Law Commission referred to many of the problems with a fault-based system (see s. 6.1), whilst acknowledging that no law can remove all feelings of conflict that may accompany a relationship breakdown.

5. **The law does nothing to save marriages**. We have already discussed to what extent a system of divorce *can* 'save' marriages, but there may be some with a prospect of reconciliation. A system in which spouses are forced either to live apart for a long period or alternatively one spouse make allegations relating to the other's conduct is a very poor model for facilitating this. The Law Commission pointed out that the low level of defended petitions should not be misconstrued as evidence that almost all divorces are consensual. The speed with which a fault-based petition can be obtained, prior to setting arrangements, means that that couples do not have to face up to the reality of the situation until after it is too late for them to change their minds.

6. **The law makes things worse for the children**. This is an extension of the 'hostility argument': the exacerbation of conflict through the use of fault damages the prospect of a cooperative parenting post-divorce, which means children may be caught in ongoing conflict between their parents.

Current calls for reform of divorce focus on the need to remove fault as a basis for adjudication of divorce.

The case for the removal of fault contains several (interlinked) sub-arguments:

1. Blaming one party of the marital breakdown may increase the level of conflict between the parties on relationship breakdown;

2. This is likely to be particularly the case where the fault allegations do not really represent the reason for the marital breakdown but instead are simply the mechanism by which the parties are able to free themselves from a marriage that has broken down;

3. Yet the current law does not only facilitate the allegations of fault but encourages them because a fact must be proved, and it is quicker to prove adultery or behaviour than to use a no-fault fact.

These arguments need further consideration.

4.1 Fault causes increased conflict

The breakdown of a relationship is likely to cause some level of conflict no matter what the legal regulation. Advocates of no-fault divorce do not suggest that the removal of fault would wave a magic wand to make marital breakdown harmonious. However, the use of fault almost inevitably promotes the appearance that the respondent is being blamed by the other for the breakdown of the marriage. Behaviour petitions under s. 1(2)(b), in particular, are cited as a source of this, because this involves listing a catalogue of conduct by the respondent, which the respondent then has to read and—unless the divorce is defended—admit before the divorce can proceed. This is at odds with the emphasis on the parties where possible mediating to agree other matters relating to the marital breakdown (see Chapter 15). It means that the parties start by looking to the past rather than focusing on making adjustments for their lives in the future.

The lawyers' organisation Resolution has long campaigned on the basis that the fault facts may make things worse between the parties. Their 2015 *Manifesto for Family Law* says making allegations of fault 'often creates conflict and makes reaching a mutually acceptable agreement much more difficult. It can fuel conflict between parents, causing significant stress and upset for their children'.[143] The Government's Mediation Task Force supported this view, arguing that 'the allegations drive the receiving party into even greater hostility and away from mediation'.[144]

Research by YouGov in 2010 found that 68% of adults agreed that people should be able to divorce without blaming each other for unreasonable behaviour or adultery.[145] Of course, this is actually the case under the current law provided that they use the separation facts, though for various reasons (see 4.3) this may not be possible.

4.2 Fault does not represent the real reasons for marital breakdown

As we have seen, parties have to 'fit' their private reasons for breakdown within a state-set framework of divorce facts under s. 1(2) Matrimonial Causes Act 1973. This has a number of potential consequences:

- A divorce may (in theory at least) be refused even where the marriage has clearly broken down—as for example in *Buffery*, and more recently in *Owens*;[146]

- A petitioner may be encouraged to exaggerate (or even fabricate) circumstances in order to satisfy the requirements. Resolution research found that 27% of divorcing couples who allege fault said their petition was not true.[147] Their *Manifesto* cites the example of 'John', who agreed with his wife that he would admit to an affair he had not had, so that their divorce could proceed quickly based on adultery. Later, this false admission damaged his relationship with his child.[148] The Mediation Task Force report said that 'Mediators, including those on the Task Force, refer often to the damage done by the requirements of what most people recognise is a charade. Some separating couples can see this and accept that to make the necessary allegations is a price worth paying. But others are not in that rational state . . .'[149]

---

[143] Resolution, *Manifesto for Family Law* (2015), 21.

[144] Family Mediation Task Force, *Report of the Family Mediation Task Force* (2014), para 36.

[145] Resolution/You Gov, *Survey into attitudes towards divorce and relationship breakdown* (12 March 2010).

[146] [2017] EWCA Civ 182.

[147] Jo Edwards, 'MPs need to get behind no-fault divorce if they're serious about reducing family conflict' (Resolution Press Release, 3 December 2015) <http://www.resolution.org.uk/news-list.asp?page_id=228&n_id=301> accessed 17 February 2017.   [148] Resolution, *Manifesto for Family Law* (2015), 21.

[149] Family Mediation Task Force, *Report of the Family Mediation Task Force* (2014), para 36.

- Linked to this is the problem that although the court is under a duty to inquire into the facts alleged, this does not happen unless the divorce is defended. This is the gap between law and practical reality that has been discussed earlier, and highlighted in the *Owens* case. James Munby, President of the Family Division, has commented: 'The reality is that we have and have had for quite some time in this country divorce by consent in the sense that if both parties wish there will be a divorce if they're able to establish the grounds for divorce which is very easy to establish. The process . . . is an essentially bureaucratic administrative process . . . '[150] The current government guidance on getting a divorce tacitly admits this, instructing the respondent: 'To agree with the divorce petition, fill in and return the acknowledgment of service form to the divorce centre within 8 days, and the divorce will go ahead'.[151] In other words, there is no suggestion that in the absence of an objection by the respondent, the divorce petition will fail. This is at odds with the court's duty to inquire into the facts as far as possible even where the divorce is not defended and places the onus of monitoring the legal test on the respondent.

- In turn, this creates what the Law Commission described as an 'unfair bargaining chip'. If the divorce is more important to one spouse than the other, then this may create a power imbalance. This might become pertinent to the behaviour fact following the case of *Owens*.

4.3 Use of the fault facts is encouraged

The problems identified earlier with use of the fault facts would perhaps be less problematic if the fault facts were not so popular. Instead, we can see from Figure 3.4 that fault facts are used in 62% of petitions, most obviously because the divorce can proceed more quickly or because of the economic difficulties in living apart. This means that the problems with fault affect significant numbers of divorcing couples.

5. Strengths of the existing law

This discussion is of course coloured by differing perceptions of the function of divorce law, and of course, by the level of understanding of the reality of divorce under the Matrimonial Causes Act 1973.

Hassan considers a spectrum of opinions amongst policy-makers in relation to the function of divorce law.[152] For example, some would argue that having fault-based grounds protects the institution of marriage, because it sends a message that marriage should not be undertaken lightly and that certain standards of behaviour are 'expected' by the state.[153] Others suggest that a strength of the current law is that it (generally) allows people to divorce quickly, and the high use of the fault facts suggests that this is what people want. In other words, the idea of prolonged waiting periods for divorce is based on a paternalistic

---

[150] Munby, Sir J. 'Judicial Office Press Conference' (London, 29 April 2014) 1–2. Available at: https://www.judiciary.gov.uk/wp-content/uploads/2014/05/munby-press-conference-290420141.pdf, accessed 1 March 2017.

[151] Available at: https://www.gov.uk/divorce/respond-to-a-divorce-petition, accessed 22 September 2017.

[152] Hassan, E. 'Setting a Standard or Reflecting Reality? The "Role" of Divorce Law, and the Case of the Family Law Act 1996' (2003) 17 *International Journal of Law Policy and the Family* 338.

[153] See, e.g., Deech, R. 'Divorce—a Disaster?' [2009] *Family Law* 1048. Hassan describes this as the 'idealist' position: Hassan, E. 'Setting a Standard or Reflecting Reality? The "Role" of Divorce Law, and the Case of the Family Law Act 1996' (2003) 17 *International Journal of Law Policy and the Family* 338, 344.

and false notion that decisions to divorce are taken lightly and irresponsibly. One lesson from the information meeting pilot for the failed Part II of the Family Law Act 1996 is that the potential for 'marriage-saving' is over-estimated.[154] Of course, support for quick divorce is as much an argument for reducing the waiting periods for the living apart facts in ss. 1(2)(d) and (e) as it is an argument for retaining fault, since the divorce process can be quick without necessarily requiring fault. Further, the advantage of speed in relation to the use of the law as it stands by petitioners is largely a result of the gap between the law and the reality; the notion that the letter of the law can be circumvented is usually not regarded as a strength.

A further argument in favour of fault is that there is may be a psychological advantage to being able to give the reasons for the marriage breakdown; that it gives a form of 'closure'. A variation of this argument is that bad conduct—principally violence by one spouse— should not be 'hidden' behind a neutral no-fault divorce process.

6. Is there a link between divorce law and divorce rates?

Concern over the rate of divorce is often cited as a factor in debates over divorce reform. This section provides some statistical context to this debate.

 CONTEXT 2: DIVORCE NUMBERS AND DIVORCE RATES

There are a number of different ways of measuring divorces. We can simply look at the number of divorces, and, provided the population is (fairly) stable, this is a valid way to assess trends over a number of years. However, it does not help us to compare jurisdictions, because it does not account for population differences (e.g. the number of divorces in England and Wales being double that of another country is no cause for surprise or concern if the population is also double).

The crude divorce rate is the number of divorces per 1000 people. This allows us to compare levels of divorce across differing populations. The UK's was 2.1 in 2011, broadly in line with the average across EU Member States (2.00) (latest figures for 2011).[155] However, the crude divorce rate is a measure against the whole population, married and unmarried.

Another measure, and one used by the Office for National Statistics (ONS), is number of divorces per 1000 of married population. This provides a useful measure both longitudinally and potentially comparatively, although figures calculated in this way are not always available for other jurisdictions. The divorce rate per 1000 married people in England and Wales was 9.3 in 2014, a fall from a high of 14.3 in 1993 to just under the rate in 1972 when the Divorce Reform Act 1969 came into effect. The ONS cites a significant fall in the number of marriages as a contributory cause to the falling divorce rate.[156]

[154] Collier, R. 'The Dashing of a Liberal Dream? The Information Meeting, the "New Family" and the Limits of Law' (1999) 11 *Child and Family Law Quarterly* 257.

[155] Eurostat, 'Marriage and Divorce Statistics' (June 2016). Available at: http://ec.europa.eu/eurostat/statistics-explained/index.php/Marriage_and_divorce_statistics, accessed 1 March 2017.

[156] ONS Statistical Bulletin, 'Divorces in England and Wales: 2014'. Available at: https://www.ons.gov.uk/peoplepopulationandcommunity/birthsdeathsandmarriages/divorce/bulletins/divorcesinenglandandwales/2014#divorces-continue-to-decline-in-2014, accessed 1 March 2017.

Debate 4: Does the Divorce Law Influence the Divorce Rate?

During the debates on the Family Law Bill 1995–6, John Patten MP commented that:

> The simple, practical fact which is undeniable, is that every time since the second world war that the House has legislated on divorce, there has been an immediate surge in the number of divorces . . . it is an empirical certainty that if we legislate again, there will be another surge in the number of divorces . . . The reforms will, alas, help turn us from the divorce capital of Europe, which we are now, to the divorce capital of the world.[157]

His statement was in the nature of a warning; his point was that in changing the law again, Parliament risked a further rise in the divorce rate. Similar concerns have been voiced in Parliamentary debates on every divorce bill from 1857 to the present, the latest example being the response of Edward Leigh MP to the No Fault Divorce Bill in 2015–16.[158]

Patten was absolutely right in his statement that there have been more divorces after every reform. This is hardly surprising, since every reform has widened access to divorce. Banning divorce altogether would be the most obvious way to make sure no divorces take place. No serious commentator, no matter how ardent a supporter of the institution of marriage, advocates this as a solution.

However, Patton also said that the rise in divorce in the past was 'apparently because of the messages sent out by the new laws has been perceived to be that divorce is meant to be easier and that the state backs marriage less and less . . . ' This represents a popular hypothesis of those who oppose divorce reform (and particularly the removal of fault): that liberalising the divorce law devalues marriage, and therefore marriages break down which with stricter divorce would have stayed together. In other words, divorce law affects not just the number of divorces but also the number of marital breakdowns.

The contrasting position is essentially that liberalising the divorce law may result in the rate of divorce rising, because it merely allows couples whose marriages have or will break down, regardless of the law, to dissolve those marriages, and that the level of family breakdown and hence divorce rises because of factors unrelated to the divorce law.

The underlying assumptions about the relationship between divorce numbers and divorce law need further critique and context about divorce numbers. We need to ask:

1. Has changing the divorce law *caused* the rise in the number of divorces? This is really another way of asking: has changing the divorce law caused a rise in the number of marital breakdowns in the past?

2. If so, would reform (particularly the removal of fault) bring about a further rise in future?

3. Finally, if it would, does this matter, and if so why?

The numbers shown in Figures 3.5, 3.6, and 3.7 give some context that will help answer these questions in the following sections.

---

[157] Hansard HC, col 482 (21 November 1995). Available at: https://www.publications.parliament.uk/pa/cm199596/cmhansrd/vo951121/debtext/51121-11.htm, last accessed 22 September 2017.

[158] Hansard HC, col 189 (13 October 2015). A very similar statement is made by Ruth Deech, 'Divorce—a Disaster?' [2009] *Family Law* 1048, 1053.

Figure 3.5 Divorce numbers and petitioner, England and Wales, 1949–2014

Source: ONS Dataset, 'Divorces in England and Wales: dataset 2014', Table 1. Available at: https://www.ons.gov.uk/peoplepopulationandcommunity/birthsdeathsandmarriages/divorce/datasets/divorcesinenglandandwales, accessed 17 February 2017.

Note: The scale (number of divorces) is different between Figures 3.6 and 3.7 because fluctuations in the first part of the twentieth century are virtually invisible when placed on the same scale as the second half of the century.

6.1 Has changing the divorce law caused a rise in the number of marital breakdowns in the past?

If we examine the trends shown in the graphs, we can make a few general observations: divorce was low until the 1920s, but then started to rise gradually, with a significant spike in the late 1940s before settling back down. There is another spike in the early 1970s, a continuing rise throughout the 1980s with a slight dip around the turn of the century, and then a steady further decline from 2005 onwards.

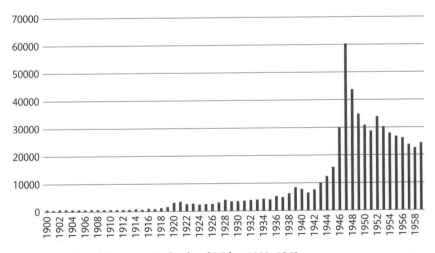

Figure 3.6 Number of Divorces, England and Wales, 1900–1960

Source: ONS Dataset, 'Divorces in England and Wales: dataset 2014', Table 1. Available at: https://www.ons.gov.uk/peoplepopulationandcommunity/birthsdeathsandmarriages/divorce/datasets/divorcesinenglandandwales, accessed 17 February 2017.

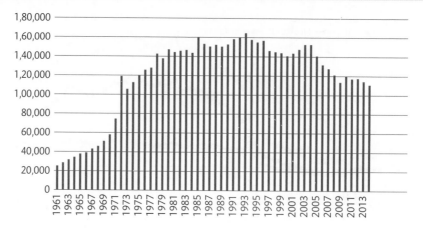

Figure 3.7 Number of Divorces, England and Wales, 1961–2014

Source: ONS Dataset, 'Divorces in England and Wales: dataset 2014', Table 1. Available at: https://www.ons.gov.uk/peoplepopulationandcommunity/birthsdeathsandmarriages/divorce/datasets/divorcesinenglandandwales, accessed 17 February 2017.

Spikes occur following divorce law reforms, most significantly following the coming into force of the 1969 Act in 1971. It is not really disputed, even by supporters of the institution of marriage, that this represented the formal end of empty shell marriages made possible by the introduction of the no-fault facts for divorce, rather than a glut of people rushing out to divorce because the reform had sent a message that marriage had been devalued.

However, the alleged link between law reform and a rise in the divorce rate cannot account for the significant spike in the late 1940s. It stretches credibility to regard this as a 'delayed reaction' to the widening of the grounds by the 1937 Act so logic suggests there must be another reason. What we see during this period is an untypically high proportion of petitions by husbands, so a much more credible explanation for the rise in divorce was caused by the disruption to family life by the Second World War. Other than in this period, petitions from wives have exceeded those by husbands ever since wives were given equal access to divorce under the 1923 Act.

Similarly, the significant rise throughout the remainder of the 1970s and 1980s cannot be accounted for by the empty shell argument; it suggests an increased number of marital breakdowns. Was this because the liberalised divorce law devalued marriage or for other reasons? Deech asserts 'it is now proven that it is the law and its administration that push the rate up'.[159] However, the Law Commission disagreed. They pointed to a number of demographic, socio-economic, and attitudinal changes in this period:

- the changing function of marriage, from 'institutionalised' to 'companionate'—in other words that people who marry now seek more emotional happiness from the union than was the case in the past, which makes the marriage tie more fragile if emotional happiness falters;

- longer lifespans means that the expected length of a marriage is much longer, and there are more opportunities for new relationships to be formed, particularly since the availability of contraception means that the couple may have a longer time to themselves after rearing a planned number of children;

- the changing position of women in society, who no longer expect to tolerate behaviour from husbands that they would have done in the past, and may now have more economic and social freedom to walk away;

[159] Deech, R. 'Divorce—a Disaster?' [2009] *Family Law* 1048, 1050.

- to some extent, a rise in the number of divorces may become self-perpetuating, since there was considerable stigma attached to divorce in the past when it was rare, which is no longer the case as it becomes more common.

The Law Commission also pointed out that there were similar rises in divorce across Europe, and an increase in marital breakdown in countries that at the time did not permit divorce at all.[160]

6.2 Would introducing no-fault divorce cause a rise in future?

A possible predictor of whether the divorce rate with the removal of fault is the experience in other countries who have already done so. However, no clear picture emerges. The Republic of Ireland has no-fault in the form of separation and has one of the lowest crude divorce rates in Europe. Russia on the other hand, also no-fault, has the highest crude divorce rate in Europe. Liz Trinder suggests that no clear causal link can be drawn between the introduction of no-fault divorce and the divorce rate. Longer-term studies suggest that impact of reform on the divorce rate may only be temporary and that it is difficult to 'disentangle' the divorce law from other factors that may affect marital breakdown (and its measurement).[161] Changes in divorce procedure, as well as divorce law, may affect the number of divorces.

One further point is that divorce is now on the decline. The Law Commission, writing in 1988, was able to say that divorce did not seem to threaten the 'institution' of marriage if the institution is judged by the number of people willing to enter into it. That picture has since changed, as there has been significant fall in the number of marriages in favour of cohabitation (see Chapter 2). This highlights the irony of measuring the strength of marriage by the number of people getting divorced. Assuming the trend away from marriage continues, it seems unlikely that no-fault divorce would have a significant effect and likely that divorce (and marriage) rates would continue to fall.

6.3 Does a rise in the divorce rate matter, and if so why?

A practical concern about the divorce rate centres on the cost to society—both financial and emotional—of 'broken families'.[162] However, the divorce rate is an incomplete measure of the number of broken families, since half of children are now born to unmarried parents and suffer equally when their parents split up regardless of whether they were married.[163] The perceived possibility of damage to children is, of course, a particular concern but this is really a cost of relationship breakdown, rather than divorce. Cohort studies investigating the effects of parental relationship breakdown on child welfare

---

[160] Law Commission, *Facing the Future: A Discussion Paper on the Ground for Divorce* (HC 479, Law Com No. 170, 1988), para 2.17.

[161] Trinder, L. 'In anticipation of a temporary blip: Would a change in the divorce law increase the divorce rate?' (2015). Available at: http://findingfault.org.uk/in-anticipation-of-a-temporary-blip-would-a-change-in-the-divorce-law-increase-the-divorce-rate/, accessed 22 September 2017.

[162] e.g., Lord Freud, former welfare reform minister suggested the cost was £46 billion in 2014. Bingham, J. '"Family breakdown" could cost taxpayers £46bn', *The Telegraph*, 4 March 2014. Available at: http://www.telegraph.co.uk/women/sex/divorce/10674267/Family-breakdown-could-cost-taxpayers-46bn.html, accessed 1 March 2017.

[163] ONS Statistical Bulletin, 'Births in England and Wales: 2015'. Available at: https://www.ons.gov.uk/peoplepopulationandcommunity/birthsdeathsandmarriages/livebirths/bulletins/birthsummarytablesenglandandwales/2015#the-percentage-of-births-outside-marriage-or-civil-partnership-continues-to-rise, accessed 6 April 2017.

show a complex picture.[164] There is no real public support for the idea that couples with children should stay together where possible to provide the children with a two-parent family. YouGov research in 2010[165] established that only 17% of people believe that unhappily married couples should stay together for the sake of their children.

It seems an inevitable consequence of the shift towards companionate relationships that there will be more breakdowns. In other words, a higher rate of divorce may be the price we pay for living in a society that places more emphasis on individual happiness, and respect for personal autonomy in relationships of all kinds.

Collier argues that divorce reform cannot be tackled effectively if discussion is rooted in an assumption that divorce itself is a problem.[166] Day Sclater and Piper point out:

> Feminist sociologists tend to argue that the changes are inevitable and that they are a welcome reflection of women's rejection of the drudgery implied by the ideals of 'hearth and home', and the fact that increasing numbers of women are leaving unsatisfactory relationships, or choosing to have children on their own, is a healthy sign that women are finding the courage, and the means, to lead autonomous lives.[167]

 DEBATE 5: SHOULD THE STATE REGULATE THE REASONS FOR DIVORCE?

The extensive criticisms of the current law that we have considered have tended to focus on the practical problems caused by fault. These arguments are part of a wider theoretical question: whether the state should regulate divorce by demanding proof of reasons at all? This is an ideological question about the relationship between state and families regarding the extent to which people should have autonomy over their personal relationships. Regulation represents public interference with the private sphere and it is important to question whether this interference is justified.

The concept of autonomy is further complicated in respect of divorce—and family law generally—as to whether autonomy should be mutual or individual (see Chapter 1). In the context of divorce, respecting mutual autonomy means allowing a couple to divorce without accounting for the reasons behind their marital breakdown, where they are both agreed that the marriage has broken down. Individual autonomy means allowing a unilateral decision by one party to divorce without giving a reason, even where the other spouse wants to continue the marriage.

The main argument in favour of interfering with the autonomy of a couple or an individual to seek a divorce in accordance with their own wishes rather than being accountable to the state is a traditional one: that marriage is an institution of value to the state; it is entered into publicly, vows are made and therefore there is a public interest in regulating its dissolution. Allowing couples to divorce without some accountability therefore risks diminishing the institution of marriage. Historically, this regulation was based around the concept that marriage was a religious sacrament, and therefore it was important to ensure that marriages were only ended where there was a genuine reason, authorised by Biblical teaching, for doing so. As well as the restriction to adultery as the sole ground until 1937, this manifested itself in provisions against collusion—in other words, where both members of a couple wanted a divorce, any suggestion that they were in agreement

---

[164]　See Helen Pearson, *The Life Project* (Allen Lane, 2016) 81–4, for an outline of birth cohort study findings showing that the effects of divorce intersect with the effects of poverty, and negative impacts of divorce have roots prior to parental separation.

[165]　Resolution/You Gov, *Survey into attitudes towards divorce and relationship breakdown* (12 March 2010).

[166]　Collier, R. 'The Dashing of a Liberal Dream? The Information Meeting, the "New Family" and the Limits of Law' (1999) 11 *Child and Family Law Quarterly* 257.

[167]　Sclater, S.D. and Piper, C. 'Re-moralising the family? Family Policy, Family law and Youth Justice' (2000) 12 *Child and Family Law Quarterly* 135.

in pursuing the divorce was a bar to the divorce taking place until 1969. This bar was a strong restriction on mutual autonomy. With increased secularisation, this has become a less significant issue. Far from being a barrier to divorce, mutual agreement over marital breakdown is now a fact that can prove breakdown under s. 1(2)(d) provided there is the required period of separation.

There is less popular value placed upon the institution of marriage in the twenty-first century than in the past. The number of marriages has fallen significantly, and cohabitation outside marriage is the fastest growing family form in the UK, although the number of cohabiting couples is still well below the number of married couples.[168] Additionally, examples from the history of divorce illustrate the practical difficulty of attempting to restrict autonomy through legal rules. Sir James Munby, in *Owens,* referred to the farce of the so called 'hotel room cases' (see 2.2) where couples colluded to obtain divorce on the ground of adultery when that was the only option, and described behaviour petitions—often the subject of negotiation and agreement between the parties—as the new situation where evidence is effectively faked for the purposes of securing a divorce.[169] In other words, the determination to divorce is not necessarily thwarted by the grounds on which it is available.

The second argument for interfering with autonomy is one of protection. We have seen the concern that divorce damages children. There is also a protection argument in respect of the adults: that without state intervention, some individuals will be put in a vulnerable position by their spouse's unilateral and unaccountable decision to divorce. In other areas of family law, protection of vulnerable family members is recognised as a valid reason for interfering with personal autonomy, for example, settlement of financial arrangements. Historically this was a valid argument in relation to divorce, because of the stigma associated it, alongside the potentially vulnerable position the financially weaker spouse might be left in (see Chapter 4). This was the motivation behind the s. 5 defence to a s. 1(2)(e) petition. Deech says:

> We expect women to jeopardise their careers by staying at home with their children and then we make their position precarious by providing for easy divorce, regardless of how well they have behaved as homemakers.[170]

However, as we have seen, this defence is rarely used, reflecting the reality that the stigma associated with divorce is much less of a factor now than it was in the past. Financial consequences of divorce can be dealt with via financial provision.

The same YouGov poll found that 75% of people agreed that 'marriages end irrespective of how hard or easy it is to get a divorce', indicating that the majority believe that marital breakdown itself is a private matter. This strengthens the case for respecting autonomy in this area of the law which could be achieved through a 'no-fault' system making autonomy a feature of the law rather than a by-product of it.

However, it is worth noting that even a no-fault system may restrict autonomy, though in a different way. The Family Law Act 1996 would have removed fault, but replaced the need to cite reasons with a requirement to go through a process including compulsory information meetings and enforced reflection. This is still a form of paternalistic model, albeit of a different kind. Eekelaar argues that the intention behind the Family Law Act framework was 'to bring it home to people that they must act responsibly; and that acting responsibly means conforming with received ideas about the desirability of marriage and undesirability of divorce'.[171]

---

[168] ONS Statistical Bulletin, 'Families and Households in the UK: 2016'. Available at: https://www.ons.gov.uk/peoplepopulationandcommunity/birthsdeathsandmarriages/families/bulletins/familiesandhouseholds/2016, accessed 17 February 2017.   [169] *Owens v Owens* [2017] EWCA Civ 182, at [95].

[170] Deech, R. 'Divorce—a Disaster?' [2009] *Family Law* 1048, 1049.

[171] Eekelaar, J. 'Family Law: Keeping us "on message"' 11 (1999) *Child and Family Law Quarterly* 387.

7. Alternatives: what could divorce law look like?

There are many different models for divorce law but the variations between them fall broadly into differences in the grounds required, and differences in the process required, including different waiting periods.

7.1 Models of divorce law

Figure 3.8 shows four broad models that may constitute grounds for divorce. Variations on these models, combined with differing process requirements, are used in jurisdictions across the world (see Context 3).

Of course, these are not exclusive alternatives. The Matrimonial Causes Act 1973 combines models 1 and 4, with an element of model 2 in respect of separation under s. 1(2)(d). The No Fault Divorce Bill 2015–16 would have added further provision for model 1 to the existing framework.

Waiting periods may theoretically be combined with any of the options for grounds. For example, Deech proposes adding a waiting period of one year to the fault grounds under the Matrimonial Causes Act 1973 to get rid of the 'quickie divorce'.[172]

The principal argument in favour of waiting periods is that it requires the parties to take time to reflect before the petition may be issued. Additionally, it is common to require arrangements for the couple's life apart, including financial matters and those for the children, to be settled during the waiting period, before the divorce can be finalised. Some jurisdictions impose different waiting periods for mutually agreed divorce from unilateral divorce, or depending on whether the couple has children. In some jurisdictions, legal separation (short of divorce) is more popularly used than it is in England and Wales, and this may be either a prerequisite to or a ground for divorce.

The 1988 Law Commission report[173] rejected the retention of fault (model 1) and considered variations on the other models:

Model 2—mutually-identified breakdown: the Law Commission pointed out that this could be an option, but it could never be the sole ground because it would not provide

MODEL 1:	**MODEL 2:**	**MODEL 3:**	**MODEL 4:**
BREAKDOWN EVIDENCED BY CONDUCT	UNILATERALLY IDENTIFIED BREAKDOWN	MUTUALLY IDENTIFIED BREAKDOWN	BREAKDOWN EVIDENCED BY A STATE OF AFFAIRS
Divorce is granted on the basis of one party committing a matrimonial fault	Divorce is granted where one party says that the marriage has broken down	Divorce is granted where both parties agree that the marriage has broken down	Divorce is granted on the basis of no-fault circumstances (usually separation)
PROCESS			
WAITING PERIODS AND/OR PROCEDURAL REQUIREMENTS			

Figure 3.8 Models of divorce

---

[172] Deech, R. 'Divorce—a Disaster?' [2009] *Family Law* 1048, 1053.

[173] Law Commission, *Facing the Future: A Discussion Paper on the Ground for Divorce* (HC 479, Law Com No. 170, 1988).

relief in cases where only one party wanted the divorce, and could therefore create a situation of breakdown without divorce, or an unfair 'bargaining chip' in settling post-divorce arrangements. They also felt that some form of reflection period would be needed.

Model 3—unilaterally-identified breakdown: the Law Commission acknowledged that the lack of scrutiny of fault petitions, for behaviour in particular, amounted to unilateral divorce on demand in many cases, yet felt that in principle unilateral demand would be unpopular with the public on the basis of removal any 'moral' element from divorce. They also pointed out the lack of protection for spouses under this model.

Model 4—separation: the Law Commission had concerns over separation as the sole ground:

- It is harder for those on low incomes to separate prior to proceedings—one possible solution here is to allow separation under the same roof, but this is unacceptable in many cases, particularly where there has been violence or abuse;

- There may be legitimate reasons why a couple is separated that do not indicate the marriage has broken down (though presumably, in that case, neither would pursue a divorce);

- The difficulty of deciding what length of separation would be indicative of breakdown.

The Law Commission's preferred option was what they called a 'process over time'. This was a combination of models 2 and 3, further combined with a waiting period. The Law Commission valued the purpose of a waiting period as a period of 'transition' in which one or both spouses could reflect on whether they really wanted to divorce and adjust their lives accordingly. They considered that 'irretrievable breakdown' should be retained, albeit on the identification of the parties, to send a message that marriages should not be dissolved lightly. In 1990, the Law Commission endorsed the 'process over time' model.[174] This influenced the government's consultation process, which eventually resulted in the Family Law Act 1996. The model that this Act would have adopted is shown in Figure 3.9.

Family lawyers' organisation Resolution propose that one or both partners should be able to give notice that the marriage has broken down irretrievably, with the divorce to be granted six months later provided one or both spouses still wants it. This provides for both mutually and individually identified breakdown, followed by a waiting period, which bears some similarity to the framework of the Family Law Act, but with fewer 'hoops' and a significantly shorter waiting period. Resolution argue that this would 'increase the chances of success for non court dispute resolution processes as it immediately puts both partners on a level footing. This will reduce the burden on the family court and help government to meet their aim for more people to resolve their problems outside of the courts'.[175]

Baroness Hale has proposed a statement of marital breakdown plus a one-year waiting period in which arrangements for finances and children would be settled.[176] This is another variation of 'process over time'.

---

[174] Law Commission, *Family Law: The Ground for Divorce* (HC 192, Law Com No. 192, 1990).

[175] Resolution, *Manifesto for Family Law* (2015), 21. See also Shepherd, N. 'Ending the Blame Game: Getting No Fault Divorce Back on the Agenda' [2009] *Family Law* 122 for the background to Resolution's reform proposal.

[176] Bentham, M. 'Top judge calls for rules which force women to take off veils when giving evidence in court' *Evening Standard*, 12 December 2014. Available at: http://www.standard.co.uk/news/uk/top-judge-calls-for-rules-which-force-women-to-take-off-veils-when-giving-evidence-in-court-9920224.html, accessed 22 September 2017.

Step 1: Information session attended by one or both parties
(both parties required prior to filing a joint petition, but could attend different sessions)
including information about counselling to save the marriage

Step 2: Three-month cooling off period (unless there are 'prescribed circumstances')

Step 3: Statement of marital breakdown filed either jointly by both parties or individually
by one party (note that in order to lead to a divorce order, this must be after the first
anniversary of the marriage)

Step 4: Period of consideration and reflection during which 'arrangements for the future
must be settled' and court give directions for further information about mediation

- Minimum 9 months if couple have no minor child
- Minimum 15 months if couple have a minor child

Step 5: Application for **divorce order,** citing irretrievable breakdown of the marriage.
This is granted provided the following requirements are satisfied:

- the marriage must have broken down irretrievavly (evidenced by a statement to that
  effect and the necessary period of consideration and reflection having lapsed);
- the couple must have satisfied the requirements as to attending information meetings,
  which have been listed erlier;
- the parties must have made the necessary arrangements for the future;
- the application must not have been withdrawn;
- there must not be an order preventing divorce in force.

Figure 3.9 What divorce in England and Wales would have looked like if Part II of the Family
Law Act 1996 had been brought into force

 CONTEXT 3: MODELS OF DIVORCE IN OTHER JURISDICTIONS

Scotland: Like England and Wales, Scotland has a mixed system, under which the ground of irretrievable breakdown must be proved by facts, some fault, and some no-fault, and was similar to the Matrimonial Causes Act 1973 until the Family Law (Scotland) Act 2006 amended the Divorce (Scotland) Act 1976. The facts are now adultery, behaviour, separation for one year where both parties consent, and separation for two years where they do not, combining models 1 and 4. There is also a further ground where an interim gender recognition certificate has been issued to either spouse.

Republic of Ireland: Under the Family Law (Divorce) Act 1996 divorce is based on no-fault grounds, namely living apart for four years out of the last five, and no prospect of reconciliation, adopting model 4. Divorce was constitutionally prohibited until 1996 (though legal separation was available before this). Ireland's low divorce rate (0.6 divorces per 1,000 people in 2011) masks the number of marital breakdowns evidenced by legal separation.[177]

Spain: Divorce law in Spain is straightforward; a three month bar after the marriage on filing (which can be waived in cases of risk) and a petition from one or both of the spouses. No

177 Eurostat, 'Marriage and Divorce Statistics' (June 2016). Available at: http://ec.europa.eu/eurostat/statistics-explained/index.php/Marriage_and_divorce_statistics, accessed 1 March 2017.

grounds are required. Where the breakdown is mutual, and arrangements for children and finances are settled, the legal process can be concluded in a matter of weeks. If the petition is unilateral, the process is longer while the finance and children arrangements are negotiated. This essentially combines models 2 and 3.

Divorce was not permitted in Spain until 1981. The divorce rate has risen steadily since its introduction, particularly so during the current century, and it is now around the EU average (and similar to the UK) at 2.2 marriages per 1,000 people in 2011.[178]

Italy: Italy requires proof of grounds, which are varied, but mainly based on the conduct of one spouse. These include being sentenced for certain serious criminal offences or two or more counts of various lesser offences including grievous bodily harm; certain circumstances relating to discontinuation or acquittal for some of the above crimes; annulment or divorce or remarriage abroad by a spouse who is a foreign national; change of sex by one spouse (either spouse can petition on this basis). Additionally, either spouse can petition in relation to a state of affairs: where the couple has been legally separated for three years (which may be based on mutual consent) or the marriage has not been consummated. Italy's divorce law therefore essentially combines models 1 and 4.

Divorce was legalised in Italy in 1970. The crude divorce rate is low compared to the rest of the EU—0.9 divorces per 1,000 people.[179]

South Africa: South Africa has a mixed system, which has some similarities to the UK. There are three grounds: irretrievable breakdown, incurable insanity, and continuous unconsciousness for six months. Like the system in England and Wales, breakdown is not self-identified as we have seen for example in Spain, and as it would have been under the Family Law Act 1996, but instead has to be proved to the court (even where the couple agree their marriage has broken down). There are circumstances that may establish breakdown, one year's separation, adultery, or imprisonment, but unlike the system in the MCA, these are indicative rather than the sole method of establishing breakdown. This is a variation of models 1 and 4.

The crude divorce rate in South Africa is low: 0.4 divorces per 1,000 population in 2013.[180]

Australia: Divorce in Australia has been no-fault since the Family Law Act 1975, based on irretrievable breakdown of the marriage, which is provable only by separation for one year (and no reasonable likelihood of cohabitation being resumed), thus corresponding to model 4. Arrangements for any children of the marriage must be settled before a divorce is granted.

The number of divorces in Australia is falling, as is the crude divorce rate, which was 2.0 per 1,000 population in 2014.[181]

New Zealand: Divorce in New Zealand is available based on irretrievable breakdown of the marriage, which is provable only by separation for two years under the Family Proceedings Act 1980. This again corresponds to model 4.

The crude divorce rate in New Zealand is 2.0.[182]

---

[178] Eurostat, 'Marriage and Divorce Statistics' (June 2016). Available at: http://ec.europa.eu/eurostat/statistics-explained/index.php/Marriage_and_divorce_statistics, accessed 1 March 2017.

[179] Eurostat, 'Marriage and Divorce Statistics' (June 2016). Available at: http://ec.europa.eu/eurostat/statistics-explained/index.php/Marriage_and_divorce_statistics, accessed 1 March 2017.

[180] Statistics South Africa, *Marriage and Divorces 2013* (2015). Available at: http://www.statssa.gov.za/publications/P0307/P03072013.pdf, accessed 1 March 2017.

[181] Australian Bureau of Statistics, *Marriages and Divorces, Australia, 2014* (2015). Available at: http://www.abs.gov.au/AUSSTATS/abs@.nsf/Previousproducts/3310.0Main%20Features122014?opendocument&tabname=Summary&prodno=3310.0&issue=2014&num=&view=, accessed 1 March 2017.

[182] OECD Family Database. Available at: http://www.oecd.org/els/family/database.htm; OECD-Social Policy Division Directorate of Employment, Labour and Social Affairs https://www.oecd.org/els/family/SF_3_1_Marriage_and_divorce_rates.pdf, both accessed 1 March 2017.

7.2 What could be done to achieve reform?

There are a number of possible options to reform the divorce law in England and Wales.

7.2.1 Implement divorce by process based on a ground of self-identified marital breakdown plus a waiting period

The most obvious reform, and the one that has received most support, is to remove fault from the divorce process. This is what the Family Law Act 1996 would have done, though as we have seen earlier, more recent proposals for reform favour a shorter process.

Advantages: It is recommended by judges and practitioners, who say that it would avoid escalating the conflict that is likely to exist around a relationship breakdown. It would complement the moves towards online, administrative divorce because it would not require adjudication. It would therefore also solve the current anomaly of a legal test that is not adjudicated in reality, unless the divorce is defended. It would recognise the reality that marriages break down for all kinds of reasons. It would bring the divorce law in England and Wales in line with many other jurisdictions in the world. It could end the 'quickie divorce'.

Disadvantages: It would require primary legislation, which might be politically difficult, given opposition to removal of fault by some MPs. It might be construed as devaluing marriage and making divorce too 'easy'. There might not be a consensus about the appropriate length of the waiting period.

7.2.2 Retain a mixed system, but reduce the time limits for the separation facts

This is the solution adopted in Scotland (see Context 3).

Advantages: An amendment to primary legislation would be required but it might be less contentious than removal of fault altogether or addition of a mutual breakdown fact. It would lessen (though not remove) the speed advantage of using fault, and thus reduce the problem of couples having to 'recriminate or separate'. It might encourage more use of the no-fault separation facts, since many couples might already have been separated for a period before one or both spouses take the final decision to divorce, or might see it as a more palatable waiting period rather than using the fault-based facts. It would reduce the number of 'empty shell' marriages resulting from an 'innocent' spouse wanting to delay or prevent a divorce.

Disadvantages: It retains fault, which many say has no place in the determination of marital breakdown, and maintains the artificiality of the relationship between marital breakdown and the facts acknowledged by law as evidencing it. The 'quickie' divorce would remain. Opponents of reform would probably object to it on the basis that it makes divorce 'easier'. It would probably cause a rise in the number of divorces, though the Scottish experience suggests that this would only be temporary.[183] It would not address the gap between the letter of the law and the reality of marital breakdown, nor the problem that unless the divorce is defended there is only lip service to the duty to test the facts of the petition. There might be concern for the protection of the 'innocent' spouse who does not want to divorce.

7.2.3 Add a further fact based on self-identified mutual breakdown (with a waiting period)

This would have been the effect of the No Fault Divorce Bill 2015–16.

Advantages: This option lessens the artificiality of the relationship between marital breakdown and the facts acknowledged by law as evidencing it by respecting the mutual

---

[183] Trinder, L. 'In anticipation of a temporary blip: Would a change in the divorce law increase the divorce rate?' (2015). Available at: http://findingfault.org.uk/in-anticipation-of-a-temporary-blip-would-a-change-in-the-divorce-law-increase-the-divorce-rate/, accessed 22 September 2017.

autonomy of a couple to decide that their marriage has broken down without having to account for why. It removes the potential discrimination that those who would prefer to divorce without alleging fault currently have to separate, which may be difficult financially. It might promote the use of no-fault divorce, and therefore whilst not removing the 'quickie divorce' might discourage it as an option. It preserves the existing protection for an 'innocent' spouse who does not want the marriage to end.

Disadvantages: This option would also retain fault in the determination of marital breakdown, and its use as an alternative to the 'quickie' divorce would depend on the length of the waiting period. As we know from the criticisms made of the No Fault Divorce Bill, Opponents of reform would probably object to it on the basis that it makes divorce 'easier' and diminishes respect for the institution of marriage. It does nothing to alleviate the lengthy separation required for a unilateral divorce in the absence of fault.

7.2.4 Procedural rather than substantive reform

This is the current focus. Of course, procedural reform can be carried out alongside substantive reforms: here we mean procedural reform in lieu of amending the legal grounds for obtaining a divorce, for example the proposals for online divorce currently being piloted (see 3.3).

Advantages: it does not require primary legislation and can therefore be implemented quickly. The process can be made more accessible by changing the language used in the divorce process, and creating a system that it easier to navigate. It acknowledges the reality that divorces happen in large numbers and administrative efficiency is needed, particularly given the increasing numbers of litigants in person. Trinder notes the potential link between procedure and use of the fault facts in Scotland: a new simplified procedure available only in separation cases had already resulted in a reduction in the reliance on fault facts prior to the amendment in the substantive law to reduce the length of separation required. More than 9 in 10 divorces in Scotland now proceed on the basis of separation rather than fault.[184]

Disadvantages: Unless accompanied by substantive reform, it does nothing to address the substantial criticisms that have been made of the existing law, in particular fault. Arguably, it increases the gap between what is supposed to happen according to the letter of the law and the actual practice.

7.3 Prospects for reform

How likely is it that the divorce law will be reformed? In February 2017, coinciding with publicity about fault in the divorce process arising from the case of *Owens v Owens*,[185] Lord Keen of Elie, in a written response on behalf of the Conservative government, reiterated that reforms other than to the substantive law were the focus:

> Whilst we have no current plans to change the existing law on divorce, we are considering what further reforms to the family justice system may be needed.[186]

However, after the *Owens* decision, when questions were again raised in the House of Lords about divorce, the government signalled that reform of the substantive law might

---

[184] Liz Trinder, 'In anticipation of a temporary blip: Would a change in the divorce law increase the divorce rate?' (2015) <http://findingfault.org.uk/in-anticipation-of-a-temporary-blip-would-a-change-in-the-divorce-law-increase-the-divorce-rate/, accessed 22 September 2017.　　[185] [2017] EWCA Civ 182.

[186] Hansard HL, WA HL5103 (13 February 2017). Available at: http://www.parliament.uk/business/publications/written-questions-answers-statements/written-question/Lords/2017-01-30/HL5103/, accessed 22 September 2017.

be under consideration after all. Baroness Buscombe suggested that divorce law would be included within a Green Paper on Family Justice to be published 'in due course'.[187] The Labour Party committed to removal of fault from the divorce process in its June 2017 Election Manifesto.[188] It seems therefore that there is greater political will to consider divorce reform, but given the result of the June 2017 election, and the likely focus on Brexit over the next Parliament, it may take time to materialise.

SUMMARY

1. Should divorce law be reformed?
   - This is the key debate in relation to divorce, and the other debates highlighted in the chapter and summarised below are important issues that arise in the context of a broader discussion of reform.
   - There is a compelling case for reform of divorce law, particularly the removal of fault from the process. The Law Commission published comprehensive criticisms of the current law in 1988, and many stakeholders in family law continue to call for no-fault divorce.
   - Key criticisms are that the use of fault increases conflict between the parties, and encourages false or exaggerated claims which do not represent the real reason for the breakdown of the marriage—the behaviour fact is particularly criticised for increasing animosity, and giving a potentially false sense of why the marriage broke down.
   - The historical context demonstrates a process of gradual liberalisation of the grounds for divorce, culminated in the (failed) attempt to introduce no-fault divorce by process under the Family Law Act 1996.
   - This reform process has been contentious, with opponents of reform arguing that removal of fault from the process undermines the institution of marriage whilst reformers argue that the experience of divorce law demonstrates that the law cannot regulate marital breakdown effectively.
   - We have seen an enormous shift from divorce being rare and socially unacceptable to being both common and commonplace. Changes in divorce procedure have been required to manage the high volume of applications, but which ironically reduces scrutiny of the divorce.
   - The current focus of reform is on making procedural changes that facilitate efficient processing of the high volume of applications. The tacit acceptance that divorce is in reality an administrative rather than judicial procedure strengthens the case for reform of the substantive law.

2. Why is adultery between people of the same sex not recognised as adultery by the law?
   - This is one aspect of the reform debate, which illustrates the discriminatory nature of divorce law as between heterosexual spouses and gay spouses.

---

[187] Hansard HL, vol 782 (29 March 2017). Available at: https://hansard.parliament.uk/lords/2017-03-29/debates/D14330EE-0828-46BA-A46E-94019953923C/DivorceLegislation, accessed 22 September 2017.

[188] Labour Party, *For the many not the few: Labour Party Manifesto 2017* (May 2017), 81. Available at: http://www.labour.org.uk/page/-/Images/manifesto-2017/Labour%20Manifesto%202017.pdf, accessed 28 June 2017.

- The anomalous position in the law reflects in part the historical definition of adultery with reference to the act of intercourse between a man and a woman; the failure to tackle this can be seen as a reluctance to accept that gay marriage is the same as heterosexual marriage.
- The issue could be avoided if fault were removed from the divorce process.

3. What does *Owens v Owens* add to interpretation of the behaviour fact?
    - *Owens* was a rare (and much-publicised) example of a defended divorce refused for failure to satisfy the test for behaviour under s. 1(2)(b) of the Matrimonial Causes Act 1973. The case appears to strengthen the objective element of the behaviour test at the expense of the subjective element, and reinforces traditional notions of marital behaviour: the petition was described as 'flimsy', and the wife characterised as 'sensitive' for objecting to her husband's 'old school' behaviour.
    - The Court of Appeal used the case to make a strong call for the removal of fault-based grounds, arguably at the expense of deciding in Mrs Owens' favour, and openly acknowledged that a lower threshold for behaviour is used in undefended cases scrutinised by a legal adviser at a divorce centre rather than a judge in court in a defended case. In other words, the legal principles are only correctly applied if the respondent refuses to admit to the behaviour alleged.
    - The ruling may lead to less cooperation between parties over behaviour petitions, stronger behaviour allegations, and/or more defended divorces, thus potentially increasing the hostility arising from the use of fault.

4. Does divorce law influence the divorce rate and does this matter?
    - This is a further aspect of the overall debate on reform, since opponents of reform argue that a liberal divorce law promotes divorce.
    - It is certainly true that divorce rates have risen in England and Wales as the law has been gradually liberalised but the factors that influence rates of marital breakdown are more complex than simply the state of the law.
    - Evidence from other jurisdictions shows that no-fault divorce does not necessarily lead to a rise in the number of marital breakdowns.
    - The divorce rate is not in any case necessarily indicative of a 'crisis' in the family but indicative of greater personal and economic freedom—particularly for women—and pursuit of more equal companionship in marriage.

5. Should the state regulate the reasons for divorce?
    - This debate represents the underpinning ideology of the reform debate: that the state has a role in regulating divorce, because the institution of marriage is a public status, and should be promoted by the divorce law and that this is more important than individual or mutual autonomy.
    - However, marital breakdown is a private matter which resists accountability, and therefore the divorce law cannot effectively restrict autonomy in respect of personal relationships—expecting divorce law to promote marriage is contradictory.
    - Criticism has also been made of the Family Law Act model of no-fault divorce for attempting to impose a perception that divorce is to be avoided via an onerous process.

Further Reading

COLLIER, R. 'The Dashing of a Liberal Dream? The Information Meeting, The "new Family" and the limits of law' (1999) 11 *Child and Family Law Quarterly* 257
- This article critiques the government's decision not to proceed with implementation of the Family Law Act 1996, and constructs a broader argument that divorce reform discourse 'problematises' divorce.

CRETNEY, S. *Family Law in the Twentieth Century, a History* (OUP, 2005)
- This text is a comprehensive review of reform in key areas of family law. Part II covers divorce reform in detail, giving context to the development of the law and procedure, and the financing of family proceedings.

DEECH, R. 'Divorce—a disaster?' [2009] *Family Law* 1048, 1049
- This article provides a contrast to much of the other material on divorce reform as Deech advocates the retention of fault as a symbol of morality.

EEKELAAR, J. 'Family Law: Keeping us "on message"' (1999) 11 *Child and Family Law Quarterly* 387
- This considers the decision not to implement the divorce provisions of the Family Law Act 1996 in the context of challenging the ability of law to regulate behaviour in personal relationships.

HASSAN, E. 'Setting a Standard or Reflecting Reality? The "Role" of Divorce Law, and the Case of the Family Law Act 1996' (2003) 17 *International Journal of Law, Policy and the Family* 338
- A detailed exploration of the spectrum of opinions on the role of the law/state in regulating divorce.

LAW COMMISSION, Facing the Future: A Discussion Paper on the Ground for Divorce (HC 479, Law Com No. 170, 1988) and Family Law: The Ground for Divorce (HC 192, Law Com No. 192, 1990)
- The Law Commission's reports provide a comprehensive analysis of the law and practice and consideration of options for reform.

SHEPHERD, N. 'Ending the Blame Game: Getting No Fault Divorce Back on the Agenda' [2009] *Family Law* 122
- Shepherd describes the Family Law Act divorce scheme, and revisits the reform debate in the context of Resolution's proposals to remove fault. See also: http://www.resolution.org.uk//endtheblamegame/?displayMode=preview, accessed 21 September 2017, for more on this.

Trinder, L. 'In Anticipation of a temporary blip: Would a change in the divorce law increase the divorce rate?' (2015), available at: http://findingfault.org.uk/in-anticipation-of-a-temporary-blip-would-a-change-in-the-divorce-law-increase-the-divorce-rate/, accessed 21 September 2017
- This article considers whether lessons can be drawn from changes to the divorce law in Scotland. See also the Finding Fault project website generally at: http://findingfault.org.uk/, accessed 21 September 2017.

4

Property Division on Divorce

Polly Morgan

–

LEARNING OBJECTIVES

After reading this chapter you will be able to:

- Explain the key legal principles and processes applied to property division on divorce;
- Identify the social concerns that legislators and courts have attempted to address through law, and evaluate how successfully the law has addressed these concerns;
- Critically discuss the extent to which there is a coherent set of underlying principles for property division.

DEBATES

After reading this chapter you should be equipped to discuss your opinion on the following central debates:

1. Should the parties have continuing financial obligations to one another that outlive the marriage?
2. Should a stellar contribution to marriage be recognised?
3. Should we compensate parties if events during the marriage cause them future disadvantage?
4. Does the law correctly balance certainty with discretion?
5. Should people be able to reach their own enforceable agreements without court approval?

1. Introduction

At the end of a marriage, it is necessary to consider the practical and financial arrangements for the parties' future: how they will share the value of the house(s), the pensions, and the savings and investments; who pays the debts; who gets personal belongings and furniture; and who has what income to live on. While the parties may think this purely a matter between them, the law will only give effect to agreements that are *objectively fair*, and if the parties cannot agree a fair settlement then courts have the power to impose a settlement on them by making a 'financial remedy' order in whatever terms *it* thinks are objectively fair. This may include the redistribution of income and assets between the parties irrespective of legal ownership. As Lord Denning said:

> The family court takes the rights and obligations of the parties all together and puts the pieces into a mixed bag. Such pieces are the right to occupy the matrimonial home or have a share in it, the obligation to maintain the wife and children, and so forth. The court then takes out the pieces and hands them to the two parties—some to one party and some to the other—so that each can provide for the future with the pieces allotted to him or to her. The court hands them out without paying any too nice a regard to their legal or equitable rights but simply according to what is the fairest provision for the future.[1]

In deciding how to exercise its powers, the courts will apply broad principles, derived mostly from case law, which tell us what fairness can look like and what rights and responsibilities should stem from married life. Yet fairness is an amorphous concept, and it will become evident that both Parliament and the judiciary have struggled to provide a coherent set of legal principles that can be applied to the wide range of family situations that come before the courts. For example, should obligations to financially support your spouse continue post-divorce? How should the law recognise the value of child-raising compared to earning money? To what extent should a couple be able to reach their own agreement even if it leaves one party on benefits and the other comfortably off? These are all aspects of one issue: what exactly does fairness look like?

This chapter looks at the courts' powers, the legal principles, the practical implications, and the problems that may arise in financial remedy practice. Although for convenience it will use the terminology 'husband' and 'wife', the same law—the Matrimonial Causes Act 1973 and all its case law—applies (with a few exceptions) to same-sex married couples. For civil partners, who can only be same-sex, the law is set out in the Civil Partnership Act 2004, which mirrors the financial provisions of the Matrimonial Causes Act 1973. It is important to note that the law described in this chapter applies only to couples who have been married or civilly partnered to one another. As discussed in Chapter 5, there are no equivalent protections in England and Wales (our jurisdiction) for unmarried couples.

Unless otherwise stated, all statutory references are to the Matrimonial Causes Act 1973, in its most current amended form.

2. Reaching a financial settlement

The parties usually seek to agree how to divide their property while the divorce itself is happening in the background. Because this can be contentious, it is good to get started early, perhaps at the same time as the divorce petition is filed.

2.1 Non court processes

The first step for a solicitor is to ask their client's spouse for *financial disclosure*—an explanation and valuation of his or her property, savings, investments, business interests, chattels, debts, incomes and outgoings, and pensions—backed up by documentary proof.

---

[1] *Hanlon v The Law Society* [1980] 1 All ER 763, 770 [g]–[h] (CA).

In most cases—60%—the parties' solicitors negotiate a settlement through correspondence, telephone conversation, or face-to-face meetings.[2] However, the parties could use mediation, collaborative law, or arbitration to reach agreement without having to enter into a contested litigation process.[3] Of these, mediation is the most popular, being responsible for resolving about 14% of cases.[4] Indeed, parties who wish to make a court application must first attend a mediation information and assessment meeting (MIAM) unless one of the limited exceptions set out in the Family Procedure Rules applies, such as evidenced domestic violence or bankruptcy.[5] The purpose of the meeting is to discuss whether the case is suitable for mediation, although a party cannot be compelled to mediate.

Where the parties have reached an agreement themselves, they can make a joint application for the court to turn their agreement into a financial remedy order.[6] Because the parties have agreed its terms, this is known as a *consent order*. The parties do not need to attend court but simply send in a draft order, an outline of their financial positions, and key information about their lives, such as their ages and those of any children, and the length of the marriage. A judge will consider the papers and decide whether to make an order in the terms sought. However, as we will see in section 8, the fact that the parties have reached agreement is highly influential in determining whether the agreement is fair. We will analyse what fairness means later in the chapter.

2.2 **The court process**

If the parties cannot reach agreement outside court, or if there are good reasons not to try, then it is open to either party to apply to court for a financial remedy order. Financial remedy is the new name for 'ancillary relief', the financial settlement being ancillary to the main suit, which is the divorce (see Chapter 3)—hence the fact that divorce proceedings must have been issued for a financial remedy application to be made.

The application triggers a contested litigation process that will ultimately result in the judge deciding who gets what, and imposing that on the parties by way of order. First, the court will issue some standard directions as to how the case is to be timetabled and managed. The parties are under an obligation to help the court to further the overriding objective to deal with cases justly—which includes proportionately.[7] In practice, this really means not letting the timetable slip or racking up huge costs, although sometimes both things happen.

The parties must first exchange financial disclosure (in form E) as well as several other documents and then attend court for the first directions appointment (FDA), the purpose of which is to identify the issues in dispute and any further information needed in order to proceed to a final hearing. This may, for example, include a valuation of the family home. The parties then obtain this information before returning to court for a financial dispute resolution (FDR) hearing (although in complex cases there may be more than one directions hearing). The primary purpose of the FDR is to try to help parties to reach their own agreement without needing to go to a final hearing. The judge therefore hears from both parties and tries to give some guidance on the parameters of an appropriate settlement and

---

[2] Hitchings, E., Miles, J., and Woodward, H. 'Assembling the Jigsaw Puzzle: Understanding Financial Settlement on Divorce' [2014] *Family Law* 209, 310.

[3] Information about these different options is available at: http://www.resolution.org.uk, accessed 23 September 2017.

[4] Hitchings, E., Miles, J., and Woodward, H. 'Assembling the Jigsaw Puzzle: Understanding Financial Settlement on Divorce' [2014] *Family Law* 209, 310.   [5] Family Procedure Rules, r. 3.8.

[6] Family Procedure Rules, r. 9.26.   [7] Family Procedure Rules, Part I.

whether one party is being unreasonable. Settlement is common at this stage because the parties are at court with (hopefully) representation, they're aware of the increasing costs, they've had a nudge from the judge about the likely outcome if the case proceeds to a final hearing, and they should by this point have all the financial information they require already to hand.[8]

If the parties still cannot reach agreement, then a final hearing is scheduled, to be heard by a different judge who has no access to the FDR positions. At a final hearing, the judge will hear evidence from both parties and representations made by their lawyers, issue a judgment, and make an order that he or she thinks is fair.

The current average time taken for a financial remedy case is just under 25 weeks.[9] Only about 10% of cases go to a final hearing, as against 69% of cases resolved by consent and 21% in which a financial remedy application is made but which settles midway through.[10]

2.3 Cost

If all this sounds expensive (and time-consuming), it is because it is. Legal aid is not available for either divorce or financial remedy proceedings, as a rule. There are exceptions: legal aid is available for mediation, and those who have certain kinds of evidence of domestic abuse can also get legal aid for solicitor-led negotiation, mediation (if suitable), or the court process. In all cases, the parties must meet stringent financial and merits criteria, meaning that even where people have the required evidence of domestic violence, they may earn too much to get legal aid, but far too little to easily afford legal representation.

The financial remedy court process is one-size-fits-all, and for very low asset cases sometimes just spending time preparing a form E is a disproportionate cost, and one that the parties can ill afford.

It is also unlikely that a party will be able to recoup their costs from their spouse. The usual order, whether this is by consent or following a contested hearing, is 'no order as to costs', that is, that each party pays his or her own costs only.[11] The rationale behind this is that 'each party has an interest in determining how the matrimonial assets should be divided or allocated, and each is usually in a position to meet costs out of his/her allotted share'.[12] However, the court can make a costs order against one party 'where it considers it appropriate to do so because of the conduct of a party in relation to the proceedings'.[13] For example, if disclosure is not full and frank, a party may be at risk of costs, or, indeed, of the final order being overturned.[14]

Although lawyer-led processes still account for the vast majority of financial settlements, the loss of legal aid, and perhaps a distrust of lawyers and courts, has led to an increasing number of people acting for themselves (known as litigants-in-person or self-represented litigants). It is a complex process to navigate without legal advice—and that is before we come to the relevant legal provisions and principles.

---

[8] Hitchings, E., Miles, J., and Woodward, H. 'Assembling the Jigsaw Puzzle: Understanding Financial Settlement on Divorce' [2014] *Family Law* 209, 314.

[9] Ministry of Justice, *Family Court Statistics Quarterly England and Wales April–June 2016*. Some will take less time and some more.

[10] Ministry of Justice, *Family Court Statistics Quarterly England and Wales April–June 2016*.

[11] Family Procedure Rules, r. 28.3(5). Cf Civil Procedure Rules. However, on an appeal a costs order where the loser pays the winner's costs is very likely.   [12] *T v T* [2013] EWHC B3 (Parker J).

[13] Family Procedure Rules, r. 28.3(6).

[14] *Sharland v Sharland* [2015] UKSC 60; *Gohil v Gohil* [2015] UKSC 61.

CONTEXT 1: WHAT FACTORS AFFECT A DECISION TO SETTLE?

We know from research that in determining whether to settle a case and on what terms, or whether to proceed to a final hearing, the parties are influenced by a number of factors, both legal and non-legal.

Robert Mnookin and Lewis Kornhouser have argued that people 'do not bargain over the division of family wealth . . . in a vacuum; they bargain in the shadow of the law'.[15] Law influences them, whether or not the matter proceeds to court, by providing a framework within which the parties must operate. While the high level of judicial discretion makes it difficult to predict the outcome even with realistic advice, this cuts both ways, encouraging or inhibiting settlement depending on the parties' attitudes to risk. When parties negotiate, they will weigh up their prospects doing better at court than through negotiation outside court, and the costs (financial, temporal, and emotional) of going to court. At the same time, each will need to consider matters from the other's perspective: what is his or her attitude to risk and prospects of success, and how much cost can they bear?

Research shows that the parties' emotional readiness to reach a settlement is also important.[16] Even if both want the divorce (which is not always the case) they may be at very different stages in their acceptance of the process. If they have begun to adjust to the divorce, it may be on the basis of an anticipated future lifestyle which is simply unrealistic. For example, they may believe that there is always a 50–50 split, or that a party who leaves forfeits the assets not taken with them.[17] They may expect the same outcome as their friend had and resist advice to the contrary. They may believe that the law has not recognised the harm being done to them by an unwanted marital breakdown, and seek to use the legal process to vindicate their position. There may be significant issues of trust, including about financial disclosure.[18] Some parties may refuse to engage with the process: perhaps they do not like the advice they are receiving or have had no advice, or mistakenly believe that nothing can happen without their consent. All of these issues can inhibit settlement.

2.4 Why an order is important

While a settlement that the parties have agreed may feel fairer to them than one that is imposed by a judge following a contested hearing, the important thing is to have an order. The claims that each party has against the other on divorce are not terminated by decree absolute (the final divorce decree), but only by so-called 'clean break' provisions in a financial remedy order (see 4.2). If there is no order, it is quite possible to be long divorced and for a former spouse to come back years later and seek financial support—even if the parties had informally agreed at the time who was to have what asset and had put that into effect. As it is the embodiment of the arrangements in a court order which renders them enforceable, *not* the agreement between the parties itself, there is nothing to stop an application being made.[19] In *Wyatt v Vince*, the wife applied for a financial remedy order

---

[15] Mnookin, R.N. and Kornhauser, L. 'Bargaining in the Shadow of the Law: The Case of Divorce' (1979) 88 *Yale Law Journal* 950.

[16] Hitchings, E., Miles, J., and Woodward, H. 'Assembling the Jigsaw Puzzle: Understanding Financial Settlement on Divorce' [2014] *Family Law* 209, 313.

[17] See Dowding, S. 'Self-Determination of Judicial Imposition? Translating the Theory into Practice', in J. Miles and R. Probert (eds), *Sharing Lives, Dividing Assets* (Hart Publishing, 2009).

[18] Hitchings, E., Miles, J., and Woodward, H. 'Assembling the Jigsaw Puzzle: Understanding Financial Settlement on Divorce' [2014] *Family Law* 209, 314.   [19] *de Lasala v de Lasala* [1980] AC 546.

nearly 20 years after decree absolute. The Supreme Court held that: '[c]onsistently with the potentially life-long obligations which attend a marriage, there is no time-limit for seeking orders for financial provision'.[20] The wife's claim may have had little value in the circumstances, but she was entitled to pursue it.

While the 20 year gap in *Wyatt* may be extreme, there have for many years been more divorces granted than financial remedy orders made, whether on a consensual or contested basis, and each of these is a potential future claim that could have a serious effect upon the financial functioning of a client's new family unit or planned retirement. A lack of knowledge of the implications, a lack of assets at the time of the divorce, and (more recently) the loss of legal aid may all have contributed this.[21]

3. The court's powers

Whether the judge is making the order on a joint application by parties who have reached agreement or the judge is rendering a decision following a contested hearing, the court can only order something if it has the power to do so under Part II of the Matrimonial Causes Act 1973, namely:

- order a party to pay the other a lump sum or sums;
- order a party to make periodical payments to the other party (spousal maintenance);
- order a party to make periodical payments for the benefit of a child (child maintenance—limited powers here because of the existence of a separate child maintenance scheme);
- order the transfer of ownership of property. Property in this context means any type of asset, not merely real property (houses);
- order the sale of property and decide how the proceeds should be shared out;
- order that property be held on trust for use by the other party or a child;
- order a pension provider to share a party's pension fund or to send a proportion of the pension income, when it is in payment, to the other party;
- vary a prenuptial or postnuptial agreement.

Leaving aside prenuptial and postnuptial agreements until 8, let us consider the rest of the courts' powers in more detail.

3.1 Lump sums

A lump sum order (s. 23(1)(c)) simply requires one party to pay an amount or amounts to the other party. This is usually within specified time after the decree absolute, often 56 days (and interest is chargeable on late payments), but you could have instalments on agreed future dates. However, do note the phrasing of the provision: it is 'an order' for the payment of a sum or sums, thus all payments must be included in the one order even if they are by instalments. Under s. 31(1) the court has power to vary or discharge an order for the payment of a lump sum by instalments 'or to suspend any provision thereof temporarily'. In doing so, the court could potentially stretch payment over such a long period that it is tantamount to reducing the amount.

---

[20] [2015] UKSC 14, at [32] (Lord Wilson).
[21] See Barton, C. and Bissett-Johnson, A. 'The Declining Number of Ancillary Relief Financial Orders' [2000] *Family Law* 94.

3.2 Periodical payments

Under s. 23(1)(a) of the Matrimonial Causes Act 1973, the court can order one party to make regular (usually monthly) payments to the other party post-divorce.[22] It is useful for ensuring each party has enough money to live on. Where there is sufficient capital to meet a party's housing and income needs, it may not be necessary to have periodical payments. This is not child maintenance, although any money coming into the household will benefit any children who live there, but is financial support between former spouses that has outlasted the marriage. Consequently, it is one of the most controversial aspects of financial remedy law.

The quantum of payments will depend on the parties' circumstances. For many centuries, the most common maintenance amount was one third of the husband's income. However, any vestiges of this approach died with *Miller/McFarlane* (Key Case 2): the principles of meeting needs and providing compensation identified in that case do not lend themselves to an arbitrary one-size-fits-all figure.[23] Accordingly, we now quantify periodical payments by reference to the claimant's budgetary needs and whether the amount identified 'represents a fair proportion of the respondent's available income'.[24]

An order can be a specified term (e.g. five years, which can be extended by further order or, under s. 28(1A), non-extendable) or—particularly where the recipient is middle-aged or older—for so long as they both shall live: a joint-lives order.[25] When considering whether to make a joint-lives or term order, with or without a s. 28(1A) bar, the Family Justice Council guidance distributed to judges recommends considering a wide range of factors about the recipient's earning capacity, childcare obligations, age, and health, as well as the payer's ability to pay.[26] 'It is almost impossible to be 'scientific'.[27]

Either party can apply for the amount of the periodical payments to be varied up or down as their circumstances change.[28] The maintenance can even be set at a nominal amount, such as one pence per year, the purpose of which is simply to keep the claim for maintenance open in case the recipient needs to apply to vary it up to a 'real' amount. It must, however, end if the recipient remarries or enters into a civil partnership, and the payer may well make an application for the payments to reduce or end upon the recipient's cohabitation, although such an application may not be successful.[29] Under s. 23(1)(b) the order can be secured against assets of the payer (usually a house) if there is a risk of non-payment, but this is not common.

If there is enough capital to do it, the payer could give the recipient a lump sum instead of ongoing periodical payments, and this would give the parties a clean break. Where the maintenance is lifetime, the parties may refer to the *Duxbury* tables to work out how big a sum is needed.[30] These are actuarial tables that take into account average life expectancy, state pension drawdown, tax rates, interest rates, and inflation to come to a guesstimated

---

[22] Orders can be made after decree nisi but will not take effect until decree absolute: Matrimonial Causes Act 1973, ss. 23(1) and (5).

[23] [2006] UKHL 24. These two cases were joined on appeal to the House of Lords.

[24] *NS v SS (Spousal Maintenance)* [2014] EWHC 4183 (Fam), at [46] (Mostyn J).

[25] Indeed, because the recipient has been maintained by the payer within the meaning of the Inheritance (Provision for Family and Dependants) Act 1975, if the payer dies while paying maintenance, the recipient has a claim against their estate.

[26] See, Family Justice Council, *Guidance on 'Financial Needs' on Divorce* (Ministry of Justice, 2016), para 68 for the full list.

[27] *Parlour v Parlour/McFarlane v McFarlane* [2004] EWCA Civ 872, at [60] (Bennett J).

[28] Matrimonial Causes Act 1973, s. 31.   [29] Matrimonial Causes Act 1973, s. 28(1).

[30] Named for *Duxbury v Duxbury* [1992] Fam 62 and located in the Family Law Bar Association's annual *At'a Glance* guide.

capital sum that, if invested, could yield the income required and be entirely used up at the end of the recipient's *actuarial* life expectancy.

3.3 Financial support for children

The Child Support Act 1991 created a scheme for the payment of child maintenance. Consequently, judges retain only limited powers to make orders under the Matrimonial Causes Act 1973, either by agreement or where the child support scheme does not apply.[31] Courts also have some powers to order financial provision for children under Sch 1 of the Children Act 1989, but as this is less generous than the Matrimonial Causes Act, it is not commonly used by married couples.

Child maintenance is discussed in more detail in Chapter 6.

3.4 Property adjustment orders

A property adjustment order is an order changing the parties' interests in property of any kind (e.g. house, savings/investments, cars, furniture) whether owned in possession or reversion. There are two types.

The first type is a property transfer order under s. 24(1)(a). This provides that a party transfer specified property into the name of the other spouse, a child of the family, or any other person specified in the order. This may be in exchange for a lump sum from the other party—for example, 'you can have the house if you take out a bigger mortgage to give me £75,000'. Where A needed the house now and could not downsize or raise a lump sum, but it is fair for B to have some money from it in the future, transfer could be made subject to a charge, that is, the matrimonial home is transferred to A subject to a charge in favour of B for £20,000 plus interest or—if you preferred to draft it this way—10% of the equity in the house. The charge would need to be redeemed on the happening of certain trigger events.

The second type is a settlement order under s. 24(1)(b). This provides that property be held on trust for the parties. For example, you could settle the house on trust for the parties as equitable tenants in common in the unequal shares of (e.g.) 90% to A and 10% to B, but B cannot realise his 10% until the happening of certain trigger events.

It is for the parties to negotiate the triggers they want, or the court to decide them. Common triggers for both types are: the youngest child turning 18 (known as a *Mesher* order[32]); the death, remarriage, or cohabitation of the occupying party, if these do not happen, the occupier potentially therefore has the use of the property for life (known as a *Martin* order[33]); or a combination of both, as in *Sawden v Sawden*.[34]

On trigger, the house will need to be sold or A will need to find some other way of raising the money to pay B. Such orders have fallen out of favour because of concerns that at the trigger event the occupying party may still not be able to rehouse themselves. It is also unfair on the party who cannot extricate his or her money from the property for some years.

Although not a property adjustment order, under the Family Law Act 1996 the court can transfer some types of 'dwelling house' tenancies between spouses or civil partners. The Act contains a list of factors to take into account in deciding whether to do this.[35]

---

[31] Child Support Act 1991, s. 8.
[32] Named for *Mesher v Mesher and Hall* [1980] 1 All ER 126 (heard 1973).
[33] Named for *Martin v Martin* [1978] Fam 12.   [34] [2004] EWCA Civ 339.
[35] Family Law Act 1996, Sch 7, para 5.

3.5 **Property sale orders**

Under s. 24A of the Matrimonial Causes Act 1973, the court has the power to order the sale of property when, in the same order or a previous order, it has ordered secured periodical payments, lump sum, or property adjustment. Property sale can be a useful back-up plan: for example, default sale of the matrimonial home can be triggered when a party fails to raise the funds to 'buy out' the other's interest.

3.6 **Pension orders**

It is never sensible to overlook pensions on divorce, even if retirement is some time away, as this is a potentially valuable resource. The court can make two kinds of orders, a pension sharing order or an attachment order. Alternatively, it is possible to offset one party's entitlement to a pension share by giving that person more of the other assets instead.

A pension sharing order (s. 24B) requires the trustees of one party's pension fund to transfer a percentage of his or her pension fund to a fund in the other party's name. The two funds will thereafter operate entirely separately, so it is a type of clean break order. This means that the recipient cannot draw their new pension before their own retirement date, even if their former spouse can draw it sooner. It also means that the pension stays in existence if the former spouse dies or if the recipient remarries. A pension sharing order cannot be made if the divorce petition was issued before 1 December 2000, the date on which pension sharing came into existence,[36] nor is it possible to share a basic state pension. It is, however, possible to share pensions that are already in payment. There are pension sharing compensation orders (s. 24E) to share compensation received from the Pension Protection Fund in relation to an insolvent scheme.

The value that is being shared is the 'cash equivalent transfer value' at the date the pension provider implements the pension share. Accordingly, the order must be expressed as a percentage rather than a fixed sum because of the way that pension funds change in value slightly from day to day; this also means that the chosen percentage will, at the time of implementation of the share, be worth slightly more or less than anticipated by the parties.

An attachment order (ss. 25B–25D of the Matrimonial Causes Act 1973) directs the pension scheme trustees to give x percent of each payment (or any lump sum) to the pensioner's ex-spouse from whenever the pension starts to be drawn. The beneficiary of the order will only receive payments once the pension holder draws the pension, and only for as long as the pension holder is alive and the recipient has not remarried (s. 28)—all things that do not affect a pension *share*. It thus leaves women, as the more likely recipients, vulnerable to the shorter life expectancy of their former husbands. Pension sharing was introduced because of these disadvantages of attachment orders.

Instead of sharing or attaching, the parties might agree to offset the difference in their pension values by giving extra capital to the party with the less valuable pensions. This can help that party meet their immediate needs, but they may have been glad for a pension when they got older. The other party may prefer to keep his or her pension unshared even if it means giving up capital now, but this may leave them less protected against the ups and downs of pre-retirement life, such as redundancy or supporting a second family.

Judges have taken various different approaches to calculating an appropriate offsetting amount, but a discount will often be applied to the cash alternative because of the potentially long period before retirement and the flexibility of capital.[37]

---

[36] With the coming into force of the Welfare Reform and Pensions Act 1999.

[37] See Taylor R. and Woodward, H. 'Apples or Pears? Pension Offsetting on Divorce' [2015] *Family Law* 1485.

3.7 Undertakings

In the event that the parties want to do something that is not within the court's powers to order, then that party may give an undertaking—put simply, a solemn promise to the court—and that undertaking can be recorded as a recital to the order. Although a party cannot be forced to give an undertaking, they are enforceable like an order.

3.8 Dealing with debts

Courts have no power to transfer sole debts between the parties or to require a non-party, such as a creditor, to release one spouse from a joint liability such as a mortgage or loan. It has to find a practical way around the issue, such as selling assets to pay off the debt. Alternatively, undertakings could be used: a party may (1) undertake to use his or her 'best endeavours to procure the release of party A from his liability under the mortgage', that is, to do their best to get the consent of the creditor; or (2) undertake to pay the mortgage 'and indemnify party A in respect thereto'.

3.9 Disposing of assets to defeat claims on divorce

It is not uncommon for a party to try to hide or dispose of assets in order to prevent the other party acquiring them on divorce. Success largely depends on the degree of prior planning involved: form E disclosure includes 12 months' bank statements, so the mysterious disappearance of some savings will generally be noticed. It is possible to get to the bottom of transactions by obtaining orders permitting oral examination of the party, production of documents, appointments, or orders preventing a party from leaving the jurisdiction. Where a party has disposed of an asset, the court can set aside (undo) that disposal. It is also possible to obtain a freezing injunction to prevent dealings with certain assets.[38]

3.10 Interim orders

The court also has the power to make some interim orders (not merely case management directions) while proceedings are ongoing. For example, the court can order interim spousal maintenance known as 'maintenance pending suit' (s. 22) and/or order that one party provides the other with money for lawyers' fees (s. 22ZA).

3.11 Orders after a foreign divorce

Under Part III of the Matrimonial and Family Proceedings Act 1984 a person who was divorced outside England and Wales can apply for financial remedy here in certain circumstances. This is discussed in Chapter 14.

 CONTEXT 2: WHAT KINDS OF ORDERS ARE MADE?

In the three-month period to June 2016, the Ministry of Justice *Family Court Statistics Quarterly*, England and Wales, recorded that 59.3% of orders included lump sum provision and 51.7% included property adjustment.[39] Just over a quarter of orders included periodical

---

[38] See s. 37 of the Matrimonial Causes Act 1973, the inherent jurisdiction of the High Court under s. 37 of the Senior Courts Act 1983, and Family Procedure Rules, r. 20.2.

[39] Ministry of Justice, *Family Court Statistics Quarterly England and Wales April–June 2016*.

payments for the benefit of a spouse and/or a child. (There is limited scope for courts still to make child maintenance orders; see Chapter 6.) Pension sharing was much more popular than pension attachment (24.5% of orders compared to 9.6%). Nevertheless, the latter figure still seems quite high considering attachment's disadvantages, but will almost certainly include cases where no sharing was possible.

4. Deciding what order to make: the statutory guidance

We have considered what orders a court could make, but not *why* the court may make an order in particular terms. It's all very well to say that the order should be fair, but what does a fair order look like? How do the negotiating parties or the court decide on an appropriate outcome in any given situation?

The answer is that there is statutory guidance in ss. 25 and 25A of the Matrimonial Causes Act 1973 (or, for civil partners, within the Civil Partnership Act 2004, which contains mirror provisions).

4.1 The general approach

Section 25(1) tells us that in deciding what it should do, the court should consider 'all the circumstances of the case'.

In doing this, the court has to give 'first consideration' to the welfare of any child of the family[40] aged under 18. 'This is a clear recognition of the reality that, although the couple may seek to go their separate ways, they are still jointly responsible for the welfare of their children.'[41] In practice, first consideration is 'invariably' interpreted as ensuring children are properly housed, but it can also affect whether or not the court should expect a primary carer to work, and, if so, for how many hours. '[T]he security and stability of children depends in large part upon the security and stability of their primary carers.'[42] Note, however, that the wording is 'first consideration' so they are not, as with child arrangements orders, the paramount consideration; the welfare of the children is not overriding.[43] The objective is fairness between the spouses.

4.2 Encouragement of a clean break

After making whatever arrangements it thinks fair, such as transfer or sale of property or pension sharing, it is usual that the financial remedy order will include a clause that permanently terminates any further claims. An order containing this type of clause is a *clean break order*. Where there are periodical payments, there is no clean break, at least of the recipient's claims against the payer's income, but you could have an order terminating the recipient's other claims (lump sum orders, property adjustment orders, pension sharing orders, and pension attachment orders) and all the claims of the payer. Note that it is not possible to clean break an obligation to support children, only claims between the parties themselves.[44]

---

[40] A child of the family is defined in s. 52 of the Matrimonial Causes Act 1973.
[41] *Miller v Miller/McFarlane v McFarlane* [2006] UKHL 24, at [128] (Lady Hale).
[42] [2006] UKHL 24, at [128] (Lady Hale).   [43] *Suter v Suter and Jones* [1987] 2 FLR 232 (CA).
[44] *Crozier v Crozier* [1994] Fam 114.

There are two relevant clauses. First, under s. 25A(1) the court has a duty to consider 'whether it would be appropriate' to exercise its powers so that 'the financial obligations of each party towards the other [i.e. periodical payments] will be terminated as soon after the grant of the decree as the court considers just and reasonable'. Second, where a court decides to make a periodical payments order anyway, s. 25A(2) requires the court to consider 'whether it would be appropriate to require those payments to be made or secured only for such term as would in the opinion of the court be sufficient to enable the [recipient] to adjust without undue hardship to the termination of his or her financial dependence on the other party'. Thus the court can impose a limited term on a maintenance order and include a clause that it is not possible to extend this.

These provisions do not operate as *presumptions* in favour of a clean break.[45] They are simply 'a powerful encouragement' to consider using capital and property to reach a clean break settlement, rather than having ongoing periodical payments. There may well be cases where a clean break will never be just and reasonable, and it 'is not to be achieved at the expense of a fair result'.[46] Periodical payments can be a valuable safety net. If one had a clean break and then fell into financial difficulties—perhaps as a result of illness or redundancy—there is no ability to return to court. The court should therefore be quite certain that independence can be achieved: 'Hope, without pious exhortations to end dependency, is not enough'.[47]

DEBATE 1: SHOULD THE PARTIES HAVE CONTINUING FINANCIAL OBLIGATIONS TO ONE ANOTHER THAT OUTLIVE THE MARRIAGE?

As Lord Scarman noted in *Minton v Minton*: '[a]n object of the modern law is to encourage each to put the past behind them and to begin a new life which is not over-shadowed by the relationship which has broken down'.[48] A clean break recognises that the marriage is at an end, and so are the mutual rights and responsibilities that existed with it.

ARGUMENTS IN FAVOUR OF A CLEAN BREAK

Continuing obligations (by way of periodical payments) can cause bad feeling between the parties. Planning for the future is difficult: the payer has indeterminable commitment: if his or her income increases, or the recipient falls into financial difficulties, s/he may face an application for increased payments. The recipient may be financially dependent on those payments to live, but a vindictive (or disorganised) ex-spouse can leave the recipient on tenterhooks every month for receipt. The payer may feel that the recipient is not taking responsibility for their own financial independence but relying on the payer's hard work. He or she may feel also that the recipient is deliberately avoiding remarriage so as to keep receiving money. While an application to terminate can be made on the basis of cohabitation (so the payer has reason to look over the recipient's shoulder to see how often the new partner is staying over) courts are reluctant to equate cohabitation with marriage.[49] This can be seem very unfair, though, where the payer observes the recipient in a new relationship that is effectively marriage in all but name.

---

[45] *SRJ v DWJ (Financial Provision)* [1998] EWCA Civ 1634 (Hale J).

[46] *Miller v Miller/McFarlane v McFarlane* [2006] UKHL 24, at [133–134] (Lady Hale).

[47] *C v C (Financial Provision: Short Marriage)* [1997] 2 FLR 26, 46 (Ward LJ).

[48] [1979] AC 593, 608.

[49] Cohabiting relationships have a higher breakdown rate, and do not have the legal signifier of commitment that is the marriage certificate. See *Kimber v Kimber* [2000] 1 FLR 383; *Grey v Grey* [2010] 1 FLR 1764 (CA).

ARGUMENTS AGAINST A CLEAN BREAK

While the legal structures for formal equality may exist, there remains substantive inequality between men and women, and financial outcomes post-divorce are worse for women (see Context 3). While there is a gender pay gap, the outcomes also reflect the allocation of roles in the marriage. This means that the consequences of a decision made within the marriage may outlast the marriage itself.

Take, for example, the situation of a woman who becomes pregnant, takes maternity leave, and thereafter returns to work part-time. The average cost of putting a child in nursery for 25 hours per week is £6,000 per year,[50] so although the most common working pattern where there are children is for the mother to work part-time,[51] financially it may not be worthwhile. Some parents may also feel social pressure not to put their children in nursery full-time.[52] As the House of Lords has recognized: '[t]he career break which results from concentrating on motherhood and the family in the middle years of their lives comes at a price which in most cases is irrecoverable'.[53] Heather Joshi found that a mother of two will lose over 40% of her lifetime earnings compared to a woman without children.[54]

A few years later, let us assume that our fictional mother and her husband divorce. It is probable that the children will have their main home with her: 86% of single parents are women.[55] She will thus continue to contribute to the marriage by parenting post-divorce. Until the children are of sufficient age for her working hours (and thus her mortgage capacity) to increase, she may well need both a majority of the available capital and regular future income from the husband. Even if she could work full-time, 'the welfare of children may not be best served by their custodial parent's self-sufficiency'.[56] It may be better for the children for a primary carer to work part-time, even if that means spousal maintenance is needed. As Connolly *et al* argue: 'British societal infrastructure still tends to promote and support a full-time breadwinner plus part-time carer model'.[57]

During the marriage and afterwards, the husband has much greater scope to build a career. This is where spousal maintenance comes in: it mitigates the effect of the decisions made during the marriage to divide roles in this way.[58]

---

[50] Rutter, J. *Childcare Costs Survey* (Family and Childcare Trust 2015). Available at: http://www.familyand-childcaretrust.org/sites/default/files/files/Childcare_cost_survey_2015_Final.pdf, accessed 15 November 2016.

[51] Park, A. *et al* (eds) *British Social Attitudes: The 30th Report* (NatCen Social Research, 2013). Available at: http://www.bsa-30.natcen.ac.uk, accessed 16 November 2016.

[52] There are conflicting studies on the effects of nursery on children, but as examples of the kinds of pressures that may impact upon parents, see Doughty, S. 'Working Mothers Risk Damaging their Child's Prospects', *Daily Mail*, 14 March 2001. Available at: http://www.dailymail.co.uk/news/article-30342/Working-mothers-risk-damaging-childs-prospects.html, accessed 23 September 2017; and Carvel, J. 'Working Mothers "Bad for Children"', *The Guardian*, 14 November 2003. Available at: https://www.theguardian.com/money/2003/nov/14/workandcareers, accessed 16 November 2016.

[53] *Miller v Miller/McFarlane v McFarlane* [2006] UKHL 24, at [118] (Lord Hope).

[54] Joshi, H. 'The Cash Opportunity Costs of Childbearing: An Approach to Estimation Using British Data' (1990) 44(1) *Population Studies* 41.

[55] ONS Statistical Bulletin, 'Families and Households in the UK'. Available at: https://www.ons.gov.uk/peoplepopulationandcommunity/birthsdeathsandmarriages/families/bulletins/familiesandhouseholds/2016, accessed 23 September 2017.

[56] Jackson, E. *et al* 'Financial Support on Divorce: The Right Mixture of Rules and Discretion?' (1993) 7 *International Journal of Law and the Family* 230, 238.

[57] See also Connolly S. *et al* 'Britain's Slow Movement to a Gender Egalitarian Equilibrium: Parents and Employment in the UK 2001–13' (2016) *Work, Employment and Society* 1, 16.

[58] Of course, if the parties had swapped traditional roles, so the husband was primary carer, then he could claim maintenance: the law is facially neutral.

You may wish to consider, however, to what extent it is appropriate to 'place that burden on the ex-spouse when it stems from the broader societal inequality of women [or parents] as much, if not more than, the couple's own financial decision-making'.[59] A society in which childcare and social care was free or much cheaper, where the pay gap was closed, and where there was a more equal division of parenting tasks would have fewer inequalities to remedy— but this would come at cost to the state, that is, the taxpayer.

Both the requirement to give first consideration to the children, and the requirement to consider a clean break were introduced into the 1973 Act by the Matrimonial and Family Proceedings Act 1984. Why do these statutory provisions promote a clean break over continuing financial obligations?

4.3 The s. 25(2) factors

Section 25 provides a non-exhaustive list of factors that 'the court shall in particular have regard to' when considering 'all the circumstances of the case', with the aim of guiding the court towards a fair outcome. The list applies whether the judge is making a decision at a contested final hearing or considering a joint consent application. It applies to families at all points on the economic spectrum too, from multi-billion pound cases to those involving parties who are impoverished. However, as the factors 'are not listed in any hierarchical order or order of importance',[60] the weight to be accorded to each one will vary depending on the circumstances of each case.[61] Some may not be relevant at all to a particular case, but where a factor is relevant it 'must be placed in the scales and given its due weight'.[62]

 Key Legislation 1: Matrimonial Causes Act 1973, s. 25

(2) [In deciding whether to exercise its powers] the court shall in particular have regard to the following matters—

(a) the income, earning capacity, property and other financial resources which each of the parties to the marriage has or is likely to have in the foreseeable future, including in the case of earning capacity any increase in that capacity which it would in the opinion of the court be reasonable to expect a party to the marriage to take steps to acquire;

(b) the financial needs, obligations and responsibilities which each of the parties to the marriage has or is likely to have in the foreseeable future;

(c) the standard of living enjoyed by the family before the breakdown of the marriage;

(d) the age of each party to the marriage and the duration of the marriage;

(e) any physical or mental disability of either of the parties to the marriage;

---

[59] Gillian Douglas, 'Simple Quarrels? Autonomy v Vulnerability' in R. Probert and C. Barton (eds) *Fifty Years in Family Law: Essays for Stephen Cretney* (Intersentia, 2012) 217, 219.

[60] *Robson v Robson* [2010] EWCA Civ 1171, at [43] (Ward LJ).

[61] *Piglowska v Piglowski* [1999] UKHL 27.

[62] *Robson v Robson* [2010] EWCA Civ 1171, at [43] (Ward LJ).

> (f) the contributions which each of the parties has made or is likely in the foresee-able future to make to the welfare of the family, including any contribution by looking after the home or caring for the family;
>
> (g) the conduct of each of the parties, if that conduct is such that it would in the opinion of the court be inequitable to disregard it;
>
> (h) in the case of proceedings for divorce or nullity of marriage, the value to each of the parties to the marriage of any benefit . . . which, by reason of the dissolution or annulment of the marriage, that party will lose the chance of acquiring.
>
> *Note*: When considering orders in respect of financial provision for children, as opposed to financial provision for a spouse (which will affect the children indirectly), there is a list of extra factors to consider at s. 25(3).

(a) the income, earning capacity, property and other financial resources which each of the parties to the marriage has or is likely to have in the foreseeable future, including in the case of earning capacity any increase in that capacity which it would in the opinion of the court be reasonable to expect a party to the marriage to take steps to acquire

The court must take into account the financial position of the parties. Sometimes this is relatively straightforward, but in other cases the parties may have complex financial arrangements, such as offshore trusts or values that are contingent on certain events, such as stock market flotation.[63] As well as legal interests, the court can take into account assets to which the parties are beneficially entitled, such as under discretionary trusts, although this does depend on the powers and practice of the trustees in distributing funds to the party.

It is important to consider the future, as well as current, position of the parties. Is one on a career track? Is there a known prospect of redundancy? Could a party undertake training to increase their earning potential? Could they work more hours? Note that the earning capacity mentioned in s. 25(2)(a) includes capacity which is currently unused—for example, it is open to you to argue that your spouse may only work 16 hours per week now, but could work 30, and agree a settlement that takes account of that. Is a party likely to inherit money imminently? One has to be careful of taking into account future inheritances other than those which are imminent, as people change their wills or live longer than expected. Nevertheless, inheritances can be a useful source of funds.

In theory, therefore, any asset is 'up for grabs' by the other party. This is why full disclosure is so important. However, it is important to explain to the parties that just because the court *could* make an order over a particular asset, it does not mean that it will. There may be very good reasons, considered in this chapter, not to do so.

(b) the financial needs, obligations and responsibilities which each of the parties to the marriage has or is likely to have in the foreseeable future

(c) the standard of living enjoyed by the family before the breakdown of the marriage

(d) the age of each party to the marriage and the duration of the marriage

A consideration of the financial needs of the parties is likely to occupy most of the attention of those advising divorcing parties. As we see in 7.1, need can encompass a wide range of different aspects. Specifically, need can be related to the standard of living enjoyed during the marriage and any disabilities of the parties.

---

[63] See e.g. *Charman v Charman (No. 4)* [2007] EWCA Civ 503 (trust); *Sharland v Sharland* [2015] UKSC 60 (flotation).

Section 25 also directs the court to look at the parties' financial obligations and responsibilities, which could include, for example, school fees or financial support for a new family, or, as in one unreported case, the need to remain in the matrimonial home because it was next door to a party's elderly parents. More commonly, financial obligations include debts that have to be repaid, such as credit cards, loans, hire-purchase agreements, and mortgages or rent. For the court's powers regarding debts, see 3.8.

(e) any physical or mental disability of either of the parties to the marriage

(f) the contributions which each of the parties has made or is likely in the foreseeable future to make to the welfare of the family, including any contribution by looking after the home or caring for the family

The duration of the marriage is relevant to the three rationales for dividing property— needs, compensation, and sharing—set out in *Miller/McFarlane*, Key Case 2. The needs arising from a short marriage are generally likely to be less than the needs arising from a long marriage, unless there are children. Similarly, relationship-generated disadvantage is less likely, and there is a weaker case for sharing the marital fruits: '[t]his reflects the instinctive feeling that parties will generally have less call upon each other on the breakdown of a short marriage'.[64] When calculating the length of the marriage, most courts include a period of prior cohabitation if it moved seamlessly into marriage.[65]

The parties' ages also reflect their needs. A younger party may have more potential to earn than someone older who has not been in the job market recently. An older party may have specific personal care needs that a younger person does not.

Contribution is to the *welfare* of the family and consequently can be financial or non-financial. In *White v White*, the House of Lords held that '[i]f, in their different spheres, each contributed equally to the family, then in principle it matters not which of them earned the money and built up the assets. There should be no bias in favour of the money-earner and against the home-maker and the child-carer'.[66]

 DEBATE 2: SHOULD A STELLAR CONTRIBUTION TO A MARRIAGE BE RECOGNISED?

Following *White v White*, some husbands began to argue that they had made a contribution to the matrimonial assets that was so considerable that it should be given significant weight as a s. 25 factor and justify them receiving the bulk of the assets after needs had been met: in other words, that their contribution went above and beyond the kind of equal-but-different contributions that the House of Lords spoke of in *White*. Such a contribution, they argued, was unmatched by the contribution of the other party. (For a discussion of the contribution of *non*-matrimonial assets, see 7.3.2.)

This has been *successfully* argued only a small number of times, although it's been argued much more frequently. Successful claimants included the husbands in *Cowan v Cowan*,[67] where it was his 'genius to perceive the potential of bin liners which would revolutionise the collection and disposal of household waste' and—the word 'genius' appearing again— *Cooper-Hohn v Hohn*,[68] where the husband, an investor, had accrued assets of between $1.35

---

[64] [2006] UKHL 24, at [24] (Lord Nicholls).   [65] *GW v RW* [2003] EWHC 611 (Fam), at [33] (Mostyn J).

[66] [2001] 1 AC 596, 605[D]–[E] (Lord Nicholls).

[67] [2001] EWCA Civ 679.   [68] [2014] EWHC 4122 (Fam), at [282]–[283] (Roberts J).

and $1.6 billion and established a charitable foundation with assets of $4.5 billion. However, the courts have sought to limit successful arguments to those 'characteristics or circumstances . . . of a wholly exceptional nature, such that it would very obviously be inconsistent with the objective of achieving fairness for them to be ignored'.[69] In *Miller/McFarlane*, Lord Nicholls said that 'parties should not seek to promote a case of "special contribution" unless the contribution is so marked that to disregard it would be inequitable. A good reason for departing from equality is not to be found in the minutiae of married life'.[70] Lady Hale thought that 'the question of contributions should be approached in the much the same way as conduct': 'Only if there is such a disparity in their respective contributions to the welfare of the family that it would be inequitable to disregard it should this be taken into account in determining their shares.'[71]

Even where an argument is successfully advanced, it is unlikely to give rise to percentages of division of matrimonial property further from equality than 66.6%–33.3%.[72] Courts have kept such awards in 'narrow bounds'[73] because of the 'inherent gender discrimination'[74] of such arguments. A good example of this is *Cooper-Hohn* in which the wife had worked, often from the early hours to after midnight, for the charitable foundation which 'demanded of her the skills and qualities which would have been needed in any CEO' and was the primary carer of four children.[75] Mrs Cooper-Hohn argued that if this was not itself also a stellar contribution, what more could she do? While theoretically possible, it is tremendously difficult to show stellar contribution other than by making (large amounts of) money.

Stellar contribution arguments do not reflect a partnership view of marriage, because they expressly argue that one party has done more for the marriage than the other. Of course, the counter argument is that some marriages are not equal partnerships in reality. One party may have done the daily grind of a marriage (whether outside the home, at home, or both) while the other party has not pulled their weight. Indeed, that may be a reason for the divorce. Morally, therefore, there could be an argument for this to be reflected in the financial settlement to a greater extent that is currently recognised.

> (g) the conduct of each of the parties, if that conduct is such that it would in the opinion of the court be inequitable to disregard it

Conduct and contribution are 'opposite sides of a coin'.[76] Both financial and non-financial misconduct can affect the appropriate financial settlement. However, we have moved away from a situation in which adultery, for example, would determine the financial outcome: 'the court should not reduce its order for financial provision merely because of what was formerly regarded as guilt or blame. To do so would be to impose a fine for supposed misbehaviour in the course of an unhappy married life' (and, of course, take up huge amounts of court time).[77] For conduct to be taken into account it has to be 'such that it would in the opinion of the court be inequitable to disregard it', and in *Wachtel v Wachtel* Ormrod J interpreted this as conduct that was 'obvious and gross'.[78] In *S v S* Burton J refers to conduct

---

[69] *Lambert v Lambert* [2002] EWCA Civ 1685 [70] (Bodey J).   [70] [2006] UKHL 24, at [67].

[71] [2006] UKHL 24, at [146] (Lady Hale).

[72] *Charman v Charman (No. 4)* [2007] EWCA Civ 503, at [90] (Sir Mark Potter P).

[73] [2007] EWCA Civ 503, at [88] (Sir Mark Potter P).

[74] [2007] EWCA Civ 503, at [80] (Sir Mark Potter P).

[75] [2014] EWHC 4122 (Fam), at [273] (Roberts J).

[76] *Miller v Miller/McFarlane v McFarlane* [2006] UKHL 24, at [164] (Lord Mance).

[77] *Wachtel v Wachtel* [1972] Fam 72 (CA), 90 (Lord Denning MR).   [78] [1972] Fam 72 (CA), 80.

as needing to have the 'gasp' factor (on the facts of the case, a hair-raising catalogue of events in which neither persons nor ornaments were safe, it merely caused a 'gulp').[79]

Most cases that do reach this 'gasp' factor standard—helpfully reviewed by Burton J—involve very serious physical attacks on the spouse, as in *H v H (Financial Relief: Attempted Murder as Conduct)*, in which the husband was serving 12 years for attempted murder, having stabbed the wife repeatedly in front of their children. She had been unable to work since the attack. The Court held that this was not merely conduct which it would be inequitable to disregard: it was conduct at the very top end of the scale. The court 'should not be punitive or confiscatory for its own sake; . . . the proper way to have regard to the conduct is as a potentially magnifying factor when considering the wife's position under the other subsections and criteria . . . it places her needs . . . as a much higher priority to those of the husband because the situation in which the wife now finds herself in is, in a very real way, his fault.'[80]

While litigation misconduct such as failing to comply with a court direction or hiding assets will usually be penalised by making a costs order against that party rather than giving them fewer of the assets, there are exceptions. In *F v F (Ancillary Relief: Substantial Assets)* the husband's conduct of the litigation was so bad that it became conduct that it was inequitable to disregard under s. 25(2)(g).[81] However, the courts can also assume that a party has assets which it has not disclosed and make an order on that basis, if that party has failed to give full and frank disclosure; and/or undo transactions that are intended to defeat the court, such as transferring assets to third parties so they are not available to be awarded to the other spouse; and/or act as though dissipated assets still exist and are available to the dissipater. For example, if the court was going to award the wife £100,000, but considered that she had dissipated £30,000 unreasonably, then the court would award her the balance of £70,000. In *McCartney v Mills McCartney*, Bennett J added £500,000 back into the wife's assets to represent her 'completely unreasonable expenditure.'[82]

> (h) in the case of proceedings for divorce or nullity of marriage, the value to each of the parties to the marriage of any benefit which, by reason of the dissolution or annulment of the marriage, that party will lose the chance of acquiring

Although this factor seems to be infrequently directly pleaded, it would be relevant to the loss of pension rights that a party would have received on his or her spouse's death had they been married at the time.

4.4 The problem with s. 25

In considering what outcome may be appropriate in a case, s. 25 tells us that we need to consider all the circumstances of the case and the listed factors and give first consideration to the welfare of the children, and consider a clean break. But then—what? Section 25 tells us what to think about, but not why. For example, it says we should consider the ages of the parties, but nowhere does it state how being older or younger should affect the outcome nor how much weight we should give to age compared to any other s. 25 factor, such as need or contribution. In fact, nowhere in the Matrimonial Causes Act 1973 is there any guidance on how each factor should affect the outcome of the proceedings. The judge has been compared to 'a bus driver who is given a large number of instructions about how to drive the bus, and the authority to do various actions such as turning left or right. There is also the occasional advice or correction offered by three senior drivers. The one piece of

---

[79] [2006] EWHC 2793 (Fam), at [57], citing *W v W* [1976] Fam 107, 110[D] (Sir George Baker P).
[80] [2005] EWHC 2911 (Fam), at [44] (Charles J).   [81] [1995] 2 FLR 45.
[82] [2008] EWHC 401 (Fam), at [179].

information which he or she is not given is where to take the bus. All he or she is told is that the driver is required to drive to a reasonable destination.'[83]

The crucial problem with s. 25 is that it offers no rationale for distributing the assets. It is axiomatic that the outcome should be fair, but absent legislative guidance as to what is fair and why, the higher courts have attempted to explain the implications of each s. 25 factor and lay down some principles for other courts to follow. One problem with this is that while the statutory factors are applicable to all divorce cases, the cases that explain them almost always involve high net-worth couples who can afford to litigate in the higher courts and whose situations 'bear no resemblance to the ordinary lives of most divorcing couples and to the average case heard, day in and day out, by district judges up and down the country'.[84] Practitioners therefore have to interpret how they may be applicable to middle and low asset couples.

The most important of all such cases is *White v White*. More recently, the House of Lords in the conjoined appeals of *Miller v Miller* and *McFarlane v McFarlane* (hereafter *Miller/ McFarlane*) provided us with three rationales for dividing the assets. To understand how important these decisions were, we need to go back to the situation before *White v White*.

5. Financial provision from the earliest divorces

For many centuries, the doctrine of coverture[85] meant that a married woman could not enter into contracts other than to prevent her starvation, and instead would have to pledge her husband's credit.[86] Until 1882, she could not legally own property. Any property she did own passed to her husband on marriage. Thus the husband had a common law duty to maintain her during the marriage and after (unless she was adulterous); this was the *quid pro quo* for the 'vital but unpaid'[87] domestic (and sexual) services the wife rendered, and the taking of her assets. 'But', said Lord Wilson in a recent speech, 'let's not be carried away by the generosity of this: *his* income may well have been generated by what prior to the marriage had been *her* property!'[88] Indeed, there was no power at all to order the transfer of assets, such as a home, to the wife, even if they had been hers to begin with.[89]

Therefore on divorce, the husband's duty to maintain her from his income continued; it was, as Beveridge said, 'a first line of defence' for the wife. In the days before the welfare state, she may otherwise have been relegated to the poor house, or resort to prostitution or other crime to avoid starvation. Family breakdown was a risk to society: it caused poverty which in turn caused social unrest. Providing for ongoing financial support mitigated this risk, although the law proved ambivalent about whether the state's interests in alleviating poverty justified 'rewarding' the wife with financial support from the husband even if she had breached the marriage contract, for example through adultery. In some cases, maintenance was payable only if the wife remained chaste thereafter—'no sex allowed, even on a

---

[83] Law Commission, *Matrimonial Property, Needs and Agreements Supplementary Consultation Paper* (Law Com No. 208, 2012) para 3.3.   [84] *Jones v Jones* [2011] EWCA Civ 41, at [69] (Wall LJ).

[85] Blackstone wrote in his *Commentaries on the Laws of England* (1765–1769) that: 'By marriage, the husband and wife are one person in law: that is, the very being or legal existence of the woman is suspended during the marriage, or at least is incorporated and consolidated into that of the husband: under whose wing, protection, and cover, she performs every thing; . . . and her condition during her marriage is called her coverture.'

[86] *James v Warren* (1706) 90 ER 956.

[87] Beveridge, Sir W. *Social Insurance and Allied Services* (the Beveridge Report) (Cmd 6404, 1942) 49.

[88] Lord Wilson, 'Changes over the Centuries in the Financial Consequences of Divorce'. Address to the University of Bristol Law Club, 20 March 2017. Available at: https://www.supremecourt.uk/docs/speech-170320. pdf, accessed 21 March 2017.

[89] Cretney, S. *Family Law in the Twentieth Century: A History* (OUP, 2003) 395–8.

non-paying basis'[90]—which is rather less about a past marriage contract and rather more about Victorian notions of womanly virtue. The obligation to maintain also existed as a disincentive for the husband to abandon the wife and thus 'triumph over the sacred permanence of marriage': 'To such a man the Court may truly say with propriety, "According to your ability you must still support the woman you have first chosen and then discarded"'[91]

In 1882, the fundamentally important Married Women's Property Act enabled a married woman to hold property (including any earnings) separately from her husband—'a system of separation of property coupled with the husband's duty to maintain his wife'.[92] (If the husband was in financial need, rather than the wife, the court had no power to order her to maintain him unless he was insane.)[93] While the Parliamentary debates record recognition of the economic importance of women's work,[94] the Act 'did little to alter the financial dependency of wives on their husbands'.[95]

It was not until the middle of the twentieth century that the wife was entitled to a share in the matrimonial home proportionate to her financial contribution—if she had made one, as opposed to given up work on marriage as most women did.[96] The court would not order provision of capital until 1963. Thus her recourse was to spousal maintenance, set at a level based on what the husband could afford and the degree to which she was morally blameless, rather than an assessment of what she needed.[97] 'The debates around divorce in the first half of the twentieth century centred on the grounds for divorce [i.e. conduct], not its economic effects'.[98]

In 1970, the Matrimonial Proceedings and Property Act gave courts, in addition to maintenance and lump sums, the power to order property adjustment.

> The law became sex-neutral, in that the same remedies and principles were applied both to husbands and to wives. . . . The law also became much kinder to homemakers and caregivers. All the actual and foreseeable resources of either party—property and income—could be shared out in whatever way the court thought just, depending on the facts and circumstances of the individual case.[99]

The 1970 Act explicitly provided that the court consider the 'contributions made by each of the parties to the welfare of the family, including any contributions made by looking after the home or caring for the family'.[100] As Lord Denning put it in the 'landmark'[101] case *Wachtel v Wachtel*, as far as the matrimonial home was concerned: '[j]ust as the wife who makes substantial money contributions usually gets a share, so should the wife who looks after the

---

[90] Lord Wilson, 'Changes over the Centuries in the Financial Consequences of Divorce'. Address to the University of Bristol Law Club, 20 March 2017. Available at: https://www.supremecourt.uk/docs/speech-170320.pdf, accessed 21 March 2017.   [91] *Sidney v Sidney* (1865) 164 ER 1485 (Sir James Wilde).

[92] Lady Hale, 'Equality and Autonomy in Family Law' (2011) 33 *Journal of Social Welfare and Family Law* 3, 8.

[93] Matrimonial Causes Act 1937, s 10(2), discussed in the *Report of the Committee on One-Parent Families* (the Finer Report) (Cmnd 5629, 1974) para 4.44.

[94] Hansard HL Deb, vol 203, cols 395–401, 18 July 1870. Available at: http://hansard.millbanksystems.com/lords/1870/jul/18/no-125-committee, accessed 23 September 2017.

[95] Pahl, J. *Money and Marriage* (Macmillan, 1989) 22.

[96] See discussion by Lord Denning in *Wachtel v Wachtel* [1972] Fam 72 (CA), 92ff.

[97] Smart, C. *The Ties that Bind: Law, Marriage and the Reproduction of Patriarchal Relations* (Routledge & Kegan Paul, 1984) 89.

[98] Eekelaar, J. 'Post-Divorce Financial Obligations', in S.N. Katz, J. Eekelaar, and M. Maclean, *Cross Currents: Family Law and Policy in the US and England* (OUP, 2000) 408.

[99] Lady Hale, 'Equality and Autonomy in Family Law' (2011) 33 *Journal of Social Welfare and Family Law* 3, 8.

[100] This is now contained in the consolidating Matrimonial Causes Act 1973 as one of the s. 25 factors (s. 25(2)(f). Section 25's wording is slightly different: it directs the court to consider contributions 'likely in the foreseeable future' aswell.

[101] Lady Hale, 'Equality and Autonomy in Family Law' (2011) 33 *Journal of Social Welfare and Family Law* 3, 8.

home and cares for the family for 20 years or more'.[102] And there were many such women—in 1975 the husband was still the primary breadwinner in 95% of marriages.[103] The court had new powers to transfer the matrimonial home to the wife, at least temporarily, for example under a *Mesher* order.[104] However, this happened in only a minority of cases.

In *Wachtel* itself, for example, the wife was awarded maintenance at one third of her husband's income and a lump sum equivalent to one third of the value of the matrimonial home, plus child maintenance. Why one third? While acknowledging that it was 'much criticised', Lord Denning found it a useful starting point because, absent the wife, the husband will have greater expense. Whereas the wife will 'do most of the housework herself' or 'remarry, in which case her new husband will provide for her', the apparently undomesticated husband 'must get some woman to look after the house—either a wife, if he remarries, or a housekeeper, if he does not. He will also have to provide maintenance for the children'.[105]

In noting that the husband needed the domestic services of 'some woman', Lord Denning was, in his chauvinistic way, at least accepting that the wife's contribution had an economic value.[106] However, in *Trippas v Trippas* he held that the husband was entitled to more because he earned it. The wife did not work in the husband's business and thus was not entitled to a share of its value, as 'all she did was what a good wife does. She gave moral support to her husband by looking after the home'.[107]

This valuing of financial contribution over a contribution in kind—a good wife is not an equal wife—led ultimately in the 1980s and 1990s to awards based on the *reasonable requirements* of the poorer spouse, that is, her needs, objectively judged by close reference to her budget, even if there was a large surplus in excess of that. It is in *Dart v Dart*[108] that we see the logical endpoint of this approach: the wife was awarded £9 million of total marital wealth estimated at £400–800 million. Her reasonable requirements were treated as determinative of her award, irrespective of the fact that the s. 25 factors are in no particular order of importance, and irrespective of any view of marriage as a partnership in which each contributes equally in cash or in kind.

As Lord Nicholls has stated: '[t]he glass ceiling thus put in place was shattered by the decision of your Lordships' House in the *White* case'.[109]

 Key Case 1: *White v White* [2001] 1 AC 596

The Whites were husband and wife farmers who had each farmed before they married in 1961. Mrs White brought into the marriage assets of £1,884 and Mr White £1,135, and together they set up a farming partnership. In 1962, they bought a farm for £32,000 with the help of a mortgage and £14,000 which Mr White's father gave to them. Over subsequent years, they acquired more land, made pension provision, and had children. In 1993, Mr White inherited a neighbouring farm whose land he and Mrs White had already been farming for some years. By the time of the first instance decision, their total assets were £4.6 million of which £1.52 million was Mrs White's half share of their partnership and her pensions. Mr White had his half share of their partnership, his pensions, and also the neighbouring farm.

---

[102] [1972] Fam 72 (CA), 94.   [103] O'Donovan, K. *Sexual Divisions in Law* (Weidenfeld & Nicolson, 1985) 151.

[104] See Eekelaar, J. 'Post-Divorce Financial Obligations', in S.N. Katz, J. Eekelaar, and M. Maclean, *Cross Currents: Family Law and Policy in the US and England* (OUP, 2000) 408, 409–13.

[105] [1972] Fam 72 (CA), 94.

[106] A more charitable view is given by Mostyn J, who refers to these comments as 'reflect[ing] the worldview of a man born in 1899': *SS v NS* [2014] EWHC 4183, at [40].   [107] [1973] Fam 134, 141.

[108] [1996] 2 FLR 286.

[109] *Miller v Miller/McFarlane v McFarlane* [2006] UKHL 24, at [8] (Lord Nicholls).

At first instance, Holman J awarded Mrs White £980,000 (21% of the assets). The judge found that this met her reasonable needs for housing and income. It was not a reasonable requirement for her to have a farm, because this would involve breaking up the existing enterprise. Mr White would be left with an amount in excess of his reasonable requirements for a home and income. But the financial contributions from his family made it reasonable for him to continue farming.[110]

The Court of Appeal increased Mrs White's award to £1.5 million. Even if the value of the inherited farm was excluded, this still equated to only about 40% of the total assets. Both parties appealed to the House of Lords, which upheld the quantum of the Court of Appeal decision, if not its reasoning. Lord Nicholls, with whom the other Lords agree, held that:

- 'The statutory provisions lend no support to the idea that a claimant's financial needs, even interpreted generously and called reasonable requirements, are to be regarded as determinative . . . the end product of this assessment of financial needs should be seen, and treated by the court, for what it is: only one of the several factors to which the court is to have particular regard.'[111]

- 'In seeking to achieve a fair outcome, there is no place for discrimination between husband and wife and their respective roles. . . . If, in their different spheres, each contributed equally to the family, then in principle it matters not which of them earned the money and built up the assets. There should be no bias in favour of the money-earner and against the home-maker and the child-carer.'[112]

- 'Before reaching a firm conclusion and making an order along these lines, a judge would always be well advised to check his tentative views against the *yardstick of equality* of division. As a general guide, equality should be departed from only if, and to the extent that, there is good reason for doing so' . . . This is not to introduce a presumption of equal division under another guise.[113]

- Assets inherited by or gifted to a party to a marriage represent a contribution made by that party, which is a relevant s. 25 factor. 'The judge should . . . decide how important it is in the particular case. The nature and value of the property, and the time when and circumstances in which the property was acquired, are among the relevant matters to be considered. However, in the ordinary course, this factor can be expected to carry little weight, if any, in a case where the claimant's financial needs cannot be met without recourse to this property . . . The initial cash contribution made by Mr White's father in the early days cannot carry much weight 33 years later.'[114]

- Lord Cooke felt that the £1.5 million awarded to Mrs White by the Court of Appeal was justified by the husband's father's contribution but was 'about the minimum that could have been awarded'.[115]

6. After *White*

In its clear focus on equality and non-discrimination *White* moved courts away from 'the 'traditional' family values of provider/dependant'[116] and into a rights-based discourse that proved fatal to the concept of reasonable requirements. 'The "yardstick of equality of

---

[110] Holman J's view as summarised by Lord Nicholls at [2001] 1 AC 596, 601[F]–602[A].
[111] [2001] 1 AC 596, 608C–D; 609A.   [112] [2001] 1 AC 596, 605B–E.
[113] [2001] 1 AC 596, 605F–G.   [114] [2001] 1 AC 596, 610F–G; 611B.
[115] [2001] 1 AC 596, 615F–G; 616A.
[116] Diduck, A. 'What Is Family Law For?' (2011) 64 *Current Legal Problems* 287, 299.

division" [instead] filled the vacuum which resulted'.[117] Notwithstanding Lord Nicholls' rejection of either a starting point or legal presumption of equal division, it did become more common thereafter for parties to share capital, if not income, equally.[118] For this reason, and for its respect for equality as between gender roles, *White* is of fundamental importance.

Of course, while the Lords tried to provide general guidance, *White* was a long marriage in which the parties had each fully contributed. But what of a short marriage in which the contributions of one were significant, or a long marriage in which the separation of breadwinner and homemaker roles meant the homemaker would be in a significantly worse position than the breadwinner post-divorce? The yardstick of equality did not seem to provide a fair approach to such situations. A few years after *White*, in two cases that were joined on appeal, *Miller v Miller* and *McFarlane v McFarlane*, the Lords had once more to provide guidance on the requirements of fairness.

 Key Case 2: *Miller v Miller* and *McFarlane v McFarlane* [2006] UKHL 24

Mr and Mrs Miller had been married for two years and nine months, with no prior cohabitation and no children. He was 39 and she 33. When they married, Mr Miller's assets were £16.7 million; post-separation they stood at about £17.5 million, plus whatever value should be attributed to his 200,000 shares in New Star, an asset management fund that he ran. Estimates for the shares, which had increased in value during their marriage, ranged from £12–18 million. Mrs Miller's assets were £100,000 but she had debts of £300,000. She had given up a job earning £85,000 once she married. The issue was how much Mrs Miller should be awarded when the assets were generated by the husband before and during the short marriage.

Mr and Mrs McFarlane had been married for 16 years with 2 years' prior cohabitation. Both were 46 years old. They had 3 children, aged 16, 15 and 9. Until 1990, when Mr McFarlane was promoted, the parties earned the same amount; indeed, Mrs McFarlane, a solicitor at a leading city law firm, at times earned more. In 1991, before the birth of their second child, the parties agreed the wife should abandon her career and bring up the children. Mr McFarlane continued in his accountancy career, becoming a partner at Deloitte. The capital in the marriage was worth around £3 million, which they agreed to split equally. However, Mr McFarlane earned £750,000 per year net, and she nothing, and only potentially £30,000 if she retrained. It was inevitable that he should pay spousal maintenance, and it was also agreed that this should be for their joint lives or further order. The issue was quantum.

The two leading judgments in *Miller* and *McFarlane* are those of Lord Nicholls, whose judgment in *White* was so important, and Lady Hale.

- 'In the search for a fair outcome it is pertinent to have in mind that fairness generates obligations as well as rights. The financial provision made on divorce by one party for the other, still typically the wife, is not in the nature of largesse. It is not a case of "taking away" from one party and "giving" to the other property which "belongs" to the former. The claimant is not a supplicant. Each party to a marriage is entitled to a fair share of the available property. The search is always for what are the requirements of fairness in the particular case.'[119]
- 'What then, in principle, are these requirements? The statute provides that first consideration shall be given to the welfare of the children of the marriage . . . Beyond this several

---

[117] *Charman v Charman (No. 4)* [2007] EWCA Civ 503, at [64] (Sir Mark Potter P).
[118] *White v White* [2001] 1 AC 596, 606[E]–[F].   [119] [2006] UKHL 24, at [9] (Lord Nicholls).

elements, or strands, are readily discernible':[120] needs, compensation, and equal sharing. (In *Charman*, Sir Mark Potter noted that the three rationales identified in *Miller/McFarlane*—needs, compensation, and sharing—each derive from s. 25 and can be linked back to s. 25 'although two of them are not expressly mentioned'.[121])

- 'The most common rationale for departing from equal division is that the relationship has generated needs which it is right that the other party should meet.'[122] 'Mutual dependence begets mutual obligations of support.'[123]
- Compensation is 'aimed at redressing any significant prospective economic disparity between the parties arising from the way they conducted their marriage'.[124] It will not be a factor in every marriage.
- The equal sharing principle 'derives from the basic concept of equality permeating a marriage as understood today. . . . When their partnership ends each is entitled to an equal share of the assets of the partnership [i.e. the matrimonial property], unless there is a good reason to the contrary'.[125] The contribution of non-matrimonial property is part of 'all the circumstances of the case' and potentially gives a reason to depart from equality in favour of the contributor.[126] (This is discussed further in 7.3.1.)
- 'In general, it can be assumed that the marital partnership does not stay alive for the purpose of sharing future resources unless this is justified by need or compensation. The ultimate objective is to give each party an equal start on the road to independent living.'[127]

Applying these principles to Mr and Mrs Miller's situation:

Mrs Miller's *needs* were 'comparatively small' and she could return to work as she had not been out of employment for long. She was entitled to 'a gentle transition' from the marital standard of living 'to the standard she could expect as a self-sufficient woman'[128] and the high standard of living enjoyed by the parties during the marriage was relevant to that.[129] She had no claim to *compensation* for relationship-generated disadvantage. The husband brought substantial wealth into the marriage at its outset, which was non-matrimonial property. 'That was a major contribution he made to the marriage'[130] that justified a departure from equal sharing. However, the wife was entitled to *share* in the matrimonial assets, and 'although the marriage was short, the matrimonial property was of great value'.[131] It included their two homes and 'the considerable increase of the husband's wealth during the marriage'.[132]

The Court awarded Mrs Miller £5 million. This represented less than one third of the value of the New Star shares, 'reflecting the amount of work done by the husband on this business project before the marriage', and was about one sixth of the husband's assets.[133]

Applying these principles to Mr and Mrs McFarlane's situation:

The parties' contributions 'were of different but equal value', as reflected in the equal division of the capital.[134] The husband's income was considerably in excess of the parties' needs and the wife was entitled to 'generous income provision'. The husband's earnings 'were the result of the parties' joint endeavours at the early stages of his professional career'. He would continue to benefit from that, not just during the marriage but also afterwards. Conversely, 'as primary carer of the three children, the wife continued to be at economic disadvantage

---

[120] [2006] UKHL 24, at [10] (Lord Nicholls). [121] [2007] EWCA Civ 503, at [69] (Sir Mark Potter P).
[122] [2006] UKHL 24, at [138] (Lady Hale). [123] [2006] UKHL 24, at [11] (Lord Nicholls).
[124] [2006] UKHL 24, at [13] (Lord Nicholls). [125] [2006] UKHL 24, at [16] (Lord Nicholls).
[126] [2006] UKHL 24, at [23] (Lord Nicholls) citing *White* [2001] 1 AC 596, 610[F]–[G] (Lord Nicholls).
[127] [2006] UKHL 24, at [144] (Lady Hale). [128] [2006] UKHL 24, at [157]–[158] (Lady Hale).
[129] [2006] UKHL 24, at [72] (Lord Nicholls). [130] [2006] UKHL 24, at [69] (Lord Nicholls).
[131] [2006] UKHL 24, at [71] (Lord Nicholls). [132] [2006] UKHL 24, at [158] (Lady Hale).
[133] [2006] UKHL 24, at [73] (Lord Nicholls). [134] [2006] UKHL 24, at [84] (Lord Nicholls).

and continued to make a contribution from which the children and, indirectly, the husband benefited. He was relieved of the day to day responsibility for their children.' She had foregone a career 'as successful and highly paid as the husband's'.[135] 'It would be manifestly unfair if her income award were confined to her *needs*. This is a paradigm case for an award of *compensation* in respect of the future economic disparity sustained by the wife, arising from the way the parties conducted their marriage.'[136] The wife was also entitled to 'a *share* in the very large surplus, on the principles both of sharing the fruits of the matrimonial partnership and of compensation for the comparable position she would have been in had she not compromised her own career for the sake of them all'.[137]

Mrs McFarlane therefore received half of the capital plus spousal maintenance of £250,000 per year from Mr McFarlane for the duration of their joint lives. Mr McFarlane also paid her child maintenance of £60,000 per year and paid the children's school fees.

7. The principles of need, compensation, and sharing

Since *Miller/McFarlane*, courts have applied the three strands, or rationales, of needs, compensation, and sharing to a wide range of cases. Each of these principles is discussed in more detail below.

7.1 Needs

Fairness almost always requires each party's needs to be met on divorce, subject to there being sufficient money to do so. This generally involves them having somewhere to live— 'there is nothing more awful than homelessness'[138]—and sufficient money to live on. But need 'is a very broad concept',[139] capable of encompassing a wide range of types of expenditure. In the majority of cases, the outcome is determined not by principle but by what is actually possible.

Most needs 'will have been generated by the marriage',[140] but some needs, such as those caused by age or disability (both s. 25 factors) will not be, and it appears these must still be met, as in *Miller/McFarlane* Lord Nicholls seems not to make a distinction between needs generated by the relationship and those external to the relationship.[141] Lady Hale similarly notes that the 'most common source of need is the presence of children, whose welfare is always the first consideration, *or of other dependent relatives, such as elderly parents*' (emphasis added). For her, however, the key is that such needs are 'linked to the parties' relationship, either causally or temporally, and not to extrinsic, unrelated factors, such as a disability arising after the marriage has ended'.[142]

While both parties' needs must be met, they are specific to the individual—based on such s. 25 factors as the standard of living during the marriage, the ages of the parties (an elderly party may have modest needs as a result of short life expectancy, for example, but conversely he or she may require a large proportion in order to meet the costs of a nursing home or carer), earning capacity, the duration of the marriage, the existence of any disability, the presence of children, and the responsibilities that each party has. Thus there

---

[135] [2006] UKHL 24, at [90]–[92] (Lord Nicholls).   [136] [2006] UKHL 24, at [93] (Lord Nicholls).
[137] [2006] UKHL 24, at [154] (Lady Hale).   [138] *Cordle v Cordle* [2001] EWCA Civ 1791 [33] (Thorpe LJ).
[139] Law Commission, *Matrimonial Property, Needs and Agreements* (Law Com No. 343, 2014) glossary.
[140] [2006] UKHL 24, at [11] (Lord Nicholls).   [141] [2006] UKHL 24, at [11] (Lord Nicholls).
[142] [2006] UKHL 24, at [137]–[138] (Lady Hale).

is ample scope for disagreement: the parties may agree that each should be housed, for example, but not the size of house or whether a party should buy or rent. They must obviously also have enough money to meet their necessary outgoings but may disagree over what standard of living is appropriate.

In low asset cases, the court's role is to 'stretch modest finite resources so far as possible to meet the parties' needs'. [143] Of course, even in cases where the assets are modest—one house, a few savings, probably a few credit card debts—meeting needs uses up all of the assets, so the other principles, compensation and sharing, simply do not come into play. The requirement to give first consideration to the welfare of any children means that the primary carer is more likely to have his or her needs met as priority:

> The invariable practice in English law is to try to maintain a stable home for the children after their parents' divorce . . . Giving priority to the children's welfare should also involve ensuring that their primary carer is properly provided for, because it is well known that the security and stability of children depends in large part upon the security and stability of their primary carers.[144]

and

> In all these cases it is one of the paramount considerations, in applying the section 25 criteria, to endeavour to stretch what is available to cover the need of each for a home, particularly where there are young children involved. Obviously the primary carer needs whatever is available to make the main home for the children, but it is of importance, albeit it is of lesser importance, that the other parent should have a home of his own where the children can enjoy their contact time with him. Of course there are cases where there is not enough to provide a home for either. Of course there are cases where there is only enough to provide one. But in any case where there is, by stretch and a degree of risk-taking, the possibility of a division to enable both to rehouse themselves, that is an exceptionally important consideration and one which will almost invariably have a decisive impact on outcome.[145]

If there are no children but competing needs, then it may be equal misery, or it may be that the court determines that one party's needs are more pressing than those of the other party. Fairness will determine the outcome.[146]

For moderate asset cases, an assessment of need usually starts with consideration of the standard of living during the marriage.[147] For most people, it is simply impossible to continue to live to the same standard once the assets are divided between two households. If, however, there are sufficient assets, then the needs will not be the fundamentals of life, but a more generous quantification. Thus the need may be for a four-bedroom detached house rather than a two-bed terrace, and a new car rather than a second-hand one. In high asset cases the standard of living experienced during the marriage means that court will cater to needs that a less wealthy person would view as luxury: for example, a house in London, a housekeeper, a wine cellar, and a holiday home,[148] or even property sufficient to continue to stable and exercise horses.[149]

---

[143] [2006] UKHL 24, at [12] (Lord Nicholls). For an extremely low asset case, see *Delaney v Delaney* [1990] 2 FLR 457. Such cases are rarely appealed because of the cost.   [144] [2006] UKHL 24, at [128] (Lady Hale).

[145] *M v B (Ancillary Proceedings: Lump Sum)* [1998] 1 FLR 53, 60 (Thorpe LJ).

[146] See Context 3 for discussion of the outcomes of divorce for men and women.

[147] Matrimonial Causes Act 2973, s. 25(2)(c); *SS v NS* [2014] EWHC 4183.

[148] All needs of Heather Mills McCartney identified in [2008] EWHC 401 (Fam).

[149] *Robson v Robson* [2010] EWCA Civ 1171.

It has been said that 'the inclusion in the section 25 factors of the marital standard of living is a statutory recognition of the relative elasticity of the concept of needs'.[150] While 'the lifestyle enjoyed during the marriage sets a level or benchmark that is relevant to the assessment of the level of the independent lifestyles to be enjoyed by the parties',[151] it is not, however, quite true to say, as Ruth Deech has, that '[i]f you marry a captain of industry, you become one yourself for all time, at least as far as the standard of living is concerned'.[152] In *BD v FD*, Moylan J said that '[t]he use of the standard of living as the benchmark emphatically does not mean that . . . in every case needs are to be met at that level either at all or for more than a defined period (of less than life)'. Particularly after a short marriage, where the standard of living has been experienced for a shorter time, or in cases where the party in need has future earning potential, the court may well use the standard of living simply as a benchmark of *short-term* needs with a subsequent tapering to enable 'a gentle transition from that standard to the standard that [he or] she could expect as a self-sufficient [person]'.[153] This reflects the fact that 'the objective of financial orders made to meet needs should be to enable a transition to independence, to the extent that it is possible'[154] and that 'the ultimate objective is to give each party an equal start on the road to independent living'.[155] Thus the court may provide more generously in the early years post-divorce or for the duration of children's minority, with a reduction some time later. It could do so by providing a lump sum that will be used up, or periodical payments with an end-date or a taper, or a house from which a party will need to downsize in the future in order to free up money to live on. A transition to independence may, of course, not be possible in some cases or at least not without interfering with the overall objective of fairness. This is particularly likely where there has been a long marriage where one party has been out of the employment market for decades. In such cases, an order would cater to lifetime needs.

 CONTEXT 3: POST-DIVORCE OUTCOMES

Obtaining a financial remedy order is not the end of the matter, as, of course, the parties must live with the consequences of it.

We noted in 4.1 that the requirement to give first consideration to the welfare of the child may mean the primary carer takes the bulk of the capital. Despite this, women usually have much worse outcomes in the long term than men both if they are primary carers of children and *even if they do not have children*. Fisher and Low, using data from the British Household Panel Survey, found that following divorce, womens' average household income falls by 31%, after controlling for household size (such as whether they have children with them), and only returns to its pre-divorce average some nine years later.[156] For women, benefits income is important, especially in the early years. Some 23% of wives move from non-receipt of benefits to receipt after separation compared to 7% of husbands.[157] The Fawcett Society found that 'women who have divorced have a higher level of debt than their male counterparts,

[150] *Juffali v Juffali* [2016] EWHC 1684 (Fam), at [145] (Roberts J).
[151] *G v G* [2012] EWHC 167 (Fam), at [136] (Charles J).
[152] Deech, R. 'What's a Woman Worth?' [2009] *Family Law* 1140, 1140.
[153] [2006] UKHL 24, at [158] (Lady Hale).
[154] Law Commission, *Matrimonial Property, Needs and Agreements* (Law Com No. 343, 2014) para 3.67.
[155] [2006] UKHL 24, at [144] (Lady Hale).
[156] Fisher, H. and Low, H. 'Who Wins, Who Loses and Who Recovers from Divorce?' in J. Miles and R. Probert (eds), *Sharing Lives, Dividing Assets: An Inter-Disciplinary Study* (Hart Publishing 2009) 228.
[157] Jarvis, S. and Jenkins, S. P. 'Marital Splits and Income Changes: Evidence from the British Household Panel Survey' 53(2) *Population Studies* 237, 251–2.

which goes against the general trend of men having higher levels of debt than women'.[158] Women have fewer savings too—68% of divorced women have less than £1,500 in savings, compared to 51% of divorced men.[159]

However, women's financial recovery is not due to their earnings, which do not change these prospects significantly, even with retraining. (In fact, where there are children, retraining 'is associated with income growth being 53% lower', which 'may indicate that retraining is undertaken to accommodate childcare responsibilities'[160] and thus more about convenient working patterns than economic advantage.) Instead, the return to pre-divorce average is most commonly due to the inclusion in the household finances of a new partner's income: within four years, 43% of women are remarried or cohabiting.[161] Older women, those in poor health, and those with children have lesser prospects of financial recovery, perhaps due to a lesser chance of repartnering.[162]

Five years from separation, men have an income that is 25% higher on average than their pre-separation income (compared to 9% lower for women).[163] Many men do repartner—about 51% remarry or cohabit within four years—but Fisher and Low suggest that 'men repartner with women whose personal income is cancelled out by the extra costs to the household', so, for men, repartnering often has a neutral financial effect.[164]

7.2 Compensation

Although not mentioned explicitly in the Matrimonial Causes Act, compensation is another of the rationales for the redistribution of assets identified in the judgments of Lord Nicholls and Lady Hale in *Miller/McFarlane*. Its purpose is in 'redressing any significant prospective economic disparity between the parties arising from the way they conducted their marriage'. This is not as simple as one giving up work to take care of children. Even where both work, there may not be 'completely equal opportunity for both'.[165] There are many kinds of decisions that could affect the parties:

> The couple may move from the city to the country; they may move to another country; they may adopt a completely different life-style; one of them may give up a well-paid job that she hates for the sake of a less lucrative job that she loves; one may give up a dead-end job to embark upon a new course of study. These sorts of things happen all the time in a relationship.[166]

Compensation therefore reflects 'the differential risk between the parties'[167] of the way in which they have ordered their lives, and their shared responsibility for the consequences.

---

[158] Westaway, J. and McKay, S. *Women's Financial Assets and Debts* (Fawcett Society, 2007) 25.

[159] Westaway, J. and McKay, S. *Women's Financial Assets and Debts* (Fawcett Society, 2007) 36.

[160] Westaway, J. and McKay, S. *Women's Financial Assets and Debts* (Fawcett Society, 2007) 242.

[161] Westaway J. and McKay, S. *Women's Financial Assets and Debts* (Fawcett Society, 2007) 239.

[162] Westaway, J. and McKay, S. *Women's Financial Assets and Debts* (Fawcett Society, 2007) 244.

[163] Jenkins, S. P. 'Marital Splits and Income Changes over the Longer Term' (2008) Institute for Social and Economic Research Working Paper. Available at: https://www.iser.essex.ac.uk/files/iser_working_papers/2008-07.pdf, accessed 9 September 2016.

[164] Fisher, H. and Low, H. 'Who Wins, Who Loses and Who Recovers from Divorce?' in J. Miles and R. Probert (eds), *Sharing Lives, Dividing Assets: An Inter-Disciplinary Study* (Hart Publishing, 2009) 240.

[165] [2006] UKHL 24, at [138] (Lady Hale).

[166] *Radmacher v Granatino* [2010] UKSC 42, at [188] (Lady Hale).

[167] John Eekelaar, 'Property and Financial Settlement on Divorce—Sharing and Compensating' [2006] *Family Law* 754, 756.

In some cases, compensation will not arise at all. In *Mills-McCartney*, for example, the wife's compensation claim was rejected as, if anything, marriage to Paul McCartney had enhanced the wife's career prospects.[168] In *Radmacher v Granatino* the majority held that 'the husband's decision to abandon his lucrative career in the city for the fields of academia was not motivated by the demands of his family, but reflected his own preference'.[169] In each case, the award was instead based on the applicant's need. In most cases, needs will, as we have considered, absorb all the assets, so there will be nothing to meet any compensation claim. Compensation, therefore, is only really relevant in cases where the other party, 'who has been the beneficiary of the choices made during the marriage, is a high earner with a substantial surplus over what is required to meet needs'.[170]

Mr and Mrs McFarlane are a paradigmatic example. Mrs McFarlane gave up work to be a full-time parent; her husband continued his career. They arranged their affairs:

> ... in a way that has greatly advantaged the husband in terms of his earning capacity but left the wife severely handicapped so far as her own earning capacity is concerned. Then the wife suffers a double loss: a diminution in her earning capacity and the loss of a share in her husband's enhanced income.[171]

When providing sufficient to meet a party's needs, you are anyway to some extent also compensating them for the fact they cannot meet those needs themselves as a result of decisions made in the relationship. So one needs to be careful of double-counting. But in *Miller/McFarlane*, Lady Hale thought that 'the economic disadvantage generated by the relationship may go beyond need, however generously interpreted'[172] and 'in some cases, compensation could justify a greater award than needs and equal sharing'. For Mrs McFarlane, for example, an award limited to her needs, even generously assessed, would leave her significantly worse than that of her former husband. She assessed her needs as carer for three children as £128,000 per year, of which her earning capacity was about £30,000. The husband assessed his needs as £60,000–80,000. His net income was £750,000. If she was awarded only the extra £100,000 she required (significant though this is by 'ordinary' standards), she would be £650,000 worse off than her former husband *per year* as a result of the choice they made that she would give up work to care for their children. Even if we interpreted her needs more generously, a purely needs-based approach will not meet the requirements of fairness.

Despite this, in a series of cases since, judges have treated compensation as falling simply within a generous assessment of needs—see *VB v JP* ('any element of compensation is best dealt with by a generous assessment of her continuing needs'),[173] *McFarlane (No. 2)*,[174] *B v S*,[175] and, most notably, *SA v PA*. In the latter case, Mostyn J thought that:

- It will only be in a very rare and exceptional case where the principle will be capable of being successfully invoked.

- Such a case will be one where the court can say without any speculation, i.e. with almost near certainty, that the claimant gave up a very high earning career which had it not been foregone would have led to earnings at least equivalent to that presently enjoyed by the respondent.

---

[168] [2008] EWHC 401 (Fam), at [84].   [169] [2010] UKSC 42, at [121] (Lord Philips P).
[170] [2006] UKHL 24, at [140] (Lady Hale).   [171] [2006] UKHL 24, at [13] (Lord Nicholls).
[172] [2006] UKHL 24, at [140] (Lady Hale).   [173] [2008] EWHC 112 (Fam), at [59] (Sir Mark Potter P).
[174] [2009] EWHC 891 (Fam) (Charles J). This was the wife's application to vary the maintenance payments for herself and the parties' children following the original House of Lords decision.
[175] [2012] EWHC 265 (Fam) (Mostyn J).

- Such a high earning career will have been practised by the claimant over an appreciable period during the marriage. Proof of this track-record is key.

- Once these findings have been made compensation will be reflected by fixing . . . the award . . . towards the top end of the discretionary bracket applicable for a needs assessment on the facts of the case. Compensation ought not be reflected by a premium or additional element on top of the needs based award.[176]

Thus, where compensation is a relevant factor, the line of cases leading to *SA v PA* indicates that it will be assessed not as a separate head of claim or premium on top of a needs-based award, but instead within generously assessed need. While this approach seems to have attracted the most judicial favour, it is not a universal view: within a month of Mostyn J's judgment, Coleridge J in *H v H* awarded an additional element for compensation on top of the wife's needs on the basis that 'there remains a very small number of cases where it stares the court in the face and to ignore it and simply approach the case on the basis of the more simplistic "needs" argument does not do full justice'.[177] This seems to reflect much better what was intended by the House of Lords in *Miller/McFarlane*, as Lady Hale spoke of 'a premium above needs'.[178] But it is very much the minority approach.

For the most part, compensation survives, barely, as a pale imitation of its creators' apparent intention. The general judicial trend was summed up rather bluntly by Valentine Le Grice QC in his response to the Law Commission's consultation on needs: 'Compensation is a useless concept in assessing spousal support. . . . Since the concept was introduced by the House of Lords it has been politely and rightly ignored by Judges at first instance'.[179] This does not mean that the courts do not take account of the aspects of marital life that give rise to compensation. It means that they treat these as part of need. The question is whether in doing so they are giving sufficient weight to this issue.

 DEBATE 3: SHOULD WE COMPENSATE PARTIES IF EVENTS DURING THE MARRIAGE CAUSE THEM FUTURE DISADVANTAGE?

Of the three rationales identified in *Miller/McFarlane*, it is compensation[180] that has been subjected to the most sustained judicial and academic attacks. There are a number of reasons why it has been so contentious, and these go both to the theoretical basis of compensation and to its practical implementation. For convenience, we will refer to the applicant for compensation as the wife.

SOME CRITICISMS OF COMPENSATION

- Lady Hale's statement that compensation is 'for the comparable position which she might have been in',[181] if taken at face value, requires the court to assess what position the wife would have been in if the parties had made different decisions during the marriage. This is extremely difficult. One cannot safely assume that the wife would have had a continuous high-earning career.[182] A great many situations could have

---

[176] [2014] EWHC 392 (Fam), [36]–[37].

[177] [2014] EWHC 760 (Fam). It is interesting to note that Coleridge J and Mostyn J have each given speeches about divorce law which seems to indicate very different views about marriage itself. Both speak, of course, from a position of privilege.   [178] [2006] UKHL 24, at [140] (Lady Hale).

[179] Law Commission, Matrimonial Property, Needs and Agreements (Law Com No. 343, 2014) para 3.27.

[180] I am grateful to Lucy Crompton for a discussion on compensation.

[181] *Miller v Miller/McFarlane v McFarlane* [2006] UKHL 24, at [154] (Lady Hale).

[182] *SA v PA* [2014] EWHC 392 (Fam), at [30] (Mostyn J).

intervened, such as redundancy, ill health, changes of career, house moves, or changes in the job market, and affected the wife's career and thus the quantification of her loss. There must also 'be a high possibility that, had the [wife] not had a relationship with the [husband] . . . she will have had one with another person'.[183] Thus her loss is based on the fact that *this* marriage failed, and the risks inherent in the decision were therefore realised. 'The most direct measure of her financial loss would compare her situation at divorce to the hypothetical situation had she married a different man.'[184] And who knows what the situation would be then? 'It is simply not possible (and highly undesirable and costly) to conduct . . . a speculative 'what if . . .?' exercise to reconstruct the parties' marriage on a different basis'.[185]

- The wife is a willing participant in the decisions that have given rise to the compensation claim. This voluntariness is at odds with most situations in which compensation arises in law, such as in personal injury. 'If each decision were part of a joint life plan, why should we presume that the now-impoverished spouse did not make those decisions for her benefit? . . . The character of the self-sacrificing wife is attributed to her retrospectively.'[186]

RESPONDING TO THESE CRITICISMS

- The parties may well be entirely happy with their respective roles. The husband may prefer his role as a breadwinner. The wife may have been happy to give up or reduce her work—perhaps she hated her job. Lady Hale thought '[t]he fact that she might have wanted to do this is neither here nor there. Most breadwinners want to go on breadwinning. The fact that they enjoy their work does not disentitle them to a proper share in the fruits of their labours.'[187]
- It is unrealistic to take the view that each individual party to a marriage is free to make a decision in a vacuum in which they only have their own self-interests to worry about— and would we want family life to be like that? Making sacrifices or compromises is a normal part of marriage. It does not follow from that that we should therefore ignore the different consequences of such decisions. Indeed, if such decisions are made as a result of a view of marriage as a joint endeavour, there is a strong moral case for recognition.
- 'It is not only in [the child's] interests but in the community's interests that parents, whether mothers or fathers and spouses, whether husbands or wives, should have a real choice between concentrating on breadwinning and concentrating on home-making and child-rearing, and do not feel forced, for fear of what might happen should their marriage break down much late in life, to abandon looking after the home and the family to other people for the sake of maintaining a career.'[188]
- There appears to be no particular justification for limiting the claims to those who have lost a high-flying career. There are all sorts of other sacrifices or compromises people make that have financial consequences post-divorce.

---

[183] Eekelaar, J. 'Property and Financial Settlement on Divorce—Sharing and Compensating' [2006] *Family Law* 754, 756.

[184] American Law Institute, *Principles of Family Dissolution: Analysis and Recommendations* para 5.05 comment e (ALI 2002). Cited by John Eekelaar in his useful discussion in 'Property and Financial Settlement on Divorce—Sharing and Compensating' [2006] *Family Law* 754, 756.

[185] *RP v RP* [2006] EWHC 3409 (Fam), at [64] (Coleridge J).

[186] Ferguson, L. 'Family, Social Inequalities, and the Persuasive Force of Interpersonal Obligation' (2008) 22 *International Journal of Law, Policy and the Family* 61, 75.

[187] [2006] UKHL 24, at [154] (Lady Hale).

[188] *SRJ v DWJ (Financial Provision)* [1999] 2 FLR 179, 182 (Hale J).

7.3 **Sharing**

The third of the rationales from *Miller/McFarlane* is sharing 'the fruits of the matrimonial partnership'.[189] Lord Nicholls refers to 'equal sharing' and the 'sharing entitlement'. In *Charman*, the Court of Appeal thought 'those phrases describe more than a yardstick for use as a check' and took it 'to mean that property should be shared in equal proportions unless there is a good reason to depart from such proportions'.[190] But what property—and what constitutes 'good' reasons?

7.3.1 Matrimonial and non-matrimonial property

Lord Nicholls and Lady Hale distinguished between matrimonial property—sometimes known as 'marital acquest' or 'family assets'—and non-matrimonial property. Although the sharing principle applies to both matrimonial and non-matrimonial assets, it does so in different ways.

Lord Nicholls' definition of matrimonial property:[191]

- Assets 'acquired during the marriage otherwise than by inheritance or gift'.
- The 'financial product of the parties' common endeavour'. (This might involve money that was received after separation but which was the product of work done during the marriage.)
- 'Even if this was brought into the marriage at the outset by one of the parties, [the parties' matrimonial home] usually has a central place in any marriage. So it should normally be treated as matrimonial property for this purpose.'

Lady Hale's definitions:[192]

- Family assets of a capital nature [such as] the family home and its contents.
- Other assets which were obviously acquired for the use and benefit of the whole family, such as holiday homes, caravans, furniture, insurance policies, and other family savings.
- Family businesses or joint ventures in which they both work.

Under both Lady Hale's and Lord Nicholls' formulations, the matrimonial home is normally a matrimonial asset.[193] In other ways, these definitions are slightly different. Whereas Lord Nicholls defines non-matrimonial property as that which the parties 'bring with them into the marriage or acquire by inheritance or gift during the marriage' (a narrow definition of non-marital property), Lady Hale takes the view that 'in a matrimonial property regime which still starts with the premise of separate property, there is still some scope for one party to acquire and retain separate property which is not automatically to be shared equally between them'.[194] It is this latter view that seemed more favoured by the other Lords and was subsequently described in *Charman* as 'perhaps the more pragmatic'.[195]

---

[189] [2006] UKHL 24, at [207] (Lady Hale).   [190] [2007] EWCA Civ 503, at [65] (Sir Mark Potter P).
[191] [2006] UKHL 24, at [21]–[22].   [192] [2006] UKHL 24, at [149].
[193] It is conceivable that there may be a rare case which involves an extremely pricey house brought into an extremely short marriage in which needs can be met without recourse to the house, where fairness would justify it not being treated as matrimonial, so it is probably not correct to say it will *always* be a matrimonial asset. *Sharp v Sharp* [2017] EWCA Civ 408 gives comfort to this view.
[194] [2006] UKHL 24, at [153].   [195] [2007] EWCA Civ 503, at [85] (Sir Mark Potter P).

7.3.2 Application of sharing of matrimonial and non-matrimonial property

Matrimonial property should be shared equally unless there is good reason not to do so. A good reason may be found in s. 25 and the principles set out in *Miller/McFarlane*: need (most commonly); compensation; conduct if inequitable to disregard; and contribution, but only if it is stellar. We know from *Charman* that a successful stellar contribution argument justifies a departure from equal sharing of matrimonial property because it is a special contribution to *matrimonial* property, not a special contribution of *non*-matrimonial property; and that 'fair allowance for special contribution within the sharing principle would be most unlikely to give rise to percentages of division of matrimonial property further from equality than 66.6%–33.3%'.

To these reasons for departing from equal sharing of matrimonial property, we can add two practical reasons linked to the nature of the assets: (1) a party taking 'copper-bottomed assets'—those that are safe from significant fluctuations in value— may receive less than someone who is taking the riskier assets such as shares, to reflect the level of risk;[196] and (2) in order to achieve a clean break, one party may take more capital instead of ongoing periodical payments from the other, higher earning, party.

Non-matrimonial property is an unmatched contribution to the marriage by one party and its source is usually outside the marriage: a pre-owned asset, or an inheritance, for example. This *potentially* gives a reason to depart from equality in favour of the contributor. Whether the court actually does this depends on the following:

- Whether the non-matrimonial assets have become mingled with the matrimonial property 'in circumstances in which the contributor may be said to have accepted that it should be treated as matrimonial property'; or because it has been used as, or to buy, a matrimonial home.[197] Thus the non-matrimonial assets may have become matrimonial.

- Even if there are non-matrimonial assets, we must still meet needs and if we cannot do that from just the matrimonial assets we will need to utilise the non-matrimonial assets too. As Lord Nicholls said in *White*, the contribution of non-matrimonial assets 'can be expected to carry little weight, if any, in a case where the claimant's financial needs cannot be met without recourse to this property'.[198] (This means that in reality we are only concerned about the distinction between matrimonial and non-matrimonial property where there is a surplus above needs to argue over.)

- It *may* be unfair to give much weight to a contribution of non-matrimonial property in the case of a long marriage. This is particularly the case if 'over time matrimonial property of such value has been acquired as to diminish the significance of the initial contribution by one spouse of non-matrimonial property'.[199] Consider that in *White* the Court approached the inheritance of a farm by the husband as justifying a division in the husband's favour, but the House of Lords took the view that it was less important a contribution than the Court of Appeal had given it.

---

[196] As in *Wells v Wells* [2002] EWCA Civ 476 and *Myerson v Myerson (No. 2)* [2009] EWCA Civ 282.
[197] *K v L* [2011] EWCA Civ 550, at [18] (Wilson LJ). Contrast with *Robson* (n 60).
[198] [2001] 1 AC 596, 610[G].   [199] *K v L* [2011] EWCA Civ 550, at [18] (Wilson LJ).

- In *Sharp v Sharp*,[200] the Court of Appeal cited Lady Hale's view that there was some scope for parties to have non-matrimonial property that was acquired during the marriage otherwise than by gift or inheritance, when considering the status of Mrs Sharp's bonuses, which she had largely kept separate. It held that 'where both spouses have largely been in full-time employment and where only some of their finances have been pooled, . . . fairness may well require a reduction from a full 50% share or the exclusion of some property from the 50% calculation'. The Court excluded Mrs Sharp's bonuses from the matrimonial assets but, crucially, this was a short, childless marriage in which these were not required to meet the husband's needs.

The court has considerable discretion to consider, in light of the above, whether to reflect non-matrimonial assets in the outcome of the case at all, and, if so, how. There are two main approaches, which Bethany Hardwick has labelled *scientific* and *artistic*. The scientific approach decides first whether the alleged non-matrimonial property should, bearing in mind mingling and the duration of the marriage, be reflected at all in the outcome. Second, if it decides it should be reflected, it then ring-fences such assets for the contributing party, and applies the sharing principle to the remainder of the assets subject to a cross-check of fairness. The artistic approach simply involves adjusting away from equal division of all the matrimonial and non-matrimonial assets to take account of the fact that non-matrimonial assets are within the pool. This is a more broad brush approach.

There are advantages and disadvantages to both methods.[201] Whichever method is used, it seems that 'there is no ground for sharing the non-matrimonial assets other than 100% to the contributor and 0% to the other'[202] under the *sharing* principle itself. It is simply that (1) there may be difficulties in establishing what is (still) non-matrimonial, and (2) there may be other reasons, such as need, justifying a different division. Perhaps the final comment should go to Wilson LJ in *Jones v Jones*: 'Application of the sharing principle is inherently arbitrary; such is, I suggest, a fact which we should accept and by which we should cease to be disconcerted.'[203]

7.4 The three principles and periodical payments

In *Miller/McFarlane*, Lady Hale rejected the application of the sharing principle to future income: 'the marital partnership does not stay alive for the purpose of sharing future resources unless this is justified by need or compensation'.[204] As Thorpe LJ thought when considering *McFarlane* in the Court of Appeal:

> The cross-check of equality is not appropriate for a number of reasons. First in many cases the division of income is not just between the parties, since there will be children with a priority claim for the costs of education and upbringing. Second Lord Nicholls [in *White*] suggested the use of the cross-check in dividing the accumulated fruits of past shared endeavours. In assessing periodical payments the court considers the division of the fruits of the breadwinner's future work in a context where he may have left the child-carer in the former matrimonial home, where he may have to meet alternative housing costs and where he may have in fact or in contemplation a second wife and a further child.[205]

---

[200] [2017] EWCA Civ 408.

[201] For a discussion of the case law and the advantages and disadvantages, see Hardwick, B. 'What's Mine Is (*Not) Yours—the Treatment of Non-matrimonial Property: No Longer a Lawless Science?'. Available at: http://www.familylaw.co.uk/news_and_comment/what-s-mine-is-not-yours-the-treatment-of-non-matrimonial-property-no-longer-a-lawless-science#.WFlcTlWLQdU, accessed 23 November 2016.

[202] *Jones v Jones* [2011] EWCA Civ 41, at [33] (Wilson LJ).   [203] [2011] EWCA Civ 41, at [35].

[204] [2006] UKHL 24, at [144].

[205] *Parlour v Parlour/McFarlane v McFarlane* [2004] EWCA Civ 872, at [106].

To this, one could add that it has never been thought advisable to disincentive a person from working and retaining the majority of what they earn for their own ends.

Given the subsequent attacks on compensation, we are left with the view expressed by Mostyn J in *SS v NS*: that an award of periodical payments 'should only be made by reference to needs, save in a most exceptional case where it can be said that the sharing or compensation principle applies'.[206] Such an assessment may, of course, be quite generous.

7.5 Needs, compensation, and sharing: how do they fit together?

You would be forgiven for being confused about how these three rationales come together.

In *Miller/McFarlane*, Lady Hale thought that 'there cannot be a hard and fast rule about whether one starts with equal sharing and departs if need or compensation supply a reason to do so, or whether one starts with need and compensation and shares the balance'.[207] Lord Nicholls thought that '[t]here can be no invariable rule on this'.[208] This is not at all helpful to the practitioner: the two approaches do lead to different outcomes, as Jo Miles has illustrated.[209]

In *Charman* the Court 'appears to favour a starting point of equal sharing modified by need, rather than meeting need and then sharing any surplus'.[210] Indeed, in purely practical terms, it is very much easier to start with an equal division of the capital (sharing) and then consider whether there is any reason to depart from that. Such an approach also sends a message: 'there may be something intangible (and, more concretely, an enhancement of bargaining position) to be gained from the idea that each party is prima facie *entitled* to an equal share of the capital and that a non-owner applicant is not merely a "needy supplicant"'.[211]

If we take equal sharing as a starting point, we should then ask ourselves whether there are reasons, found in s. 25, for departing from that and giving one party more of the assets. In the majority of cases, there is likely to be a reason, which could be:

- to meet needs (see 7.1);

- conduct, if inequitable to disregard (see 4.3);

- stellar contribution to matrimonial assets, within the limits outlined in *Charman* (see 7.3.2 and Debate 2);

- the presence of non-matrimonial assets (see 7.3.2);

- to provide a party with compensation for relationship generated disadvantage (see 7.2 and Debate 3);

- to capitalise a periodical payments claim to enable a clean break (see 3.2);

- to provide an offsetting lump sum instead of a pension share (see 3.6);

- because one party has taken riskier assets than the other (see 7.3.2);

- because of the presence of a prenuptial agreement (see section 8).

---

[206] [2014] EWHC 4183, at [46]. See also his comments in *B v S* [2012] EWHC 265 (Fam), at [79].

[207] [2006] UKHL 24, at [144].   [208] [2006] UKHL 24, at [29].

[209] Miles, J. '*Charman v Charman*: Making Sense of Need, Compensation and Equal Sharing after *Miller/McFarlane*' (2008) 20 *Child and Family Law Quarterly* 378, 389. For further discussion, see George, R. *Ideas and Debates in Family Law* (Hart Publishing 2012) 96–9.

[210] Miles, J. '*Charman v Charman*: Making Sense of Need, Compensation and Equal Sharing after *Miller/McFarlane*' (2008) 20 *Child and Family Law Quarterly* 378, 389.

[211] Miles, J. '*Charman v Charman*: Making Sense of Need, Compensation and Equal Sharing after *Miller/McFarlane*' (2008) 20 *Child and Family Law Quarterly* 378, 389.

Need is likely to be the most common. However, if by sharing the assets equally we have also succeeded in meeting each party's needs, then great: 'While need is often a sound rationale, it should not be seen as a limiting principle if other rationales apply.'[212] Thus if equal sharing gives you more than meets your needs, you should get equal sharing. If needs gives you more, you get needs.[213] Compensation, following *SA v PA*, is usually treated as within a generous assessment of need, so there is an overlap there and a risk of double-counting.

Therefore, these three strands or rationales should not be treated as separate heads of claim as they would in a personal injury case, for example, by adding one to the other.[214] 'The outcome of ancillary relief cases depends upon the exercise of a singularly broad judgment that obviates the need for the investigation of minute detail and equally the need to make findings on minor issues in dispute.' Courts should instead 'paint their canvas with a broad brush rather than a fine sable', and the judge should conclude his or her consideration by assessing whether, in light of all elements of the case, the outcome is fair.[215]

 DEBATE 4: DOES THE LAW CORRECTLY BALANCE CERTAINTY WITH DISCRETION?

As we have seen, lawyers advising couples on financial settlement have to take into account a huge number of factors before giving their opinion—all the circumstances of the case, filtered through the prism of the s. 25 factors, the three principles from *Miller/McFarlane*, the encouragement of independence, and what is actually possible with the assets one has. This is a highly discretionary system, a 'luxury discretion',[216] in which no single factor is always weighted more heavily, no mathematical formula is applied, and judges make comments like these:

- 'The quantification of periodical payments is more an art that a science. The parameters of s 25 are so wide that it might be said that it is almost impossible to be "scientific" . . . no family judge in exercising this jurisdiction can achieve perfection given the width of s 25. He or she can only do his best to get as near to it as is possible in the circumstances of any particular case.'[217]
- 'Application of the sharing principle is inherently arbitrary; such is, I suggest, a fact which we should accept and by which we should cease to be disconcerted.'[218]
- 'There can be no invariable rule on this. . . . Needless to say, it all depends upon the circumstances.'[219]
- 'In reading and re-reading all the now familiar authorities, attempting to expose and explain the underlying principles, one is reminded of a frenzied butterfly hunter in a tropical jungle trying to entrap a rare and elusive butterfly using a net full of holes. As soon as it appears to have been caught it escapes again and the pursuit continues.'[220]

Given both the legal uncertainty and the wide range of potentially fair case outcomes, research by Davis *et al* found that it was impossible to tell from the case files what the outcome of a finan-

---

[212] [2006] UKHL 24 (Lady Hale).   [213] See *Charman v Charman (No. 4)* [2007] EWCA Civ 503, at [73].
[214] *RP v RP* [2006] EWHC 3409 (Fam).   [215] *Parra v Parra* [2002] EWCA Civ 1886, at [22] (Thorpe LJ).
[216] Cooke, E. '*Miller/McFarlane*: Law in Search of Discrimination' (2007) 19 *Child and Family Law Quarterly* 98.   [217] *Parlour v Parlour/McFarlane v McFarlane* [2004] EWCA Civ 872.
[218] *Jones v Jones* [2011] EWCA Civ 41.   [219] [2006] UKHL 24, at [29] (Lord Nicholls).
[220] *Charman v Charman* [2006] EWHC 1879 (Fam) (Coleridge J).

cial remedy case was to be.[221] Indeed, it has been suggested that the extent of the discretion may be so wide as to 'enable a judge to elect between outcomes'. 'In such cases . . . it is not necessarily healthy to pretend that the conclusion has been inexorably determined by prior principle'.[222]

In Context 1, we noted that people bargain in the shadow of law; that is, they consider what would happen if they went to court when considering whether to settle and on what terms. A more certain outcome, whether through clearer rules or even a mathematical formula, could also help ensure that like cases were treated alike. If the law is unpredictable, then parties may be more likely to litigate, as there is everything to 'play for'. Discretionary systems are expensive, for the parties and the court system. At a time when legal aid is mostly unavailable and people are attempting to represent themselves, it is even more important that they should be able to identify, understand, and apply the relevant legal principles.

But the price of predictability is fairness in some cases. A one-size-fits-all approach would mean some parties had 'harsh or unfair' outcomes that should not exist if the parties' exact circumstances are taken into account. The 'flexibility and sensitivity' our legal system provides enables a judge or practitioner to consider each couple's unique situation and tailor an outcome that is fair for them.[223] While like situations should be treated alike, our discretionary system understands that every case is unique and consequently that there is no such thing as a truly 'like' case.

In recent years, there has been a general trend away from discretion and towards rule-based outcomes in a number of legal systems.[224] In England, successive governments have sought to limit judicial discretion by providing more certainty of outcome.[225] One example is the introduction of a statutory child maintenance scheme with a mathematical formula to calculate the appropriate level of child maintenance. In 1998 the government consultation document *Supporting Families* proposed that there should be a hierarchy of principles that could be applied on divorce; the same document also proposed that prenuptial agreements be recognised subject to a number of safeguards.[226] However, these proposals were never actioned and indeed the Lord Chancellor's Ancillary Relief Advisory Group rejected the idea, although it was in favour of the codifying of case law principles.[227]

Since then, the Law Commission has also considered whether the law should be reformed to be more certain. They considered mathematical formulae for periodical payments and binding nuptial agreements.[228] Most academic and judicial respondents to the consultation favoured limiting discretion by providing guidelines but not dispensing entirely with judicial discretion. As a result the Family Justice Council has developed guidelines for judges and members of the public in an attempt to encourage consistency in decision-making and make the law more accessible to the public.

Most recently, Baroness Ruth Deech has introduced a Private Member's Bill into Parliament which seeks to amend the Matrimonial Causes Act 1973 by reducing discretion in the

---

[221] Davis, G. *et al* 'Ancillary Relief Outcomes' (2000) 12 *Child and Family Law Quarterly* 43.

[222] Cretney, S. 'The Family and the Law—Status or Contract?' (2003) 15 *Child and Family Law Quarterly* 403, 416. [223] [2006] UKHL 24, at [122] (Lady Hale).

[224] Jackson, J. *et al* 'Financial Support on Divorce: The Right Mixture of Rules and Discretion?' (1993) 7 *International Journal of Law and the Family* 230.

[225] See Douglas, G. and Perry, A. 'How Parents Cope Financially on Separation and Divorce—Implications for the Future of Ancillary Relief' (2001) 13 *Child and Family Law Quarterly* 67.

[226] Home Office, *Supporting Families* (The Stationery Office, 1998).

[227] Ancillary Relief Advisory Group, *Possible Reforms to the Substantive Law on Ancillary Relief* (Lord Chancellor's Department, 1998).

[228] Law Commission, *Matrimonial Property, Needs and Agreements* (Law Com No. 343, 2014) para 3.129.

way courts dealt with periodical payments, non-matrimonial property, and nuptial agreements.[229] Lord Wilson has suggested that the Bill's supporters:

> believe too readily what they see in the papers and . . . regard the exceptional cases as the norm . . . This leads them to exaggerate the difficulties of our current system and to ignore the virtue of principles which have a sufficient degree of elasticity to enable a reasonable result to be fitted to each case. Some of the rigid provisions which the group have included in their proposed reform bill . . . would have had grotesque consequences if they were to have been applied to a number of the cases in which I have participated.[230]

Like all Bills that lack government support, its purpose is to raise awareness of the issue and it has little chance of becoming law.

8. Nuptial agreements

A nuptial agreement is an agreement between the parties that provides for the financial consequences of marital breakdown. There are various different kinds, depending on when the agreement is reached. An agreement made before the marriage is a *prenuptial agreement*, sometimes called an 'antenuptial' agreement. An agreement made during the marriage but before it has broken down is a *postnuptial agreement*. They are not very common, but might be drawn up because the parties ran out of time to draw up a prenuptial agreement, or had a crisis in their marriage, as in *NA v MA*.[231] An agreement made once the marriage has broken down could be a *separation agreement* if they're not divorcing right away but still want to sort out the money, or *an agreement for the compromise of financial remedy claims* if they are in divorce proceedings. Separation agreements were more common in the past when divorce was less easily available. These days, they are mostly used if the parties wish to wait two or five years to divorce on a no-fault basis, but need to resolve financial matters in the meantime.

Traditionally, agreements which anticipated a possible future breakdown of the marriage—prenuptial agreements and postnuptial agreements—were void because they may act as an incentive to separate and that was contrary to public policy. This did not apply where the marriage had already broken down, so separation agreements and agreements for the compromise of a financial remedy claim were, and still are, lawful.

There is of course no problem at all with this distinction if on divorce they are both happy to apply to court for a financial remedy agreement in the same terms as their prior agreement. But what if one party seeks to resile from the agreement before its terms can be approved by the court? In such a case, the courts will approach each type of agreement in different ways.

8.1 Agreements made after the breakdown of the marriage

Let us assume that the parties have negotiated the terms of a financial settlement between them, perhaps through an exchange of offer and acceptance-type letters, or they might have got as far as embodying the terms in a draft financial remedy order or a separation agreement. What happens if one party then changes his or her mind?

---

[229] Divorce (Financial Provision) Bill [HL].

[230] Lord Wilson, 'Changes over the Centuries in the Financial Consequences of Divorce'. Address to the University of Bristol Law Club, 20 March 2017. Available at https://www.supremecourt.uk/docs/speech-170320.pdf, accessed 21 March 2017.   [231] [2006] EWHC 2900 (Fam).

In this situation, the response of the other side may well be 'tough—we have a concluded agreement and you're stuck with it'. But things are a little more complicated than that. As stated in *Xydhias v Xydhias*:

> an agreement for the compromise of an ancillary relief application does not give rise to a contract enforceable in law. The parties seeking to uphold a concluded agreement for the compromise of such an application cannot sue for specific performance. The only way of rendering the bargain enforceable, whether to ensure that the applicant obtains the agreed transfers and payments, or whether to protect the respondent from future claims, is to convert the concluded agreement into an order of the court.[232]

In other words, and rather confusingly, the position even if the agreement is valid in the sense that no standard contract vitiating factors are present—mistake, duress, incapacity, undue influence, etc.—and the parties are thus bound by it, the agreement cannot be enforced unless approved by a court. At that point, its authority stems from the court order itself not the prior agreement: *de Lasala v de Lasala*.[233] Thus in the event of a dispute about the agreement (or if one party is claiming there's no agreement at all), one party—probably the one seeking to uphold the agreement—should apply to court. Any clause that seeks to prevent this is ineffective for public policy reasons, a longstanding principle deriving from *Hyman v Hyman*[234] and now found in s. 34(1) of the Matrimonial Causes Act 1973.[235]

There are two potential court routes:

1. The easiest and most common way is to apply to court and make the resiling party 'show cause' why an agreement reached should not be converted into an order. This places the burden onto whoever is seeking to get out of the agreement to justify why they should not be held to it (perhaps they say there was never an agreement at all).

2. Alternatively, if it is a written agreement, then it may be valid under s. 34 of the Matrimonial Causes Act 1973 as a 'maintenance agreement': an agreement *between parties to a marriage*, in *writing*, which contains *financial arrangements*, whether made during marriage or after the dissolution or annulment of the marriage. (Note therefore that this does not mean 'maintenance' in the sense of periodical payments. It means financial settlement generally.)

Whichever route is used, the court cannot shirk its statutory obligation to consider all of the s. 25 factors. 'The determination of an application by a court which has failed to have regard to them is unlawful'.[236] The fact of a prior agreement is a s. 25 factor (conduct) as well as being part of all the circumstances of the case. So how important is it as a s. 25 factor? The case of *Edgar v Edgar* tells us that:

> in deciding the weight to be given [to the prior agreement], regard must be had to the conduct of both parties leading up to the prior agreement, and to their subsequent conduct in consequence of it. It is not necessary in this connection to think in formal legal terms, such as misrepresentation or estoppel; *all* the circumstances as they affect each of two human beings must be considered in the complex relationship of marriage. So the

---

[232] [1999] 2 All ER 386.

[233] [1980] AC 546. Cf civil litigation where an agreed settlement derives its authority from the contract made between the parties: *Purcell v FC Trigell Ltd* [1971] 1 QB 358.

[234] [1929] AC 601 (HL).

[235] The rest of the agreement is unaffected. This inability to oust the jurisdiction of the court would affect an arbitration clause although one assumes that given the circumstances of an arbitration any decision reached by the arbitrator would be likely upheld.

[236] Lord Wilson delivering the Supreme Court's single judgment in *Wyatt v Vince*, citing as authority Lord Brandon of Oakbrook in *Livesey (formerly Jenkins) v Livesey* [1985] AC 424, 437.

circumstances surrounding the making of the agreement are relevant. Undue pressure by one side, exploitation of a dominant position to secure an unreasonable advantage, inadequate knowledge, possibly bad legal advice, an important change of circumstances, unforeseen or overlooked at the time of the making of the agreement, are all relevant to the question of justice between the parties.[237]

These factors help us to consider whether the agreement was properly and fairly arrived at. If it was, as Ormrod LJ also said (and this is much quoted in subsequent cases):

> Important too is the general proposition that formal agreements properly and fairly arrived at with competent legal advice should not be displaced unless there are good and substantial grounds for concluding that an injustice will be done by holding the parties to the terms of their agreement. There may well be other considerations which affect the justice of this case; the above list is not intended to be an exhaustive catalogue.

Thus, the existence of an agreement is potentially a very weighty s. 25 factor, or even of 'magnetic importance'[238]: 'clearly when people make an agreement like this it is a very important factor in considering what is the just outcome of the proceedings . . . what they themselves felt to be fair'.[239] This means that the court would want to have 'good and substantial' grounds for not holding the parties to that agreement, namely a change in the parties' circumstances since the agreement was made that renders it unfair (it is not enough to show that you made a bad bargain);[240] and/or that the agreement does not make proper provision for any child of the family;[241] and/or it casts 'onto the public purse an obligation which ought properly to be shouldered within the family', which is contrary to public policy.[242]

As the type of agreement to which this test applies is one made after the breakdown of the marriage, the opportunity for the circumstances to change is fairly limited, and, while parties may feel under pressure at the point of divorce, there is not a great deal of leverage that one party can exercise to force another to accept terms that fail to provide adequately for children or which leaves them on benefits unnecessarily. Absent these criteria, anyone seeking to get out of a separation agreement or an agreement the compromise of a financial remedy claim faces an uphill struggle. This approach survives the Supreme Court decision in *Radmacher v Granatino*, for reasons discussed in the following sections.

8.2 Agreements made before or during the marriage

Given that prenuptial and postnuptial agreements were traditionally contrary to public policy and thus invalid, the *Edgar* approach was never applied to such agreements. However, in *Macleod v Macleod* the Privy Council, considering a postnuptial agreement, rejected such policy reasons outmoded.[243] Once they were out of the way, the Board then had to consider how to treat such an agreement. It held that the *Edgar* approach should be applied to postnuptial agreements in the same way as separation agreements and agreements for the compromise of financial remedy proceedings. It did not extend this approach to prenuptial agreements, however, taking the view that they were 'very

---

[237] [1980] 3 All ER 887 (CA) (Ormrod LJ).

[238] *Crossley v Crossley* [2007] EWCA Civ 1491, at [15] (Thorpe LJ).

[239] *Brockwell v Brockwell* [1975] CAT 468 (CA) (Ormrod LJ).

[240] Derived from *Edgar* and ss. 34–35 of the Matrimonial Causes Act 1973.

[241] Derived from *Edgar* and ss. 34–35 of the Matrimonial Causes Act 1973.

[242] *Macleod v Macleod* [2008] UKPC 64 (Lady Hale). By public purse, Lady Hale means social housing and social security benefits. See also *Hyman v Hyman* [1929] AC 601 (HL).

[243] [2008] UKPC 64. The Privy Council is the highest court of the Isle of Man. The Manx legislation under discussion in the case mirrored that of England and Wales. The Board of the Council is made up of Supreme Court judges. This means their decision, while not directly binding, is highly influential.

different from' postnuptial agreements. It may well, of course, have been that the Board preferred that Parliament legislate if it wanted to change the status of prenuptial agreements. However, given that Parliament failed to do so, the Supreme Court had to address the issue of prenuptial agreements subsequently, in *Radmacher v Granatino*. In doing so, it provided guidance on the current approach to all four types of agreement, and held that the approach taken in *Macleod* was wrong.

 Key Case 3: *Radmacher v Granatino* [2010] UKSC 42

This case involved a prenuptial agreement between a very wealthy German heiress and a French banker. The agreement provided that if the marriage ended each would retain his or her own assets and make no claim on the other. It was drawn up by the Radmacher family's usual German notary. The husband probably first saw a draft of the agreement on 24 July 1998. It was in German, which the husband did not understand, but he did not seek a translation or independent legal advice. Instead, on 1 August 1998 the notary provided him with a verbal translation and the parties then signed the agreement. They married in November 1998 in England and thereafter lived in England.

After eight years of marriage, Ms Radmacher issued divorce proceedings in London. The parties' position had changed significantly since marriage. Mr Granatino had retrained as a biochemist and was earning £30,000 per year as against $US 470,000 when they married. Ms Radmacher's father had given her additional monies during the marriage, bringing her annual income to £2.6 million and her total wealth to £100 million. The parties also had two daughters who were to divide their time between their parents.

The matter came before Baron J.[244] She held that the circumstances surrounding the agreement's creation meant that the agreement was flawed. Nevertheless, she thought that the award 'should be circumscribed to a degree' to reflect the agreement. Its existence acted as a 'discounting factor' pointing her to 'the lower end of the bracket' when meeting Mr Granatino's needs.[245] She awarded him £2.5 million to buy a house; £700,000 to pay most of his debts; £25,000 for a car; and £2.34 million being capitalised maintenance of £100,000 per year for life. In addition to this, Ms Radmacher was to buy a house in Germany (in her name) for Mr Granatino to use when he visited the children there, and pay child maintenance of £35,000 per annum per child to cover the time when the children were with him. (The court had jurisdiction regarding child maintenance because Ms Radmacher's income exceeded the statutory child maintenance scheme cap: see Chapter 6.)

The Court of Appeal felt that Baron J had made only a 'negligible' discount to reflect the agreement. It did not interfere with most of Baron J's award but held that the house should revert to Ms Radmacher when the children left home, and the lump sum in lieu of spousal maintenance should be sufficient only to last Mr Granatino until the youngest child was 22, not for the spouses' joint lives. 'Essentially the major funds (housing and income for the husband) should be provided for him in his role as father rather than as former husband . . . this approach is necessary to give proper weight to the ante-nuptial contract.'[246]

Mr Granatino appealed to the Supreme Court, which upheld the quantum of the Court of Appeal decision, but for slightly different reasons. The majority of judges (Lady Hale dissenting) decided that:

---

[244] As *NG v KR (Pre-Nuptial Contract)* [2008] EWHC 1532. [245] [2008] EWHC 1532, at [93].
[246] [2009] EWCA Civ 649, at [50]–[51] (Thorpe LJ).

the court should give effect to a nuptial agreement that is freely entered into by each party with a full appreciation of its implications unless in the circumstances prevailing it would not be fair to hold the parties to their agreement.[247]

Their reasoning was that:

there should be respect for individual autonomy. The court should accord respect to the decision of a married couple as to the manner in which their financial affairs should be regulated. It would be paternalistic and patronising to override their agreement simply on the basis that the court knows best.[248]

8.3 **Nuptial agreements after** *Radmacher*

Following the majority's formulation, we should therefore assess a nuptial agreement by reference to two questions:

1. Was the agreement freely entered into by each party with a full appreciation of its implications?

   - Intention to create legal relations. '[I]n future it will be natural to infer that parties who enter into an antenuptial agreement to which English law is likely to be applied intend that effect should be given to it.'[249]

   - Standard vitiating factors, for example, duress, fraud, misrepresentation. If these are found, they 'negate any effect the agreement might otherwise have'.[250]

   - Unconscionable conduct. This is not merely undue pressure,[251] which can fall short of duress, but 'other unworthy conduct, such as exploitation of a dominant position to secure an unfair advantage, would reduce or eliminate' the weight given to the agreement.[252]

   - Independent legal advice is 'obviously desirable' and would make it harder to show that a party was pressured into the agreement or did not understand its implications.[253]

   - Full financial disclosure may be necessary but 'if it is clear that a party is fully aware of the implications of an antenuptial agreement and indifferent to detailed particulars of the other party's assets, there is no need to accord the agreement reduced weight because he or she is unaware of those particulars. What is important is that each party should have all the information that is material to his or her decision' to enter into an agreement on those terms.[254] Thus in *Radmacher* it was enough simply for Mr Granatino to know that Ms Radmacher was extremely wealthy—a precise figure was unnecessary.

2. What prevailing circumstances might mean that it was unfair to hold the parties to their agreement?

   - Does it leave a party in real need while the other enjoys a sufficiency or more? 'Where each party is in a position to meet his or her needs, fairness may well not

---

[247] [2010] UKSC 42, at [75] (Lord Philips for the majority).   [248] [2010] UKSC 42, at [78].

[249] [2010] UKSC 42, at [70].   [250] [2010] UKSC 42, at [71].

[251] As in *NA v MA* [2006] EWHC 2900 (Fam) when, after a seven-year marriage, the distressed wife signed a postnuptial agreement when the husband gave her an ultimatum: sign it today, or the marriage is over and you cannot return home.   [252] [2010] UKSC 42, at [71].

[253] [2010] UKSC 42, at [69].   [254] [2010] UKSC 42, at [69].

require a departure from their agreement.'[255] If it does leave a party in real need at the point of divorce, the agreement should be departed from to the extent required to meet needs.

- Does it discriminate against a homemaker? '[I]f the devotion of one partner to looking after the family and the home has left the other free to accumulate wealth, it is likely to be unfair to hold the parties to an agreement that entitles the latter to retain all that he or she has earned.' [256]

- Does it provide for children adequately? 'A nuptial agreement cannot be allowed to prejudice the reasonable requirements of any children of the family'.[257]

Radmacher therefore makes a distinction between:

- Agreements which are intended to be implemented immediately (i.e. agreements for the compromise of a financial remedy claim and separation agreements), for which the strict *Edgar* approach continued to be appropriate. This is because they deal with the current reality and the parties therefore knew what effect they would have when they agreed to the terms.

- Those made before or during the marriage (prenuptial and postnuptial agreements). The majority in *Radmacher* thought that *Macleod* was wrong to always draw a distinction between these two types of agreement. The *Edgar* approach of looking for a change in circumstances could be appropriate for some postnuptial agreements made towards the end of the marriage (because the assets may not have changed much by the time of the divorce) 'or at the start of a marriage if one or both parties bring significant property to it' (because you're protecting non-matrimonial assets).[258] But for other cases looking for a change in circumstances is not a very helpful test because the situation will have changed. It's more important to consider the current prevailing circumstances.

8.4 *Radmacher* and needs, compensation, and sharing

The Court's decision in *Radmacher* gives us as a starting point that the nuptial agreement will be followed unless it is unfair to hold a party to their agreement. If the agreement was not entered into with a full appreciation of its implications, the court may give little or even no weight to it as a s. 25 factor. If the agreement *was* properly entered into, but it is unfair in the circumstances prevailing, the court is unlikely to hold it is totally irrelevant. Rather, the court will depart from it to the extent necessary to meet the requirements set out in 8.3.

Remember that the court is not applying the principles derived from *White* and *Miller/ McFarlane* as though the agreement had never existed. The agreement's existence 'is capable of affecting the overall balance of what is fair as one of the factors or rationales to be taken into account in the application of the statutory discretion', so that a fair outcome where there is a nuptial agreement may be less generous than a fair outcome where there was no agreement at all.[259] As Lord Wilson has pointed out, 'clearly a contract which

---

[255] [2010] UKSC 42, at [82].

[256] [2010] UKSC 42, at [81]. Note that the majority took the view that there was no compensation factor in this case. 'The husband's decision to abandon his lucrative career in the city for the fields of academia was not motivated by the demands of his family, but reflected his own preference', at [121]. Lady Hale viewed this differently, at [194].   [257] [2010] UKSC 42, at [77].   [258] [2010] UKSC 42, at [65].

[259] *V v V (Pre-Nuptial Agreement)* [2012] 1 FLR 1315, 1329 (Charles J). See also *Radmacher v Granatino* [2010] UKSC 42, at [75].

makes less provision for a party than he or she would have secured under the ordinary law does not, on that account, generate an unfair outcome; any contrary conclusion would make the prenuptial contract not worth the paper on which it was written'.[260] Consider the language used in *Radmacher*. Needs must still be met, but so as not to leave a party in 'a predicament of real need'. As Jo Miles has pointed out,[261] *Radmacher* does not tell us what is meant by the term 'real need' but in *Kremen v Agrest* it was interpreted as 'that minimum amount required to keep a spouse from destitution'.[262] For the public policy reasons articulated in *Macleod*, an agreement that left one party with recourse to benefits only is unlikely to be held to meet their real needs.

To some extent any compensation claim must also still be met, but the phrase used in *Radmacher*—'[I]f the devotion of one partner to looking after the family and the home has left the other free to accumulate wealth, it is likely to be unfair to hold the parties to an agreement that entitles the latter to retain all that he or she has earned'—is not an unqualified assertion that in such circumstances the agreement would be ignored. It is perhaps more likely that the agreement will be deviated from to the extent required to ensure that one party does not retain all that he or she has earned. Thus while 'of the three strands identified in *White v White* and *Miller v Miller*, it is the first two, needs and compensation, which can most readily render it unfair to hold the parties to an ante-nuptial agreement', the assessment of those strands may be significantly less generous than would otherwise be the case. '[I]t is in relation to the third strand, sharing, that the court will be most likely to make an order in the terms of the nuptial agreement in place of the order that it would otherwise have made.'[263]

Thus the agreement can make 'provisions that conflict with what the court would otherwise consider to be the requirements of fairness'.[264] That is, after all, the purpose of a nuptial agreement—if you'd get the same outcome going to court, why enter into one?

 DEBATE 5: TO WHAT EXTENT SHOULD THE PARTIES BE ABLE TO REACH THEIR OWN AGREEMENTS WITHOUT COURT APPROVAL?

In her dissent in *Radmacher*, Lady Hale noted that this was 'a complicated subject upon which there is a large literature and knowledgeable and thoughtful people may legitimately hold differing views'.[265] The majority decision was based on respect for individual autonomy: the freedom to control, insofar as possible, one's own future. Part of this is the freedom to enter into contracts governing aspects of one's life, both public and private. Why should an adult not enter into such a contract? Part of being an autonomous adult is the freedom to make bad decisions and live with the consequences. There are other arguments in favour of enforceable marital agreements. They may reduce litigation and costs. Given the high divorce rate and the uncertainty of the existing law, the ability to enter into an enforceable agreement may even encourage more people to marry—particularly, perhaps, those who have been married before and who have property from that marriage that they want to preserve.

[260] Lord Wilson, 'Changes over the Centuries in the Financial Consequences of Divorce'. Address to the University of Bristol Law Club, 20 March 2017. Available at https://www.supremecourt.uk/docs/speech-170320.pdf, accessed 21 March 2017.

[261] Miles, J. 'Marriage and Divorce in the Supreme Court and the Law Commission: For Love or Money?' (2011) 74 *Modern Law Review* 430, 443. See also Murray, A. 'Pre-Nuptials, LSPs and Compensation Guidance: Before and After the Law Commission Report' [2014] *Family Law* 491.

[262] [2012] EWHC 45 (Fam), at [72] (Mostyn J).   [263] [2010] UKSC 42, at [81]–[82].

[264] [2010] UKSC 42, at [75].   [265] [2010] UKSC 42, at [135].

Yet the Court did not hold that such contracts were automatically enforceable. While it certainly moved in that direction, it provided a number of safeguards. Given that in other areas of life the law provides very limited relief to those who enter into unwise contracts, is there something special about the marital context that justifies this different approach?

There are three main arguments, which are strongest when it comes to prenuptial agreements rather than agreements at the end of a marriage:

1. *People in relationships need protecting.* Parties enter into prenuptial agreements when— one assumes—they are in the full flush of love. 'The court . . . should not be blind to human frailty and susceptibility when love and separation are involved'.[266] The economically weaker party may not have equal bargaining power, or the clarity, foresight, and conviction to 'make rational choices in the same way that businessmen can'.[267] Notwithstanding a 42% divorce rate,[268] they may not believe that the prenuptial agreement will ever be triggered or they may not anticipate a future change in circumstances—a career change; the birth of children; an illness or disability; years out of the job market—that renders it less favourable. In such circumstances, is it appropriate for the law to intervene to protect that party? There are examples of laws framed so as to 'redress inequality of bargaining power in other long running relationships, notably between landlord and tenant, employer and employee. Are they not a closer analogy with marriage than an ordinary commercial bargain between economic equals?'[269] Or is this patronising, as the majority of the Supreme Court considered?

2. *The wider social interest in marriage.* A second argument is that the court is not merely ensuring fairness between the parties but representing a wider societal interest in ensuring that the parties cannot bargain their way out of supporting one another. As the House of Lords said in *Hyman*, the parties' claims are 'a matter of public concern which they cannot barter away'. By marrying, the parties 'contract into the package which the law of the land lays down'. The state recognises your marriage and provides certain legal advantages to married couples that it does not provide for the unmarried. One cannot pick and choose among these rights and responsibilities. If marriage 'simply means what the parties want it to mean'[270] there is no justification for privileging marriage in law.

3. *The gender dimension.* As Lady Hale recognised in her dissent in *Radmacher*, women are usually the economically weaker party,[271] and the purpose of a prenuptial agreement is to deny that person the 'provision to which she . . . would otherwise be entitled'[272] at the end of the marriage. In other words, it is about the autonomy to contract out of concepts such as equality, partnership, and marriage as a joint endeavour in which each contributes equally and supports the other—'standards that are intended to be of universal application throughout our society'.[273] As Herring points out, 'there is no other area of discrimination law you can contract out of'.[274] Indeed, the autonomy that the majority was concerned about is, as the Law Commission pointed out, 'not simply the freedom to make an agreement' but also 'the freedom to force one's partner to abide by an agreement when he or she no longer wishes to do so . . . it is

---

[266] *NG v KR (Pre-Nuptial Contract)* [2008] EWHC 1532, at [129] (Baron J).

[267] *Radmacher v Granatino* [2010] UKSC 42, at [135] (Baroness Hale).

[268] *Radmacher v Granatino* [2010] UKSC 42, at [135] (Baroness Hale).

[269] Lady Hale, 'Equality and Autonomy in Family Law' (2011) 33 *Journal of Social Welfare and Family Law* 3, 12.

[270] Herring, J. (2010) 'On the Death Knell of Marriage', 160 *New Law Journal* 1551.

[271] *Radmacher* was unusual in that if it was the wife who was the wealthier.

[272] *Radmacher v Granatino* [2010] UKSC 42, at [137].   [273] *F v F* [1995] 2 FLR 45, 66 (Thorpe J).

[274] Herring, J. 'On the Death Knell of Marriage' (2010) 160 *New Law Journal* 1551.

therefore freedom to use a contract to restrict one's partner's choices'.[275] It is troubling that the steps towards gender equality that the Supreme Court took in *White* and *Miller/McFarlane*—decisions that had potentially lifelong real-world consequences for those divorcing after them—were put at risk by the decision in *Radmacher*. Will it be, as Lady Hale wondered, 'a retrograde step likely only to benefit the strong at the expense of the weak'?

9. After the order

Obtaining the order is not the end of matter. There is further work for the lawyers and the parties to do.

9.1 Implementing the terms

First, if they have not already done so, the parties must obtain decree absolute. They may have paused the divorce proceedings at decree nisi stage and not applied for decree absolute so as to enable them to remain married while financial matters were resolved. (A spouse is in a much stronger position than an ex-spouse if one of the parties dies in the interim.) The parties then have to implement the terms of the order. This may mean transferring title to a house, closing joint bank accounts, transferring shares, making lump sum payments, or starting to make regular payments to the former spouse.

9.2 Enforcement

The Law Commission has estimated that on average 9% of financial remedy orders will be the subject of enforcement action, and this does not include those orders being breached but where there is no enforcement action.[276] The court has a range of powers to compel compliance with an order. What is appropriate will depend on the aspect of the order that needs to be enforced. Where a party refuses to sign documents to effect a house sale or transfer, a judge can do this instead. In the case of lump sums or unsecured periodical payments, the court has the power to make an order for attachment of earnings (whereby the periodic payments are deducted directly from wages by the employer), or a judgment summons which could result in a deliberate non-payer's imprisonment for contempt of court; it is also to use third party debt orders and warrants of control over assets.[277] However, on the basis that prevention is better than cure, the Law Commission has recommended that judges are directed to consider whether any terms as to enforcement should be included whenever a family financial order is made.[278] Thus, the court could make a secured periodical payments order rather than an unsecured one, so that in the event of non-payment the secured property is sold.

9.3 Appeals and applications to set aside an order

The principle that there should be finality of litigation weighs heavily on the court. Nevertheless, the parties can appeal (within strict time limits) on the following grounds.

---

[275] Law Commission, *Matrimonial Property Agreements* (Law Com No. 198, 2011) para 5.31.

[276] Law Commission, *Enforcement of Family Financial Orders* (Law Com No. 370, 2016) para 1.21.

[277] See Oliver, S., Brown, D., and Schofield, G. *Enforcing Family Finance Orders* (2nd edn, Jordans, 2017). See also the methods discussed by Saunders, Z. in a series of articles: [2016] *Family Law Journal* 740, 787, 931.

[278] Law Commission, *Enforcement of Family Financial Orders* (Law Com No. 370, 2016) Chapter 18.

9.3.1 Where the order is wrong

The Appeal Courts have deliberately refused to define 'wrong' but in this context it essentially means this: either the District Judge has ordered something that he had no power to order, or arrived at a conclusion on the basis of no evidence, those being two examples, or in exercising the discretionary powers under the Matrimonial Causes Act in identifying the parties' assets and incomes and in carrying out the re-distributed phase of the exercise, he has come to a conclusion that is so wide of the mark as to be outside the wide ambit of reasonable conclusions that would amount to a fair outcome. It is not sufficient that I might have reached a different conclusion—that is no test of the measure of the order being wrong.[279] The wide discretion that judges have means it is unlikely that an order will be held to be wrong.

9.3.2 Where there has been misrepresentation, fraud, duress, or mistake

'Even innocent misrepresentation as to a material fact can be a vitiating factor if the undisclosed fact was material to the decision which the court made at the time and/or if it undermines the basis on which the order was made'.[280] The parties can challenge an order either by way of an appeal or by way of an application to a first instance judge to set aside the order.

9.3.3 Where the rationale for the order has been invalidated by a supervening event

In the leading case, *Barder v Barder (Caluori Intervening)*, the order provided that the matrimonial home be retained by the wife for herself and the two children.[281] Approximately one month after the consent order was approved, the wife killed herself and the children, and the husband applied for leave to appeal out of time against the terms of the order. The House of Lords set four conditions for a successful application out of time: (1) new events have occurred since the making of the order which invalidate the basis, or fundamental assumption, upon which the order was made, so that, if leave to appeal out of time were to be given, the appeal would be certain, or very likely, to succeed; (2) the new events should have occurred within a relatively short time of the order having been made; (3) the application for leave to appeal out of time should be made reasonably promptly in the circumstances of the case; (4) the grant of leave to appeal out of time should not prejudice third parties who have acquired, in good faith and for valuable consideration, interests in property which is the subject matter of the relevant order.

Note that a common type of mistake—mistake as to the value of an asset—is no longer regarded as falling within the *Barder* principle. Fluctuations in the value of assets such as shares and houses are normal and predictable, even if the consequences can be severe: in *Myerson v Myerson (No. 2)*, a fall in the value of the shares taken, willingly, by the husband as the bulk of his settlement meant that the split of the assets went from 43% to the wife to the equivalent of 105% to the wife by the time of the husband's unsuccessful appeal.[282]

10. Conclusion: what conception of fairness underlies financial remedy law?

The objective that courts have identified—'to do that which is fair, just and reasonable between the parties in rearranging the family finances'[283]—has developed over decades of case law. Fairness itself is not mentioned in the Matrimonial Causes Act 1973 or its

---

[279] *Andrew C v Rebecca C* [2015] EWFC 236 per Booth J. This is a rare example of a reported modest asset case.

[280] *AB v CD* [2016] EWHC 10 (Fam) (Roberts J). See also, for deliberate fraud, *Sharland v Sharland* [2015] UKSC 60 and *Gohil v Gohil* [2015] UKSC 61.   [281] [1988] AC 20.

[282] [2009] EWCA Civ 282.

[283] *Page v Page* [1981] 2 FLR 198 (CA) 206 (Wood J), which, ironically, had an extraordinarily unfair outcome by modern standards.

antecedents. Yet the idea that a financial settlement should be fair is not contentious. As a concept, it has considerable 'rhetorical force'.[284]

However, as we have seen, pinning down what fairness requires has proven extremely difficult. As Lord Nicholls recognised in *Miller/McFarlane*, it 'is grounded in social and moral values [that] change from one generation to the next'.[285] Faced with an almost total absence of legislative input, the courts have sought to identify and expound on underlying principles to ensure that financial remedy decisions continue to be made 'in a climate which reflects society's current attitudes'.[286] In the case law considered in this chapter, we can see four different conceptions of fairness at work: fairness as responsibility to provide for dependants (pre-*White*); fairness as valuing different roles equally (*White*); fairness as acknowledging the different consequences of those roles (*Miller/McFarlane*); and, most recently, fairness as autonomy (*Radmacher*). We have moved from responsibility towards others to responsibility for oneself.

As far back as the Poor Laws, the state sought to look first and foremost to the resources within the family to provide for all members of the family, rather than the burden falling on the state—'an ethic of family responsibility'.[287] So, too, divorce laws reflected a social interest in the wife's continued economic needs being met, however inadequately, by the husband rather than the state. Marriage is 'its own little security system' . . . '[t]he more the private family can look after its own, the less the state will have to do so'.[288]

As recently as *Dart*, the court's judgment was still 'firmly located within the traditional discourse of the provider's responsibility to his dependant—to meet needs'[289] (for what were reasonable requirements but moderately assessed needs?).[290] 'The idea that a wife might have a little extra to save for a rainy day or to leave to her family if she died was seen as going beyond what she reasonably required.'[291] As Alison Diduck points out, that is the role of the provider,[292] and the wife is not the provider—on the contrary:

> in the breadwinner/dependant ideology of marriage the claimant wife (and approximately seventy per cent of claimants are wives) comes to law not as the autonomous rights-bearing individual, but as dependant and supplicant (or potential plunderer of her husband's fortune). . . . It was as if the courts felt similar to the way in which many husbands and wives feel when they are negotiating ancillary relief – that it is the husband's money and assets that are being dealt with.[293]

White 'altered the narrative'[294] in its language—the 'yardstick of equality', 'no place for discrimination between husbands and wives', 'no bias in favour of the money-earner'—and the idea that a non-financial contribution could be equal to a financial one. Fairness here meant equality. In *Miller/McFarlane*, equality had three strands.

First, it involved understanding that formal equality of division is not the same as substantive equality if decisions made by the parties during the marriage have disparate

---

[284] Diduck, A. 'Ancillary Relief: Complicating the Search for Principle' (2011) 38 *Journal of Law and Society* 272, 273.   [285] [2006] UKHL 24, at [4].

[286] *Co v Co (Ancillary Relief: Pre-Marriage Cohabitation)* [2004] EWHC 287 (Fam), at [43] (Coleridge J).

[287] Eekelaar, J. 'Family Law and Social Control', in J. Eekelaar and J. Bell (eds), *Oxford Essays in Jurisprudence* (Clarendon Press, 1987).

[288] Lady Hale, 'Equality and Autonomy in Family Law' (2011) 33 *Journal of Social Welfare and Family Law* 3, 4.

[289] Diduck, A. 'What Is Family Law For?' (2011) 64 *Current Legal Problems* 287, 295.

[290] See discussion by Lord Nicholls in *White v White* [2001] 1 AC 596, 607, 608.

[291] Lady Hale, 'Equality and Autonomy in Family Law' (2011) 33 *Journal of Social Welfare and Family Law* 3, 8.

[292] Diduck, A. 'What Is Family Law For?' (2011) 64 *Current Legal Problems* 287, 295.

[293] Diduck, A. 'Fairness and Justice for All? The House of Lords in *White v White*' (2001) 9 *Feminist Legal Studies* 173, 175.

[294] Diduck, A. 'What Is Family Law For?' (2011) 64 *Current Legal Problems* 287, 303.

consequences post-divorce: 'Giving half the present assets to the breadwinner achieves a very different outcome from giving half the assets to the homemaker with children'.[295] Second, both parties are responsible for these disparate consequences—'mutual dependence begets mutual obligations of support'.[296] This is a new responsibility ethic to replace the responsibility of the breadwinner to his dependant, but it has old roots in the idea that parties should look first to one another and not to the state. Third, marriage is an equal partnership (albeit one in which the parties can retain non-matrimonial property), at the end of which each party is *entitled* to a fair share of the available property.

Yet we also see another theme emerging: autonomy, individual choice. We can see it in the statutory encouragement of a clean break. We see it in Lady Hale's reference to giving each party 'an equal start on the road to independent living'.[297] We see it in Mostyn J's attacks on compensation: 'No one forced her to give up work . . . what cannot be disputed is that the reason Mrs McFarlane gave up work was because she, and intelligent liberated autonomous adult woman, decided to give up work'.[298] 'In the new discourse the individual becomes responsible for herself and her familial choices'.[299] We see it too in *Radmacher*, with its explicit statement that there should be respect for individual autonomy. Here, once more, we see responsibility: this time, responsibility for oneself. Anne Barlow situates such decisions in a social context in which adult couples are increasingly given the 'liberty jointly to exercise their autonomy around decision-making', such as with the 'replacement of statutory child support obligations with parent-negotiated child maintenance; strong regulatory encouragement for family mediation; and rejection of calls for family law regulation of cohabitant separation'.[300]

So, is this what fairness is now? Lady Hale thought that respecting individual autonomy reflects a different kind of equality.[301] But we must be careful with autonomy. On the face of it, it's a very attractive principle.[302] But it underestimates the gendered social, economic, and structural constraints affecting decision-making in a marriage. Even if this were not the case, would we want people to act as autonomous individuals rather than as families?

For us, the discussion is academic. But the Wachtels, the Darts, the Whites, the Millers and McFarlanes, the Radmachers and Granatinos saw their marriages reduced, years hence, to footnotes to a textbook. For them, the law's reasoning is anything but academic: judgments in their cases directed the future course of their lives. The theories and principles we consider were their lived experience.

SUMMARY

1. Should people have continuing financial obligations to one another that outlive the marriage?
   - On divorce, the parties have financial claims against one another, which can only be terminated by a 'clean break' financial remedy order.
   - An object of the modern law is to encourage the parties to move on, recognising that the marriage is at an end. Despite this, a party may be ordered

---

[295] [2006] UKHL 24, at [136] (Lady Hale).   [296] [2006] UKHL 24, at [11] (Lord Nicholls).

[297] [2006] UKHL 24, at [144] (Lady Hale). In, 'Equality and Autonomy in Family Law' (2011) 33 *Journal of Social Welfare and Family Law* 3, she asks whether equality of opportunity is the key.

[298] *SA v PA* [2014] EWHC 392 (Fam), at [28].

[299] Diduck, A. 'What Is Family Law For?' (2011) 64 *Current Legal Problems* 287, 306–8.

[300] Barlow, A. 'Solidarity, Autonomy and Equality: Mixed Messages for the Family?' (2015) 27 *Child and Family Law Quarterly* 223.   [301] [2010] UKSC 42, at [178].

[302] Barlow, A. 'Solidarity, Autonomy and Equality: Mixed Messages for the Family?' (2015) 27 *Child and Family Law Quarterly* 223, 225.

to make periodical payments to the other party, potentially for as long as they both live. This is highly contentious because it outlasts the marriage. As such, it can cause bad feeling between the parties and hinder planning for the future. There is considerable scope for the parties to interfere with one another's lives or to arrange their situation to affect the periodical payments.

- Periodical payments can be an important safety net, especially because financial outcomes post-divorce are worse for women than men. However, we need to consider how much the responsibility for resolving this lies with the parties, as opposed to society as a whole.

2. Should stellar contribution to marriage be recognised?

- Whether the parties reach agreement themselves as to terms, or whether they use the contested court process, the court has to determine that the outcome is objectively fair before it makes an order. The court must consider all the circumstances of the case, as well as a checklist of considerations in s. 25 of the Matrimonial Causes Act 1973.

- In Key Case 1, *White v White*, the House of Lords held that there should be 'no bias in favour of the money-earner and against the home-maker and child-carer'. Therefore equality should only be departed from if there is good reason. Following *White*, more parties shared capital equally.

- A stellar contribution is an argument that one party's contribution to the marriage has been so great that it justifies a departure from equality in favour of the contributor. There have been very few cases where stellar contribution has been successfully argued, and all involve very high assets and an exceptional quality or spark of genius in the contributor. Even then, a successful argument is not likely to change the split of assets beyond 66.6%–33.3%. This is because courts are alert to the risk of gender discrimination.

3. Should we compensate parties if events during the marriage cause them future disadvantage?

- In Key Case 2, *Miller/McFarlane*, the House of Lords held that there are three rationales for property division on divorce: meeting the parties' needs, and the needs of any children of the family; compensating a party for any economic disadvantage they may experience as a result of decisions made in the relationship; and (as a reflection of the idea of marriage as a partnership) sharing the marital fruits.

- Compensation reflects the fact that decisions made during the marriage may have a long-term effect on the parties' prospects after the end of the marriage. For example, a woman may have given up work to raise children, to the detriment of future earnings. It may be in society's interests for people to be able to make such decisions without regard to their future self-interest. However, matrimonial compensation is different to compensation for loss recognised in other areas of law. It has therefore been the subject of a number of judicial and academic attacks.

4. Does the law correctly balance certainty with discretion?

- Lawyers advising couples on financial settlement have to take into account a huge number of factors when giving an opinion—all the circumstances of the case, filtered through the prism of the s. 25 factors, the three principles from *Miller/McFarlane*, the encouragement of independence, and what is actually possible with the assets one has. The evaluation of these factors creates a great deal of discretion.

- Discretion means that courts are able to reach an outcome that is fair in a particular case and recognises that every family's situation is slightly different. This also means that outcomes can be unpredictable and the relevant principles difficult to find and apply, especially for people who don't have a lawyer. This can encourage litigation, and costs. A more certain system would mean that some cases had unfair or harsh outcomes, but these may be outweighed by the benefit of having more predictable outcomes.

- In recent years, there has been a general trend away from discretion and towards rule-based outcomes.

5. Should people be able to reach their own enforceable agreements without court approval?
   - At present, it is not possible for the parties, through a nuptial agreement, to oust the jurisdiction of the court to exercise its powers.
   - In Key Case 3, *Radmacher v Granatino*, the Supreme Court decided that the court should give effect to a nuptial agreement that is freely entered into by each party with a full appreciation of its implications unless in the circumstances prevailing it would not be fair to hold the parties to their agreement. They said that the court should accord respect to the decision of a married couple as to the manner in which their financial affairs should be regulated.
   - There are three main arguments against the automatic recognition of nuptial agreements. These are that people in relationships need protecting from the consequences of bad decisions or unexpected life changes; that there is a wider social interest in parties supporting one another; and that prenuptial agreements are about opting out of concepts such as equality, partnership, and marriage as a joint endeavour, which are socially important and which protect the weaker (usually female) party.

Further Reading

BARLOW, A. 'Solidarity, Autonomy and Equality: Mixed Messages for the Family?' (2015) 27 *Child and Family Law Quarterly* 223

DIDUCK, A. 'What Is Family Law For?' (2011) 64 *Current Legal Problems* 287

LADY HALE, 'Equality and Autonomy in Family Law' (2011) 33 *Journal of Social Welfare and Family Law* 3
   - These three articles are excellent discussions of the principles underlying family law.

CRETNEY, S. *Family Law in the Twentieth Century: A History* (OUP, 2003)
   - A comprehensive, scholarly, much-respected history of marriage, divorce, finances, and children. Read it to understand where the law has come from, and thus to better understand the law today.

MILES J. and PROBERT, R. (eds) *Sharing Lives, Dividing Assets: An Inter-Disciplinary Study* (Hart Publishing, 2009)

- For those wanting empirical research on the financial consequences of relationships and relationship breakdown, this is a useful book.

THE LAW COMMISSION's Matrimonial Property, Needs, and Agreements project

- The Law Commission's consultations, summaries of responses, and recommendations are admirably clear discussions of the current law, its merits and problems. Their work on matrimonial property, needs, and agreements can be found on their website at: http://www.lawcom.gov.uk/project/matrimonial-property-needs-and-agreements/.

White v White [2001] 1 AC 596; *Miller v Miller/McFarlane v McFarlane* [2006] UKHL 24; *Charman v Charman (No. 4)* [2007] EWCA Civ 503; and *Radmacher v Granatino* [2010] UKSC 42

- These are the leading cases, and there is really no substitute for reading them.

5

Property Division on the Breakdown of Non-Matrimonial Relationships

Warren Barr

LEARNING OBJECTIVES

After reading this chapter you will be able to:

- Appreciate the mechanisms used in property law to provide proprietary or other entitlements for cohabitants, namely trusts of the family home (constructive and resulting) and proprietary estoppel, and the limits of those rules;

- Provide a critical analysis of the impact of the application of different rules to the rights of cohabitants;

- Understand the distinction between property law based rights and the impact of family relationships and obligations;

- Show an awareness the history of law reform in this area, and appreciate the reasons for the failure to produce a legislative solution.

DEBATES

After reading this chapter you should be equipped to discuss your opinion on the following central debates:

1 Is there a single approach to imputation of common intention in sole and joint legal ownership cases?

2 Should property division on non-marital breakdown be based on family law or property law principles?

3 Are common intention constructive trusts in the family home a new construct?

4 What are the limits of estoppel remedies?

1. Introduction

The family home is the key property asset that most family members will own in their lifetimes.[1] It is often not thought of as an asset in this sense, except perhaps at the time of purchase, as owners tend to have an emotive relationship with the place in which they live their lives, and raise any children. The home has a high financial value, but that is not the principal value attached to it.[2] The financial value of the property, and the ownership entitlements of those who live there, tends only to become a reality when a relationship ends, and one or both parties to the relationship want to leave the family home or have the property sold.

Unfortunately, many people living together in a home do not give any real thought to whether the property is owned between them, or what would happen if they separated. It is here that 'the unattainable precision of property law collides with the casual inarticulacy of home sharing'.[3] In the absence of any formal, legal agreement between the parties as to how the home is shared, strict property principles are applied. Hence, if only one person appears on the legal title to the home, that person is considered to own the home, to do with what they like, irrespective of who else lived with them. If the cohabiting couple are married or registered as civil partners, the court has distributive powers to provide a financial settlement or divide the ownership of the home (see Chapter 4). To the surprise of many, there is no concept of 'common law marriage' in English law,[4] so that a couple who are simply cohabiting have no rights or entitlements to the property at common law when the relationship ends. This is so even where they have lived together in a relationship for many years and spent considerable sums of money on making a home together and/or raising children. Matters of the family economy, such as who paid for food bills, family holidays, furnishings, and decorations, are all irrelevant. Without more, on the ending of a relationship the party named as the legal owner of the family home could make his or her former partner homeless, and would be under no obligation to provide any financial settlement from the home to benefit the partner. If there are children from the relationship, there is a duty to maintain any children and either of the cohabiting couple can apply for a property adjustment order to be made under the Children Act 1989 (see Chapter 6).

The nature of home sharing means that even where both cohabitants appear on the legal title to the property, they may own it together but be unclear as to their respective entitlements to the property. Do they own it equally or in unequal shares? What if one party to the relationship has borne the brunt of the financial side of the relationship while the other has assumed the burdens of daily family life? Should that alter any division of ownership between them, and, if so, to the benefit of whom?

The law of equity has come to the rescue of cohabiting couples and provided a series of mechanisms by which it seeks to provide rights in the home for the non-legal owner, or to decide the precise entitlements of joint legal owners. The principal mechanisms employed are the trust, particularly the constructive trust of common intention, and, more recently, the doctrine of proprietary estoppel. The fact that these rules are property rather than rights based is important; there is no right to property derived from being part of a relationship. Such a right only exists where settled rules and principles grant it

---

[1] Aspects of this chapter draw on the author's work in Pearce, R. and Barr, W. *Pearce and Stevens' Trusts and Equitable Obligations* (6th edn, OUP, 2014).

[2] See Fox O-Mahoney, L. *Conceptualising Home: Theories, Laws and Policies* (Hart Publishing, 2007).

[3] Briggs, A. 'Co-ownership and an Equitable Non Sequitur' (2012) 128 *Law Quarterly Review* 183, 183.

[4] Probert, R. 'Common Law Marriage: Myths and Misunderstandings' (2008) 20 *Child and Family Law Quarterly* 1.

(see Chapter 4 on property division on divorce and Chapter 6 on child support). Hence, in the cases where there is only one person in the relationship named on the legal title, there is an additional hurdle for a cohabitant to overcome before equity can consider the extent and nature of the entitlement—the creation, through property law principles, of a right in the home. This is known, as we shall see, as the *acquisition* phase of analysis. The entitlements granted in equity vary from a share of what is called the beneficial ownership of the property under a trust, which has a financial value and other rights attached to it, to occupational rights to live in the property for life, down to a simple financial entitlement to a share of the purchase monies of the home when sold. Identifying the nature of the cohabitants' respective rights to the family home is referred to as the *quantification* phase.

The circumstances in which common intention constructive trust and proprietary estoppel are employed, the nature of the rules applied and outcomes they produce are often open to criticism and can be confusing both in theory and in application. For example, despite clear comments in support from the highest judiciary in the land, matters of the family economy are still often overlooked in quantifying what the entitlements of cohabitants are and, as a result, the decisions reached are often (correctly) criticised as not doing justice between the parties. The law is constantly evolving through the cases, and, as we shall see, attempts at finding a legislative solution to the rights of cohabitants, have failed to date and show little prospect of success.

In this chapter, we will explore the reasons why cohabitants do not often think through their entitlements to the property and why the law has been slow to provide redress to them. We will consider the rules applicable to the application of trusts and proprietary estoppel to aid cohabitants, as well as critique them. We will also consider the practical impact of the remedies provided by outlining what happens when property is to be sold, before concluding by considering the many attempts at law reform and why they have, to date, failed to reach the statute books.

2. The family home: the issues stated

This chapter will primarily consider cohabiting couples, referred to as cohabitants, in situations where property is being shared by two people in an intimate relationship, normally of a sexual nature and the property is regarded as the family home. Of course, the members of a family are much more varied than this. Children do not feature directly in the context of the acquisition of rights in the family home. It is worth remembering that this is what this area is about: the acquisition of rights in property, as entitlements do not derive from the status of a family member, or any sense that they should be so entitled to an interest in the home simply on the basis of their status as a family member. Hence, the costs of caring for children, financial and in time, may factor into deciding the extent of an already established entitlement to a right in the family home for the adult cohabitant. There is no system of allocation of rights through equitable intervention to provide rights in the family home for the children themselves.

Changing patterns of home ownership, and the rising cost of entry to the property ladder, mean that adult children may now live in the family home, or contribute to the cost of it, so that they too may benefit from a chance to acquire rights. Similarly, elderly relatives might be living in the family home, and may have helped finance the purchase, or contribute to the expenses of life in the family home. They may also be entitled to an interest in equity. The focus of this chapter, as stated, is on the two adult partners in the relationship. There are, however, many reported cases in which different relationships are considered, especially in relation to proprietary estoppel. There are a number of cases where someone has been persuaded to provide support for an older person by providing unpaid personal care, or by working on their farm without being fairly paid. They may be able to acquire rights using the same principles as those that apply between couples.

Before the Second World War, most people in Britain rented the house in which they lived. Nowadays most people aspire to live in homes that are owned by at least one of the people living there.[5] The increasing recognition of the equal place of women, their growing economic contribution to marriage through their participation in the labour market, and especially the growth in, and acceptance of, divorce, made it essential to determine when a wife enjoyed a share of the ownership of her matrimonial home.[6] The issues have been the same for female cohabitants, but they have not seen the same recognition of entitlement, other than through the application of equitable property law principles.

2.1 No special category of family property at common law

The starting point is that the property rights of people living in the family home are determined by the ordinary laws of property in England and Wales. English law has resisted any civil law conception of 'community of property' between spouses, vesting ownership of family property, equally in both. This concept has also been adopted in most of the Commonwealth, in the common law world.[7] Instead, the English common law originally vested all property in a marriage in the hands of the husband.

Statutory reform for married couples was a painfully slow process. The Married Women's Property Act 1882 had, broadly, the effect that all wives were capable of acquiring and owning their own property free from their husband's control. This looked like a significant blow for equality of rights in marriage, but just because it removed barriers so that wives could own family property, it did not mean that they did in practice. Given the lack of such equality in the workforce, it was still the husband who was the breadwinner and had the financial means to purchase property. The most significant provision in the 1882 was s. 17, which empowered the courts to resolve disputes as to ownership and possession of the family home, and to make such order as they 'thought fit'. This sounded more impressive in theory than it was in practice, as many judges interpreted the provision in a narrow sense of declaring what rights the husband and wife already had in the property, rather than allowing distribution of property between the parties. Others thought it gave effect to division of family assets. It was subsequently confirmed that the court could only declare rights under s. 17, not vary or adjust them.[8]

It was not until the passing of the Matrimonial Causes Act 1973,[9] itself subsequently amended, that wide-ranging powers were conferred on the divorce court to reallocate a married couple's assets on divorce. Spousal rights have been since been further enhanced—following the Matrimonial Homes Act 1967 (now contained in s. 30(1) of the Family Law Act 1996), spouses were given an automatic, statutory right of occupation in the family home (or home right). Similarly, the Inheritance (Provision for Family and Dependents) Act 1975 gave the courts wide powers to make reasonable provision for spouses and family out of the deceased's estate. Cohabiting same-sex couples, like heterosexual couples, have no rights to the family home arising from their status as cohabitants. Same-sex cohabitants

---

[5] See Law Commission, *Cohabitation: The Financial Consequences of Relationship Breakdown* (Law Com No. 207, 2007, Parts I and II.

[6] See Cretney, S. *Family Law in the Twentieth Century* (OUP, 2003); Barlow, A. and James, G. 'Regulating Marriage and Cohabitation in 21st Century Britain' (2004) 67 *Modern Law Review* 143.

[7] See Law Commission, *Sharing Homes* (Law Com No. 278, 2002) Pt IV.

[8] *Gissing v Gissing* [1971] AC 886.

[9] Technically, this was a re-enactment of the Matrimonial Proceedings and Property Act 1970.

are subject to the same property law rules as opposite-sex cohabitants. It is only where they become registered civil partners under the Civil Partnerships Act 2004 that they have rights akin to married couples on the dissolution of the relationship, or if they marry under the Marriage (Same Sex Couples) Act 2013.

Context 1: Rights for Non-Married Couples

There has traditionally been significant opposition to providing similar rights to unmarried couples as married couples or civil partners enjoy. The Law Commission argued strongly for a concept of community of property in its discussion paper, 'Sharing Homes'.[10] This would have meant that there was a requirement to provide for families, giving entitlements to non-married cohabitants as of right. Consultees responded forcefully and negatively, and the proposal was dropped. There is also evidence that social attitudes may have changed, and that the law should treat married and unmarried couples in the same way when relationships break down, particularly where children are present.[11] The opportunity, though, has passed.

Such rights exist following legislative reform in other common law countries. In Australia, property rights of unmarried couples, including same-sex couples, are recognised through primary legislation—Family Law Amendment (De Facto Financial Matters) 2008 (amending the Family Law Act 1975).[12] Similar rights also exist in New Zealand, which passed the New Zealand Property (Relationships) Amendment Act 2001 to enable them. Closer to home, our civil law cousins in Scotland have introduced a statutory scheme dealing with the property rights of cohabiting couples in Scotland; the Family Law (Scotland) Act 2006.[13]

It remains a frustrating point that there has been no legislative reform in England and Wales, but, as we shall see, a private Members Bill, the Cohabitation Rights Bill, has offered some limited hope of legislative action.

It is worth repeating that none of these statutory rights are available to unmarried cohabiting couples. It is also a regrettable fact that the majority of cases that come before the courts to determine rights in the family home involve unmarried cohabitants.[14] Unless they are both named in the legal title to the property, the non-legal owning cohabitant has no rights in common law or statute to an entitlement to property beyond limited protection for the maintenance of a cohabitant on the death of their partner under the Inheritance (Provision for Family and Dependants) Act 1975. The title will be in the name of one person only either because at the time the home was purchased, it had been expressly conveyed into the name of one of them only, or where one partner already owns a home, and the other moved into it. In both cases, the common law offers no assistance. It does not matter that the cohabitant might have contributed to the cost of acquiring the family home or to the expenses of life in the family home. It even does not matter where these actions were motivated by a belief, encouraged by the legal owner, that the cohabitant would acquire a stake in the home.

---

[10] See Law Commission, *Sharing Homes* (Law Com No. 278, 2002) Pt IV.

[11] Barlow, A. *et al* 'Cohabitation and the Law: Myths, Money and the Media' in A Park *et al* (eds), *British Social Attitudes: The 24th Report* (Sage, 2008).

[12] See Baker, H. 'New Cohabitation Law in Australia' [2009] *Family Law* 1201.

[13] For a good commentary, see Hess, E. 'The Rights of Cohabitants: When and How Will the Law be Reformed?' [2009] *Family Law* 405.

[14] Law Commission, *Cohabitation: The Financial Consequences of Relationship Breakdown* (Law Com No. 179, 2006) 47.

CONTEXT 2: THE GROWTH IN COHABITATION

There is a clear move away from parties occupying the family home as married couples, whether opposite-sex or same-sex couples, or as registered civil partners. In 2016, the Office of National Statistics (ONS) noted that there were some 18.9 million families in the UK, of which 12.7 million were married or civil partner couple families.[15] So, marriage remains the dominant form of family relationship. Nonetheless, the same report found that cohabiting couple families were the fastest growing family type between 1996 and 2016, more than doubling from 1.5 million families to 3.3 million families. Of these, around 87,000 were same-sex couple families. This may be a generational issue, and The Marriage Foundation in June 2014, building on ONS, found that there was a generation gap in marriage, which revealed that 47% of women and 48% of men aged 20 said they intend never to marry.

However, rather than any breakdown of the family unit often talked about in the popular media, these findings may simply be a reflection that people are happy to spend their life with a partner without feeling a need to formalise the relationship either religiously or in law. This presents a problem, legally, when the relationship between cohabitants ends if the rights to property are not clearly defined. In the family law context, it also creates practical problems of housing post-relationship breakdown and the financial resources necessary to establish the parties as individuals.

2.2 The intervention of equity

The law of equity exists to fill gaps in the common law, and it is best thought of as a separate body of rules that supplement the law, even though courts now administer both law and equity together.[16] Equity recognises rights that the common law did not, and, as we shall see, the principal method used to give a cohabitant a right in the family home is the trust. This is a device for separating control and benefit over any type of property, which we consider in 3.1. A right recognised by equity means that the cohabitant is not left without some redress against the legal owner of the family home on separation.

2.3 A simple solution: declaring interests

It is easy to understand why couples, embarking on a relationship together, and buying their first home may not think about what would happen on breakdown of the relationship and if they separated. It is uncomfortable to consider the end of the relationship at any time, particularly at the outset of it. Life rarely follows the legal conception of what people are supposed to do in their lives, so it is not surprising that couples do not necessarily think to declare their legal interests in the property. It is even less surprising that where people move in to a property that is already owned by one of the partners to the relationship, legal rights are rarely at the top of the discussion agenda. Of course, such discussions can and often do take place over time, and, as we shall see, it is the fact of these conversations which has provided a way for equity to allow interests to be granted under a trust, as they provide the 'common intention' necessary for equity to intervene in the affairs of the parties. This still does not answer the question as to why many cohabiting

---

[15] ONS Statistical Bulletin, 'Families and Households in the UK: 2016'. Available at: https://www.ons.gov.uk/peoplepopulationandcommunity/birthsdeathsandmarriages/families/bulletins/familiesandhouseholds/2016, accessed 24 September 2017.

[16] See further, Pearce R. and Barr W. *Pearce & Stevens Trusts and Equitable Obligations* (6th edn, OUP, 2014) Chapter 1.

couples do not legally formalise the property rights arising as a consequence of their relationship.

Part of this may be ignorance of the legal principles involved, and the (perceived and real) costs and complexity of legal advice and action. It may also be that couples assume that both parties would behave reasonably on relationship breakdown, though this is often misplaced optimism, as the cases demonstrate.[17] The other part is, as discussed in Chapter 2 of this book, the enduring myth of common law marriage, or, put more strongly, the sustained and mistaken belief of a large proportion of the population that cohabiting relationships of a certain quality or duration are given special recognition. The British Social Attitudes survey in 2006 found that 51% of respondents believed that an unmarried couple who live together for some time 'definitely' or 'probably' have a 'common law marriage' which gives them the same legal rights as married couples.[18]

The formal actions that cohabiting couples can take to declare their property rights in the family home are tolerably clear and relatively inexpensive. In most of the reported case law, the problem that required litigation would not have arisen if the parties had given sufficient thought to the issue and had chosen to create an express trust, declaring how the beneficial interests in the property would be held. This can be declared at any time during the relationship, and the formalities are considered briefly in 3.2. Likewise, if the purchase of the family home is co-financed by both parties to the relationship, it is a simple matter of conveyancing practice by the acting solicitors to ensure that both parties are entered on the legal title and to explain the different methods by which a family home can be owned.[19]

It would be better for all concerned if couples living together did not have to rely upon the assistance of equity. The courts have stressed the need for parties who decide to live together in a family home to make express provision, setting out their rights and entitlements to the property. Legal practitioners who are involved in home purchases also bear a responsibility to try to ensure that the parties are clear about their intentions with respect to the ownership. This is perhaps most clearly stated by Ward LJ in *Carlton v Goodman*:[20]

> I ask in despair how often this court has to remind conveyancers that they would save the clients a great deal of later difficulty if only they would sit the purchasers down, explain the difference between a joint tenancy and a tenancy in common, ascertain what they want and then expressly declare in the conveyance of transfer how the beneficial interest is to be held because that will be conclusive and save all argument. When are conveyancers going to do this as a matter of invariable standard practice? This court has urged that time after time. Perhaps conveyancers do not always read the law reports. I will try one more time: ALWAYS TRY TO AGREE ON AND THEN RECORD HOW THE BENEFICIAL INTEREST IS TO BE HELD. It is not very difficult to do.

This, however, is rarely done, as the constant stream of cases involving the family home coming before the courts demonstrates.

---

[17] Barlow, A., Burgoyne, C., and Smithson, J. *The Living Together Campaign—An Investigation of its Impact on Legally Aware Cohabitants*, Ministry of Justice Research Series 5/07 (2007) 32–8. Available at: http://www.lawcom.gov.uk/wp-content/uploads/2015/06/living-together-research-report.pdf, accessed 20 June 2017.

[18] See Barlow, A. *et al* 'Cohabitation and the Law: Myths, Money and the Media', in A. Park *et al* (eds), *British Social Attitudes: The 24th Report* (Sage, 2008) 40–2.

[19] A format exists to allow this: see Land Registration Rules 2003, TR 1 and Declarations form. There is also a form (JO), which in Land Registry practice allows a declaration of trust interests.

[20] [2002] EWCA Civ 545, at [44].

3. Trusts in the family home

Here, we will consider the operation of the trust as it is used to benefit cohabitants. We will consider express trusts, which are used in the (rare) situations where cohabitants decide to formally declare their interests in property, then the common intention constructive trust, before ending with the resulting trust, a type of implied trust which has fallen out of favour in the family home with the continued evolution of the constructive trust.

3.1 **An introduction to trusts**

We have come this far into this chapter without any clear understanding of what a trust is. The answer to that question is a textbook in its own right,[21] but we can describe some of the key features of the trust mechanism, so that we can understand its application to ownership of the family home.

Put simply, trusts allow the ownership of property to be separated from its management. Where property is subject to a trust, there is a duality of ownership, and a distinction must be drawn between the legal ownership and the equitable ownership. A person enjoying the legal ownership of the trust property is referred to as a 'trustee', and a person enjoying the equitable ownership is a 'beneficiary'. Equity imposes multiple duties on the legal owner, the trustee, to ensure that they control the property, not for their own benefit, but for the benefit of the beneficiary or beneficiaries. For that reason, we think of the beneficiaries of a trust as being the owners of the property, as they receive the benefits of ownership, even though the legal control of the property rests with the trustees.

Let's consider an example. Mary and John are unmarried cohabitants in the family home. John already owned the home when the relationship started, so he was the sole legal owner. If there is no trust, John is the only person in the relationship with rights over the home, and, if the relationship between Mary and John breaks down, Mary has no legal entitlements to the family home. John could cast Mary out into the street, or sell the home and retain all of the proceeds of sale himself. If, however, a trust is found to exist in this situation, matters are very different. John is still the sole legal owner, as he is the only person whose name will appear on the land ownership documents. However, John now has the legal title as a trustee. This means that while he has control of the home (he is the person, for example, who could sell the home to another), he can no longer simply act in his own interests. In this situation, John will have to consider Mary's rights, as Mary, as the beneficiary, is entitled to the benefits of any property ownership. If the relationship breaks down, Mary will be entitled to some say in whether she should be able to stay in the property, and, if the property is sold, Mary will be entitled to share in the proceeds of sale. Figure 5.1 illustrates the definition of a trust of the family home.

Apart from whether or not a trust exists so that Mary has an entitlement to the home as a beneficiary of a trust, it becomes important to know the extent of the beneficial ownership in a trust. In our example, this would determine the share of the proceeds of sale of the family home that Mary would be entitled to. If Mary had a 30% share of the beneficial interest, on sale they will obtain 30% of the sale price. Whether or not an entitlement to a beneficial interest under a trust exists is referred to as the 'acquisition' of an interest by cohabitants like Mary. Determining the extent or size of the beneficial interest, once established, is referred to as the 'quantification' of the interest held under a trust. The actual rights that a beneficial interest might confer on a cohabitant like Mary are as much a matter of land law as they are of trusts, but the basic nature of these rights is outlined at section 6.

---

[21] See, e.g., Pearce, R. and Barr, W. *Pearce & Stevens Trusts and Equitable Obligations* (6th edn, OUP, 2014), Chapter 10.

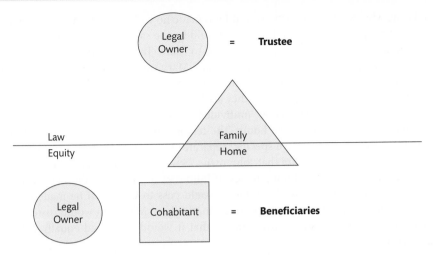

Figure 5.1 A trust of the family home

3.2 **Express trusts**

Express trusts are the method by which cohabitants can declare their express interests in the family home, but, as already discussed this rarely happens in practice. In an express trust, the beneficial shares are set out in the document creating the trust (known as the 'trust instrument'). Cohabitants can declare an express trust at the time the home is bought, or at any later date (as, for instance, where one party moves in with the other).

An express trust of the family home must be declared or evidenced in writing[22] and it must comply with the general rules that apply to the creation of any express trust of certainty and constitution.[23] There is, unfortunately, no requirement that where two or more parties purchase a property together a trust should be declared, even though a simple form (J0) exists for legal advisers to facilitate this.[24]

One complication arises from the fact that a beneficial interest in the family home is an interest in land. The nature of the beneficial shares in land will depend on the method of co-ownership declared under an express trust. There are two possibilities in equity, either that the beneficiaries hold under a 'joint tenancy' or a 'tenancy in common'.[25]

The difference between the two is important. Let's return to John and Mary, who since we left them are still unmarried, but now have a baby girl, Clara. If John and Mary declare themselves joint tenants in equity, they are viewed together as owning the whole of the property.[26] Separately, they own nothing. If John were to die, Mary would

---

[22] Law of Property Act 1925, s. 53(1)(b); Law of Property (Miscellaneous Provisions) Act 1989, s. 2.

[23] There must be a clear intention to create a trust, and the terms of the trust must be clear as to how the home is to be held between the parties. This is known as the 'three certainties' of an express trust. The property must be vested in the legal owner as trustee, which is referred to as the fact that the trust must be completely constituted. See, e.g., Pearce, R. and Barr, W. *Pearce & Stevens Trusts and Equitable Obligations* (6th edn, OUP, 2014) Chapter 7.

[24] See Moran, A. 'Anything to Declare? Express Declarations of Trust on Land Registry Form TR1: The Doubts Raised in *Stack v Dowden*' [2007] *The Conveyancer and Property Lawyer* 364; Cooke, E. 'The Wake of *Stack v Dowden* in the House of Lords' (2008) 20 *Child and Family Law Quarterly* 255.

[25] There can only ever be a joint tenancy at law, simply as a process to allow land to be easily bought and sold—see, e.g., Smith, R. *Property Law* (Longman, 2011) Chapters 14 and 15.

[26] See, e.g., *AG Securities v Vaughan* [1990] 1 AC 417 (HL).

receive the whole of the property, even if John made no will. This has the benefit of certainty and simplicity. However, the result would be the same even if John had made a will leaving his beneficial interest in the home to Clara. This right, which takes effect at the moment of death, is called 'survivorship', and Mary would become the sole owner of the property, as there is no longer anyone to be a co-owner with. If John and Mary are instead tenants in common in equity, they are both viewed as having 'undivided shares' in the property. They are classed as 'undivided', as they are shares of the value, not of particular rooms or areas in the home. The tenancy in common is the only method where John and Mary can have specific, separate shares in their home. For example, the express trust might declare that John owns 75% of the home, Mary the remaining 25%.[27] This cannot create a joint tenancy. If John dies in this situation, his will would take effect as normal and his 75% interest would pass to Clara.[28] If he made no will, however, John's interest would not pass automatically to Mary, but would instead pass under the statutory intestacy provisions so that it would be shared equally between Mary and Clara.[29]

It follows that, in most family relationships, where there is an express trust, the cohabitating couple should declare themselves tenants in common in specific shares. This allows maximum flexibility and reduces the scope for arguments over the extent of the interest when the relationship between the cohabitants breaks down. There are good reasons to make a will beyond any concerns of the family home, which include savings in estate duty and distributing one's property on death as one sees fit.

Where a joint tenancy has instead been preferred, it is worth noting that a joint tenancy can be converted by deeds or action into a tenancy in common by a process known as 'severance'.[30] If the relationship between the joint tenants in the family home breaks down irreparably, the cohabitants would be well advised to serve a written notice of severance to allow entitlement to specific shares in the property by converting the joint tenancy into a tenancy in common.[31] In practice, this will only happen where the cohabiting couple seek legal advice on what action to take on the ending of the relationship.

It is worth nothing that even where a tenancy in common is created, there is no requirement that the extent of the shares in the property is expressly defined in the trust instrument. So, the document creating the trust may state that the cohabitants hold the property as 'tenants in common' in equity, but not whether they each own 50%, or other division. In those cases where a tenancy in common exists, but no demonstrable shares have been stated in the trust instrument, there is a presumption of equality in terms of the size of the beneficial interests, that is, 50–50, but this presumption may be displaced by a contrary common intention of the parties. There must be some evidence during the course of the relationship that the parties had an intention that the extent of their share in the property would not be an equal split. This is, as we shall see, the factual situation which presented itself in both *Stack v Dowden* and *Jones v Kernott*, and the variation takes effect through a constructive trust of common intention.

---

[27] See, e.g., *AE Jones v EW Jones* [1977] 1 WLR 438 (CA).

[28] Interestingly, as Clara is a minor, she would not be able to own the beneficial interest herself anyway. It would be held on trust for Clara until she reached the age of legal majority.

[29] See Inheritance and Trustees' Powers Act 2014.

[30] It is not possible to so convert a tenancy in common into a joint tenancy. If all the tenants in common agree, they could change the nature of their ownership of property by creating an express trust declaring that they now hold the property as joint tenants.

[31] See Law of Property Act 1925, s. 36(2).

3.3 **Constructive trusts of common intention**

Constructive trusts are referred to 'implied trusts', because they are implied from the factual circumstances by the courts, rather than deliberately created by the parties concerned. This means that a trust dividing the beneficial ownership between the cohabitants can arise, even if they did not expressly state that they wanted to share the property through an express trust. Constructive trusts are not implied on the whim of the courts, but on settled principles identifying factual circumstances where a trust dividing the ownership of the property is deemed to have arisen. The effect of the relationship between cohabitants, and their intentions in sharing the property as a home, is one of these factual circumstances. The form of constructive trust that has been used in the context of the family home is known as the 'common intention constructive trust'. The trust is so called because Lord Diplock in *Pettitt v Pettitt*[32] said that the approach to be adopted in cases involving the family home should be based upon seeking the 'common intention' of the parties to the relationship in owning the home.

 Key Legislation 1: Law of Property Act 1925, s. 53

(1) Subject to the provision hereinafter contained with respect to the creation of interests in land by parol—

    (a) no interest in land can be created or disposed of except by writing signed by the person creating or conveying the same, or by his agent thereunto lawfully authorised in writing, or by will, or by operation of law;

    (b) a declaration of trust respecting any land or any interest therein must be manifested and proved by some writing signed by some person who is able to declare such trust or by his will;

    (c) a disposition of an equitable interest or trust subsisting at the time of the disposition, must be in writing signed by the person disposing of the same, or by his agent thereunto lawfully authorised in writing or by will.

(2) This section does not affect the creation or operation of resulting, implied or constructive trusts.

The family home is an estate in land,[33] so the acquisition of a beneficial interest under a trust by a cohabitant is the creation of an interest in land. Normally, this section requires that the creation of most interests in land must be evidenced in writing, as provided by s. 53(1)(b). An expressly created trust over the family home must meet this requirement but, as we have seen, many cohabitants do not complete this formality.

    By contrast, a constructive trust of the family home, which is based on a common intention between the cohabitants to share ownership of the property, does not require writing to be effective. This is only possible because s. 53(2) provides that the requirement of writing imposed by the statute is not applicable in the case of a constructive trust. Without this, the mechanism would have no application in the family home to help cohabitants, whether they were seeking to acquire an interest in the home, or declare the size of an existing beneficial share in the home. The effect of s. 53(2) is to enable cohabitants to avoid the formality of writing for the creation of a trust over the family home, if the requirements for establishing a 'common intention' are made out as the basis for a constructive trust.

---

[32] [1970] AC 777.

[33] In English law, all ownership rights are expressed as 'estates', which describe bundles of rights exercised over the relevant areas of land (described as 'parcels' of land).

There are two elements for establishing a common intention constructive trust over the family home:

1. The cohabitant who is the legal owner has said or done something regarding ownership of the family home that makes it inequitable to deny a beneficial interest in the property to the non-legal owner;

2. The non-legal owner must have acted to their detriment, relying on the words or deeds regarding ownership of the property to acquire a beneficial interest.[34]

There are two major issues that arise from this definition:

1. What evidence is necessary to demonstrate a common intention?

The finding of a common intention is an artificial exercise. If the parties concerned had given real thought to the ownership of the home, they would have made express provision as to their entitlements. The court is construing the words and deeds of the parties, particularly the legal owner, in a context they might never have truly intended, to infer a common intention that in fact both partners might never have recognised themselves as having.

2. What is the nature of the detriment that the law accepts to allow a trust interest to be created?

The requirement of detriment was interpreted in an extremely narrow sense, on the basis that what was at dispute was an interest in property, so, necessarily some form of financial contribution to the property was the most obvious form of detriment. Even in relation to financial contributions, debate raged as to whether only direct contributions to the purchase price, or monetary contributions which added value to the financial value of the home such as renovation or extension work, were sufficient. Indirect payments by the non-legal owner, such as meeting household expenses so that the legal owner could meet mortgage repayments, might not be classified as detriment. Other, wider elements of the relationship, such as the cohabitant taking sole or major responsibility for running the home or looking after the children were of extreme importance in terms of the family relationship and the creation of the sense of 'family home', but were much harder to quantify, and also much more difficult to relate to the creation of a property interest in the home.

Nevertheless, in quantifying the extent of the interest, the law quickly moved beyond a simple calculation based on any financial contribution to a wider sense of factors to give effect to the 'common intentions' of the parties. This means that the value of the interest the non-legal owner acquired under the trust could be greater than the value of their financial contributions to the property, for example, even if they had contributed only 5% of the value of the purchase price of the property, the extent of their beneficial interest could be much higher, based on the parties 'common intention'. The decision over the division of the cohabitants' respective beneficial interests under a common intention constructive trust is now based of a wide range of factors, taking into account most aspects of family law in the home.

For many years, the leading case in determining these questions has been *Lloyds Bank plc v Rosset*,[35] where Lord Bridge sought to rationalise and restate all of the case law into a framework that could be applied in future cases.

---

[34] [1971] AC 886, 905.   [35] [1991] 1 AC 107.

Key Case 1: *Lloyds Bank v Rosset* [1991] 1 AC 107 (HL)

Unusually, this concerned a married couple, and the issue was whether Mrs Rosset had a beneficial interest that could take priority to the interests of the mortgage lender on the sale of the property, that is, she had acquired a beneficial interest under a trust before the mortgage company had granted a mortgage over the property. Mr and Mrs Rosset were married in 1972. In 1982, Mr Rosset became entitled to a substantial sum of money under a family trust fund and the couple found a house that required complete renovation. It was purchased for £57,500 in the sole name of Mr Rosset, on the basis that the trustee of the fund had refused to advance the money for a purchase in joint names. The cost of the renovation work was provided by Mr Rosset alone. Mrs Rosset had, however, helped with the renovation work. She had decorated some bedrooms and prepared others for decoration, as well as supervised the work of the builders who were carrying out the renovation work. She claimed to be entitled to a share of the ownership by way of a constructive trust, even though Mr Rosset was the sole legal owner of the property.

The judge at first instance held that, although there was no express agreement that Mrs Rosset was intended to enjoy a share of the beneficial ownership, he could infer a common intention to share from the fact that she had assisted with the renovations, as this had been work that she would not have undertaken unless she was to have an interest in the house. The Court of Appeal agreed that Mrs Rosset had acquired an interest in the home. However, the House of Lords held that no such intention could be inferred from the work she had done, and that, in the absence of an express common intention stating that the parties intended to share ownership of the house, no constructive trust had arisen in Mrs Rosset's favour. Mr Rosset remained the absolute owner of the house and Mrs Rosset had not acquired a beneficial interest in the property under a trust.

Lord Bridge made a division between two situations in which a cohabitant could acquire an interest in the family home under a common intention constructive trust. In the first situation, the parties could expressly agree to share the home. If there was an express agreement to share, no financial contribution to the purchase property was required by the non-legal owner to acquire a beneficial interest under a trust. There had to be some act done on the basis of the agreement which demonstrated some form of detriment by the non-legal owner.

In the second situation, the parties' 'common intention' to share ownership of the home was to be inferred purely from the conduct of the parties. In this situation, where the intention to share was inferred from conduct, only something in the nature of a financial contribution to the purchase of the family home would demonstrate detriment by the non-legal owner. Without this detriment, a constructive trust would not be implied to give the non-legal owner a beneficial interest in the home.

At the end of the cohabitation relationship, to demonstrate acquisition of a property right in the family home, the non-legal owner either had to show evidence of an express agreement to share ownership, or a financial contribution to the purchase of the family home. If this could not be demonstrated, they had no right of ownership over the family home they had lived in with their partner, whatever other contributions they may have made to the maintenance of the family, support of their partner's career, and care of children or other relatives.

The decision in *Rosset* was the reference point in situations where a cohabitant, who was not the legal owner of the property, had to demonstrate a right to acquire an interest in the family home. Matters were always different where both cohabitants already had a beneficial interest in the family home, as they were joint legal owners. In this situation, where there was no express trust declaring that they held the equitable title as joint tenants or tenants in common (see 3.2), it was always assumed that the equitable title was held jointly.

Where legal ownership is joint, it is normally assumed that, since the cohabitants have not expressly stated what the division of ownership is, it should be shared 50–50.[36] Following *Stack v Dowden*[37] and *Jones v Kernott*,[38] a new approach was suggested. It is now clear that the initial presumption of equal joint ownership can be displaced by evidence of a different common intention as to the division of ownership. This intention could change over the course of the relationship, and it would be up the court to infer this intention as to the size of the beneficial shares from the deeds and actions of the parties, or, if that was not possible, to impute an intention on the basis of fairness.

> ### ❓ DEBATE 1: IS THERE A SINGLE APPROACH TO IMPUTATION OF COMMON INTENTION IN SOLE AND JOINT LEGAL OWNERSHIP CASES?

The approach taken to finding a common intention in *Stack v Dowden* and *Jones v Kernott* begged the question whether, in fact, the courts still had to follow the approach to acquisition of an interest in *Lloyds Bank v Rosset* in sole ownership cases. Instead of requiring an express agreement between the legal and non-legal owner, or a contribution to the purchase price by the non-legal owner, should it be possible to simply infer or even impute a common intention where the parties have cohabited, on the basis that the home is shared and so the property rights should be shared also? This would be a very important development of the law for non-legal owner cohabitants. Effectively, their right to own the family home would be imputed from the fact they had shared a home with the legal owner, removing the requirement to demonstrate an agreement or detriment such as a financial contribution.

This issue is still unsettled, but there is strong reason to argue that, as a matter of law, the *Rosset* approach to acquire an interest remains. Neither *Stack* nor *Kernott* sought to overrule *Rosset*, and they were both decisions concerning the entitlements of cohabitants who were already joint legal owners of the family home. The only issue to be directly considered in those cases was the size of the beneficial share each cohabitant was entitled to (the quantification of their beneficial interests). There was no need to address whether a cohabitant was entitled to a beneficial interest in the family home (the acquisition of interests). Indeed, in *Jones v Kernott* itself, Lord Wilson felt the issue was open for consideration, as it did not fall on the facts before the Supreme Court, but that it would 'merit careful thought'.[39] Lady Hale and Lord Walker, who together gave the leading speech, noted that 'sole legal owner cases have a different starting point . . . because the claimant . . . has the burden of establishing some sort of implied trust . . .'[40] Having outlined the factors applicable to determining the size of a beneficial share, they also said of single owner cases:

> The first issue is whether it was intended that the other party have any beneficial interest in the property at all. If he does, the second issue is what that interest is. There is no presumption of joint beneficial ownership. But their common intention has once again to be deduced objectively from their conduct.[41]

Read together, these statements suggest that the impact of the Supreme Court decision to sole legal owner in the family home does not extend or alter the principles upon which an entitlement to an interest in the home is acquired. The two-stage approach of establishing a beneficial interest under a trust either by express agreement, or by financial contribution by

---

[36] *Jones v Kernott*, at [15] (Lord Walker and Lady Hale, confirming existing law). [37] [2007] 2 AC 432.
[38] [2011] UKSC 53. [39] [2011] UKSC 53, at [84]. [40] [2011] UKSC 53, at [17].
[41] [2011] UKSC 53, at [52].

the non-legal owner set out in *Lloyds Bank v Rosset*, still applies. This interpretation of the law has been followed in many of the later cases, such as *Geary v Rankine*:[42]

> Whether the beneficial interests are to be shared at all is still a question of a party's actual shared intentions. An imputed intention only arises where the court is satisfied that the parties' actual common intention, express or inferred, was that the beneficial interest would be shared, but cannot make a finding about proportions in which they were to be shared.

It also speaks to the property law nature of the constructive trust, rather than focusing on the family relationship between the parties as the basis of any entitlement. There is a role for certainty and predictability in the property entitlements of parties, and, viewed from this perspective:

> Problems of uncertainty might well abound if a more holistic approach were taken to the acquisition question, and the answer to the fundamental question whether a legal non-owner does or does not have an interest in a given piece of property could become extremely difficult to predict before litigation.[43]

Moreover, inferring an interest without first showing that it had been acquired would remove the need for a cohabitant to demonstrate that they had acted to their detriment in some way. This would be a move to entitlements arising from intentions of the parties derived from their familial relationship, rather than through recognised principles of property law. There is no mention of detrimental reliance in either *Stack v Dowden* or *Jones v Kernott*, but, of course, in those cases the cohabitant was already entitled to some interest in equity by being named on the legal title of the property.

Not all decisions are so consistent. The emphasis remains on establishing an entitlement by the non-legal owner on property law principles, rather than deriving their interest from the existence of the cohabitation relationship. So, in *Capehorn v Harris*[44] the Court of Appeal clearly stated that it was not open in sole legal owner cases for the court to impute an intention to acquire an interest, and because the trial judge had done just that when no agreement was evident between the parties, Mr Harris was deprived of an interest behind a constructive trust.[45] The case law, nevertheless, demonstrates confusion and the temptation to adopt a simpler approach to establishing an interest in the family home.[46] In *Bhura v Bhura*,[47] Mostyn J simply asked: what are the parties' beneficial shares? There was no distinction made between acquiring an interest and quantifying it, once acquired. The Privy Council in *Abbott v Abbott*[48] expressly disapproved of the approach in *Rosset* and found that the approach of inference of a common intention should be enough to allow joint division of assets on the facts of that case. This, of course, is persuasive only.

The risk for sole legal owners is that, when their partner moves into their property, they lose part of their interest to the cohabitant, without any express statement acknowledging this, or any financial contributions made by their partner. However, it is arguable that imputing an intention to share ownership of the property when the parties are sharing a home, irrespective of the names on the legal title, is a more realistic reflection of the relationship and

---

[42] [2012] EWHC 1387, at [19] (Lewison J). See also *Aspden v Elvy* [2012' EWHC 1387; *Capehorn v Harris* [2015] EWCA Civ 955 (CA); *Barnes v Philips* [2015] EWCA Civ 1056 (CA).

[43] Sloan, B. 'Keeping Up With the Jones Case: Establishing Constructive Trusts in "Sole Legal Owner" Scenarios' (2015) 35 *Legal Studies* 226.

[44] 2015] EWCA Civ 955 (CA).   [45] See, also, *Barnes v Philips* [2015] EWCA Civ 1056 (CA).

[46] See Gardner, S. 'Heresy—or Not?—in Family Property?' (2015) 79 *The Conveyancer and Property Lawyer* 332.

[47] [2014] EWHC 727 (Fam).   [48] [2012] EWHC 1387.

the nature of family life, even if it gives rise to uncertainty of ownership in some cases. On the weight of authority, without a decision of the Supreme Court to the contrary, the approach to common intention constructive trusts still falls into either one or two stages, depending on whether the cohabitant is seeking to simply declare the size of their existing beneficial entitlement (joint legal owners), or acquire a beneficial interest before that entitlement can be decided (sole legal owners).

What is clear, after both *Stack v Dowden* and *Jones v Kernott*, is that the principles applicable to deciding the extent of each parties' beneficial interest, the division of the property between the parties, are the same in sole and joint legal owner cases. So, if a sole legal owner demonstrates that they have acquired a beneficial interest, the precise extent of the beneficial share will be inferred from the deeds or actions of the parties, or, where that is not possible, will be imputed by the courts.

The legal steps applicable are as follows:

1. Acquisition of a property interest by claimant; (only relevant to sole legal owner cases).
2. Quantification of the property interest (same rules applicable, to sole and joint legal owner cases, no matter how the interest is acquired).[49]

We now turn to some more detailed examples of how these steps operate in practice.

3.3.1 Acquisition of a beneficial interest: sole legal owner cases

Lord Bridge in *Lloyds Bank v Rosset*, as we have seen, made a distinction between situations in which the parties had an express common intention to share the family home demonstrated through an agreement, and those where it was raised by conduct alone. It is clear that either pathway to an interest requires both establishing the common intention and an element of detriment on the part of the claimant cohabitant on the basis of that common intention.

What has not been mentioned before, is that the search is supposed to be for the actual common intentions that the parties have manifested, not a common intention created for them by the courts. In the words of Lord Morris of Borth-y-Guest in *Gissing v Gissing*,[50] cited with approval by Lord Bridge:[51]

> The courts cannot devise agreements which the parties never made. The court cannot ascribe intentions which the parties in fact never had.

The court says it is 'discovering' an agreement either from the words used, or the conduct of the parties, which the parties would recognise if they had been forced to sit down and articulate how they thought the home would be owned between them. This is despite the legal title being in one name only. By requiring consideration of whether a common intention can be established, it is not the court imposing a view of what it considers fair in the circumstances of a particular case by giving the cohabitant without legal title an interest in the home. This has shaped the development of the law, as we shall see.

Nature of an agreement

Looking at the nature of an agreement first, Lord Bridge stated that an agreement could be found from partially remembered discussions and imprecise terms, such as may occur

---

[49] These two stages, which have often been used to classify and analyse the law, were given express judicial approval in *Geary v Rankine* [2012] EWCA Civ 55 (CA).   [50] [1971] AC 886, 898.

in an intimate relationship. It is a matter of evidence of what the parties said to each other at the time that the property was purchased and thereafter.[52] In reality, the only 'common' part of the intention is that the cohabitant does not have a contrary intention about ownership,[53] which, if they have acted to their detriment on reliance of the statements of the legal owner, is extremely unlikely. In effect, the court is looking for a representation or assurance by the sole legal owner, on which the cohabitant can act to their detriment.[54]

That certainly appears to have been the case in *Eves v Eves*[55] and *Grant v Edwards*,[56] cases which Lord Bridge considered were 'outstanding examples'[57] of constructive trusts created through an express common intention. In *Eves v Eves*[58] an unmarried couple, Janet and Stuart Eves,[59] purchased a new home solely in the name of Stuart. Stuart told Janet that it was to be their house, and a home for themselves and their children. He also said that the purchase could not be completed in their joint names because she was under 21, but that if she had been of age it would have been purchased in their joint names. This was untrue. In *Grant v Edwards*[60] Mr Edwards purchased a house in his name alone to provide a home for himself and his lover, Mrs Grant. He told Mrs Grant that he had not purchased it in their joint names because that would prejudice her divorce proceedings. This was held to be a common intention on the basis that there would have been no need for an excuse unless he intended her to have an interest in the property.

Common intention, in practice, is an artificial construct and the words of the legal owner are being construed in a forensic manner, despite being said in a domestic context. Mr Edwards (and arguably, also, Stuart Eves) never genuinely intended their partners to enjoy a share of the ownership of their respective houses, but the courts were able to construe their words to demonstrate that such an intention existed. Comments made during everyday life, which may have been uttered for numerous reasons, are now being taken as clear evidence in relation to ownership of the home. Conversations in family life rarely follow that pattern; often things are said with the simple purpose of ending the conversation, rather than to determine existing (or future) rights in how the property is shared in legal terms. This is one set of reasons that the concept of the express common intention constructive trust has attracted considerable criticism as a result.[61] Nevertheless, it does demonstrate that the courts are keen to try and assist the non-legal owner in these situations.

Let's introduce a new couple, as our example for this section discussion. Roger and David were cohabiting in the family home, as a same-sex couple. The home is in David's name as sole legal owner. The relationship has now ended, following a serious disagreement between them. David is now selling the home.

So, if Roger is to try and establish that he has an equitable interest in the home, there must be evidence that he and David at least has some discussions about the ownership. On a number of occasions, Roger asked David what would happen if they ever ceased to be a couple. David was generally dismissive, but often said 'the house is ours together—we share it equally', or words to similar effect. Roger often raised the issue when David was

---

[51] Numerous other judges have cited this passage with approval, including Lady Hale in *Stack v Dowden*.

[52] [1991] 1 AC 107, 132.

[53] See Glover N. and Todd, P. 'The Myth of Common Intention' (1996) 16 *Legal Studies* 325.

[54] See *Morris v Morris* [2008] EWCA Civ 257 (no representation, so no common intention). See also *James v Thomas* [2007] EWCA Civ 1212 (express agreement could not be imputed from conduct); *Re Ali* [2012] EWHC 2302 (no credible evidence given of representations on which to found a common intention).

[55] [1975] 1 WLR 1338.   [56] [1986] Ch 638.

[57] [1991] 1 AC 107, 133. See also *Hammond v Mitchell* [1992] 2 All ER 109.   [58] [1975] 1 WLR 1338.

[59] Although they shared the same name, this was because Janet had changed her surname to his by deed poll.

[60] [1986] Ch 638.

[61] See, e.g. Gardner, S. 'Rethinking Family Property' (1993) 109 *Law Quarterly Review* 263; Mee, J. *The Property Rights of Cohabitees* (Hart Publishing, 1999) 117–73.

trying to settle down to watch TV, and, experience showed, saying that Roger should not worry about it was a quick way to end the discussion. In the situation, the court may well infer an agreement to share the family home from what David has said.

However, Roger, like all cohabitants in this situation, does not acquire a beneficial interest in the family home simply because he can demonstrate a common intention that ownership should be shared. Roger needs to demonstrate some element of detrimental reliance to be granted an interest in the family home. This need not involve the expenditure of money, but there must be some link between the act Roger claims as detrimental reliance and the common intention to share in the beneficial ownership of the home. In *Eves v Eves*,[62] extensive gardening by Janet Eves was held to be sufficient detriment. Similarly, in *Grant v Edwards*,[63] while Edwards paid the mortgage instalments, Grant made a substantial contribution from her own wages to the housekeeping and bringing up the children. The Court of Appeal held that her conduct amounted to sufficient detriment to justify a constructive trust and the acts can be part of 'the joint lives of the parties . . . The acts do not have to be referable to the house.[64] So, if Roger can show similar acts of detriment, he will have acquired an interest in the family home.

Conduct

The second method Lord Bridge suggested for discovering a common intention was inferring it from conduct, where no express words had been used. Effectively, in this situation, the only conduct that would allow a cohabitant to acquire an interest is a direct contribution to the purchase price. Only where there is a payment that is referable to the purchase of the home will a claim be successful. In such cases, the payment to the purchase price will raise the common intention, on the basis that the cohabitant would not have advanced the money without an expectation of an interest, and provide the detriment. This will also happen where the cohabitant has enabled the property to be purchased at a discounted price,[65] or had increased the value of the property by undertaking or contributing to the cost of significant, structural improvements to the home. Not every payment of money during a relationship is attributable to the purchase of the home. The parties may have merely done what spouses or partners would ordinarily do in any relationship. Payments that do not contribute to the purchase price of property, for example the payment of removal costs or solicitors' fees,[66] will clearly be insufficient to generate an inferred common intention, as they are not regarded as a contribution to the purchase price. Similarly, if the money was intended to be a gift, or was advanced as a loan, that would also stop a common intention as to shared ownership of the home arising, as the monetary payment would be explicable on a different basis.

So, returning to David and Roger, this time there is no evidence of any conversation between them as to ownership of the family home. Roger is therefore seeking to establish an equitable interest in the home through a common intention inferred from conduct alone. Roger did not pay towards the purchase of the home, but he has redecorated some of the rooms at high expense, both in time and money. This will not be enough to establish a beneficial interest, as redecoration is not a structural improvement adding to the financial value of the home, so it is not a contribution to the purchase price. What, however, if Roger has contributed to mortgage payments on the family home?

Making mortgage contributions may be thought of as a clear way of making a contribution to the purchase price of the home, particularly as most houses are bought with mortgage finance. Despite this, in *Curley v Parkes*,[67] the Court of Appeal suggested that

---

[62] [1975] 1 WLR 1338.   [63] [1986] Ch 638.   [64] [1986] Ch 638, 657.
[65] See *Oxley v Hiscock* [2005] Fam 111.   [66] *Curley v Parkes* [2004] EWCA Civ 515.
[67] [2004] EWCA Civ 1515.

making mortgage payments, directly or indirectly, were not contributions to the purchase price as they were simply payments of the debt due on the mortgage loan. This case has not been often followed,[68] and it would be both an undue and unfair curtailment of the law if it were, even though, at a technical level, the point has some merit as to the discharge of a debt.

What if Roger has been the person who manages the domestic responsibilities in the relationship, doing the food shopping and cooking, paying for the cleaning and laundry to be done. Would this be a contribution to the purchase price? The answer is most likely no. It is clear that a constructive trust will not be created from conduct that, though costly in time and effort, does not contribute financially at all to the purchase price of the property. A constructive trust will not be inferred in favour of a person who undertakes domestic responsibilities, bears children, provides childcare, or looks after sick or elderly relatives.[69]

Again, it is essential to appreciate that the law is seeking to create property rights for cohabitants like Roger, not give effect to a sense of social justice between families. This can act to disadvantage cohabitants who have performed a domestic role caring for children and the household, supporting their partners' career aspirations, but not making direct financial contributions. At times the courts have sought to take a more expansive view of contributions. In *Le Foe v Le Foe*,[70] for example, Nicholas Mostyn QC held that the financial contributions of a couple to the acquisition of their home should be viewed as a whole, so that a wife's contributions towards the household expenses could be regarded as an indirect contribution to the purchase price of the property as they enabled the other party to make a direct contribution.[71] This has not been a consistent approach.

 CONTEXT 3: THE IMPACT OF FINANCIAL CONTRIBUTIONS

Criticisms have often been levelled that the current property rules for cohabitants work to the manifest disadvantage of the woman, particularly with the clear value that is given to financial contributions as a form of detriment by the law. It is an uncontested fact that men are much more likely to be owner-occupiers than women: 75% of men own their own home, as compared to only 60% of women.[72] Similarly, continuing workplace inequality means that either woman are often in low status, low paid jobs or are in lower grade equivalents to their male counterparts. The pay gap remains too, with women earning statistically about 9.4% less than men doing the same work.[73] Moreover, women are more likely to work part-time than men.[74] When translated into contributions to the household finances, 'men still earn

---

[68] See *Lightfoot v Lightfoot-Browne* [2005] EWCA Civ 201, *Abbott v Abbott* [2008] Fam Law 215 (PC). Compare *Driver v Yorke* [2003] 2 P & CR 210 (occasional contributions to the mortgage instalments made by the two sons of the purchaser of a flat would not give rise to an inference of a common intention because the payments did not have sufficient connection with the purchase to be treated as a contribution to the purchase price).

[69] *Burns v Burns* [1984] Ch 317, 344 (May LJ).   [70] [2001] 2 FLR 970.

[71] See also *Aspden v Elvy* [2012] EWHC 389, at [123] (Behrens J).

[72] ONS, 'Focus on Gender' (2008). Available at: http://webarchive.nationalarchives.gov.uk/20160129200859/http://www.ons.gov.uk/ons/publications/re-reference-tables.html?edition=tcm%3A77-51144, accessed 9 October 2017. While figures will have changed since this survey, they will not have altered in a transformative way.

[73] ONS Statistical Bulletin, 'Annual Survey of Hours and Earnings: Provisional Results: 2016'. Available at: https://www.ons.gov.uk/employmentandlabourmarket/peopleinwork/earningsandworkinghours/bulletins/annualsurveyofhoursandearnings/2016provisionalresults, accessed 24 September 2017.

[74] ONS Statistical Bulletin, *Labour Market Statistics* (2014). Available at: http://webarchive.nationalarchives.gov.uk/20160105181550/http://www.ons.gov.uk/ons/rel/lms/labour-market-statistics/september-2014/statistical-bulletin.html, accessed 9 October 2017.

about two-thirds of couples' joint earnings across all age groups'.[75] It is also still the case that women are most likely to perform most of the unpaid work within the home, such as cooking meals, which can exclude or interfere with access to the labour market.[76]

In terms of purchasing a family home, the increase in house prices in England and Wales means that two incomes are often necessary to secure a mortgage to purchase the family home. While it is now true that most women will be in a position to make a financial contribution to the home, the nature of that contribution (in legal terms, whether direct or indirect) will be a matter of the individual family economy. In other words, how individual couples have decided to organise their finances.

Hence, this inequality is repeated in a set of legal rules which value financial contribution above other factors.

This element of the legal framework established in *Rosset* has drawn considerable criticism, even though Lord Bridge was clear that more than a change of position was needed, and he was reviewing a large corpus of case law in doing so. However, the relative ease with which it is possible to demonstrate an express common intention, and the difficulties of making a distinction between words and conduct as two separate elements of proving a common intention, mean that the issue may not often appear in practice. Often, there will be some form of payment of some type, and something said between the parties that will allow acquisition of an interest.

 Debate 2: Should Property Sivision on Non-Marital Breakdown be Based on Family Law or Property Law Principles?

Ownership of the family home lies at the intersection of two areas of legal analysis: property law and family law. Family law and property law adopt different approaches on the issues associated with property division on relationship breakdown. Property law is about identifying and protecting competing property rights between different rights holders. Family law, by contrast, is often discretion based and concerned about familial status, and the consequences of relationship breakdown.[77] Lord Neuberger, in the approach of lawyers to cohabitation issues, said:

> Chancery law—in particular, company and property law—and family law—in particular, financial remedies—are not happy cohabitants either. Indeed, some might say that property lawyers and family lawyers have something of an oil-and-vinegar quality.[78]

Seen through the lens of a property lawyer, particularly in the sole legal owner cases, equity is being used to give a cohabitant an interest in the home, by depriving the legal owner of what is otherwise his or her interest alone. It is as much about deprivation of property for one cohabitant, as it is about the creation of an interest for the non-legal owner. This has necessarily coloured the development of the law, as it is not about working from a position of

---

[75] See Price, D. 'Pension Accumulation and Gendered Household Structures: What are the Implications of Changes in Family Formation for Future Financial Inequality?' in Miles J. and Probert, R. (eds), *Sharing Lives, Dividing Assets* (Bloomsbury, 2009) 262.

[76] See Bryan, M.L. and Sanz, A.S. 'Does Housework Lower Wages and Why? Evidence for Britain', ISER Working Paper (2008).

[77] Miles, J. 'Property Law v Family Law: Resolving the Problems of Family Property' (2003) 23 *Legal Studies* 624, 627.

[78] Lord Neuberger, 'The Plight of the Unmarried', Keynote Speech for 'At a Glance' Conference 2017, 21 June 2017, at [2].

entitlement in the case of the cohabitant as a partner in a relationship, but about demonstrating that this person is entitled because of a combination of the words and deeds of the legal owning partner, on which the cohabitant had acted to his or her detriment. This approach is not expressly concerned with balancing the contributions to family life which could not be related to ownership of a house, such as child-rearing or the performance of the usual domestic tasks that partners ordinarily undertake in the home. These are valuable contributions, but property law, which is about managing people's competing interests in and over property, is designed to promote certainty, to allow decisions to be predicted. To stray too far into situations which depend almost exclusively on their facts, as would be necessary to do real justice between individual parties in the family home, would:

> produce unacceptable uncertainty, especially as regards the structure of negotiations between the parties following the breakdown of their relationship. There is a need for legal certainty to enable legal advisors to advise their clients clearly and to prevent the dispute from being litigated.[79]

Family law, by contrast, would prefer to treat the issue of entitlements to the family home in terms of a 'materially communal relationship'.[80] It is important to appreciate that the use of trusts (and, as we shall see, proprietary estoppel) is a property law solution to a family law issue. The status of the family home provides the reason for equity to intervene, as it is more than simply another part of an individual's property portfolio; there is an emotional connection in the home that is not captured in traditional property-based thinking.[81]

The lack of a regime giving discretion to the court to adjust the property rights of individuals, instead of declaring how the property is held, means that the trust concept will never be a satisfactory vehicle for the resolution of disputes.[82] The trust is a method of managing wealth, and often of providing tax advantages to the owner of property by manipulation of the separation of ownership and control of assets.[83] It is not a mechanism which lends itself easily to determining entitlements in the family home, beyond allowing some simple sharing of the home as an asset.

Other criticisms of the current approach centre on the inadequacies of common intention as a concept to capture and compensate a domestic cohabiting relationship 'because authority precludes the most significant form of domestic behaviour as evidence to establish such intentions, and partly because the character of the intentions attributed to the parties in the domestic sphere is unreal'.[84]

The law has been changed, following *Stack v Dowden* and *Jones v Kernott*, so that when quantifying the size of the beneficial share, the approach of the court is closer to a family law conception of redistributive justice in the factors it considers and the fact-based approach that it undertaken. The courts have struggled to apply and balance this approach, which, in the end, is designed to achieve fairness between the parties. Whatever the issues, it is clear the approach is far away from what property lawyers value. Indeed, predicting the size of the share a cohabitant would be entitled to has proved difficult in practice, meaning that giving good advice in this area has been challenging.

---

[79] Davies, P. and Virgo, G. *Equity & Trusts Text, Cases and Materials* (OUP, 2016) 460.

[80] Gardner, S. 'Family Property Today' (2008) 124 *Law Quarterly Review* 422.

[81] See generally, Fox O'Mahony, L. *Conceptualising Home: Theories, Laws and Policies* (Hart Publishing, 2007).

[82] See Cretney, S. *Family Law in the Twentieth Century: A History* (OUP, 2003) 113.

[83] For criticism of the trust concept, see, e.g., A Knobel, A. 'Trusts: Weapons of Mass Injustice?' (2013) *Tax Justice Network*. Available at: http://www.taxjustice.net/reports-2/, accessed 9 October 2017.

[84] Eekelaar, J. 'A Woman's Place—A Conflict between Law and Social Values' [1987] *The Conveyancer and Property Lawyer* 93, 101.

3.3.2 Quantification of beneficial interests: Sole and joint legal owner cases

Once an interest in the property has been established, either through agreement or conduct in sole legal owner cases, or through joint legal ownership, the extent of the interest must be quantified. The approach that should be applied to determine this is clear in theory, following the House of Lords decision in *Stack v Dowden* and the Supreme Court case of *Jones v Kernott*, which together rationalised earlier inconsistent decisions as to the approach to be adopted.[85] However, as we shall see, applying that theory in practice has led to some difficulties.

 Key Case 2: *Stack v Dowden* [2007] 2 AC 432

A couple had lived together for 25 years, and had four children. The original family house had been purchased by Ms Dowden alone, through a combination of savings and mortgage finance. Ms Dowden paid all the mortgage repayments and Mr Stack helped with improvements to the home. On sale, title to the new house was registered in both names. The purchase was funded 65% from Ms Dowden (proceeds of sale and savings) and the remainder from an endowment mortgage loan. Mr Stack paid the interest on the loan. Capital was repaid by lump sums, of which Mr Stack contributed £27,000, and Ms Dowden the remaining £38,000. The parties kept their financial affairs entirely separate throughout their relationship together. On the breakdown of the relationship, Mr Stack sought an order for sale and equal division of any proceeds of sale.

In the past, in joint legal ownership cases, there has been a presumption that the ownership of the property was shared equally, 50–50, or, where purchase money had been provided, but in unequal shares, that the ownership followed the financial contributions. Following the decision in *Oxley v Hiscock*,[86] the Court of Appeal had divided the proceeds of sale 65% to Ms Dowden, 35% to Mr Stack as representing a fair share of the course of dealings between the parties, with which the House of Lords agreed. Baroness Hale concluded that this was an unusual case[87] and that Ms Dowden had successfully rebutted the strong presumption of joint beneficial ownership. The couple kept their affairs 'rigidly separate'[88] and Ms Dowden had contributed much more to the financial acquisition of the property than Mr Stack had done:[89]

> This is not a case in which it can be said that the parties pooled their separate resources, even notionally, for the common good . . . they undertook separate responsibility for that part of the expenditure which each had agreed to pay.[90]

The task of the court was to 'to ascertain the parties' common intentions as to what their shares in the property would be, in the light of their whole course of conduct in relation to it'. It was not simply to impute the court's view of fairness, so that while they House of Lords reached the same conclusion as to the size of the beneficial shares awarded to Mr Stack and Ms Dowden, they did so for different reasons.

The list of factors which were to be taken into account to quantify the interest were necessarily much wider than those that would allow someone to acquire an interest in the family

---

[85] See, e.g., *Midland Bank v Cooke* [1995] All ER 562 (basis was assumed agreement); *Oxley v Hisock* [2004] EWCA Civ 546 (CA) (basis was fairness).   [86] [2004] EWCA Civ 546 (CA).

[87] See, however, the contrary argument that such matters of the family economy are more common than the House of Lords thought—see Douglas, G. Pearce, J., and Woodward, H. 'Cohabitants, Property and the Law: A study of injustice' (2009) 72 *Modern Law Review* 24.

[88] [2007] 2 AC 432, at [92].   [89] [2007] 2 AC 432, at [89].   [90] [2007] 2 AC 432, at [90]–[91].

home. Baroness Hale said that in determining the size of a beneficial share in the property, the court should have recourse to the following indicative list of factors:

> any advice or discussions at the time of transfer which cast light on their intentions then; the reasons why the home was acquired in their joint names; the reasons why (if it be the case) the survivor was authorised to give a receipt for the capital moneys; the purpose for which the home was acquired; the nature of the parties' relationship; whether they had children for whom they both had responsibility to provide a home; how the purchase was financed, both initially and subsequently; how the parties arranged their finances, whether separately or together or a bit of both; how they discharged their outgoings on the property and their other household expenses.[91]

These were not intended to be an exhaustive list of factors, just to provide useful guidelines. This was a sea change in the law for joint legal owners, as it demonstrated that the common intentions of the parties could change over the course of the relationship. It was, however, unclear when and whether it was permissible for the court to simply impute a common intention to the parties as to the size of their beneficial share in the home, rather than infer it from the conduct of the parties. It was also unclear how to apply the various factors listed by Lady Hale in reaching a conclusion as to the size of the beneficial shares, and, how they should be weighted.[92] These issues were addressed by the Supreme Court in *Jones v Kernott*.

Key Case 3: *Jones v Kernott* [2011] UKSC 53

Ms Jones and Mr Kernott started living together in 1983, initially living together in a mobile home which Ms Jones had bought in her own name two years earlier. In 1985 the mobile home was sold, and the proceeds of sale were used as a deposit for a house in Thundersley, Essex, which was bought in their joint names. Whilst Ms Jones paid the mortgage (which was in joint names), Mr Kernott met most of the cost of an extension which significantly increased the value of the house. He also made a significant contribution towards the family's household expenses. The couple, who by now had two children, separated in 1993. Mr Kernott made no further contribution towards the house or household expenses, and no significant financial or other contributions towards the support of the children. An attempt was made to sell the Thundersley house, and when this proved unsuccessful, the parties cashed in an insurance policy, and Mr Kernott used his share of the proceeds as the down payment of another home of his own. There was no discussion about how the parties' affairs should be resolved until Mr Kernott in 2008 claimed a half share of the Thundersley property.

There had been some difficulty in the lower courts in applying the principles set out in *Stack v Dowden*. On the basis of fairness, the trial judge and high court gave Mr Kernott only a 10% share of the home, as he had not been involved in the family since 1993. The Court of Appeal disagreed, holding that there was no evidence to depart from the inference of equal distribution and it was not for the court to impute what it thought was fair in this case. Lord Walker and Lady Hale, giving the leading speech in the Supreme Court, said that the parties could be said to have intended to determine their respective entitlements in the Thundersley home in 1993 when they separated. On this basis, the outcome on the parties' entitlements to the home was so similar to that reached by the trial judge that it was upheld.

---

[91] [2007] 2 AC 432, at [69] and [70].

[92] See *Fowler v Barron* [2008] EWCA Civ 377 (equal division, though no financial contributions on the mortgage by claimant); *Abbot v Abbot* [2008] Fam Law 215 (PC) (equal distribution, despite a less than 10% financial contribution).

Lady Hale and Lord Walker explained that the court can only impute a common intention where it is not possible to infer a common intention from the words or conduct of the parties, and that imputation is made on the basis of fairness.[93] Determining how the parties' intended to share the property is the starting point. If this cannot be determined on the facts, the court will decide the division of the beneficial interest between the parties, based on what is adjudged fair in the circumstances.

What about sole name cases, where, of course, there is no presumption of equality of division of the beneficial interest? What is the approach there? The matter appears to have been settled by *Capehorn v Harris*.[94] In reviewing the applicable law, the Court of Appeal said that unless there was an agreement as to the extent of the interest, the court may impute an intention that a fair share was intended.[95] So, the approach is the same approach as adopted in the joint name cases, and the same factors apply.

So, in our example, where does that leave Roger and David? Well, it should mean that, provided Roger has an interest, the court will seek to quantify it in a liberal manner. The first port of call would be to consider the words and conduct of the parties to see if it was possible to find some common intention as to the size of Roger's beneficial share of the home. If that was not possible, the court could ultimately impute what it thought was a fair share on the basis of how Roger and David conducted family life in the home.

In fact, despite the clarity on paper of the approach in *Jones v Kernott*, and the breadth of factors that should be considered when determining shares in *Stack*, the courts have continued to have difficulty with the quantification of interests in the family home in both sole and joint legal owner cases. Judges have struggled with new factors introduced in inference and imputation[96] and have instead tended to fall back on financial contributions, rather than deal with the 'messier' issues of the nature of the relationship or the character of the parties in imputing an intention as to what is a 'fair' award between the parties.

Graham-York v York[97] provides a good illustration of the issues.[98] Miss Graham-York contested a finding that she was entitled to a 50% beneficial interest in the family home behind a constructive trust. It was beyond argument that the sole legal owner of the home, Mr Norton York, had been abusive and controlling in his dealings with his partner, and that she had lived with him for 33 years until his death. Nevertheless, the Court of Appeal found that, on the basis of her financial contributions to the property and joint contributions to household expenditure and bringing up the couple's daughter, Miss Graham-York was entitled to a 25% share of the beneficial ownership of the home. Tomlinson LJ said:

> It is essential, in my judgment, to bear in mind that, in deciding in such a case what shares are fair, the court is not concerned with some form of redistributive justice. Thus it is irrelevant that it may be thought a "fair" outcome for a woman who has endured years of abusive conduct by her partner to be allotted a substantial interest in his property on his death. The plight of Miss Graham-York attracts sympathy, but it does not enable the court to redistribute property interests in a manner which right-minded people might think amounts to appropriate compensation.

It is unclear, however, from the judgment just exactly what factors, beyond the financial, made up the share. Tomlinson LJ noted that Miss Graham-York had made as much of a financial contribution as she possibly could. This is a return to focusing on financial matters, while placing non-financial factors in the background.[99]

---

[93] [2011] UKSC 53, at [51]. [94] [2015] EWCA Civ 955 (CA). [95] [2015] EWCA Civ 955, at [16].
[96] See *Aspden v Elvy* [2012] EWHL 3570 (arbitrary figure reached); *S v J and Others* [2016] EWHC 559 (Fam) (mixed up inference and imputation).
[97] [2015] EWCA Civ 7. [98] See also *Sandhu v Sandhu* [2016] EWCA Civ 1050.
[99] Greer S. and Pawlowski, M. 'Imputation, Fairness and the Family Home' [2015] *The Conveyancer and Property Lawyer* 512, 521.

3.3.3 Assessing the operation of the constructive trust of common intention

The approach to the acquisition and quantification of interests under a common intention constructive trust is not without significant issues. Despite a constant stream of cases, and the guidance provided by the three leading cases in this area of law, the results are rarely satisfactory.

It is also apparent that, for many family lawyers, the equitable mechanisms are inappropriate. Even when it comes to quantifying an interest gained through an equitable solution, there are problems. Miles, for example, argues that economic difficulties following relationship breakdown 'cannot be solved without express reference to the nature, or effects of, the relationship between the parties and an express policy aimed at dealing specifically with the problems encountered in such relationships'.[100] Property lawyers are no less critical. Mee concludes that the doctrine remains 'stubbornly half baked'. Clearly, this ill-conceived doctrine should find no place in the law of England.'[101]

Nonetheless, there is reason to defend the attempts at principle evident in the work of the judges, while still being mindful of the issues that exist. Clarity is important when dealing with proprietary interests. In developing an set of methods to provide for cohabitants seeking an interest in the family home, English law is involved in a search for fairness balanced by clarity, however flawed that search may be. If the balance swings too far in favour of fairness, there is not only a problem in deciding what factors are relevant and what weight they should carry, there is also a problem of lack of clarity and certainty. Without certainty in an outcome, legal advice is difficult to provide, and matters would need to go to court for determination, which is expensive in time and money and is not a sensible outcome. This use of trusts in the family home is still very much work in progress, and as Lord Neuberger remarked:

> For the time being at least, and in the absence of legislative intervention, I think that the unmarried can expect a rougher ride than their married counterparts, at least when relying on the law to deal with the fall-out of their falling out.[102]

 DEBATE 3: ARE COMMON INTENTION CONSTRUCTIVE TRUSTS IN THE FAMILY HOME A NEW CONSTRUCT?

The courts have insisted that they have not developed new or special rules for acquiring an interest in the family home, and that they have simply applied existing property rules to new situations. It is, however, possible to say one thing and in fact do another. It could be argued that equity has allowed the creation of a special set of rules under the cloak of the constructive trust mechanism, which only operate in the context of the family home. We have seen this in how the court will construe evidence, words and deeds, to find a common intention—the 'agreement' to find a constructive trust where only one of the cohabitants is the legal owner is not an agreement that the parties themselves would often recognise as having been reached. It is also far removed from the level of certainty normally expected to find agreements relating to contracts between parties. Equity is responding here to a social and legal problem which needs to be addressed—the fact that there are no rights for cohabiting couples who are neither married nor registered as civil partners. In so doing, it has found a

---

[100] Miles, J. 'Property Law v Family Law: Resolving the Problems of Family Property' (2003) 23 *Legal Studies* 624, 648.

[101] Mee, J. *The Property Rights of Cohabitees* (Hart Publishing, 1999) 173–4.

[102] Lord Neuberger, 'The Plight of the Unmarried', Keynote Speech for 'At a Glance' Conference 2017, 21 June 2017, at [26].

method to give an interest under a trust which would not be recognised in other areas of the law. There is strong judicial support for this approach at the very highest level in the latest Supreme Court decision in *Jones v Kernott*[103] and subsequent decisions of the first instance and appellate courts.

Indeed, the changes to a liberal approach to quantifying the beneficial shares in the family home under a constructive trust can, as we have seen, be based on the concept of doing justice between the parties on the basis of determining the fair shares for each partner by imputation of the court. This is similar to the adjustment of property rights under s. 25 of the Matrimonial Causes Act 1973 (see Chapter 4), though those rights go further. Here, ostensibly equal division is the norm, but, in practice, in using their powers, the courts focus on the immediate housing needs of the parent with care of dependent children.[104] The factors listed when quantifying an interest do not go so far, and the needs of the parties are only one factor considered, and, as we have seen, are often not given the same value or weight as financial considerations. Nonetheless, the width of the factors and an approach which allows inference and, if necessary imputation of intention, is further evidence of a willingness to engage with the social justice of the situation between the parties, rather than simply to determine property rights and entitlements.

So, do we have a new concept of constructive trust? It is difficult to be certain, but, it is patent that existing trusts principles have been strained to their absolute limits to provide solutions in this difficult area. The issues with which the courts are dealing are complex, so it is not surprising that there have been some false starts, and that there has been uncertainty or inconsistency. Whether we are moving to a future where the constructive trust is simply a vehicle for doing justice between family members remains to be seen. The fact that, in sole legal owner cases, there remains a need to acquire an interest, means we have not reached that point yet. If the law moves to allow the courts to simply impute that the non-legal owner should be entitled to an interest in the home on the basis of their conduct, then the constructive trust of common intention will indisputably be an entirely different concept than it is currently. It will become the remedy used by the court to do justice between the parties.

Perspectives will be divided on whether that point should ever be reached. For the author's part, it would be an abuse of certainty and property law principles for equity to go this far. This would be social engineering by the judiciary, conferring a status on cohabitants divorced from any legal rules or legal basis. Parliament has seen fit to award a special status to married couples and registered civil partners, which was not conferred on cohabitants. This is not to ignore that there are significant issues which need to be addressed. It should instead be recognised that trusts are not the mechanism to achieve fairness between unmarried cohabitants. Such issues would be better addressed through legislative intervention, a topic considered at the end of this chapter.

3.4 Resulting trusts

A purchase money resulting trust was the first type of implied trust used to allow a cohabitant to acquire an interest in the home of a sole legal owner.[105] It is based on a presumption that, where there is a joint acquisition of the family home, a purchaser would not have financed the purchase of the home without wishing to retain a share of the beneficial ownership.[106] The acquisition of the interest under a presumed resulting trust is based on a direct

---

[103] [2011] UKSC 53 (Lord Walker and Lady Hale); Lord Collins at [60]; Lord Kerr at [68].

[104] Hitchings, E. 'Everyday Cases in the Post-White Era' [2008] *Family Law* 873, 877.

[105] See further, Pearce, R. and Barr, W. *Pearce & Stevens Trusts and Equitable Obligations* (6th edn, OUP, 2014) Chapter 8.   [106] *Pettitt v Pettitt* [1970] AC 777, at 794. See also *Gissing v Gissing* [1971] AC 886.

contribution to the purchase price of land, which is necessary to be classed as a purchaser of the property. The presumption could apply where a family home is bought in the name of one of the couple only, or where it is bought in their joint names and there is no express declaration of the beneficial interests. The normal method of quantifying an interest arising out of a resulting trust was an arithmetical calculation, so that the share of the beneficial ownership attained was proportionate to the share of the purchase price contributed.[107]

Over the years, in an attempt to broaden both the situations in which the trust would arise, and also to allow quantification of interests on a broader basis, the resulting trust had slowly began to morph in the hands of certain judges into the constructive trust. Indeed, it was largely overtaken by the constructive trust analysis put forward by Lord Bridge in *Lloyds Bank v Rosset* where a common intention is found only from conduct alone (see 3.3.1). Following clear dicta in *Stack v Dowden* and *Jones v Kernott*, this use of resulting trusts has fallen out of favour in the family home:

> The assumptions as to human motivation, which led the courts to impute particular intentions by way of the resulting trust, are not appropriate to the ascertainment of beneficial interests in a family home.[108]

The resulting trust nevertheless refuses to fade into the annals of legal history in relation to the family home. Lord Neuberger, who was in dissent in *Stack v Dowden*, felt that resulting trusts should have a place to play in the family home. Later, in *Laskar v Laskar*,[109] where he sat as a Lord Justice of Appeal in the Court of Appeal, he drew a distinction between cohabitants buying a family home, and simply buying property together. If property was simply bought as a family investment, an asset, it was more akin to a commercial transaction and normal resulting trust principles should apply.[110] More significantly, the Privy Council in *Marr v Collie*,[111] held that a resulting trust would apply to a traditional family home situation, and that the constructive approach in *Stack* might also apply to houses bought by a couple as investment assets. It was, according to Lord Kerr, all a matter of context.[112] The facts were atypical, and concerned a number of properties between Mr Marr and Mr Collie, as well as collection of other items of property, such as a boat and an art collection. This is nonetheless a surprising conclusion, and might suggest that there is still life in the resulting trust for cohabitants.[113]

4. Estoppel remedies in the family home

Proprietary estoppel is an entirely different equitable mechanism from either the constructive or resulting trust. It is not a form of trust, but is instead an equitable remedy that may allow someone to acquire an interest in property which they do not currently have. In terms of the family home, it provides another means by which a cohabitant who is not on the legal title or already a beneficiary under an express trust may get some interest in the home.

Proprietary estoppel is based on conscience, so it will come to the aid of a cohabitant where the circumstances are such that it would be unfair (or unconscionable) for the legal

---

[107] *Bull v Bull* [1955] 1 QB 234.

[108] *Jones v Kernott* [2011] UKSC 53 at [53]. See also *Stack v Dowden* [2007] 2 AC 432, at [60] (Baroness Hale, citing with approval Lord Walker's discussion at [19]–[31]).   [109] [2008] EWCA Civ 347.

[110] See *Erlam v Rahman* [2016] EWHC 11 (Ch) (resulting trusts used in a 'buy to let' house purchase). See also *Wodzicki v Wodzicki* [2017] EWCA Civ 95 (resulting trust used where no close relationship between the parties).

[111] [2017] UKPC 17.   [112] [2017] UKPC 17, at [54].

[113] See George, M. and Sloan, B. 'Presuming Too Little About Resulting and Constructive Trusts?' [2017] *The Conveyancer and Property Lawyer* 303.

owner to deny that the cohabitant should be entitled to some rights in the family home. To determine the circumstances in which it will be unconscionable, there are clear principles to be followed and estoppel cannot simply be pleaded or recognised on the basis of what an individual judge believes is 'fair in any particular case'.[114]

So, what are those circumstances? For the purposes of this section, it's time for another example. Wilma and Burt have been living together in the family home for 16 years as unmarried cohabitants. Wilma is the legal owner of the home. They have now decided to separate, and Wilma is claiming that Burt is not entitled to any interest whatsoever in the family home. Burt would have to show that Wilma, as the legal owner of the home, has by encouragement or representations made to Burt, led him to believe that he has, or will obtain, some rights in respect of the family home. Burt would also have to demonstrate that he acted to his detriment on the basis of this belief, so much so that it would be considered unconscionable for Wilma to assert her legal entitlement to the property alone. Equity will intervene and stop Wilma from denying that Burt should be entitled to some rights in the home.

From this outline of how estoppel operates, it is clear that there is a substantial overlap between constructive trusts and proprietary estoppel. This means that the same facts might give rise either to the recognition of a constructive trust, or to the award of an estoppel remedy. The overlap has in the past led the judiciary to enquire whether there is any substantive difference between the two,[115] but the fact of the different remedies available under proprietary estoppel means it is a very different claim.

This leads us to consider what Burt's rights in the home will be. This is very different from the approach in trusts, where the issue was about quantifying a beneficial share in the property under a trust. If Burt can demonstrate an estoppel claim, he would be entitled to a right referred to as a 'mere equity'. This mere equity has to be 'satisfied' (completed) by the grant of an appropriate remedy by the court and a range of remedies are available to the courts. This may order that the family home is Burt's alone, or they may give considerably less, such as a licence (permission) for Burt to live in the family home for life or a simple monetary payment. The manner through which the court decides on the appropriate remedy is a matter of considerable debate, as we shall see.

What follows is an outline of the salient features of proprietary estoppel. The discretionary nature of the remedy means that there are many more cases than would fit into this treatment, but the key aspects will be covered here.

4.1 Acquisition of an interest by proprietary estoppel

Proprietary estoppel was not utilised in the family home for a long period of time, due to the restrictive approach of *Willmott v Barber*.[116] However, Oliver J restated the criteria in *Taylor Fashions Ltd v Liverpool Victoria Trustees Co Ltd*,[117] which provides a much broader understanding of the operation of proprietary estoppel. The case was commercial in nature, but the actual facts are not relevant. Oliver J restated the requirements of estoppel in broad terms, noting that the basis lay in stopping unconscionable activity. A claimant would be able to establish an estoppel if they could prove an assurance, reliance and detriment in circumstances in which it would be unconscionable to deny a remedy to the claimant. These criteria are not to be viewed as a rigid formula, though they provide a useful framework for analysis, and the courts must take a 'holistic approach' to these factors to establish, in the end, whether the legal owner should be able to go back on his assurance to

---

[114] *Jennings v Rice* [2002] NPC 28 (Robert Walker LJ).
[115] See, e.g., the obiter statements of Chadwick LJ in *Oxley v Hiscock* [2005] Fam 211, at [66].
[116] (1880) 15 Ch D 96.   [117] [1982] QB 133.

the claimant about the use of the property.[118] This refreshed formulation gave the doctrine utility on the breakdown of relationships in the family home.

4.1.1 Representation or assurance

Let's return to Wilma and Burt. Burt will only be able to claim a 'mere equity' in the family home if, as a cohabitant, he can establish that Wilma, as legal owner of the family home made a representation, or created or encouraged an expectation that Burt was presently entitled, or would become entitled, to an interest in the home. An assurance may be given 'actively' through the acts of Wilma as legal owner, or 'passively' through her silence and failure to disabuse Burt of his belief that he is entitled to an interest in the land.

To be valid, an assurance must be unambiguous and must appear to have been intended to be taken seriously. If Wilma said to Burt something like 'the home is as much yours as mine', that would probably suffice. Taken in its context, it must have been a promise which one might reasonably expect to be relied upon by the person to whom it was made.[119] Given the similarity of an assurance with the requirements of constructive trusts of common intention, it would be rare for circumstances which give rise to the finding of an express common intention to not also give rise to an assurance in proprietary estoppel.[120] However, it is possible to establish a claim to an estoppel in a situation where there would be insufficient evidence to demonstrate a common intention to support a constructive trust on the basis of an agreement. In *Southwell v Blackburn*,[121] for example, there was clearly no common intention as to the ownership of the family home on the evidence which suggested that the property had been purchased purely by one party alone. Nevertheless, the cohabitant was able to demonstrate that there had been a representation or assurance on the basis that he had given her assurance that she would 'always have a home and be secure'.[122]

 Key Legislation 2: Law of Property (Miscellaneous Provisions) Act 1989, s. 2

(1) A contract for the sale or other disposition of an interest in land can only be made in writing and only by incorporating all the terms which the parties have expressly agreed in one document or, where contracts are exchanged, in each.

(2) The terms may be incorporated in a document either by being set out in it or by reference to some other document.

(3) The document incorporating the terms or, where contracts are exchanged, one of the documents incorporating them (but not necessarily the same one) must be signed by or on behalf of each party to the contract.

(4) ...

(5) ... and nothing in this section affects the creation or operation of resulting, implied or constructive trusts.

This section requires all contracts for the 'sale or other disposition' of an interest in land to be in writing, and it sets out the form that writing must take. There is a well-known exception governing conduct which gives rise to a constructive trust (s. 2(5)), but there is nothing to authorise the use of estoppel in similar situations. This lead to some element of debate as to whether an estoppel claim could succeed in the family home.

---

[118] See *Gillet v Holt* [2001] Ch 210; *Thorner v Major* [2009] UKHL 18.

[119] *Thorner v Major* [2009] UKHL 18, at [56] (Lord Walker).

[120] Dixon, M. 'Invalid Contracts, Estoppel and Constructive Trusts' [2005] *The Conveyancer and Property Lawyer* 247.

[121] [2014] EWCA Civ 1347. See Hayward, A. 'Cohabitants, Detriment and the Potential of Proprietary Estoppel: *Southwell v Blackburn* [2014] EWCA Civ 1347' (2015) 27 *Child and Family Law Quarterly* 303.

[122] [2014] EWCA Civ 1347, at [4].

Lord Scott suggested in *Yeoman's Row v Cobbe*,[123] that 'proprietary estoppel cannot be prayed in aid in order to render enforceable an agreement that statute has declared to be void',[124] such as a contract to grant an interest in land which has not been made in writing. At face value, this would have led to proprietary estoppel being of little use in the family home,[125] since the creation of an interest in the family home, is technically the grant of an interest in land. The decision, it is worth noting, was one that dealt with a commercial set of facts, not the family home. The difference in the domestic context was addressed in *Thorner v Major*,[126] where Lords Walker and Neuberger both indicated that the assurance or understanding on which a claimant relied in the family home did not need to be expressed with precise and exact definition.[127] Moreover, Lord Neuberger was clear in his view that Lord Scott's observations on estoppel and void contracts in *Cobbe* had no relevance in a case with no contractual connection, such as in family cases.[128]

4.1.2 Reliance

Burt must demonstrate that, as cohabitant, he acted in reliance upon the assurance (here, that the home 'is as much yours as mine') in relation to which the claim is being made.[129] It is not unconscionable to make an assurance if it is not acted upon. Whether there has been a valid reliance will therefore be a question of fact in every case, and it is relatively easy to find apparent inconsistencies in the approach of individual members of the judiciary. In *James v Thomas*,[130] the Court was unwilling to accept that the motivation for the claimant's behaviour was reliance on an assurance relating to ownership of the family home, but instead arose from a desire to make a life together as a couple. Contrast this with the more relaxed approach evident in *Matharu v Matharu*,[131] where installing a kitchen in the property by the cohabitant was constituted as sufficient reliance on the assurances made. What is clear is that it is sufficient that the cohabitant relies on the assurance, even if the legal owner did not intend them to rely on it. In our example, Burt moved into the home, having given up a chance to buy a home of his own at a heavily discounted rate. That would probably suffice as an act of reliance. Wilma would not be able to argue that she did not intend her assurance about the ownership of the home to be acted upon.

4.1.3 Detriment/change of position

Reliance alone is not sufficient. Burt, in relying on what Wilma said, must demonstrate some element of detriment in the acts claimed as reliance on the assurance made. Rights over land are not created by mere representations, which do not amount to either a contract or a declaration of trust.[132] It is for this reason that detriment is required.[133]

Very much like detriment in a constructive trust based on express agreement, the action required of the cohabitant need not require the expenditure of money, though financial contributions could provide clear evidence of detriment. Hence, paying for an extension to the property which adds to the value of the home would be sufficient detriment.[134] The category is even wider here than the acts that would be valid for a constructive trust,

---

[123] [2008] UKHL 55.   [124] [2008] UKHL 55, at [29].

[125] Etherton, S. 'Constructive Trusts and Proprietary Estoppels: The Search for Clarity and Principle' [2009] *The Conveyancer and Property Lawyer* 104, 120.

[126] [2009] UKHL 18.   [127] See, e.g., [2009] UKHL 18, at [98].

[128] [2009] UKHL 18, at [96]–[98] (Lord Neuberger). Followed in *Thompson v Foy* [2009] EWHC 1076 (Ch); *Gill v Woodall* [2009] EWHC 834; *Ghazanni v Rowshan* [2015] EWHC 1922 (Ch).

[129] See further, Robertson, A. 'The Reliance Basis of Proprietary Estoppel Remedies' [2008] *The Conveyancer and Property Lawyer* 295.   [130] [2007] EWCA Civ 1212.

[131] (1994) 68 P & CR 93.   [132] See Key Legislation 1: Law of Property Act 1925, s. 53.

[133] *Gillet v Holt* [2001] Ch 210, adopted in *Suggitt v Suggit* [2012] EWCA Civ 1140.

[134] *Gillet v Holt* [2001] Ch 210.

as proprietary estoppel is concerned with the conscience of the legal owner. For example, working in the home without adequate payment is sufficient detriment. In *Thorner v Major*[135] the House of Lords held that the claimant had acted to his detriment by doing substantial farm work for 30 years without pay, for most of that time in reliance on an assurance that he would inherit the farm.[136] Along similar lines, giving up a job and moving to a new area has been held to be a sufficient change of position.[137] In a number of cases, being 'deprived of the opportunity of a better life elsewhere'[138] has been held to be detriment, as in *Greasley v Cooke*.[139] Burt, in giving up an opportunity to buy his own home at a heavily discounted rate, would likely suffice as appropriate detriment.

4.1.4 Unconscionability

Detriment must be considered together with the additional requirement of unconscionability. This means that a change of position will only be sufficiently substantial if it means, in all the circumstances of the case, it would be unjust or inequitable to withdraw the assurance or expectation. This step been criticised by Wells, on the basis that it is creating uncertainty by requiring something additional to detriment,[140] but it is arguably part of an holistic approach to founding an estoppel claim. It means that the interests of Wilma, as legal owner, are balanced against the actions of Burt as the claimant, which is not possible under the trusts approach.

In essence, the more detrimental reliance undertaken by the cohabitant on the basis of the assurance, the more likely it is that it would be unconscionable for the legal owner to withdraw the assurance. It would be a matter of argument as to whether Burt's giving up an opportunity to purchase another home at a discounted rate would be sufficient to make it unconscionable for Wilma to withdraw the expectation that Burt was to have an interest in the home. If, for example, Burt had paid for an extension of the home, which would have involved financial expenditure by Burt and which would have added value to the property, this would be a more likely to meet this criteria. If successful in an estoppel claim, Burt would be granted a 'mere equity' in the family home.

4.2 Quantification of an interest by proprietary estoppel

It is for the court to determine, in its discretion, the type of remedy that would be appropriate to achieve justice between the parties and satisfy the 'mere equity' that cohabitants like Burt have established. The rights given may be more or less than either Burt or Wilma expected or might have wished. Remedies have included the outright transfer of land to the claimant,[141] the grant of a lease (meaning that the claimant has had to pay a rent for occupation),[142] a right of occupancy in the home,[143] and simple, financial compensation.[144] The range of remedies is open-ended, and this can mean there is real uncertainty as to the nature of the right granted. It also means that both Burt and Wilma will either have to agree the right that Burt has in the family home between them, or take the action to court for the court to formally decide on the appropriate award.

The most significant issue is how the court decides on the appropriate remedy to satisfy the equity.[145] Many different approaches have been suggested and employed by the courts.

---

[135] See [2009] UKHL 18.   [136] See also *Davies v Davies* [2016] EWCA Civ 463.

[137] See *Jones v Jones* [1977] 1 WLR 438.   [138] *Henry v Henry* [2010] UKPC 3, at [61].

[139] [1980] 1 WLR 1306.

[140] Wells, R. 'The Element of Detriment in Proprietary Estoppel' [2001] *The Conveyancer and Property Lawyer* 13.

[141] *Pascoe v Turner* [1979] 1 WLR 431; *Gillet v Holt* [2001] Ch 210.

[142] *Grant v Williams* (1977) 248 EG 947.   [143] *Inwards v Baker* [1965] 2 QB 29.

[144] *Dodsworth v Dodsworth* (1973) 228 EG 115.

[145] See, e.g., Bright, S. and McFarlane, B. 'Proprietary Estoppel and Property Rights' (2005) 64 *Cambridge Law Journal* 449.

DEBATE 4: WHAT ARE THE LIMITS OF ESTOPPEL REMEDIES?

The underlying principle is supposed to be, whatever the approach adopted, that the court awards the minimum equity necessary to do justice between the parties.[146] Two main opposing views have been advocated to explain the function of the court in the determination of the appropriate remedy. The 'narrow approach' considers that the court is simply required to carry into effect the parties' own 'reasonable expectations'. Under this view, the court is left with a very structured discretion as to the remedy that is appropriate. The 'flexible approach' argues that the court has a wide discretion to decide the appropriate remedy in all the circumstances of the case. In *Jennings v Rice*[147] the Court of Appeal considered the merits of these alternatives and concluded that a 'composite approach' should be adopted which would ensure that there was proportionality between the remedy awarded and the detriment experienced.

Much academic ink has been spilt on trying to advocate for, or against, the approach the courts should take. For those who think the basis of action should be related to the reasonable expectations of the claimant,[148] the outcome of many cases do not easily fit within it (such as monetary awards). An approach founded on reasonable expectations is inconsistent with judicial statements which emphasise the court's inherent flexibility in determining the remedy. On a more practical level, what amounts to a reasonable expectation as to the remedy is unlikely to be clear from the assurance or representation made, and will require some inference or imputation by the court. On the positive side, this approach would be fairer to the legal owner in the family home situation, as the remedy granted would reflect what the claimant anticipated from what was said and done.

For those who argue that the approach is based on broad discretion,[149] so that the court is unfettered in choosing a remedy to meet the needs of the case before it, the key criticism is that of uncertainty in the outcome, and a lack of predictability in advising claimants as to the remedy they are likely to receive. The attraction of this approach in the family home is that reviewing all the circumstances and particular facts of a case is likely to result in a more fair assessment in the overall situation of the family life and contributions made within it.

What lies behind the so-called composite approach is a recognition that the narrow and wide discretions are not opposed approaches, but that elements of both are evident in any decision the court makes as to the remedy available. The key point is that the unconscionability is remedied, whatever the approach adopted, and that the standard is the minimum right to do justice between the parties, not the most appropriate right in the eyes of the court or claimant. This approach has been adopted in a number of cases. In *Gillett v Holt*,[150] Robert Walker LJ stated that the court does not possess an unbridled discretion, but is required to exercise its discretion to determine an appropriate remedy within the limits of the expectations that have been created by the assurances. This was also the approach of Arden LJ in *Suggitt v Suggitt*.[151] This must represent the settled approach, and this reasoning balances the rights of both cohabitants in the family home in reaching an appropriate remedy.

The greater flexibility in approach and remedy under proprietary estoppel should be of interest to both the cohabitant seeking an interest, and the legal owner, for different reasons. With the claimant, there could be an entitlement to more than a beneficial interest; to the legal owner they may have to give some right to the cohabitant on relationship breakdown,

---

[146] *Crabb v Arun DC* [1976] Ch 179.   [147] [2002] EWCA Civ 159.

[148] See, e.g., Cooke, E. 'Estoppel and the Protection of Expectations' (1997) 17 *Legal Studies* 258.

[149] See, e.g., Dewar, J. 'Licences and Land Law: An Alternative View' (1986) 49 *Modern Law Review* 741.

[150] [2001] Ch 210.   [151] [2012] EWCA Civ 1140.

but not necessarily surrender a right in their home. Nevertheless, this inherent flexibility has led to some strange results, which are depressingly familiar from the constructive trusts cases as to the nature of what is valued in a relationship when deciding rights once that relationship has ended.

Arif v Anwar[152] provides an example of generosity to the cohabitant. Here, the remedy granted under a claim by proprietary estoppel was a 25% share of the beneficial interest on the property. This was arrived at, it appears, on the basis that the claimant had been promised a share in the premises and the detriment was incurred on the basis of this specific promise. The same could be said, it is suggested, for many cases where there is an assurance about the ownership; there is little unique on the facts. It is also instructive that this representation would not have been sufficient to found an action through a common intention constructive trust via an express agreement. The award also seems generous when viewed in terms of the minimum equity necessary to do justice between the parties, as the financial detriment incurred was £280,000 of a house worth £1.75 million.

Davies v Davies[153] provides a salutary tale of a lack of generosity to a claimant. This case is not the classic family homes situation, as it involved the claim of a daughter against her parent's farm, but the reasoning is equally applicable as to the equitable remedy reached. The parents owned a farm which they wished to remain in the family, but the claimant daughter was the only family member interested in running it. In consequence, she lived and worked on the farm for very low pay, and it was clear that her parents had made various representations over the course of many years that she would have an interest in the farm business and would be left it in the will. There were many disagreements over the years too, and the daughter left the farm many times, finally leaving in 2012 for good, at which point the parents changed their will to leave the farm to all siblings equally. The claimant's two heads of detrimental reliance were that she had worked for low pay, and had lost the opportunity to pursue a career of her choosing elsewhere on reliance on the expectations of ownership of the farm. At first instance, the daughter was awarded £1.3 million pounds to satisfy her equity, though her parents had offered £350,000 in compensation for her work on the farm.

In reversing this award, the Court of Appeal held that the claimant was only entitled to £500,000. The reasons were twofold: first, in leaving the farm at various times, the various expectations had been brought to an end, and it was clear that the nature of the promise by the parents to the claimant had also changed over time. Second, the non-financial detrimental reliance, the loss of opportunity, was not irretrievable and did not amount to sufficient to supply the extra award beyond the £350,000 offer from the parents, which was adequate compensation for the work done on the farm. This was very much a forensic analysis of the financial contributions to the farm discounting the other factors, and leads to a manifestly inequitable result. As noted by Tattersall:

> The stark reality of the Court of Appeal's judgment is that Eirian Davies suffered detriment; such detriment was acknowledged by the courts and then thereafter worsened. Eirian's sisters, the unwitting beneficiaries, have prospered by having their 33% share of the estate increased to 50%. Subsequently, Eirian's detriment is worsened further by having to pay substantial legal fees. The facts of the case lead one to question whether it is good law for a claimant in a proprietary estoppel claim to have their injustice recognised by the courts and then made worse — such an approach would seem to represent the antithesis of equity's role within the English legal system.[154]

---

[152] [2015] EWHC 1384 (Ch).   [153] [2016] EWCA Civ 463 (CA).
[154] Tattersall, L. 'A Portable Palm Tree: Proprietary Estoppel in *Davies v Davies* (CA)' (2006) 30 *Trusts Law International* 237, 242.

This uncertainty as to the remedy, and the lack of a coherent structure in which the courts can operate, does rob proprietary estoppel of some of its utility as an effective replacement for the constructive trust of common intention to assist cohabitants. Similar problems in quantifying interests, such as the primacy afforded to financial contributions, pervade the operation of the doctrine.

5. Property entitlements

Until now, this chapter has focused on the acquisition and quantification of an interest in the family home. There is another dimension, normally covered in land law texts, which concerns the entitlements that arise from having an interest in the land (where such an interest is, in fact, granted under an estoppel claim). What follows is a brief summary of the pertinent rules for trust interests. Whether the interest of the cohabitant would bind a third party on sale is also relevant, but that is a matter for land law texts, as it is not straightforward to explain, as it depends on a variety of factors and whether title to the family home is part of the unregistered or registered land system. At the very least, where property is sold, the equitable owner will be entitled to a share of the proceeds of sale proportionate to the size of their equitable interest.[155]

It is also worth noting that an express (or implied) trust of the family home will be classed as a trust of land, which is a statutory construct under the Trust of Land and Appointment of Trustees Act 1996, s. 36(1). One issue that needs to be addressed is, if the legal owner wants to sell the property, can the cohabitant with an interest in trust stop sale, or remain in the property?

The answer to these questions is provided by an analysis of the rights of each cohabitee and then by applying the rules and principles set out in the Trusts of Land and Appointment of Trustees Act 1996 (TOLATA) and the Land Registration Act 2002. Under TOLATA, a person with a beneficial interest in the property has a right of occupation which can be regulated by the courts, and can also apply to court to prevent a sale taking place under s. 14. In making a decision on, say, the question of sale, the court has regard to various factors set out in s. 15(1).

 Key Legislation 3: Trusts of Land and Appointment of Trustees Act 2002, s. 15(1)

Matters relevant in determining applications.

(1) The matters to which the court is to have regard in determining an application for an order under section 14 include—
  (a) the intentions of the person or persons (if any) who created the trust,
  (b) the purposes for which the property subject to the trust is held,
  (c) the welfare of any minor who occupies or might reasonably be expected to occupy any land subject to the trust as his home, and
  (d) the interests of any secured creditor of any beneficiary.

While this looks comprehensive, the section does not give the court any guidance about the weighting or application of the factors, and therefore how disputes should be resolved or the protection of use and occupation weighed against the other interests.

---

[155] See, generally, Dixon, M. *Modern Land Law* (10th edn, Routledge, 2016).

In the domestic context, it would be difficult to argue that the 'purpose' of the trust continues through a relationship breakdown, and the court would normally order sale in such circumstances. Decisions are not always consistent, so in *Holman v Kingston Howes*,[156] the purchase of the property as a home for one of the beneficiaries led to the court postponing sale. The fact that the family home may be required for the maintenance of any children of a relationship is not a sufficient reason for the court to refuse an order for sale, unless there is a real threat of harm to the children.[157]

More problematic is the situation where it is not the other party in the relationship seeking sale, and a mortgagee or other secured creditor is asking that the home be sold to pay off existing debts. Here, it appears that the use and occupation of land by the home owners is not protected. Indeed, in the absence of hardship to children as a factor to be taken into consideration, it seems from the case law that the rights of mortgagees and other creditors will be given precedence, and at best sale will only be postponed to allow for alternative arrangements for accommodation to be made. In *Mortgage Corporation v Shaire*,[158] for example, sale was not immediately ordered, but the creditor mortgagee was entitled to be paid interest as the price of not making an order for sale. The order was postponed, not suspended for all time. Nevertheless, it remains true that a party granted an interest in land is still better off than someone without a proprietary interest in the home, as no such discussion even arises in relation to personal interests such as a licence to occupy the home.

6. Reforming the law: challenges and perspectives

We have seen that neither constructive trusts nor estoppel are necessarily fit for purpose in relation to deciding questions of ownership of the family home for cohabitants. It is understandable that other legal jurisdictions have adopted a legislative solution, granting the courts a discretion to adjust the property rights of cohabitants, in much the same way as the courts in England have been granted the right to adjust the property rights of married couples on divorce (see Chapter 4).

The lack of a legislative solution in England and Wales has not been for the want of effort. The Law Commission has expended considerable time, and public monies, on numerous, elaborate proposals for automatic joint ownership of the matrimonial home during marriage.[159] They failed to gain support, as many suggested that this was an issue that could be addressed in practical terms, rather than through legislative intervention. Conveyancing practice could allow joint legal ownership, as we have seen, and many felt that the existing equitable rules, through implied trusts, were sufficient to deal with the situation.

In 1995, the Law Commission began an expansive project to review the law with the aim to develop a scheme applicable to all home-sharers, whether sexual partners or friends. The Commission was unable to propose any scheme to cover all relationships, and, again met with resistance in consultation, on the basis that such proposals undermined the sanctity of marriage, which Parliament had seen fit to protect separately from unmarried cohabitation. The *Sharing Homes* project was not a success, and the final report contained no legislative suggestions for reform, but provided the basis for debate for that reform.[160]

---

[156] [2005] EWHC 2824 (Ch).

[157] See *First National Bank plc v Achampong* [2003] EWCA Civ 487, [2004] 1 FCR 18.

[158] [2000] 1 FLR 273.

[159] See Law Commission reports: Law Com No. 5, 1973; Law Com No. 86, 1978; Law Com No. 115, 1982; and Law Com No. 175, 1988.

[160] See Law Commission, *Sharing Homes* (Law Com No. 278, 2002); Law Commission, *Cohabitation: The Financial Consequences of Relationship Breakdown* (Law Com No. 179, 2006).

The latest attempt at reform by the Commission was to suggest a statutory scheme for cohabiting couples that would allow for the determination of the property rights of cohabitants on a similar basis to married couples and registered civil partners.[161] This proposed a scheme which would apply to cohabitants who either had children or met a minimum qualifying period of cohabitation in the home and who had made some sort of lasting contribution to the family. The scheme was to be voluntary, in that it could be excluded by a written agreement between the parties. If it applied, on relationship breakdown, the court could make a property adjustment award, which reflects not only the contributions of the parties during the relationship, but also the financial needs and resources the parties could call upon in the future and the welfare of any children living with, or expected to live, with either party.

This scheme would represent a vast improvement on the current position available through the intervention of equity. Unfortunately, though a similar scheme now exists in Scotland under the Family Law (Scotland) Act 2006, there is no indication that it will ever be enacted in England and Wales. In September 2011, the then government announced that it did not plan to implement the Law Commission's proposals during the session. Nothing has happened since.

Despite this, calls for reform have also come from the judiciary, including Lord Wilson in *Jones v Kernott*, and Lady Hale in *Gow v Grant*.[162] In June 2014, Lord Mark introduced a Private Members Bill, the Cohabitation Rights Bill, which seeks to provide basic protections for cohabitants and for the provision of their property upon death. Under the Bill, the court is able to make a financial settlement order where there is a 'retained benefit' or an 'economic disadvantage' dependent on any 'qualifying contributions' made—either financial or other. It is similar to, but not the same as, the Commissions Bill. It received a first reading in the House of Lords, but the second reading remains unscheduled. The Bill, in substantially the same form, was introduced again in 2017.

The plight of cohabitants remains in the hands of the judiciary and their equity-based solutions. It remains to be seen whether further evolution will address the concerns of these devices, but, in the absence of legislation, cohabitants have reason to be thankful for the intervention in the family home.

SUMMARY

1. Is there a single approach to imputation of common intention in sole and joint legal ownership cases?
   - There is an argument that a common intention should be inferred or imputed, whether or not the cohabitant is already entitled to an interest in land by being named on the legal title and seeks to determine the size of their beneficial entitlement, or has no existing entitlement in the home and needs to acquire an interest.
   - Dicta in the leading cases support a different approach in sole legal owner cases, as the cohabitant has to demonstrate an entitlement by means of a traditional constructive trust of common intention demonstrated through express agreement or conduct, on which she or he relied to their detriment.

---

[161] Law Commission, *Cohabitation: The Financial Consequences of Relationship Breakdown* (Law Com No. 179, 2006).   [162] [2012] UKSC 29, at [47].

- The latest decisions in the Supreme Court have not overruled existing precedents, and the requirement to both prove an entitlement to an interest and demonstrate an element of detriment are both requirements of property law.
- Some cases have been inconsistent, nonetheless, and sought to infer a right on the basis of a common intention alone. While these are cited with approval by some commentators, they do not represent the current state of the law.
- Once an interest has been established, the quantification of that interest follows the same set of rules, whether or not the cohabitant was entitled through a constructive trust of common intention or by being named on the title of the family home.
- There is a clear role for imputing the size of an interest, in either case, when the common intention cannot easily be inferred from the facts.

2. Should property division on non-marital breakdown be based on family law or property law principles?
   - Rights of unmarried cohabitants on relationship breakdown lie at an intersection between property rights and family law rights.
   - Property rights are concerned with certainty and predictability, and the way property law perceives the family home situation in sole legal owner cases is that the legal owner should not be deprived of his or her entitlement to the whole of the property without rights being established by the cohabitant on settled principles.
   - Family law is discretion based, and the use of property concepts does not sit easily with a wish for resource distribution.
   - That courts struggle in areas such as identifying factors beyond financial considerations, either in establishing interests for cohabitants in the sole legal owner cases, or quantifying interests in the home on the basis of matters of family life.

3. Are common intention constructive trust in the family home a new construct?
   - In developing the constructive trust of common intention, the courts have been adamant that they are not creating new rules, just adapting existing ones to a new, social situation.
   - There is reason to suspect that there is a difference between what the courts say they are doing, and what they are actually doing.
   - The approach of the law, particularly in quantifying the interest of cohabitants, is closer to the position of married couples who divorce under the Matrimonial Causes Act 1972 than basic property rights.
   - If new concepts have not yet been developed, existing principles have been strained to their absolute limits. If imputation of an interest, rather than the size of the interest, ever becomes part of the law, any debate will be removed and a new category of right will have been created by equity.

4. What are the limits of estoppel remedies?
   - An estoppel claim arises in similar situations to a constructive trust of common intention, but the requirements are more fluid as they are based on unconscionability, and this means that a claim in estoppel may arise in situations where it would not be possible in a constructive trusts based claim.

- A claim in estoppel does not automatically lead to a remedy. The remedy must be supplied. This is supplied by court order, and the court has a range of remedies available, which can give more or less than both what a cohabitant might expect, or than would be given under a constructive trust of common intention.
- There has been some disquiet expressed as to process by which the courts decide on the appropriate remedy under estoppel. It is accepted, though, that the end point is supposed to be a right which is the minimum right required to do justice to the claimant.
- Rather than categorise the exercise of this discretion into narrow or wide categories, the truth is that the courts should take a composite approach which recognises that these approaches are elements in making sure that unconscionability is remedied. There should be some link to the assurances made which allowed the claim in proprietary estoppel in the first place.
- The courts are capable of reaching strange decisions on the facts, and, again, can be too influenced by financial factors.

Further Reading

COWAN D., FOX-O'MAHONEY, L., and COBB, N. *Great Debates in Land Law* (2nd edn, Palgrave McMillan, 2016) Chapter 11
- An excellent and readable overview of cohabitation in the family home.

DIXON, M. 'The Still Not Ended, Never Ending Story' [2007] *The Conveyancer and Property Lawyer* 83
- A lively account of the impact of *Jones v Kernott* on the family home.

GARDNER S. 'The Remedial Discretion in Proprietary Estoppel—Again' (2006) 122 *Law Quarterly Review* 438
- Together considers all of the key decisions on feeding an estoppel.

PAWLOWSKI, M. 'Imputing Intention and the Family Home' [2016] *Family Law* 189
- A compelling analysis of the rules and limits on imputing intention by the courts, as opposed to inferring intention.

Probert, R. 'Equality in the Family Home? *Stack v Dowden* (2007)' (2007) 15 *Feminist Legal Studies* 314, 348
- Good critique of the inequalities in the approach of the courts, particularly around financial contributions.

SWADLING, W. 'The Common Intention Constructive Trust in the House of Lords: An Opportunity Missed' (2007) 123 *Law Quarterly Review* 511
- A critical account of the development of constructive trusts in the family home, and *Stack v Dowden*.

THOMPSON, 'Constructive Trusts, Estoppel and the Family Home' [2004] *The Conveyancer and Property Lawyer* 496
- Provides a good analysis of the relationship between the different mechanisms in the family home.

6

Child Support

Lara Walker

LEARNING OBJECTIVES

After reading this chapter you will be able to:

- Understand the different debates surrounding child support, including those on who should pay and the role of private agreements;

- Identify the rules for calculating child support under the Child Support Act 1991 and recognise the role of the courts in the context of child support;

- Critically analyse the government's child support policy and the rules relating to it.

DEBATES

After reading this chapter you should be equipped to discuss your opinion on the following central debates:

1. Who should support children financially?

2. Should we rely on private agreements for child support?

3. How should child support obligations be enforced; through a state body or privately?

1. Introduction

Child support in England and Wales is predominantly dealt with by the Child Support Act 1991. However the Children Act 1989 and the Matrimonial Causes Act 1973 are also relevant. Child support is important for many reasons. In particular, studies indicate that, in general, children in single parent families are more likely to be worse off than children in two parent families with many living below the poverty line. It is clear that many children in single parent families need additional financial support, but it is unclear where this money should come from. Should the parents pay for the child, should the taxpayer pay, or should there be a contribution from both the state and the parents to help alleviate child poverty? There are many difficult questions to be answered.

Another concern is that it is often parents on low incomes who fail to pay child support.[1] The small amount they can pay towards child support is unlikely to raise the primary caretakers income to a suitable level and it reduces the money the paying parent has to live off. The paying parent may be relying on the support of their own family or they may have started a new family with a new partner, or taken on the care of the children of their new partner, who they will then also have to support. If the money is spread too thinly between the relevant children then this might not do enough to resolve the issue of poverty, so policy-makers need to think carefully about who the law should require to pay child support. There are, of course, children who receive child support who are not at risk of poverty but nonetheless the primary caregiver needs some additional support. There is also the question of whether particularly well-off absent parents should pay more. These complicated issues have troubled policy-makers for years and they have struggled to find a suitable theory on which to place a duty of child support. This chapter will begin by looking at some theories and problems associated with the theories, before moving on to look at the English policy and law in greater detail.

2. Theory

There is no question that when asked many people would consider that parents should provide support for their children, that separated parents should continue to provide support, and that single parents are entitled to support for the child from the non-resident parent (usually, but not always, the father).[2] However the difficult factor is finding a theoretical underpinning for this duty which is believed, by many, to exist. Without a theoretical underpinning that suggests that this duty should belong to parents, some consider that the duty should belong to the state which has higher funds.

 DEBATE 1: WHO SHOULD SUPPORT CHILDREN FINANCIALLY?

The general presumption might be that parents should support their children financially, however, some argue that this should not always be the case. Consequently there are different theories which have been advanced which try to underpin why certain people should pay child support and these depend on the purpose of the child support payment. For example, is the purpose of the child support payment to hold those who created the child responsible for funding the upbringing of that child, or is child support designed to promote child welfare and prevent poverty? If the sole purpose of child support is to prevent child poverty then it is arguable that the state should take responsibility for this, as the funds available are often higher. If however the payment of child support has a broader function then it is arguable that the support should be paid by parents, or parents in conjunction with the state in order to prevent child poverty and serve other functions, such as holding parents responsible for their children. If the state was solely responsible for every child then they would not be able to control state welfare payments, and they would need to use money collected from taxpayers to fund this.

---

[1] Takayesu, M. and Eldred, S. 'Setting appropriate Child Support Orders and Addressing Barriers: Research and Policy Implications to Improve Payments and Compliance' in P. Beaumont *et al* (eds) *The Recovery of Maintenance in the EU and Worldwide* (2014, Hart Publishing) 137.

[2] Ellman, I.M. *et al* 'Child Support Judgments: Comparing Public Policy to the Public's Policy (2014) *International Journal of Law, Policy and the Family* 274; Wikeley, N. *et al* Department for Work and Pensions Research Report No. 503 'Relationship separation and child support study' (Corporate Document Services, 2008).

Some of the theories that have been advanced will be explored briefly here.[3] The causation theory recognises that the parents created the child so they should therefore pay for that child's upbringing. This is similar to the parental consent theory, which is based on the idea that the parties choose to procreate, or at least risk procreation. However this may not be the case where there was a lack of consent to the sexual relationship, such as rape, or one party was deceived about contraception. Gender equality is also relevant in the sense that women suffer the risks of pregnancy, and absence from work during maternity leave is likely to damage their career progression, therefore requiring fathers to pay child support is one way of trying to promote equality. Child support could also be used to encourage family planning, by encouraging those who do not want to have a child to take steps to prevent this happening.

On the other hand the insurance and distributive justice theories require people to pay for things which benefit them. For example if children produce external benefits then it could be argued that the wider population should support children. When these children are older and form the working population, the generation which previously supported them will be reliant on pensions which are generated by the current fee earners.[4] Although all these theories have some merits, they also have some downsides.[5] Therefore four, arguably more persuasive, theories will be considered in greater detail. These are:

- moral understanding and obligations;
- prevention from harm;
- family responsibilities;
- children's rights.

You will see as this chapter unfolds that the law primarily places the responsibility to pay child support on the child's parents. However you will see that the persons who might be required to pay differ depending on the Act applicable.

It can be argued that parents have a moral duty to support their child. This is underpinned by the general presumption that this is what society expects.[6] The parents conceived the child therefore they have a moral obligation to care for that child which includes providing financial support. However because there is a moral obligation does that mean this should be converted into a legal duty? If so, how should this be done? There are perfectly good arguments for converting certain moral obligations into legal duties in order to protect society, in this case children. The problem is that they can only be converted into a legal obligation in regard to the social rules in the country, state, area or even religion in which the rules are made.[7] The moral duty can be understood as a requirement for nurturing and protecting children which falls on everyone, and the community can then create social rules which best fulfil the obligation.[8] This could be parents, but if the child's parent

---

[3] See, e.g. Altman, S. 'A Theory of Child Support' (2003) 17 *International Journal of Law, Policy and the Family* 173.

[4] For further information on these theories, see Altman, S. 'A Theory of Child Support' (2003) 17 *International Journal of Law, Policy and the Family* 173, 176–89.

[5] For some criticisms, see Altman, S. 'A Theory of Child Support' (2003) 17 *International Journal of Law, Policy and the Family* 173.

[6] Ellman, I.M. *et al* 'Child Support Judgments: Comparing Public Policy to the Public's Policy (2014) *International Journal of Law, Policy and the Family* 274.

[7] Eekelaar, J. 'Are Parents Morally Obliged to Care for their Children?' (1991) *Oxford Journal of Legal Studies* 340, 351.

[8] Eekelaar, J. 'Are Parents Morally Obliged to Care for their Children?' (1991) *Oxford Journal of Legal Studies* 340, 353.

abandons them then someone else takes on the moral duty to look after that child whether this is the wider family, a specific community, or the state. Research indicates that parents who have lived in the same house as their child prior to a break down in relationship are more likely to pay child support than those who have not,[9] suggesting that those who have not may consider that they have less of a moral obligation to support their child.

Altman argues that the best theoretical underpinning for the argument that child support should be paid by parents is the prevention from harm theory.[10] He contends that the payment of child support is a method for parents to demonstrate love for their children, and the demonstration of love can help to protect children from psychological harm. Studies have shown that non-resident parents who pay child support tend to visit their child more and have less conflict with the resident parent.[11] Research also shows that children who receive support feel less rejected, have fewer problems, and perform better in school.[12] Therefore child support paid by the non-resident parent is one way of protecting children from harm, by demonstrating love. 'Non-support is a culpable demonstration of indifference, not because money is the central means of showing love, but because those who do not support their children often show their indifference in this and many other less patent ways, all of which harm children.'[13] Unlike some other theories this one demonstrates why it should be the parent in particular who should pay child support. The child does not need to be loved by the state but by their parents and family.

One problem with this theory, which is on the whole very persuasive, is that it does not take account of the inability of parents to pay, either because they have limited funds and/or because child support is set too high. Research indicates that non-resident parents earning minimum wage are less likely to pay child support than those earning above minimum wage.[14] The rate of compliance increases in line with wage category.[15] Research also shows that inappropriate orders lead to inconsistent payments and high arrears.[16] Therefore, although the theory is persuasive, it would have to be implemented into policy in a sensible way which accounted for ability to pay in order to prevent further harm, as failure to pay can increase conflict between parents.[17]

Another theoretical underpinning is responsibility,[18] more specifically family responsibilities.[19] This theory is advocated by many academics researching family law,

---

[9] Skinner, C. 'Child Maintenance Reforms: Understanding father's Expressive Agency and the Power of Reciprocity' (2013) 27 *International Journal of Law, Policy and the Family* 242, 244; Douglas, G. *et al* 'Contact is not a Commodity to be bartered for money' [2011] *Family Law* 491, 493.

[10] Altman, S. 'A Theory of Child Support' (2003) 17 *International Journal of Law, Policy and the Family* 173, 189–200.

[11] Bryson, C. *et al Kids aren't free: the child maintenance arrangements of single parents on benefit in 2012* (Gingerbread).

[12] Altman, S. 'A Theory of Child Support' (2003) 17 *International Journal of Law, Policy and the Family* 173, 190.

[13] Altman, S. 'A Theory of Child Support' (2003) 17 *International Journal of Law, Policy and the Family* 173, 192.

[14] Takayesu, M. and Eldred, S. 'Setting appropriate Child Support Orders and Addressing Barriers: Research and Policy Implications to Improve Payments and Compliance' in P. Beaumont *et al* (eds) *The Recovery of Maintenance in the EU and Worldwide* (2014, Hart Publishing) 137, 145 (fig 3).

[15] Takayesu, M. and Eldred, S. 'Setting appropriate Child Support Orders and Addressing Barriers: Research and Policy Implications to Improve Payments and Compliance' in P. Beaumont *et al* (eds) *The Recovery of Maintenance in the EU and Worldwide* (2014, Hart Publishing) 137, 145 (fig 2). For those earning minimum wage the compliance rate was 19.9% compared to 75.3% for the high income category.

[16] Takayesu, M. and Eldred, S. 'Setting appropriate Child Support Orders and Addressing Barriers: Research and Policy Implications to Improve Payments and Compliance' in P. Beaumont *et al* (eds) *The Recovery of Maintenance in the EU and Worldwide* (2014, Hart Publishing) 137, 143.

[17] Seltzer, J. 'Consequences of marital dissolution for children' (1994) 20 *Annual Review of Sociology* 235, 250–2.

[18] See, e.g., Eekelaar, J. *Family Law and Personal Life* (OUP, 2007) ch 5.

[19] Bridgeman, J. *et al* (eds) *Regulating Family Responsibilities* (Ashgate, 2011) 3.

and it is also supposed to underpin government policy in this area (3.3). Much like moral obligations, not all responsibilities are legal duties, but nevertheless they are responsibilities that parents owe to their child or family members owe each other. Responsibility can be used as a framework for shaping the law in order to take account of specific issues relating to families. This could be used to foster more responsible care and to support responsible caring,[20] in this case in relation to the payment of child support. Responsibility can also be thought of in broader terms than family responsibility. Supporting children financially is the responsible thing to do and this burden can fall firstly on parents, in relation to responsible parenting, and be extended to the state to take financial responsibility for these children where the parents are financially unable to provide enough support.

An alternative justification, or theory, is a rights justification. Children's rights originate from the United Nations Convention on the Rights of the Child 1990 (UNCRC), and any legal right relating to child support taken from that Convention is dependent on the status of the UNCRC in the country in which the child resides. The UK has ratified the UNCRC, however as a general principle the UK does not incorporate international treaties into domestic law.[21] In the context of the UNCRC ministers in England have committed to giving the Convention due consideration when making policy and legislation, and legislation is assessed to ensure compatibility with the UNCRC.[22] The relevant provision of the UNCRC is Article 27, but Article 18 also deserves mention. Article 27(1) recognises the right of every child to an adequate standard of living. The responsibility for securing this standard of living to ensure the child's development, lies predominantly with the parents.[23] However states should take measures to assist parents in cases of need.[24] The provision also requires that state parties take measures to ensure the recovery of maintenance for the child, from the people who have financial responsibility for the child. So the UNCRC essentially creates a right to child support for all children and it places primary responsibility for this with parents, or anyone else 'responsible' for the child.

UNICEF recognise that child support often carries wider social benefits than simply improving the living standards of children and it can also address the issue of single parent families by encouraging the non-resident parent to play a more active role in the child's upbringing.[25] Article 18 indicates that both parents have common responsibilities for the upbringing and development of the child. This goes beyond financial responsibilities with the aim being that both parents should play an active role in their child's upbringing.[26] In order to help achieve this, the state can adopt employment, tax, and welfare measures to encourage both parents' active involvement in child rearing.[27] These employment measures could encourage more flexible hours to allow parents to adapt their working hours to allow them to spend time with their children, or include tax credits or childcare vouchers for working parents. Therefore the rights analysis, like the

---

[20] Bridgeman, J. *et al* (eds) *Regulating Family Responsibilities* (Ashgate, 2011) 5.

[21] Committee on the Rights of the Child, 'List of issues in relation to the fifth periodic report of the United Kingdom of Great Britain and Northern Ireland, Addendum, Replies of the United Kingdom of Great Britain and Northern Ireland to the list of issues' (March 2016) CRC/C/GBR/Q/5/Add.1, para 5.

[22] Committee on the Rights of the Child, 'List of issues in relation to the fifth periodic report of the United Kingdom of Great Britain and Northern Ireland, Addendum, Replies of the United Kingdom of Great Britain and Northern Ireland to the list of issues' (March 2016) CRC/C/GBR/Q/5/Add.1, para 6.

[23] Article 27(2) UNCRC.   [24] Article 27(3) UNCRC.

[25] Hodgkin, R. and Newell, P. *Implementation Handbook for the Convention on the Rights of the Child* (UNICEF, 2007) 401.

[26] Hodgkin, R. and Newell, P. *Implementation Handbook for the Convention on the Rights of the Child* (UNICEF, 2007) 235.

[27] Hodgkin, R. and Newell, P. *Implementation Handbook for the Convention on the Rights of the Child* (UNICEF, 2007) 236.

responsibilities theory (and using similar language in terms of the responsibility to pay), places primary responsibility with the parents but recognises that the state also has responsibility. This could be a financial responsibility where the parent can only contribute a small amount or a responsibility to initiate additional welfare measures to ensure that both parents can participate in the child's life.

These theories create theoretical underpinnings for the creation of a duty of child support. All, apart from the harm theory, require both the parents and the state to take responsibility for the child. The harm theory clearly demonstrates why the obligation should primarily lie with the parent, but it fails to account for situations where the non-resident parent is unable to provide a suitable amount of child support and does not explain why the state should step in in such cases. The government policy in this area, which this chapter will now consider, seems to focus on family responsibilities but the government method of regulating this responsibility has altered through time.

3. Policy

Now that we have considered the key theories, the chapter will look at the government policy on child support in order to establish whether the policy is built on any of these theories and, if so, how closely it actually relates to the theory.

3.1 Background

Prior to 1991 child support was dealt with by the courts. Initially children born outside of marriage had no rights and at common law neither the father, nor the mother, were liable for maintenance.[28] The Poor Law did place an obligation on mothers to support their illegitimate children, but it was not until 1884 that the Poor Law provided the mother with the power to apply for maintenance.[29] However the right of unmarried mothers to make a claim was limited, for example, claims had to be brought within three years of the child's birth. Despite a number of changes to the legislation this restriction was not removed until 1987 through the Family Reform Act. The provisions that now cover applications to court are found in Sch 1 of the Children Act 1989, discussed later (5.3.2). However, between the 1970s and the early 1990s there was a large increase in the number of single parents and, there were many applications for child support going to court and child support orders given by courts were deemed to be inconsistent. Consequently the government decided to establish an administrative system for the recovery of child support.

3.2 The Child Support Act 1991 and the Child Support Agency

In 1991 the Conservative government introduced the Child Support Act along with the Child Support Agency (CSA). The rise in single parent families had prompted the review and subsequent overhaul of the law. The change in policy was initially driven by Prime Minister Mrs Thatcher who adopted the catchphrase 'parenthood is for life',[30] and the aim was to ensure that parents paid for their children. The review of policy and law began with the publication of the White Paper 'Children Come First'.[31]

---

[28] *Ruttinger v Temple* (1863) 4 B & S 491.   [29] Poor Law Amendment Act 1884.

[30] See, e.g., Eekelaar, J. 'Are Parents Morally Obliged to Care for their Children?' (1991) 11 *Oxford Journal of Legal Studies* 340, 340.

[31] *Children Come First: The Government's Proposals on the Maintenance of Children* (White Paper, Cm 1264, 1990).

CONTEXT 1: SOCIAL ISSUES WHICH INFLUENCED THE 1991 ACT

Between the 1970s and the early 1990s the proportion of children born to unmarried mothers in the UK trebled from around 10% to 30%. This social change influenced changes in child support policy and the move to an administrative system through the Child Support Act 1991.

Prior to the inception of the 1991 Act the government collected data on families within the UK. The information collected was contained in the government's White Paper. Data collected showed that the percentage of lone parent families on benefit who were also receiving maintenance fell from 50% in the early 1980s to 23% by the end of the decade.[32] Data also showed that the recovery rate of maintenance was higher for lone parents not receiving income support, than for those who were receiving income support (44% compared to 22%).[33] Other notable findings were that 94% of maintenance recipients were women;[34] and 71% of absent parents were in full time employment,[35] albeit earning less on average than the general population.[36] The White Paper also looked into new policies in other countries, and claimed that the trend of large dependence on public support had led to legislation aimed at obtaining child support from absent parents.[37] 'The legislation has reflected the two main principles; of requiring parents to take responsibility for their children even if they were no longer living with them, and the need for the government to intervene to ensure that this occurs.'[38]

The proposals within the White Paper included formulas to help with the calculation of maintenance payable, on the basis that current maintenance orders varied widely,[39] and the international study had indicated that the introduction of a formula increased payments.[40] The proposal included the creation of an agency to handle all child support applications known as the Child Support Agency. The aim was that all the services could be delivered by one single authority, rather than spread across different bodies, so that parents knew where to go for help and advice.[41] The agency was to have a variety of duties from calculating the maintenance payable through to securing enforcement of the payment. The agency was introduced in a flexible way in the White Paper which provided that where maintenance was being paid directly to the caring parent there would be no

---

[32] *Children Come First: The Government's Proposals on the Maintenance of Children* (White Paper, Cm 1264, 1990) Vol II, 1.4.1.

[33] *Children Come First: The Government's Proposals on the Maintenance of Children* (White Paper, Cm 1264, 1990) Vol II, 1.4.4.

[34] *Children Come First: The Government's Proposals on the Maintenance of Children* (White Paper, Cm 1264, 1990) Vol II, 3.2.2.

[35] *Children Come First: The Government's Proposals on the Maintenance of Children* (White Paper, Cm 1264, 1990) Vol II, 3.3.2.

[36] *Children Come First: The Government's Proposals on the Maintenance of Children* (White Paper, Cm 1264, 1990) Vol II, 3.3.4.

[37] *Children Come First: The Government's Proposals on the Maintenance of Children* (White Paper, Cm 1264, 1990) Vol II, 7.2.

[38] *Children Come First: The Government's Proposals on the Maintenance of Children* (White Paper, Cm 1264, 1990) Vol II and see Hansard HL vol 522, cols 1695–6 (29 October 1990).

[39] *Children Come First: The Government's Proposals on the Maintenance of Children* (White Paper, Cm 1264, 1990) Vol I, para 1.5.

[40] *Children Come First: The Government's Proposals on the Maintenance of Children* (White Paper, Cm 1264, 1990) Vol II, para 7.6.

[41] *Children Come First: The Government's Proposals on the Maintenance of Children* (White Paper, Cm 1264, 1990) Vol I, 5.2.

need for the agency to interfere.[42] The White Paper indicated that it should be up to parties to choose whether to use the agency and which of its services they wanted to use; such as using the agency for enforcement purposes, or using the agency to calculate maintenance then reaching a private agreement and dealing with enforcement independently.[43] However, where the lone parent was receiving income support there would be a requirement for that parent to use the agency.[44] Finally the courts were no longer to be involved in child support applications, and all applications, apart from private agreements, were to be directed through the agency.

The proposal came at the same time as other major amendments were made to the law in relation to families by the Children Act 1989, which focused on parental responsibility. It also followed various new measures in relation to social security, such as the Social Security Act 1990, which supported the Department for Social Security (DSS) recovering money paid in benefits from absent parents. The underlying policy behind the proposal was to reduce the welfare bill by recovering child support from non-resident parents, however the original proposal did also have social and moral claims such as lifting more single mothers and their children out of poverty and forcing absent fathers to honour their responsibilities towards their children.[45]

The White Paper, and the ideas contained in it, received wide support.[46] The Child Support Bill was published in February 1991, just two months after the closing date for responses to the White Paper and the Bill was passed by July 1991.[47] During this time the Treasury and the DSS had disagreements about the purpose of the Bill. The Treasury wanted to cut public expenditure and they considered that recovering money from absent parents (normally fathers) would be a good way to do this. The DSS, on the other hand, wanted to 'do good' and promote the welfare of children by making additional money available for single parents through the recovery of child support. The DSS also wanted access to the Service to be flexible, but the Treasury wanted to force as many people as possible to use the Service so that they could recover more funds. The Treasury won the debate and the Act became solely about reducing state welfare payments and reclaiming public funds.[48] Several measures were pushed through that were contrary to those recommended in the White Paper and to the advice of the DSS.

The new agency was to be faced with dealing with all new child support arrangements, applying the complicated formulas designed by the DSS, the enforcement of these obligations, and the enforcement of current maintenance obligations, including any arrears. This was a huge task, and all of these changes were to be implemented at the same time, in contrast to some of the countries studied which had implemented their changes in stages and not on such a vast scale.[49]

Unsurprisingly the Child Support Agency failed. The idea of parents being responsible for their children and their upbringing was acknowledged, but it was overshadowed by

---

[42] *Children Come First: The Government's Proposals on the Maintenance of Children* (White Paper, Cm 1264, 1990) Vol I, 5.15.

[43] *Children Come First: The Government's Proposals on the Maintenance of Children* (White Paper, Cm 1264, 1990) Vol I, 5.26.

[44] *Children Come First: The Government's Proposals on the Maintenance of Children* (White Paper, Cm 1264, 1990) Vol I.

[45] King, A. and Crewe, I. *The Blunders of our Governments* (Oneworld, 2014) ch 6.

[46] See, e.g. Hansard HL vol 522, cols 1695–708 (29 October 1990); Roll, J. Child Support Research Paper 94/20 (1994) 2.

[47] Roll, J. Child Support Research Paper 94/20 (1994) 11; King, A. and Crewe, I. *The Blunders of our Governments* (Oneworld, 2014) ch 6.

[48] King, A. and Crewe, I. *The Blunders of our Governments* (Oneworld, 2014) ch 6.

[49] *Children Come First: The Government's Proposals on the Maintenance of Children* (White Paper, Cm 1264, 1990) Vol II, 7.4–7.5.

the government's drive to save public expenditure by reducing welfare payments. The Act instead removed responsibility from people capable of managing their own arrangements by directing all cases through the Child Support Agency. This increased the workload of the agency. The agency was very costly and it was also claiming back benefits from the child support collected, rather than paying the child support to the parent. This was not doing anything to reduce poverty because the lone parent was not receiving any additional money, just a substitution. The Child Support Act was updated in 1995, but there was no notable improvement on the 1991 Act.

3.3 Current policy and the move towards private agreements

In 2006 action was taken to replace the failed child support system and Child Support Agency. By this time New Labour were in power and they had a very different political approach to state benefits than the previous Conservative government. In 2006 the Henshaw report was published which had new ideas and a new philosophy. The report emphasised that the reason the state is involved in child support is to ensure the welfare of children.[50] The report suggested a change of approach that focused on children, responsibilities, and compliance. In particular under the new policy parents on benefits were to be allowed to keep the child support they received. This change 'would make a significant contribution to meeting the Government's child poverty objective'.[51] The policy aimed to improve the welfare of children and saw a role for both parents and the government in reducing child poverty.

 CONTEXT 2: FOCUS ON PRIVATE AGREEMENTS

A major theme in the Henshaw report, and the resulting policy, was an emphasis on private agreements. The report indicated that any new regime should focus on private agreements, which parents should be encouraged and supported to make, and the state was only to become involved when parents could not reach an agreement.[52] Rather than relying on the actions of the Child Support Agency, a government service was to become a backup option, rather than the main option. This major change was designed to allow the government service to focus on resolving a smaller number of more difficult cases, and it was hoped that the change would also encourage parents to cooperate with the system.[53] The policy behind the new approach was that parents should take responsibility and financial responsibility was to be recognised as a key element of parental responsibility.[54] One way of encouraging parents to take responsibility was to allow parents to reach their own agreements and organise enforcement between themselves.

Over recent years this approach has been reflected in wider government policy in family law. There is now an emphasis on autonomy and private agreements rather than state funded access to legal services. Self-reliance has become a dominant theme in social policy, and autonomy and independence have become key policy goals.[55] The Legal Aid, Sentencing, and Punishment of Offenders Act 2012 (LASPO) greatly reduced access to legal aid for private family law disputes, and the first year of LASPO saw a 60% drop in family legal aid.[56] These changes apply to applications for child support under the court system, rather than the CSA

---

[50] Henshaw Report 2006.   [51] Henshaw Report 2006, 2.   [52] Henshaw Report, 2006, 5.
[53] Henshaw Report, 2006, 7.   [54] Henshaw Report, 2006, 12.
[55] Herring, J. 'Making Family Law more Careful' in J. Wallbank and J. Herring (eds) *Vulnerabilities, Care and Family Law* (Routledge, 2013) 43.
[56] Ministry of Justice, *Legal Aid Statistics in England and Wales 2013–2014*, 20.

(see section 5). The initial changes introduced sought to reduce legal aid for private disputes but retained legal aid for public child law cases and disputes involving domestic violence. However the most recent measures have also vastly decreased access to legal aid for domestic violence victims by introducing a means test which limits access to legal aid to those with very low means.[57] Therefore the current social-legal context focuses on autonomy and private ordering regardless of the status of those involved in the dispute, their ability to make private agreements, and the balance of power within the relationship.

The policy expressed in the Henshaw report was undoubtedly better than the old approach relying solely on the Child Support Agency. The aim was about protecting children and their primary carers, rather than just clawing back money paid out through the benefits system from absent parents, with the state accepting 'a full role in alleviating child poverty following parental separation'.[58] The new policy can be linked to the responsibility theory beginning with a 'family responsibility' for parents to look after their children financially, with state intervention and assistance where the parents are unable to agree on this and/or maintain their child to a suitable standard. It also has resonance with children's rights and the approach of the UNCRC which again places primary responsibility with the parents, but also recognises that the state also has a role in alleviating child poverty and should provide back up where necessary. This policy came into force under the Child Maintenance and other Payments Act 2008 and the new government body in charge was called the Child Maintenance Service.

The system was revised again slightly when the Coalition government of Conservatives and Liberal Democrats came into power in 2010 and the name and the position of the agency was revised again. Maintenance is now collected through the Department for Work and Pensions. For ease the administrative body will generally be referred to as the government service; but when referring to provisions in the legislation it will be referred to as the Secretary of State, from whom the service gets its legal authority, as per the legislation. Unfortunately the new system has not worked as efficiently and effectively as planned. The new service is still very expensive to run, child support continues to be unrecovered, and the department charges for its services.

4. Law under the child support scheme

The core part of the current law entered into force from August 2012 and the main part is found under the Child Support Act 1991, as amended. The two key characteristics of the child support scheme are that maintenance is calculated via a formula, and there is a government service that is entrusted with the role of applying the formula and collecting child support. The initial formula was extremely complicated, taking into account the income of both parents and the needs of their children (but not necessarily step-children).[59] The formula was developed and simplified over the years and now only takes account of the non-resident parent's income, however it does account for all dependent children. The government service is now managed by the Department for Work and Pensions but

[57] See https://www.gov.uk/legal-aid/domestic-abuse-or-violence, accessed 3 February 2017.

[58] Miles, J 'Responsibility in Family Finance and Property Law' in J Bridgeman *et al* (eds) *Regulating Family Responsibilities* (Ashgate, 2011) 91, 101.

[59] *Children Come First: The Government's Proposals on the Maintenance of Children* (White Paper, Cm 1264, 1990) Vol I, Ch 3.

certain obligations are still dealt with under previous systems, depending on when the maintenance calculation was first established. The aim is to move all maintenance cases to the new system by 2018.

4.1 **Relevant parties**

The relevant parties for the purpose of the Act are: qualifying children, non-resident parents, and persons with care. A qualifying child is a person under the age of 16,[60] or a person under the age of 20 in prescribed circumstances, in cases which fall under the regime in the 2008 Act.[61] A child is a qualifying child where either, 'one of his parents, in relation to him is a non-resident parent;[62] or both of his parents are, in relation to him, non-resident parents'.[63] A parent is considered to be a non-resident parent where 'that parent is not living in the same household with the child;[64] and the child has his home with a person who is, in relation to him, a person with care'.[65] A person with care is a person with whom the child has his home and who usually provides day-to-day care for the child.

 DEBATE 2: WHO SHOULD SUPPORT CHILDREN FINANCIALLY?

For the purpose of this Act only those with the legal status of parent will be liable to pay child support. A parent is defined as 'any person who is in law the mother or father of the child'.[66] This definition covers birth parents (unless the child was legally adopted or born as a result of a surrogacy agreement), adoptive parents, and parents by virtue of the Human Fertilisation and Embryology Acts 1990 and 2008. The focus on legal parents, rather than social parents makes the Act easier for the government service to apply. By making it clear who should pay, regardless of the family situation, the Child Support Act creates consistency.

However it is questionable whether this actually accounts for the reality of people's lives, which are indeed far more complicated than the Act and its formula necessarily allows for.[67] In the context of step families, in particular, people have different perceptions about which children should take priority as the family expands and changes. This is not to say that the children from the first family do not need financial support, but the mother might have a new partner who can support the child and the father may now be supporting step-children. Although the formula now does take account of step-children (see 4.2.1), its rigid application may not be suitable in all cases, and it may result in situations where families are in a chain of households in which money is passed, with the reductions meaning money is spread thinly across the children. In contrast the legal provisions in the Matrimonial Causes Act 1973 and the Children Act 1989 take account of social parents and different family relationships, and are more flexible (see section 5). These provisions allow the court to give an order that should work for a particular family, however the introduction of the courts' discretion obviously removes the consistency created by the Child Support Act.[68]

Families also have the option of reaching private agreements which work for them, in order to avoid the rigid application of the child support formula for complex families

---

[60] Child Support Act 1991, s. 55(1)(a), as amended.

[61] Child Support Act 1991, s. 55(1)(b) and see Child Maintenance and other Payments Act 2008, s. 42 and accompanying note.   [62] Child Support Act 1991, s. 3(1)(a).

[63] Child Support Act 1991, s. 3(1)(b).   [64] Child Support Act 1991, s. 3(2)(a).

[65] Child Support Act 1991, s. 3(2)(b).   [66] Child Support Act 1991, s. 54 (1).

[67] Millar, J. 'Family Obligations and Social Policy: The Case of Child Support' (1996) 17 *Policy Studies* 181.

[68] See Chapter 4 for debates surrounding the wide discretion of the courts in relation to property division on divorce.

(see section 6). This could be seen as an advantage of the current system, which focuses on autonomy and private agreements, because it allows individuals to determine who is responsible, increases flexibility, and it could be seen to promote autonomy. However the disadvantage of this is that it allows individuals to negotiate out of agreements, so they may not fulfil their responsibility and this may also cause harm to the child (see section 2). Further individuals may not be able to act autonomously in the way the government intended due to the structure of family relationships and the emotional factor involved.[69]

A person with care is the person with whom the child lives. That person should provide the day-to-day care of a child. Certain categories of persons are excluded from being considered as a person with care. These are local authorities and foster parents with whom the child has been placed by the local authority.[70] This is likely to be because the foster family is provided with an allowance from the local authority for the period of foster care, therefore they do not have an additional claim for child support from the child parents.[71]

 Key Legislation 1: Child Support Act, s. 3

(3) A person is a *'person with care'*, in relation to any child, if he is a person—
   (a) with whom the child has his home;
   (b) who usually provides day to day care for the child (whether exclusively or in conjunction with any other person); and
   (c) who does not fall within a prescribed category of person.

(4) The Secretary of State shall not, under subsection (3)(c), prescribe as a category—
   (a) parents;
   (b) guardians;
   (c) persons named, in a child arrangements order under section 8 of the Children Act 1989, as persons with whom a child is to live; . . .

(5) For the purposes of this Act there may be more than one person with care in relation to the same qualifying child.

A person with care is a person with whom the child has his home and who usually provides day-to-day care for the child. However, more than one person may be a person with care in relation to the child.[72] What should happen where care is shared between both parents? How do we determine which parent is the non-resident parent, who should pay, and how much they should pay? This is not something that was necessarily an issue when the Act was first introduced and the aim was to protect single parents. Now if parents share care equally, there will be no non-resident parent and therefore the Child Support Act will not be applicable.[73] However one parent may still be able to claim child support under Sch 1 of the Children Act through a judicial process, to ensure that children have an adequate standard of living in both households (see section 5).

---

[69] Diduck, A. 'Autonomy and Family Justice' (2016) 28 *Child and Family Law Quarterly* 133.
[70] Child Support Maintenance Calculation Regulations 2012 (SI 2677/2012), Reg 78.
[71] However, see also Child Support Maintenance Calculation Regulations 2012 (SI 2677/2012), Regs 51 and 53.
[72] Child Support Act 1991, s. 5.
[73] Child Support Maintenance Calculation Regulations 2012 (SI 2677/2012), Reg 50.

For unequal shared care, in the day-to-day upbringing of the child, where the child is to spend at least one night a week with the non-resident parent, at the address where they reside, a deduction will be made to the amount of child support payable.[74] The person with care should receive maintenance on behalf of the child, but what does the statute mean by 'provides the day to day care for the child'? This will mean that the child is residing at the same address as the parent providing care, but a legal order requiring the child live with a particular person will not in itself be enough. The child must actually reside with that person and that person should carry out household tasks which involve the practical care of the child, so the person who 'puts food on the table, washes the child's clothes, deals with letters from the school and reads a bedtime story'.[75]

The Child Support Act 1991 requires that each parent supports their child.[76] Where the person with care is the child's other legal parent then they are deemed to be supporting their child by providing housing and day-to-day care, which will usually involve some financial input. However a person with care will not necessarily be the child's parent which is why the terminology person with care is used rather than parent with care.

4.1.1 Disputes about parentage

It might be questioned whether the non-resident parent is actually the parent of the qualifying child (this is most likely to be about whether the father is the biological father). Where the non-resident parent disputes parentage, the child support officer should only make a maintenance assessment if the case falls within one of the specific categories listed in section 26 of the Act.

 Key Legislation 2: Child Support Act 1991, s. 26

A1: the child is habitually resident in England and Wales; the Secretary of State is satisfied that that parent was married to the child's mother at some point in the period beginning with the conception and ending with the birth of the child; and the child has not been adopted.

A2: the child is habitually resident in England and Wales; the parent has been registered as the child's father in accordance with the relevant legislation for England and Wales, Scotland or Northern Ireland; and the child has not subsequently been adopted.

A3: where the result of a scientific test would be relevant for determining parentage and either the alleged parent refuses to take the relevant test; or has taken the test and the test shows that there is no reason to doubt that the alleged parent is the parent of the child.

A: the parent has adopted the child

B: the parent has a parental order under s 30 of the HFEA 1990 or s 54 of the HFEA 2008

B1: Where the Secretary of State is satisfied that the person is a parent of the child by virtue of s 27 or 28 of the HFEA 1990 or any of s 33 to 46 of the HFEA 2008.

C: There is a declaration that the parent is a parent of the child in question (or a declaration which has that effect) is in force under s 55A or 56 of the Family Law Act 1986 and the child has not subsequently been adopted.

F:[77] The parent has been found to be the father of the child in relevant proceedings in England and Wales, the finding still subsists, and the child has not been subsequently adopted.

---

[74] Child Support Act 1991, Sch 1, paras 7–9 (as amended).
[75] *GR v CMEC* [2011] UKUT 101(AAC); [2011] 2 FLR 962 (Wikeley J), at [48].
[76] Child Support Act 1991, s 1.

Where the alleged parent has denied parentage and does not fall within one of the categories listed then the agency will ask the parties to undergo a DNA test. If the alleged parent refuses then parentage is presumed. The child also needs to be tested and may also refuse to participate in the test. In *L v P*, the refusal by a 15 year old to provide DNA was upheld by the court and the alleged father remained liable to pay the maintenance.[78] The party disputing parentage is obliged to pay for the DNA test, however the fee is refunded if it is discovered that the party is not actually the child's parent.

4.2 The child support formula

As explained previously, the new formula is much simpler than the initial formula. The discussion in this chapter will focus on the current formula. The formula is set out in Sch 1 of the amended Act. The key information that the formula is based on is the gross income of the non-resident parent and the number of dependent children. The gross income of the parent is determined by reference to historical income, and therefore the amount used by the formula is based on the gross income from the previous tax year.[79] Historic income may, however, be very different to the parent's current income. Where the current income varies from the historic income by 25% or more, current income can be used instead.[80]

4.2.1 The basic rate

The general rule is that the non-resident parent should pay 12% of his gross weekly income for one qualifying child; 16% for two children, and 19% where there are three or more qualifying children.[81] The non-resident parent will pay this amount on gross earnings of up to £800 per week. If the parent has income above this amount then the parent will pay 9% for one child, 12% for two children, and 15% for three or more on any gross income in excess of £800.[82] However the total income that can be included in the assessment is capped at £3,000 a week.[83] Any gross income in excess of that £3,000 cannot be included in the child support assessment. This is to prevent wealthy parents having income taken which is far in excess of the child's needs, however the formula does not make any attempt to assess what the child's needs might be. This is in contrast to the first formula where the child's needs were taken into account, albeit to a very basic standard. It is possible to make an application to the court for 'top up maintenance' in cases where this is considered to be appropriate (see section 4).

The formula also takes account of other relevant children, including step-children, of the non-resident parent. It does this by making a deduction from the gross income before the basic rate assessment is applied, thus reducing the income available through the formula. In such cases a reduction of 11%, 14%, or 16% (depending on the number of other dependent children) is to be made to the gross income before the formula is applied in favour of the qualifying children.[84] So for example if a non-resident parent, with a gross income of £600 per week, had three relevant children and one qualifying child, then the

---

[78] *L v P (Paternity Test: Child's Objection)* [2010] EWCA Civ 1145.

[77] Case D has been repealed and Case E only applies in Scotland.

[79] See Child Support Act 1991, Sch 1, para 10 and Child Support Maintenance Calculation Regulations 2012 (SI 2677/2012), Regs 34–42. Periodic income checks and regular annual reviews should be carried out in accordance with Regs 19–22.

[80] Child Support Maintenance Calculation Regulations 2012 (SI 2677/2012), Reg 23. Employed non-resident parents have a duty to report and increases in income (Child Support Information Regulations, Reg 9A).

[81] Child Support Act 1991, Sch 1, para 2(1).   [82] Child Support Act 1991, Sch 1, para 2(2).

[83] Child Support Act 1991, Sch 1, para 10(3).

[84] Child Support Act 1991, Sch 1, para 2(3), as modified by the Child Support Maintenance (Changes to Basic Rate Calculation and Minimum Amount of Liability) Regulations 2012 (SI 2678/2012).

money available would be reduced by £96 per week (to £504) and the money payable to the qualifying child would be £60.48 per week.

4.2.2 Reduced rate

The reduced rate begins to apply where the non-resident parent's gross income is less than £200 per week. Where the income is above £100 and below £200 then the parent will pay a reduced rate, determined in accordance with the Regulations,[85] which will be at least £7 per week.[86] The £7 payable is to cover the first £100 of income, the non-resident parent will then pay a set percentage on any income over £100, starting at 19% where there is one qualifying child and no other relevant qualifying children.[87] So if the non-resident parent with only one qualifying child (and no other relevant children) earns £180 a week, the maintenance payment will be calculated as 19% of £80 (£15.20) plus the remaining £7; he will owe £22.20.

4.2.3 Flat rate

A flat rate of £7 per week is payable where the non-resident parents gross weekly income is £100 per week or less, the non-resident parent receives any benefit, pension, or allowance or the parent or his partner receive any benefit.[88]

4.2.4 No support payable (nil rate)

No child support is payable if the non-resident parent has a gross income of less than £7 per week, or he is of a prescribed description, such as a child, prisoner (including someone detained in hospital), or person living in a care home.[89]

4.2.5 Reduction for shared care

As mentioned earlier the amount payable is reduced if the child has overnight stays with the non-resident parent. The number of nights that the child spends at the non-resident parent's home is determined by the Secretary of State over a 12-month period. The reduction is calculated as a fraction to subtract from either the basic or reduced rate depending on the number of nights spent at the non-resident parent's house.[90] This is shown in Table 6.1.[91]

Table 6.1 Reductions to child support for shared care

Number of nights	Fraction to subtract
52 to 103	one seventh
104 to 155	two sevenths
156 to 174	three sevenths
175 or more	one half

---

[85] Child Support Maintenance Calculation Regulations 2012 (SI 2677/2012), Reg 43.

[86] Child Support Act 1991, Sch 1, para 3.

[87] See Child Support Maintenance Calculation Regulations 2012 (SI 2677/2012), Reg 43 for more details.

[88] Child Support Act 1991, Sch 1, para 4(1).

[89] Child Support Act 1991, Sch 1, para 5 and Child Support Maintenance Calculation Regulations 2012 (SI 2677/2012), Reg 45.

[90] Child Support Act 1991, Sch 1, para 7.

[91] Child Support Act 1991, Sch 1, para 7(4). If the applicable fraction is one -half in relation to any qualifying child in the care of the person with care, the total amount payable to the person with care is then to be further decreased by £7 for each such child (para 7(6)). The nights are based on nights per year, but can be amended to shorter periods if necessary, in which case the number of nights should be reduced proportionately.

So if the amount payable is calculated as £210 per week, using the basic rate of 12%, and the child spends 102 nights at the non-resident parent's house then the amount payable will be reduced to £180 per week. In contrast if the child spent two more nights there (per year) the amount payable would reduce to £150 per week. These, arguably, artificial cut off points can cause disputes about overnight stays and contact arrangements. The number of nights is to be determined in relation to the number of nights that the second parent is expected to care for the child.[92] Where this is unclear the Secretary of State can make an assumption.[93] The amount payable should never fall below £7 a week; this amount is always applied as a minimum rate to all calculations (unless the nil rate applies).[94]

4.2.6 Apportionment

This provision applies where the non-resident parent has more than one child and not all those children live together. The basic rate percentages work on the assumption that all the children live together, and therefore the person with care will not need as much money again for each child. In cases where the children have different persons with care, the total amount of maintenance is calculated in accordance with the basic rate but then the money is divided between the persons with care in a proportionate way.[95] For example if the non-resident parent had two children each living with a different person with care, the amount payable would still be 16% of gross income but the money would be divided equally between the two persons with care, so they would receive 8% each. This can make a big difference in terms of income for the person with care. For example if a non-resident parent earning £250 gross per week has one child then the person with care will receive £30, but if they have two children living in different households then each person with care will only receive £20 per week (a difference of over £40 per month or £520 per year).

4.3 **Making an application**

Either a person with care or a non-resident parent can make an application for a mainte-nance calculation in relation to a qualifying child under s. 4(1) of the Child Support Act 1991, as amended. However a key policy of the new scheme is that parents should make their own family based arrangement for support, where possible. Therefore before accept-ing an application the government service can invite the applicant to consider whether it is possible to make a family agreement.[96] Parents are assisted by the information provided by the Child Maintenance Options website, which includes an online calculator to determine how much maintenance is due.

Where applicants need to use the government service, parents are prevented from re-questing a new calculation within a year of a maintenance agreement or order, which is in force, being entered into or made.[97] The parent making the application must supply the government service with as much information as possible, in order to assist the service to locate the non-resident parent and make the correct maintenance calculation. Non-resident parents and their employers are expected to provide accurate information on that parent's earnings, and an offence is committed if false information is knowingly supplied, or the individual does not comply with the request.[98] Information can also be obtained from HM Revenue and Customs (HMRC) and all calculations falling under the system in place since 2008 require information from PAYE and/or self-assessment returns.

---

[92] Child Support Maintenance Calculation Regulations 2012 (SI 2677/2012), Reg 46. It is possible to make this assessment for a period of less than a year.
[93] Child Support Maintenance Calculation Regulations 2012 (SI 2677/2012), Reg 47.
[94] Child Support Act 1991, Sch 1, para 7(7).   [95] Child Support Act 1991, Sch 1, para 6 and 5A.
[96] Child Support Act 1991, s 9(2A).   [97] Child Support Act 1991, s. 4(10)(aa) and (ab).
[98] Child Support Act 1991, s 14A(2) and (3).

Key Case 1: *Gray v Secretary of State for Work and Pensions* [2012] **EWCA Civ 1412**

In *Gray* the father was self-employed, therefore the self-assessment return was required to assist with the maintenance calculation. The CSA had accepted his own evidence of his income as shown on his income and expenditure accounts prepared by his accountants without carrying out an audit for submission to the HMRC. The mother appealed to the First Tier Tribunal, on grounds that the father had misstated his weekly income. The Tribunal held that the father had indeed failed to declare his full income and the Tribunal judges made their own finding as to his true income. The father appealed this decision and the case eventually went to the Court of Appeal. The question was whether the child support calculation should be made on the basis of HMRC assessments, or whether the authorities could look beyond these in certain cases.

Ward LJ stated that:

[24] [T]he Regulations do not go so far as to state that a father's earnings for income tax purposes shall be treated as his earnings for child support purposes. There is no such deeming provision.

[28] I must, therefore, give effect to the ordinary meaning of the words and conclude that the answer to the question posed in this appeal is that the decision maker is entitled to rely on an evaluation of the father's actual profits from self-employment in the relevant period rather than the figures submitted to HMRC in his tax return

This case was extremely important as it recognised that the figures submitted to HMRC might not be accurate, or may differ from actual profit on the basis of what needs to be submitted. Unfortunately it was considered that this was too complicated and the law was amended to provide clarity.[99] The current law indicates that only HMRC assessments can be taken into account, unless of course the income being considered was earned prior to these changes.

As a result of the changes made after the Henshaw report, there is no longer a requirement for particular categories of people to use the child support system. However research found that in 2012 child support arrangements (rather than family agreements) still accounted for two thirds of all maintenance arrangements which single parents on benefit reported as having.[100]

4.4 Default maintenance decision

Where the Secretary of State does not have enough information to make a maintenance decision on the basis of a maintenance calculation then it can make a default decision until adequate information is obtained.[101] The default rate imposes a flat rate figure which depends on the number of qualifying children. The rate is £39 per week for one qualifying child, £51 for two, and £64 for three or more.[102] Based on the basic rate a person earning £325 per week will have to pay £39 per week for one child, so the default rate will benefit some parents but will penalise lower earners.

---

[99] Ward LJ was considering the previous law under the 1992 Statutory Instrument: Child Support (Maintenance Assessments and Special Cases) Regulations 1992 (SI 1815/1992).

[100] Bryson, C. *et al Kids aren't free: the child maintenance arrangements of single parents on benefit in 2012* (Gingerbread) 10.

[101] Child Support Act 1991, s. 12.

[102] Child Support Maintenance Calculation Regulations 2012 (SI 2677/2012), Reg 49.

4.5 **Variations**

In certain circumstances it is possible to apply for a variation on the maintenance calculated if the formulas do not result in a calculation that is appropriate in relation to that family's particular circumstances. The person making an application for variation must state what grounds the application is made on.[103] There are two cases on which an application can be made. One relates to special expenses of the non-resident parent, which includes expenses like: travel and accommodation costs related to maintain contact with the qualifying child, the payment of the maintenance element of boarding fees, and mortgage payments for the home occupied by the parent and child.[104] A successful application on this ground will likely lead to a reduction in the child support calculation. The other case relates to unearned and diverted income, and can apply where the non-resident has the ability to control their income, for example they own a small company, and have unreasonably reduced their income in order to lower their child support calculation.[105] A successful application on this ground will likely lead to an increase in the child support calculation. Where one of the grounds apply, the government service has discretion to decide whether to make a variation.[106]

When deciding whether to make a variation the general principles to be taken into account are that: parents should be responsible for maintaining their children when they can afford to do so and where a parent has more than one child they are responsible for maintaining them all equally.[107] Before deciding whether to make a variation the Secretary of State must consider that the variation is fair and equitable and is in accordance with the welfare of the child.[108] Situations in which variation may be given are laid out in Sch 4B,[109] and further guidance is given in the Child Support Maintenance Calculation Regulations 2012 (SI 2677/ 2012). The ability to make variations allows for more flexibility in the system. The lack of flexibility was one of the key criticisms of the original Act,[110] despite the fact that the main aim was to create consistency between orders.

4.6 **Revision and termination of calculations**

All maintenance calculations that were established after the changes came into force in 2012 are subject to an annual case check to determine if the circumstances have changed and a revision is needed.[111] Because these cases are reviewed annually, no changes will be made outside the annual review unless the non-resident parent's gross income has changed by at least 25%.[112] Where a change is required the Secretary of State can revise the decision under s. 16 on the application of either party or of its own motion. Under s. 17 a decision may be superseded due to a change of circumstances. A change of circumstances can result from a change in the earning capacity of the non-resident parent due to a change of job which results in an increase or decrease in wages, or the non-resident parent becoming unemployed. The non-resident parent may become a step-parent to the children of their new partner or they may have had another child of their own. Therefore it is clear that there needs to be a mechanism in place to revise the formula as necessary, but the 25%

---

[103] Child Support Act 1991, s. 28A(4)(b).

[104] See Child Support Maintenance Calculation Regulations 2012 (SI 2677/2012), Regs 63–68 and Child Support Act 1991, Sch 4B(2).

[105] See Child Support Maintenance Calculation Regulations 2012 (SI 2677/2012), Regs, 69–71 and Child Support Act 1991, Sch 4B(3).   [106] Child Support Act 1991, s. 28E-F.

[107] Child Support Act 1991, s. 28E(2).   [108] Child Support Act 1991, s. 28F.

[109] Child Support Act 1991, s. 28F.   [110] Roll, J. Child Support Research Paper 94/20 (1994) 27.

[111] Child Support Maintenance Calculation Regulations 2012 (SI 2677/2012), Regs 19–22.

[112] Child Support Maintenance Calculation Regulations 2012 (SI 2677/2012), Reg 23.

safety net means that the maintenance calculation will not have to be changed every couple of months because of a slight increase or decrease in the non-resident parent's wage.

Maintenance calculations cease to have effect on the death of the non-resident parent or the person with care. They also end if the non-resident parent ceases to be the child's parent, either because the child is adopted or made the subject of a parental order, or where there is no longer any qualifying child with respect to whom the order would have effect.[113] This would include the death of the child or the child becoming an adult and being self-sufficient, either by completing education and/or getting married for example. The maintenance calculation will also be terminated where the non-resident parent and caring parent reconcile and cohabit for a continuous period of at least six months, where the person with care ceases to be the person with care and where the calculation has been revised.[114]

4.7 **Appeals**

A non-resident parent or a person with care can appeal to the First Tier Tribunal against a decision of the Secretary of State regarding a child support calculation (including a refusal to make an assessment).[115] If the appeal is successful the Tribunal is open to make its own maintenance decision or it can remit the case to the Secretary of State for a new calculation in light of its ruling. It is obviously preferable for the First Tier Tribunal to use the power afforded to it and establish its own decision in order to make the system as smooth and efficient as possible. Appeals on points of law can be made to the Upper Tribunal[116] and then to the Court of Appeal.[117] The ability to appeal is an important element of the system and the need for this was discussed from the outset.[118]

4.8 **Collection and enforcement**

There are now two methods for collection and enforcement available: collection through the government service 'collect and pay' route, and 'maintenance direct' which is direct payments between the parties. The government service may be responsible for the collection of maintenance when this is requested by the applicant,[119] under s. 4, however, the Secretary of State can only make arrangements for the collection of maintenance, under the collect and pay service, if the non-resident parent agrees to the involvement of the Service or if the Commission is satisfied that without the arrangements the maintenance is unlikely to be paid.[120]

 DEBATE 3: HOW SHOULD CHILD SUPPORT OBLIGATIONS BE
ENFORCED; THROUGH A STATE BODY OR PRIVATELY?

The general approach under the current system is that everyone should fall under 'maintenance direct' unless the government service is convinced that 'collect and pay' is necessary. Therefore parties who have been unable to reach private agreements are usually responsible for enforcing their own maintenance obligations directly. Where parties are put on the 'collect and pay' service then this comes at a cost, so they are penalised for requiring this service. Paying parents are now charged a fee of 20% of the maintenance calculation which

---

[113] Child Support Act 1991, Sch 1, para 16. [114] Child Support Act 1991, Sch 1, para 16.
[115] Child Support Act 1991, s. 20. [116] Child Support Act 1991, s. 24.
[117] Tribunals, Courts and Enforcement Act 2007, s. 13.
[118] Hansard HL vol 522, cols 1695–708, 1702 (29 October 1990). [119] Child Support Act 1991, s. 29.
[120] Child Support Act 1991, s. 4(2A).

is payable in addition to the amount payable under the calculation, and persons with care, including domestic violence survivors, have 4% deducted from the money they are due.[121]

REASONS BEHIND THE CHARGE AND THE MOVE TO MAINTENANCE DIRECT

The government has argued that the Service is costly and therefore needs to be paid for by its users. They also consider that parents will become more responsible if they have to organise their own enforcement, relying on the emphasis on responsibility in the Henshaw report.

PROBLEMS WITH THE CHARGE

Parents will only be diverted to collect and pay where it is clear this is necessary. This is likely to be because the non-resident parent is not meeting their child support obligations. Where the parent is struggling to pay their child support the additional 20% fee will be problematic, and the 4% deduction is taking money from the child, which may contribute to child poverty. The fees may also act as a disincentive to seeking maintenance. The introduction of fees for enforcement has been widely criticised, and it is not in line with the approach in other countries where the government service is responsible for enforcement and this does not come at an additional cost (see 7.1). The UNCRC requires that state parties take all appropriate measures to secure the recovery of maintenance,[122] but it does not provide any further guidance on what these measures might be nor whether fees are acceptable.

IS COLLECT AND PAY A REAL OPTION?

Evidence suggests that it is very difficult for persons with care to convince the government service that they should be put on the collect and pay service, even when the non-resident parent is clearly defaulting.[123] This is problematic because this will not secure enforcement of the order, and it could be argued that the state is failing to take appropriate measures. Although the aim is to reduce the involvement of the government service, so that it can focus on more difficult cases and allow parents to make their own arrangements, if cases are not being redirected to collect and pay, then the government service is not actually providing extra assistance in these difficult cases and the additional enforcement powers are not being used. Further the charge turns the system into a pay for hire service.[124] If parents are willing to pay but they are not permitted to use the service, then the whole system could fall into question (see also *Kehoe*: Key Case 2). The experimental statistics indicate that only 30% of maintenance calculations have been put on the collect and pay system.[125] This seems to mean 30% of cases where the Service know there is a liability, so where there is a maintenance calculation, the data does not include purely private agreements. If 70% of these parents are unable to reach private agreements then they might have difficulty dealing with the private enforcement of the maintenance calculation.

Private enforcement can work well in some cases, but it is arguable that state support is required to ensure that child support obligations are enforced and children can benefit from child support.

In cases where parents do not pay child support, there are two stages for securing collection and then enforcement, where necessary, through the government service. The Secretary of State has certain powers for collection that they can apply automatically,

---

[121] See https://www.gov.uk/child-maintenance/how-to-pay, accessed 3 October 2016.

[122] Article 27(4) UNCRC.

[123] Evidence to the Work and Pensions Committee, Child Maintenance Services. Available at: http://www.parliamentlive.tv/Event/Index/f9179aaf-bb9a-425a-8eea-26fc9fb5a94a, accessed 17 November 2016.

[124] Diduck, A. 'Autonomy and Family Justice' (2016) 28 *Child and Family Law Quarterly* 133.

[125] Child Maintenance Service 2012 Scheme Experimental Statistics (Aug 2013–Nov 2016) 8.

whereas they need to seek an order from court before proceeding with other enforcement measures. In order to ensure collection the Secretary of State can make a deduction from earnings order against the non-resident parent.[126] The order can be made against future payments due, arrears, or against both payments due and arrears. The order is sent to the employer of the paying parent. Their employer deducts the money from the PAYE wage through the taxation system and sends the deducted money to the government service so the paying parent never receives the money in their wage. This operates in the same way as other deductions such as student loan and pension deductions.

However, it is clear that this method only works for those who are in regular employment, so for example it cannot apply to non-resident parents who are self-employed. The collection of child support from self-employed non-resident parents has always proved much more difficult; it is also more difficult to make an earnings assessment. Consequently the Secretary of State can now also make deduction orders in relation to bank accounts (or other similar accounts) belonging to the non-resident parent.[127] These orders can again be made in relation to arrears and/or future payments and the order can require that the payments are made either periodically or by lump sum.[128] If the account is a joint account the Secretary of State must allow each party to the account to make representations.[129] Despite this power it is still more difficult to collect payments from self-employed parents. In special cases collection can also be secured through deduction from benefits,[130] and the Secretary of State also has the power to recover arrears from a deceased's estate for maintenance which the deceased was liable, immediately before death.[131]

Where the non-resident parent misses one or more payments, the Secretary of State can apply for a liability order in order to take enforcement action for enforcement of the obligation to pay child support.[132] The Secretary of State should apply to the magistrates' court for the liability order against the defaulting parent.[133] Where a liability order has been made, the Secretary of State can take enforcement action through a variety of mechanisms. The Secretary of State can instruct bailiffs to take control of goods to the value of the amount of maintenance unpaid, and the value of costs connected with the proceedings.[134] The Secretary of State can request a charging order from the county court for the amount unpaid.[135] An application can also be made to the court for a measure preventing avoidance, such as preventing a property transfer.[136] The Secretary of State can provide information on the unpaid sums to a credit referencing agency, which will adversely affect any credit checks run on the non-resident parent.[137] If none of these measures work then the Secretary of State can apply for more punitive measures such as a disqualification from driving or licence withholding.[138] The most punitive measure available is imprisonment,[139] which should only be used as a measure of last resort.[140]

---

[126] Child Support Act 1991, s. 31. This also comes at a cost, currently £50 (https://www.gov.uk/child-maintenance/nonpayment-what-happens, accessed 3 October 2016).   [127] Child Support Act 1991, s. 32A.

[128] A lump sum deduction order is charged at £200 (https://www.gov.uk/child-maintenance/nonpayment-what-happens, accessed 3 October 2016).   [129] Child Support Act 1991, s. 32B.

[130] Child Support Act 1991, s. 43.   [131] Child Support Act 1991, s. 43A.

[132] Child Support Act 1991, s. 4 and s. 33. A liability order is charged at £300 (https://www.gov.uk/child-maintenance/nonpayment-what-happens, accessed 3 October 2016).

[133] Child Support Act 1991, s. 33(2).   [134] Child Support Act 1991, s. 35.

[135] Child Support Act 1991, s. 36.   [136] Child Support Act 1991, s. 32L.

[137] Child Support Act 1991, s. 49D.   [138] Child Support Act 1991, s. 39A and 40B.

[139] Child Support Act 1991, s. 39A and s. 40.

[140] *Karoonian v CMEC; Gibbons v CMEC* [2012] EWCA Civ 1379.

? DEBATE 4: HOW SHOULD CHILD SUPPORT OBLIGATIONS BE
ENFORCED; THROUGH A STATE BODY OR PRIVATELY?

METHODS OF ENFORCEMENT

The use of punitive measures such as license withholding and imprisonment, is a matter
for debate. If the obligations are enforced privately then there is no option to use punitive
measures. If the state is therefore going to get involved then there is an argument that they
should use all the enforcement measures that they have available to them, including punitive measures to secure enforcement. However the alternative argument is that orders which
require punitive measures are taken, restrict the fundamental rights of the non-resident parent. These measures may also be counterproductive if they affect the non-resident parent's
earning potential. If the non-resident parent can no longer earn money as a result of the
measures then they will be unable to pay child support.

Courts should take account of the non-resident parent's employment as a driving disqualification may be counterproductive if their current employment requires them to drive.
Of course it may result in the immediate payment of child support so that they can work
again, but generally unemployment is not going to assist with the collection of child support.
Further the inability to drive could also have adverse effects on contact.

The use of imprisonment as punishment is very severe and it has similar problems to
driving disqualifications in that it will most definitely have an adverse effect on employment,
earning potential, and contact. Because of these problems prison sentences are often issued
as suspended sentences on the condition that the non-resident parent pays a certain amount
of maintenance per week. If the non-resident parent defaults then there is the risk that they
will go to prison. These measures should only be used where the parent is wilfully refusing or
culpably neglecting to pay.[141] In this situation culpable neglect could occur where the parent
has not paid the priority debt—child support—and has instead decided to use his bonus to
take his new family on a fancy holiday.

All other mechanisms should be used to try to recover the money before such drastic
measures are taken, and data indicates that these punitive measures are rarely sought.[142] It
is better to use alternative enforcement measures which can actually assist with the ongoing
enforcement of the maintenance obligation, rather than to take these draconian measures
which are likely to hamper the parent's ability to pay and are therefore less effective.

Where an application is made to the court, following a request by the Secretary of State
for a liability order, the court cannot question the liability order nor the maintenance calculation. So the parent cannot raise these issues as a defence during the proceedings, they
have to raise any queries about the maintenance calculation through the appeals system
discussed earlier. An alleged failure to consider the welfare of the child is also not a ground
for granting an appeal against a deduction from earnings order, or other measure of enforcement. However in *Bird* the non-resident parent successfully argued that he had made
the payment via an alternative method.[143] In *Bird* this was through mortgage instalments,
but school fees are another thing that have been deemed to have this effect.[144]

---

[141] *Karoonian v CMEC; Gibbons v CMEC* [2012] EWCA Civ 1379.

[142] Latest statistics suggest that there were only five suspended committal sentences from April 2015 to
March 2016. There is no data on other types of committals. See Child Support Agency Quarterly Summary of
Statistics (June 2012) (data tables, Table 22). However these are all old cases which are being phased out or ceas-
ing to exist, there is no data on cases using the 2012 system (the experimental statistics do not include data on
enforcement).   [143] *Bird v Secretary of State for Work and Pensions* [2008] EWHC 3159 (Admin).

[144] *R (Green) v Secretary of State for the Department of Work and Pensions* [2010] EWHC 1278 (Admin).

> **Key Case 2: *R Kehoe v Secretary of State for Work and Pensions* [2005] UKHL 48**
>
> An interesting point to note is that the person with care cannot challenge the decisions of the Child Support Agency in relation to enforcement. In *R Kehoe v Secretary of State for Work and Pensions*[145] it was held that a parent has no right to challenge how the Child Support Agency chooses or does not choose to enforce a calculation. This was because the 1991 Act did not create civil rights and obligations in regard to enforcement so Article 6(1) of the European Convention on Human Rights (ECHR), the right to a fair trial, was not engaged.[146] The majority of the House of Lords considered that the Act had replaced any pre-existing rights of either a child or a parent to periodical payments for maintenance of that child. This was a narrow approach, which took a literal interpretation of the provisions as expressly stated in the Act. In contrast Baroness Hale, dissenting, took a different approach, noting that although the scheme deprived parents of their right to enforce maintenance, the underlying right to receive maintenance remained, and thus therefore raised an issue under Article 6 ECHR.[147] It is questionable whether the decision was correct given that the 1991 Act is not the sole remedy and an alternative or additional system remains in place.[148] Mrs Kehoe made an application to the European Court of Human Rights for an alleged breach of the right to a fair trial but it was unsuccessful.[149]
>
> The continued significance of the decision under the current system also needs to be explored. The decision was given when all calculations and agreements had to be enforced through the government service. Now that there is no obligation to use the Service it is questionable whether the Act still replaces any pre-existing rights to periodical maintenance payments, surely those that choose to make their own private arrangements now have their own right to child support payments. Despite this those who want help with enforcement will only be put on the collect and pay service if the government service decides that this is appropriate, so unless there is a workable private agreement in place, parents with care remain at the behest of the Service who decide whether assistance is needed with enforcement regardless of the wishes of the parent, and *Kehoe* will continue to apply to those cases. If the maintenance arrangement, or agreement, is not enforced, then the child's right to support is not fulfilled.

4.9 Criticisms of the child support scheme

Several problems remain with the child support scheme under the amended Child Support Act:

- First, despite the fact that a main aim was to achieve consistency it can be argued that the system is still not flexible enough. The rigid application of the formula, the formal approach to modification, and the limits on the role of the government service prevents a more flexible approach which takes account of parent's ability to pay. This can be contrasted with the approach in Norway, discussed in 7.1.

- Second, the focus on child support rather than family responsibilities, or child rights more broadly prevents the government from looking at the underlying problems in relation to payment and orders. This is different to the approach in other legal systems (see 7.2). The system seems to presume a wilful refusal to pay rather than offering support to children and their families.

---

[145] [2005] UKHL 48.   [146] [2005] UKHL 48, at [43].   [147] [2005] UKHL 48, at [70]–[71].

[148] Wikely, N. 'A Duty but not a Right: Child Support after *R (Kehoe) v Secretary of State for Work and Pensions*' (2006) 18 *Child and Family Law Quarterly* 287.

[149] *Kehoe v United Kingdom* App. No. 2010/06 [2008] FLR 1014.

- Third, the introduction of charges for the use of the collect and pay service fails to show a proper understanding of barriers to enforcement. The aim of the government service since the policy changes initiated by the Henshaw report has been to focus on the most difficult cases. These cases are difficult because there are deeper issues, which affect payment such as: ability to pay, ability to work, and domestic violence. These issues are unlikely to be resolved by charging the paying parent extra and reducing the amount of child support paid to the person with care. This approach is penalising those that need help instead of helping them.

- Fourth, many people still do not have a maintenance agreement. 43% of single parents on benefit had no maintenance agreement, whether CSA or private, and 58% of these parents did not want an agreement.[150] This was often in cases where there was no contact between the child and the non-resident parent, particularly in domestic violence cases where the caring parent did not want contact or a financial contribution from someone who had previously damaged the family.[151]

- Fifth, despite changes to enforcement mechanisms, child support agreements remain unenforced.

- Sixth, the government service still costs more money to run compared to the money it recovers.

5. The residual role of the courts

Most child support cases are dealt with through the government service or through private agreements. However, there remains a limited role for the courts in this area in certain circumstances. The role of the courts is limited because the aim was to direct all applications through the administrative system which was supposed to be more effective than the court system. Although the child support scheme did not work as well as was intended, the general approach of the family justice system, now, is to keep family disputes out of court, so that these disputes can be resolved through private agreements. This is exemplified by the cuts to legal aid, which make it almost impossible to get legal aid for private family disputes (see Chapter 15).

This section will now discuss the particular circumstances in which the court can make a child support order.

5.1 No jurisdiction under the child support scheme

Where the Secretary of State has jurisdiction to make a maintenance calculation with respect to a child, no court shall exercise any power which it would otherwise have to make, vary, or revoke a maintenance order in respect of the child and non-resident parent concerned.[152] So the general rule is that the court cannot make an order where there is jurisdiction under the child support scheme. However, there will not always be jurisdiction under the child support scheme, so in certain circumstances where the scheme does not apply, the courts have jurisdiction to make child support orders:

- Firstly, the Secretary of State only has jurisdiction if *all* relevant parties (the qualifying child, person with care, and non-resident parent) are habitually resident in the

---

[150] Bryson, C. *et al Kids aren't free: the child maintenance arrangements of single parents on benefit in 2012* (Gingerbread) 10.

[151] Bryson, C. *et al Kids aren't free: the child maintenance arrangements of single parents on benefit in 2012* (Gingerbread) 107.   [152] Child Support Act 1991, s. 8(3).

UK.[153] Where the non-resident parent is not habitually resident in the UK but is employed by the civil service, is a member of the armed forces, or is employed by another body of a prescribed description then there will be jurisdiction under the child support scheme in these specific circumstances.[154]

- Second, a child support calculation can only be made against a non-resident parent who is the legal parent of the qualifying child. It cannot be made against step-parents who have previously supported the child. In such cases the person with care can make an application to the courts for maintenance from a non-resident step-parent. Any maintenance will be awarded by the court in accordance with the concept of the child of the family (see 5.3.1).

- Third, child maintenance can be sought from the courts where the child in question is not a qualifying child for the purpose of the Child Support Act.[155] This could be because the child is over 16 and is not in full-time education.

- Fourth, the court can make a maintenance order where the parents have agreed that it should.[156] This includes cases where parties agree that maintenance should be paid but cannot agree on the amount to be paid.

 Key Case 3: *V v V (Child Maintenance)* [2001] FLR 799

In *V v V*, Wilson J looked at what it meant for parties to agree not to use the government service. Where there is a consent order then parties can avoid the mainly inflexible rules in the Child Support Act. In *V v V*, Wilson J took a broad view of what was meant by a consent order. In these cases a practice to avoid the CSA has emerged, whereby the court initially makes a nominal order, with the parties consent, and then the court later varies that order as appropriate. Wilson J considered that it was entirely legitimate for the nominal order to be as little as five pence and indicated that this was a practice that had been ongoing for eight years at the time of the decision. However he didn't even think it was necessary to even state an amount in the order.

> [21] . . . My view is that, if the words 'by consent' appear above the nominal order, they satisfy the requirement of a written agreement and that any requirement for the issue of notice of application can and should be waved.

In the case, an order was made which would apply until the children were 22. Wilson J therefore considered that the parties would not be able to make use of the CSA, in this case. This case takes a broad approach to the use of consent orders and makes it easy for parties to avoid the government service, at least initially.

In these cases because no calculation has been made then the court is open to vary any order it makes.[157] However, after the consent order has been in force for one year then either party is free to go to the government service and request a maintenance calculation, which will bring an end to the consent order. Finally, the court also has jurisdiction where there is a maintenance order which was made before 3 March 2003, or there is one made on or after that date which has been in force for less than a year.

---

[153] Child Support Act 1991, s. 44. For more on the meaning of habitual residence, see Chapter 15.
[154] Child Support Act 1991, s. 44(2A).   [155] In accordance with Child Support Act 1991,s. 3(1).
[156] Child Support Act 1991, s. 8(5).   [157] Child Support Act 1991, s. 8(3A).

5.2 Orders instead of, or in addition to, child support

As well as the ability to make orders where there is no jurisdiction under the child support scheme, the court can also make orders instead of, or in addition to, child support under the 1991 Act. Where orders are made in addition to the maintenance calculation these are known as 'top up' orders. A so called top up order can be applied for where there is a maintenance calculation in place which was set at the ceiling fixed by Sch 1, discussed earlier. The court may make an order for additional maintenance where it 'is satisfied that the circumstances of the case make it appropriate for the non-resident parent to make or secure the making of periodical payments under a maintenance order in addition to child support maintenance'.[158] Therefore if the non-resident parent is particularly wealthy it is still possible to increase the amount of maintenance payable through the courts despite the cap on assessable income in the Act. There are also powers which allow the court to make a maintenance order which is designed to meet expenses in relation to education and training,[159] or to meet expenses related to a child's disability.[160]

The Child Support Act 1991 only deals with orders that require the making of periodical payments. Orders for the payment of a lump sum and orders made in relation to property adjustment are not covered by the Act, so the court maintains the power to make such orders in relation to children.

5.3 Power of the court to make additional orders

It is clear that the court has the ability to make orders in relation to child maintenance in particular circumstances, but what types of orders can it make and which provisions can these be made under? There is provision under the Matrimonial Causes Act 1973 for children whose parents were married (but are in the process of ending the marriage), and provisions in Sch 1 of the Children Act 1989 for other applications. These provisions can be used to provide top up maintenance, fill any gaps created under the Child Support Act, and apply where a relationship between cohabiting couples breaks down. Both Acts apply to a wider category of people than those falling under the jurisdiction of the Child Support Act 1991.

5.3.1 Matrimonial Causes Act 1973

Under Part II of the Matrimonial Causes Act 1973 (see further section 3, in Chapter 4), on or after the grant of a decree of divorce or nullity the court has power to make various orders for the benefit of a child of the family. This provision is very useful because unlike the Child Support Act 1991 it does not restrict children to legal children but also uses the broader term 'child of the family', which can include step-parents, or other types of social or de facto parents (providing the parties were married).

 Key Legislation 3: Matrimonial Causes Act, s. 52

A child of the family in relation to the parties of a marriage, means:

(a) a child of both of those parties; and
(b) any other child, not being a child who has been boarded-out with those parties by a local authority or voluntary organisation, who has been treated by both of those parties as a child of their family;

---

[158] Child Support Act 1991, s. 8(6)(c).   [159] Child Support Act 1991, s. 8(7).
[160] Child Support Act 1991, s. 8(8). See also Roll, J. Child Support Research Paper 94/20 (1994) 15.

Before any order can be made it has to be established that the non-parent did in fact treat the child as a child of the family. Where the child lives in the same household with the parent for a considerable period of time that child will most likely be treated as a child of the family. The question gets more difficult where the child spends time between two households or the marriage has only lasted for a short time. These questions would be very difficult for an administrative body to deal with, which is why they are reserved for the court and the 1991 Act confines itself to legal parents. If the child is considered to be a child of the family any order has to take account of any support that might be payable under the Child Support Act 1991.[161]

The orders available to the court are set out in ss. 23 and 24 of the Matrimonial Causes Act 1973. The court can essentially order periodical payments, secured periodical payments, lump sum payments, transfers of property, and settlements of the property for the benefit of any child of the family. When deciding whether to make an order the court must have regard to issues listed in s. 25. In particular the court should give regard to: the financial needs of the child; the income, earning capacity, property, and other financial resources of the child; any physical or mental disability of the child; and the manner in which he was being, or expected to be, educated.[162]

5.3.2 Children Act 1989

If the Matrimonial Causes Act 1973 is not applicable because the parties are not divorcing, then relevant persons will need to use Sch 1 of the Children Act 1989 to seek financial provision beyond that made in the Child Support Act 1991. The court can make financial provision for children under the Children Act 1989 either on application,[163] upon its own motion when varying or discharging a child arrangements order, or a special guardianship order,[164] or when the child is a ward of court.[165]

Applications for financial provision under the Children Act can be made by parents, guardians, special guardians, and any person who is named in a child arrangements order as a person whom the child should live with.[166] For the purpose of these provisions parent includes both married and unmarried parents, second female parents, and any party to a marriage, or any civil partner in relation to whom the child is a child of the family.[167] The reference to second female parents seeks to include those with legal parentage under s. 43 of the Human Fertilisation and Embryology Act 2008 (see 3.1.2 in Chapter 8). Orders can be made against either or both parents of the child;[168] the same definition of parent applies.[169] An order could be made against both parents in a situation where the child lives with a legal guardian or another family member such as their grandparents. Both parents may then have an obligation to pay child support to the grandparents. No orders can be made against guardians, special guardians, or those, other than parents, who have a child arrangements order in their favour. This is in line with the general policy of not making these persons liable to make financial provision in the same way as a parent,[170] simply because they are taking on the responsibility of caring for the child.

The family court can make orders for unsecured periodical payments for the benefit of the child or to the child themselves, for as long as is specified in the order.[171] The court can also order lump sum payments.[172] Lump sum orders can be made outright or can be

---

[161] See Matrimonial Causes Act 1973, s. 25(4). [162] Matrimonial Causes Act 1973, s. 25(3).
[163] Children Act 1989, Sch 1 para 1(1). [164] Children Act 1989, Sch 1, para 1(6).
[165] Children Act 1989, Sch 1, para 1(7). [166] Children Act 1989, Sch 1 para 1(1).
[167] Children Act 1989, Sch 1, para 16(2). [168] Children Act 1989, Sch 1 para 1(2).
[169] Children Act 1989, Sch 1, para 16(2).
[170] Law Commission, *Guardianship and Custody* (Law Com No. 172) para 2.25.
[171] Children Act 1989, Sch 1, paras 1(1)(a), (b), and 1(2)(a).
[172] Children Act 1989, Sch 1, paras 1(1)(a), (b), and 1(2)(c).

ordered as payable by instalments.[173] The term 'benefit for the child' has been interpreted broadly. The benefit for the child does not need to be direct, for example, orders can be made to cover the applicant's legal expenses for the proceedings, if the purpose of the proceedings is to benefit the child.[174] It has also been held that payments to allow one parent to travel to another country in order to bring proceedings there for the return of the child, could be ordered as payments for the benefit of the child under the Children Act 1989.[175]

The court has the power to order secured periodical payments, settlements of property, and property transfers under the Children Act 1989.[176] As with lump sum payments property transfers are not limited to financial benefit. For example, in *K v K* it was held that there was power to order an unmarried father to transfer a joint council tenancy to the mother so that the children could live with the mother in the family home.[177] Generally the court will order the transfer of property for a limited time, and the property will transfer back to the non-resident parent at a designated time such as when the youngest child turns 18 or when the children have completed full-time education.

The orders available are similar to those under the Matrimonial Causes Act 1973. Similarly when deciding whether or not to make an order under the Children Act 1989 the court should have regard to: the income, earning capacity, property, and other financial resources which any parent, the applicant, and any other person in whose favour the court proposes to make the order, has or is likely to have in the foreseeable future;[178] the financial needs, obligations, and responsibilities which any parent, the applicant, and any other person in whose favour the court proposes to make the order, has or is likely to have in the foreseeable future;[179] the financial needs of the child;[180] the income, earning capacity, property, and other financial resources of the child;[181] any physical or mental disability of the child;[182] and the manner in which the child was being, or was expected to be, educated or trained.[183]

The list makes no reference to the child's welfare, maintenance is expressly excluded as a matter concerning the child's upbringing by s. 105(1) of the Act. This is slightly peculiar as the amount of money parents have to spend on a child will most likely form an integral part of that child's upbringing, particularly where the child is living in poverty. The courts, however, have held that the welfare of the child is one of the circumstances to be taken into account when making an assessment under Sch 1.[184] In addition, there is no reference to standard of living in this list.[185] This in turn leaves open the question of whose standard of living an order should reflect, which is particularly difficult where the parties have never lived together. In cases where one parent is rich this may mean that the caring parent is also indirectly benefiting from on order made for the benefit of the child. In some cases parents who have had short relationships may indeed benefit, whereas cohabitants that have no children may gain no financial benefit on separation. The courts have however accepted this as a necessary evil, recognising that the child must be looked after and therefore the primary carer must receive an allowance that allows them to do this at the appropriate level in relation to the other aspects of the standard of living that the child is to enjoy.

---

[173] Children Act 1989, Sch 1, para 5(5).   [174] *M-T v T* [2006] EWHC 2492 (Fam).

[175] *Re S (Child: Financial Provision)* [2004] EWCA Civ 1685.

[176] Children Act 1989, Sch, 1, paras 1(1)(a) and 1(2)(b),(d), and (e).

[177] *K v K (Minors: Property transfer)* [1992] 2 All ER 727, CA.

[178] Children Act 1989, Sch 1, paras 4(1)(a) and 4(4).

[179] Children Act 1989, Sch 1, paras 4(1)(b) and 4(4).   [180] Children Act 1989, Sch 1, paras 4(c).

[181] Children Act 1989, Sch 1, paras 4(d).   [182] Children Act 1989, Sch 1, paras 4(e).

[183] Children Act 1989, Sch 1, paras 4(f).   [184] *J v C (Child: Financial Provision)* [1999] 1 FLR 152.

[185] Cf. Domestic Proceedings and Magistrates Court Act 1978, s 3(2)(c) and 3(3)(d).

Key Case 4: *Re P (Child: Financial Provision)* [2003] EWCA Civ 837

In *Re P* the parents had an intermittent sexual relationship, for four years, which resulted in the birth of their child.[186] The father was extremely wealthy and the mother came from an affluent background, but did not have her own career. She depended on her parents to maintain her own standard of living.

The Court of Appeal held that in cases where 'one or both parents lie somewhere on the spectrum from affluent to fabulously rich'[187] the court must decide what kind of home the respondent should provide for that child. This should be a realistic assessment of what the standard of living should be. After determining this the court should assess the costs of furnishing the home along with the cost of a family car. The court must then determine how much it would cost to maintain the home and meet other livings costs. Finally, the court must assess the allowance to be made for the care of the child by the caring parent. When making this assessment the court must recognise the responsibility, and the sacrifice, that the unmarried parent (generally the mother) who is to be the primary carer for the child, perhaps the exclusive carer, takes on. In order to discharge this responsibility the carer must have control of a budget that reflects both the social and financial position of her and the father.[188]

The father was ordered to pay a lump sum of £1 million for the purchase of a house, a further lump sum of £100,000 for furnishings etc., and ordered to pay yearly periodical payments of £70,000 to meet other living costs and to pay the allowance for the mother's care. The periodical payments were ordered as top up maintenance over and above the child support assessment made in accordance with the Child Support Act 1991.

There is a limit to the extent of the periodical payments. If high periodical payments have not been sufficient to support both mother and child then the mother must adjust her lifestyle so that she is able to bring up her child within the budget allocated in the periodical payments.[189] In *GN v MA* the mother's application to raise the periodical child support payments from £204,000 to £780,000 per annum was struck out because there was no legal basis for making the application.[190]

Orders for periodical payments can begin on the date of the making of the application, or on any later date.[191] The general rule is that the payments should not extend beyond the child's 17th birthday,[192] however the court may specify a later date if this is considered to be appropriate but this should not extend beyond the child's 18th birthday,[193] unless the child is attending an educational establishment, undergoing training, or there are other special circumstances that justify extending the payments.[194] In cases where there has been a property transfer or settlement, the property should revert back to the owner at the same time as periodical payments cease, unless there are special or exceptional circumstances. This would include the education of the child.[195] There is also a special provision which allows children over 18 to make an application before the court.[196] The court also retains the power to vary, suspend, or revoke any order.[197]

---

186 [2003] EWCA Civ 837.   187 [2003] EWCA Civ 837, at [45] (Thorpe LJ).
188 [2003] EWCA Civ 837, at [48]–[49].   189 *GN v MA* [2015] EWHC 3939 (Fam).
190 [2015] EWHC 3939 (Fam), and see the Family Procedure Rules 2010, r. 4.4.
191 Children Act 1989, Sch 1, para 3(1).   192 Children Act 1989, Sch 1, para 3(1)(a).
193 Children Act 1989, Sch 1, paras 3(1)(a) and (b).   194 Children Act 1989, Sch 1, para 3(2).
195 *Re N (Payments for Benefit of Child)* [2009] EWHC 11 (Fam).   196 Children Act 1989, Sch 1, para 2.
197 Children Act 1989, Sch 1, paras 1(6) and 6.

Where the court is considering making an order against a step-parent the court must have regard to:

- whether that person had assumed responsibility for the maintenance of the child and, if so the extent to which and on the basis on which he assumed responsibility, including the length of the period during which he met that responsibility;[198]

- whether he did so knowing that the child was not his child;[199] and

- the liability of any other persons to maintain the child.[200]

Where the court makes such an order it must be recorded in the order that it was made against someone who is not the mother or the father of the child.[201]

6. Private agreements

There are different types of private agreements that can be made. Binding agreements made between spouses or civil partners can include provision for their children. The Supreme Court has ruled that both pre and postnuptial agreements can be given effect unless it would not be fair to do so [202] (see section 4, in Chapter 8). The parties can make an agreement that falls within s. 34 of the Matrimonial Causes Act 1973 (see Chapter 4). In the alternative parents can make binding agreements solely for the benefit of their children. Both the Children Act 1989 and the Child Support Act 1991 recognise that parents might want to make private agreements and provide provision for these.

The Children Act 1989 defines a maintenance agreement as any agreement in writing made with respect to a child which was made between the father and mother of the child[203] (or between the mother and second female parent);[204] and contains provision with respect to the making or securing of payments, or the disposition or use of any property, for the maintenance or education of the child.[205] The Child Support Act 1991 defines a maintenance agreement as any agreement for the making, or for securing the making, of periodical payments by way of maintenance to or for the benefit of any child.[206] The Children Act 1989 provides for a wider range of payments but it does have the proviso that the agreement is in writing, which is not necessary for an agreement made in relation to the Child Support Act 1991. There is also no requirement that it was the parents of the child that made the agreement in the context of the Child Support Act 1991.

Private maintenance agreements as defined in the Child Support Act 1991 are not restricted by the operation of that Act,[207] however the existence of such an agreement does not prevent a party, or any other person, from seeking a maintenance calculation under the Act.[208] Any provision in an agreement which restricts the right to a party seeking a maintenance application, will be void.[209] This is problematic in cases where non-resident parents have 'hidden income' because the private agreement can reflect this, but the paying parent may then ask for a maintenance calculation based on traceable income which is much lower than actual income and would result in a low calculation.

However, as mentioned in 4.3, the Act also provides that the Secretary of State may take steps to encourage the making and keeping of agreements.[210] In particular the Secretary of

---

[198] Children Act 1989, Sch 1, para 4(2)(a).   [199] Children Act 1989, Sch 1, para 4(2)(b).
[200] Children Act 1989, Sch 1, para 4(2)(c).   [201] Children Act 1989, Sch 1, para 4(3).
[202] *Radmacher v Granatino* [2010] UKSC 42.   [203] Children Act 1989, Sch 1, para 10(1)(a).
[204] Children Act 1989, Sch 1, para 10 (8).   [205] Children Act 1989, Sch 1, para 10(1)(b).
[206] Child Support Act 1991, s. 9(1).   [207] Child Support Act 1991, s. 9(2).
[208] Child Support Act 1991, s. 9(3).   [209] Child Support Act 1991, s. 9(4).
[210] Child Support Act 1991, s. 9(2A).

State may even invite the parent to consider whether it is possible to make an agreement, before accepting the application.[211] This is in order to reduce the need for applications to be made under the Act and therefore reduce the pressure on the government service. As we have seen the reduction in the number of cases going through the Service was one of the recommendations in the Henshaw report, in order to allow the Service to focus on more difficult cases. So although it is still possible to request an indicative calculation on which to then base a private agreement,[212] the general approach is to steer all applicants away from the government service as far as possible. This is a vast contrast to the initial policy and the actions of the Child Support Agency under the original conception of the Act, which tried to direct as many applications through the Service as possible.

The court may alter a privately arranged maintenance agreement in accordance with the Children Act 1989. Before altering the agreement the court must be satisfied that by reason of a change of circumstances in the light of which any financial arrangements contained in the agreement were made (including a change foreseen by the parties when making the agreement) the agreement should be altered so as to make different financial arrangements;[213] or that the agreement does not contain proper financial arrangements with respect to the child.[214] This provision should only apply where the court's jurisdiction is not restricted by the Child Support Act 1991. As discussed earlier in 5 the role of the court only kicks in when certain conditions are met. Therefore the 1991 Act provides that no court can vary a maintenance agreement where it is prevented from doing so by s. 8 of the same Act.[215] This only limits the court's jurisdiction to make an order for periodical payments, and does not apply where the parties have reached an agreement and are seeking a consent order. Once the consent order has been made the court then has jurisdiction to vary the consent order.

 ## DEBATE 5: SHOULD WE RELY ON PRIVATE AGREEMENTS FOR CHILD SUPPORT?

There has been a vast change in direction with private child support agreements now being the preferred method of determining and arranging for the payment of child support. The law and policy aims to try and get families to make child support agreements privately, without the assistance of the government service or the court system. Is this the correct approach?

ARGUMENTS IN FAVOUR OF PRIVATE AGREEMENTS

The perceived advantages of private agreements are that they empower individuals to act autonomously and encourage them to work collaboratively.[216] Private agreements can also be flexible. A study by Andrews *et al* found that parents prefer to use private agreements where possible because they find the agency inflexible.[217] Bryson *et al* found that where there is a functioning private child support agreement in place then these can work well, and it is more likely that contact will also take place.[218]

---

[211] Child Support Act 1991, s. 9(2A).   [212] Child Support Act 1991, s. 9A(1).

[213] Children Act 1989, Sch 1, para 10(3)(a).   [214] Children Act 1989, Sch 1, para 10(3)(b).

[215] Child Support Act 1991, s. 9(5).

[216] See Diduck, A. 'Autonomy and Vulnerability in Family Law: The Missing Link' in J. Wallbank and J. Herring (eds) *Vulnerabilities, Care and Family Law* (Ashgate, 2013) 95.

[217] Andrews, S. *et al* 'Promotion of child maintenance: research on instigating behaviour change volume I: Main Report', CMEC Research Report No. 1, London: Child Maintenance and Enforcement Commission.

[218] Bryson, C. *et al Kids aren't free: The child maintenance arrangements of single parents on benefit in 2012* (Gingerbread).

Further Ellman *et al* found that the general public consider that the maintenance awarded by the agency is too low and that the mother's income should also be taken into account when determining maintenance.[219] Therefore private agreements, although varied, might be more realistic (and possibly higher) than the calculations made through the formula and are likely to take account of both parents earning capacity.

It is also important to remember that families can use the online calculator on the maintenance options website to reach a private agreement which is in line with the maintenance calculation which would be provided by the government service. So individuals can reach private agreements which work for them, independent of the law under the Child Support Act, or reach a private agreement which is in line with the rules in the Child Support Act. Therefore private agreements create a lot of flexibility for families.

Private agreements can have positive features, but it has to be recognised that not all family breakdowns are amicable and not all families are capable of reaching workable private agreements.

ARGUMENTS AGAINST PRIVATE AGREEMENTS

There are several disadvantages of private agreements. Not everyone has a working relationship whereby they are capable of making a suitable agreement with their ex-partner, and there is no way of ensuring that private agreements are in place. A study carried out in 2012 found that 43% of single parents on benefit had no maintenance agreement in place.[220] There is no need for private agreements to be consistent so children in similar circumstances might receive different payments, and there is an increased risk of one of the parties being coerced or manipulated in the negotiations.[221] These elements were problems which the child support system sought to eradicate.[222] Some of these problems could be managed if parties make use of the agency for an indicative calculation. It currently costs £20 to make an application through the government service.[223] Another important issue is that private agreements are not legally enforceable, unless the parties seek a consent order from the court. Therefore these agreements may not be followed up with child support payments and could fall apart relatively quickly.

Where parties do not seek an indicative calculation, then of course there is the risk of both manipulation and inconsistent agreements. In particular manipulation may be used in regard to contact. One parent may agree to child support on the basis that the caring parent allows them to have contact with their child. This is controversial because there might be reasons for no contact, supervised contact, or reduced contact, but child support is always necessary.[224] The paying parent may also withhold the money due each month making the person with care have to go through additional hoops in order to get the money. This is a form of coercive control and allows the paying parent to continue making life difficult for the person with care. There is no guarantee that the arrangement will be diverted to the collect and pay system, and even if it is the parties will still have to pay the additional costs

---

[219] Ellman, I.M. *et al* 'Child Support Judgments: Comparing Public Policy to the Public's Policy (2014) *International Journal of Law, Policy and the Family* 274.

[220] Ellman, I.M. *et al* 'Child Support Judgments: Comparing Public Policy to the Public's Policy (2014) *International Journal of Law, Policy and the Family* 274.

[221] Skinner, C. 'Child Maintenance Reforms: Understanding Father's Expressive Agency and the Power of Reciprocity' (2013) 27 *International Journal of Law, Policy and the Family* 242, 246.

[222] *Children Come First: The Government's Proposals on the Maintenance of Children* (White Paper, Cm 1264, 1990).

[223] See https://www.gov.uk/child-maintenance/how-to-apply, accessed 3 October 2016. Victims of domestic violence, persons under 19, and persons living in Northern Ireland do not have to pay this fee.

[224] See, e.g., Douglas, G. 'Contact is not a Commodity to be bartered for money' [2011] *Family Law* 491.

regardless of whether there is domestic violence. Where parents reach private agreements across different areas of family law there is no guarantee that the child's welfare will be considered nor that other legal principles will be upheld.[225] The problem of manipulation is of concern across all areas of family law now that there is a focus on private agreements rather than court orders.[226]

Another important element is compliance or enforcement. There is limited point in having consistent maintenance calculations if they are rarely complied with or enforced. If private arrangements are more likely to be complied with then they have to be preferred, even if they are inconsistent. However is there any evidence which confirms that private agreements are more likely to be complied with?

 CONTEXT 3: DO PRIVATE AGREEMENTS WORK?

Research on single parents on benefit indicates that where a functioning private agreement is in place then these work well.[227] Regular payments are usually made,[228] the caring parent is also more likely to receive an informal payment than those with a government agreement,[229] and it is more likely that contact will take place.[230] In general a functioning child support agreement is the sign of a working relationship between the two parents across all areas. However, some parents received less money than they would through the government service and payments may be more ad hoc.[231] This flexibility is seen as a positive side of private agreements, and a way to make all parts of the parent–child relationship function effectively.[232]

One key problem, however, was that where private arrangements had stopped working the caring parent made the decision to switch to the government service or accepted the situation by default and it was considered that there was no arrangement in place.[233] This is in contrast to arrangements under the original provisions of the Child Support Act 1991, where the arrangement remained in place even though it was not working.[234] Therefore although

[225] Diduck, A. 'Autonomy and Family Justice' (2016) 28 *Child and Family Law Quarterly* 133.

[226] A recent study in Australia, where mediation is also encouraged highlights some of the difficulties inherent in these systems. Laing, L. 'Secondary Victimization: Domestic Violence Survivors Navigating the Family Law System' (2016) *Violence Against Women* 1.

[227] Bryson, C. *et al Kids aren't free: The child maintenance arrangements of single parents on benefit in 2012* (Gingerbread).

[228] Bryson, C. *et al Kids aren't free: The child maintenance arrangements of single parents on benefit in 2012* (Gingerbread) 44 et seq.

[229] Bryson, C. *et al Kids aren't free: The child maintenance arrangements of single parents on benefit in 2012* (Gingerbread) 53.

[230] Bryson, C. *et al Kids aren't free: The child maintenance arrangements of single parents on benefit in 2012* (Gingerbread) 61.

[231] Bryson, C. *et al Kids aren't free: The child maintenance arrangements of single parents on benefit in 2012* (Gingerbread) 90.

[232] Bryson, C. *et al Kids aren't free: The child maintenance arrangements of single parents on benefit in 2012* (Gingerbread) 90.

[233] Bryson, C. *et al Kids aren't free: The child maintenance arrangements of single parents on benefit in 2012* (Gingerbread) 97.

[234] Bryson, C. *et al Kids aren't free: The child maintenance arrangements of single parents on benefit in 2012* (Gingerbread) 87.

73% of those who *recognised* that they had a private agreement in place reported that they received regular payments,[235] the researchers found it difficult to determine whether private arrangements were in fact more reliable as only working private arrangements were considered to be arrangements by the parents. In contrast only 40% of those with a Child Support Act arrangement reported receiving regular maintenance.[236] It is difficult to compare these figures because it is clear when there is a government arrangement in place, but individuals were not always clear about whether there was a private agreement in place. It is clear that private arrangements can be very effective in some cases, however, they only worked for certain categories of people.[237]

It would seem that parents prefer to use private agreements where possible, because they find the government service inflexible. Consequently only those who have already been using the Service, or those who are unable to make or maintain a private agreement will revert to the Service. Given that private agreements seem to be the preferred option by all it is questionable whether it is necessary to impose such harsh penalties on those who are forced to use the government service, by charging them extra or taking money from their child support.

7. Comparative context

This section briefly considers the child support systems in Norway and the USA. The comparative analysis allows consideration of how other countries deal with some of the problems outlined during the course of this chapter.

7.1. Norway

Norway has a very efficient administrative system in place for the collection of maintenance. The recovery rate is 80%.[238] The administrative system is cheaper for parties who cannot reach an agreement because they do not have to pay court fees and they do not need legal representation. The administrative system is thought to have lowered the level of conflict between the parents, particularly since the law was changed in 2003 so that maintenance is now calculated on the basis of the income of both parties.[239] As a starting point the Norwegian system provides a table of costs for supporting a child, which is

---

[235] Bryson, C. *et al Kids aren't free: The child maintenance arrangements of single parents on benefit in 2012* (Gingerbread), emphasis added.

[236] Bryson, C. *et al Kids aren't free: The child maintenance arrangements of single parents on benefit in 2012* (Gingerbread).

[237] Bryson, C. *et al Kids aren't free: The child maintenance arrangements of single parents on benefit in 2012* (Gingerbread) 63.

[238] Suae, J. *et al* 'Administrative Establishment and Enforcement of Child Support in Norway' in P. Beaumont *et al* (eds) *The Recovery of Maintenance in the EU and Worldwide* (Hart Publishing, 2014) 161, 161. It is difficult to find comparative data. The experimental statistics suggest that only 17% of maintenance is unpaid, so a recovery rate of 83%, but the statistics presume *that those using maintenance direct are receiving maintenance* (emphasis added). There is no evidence that they are (Child Maintenance Service 2012 Scheme Experimental Statistics (Aug 2013–Nov 2016). Actual data on the Child Support Agency, from March 2013 (before the bulk of cases were transferred) shows that only 59.4% of cases were paying the full maintenance liability (Child Support Agency Quarterly Summary of Statistics for Great Britain), but again this is not directly comparable as the Norwegian statistic relates to overall maintenance collected.

[239] Suae, J. *et al* 'Administrative Establishment and Enforcement of Child Support in Norway' in P. Beaumont *et al* (eds) *The Recovery of Maintenance in the EU and Worldwide* (Hart Publishing, 2014) 161, 163.

updated annually in line with average expenses. The cost allocated increases with the age of the child.[240] The maintenance costs are divided between the parents in relation to their income.[241] Deductions are then made from the non-resident parent's contribution based on contact,[242] in order to get the final calculation.

The main difference between the Norwegian formula and the UK formula is that the Norwegian formula tries to establish the cost of a child, whereas the UK formula just requires a proportion of income is paid without consideration of what a child needs in order to escape poverty. The Norwegian system also takes account of both parents' wages which is more in keeping with public perceptions according to recent studies.[243] Interestingly these two features were part of the original formula in the UK (see 3.2). In the UK these features were phased out for being too complicated, whereas the Norwegian system began with a simple formula and phased in these changes in order to provide a better calculation. One downside to the Norwegian system could be that it does not require high-earning non-resident parents to pay more, and this goes against current public opinion in the UK.[244]

Private agreements are common in Norway. Information to assist parties in reaching a private agreement is publicly available on the Labour and Welfare Administration's website and a web based child support stipulation calculator is also available.[245] The calculator provides the same assessment as applicable under the law, so provided the information is entered correctly parents should get the same result as they would through the agency. Private agreements save the government time and money and are therefore encouraged.[246] The Norwegian experience indicates that private agreements are the most effective mechanism for resolving child support questions when parents separate.[247] If the parties cannot reach a private agreement a fee of 115 euros per person is charged for the administrative establishment or modification of a decision,[248] which is just over £100. The fee does not apply to those who earn less than 27,000 euros per year (£24,316).[249] This figure varies in line with expected wages.[250] Although the fee may appear quite high, it only applies to certain categories of the population and therefore if this was applied in the UK it would not apply to single parents on benefit whom the system was initially designed to help.

---

[240] Suae, J. *et al* 'Administrative Establishment and Enforcement of Child Support in Norway' in P. Beaumont *et al* (eds) *The Recovery of Maintenance in the EU and Worldwide* (Hart Publishing, 2014) 161, 166–7.

[241] Suae, J. *et al* 'Administrative Establishment and Enforcement of Child Support in Norway' in P. Beaumont *et al* (eds) *The Recovery of Maintenance in the EU and Worldwide* (Hart Publishing, 2014) 161, 166.

[242] Suae, J. *et al* 'Administrative Establishment and Enforcement of Child Support in Norway' in P. Beaumont *et al* (eds) *The Recovery of Maintenance in the EU and Worldwide* (Hart Publishing, 2014) 161, 167.

[243] See, Ellman, I.M. *et al* 'Child Support Judgments: Comparing Public Policy to the Public's Policy (2014) 28 *International Journal of Law, Policy and the Family* 274.

[244] Ellman, I.M. *et al* 'Child Support Judgments: Comparing Public Policy to the Public's Policy (2014) 28 *International Journal of Law, Policy and the Family* 274.

[245] Suae, J. *et al* 'Administrative Establishment and Enforcement of Child Support in Norway' in P. Beaumont *et al* (eds) *The Recovery of Maintenance in the EU and Worldwide* (Hart Publishing, 2014) 161, 172.

[246] Suae, J. *et al* 'Administrative Establishment and Enforcement of Child Support in Norway' in P. Beaumont *et al* (eds) *The Recovery of Maintenance in the EU and Worldwide* (Hart Publishing, 2014) 161, 166.

[247] Suae, J. *et al* 'Administrative Establishment and Enforcement of Child Support in Norway' in P. Beaumont *et al* (eds) *The Recovery of Maintenance in the EU and Worldwide* (Hart Publishing, 2014) 161, 173.

[248] However collection is free.

[249] Suae, J. *et al* 'Administrative Establishment and Enforcement of Child Support in Norway' in P. Beaumont *et al* (eds) *The Recovery of Maintenance in the EU and Worldwide* (Hart Publishing, 2014) 161, 171–2.

[250] Suae, J. *et al* 'Administrative Establishment and Enforcement of Child Support in Norway' in P. Beaumont *et al* (eds) *The Recovery of Maintenance in the EU and Worldwide* (Hart Publishing, 2014) 161, 171–2. It is set in line with what is considered to be a low income.

Research indicates that private agreements work better for certain categories of people, which includes those who earn a regular income,[251] therefore the people required to pay are largely those who private agreements are expected to work for. An ideal system should also include an exception in domestic violence cases, since these are also cases where it can be difficult to reach a private agreement.

In Norway state enforcement, or collection, of child support is paid for by the government. However unlike the UK system, the work done by the Norwegian collection agency is very cost effective. For every euro spent, around 33 euros are collected.[252] Nearly 40% of the child support collected in Norway in 2013 was paid voluntarily by the non-resident parent.[253] Where the parent has accrued debt the collection agency will begin a conversation with the parent and enter into an agreement with them. This will often result in a monthly payment lower than the calculation.[254] Where payment is not made voluntarily the two main enforcement measures are wage withholding and deduction from social security and pensions benefits.[255] Other methods used are: the withholding of tax and VAT refunds; withholding agricultural grants and other governmental contributions; garnishment of bank accounts; and the forced sale of immoveable property and other personal property.[256] The agency can apply to the court for travel restrictions to be imposed on the defaulting parent. Where successful the passport is impounded, and the restrictions are not usually lifted until the parent has paid the full amount. However this measure is rarely utilised by the agency and rarely imposed by the court.[257] Finally the agency can inform the police of non-compliance with the obligation. The police can charge the parent, but only if the non-resident parent has the ability to pay.[258] Since 2008 referrals to the police have dropped and so have conviction rates.[259]

7.2 USA

Child support in the USA is complicated because each state has its own formulas, and some states' formulas are more complicated than others.[260] The USA also has an interstate system, to ensure collection of child support where children live in different states from the non-resident parent, under the Uniform Interstate Family Support Act. Therefore rather than look at how maintenance is calculated in each state this section will focus on the general policy and approach in the USA.

---

[251] Bryson, C. *et al Kids aren't free: The child maintenance arrangements of single parents on benefit in 2012* (Gingerbread) 67.

[252] Suae, J. *et al* 'Administrative Establishment and Enforcement of Child Support in Norway' in P. Beaumont *et al* (eds) *The Recovery of Maintenance in the EU and Worldwide* (Hart Publishing, 2014) 161, 175.

[253] Suae, J. *et al* 'Administrative Establishment and Enforcement of Child Support in Norway' in P. Beaumont *et al* (eds) *The Recovery of Maintenance in the EU and Worldwide* (Hart Publishing, 2014) 161, 176.

[254] Suae, J. *et al* 'Administrative Establishment and Enforcement of Child Support in Norway' in P. Beaumont *et al* (eds) *The Recovery of Maintenance in the EU and Worldwide* (Hart Publishing, 2014) 161, 176–7.

[255] Suae, J. *et al* 'Administrative Establishment and Enforcement of Child Support in Norway' in P. Beaumont *et al* (eds) *The Recovery of Maintenance in the EU and Worldwide* (Hart Publishing, 2014) 161, 177.

[256] Suae, J. *et al* 'Administrative Establishment and Enforcement of Child Support in Norway' in P. Beaumont *et al* (eds) *The Recovery of Maintenance in the EU and Worldwide* (Hart Publishing, 2014) 161, 177–8.

[257] Suae, J. *et al* 'Administrative Establishment and Enforcement of Child Support in Norway' in P. Beaumont *et al* (eds) *The Recovery of Maintenance in the EU and Worldwide* (Hart Publishing, 2014) 161, 178.

[258] Suae, J. *et al* 'Administrative Establishment and Enforcement of Child Support in Norway' in P. Beaumont *et al* (eds) *The Recovery of Maintenance in the EU and Worldwide* (Hart Publishing, 2014) 161, 178.

[259] Suae, J. *et al* 'Administrative Establishment and Enforcement of Child Support in Norway' in P. Beaumont *et al* (eds) *The Recovery of Maintenance in the EU and Worldwide* (Hart Publishing, 2014) 161, 179.

[260] Takayesu, M. and Eldred, S. 'Setting appropriate Child Support Orders and Addressing Barriers: Research and Policy Implications to Improve Payments and Compliance' in P. Beaumont *et al* (eds) *The Recovery of Maintenance in the EU and Worldwide* (2014, Hart Publishing) 137.

Figure 6.1: Family-centered strategies (bubble chart)

Source: Office of Child Support Enforcement. Available at: www.acf.hhs.gov/css, accessed 2 September 2016.

The USA has had a child support system in place since 1975. Keith explains that it took the USA around '35 years to establish a truly integrated, largely automated, efficient and effective child support system'.[261] The programme has evolved steadily alongside its scope and its services.

The establishment and collection of child support is now seen as an integrated part of the family which should be developed alongside other family matters rather than a stand-alone issue, not interlinked with other areas simply because it is managed by a different agency. Although in many cases the collection of child support is still be treated as a purely administrative matter, this is not true for all cases particularly 'problem cases'. As such the programme is now much more flexible and the scope of its services has expanded. The programme does not simply penalise non-compliant parents for failure to pay, but aims to assist non-resident parents and support their needs (whether through education, training, or work support) in order to increase their ability to pay and promote economic stability.[262] As is clear from Figure 6.1[263] the programme aims to support healthy family relationships including the engagement of fathers in the child's life from birth, which recognises that the child has both emotional and financial needs. The programme also includes support for family violence collaboration which requires efforts to reduce the risk of family violence and also requires that domestic violence survivors are helped to pursue

[261] Keith, R. 'Enforcement in the US and Globally: 1975–2025' in P. Beaumont *et al* (eds) *The Recovery of Maintenance in the EU and Worldwide* (2014, Hart Publishing) 21, 43.

[262] See, e.g., https://www.acf.hhs.gov/css/resource/improving-child-support-outcomes-through-employment-programs, accessed 2 September 2016 and Keith, R. 'Enforcement in the US and Globally: 1975–2025' in P. Beaumont *et al* (eds) *The Recovery of Maintenance in the EU and Worldwide* (2014, Hart Publishing) 21, 43.

[263] Figure taken from the Office of Child Support Enforcement. Available at: http://www.acf.hhs.gov/css/child-support-professionals/fact-sheets/family-centered-strategies, accessed 2 September 2016. The figure was also used by V. Turetsky at The Hague Asia Pacific Week Conference on Maintenance and Child Support (2015) to explain the latest strategies of the US government.

their child support safely. Therefore this holistic approach tries to support successful relationships between children and their parents, whilst recognising the risks of domestic violence and the need for support to gain employment in order to increase ability to pay. This is not the same as saying that child support and contact goes hand in hand, but is much more holistic than this recognising the benefits of healthy family relationships alongside the risks of forced relationships and forced contact. This combined approach with further considerations than simply the collection of child support enables more personalised and more focused remedies to be employed.

SUMMARY

1. Who should support children financially?
   - Parents have primary responsibility for supporting their children financially, but the state will step in and provide financial support where necessary. The state no longer uses child support as a method for recovering benefits paid, instead parents can keep all money that is paid in relation to child support in addition to any benefits received.
   - Under the Child Support Act only biological parents, those with a parental order, or those who have formally adopted a child qualify as parents for the purpose of the Act. In addition the formula under the Child Support Act is applied in a rigid inflexible manner, which may not fully take account of individual circumstances. There are some benefits to this approach; the Child Support Act provides clarity and legal certainty. It also means that non-resident parents in similar financial circumstances will have the same liability.
   - Under the Children Act and the Matrimonial Causes Act more people may be liable for child support payments and the focus is on whether the child is a child of the family. The law under the Children Act and the Matrimonial Causes Act also provides more flexibility than that under the Child Support Act, and can be used in certain circumstances to fill any gaps left by the inflexibility of the formula.

2. Should we rely on private agreements for child support?
   - The government's current policy focuses on private agreements and encourages individuals to take responsibility for their private family disputes. However, this also permits the government to sidestep their responsibilities by pushing child support into the private sphere.
   - Private agreements do not work for everyone, and many families do not have a private agreement in place. Therefore it is difficult to determine whether parents are fulfilling their responsibilities to their child if they choose not to have a private agreement. It is also difficult to determine how effective private agreements are when enforcement is also a private matter.

3. How should child support obligations be enforced; through a state body or privately?
   - There are two mechanisms for enforcement—maintenance direct and collect and pay—however 70% of people, who have a calculation from the

government service, are on maintenance direct and it is difficult to be placed on the collect and pay scheme. The current government statistics simply presume that all maintenance under maintenance direct is collected and there is no mechanism in place to determine whether the system actually works. Although the aim is to reduce the involvement of the government service, so that it can focus its time on more difficult cases and allow parents to make their 'own arrangements, if cases are not being redirected to collect and pay, then the government service is not actually providing extra assistance in these difficult cases and are not making use of the enforcement powers available.

- The collect and pay service costs the paying parent an additional 20% over and above the maintenance calculation. It also means that the person with care sees a 4% reduction in the money received in comparison to the maintenance calculation. In cases where the parents have limited means this additional money may be difficult to find and the reduction in child support is unlikely to be in the best interests of the child. Further where parents are happy to pay the fee this effectively turns the system into a pay for hire service. If parents are willing to pay but they are not permitted to use the collect and pay service, this is not logical and goes against party autonomy, which the system apparently supports.

- The state body has a number of enforcement powers and mechanisms available, but these are not widely used. Further as a result of *Kehoe* parent's cannot rely on the Service to utilise these options and do not have the ability to request the Service to take a certain route. The other problem is that some of the enforcement mechanisms are severe and could be counterproductive if they reduce the non-resident parents earning potential.

Further Reading

ALTMAN, S. 'A Theory of Child Support' (2003) 17 *International Journal of Law, Policy and the Family* 173–210
- For further information on different theories of child support and the private public debate.

BRYSON, C. *et al Kids aren't free: The child maintenance arrangements of single parents on benefit in 2012* (Gingerbread)
- This is an empirical study of the types of child support arrangements that were in place, and how successful they were.

EEKELAAR, J. 'Are Parents Morally Obliged to Care for their Children' (1991) 11 *Oxford Journal of Legal Studies* 340
- A theoretical discussion on moral obligations and further information about government policy at the time the Child Support Act was first introduced.

ELLMAN, I.M. *et al* 'Child Support Judgments: Comparing Public Policy to the Public's Policy' (2014) 28 *International Journal of Law, Policy and the Family* 274–301
- For general views from the public on what child support calculations should consider and how much child support should be paid.

FEHLBERG, B. and MACLEAN, M. 'Child Support Policy in Australia and the United Kingdom: Changing Priorities but a similar tough deal for Children?' (2009) 23 *International Journal of Law, Policy and the Family* 1–24.

- For a comparative analysis with another jurisdiction and a summary and critique of the policy in both countries.

TAKAYESU, M. and ELDRED, S. 'Setting appropriate Child Support Orders and Addressing Barriers: Research and Policy Implications to Improve Payments and Compliance' in P. BEAUMONT et al (eds) *The Recovery of Maintenance in the EU and Worldwide* (Hart Publishing, 2014) 137

- Information on a study of barriers to child support enforcement and an analysis of changes that could be made to improve payments and compliance.

7

Domestic Violence and Abuse

Anna Carline and Roxanna Dehaghani

LEARNING OBJECTIVES

After reading this chapter you will be able to:

- Critically evaluate the notion of 'domestic violence and abuse'. This will include a discussion of what amounts to domestic violence and abuse;

- Appreciate the prevalence and nature of domestic violence and abuse, and the extent to which it is a gendered phenomenon;

- Understand how family law responds to domestic violence and abuse. More specifically, you will understand the three key family law remedies: non-molestation orders, occupation orders, and forced marriage protection orders;

- Identify, and critically reflect upon, some of the wider justice issues relating to family law's response to domestic violence and abuse;

- Identify, and critically reflect upon, some of the key criminal law and criminal justice responses to domestic violence and abuse.

DEBATES

After reading this chapter you should be equipped to discuss your opinion on the following central debates:

1. How should domestic violence be defined?

2. To what extent is domestic violence a gendered phenomenon?

3. Should the concept of 'associated person' more accurately reflect the reality of domestic violence?

4. Should the breach of a family law order be a criminal offence?

5. Does the introduction of the domestic violence disclosure scheme 'responsibilise' the victim?

1. Introduction

Domestic violence and abuse impacts the lives of millions every year. Such conduct generally takes place behind closed doors, and involves individuals who are close and emotionally connected to each other. Consequently, developing an effective legal response—which will protect victims and ultimately reduce prevalence—is challenging. While many of the acts involved in domestic violence and abuse are of a criminal nature, family law plays a very important role in providing protection for the victim. In addition to exploring the prevalence of domestic violence and abuse, the chapter will examine how, historically, domestic violence was considered to be a private matter that was none of the law's concern. While domestic violence is now recognised to be an important social issue, the historical acceptance of such abuse provides a context to understand some of the difficulties that victims face today.

This consideration of the historical context highlights that it is also important to examine what is meant by the term 'domestic violence': what conduct is recognised as amounting to domestic violence? How should domestic violence be defined? As the chapter will demonstrate, the definition of domestic violence has changed considerably over the years, and it is now generally accepted that domestic violence is by no means limited to physical and sexual abuse, but also encompasses coercive and controlling behaviour.

In line with this broader definition, it is now also recognised that forcing a person to marry against their will is a form of domestic violence. Accordingly, the chapter will explore how the family law has been reformed to respond to the phenomena of forced marriage. This includes aiming to provide protection for potential victims, as well as remedies for those who have already been forced into marriage.

In addition to exploring the relevant statistics, the chapter will consider the debates regarding the gendered nature of domestic violence: to what extent is domestic violence primarily committed by men against women? Is the violence that women use against men of a different nature to that which men use against women? Related to these debates, the chapter will explore some of the theories behind the causes of domestic violence. Why do some people abuse their partners? And why do more men than women abuse their partners?

A key focus of the chapter will be the family law remedies that are available for domestic abuse victims. Three key remedies will be examined: non-molestation orders, occupation orders, and forced marriage protection orders. The chapter will explore the various eligibility criteria of these orders, along with their content and duration. In general, these orders prevent the respondent—the perpetrator—from engaging in certain conduct and may require that s/he vacates the family home. The chapter will explore some of the pivotal aspects of these orders, such as the notion of 'associated person'. How is 'associated person' defined? To what extent does this definition correspond with the reality of domestic violence and abuse? Of further importance is how the orders are enforced. How effective are these orders at preventing abuse and protecting the victim? What powers does the court have if the respondent breaches an order? As will be seen, it is now a criminal offence to breach some of the family law orders, but to what extent should it be a criminal offence to breach a family law order?

In addition to examining the key family law orders, the chapter will also explore some of the wider factors pertaining to the family justice system's response to domestic violence. It is important to recognise the impact of the changes to legal aid, as introduced by the Legal Aid, Sentencing and Punishment of Offenders Act 2012 (LASPO) (see Chapter 15), and the extent to which victims of domestic violence may feel threatened during family law proceedings, particularly in cases involving the arrangements for children after separation. What challenges do domestic violence victims face during family law proceedings? How can these difficulties be remedied?

In order contextualise the importance of family law, and how family law remedies have developed to respond to the domestic violence and abuse, it is necessary to examine aspects of criminal law and criminal justice. It is important to remember that family law is private law. As such, the case is between the victim and the perpetrator, and it is the victim who must apply to the courts for an order. Further, private law remedies are concerned with protecting the victim, as opposed to punishing the offender. In contrast, with the criminal law, the case is between the state and the perpetrator. Accordingly, while a victim may report the perpetrator to the police, it is ultimately the police and the Crown Prosecution Service (CPS) who will decide whether the perpetrator should be charged and prosecuted for an alleged offence. If found guilty, by either a magistrate or a jury, the offender will receive a criminal conviction and then be punished, the severity of which (i.e. whether s/he receives a prison sentence) would depend upon the crime committed. In exploring the criminal law developments, the chapter will provide a critical analysis of the new offences of 'coercive control' and that of stalking. What are the arguments for and against developing new criminal offences to respond to domestic violence and abuse? Other pivotal initiatives that will be discussed include the powers given to the police to exclude a perpetrator from the premises, and what is known as 'Clare's Law'—a scheme which enables an individual to find out if their partner has been convicted for a domestic violence related offence. Following on from this, the chapter will explore the potential of joint specialist domestic violence courts, which deal with both family and criminal law remedies, and introduce the concept of 'therapeutic jurisprudence'. To what extent do these developments and reforms improve the criminal justice system's response to domestic violence?

2. Exploring domestic violence

This section provides a critical analysis of the concept of domestic violence and abuse. In order to contextualise recent developments and debates, the section commences with an historical overview and highlights the impact of feminist activism upon society's perspective of, and legal responses to, domestic violence. Thereafter, the section explores the definition of domestic violence, along with the prevalence, nature, and perceived causes of such abuse.

2.1 Domestic violence, patriarchy, and the public/private divide: the historical context

A critical evaluation of the family law's response to domestic violence requires an understanding of the feminist debates regarding the role of patriarchy, the public/private divide, and how, historically, the law accepted male violence against women. These debates help to contextualise the development of family law remedies, along with the ongoing difficulties that many victims face today. The law continues to be exceptionally unsuccessful at protecting women from domestic abuse. One suggested reason for this is that the law is inherently patriarchal: it maintains men's power over women—it allows men to dominate the legal system and thereby subordinate women.

The historical patriarchal nature of law can be seen through the Doctrine of Coverture. As stated in Blackstone, this doctrine rendered the wife subject to the control of her husband:

> By marriage, the husband and wife are one person in law: that is, the very being or legal existence of the woman is suspended during the marriage, or at least incorporated and consolidated into that of her husband: under whose wing, protection and cover, she performs everything.[1]

---

[1] Blackstone, W. *Commentaries on the Laws of England* (Clarendon Press, 1778) 442.

Once married, a woman became completely tied to her husband. A husband was permitted to chastise his wife by beating her with a stick no wider than his thumb (known as the 'rule of thumb'). Furthermore, it was not until 1991 that it became a crime for a husband to rape his wife.[2] Feminist scholars have argued that this historical acceptance of domestic violence maintains and perpetuates a public/private distinction—while the public sphere is regulated by the law, the private sphere is not. Consequently, what occurs in private is none of the state's concern.

As such, domestic violence has not readily been recognised as a social problem, which renders it difficult to tackle effectively. In the nineteenth century, the womens' suffrage movement initially used the term 'wife-beating' in order draw attention to the abuse women suffered at the hands of their husbands.[3] In the late nineteenth century, first wave (1830s–early 1900s) feminist Frances Power Cobbe adopted the phrase 'wife-torture' in order to emphasise the degree of harm women suffered. Cobbe argued that wife-beating turned into wife torture, which eventually led to wife-maiming, wife-blinding, or wife-murder.[4] However, Howe notes that second wave (1960s–1980s) feminists strategically adopted the phrase 'domestic violence', as part of the continued efforts of the feminist movement to compel the state to acknowledge and respond to violence against women in the home.[5] Nevertheless, the prefix 'domestic' has been critiqued for minimising and dismissing the violence suffered by victims.[6] Douglas and Godden have also argued that the use of family law continues to construct domestic violence as a matter of private, and not public, concern:

> . . . the effect of domestic violence legislation has been to separate 'intimate partner' violence out from other forms of assault. The repositioning of violence between intimate partners within the private, less publicly accountable sphere has been to subtly construct it against the 'more serious' categories of criminally vilified violence.[7]

Significantly, as we explore in further detail in 6, many of the problems with enforcement that were evident in the mid-1800s still exist today: maximum penalties are rarely enforced and punishment of the perpetrator can indirectly punish the wife/female partner and children. Women could face hardship if their partner is issued a fine or sent to prison. Such factors are likely to deter a woman from reporting, as could the fear of being reprimanded by the abuser. Hence, domestic violence poses quite a quandary; while campaigners want perpetrators to be punished, it is also recognised that this might impact negatively upon the victim and any children. Consequently, feminists in the nineteenth century focused upon helping women leave abusive relationships. Here, we can contextualise the development of family law remedies. A campaign led by Frances Power Cobbe resulted in the inclusion of separation orders in the Matrimonial Causes Act 1878. Subsequently, a court had the power to grant a wife judicial separation with maintenance when the husband had been convicted of aggravated assault. Women were gradually provided more rights over their property, and the courts were able to grant and enforce maintenance orders.[8] The current family law orders are contained in the Family Law Act 1996. However, prior to examining the relevant provisions, it is important to explore the definition, nature, and causes of domestic violence.

---

[2] *R v R* [1991] 3 WLR 767.   [3] Mooney, J. *Gender, Violence and the Social Order* (MacMillan, 2000) 68.

[4] Cobbe, F. P. 'Wife-Torture in England' [1878] 55 *The Contemporary Review* 72.

[5] Howe, A. *Sex Violence and Crime: Foucault and the 'Man' Question* (Routledge, 2008) 181.

[6] Howe, A. *Sex Violence and Crime: Foucault and the 'Man' Question* (Routledge, 2008) 181.

[7] Douglas, H. and Godden, L. 'The Decriminalisation of Domestic Violence' (2003) 27 *Criminal Law Journal* 32, 32.

[8] See Married Woman's Property Act 1870 and Summary Jurisdiction (Married Woman) Act 1895.

2.2. **Defining domestic violence**

The phrase 'domestic violence and abuse' is generally deployed to refer to abusive behaviour that takes place within the home and/or family. The majority of abuse takes places between intimate partners, such as husband and wife, or those who live together as if they were husband and wife. However, as we examine later, the current government definition encompasses violence between a wide range of familial members. An exploration of the history of the law's response to domestic violence also demonstrates how the definition has evolved over time to encompass a wide range of abusive behaviour. Nevertheless, as will be discussed in further detail in 6, evidence illustrates that the state and the legal system continues to treat violence within the privacy of the home less seriously than that which occurs in the public sphere. A further concern relates to the use of the word 'violence', which tends to connote physical injury only and, as such, fails to recognise the breadth of abuse that victims suffer. Two recent developments, however, indicate an acknowledgement within law and policy that domestic violence encompasses non-physical abuse.

 Key Case 1: *Yemshaw v Hounslow London Borough Council* [2011] UKSC 3

The Supreme Court examined the definition of domestic violence for the purposes of the Housing Act 1996. Ms Yemshaw was married and had two children, aged 6 and 8 months. She was fearful of her husband: there was no physical abuse but her husband had inflicted upon her, emotional, psychological, and financial abuse. She applied to the local housing authority for accommodation but the authority refused to rehouse her, stating that they only had to rehouse someone who had a house if it was not reasonable for them to live there. It was not reasonable if that person was a victim of domestic violence. The housing authority said that, as there was no physical violence or violent touching and no probability of it, there was no domestic violence. Ms Yemshaw sought judicial review. Whilst the Court of Appeal supported the approach by the housing authority, the Supreme Court did not. The case was remitted back to the local authority to approach the case on this new understanding of domestic violence:

> Was this, in reality, simply a case of marriage breakdown in which the appellant was not genuinely in fear of her husband; or was it a classic case of domestic abuse, in which one spouse puts the other in fear through the constant denial of freedom and of money for essentials, through the denigration of her personality, such that she genuinely fears that he may take her children away from her however unrealistic this may appear to an objective outsider? This is not to apply a subjective test. The test is always the view of the objective outsider but applied to the particular facts, circumstances and personalities of the people involved.[9]

In 2011, the then Coalition government held a consultation on the definition of domestic violence.[10] During the consultation process, concern was expressed that any definition should appropriately acknowledge the role of 'coercive control' in an abusive relationship. The concept of 'coercive control' was developed by Stark in order to highlight how abusers engage in 'a pattern of behaviour which seeks to take away the victim's liberty or freedom, to strip away their sense of self'.[11] This includes the 'micro-regulation' of a victim's

[9] Baroness Hale, at [36].

[10] Home Office, *Cross-Government Definition of Domestic Violence: A Consultation* (Home Office, 2011); Home Office, *Cross-Government Definition of Domestic Violence—A Consultation: Summary of Responses* (Home Office, 2012).

[11] Stark, E. *Coercive Control: How Men Entrap Women in Personal Life* (OUP, 2009).

everyday life, so they become entrapped within the relationship. Further to this, the consultation highlighted the plight of victims between the ages of 16 and 18: they were too old to fall within the ambit of child protection agencies, but were too young to be recognised as victims of domestic violence, which at that time was restricted to adults.[12]

Subsequently, the government now defines domestic violence as: [13]

- Any incident or pattern of incidents of controlling, coercive, threatening behaviour, violence or abuse between those aged 16 or over who are or have been intimate partners or family members regardless of gender or sexuality. The abuse can encompass but is not limited to:
  - psychological;
  - physical;
  - sexual;
  - financial;
  - emotional.

This new definition also elaborates on the meanings of 'controlling' and 'coercive':

- Controlling behaviour is: a range of acts designed to make a person subordinate and/ or dependent by isolating them from sources of support, exploiting their resources and capacities for personal gain, depriving them of the means needed for independence, resistance, and escape and regulating their everyday behaviour.
- Coercive behaviour is: an act or a pattern of acts of assault, threats, humiliation, and intimidation or other abuse that is used to harm, punish, or frighten their victim.

It is also important to emphasise that domestic abuse does not necessarily come to an end because the victim has managed to leave the relationship. Consequently, the term 'post-separation abuse' has been developed to acknowledge that abuse may endure—and even escalate—after a relationship has been terminated.

 DEBATE 1: HOW SHOULD DOMESTIC VIOLENCE BE DEFINED?

Lady Hale in *Yemshaw v Hounslow London Borough Council* stated that the word violence 'is capable of bearing several meanings and applying to many different types of behaviour', and that 'these can change and develop over time'.[14] Subsequently, the Supreme Court recognised that it was no longer appropriate to limit violence to physical acts, but rather a wider definition should be adopted which encompassed psychological, emotional, and financial abuse. A similar broad approach is adopted by the Council of Europe's Convention on combating and preventing violence against women and girls (known as the Istanbul Convention) which states:

'domestic violence' shall mean all acts of physical, sexual, psychological or economic violence that occur within the family or domestic unit or between former or current spouses of partners, whether or not the perpetrator shares or has shared the same residence with the victim.[15]

---

[12] Home Office, *Cross-Government Definition of Domestic Violence: A Consultation* (Home Office, 2011).
[13] Home Office, *Cross-Government Definition of Domestic Violence—A Consultation: Summary of Responses* (Home Office, 2012) 19.   [14] [2011] UKSC 3, at [27].
[15] Council of Europe Convention on combating and preventing violence against women and girls (Council of Europe, 2011), Article 3(b). The UK is a signatory to the Istanbul Convention, but has still to ratify it.

The official governmental definition further develops the notion of domestic violence by including coercive and controlling behaviour. These advances are significant as they emphasise the importance, impact, and range of non-physical abusive tactics, which are often a large part of abuse within relationships. Many victims and perpetrators, as well as frontline practitioners (such as police officers and social workers), tend not to view controlling and coercive activities as amounting to abuse. On this basis, it can be argued that the government's definition has an important educational and symbolic role: it sends out a clear message to the public and practitioners. This could potentially enable victims to recognise that they have been subject to abuse and encourage them to act, as well as improve the responses of frontline agencies. Nevertheless, such positives require widespread awareness of the new definition. In addition, it is likely to be very difficult to change long-standing perceptions of what amounts to domestic violence.

The government's new definition, however, did not receive unanimous support. Some respondents to the consultation argued against the inclusion of coercive control on the basis that:

- it would be difficult to police such a definition;
- it may result in a broader category of victims;
- there may be confusion as to what constitutes abuse and what does not where there is not an act of violence, and;
- it may result in people being labelled as violent when they are not.[16]

From a different perspective, Kelly and Westmarland argue that the definition misrepresents the reality of domestic violence and abuse, on the basis that the focus on 'incidents' fails to recognise that domestic violence 'is a pattern of coercive control'.[17] They further emphasise:

the notion that 'domestic violence' can be broken down into single standalone 'incidents' has skewed not only knowledge, since any incident counts the same as repetition in prevalence surveys, but also which interventions are deemed appropriate, and who would be prioritised to receive support.[18]

Kelly and Westmarland also argue that the definition marginalises sexual violence and rape and 'downgrades forms of violence disproportionately experience by minority women',[19] in particular female genital mutilation. They are also critical of the gender-neutral definition that is adopted by the government, which can be contrasted with the approach adopted by the Council of Europe. The Istanbul Convention explicitly recognises that women are disproportionately affected by domestic violence and further states that 'violence against women is one of the crucial social mechanisms by which women are forced into a subordinate position compared with men'.[20] The gendered nature of domestic violence will be explored further in 2.3.

[16] Home Office, *Cross-Government Definition of Domestic Violence—A Consultation: Summary of Responses* (Home Office, 2012) 17.

[17] Kelly, L and Westmarland, N. 'Time for a rethink—why the current government definition of domestic violence is a problem', *Trouble & Strife,* 14 April 2014. Available at: http://www.troubleandstrife.org/2014/04/time-for-a-rethink-why-the-current-government-definition-of-domestic-violence-is-a-problem/, accessed 5 May 2017.

[18] Kelly, L and Westmarland, N. 'Naming and Defining "Domestic Violence": Lessons From Research With Violent Men' (2016) 112 *Feminist Review* 113–27.

[19] Kelly, L and Westmarland, N. 'Time for a rethink—why the current government definition of domestic violence is a problem', *Trouble & Strife,* 14 April 2014. Available at: http://www.troubleandstrife.org/2014/04/time-for-a-rethink-why-the-current-government-definition-of-domestic-violence-is-a-problem/, accessed 5 May 2017.

[20] Council of Europe Convention on combating and prevention violence against women and girls, 6.

2.2.1 Forced marriage and domestic abuse

Forced marriage is a form of domestic violence against women and men, a serious abuse of human rights and, where a minor is involved, child abuse. As the Universal Declaration of Human Rights, Article 16(2) states, marriage should only be entered into with the free and full consent of both intending spouses. The right to marry, and the right not to marry, is contained under Article 12 of the European Convention on Human Rights and Fundamental Freedoms 1950. Such requirements are informed by the principles of self-determination and human dignity.

Forced marriage can be defined as a marriage where one or both people do not (or in the case of some people with learning or physical disabilities, cannot) consent to marriage and pressure or abuse is used. This pressure can be physical, emotional, and psychological (including when someone is made to feel like they are bringing shame on their family) and/or financial. Some people are taken abroad unaware that they are to be married and, when they arrive in the country, their passports may be taken from them to stop them returning home. Forced marriage has been distinguished from arranged marriage—where the family take a leading role in choosing the marriage partner, but the choice to enter the marriage is left to the intended spouses. However, it can also be argued that this distinction fails to recognise the complexities involved in forced marriages.

It is also important to note that, under s. 12 of the Matrimonial Causes Act 1973, a marriage is voidable if either party was unable to consent to it, due to duress. This issue is discussed further in Chapter 2, which explores the law of nullity.

2.3 Domestic violence: statistics and causes

In order to comprehend the vital role family law has to play in dealing with domestic violence, and the importance of developing effective remedies, it is necessary to appreciate the nature, extent, and causes of the abuse. As we explore in this section, domestic violence is very prevalent—impacting on millions of individuals and families in England and Wales every year.

 CONTEXT 1: DOMESTIC VIOLENCE KEY STATISTICS

- The Office for National Statistics (ONS)[21] highlights that, in the year ending March 2016, in England and Wales an estimated 1.8 million adults aged 16 to 59 had experienced domestic abuse in the previous year. This amounts to 6 in 100 adults.
- In the year ending March 2016, 7.7% of women and 4.4% of men reported having experienced domestic abuse. Female victims were estimated at 1.3 million, compared with 716,000 male victims.
- Overall, 26% of women and 14% of men had experienced some form of domestic abuse since the age of 16, equivalent to an estimated 4.3 million female victims of domestic abuse and 2.2 million male victims.
- For women, the most commonly experienced types of intimate violence since 16 were non-sexual partner abuse (20.1%), stalking (20.9%), and sexual assault (19.9%). For men, the most commonly experienced types of abuse were stalking (9.9%) and non-sexual partner abuse (8.8%).

---

[21] The statistics are taken from: ONS, *Domestic abuse in England and Wales: year ending March 2016* (ONS, 2016) and ONS, *Crime Statistics, Focus on Violent Crime and Sexual Offences, Year ending March 2016* (ONS, 2017); Home Office and Foreign & Commonwealth Office. *Forced Marriage Unit Statistics* (Home Office, 2016).

- Female homicide victims were far more likely than male victims to be killed by a partner or ex-partner (46% and 7% respectively) and less likely to be killed by friends/acquaintances (8% compared with 40%).
- Of the 432 domestic homicides reported by the police in England and Wales between April 2012 and March 2015, 27% of victims were male and 73% were female. For all homicides, the gender breakdown of victims is 67% male and 33% female.
- Female domestic homicide victims were more likely to be killed by a partner or ex-partner (77%) than a family member (23%). With male domestic homicide victims, 51% were killed by a partner or ex-partner and 49% by a family member.

Forced marriage statistics:

- In 2015 the Forced Marriage Unit provided advice or support with a possible forced marriage in 1,220 instances.
- In most forced marriage cases, the victim was female as opposed to male: 980 (80%) and 240 (20%) respectively.
- Where age was known, the victim was aged 18 to 25 in 427 (35%) of cases and between 16 and 17 in 155 (13%). The victim was under the age of 16 in 174 (14%) of instances.
- In 141 (12%) of these instances, the victim had either a physical or learning disability.
- In 29 cases (2%), the victim identified as lesbian, gay, or transgender.

These statistics indicate that domestic violence is gendered. The majority of victims are female, and violence is mostly perpetrated by men on women. This is not to say that men are not victims of domestic violence; instead, it is stated to highlight that it is a problem that disproportionally impacts upon women. In Debate 2, we will explore further some of the debates relating to the extent to which domestic violence is a gendered phenomenon.

 DEBATE 2: TO WHAT EXTENT IS DOMESTIC VIOLENCE A GENDERED PHENOMENON?

While women are more adversely affected by domestic violence, the terms 'domestic violence' or 'family violence' are gender neutral, thus ignoring the gendered dynamics of violence within the home. This gender-neutral perspective of domestic and sexual violence has emerged alongside a field of research which maintains that women are just as, if not more, violent then men.[22] The 'symmetrical' and gender-neutral conceptualisation has been vigorously contested by researchers who adopt a 'violence against women' perspective. Dobash and Dobash highlight how those who maintain that women and men are equally violent, use an 'act-based'/'conflict tactic scale' approach to estimate the frequency of intimate partner violence, which counts each individual act of violence and abuse. This method, however, fails to take account of the circumstances, motivations, and the impact of the violence. It renders equal what is qualitatively different. In contrast:

> [r]esearchers who study the whole event, rather than a list of 'acts' that may have occurred across many such events, find that women's violence (lethal and non-lethal) is often associated with self-defence, and/or retaliation against a male partner. This frequently occurs after years of physical abuse from the male partner.[23]

[22] See, e.g., Straus, M.A. and Gelles R.J. 'Societal Change and Change in Family Violence from 1975 to 1985 as Revealed by Two National Surveys' (1986) 48 *Journal of Marriage and the Family* 465.

[23] Dobash, P.R. and Dobash, R.E. 'Women's Violence to Men in Intimate Relationships: Working on a Puzzle' (2004) 44 *British Journal of Criminology* 324, 328.

An appreciation of the gendered nature of domestic violence leads to a consideration of the causes of abuse. Why do more men than women abuse their partners? Various theories have been presented to explain the causes of domestic violence, these include:

1. *Psychopathological theories.* These theories maintain that domestic violence is committed by deviant individuals, who are predisposed to violent behaviour. In this model, the causes of domestic violence are individualised. A 2003 study conducted by the Home Office highlighted the following risk factors:

   witnessing domestic violence in childhood, disrupted attachments patterns, high levels of interpersonal dependency and jealousy, attitudes condoning domestic violence and lack of empathy.[24]

There is also a connection between the consumption of intoxicants and domestic violence, with research indicating that, in 32% of cases, the violence was committed whilst the perpetrator was under the influence of alcohol.[25] However, the link between alcohol and abusive behaviour is not limited to domestic violence. In the 2015 Crime Survey, the victim perceived the offender to be under the influence of alcohol in 47% of cases involving intimate violence (which includes violence committed by strangers).[26]

2. *Social and economic deprivation theories.* This approach maintains that domestic violence is caused by wider social and economic factors, including, lack of employment, financial difficulties, and poor housing. While such issues may be a cause of stress within a family unit, such an approach suggests that domestic violence primarily occurs in lower and working class families. This, however, is a misconception, as domestic violence occurs in all socio-economic groups.[27]

3. *The patriarchal nature of society.* This theory highlights the pervasive nature of gender inequality and argues that domestic violence forms part of the way in which men maintain their power and control over women. For example, the Declaration on the Elimination of Violence Against Women states:

   . . . violence against women is a manifestation of historically unequal power relations between men and women, which have led to domination and discrimination against women by men and to prevent the full advancement of women, and that violence against women is one of the crucial social mechanisms by which women are forced into a subordinate position compared with men.[28]

4. *Social-ecological theories.* Under this approach, violence (and behaviour more generally) is recognised to be 'the outcome of multiple risk factors and causes, interacting at four levels of a nested hierarchy'.[29] The theory is based on a four-part model, which comprises: microsystem (individual personal history); exosystem (family and peer

[24] Home Office, *Domestic Violence Offenders: Characteristics and Offending Related Needs* (Home Office, 2003) 1.

[25] Mirrlees-Black, C. *Domestic Violence: Findings from a New British Crime Survey Completion Questionnaire,* Home Office Research Study 191 (Home Office, 1999).

[26] ONS, *Focus on Violent Crime and Sexual Offences: Year ending March 2015* (ONS, 2016) 21.

[27] For a detail breakdown of demographics and domestic violence, see ONS. *Focus on Violent Crime and Sexual Offences: Year ending March 2016.* (ONS, 2017) 89–92.

[28] Declaration on the Elimination of Violence against Women, General Assembly Resolution 48/104 (December 2004).

[29] World Health Organisation (WHO) and the London School of Hygiene and Tropical Medicine, *Preventing intimate partner and sexual violence against women: Taking action and generating evidence* (World Health Organisation, 2010) 7.

influences); mesosytem (community level influences); and macrosystem (societal/structural level influences).[30] Consequently, this approach identifies individual factors while also according with feminist perspectives, which emphasise the broader cultural, social and structural factors, including gender relations, in the perpetration of violence against women.

These discussions regarding the gendered nature of domestic violence and the exploration of the causes of abuse, are not simply matters for academic debate and analysis. They have significant strategic, policy, resource, and legal implications. If domestic violence is overwhelmingly perpetrated by men against women, and it is part of a wider pattern of gender discrimination, this needs to be recognised and incorporated in to legal and policy responses. For example, when the government and local authorities are allocating funding for refuges, to enable victims to flee domestic violence, it is important that the allocation of funding takes into account that more women are victims than men, that women are more likely to be killed by their partner upon attempting to leave, that women are overwhelmingly the primary carers for children, and tend to have less financial resources. Likewise, it is important that family lawyers, judges, and law reformers, are aware of these factors. These factors will need to be taken into consideration when advising a victim on the most effective—and safe—course of action to take; when a judge is making decisions with regards to which orders should be granted; and when determining the nature and content of future legal reforms. Producing remedies that are effective in protecting victims, and that aim to prevent occurrences of abuse, requires an informed understanding of the nature and causes of the phenomena.

This section has examined how domestic violence is defined—exploring the historical context and the current definition—and has debated what the definition of domestic violence should be. The gendered nature of domestic violence has also been examined and debated, in light of the statistical data. In the following section, we will explore the key family law orders available to victims of domestic violence.

3. Family law orders

A victim of abuse has recourse to three key family law orders, which aim to prevent the occurrence of future incidences. As these family law orders are within the realm of private/civil law, it is the victim who decides whether or not to instigate proceedings. In contrast, with criminal law remedies the decision whether or not to take action lies with the police and the CPS. In 1992, the Law Commission made recommendations to replace the previous system of civil remedies, which were described as 'complex, confusing and lack[ing] integration'.[31] The subsequent Family Law Act 1996 implemented two orders: non-molestation orders, which aim to protect a victim from molestation; and occupation orders, which regulate the occupation of the family home.

With regards to forced marriage, forced marriage protection orders, which aim to both prevent a forced marriage from occurring and provide for an individual who has already been forced into marriage, were inserted in to the Family Law Act 1996 by the Forced Marriage (Civil Protection) Act 2007.

---

[30] Bronfenbrenner, U. *The Ecology of Human Development: Experiments by Nature and Design* (Harvard University Press, 1979).

[31] Law Commission, *Family Law, Domestic Violence and Occupation of the Family Home* (Law Com No. 207, 1992).

3.1 **Non-molestation orders**

Section 42 of the Family Law Act 1996 provides:

[1] non-molestation order means an order containing either or both of the following provisions:

   (a) provision prohibiting a person ('the respondent') from molesting another person who is associated with the respondent;

   (b) provision prohibiting the respondent from molesting a relevant child.

Molestation is a very broad concept, which encompasses a wide range of behaviour. The Law Commission recognised that domestic violence was not limited to physical or sexual assaults, but also included 'psychological molestation or harassment which has a serious detrimental effect upon the health and well-being of the victim'.[32] Subsequently, molestation is considered to include, in addition to physical and sexual violence, 'any form of serious pestering or harassment and applies to any conduct which could properly be regarded as such a degree of harassment as to call for the intervention of the court'.[33] However, the introduction of a statutory definition was thought to be inappropriate, on the basis that any delineation of the term may become 'overly descriptive' or generate disputes in marginal cases; and unnecessary, as the term was already 'well established and recognised by the courts'.[34]

The Law Commission noted that 'common instances' of molestation included:

Persistent pestering and intimidation through shouting, denigration, threats or arguments, nuisance telephone calls, damaging property, following the applicant about and repeatedly calling at her home or place of work.[35]

In some circumstances, context will be pivotal. For example, calling at a person's house during the day time *could* amount to molestation, if, for example, it formed part of a pattern of abusive behaviour. By contrast, an act of physical violence will inevitably constitute molestation. A non-molestation order may be drafted to prohibit specific behaviour and/or may prohibit molestation in general. The Law Commission highlighted the importance of this 'dual capability':

Where it is obvious that there should be a limitation on a particular sort of behaviour, the order should be specific so that the respondent is left in no doubt about what he must stop doing. However, the order also needs to be sufficiently general to cover any other objectionable behaviour in which the respondent may subsequently decide to indulge.[36]

As a breach of a non-molestation order is now a criminal offence (as discussed in further detail in 3.6.1), the way in which an order is drafted has increased in significance, and guidance from the Court of Appeal indicates that orders should be phrased using precise, as opposed to generic, terms.[37] Nevertheless, a tendency to invoke generic drafting has

---

[32] Law Commission, *Family Law, Domestic Violence and Occupation of the Family Home* (Law Com No. 207, 1992) 4.

[33] Law Commission, *Family Law, Domestic Violence and Occupation of the Family Home* (Law Com No. 207, 1992) 19.

[34] Law Commission, *Family Law, Domestic Violence and Occupation of the Family Home* (Law Com No. 207, 1992).

[35] Law Commission, *Family Law, Domestic Violence and Occupation of the Family Home* (Law Com No. 207, 1992) 3.

[36] Law Commission, *Family Law, Domestic Violence and Occupation of the Family Home* (Law Com No. 207, 1992) 19.   [37] *R v Shane P* [2004] EWCA Crim 287; *Bones v R* [2005] EWCA 2395.

been noted by James: 'if one were to sample the non-molestation orders made on any given day throughout the country, one imagines that the majority of them would be drafted in exactly the same way'.[38] James suggests that the reluctance to use more specific terminology is due 'to a lack of judicial enthusiasm . . . [to create] specific criminal offences of otherwise non-criminal behaviour', along with 'a lack of time and culture of thinking that speed and effectiveness are not mutually exclusive'.[39] However, while generic wording may be sufficient in many cases, in others, the needs of the victim will require precision.

With regards to duration, under s. 42(7), a non-molestation order may be made for a specified period or until further order. Fixed time limits were considered by the Law Commission to be 'arbitrary' and would impede the court's ability to 'react flexibly to problems arising within the family'.[40] A non-molestation order, hence, can provide both short- and longer-term protection, and continue beyond the end of a relationship.

3.1.1 What factors will the court consider when deciding whether to make a non-molestation order?

The Law Commission contemplated three different approaches to defining the factors a court would consider when determining an application for a non-molestation order. First, precise criteria could be adopted which, for example, limited orders to cases involving the use or threat of actual violence. However, this approach would place a 'premium upon alleging violence' and contradicts the recognition that domestic violence encompasses many forms of non-physical forms of abuse.[41] Second, the criteria could be left undefined, as was the then approach in the magistrates' court. The Law Commission noted that there was no evidence to suggest that this caused any difficulties in practice. Nevertheless, it was felt that a definition would ensure consistency and firmly establish that physical violence was not a prerequisite for an order. The Law Commission consequently preferred the adoption of a 'broad statutory criteria', and this is the approach which has been adopted in the Family Law Act 1996.

 Key Legislation 1: Family Law Act 1996, s. 42(5) and s. 63(1)

Section 42(5) states that the court:

> . . . shall have regard to all the circumstances including the need to secure the health, safety and well-being (a) of the applicant; and (b) of any relevant child.

Section 63(1) defines 'health' to include mental as well as physical health.

In applying the statutory criteria, the court is to adopt a holistic and forward-looking approach, and thus it is not limited to past conduct of the respondent. Nor is evidence of physical injury required. This approach reflects the fact that family law is concerned with protecting the victim from harm, as opposed to punishing the perpetrator. Accordingly, the court is concerned with the *effect* on the victim, as opposed to the *culpability* of the

---

[38] James, B. 'Drafting non-molestation orders: going beyond the blanket ban' (2009) *Family Law Weekly*. Available at: http://www.familylawweek.co.uk/site.aspx?i=ed30795, accessed 25 September 2017.

[39] James, B. 'Drafting non-molestation orders: going beyond the blanket ban' (2009) *Family Law Weekly*. Available at: http://www.familylawweek.co.uk/site.aspx?i=ed30795, accessed 25 September 2017.

[40] Law Commission. *Family Law, Domestic Violence and Occupation of the Family Home* (Law Com No. 207, 1992), 27.

[41] Law Commission. *Family Law, Domestic Violence and Occupation of the Family Home* (Law Com No. 207, 1992) 20.

perpetrator. However, two cases appear to conflict with this approach, and indicate that at times the court may place emphasis upon the intention of the respondent.

In *C v C (Non-molestation Order: Jurisdiction)*,[42] after the publication of two newspaper articles that portrayed the applicant in a very unflattering light, the husband obtained a non-molestation order against the wife, in order to prevent her providing any information to the press. The Court of Appeal, however, upheld the wife's appeal against the order. Sir Stephen Brown P stated that the term molestation: 'implies some quite deliberate conduct which is aimed at a high degree of harassment at the other party, so as to justify the intervention of the court.'[43] It can, however, be argued that this approach imposes a higher threshold than was anticipated by the Law Commission. Moreover, as the Court noted the applicant was more concerned about any 'damage to his reputation', as opposed to any molestation—which relates to the *effect* of the behaviour—it seems that the reference to deliberate conduct was unnecessary.

The issue of unintentional conduct also arose for consideration in the case of *Banks v Banks*.[44] Mrs Banks, who was 79 and suffered from mental health issues and advanced dementia, was due to return to the matrimonial home after being admitted to hospital under the Mental Health Act 1983. Mr Banks applied for a non-molestation against his wife, on the basis that her verbal and physical abuse was a threat to his well-being. A consultant psychologist, however, also informed the Court that it was unlikely that Mrs Banks' behaviour would pose a threat to Mr Banks' health. In rejecting the application, Judge Geddes emphasised that Mrs Banks' physical and verbal abuse was a 'symptom of her mental condition' and beyond her control; it was not deliberate and intentional. Consequently, an order prohibiting such behaviour, even if the order could be understood by Mrs Banks, would 'serve no practical purpose', as she would be unable to comply with its terms.[45]

It is, however, possible to agree with the outcome of *Banks v Banks* without invoking the high threshold that the Court appeared to apply in *C v C*. Conduct that is not deliberate spans a very wide spectrum, to encompass, for example, reckless and thoughtless behaviour; and a distinction can be drawn between behaviour that is thoughtless, and that which is uncontrollable, due to mental incapacity. While the former is capable of being deterred, the latter is not. However, difficulties could arise in other cases, particularly those involving alcoholics, who may argue that their drinking and/or their violence is beyond their control. Given the connection between alcohol consumption and domestic violence, it is important that drunken abusive behaviour is not considered to fall outside the purview of s. 42. Nevertheless, given that the courts have a wide discretion and take into account all the circumstances of the case, it is possible for fine distinctions to be drawn in order to provide the protection that is needed in a specific case.

Despite the forward-looking approach adopted by s. 42, concerns have been expressed that clients are often discouraged by their lawyers from applying for a non-molestation order, particularly in cases in which there is a lack of violence. Indeed, some practitioners have indicated that courts require evidence of physical violence before they will grant an order. Research indicates that some solicitors can also be unsympathetic and at times have suggested that the victim may have precipitated the abuse.[46] Hence, the adoption of a victim-focused statutory criteria may be undermined in practice.

3.1.2 Associated persons and relevant children

As set out in s. 42, a non-molestation order prevents the respondent from molesting an 'associated person' and/or a 'relevant child'. Hence, there must be some form of connection

---

[42] [1998] Fam 70.   [43] [1998] Fam 73.   [44] [1999] 1 FLR 726.   [45] [1999] 1 FLR 729.
[46] Burton, M. *Legal Responses to Domestic Violence* (Routledge-Cavendish, 2008) 40.

between the person protected by the order and the respondent, which operates to limit the applicability of non-molestation orders.

Key Legislation 2: Family Law Act 1996, s. 62: Associated persons and relevant child

In developing the concept of the 'associated person' the Law Commission aimed to adopt a middle ground between a completely unrestricted eligibility criteria and a more exclusive gateway, which would limit orders to more immediate family members, specifically spouses and cohabitants (whether current or otherwise), parents, and those with parental responsibility.

Section 62(3) of the Family Law Act 1996 (as amended) provides that '. . . a person is associated with another person if—

(a)　they are or have been married to each other;

(aa)　they are or have been civil partners of each other;

(b)　they are cohabitants or former cohabitants;

(c)　they live or have lived in the same household, otherwise than merely by reason of one of them being the other's employee, tenant, lodger or boarder;

(d)　they are relatives [s. 63(1): the father, mother, stepfather, stepdaughter, son, daughter, stepson, stepdaughter, grandmother, grandfather, grandson, or granddaughter or the brother, sister, uncle, aunt, niece or nephew of that person or of that person's spouse or former spouse];

(e)　they have agreed to marry one another;

(eza)　they have entered in to a civil partnership agreement (engagement);

(ea)　they have or have had an intimate personal relationship with each other which is or was of significant duration [as inserted by the s. 4 of the Domestic Crime and Victims Act 2004];

(f)　in relation to any child, [parent of a child or has or has had parental responsibility for the child, s. 4];

(g)　they are parties to the same family proceedings.

With regards to the concept of a 'relevant child', a similarly wide approach is adopted. Section 62(2) provides the definition of a relevant child to encompass:

(a)　any child who is living with or might reasonably be expected to live with either party to the proceedings;

(b)　any child in relation to whom an order under the Adoption Act 1976, the Adoption and Children Act 2002 or the Children Act 1989 is in question in the proceedings; and

(c)　any other child whose interests the court considers relevant.

Under s. 42(2)(b) the court also has the power to make a non-molestation order against a respondent in any family proceedings, 'if it considers that the order should be made for the benefit of any other party to the proceedings or any relevant child even though no such application has been made'.

The definition of 'associated persons' is the product of numerous amendments, as family law has evolved to recognise and protect various familial and intimate relationships. Accordingly, the concept encompasses same-sex couples, through the inclusion of civil partnerships and the definition of cohabitants as 'two persons who, although not married to each other, are living together as husband and wife or (if of the same sex) in an equivalent relationship', as introduced by the Domestic Violence, Crime and Victims Act 2004. Prior to 2004, those who were, or had been, in a serious relationship, but had not cohabited, did not fall into the remit of 'associated persons'. Nevertheless, the Court of Appeal in *G v F (Non-Molestation Order: Jurisdiction)*[47] stressed that, when interpreting s. 62, courts 'should give the statute a purposive construction and not decline jurisdiction, unless the facts of the case before them are plainly incapable of being brought within the statute'.[48] In declaring that the parties were cohabiting for the purposes of s. 62, Wall J drew upon the six 'signposts' of cohabitation, set out in *Crake v Supplementary Benefits Commission*: '(1) whether they are members of the same household; (2) whether the relationship is stable; (3) whether there is financial support; (4) whether there is a sexual relationship; (5) whether they have children; (6) whether there is public acknowledgment.'[49] Of these, three were considered to be present: the parties had engaged in a sexual relationship, they shared the same household as they frequently spent the night together, and for a period of time they operated a joint bank account.

The law was amended in 2004 to include those couples who have, or have had, an 'intimate personal relationship' of a 'significant duration'. While no further guidance has been provided on the definition of these terms, the approach adopted by Wall J in *G v F* suggests that an inclusive approach must be adopted: 'It would, I think, be most unfortunate if section 62(3) was narrowly construed so as to exclude borderline cases where swift and effective protection for the victims of domestic violence is required.'[50]

Case law also indicates that it is the association between the parties which is pivotal, as opposed to the nature of the dispute. *Chechi v Bashier*[51] involved a bitter dispute between two brothers over land in Pakistan. The judge declined to grant a non-molestation order, on the basis that, *inter alia*, the relationship between the parties was incidental to the dispute and the issue should be dealt with by the civil, not the family, courts. While the Court of Appeal agreed that an order should not in this instance be granted, Butler Sloss LJ nevertheless stressed that the judge was wrong to state that the relationship was incidental to the dispute. Prima facie, the circumstances fell within the remit of s. 42:

> Although the dispute between the parties is in origin about land, it is patently overlaid and magnified by the family relationship, which has fuelled and kept alive the original disagreement. The depth of the dissension and the violent reaction of both sides must owe a great deal to family ill-feeling.[52]

> **?** DEBATE 3: SHOULD THE CONCEPT OF 'ASSOCIATED PERSON' MORE ACCURATELY REFLECT THE REALITY OF DOMESTIC VIOLENCE?

It could be argued that the gateway of 'associated persons' sits in tension with the underlying objective of non-molestation orders—which is to protect individuals from violence and harassment. There seems to be little justification to prevent a victim of molestation from obtaining an order on the basis that their relationship with the respondent lacked a particular nexus. Further, an applicant is required to establish facts which are peripheral to their need for protection. However, whilst acknowledging these disadvantages, the Law Commission commented that the introduction of a protective order absent of any eligibility restrictions would effectively create a new tort of harassment or molestation. Concomitantly, the family law system was also not considered to the appropriate forum in which to respond to disputes between other groups of individuals, such as neighbours, landlord and tenants, and

---

[47] [2000] Fam 186.   [48] [2000] Fam 198.   [49] [1982] 1 All ER 498.
[50] [2000] Fam 186, 198.   [51] [1999] 2 FLR 489.   [52] [1999] 2 FLR 493.

employers and employees. In addition, alternative remedies are available for non-familial cases. For example, a victim may apply for an injunction to prohibit the respondent from 'pursing any conduct which amounts to harassment' under s. 3A of the Prohibition of Harassment Act 1997.

The Law Commission contemplated that that the 'special nature of family relationships' justified the creation of a distinct and discrete family law remedy: 'When problems arise in close family relationships, the strength of emotions involved can cause unique reactions which may at times be irrational or obsessive'.[53] Further, it may not always be possible for family members to completely terminate their relationship, and consequently the objective of the law 'should be to provide a framework to enable people in this situation to continue their relationship in a civilised fashion'.[54]

While it is appropriate that the concept of 'associated person' now encompasses same-sex and non-cohabiting couples, criticisms remain. In particular, the broadness of the concept misrepresents the reality of domestic violence. First, subsection (c) potentially covers a broad spectrum of relationships, extending far beyond familial proximity. The Law Commission acknowledged that this category may generate peculiar distinctions—for example, friends who share a flat as joint tenants would fall with the remit of s. 62, however, an individual who sublet a room from a friend would not—but highlighted the category was necessary in order to capture 'close friends who have lived together on a long term basis, whatever the precise nature of their relationship'.[55] This reasoning can, however, be disputed, as the Law Commission justified the imposition of the 'associated persons' gateway because familial relationships produce unique tensions. Hence, it could be argued that it is the nature of the relationship that is fundamental, as opposed to the fact that the parties live together.

Furthermore, the inclusion of the very large range of relatives, courtesy of subsection (d), fails to acknowledge the gendered reality of domestic violence and the very specific factors that characterise male violence against female partners. Reece argues that, further to financial dependence and barriers to leaving the relationships, domestic violence against women is characterised by the following factors:[56]

Proximity coupled with isolation.

In addition to the existence of an intimate relationship between the parties, research indicates that the isolation of the victim, particularly from family and friends, plays a key factor in the perpetration of abuse.

Controlled emotions in the context of unequal power.

Far from being the result of uncontrolled or heightened emotions, evidence demonstrates that domestic abuse is a deliberate course of conduct which tends to occur in relationships where there is in imbalance of power. Accordingly, abuse tends to be perpetrated by the more powerful and dominant partner in the relationship.

Significantly, these factors are unlikely to feature in the wide range of other relationships included within the definition of associated persons. Consequently, Reece argues that, by constructing domestic violence as something that potentially occurs in a broad range of relationships, the concept of 'associated person' paradoxically operates to minimise abuse:

---

[53] Law Commission. *Family Law, Domestic Violence and Occupation of the Family Home* (Law Com No. 207, 1992) 24.

[54] Law Commission. *Family Law, Domestic Violence and Occupation of the Family Home* (Law Com No. 207, 1992) 24.

[55] Law Commission. *Family Law, Domestic Violence and Occupation of the Family Home* (Law Com No. 207, 1992) 29.   [56] Reece, H. 'The End of Domestic Violence' (2006) 69 *Modern Law Review* 770.

'The claim that domestic violence occurs in every type of relationship seems to be the reverse of minimising domestic violence, but in fact it is another method, because if domestic violence occurs everywhere then domestic violence occurs nowhere.'[57] As Reece notes, minimising domestic violence enables the state to continue to 'preserve the status of the traditional nuclear family',[58] over and above protecting victims. This, in turn, leads to the production of remedies which do not adequately recognise and respond to the very specific difficulties victims face.

3.2 Occupation orders

An occupation order can give a victim a right to enter or remain in the home, and can order the respondent to leave the home. As occupation orders interfere with property rights, they are considered to be draconian, and provisions relating to occupation orders are somewhat more complex than the law pertaining to non-molestation orders. The law is set out across ss. 33 to 38 of the Family Law Act 1996, and a distinction is drawn between those who have a pre-existing right to occupy the family home—known as entitled applicants—and those who do not—the non-entitled applicant. An entitled applicant may obtain an occupation order against a broad category of persons. In contrast, non-entitled applicants are only able to apply for an occupation order against a partner or former partner.

The Law Commission explained that they supported distinguishing between entitled and non-entitled applicants for two reasons: first, in contrast to a non-molestation order, the consequences of an occupation order are potentially substantially 'more serious' for the respondent, as such an order 'can severely restrict property rights', while s. 42 only prevents the respondent from engaging in behaviour that is in the least anti-social, if not illegal. Second, the purpose of the occupation order is different in the two circumstances. For non-entitled applicants, an order offers short-term protection while the applicant secures suitable alternative accommodation or the court determines the outcome of a property law application. In contrast, with entitled applicants, the occupation order may not simply be about short-term protection, but may 'regulate the occupation for the home until its medium or long term destiny' has been determined.[59]

3.2.1 Occupation orders and 'entitled applicants': Family Law Act 1996, s. 33

Under s. 33, certain individuals are 'entitled applicants', and 'entitled applicants' may apply for an occupation order against any associated person with whom s/he shares, or intended to share, the property with. The concept of associated person is the same as that discussed earlier in 3.1.2 in relation to non-molestation orders.

Entitled applicants are divided into two categories:

- Those who are entitled to occupy a house by virtue of a legal or beneficial interest in the property or by contract. This encompasses individuals who own or rent a property.

- Those who have what is known as 'home rights' under s. 30 of the Family Law Act 1996: if 'A' is not entitled by virtue of a beneficial interest or contact, but their spouse or civil partner is, 'A' nevertheless has a right to occupy the family home.

---

[57] Reece, H. 'The End of Domestic Violence' (2006) 69 *Modern Law Review*, 791.

[58] Reece, H. 'The End of Domestic Violence' (2006) 69 *Modern Law Review*, 791.

[59] Law Commission. *Family Law, Domestic Violence and Occupation of the Family Home* (Law Com No. 207, 1992) 30.

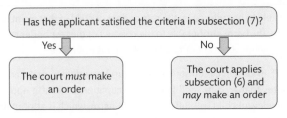

Figure 7.1: Relationship between subsections (7) and (6)

Accordingly, if a victim's spouse or civil partner is the sole owner of the family home, the victim nevertheless has a right to occupy the family home. Note, however, that the same 'home right' does not extend to cohabiting couples.

What orders can a court make?

Under s. 33 there are two types of order available to the courts: declaratory and regulatory. Subsections (4) and (5) enable the court to make an order which is declaratory in nature: the court declares that the applicant has an existing right to occupy and remain in the property. The wider reaching orders are those under s. 33(3), as they enable the court to regulate the occupation of the dwelling house. Under s. 33(3), a court can, for example, prevent the respondent from evicting the applicant; regulate how the applicant and respondent occupy the premises; or require a respondent to vacate the home, while allowing the victim to take up, or remain in, residence.

In terms of duration, under s. 33(10), an order may be made for a specified period, until the occurrence of a specified event or until further order, or until the court next hears the issue. This reflects the sentiment that an occupation for an entitled applicant may not necessarily be about providing short-term protection, but may offer a medium or even long-term solution.

What factors will the court consider when deciding whether to grant a s. 33 occupation order?

Two key subsections set out the approach the court must adopt when determining an application for an occupation order under s. 33: subsection (6) and (7). It was, however, established by the Court of Appeal in *Chalmers v Johns*[60] that the court should start with s. 33(7) before considering the factors in s. 33(6). This is because while subsection (6) gives the court the *discretion* to make an order, subsection (7) places a *duty* on the court to make an order. The relationship between subsections (7) and (6), and the approach to be adopted by the court, is displayed in Figure 7.1.

 Key Legislation 3: Family Law Act 1996, s. 33(7)

The balance of harm test:

> If it appears to the court that the applicant or any relevant child is likely to suffer significant harm attributable to conduct of the respondent if an order under this section is not made, the court shall make the order unless it appears to it that—

> (a) the respondent or any relevant child is likely to suffer significant harm if the order is made; and

---

[60] [1999] 1 FLR 392.

(b) the harm likely to be suffered by the respondent or child in that event is as great as, or greater than, the harm attributable to the conduct of the respondent which is likely to be suffered by the applicant or child if the order is not made.

By virtue of s. 33(7), in certain circumstances the court has a *duty* to make an occupation order. Subsection (7) states that a court *shall* grant an occupation order if it appears likely that the applicant and any relevant child will suffer significant harm, which is attributable to the respondent, if an order is not made. The word *shall* in subsection (7) imposes a mandatory duty upon the court. 'Harm' is given the same meaning as in relation to non-molestation orders, and thus encompasses physical and mental harm and, in relation to any child, includes ill-treatment and the impairment of health or development. However, there is the additional requirement that, in order to fall within s. 33(7), the harm must be *significant*, which has been held to mean 'considerable, noteworthy or important'.[61] The Law Commission considered that, while it was important for the court to have a general discretion to grant an occupation order, the court should be directed to impose an order in cases involving significant harm.

However, s.33(7) (see Key Legislation 3) continues to state that an order shall only be made, if the balance of harm test is made out. The correct approach to be adopted by the courts to applying the balance of harm test was clarified by the Court of Appeal in *Chalmers v Johns*:[62]

> [I]n approaching its function under [section 33] the court has first to consider whether the evidence establishes that the applicant or any relevant child is likely to suffer significant harm attributable to the conduct of the respondent if an order is not made. If the court answers in the affirmative, then it knows it must make an order unless balancing one harm against another, the harm to the respondent or child is likely to be as great (Thorpe LJ, at 396).

Accordingly, the first step is for the court to assess whether the applicant (and any relevant child) is likely to suffer harm which is (a) significant and (b) attributable to the conduct of the respondent, if an order *is not* made.

- If the answer is no, the court does not have a duty under s. 33(7) to make an order. The court will then consider whether an order should be made under s. 33(6).
- If the answer is yes, the second step is for the court to consider whether the respondent and any relevant child is likely to suffer harm if the order *is* made.
  - If this harm is *in the least as great* as the harm that is likely be suffered by the applicant (and any relevant child) if an order is not made, the court does not have a duty under s. 33(7) to make an order. The court will then consider whether an order should be made under s. 6.
  - But, if the applicant (and any relevant child) is likely to suffer harm that is *greater than* that likely to be suffered by the respondent (and any relevant child), s. 33(7) is satisfied and the court *must* grant an order.

Establishing 'significant harm' under Family Law Act 1996, s. 33(7)

In *Chalmers v Johns*, the Court of Appeal provided further indication of what may amount to significant harm. The husband and wife had what the Court described as being a 'tempestuous' relationship. Both parties had made allegation against each other and, while the police had been called out four times, the injuries inflicted were of a minor nature. The judge at first instance noted that 'it is not a domestic violence as

---

[61] *Humberside CC v B* [1993] 1 FLR 257 (Booth J).   [62] [1999] 1 FLR 392.

so frequently comes before these courts', but nevertheless the Court granted the wife an occupation order to exclude the husband from the family home. In upholding the husband's appeal against the order, Otton LJ stated: 'the evidence fell very far short of establishing that A was likely to suffer considerable or noteworthy or important harm if the order was not made'.[63]

Evidencing that the harm suffered is significant is necessary, but not sufficient to meet the requirements of s. 33(7). The applicant must also demonstrate that it is 'attributable to the respondent', a factor that was explored by the Court of Appeal in the case of *G v G (Occupation Order)*.[64] This case involved a married couple who had two children, aged 15 and 12. During their divorce proceedings, the parties lived together in the same house in 'an atmosphere of tension and strain', which was caused, to some extent, by the conduct of the husband. While the judge at first instance held that the children would suffer significant harm if the mother was not granted an occupation order, her application was denied on the basis that the judge held that the harm could not be said to be attributable to the husband, as his conduct was, largely, unintentional. However, Thorpe LJ disagreed that unintentional conduct could not be attributable to respondent, on the basis that the focus should be upon the effect of the conduct:

> Plainly the court's consideration must be upon the effect of the conduct rather than on the intention of the doer. Whether conduct is intentional or unintentional is not the question. . . . Tiny wounds may be inflicted with great malice: great blows may be struck unintentionally. Of course, lack of intent might support a plea of accidental injury. But where something is not done accidentally it is not to be dismissed on the ground that it was not done deliberately [27].

Nevertheless, the Court of Appeal dismissed the wife's appeal on the basis that the circumstances of the case did not reach the initial threshold of significant harm. Thorpe LJ commented that the case did not involve physical violence, but rather the tension and atmosphere was due to the 'incompatible personalities and the heightened tensions' that inevitably arise during divorce proceedings.[65]

The need for the conduct to be attributable to the respondent was also an issue in the case of *Y (Children)*.[66] The husband and wife, who had separated after 20 years of marriage, resided in the family home with two of their four children: a 13-year-old boy (J) and a 16-year-old girl (R), who was pregnant. During the lengthy divorce proceedings, the parties separated into two camps comprising the father and J in one, and the mother and R in the other. The father, who had significant health difficulties due to his diabetes, was granted an occupation order, to the exclusion of the wife. The Recorder, who described the family as being 'divided among itself and at war with itself',[67] indicated that significant harm would occur if an order was not granted, and commented that the father's illness tipped the balance in his favour. However, the Court of Appeal emphasised that, even if significant harm could be said to exist—which it doubted—the Recorder failed to 'address the questions to whom will harm be caused, and by whom it will be caused'.[68] The Court of Appeal held that there was no 'finding that the harm was attributable to the conduct of the mother',[69] and accordingly s. 33(7) did not apply.

Balancing the harm under Family Law Act 1996, s. 33(7)

If the applicant fulfils the requirements that they (and any relevant child) will suffer significant harm attributable to the respondent if an order is not made, the court is then

---

[63] [1999] 1 FLR 392, at [398].   [64] [2000] 2 FLR 36.   [65] [2000] 2 FLR 36, at [30].
[66] [2000] 2 FCR 470.   [67] [2000] 2 FCR 470, at [6].   [68] [2000] 2 FCR 470, at [23].
[69] [2000] 2 FCR 470.

required to balance this against any harm that will be caused to the respondent (and relevant child) if the order is made. The Law Commission speculated that, while in many cases the respondent may be able to 'establish a degree of hardship' if an occupation order was granted, s/he would be 'unlikely to suffer significant harm, whereas [the applicant] and children who are being subjected to his violence or abuse may very easily suffer harm if he remains in the house'. [70]

However, the case of *B v B*[71] indicates how the balance may tip towards favouring the respondent, particularly when a child is involved. The wife (Mrs B) moved out of the council house with the 2-year-old daughter (YB), after suffering serious violence from the husband (Mr B). Mrs B and YB were provided unsatisfactory bed and breakfast accommodation, whilst the husband remained in the house with his son (MB). The husband's appeal, against a s. 33 occupation order requiring him to vacate the property, was upheld by Court of Appeal. It was noted that the son would have to move schools if an order were made, and that separating the son from his father was not an option. The Court concluded: 'In our judgment, if, on the facts of this case, the respective likelihoods of harm are weighed so far as the two children are concerned, the balance comes down clearly in favour of MB suffering the greater harm if an occupation order is made.' (Butler-Sloss LJ, at 724).

This judgment has been criticised, since the balancing act performed by the court focused solely upon the harms that would be suffered by the children, to the exclusion of the harms caused by Mr B's violence. This may be because Mrs B and YB, having already moved into alternative accommodation, were no longer perceived to be at risk of harm from Mr B. This, however, places a victim of abuse in a difficult scenario. To fall within s. 33(7) the applicant must prove that any harm they are likely to suffer stems from the respondent, as opposed to wider circumstances, such as inappropriate housing. Hence, if the applicant has managed to remove themselves (and any relevant children) from the home and into alternative accommodation, albeit temporary and/ or unsuitable, then the court may consider that they are no longer at risk of suffering significant harm that can be attributed to the respondent. However, as Kaganas argues:

> To assess the likelihood of significant harm once the victim has already taken steps to protect herself by fleeing would deprive the provision of much of its force. It was surely not Parliament's intention that, if the victim leaves she should no longer be considered to be likely to suffer significant harm at the hands of the abuser.[72]

The Court of Appeal stated that 'the message of this case is emphatically *not* that fathers who treat their partners with domestic violence and cause them to leave the home can expect to remain in occupation of the previously shared accommodation'.[73] Nevertheless, this is what seems to have occurred in *B v B*.

In all the cases discussed, the Court of Appeal held that s. 33(7) was not satisfied, and therefore the Court did not have a *duty* to make an occupation order. Nevertheless, even if an order is not mandatory under s. 33(7), the court retains a general *discretion* to grant an order, and is required to consider all the relevant circumstances and the 'general factors' as set out in s. 33(6). As Thorpe LJ noted in *Chalmers v Johns*: 'If, however, the court answers [s. 33(7)] in the negative, then it enters the discretionary regime provided by subsection (6).'

---

[70] Law Commission. *Family Law, Domestic Violence and Occupation of the Family Home* (Law Com No. 207, 1992) 38.   [71] [1999] 1 FLR 715.

[72] Kaganas, F. 'B v B (Occupation Order) and Chalmers v Johns: Occupation Orders under the Family Law Act 1996' (1999) 11 *CFLQ* 193, 201.   [73] [1999] 1 FLR 715, 724.

Key Legislation 4: Family Law Act 1996, s. 33(6)

The discretionary regime:

> In deciding whether to exercise its powers under [s. 33(6)] and in what manner, the court shall have regard to all the circumstances, including—
>
> (a) the housing needs and housing resources of each of the parties and of any relevant child;
> (b) the financial resources of each of the parties;
> (c) the likely effect of any order, or of any decision by the court not to exercise its powers, on the health, safety or well-being of the parties and of any relevant child; and
> (d) the conduct of the parties in relation to each other and otherwise.

These general factors are both forward and backward looking: they require the court to take into consideration the conduct of the parties, as well as factors such as the health, safety, or well-being of the parties involved. In *Y (Children)*[74] Ward LJ approached s. 33(6) by examining each factor individually: First, with regards to the parties housing needs and resources, it was noted that 'the matrimonial home could reasonably be divided to meet the housing needs of each of them'.[75] Second, there was nothing to suggest that the financial resources of the wife placed her in a better position to rent privately. Third, with regards the likely effect of the order, the Court of Appeal commented that the husband's ill-health and unhappiness stemmed from the relationship with R, as opposed to the wife, and thus excluding the latter was unlikely to have a positive impact. And fourth, with regards to the conduct of the parties, it was noted that 'they are perhaps one as bad as the other', and consequently the wife's appeal against the order was upheld.[76]

Further factors that may fall within the broader remint of 'all the circumstances' include the timing of a substantive hearing to determine ancillary relief matters. For example, in *G v G* Dame Butler-Sloss stressed that as the hearing was due to take place in three weeks, an order was 'undesirable'.[77]

The Court of Appeal has highlighted on numerous occasions that the threshold for fulfilling the criteria for an occupation order is set at a high standard; indeed, in all the previously discussed cases it was held that an occupation order was not warranted. Thorpe LJ in *Chalmers v Johns* stated that an order that requires 'a respondent to vacate a family home' and 'overrides property rights' was a 'draconian order' that was 'only justified in exceptional circumstances'.[78] His Lordship noted that an order may be warranted where there is actual, or a risk of, violence or harm to the victim, but that this was not the situation in *Chalmers v Johns*. The circumstances amounted to 'domestic disharmony' which could have been controlled through the imposition of a non-molestation order. Similarly, in *Y (Children)* Sedley LJ stressed that an order was to be seen 'a last resort' in an 'intolerable situation', as opposed to 'a move in a game of matrimonial chess'.[79] The reasoning adopted by the Court of Appeal initially appeared to suggest that only cases that involved physical violence would be sufficiently 'exceptional'. In *G v G*, for example, Thorpe LJ further stated:

> . . . this was not a case in which the wife had suffered any violence at the hands of the husband, and it has been said time and time again that orders of exclusion are draconian and only to be made in exceptional cases.[80]

---

[74] [2000] 2 FCR 470. [75] [2000] 2 FCR 470, at [28]. [76] [2000] 2 FCR 470.
[77] [2000] 2 FLR 36, at [41]. [78] [1999] 1 FLR 392, 397.
[79] [2000] 2 FCR 470, at [46]. [80] [2000] 2 FLR 36, at [36].

Such an approach clearly conflicts with the rationale of the Law Commission, which emphasised the need for a remedy, as opposed to allegations of violence. Moreover, it fails to acknowledge that the concept of 'harm' as defined under s. 63(1) of the Family Law Act 1996 is not confined to physical violence.

However, in more recent cases the Court of Appeal has adopted a broader interpretation of what amounts to an 'exceptional' case. In *Grubb v Grubb*[81] the Appeal Court upheld a wife's occupation order under s. 33(6) to enable herself—and the five children—to reside in the six-bedroomed family home, which was part of the husband's large estate, during a bitter and defended divorce. The judge found that the wife was 'under stress and needs to be separated from the husband if possible',[82] and she was found to be suffering from a moderately severe depressive disorder. What appears key to the Court of Appeal's decision was the fact that the husband had suitable alternative accommodation available to him, in the form of a one-bedroomed flat, which would have been insufficient to accommodate the applicant and their children. While recognising that an occupation order is 'always serious', Wilson LJ commented: 'the occupation order is likely to carry its greatest level of seriousness when it is made against a spouse to whom alternative accommodation is not readily available.'[83] The case has been criticised for placing too much weight on the respondent's housing resources.[84] It could, nevertheless, be argued that husband's behaviour throughout the separation bordered on being coercive and controlling. For example, he was found to have verbally abused the applicant on numerous occasions and that, after the wife's divorce petition, he 'continued to be domineering and controlling'.[85] Further, the wife had presented alternative solutions to the housing situation. However, the husband failed to take them into consideration.

 Key Case 2: *Dolan v Corby* [2011] EWCA Civ 1664

The applicant in this case, Ms Dolan, had made allegations of physical and sexual violence against Mr Corby. However, these had not been proved, and there was much disagreement regarding the history of the relationship. Mr Corby, however, was stated to have a 'dominating disposition', and that he had verbally abused and 'frequently belittled' the applicant.[86] At the same time, Ms Dolan was not beyond reproach. The Recorder noted that her 'conduct to towards [the respondent] over the years must have been difficult to put up with',[87] and this was linked to her history of drug abuse. Nevertheless, Ms Dolan was considered to be 'a vulnerable woman' who was 'unable to live with the respondent', and an order was granted under s. 33(6).[88]

In dismissing Mr Corby's appeal, the Court of Appeal clearly stated that it was wrong to construe s. 33 as requiring violence; but that other factors, and in the present instance Ms Dolan's psychiatric state and her vulnerability, were 'capable of making the case exceptional'. Black LJ explained:

> I do not read *Chalmers v Johns* or *G v G* as saying that an exclusion order can only be made where there is violence or a threat of violence. That would be to put a gloss on the statute which would be inappropriate. . . . [E]xceptional circumstances can take many forms . . . the important thing is for the judge to identify and weigh up all the relevant factors of the case whatever their nature (Black, LJ, at [24]).

[81] [2009] EWCA Civ 976.   [82] [2009] EWCA Civ 976, at [15].   [83] [2009] EWCA Civ 976, at [26].
[84] James, B. 'Occupation Orders after *Grubb*' (2009) *Family Law Week*. Available at: http://www.familylaw-week.co.uk/site.aspx?i=ed43513, accessed 25 September 2017.
[85] [2009] EWCA Civ 976, at [14].   [86] [2011] EWCA Civ 1664, at [11].
[87] [2011] EWCA Civ 1664, at [11].   [88] [2011] EWCA Civ 1664, at [9].

In *Re L (Occupation Order)*[89] the Court of Appeal upheld an order to exclude the husband. It was found that the poor relationship and constant shouting between the husband and wife was causing the twin boys, aged 8, to suffer significant harm. However, as the harm was attributable to both the parties, the judge granted an order under s. 33(6), as opposed to s. 33(7). The husband's argument that the order was 'too draconian a response to the situation at home' was rejected by the Court of Appeal. Black LJ stressed that there was 'nothing in section 33(6) to limit the discretion to make an occupation order to cases in which there has been physical violence'; and but rather the focus on the 'effect on the health, safety and well-being' encompassed 'all manner of other problems that can occur when a relationship has run into difficulties'.[90] Her Ladyship also emphasised that 'significant harm' under s. 33(7) was by no means limited to physical violence.

3.2.2 Occupation orders: Non-entitled applicants

A non-entitled applicant may still apply for an occupation order, but only against their current or former partner. The section that governs the application depends upon (a) whether the respondent is entitled to the property and (b) the relationship between the respondent and the applicant. This leads to the delineation of four different categories and sections, as set out in Table 7.1:

Table 7.1 Non-entitled applicants—categories and sections

Respondent	Nature of relationship with non-entitled applicant	Section
Entitled	Former spouse or civil partner	35
Entitled	Cohabitant or former cohabitant	36
Non-Entitled	Current or former Spouse or Civil partner	37
Non-Entitled	Cohabitant or former cohabitant	38

A distinction is drawn between entitled and non-entitled respondents as, with the latter 'the court is only adjusting occupation rights between the parties themselves'.[91] It is important to note that 'home rights' for spouses or civil partners come to an end upon divorce or dissolution. In contrast, the interference with the property rights of an entitled respondent is potentially more acute, as s/he could, for example, be required to vacate their home, while the non-entitled applicant takes up residence. The distinction based on the nature of the relationship between the applicant and respondent is, however, increasingly difficult to justify, given the exponential growth in the number of cohabiting couples. As will be seen, cohabiting couples are provided less protection than former or current spouses and civil partners.

What Orders can be made?

Entitled respondents and non-entitled applicants: In a case involving a non-entitled applicant and an entitled respondent, the court can make two types of orders: declaratory and regulatory, similar to those under s. 33(3). However, for non-entitled applicants, declaratory orders are more instrumental, as they provide the applicant the right to occupy, and not be evicted or excluded from, the family home.[92] Further to granting the applicant occupation rights, the court may then make a regulatory order. While these are less far-reaching than those contained in s. 33(3), the court can nevertheless regulate how the

---

[89] [2012] EWCA 721.   [90] [2012] EWCA 721, at [21].
[91] Law Commission. *Family Law, Domestic Violence and Occupation of the Family Home* (Law Com No. 207, 1992) 31.   [92] See ss. 35(5) and 36(5) of the Family Law Act 1996.

applicant and respondent occupy the dwelling house, and may require the respondent to leave all or part of the family home. In terms of duration, under ss. 35(10) and 36(10) the court in the first instance may only grant an order for no longer than six months, reflecting the fact that it is a short-term solution. Under s. 35(10), the court can extend the order on one or more occasions, again for a term not exceeding six months. However, with cohabitating couples, the court is only entitled to extend the order on one more occasion, thus providing less protection.

Non-entitled respondents and non-entitled applicants: Cases where neither the applicant nor the respondent are entitled to occupy the dwelling house are noted by the Law Commission to be 'comparatively rare, but may arise where they are squatters or bare licensees'.[93] Consequently, they are considered to be less draconian, as property rights are not being overridden. As outlined in ss. 37(3) and 38(3), an order may regulate the occupation of the dwelling house, require the respondent to allow the applicant to enter and remain in the premises, and exclude the respondent from all or part of the house. With regards to duration, the same model as used in ss. 35 and 36 is adopted. Hence, the initial order may not exceed six months, and while this may be extended on one or more occasion in cases involving current or former spouses or civil partners, only one extension period may be granted in cases involving current or former cohabitants.

What factors will the court take into account?

Entitled respondents and non-entitled applicants: When dealing with the cases involving an entitled respondent and a non-entitled applicant, different criteria apply in relation to the declaratory and regulatory orders. Furthermore, the criteria also differ depending upon the relationship between the applicant and the respondent.

With regards to former spouses or civil partners, under s. 35(6), in deciding whether to make a *declaratory* order, the court must take into account all of the circumstances, including:

(a) the housing needs and housing resources of each of the parties and of any relevant child;

(b) the financial resources of each of the parties;

(c) the likely effect of any order, or of any decision by the court not to exercise its powers, on the health, safety or well-being or the parties and of any relevant child;

(d) the conduct of the parties in relation to each other and otherwise;

(e) the length of time that has elapsed since the parties ceased to live together;

(f) the length of time that has elapsed since the marriage or civil partnership was dissolved or annulled; and

(g) the existence of any pending proceedings between the parties [for property adjustment orders, orders for financial relief against parents, or relating to the legal or beneficial ownership of the dwelling-house].

With regards to former cohabitants, under s. 36(6) the criteria for a *declaratory* order replicates factors s. 35(6)(a)–(d) above (hereafter 'the general factors'), and continues to include the following:

(e) the nature of the parties' relationship and in particular the level of commitment involved in it;

(f)   the length of time during which they have cohabited;

(g) whether there are or have been any children who are children of both parties or for whom both parties had parental responsibility;

---

[93] Law Commission. *Family Law, Domestic Violence and Occupation of the Family Home* (Law Com No. 207, 1992) 30.

(h)   the length of time that has elapsed since the parties ceased to live together; and

(i)   the existence of any pending proceedings between the parties [for financial relief against parents or relating to the legal or beneficial ownership of the dwelling house].

The Law Commission highlighted that, while cohabitants had chosen not to enter the *'mutual commitment'* of marriage, the passage of time and the presence of children may nevertheless give rise to certain obligations.[94]

With regards to the factors the court will take into account when deciding whether to make a regulatory order, we once again see how the law offers less protection to cohabitants. In cases involving a former spouse or civil partner, the balance of harm test applies and, accordingly, if satisfied, the court is under a *duty* to make a regulatory order. If the test is not fulfilled, the court retains a discretion to make an order, taking into account all the circumstances of the case and the 'general factors', as well as the length of time that has elapsed since the parties ceased to live together.[95] However, in relation to cohabitants, the balance of harm criteria is posed as a *question*, which is to be taken into account by the court in addition to the 'general factors':

 Key Legislation 5: The balance of harm question: Family Law Act 1996, s. 36

(7)   In deciding whether to exercise its powers to include one or more of the provisions referred to in subsection (5) [a regulatory order] and (if so) in what manner, the court shall have regard to all the circumstances including—
   (a)   the matters mentioned in subsection (6)(a) to (d) [the general factors]; and
   (b)   the questions mentioned in subsection (8).

(8)   The questions are—
   (a)   whether the applicant or any relevant child is likely to suffer significant harm attributable to conduct of the respondent if the subsection (5) provision is not included in the order; and
   (b)   whether the harm likely to be suffered by the respondent or child if the provision is included is as great as or greater than the harm attributable to conduct of the respondent which is likely to be suffered by the applicant or child if the provision is not included.

Even in cases involving significant harm, the court is not under a duty to grant a regulatory order.

Non-entitled respondents and non-entitled applicants. When determining whether to grant an order under s. 37, which relates to current or former spouses or civil partners, subsection 37(4) states that s. 33(6) and (7) apply. Hence, a duty to grant an order will arise if the balance of harm test is satisfied, and in other cases the discretionary regime applies. With regards to cohabitants, once again the balance of harm criteria is posed as a question, which is to be considered in addition to the 'general factors'.

3.3 Forced marriage protection orders

Prior to the introduction of forced marriage protection orders in 2007, protection was offered via 'a patchwork of laws that were not specifically designed to tackle forced

---

[94] Law Commission. *Family Law, Domestic Violence and Occupation of the Family Home* (Law Com No. 207, 1992) 31.   [95] Family Law Act 1996, s. 35(7).

marriage'.[96] These included, amongst other provisions, non-molestation orders under s. 42 of the Family Law Act 1996 and injunctions under s. 3 of the Prohibition of Harassment Act 1997 and an injunction to prohibit the commission of a tort under s. 37 of the Senior Courts Act 1981.

A forced marriage protection order can now be made under s. 63A of the Family Law Act 1996, which states:

(1) The court may make an order for the purposes of protecting—

   (a) a person from being forced into a marriage or from any attempt to be forced into a marriage; or

   (b) a person who has been forced into a marriage.

A forced marriage is a marriage which occurs without the victim's 'free and full consent'.[97] Force is not limited to physical violence, but encompasses 'coerce by threats or other psychological means', and may be directed against the victim and/or another person.[98] An order may be made against persons other than those named as respondents in the application, and may contain 'such prohibitions, restrictions or requirements' and 'such other terms' as considered appropriate by the court. Examples include an order to: 'prevent a forced marriage from occurring; hand over *all* passports (where there is dual nationality) and birth certificates and not to apply for a new passport; stop intimidation and violence; to reveal the whereabouts of a person; to stop someone from being taken abroad; facilitate or enable a person to return to the UK within a given time period.' [99]

In deciding whether to impose an order, the court 'must have regard to all the circumstances including the need to secure the health, safety and well-being of the person protected'. Further s. 63A(3) states that, with regards to the issue of well-being, the court 'should have regard to the person's wishes and feelings (so far as they are reasonably ascertainable) as the court considers appropriate in the light of the person's age and understanding'. This reflects the fact that various third parties may apply for an order, as discussed in 3.5 below.

A case which illustrates when a court will grant an order is that of *A v SM*.[100] The applicant, Z, applied for forced marriage protection orders against her parents to protect herself and her six siblings. The parents had taken the children to Bangladesh for a holiday but, fearing that she would be forced into marriage, Z managed to escape with help from the forced marriage unit at the British High Commission. However, when in Bangladesh, Z's sister B entered in to a marriage. While B initially maintained that she had married voluntarily, she subsequently stated that the marriage had been forced by her parents, but that she was pressurised to say otherwise by her father. There was also evidence that B had been dragged into a car by her parents and taken away to an unknown location. In such a situation, the Court agreed that the children were at risk of being forced into marriage, and granted the applications.

3.4 **Other orders**

In addition to the family law orders, a victim of domestic violence may also use the civil remedies that are available under the Protection from Harassment Act 1997 and these are not restricted to 'associated persons'. In particular, the court has the power to issue a

---

[96] Gaffney-Rhys, R. 'The Implementation of the Forced Marriage (Civil Protection) Act 2007' (2009) 31 *Journal of Social Welfare and Family Law* 245, 247.

[97] Family Law Act 1996, s. 63A(4).   [98] Family Law Act 1996, s. 63A(5)–(6).

[99] Ministry of Justice. *One year On: The initial impact of the Forced Marriage (Civil Protection) Act 2007 in its first year of operation.* (Ministry of Justice, 2009) 15.

[100] [2012] EWHC 435 (Fam).

restraining order under s. 5, in order to prevent the respondent from harassing the victim and/or causing the victim to fear violence. Initially, restraining orders were restricted to cases in which the respondent was found guilty of an offence of harassment or putting the victim in fear of violence, as set out in ss. 2 and 4 of the Protection from Harassment Act 1997, and thus were limited in scope. However, following the Domestic Violence, Crime and Victims Act 2004, the court can now make a restraining order in cases where the defendant is acquitted of a criminal charge, but an order is considered appropriate 'to protect a person from harassment by the defendant'. Whilst this extension has generally been welcomed,[101] it is dependent upon a case proceeding to trial and, as we discuss in further detail later, domestic violence victims frequently face significant difficulties when turning to the criminal law.

3.5 *Ex parte* orders, third party applications, and number of orders made

3.5.1 *Ex-parte orders*

The orders considered in this section: non-molestation, occupation, and forced marriage protection, can be made *ex parte*—without the respondent being notified of, nor present at, the proceedings. *Ex parte* orders are granted in exceptional circumstances, in order to provide vital protection in an emergency. There are, however, various disadvantages to *ex parte* proceedings, as outlined by the Law Commission. First, there is an increased risk of a 'misconceived or malicious application being granted' or 'the perpetration of some other injustice', in a case in which the respondent has not been afforded the opportunity to reply. Second, the court is prevented from trying to 'reduce the tension of the dispute'. Third, the judge is also unable to 'bring home the seriousness of the situation to the respondent to underline the importance of complying with the order or undertaking'.[102] Nevertheless, it was recognised that *ex parte* orders may at times be 'necessary and desirable'. The Law Commission emphasised that urgent action may be required in two scenarios: first, 'cases in which the remedy is needed urgently in itself'; and second, where the applicant requires to be safeguarded from the respondent in order to apply for a protective order.[103]

Section 45 of the Family Law Act 1996 states that the court can make an *ex parte* order 'in any case where it considers that it is just and convenient to do so', and must take into consideration all the circumstances of the case, including:

(a) any risk of significant harm to the applicant or a relevant child, attributable to conduct of the respondent, if the order is not made immediately;

(b) whether it is likely that the applicant will be deterred or prevented from pursuing the application if an order is not made immediately; and

(c) whether there is reason to believe that the respondent is aware of the proceedings but is deliberately evading service and that the applicant or a relevant child will be seriously prejudiced by the delay involved—

   (i) where the court is a magistrates' court, in effecting service of proceedings; or

   (ii) in any other case, in effecting substituted service.[104]

---

[101] Hester, M. *et al Early Evaluation of the Domestic Violence, Crime and Victims Act 2004*, (Home Office, 2008) 30–1.

[102] Law Commission. *Family Law, Domestic Violence and Occupation of the Family Home* (Law Com No. 207, 1992) 42.

[103] Law Commission. *Family Law, Domestic Violence and Occupation of the Family Home* (Law Com No. 207, 1992) 42.

[104] See s. 45 of the Family Law Act 1996 (non-molestation and occupation orders) and s. 63D of the Family Law Act 1996 (forced marriage protection order).

The issue of 'evasion of service', as covered in s. 45(2)(c), was highlighted by the Law Commission as being a key problem. In addition to the time and expense incurred, evasion was often used as a ploy by respondents to 'wear down the applicant's resolution by causing delay and making the process even more difficult', which would result in an application being withdrawn or abandoned.[105]

If granted, the respondent must be provided the opportunity to make representations at a full hearing, as 'soon as just and convenient'. With regards to duration, guidance issued to the courts states that an *ex parte* order must have a determinate end date and 'should not normally exceed 14 days'.[106] Evidence indicates that courts are more reluctant to grant an occupation order *ex parte,* in contrast to a non-molestation order, which is perhaps unsurprising given the perceived draconian nature of the former.[107]

3.5.2 Third party applications

Given the nature of domestic abuse, various barriers may preclude a victim from applying for a protective order. Consequently, some provision has been made to enable third parties, other than the victim themselves, to apply for an order. In relation to a forced marriage protection order, in addition to the person to be protected, under s. 63C of the Family Law Act 1996, an application may be made by either a relevant third party (specified to be local authorities)[108] or by any other person by leave of the court. In deciding whether to grant leave, s. 63C(4) states that the court must have regard to all the circumstances of the case, including:

(a) the applicant's connection with the person to be protected;

(b) the applicant's knowledge of the circumstances of the person to be protected; and

(c) the wishes and feelings of the person to be protected so far as they are reasonably ascertainable and so far as the court considers it appropriate, in the light of the person's age and understanding, to have regard to them.

Official statistics indicate that applications by third parties represent a significant proportion of cases, as set out in Table 7.2. This is, perhaps, unsurprising given the dynamics of forced marriage, particularly when children are involved.[109]

In relation to non-molestation and occupation orders, provision had been made for third party applications, although s. 60 of the Family Law Act 1996 is currently not in force. The Law Commission outlined the benefits that may accrue from allowing a third party, particularly the police, to apply for an order:

> in many cases the victim is in a state of helplessness because of the violence and is unable to take any initiative herself. Giving this power to the police removes the burden of taking action from her, reduces the scope for further intimidation by the perpetrator and leads to fewer cases being withdrawn.[110]

---

[105] Law Commission. *Family Law, Domestic Violence and Occupation of the Family Home* (Law Com No. 207, 1992) 43.

[106] President of the Family Division, *Practice Guidance: Family Court—Duration of Ex Parte (Without Notice) Orders* (13 October 2014). Available at: https://www.judiciary.gov.uk/wp-content/uploads/2013/03/practice-guidance-family-court-duration-of-ex-parte-orders.pdf, accessed 25 September 2017.

[107] Barron, J. *Five Years On: A Review of Legal Protection from Domestic Violence* (Women's Aid, 2002).

[108] The Family Law Act 1996 (Forced Marriage) (Relevant Third Party) Order 2009.

[109] HM Government. *Family court tables (July to September 2016)* Table 15. Available at: https://www.gov.uk/government/statistics/family-court-statistics-quarterly-july-to-september-2016, accessed 25 September 2017.

[110] Law Commission. *Family Law, Domestic Violence and Occupation of the Family Home* (Law Com No. 207, 1992) 46.

Table 7.2 Number of forced marriage protection orders by age and applicant type, 2010–15.

Year	FMPO: Age of Applicant			FMPO: Applicant Type			
	17 & under	Over 17	Unknown	Person to be protected	Relevant 3rd party	Other 3rd Party	Other
2010	57	55	4	37	30	45	4
2011	65	50	8	38	44	41	0
2012	51	38	27	44	31	41	0
2013	112	57	4	72	51	50	0
2014	115	53	4	40	72	60	0
2015	165	76	20	51	77	133	0

The involvement of the police was considered to have the further advantage of emphasising to the respondent the seriousness of the issue, and the likely reduction in violence would have a positive impact upon their workload. However, despite receiving support from practitioners, the government declined to implement s. 60.

 CONTEXT 2 : TABLE 7.3 DETAILS THE NUMBER OF APPLICATIONS AND ORDERS MADE, IN RELATION TO NON-MOLESTATION AND OCCUPATION ORDERS:[111]

Table 7.3 Number of non-molestation and occupation orders made, 2009–15.

Year	Applications		Orders made	
	Non-molestation	Occupation	Non-molestation	Occupation
2009	20,649	7,788	22,881	4,662
2010	18,358	6,193	21,194	3,715
2011	16,135	5,189	19,556	3,172
2012	16,288	4,969	19,405	2,759
2013	18,749	5,136	22,284	2,748
2014	19,467	5,022	24,000	2,591
2015	18,700	4,555	23,626	2,347

The figures for non-molestation orders are significantly higher than those for occupation orders. While the number of occupation orders made decreased by about 50% from 2009 to 2012, they have remained relatively steady thereafter. With regards non-molestation orders, a decrease in both applications and orders made occurred between 2009 and 2012, with slight increases in 2013 and 2014. It is also interesting to note that the number of non-molestation orders made is higher than the number of applications; this is due to the power of the court to make an order in lieu of an application, under s. 42(2)(b).

---

[111] HM Government. *Family court tables (July to September 2016)* Table 14. Available at: https://www.gov.uk/government/statistics/family-court-statistics-quarterly-july-to-september-2016, accessed 25 September 2017.

When we turn to forced marriage protection orders, we can see that the figures are much lower, as set out in Table 7.4.[112] Nevertheless, in general there has been a gradual increase over the years. As with non-molestation orders, the court can make an order in the absence of an application if it is needed to protect an individual (s. 63C(6)).

Table 7.4 Number of forced marriage protection orders made, 2009-15

Year	Total applications made	Number of orders made
2009	96	101
2010	116	149
2011	123	157
2012	116	124
2013	173	108
2014	172	176
2015	261	217

3.6 Enforcing orders and undertakings

In order to be effective, protective orders must be enforceable by the victim if there is a breach of the order by the perpetrator. Initially, orders could only be enforced by contempt of court proceedings, with the court being able to attach a power of arrest in certain circumstances. However, the breach of non-molestation and forced marriage protection orders has now been criminalised. Alternatively, as opposed to imposing an order the court may accept what is known as an 'undertaking'.

3.6.1 Criminalising the breach of non-molestation and forced marriage protection orders.

With regards to non-molestation orders, s. 42A(1) of the Family Law Act 1996, inserted by s. 1 of the Domestic Violence, Crime and Victims Act 2004, now states that: 'A person who without reasonable excuse does anything that he is prohibited from doing by a non-molestation order is guilty of an offence.' As an order may be made *ex parte*, s. 42A(2) states that a person will be guilty 'only in respect of conduct engaged in at a time when he was aware of the existence of the order'. Significantly, the order does not need to be served upon an individual in order for an offence to be committed. During the Parliamentary debates, concern was expressed regarding the evasion of service, which could undermine the offence. Baroness Scotland explained that 'by refusing to open their doors to processors, respondents can continue to harass the applicant while truthfully claiming not to have been served the order. This makes a mockery of court orders and the protection they are supposed to provide.'[113] If an offender is convicted on indictment s/he may be sentenced to a maximum of five years imprisonment and/or a fine under s. 42A(2), reducing to 12 months maximum and/or a fine, upon summary conviction.

---

[112] HM Government. *Family court tables (July to September 2016)* Table 15. Available at: https://www.gov.uk/government/statistics/family-court-statistics-quarterly-july-to-september-2016, accessed 25 September 2017.

[113] Hansard HL vol 656, cols 225–6GC, 19 January 2004. Cited in House of Commons Research Paper 04–44, 27.

Prior to the Anti-social Behaviour, Crime and Policing Act 2014, a forced marriage protection order was only punishable as contempt of court. As Gaffney-Rhys highlights, this led to the application of different responses to the breach of a non-molestation order and the breach of a forced marriage order. Whereas the former was deemed to be a criminal offence, the latter was not. This distinction, however, could not be justified, particularly as the rationale behind the amendments to the Family Law 1996 made by the Forced Marriage (Civil Protection) Act 2007 'was to emphasise that forced marriage is a form of domestic violence'.[114] Accordingly, the breach of a forced marriage protection order is now a criminal offence under s. 63CA of the Family Law Act 1996, the maximum penalty for which is five years imprisonment on indictment. Concern, however, has been expressed with regards to the extent to which orders can be monitored, and therefore breaches acted upon. As highlighted by Sanghera:

> I am not aware of any other injunction in this country under which the individual is returned to the perpetrators. In these cases, forced marriage protection orders are issued to our victims, in the main minors, then those victims are returned to multiple perpetrators in that house. Once that front door closes, I am not aware of who is monitoring the implementation of that order because the named people may not be intimidating them but, believe me, there are many other family members that are. Then our victim is put under great pressure and that is a huge concern to us.[115]

 DEBATE 4: SHOULD THE BREACH OF A FAMILY LAW ORDER BE A CRIMINAL OFFENCE?

The move to criminalise the breach of a non-molestation order generally received the support of practitioners and domestic violence victims, as it was noted that a non-molestation order without a power of arrest was pointless.[116] There was also concern that, as a power of arrest can be attached to a specific part of the order, police officers may be unsure whether they are able to arrest the respondent.[117]

However, some disquiet was also expressed. It was feared that the reform may lead to victims facing increasing pressure—by the respondent and/or their legal advisers—to accept what is known as an 'undertaking'. An undertaking is a promise by the respondent to behave as requested by the court, and may be made instead of a non-molestation or occupation order. However, as we examine in further detail later, if the perpetrator breaches an undertaking, the court has very limited powers of response.[118] Relatedly, Platt has argued that the move towards increased criminalisation may deter victims from applying for an order, as they may not wish to criminalise their partners.[119] They may also feel disempowered as it will be the police and the CPS, as opposed to the victim, who will decide whether criminal

---

[114] Gaffney-Rhys, R. 'The Criminalisation of Forced Marriage in England and Wales: One Year On' [2015] *Family Law* 1378, 1379.

[115] House of Commons and Home Affairs Committee. *Forced Marriage*, Eighth Report of Session 2010–12, (House of Commons, 2011) 6.

[116] Barron, J. *Not Worth the Paper . . . ? The Effectiveness of Legal Protection for Women and Children Experiencing Domestic Violence* (Women's Aid, 1990) cited in House of Commons and Home Affairs Committee. *Forced Marriage*, Eighth Report of Session 2010–12, (House of Commons, 2011) 19.

[117] House of Commons Research Paper 04/44, 26.

[118] House of Commons *Safety and Justice: The Government's Proposals on Domestic Violence* (Home Office, 2003) 33.

[119] Platt, J. 'The Domestic Violence, Crime and Victims Act 2004 Part 1: Is It Working?' (2008) 38 *Family Law* 642, 642.

action is taken against the perpetrator for breaching the order.[120] Indeed, it is significant that, following enactment of the Domestic Violence, Crime and Victims Act 2004, there was a fall in application numbers for non-molestation orders, which is surprising given the victim-focused nature of the reforms.[121] From a different perspective, the human rights organisation Liberty argued that criminalising the breach of a non-molestation order involved the 'blurring of the criminal law and civil law', and produced a '"personal criminal law", where the defendant is punished not for breaking the law of the land but for breaking a law which applies to him personally'.[122]

Victims stressed that their support for criminalising the breach of a non-molestation order was based upon the presumption that the order would be effectively enforced and lead to the imposition of a significant punishment, as opposed to just a 'little fine'.[123] It is important to note that when sentencing a case, the court is concerned with the conduct that breached the order, as opposed to the behaviour which led to the imposition of an order. It is also important that courts are required to apply the sentencing guidance issued by the Sentencing Council.[124] This guidance sets out those factors that the court is required to take into account when determining the sentence, and sets out the appropriate penalty that the court may pass; for example, whether the perpetrator should pay a fine or receive a prison sentence, and how much the fine or how long the prison sentence should be. It is significant to note that the guidelines pertaining to domestic violence appropriately acknowledge that the domestic nature of a case can operate as an *aggravating* factor. As such, the court should only ever allow the fact that the case involved intimate partners to increase, and not decrease, the severity of the sentence; for example, lead to a higher fine or a longer prison sentence.[125] However, the mitigating factors—those that will lead to a reduction in the sentence—include provocation by the victim, which may reinforce victim-blaming stereotypes. Indeed, the following comments were made by magistrates when sentencing domestic violence cases involving actual bodily harm:[126]

- 'Are there any courses the woman can attend to learn how to avoid being hit?';
- 'If a woman knows what is going to happen, why does she carry on winding up the man?';
- 'I would say that the husband [is] justified in being aggrieved at things not being ready';
- 'The man was under stress'.[127]

[120] Platt, J. 'The Domestic Violence, Crime and Victims Act 2004 Part 1: Is It Working?' (2008) 38 *Family Law* 642, 642.

[121] Platt, J. 'The Domestic Violence, Crime and Victims Act 2004 Part 1: Is It Working?' (2008) 38 *Family Law* 642, 642.

[122] House of Commons. *The Domestic Violence, Crime and Victims Bill [HL]: Domestic Violence Provisions*, Research Paper 04/11 (House of Commons, 2004) 28.

[123] Hester, M. *et al Early Evaluation of the Domestic Violence, Crime and Victims Act 2004*, Ministry of Justice Research Series 14/08 (Ministry of Justice, 2008) 23.

[124] See Sentencing Council. *Overarching Principles: Domestic Violence—Definitive Guideline* (Sentencing Council, 2006); Sentencing Council. *Breach of a Protective Order: Definitive Guideline* (Sentencing Council, 2006).

[125] See Sentencing Council, *Overarching Principles: Domestic Violence—Definitive Guideline* (Sentencing Council, 2006).

[126] Gilchrist, E. and Blissett, J. 'Magistrates' Attitudes to Domestic Violence and Sentencing Options' (2002) 41 *British Journal of Criminology* 348.

[127] Gilchrist, E. and Blissett, J. 'Magistrates' Attitudes to Domestic Violence and Sentencing Options' (2002) 41 *British Journal of Criminology* 359.

As Burton argues: 'the courts will need to be very sensitive in their handling of the criterion if to free themselves from criticism that alleged "nagging" of a low-level nature is regarded as provocation for serious domestic violence.'[128] The defendant's 'positive good character' is also included as a mitigating factor. However, 'perpetrators regularly appear charming and in control and often win over officials in the system when compared with women.'[129]

With regards occupation orders, the government decided against criminalising a breach of an occupation order, on the basis that 'history of violence or molestation' was not a prerequisite for the granting of an order.[130] The reforms also require courts 'to consider granting a non-molestation order when it considers making an occupation order'.[131] Accordingly, if the respondent breaches the occupation order, s/he is also likely to have breached the non-molestation order. However, this reasoning can be subjected to critique. As explored earlier, criteria for a non-molestation order is more forward-looking than that in relation to occupation orders, with the latter requiring a consideration of the conduct of the parties if, on the facts, the balance of harm test is not satisfied. Furthermore, we have seen that courts are often reluctant to grant an occupation order in the absence of physical violence. Subsequently, a domestic violence victim could be required to be present at two separate court hearings, if a perpetrator breaches both orders.

3.6.2 Power of arrest and contempt of court

Courts may attach a power of arrest to an order, which enables a constable to arrest without a warrant 'any person whom he has reasonable cause for suspecting to be in breach' of an order.[132] In lieu of a power of arrest, a victim is required to apply to the court for a warrant to arrest the respondent. Section 47(9) states that a warrant will not be issued unless '(a) the application is substantiated on oath; and (b) the [court] has reasonable grounds for believing that the respondent has failed to comply with the order'. Accordingly, a power of arrest offers significant support and protection for a victim at a time when it is most needed. When deciding whether to attach a power of arrest, the court *shall* attach a power of arrest if 'it appears to the court that the respondent has used or threatened violence against the applicant or a relevant child' unless it is 'satisfied that in all the circumstances of the case the applicant or child will be adequately protected' without it.[133]

Prior to 2004, the courts could attach a power of arrest to both non-molestation and occupation orders. However, subsequent to criminalising the breach of a non-molestation order, a power of arrest may now only be attached to an occupation order.

Upon arrest for a suspected breach, the respondent must be brought before the family court within 24 hours. If the evidence permits, the court may decide there and then if the respondent has breached the order. The breach of a court order amounts to contempt of court, and while this is not a criminal offence, the court can impose a sentence of up to 24 months imprisonment. If further evidence is required, the respondent can be remanded in custody or released on bail, and the case will be adjourned for what is known as a full

---

[128] Burton, M. *Legal Responses to Domestic Violence* (Routledge-Cavendish, 2008) 64.

[129] Women's National Commission. *Unlocking the Secret: Women Open the Door on Domestic Violence*, 2003, cited in Burton, M. *Legal Responses to Domestic Violence* (Routledge-Cavendish, 2008) 64.

[130] House of Commons. *Domestic Violence, Crime and Victims Bill Explanatory notes Bill 83 EN* (House of Commons, 2004) para 17.

[131] House of Commons. *Domestic Violence, Crime and Victims Bill Explanatory notes Bill 83 EN* (House of Commons, 2004) para 27.

[132] See ss. 47 and 63H of the Family Law Act.   [133] See ss. 47 and 63H 1996.

committal hearing. In the absence of either a power of, or a warrant for, the respondent's arrest, the applicant may also apply to the court for 'an order to commit the respondent to prison for contempt of court'.

The Court of Appeal has emphasised that the sentencing objectives and principles in cases of contempt differ to those in 'ordinary criminal cases'. Whilst there is a 'shared deterrent objective in the punishment of domestic violence by imprisonment', with a contempt case, 'an important objective . . . is to uphold the authority of the court by demonstrating that its orders cannot be flouted with impunity'.[134] The following guidance was developed by Hale LJ in *Hale v Tanner*:[135]

- The full range of criminal sentencing options is not available for contempt of court.
- Custody is not automatic.
- If imprisonment is appropriate, the length of committal should be decided without reference to whether or not it is to be suspended.
- The length of the sentence depends on the court's objectives. There are two objectives . . . One is to mark the court's disapproval of the disobedience of its order. The other is to secure compliance with that order in the future.
- The length of the committal has to bear some relationship to the maximum statutory sentence of 2 years.
- Suspension is possible in a much wider range of circumstances than it is in criminal cases.
- The length of the suspension requires separate consideration.
- The court has to bear in mind the context. This may be aggravating or mitigating.

Conduct which results in the breach of a protective order may also give rise to criminal proceedings, and hence Hale LJ stressed that it is important a person guilty of contempt is not punished 'twice for the same events'.[136] Additional guidance on the issue of parallel proceedings is provided in *Lomas v Parle*:

> the first court to sentence must not anticipate nor allow for a likely future sentence. It is for the second court to reflect the prior sentence in its judgment in order to ensure that the defendant is not punished twice for the same act. It is essential that the second court should be fully informed of the factors and circumstances reflected in the first sentence (Thorpe LJ, at [48]).

However, it is also important to note that, in relation to both non-molestation and forced marriage protection orders, conduct which constituted the breach can be punished either as contempt of court or as the relevant criminal offence under ss. 42A and 63CA, but not both.[137]

While the court has the power to pass a custodial sentence of up to 24 months, the Court of Appeal in *Ansah v Ansah* stipulated that in cases involving families, a custodial sentence—suspended or otherwise—was a remedy of the 'very last resort', only to be made 'very reluctantly and only when every other effort to bring the situation under control has failed or is almost likely to fail'.[138] The Court discharged a suspended committal order against the wife for breaching an *ex parte* injunction which prohibited her from visiting the matrimonial home. This is, however, not to state that a court will not impose a

---

[134] *Lomas v Parle* [2003] EWCA Civ 1804, at [47].
[135] [2000] 1 WLR 2377, 2381.   [136] [2000] 1 WLR 2377, 2381.
[137] See ss. 42A(3) and (4) of The Family Law Act 1996 (non-molestation orders) and ss 63CA(3) and (4) of the Family Law Act 1996 (forced marriage protection orders).   [138] [1977] Fam 138, 144.

custodial sentence. In *Lomas v Parle*, two concurrent sentences of eight months were held to be warranted when the defendant breached the non-molestation order while he was on bail for threats to kill and common assault. Similarly, in *H v O* a nine months immediate custodial sentence was considered appropriate when the breach of the non-molestation order involved actual and threatened violence, which included attacking the victim in the street, grasping her throat, and forcing her on to the bonnet of a car.[139]

3.6.3 Undertakings

A court may accept what is known as an 'undertaking' from a respondent, as opposed to imposing a non-molestation, occupation, or forced marriage protection order. An undertaking is a promise from the respondent to behave as requested by the court. The breach of an undertaking amounts to contempt of court, however, no power of arrest may be attached. With regards to occupation s. 46(3) of the Family Law Act 1996 states that the court cannot accept an undertaking in cases where a power of arrest would have been attached to the order. With regards to non-molestation and forced marriage orders, ss. 43(3A) and s. 63E set out that an undertaking may not be made if 'the respondent has used or threatened violence against the applicant or child [or person to be protected]' and for their protection 'it is necessary to make [an order] so that any breach may be punishable under [sections 42A and 63CA]'. In domestic violence cases undertakings are controversial, as apologies and promises to improve are not an unusual aspect of abusive behaviour. Applicants may also be pressurised to accept an undertaking, as it favours the respondent as no finding of fact is made.

4. Domestic violence and family justice

In addition to the protective orders, there are various wider factors that relate to the family justice system's response to abuse victims. It is important to note that domestic violence may arise as a factor for the courts in various family law proceedings, particularly in cases involving disputes between parents regarding arrangements for children following separation. It is vital that a victim can access high quality legal advice and representation. However, recent reforms have significantly restricted the availability of legal aid in family law cases, which has significant ramifications for cases involving domestic abuse. Relatedly, there have been recent calls to ensure that domestic violence victims are sufficiently protected and supported during court proceedings, and not subjected to further abuse.

4.1 Domestic violence and legal aid

Legal aid is a vital resource for individuals who would otherwise be unable to obtain legal advice and representation. However, LASPO 2012 significantly reduced its availability for private law family proceedings. While an applicant for a non-molestation, occupation, and forced marriage orders may still access publicly funded legal representation, legal aid for all other private family law remedies will only be available in exceptional circumstances (see Chapter 15). As domestic abuse is recognised as an exceptional circumstance, prima facie, victims can access legal aid. However, in order to be eligible, prescribed evidence of the abuse must be produced and, in practice, this has caused difficulties for many victims. The evidence permitted is set out in the Civil Legal Aid (Procedure) Regulations 2012 (as amended), and includes: the existence of a protective order or an undertaking; letters from social services, medical practitioners, a MARAC (multi-agency risk assessment conference) confirming the presence or risk of abuse; a letter from a domestic violence support

---

[139] [2004] EWCA Civ 1691.

agency confirming that the victim was admitted to a refuge, or refused admission due to insufficient accommodation; a domestic violence protection notice; and that the perpetrator has a relevant unspent conviction or police caution, or is on bail, or is bound over by a court order. These provisions have, however, been criticised by feminist campaign groups and commentators:[140]

> Asking for proof in this way colludes with and reinforces the idea that a) if there's no physical violence then it's not actually abusive and b) that a large number of women who allege abuse are lying.[141]

In addition, campaign group Rights for Women argued that the regulations frustrated the purpose of LASPO 2012, on the basis that many victims of domestic violence were unable to provide the evidence required. Of particular concern was the fact that, as initially drafted, the evidence provided had to be less than 24 months old, and that those who suffered financial abuse were not adequately covered.

 CONTEXT 3 : LEGAL AID AND DOMESTIC VIOLENCE

In their 2016 report *Evidencing Domestic Violence: Nearly Three Years On*, Rights of Women highlighted that:

- 37% of women responding to the survey who had experienced or were experiencing domestic violence did not have the prescribed forms of evidence to access family law legal aid.
- 23% of women responding would have had one or more of the prescribed forms of evidence if the two-year time limit on those forms of evidence was not in place.
- 53% of respondents took no action in relation to their family law problem as a result of not being able to apply for legal aid. 29% paid a solicitor privately and 28% represented themselves at court.[142]

Accessing legal aid has been described as a 'life-line' for victims of abuse, particularly in cases involving contact arrangements for children post separation. Rights of Women highlighted that:

- Victim-survivors are not enabled to give their best evidence about histories of abuse, which may be crucial to determining whether contact, and in what form, is deemed appropriate.
- The difficulties of cross-examining their perpetrators may mean they do not ask sufficiently probing questions or challenge responses, which again informs what evidence is available to the court.
- They are rarely equipped with the legal knowledge and experience to prepare documentation and negotiate family law processes e.g. requesting finding of fact hearings.
- Pressure to reach speedy resolution may mean that women accede to arrangements which are not necessarily in their own or their children's best interests.[143]

Rights of Women consequently initiated judicial review proceedings, and the Court of Appeal in *R (On the Application of Rights of Women) v The Lord Chancellor and Secretary of*

---

[140] See Hunter, R. 'Doing Violence to Family Law' (2011) 33 *Journal of Social Welfare and Family Law* 343.
[141] Rights of Women, *Women's Access to Justice: A Research Report* (Rights of Women, 2011) 30.
[142] Rights of Women, *Evidencing Domestic Violence: Nearly Three Years On* (Rights of Women, 2016) 1.
[143] Rights of Women, *Picking up the Pieces: Domestic Violence and Child Contact* (Rights of Women, 2012) 40.

State held that Reg. 33—which detailed the prescribed evidence—was invalid. Longmore LJ stated that:

> Regulation 33 does frustrate the purposes of LASPO insofar as it imposes a requirement that the verification of domestic violence has to be dated within a period of 24 months before the application for legal aid, indeed, insofar as it makes no provision for victims of financial abuse.[144]

Following this decision, the time period for the verifying evidence was initially extended to five years.[145] However, following ongoing criticism, the government has announced that it will abolish the time limit, and accept a wider range of supporting evidence.[146] This positive development may enable more victims of domestic violence to access legal aid. However, proving non-physical forms of abuse is likely to be challenging. In addition, as the domestic violence exception only applies to victims, and not perpetrators, concerns remain, as the victim will then potentially face being questioned by her abuser during the court process, a point we address further in the next section.

4.2 Family law litigation as domestic violence and special measures

In many cases, terminating a relationship will not bring about an end to the abuse. Indeed, as noted in the introduction, it can lead to an escalation in violence. Relatedly, research has also indicated that abusive men will often take advantage of family law litigation, particularly in relation to post-separation arrangements for children, as a means of continuing their abuse:

> Some perpetrators get the message that the relationship is over and are genuinely interested in seeing their children. Others use it as a mechanism to keep back into the relationship, others to undermine the victim's confidence and self-esteem, others to make the victim feel trapped and some to 'get at them' further by undermining them as a parent.[147]

It has been argued that a perpetrator's persistent application for orders over children of the relationship amounts to harassment of the victim,[148] which is enabled by the existence of a 'pro-contact' culture, which assumes that it is in the child's best interest to have a relationship with both parents (see Chapter 9), even in cases involving violence. Victims have also highlighted the subtle ways a perpetrator may continue their violence in the courtroom, but that such tactics may not be obvious to others, nor considered to amount to abuse. This includes 'invasive surveillance', whereby the perpetrator stares at the victim throughout proceedings.[149] Indeed, victims have highlighted how they frequently feel intimidated and unsafe during court cases.

Of particular concern is the likelihood that their abuser will question them personally during court proceedings. The reduction in legal aid has inevitably increased the numbers of litigants in person, as individuals are unable to afford legal representation. Consequently, while a victim *may* be able to access legal aid, a perpetrator could be required to represent

---

[144] [2016] EWCA Civ 91, para 47.

[145] The Civil Legal Aid (Procedure) (Amendment) Regulations 2016 (SI 516/2016).

[146] See House of Commons (2017) *Legal Aid Scheme: Domestic Violence: Written Question—66948*. Available at: http://www.parliament.uk/business/publications/written-questions-answers-statements/written-question/Commons/2017-03-07/66948, accessed 8 May 2017.

[147] Rights of Women, *Picking up the Pieces: Domestic Violence and Child Contact* (Rights of Women, 2012) 34 (R52 barrister).

[148] Miller, S.L. and Smolter, N.L. '"Paper abuse": When All Else Fails, Batterers Uses Procedural Stalking' (2011) 17 *Violence Against Women* 637.

[149] Rights of Women. *Picking up the Pieces: Domestic Violence and Child Contact* (Rights of Women, 2012) 42.

themselves during private family law proceedings, if they unable to pay for a lawyer, and research has shown that up to 25% of domestic abuse victims will be personally cross-examined by their abuser during proceedings. It has been recognised by the All Party Parliamentary Group on Domestic Violence that this provides the opportunity for a perpetrator to continue his abuse:

> Litigants in person are a major problem and when cross examination of a victim by an abuser takes place that is very concerning. Coercive control can be played out in the court arena.[150]

Such practice has been condemned by Mumby P, and subsequently the government has committed to reforming the law in order prohibit the questioning of victims by their abusers in family law proceedings.[151] Significantly, in the criminal courts a person accused of a sexual offence is not permitted to personally cross-examine a complainant during a criminal law trial. Indeed, numerous 'special measures' are in place to support a victim/witness through a criminal trial. Set out in ss. 23–29 of the Youth Justice and Criminal Evidence Act 1999, these include: screens to shield the witness from the accused; giving evidence via a live link; giving evidence in private (this does not involve removing the accused from the court, but rather relates to the members of the public); removal of wigs and gowns; video recorded evidence-in-chief; video recorded cross-examination or re-examination; and examination through an intermediary.

While there is provision for special measures to be put in place during a family law case, their use is haphazard and the policy framework is unclear.[152] During the recent Parliamentary debate on the cross-examination of domestic violence victims in 2017, the government indicated that it would consider how the law could be reformed to ensure the better provision of special measures in the family law courts.[153]

5. Criminal law and criminal justice responses

Given the complexity of domestic abuse, an understanding of the family law's response needs to be contextualised within a broader consideration of the developments within the criminal justice system. This section will therefore address how the criminal law and criminal justice system have responded to domestic violence or, perhaps more accurately, how the criminal law and criminal justice system have *failed* to respond to domestic violence.

5.1 The failure of the state to respond to domestic violence

In theory, the criminal law should be able to respond to domestic and sexual violence: certain aspects of domestic violence fall under the Offences against the Person Act 1861 and sexual violence is prohibited by the Sexual Offences Act 2003. The reality is, however, much different: whilst these Acts should provide a sufficient remedy, in practice the criminal law and criminal justice system have generated unsatisfactory results. Furthermore, the courts and the police have, historically, shown little sympathy for women who suffer

---

[150] All Party Parliamentary Group on Domestic Violence (APPG). *Domestic Violence, Child Contact and the Family Courts: All Parliamentary Group on Domestic Violence Parliamentary Briefing* (APPG, 2016) 14.

[151] Prison and Courts Bill 2017, cl. 47; House of Commons. *Domestic Violence Victims: Cross Examination* (House of Commons, Hansard, 2017).

[152] Coy, M. *et al* 'It's like going through the abuse again': domestic violence and women and children's (un) safety in private law contact proceedings' (2015) 37 *Journal of Social Welfare and Family Law* 53.

[153] House of Commons. *Domestic Violence Victims: Cross Examination* (House of Commons, Hansard, 2017).

domestic violence. The state's response has suggested that domestic violence is unworthy of attention; the result of which has been a failure of the state to adequately protect victims of domestic violence.

A more proactive police approach started to emerge in the 1990s with the introduction of Domestic Violence Units: these units were developed, in part, in response to the criticisms levied at the state for its failure to intervene in domestic violence cases. The aim of the units was to 'help ensure the safety of women and children by intervening with offenders and supporting victims. That is, to protect specific abused women as well as potential victims.'[154] Other relevant initiatives include the introduction of Independent Domestic Violence Advocates (IDVAs). IDVAs are caseworkers who assist victims of domestic violence to access help and support victims through the criminal justice process.[155] Although the changes would seem to suggest that domestic violence is being tackled within the criminal justice system, evidence indicates that domestic violence is still largely considered to be less serious than other comparable assaults. Charges in domestic violence cases tend to be reduced from s. 47 Offences Against the Person Act 1861 (assault occasioning actual bodily harm) to s.39 Offences Against the Person Act 1861 (assault), and disproportionately so. Furthermore, such cases tend to be confined to the magistrates' courts: 94% of domestic assault cases are dealt with by a magistrate, as opposed to 79% of non-domestic assault cases.[156] Additionally, the sentences passed in domestic assault cases are disproportionately more lenient than non-domestic assault cases. Overwhelmingly, perpetrators of domestic violence are likely to receive a conditional discharge or a small fine. Such responses have a twofold effect: they fail to protect the victim and, at the same time, construct domestic violence as 'trifling and non-criminal'.[157]

More recently, steps have been taken to improve the criminal justice response to domestic violence. In September 2013, the Home Secretary, Theresa May, commissioned Her Majesty's Inspectorate of Constabulary (HMIC) to inspect the police response to domestic violence. The findings indicated that:

- Overall, the police response to domestic violence was inadequate.

- Most forces suggest that domestic violence is a priority. However, what appears on paper does not translate into practice.

- Acquisitive crime and serious organised crime appear as priorities: tackling domestic abuse too often remains a poor relation.

- Some areas of core policing exhibited alarming and unacceptable weaknesses, in particular, the collection of evidence by officers.

- A failure to 'reinforce right behaviours, attitudes and actions of officers' due to 'poor management and supervision'.

- A failure amongst police forces to prioritise actions that will tackle domestic abuse.

- Variable arrest rates were evident across police forces in England and Wales, ranging from 45% to 90%.[158]

---

[154] Lewis, R. *et al* 'Law's Progressive Potential: The Value of Engagement with the Law for Domestic Violence' (2001) 10 *Social and Legal Studies* 105, 108.

[155] See further https://www.gov.uk/guidance/domestic-violence-and-abuse, accessed 25 September 2017.

[156] Cretney, A. and Davis, A., 'Prosecuting Domestic Assault: Victims Failing Courts, or Courts Failing Victims' (1997) 36 *The Howard Journal* 146, 149.

[157] Cretney, A. and Davis, A., 'Prosecuting Domestic Assault: Victims Failing Courts, or Courts Failing Victims' (1997) 36(2) *The Howard Journal* 146, 152; Edwards, S. *Policing Domestic Violence: Women, the Law and the State* (SAGE, 1987) 232.

[158] HMIC. *Everybody's Business: Improving the Police Response to Domestic Abuse* (HMIC, 2014).

5.1.1 Criminalising coercive control

As noted earlier, aspects of domestic violence can be charged under the Offences against the Person Act 1861 and sexual violence can similarly be charged under the Sexual Offences Act 2003. However, as also noted earlier, there have been numerous inadequacies in this approach within the criminal justice system. Section 76 of the Serious Crime Act 2015 sought to address this issue.

 Key Legislation 6: Serious Crime Act 2015, s. 76

- *Section 76(1)*: A person (A) commits this offence if (s)he engaged in repeated and continuous coercive or controlling behaviour towards another person (B). A and B must be personally connected, A's behaviour must have a serious effect on B, and A knows or ought to know that the behaviour will have such an effect.
- *Section 76(4) serious effect*: A's behaviour has a serious effect on B if it causes B to fear, on at least two occasions, that violence will be used against B; or it causes B serious alarm or distress which has a substantial adverse effect on B's usual day-to-day activities.
- *Section 76(2) personally connected*: A and B are personally connected if A is in an intimate personal relationship with B; or A and B live together and they are members of the same family; or they have previously been in an intimate personal relationship with each other.
- *Section 76(6) members of the same family*: A and B are members of the same family if they are, or have been, married to each other; they are, or have been, civil partners of each other; they are relatives; they have agreed to marry one another (whether or not the agreement has been terminated); they have entered into a civil partnership agreement (whether or not the agreement has been terminated); they are both parents of the same child; or they have, or have had, parental responsibility for the same child.

There are, however, the Home Office has highlighted various arguments for and against a specific domestic abuse offence, as set out in Table 7.5:[159]

In a 2015 Report, *Increasingly everyone's business: A progress report on the police response to domestic abuse*, HMIC highlighted some problems with the police response to domestic violence. In particular, there was inconsistent awareness among response staff of what was

Table 7.5 Arguments for and against a specific domestic abuse offence

For	Against
The HMIC makes clear that police fail to see domestic abuse, particularly its non-violent form, as a serious crime.	Victims often fear the consequences for their families and perpetrators
Acts that are clearly criminal are not referred for prosecution and the arrest rate varies widely.	Accessing the criminal justice system can be intimidating.
Creating a specific offence may send a clear, consistent message to frontline agencies. It may also help victims identify the behaviour as wrong and encourage reporting, and cause perpetrators to rethink their controlling behaviour	A new offence may be seen as duplicating existing legislation and distracting frontline agencies.

---

[159] Home Office. *Strengthening the Law of Domestic Abuse—A Consultation* (Home Office, 2014) 11.

meant by coercive and controlling behaviour. Further, officers' attitudes to victims of domestic violence were mixed: 'some response officers fail to understand and appreciate the dynamics of domestic abuse, particularly in relation to coercive control.'[160] Police officers also had a tendency to focus on physical injury and to neglect psychological harm: physical injury garnered a more positive response when compared with emotional abuse. The offence had, and has, the potentiality for adding to a 'hierarchy of harm', whereby physical harm is considered to be more serious than psychological harm.[161] It has also been recognised that some of the issues with the offence have resulted from, at least in part, a lack of or inconsistent training. HMIC were hopeful that the College of Policing training on coercive control would help rectify this issue.[162] Stark has highlighted the fundamental nature of police support and cites the support of the College of Policing as crucial to the success of policing the new offence under s. 76.[163] He suggests that, *inter alia*, responses to domestic violence could be improved if England and Wales were to have one police force, as is the case in Scotland. This, Stark believes, would lead to 'greater local consistency, coordination, data sharing, review, and department accountability'.[164] He also highlights how police in Scotland have adopted an offender-centred approach, something which he believes could improve the success of s. 76. A change in police culture is also required.[165] Put simply, whilst the introduction of the offence of coercive control in England and Wales has been a 'progressive step'[166] and something that filled a legislative gap,[167] it is simply not enough to criminalise coercive control; success in protecting victims of domestic violence requires that those on the frontline—that is, police officers—are able to understand and thereby enforce the law.

5.1.2 Criminalising stalking

Of all intimate partner violence, stalking has been recognised as the most common in England and Wales,[168] with a partner or ex-partner as the most common perpetrator (in 39% of cases).[169] Until very recently, victims were forced to rely on the Protection from Harassment Act 1997; however, in 2012 the failures of this law were recognised by an independent inquiry: it noted that 'too many perpetrators fall through the net'.[170] Although the Protection from Harassment Act's key aim was to deal with stalking, the notion of harassment has not been defined.[171] This definitional void subsequently led to a wide range

---

[160] HMIC. *Increasingly Everyone's Business: A Progress Report on the Police Response to Domestic Abuse* (HMIC, 2015) 42.

[161] Bettinson, V. and Bishop, C. 'Is the Creation of a Discrete Offence of Coercive Control Necessary to Combat Domestic Violence?' (2015) 66 *Northern Ireland Legal Quarterly* 179.

[162] HMIC, *Increasingly Everyone's Business: A Progress Report on the Police Response to Domestic Abuse* (HMIC, 2015) 21 and 38.

[163] Stark, E. 'Policing Partner Abuse and the New Crime of Coercive Control in the United Kingdom' (2016) 8 *Family and Intimate Partner Violence Quarterly* 345, 347 and 351.

[164] Stark, E. 'Policing Partner Abuse and the New Crime of Coercive Control in the United Kingdom' (2016) 8 *Family and Intimate Partner Violence Quarterly* 345, 349.

[165] Stark, E. 'Policing Partner Abuse and the New Crime of Coercive Control in the United Kingdom' (2016) 8 *Family and Intimate Partner Violence Quarterly* 345, 350–1.

[166] Bettinson, V. 'Criminalising Coercive Control in Domestic Violence Cases: Should Scotland Follow the Path of England and Wales?' (2016) 3 *Criminal Law Review* 165, 166.

[167] Bettinson, V. and Bishop, C. 'Is the Creation of a Discrete Offence of Coercive Control Necessary to Combat Domestic Violence?' (2015) 66 *Northern Ireland Legal Quarterly* 179.

[168] Home Office, *Consultation on Stalking*, (Home Office, 2011) 5.

[169] Home Office, *Consultation on Stalking*, (Home Office, 2011) 5, citing Smith K. *et al Homicides, Firearm Offences and Intimate Violence 2009/10*, Home Office Statistical Bulletin 01/11 (Home Office, 2011).

[170] Justice Unions' Parliamentary Group. *Independent Parliamentary Inquiry into Stalking Law Reform: Main Recommendations and Findings* (Justice Unions' Parliamentary Group, 2012) 4.

[171] Harris, J. *An Evaluation of the Use and Effectiveness of the Protection from Harassment Act 1997* (Home Office, 2000) 1.

of disparate behaviour falling within the ambit of the Act, varying from disputes between neighbours to domestic violence.[172] It was argued by victims, in the inquiry, that stalking should be 'treated distinctly from other forms of harassment'.[173]

Problems also arose due the Protection from Harassment Act's differentiation between two offences. Under s. 2 of the Protection from Harassment Act 1997 it was an offence to engage in a course of conduct which amounts to harassment. This was a 'less' serious offence and, as it was summary, it could only be tried at the magistrates' court. By contrast, s.4 of the Protection from Harassment Act 1997 made it an offence to engage in a course of conduct which causes another person to fear that violence will be used against them. This was a more serious, triable either way offence. Unsurprisingly perhaps, evidence submitted to the independent inquiry demonstrated that the s. 4 offence was 'rarely used and when it was short custodial sentences were the norm, which were not long enough for treatment'.[174] Respondents to the Home Office's consultation on stalking commented upon the tendency of the CPS to downgrade prosecutions 'to a lesser offence in order to increase chances of obtaining a conviction'.[175] This was done to alleviate the difficulties associated with proving that the victim feared that violence would be used against them. Baroness Royall pointed to the 'overwhelming evidence from the independent inquiry . . . that the law is currently a barrier to just sentencing because the evidence required for stalking to be tried as an indictable offence is, in practice, too difficult to prove'.[176] Consequently, '[b]ecause of the near impossibility of proving fear of violence, perpetrator after perpetrator has been given ludicrously lenient sentences in the Magistrates' Court and has consistently broken restraining orders'.[177] The independent inquiry therefore proposed the following: render s. 2 of the Protection from Harassment Act 1997 a triable either way offence (that is an offence that can be tried either at the Magistrates' or the Crown court); abolish s. 4; and introduce a new stalking offence which contains a non-exhaustive list of stalking behaviour.[178] Such an approach would replicate the law in Scotland.[179]

Explicit stalking offences were subsequently introduced by s. 111 of the Protection of Freedoms Act 2012. Examples of what amounts to stalking were also provided under Protection from Harassment Act 1997. s. 2A, as introduced by s.111 of the Protection of Freedoms Act 2012 (England and Wales). These include: (a) following a person; (b) contacting, or attempting to contact, a person by any means; (c) publishing any statement or other material—(i) relating or purporting to relate to a person, or (ii) purporting to originate from a person; (d) monitoring the use by a person of the internet, email or any other form of electronic communication; (e) loitering in any place (whether public or private); (f) interfering with any property in the possession of a person; (g) watching or spying on a person.

The reforms of the Protection of Freedoms Act significantly mirrored much of the Protection from Harassment Act offences: in particular, the divide between the summary

---

[172] Justice Unions' Parliamentary Group. *Independent Parliamentary and Intimate Violence 2009/10* (Home Office, 2011) 15.

[173] Justice Unions' Parliamentary Group. *Independent Parliamentary and Intimate Violence 2009/10* (Home Office, 2011) 15.

[174] Justice Unions' Parliamentary Group. *Independent Parliamentary and Intimate Violence 2009/10* (Home Office, 2011) 12.

[175] Home Office. *Review of the Protection from Harassment Act 1997: Improving Protection for Victims of Stalking—Summary of Consultation Responses and Conclusions* (Home Office, 2012) 10.

[176] Protection of Freedoms Bill. House of Lords, Third Reading, 12 March 2012, col 21.

[177] Protection of Freedoms Bill. House of Lords, Third Reading, 12 March 2012, col. 22.

[178] Justice Unions' Parliamentary Group. *Independent Parliamentary Inquiry into Stalking Law Reform: Main Recommendations and Findings* (Justice Unions' Parliamentary Group, 2012), 30–1.

[179] See Criminal Justice and Licensing (Scotland) Act 2010 (Scot), s. 39.

and triable either way offences[180] whereby the Act brings in a 'lower level' (summary only) stalking offence under s. 2A and a triable either way offence under s. 4A, which is concerned with further impact upon the victim. As initially phrased, a victim had to, once again, demonstrate suffering from fear of violence, in order for the act to fall under the more serious offence. During the reform process, this was eventually changed to encompass stalking behaviour which caused the victim 'serious alarm or distress which has a substantial adverse effect on [their] usual day to day activities', in addition to fearing violence.[181] Concerns nevertheless remain, particularly with regard to the fact that the new s. 2A stalking offence is a summary offence. This replication of the Protection from Harassment Act's problematic divide has the potential to suggest once again that stalking is not a serious issue. It also fails to deal with concerns that the police and the CPS may more readily go for the summary offence in the magistrates' court in order to secure a conviction, which will consequently impact upon the sentence. Furthermore, a conviction for the serious offence requires that a victim changes their daily routine. By requiring the victim to alter his or her daily life, the focus shifts away from the nature of the conduct itself and towards the *victim's response* to the stalking conduct. Given the perpetuation of the 'ideal victim types' (i.e. stereotypical notions of what amounts to domestic violence and how a victim would react) and the manner in which the behaviour of an abused woman is frequently judged against such problematic notions, these concerns are indeed justified.

5.1.3 Criminalising forced marriage

In addition to criminalising the breach of a forced marriage protection order, the Anti-Social Behaviour, Crime and Policing Act 2014 introduced the specific offence of forced marriage, as outlined in s. 121. The criminalisation of forced marriage is, however, a thorny issue: there are arguments both for and against making forced marriage a criminal offence. Table 7.6 outlines the arguments as put forward by the House of Commons.[182]

Table 7.6 Arguments for and against criminalising forced marriage

For	Against
A new offence could have a deterrent effect and send a clear signal (domestically and abroad) that forcing a person to marry is unacceptable.	Victims may stop asking for help and/or applying for civil remedies due to a fear that their families will be prosecuted and/or because of the repercussions from failed prosecutions.
A new offence could empower young people to challenge their parents or families.	Parents may take their children abroad and force them to marry or hold them there, to avoid prosecution taking place in the UK.
A new offence could make it easier for the police, social services, and health services to identify that a person has been forced into marriage as existing legislation may not easily be linked with forced marriages.	An increased risk that prosecution, or threat of prosecution, may make it more difficult for victims to reconcile with their families.
A new offence would provide punishment to the perpetrator.	The existing behaviour may overlap with existing offences.

---

[180] Section 111 introduces into the Protection from Harassment Act 1997, s. 2A, the offence of stalking and s. 4A, the offence of stalking involving fear of violence or serious alarm or distress.

[181] Protection from Harassment Act, s. 4A(1)(a)(ii). See Protection of Freedoms Act 2012 (E/W), s. 111.

[182] House of Commons. *Forced Marriage* (House of Commons Library, 2015) 9–10.

CONTEXT 4: CRIMINALISATION OF FORCED MARRIAGE

A 2015–16 CPS report highlighted the rise of the rate of referrals from the police, the number of referrals charged, and the volume of prosecutions completed between 2014–15 and 2015–16. However, the report also highlighted a fall in the success rate of prosecutions: 63.0% in 2014–15 to 60.4% in 2015–16. It also reported on the gender of the defendant: perhaps unsurprisingly, of the 53 defendants, the majority were male (81.1%). In 2015–16, there were five prosecutions under the specific forced marriage offence and six for breach of a forced marriage protection order. The data includes all cases flagged as 'forced marriage' and not only those relating to the new specific criminal offence under s. 121 of the Anti-Social Behaviour, Crime and Policing Act 2014.[183] In relation to this specific offence, the report highlighted an issue with prosecution: of the five defendants prosecuted in 2015–16, not one was convicted. This issue arose due to victim withdrawal and refusal to attend the hearings.[184] There was greater success in prosecuting the offence of a breach of a Forced Marriage Protection Order—of six cases prosecuted, one defendant was successfully prosecuted and another was convicted of more serious offences; two cases were unsuccessful due to victim issues (one case had two defendants) and another was unsuccessful at trial.[185] Issues with attrition and conviction rates could be, in part, due to the relative recentness of this offence.

As Gaffney-Rhys highlights, in identifying a marriage as 'forced' for the purposes of s. 121, there can be difficulty distinguishing between consent to marriage given freely and consent to marriage given out of duress or a feeling of obligation. Indeed, 'consent and coercion are not binaries; the social context within which consent is constructed is crucial to understanding coercive constraints'.[186] This raises a significant issue for families: when pressure is placed on an individual to marry, the family, and in particular the parents, may not be aware that their actions constitute force. This is particularly so given the prevalence of obedience within certain communities.[187] Despite difficulties, the law has been ostensibly more successful in England and Wales than in Denmark (where no cases have reached the courts since the criminalisation of forced marriage in 2008).[188] Whilst the offence of forced marriage may go some way to protecting victims, problems nevertheless remain: thought needs to be given as to how these offences may be prosecuted and questions could be raised regarding the utility of this specific criminal offence.

5.2 Domestic violence protection notices and orders

Domestic violence protection notices and orders ('DVPN' and 'DVPO') were implemented throughout England and Wales in 2014. Under Crime and Security Act 2010, s. 24, a senior officer may issue a DVPN if (s)he reasonably believes that the perpetrator 'has been violent towards or has threatened violence towards, an associated person' and the DVPN 'is necessary to protect that person from violence or a threat of violence'. Whilst

---

[183] CPS, *Violence against Women and Girls: Crime Report 2015–16* (CPS, 2015–16) 8–9. See also 66–7.

[184] CPS, *Violence against Women and Girls: Crime Report 2015–16* (CPS, 2015–16) 67.

[185] CPS, *Violence against Women and Girls: Crime Report 2015–16* (CPS, 2015–16) 67.

[186] Anitha, S. and Gill, A.K. 'A Moral Panic? The Problematization of Forced Marriage in British Newspapers' (2015) 21 *Violence Against Women* 1123, 1124.

[187] Gaffney-Rhys, R. 'The Criminalisation of Forced Marriage in England and Wales: One Year On' [2015] *Family Law* 1382–3.

[188] Gaffney-Rhys, R. 'The Criminalisation of Forced Marriage in England and Wales: One Year On' [2015] *Family Law* 1384.

the officer must consider, amongst other things, the victim's opinion regarding the DVPN, one can be issued without her consent. Once issued, the officer must apply to the magistrates' court within 48 hours for a DVPO. In addition to prohibiting molestation (which is mandatory), both the notice and order may prohibit the perpetrator from entering any relevant premises if he cohabits with the victim. A breach of a DVPO is contempt of court.

Drawing upon similar provisions in Austria, Germany, and Switzerland, these orders were considered necessary due to a 'dangerous "gap" in the criminal and civil justice systems'.[189] As the orders are taken out by the police, as opposed to the victim, and indeed do not require the victim's involvement, they provide 'police led immediate protection, where, currently, immediate protection does not exist to enable victims of domestic violence to have the time and support needed to consider their future options, including longer-term civil injunctions'.[190] Without a doubt, such measures are to be welcomed, and the pilot indicated that the orders resulted in reduced re-victimisation when compared with arrests where 'no further action' was taken.[191] The Home Office are taking further steps to improve the use of and enforcement of DVPOs, such as working with the Ministry of Justice to improve guidance for magistrates. Furthermore, the College of Policing launched a training package on domestic violence protection orders for police officers.[192]

Although these are most certainly positive steps, issues nevertheless remain. Both Refuge and the Fawcett Society cautioned that in Austria, Germany, and Switzerland, the equivalent measures are 'linked to wider systems of intervention',[193] hence their effect may be somewhat limited in England and Wales. During the pilot 'no perpetrator had engaged, via a DVPO, in interventions designed to end their abusive behaviour',[194] although this may be due to the fact that programmes were not available.[195] Their application also relies on police involvement, which is at times lacking: the pilot evaluation indicated varying levels of police officer support, with a minority of officers considering the order to be disproportionate, particularly in cases involving what was perceived to be '"low-level" violence'.[196] This may lead to minimisation where there is no serious physical assault and may also lead to coercive control being ignored. The HMIC 2015 report also highlighted issues with the enforcement of DVPOs: action was lacking when orders were breached, impacting upon victims and their confidence in the criminal process.[197] Staff also exhibited a

[189] House of Commons Library. *Crime and Security Bill: Bill No 3 2009/10*, Research Paper 09/97 (House of Commons Library 2009) 28. See also ACPO, *Tackling Perpetrators of Violence Against Women and Girls* (ACPO, 2009).

[190] Home Office. *Impact Assessment of Domestic Violence Protection Orders (DVPO)—A Pilot Scheme* (Home Office, 2009) 1.

[191] Home Office. *Evaluation of the Pilot of Domestic Violence Protection Orders*, Research Report 76 (Home Office, 2013) 6.

[192] Home Office. *Domestic Violence Protection Orders (DVPO): One Year On—A Home Office Assessment of National Roll-Out* (Home Office, 2016).

[193] Refuge. *Together We Can End Violence Against Women And Girls: A Consultation Paper* (Refuge, 2009) cited in House of Commons Library, *Crime and Security Bill: Bill No 3 2009/10*, Research Paper 09/97 (House of Commons Library 2009) 32. See also Fawcett Society. *Consultation Response from the Fawcett Society to HM Government Together We Can End Violence Against Women and Girls* (Fawcett Society, London: 2009) cited in House of Commons Library, *Crime and Security Bill: Bill No 3 2009/10*, Research Paper 09/97 (House of Commons Library 2009) 32; Burton, M. 'Emergency Barring Orders in Domestic Violence Cases: What Can England and Wales Learn From Other European Countries?' (2015) 27 *Child and Family Law Quarterly* 25.

[194] Home Office, *Evaluation of the Pilot of Domestic Violence Protection Orders*, Research Report 76 (Home Office, 2013) 5.

[195] Home Office. *Evaluation of the Pilot of Domestic Violence Protection Orders*, Research Report 76 (Home Office, 2013) 5.

[196] Home Office. *Evaluation of the Pilot of Domestic Violence Protection Orders*, Research Report 76 (Home Office, 2013) 20.

[197] HMIC. *Increasingly Everyone's Business: A Progress Report on the Police Response to Domestic Abuse* (HMIC, 2015) 18.

lack of knowledge on how to obtain DVPOs and other civil orders. This, too, was seen to have a potentially negative impact on the confidence of victims in the criminal process.[198] There are further difficulties within the court, particularly in terms of the level of evidence required before an order was granted, which was often on-par with that required for a criminal charge.[199]

The aim of DVPOs not requiring the involvement of the victim also seemed not to have been met: some victims had been compelled to attend court.[200] Victims may also have to apply for a civil protection order as a DVPO lasts a maximum of 28 days. An alternative solution, in England and Wales, might be to bring into force s. 60 of the Family Law Act 1996, discussed earlier, under which a third party is allowed to apply for a civil protection order on behalf of a victim.

5.3 A domestic violence disclosure scheme

Another approach which has recently been implemented in England and Wales is the domestic violence disclosure scheme, under which individuals had a 'right to ask' and 'a right to know' about another person's history of domestic violence. Whereas with the former, the member of the public applies to the police for a disclosure, with the latter, the police take the proactive decision to disclose information to a potential victim.[201] The proactive decision to make a disclosure can be made where the police or a partner agency come across information that indicates that an individual may be at risk of domestic violence. This would, however, require that the police or a partner agency become aware of this information,[202] and abusers are now being required to inform the police when they get a new partner.[203] The rationale behind these schemes focused upon enabling 'a potential victim to make choices about her safety and that of her children'.[204] To this end, the scheme introduced a 'recognised and consistent procedure'[205] for the police to exercise their existing common law powers to 'disclose information relating to previous convictions or charges to A where there is a pressing need for disclosure of the information concerning B's history in order to prevent further crime'.[206] Prima facie, such an approach has received support from those police and partner agencies who participated in the pilot.[207] However, disclosure rates varied amongst the pilot areas: the assessment suggests that this may be a result of the different interpretations given to the phrase 'pressing need', which was considered by practitioners to be unclear and too subjective.[208]

As is well documented, many violent men are initially very loving and charming. The abuse does not necessarily commence from the beginning of the relationship and many

---

[198] HMIC. *Increasingly Everyone's Business: A Progress Report on the Police Response to Domestic Abuse* (HMIC, 2015) 41.

[199] HMIC. *Increasingly Everyone's Business: A Progress Report on the Police Response to Domestic Abuse* (HMIC, 2015) 21.

[200] HMIC. *Increasingly Everyone's Business: A Progress Report on the Police Response to Domestic Abuse* (HMIC, 2015) 22.

[201] Home Office. *Domestic Violence Disclosure Scheme (DVDS) Guidance* (Home Office, 2016).

[202] Home Office. *Domestic Violence Disclosure Scheme (DVDS) Guidance* (Home Office, 2016) 5.

[203] Walker, M, *Domestic abuser must tell police if he gets a new girlfriend*, The Guardian, 4 April 2017. Available at: https://www.theguardian.com/society/2017/apr/04/domestic-abuser-must-tell-police-if-he-gets-a-new-girlfriend, accessed 25 September 2017.

[204] ACPO. *Tackling Perpetrators of Violence against Women and Girls* (ACPO, 2009) para. 2.1.5; see Home Office, *Domestic Violence Disclosure Scheme—A Consultation: Summary of Responses* (Home Office, 2012) 3.

[205] Home Office. *Domestic Violence Disclosure Scheme (DVDS) Pilot Assessment* (Home Office, 2013) 9.

[206] Home Office. *Domestic Violence Disclosure Scheme—A Consultation: Summary of Responses* (Home Office, 2012) 6.

[207] Home Office. *Domestic Violence Disclosure Scheme (DVDS) Pilot Assessment* (Home Office, 2013).

[208] Home Office. *Domestic Violence Disclosure Scheme (DVDS) Pilot Assessment* (Home Office, 2013) 18–20.

women may be unaware of the violent tendencies of a new partner. However, concerns need to be noted. The move towards the introduction of such a scheme followed the murder of Clare Wood, killed by her ex-partner, George Appleton, who had a history of domestic violence.[209] Her family commented that she would not have become involved with Appleton had she been aware of his record. However, the Independent Police Complaints Commission (IPCC) report clearly highlights numerous failures by the Greater Manchester Police (GMP) in their dealings with both Clare Wood and George Appleton.[210] This suggests that the state's response to domestic violence must also be improved: more must be done to protect those who are at risk. This was, indeed, highlighted by police and support workers in the assessment of the pilot scheme when they expressed concerns as to whether 'an appropriate level of support could always be provided if the scheme was rolled out'.[211] As one support worker noted: 'If we delivered a disclosure without a support worker there, we would be "setting the potential victim up to fail"'.[212] Some of the pilot areas opted against active publication of the scheme due to fear of inadequate resources should there be a high number of applicants.[213] Hence, even if potential victims take steps to find out more about their partner's (potential) history of domestic violence, this does not solve the entire problem: there must also be adequate protection for those who may be or are victims of domestic violence. The pilot assessment also highlights that a non-disclosure does not necessarily translate into the absence of risk.[214] It was thus also felt important to ensure the provision of support services to individuals in cases of non-disclosure.[215] This is particularly noteworthy given that a Home Office assessment conducted in 2016 demonstrated out of 4,724 applications, disclosures were made in a total of 1,938 cases.[216] Further caution was noted in relation to the remit of the scheme: whilst it was potentially 'another important "tool in the box" for professionals', it should not be considered to be a '"catch-all" for domestic abuse protection work'.[217]

 DEBATE 5: DOES THE INTRODUCTION OF THE DOMESTIC VIOLENCE DISCLOSURE SCHEME 'RESPONSIBILISE' THE VICTIM?

During the piloting of Clare's Law, the Association of Chief Police Offices (ACPO) commented: 'A right to know and a right to ask will empower women to make informed decisions to protect themselves and their children when getting involved with a new partner.'[218] Accordingly, it is contemplated that the provision of information regarding a partner's abusive past will enable and empower women to adopt appropriate protective measures. However, this

---

[209] See IPCC, *IPCC Independent Investigation: Greater Manchester Police Contact With Clare Wood Prior to Her Death* (IPCC, 2010).

[210] IPCC, *IPCC Independent Investigation: Greater Manchester Police Contact With Clare Wood Prior to Her Death* (IPCC, 2010).

[211] Home Office. *Domestic Violence Disclosure Scheme (DVDS) Pilot Assessment* (Home Office, 2013) 15.

[212] Support Worker, Gwent, as cited in Home Office. *Domestic Violence Disclosure Scheme (DVDS) Pilot Assessment* (Home Office, 2013).

[213] Home Office. *Domestic Violence Disclosure Scheme (DVDS) Pilot Assessment* (Home Office, 2013) 22.

[214] Home Office. *Domestic Violence Disclosure Scheme (DVDS) Pilot Assessment* (Home Office, 2013) 19.

[215] Home Office. *Domestic Violence Disclosure Scheme (DVDS) Pilot Assessment* (Home Office, 2013) 20–1.

[216] Home Office. *Domestic Violence Disclosure Scheme (DVDS): One Year On—Home Office Assessment of National Roll-out* (Home Office, 2016) 4.

[217] Home Office. *Domestic Violence Disclosure Scheme (DVDS): One Year On—Home Office Assessment of National Roll-out* (Home Office, 2016) 15.

[218] See: https://www.gov.uk/government/news/new-domestic-violence-disclosure-scheme-piloted-by-police, accessed 13 July 2017.

empowerment discourse fails to acknowledge that victims of domestic abuse face significant risks and encounter substantial barriers when attempting to leave a violent relationship. In contrast, it has been argued that as opposed to promoting victim empowerment, Clare's Law problematically amounts to a 'policy of responsibilization',[219] which is 'one of the distinctive techniques of governing in the neo-liberal welfare state'.[220] Neo-liberal governance requires that citizens are 'active [and] . . . self-regulate according to the norms of risk management'.[221] Under this approach, citizenship and state protection are only afforded to those who engage in 'responsible' practices, while those who do not are left without protection and support. Significantly, this approach also individualises problems and does not address the myriad ways in which the state frequently fails to deal with male violence against women.[222] It can be argued that the 'right to ask' and 'right to know' scheme places responsibility on the victim to protect themselves from domestic violence, rather than compelling the state and its agencies (such as the police) to better respond to and better protect victims. Indeed, it has been argued that, conversely, the disclosure scheme may 'promote police inaction', as authorities assume that 'post-disclosure, the situation is being managed by the victim themselves'.[223]

In addition, those who fail to engage in 'a right to know' or adopt an 'inappropriate' response to any information they may receive may find themselves increasingly judged and consequently at greater risk in a system that is already prone to victim-blaming. There is therefore scepticism with regard to how much this scheme will effectively protect people from domestic violence; perhaps it is more important for police to take seriously and respond effectively to allegations of domestic violence. For example, the IPCC found failings in the way in which Greater Manchester Police had dealt with Clare Wood in the months preceding her murder—she had reported Appleton to the police for criminal damage, harassment, threats to kill, and sexual assault. Consequently, it was found that Greater Manchester Police could have done more to protect her. Significantly, the extent to which the disclosure scheme is an effective response to the problems identified by the IPCC has been disputed. As Fitz-Gibbon and Walklate argue:

> The IPCC review points to the important of ensuring adequate support for women attempting to extricate themselves from high-risk relationships, and the need for better risk assessment and case management at the frontline police stage. Clare's Law arguably addresses neither of these critical issues but rather, in diverting police resources away from frontline case management may exacerbate failing identified in the IPCC review.[224]

This raises a number of questions: should individuals be held responsible for their victimisation? Should the state be required to do more to tackle the causes of domestic violence on a macro and/or meso level?

---

[219] Carline, A. and Easteal, P. *Shades of Grey—Domestic and Sexual Violence Against Women: Law Reform and Society* (Routledge, 2014); Fitz-Gibbon, K. and Walklate, S. 'The Efficacy of Clare's Law in Domestic Violence Law Reform in England and Wales' (2017) 17 *Criminology and Criminal Justice* 284. See also Duggan, M. 'Using Victims' Voices to Prevent Violence Against Women: A Critique' (2012) 10 *British Journal of Community Justice* 25.

[220] Scoular, J. and O'Neill, M. 'Regulating Prostitution: Social Inclusion, Responsibilization and the Politics of Prostitution Reform' (2007) 47 *British Journal of Criminology* 764, 771.

[221] Scoular, J. and O'Neill, M. 'Regulating Prostitution: Social Inclusion, Responsibilization and the Politics of Prostitution Reform' (2007) 47 *British Journal of Criminology* 764, 772.

[222] Scoular, J. and O'Neill, M. 'Regulating Prostitution: Social Inclusion, Responsibilization and the Politics of Prostitution Reform' (2007) 47 *British Journal of Criminology* 764, 772.

[223] Fitz-Gibbon, K. and Walklate, S. 'The Efficacy of Clare's Law in Domestic Violence Law Reform in England and Wales' (2017) 17 *Criminology and Criminal Justice* 284, 295.

[224] Fitz-Gibbon, K. and Walklate, S. 'The Efficacy of Clare's Law in Domestic Violence Law Reform in England and Wales' (2017) 17 *Criminology and Criminal Justice* 284, 291.

6. The potential of joint domestic violence courts

Domestic violence is a complex problem involving psychological and emotional violence as well as physical violence. Victims are often reluctant to come forward because of their relationship with the perpetrator and the impact that criminal proceedings may have on any children involved. Victims may also be vulnerable and may feel intimidated, particularly as a result of the abuse. They may find the court process traumatic and this may add to their reluctance to pursue a case in either the criminal courts or the civil courts. A separate court system requires that the victim undergoes both criminal and civil proceedings should s/he wish to avail of remedies in both courts. The complexity of the problem of domestic violence, which encompasses different types of harm and different legal matters, requires a multidimensional approach to domestic violence in the courts. This section will follow on from the previous by exploring the potential of joint specialist domestic violence courts, which deal with both family and criminal law remedies. This will include a discussion of the concept of 'therapeutic jurisprudence'.

6.1 Specialist domestic violence courts and fast track systems

A report produced in 2004 on behalf of the CPS highlighted the need for specialist domestic violence courts (SDVCs) and also recognised that the effectiveness of specialist courts needed to be addressed within the context of the dynamics of domestic violence.[225] The report identified how the establishment of specialist domestic violence courts would enable domestic violence to be tackled within a multi-agency framework and could be designed with the specific needs of domestic violence victims in mind. The government's White Paper for criminal justice reform 'Justice for All' stated:

> Specialisation could increase the throughput of cases, secure more effective outcomes, allow more convenient and less burdensome arrangements to be made for victims, witnesses and lawyers, and use court time more effectively. But it does depend on having sufficient cases to justify the special arrangements, and on the availability of suitably trained judges, magistrates, and staff.[226]

In addition, the White Paper also stated that victims should be at the heart of the system:

> We will put the victims, who suffer most from crime, at the heart of the system and do everything we can to support and inform them, and we will respect and protect the witnesses without whom the CJS would not function.[227]

Five specialist courts were established in Cardiff, Derby, Leeds, West London, and Wolverhampton, and each of these operated at magistrates' court level.[228] In 2011, the specialist courts were extended to include: Wales, East Midlands, Eastern, London, Merseyside/Cheshire, North East, North West, South East, South West, Thames and Chiltern, Wessex, West Midlands, and Yorkshire and Humberside.[229] In lieu of a specialist court, cases will be heard in the standard magistrates or Crown Court, as appropriate.

In addition to dealing with the running of the trial and organising pre-trial hearings and fast-tracking cases (often dedicating a specific day or time for domestic violence

---

[225] Cook, D. *et al Evaluations of Specialist Domestic Violence Courts/Fast Track Systems* (CPS, 2004).

[226] Home Office. *Justice for All* (White Paper, Cm 5563, 2002) para 4.45, 78.

[227] Home Office. *Justice for All* (White Paper, Cm 5563, 2002) para 0.2, 13.

[228] Cook, D. *et al Evaluations of Specialist Domestic Violence Courts/Fast Track Systems* (CPS, 2004) 4.

[229] CPS. *Specialist Domestic Violence Courts,* (CPS, 2013). Available at: https://www.cps.gov.uk/publications/equality/vaw/sdvc.html, accessed 17 January 2014.

cases to be heard), the specialist courts also offer specialist advocacy support and/ or police domestic violence officers at court to provide relevant information and to advise and support victims. They may also provide specially trained magistrates, police officers, and prosecutors, and may ensure that there are separate entrances, exits, and waiting areas to ensure that victims do not come into contact with the perpetrator or related persons.[230] The advocacy support involves: reporting progress to the victims, informing courts on behalf of victims, supporting victims, coordinating information sharing, and the development of protocols and engaging in outreach in the community.

The report did recognise that victim withdrawals continued to be a problem because of the nature of the offence—however research also indicated that a lower proportion of women are likely to retract if they feel properly supported and fully informed. The report notes that victim withdrawal should not be used to measure the success of the specialist courts, and what should be concentrated upon is the ability to build cases using evidence other than that from the victim. One area of concern was the way in which evidence was collected: in domestic violence cases, there are many lost opportunities for evidence collection. Good practice to be encouraged included the use of medical statements, forensic evidence, and photographic evidence.[231] Other important recommendations include developing specialist arrangements for all trials, particularly in the Crown Court and the provision of specially trained, dedicated prosecutors. Links with civil courts should also be made.

A 2008 report highlighted a number of key factors in the success of SDVCs. With regard to the aim of bringing perpetrators to justice, the report highlighted how effective systems for identifying cases, good training and dedicated staff, cluster or cluster and fast-track court listings, strong multi-agency partnerships, and perpetrator programmes could improve the success of a SDVC. It also highlighted how success in supporting and ensuring the safety of victims could be improved or achieved: this was done by, *inter alia*, a focus on engaging with victims and safe court facilities.[232]

6.2 Joint specialist courts

Whereas the specialist courts in this jurisdiction are only concerned with criminal issues, other jurisdictions have domestic violence courts which deal with both civil and criminal remedies. Specialist domestic violence courts have developed across the USA in both the civil and criminal sphere, with the first joint court established in Washington in 1998.[233] Here it was felt that the traditional judicial response to domestic violence was not adequately protecting victims: although they had pro-arrest and pro-prosecution policies, victims were put in jeopardy when the court response was uneven. Thus, the courts now bring together all criminal appearances whilst also dealing with family law remedies. These courts were seen to incorporate a 'therapeutic' approach.[234]

Overall the main benefit of such courts is that they are a:

> . . . one stop shop; a single entry point for civil and criminal remedies and a place where victims of domestic violence may obtain all forms of relief from a judge who is

[230] CPS. *The Prosecution of Domestic Violence Cases* (CPS, 2014) 44.

[231] Cook, D. *et al Evaluations of Specialist Domestic Violence Courts/Fast Track Systems* (CPS, 2004) 7–9.

[232] Home Office. *Justice with Safety: Specialist Domestic Violence Courts Review 2007–08* (Home Office, 2008) 6.

[233] Cook, D. *et al Evaluations of Specialist Domestic Violence Courts/Fast Track Systems* (CPS, 2004) 41.

[234] Cook, D. *et al Evaluations of Specialist Domestic Violence Courts/Fast Track Systems* (CPS, 2004) 42.

knowledgeable about domestic violence . . . [T]his may prevent frustration to victims caused by inconsistent and insensitive judicial rulings . . .[235]

6.2.1 The need for joint courts: the case of *Lomas v Parle*

The need for joint courts was recognised by the judiciary in the case of *Lomas v Parle*.[236] In this case the husband had been arrested numerous times for assault and had convictions for both assault and harassment. There were numerous breaches of bail and non-molestation orders; he continually flouted the court orders and used leniency as an opportunity to continue his abuse. He was committed for contempt of court and his sentence was increased from four months to eight months. Thorpe LJ recognised the 'unsatisfactory nature of the present interface between the criminal and family courts in such cases', adding the current approach was 'expensive, wasteful of resources and time-consuming'.[237] Furthermore, it was recognised that the disconnected approach between criminal law and family law courts could generate stress for the victim as she would be required to move between courts when seeking protection from her husband.

6.2.2 An integrated domestic violence court

An integrated domestic violence court (IDVC) was set up in Croydon in October 2006 as a means of bringing together, at magistrates' level, criminal issues and concurrent Children Act 1989 or civil injunction proceedings. The IDVC sought to build upon the success of the SDVCs, whilst also seeking to improve upon the current model by building links with civil family courts and addressing issues of information-sharing. In recognition of these issues, the IDVC was seen to be a 'logical extension' whereby specially trained personnel could be present, and civil and criminal elements could be dealt with in the same setting. The American model was viewed as an ideal system upon which to base the pilot IDVC: this SDVC model emerged in the US criminal court system in the mid-1990s and, by 2008, was widely established throughout America. The IDVC adopted the SDVC model but also built upon this by incorporating civil elements. A transplant of an American model is not, of course, without its problems, particularly given the differences between the two jurisdictions, most notably, a lack of equivalent American human rights legislation which prevents criminal charges after civil charges are made, and the higher prevalence of plea bargaining in the USA. The US model was based upon the concept of 'therapeutic jurisprudence', which 'focuses on the extent to which the legal process promotes the psychological and physiological well-being of those it affects'.[238] The court, rather than finding guilt or innocence, attempts to work with relevant agencies to address the family's problems. This problem-solving approach seeks to counteract the issue with repeat appearances at court, as highlighted in the *Lomas*[239] case.

 CONTEXT 5: THE INTEGRATED DOMESTIC VIOLENCE COURT—AN EVALUATION

- During the first year, the IDVC only dealt with five cases. The expectation was 75 cases.
- The small number made it difficult to assess whether the court had met its aims.
- The small numbers may have been due to either to a lack of cases with overlapping issues or because the criteria was too restrictive.

---

[235] Cook, D. *et al Evaluations of Specialist Domestic Violence Courts/Fast Track Systems* (CPS, 2004) 42.
[236] [2003] EWCA Civ 1804.   [237] [2003] EWCA Civ 1804, at [42].
[238] Hester, M., Pearce, J., and Westmarland, N. *Early Evaluation of the Integrated Domestic Violence Court, Croydon*, Ministry of Justice Research Series 18/08 (Ministry of Justice, 2008) 3.
[239] [2003] EWCA Civ 1804.

- Some respondents considered the lack of cases to indicate that the need did not exist for a joint court. However, others expressed commitment to the development of IDVCs. [240]

The researchers urged, *inter alia*, that cases should be tracked through the courts to ascertain whether there was sufficient overlap to provide justification for continuing with the IDVC. They felt that, in line with the work of the American courts, there *was* need for the IDVC but argued that cases may simply not be reaching the court.[241]

6.3 Therapeutic jurisprudence

As noted earlier, the American domestic violence court model was founded on the principle of therapeutic jurisprudence.[242] Therapeutic jurisprudence, as Wexler highlights, explores how the law can act as a therapeutic agent. In particular, it examines how the law, and more specifically, the law in action, can impact on the individual's emotional and psychological well-being. The focus within therapeutic jurisprudence is on the human aspects of the law: it approaches the law as having the potential to produce certain behaviours and outcomes. Therapeutic jurisprudence urges scholars and practitioners to find ways in which the law can be applied in a more therapeutic manner, whilst also respecting other values such as justice and due process. It involves specialist courts adjudicating on specific issues and highlights the importance of legal roles: the manner in which justice actors behave during the process can impact upon the outcome.[243] In the case of domestic violence, the treatment of the victim or the perpetrator by the judge, prosecutor, or police could impact upon recovery (in the case of the victim) or recidivism (in the case of the perpetrator).

Taking the example of criminal trials, the fact that the prosecutor is employed by the state and not by the victim can result in the victim being sidelined. In particular, as domestic violence can be viewed as a crime against the state, the voice of the victim is often ignored or forgotten.[244] In many instances, the focus of the case results in a silencing of the victim. Within a framework of therapeutic jurisprudence, the justice system could adopt a victim-centred model with, at its centre, a focus on empowerment.[245] A victim or client-centred model employed at different stages of the court process, such as one adopted in the SDVCs, could provide a form of therapeutic jurisprudence for the victim by improving the victim's well-being.[246] Increased cohesion between the criminal and civil courts could have an even greater therapeutic effect for the victim and, with greater support during the judicial process(es), victims may be better assisted when facing abuse and violence from their partners.

---

[240] Hester, M., Pearce, J., and Westmarland, N. *Early Evaluation of the Integrated Domestic Violence Court, Croydon*, Ministry of Justice Research Series 18/08 (Ministry of Justice, 2008) 39.

[241] Hester, M., Pearce, J., and Westmarland, N. *Early Evaluation of the Integrated Domestic Violence Court, Croydon*, Ministry of Justice Research Series 18/08 (Ministry of Justice, 2008) 39.

[242] Winick, B.J. 'Therapeutic Jurisprudence and Problem Solving Courts' (2002) 30 *Fordham Urban Law Journal* 1055, 1057.

[243] Wexler, D.B. 'Therapeutic Jurisprudence: An Overview' (2000) 17 *Thomas M. Cooley Law Review* 125, 125–6.

[244] Esptein, D. 'Effective Intervention in Domestic Violence Cases: Rethinking the Roles of Prosecutors, Judges, and the Court System' (1999) 11 *Yale Journal of Law and Feminism* 3, 17.

[245] Hartley, C.C. 'A Therapeutic Jurisprudence Approach to the Trial Process in Domestic Violence Felony Trials' (2003) 9 *Violence against Women* 410, 418–19.

[246] Hartley, C.C. 'A Therapeutic Jurisprudence Approach to the Trial Process in Domestic Violence Felony Trials' (2003) 9 *Violence against Women* 410, 418–19. See also Bennett Cattaneo L. and Goodman, L.A. 'Positive Experiences Within the Justice System can Improve a Domestic Violence Victim's Wellbeing and Mental Health' (2010) 25 *Journal of Interpersonal Violence* 481, 497.

SUMMARY

1. How should domestic violence been defined?
   - The phrase domestic violence and abuse relates to abusive behaviour that takes place within the home and/or a familial relationship. However, the terms used and the precise definition has evolved considerably over the years. Nevertheless, contentions remain, and the prefix of 'domestic' can be criticised for minimising and dismissing the violence suffered by victims.
   - Far from being academic, understanding what amounts to domestic violence is key to understanding the difficulties many victims face when applying for legal remedies. It is now accepted that domestic violence and abuse covers a wide range of behaviour. It is by no means limited to physical violence, but also encompasses psychological, emotional, and financial abuse.
   - The government's most recent definition recognises that 'coercive' and 'controlling' behaviour amounts to domestic violence. It is also important to highlight that abusive conduct may endure, and even escalate, beyond the end of a relationship. In addition, forcing a person into marriage also amounts to a form of domestic abuse.

2. To what extent is domestic violence a gendered phenomenon?
   - The statistics indicate that domestic violence is gendered: the majority of victims are female, and the majority of perpetrators are male. This is not to say that men are not victims of domestic violence; rather, it highlights that it is a problem that overwhelmingly impacts upon women.
   - However, the term 'domestic violence' is gender neutral, and it can be argued that this obscures the gender dynamics of violence. This gender-neutral perspective has developed alongside research which maintains that women are just as violent as men.
   - In contrast, scholars who adopt a 'violence against women' perspective highlight the importance of the wider context within which women tend to use violence. It has been argued that women tend to use violence in retaliation or self-defence. It is also less frequent and severe than that inflicted on women by men.

3. Should the concept of 'associated person' more accurately reflect the reality of domestic violence?
   - The notion of the 'associated person' is a key concept within family law. In order to apply for a non-molestation order, the applicant must be associated in some way to the respondent. With regards to occupation orders, an entitled applicant under s. 33 may likewise only apply for an order against a person with whom they are associated.
   - It can be argued, however, that the 'associated person' requirement conflicts with the aim of providing protection to those who are in need. However, the Law Commission highlighted that the 'special nature' of family life justified the creation of a discrete remedy, which would only be available to those who are intimately connected.

- The concept has been reformed over the years to recognise various forms of relationships, in particular same-sex couples and those who are in a serious relationship, but have not cohabited. However, at the same time it was been argued that the definition is overly broad, and encompasses a very wide range of relationships, which fails to recognise the gendered nature of domestic violence.

4. Should the breach of a family law order be a criminal offence?
   - In order to be effective, it is important that family law orders can be enforced by the court. Initially, a breach of an order could only be punished as contempt of court, and consequently the court had limited sentencing powers.
   - Relatedly, a respondent could only be arrested for breaching an order if the court attached a power of arrest to an order. Without this, an applicant would be required to apply to the court for an arrest warrant, at a moment when they were particularly vulnerable.
   - The breach of a non-molestation and a forced marriage protection order is now a criminal offence, a move which has been overwhelmingly supported by victims' groups. However, others have argued that this amounts to a blurring of the criminal and civil law, and the creation of 'personal criminal offences'.
   - Conversely, criminalising the breach of an order may effectively reduce the range of options available to, and disempower, a victim, particularly if they do not wish their partner/family member to be criminalised. It may be that the family will suffer negative consequences, such as the loss of income, if a perpetrator is criminalised. A delicate balancing act is required.

5. Does the introduction of the domestic violence disclosure scheme 'responsibilise' the victim?
   - The domestic violence disclosure scheme was introduced following the death of Clare Wood, who was killed by her ex-partner George Appleton. Under this scheme, an individual has a right to be informed if their partner has a conviction for a relevant domestic violence offence.
   - There is, however, scepticism with regards to the extent to which this scheme will be effective in protecting people from domestic violence. Further, it should not be assumed that a non-disclosure translates into the absence of risk.
   - It can be argued that the scheme individualises the problem of domestic violence and constructs the individual as responsible for managing the risk posed by domestic violence, as opposed to the state and the police. In contrast, it is perhaps more important to improve the police responses to domestic violence.

Further Reading

BETTINSON, V. 'Criminalising Coercive Control in Domestic Violence Cases: Should Scotland follow the path of England and Wales?' (2016) 3 *Criminal Law Review* 168
- Provides a critical analysis of the development of the offence of coercive control in England and Wales and considers the extent to which a similar offence should be introduced in Scotland.

BURTON, M. 'Emergency Barring Orders in Domestic Violence Cases: What can England and Wales Learn From Other European Countries?' (2015) 27 *Child and Family Law Quarterly* 25
- Provides a critical evaluation of the introduction of the domestic violence protection notices and orders.

CARLINE, A. and EASTEAL, P. *Shades of Grey—Domestic and Sexual Violence Against Women: Law Reform and Society* (Routledge, 2014)
- Provides a critical analysis of the legal and policy responses to domestic and sexual violence in England and Wales and Australia.

DOBASH, P.R. and DOBASH, R.E. 'Women's Violence to Men in Intimate Relationships: Working on a Puzzle' (2004) 44 *British Journal of Criminology* 324
- Drawing upon a quantitative and qualitative research project, this article examines the extent to which domestic violence is gendered.

FITZ-GIBBON, K. and WALKLATE, S. 'The Efficacy of Clare's Law in Domestic Violence Law Reform in England and Wales' (2017) 17 *Criminology and Criminal Justice* 284
- Provides a critical examination of the introduction of the Domestic Violence Disclosure Scheme: 'Clare's Law'.

IDRISS, M.M. 'Forced Marriages—The Need for Criminalisation' (2015) 9 *Criminal Law Review* 689
- Examines the arguments for and against the criminalization of forced marriages.

MUSGROVE, A. and GRAVES, N. 'The Domestic Violence, Crime and Victims Act 2004: Relevant or "Removed" Legislation?' (2008) 29 *Journal of Social Welfare and Family Law* 233
- Drawing upon a case study involving women who suffered domestic violence victims in the Midlands, this article examines the extent to which the Domestic Violence, Crime and Victims Act 2004 appropriately responds to the needs of victims.

STARK, E. *Coercive Control: The Entrapment of Women in Personal Life* (OUP, 2007)
- Develops the concept of 'coercive control' in order to illustrate how domestic violence involves a pattern of controlling behaviours.

8

Legal Parenthood and Parental Responsibility

Kirsty Horsey

LEARNING OBJECTIVES

After reading this chapter you will be able to:

- Identify the common law rules and presumptions that determine legal parenthood;
- Understand how legal parenthood is awarded following the use of different forms of assisted conception, and the differing rules that apply to each of these;
- Critically analyse different concepts and understandings of parenthood and the way these inform and underpin legal rules;
- Appreciate who may obtain parental responsibility for a child, and its impact and importance.

DEBATES

After reading this chapter you should be equipped to discuss your opinion on the following central debates:

1. Does the law on assisted conception appropriately and effectively deal with the multiple different permutations of family creation that technology affords us?

2. Should legal parenthood be based on genetic links, gestational relationships, intention, or something else?

3. Who should, and who should not, be given parental responsibility for children?

1. Introduction

Families are all different. In the twenty-first century, they may be created in a vast number of ways, by a variety of people, each performing different roles. Families change: they may start life as one unit but this unit may, through a variety of different relationships and circumstances, expand, contract, divide, reform, or dissolve, so defining who or what a family is—or who parents are—has become increasingly complicated. There is no longer such a thing as the 'traditional' or 'normal' family. Undoubtedly, the relative fluidity of family forms in the current time derives in some way from an increased and increasing social acceptance of familial difference and diversity, including attitudes (and availability) in relation to divorce and remarriage, to single parenthood, and to same-sex relationships, among other things. However, a person always has legal parents—at present limited to a maximum of two people in this jurisdiction. These people may be different from a child's 'natural', 'social', or 'psychological' parents, as we shall see, though very often one person may perform a combination of two or more of these parent 'roles'. Some other jurisdictions might recognise more than two people as parents. For example, s. 30 of British Columbia's (Canada) Family Law Act 2013 allows for more than two parents in an exception to the usual rules when a written agreement is made between either intended parents (surrogacy), in a relationship with each other, and a birth mother who wants to be a parent, or a birth mother and the person she is in a relationship with, and a donor who also wants to be a parent.[1]

This chapter starts by exploring how the law in England and Wales defines legal parenthood. That is, who is recognised in law as the parents of any given child? This is important, not only because it makes the child a member of that person's family, but also because only the legal parents of a child have the standing to bring or defend proceedings about them.[2] It also matters in terms of citizenship rights, restrictions on who may marry, death in intestacy, and the duty to financially maintain a child (see Chapter 6).[3] The concept or status of legal parenthood thus represents the choice the law has made about who should hold this role. Legal parenthood is an inalienable status, and can only be removed by adoption (see Chapter 12), or the granting of a parental order in the context of surrogacy (see section 3.3). There are obviously many ways in which parenthood *could* be determined: by biological (including genetic and gestational) links, by social ties, by intentionality, or psychologically (who looks after the child and who does the child believe its parents to be?).[4] However, it should be noted that legal paren*thood* can be said to differ from paren*tage* (which denotes the biological or genetic connection), and it is also clearly different from parental *responsibility* (see section 4).[5] It is entirely possible that legal parents do not have parental responsibility. Conversely, parental responsibility may be held by people who neither are legal parents, nor are even biologically related to the child—and it might be held by more than two people, each of whom can exercise it independently of the other(s). The concept derives from s. 3 of the Children Act 1989 and defines 'the rights, duties, powers and authority' held by adults in respect of particular children and their property.

The main focus of this chapter is on legal parenthood. The chapter first considers how legal parenthood is determined when children are born following 'natural' conception. It then considers developments in assisted reproductive technologies, which often leave us

---

[1] See also 'Historic ruling grants 'tri-custody' to trio who had threesome', *New York Post*, 10 March 2017.

[2] See *Re G (Children) (Residence: Same Sex Partner)* [2006] UKHL 43, at [32] (Baroness Hale).

[3] Child Support Act 1991, s. 1.

[4] *Re G (Children) (Residence: Same Sex Partner)* [2006] UKHL 43, at [33]–[37] (Baroness Hale). See also Johnson, M., 'A Biomedical Perspective on Parenthood' in A. Bainham, S. Day Sclater, and M. Richards *What is a Parent?* (Hart Publishing, 1999). For an excellent critique of Baroness Hale's judgment in *Re G*, especially her seeming prioritisation of the genetic and (especially) gestational links, see Diduck, A, '"If Only we can Find the Appropriate Terms to Use, the Issue Will be Solved": Law, Identity and Parenthood' (2007) 19 *Child and Family Law Quarterly* 458. For a rewritten version of the judgment itself, see Diduck, A. '*In re G (Children) (Residence: Same Sex Partner)*—Judgment', in R. Hunter, C. McGlynn, and E. Rackley (eds), *Feminist Judgments: From Theory to Practice* (Hart Publishing, 2010).

[5] Bainham, A. 'Parentage, Parenthood and Parental Responsibility: Subtle, Elusive, Yet Important Distinctions' in A. Bainham, S. Day Sclater, and M. Richards *What is a Parent?* (Hart Publishing, 1999). Also see Collier, R. and Sheldon, S. *Fragmenting Fatherhood: A Socio-Legal Study* (Hart Publishing, 2008) 3–7 on the different meanings of *paternity* and *fatherhood*.

with a wider pool of people who might potentially be parents, due to the separation of the biological processes of parenting as well as the social ones. And, it is often a hotly argued topic, as people can have widely diverging views about who the parents in such circumstances should be, depending on their own perspective of what a parent is. However, the notions of parenthood and family are largely legally constructed. In different societies, parenthood and family relationships may be determined differently, based on wider notions of kinship and relatedness. Though there are both biological relationships and social family constructs at play, these are not necessarily reflected in the law. As with other aspects of family law, much of the existing law on parenthood—though it has to some extent evolved as social constructions of the family have evolved over time—is rooted in the long-standing primacy of the notion of the traditional heterosexual, monogamous couple, that which was labelled 'the sexual family' by Martha Fineman.[6] When families are created in all kinds of different ways, we need to be able to determine who the law will define as the 'parents' of the children. Does the method of conception affect the 'normal' rules of legal parenthood and, if so, how?

Legal parenthood has, in relation to assisted reproductive technologies, been determined by statute: the Human Fertilisation and Embryology Acts of 1990 and 2008, hereafter referred to in this chapter as the HFA Acts of 1990 and 2008. However, there have been challenges to the 'status provisions' under the Acts, both academic and, more recently, on human rights grounds. In this chapter we will explore the different permutations of legal parenthood that arise from the use of different methods of conception. We will identify the occasions where the law on parenthood departs from the usual presumptions and why, while also considering whether the law has got this right in all instances.

The final part of the chapter looks at the legal concept of parental responsibility. This is different from and potentially wider than legal parenthood, which defines a relationship between children and their parents. Parental responsibility creates—as the name suggests—certain responsibilities in respect of the child, such as to provide a home for the child, and to protect and maintain them. Aspects of a child's life, such as choices in relation to education and medical care, also fall within the ambit of parental responsibility. It is the law's job to determine who should, and who should not, have parental responsibility for a child.

2. Who is a legal parent?

For the majority of families, the issue of legal parenthood is not contentious. Most of the time, those adults with an actual or presumed biological connection to a child (parentage) are also the legal parents. In English common law, the starting point has always been clear, following the Roman maxim 'mater semper certa est', the mother is always certain, a demonstrable fact, proved by birth ('mater est quam gestatio demonstrat').[7] However conception occurred, the woman who gave birth to a child was legally defined as its mother. At the time this principle was established, it would not have been possible to separate the two biological matters of genetics and gestation in women. Yet, even though this is now possible (e.g. in IVF with egg donation, or in surrogacy arrangements), the maxim holds true today and the birth mother is always regarded as the legal mother.

---

[6] Fineman, M.A. *The Neutered Mother, the Sexual Family, and Other Twentieth Century Tragedies* (Routledge, 1995).

[7] See the *Ampthill Peerage Case* [1977] AC 547, where Lord Simon of Glaisdale referred to motherhood as a fact, being 'proved demonstrably by parturition' (at 577).

The common law presumption that ran alongside this rule is that, when a woman was married, her husband was the father ('pater est quem nuptiae demonstrant') of any child she gave birth to, even with indications or suspicions to the contrary. Only with evidence establishing beyond doubt that the husband was not the father could the principle be overturned. Thus, husbands assumed all the responsibilities of fatherhood, while the child was ensured both a legal father and mother. This rule has its origins in times when being born 'out of wedlock' had potentially disastrous consequences (such as in relation to title, inheritance, or burial rights) and had one very clear advantage in that it brings certainty—for both the children concerned and for the local parishes who would otherwise potentially be financially responsible for bastard children. Though the fatherhood presumption is now rebuttable in certain situations,[8] it still exists, in the context of heterosexual marriage, and both parents must be registered within 42 days of a child's birth.[9] The treatment of parenthood in same-sex marriage and civil partnerships can differ depending on whether the couples are women or men, as we shall see.[10]

2.1 **Unmarried parents**

For unmarried couples, the law is different—there is no automatic presumption of paternity attached to a woman's unmarried partner. In 2015, just under 48% of all babies born were born outside of marriage or civil partnerships. 60% of these were born to cohabiting couples.[11] There is, however, a lesser presumption based on the registration of birth. Naming a man on the birth certificate is taken to be a good indication that he is (or is at least believed to be) the natural father of the child. Despite being a 'natural' (biological) parent, the father of a child born to unmarried parents was not able to be legally recognised as a parent until the Family Law Reform Act 1987. Now, who the second parent is/can be (alongside the woman who gives birth, who has a duty to register the child[12]) often depends on whether a child was conceived naturally or via licensed fertility treatment, as we shall see later in section 3. If conceived naturally, then there is a difference when unmarried parents agree that the male partner should be registered, and when they are not registered as the father, or when there is a dispute about who the 'real' father is.

For unmarried parents to jointly register the birth of a child, either an agreement between them to do so is required, or a court order compelling the father to be so registered.[13] If a child's mother does not want to name a man on her child's birth certificate she can simply refuse to do so. However, there has long been a strong policy concern that this kind of behaviour should be discouraged (see the never implemented sections relating to birth registration of unmarried fathers in the Welfare Reform Act 2009).[14]

---

[8] See s. 26 of the Family Law Reform Act 1969, which allows the presumption to be rebutted where, on the balance of probabilities, it is more likely than not that the husband is not the biological father.

[9] See s. 2 of the Births and Death Registration Act 1953. However, note that Bainham contends that somewhere between 2 and 10% of children are wrongly registered as the children of their mother's husband ('What is the Point of Birth Registration?' (2008) 20 *Child and Family Law Quarterly* 449).

[10] Note that the Court of Appeal has recently confirmed that civil partnerships are unavailable to opposite-sex couples: *Steinfeld and Keidan v Secretary of State for Education* [2017] EWCA Civ 81. The couple pursuing the case, Rebecca Steinfeld and Charles Keidan, intend to appeal the decision to the Supreme Court.

[11] ONS Statistical Bulletin, *Births in England and Wales: 2015*. Available at: https://www.ons.gov.uk/peoplepopulationandcommunity/birthsdeathsandmarriages/livebirths/bulletins/birthsummarytablesenglandandwales/2015, accessed 26 September 2017.   [12] Under s. 10 of the Births and Deaths Registration Act 1953.

[13] Under s. 10 of the Births and Deaths Registrations Act 1953.

[14] For a sustained critique of these proposed reforms, as part of a wider regulatory policy on fatherhood and the assumptions on which this was premised, in particular the prioritisation of genetic fatherhood 'with no seeming awareness that the word is also often used in other ways' see Sheldon, S., 'From "Absent Objects of Blame" to "Fathers who Want to Take Responsibility": Reforming Birth Registration Law' (2009) 31 *Journal of Social Welfare and Family Law* 373, 374.

Where the genetic paternity of a child is disputed, various people and agencies are entitled to apply to the Family Division of the High Court to have the biological parentage declared (i.e. via a DNA test). This application may be made by parties including the child, the mother of the child, the putative father, an interested person (including a person caring for the child), and the Child Support Agency or Child Maintenance Group within the Department for Work and Pensions (formerly the Child Maintenance and Enforcement Commission until 2012).[15] Such a declaration is binding on all concerned. If a father wants to prove paternity (where he is not recorded on the register of births), or challenge it (where a presumption that someone else is the father applies) then he must rebut the presumption on the balance of probabilities, producing such evidence as is required to do so.[16] Obviously, while once this may have proved difficult, it has become much easier to do in an era where reliable DNA tests are readily available. When there is a dispute over parentage, the court has the power to direct that tests are undertaken, including directing that bodily samples must be provided,[17] and the ability to infer whatever it likes if consent to take such samples is refused.[18]

In choosing whether to exercise this power the court needs to decide whether it would be in the child's best interest to do so—though this may be affected by considerations of whether it is the child's right to know their genetic parents (as indicated by those who favour an approach under the 1989 United Nations Convention on the Rights of the Child),[19] or whether the rights of the putative father to prove his parental status prevail. In *Re H (Paternity: Blood Tests)*,[20] for example, it was found, with reference to the United Nations Convention, that all children have the 'right to know the truth' unless this is outweighed by any considerations for their welfare (see Ward LJ, at [80]).[21] For a long time, no particular approach seems to be prioritised over any other—though more recently we can probably say that there is more of a tendency *to* direct tests, in the interests of children being able to know their 'true' genetic identity.[22] This favouring of 'truth' is perhaps connected to other background policy decisions, including the decision to remove anonymity from gamete donors in 2005, while at the same time encouraging previously anonymous donors to voluntarily enter their details on a register accessible by donor-conceived children at the age of majority. Evidently, for some time, the genetic relationship (as a record of 'truth' and 'identity') has been held to be of high importance.

3. Parenthood and assisted reproductive technologies

It has only been since the birth of Louise Brown in 1978 that people have been able to use *in vitro* fertilisation (IVF) to have children. Despite the relative youth of this medical technique it is now estimated that there are more than 5.4 million people born from IVF worldwide.[23] In 2014, 52,288 women had a total of 67,708 cycles of IVF or ICSI

---

[15] Under s. 55A of the Family Law Act 1986.   [16] Family Law Act 1986, s. 58(1).
[17] Family Law Reform Act 1969, s. 20(1).   [18] Family Law Reform Act 1969, s. 23.
[19] Also see similar considerations regarding a child's interest in discovering the identity of their genetic parent under Article 8(1) ECHR (the right to private and family life), as in *Mikulic v Croatia* App. No. 53176/99 [2002] FCR 720.   [20] [2001] 2 FLR 65.
[21] For instances of this, see *Re D (Paternity)* [2007] 2 FLR 26 and *Re J (Paternity: Welfare of Child)* [2007] 1 FLR 1064.
[22] See, e.g., *Re H (A Minor) (Blood Tests: Parental Rights)* [1997] Fam 89 (CA); *Re T (A Child) (DNA Tests: Paternity)* [2001] 3 FCR 577.
[23] European Society of Human Reproduction and Embryology (ESHRE), *ART Fact Sheet* October 2016. Available at: https://www.eshre.eu/en/Press-Room/Resources.aspx, accessed 26 September 2017.

in the UK.[24] Of course, no technology has ever been required for some other assisted reproductive technologies—for example, 'artificial' insemination (now more commonly called donor insemination (DI)), which involves the collection of semen outside of the body and its transfer into a woman. Though clinical applications of DI are common—and come with the added benefit that the samples collected will be both sterile and will have been tested for a range of diseases—DI always could be—and often still is—performed privately, outside of licensed clinics and without the help of professionals. Similarly, surrogacy, except when IVF is used, can also be a totally private arrangement, involving the home insemination of a surrogate who uses her own egg. The question is, when multiple people contribute to the creation of a child, who are (or who should be) its parents?

The demand for assisted reproductive technologies is unlikely to decline in coming years. The Human Fertilisation and Embryology Authority (HFEA), the agency that regulates the provision of fertility treatments through licensed clinics in the UK, says that one in seven couples of reproductive age will experience infertility at some point.[25] In this context, 'infertility' means medical infertility, defined as a disability by the World Health Organisation and relating to heterosexual couples who cannot conceive within one year of trying to through regular unprotected sexual intercourse.[26]

Evidently the HFEA's figure or the World Health Organisation's definition do not take into account those who cannot have children 'naturally' for non-medical reasons, such as a same-sex male couple. It is likely that, with changes to who may be recognised as legal parents under the Human Fertilisation and Embryology Act 2008, as well as the legitimation of same-sex marriage by the Marriage (Same Sex Couples) Act 2013, increasing numbers of same-sex couples will seek to become parents using assisted reproductive technologies. Though the law has got past the 'should same-sex couples be allowed to become parents?' question,[27] there are still questions about when, how, and in what circumstances two people of the same sex can both become the legal parents of the same child(ren), outside of adoption, though the law does now allow the deliberately intended creation of two same-sex legal parents at birth, subject to certain and specific considerations having been met. Further issues arise in relation to multiple parents, 'co-parenting' and transgender people.[28] As technology advances even further, we may find ourselves considering parenthood in ever more complex situations—for example, if uterine transplants ever become a real possibility, this will raise different kinds of biological issues, and even more so if pregnancy can ever be

---

[24] Human Fertilisation and Embryology Authority, *Fertility treatment 2014—Trends and figures*, 11. Available at: https://www.hfea.gov.uk/about-us/publications/, accessed 9 October 2017. ICSI stands for intracytoplasmic sperm injection, and is a later variation of IVF procedures, producing the first live birth in 1991. In ICSI, a single sperm is injected directly into an egg to fertilise it. It is usually used to overcome problems associated with male infertility.

[25] Human Fertilisation and Embryology Authority, *Fertility treatment 2014—Trends and figures*, 6. Available at: https://www.hfea.gov.uk/about-us/publications/. ESHRE, *ART Fact Sheet* October 2016, available at: https://www.eshre.eu/en/Press-Room/Resources.aspx, accessed 26 September 2017, gives the figure as one in six, elaborating that this is about 9% prevalence worldwide for women aged 20–44.

[26] World Health Organisation International Committee Monitoring Assisted Reproductive Technologies 'Glossary', revised 1999. Available at: http://www.icmartivf.org/ivf-glossary.html, accessed 9 October 2017.

[27] Same-sex couples have been able to adopt since the Adoption and Children Act 2002.

[28] See e.g. *X, Y and Z v UK* App no 21830/93; *J v C (Void Marriage: Status of Children)* [2006] EWCA Civ 551 (in relation to a deception); *R (on the application of JK) v Registrar General for England and Wales* [2015] EWHC 990 (Admin) (regarding whether a person who changed gender after the birth of a child could alter the birth record especially in relation to keeping their transgender status private).

established in a man; or 'artificial' gametes (sperm and egg cells) can be created from other body cells.[29]

 CONTEXT 1: THE WARNOCK REPORT 1984

The Warnock Committee was established by the government in 1982, to consider the moral, ethical, legal, and other issues around IVF, donation of sperm and eggs, and surrogacy, as well as the related science of embryology.[30] This was felt necessary at the time because of concerns at the speed with which these technologies were developing, and also as a reaction to the 1978 birth of Louise Brown. The Committee's remit was to consider and develop principles for the proper regulation of these technologies in the light of these concerns. Chaired by moral philosopher Mary Warnock (later Baroness Warnock), the Committee's terms of reference were:

> To consider recent and potential developments in medicine and science related to human fertilisation and embryology; to consider what policies and safeguards should be applied, including consideration of the social, ethical and legal implications of these developments; and to make recommendations.[31]

The findings of the Committee were published in 1984, in what is now referred to as the Warnock Report. The Warnock Committee concluded that the human embryo should be protected, to a point, but that continued research on embryos and on IVF and related technologies (for the purposes of improving fertility treatments) would be permissible, if regulation struck an appropriate balance and provided appropriate safeguards. In its report, the Committee proposed the establishment of a regulatory authority which would license the use of human embryos outside the body in treatment, storage, and research.

In many ways, the Warnock Report formed the basis for the HFE 1990. Following the Warnock Report, the UK produced some of the most liberal regulation of assisted reproduction and embryology in the world, in legislation that has been mirrored—in parts if not always as a whole—in other jurisdictions since. The HFE Act 1990 was passed after incredibly detailed Parliamentary debate and—tellingly—much persuasion and lobbying by the scientific and medical community, aiming to allow politicians to understand the realities and limitations of the science. The 1990 Act also established a licensing system that applies to both NHS and private clinics, and the HFEA to oversee clinics' treatments.

The 1990 Act was not perfect by any means and certainly, as science and society continued to advance, began to show its age by the time we entered the twenty-first century.[32] Following

---

[29] As can be evidenced by the debates on mitochondrial transfer—mitochondria are the 'batteries' of a cell, found in the cytoplasm surrounding the nucleus, and passed on by the maternal link). Using advanced IVF procedures to remove a nucleus from an egg (or embryo) that contains faulty mitochondria, and placing it into an enucleated donated egg (or embryo) that is 'healthy', then using the resulting egg/embryo in fertility treatment, allows the inheritance of the faulty mitochondria, which can cause serious and devastating disease in children, to be avoided. The UK became the first country in the world to approve the procedure (The Human Fertilisation and Embryology (Mitochondrial Donation) Regulations 2015 (SI 572/2015), but one question that kept arising in the debates (especially in the press) was whether a baby created this way would be a 'three-parent baby' or whether this was 'three-parent IVF'. Clearly, however, despite the biological material coming from three people, the nuclear DNA would still only come from two, meaning the child only has two 'parents'.

[30] It reported in 1984: *Report of the Committee of Inquiry into Human Fertilisation and Embryology* (Cmnd 9314, 1984) ('the Warnock Report').   [31] The Warnock Report (Cmnd 9314, 1984) para 1.2.

[32] For an evaluation of the Act's effectiveness in the early twenty-first century, and conclusions on how it needed to be updated, see Biggs, H., and Horsey, K. (eds), *Human Fertilisation and Embryology: Reproducing Regulation* (Routledge-Cavendish, 2007).

various consultations, an amending statute—the Human Fertilisation and Embryology Act 2008—was passed. This was not a wholesale re-write of the law (which arguably it should have been), thus the two pieces of legislation have to be read together, alongside various pieces of secondary legislation.[33]

Assisted reproductive technologies enable the biological processes of conception and the social practice of parenting to be spread among multiple different parties. With the law only allowing two legal parents, this means some choices have had to be made. The HFE Act 2008 contains the current provisions on parenthood in this context and sets out who may be legal parents in a wide range of different circumstances. The law is very complicated due to the many permutations of different people who may receive fertility treatments (married or unmarried, same-sex or opposite-sex couples, even single people) and the variation of sources and combinations of the biological material used (some of which may have come from donors). The HFE Act 1990 established the HFEA and also established a regime under which clinics may be granted (and keep) licenses to provide treatments. The use and storage of genetic materials (gametes and embryos) from both patients and donors is subject to strict written consent requirements.[34] In addition, clinics must provide prospective patients (and their partners) suitable opportunities to receive appropriate counselling before valid consent can be given.

There is no limit set by law on who can access or use assisted reproductive technologies, though licensed clinics that provide these services are required to undertake an assessment of the welfare of the putative child (s. 13(5) of the HFE Act 1990 as amended by s. 14(2)(b) of the HFE Act 2008) before deciding whether or not to provide treatment.[35] This is not uncontroversial. Under the original formulation of the HFE Act 1990, part of this assessment required clinic decision-makers to have regard of the need of the child *for a father*. Thus, this section provided the justification for many clinics to deny treatment to single women and lesbian couples. While these kind of treatment denials might have been more prevalent in the earlier days of IVF and other clinical treatments than in the time immediately before the wording of the section was changed in 2008, the very fact that the law seemed to suggest both that access to (potential) parenthood should be policed in this way, and that fatherless families were more problematic came under heavy criticism.[36]

Since 2008, clinics are asked to consider putative children's welfare by considering their future need for 'supportive parenting', rather than for a father. Empirical work undertaken by McCandless and Sheldon suggests, however, that the enactment of this new provision changed very little in clinical practice.[37] By 2008, they showed, the majority of clinics were already fairly permissive in their interpretations of the welfare requirement, and only something that really raised eyebrows among clinic staff would be likely to result in treatment being refused, either before or after the section was amended. The HFEA Code of Practice supports this kind of permissive interpretation of the statutory requirement (guidance note 8.11), stating that supportive parenting is, in effect, presumed among prospective parents unless there is evidence to the contrary.[38]

---

[33] And other related statutes, such as the Surrogacy Arrangements Act 1985.   [34] HFE Act 1990, Sch 3.

[35] In addition, the provision of some treatments requires patients to undergo mandatory counselling (s. 13(6)).

[36] Jackson, E., 'Conception and the Irrelevance of the Welfare Principle' (2002) 65 *Modern Law Review* 176.

[37] McCandless, J. and Sheldon, S. 'No Father Required'? The Welfare Assessment in the Human Fertilisation and Embryology Act 2008' (2010) 18 *Feminist Legal Studies* 201.

[38] HFEA Code of Practice (8th edn, 2009) (latest revision July 2016).

3.1 Conception using donated gametes or embryos

Conception using donated gametes (sperm or eggs) or embryos further challenges the notion of who or what a parent should be. The use of donor sperm,[39] for example by a heterosexual couple who have found themselves unable to conceive, brings a question about who should be recognised as the legal father. Should it be the man who provided the sperm, or the man who intended to conceive the child with his partner (married or otherwise), and intends to raise and nurture that child? Furthermore, the use of donor insemination by a same-sex female couple, or by a single woman, raises a different question entirely—does there have to be a legal father at all, when this is obviously not what was intended?

Pregnancy can also be achieved by using donor eggs. Some women, who are able to carry a child and give birth, but are not able to conceive, may be helped by this method. They may have donated eggs either transferred to the uterus and then have fertilisation attempted by insemination using sperm from her husband or partner (or a sperm donor), or donated eggs fertilised using IVF techniques (again, with sperm either from the husband/partner, or from a donor) and the resulting embryos transferred to the uterus. Who, in these circumstances, is the legal mother? Should it be the woman who provides the egg? The woman who carries the baby and gives birth? The woman who intends to be the parent of the resulting child?[40] Further, where both donated egg and sperm are used, or if an entire embryo is donated, similar questions arise about *both* motherhood and fatherhood. And, if an egg or embryo is donated to a same-sex male couple, who engage a surrogate to carry the child for them, additional questions arise—does there even have to be a legal mother? As we shall see, the law has given us answers to some of these questions.

3.1.1 Motherhood

 Key Legislation 1: HFE Act 2008, s. 33(1)

> The woman who is carrying or has carried a child as a result of the placing in her of an embryo or of sperm and eggs, and no other woman, is to be treated as the mother of the child.

This section applies to all treatments involving egg or embryo donation, whether this takes place in clinics licensed by the HFEA, or elsewhere (e.g. in another country).[41] Though the same is true of natural conception, as we have seen in the common law, the legislation determines that in any circumstances where treatment is carried out in a licensed clinic, and the genetic and gestational components of a child differ, the gestational mother will be the legal mother, as the Warnock Committee had recommended.[42]

Thus, however a child is conceived, and no matter where the genetic material comes from, the woman who carries the child and gives birth to it is regarded in law as the child's mother. Conversely, any woman who donates an egg to another woman will not be the legal mother, despite being the biological or genetic mother (this is clearly specified in s. 47). The same is true when an embryo is donated.

---

[39] A note about terminology here. Though this has often been referred to as 'artificial' insemination by donor (AID), this author dislikes the connotation of artificiality, and prefers instead the term 'donor insemination', which will be used through the remainder of the chapter.

[40] This third possibility is particularly relevant in the context of surrogacy.

[41] Note that an identical provision exists in s. 27(1) of the HFE Act 1990, which applies to conceptions that occurred before the provisions of the 2008 Act came into force.

[42] The Warnock Report (Cmnd 9314, 1984) para 6.8.

Usually, such formulation is unproblematic. A woman who *donates* an egg or embryo to another woman does not intend to be the mother of any child that results from her donation. A woman undergoing IVF treatment for infertility who requires a donated egg or embryo to be provided in order for her to achieve pregnancy does intend to be the mother. However, as we shall see when we consider surrogacy (in 3.3), this is not always the case—as it might be that a woman has offered to carry a baby for another person or couple using their own or a donor egg/embryo. In such situations the intentions of the parties towards parenthood do not match a definition of motherhood that centres on the act of giving birth, and is therefore sometimes problematic.

3.1.2 Fatherhood and second parents

The situation is different—and even more complicated—when it comes to determining who the second legal parent is (where there is one). This could be, and most usually is, a father. However, in the case of two women who have a child together, a father is not necessarily desired, and a mechanism under which a woman's female partner can become the second legal parent (though, interestingly, not a second 'mother') has been created, as we shall see. The starting point of the common law is that, subject to any other provisions that might apply (such as those from the HFE Acts) which determine legal fatherhood in particular situations, the genetic father is the legal father. Obviously this would have big implications for sperm donation, and we will consider how this has been dealt with in detail later.

Though it is hard to imagine now, there was once a time when the use of sperm donation was thought by some to amount to adultery. For example, in 1960 the government commissioned the Feversham Committee to consider 'artificial' insemination. In its Report, the Committee found that the majority of society (including the medical profession) opposed donor insemination. It therefore concluded that donor insemination was an undesirable practice, which was to be strongly discouraged.[43] The Warnock Committee found that there were no moral objections to the practice of 'artificial' insemination when the husband's sperm was used, and recognised that there were some moral objections to the use of sperm donation but also considered that, over time, attitudes had changed, and there was growing acceptance of the use of donor insemination. However, at the time of the Warnock Report, children born from donated sperm were still deemed to be illegitimate:

> A child born as a result of AID [artificial insemination by donor], on the other hand, is illegitimate, and so is liable to suffer all the disadvantages associated with that status. In theory the husband of the woman who bears an AID child has no parental rights and duties in law with regard to that child; these in principle lie with the donor, who could be made liable to pay maintenance, and who could apply to a court for access or custody.[44]

The Warnock Committee concluded 'that AID should no longer be left in a legal vacuum but should be subject to certain conditions and safeguards, and receive the protection of the law'.[45] Law Commission recommendations at the time regarding illegitimacy said that the husband of a woman receiving donor insemination treatment, rather than the donor, should be the legal father for all purposes. The Warnock Committee unanimously agreed and:

---

[43] Home Office and Scottish Home Department, *Departmental Committee on Human Artificial Insemination* (Cmnd 1105, 1960) (Chairman: The Earl of Feversham).

[44] The Warnock Report (Cmnd 9314, 1984) para 4.9.

[45] The Warnock Report (Cmnd 9314, 1984) para 4.16.

accordingly recommend[ed] that the AID child should in law be treated as the legitimate child of its mother and her husband where they have both consented to the treatment. This will require legislation.[46]

In response to the Warnock Committee's recommendation, the Family Law Reform Act 1987 first recognised that a married man could be the legal father of a child born to his wife following insemination using another man's sperm under s.27(1), subject to his having provided consent to the insemination. This position was also enshrined in s.28(2) of the HFE Act 1990, which determined that the husband of any woman who had a child after donor insemination would become the legal father, providing he had consented to her being so treated.[47]

Later, however, changes in science, society, and the common law in the years since 1990 made it necessary for the legislation, including its parenthood provisions, to be reviewed. To pull out just some examples, since 1990 it had become possible for same-sex couples to enter civil partnerships from 2004, possible for unmarried and same-sex couples to jointly adopt children, and possible for unmarried men to acquire parental responsibility via joint birth registration with the mother. In 2005, the ability of gamete donors to retain anonymity had been removed. In 1997, the Court of Appeal allowed Diane Blood's challenge against the HFEA to be allowed to export her dead husband's sperm for use in fertility treatment (the treatment having been refused here), creating the idea of 'posthumous parenthood' (see 3.1.3). In 2001, following developments in mammalian cloning procedures, human reproductive cloning had been banned.[48]

A public consultation on the 1990 Act was issued by the Department of Health,[49] which was supplemented by smaller consultations conducted by the HFEA on key individual issues. In the consultation document, it was said that the (then) government:

> aimed to consider the extent to which changes may be needed to better recognise the wider range of people who seek and receive assisted reproduction treatment in the early 21st Century. The Government has also considered the impact of other legal changes that have occurred since the HFE Act came into force in 1991. For example, the coming into force of the Civil Partnership Act 2004 created a new legal relationship which two people of the same sex can form by registering as civil partners of each other ...[50]

A White Paper[51] led to a draft Bill which was then subjected to extensive pre-legislative scrutiny and much debate.[52] Despite this detailed attention given to the new legislation, other than some minor clarifications to some existing provisions, the current parenthood provisions mirror the content of the 1990 Act, with some notable extensions. It is therefore useful to understand the history of the provisions (notwithstanding the fact that the 1990 Act still applies to children born before the 2008 Act's provisions came into force) and the case law that derived from them, as this may provide indications of how future cases will be decided.

---

[46] The Warnock Report (Cmnd 9314, 1984) para 4.17.

[47] As in relation to legal motherhood, the time of conception is relevant for determining which statutory provision to use.   [48] Human Reproductive Cloning Act 2001 (now repealed).

[49] Department of Health, *Review of the Human Fertilisation and Embryology Act—A Public Consultation* (Department of Health, 2005). The House of Commons Science and Technology Committee also conducted its own consultation, with its findings published in its fifth report (session 2006–7).

[50] Department of Health, *Review of the Human Fertilisation and Embryology Act—A Public Consultation* (Department of Health, 2005) para 2.67.

[51] *Review of the Human Fertilisation and Embryology Act: Proposals for Revised Legislation (including establishment of the Regulatory Authority for Tissues and Embryos)* (Cm 6989, 2006).

[52] Human Tissue and Embryos (Draft) Bill (Cm 7087). See scrutiny report of the Joint Committee on the Bill, *Human Tissue and Embryos (Draft) Bill Volume 1: Report* HL Paper 169–1, HC Paper 630–1 (1 August 2007).

Fatherhood after assisted reproductive technologies

The recognition of a married man as the father of a child born to his wife following donor insemination, following the Family Law Reform Act 1987 and later the HFE Act 1990, mirrored the common law presumption of paternity and legal parenthood. The HFE Act 1990 had a wider scope than the earlier legislation. It established an entire regulatory framework for the licensed provision of assisted reproductive technologies, and created comprehensive rules for establishing parenthood following all forms of fertility treatments and specifically in the case of sperm, egg and embryo donation. These rules came into force on 1 August 1991 with the provisions in relation to the use of donated sperm in the context of a marital relationship under s. 28(2) of the HFE Act 1990 'overtaking' those in the 1987 Act.[53] However, the HFE Act 1990 also, for the first time, contained a provision under s. 28(3) that recognised the legal fatherhood of a non-married male partner of a woman who was inseminated with donated sperm, provided that the woman and her partner were receiving 'treatment together' in licensed facilities, subject to the consent requirements.[54]

The provisions under ss. 27–29 of the HFE Act 1990 lasted until new provisions in the HFE Act 2008 came into force, after a review of the parenthood provisions in the 1990 Act (and still apply to conceptions that took place between the coming into force of the two different Acts). The relevant sections of the 2008 Act (ss. 33–48) lay out the ways that legal parenthood is determined for children born after this part of the Act came into force in April 2009.

 Key Legislation 2: Fatherhood under the HFE Act 2008, ss. 35–37

These sections apply only in the circumstances where a child:

is being or has been carried by a woman as a result of the placing in her of an embryo or of sperm and eggs or her artificial insemination (HFE Act 2008, s. 34).

This means that any conception by sexual intercourse (which may happen in privately arranged (i.e. non-clinical) donation or surrogacy situations, though is likely to be rare, given the relative ease of self-insemination) is not included under the parenthood provisions under the Act, leaving parenthood in these situations to be determined by ordinary common law principles (see section 2).

Section 35 of the HFE Act 2008 is similar to the provision in s. 28(2) of the 1990 Act. It applies if a woman was married to a man at the time of her treatment and 'the embryo carried by her was not brought about with the sperm of the other party to the marriage', then (subject to s. 38 where the common law presumption of legitimacy is written in to the legislation):

the other party to the marriage is to be treated as the father of the child unless it is shown that he did not consent to the placing in her of the embryo or the sperm and eggs or to her artificial insemination (HFE Act 2008, s. 35(1)(b)).

Consent of the putative father is therefore important, though the burden falls on any husband who says he did not give consent to prove it. If the treatment took place in a licensed clinic then there should be measures in place to ensure that the relevant required consents are obtained.

---

[53] Made explicit by s. 49(4) of the HFE Act 1990. Thus s. 27 of the Family Law Reform Act 1987 only (and still) applies to inseminations that took place prior to the HFE Act 1990 coming into force. See *J v C and another* [2006] EWCA Civ 551.   [54] See *Re R (IVF: Paternity of Child)* [2005] UKHL 33.

However, in private arrangements no such measures apply and, in any case, as we shall later see, mistakes can happen. There has recently been lots of criticism of failings to do this properly.[55]

The position of men who are *not* married to the woman having treatment is covered under ss. 36–37. Section 36 applies where 'the agreed fatherhood conditions' drawn from s. 37 apply:

> If no man is treated by virtue of section 35 as the father of the child and no woman is treated by virtue of section 42 as a parent of the child,[56] but—
>
> (a) the embryo or the sperm and eggs were placed in W [the woman], or W was artificially inseminated in the course of treatment services provided in the United Kingdom by a person to whom a licence applies,
>
> (b) at the time when the embryo or the sperm and eggs were placed in W, or W was artificially inseminated, the agreed fatherhood conditions were satisfied in relation to a man, in relation to treatment provided to W under the licence,
>
> (c) the man remained alive at the time, and
>
> (d) the creation of the embryo carried by W was not brought about with the man's sperm,then, subject to section 38(2) to (4), the man is to be treated as the father of the child.

This is a relatively radical position, as it means that a man can become the legal parent of a child to whom he is not biologically related, alongside a woman to whom he is not married (though note that via birth registration, this could have happened in any case in a natural conception). It is a real recognition of the concept of 'intended parenthood', even in the absence of a genetic connection.

The 'agreed fatherhood conditions' as outlined in s. 37 are met by a man ('M') in relation to the woman ('W') where:

> (a) M [the man] has given the person responsible a notice stating that he consents to being treated as the father of any child resulting from treatment provided to W under the licence,[57]
>
> (b) W has given the person responsible a notice stating that she consents to M being o treated,
>
> (c) neither M nor W has, since giving notice ... given the person responsible notice of the withdrawal of M's or W's consent to M being so treated,
>
> (d) W has not, since the giving of the notice under paragraph (b), given the person responsible—
>
> > (i) a further notice under that paragraph stating that she consents to another man being treated as the father of any resulting child, or
> >
> > (ii) a notice under s44(1)(b) stating that she consents to a woman being treated as a parent of any resulting child, and
> >
> > (iii) W and M are not within prohibited degrees of relationship in relation to each other.

Such 'notices' must be in writing and must be signed by the relevant party to have effect under s. 37(2). As we shall see, however, the provision of notices has not always managed to lead to legal parenthood being conferred on those parties by whom it was intended. However, when it does, s. 48(1) determines that the man will become the legal father of the child for all purposes.

---

[55] See *In the matter of the Human Fertilisation and Embryology Act 2008 (Case K)* [2017] EWHC 50 (Fam) and other cases discussed later in this section.   [56] See 'second female parents', later in this section.

[57] The 'person responsible' is a technical term under the legislation, meaning the member of clinical staff with legal responsibility for ensuring a clinic's compliance with the requirements of the HFE Acts 1990 and 2008.

The combined effects of ss. 36 and 37, therefore, are that when a woman receiving licensed treatment in a UK clinic, using the sperm of someone who is not the man who intends to be the father (i.e. donor sperm), and who does not have a husband, a same-sex spouse, or a civil partner who would be made a parent by the provisions of s. 35 or s. 42, respectively, and both those parties ('M' and 'W') have satisfied the notice requirements under s. 37 for 'agreed fatherhood conditions', without later revoking them, and provided the relevant consent,[58] then she and the intended father will become the legal parents. Though this is complicated, it does represent a step forward, in that it recognises that people may choose to have children outside of marriage/civil partnerships, even via the use of assisted reproductive technologies. However, the criticism is that it still sets a different standard for married and civilly partnered people as compared to unmarried couples.

As we saw earlier, when a couple is married, the provisions in s. 35 mean that insemination *outside* of a licensed clinic, or the placing of an embryo or of eggs and sperm in a woman in a non-UK clinic, would not negate the married husband's claim to parenthood, in the absence of his being able to show that he did not consent to those procedures. However, if a non-married couple achieved pregnancy by self-insemination using donor sperm outside of a licensed clinic, the male partner—no matter what he consented to—would not be recognised as the legal father. Instead, the common law would apply and would render the *donor* the legal father by virtue of his genetic connection. Whether or not it makes sense to maintain such a distinction in the modern day is certainly questionable, though of course some of the reasoning behind the legislative provisions may be as much down to pragmatic considerations (regarding proof) as anything else.

We should also note that if consent is withdrawn by either party in relation to a particular man being identified as the child's father, after the point of insemination or embryo transfer, then this does not render the treatment unlawful, it just (technically) means that there will be no legal father. However, if consent is withdrawn *prior* to treatment, no treatment can be given, as illustrated by *Evans v UK*.[59] In this case, Natallie Evans was told that her ovaries needed to be removed following a cancer diagnosis, and that she should harvest some of her eggs should she wish to consider having children in the future, as the cancer treatment she needed would render her infertile. She was advised that she would have a better chance of future fertility treatment being successful if embryos were frozen, rather than eggs (egg freezing and treatment from this was in relative infancy at this point). Because of this, and relying on her then partner Howard Johnston's promise that they would stay together, embryos created by mixing their sperm and eggs were frozen and stored subject to the relevant consents by both parties. Later, Evans and Johnston's relationship broke down, and he asked the clinic to destroy the stored embryos. Natallie Evans asked the Court to say that he could not withdraw or vary his earlier consent, and contended that not to do so would violate her Article 8 right to respect for her private and family life, Article 12 right to marry and found a family, and Article 14 non-discrimination right under the European Convention on Human Rights and Fundamental Freedoms 1950 (ECHR), as well as claiming that the right to life of the embryos themselves were protected by Article 2.

The Court of Appeal found against her, and permission to appeal to the House of Lords was refused, so Ms Evans appealed to the European Court of Human Rights. In due course

---

[58] Schedule 3 to the Act makes it clear that written consent is required for the use or storage of genetic material. Sch 3, para 5 says that gametes may not be used in treatment unless an effective consent is in place, other than when they are used for the recipient and another who receive treatment services together.

[59] [2007] 2 FCR 5 (ECtHR).

her case was heard in the Grand Chamber, which unanimously held that there was no violation of Article 2 ECHR. In respect of Article 8, a majority found that that her right to respect for her private and family life was engaged—though also that her former partner's rights were engaged, and the two sets of rights were in direct competition—one or other of them would be affected, no matter what happened. Ultimately, the Grand Chamber found that there was no violation of Article 8, because other factors had to be taken into account, including the foundational principle of consent as required by the statutory framework. Also, because there was no one way of dealing with such issues across the Member States, the United Kingdom had to be granted a wide margin of appreciation. Similarly, the majority held that there was no discrimination against Natallie Evans. However, the dissenting minority found that the 'bright-line' nature of the consent rules meant that there could be no proper balancing of the interests of competing parties, and that this had a disproportionate impact on Evans, who had lost her only chance of ever having a child biologically related to her.

The consent provision had existed under HFE Act 1990 Act under s. 28(2), and was examined and strictly applied in the case of *Leeds Teaching Hospital NHS Trust v A*.[60] Mr and Mrs A were undergoing fertility treatment in the Leeds clinic. Mr and Mrs B were also having treatment in the same clinic. Both couples were using their own gametes in the treatment, so neither couple had consented to the use of donor gametes. Due to a mix-up in the clinic, the wrong sperm was provided to Mrs A—her eggs were fertilised with a sample of Mr B's sperm, and she carried the resulting embryo to term. Mrs A, who was white, as was her husband, gave birth to mixed race twins. DNA tests established that Mr B was the biological father of the twins. Mr B applied for a declaration of parentage. According to the legislation, because she had given birth, Mrs A was the mother. Because Mr A had not given his consent to an embryo created using 'donor' sperm being placed in Mrs A, he could not be recognised as the father under s. 28(2), meaning that the common law would apply and Mr B would be the legal father.

Mr and Mrs A tried to argue that appropriate consent had in fact been given but, in giving judgment, then President of the Family Division, Dame Elizabeth Butler-Sloss found that Mr A would have had to have given his consent for the actual procedure (i.e. the use of another man's sperm) that had taken place, in order for the consent to be effective. She said:

> On the clear evidence presented in the consent forms Mr A plainly did not consent to the sperm of a named or anonymous donor being mixed with his wife's eggs. This was clearly an embryo created without the consent of Mr and Mrs A (at [28]).

Thus, despite his willingness to take on the fatherhood role, and the fact that he would have been the legal father had the intention been to use donor sperm, Mr A was unable to be recognised as the legal father. It was, however, agreed by both couples that the children should continue to live with and be brought up by Mr and Mrs A.

What we can take from these case examples, is that consent—not only consent to one's own treatment, but the appropriate consent for the treatment of one's partner in order to be able to secure legal parenthood for those who intend to be the parents—is a very important concept within the law, including in relation to establishing legal parenthood. It has also become increasingly apparent that obtaining the proper consent—in the right way—has become even more important than ever, following a string of recent cases dealing with licensed fertility clinics' shortcomings in relation to obtaining the appropriate consents needed for fertility treatment post-implementation of the HFE Act 2008.

---

[60] [2003] EWHC 259 (Fam).

Key Case 1: *In the matter of the Human Fertilisation and Embryology Act 2008 (Case K)* [2017] EWHC 50 (Fam).

This was the latest in a series of similar cases where consent was at issue and had affected the legal parenthood situation.[61] It was the 24th such case to come before the (now recently retired) President of the Family Division, Sir James Munby. *Case K* concerned an application brought by a father (with the mother's support) for a declaration of parentage under s. 55A of the Family Law Act 1986, that he is, in accordance with ss. 36–37 of the HFE Act 2008, the legal parent of the twins born to the couple following the use of donated sperm in treatment at a licensed clinic. The Registrar had refused to register the man as the children's father, because the necessary consent documents could not be produced. The Registrar required 'Form WP' and 'Form PP', but the couple had each signed 'Form IC'. While the Registrar General, who was joined as an interested party, could have issued an amended birth certificate, this would have had the wording 'Pursuant to section 14A of the Births and Deaths Registration Act 1953 on the authority of the Registrar General' on its face. The couple had not yet decided whether or when to tell their children that they were conceived using donated sperm, and did not, therefore, want such a reissued certificate, as the amended entry would indicate the children's method of conception.

The couple had instigated the fertility treatment together, and had gone through the whole process together.[62] From the beginning, both partners had intended that the man would be the legal parent of any child(ren) born. Once their pregnancy was achieved, and up until and after the birth of the twins, both partners believed that the man was the other legal parent. They thought they had signed all the appropriate forms as required by the 2008 Act, so assumed that they had undertaken all necessary preparations to ensure that they would both become the legal parents of any child born though the treatment. They did not discover that anything was 'wrong' until they attempted to register the births.

The couple contended that the Registrar had made an error of law due to a lack of understanding or knowledge of the decision in an earlier case,[63] having followed a handbook that had not been updated since that case. The Registrar General had no statutory power to register the children afresh; to do so would require their initial birth registration to be quashed via a judicial review. The case was adjourned so that the couple could decide if this was what they wanted. The father later applied for a judicial review on the basis of an error of law made by the Registrar. The local authority acknowledged that the handbook used by the Registrar was incorrect and confirmed that it did not intend to contest the man's claim, anticipating that a consent order could be agreed.

Munby P later made a declaration (in the Family Division) in favour of the couple and (in the Administrative Court) quashed the original birth registration, thus allowing the children to be registered as the children of both of the couple. He found that (though unintentionally):

---

[61] The appropriate consent forms in each of the cases had either been lost, or were not the consent forms mandated for use by the HFEA (Forms WP and PP) under the 2008 Act. See, previously, eg *AB v CD and the Z Fertility Clinic* [2013] EWHC 1418 (Fam); *X v Y v St Bartholomew's Hospital for Reproductive Medicine* [2015] EWFC 13; *F v M and others* [2015] EWHC 3601 (Fam); *In the matter of the Human Fertilisation and Embryology Act 2008 (Cases A, B, C, D, E, F, G and H)* [2015] EWHC 2602 (Fam); *D v D (Fertility Treatment: Paperwork Error)* [2016] EWHC 2112 (Fam); *Re A and others (Legal Parenthood: Written Consents)* [2016] 1 WLR 1325; *Re the Human Fertilisation and Embryology Act 2008 (Case O)* [2016] EWHC 2273 (Fam); *In the matter of the Human Fertilisation and Embryology Act 2008 (Case L)* [2016] EWHC 2266 (Fam); *Case V (Human Fertilisation and Embryology Act 2008)* [2016] EWHC 2356 (Fam); *In the Matter of the Human Fertilisation and Embryology Act 2008 (Cases P, Q, R, S, T, U, W and X)* [2017] EWHC 49 (Fam); *Re Human Fertilisation and Embryology Act 2008 (Cases AD, AE, AF, AG and AH)* [2017] EWHC 1026 (Fam).

[62] See [2017] EWHC 50 (Fam), at [7] (Mumby P).

[63] *Re A and others (Legal Parenthood: Written Consents)* [2016] 1 WLR 1325.

> put starkly, the state by its actions has denied these parents the right to decide for them-
> selves, within the privacy of the family, what in their view, as devoted parents, is in the best
> interests of their children – a matter which, to speak plainly, is no business of the state.[64]

It is clear that the bureaucratic version of consent and notice required by the HFE Act 2008 can have effects on people's lives well beyond that which was (presumably) intended. Because of administrative errors, legal parenthood becomes difficult to achieve, despite people entering into treatments together and intending to become parents together (and in fact performing the social role of parent). The series of cases that have arisen from these errors show that the courts are now willing to put right such mistakes. In fact, in *Case V (Human Fertilisation and Embryology Act 2008)*,[65] which concerned a female same-sex couple (see the following section), Munby P observed that:

> The bureaucrats, administrators and lawyers involved need to understand the immense emotional impact on the ordinary people unwillingly caught up in these cases of the seem-ingly and profoundly disturbing discovery that something has gone 'wrong'.[66]

Second female parents

In relation to same-sex female parenthood really all that changed under the HFE Act 2008 was the necessary extension of the presumption of legal parenthood to female civil partners (in the same way as to husbands)[67] and of the provisions relating to unmarried female part-ners (in the same way as to unmarried heterosexual partners) of a woman who had a child after using donated sperm.[68] Though it was therefore made easier for same-sex (female) couples to jointly obtain legal parenthood under the Act, the changes did not radically alter who or what a parent could be—though clearly more inclusive of same-sex parent families, there remain issues, for example in relation to nomenclature (i.e. can there be two 'mothers'?), to those who choose to become parents by themselves, or to those who would—if they could—opt to have more than two people legally recognised as parents.[69]

 Key Legislation 3: HFA Act 2008, ss. 42–47

Where the HFE Act 2008 clearly did go beyond well beyond what had gone before is in relation to parenthood being shared between same-sex female partners. Given the reality that the law allows civil partnerships and same-sex marriage, coupled with the fact that a woman could give birth in this context, it is hard to see that the legislation could not have done so, without risking a claim of discrimination on grounds of sexuality. The sections of the Act that confer 'second parent' status on a mother's female partner mirror exactly the substance of the provisions for fatherhood under ss. 35–37.

Thus, s. 42 applies if a woman ('W') was married or in a civil partnership with another woman at the time of 'the placing in her of the embryo or the sperm and eggs or of her artificial insemination', then (subject to s. 45 where the common law presumption of legitimacy is written in to the legislation):

---

[64] [2017] EWHC 50 (Fam), at [21].   [65] [2016] EWHC 2356 (Fam).

[66] [2016] EWHC 2356 (Fam), at [27].   [67] And since the 2013 Act, female same-sex spouses.

[68] Note, the Sch 3 consent requirement still applies, and also the female partner of a woman who undergoes treatment becomes defined as the 'second parent', not a mother, which continues to be defined (by s. 33) as the woman who gives birth 'and no other woman'.

[69] See section 1 at the beginning of the chapter re British Columbia, Canada.

the other party to the civil partnership or marriage is to be treated as a parent of the child unless it is shown that she did not consent to the placing in W of the embryo or the sperm and eggs or her artificial insemination (s. 42(1)).

Consent of the putative second parent is therefore important, though the burden falls on any spouse or civil partner who says they did not give their consent to prove it. This too is a real recognition of the concept of 'intended parenthood', even in the absence of a genetic connection and even in the absence of a heterosexual relationship, where even the pretence of there being two biological connections cannot be maintained.

The position of women who intend to be the second parent is covered under ss. 43–44 in a similar way to that in ss. 36–37 for men. Section 43 applies where 'the agreed female parenthood conditions', given in s. 44, apply, and states:

If no man is treated by virtue of section 35 as the father of the child and no woman is treated by virtue of section 42 as a parent of the child, but—

(a) the embryo or the sperm and eggs were placed in W, or W was artificially inseminated, in the course of treatment services provided in the United Kingdom by a person to whom a licence applies,

(b) at the time when the embryo or the sperm and eggs were placed in W, or W was artificially inseminated, the agreed female parenthood conditions (as set out in section 44) were satisfied in relation to another woman, in relation to treatment provided to W under that licence,

(c) the other woman remained alive at the time,then, subject to section 45(2) to (4), the other woman is to be treated as a parent of the child.

The 'agreed female parenthood conditions' as outlined in s. 44 are met by 'another woman' ('P') in relation to W (the treated woman/mother) *if, but only if,* (my emphasis)—

(a) P has given the person responsible a notice stating that P consents to P being treated as a parent of any child resulting from treatment provided to W under the licence,

(b) W has given the person responsible a notice stating that she consents to P being so treated,

(c) neither M nor P has, since giving notice . . . given the person responsible notice of the withdrawal of P's or W's consent to P being so treated,

(d) W has not, since the giving of the notice under paragraph (b), given the person responsible—
   (i) a further notice under that paragraph stating that W consents to a woman other than P being treated as the parent of any resulting child, or
   (ii) a notice under s37(1)(b) stating that W consents to a man being treated as the father of any resulting child, and

(e) W and P are not within prohibited degrees of relationship in relation to each other.

Again, all 'notices' must be in writing and must be signed by the relevant party to have effect (s. 37(2)). When the notices do have effect, s. 48(1) determines that the 'other woman' will become the second legal parent of the child for all purposes. Section 46(1) makes clear that where there is a second female parent, no man can be treated in law as the father. Thus, ss. 43 and 44—somewhat controversially—allow legal recognition of the deliberate creation of 'fatherless families'.

AB v CD and the Z Fertility Clinic [2013] EWHC 1418 (Fam) illustrates just how this can go wrong. In this case, the mother of children born following donor insemination in a licensed clinic disputed that her female ex-partner was the children's second parent. The issue in this case was whether the necessary consents had been put in place. It was established that the treatment had taken place over two days and the consent forms had only been signed on the second day, thus they were not effective. In addition, a sequence of other failures at the clinic concerned (this was just as the HFE Act 2008 was coming into effect, bringing with it new procedures) meant that the clinic had breached its licence conditions. Cobb J held that the ex-partner was not the second legal parent. It was this case that sparked the audit of clinics' practices and procedures which identified the numerous problems affecting consent in the case outlined in *Case K* and related cases, discussed earlier.

> **❓ DEBATE 1: DOES THE LAW ON ASSISTED CONCEPTION APPROPRIATELY AND EFFECTIVELY DEAL WITH THE MULTIPLE DIFFERENT PERMUTATIONS OF FAMILY CREATION THAT TECHNOLOGY AFFORDS US?**

The HFE Act 2008 has—but only to an extent—formalised acceptance of and reflected in law some more modern understandings of parenthood and family types that incorporate social and intentional aspects of parenting, disconnected it (in some cases) from the biological link and goes well beyond the old common law presumptions. Nevertheless, the changes it has brought are perhaps not as radical as at first it may have seemed and, in fact, may not go far enough.

The HFE Act 2008 could hardly have failed to incorporate same-sex partners in the wake of the Civil Partnership Act 2004 (and latterly the availability of same-sex marriage, which has resulted in later amendments to the HFE Act 2008), and the fact that same-sex couples could adopt. Nor could it maintain a real distinction (though it has continued to maintain some differences) between married and unmarried couples, again particularly given the fact that unmarried couples can jointly adopt, and obviously can—and do—also have children together outside of the context of fertility treatment. Despite this, both the Act and its preceding consultation failed in any way to question the notion that the birth mother is always the legal mother.

What this leaves us with is the differentiated treatment of certain parties—so at the same time as an attempt was made to liberalise and modernise concepts of parenthood, some people continue to find themselves excluded. While it is possible, for example, for two women to share legal parenthood status (ss. 43–44), it is not possible for two men to do so at birth. Obviously, two men seeking to have a child would need to use surrogacy to do so (see 3.3), meaning that a woman carries the child and gives birth—more involvement than is required by egg, sperm, or embryo donors. However, she will always be the legal mother, despite not intending to be so. The provisions of the HFE Act 2008 recognise that egg and sperm donors do not intend to be parents of the child that their genetic material brings into the world (though it bizarrely does *not* recognise this in the situation where an unmarried heterosexual or same-sex female couple conceives via donation outside of a licensed clinic), while recognising the intentions of those that do intend to be parents, via the medium of the 'notice' provisions and consent requirements. It would not be so difficult to do the same for male same-sex partners (or single men) having children using surrogacy.

Part of this debate—perhaps inevitably—relates to terminology. The other issue raised by these supposedly liberalising principles is the idea of what 'motherhood' can be. Despite being recognised by the HFE Act 2008, a female partner of a woman who gives birth can in law only be a 'second parent'—and not a 'mother', even if her egg was used. Where both female partners are capable of carrying a child, and both wish to do so for the completion of the intended family unit, this could bizarrely result (and possibly already has) in households where one woman is mother to one child and second parent to another, later child, and the other female partner's parenthood status is the reverse of this. This seems somewhat counterintuitive and again results from the wholesale reluctance to challenge or deconstruct what 'a mother' is or can be when the legislation was updated.

3.1.3 Posthumous conception and parenthood

Sections 39 and 40 of the HFE Act 2008 allows fatherhood to be attributed to a man who has died, in situations where his sperm or an embryo created using his sperm was used after his death (s. 39) and where an embryo created 'with' him in the receipt of 'treatment together', but not using his sperm (s. 40) is used. These sections allow this as long as the consent requirements were met before the death occurred, but only for the 'purpose of enabling the man's particulars to be entered as the particulars of the child's father in a relevant register of births', and for no other purpose.[70] Section 46 replicates this situation for a second female parent where the woman has become deceased subsequent to giving consent. Thus, we see again the importance of consent to the attribution of legal parenthood.

The idea of 'posthumous conception' originated from the case of Diane Blood.[71] The Bloods had been trying to start a family but Stephen Blood contracted meningitis and lapsed into a coma—his sperm was collected at the hospital shortly before he died in 1995. The HFEA refused Mrs Blood authorisation to use the sperm as she did not have written consent from her husband. The High Court upheld the authority's decision because the HFE Act 1990 did not give any discretionary powers to waive the consent requirements. The Court of Appeal agreed that Mrs Blood could not lawfully be treated in this country, but also decided that the HFEA should reconsider whether Mrs Blood should be allowed to export the sperm to Belgium for treatment, given that a discretion was conferred on the HFEA by s. 24(4) of the HFE Act 1990 to authorise the import or export of gametes subject to such conditions as the Authority thinks fit.

In *ex parte Blood*, Lord Woolf MR noted that the sperm's storage was unlawful without the requisite written consent. However, given the unprecedented circumstances, he realised it was necessary for the clinic to store the sperm first and decide the legality of doing so later. Pointedly, he said that he did not foresee the courts having to consider the legality of exporting unlawfully stored sperm again, as the decision clarified the law by emphasising that a person's gametes must not be stored in this country (whether or not for export) without that person's written effective consent (under Sch. 3 to the 1990 Act). However, Mrs Blood's appeal was allowed because the HFEA:

> was not properly advised as to the importance of [European] Community law as to treatment in Belgium. Mrs Blood has the right to be treated in Belgium with her husband's sperm unless there are good public policy reasons for not allowing this to happen.[72]

A decade later, however, a similar case raised new legal arguments. In *L* [2008],[73] a widow sought authorisation from the High Court to undergo IVF abroad using her dead husband's sperm. She had obtained emergency court permission, pending later legal resolution, to have sperm collected from her 31-year-old husband's body hours after he died in June 2007 from unexpected complications following a routine appendix removal. The sperm was transferred to a clinic for storage. L sought a declaration in respect of the HFE Act 1990 to allow the sperm to be lawfully stored and then used either in the UK or exported for storage and use in another country. L pleaded that the couple had wanted another child, had discussed this with family and friends, and had been in the preliminary stages of seeking IVF together (this was confirmed in a statement from her gynaecologist). L explained that they had not thought to have him provide written consent at this stage, because they had not feared that the minor surgery would be fatal. Her lawyer also argued

---

[70] Section 40(4) of the HFE Act 2008. A similar provision had existed in s. 28 of the 1990 Act.

[71] *R v Human Fertilisation and Embryology Authority, ex parte Diane Blood* [1997] 2 All ER 687.

[72] [1997] 2 All ER 704.

[73] *L v Human Fertilisation & Embryology Authority & Secretary of State for Health* [2008] EWHC 2149 (Fam).

that *disposal* of his sperm would contravene her human right to respect for her private and family life protected under Article 8 ECHR enshrined in UK law by the Human Rights Act 1998 (not in force and so not available to Diane Blood at the time) and rights under European Union law—dictating free movement of persons, services, and goods across national boundaries.

The Court dismissed the claimant's application. Giving judgment, Charles J ruled that it was probably unlawful for her to have removed her husband's sperm without his prior written consent. He also found that the HFEA's absolute requirement of effective consent for use of continued storage and use of sperm is not incompatible with the protected right under Article 8 ECHR. However, in respect of storage for use and such subsequent use outside the UK, Charles J found the position to be less clear, given the discretion conferred by s. 24(4) of the HFE Act 1990.

3.2 **Transsexual parenthood**

Unless a person's gender has been changed post-birth according to the provisions of the Gender Recognition Act 2004 (see Chapter 2), the law maintains that their sex is determined by the biological criteria as defined at birth. As a gender recognition certificate granted under the Gender Recognition Act 2004 does not have retrospective effect, it will not affect any parenthood status obtained at any time before the certificate was issued,[74] but will impact on any treatments undertaken after its issue. This can result in a variety of complex and seemingly contradictory situations regarding legal parenthood.

For example, a female-to-male transsexual person could become a father under the provisions of ss. 35 and 36 of the HFE Act 2008, if he had been issued with a gender recognition certificate. If, as is now possible under the Gender Recognition Act 2004 (see Chapter 2), he was married to a woman who received treatment then (subject to the consent provisions) he would become the father of any child conceived. Even if not married, if he undertook treatment services 'together' with a female partner at a licensed clinic, he could be the father. And, in the absence of a gender recognition certificate, as they would still be regarded as a woman according to the law, that person could still become a second legal parent (though not a father), under the provisions in ss. 42–44 of the HFE Act 2008. Imagine the situation, for example, where a female-to-male transsexual person had given birth to a child prior to gender reassignment and the issue of a gender recognition certificate, and later had another child following treatment of their married partner with donor sperm under the provisions of ss. 35 and 36 of the HFE Act 2008—that person would then be a mother to one child, but a father to the other. Also, though it is not yet possible for a male-to-female transsexual person to carry and deliver a child, this may become possible in the future. As giving birth is the defining fact of 'motherhood', she would in that situation be a mother. However, the same person may have previously been a father. In fact there are potential questions about whether a male-to-female transsexual person should be permitted to use sperm collected and frozen when she was a man in order to have a child—could she be both the biological father and the legal mother? Or would she be regarded as her own sperm donor? Or must/should she only be allowed to use the sperm of her male partner, if there is one, or donor sperm? These and other questions may prove to challenge the understandings of legal parenthood still further in the future.

---

[74] Gender Recognition Act 2004, s. 12 and see *R (on the application of JK) v Registrar General for England and Wales* [2015] EWHC 990 (Admin).

3.3 **Surrogacy arrangements**

Surrogacy is an arrangement in which a woman (the surrogate) agrees to become pregnant, carry, and give birth to a child (or children) for another person or couple, who ultimately intend to be the parent(s). Surrogacy arrangements fall into one of two types, though the terminology used by different people to describe these arrangements varies considerably. 'Full', 'IVF', 'host', 'carrier', or 'gestational' surrogacy is when a surrogate is genetically unrelated to the child she carries (i.e. she is implanted with sperm and eggs or an embryo created either by the intended parents' egg and sperm, or one created using donated gametes). This kind of surrogacy obviously requires specialist medical involvement as IVF techniques are used to bring about pregnancy. 'Partial', 'straight', 'genetic', or 'traditional' surrogacy occurs where the surrogate's own egg is used (so she is also genetically related to any resulting child(ren)). While this may involve medical treatment (e.g. insemination at a licensed clinic), pregnancy might also be established 'informally', via self-insemination. The bulk of the UK's law on surrogacy is found in the Surrogacy Arrangements Act 1985, with some additional regulation coming from the HFE Act 1990 (as amended by the HFE Act 2008). Surrogacy arrangements are unenforceable either by or against any of the parties, meaning that no party can be bound to their agreement.[75] Specifically, at its starkest, this means that the woman acting as surrogate can change her mind about handing over the baby, or the intending parent(s) could refuse to take the child and/or to pay anything they had agreed to pay for the surrogate's expenses.

Surrogacy arrangements may be entered into by strangers, sometimes facilitated by a surrogacy agency,[76] or by family or friends. For example, sisters can—and do—act as surrogate for their sisters, and there are instances of mothers being surrogates for their own daughters,[77] or vice versa. Clearly, this makes determining who the parents of children born through surrogacy are of paramount importance. As indicated in section 3.1.1, a woman who gives birth to a child will always be that child's legal mother. This means, to elaborate on just one example of the familial surrogacy relationships given, that if a woman acts as a surrogate for her own daughter (even where the pregnancy is established using her daughter's eggs), she will be the legal mother (and not the grandmother) of that child. If she was married, her husband (the grandfather) would in fact be the legal father.

Until the 1990 Act, the only way to transfer legal parenthood to the intended parents was by adoption. The HFE Act 1990 introduced the 'parental order', under which eligible intended parents can apply to have legal parenthood transferred to them and a new birth certificate issued for the child(ren). Parental orders came about via a late amendment to the HFE Bill as it was being debated in Parliament, submitted by Michael Jopling, then a Cumbrian MP, on behalf of a couple from his constituency, who had undertaken 'full' surrogacy using their own gametes and who objected to having to adopt their own biological children.[78] As we shall see, however, despite the availability of parental orders, there have been a number of problems with the eligibility criteria, and many cases have reached the courts in recent years, challenging some of the provisions.

In the 1990s, the government commissioned a further inquiry, chaired by Professor Margaret Brazier, to look specifically into surrogacy. The inquiry was to look at the regulation of surrogacy, specifically in regard to payments, in the light of various cases and the spectre of commercial agencies seeking to operate in the UK. The inquiry report was

---

[75] Surrogacy Arrangements Act 1985, s. 1(A) as inserted by HFE Act 1990, s. 36.

[76] Which can only operate on a non-profit basis according to the law as any commercial agencies or brokers have been prohibited since the Surrogacy Arrangements Act 1985. It is also illegal to advertise for or as a surrogate.　　　　　　　　　　[77] And even sons—see *Re B v C (Surrogacy: Adoption)* [2015] EWFC 17.

[78] Hansard HC vol 170, col 944 (2 April 1990). The couple's case became *Re W (Minors)(Surrogacy)* [1991] 1 FLR 385.

published in 1998.[79] It recommended that a new Surrogacy Act should be passed, based on openness and understanding of the agreements between parties, as well as a surrogacy Code of Practice to provide guidance to surrogates and intended parents. The report also recommended that payments to surrogates should be prohibited, other than to allow compensation to the surrogate for reasonably incurred expenses as a result of the pregnancy. None of the report's recommendations were acted upon and the law has therefore remained largely the same since that time, subject to the small amendments made regarding who may obtain a parental order following the HFE Act 2008.

There was very little court activity on surrogacy for quite some time through the 1990s and into the early twenty-first century. However, in more recent years—perhaps the last decade—another aspect of surrogacy and the way it is practised has generated a considerable amount of case law: 'cross-border' or 'international' surrogacy arrangements. This describes the situation whereby intended parents from the UK travel to destinations in other countries in order to enter an arrangement with a surrogate there. The USA has always been a popular destination for British intended parents, but in the past decade or so, various other countries have proved to be popular surrogacy destinations, including India, Thailand, Nepal, Mexico, Cambodia, Russia, the Ukraine, Georgia, and Canada (though some of these destinations have since been shut down to foreign intended parents). Because most cross-border surrogacy is commercial in nature, a number of cases have reawakened the issue of payments, as this is potentially a factor in determining who can, and who cannot, obtain legal parenthood following surrogacy.

Further, perhaps even because of this reawakened interest, as well as other issues flowing from the nature of cross-border surrogacy arrangements, such as domicile and citizenship issues conflict of laws issues, delays in or failures to apply for a parental order within the specified timeframe, and more, other 'domestic' cases have also begun to emerge. Many of these challenge the legal parenthood provisions of the HFE Act 2008 and, it seems, some may have the effect of changing the definition of who can become a legal parent following surrogacy.

3.3.1 Parental orders

A parental order is a court order that 'reallocates' legal parenthood after a surrogacy arrangement, removing this status from the original legal parents at birth and giving it to the intended parents. However, not everyone who has a child through surrogacy is able to apply for an order, and the rules and limitations about when and to whom an order may be granted are quite complicated—and often controversial—as we shall see.

 Key Legislation 4: HFE Act 2008, s. 54

(1) On an application made by two people ('the applicants'), the court may make an order providing for a child to be treated in law as the child of the applicants if—

   (a) the child has been carried by a woman who is not one of the applicants, as a result of the placing in her of an embryo or sperm and eggs or her artificial insemination,

   (b) the gametes of at least one of the applicants were used to bring about the creation of the embryo,[80] and

   (c) the conditions in subsections (2) to (8) are satisfied.

---

[79] *Surrogacy: Review for Health Ministers of Current Arrangements for Payments and Regulation, Report of the Review Team* (Cm 4068, 1998).

[80] Note that since The Human Fertilisation and Embryology (Mitochondrial Donation) Regulations 2015, this specifically excludes (by virtue of the insertion of s. 54(1A)) an egg donor who contributed only mitochondrial DNA, not nuclear DNA, for the purposes of avoiding inherited (via mitochondria) genetic disease.

(2) The applicants must be—

   (a) husband and wife,

   (b) civil partners of each other, or

   (c) two persons who are living as partners in an enduring family relationship and are not within prohibited degrees of relationship in relation to each other.

(3) ... the applicants must apply for the order during the period of 6 months beginning with the day on which the child is born.

(4) At the time of the application and the making of the order—

   (a) the child's home must be with the applicants, and

   (b) either or both of the applicants must be domiciled in the United Kingdom or in the Channel Islands or the Isle of Man.

(5) At the time of the making of the order both the applicants must have attained the age of 18.

(6) The court must be satisfied that both—

   (a) the woman who carried the child, and

   (b) any other person who is a parent of the child but is not one of the applicants (including any man who is the father by virtue of section 35 or 36 or any woman who is a parent by virtue of section 42 or 43), have freely, and with full understanding of what is involved, agreed unconditionally to the making of the order.

(7) Subsection (6) does not require the agreement of a person who cannot be found or is incapable of giving agreement; and the agreement of the woman who carried the child is ineffective for the purpose of that subsection if given by her less than six weeks after the child's birth.

(8) The court must be satisfied that no money or other benefit (other than for expenses reasonably incurred) has been given or received by either of the applicants for or in consideration of—

   (a) the making of the order,

   (b) any agreement required by subsection (6),

   (c) the handing over of the child to the applicants, or

   (d) the making of arrangements with a view to the making of the order, unless authorised by the court.

This section allows certain people to apply for a parental order after the birth of a child to a surrogate. Apart from perhaps more obvious requirements like establishing a minimum age of 18, and requiring domicile in the UK, Channel Islands, or the Isle of Man, it can be seen from the provisions that parental orders are not available to everyone.

Section 54(1), for example, specifies that applicants must be a couple, in that it requires 'two people', thus single people are unable to apply. Section 54(1)(b) tells us that at least one member of the couple applying must have supplied genetic material, so any couple unfortunate enough to require 'double donation' because they are both medically infertile are unable to apply.[81]

---

[81] That is, where neither party is able to produce gametes. If this occurred in 'ordinary' IVF then the provisions outlined in 3.1 would operate, making the woman who gives birth the mother and her male or female spouse or partner could also be automatically recognised as the father/second parent. If such a couple *also* require a surrogate, because the female partner (if there is one) is unable to or medically advised against carrying a pregnancy, then they cannot obtain a parental order if they use donated gametes or a donated embryo carried by a surrogate—they would have to adopt the child(ren) to become legal parents.

Section 54(2) requires the couple to be in a marriage, civil partnership, or 'enduring family relationship' (whatever that is—it is largely undefined here) when they make the application. Sections 54 (6) and (7) have the combined effect of requiring full and unconditional consent to the making of the order from not only the surrogate, but also her husband or partner, if they too are a legal parent of the child at birth by virtue of their relationship with her, unless those people cannot be located or are otherwise incapable of giving consent. As can be seen from s. 55(7), consent cannot be given within the first six weeks of a child's life—in addition, according to s. 54(3), applications for a parental order can only be made until the child(ren) concerned reaches six months old. Finally, s. 54(8) allows only 'reasonable expenses' to be paid or received in relation to a surrogacy arrangement.

Despite all the detailed provisions and limitations on who may apply for or obtain a parental order contained within s. 54 of the HFE Act 2008, there have been a number of exceptions made by the courts all in the name of promoting the best interests of the children concerned. The increasing number of exceptions to the parental order requirements, and the reasons given for them, has led some to view the legislation on surrogacy as increasingly out-dated, and an imperfect reflection of the realities of modern surrogacy as practised.[82] Since 2010, the court, in considering whether to grant a parental order, must make the child's (lifelong) welfare the paramount consideration.[83] This has led to various decisions that seemingly contravene the actual wording of the provisions. Various situations faced by applicants have given rise to challenges to almost every single provision and—in part as a result of this—have led various campaigners mobilising to see the law reformed.

 CONTEXT 1: SURROGACY LAW REFORM

As a result of many representations made about reform, as well as the various and increasing legal anomalies thrown up in court cases over the past decade or so, there has been a growing call for reform of surrogacy laws, not only from academics, but also from legal practitioners working with those who they have advised in surrogacy cases, as well as non-profit organisations that deal with surrogacy. More recently, the voices of surrogates and intended parents have also been heard.[84] Interestingly, Mary Warnock, who might be said to be the 'architect' of the law, has publicly spoken and has written about the fact that her perception of surrogacy in the 1980s led her to get it 'wrong'.

[82] See, e.g., Horsey, K. and Sheldon, S., 'Still hazy After All These Years: The Law Regulating Surrogacy' (2012) 20 *Medical Law Review* 67; Horsey, K. 'Fraying at the Edges—UK Surrogacy Law in 2015' (2016) 24 *Medical Law Review*; Alghrani, A and Griffiths, D., 'The Regulation of Surrogacy in the United Kingdom: The Case for Reform' (2017) 29 *Child and Family Law Quarterly* 165.

[83] The Human Fertilisation and Embryology (Parental Orders) Regulations 2010 (SI 985/2010) apply s. 1 of the Children and Adoption Act 2002 to parental order applications, including the 'welfare checklist'.

[84] See, e.g., Horsey, K. 'Surrogacy in the UK: Myth busting and reform' Report of the Surrogacy UK Working Group on Surrogacy Law Reform (Surrogacy UK, 2015); Natalie Gamble Associates, 'House of Lords debates surrogacy law reform' (blog post, December 2016). Available at: http://www.nataliegambleassociates. co.uk/blog/2016/12/, accessed 26 September 2017. See also a special issue of the *Journal of Medical Law and Ethics* (vol 4, December 2016), which contained the papers presented at a conference on surrogacy law reform in May 2016, including papers advocating reform written by, *inter alia*, Baroness Mary Warnock, Professor Margaret Brazier, chair of the 1998 surrogacy review (see *Surrogacy: Review for Health Ministers of Current Arrangements for Payments and Regulation, Report of the Review Team* (Cm 4068, 1998)) and Kim Cotton, the 'first' UK surrogate, who also established one of the UK's main non-profit surrogacy agencies.

Alongside the remedial order being introduced to address the issue of single parents by surrogacy (see the following section), the Law Commission consulted in 2016 on whether to include surrogacy law reform in its 13th programme of reform. In a House of Lords debate in December 2016 it was confirmed that the government supported such a review of the law.[85] By March 2017, we knew that surrogacy had passed the Law Commission's 'first sift', with it having received over 1300 submissions from interested parties on its consultation. A final decision on the whether a programme of reform of surrogacy law will be taken forward was expected in autumn 2017, having been delayed from its originally timed schedule by the calling of the snap general election in June 2017, but at the time of writing, no announcement had yet been made.

A number of parental order cases have been decided outside of the parameters of s. 54 in relation to the time in which the application was made. However, here as elsewhere, as we shall see, the consent requirement seems to be holding strong—though may be problematic in this context.

Problematic parental order situations: time limits

In *X (A Child) (Surrogacy: Time Limit)* [2014], Munby P granted a parental order to intended parents who applied outside of the six month time limit specified in s. 54(3) of the HFE Act 2008. He asked:

> Can Parliament really have intended that the gate should be barred forever if the application for a parental order is lodged even one day late? I cannot think so . . . Given the subject matter, given the consequences for the commissioning parents, never mind those for the child, to construe section 54(3) as barring forever an application made just one day late is not, in my judgment, sensible.[86]

  Key Case 2: *A & B (Children) (Surrogacy: Parental Orders: Time Limits)* [2015] EWHC 911 (Fam).

British parents had two children—at the time of the case aged 5 and 8 years old—via a surrogate in California, USA. Pre-birth court orders issued in California had allowed birth certificates to be issued with both intended parents' names on them. Under Californian law, therefore, the intended parents were the parents. However, under English law, without a parental order, the surrogate would be considered the legal mother because she had given birth to the child. The intended (social) parents did not find this out until 2012, when they then applied for an order to be made.

The approach adopted by Munby P in *X (A Child) (Surrogacy: Time Limit)* was followed by Russell J, who found that it would be 'manifestly unjust' to give such a delay, even if very long 'greater weight than the welfare of these children' (at [71]). She also determined that the welfare of any children concerned should outweigh any public policy concerns, except in cases where there was a grave abuse of public policy, which this case was not (at [46]–[47]). The parental orders were granted.

It therefore appears from this decision that there is now no real time limit in the law within which a parental order application must be made, making the provision in s. 54(3) HFE Act 2008 seem somewhat obsolete.[87]

---

[85] Hansard HC vol 777, col 1331 (14 December 2016).

[86] *X (A Child) (Surrogacy: Time Limit)* [2014] EWHC 3135 (Fam), at [55].

[87] See also *AB v CD (Surrogacy—Time Limit and Consent)* [2015] EWFC 12 (Fam) and *A and B (Children: Surrogacy: Parental Orders: Time limit)* [2015] EWHC 911 (Fam).

In *A & B (No. 2—Parental Order)* [2015] EWHC 2080 (Fam), the intended parents were also granted parental orders having similarly been unaware that a parental order was necessary, having had their names recorded on the Indian birth certificates after their (at the time of the hearing) 3-year-old twins were born to an Indian surrogate. In this case, as well as the time delay, there were additional complicating factors. By the time of the application, the couple had separated (s. 54(4)(a) requires that 'the child's home must be with the applicants' at the time an application is made), and there were also issues relating to domicile, consent, and payments made to the surrogate.

In *A & Anor v C & Anor*, Theis J granted parental orders to applicants who had three children aged 12 (twins) and 13, born to a surrogate in the USA.[88] Again, the couple had obtained pre-birth orders, which established their legal relationship in the state where they were born, and had no idea that they needed to take further legal steps to ensure their parenthood status in England, until reading an article in 2016. The applicants, who represented themselves in the hearing, (see Chapter 15) asked that:

> . . . this short judgment is put in the public domain, as they want to ensure that other people in the same position as them are encouraged to make applications to secure their legal relationship with children born through surrogacy arrangements. By not doing so risks complications later on, for example if there is a need to demonstrate they are the legal parent of a child, or a need to show they have parental responsibility for the child concerned (at [11]).

In fact, such a case might lead us to doubt whether there should continue to be any time limit on applications at all, and this might be one consideration if and when the law on surrogacy is reformed in the future. However, as Theis J said in the case, the reason these decisions are (currently) made on a case by case basis is in part so as 'not to discourage commissioning parents in surrogacy arrangements from making applications for parental orders promptly', in the best interests of children in securing their legal relationship with their parents.[89]

Problematic parental order situations: reasonable expenses

Despite what the provision in s. 54(8) of the HFE Act 2008 says, it is now in fact quite common for a court to retrospectively authorise payments made in a surrogacy arrangement, in order to grant a parental order to the intended parents.

 Key Case 3: *Re X & Y (Foreign Surrogacy)* [2008] EWHC 3030.

British parents had twins using a Ukrainian surrogate. The payment they made to the surrogate included a lump sum payment of 25,000 euros to enable her to buy a flat, as well as 235 euros per month. Hedley J retrospectively authorised the payments and granted the intended parents the parental order. In his judgment, he said that:

> ... it is almost impossible to imagine a set of circumstances in which by the time the case comes to court, the welfare of the child (particularly a foreign child) would not be gravely compromised (at the very least) by a refusal to make an order (at [24]).

This decision, though prior to the introduction of the 2010 Surrogacy Regulations, seems to have set the tone for future decisions on payments. As the welfare of the child is the court's paramount consideration, it is unlikely that there will be a case where the child's welfare is better served by removing it from the care of the intended parents, because they paid what might be considered to be a sum exceeding 'reasonable expenses' to a surrogate.

---

[88] [2016] EWFC 42.   [89] [2016] EWFC 42, at [8].

Cases following *Re X & Y* continued the trend of retrospective authorisation of payments—and the subsequent granting of parental orders—in the child's best interests. In *Re L (A Minor)*,[90] Hedley J referred to the paramountcy principle in doing so. In *X and Y (Children)*,[91] the late Sir Nicholas Wall, then President of the Family Division, found that despite payments made to two Indian surrogates clearly representing more than reasonable expenses, they were not 'disproportionate', and the intended parents had acted in good faith in making them.

It seems now that we have reached a point where payments made to surrogates and to agencies in overseas arrangements have become relatively uncontroversial, and do not stand in the way of legal parenthood being transferred to the intended parents via a parental order. Indeed, in *Re AB (Surrogacy; Domicile)*, Theis J referred to the payments that had been made in a Nepalese surrogacy arrangement as a 'non-controversial matter' in the context of the granting of a parental order.[92] As well as the agency fee, and about $9,500 in expenses, the surrogate had been paid $42,993 (amounting to approximately £29,500) *over and above* her reasonable expenses. In authorising the payments, Theis J said they were 'well within the figures this Court has seen in similar cases' (at [11]).

Problematic parental order situations: single applicants

As we have seen, s. 54(1) HFE Act 2008 stipulates that parental orders may be granted following 'an application made by two people . . .' Given that single women may access fertility services, and the fact that single people can adopt (see Chapter 12), the wording of this section appears to be somewhat problematic.

Key Case 4: *Re Z (A Child: Human Fertilisation and Embryology Act: Parental Order)* [2015] EWFC 73

In this case the application for a parental order was made by a single man, who had a child by a surrogate in the USA and was performing the social fatherhood role. The surrogate had given notarised consent to the making of the order, which was also supported by CAFCASS.[93] The court was asked two questions: first, whether it was open to it to make a parental order under s. 54 (1) of the HFE Act 2008 to a single applicant and, secondly, if not, whether it could 'read down' the section in accordance with the Human Rights Act 1998. Counsel argued that not to do so would be discriminatory interference with the man's right to respect for his private and family life under Articles 8 and 14 ECHR on the grounds of his single person status. They also pointed out that such 'reading down' had already occurred in other cases in relation to ss. 55(3) and 54(4).[94]

It was clear from the judgment given by Munby P that, had he considered himself able to, he would have 'read down' the section and allowed the parental order to be granted. In some cases previously decided by him, relating to applications made outside of the six month 'time limit', he had found that it could not possibly have been Parliament's intention that if an

---

[90] [2010] EWHC 3146 (Fam).   [91] [2011] EWHC 3147 (Fam).

[92] *Re AB (Surrogacy; Domicile)* [2016] EWFC 63.

[93] The Children and Family Court Advisory Service. Cafcass has designated 'parental order reporters' who conduct assessments of intended parents, including making home visits, and make recommendations to the courts as to the suitability of the granting of a parental order.

[94] See, e.g., *A v P (Surrogacy: Parental Order: Death of Applicant)* [2011] EWHC 1738 (Fam), [2012] 2 FLR 145; *Re X (A Child) (Parental Order: Time Limit)* [2014] EWHC 3135, [2015] Fam 186, [2015] 1 FLR 349; *Re A and B (Children) (Surrogacy: Parental Orders: Time Limits)* [2015] EWHC 911 (Fam); and *A and B v X and Y* [2015] EWHC 2080 (Fam).

application was made one day later than six months, this would preclude the making of an order, particularly as this would not be in the child's best interests, and had 'read down' the relevant section (see Key Case 2). Here, however, he felt himself constrained by the wording of the HFE Act 2008, and he had also been directed to part of the debate on the passage of the legislation where the minister concerned had justified the restriction to couples.[95]

Since the decision in *Re Z (A Child: Human Fertilisation and Embryology Act: parental order)*, the President of the Family Division held in *In the matter of Z (A Child) (No. 2)* that the current law discriminates unfairly against single parents and their children, and is in breach of the Human Rights Act 1998.[96] In a debate on surrogacy law reform in the House of Lords in December 2016, Lady Chisholm of Owlpen, speaking on behalf of the government, said:

> [We have decided] the Government's response to the recent High Court judgment that declared that a provision in the Human Fertilisation and Embryology Act 2008—which enables couples but not single people to obtain a parental order following surrogacy—is incompatible with the Human Rights Act. We will, therefore, update the legislation on parental orders to ensure that it is compatible with the court judgment. I can confirm that the Government will introduce a remedial order to achieve this, so that single people can apply for parental orders on the same basis as couples.[97]

This remedial order was expected to be issued in May 2017, but was delayed by the calling of a snap general election and at the time of writing was expected to be laid in late 2017/ early 2018, potentially therefore coming into effect, at the earliest, in mid-2018. If it is passed, it will operate retrospectively to allow those single people who are already (social) parents by surrogacy to apply for a parental order, such as the biological father in *Re Z (A Child: Human Fertilisation and Embryology Act: parental order)*. Therefore, we know that the position on biologically-related single parents through surrogacy is likely to change, whether or not there is full-scale review of the legislation on surrogacy following the Law Commission's considerations. Single people who become parents this way will no longer have to adopt to achieve legal parenthood, but will be able to obtain a parental order. It should be noted, however, that although Lady Chisholm mentioned 'single people', only those who are genetically related to the child born by surrogacy will be able to apply. In the rare situation where this might not be the case, such as in the case of a single woman who, for example, is unable to store eggs before a radical hysterectomy as part of cancer treatment, and uses another woman to carry her child for her, it would appear that this too might contravene the single woman's human rights.

Problematic parental order situations: consent and the fallback to adoption

A number of cases have dispensed with the requirement for free and informed consent of the surrogate and any other legal parent after the birth in situations where, for example, the surrogate cannot be found when the application for the parental order is made. This is allowed by s. 54(7) and applied, for example, in two cases where an Indian surrogate was unable to be found in order to give consent[98] and another where a Ukrainian surrogate

---

[95] [2015] EWFC 73, at [16].   [96] *In the matter of Z (A Child) (No. 2)* [2016] EWHC 1191 (Fam).

[97] Hansard 14 December 2016 Vol. 777, col. 1332.

[98] *D and L (Surrogacy)* [2012] EWHC 2631 (Fam) and *AB v CD (Surrogacy—Time Limit and Consent)* [2015] EWFC 12.

could no longer be located by the clinic involved by the time the parental order application was made.[99] However, in *Re AB (Surrogacy: Consent)*,[100] the intended parents of twins born to a surrogate, who were both genetically related to the children, were unable to obtain a parental order where the surrogate actively refused to give her consent to the making of the order. The relationship between the surrogate, her partner, and the intended parents had broken down during the course of the pregnancy. However, the surrogate still handed the twins to the intended parents soon after their birth and the twins had been in their care since that point. The surrogate did not wish for any active involvement in the children's lives. Without a parental order, the intended parents would have to adopt their own biological children in order to become their legal parents, something they wished to avoid doing. The surrogate and her husband had confirmed that they would not object to the making of an adoption order.

Despite various requirements within s. 54 of the HFE Act 2008 having been put aside in the best interests of children, or ruled incompatible with human rights, as seen earlier in the chapter, Theis J found herself unable, in *Re AB (Surrogacy: Consent)*, to dispense with the surrogate's consent in the same way.[101] The consequence of this was, as she pointed out, that:

> Without the respondent's consent the application for a parental order comes to a juddering halt, to the very great distress of the applicants. The result is that these children are left in a legal limbo, where, contrary to what was agreed by the parties at the time of the arrangement, the respondents will remain their legal parents even though they are not biologically related to them and they expressly wish to play no part in the children's lives (at [9]).

Instead she granted the application to adjourn the matter generally (supported by all the parties), acknowledging the exceptional circumstances of the case. Therefore, unless and until the surrogate and her partner change their minds about giving consent (or the biological parents adopt), the:

> … consequences for the children of the parental orders not being made are as follows:
>
> (1) They remain living with the applicants, who are their biological and psychological parents, but not their legal parents. The child arrangements order, which gives the applicants parental responsibility, lasts until they are 18 years old.
>
> (2) The respondents, who wish to play no part in the children's lives, remain the children's legal parents throughout their lives by virtue of ss 33 and 35 HFEA. (at [10]).

 DEBATE 2: SHOULD LEGAL PARENTHOOD BE BASED ON GENETIC LINKS, GESTATIONAL RELATIONSHIPS, INTENTION, OR SOMETHING ELSE?

Why should biological parents ever have to adopt their own children? That is not the right outcome for a surrogacy arrangement but comes about because of the law's insistence on motherhood as being based on gestation and birth to the exclusion of all else. Perhaps it is time, therefore, to create an exception to this rule in the context of surrogacy.

It is worth thinking about why gestational relationships have more importance than other parental (or maternal) relationships. Largely, this is historical and goes back to the indisputa-

---

[99] *RS v T (Surrogacy: Service, Consent and Payments)* [2015] EWFC 22.   [100] [2016] EWHC 2643 (Fam).
[101] Note—in adoption proceedings, the consent of the birth parents to the proposed adoption can be dispensed with by the court where it is unreasonably withheld (see Chapter 12). No such provision exists in relation to surrogacy, though it is arguably something that should be considered in law reform.

bility of the fact that, once, if a child was given birth to by a woman, she had to be that child's mother (see section 3). From today's perspective, however, it seems distinctly odd that gestation holds more importance than genetics—and then there is also the question of choice, or intention to become a parent. Given that reproductive processes can now be so widely fragmented, there are obviously now questions about whether genetics, gestation, intention, or what's happening in practice should be regarded as the most important determinant of legal parenthood. Given that the focus on gestation is historical, are there good reasons that people still rely on it to determine motherhood?

In a previous case (about time limits), Russell J called adoption following surrogacy 'a square peg for a round hole'. She added that the 'very existence of parental orders is a testament to the decision of Parliament that adoption orders do not befit children born through surrogacy'. Theis J found similarly in *Re AB* that:

> A parental order was devised specifically for a surrogacy arrangement, recognising the biological connection of the applicants as intended parents of the child. Whilst the respondents have indicated they would not object to an adoption order being made that does not reflect the reality, these children are the biological children of the applicants. An adoption order treats the children as if they were the children of the applicants, which they already are (at [29]).

Concluding her judgment, she added:

> The court can only express the hope that [the surrogate] will be able to rediscover what led her to undertake such a selfless role and see the situation from the view point of these young children. From the perspective of these children's lifelong emotional and psychological welfare parental orders are the only orders that accurately and properly reflect the children's identity as surrogate born children (at [32]).

However, it seems, despite biological connections, the children's 'identity' and the original intentions of the parties entering surrogacy arrangements, what actually makes a parent in the end following surrogacy is the consent of the surrogate and her partner. There are various ways that the law could get around this, which range from small reforms to very large ones—though it is likely that all would be controversial as they challenge the notion of motherhood. It is notable that the adjournment was asked for and granted in this case in part in the hope that there 'may be some change in the current statutory regime governing parental orders' (at [13]).

The first change that could be made is to the consent requirement in s. 54 (6) and (7) of the HFE Act 2008. This could be altered, so that it would allow a judge to make an order in the absence of consent where it is unreasonably withheld, bringing surrogacy into line with adoption. Secondly, the consent requirement could be removed altogether, or 'done away with' for the purposes of parental order applications.[102] Thirdly, the definition of who a legal mother is following surrogacy could be changed entirely. Section 33 of the HFE Act 2008 *could* say:

> *Except in cases of surrogacy*, the woman who is carrying or has carried a child as a result of the placing in her of an embryo or of sperm and eggs, and no other woman, is to be treated as the mother of the child.

---

[102] As argued by Alghrani, A. and Griffiths, D., 'The Regulation of Surrogacy in the United Kingdom: The Case for Reform' (2017) 29 *Child and Family Law Quarterly* 165.

This would leave room for the law to recognise the intended (or biological—though they may not be the same person) mother as the legal mother of the child following surrogacy, leaving the surrogate to be the one who would dispute this, should she wish to, upon the birth of the child. The courts would be left to determine such challenges according to the principle of the paramountcy of the child's welfare.

Fourthly, we could determine parenthood following surrogacy—or all parenthood following assisted reproductive technologies—differently; that is by the intention of the parties.[103] Little would change in respect of 'ordinary' assisted reproductive technologies like IVF, and even with donor insemination: this would represent the position that the law already adopts, including taking into account same-sex partnerships. In surrogacy it would represent the true nature of the relationship, while recognising that surrogates do not in fact regard themselves as mothers.[104]

It can be seen, then, that surrogacy—as with the use of assisted reproductive technologies in other contexts—raises numerous issues regarding the determination of legal parenthood. As assisted reproductive technologies develop even more complexities in the future, as they inevitably will, it will be interesting to watch further debates about parenthood develop.

4. Parental responsibility

There has been a general move in family law over time, away from parents and adults having rights over children, to them having responsibilities towards them. There is a big difference between being the legal parent of a child, and having parental responsibility *for* a child. The law regarding who has—and who does not have—parental responsibility is found in the Children Act 1989 and related case law. Some people gain parental responsibility automatically, according to who they are, while others do not and can only achieve it by being granted it.

 Key Legislation 5: Children Act 1989, s. 3(1)

'In this Act 'parental responsibility' means all the rights, duties, powers, responsibilities and authority which by law a parent of a child has in relation to the child and his property'

This section outlines and defines, in broad terms, the concept of parental responsibility.[105] There is, however, no further definition given within the statute. The concept was introduced by the Children Act 1989 and exemplified a change in underlying public policy in relation to children,[106] and marked an understanding that the relationship between children and their parents (or the other adults who care for them) should be defined by the responsibilities of the *adults*, not the rights, powers, or control they have in respect of children. Parental responsibility exists *for the benefit of the child* not for the benefit of parents/adults.

---

[103] As argued by Horsey, K. 'Challenging Presumptions: Legal Parenthood and Surrogacy Arrangements' (2010) 4 *Child and Family Law Quarterly* 449. Intentional parenthood is already recognised in some jurisdictions.

[104] See Horsey, K. 'Surrogacy in the UK: Myth busting and reform' Report of the Surrogacy UK Working Group on Surrogacy Law Reform (Surrogacy, 2015).

[105] That the concept is a broad one was highlighted by the Court of Appeal in *T v T* [2010] EWCA Civ 1366 (see especially Black LJ, at [23]).

[106] The Act followed a review of the law by the Law Commission, *Family Law, Review of Child Law: Guardianship and Custody* (Law Com No. 172, 1988). The 'new' understanding of parental responsibility was informed by the (then) recent case *Gillick v West Norfolk and Wisbech Area Heath Authority* [1986] AC 112 (see Law Commission, *Family Law, Review of Child Law: Guardianship and Custody* (Law Com No. 172, 1988) para 2.4).

While the number of legal parents is restricted to a maximum of two, there is no such limitation in relation to the number of people who might hold parental responsibility at any one time,[107] and there may be situations where those who are the legal parents do not in fact have parental responsibility. For the majority of families, the question of who has parental responsibility is largely unproblematic—it will usually be the legal parents who initially hold this responsibility. In situations where this is not the case, it may be the social parents—those who do the day-to-day job of being a parent—who have it. Or, it could be a mixture of both. Parental responsibility brings with it certain decision-making capacities in relation to a child's upbringing, such as in the context of choosing (and being responsible for ensuring the child attends) education, and the ability to make medical treatment decisions.

As well as those legal parents to whom parental responsibility is automatically conferred, or who may later acquire it (see 4.1), parental responsibility may be held (at the same time, according to s. 2(5) of the Children Act 1989) by a variety of other people, including social parents such as step-parents, guardians, and even by the state (see Chapter 11). Step-parents (but not mere cohabitants) can also acquire parental responsibility for the children of their spouse or partner, in agreement with the child's parents, following amendments made to the Children Act 1989 (introducing s. 4A) by the Adoption and Children Act 2002 and Civil Partnership Act 2004. This removed the need to resort to 'step-parent adoption', which in many cases was a less than appropriate solution, as it terminated and erased the child's existing legal relationship with one of their legal parents. Adoption orders give the adopters parental responsibility, but when adoption occurs, any responsibility held by the original parents or anyone else is terminated because adoption entails a complete transfer of parenthood (Adoption and Children Act, s. 46(2)(a)). Guardians have parental responsibility for the duration of their guardianship (Children Act 1989, s. 5(6)). Special guardians also acquire parental responsibility for as long as the special guardianship order (see Chapter 12) exists. Unlike other forms of parental responsibility, however, special guardians can exercise their parental responsibility to the exclusion of others (Children Act 1989, s. 14C(1)(b)).

Evidently, when a range of people hold parental responsibility, it is important to know who and how many of them are needed in order to make decisions about the child's upbringing. For example, if a child needs to have consent given on their behalf for a medical procedure, is it sufficient to get a decision from one party with parental responsibility or do all of them have to give this? What if different parties with parental responsibility disagree about the decision? (see Chapter 12).

 CONTEXT 3: THE RELATIONSHIP BETWEEN CHILDREN, PARENTS, AND THE STATE

It was mentioned earlier that there were wider public policy concerns underpinning the enactment of the Children Act 1989. The Act came at a time when there were widespread and increasing social and political concerns about families in a broad sense, brought about by decreasing rates of marriage, increasing rates of (and the perceived ease of) divorce (see Chapter 3) and the concomitant increase in the number of single-parent families (see Chapter 6). The view of the Conservative government of the time, led by Margaret Thatcher as Prime Minister, was that parenting was the responsibility of parents and not of the state, which was seen as having had increasing responsibility (and costs) in relation to some children as a

---

[107] Children Act 1989, s. 2(5).

result of these social changes in the post-war period. Parents, it was thought, should be *held* to these responsibilities—and in particular, *fathers* (including absent ones) should.

In this way, the very concept of parental responsibility is understood by some scholars not only as signalling the move away from parental 'rights' and towards their duties or obligations in respect of the care and upbringing of children, as having a subtext about *ensuring* that parents 'do their job'. Parental responsibility is a way, outside of the marriage relationship, of attaching these duties to parents who might otherwise seek to evade them.[108] This state mistrust of unmarried families and 'feckless' fathers continued for many years. There was a slight policy shift exemplified by the Labour government after 1997: not only did that government want unmarried fathers to continue to be financially responsible for their children, but believed that they should be engaged and involved, too, as part of the children's best interests. Hence, for example, the changes made to the birth registration process during that period of government, allowing (and indeed actively encouraging) the joint registration of unmarried parents, giving both parents parental responsibility (see 2.1).

4.1 Who gets parental responsibility?

Parental responsibility is either automatically conferred, or it can be acquired under the Children Act 1989. Automatic parental responsibility for two parents used to only occur when a child was born within a heterosexual marriage relationship. However, the number and types of people who may automatically gain parental responsibility has increased in recent years because of other related developments to the law, such as the introduction of civil partnerships and later, same-sex marriage, as well as changes made by the HFE Act 2008 in relation to legal parenthood following the use of assisted reproductive technologies. All mothers—married or otherwise—continue to automatically have parental responsibility for their children at birth. The same is true for mothers' male or female spouses and their female civil partners who have gained second legal parent status under s. 42 of the HFE Act 2008 (see 3.1.2), as long as they are married to or civil partners with the mother at the time of the child's birth.[109]

Unmarried male fathers, and female partners to whom the mother is not married or civilly partnered (even if she has acquired second legal parent status under s. 43 HFE of the Act 2008) do not have parental responsibility automatically conferred upon them; it must be granted *to* them. This is true even though these partners may be genetically related to the child concerned and/or performing a social parenting role. Unless they acquire parental responsibility, therefore, the ability of these people to take certain decisions on behalf of the child is limited—including the fact that the child may be adopted without their consent.

 Key Legislation 6: Children Act 1989, s. 4

Acquisition of parental responsibility by father.

  (1) Where a child's father and mother were not married to each other at the time of his birth, the father shall acquire parental responsibility for the child if—

      (a) he becomes registered as the child's father under any of the enactments specified in subsection (1A);

---

[108] Though at the same time, the courts have brought back in ideas of parental rights, for example, in duties to consult others who hold parental responsibility about particular decisions—despite the fact that the Children Act 1989 provides that parental responsibility can be exercised jointly and severally.

[109] 'At the time of birth' in this context includes time between conception and birth, according to Family Law Reform Act 1987, s. 1(4).

> (b) he and the child's mother make an agreement (a 'parental responsibility agreement') providing for him to have parental responsibility for the child; or
> (c) the court, on his application, orders that he shall have parental responsibility for the child.
>
> This section details how a man not married to the mother of a child at the time of birth may acquire parental responsibility. Section 4ZA lays out in the same terms how second female parents may do so.

Clearly this position is somewhat controversial, especially as it means that some *legal* parents do not have parental responsibility for their own children at birth. The policy reasoning behind not allowing automatic responsibility to be conferred on unmarried fathers includes the variety of relationships between such men and mothers who had children—the relationship might be close, mirroring a traditional marriage relationship, or the two may barely even know each other. The child may even have been born following the mother's rape.[110] Such a policy position has been longstanding and the fact that parental responsibility is not automatically conferred on unmarried fathers has been even been challenged in the European Court of Human Rights, though it was deemed not to be an interference with unmarried fathers' human rights.[111] However, over time there was increasing concern about the situation, and some widespread and very public campaigning by some fathers who found themselves in this position, resulting eventually in a change to the law with the passage of the Adoption and Children Act 2002, taking effect in 2003.

Since 2003 unmarried fathers who are jointly entered with the mother on the birth register acquire parental responsibility at that point (unless he has previously been unsuccessful in an application to the court for a parental responsibility order, or he has lost parental responsibility that he previously held), but *not from birth*.[112] Alternatively (but in decline since the changes to birth registration in 2003), an unmarried father may enter and register with the Central Family Court a 'parental responsibility agreement', whereby he agrees to share parental responsibility with the mother. Without joint birth registration or a parental responsibility agreement, a man may only gain parental responsibility by a court order.[113] This can be the result of an application made on his own behalf (which can be opposed by the mother), or may come about automatically alongside a child arrangements order in which the court determines the child should live with their father.[114] This position is now the same for a woman who is a second legal parent according to s. 43 of the HFE Act 2008. When a court considers making a parental responsibility order under s. 4(1)(c) of the Children Act 1989, it must obviously do so according to a consideration of the child's best interests.[115] Numerous cases have interpreted the material factors that a court ought to take into account in so doing, including, as a starting point, the 'degree of commitment' shown by the father to the child,[116] the 'degree of attachment' between them, and a consideration of the reasons why the father/second legal parent wants the order to be made.[117] That these principles are a starting point and that there may be other

---

[110] See, e.g., the explanation in *Re H (Illegitimate child: Father: Parental Rights) (No. 2)* [1991] 1 FLR 214 (Balcombe LJ).   [111] *B v UK* [2000] 1 FLR 1.

[112] Adoption and Children Act 2002, s. 111.   [113] Granted under s. 4 of the Children Act 1989.

[114] Children Act 1989, s. 12(1).

[115] *Re W (Parental Responsibility Order: Inter-relationship with Direct Contact)* [2013] EWCA Civ 335.

[116] And presumably also, now, a second legal parent.

[117] See *Re H (Minors) (Local Authority: Parental Rights) (No. 3)* [1991] Fam 151 (CA), especially Balcombe LJ at 158. The case related to the earlier 'parental rights order' under the Family Law Reform Act 1987 which were in place prior to parental responsibility orders, but the principles have held.

relevant factors was confirmed by Balcombe LJ in *Re G (A Minor) (Parental Responsibility Order)*,[118] and Butler-Sloss LJ in *Re RH (A Minor) (Parental Responsibility)*.[119] Indeed, even where the principles are satisfied, there may be other reasons why making an order might not be deemed to be in the child's best interests.[120]

Though acquiring parental responsibility gives the parents who do so the same rights and obligations as those who automatically had parental responsibility from birth, the two main differences between those groups of parents are that there is a period of time between the child's birth and the making of the order where parental responsibility is not held by that person, and that acquired parental responsibility may be taken away again (by the court) unless it is obtained via adoption.

Any child arrangements order that states that a child is to live with a person (formerly known as a residence order) automatically gives that person parental responsibility if they do not already have it. There was a period of time where the courts had to consider issuing child arrangements orders even where there was no dispute about where the child was to live, in order for it to be followed by parental responsibility, merely because the provisions of the Children Act 1989 did not apply to a particular situation, including that where a same-sex couple had children following insemination outside of premises licensed by the HFEA. The appropriateness of this was somewhat questionable, but the situation has been ameliorated by the Children and Families Act 2004, which inserted s. 12(2A) in the Children Act 1989 allowing a free-standing parental responsibility order to be granted to someone under a child arrangements order that does not stipulate that the child is to live with them. The court is also obliged to consider, in the context of a child arrangements order under which the child is likely to spend time or have contact with their father or second female legal parent (who does not have parental responsibility), whether it would be appropriate for him/her to have parental responsibility and, if so, to make an order.

 DEBATE 3: WHO SHOULD, AND WHO SHOULD NOT, BE GIVEN
PARENTAL RESPONSIBILITY FOR CHILDREN?

We know that courts must take into account the welfare of the child(ren) concerned when considering whether or not to grant a parental responsibility order. Among the reasons sometimes given by the court for the refusal to make an order include the father's lack of capacity, his abusive behaviour, or his criminal behaviour, especially when this results in multiple convictions.[121] Interestingly, however, though such behaviour might constitute grounds for divorce (see Chapter 3), or in extreme situations convince a court to terminate parental responsibility (see 4.3), the very fact of parental separation or divorce, or the dissolution of a marriage or civil partnership, does not terminate any existing parental responsibility already held.

But what about 'unusual' or 'extraordinary' family situations? To what extent should the consideration of a child's welfare by a court depend on its assessment of how 'normal' (or even 'correct') a child's family circumstances are? Some of these potential problems are illustrated by cases related to known sperm donors—for example when a female couple use

---

[118] [1994] 1 FLR 504. [119] [1998] 2 FCR 89 (CA).

[120] See *Re H (Parental Responsibility)* [1998] 1 FLR 855; *Re P (Parental Responsibility)* [1998] 2 FLR 96; *Re B (Role of Biological Father)* [2008] 1 FLR 1015.

[121] See, e.g., *Re H Parental Responsibility)* [1998] 1 FLR 855 and *Re P (Parental Responsibility)* [1998] 2 FLR 96. But compare *Re S (A Minor) (Parental Responsibility)* [1995] 3 FCR 225 (CA), where an order *was* granted in respect of a 7-year-old girl, despite the father's conviction for possession of child and other pornography.

sperm donated by a male friend in order to conceive, and the male friend later wants to establish a 'fatherly' or otherwise paternal relationship with the child.

There is an argument that a child created in this way should certainly be able to know (or find out) who their genetic father is, and indeed this has been written into the law since 2005, reflecting a policy shift towards non-anonymous donations. Donor anonymity was removed for all donations taking place after 1 April 2005, giving children born from egg or sperm donation the right to find out who their genetic parent is at the age of majority (or at 16, if seeking to marry). However, anyone who donated before that date is able to 're-register', meaning that they may choose to remove their anonymity retrospectively—and become potentially identifiable to any children born from their donation.[122] Welcoming the government's decision to remove donor anonymity, following a Department of Health consultation, Suzi Leather, then chair of the HFEA, said:

> We consider that sharing information about origins with our children is part of responsible parenting. Although it is right to respect the guarantees of anonymity that have been given to donors in the past, it also seems to me wrong that the state has information about someone's origins which they want and cannot have. Secrecy in adoption has been discredited and secrecy in assisted reproduction will come to be too.

However, this is very different from a donor (with all the connotations that word holds) wanting to be involved in the life—and bringing up—of a child, and especially their holding parental responsibility.

In *Re D (Contact and PR: Lesbian Mothers and Known Father) (No. 2)*[123] Mr B, the genetic father of a five-year-old girl applied for parental responsibility. The girl had been born in 2000 to two female parents. The women wanted to have a child together and, because they also wanted her to have a 'father figure', advertised for a man who would be interested in fathering a child. The child was conceived after discussion and agreement and—crucially— following sexual intercourse with Mr B, the sperm donor. Mr B had understood from the agreement that he was to have a continued and involved role in the girl's life, sharing her time and with his equal participation in decisions about her upbringing. The female couple, however, had a different idea—they understood that Mr B would only visit the girl once in a while, and would not have any role in decisions about her upbringing. They did not want him to share parental responsibility with them as this would undermine their efforts to be seen as a real family unit and they did not want to give him legitimacy as 'a parent'.

Mr B offered to undertake not to exercise his parental responsibility (if granted) to involve himself, without the mother and her partner's consent, in areas of the child's life where they might anticipate problems with his involvement, namely relating to her medical treatment and schooling. Black J deliberated on whether making a parental responsibility order would be in the child's best interests, given the potential threat to the stability of her immediate family, as well as society's perception of the family if he were to use it to become more visible in the child's life, but ultimately granted Mr B parental responsibility, on the basis of the undertakings he had made. Black J was swayed by authorities that stressed the inappropriateness of refusing an order because of a feared misuse by the father. She was also influenced by the fact that the applicant was the child's biological father.

Black J recognised that the application arose at a time of considerable change in law in relation to same-sex couples, and that the law was possibly advancing faster than the views of

---

[122] For a critique of the changed policy, see Turkmendag, I., Dingwall, R., and Murphy, T. 'The Removal of Donor Anonymity in the UK: The Silencing of Claims by Would-Be Parents' (2008) 22 *International Journal of Law, Policy and the Family* 283. See also Wardle, P. 'The Real Impact of the Removal of Donor Anonymity' *BioNews* 445, 18 February 2008.   [123] [2006] EWHC 2 (Fam).

society in general, where 'new' ways of living were evolving but language had not yet developed to accommodate them (at [33]–[34]).[124]

It is perhaps the case that perceptions of who and what a family is—including the relevance of genetic parentage—have developed even further since 2006. For example, in *TJ v CV*,[125] Hedley J fund that it would not be in a child's best interests for the known sperm donor to have more than a contact relationship with the child and that to grant him a parental responsibility order would be inappropriate, even though he was the genetic father.[126] Similarly, in *R v E and F (Female Parents: Known Father)*,[127] a child was born to a woman in a civil partnership, and had lived with her mother and mother's partner from birth. The mother's female partner acquired parental responsibility for the child as a step-parent, under a written agreement with the mother. The biological father was an American man in a same-sex marriage. Although his name was on the birth certificate, he had not acquired parental responsibility for the child as the birth was prior to the change in the law in relation to parental responsibility and unmarried fathers. Bennett J refused the father's application for parental responsibility and shared residence on the grounds that it had never been intended that he would take responsibility or have decision-making powers about the child's life and, in any case, he was already consulted by the mother and her partner over big decisions. There was no evidence to suggest that he had co-parented the child and critically the evidence did show that the child did not view him as a parent, even though he had extensive contact, was named on the birth certificate, his surname was one of the child's names, he was consulted about big decisions, and was referred to as 'Daddy'.

In *A v B and C (Contact: Alternative Families)* [2012] the Court of Appeal returned to the fact that the guiding principle of the law in all cases is the best interests of the child concerned.[128] In that case, Thorpe LJ recognised that there may be advantages for the child in having a legally recognised relationship with more than two parents.

These decisions show that the courts seem to take a different view about what or who a parent is, compared to who should hold parental responsibility, and that a biological connection does not even raise the presumption that a parental responsibility order might follow. It is difficult, as these cases prove, to separate the concepts of a child's need for knowledge of their genetic *identity* from their understanding of who their *parents* are or should be. But the very nature of—and intentions behind—donation ought, it seems, to preclude not only parenthood but also parental responsibility. Certainly, because language has not evolved to adequately cover these cases, those parties entering such arrangements need to be absolutely clear *prior to conception* of all of the roles to be played.

4.2 Exercising parental responsibility

Unless the law specifically requires the consent of the parents and/or all of those who hold responsibility, those who have parental responsibility can exercise it jointly and severally (s. 2(7) of the Children Act 1989). This means that each one of them can make decisions that meet their responsibility independently of the other(s). The situations where the law deems it necessary to have the agreement of all the parties who hold parental responsibility include removing the child from the jurisdiction, changing the child's name, consenting to serious or irreversible medical treatment, or consenting to marriage or the entering of a civil partnership if the child is under the age of 18.

---

[124] On language difficulties in this type of case, see also *MA v RS (Contact: Parenting Roles)* [2011] EWHC 2455, at [9]–[10] (Hedley J).   [125] [2007] EWHC 1952.

[126] Hedley J may have been swayed by the fact the applicant was the brother of one of the female civil partners, so also, therefore, the child's uncle.   [127] [2010] 2 FLR 383.

[128] [2012] EWCA Civ 285.

According to s. 2(8) of the Children Act 1989, no party with parental responsibility is able to exercise it in a way that is contrary to any court order issued under the Act. If the parties who hold parental responsibility are intractably in disagreement with how the responsibility should be exercised in a particular situation, a 'section 8 order' may be applied for or the child may even be made a ward of court or placed under its inherent jurisdiction. Some or all of a person's responsibility, however, may be exercised by a nominated person or people acting on the holder's behalf, such as in a childcare context (s. 2(9) of the Children Act 1989). And this person might already be someone who has parental responsibility for that child (e.g., imagine the transfers of childcare that may occur between separated or divorced couples). However, the responsibility is not *delegated* to that other person for the purposes of civil or criminal law, thus part of the exercise of parental responsibility is to ensure that arrangements are properly made.

4.3 Losing parental responsibility

Those who do have parental responsibility automatically conferred cannot 'get rid' of it—it can only be removed by adoption, or the making of a parental order following a surrogacy arrangement (see 3.3.1). Parental responsibility also comes to an end automatically once any order it is 'attached' to (such as a child arrangements order) ceases to have effect. It comes to an end naturally, whether gained automatically or later acquired, when the child concerned reaches the age of 18.

Parental responsibility held by those who only later acquire it may also be terminated by the court (not by another person with parental responsibility) or revoked by the court on an application under s. 4(2A) of the Children Act 1989 made by any other person who has parental responsibility for the child concerned. An application may even be made, with the court's leave, by the child (s. 4(3) of the Children Act 1989). Termination is a rare occurrence and is only granted in the most extreme circumstances. In the first case where parental responsibility was terminated, the father had been imprisoned for deliberately injuring the child.[129] In *Re F (Indirect Contact)*,[130] the father's history of severe violence justified the removal of his parental responsibility, and in *CW v SG* the issues were the father's drug use and convictions and imprisonment for sexual offences involving minors including his step-children.[131] In that case, Baker J found that a relevant consideration was that 'if the father did not have parental responsibility it is inconceivable it would now be granted to him' (at [59]). In *A v D (Parental Responsibility)*,[132] the father's parental responsibility was terminated after it was established that he had a long criminal history involving many violent offences, including severe domestic violence against the mother, which had left her with post-traumatic stress disorder. At the time of the hearing he was in prison for causing the mother grievous bodily harm. The 4-year-old child, A, had witnessed the violence and had many complex needs as a result. The mother, A and another of her children were living at a confidential address. She had also applied to the court to be able to change the child's name, so that when the father left prison, he would not easily find them. The police had made the assessment that should he locate A's mother, she would 'face a real risk to her life and limb' (at [13]).

Returning to Debate 3, it should be noted that termination of parental responsibility—even for the kinds of reasons outlined here—is not possible for a *married* parent. One of the arguments made by the father in *CW v SG* [2013] was that the fact his rights could be terminated, but a married father's could not be, meant that the application of

---

[129] *Re P (Terminating Parental Responsibility)* [1995] 1 FLR 1048.   [130] [2007] 1 FLR 1015.
[131] [2013] EWHC 854 (Fam).   [132] [2013] EWHC 2963 (Fam).

s. 4(2A) of the Children Act 1989 was incompatible with Articles 8 and 14 ECHR, since it discriminates against unmarried fathers in a way that infringes their right to family life. This idea had previously been considered in *Smallwood v UK*,[133] where an unmarried father had contended that he was discriminated against by having his parental responsibility terminated by virtue of his marital status. However, the European Court of Human Rights found that although the father's Article 8 rights were engaged, they had not been violated, as there remained an objective and reasonable justification for the difference in legislative treatment between unmarried and married fathers. Part of its reasoning was the variety of different relationships that unmarried fathers might have with their children, the fact that parental responsibility does not necessarily give contact rights, and the fact that even after termination of parental responsibility, an application could be made to re-obtain it. All decisions would be based on the child's best interests at the time. In *CW v SG*, the father's lawyers sought to distinguish *Smallwood* because the social and legal context of unmarried fathers in society had changed, as demonstrated by the change in public policy and law as seen in the Adoption and Children Act 2002, which allowed unmarried fathers to jointly register the birth of a child alongside the mother, thereby acquiring parental responsibility. However, the Court found that *Smallwood* was still good law, despite the societal changes. While this may answer the question why unmarried fathers who are entered on the birth register or otherwise acquire parental responsibility are treated differently, it begs another question: why can parental responsibility of a married father *not* be terminated in the same kinds of situations? Not to allow this surely indicates that the law rates the status of marriage (where fathers' relationships with children and wives can surely vary as much as those of unmarried fathers) as a higher consideration in children's best interests than anything else.

SUMMARY

1. Should legal parenthood be based on genetic links, gestational relationships, intention, or something else?
   - A woman who gives birth to a child is always its legal mother, even if she is acting as a surrogate to enable another person or couple to have a child, and even if she is genetically unrelated to a child she carries.
   - The law recognises the position of sperm and egg donors, and does not regard them as legal parents, though a sperm donor who donates sperm outside of the remit of the Human Fertilisation and Embryology Act 2008 might still be the legal father.
   - Legal parenthood can be transferred from the legal parents at birth by virtue of a parental order following surrogacy, or by adoption. However, only certain people are able to apply for parental orders, and the law stipulates certain conditions that must be met before an order can be granted.
   - In recent years, some of the provisions relating to the granting of a parental order have been circumvented by the courts in the interests of the paramountcy of the child(ren)'s welfare. One of the requirements, relating to single fathers, has been found to be in contravention of human rights law.

---

[133] (1999) 27 EHRR 155.

2. Does the law on assisted conception appropriately and effectively deal with the multiple different permutations of family creation that technology affords us?
   - The Human Fertilisation and Embryology Acts of 1990 and 2008 have defined who is—and who is not—a legal parent following the use of assisted reproduction technologies. A woman who gives birth to a child will always be its legal mother.
   - To an extent, the legislation now recognises the different permutations of family that may be created by these technologies.
   - Same-sex spouses and civil partners can become parents of children born within their relationship, in a reflection of how this happens for heterosexual married partners. Two women may therefore share parenthood status, but the situation for two men—who must use surrogacy to have a child—is different.
   - However, parenthood following assisted conception is affected by where and how conception takes place—that is, under a licence issued by the HFEA, or not, or if it follows a surrogacy arrangement.

3. Who should, and who should not, be given parental responsibility for children?
   - Mothers always have parental responsibility and, if they are married or have a partner who has acquired 'second legal parent' status within a civil partnership at the time of the child's birth, hold this jointly with the other legal parent.
   - Unmarried fathers who jointly register the child with the mother also acquire parental responsibility from the point of the registration.
   - Other people with relationships with the child can apply to be granted parental responsibility by the court. This may be opposed by the mother. Courts must only grant an order if it is in the child's best interest to do so.
   - Parental authority can be terminated by a court, but this is rare and happens only in the most extreme of circumstances.

Further Reading

BRAZIER, M. and WAXMAN, S. 'Reforming the Law Regulating Surrogacy: Extending the Family' (2016) 4 *Journal of Medical Law and Ethics* 159
   - Considers the current law relating to surrogacy and emphasises the need for urgent reform. Argues for surrogacy regulation to reflect a fiduciary model recognising relationships between families, extended families and surrogates.

D'ALTON-HARRISON, R. 'Mater semper incertus est: who's your mummy?' (2014) 22 *Medical Law Review* 357
   - Makes the argument that the time has come to move away from a legal definition of 'mother' that is based on biology to one that recognises different forms of motherhood.

HORSEY, K. (2010) 'Challenging Presumptions: Legal Parenthood and Surrogacy Arrangements' (2010) 4 *Child and Family Law Quarterly* 449
   - Argues that the law regarding the acquisition of legal parenthood should be based on intention.

HORSEY, K. and SHELDON, S. 'Still Hazy After All These Years: The Law Regulating Surrogacy' (2012) 20(1) *Medical Law Review* 67–89
- Revisits the 1998 Brazier Report in the light of subsequent developments in surrogacy and assesses to what extent its key findings remain salient. Brazier's recommendations provide focus for a critical analysis of the law regarding surrogacy.

HORSEY, K. 'Surrogacy in the UK: Myth busting and reform' Report of the Surrogacy UK Working Group on Surrogacy Law Reform (Surrogacy UK, 2015)
- A report published by one of the UK's non-profit surrogacy agencies which points out a number of myths about surrogacy, and the way it is practiced and understood in the UK, and calls for legal reform.

HORSEY, K. 'Not Withered on the Vine: The Need for Surrogacy Law Reform' (2016) 4 *Journal of Medical Law and Ethics* 181
- Argues that surrogacy law reform is much needed in the wake of new understandings of how it is practised, as well as case law showing that the law in its current form is inadequate.

HORSEY, K. 'Fraying at the Edges: Surrogacy Law in 2015' (2016) 24(4) *Medical Law Review* 608
- Analyses a series of 2015 surrogacy cases that indicate that the law regulating surrogacy in the UK is increasingly out of date and failing to adequately protect the best interests of children and families.

JONES, C. 'Parents in Law: Subjective Impacts and Status Implications around the use of Licensed Donor Insemination' in A. DIDUCK, and K. O'DONOVAN (eds) *Feminist Perspectives on Family Law* (Routledge-Cavendish, 2006) 75
- Deconstructs the idea of kinship and the norms of bio-genetic relatedness, and on parental responsibility within donor-created families.

LEE, E., MACVARISH, J., and SHELDON, S. 'Assessing Child Welfare under the Human Fertilisation and Embryology Act 2008: A Case Study in Medicalization?' (2014) 36 *Sociology of Health & Illness* 500–515
- Reports findings from a study of interviews with staff working in assisted conception clinics in the UK about their experience of making preconception 'welfare of the child' assessments.

LEE, E., MACVARISH, J., and SHELDON, S. (2015). 'After the "need for.a father": "The welfare of the child" and "supportive parenting" in UK assisted conception clinics' Families, Relationships and Societies. Available at: http://dx.doi.org/10.1332/204674315X14303090462204, accessed 26 September 2017
- Critiques the idea that the move from a child's 'need for a father' to the idea of 'supportive parenting' is progressive, and evaluates the perceptions of clinic staff in the meanings they ascribe to 'supportive parenting'.

McCANDLESS, J. and SHELDON, S. 'No Father Required'? The Welfare Assessment in the Human Fertilisation and Embryology Act (2008)' (2010) 18 *Feminist Legal Studies* 201
- An empirical and academic analysis of the change to clinics to consider a child's 'need for "supportive parenting"', rather than 'for a father', after the HFE Act 2008.

McCANDLESS, J. and SHELDON, S. 'The Human Fertilisation and Embryology Act (2008) and the Tenacity of the Sexual Family Form' (2010) 72 *Modern Law Review* 175
- Discusses in depth the parenthood provisions under the 2008 legislation and critiques their adherence to the norms of the 'sexual family'.

WALLBANK, J. 'Reconstructing the HFEA 1990: Is Blood Really Thicker Than Water?' (2004) 16 *Child and Family Law Quarterly* 387
- Considers the role of the HFEA 1990 in relation to homosexual couples and single women and the review of the operation of the legislation.

9

Private Child Law

Annika Newnham

LEARNING OBJECTIVES

After reading this chapter you will be able to:

- Explain how courts decide disputes about an aspect of a child's upbringing using the paramountcy test in s. 1(1) of the Children Act 1989 and the other guidelines within s. 1, particularly the s. 1(3) welfare checklist and the s. 1(2A) parental involvement presumption;

- Understand the practical use of the different orders under s. 8 of the Children Act 1989 and apply the relevant law;

- Critically evaluate how the law has developed through the case law and understand how the wider context impacts on outcomes in s. 8 disputes.

DEBATES

After reading this chapter you should be equipped to discuss your opinion on the following central debates:

1. Is the court the best place for private child law disputes?

2. What is shared parenting and when is it good for children?

3. Should courts be doing more to promote contact with fathers?

1. Introduction

This chapter looks at the law that is used to resolve disputes about where children should live, who they should have contact with, and other aspects of parental responsibility (see Chapter 8). The majority of such disputes are between two parents, but they can also involve grandparents, other relatives, or even people like friends and neighbours (a separate regime is provided for cases where the state intervenes to assist parents or protect children (see Chapter 11)). The subject matter of these disputes can, for example, be where a child should live, whether children should spend time with a parent, where a child should go to school, or whether a parent should be allowed to move hundreds of miles away from the other parent and take the children with them.

Historically, the law did not involve itself in these disputes; instead fathers were trusted to make decisions for their wives, children, and other members of their household. Judges felt that to interfere with this 'sacred duty' would cause more harm than good in the long run.[1] There are still traces of this reluctance to interfere in private family affairs in the current legislation (a clear example is s. 1(5) which is discussed in 4.5), but courts can and will go against the wishes of both fathers and mothers where this is held to be in the child's best interests.

The Children Act 1989 is the main piece of legislation for the regulation of disputes between parents. This Act was an ambitious and largely successful attempt to modernise, simplify, and improve the law. As part of this reform, the old orders of custody and access, which had stoked conflicts by creating winners and losers, were scrapped. Instead, to 'lower the stakes' the Act introduced parental responsibility to regulate parents' legal status, and a set of orders in s. 8, which were designed to only affect practical arrangements.[2] In this chapter, they are referred to as s. 8 orders. Parents' relationships with their children would remain unaffected by such practical changes, ensuring that children did not lose touch with a non-resident parent.

How do courts make decisions? These disputes, like public law cases, are decided solely on the basis of what will be best for the child. This unavoidably involves an element of guesswork, but judges and magistrates can seek help from the general principles developed in the case law, from the court's social workers (Children and Family Court Advisory and Support Service, known as Cafcass), and in difficult cases from expert witnesses including child psychologists, doctors, or other experts. If the question is where a child should live, then the decision will depend on where the child is most likely to thrive; if the question is about contact, then the court will consider whether the risks outweigh the benefits; and if a question is about healthcare, education, religion, or other important aspects of a child's life, the court will have the help of expert evidence to decide what will be for the best. In this area of family law, certainty is far less important than flexibility and a pragmatic focus on finding the best solution, or in many cases the least bad solution. There is a lot of judicial discretion. For example, under s. 10(1)(b) of the Children Act 1989, the court can make an order even though that neither party had asked for that particular order.

This chapter will begin with introducing the orders and the wider context of the family justice system. It explains how decisions are made, and who can apply. Cases are then broken down into: disputes about where a child should live; with whom there should be contact; disputes about one specific point; and finally whether a parent should be entitled to take a child out of the country or change his/her name when there is an order in place. At the end of the chapter there is a brief outline of the High Court's inherent jurisdiction.

2. The framework of orders

When two parents (or sometimes a parent and another adult who is close to the child) have a disagreement about something related to that child's upbringing, they can ask the court for help. The orders used by the court are found in s. 8 of the Children Act 1989, which is why they are known as s. 8 orders. They were designed to deal with practical disputes without affecting the long-term rights and responsibilities that are contained within parental responsibility. As we will see in this chapter, the courts have sometimes departed from that original idea.

---

[1] *Re Agar-Ellis* (1883) 24 Ch D 317, at 329 (Brett MR).
[2] Law Commission, *Family Law Review of Child Law: Custody* (Law Com Working Paper No. 96, 1986) para 7.18; Department of Health, *The Children Act 1989: Guidance and Regulations, Vol 1, Court Orders* (1991) para 2.25.

There are three orders available to the court to resolve these disputes. There were originally four, but the residence order and the contact order were replaced with the child arrangements orders in 2014 by s. 12 of the Children and Families Act 2014. Even before this change was made, there was no clear distinction in law between residence and contact. Contact often includes overnight contact, and can range from the occasional visit to three nights per week and half of all holidays. There are many arrangements for children to spend time with a parent that could equally comfortably be labelled 'living with' or 'having contact with'. The courts see this as a positive thing, which allows them to tailor both the schedules and the formal orders to best benefit every unique child.[3]

The three orders are all set out in the same section of the Children Act.

 Key Legislation 1: Children Act 1989, s. 8(1)

In this Act—

'a child arrangements order' means an order regulating arrangements relating to any of the following—

(a) with whom a child is to live, spend time or otherwise have contact, and

(b) when a child is to live, spend time or otherwise have contact with any person;

'a prohibited steps order' means an order that no step which could be taken by a parent in meeting his parental responsibility for a child, and which is of a kind specified in the order, shall be taken by any person without the consent of the court;

'a specific issue order' means an order giving directions for the purpose of determining a specific question which has arisen, or which may arise, in connection with any aspect of parental responsibility for a child.

The orders will be discussed in more detail in 5, once we have looked at when these orders can be made, and who can and cannot apply. However, it is first important to introduce the context in which these cases are heard.

3. The family justice system

Section 8 disputes are heard by the Single Family Court, and are allocated according to the complexity of the case to magistrates, district judges, circuit judges, or High Court judges if particularly complex. The rules on how the courts should deal with these cases are set out in the Child Arrangements Programme (CAP).[4] CAP has two main aspects. The first is the promotion of out of court dispute resolution (not just an aim of CAP but of government policy more widely, see Chapter 15). Applicants are now required to attend a Mediation Information Assessment Meeting (MIAM) before an application can be made to court, unless certain exceptions apply, such as a history of domestic violence or a serious, immediate risk to life or health. The second aspect of CAP is the insistence that when cases do go to court, they should be resolved swiftly and efficiently (ideally with no more

---

[3] *Re K (Shared Residence Order)* [2008] EWCA Civ 526; [2008] 2 FLR 380, at [6] (Wilson LJ).

[4] Practice Direction 12(B)—Child Arrangements Programme, issued 22 April 2014. Available at: https://www.justice.gov.uk/courts/procedure-rules/family/practice_directions/pd_part_12b, accessed 12 August 2017.

than three hearings). Both these aims can conflict with the need to ensure that allegations are investigated and cases are resolved as fully as possible, and with making sure that the parties are in a good position to negotiate their own solutions when new problems crop up in the future.[5]

Cafcass exists to 'make sure that children's voices are heard and decisions are taken in their best interests'.[6] Cafcass reporters are trained social workers who are independent of both the courts and local authority social services. They carry out basic safeguarding checks by asking parents if they can identify any risks to the child and contacting both the police and the local authority social services. Cafcass are also often in court to meet with parents before their first hearing, to understand the dispute and try to find ways to compromise before the parties see the judge. Cafcass can also be asked by the court to write detailed reports under s. of the Children Act 1989. Sometimes, when the local authority's children's services are already involved with the family, they will write the s. 7 report.

4. How is a decision made? The welfare test

The approach to deciding disputes between two private adults about questions relating to a child's upbringing is set out in s. 1(1) of the Children Act 1989, and given further detail through the other subsections to s. 1. The most controversial of these is the latest addition, the parental involvement presumption, which is explained in 4.3.

4.1 The paramountcy principle

The paramountcy test is a very distinct way of deciding cases. The court does not follow the usual approach of weighing up the rights and duties of both parties (usually the parents), nor does it look back at past conduct to determine who wins the case. Instead, the paramountcy principle is forward looking, and it looks past the parents to focus solely on the child.

 Key Legislation 2: Children Act 1989, s. 1(1)

When a court determines any question with respect to—

   (a) the upbringing of a child; or
   (b) the administration of a child's property or the application of any income arising from it,

the child's welfare shall be the court's paramount consideration.

This is known as the paramountcy principle, the welfare test, or the best interests principle. The terms are interchangeable, but for clarity, in this chapter the test will be referred to as the paramountcy principle.

---

[5] Barlow, A. 'Rising to the Post-LASPO Challenge: How Should Mediation Respond?' (2017) 39 *Journal of Social Welfare and Family Law* 203; Harding, M. and Newnham, A. 'How do County Courts share the care of children between parents? Full report' (University of Warwick, 2015). Available at: http://www.nuffieldfoundation.org/share-care. Accessed 1 July 2017.

[6] Cafcass. *About Cafcass*. Available at: https://www.cafcass.gov.uk/about-cafcass.aspx, accessed 14 August 2017.

In *J v C*,[7] the House of Lords interpreted 'first and paramount consideration' to mean that the child's welfare was not just the top item in a list of relevant matters, but should always determine the outcome. Other people's rights, needs, and wishes should only be considered by the court if they are likely to impact on the child. Although the case pre-dates the Children Act 1989, the paramountcy test was already in place, contained in s. 1 of the Guardianship of Infants Act 1925. In this case, the parents and foster parents were in a dispute about a 10-year-old boy, who had been living with his English foster parents for most of his life, initially because his mother was seriously ill with tuberculosis. His father now had steady employment in Spain, his mother was in good health, and when the foster parents wanted to change the boy's religion, the parents wanted their son back. He was, by now, fully integrated in his foster parents' family. It was made clear that the rights of parents who had done nothing wrong could still be outweighed by the child's best interests. The 10-year-old stayed with his English foster family.

On paper, this focus solely on the child seems incompatible with the fact that both parents and children have rights to family life with each under Article 8(1) of the European Convention on Human Rights and Fundamental Freedoms 1950 (ECHR), the right to respect for private and family life. However, the European Court of Human Rights has maintained compatibility by categorising the need to promote the child's welfare as legitimate and proportionate interference with parents' rights under Article 8(2). This approach allows the child's best interests to determine the outcome.[8] Our own judges have on several occasions opined that 'there is no inconsistency of principle or application between the English rule and the Convention rule'.[9] Differences between the two approaches are said to be 'merely semantic', a matter of words.[10] This approach has been criticised.[11] However, in practice, it is the adults who make applications and argue for or against an order and it is all too easy for the court's focus to drift onto what parents want. The paramountcy principle is necessary to push against this.

The paramountcy principle is used in many jurisdictions and has great symbolic appeal: it is difficult to disagree with the notion that children are precious, yet vulnerable, and that law should focus on helping them mature into well-adjusted adults.[12] It is easy to endorse this general principle, but, it is much more difficult to give it content; to agree on how children's interests are best promoted. Since each case is determined on its own facts, the paramountcy principle can be criticised as being indeterminate and unpredictable. There is often more than one 'right' outcome, and judges are given discretion to balance the potential risks and benefits in any given case. Therefore, an appeal will never succeed simply because the appellate judge would have reached another decision; it must be shown that the first instance judge has either failed to apply the correct principles, or failed to balance all the relevant factors, and has 'erred in law' to such an extent that his conclusion cannot be trusted.

Despite this emphasis on flexibility, rules of thumb, assumptions, and presumptions have developed which make decisions more predictable, but far less focused on what is best for this particular, individual child.

---

[7] [1970] AC 68.   [8] *Yousef v Netherlands* App. No. 33711/96 [2003] 1 FLR 210.

[9] *Re KD (A Minor) (Ward: Termination of Access)* [1988] AC 806, 812 (Lord Templeman). See also. e.g., *Re B (Adoption by One Natural Parent to Exclusion of Other)* [2002] 1 FLR 196.

[10] *Re KD (A Minor) (Ward: Termination of Access)* [1988] AC 806 (Lord Templeman), at 825.

[11] Tolson, R. 'The Welfare Test and Human Rights: Where's the Beef in the Sacred Cow?' *Family Law Week* (2005). Available at: http://www.familylawweek.co.uk/site.aspx?i=ed307, accessed 14 August 2017; Choudry, S. and Fenwick, H. 'Taking the Rights of Parents and Children Seriously: Confronting the Welfare Principle under the Human Rights Act' (2005) 25 *Oxford Journal of Legal Studies* 453; Harris-Short, S. 'Family law and the Human Rights Act 1998: Judicial Restraint or Revolution?' (2005) 173 *Child and Family Law Quarterly* 29.

[12] Herring, J. 'Parents and Children' in J. Herring (ed) *Family Law: Issues, Debates, Policy,* (Willan Publishing, 2001) 165.

4.2 **The welfare checklist**

As the previous section explains, judges hearing s. 8 disputes have considerable discretion, and there is often more than one 'right' outcome. However, judicial discretion is not limitless. The welfare checklist in s. 1(3) was included in the statute to help judges and magistrates focus on the things that are likely to be of importance in most cases.

 Key Legislation 3: Children Act 1989, s. 1(3)

[Where the court is considering whether to make, vary or discharge a s. 8 order] a court shall have regard in particular to—

(a) the ascertainable wishes and feelings of the child concerned (considered in the light of his age and understanding);
(b) his physical, emotional and educational needs;
(c) the likely effect on him of any change in his circumstances;
(d) his age, sex, background and any characteristics of his which the court considers relevant;
(e) any harm which he has suffered or is at risk of suffering;
(f) how capable each of his parents, and any other person in relation to whom the court considers the question to be relevant, is of meeting his needs;
(g) the range of powers available to the court under this Act in the proceedings in question.

The list is non-exhaustive and non-hierarchical. This means that a court is free to take into account some other factor, which is important in that case, even though it is not on the s. 1(3) list. The different factors listed are all equally important, or, it could also be said, their relative importance will vary from one case to the other. If the question is whether a 14-year-old girl should have contact with a violent alcoholic parent, then her wishes under s. 1(3)(a) will carry considerable weight. If she has a 14-month-old half-brother, then his needs under s. 1(3)(b) and the risks of harm under s. 1(3)(e) will probably determine the outcome for him.

The complexity of disputes over children often means that the factors listed in the checklist pull in different directions. The 14-month-old boy could have his emotional needs met by contact, but the risks of harm and that parent's inability to meet his needs will weigh against contact. The 14-year-old girl could be harmed in the short term if forced into contact against her wishes, but in the long term it may help her to have some positive memories of this parent.

Baroness Hale has said that 'In any difficult and finely balanced case … it is a great help to address each of the factors in the list, along with any others which may be relevant, so as to ensure that no particular feature of the case is given more weight that it should properly bear'.[13]

This is also very good advice for any student answering a problem question in this area. Just like the judge who is trying to 'appeal-proof' their judgment by expressly linking all the appropriate considerations to their conclusions, frequent mentions of the factors in the welfare checklist demonstrate your skill in applying the law to the facts.

---

[13] *Re G (Children) (Residence: Same-Sex Partner)* [2006] UKHL 43; [2006] 2 FLR 629, at [40].

4.2.1 Children's wishes and feelings

Under s. 1(3)(a) a court must consider a child's wishes and feelings. '[T]he direct evidence of children is seldom heard or rarely available in the family courts.'[14] This is due to a wish to protect children from the stresses of going to the court, or the pressure of feeling that they have to make a decision they see as choosing between their parents. Judges also rarely talk directly to children; they have no training to do this, and the rules of evidence mean that judges 'cannot promise a child that any conversation with the child will be entirely confidential'.[15] Instead, specially trained social workers employed by Cafcass present children's wishes to the court. In difficult or high conflict cases a children's guardian may also be appointed, to make sure someone is always focused on what is best for the child rather than what the parents want. It is rare for children to make their own applications to court (see 5.2.2). However, Cafcass must both present children's wishes *and* make recommendations on what is best for children, even when these are two different things.

4.3 The parental involvement presumption

Briefly summarised, it can be argued that because parental separation is traumatic for many children, and can have negative impacts throughout the child's life, children's time after separation should be divided as equally as possible between the parents, because this limits the child's sense of loss, and is the option that most resembles the intact nuclear family. All this sounds like common sense, but it is dangerous to take an observation about what is often best for most people and turn it into a rule about what is always best for everyone.

A new presumption, originally titled the shared parenting presumption, was introduced to Parliament as clause 12 of the Children and Families Bill 2013–14. The objective was to prevent children being used as pawns in a 'winner takes all' game, and encourage continuing parent–child bonds.[16]

The Children Act 1989, s. 1(2A)

> A court … [which is considering whether to make, vary or discharge a section 8 order] is as respects each parent within subsection (6)(a) to presume, unless the contrary is shown, that involvement of that parent in the life of the child concerned will further the child's welfare.

The government had taken note of Australian research findings demonstrating how a shared parenting presumption can put children at risk of harm if unsuitable fathers start insisting on what they see as their rights to an equal share of their children's time. Mothers often agree, and children are put at risk.[17] Therefore, s. 1(2A) was complemented with a new s. 1(6):

Children Act 1989, s. 1(6) states:

… a parent of the child concerned—

(a) is within this paragraph if that parent can be involved in the child's life in a way that does not put the child at risk of suffering harm; and

---

[14] Judiciary of England and Wales, *Final Report of the Vulnerable Witnesses and Children Working Group* (2015) 5. Available at: https://www.judiciary.gov.uk/publications/final-report-of-the-vulnerable-witnesses-and-children-working-group/, accessed 18 July 2017.

[15] *Mabon v Mabon and others* [2005] EWCA Civ 634; [2005] 2 FLR 1011, at [38] (Wall LJ).

[16] Tim Loughton, the then Minister for Children and Families, in a letter to the *The Times* published 13 June 2012 and cited in 'Children's Minister Clarifies Nature of Proposals for Shared Parenting after Divorce' *Family Law Week* (2012) available at http://www.familylawweek.co.uk/site.aspx?i=ed98501, accessed 14 August 2017.

[17] Fehlberg, B. 'Legislating for Shared Parenting: How the Family Justice Review got it Right' [2012] *Family Law* 709; Trinder, L. 'Shared Residence: A Review of Recent Research Evidence' (2010) 22 *Child and Family Law Quarterly* 475.

(b) is to be treated as being within paragraph (a) unless there is some evidence before the court in the particular proceedings to suggest that involvement of that parent in the child's life would put the child at risk of suffering harm whatever the form of the involvement.

How this provision will work in practice will depend on how difficult it will be for the other parent, to produce 'some evidence' that will satisfy the court, particularly given the restrictions on legal aid brought in by the Legal Aid, Sentencing and Punishment of Offenders Act 2012 (LASPO) (see Chapter 15).[18] Parties in s. 8 cases can now only get legal aid if they can produce some evidence of domestic violence, or if their circumstances are truly exceptional.

CONTEXT 1: WHY WAS THE NEW PARENTAL INVOLVEMENT PRESUMPTION INTRODUCED?

Groups such as Families Need Fathers and Fathers for Justice have for a long time been campaigning for a presumption in favour of equal sharing of children's time, claiming that courts have a bias in favour of mothers who can marginalise fathers for their own selfish reasons.[19] The government wanted to send a strong warning to parents against unnecessary conflicts around children. They also acknowledged that the reform was not intended to change how courts used the paramountcy principle to decide disputes.[20] This is right, since a number of research studies have shown that the courts were already focused on promoting as much contact as possible.[21]

Instead, the Minister for Children and Families said during the passage of the Children and Families Act 2014 that '[t]he most important element of this is to ensure that there is real confidence in the family justice system.'[22] A second aim was to 'encourage the resolution of agreements outside court by making clear the basis on which courts' decisions are made and by ensuring that parents' expectations are realistic when deciding whether to bring a claim to court.'[23] At first glance, these two aims seem to pull in opposite directions. If you increase confidence in an institution this usually leads to an increase in use. Whereas if public confidence in an institution is low, that normally dissuades use. If there is an outbreak of diarrhoea linked to a sandwich shop, for example, people would lose confidence, and not shop there again until there was a successful hygiene inspection. Yet the government were hoping

---

[18] *R (Rights of Women) v Secretary of State for Justice* [2016] EWCA Civ 91; [2017] 1 FLR 615.

[19] Kaganas, F. 'A Presumption that "Involvement" of Both Parents is Best: Deciphering Law's messages' (2013) 25 *Child and Family Law Quarterly* 270, 283. See, e.g., Families Need Fathers, 'Shared Parenting Research'. Available at: https://fnf.org.uk/publications/shared-parenting-research#faqnoanchor, accessed 1 July 2017; Fathers 4 Justice, 'About Fathers 4 Justice'. Available at: http://www.fathers-4-justice.org/about-f4j/campaign-faqs/, accessed 1 July 2017.

[20] Department for Education, *Children and Families Bill 2013: Contextual Information and Responses to Pre-Legislative Scrutiny* (Cm 8540, 2013) para 63, Annex 1 of Annex B.

[21] Smart, C. *et al Residence and Contact Disputes in Court: Volume 1* (University of Leeds, 2003); Hunt, J. and Macleod, A. *Outcomes of Applications to Court for Contact Orders after Parental Separation or Divorce* (Ministry of Justice, 2008); Harding, M. and Newnham, A. 'How do County Courts share the care of children between parents? Full report' (University of Warwick, 2015). Available at: http://www.nuffieldfoundation.org/share-care, accessed 1 July 2017.

[22] Edward Timpson's evidence before the Justice Committee: Justice Committee, *Fourth Report: Pre-Legislative Scrutiny of the Children and Families Bill* (TSO, 2012) para 149. http://www.publications.parliament.uk/pa/cm201213/cmselect/cmjust/739/73907.htm#a10, accessed 11 August 2017.

[23] Department for Education, *Children and Families Bill 2013: Contextual Information and Responses to Pre-Legislative Scrutiny* (Cm 8540, 2013) para 63, Annex 1 of Annex B.

to achieve the opposite: increase confidence but decrease use. The best way for this to make logical sense is if the reform was designed to increase fathers' and the general public's confidence in the family courts (at a very low cost) while also discouraging mothers from using the courts to resist fathers' applications for contact. As will be discussed later in relation to both contact and shared residence, this is worrying.

As the Children and Families Bill proceeded through Parliament, changes were made. In the House of Lords, Baroness Butler-Sloss, a former senior judge and President of the Family Division, successfully introduced an amendment that stressed there was no presumption of equal division, or any particular proportion of a child's time. This is now contained in s. 1(2B) of the Children Act 1989 and states that 'involvement' means involvement of some kind, either direct or indirect, but not any particular division of a child's time.

This has been criticised by fathers' groups, as watering down the presumption and making it meaningless. It is, however, an important reminder that the child's welfare is the paramount consideration, that is, the first and only thing the court should think about.

4.4 The 'no delay' principle

The Children Act 1989, s. 1(2) states that:

> In any proceedings in which any question with respect to the upbringing of a child arises, the court shall have regard to the general principle that any delay in determining the question is likely to prejudice the welfare of the child.

Children have a different sense of time. When you are a small child, Christmases and birthdays feel very far apart. Having to wait for a decision for two months can feel unbearable. A contested court case is stressful for all parties involved, but it can be particularly damaging for the children if that stress drags on for longer than is necessary. Another reason is that if a court case takes too long, then what was a temporary thing can become a settled situation. Say, for example, that a mother has kept a 4-year-old child with her at the end of a contact visit because she claims the father uses drugs. If the case takes a year, only to find that the mother's allegations are groundless and she is unreasonably hostile against the father, then the court is in a difficult situation. The benefits of a move back to the father, who is the better primary carer, must be balanced against the risks of uprooting the child from what has quite quickly become a settled school and home environment.

 CONTEXT 2: DELAY AND THE FAMILY JUSTICE SYSTEM

In recent years, there has been a big push to reduce delay in the family court system. Delays have often been caused by there being too many cases, and not enough court rooms, qualified judges, and other personnel. Following the Family Justice Review in 2011, in care proceedings, the ambitious 26-week deadline was brought in (see Chapter 11). In relation to s. 8 cases, CAP was brought in to improve efficiency (see section 3) and make sure that cases which cannot be diverted away from court (e.g. into mediation) will be resolved as swiftly as possible. The average time a case took to get through court had been increasing up until 2014 when it was 16.8 weeks. In 2015, that had been reduced to 14.3 weeks, and by 2016 the average was down to 13.6 weeks.[24] Harding and Newnham have been critical of this focus on speed, arguing that 'Time taken in the courts process should not always be viewed as unnecessary delay'. In their 2011 sample of cases, courts used a series of short hearings, interim orders, and review hearings to gradually introduce and increase contact and resolve positions that initially seemed entrenched.[25] In the family courts, as in most areas of life, there is a tension between doing things quickly and doing them properly.

4.5 The 'no unnecessary order' principle

This is often paraphrased as the no order principle, but as Andrew Bainham has pointed out, is better described as the no unnecessary order principle.[26]

The Children Act 1989, s. 1(5) states that:

> Where a court is considering whether or not to make one or more orders under this Act with respect to a child, it shall not make the order or any of the orders unless it considers that doing so would be better for the child than making no order at all.

Section 1(5) was introduced in response to concerns that courts were routinely making orders even where divorcing parents were in full agreement about arrangements, and that this was taking parents' sense of agency away from them by issuing orders in formal, legal language that they could not relate to their own situations. It requires judges and magistrates to think before making an order: is this necessary, and can I be reasonably confident that it will not prove counterproductive or have unintended side effects (e.g. by increasing conflict)? This does not mean there has to be a real dispute for there to be an order. Orders can be made to confirm existing arrangements where this gives stability and reassurance to a parent and consequently has a positive impact on the child.[27]

5. Section 8 orders: when can they be made and who can apply?

Ideas about how children should be raised vary, and people also often have strongly held views, for example on discipline (is smacking cruel and counterproductive?) and education (should homework be banned to give children more time for free, creative play?) or even relatively trivial things like haircuts (should boys have short hair and girls have long hair?). Parents are allowed considerable freedom on most aspects of childrearing, and it is important that s. 8 orders are not misused and that children and their primary carers are protected from unnecessary, stressful interference from busybodies. Therefore, are limits to the way s. 8 orders can be sought and used.

---

[24] Ministry of Justice, *Family Court Statistics Quarterly: Annual 2016 including October to December 2016*. Available at: https://www.gov.uk/government/statistics/family-court-statistics-quarterly-october-to-december-2016, accessed 14 August 2017.

[25] Harding, M. and Newnham, A. 'How do County Courts share the care of children between parents? Two Page Briefing' (University of Warwick, 2015). Available at: http://www.nuffieldfoundation.org/how-do-county-courts-share-care-children-between-parents, accessed 14 August 2017.

[26] Bainham, A. 'Changing Families and Changing Concepts—Reforming the Language of Family Law' (1998) 10 *Child and Family Law Quarterly* 1.

[27] *Re G (Children)* [2005] EWCA Civ 1283; [2006] 1 FLR 771.

5.1 **The order must relate to a child's upbringing**

Parents, and other interested parties, can only use applications for s. 8 orders to ask the court to determine something that is linked to the exercise of parental responsibility, that is, the sorts of decisions that are usually made by holders of parental responsibility: where the child should live, go to school, or travel on holiday; whether the child should have medical treatment or be brought up in a particular religion. Courts can also make s. 8 orders on other, less common, questions, provided they relate to the child's welfare. A father can ask the mother not to consume drugs or alcohol when the child is around, but cannot demand that she gives up a potentially dangerous hobby of her own, such as mountain climbing or horse riding.

A newspaper can print a story about alleged shortcomings in the fostering system, but the newspaper's right to publish information which is in the public interest cannot override the need to maintain anonymity for any particular child, if this is in his or her best interests (which are paramount).[28]

As was discussed in relation to the *Gillick* case, parents' powers over children wane with the child's increasing maturity (see Chapter 10).[29] As they get older, children are increasingly able to 'vote with their feet' and courts often recognise that is likely to be counterproductive, in the long term, to force them into arrangements. In such circumstances, orders for indirect contact are used to 'keep the door open'.[30] Under s. 9(6) of the Children Act 1989, 'no court shall make a section 8 order which will end after the child has reached the age of 16 unless it is satisfied that the circumstances of the case are exceptional'.

 DEBATE 1: IS THE COURT THE BEST PLACE FOR PRIVATE CHILD LAW DISPUTES?

In both news and fiction, we see stories about bitter parents who use the courts to prolong their own battles or punish each other, while their lawyers use aggressive negotiations to drag everything out and make more money. It is not surprising that many people, including family policy-makers, think this is the reality of most cases.[31] The campaign group 'Fathers 4 Justice', for example, claim that legal professionals deliberately stoke conflict to make cases last longer and increase their income.[32] Their factsheet ends with an unattributed quote, presumably from a father: 'If divorce is like a burning house then going into the family courts is like emptying a plane-load of napalm onto the situation.'[33] There are a small number of long-running high-conflict cases, but there is no evidence of any cases being prolonged by family lawyers trying to get rich quick. Several studies in this jurisdiction have shown that specialist family solicitors see it as a large part of their role to reduce and resolve conflicts, to persuade their clients to compromise

---

[28] *Re X (A Child) (Injunctions: Restraining Publications)* [2001] 1 FCR 541; [2000] All ER (D) 1403.

[29] *Gillick v West Norfolk and Wisbech Area Health Authority* [1986] AC 112; [1986] 1 FLR 224.

[30] Harding, M. and Newnham, A. 'How do County Courts share the care of children between parents? Full report' (University of Warwick, 2015) 100–1. Available at: http://www.nuffieldfoundation.org/share-care, accessed 1 July 2017; Hunt, J. and Macleod, A. *Outcomes of Applications to Court for Contact Orders after Parental Separation or Divorce* (Ministry of Justice, 2008) 75.

[31] Lewis, P. *Assumptions about lawyers in policy statements: A survey of relevant research* (Lord Chancellor's Department, 2000).

[32] Fathers 4 Justice, 'Frequently Asked Questions: 'Why are so many Solicitors, Barristers and Judges opposed to the Fathers4Justice proposals?'. Available at: http://www.fathers-4-justice.org/about-f4j/campaign-faqs/, accessed 1 July 2017.

[33] Fathers 4 Justice, 'Factsheet'. Available at: http://www.fathers-4-justice.org/about-f4j/fact-sheet/, accessed 1 July 2017.

or conform to the courts' idea of how reasonable, sensible parents behave.[34] Most family courts will have a few files which are so big that they have to be wheeled into the court on a trolley, because the litigation has been going on for ten years or more, but in those cases it is the parents themselves who are driving the conflict for complicated reasons that are sometimes not even clear to them.[35] The removal of legal aid from most s. 8 disputes by LASPO 2012 (see Chapter 15) is likely to have meant that more of the courts' time is taken up with hostile litigants in person who are focused on the getting the judge to hold that they are right and that their ex-partner is terrible, rather than on doing what is best for their children.

Recent reforms to the law, the court process, and family law policy have all aimed to divert parents away from courts and towards mediation. Mediation is said to have many advantages over litigation; it is quicker, cheaper and less stressful for both the parties and their children. It can help to improve communication. It gives parents more control, allowing them to work out their own solutions; that should also make it easier for them to implement their agreements in the years to come.[36] Yet, '[i]t is clear', as Rosemary Hunter has observed, 'that the supply of and … enthusiasm for family mediation has always outstripped demand for mediation on the part of potential clients'.[37] Many parents prefer to go to court, with the assistance of a solicitor if they can afford one, or as self-representing litigants in person. Why? In some cases, there might underlying bitterness about other things that drives the s. 8 dispute, but research suggests that most cases in the family courts 'could not have been successfully diverted to mediation'.[38]

A very important point to make is that approximately 90% of separating parents work out the arrangements for their children without involving the courts.[39] This means that, where an order is applied for, the case is likely to be bitter or long-running, and involve complicating factors such as domestic violence, neglect, or addiction. Compare it to a winter flu epidemic. Some people will only be mildly affected and 'soldier on' at work or looking after their children. Most people will take a few days off work to curl up under a duvet with a hot drink. However, people with underlying health problems, babies, and frail old people will end up in hospital. We would never blame doctors for the fact that the people in hospital are sicker, and that a few will even die there. Those people are in a bed on a ward because they need to be, or they would never get better, and the hospital helps most of them. Similarly, we should not blame the family courts for the fact that many cases that reach them are bitter or difficult to resolve. Most cases are in the family courts because they need that help to investigate and resolve their problems, or because they need a formal order.[40]

---

[34] Neale, B. and Smart, C. '"Good" and "Bad" Lawyers? Struggling in the Shadow of the New Law' (1997) 19 *Journal of Social Welfare and Family Law*, 377, 387; Piper, C. 'How Do You Define a Family Lawyer?' (1999) 19 *Legal Studies* 93, 106; King, M. 'Being Sensible: Images and Practices of the New Family Lawyer' (1999) 28 *Journal of Social Policy* 249, 272.

[35] Laing, K. 'Doing the Right Thing: Cohabiting Parents, Separation and Child Contact' (2006) 20 *International Journal of Law, Policy and the Family*, 169, 173; Kaganas, F and Day Sclater, S. 'Contact Disputes: Narrative Constructions of "Good" Parents' (2004) 12 *Feminist Legal Studies*, 1, 22.

[36] See, e.g., the Family Mediation Council's Website, available at: https://www.familymediationcouncil.org.uk/family-mediation/ and Ministry of Justice leaflets available at: https://www.gov.uk/government/publications/family-mediation, both accessed 14 August 2017.

[37] Hunter, R, 'Inducing Demand for Family Mediation—Before and After LASPO' (2017) 39 *Journal of Social Welfare and Family Law* 189.

[38] Smart, C. *et al Residence and Contact Disputes in Court: Volume 1* (University of Leeds, 2003); Harding, M. and Newnham, A. 'How do County Courts share the care of children between parents? Full report' (University of Warwick, 2015) 129. Available at: http://www.nuffieldfoundation.org/share-care, accessed 1 July 2017.

[39] Blackwell, A. and Dawe, F. *Non-Resident Parental Contact* (ONS, 2003) 39.

[40] Harding, M. and Newnham, A. 'How do County Courts share the care of children between parents? Full report' (University of Warwick, 2015) 35, 129–31. Available at: http://www.nuffieldfoundation.org/share-care, accessed 1 July 2017.

5.2 Who can apply?

The Children Act 1989 contains a 'filtering mechanism' which seeks to protect children and their families from unnecessary interference. Litigation causes uncertainty and can be stressful for all involved, including children.

5.2.1 Entitled applicants

Section 10(4) of the Children Act 1989 gives defined types of applicants the right to apply for s. 8 orders without first having to seek the court's permission:

- parents;
- guardians, including special guardians (see Chapter 12);[41]
- step-parents who have acquired parental responsibility under s. 4A of the Children Act 1989 (see Chapter 8); and
- anyone who has the relevant child living with him/her under an existing child arrangements order.

These categories of persons have parental responsibility over the child concerned, and are presumed to have a legitimate interest in the child's welfare and good reasons to request the court's help. Restrictions can be imposed in appropriate cases (see 5.3) and once an application has been made the parties will still be encouraged to resolve their dispute through compromise rather than a contested hearing.

Section 10(5) of the Children Act 1989 also lists groups of applicants who are entitled to apply for child arrangements orders. These groups are presumed to have enough involvement with the child to make applications for the child to live with them, or to have contact with the child, but it would not be appropriate to give them the right to make applications to go against or override the decision-making powers of those who hold parental responsibility (e.g. by making an application that a boy should be circumcised and brought up in the Jewish religion). These groups are:

- anyone to whom the child is, or was, 'a child of the family', because they were in a marriage or civil partnership with a parent of the child;
- any person with whom the child has lived for a period of at least three years; not necessarily continuously, but the period cannot have ended more than three months ago;
- any person who:
- where a child arrangements order is in place, has the consent of everyone named in that order as someone with whom the child lives;
- where the child is in the care of a local authority, has the consent of that authority;
- in any other case, has the consent of each of those who have parental responsibility for the child;
- where a court making a child arrangements order for the child to have contact with the applicant has also granted the applicant parental responsibility under s. 12(2A).

There are further groups of applicants who can only apply for the child to live with them under a child arrangements order:

- Under s. 10(5A), a local authority foster parent if the child has lived with him or her for at least one year immediately before making of the application, or

[41] Children Act 1989, s. 14A.

- Under s. 10(5B), a relative with whom the child has lived for at least one year immediately before making the application.

5.2.2 An application by the child

Under s. 10(8) of the Children Act 1989 the child concerned can make an application, but only if the court is satisfied that he or she has sufficient understanding. This is determined by taking the gravity and complexity of the issues involved into account, as well as the child's age and maturity. Courts require a high level of understanding from children, predominantly to shield them from the more stressful aspects of contested proceedings, and prefer for children's views to be presented by Cafcass or the National Youth Advocacy Service (NYAS).

In *Mabon v Mabon and others*, the judge had refused an application for their own solicitor by the three eldest children (aged 17, 15, and 13). The judge felt that independent representation would have almost no advantages to outweigh the disadvantages of further delay, emotional damage, and exposure to the harshness of the litigation process. The Court of Appeal, however, identified a number of factors which pointed strongly towards the grant of separate representation and, given the adolescents' documented maturity and understanding, it was 'simply unthinkable to exclude young men from knowledge of and participation in legal proceedings that affected them so fundamentally.'[42]

However, research shows that separate representation is, in practice, very rare.[43]

5.2.3 All other applicants—leave to apply required

If anyone outside of the categories listed earlier wants to make an application they can do so, but they must first seek permission (leave of the court) to apply. If leave is granted, an application can be made for a s. 8 order.

Under s. 10(9) of the Children Act 1989 a court hearing a leave application has to consider:

- the nature of the proposed application;
- the relationship between the child and the applicant;
- any risk of harm to the child from the disruption caused by the court case; and,
- where the child is being looked after by a local authority, the plans of that authority as well as the parents' wishes and feelings.

The child's welfare is not paramount in leave applications,[44] and nor must the applicant show that they have a reasonable chance of success,[45] but both of these factors may be relevant to the leave application. For example, a grandmother who would like to put her regular overnight contact with her grandson on a more formal footing is very likely to be granted leave, but another grandparent who has not seen the child for years, and has fallen out with both of the parents, is far less likely to be successful. In *Re G and Re Z* two men who had acted as sperm donors for two lesbian couples, and who were not legally recognised as parents, wanted leave to apply for a s. 8 order. Baker J granted

---

[42] *Mabon v Mabon and others* [2005] EWCA Civ 634; [2005] 2 FLR 1011, at [23] (Thorpe LJ).

[43] Fortin, J. Hunt, J., and Scanlan, L. *Taking a longer view of contact: The perspectives of young adults who experienced parental separation in their youth* (Sussex Law School, 2012) xix; Harding, M. and Newnham, A. *How do County Courts share the care of children between parents? Full report* (University of Warwick, 2015) 47, 50. Available at: http://www.nuffieldfoundation.org/share-care, accessed 1 July 2017.

[44] *Re A (Minors) (Residence Orders: Leave to Apply)* [1992] Fam 182; [1992] 3 All ER 872.

[45] *Re J (Leave to issue Application for Residence Order)* [2002] EWCA Civ 1346; [2003] 1 FLR 114;

leave because there had been frequent contact before the parties fell out; the lesbian couples had encouraged relationships between the sperm donors and their biological offspring.[46]

5.3 Restrictions on applications

The need to give families freedom from unwarranted interference is a strong theme in the Children Act 1989; it can be seen in the following restrictions on who can apply, and when.

5.3.1 Local authorities

One of the aims behind the Children Act 1989 was to clearly separate public and private child law. Children can only be removed from their parents against the latter's wishes if the local authority has established either: that the child is suffering, or is likely to suffer, significant harm attributable to the parents' care; or because the child is beyond parental control (see Chapter 11).[47] Therefore, s. 9(2) of the Children Act 1989 prohibits the making of a child arrangements order under s. 8 in favour of a local authority, to prevent circumvention of this significant harm test in favour of the less demanding paramountcy principle.

Similarly, a local authority foster parent cannot apply for leave unless he either has the local authority's consent to the application, he is the child's relative, or the child has lived with him for at least one year when he is seeking leave.[48] Parents who voluntarily place their children with local authority[49] foster parents while they are going through a difficult time should not have to worry about the foster family keeping their children simply because they make better parents. Local authorities, too, should be able to make long-term plans for children free from the distraction of litigation brought by foster parents, who have perhaps only had the child living with them for a few weeks.

5.3.2 Requiring parents to seek leave before applying

As mentioned in the Debate 3, there are a small number of parents who are so caught up in their own long-running bitter conflicts that they lose sight of what is best for their children. Application after application is made as new allegations are aired, interim orders are thwarted, and every minor incident is used as an opportunity to escalate tensions. Such cases waste the courts' and Cafcass' time and, more importantly, put children at risk of significant harm until they eventually turn 16 and 'age out' of the family justice system.

Therefore, s. 91(14), the Children Act 1989 gives a court the power to make an order, which forces one or both parties to seek leave before they make any more applications to the court.

The courts have described orders under s. 91(4) as a 'weapon of last resort' which should be used sparingly, either because of a history of 'repeated and unreasonable applications', or where the facts of the case go beyond the commonly encountered need for a time to settle to a regime and there is a serious risk that, without the imposition of the restriction, the child or the primary carers will be subject to unacceptable strain'.[50] Orders can be made for a set time or indefinitely; they can be made against one or both parties; in response to an application by one of the parties, or of the court's own motion. A judge must give clear reasons for the order,[51] and it is imperative that those who will be affected by the order

---

[46] *Re G and Re Z (Children: Sperm Donors: Leave to Apply for Children Act Orders)* [2013] EWHC 134 (Fam); [2013] 1 FLR 1334.   [47] Children Act 1989, s. 32(2).

[48] Children Act 1989, s. 9(3).   [49] Children Act 1989, s. 20.

[50] *Re P (Section 91(14) Guidelines) (Residence and Religious Heritage)* [1999] 2 FLR 573, at 592–3.

[51] *Re T (A Child) (Suspension of Contact: Section 91(14) CA 1989)* [2015] EWCA Civ 719; [2016] 1 FLR 916.

understand what is being proposed and have a real effective opportunity to put forward arguments against the order.[52]

It is important to note that a s. 91(14) order does not ban parents from applying for a s. 8 order. It only requires them to seek leave first, putting them on an equal footing with, for instance, grandparents. As one barrister has commented: 'the hurdle is not formidable and in essence all the applicant has to demonstrate is that his substantive application is not hopeless.'[53]

In *Re A and B* there was a long-running and bitter conflict between a lesbian couple, with whom the two children were living, and the father and his partner, with whom contact had broken down. The dispute was complicated by the mother's long-standing mental health problems which left the whole family less able to cope with stress. The situation had been so serious that the local authority children's services had been asked to help support the family. This had provided increased stability, but the children, aged 10 and 14, remained resistant to any form of contact with their father and his partner. An order was made for indirect contact to continue, and Cobb J also upheld a s. 91(14) order on appeal, since 'any further application to the court in the near future by either party is likely to be harmful to the children, and in particular to the stability of their family life; any resumption of litigation would be likely to have a deleterious effect on [the biological mother] whose fragile mental health can withstand few challenges. Moreover, as things stand it seems to me that no court order is likely to achieve any change in the current situation.'[54]

6. Child arrangements 'live with' orders

There has never been a clear-cut line between residence and contact orders, since contact can be overnight contact for several nights a week, or for a few solid weeks during the school holidays. Many schedules could equally be labelled residence or contact. A court has to first decide what arrangements will be best for the child, and then decide whether to label it contact or residence (on the same basis of what is in the child's best interests).[55]

In 2014, both residence and contact orders were replaced with the single child arrangements order; the residence order was replaced with a child arrangements order for the child to live with the person named in the order. This change was clearly not made for linguistic convenience, a 'residence order' is much easier to say than 'a child arrangements order stipulating with whom the child is to live', or similar.

 CONTEXT 3: TRYING TO REDUCE HOSTILITY

As was mentioned in Debate 1, there are a small number of bitter, complex s. 8 cases that run for years and even decades. Many things have been tried to decrease conflict in residence and contact cases, but with little or no results.

One example is the replacement of residence and contact orders with child arrangements orders. The change of terminology was designed to remove any perception among litigating

---

[52] *Re C (Litigant in Person: Section 91(14) Order)* [2009] EWCA Civ 674; [2002] 2 FLR 1461.

[53] Reed, L. 'Section 91(14) Orders—A Never Ending Story?' (2011) *Family Law Week*. Available at: http://www.familylawweek.co.uk/site.aspx?i=ed84124, accessed 14 August 2017.

[54] *Re A and B (Contact) (No. 4)* [2015] EWHC 2839 (Fam); [2016] 2 FLR 429. However, Cobb J reduced the duration of the s. 91(14) order from six to two years.

[55] *Re K* [2008] EWCA Civ 526; [2008] 2 FLR 380, at [6] (Wilson LJ).

parents that a parent with a residence order in some way had the 'upper hand'. The Coalition government, in proposing the name change, said that: ' ... the amendment will, in time, encourage separated parents to adopt less rigid and confrontational positions with regard to arrangements for their children.'[56] Liz Trinder dryly observed that: 'No empirical evidence was offered to support those views'.[57]

This kind of change has been tried before. The use of the term 'custody' was abolished in the Children Act 1989, and replaced with parental responsibility and residence orders, to separate abstract legal rights from practical arrangements, and reduce hostility between parents.[58] Yet, the numbers of cases in the courts continued to rise.[59] The use of shared residence orders was expanded for similar reasons: 'they avoid the psychological baggage of right, power and control that attends a sole residence order'.[60] Unfortunately, this second change of terminology also failed to reduce hostility between parents, and this was increasingly recognised by judges. In Re D[61] in 2011, Thorpe LJ described the parents' 'bitter dispute', which had been running almost continuously for nine years, as both 'very sad' and 'a commonplace story', having no doubt encountered many similar cases during his long career. He noted that although '[p]rogress seemed to have been achieved' when a shared residence order was made, it only lasted three years, which were all marred by 'continuing returns to court'.[62] This is the reality for many cases where shared residence is tried to reduce hostility.

In this chapter the term 'live with' order, adopted by practitioners for convenience, will be used.

There are three main ways a 'live with' order can be made:

- to one parent (what used to be known as a sole residence order);
- to two adults who live together (previously known as a joint residence order);
- to two adults who live in different households (previously known as a shared residence order).

A 'live with' order has several important consequences. Under s. 13(1) of the Children Act 1989, where such an order is in force, no-one can change the child's surname, or remove the child from the UK for more than a month without the written consent of everyone who has parental responsibility (see 9.2).

Finally, if the person with whom the child is to live did not already have parental responsibility, then parental responsibility is conferred for the duration of the order under s. 12(2) of the Children Act 1989. Under s. 12(1A) of the Children Act 1989, if the person in whose favour the 'live with' order is made is an unmarried father or a second parent under the Human Fertilisation and Embryology Act 1991 who did not already hold parental responsibility, the court must consider whether to make a separate parental responsibility order under s. 4 or s. 4ZA of the Children Act 1989.

---

[56] Department for Education, *Children and Families Bill 2013: Contextual Information and Responses to Pre-Legislative Scrutiny* (Cm 8540, 2013) 30–1.

[57] Trinder, L. 'Climate Change? The Multiple Trajectories of Shared Care Law, Policy and Social Practices' (2014) 26 *Child and Family Law Quarterly* 30, 44.

[58] Law Commission, *Family Law Review of Child Law: Custody* (Law Com Working Paper No. 96, 1986) para 7.18; Department of Health, *The Children Act 1989: Guidance and Regulations, Vol 1, Court Orders* (HMSO, 1991) para 2.25.

[59] Ministry of Justice, *Judicial and Court Statistics 2008* (TSO 2009).

[60] *Re A R (Children)* [2010] EWHC 1346 (Fam); [2010] 2 FLR 1577, at [52] (Mostyn J).

[61] *Re D* [2011] EWCA Civ 1497.   [62] *Re D* [2011] EWCA Civ 1497, at [2] (Thorpe LJ).

6.1 Choosing one main home: sole residence

In most cases, the court has to do decide on one home, with one party, where the child will live for most of the time. In many cases, the parties agree on this point, but disagree over contact; but in some cases there is a genuine dispute about who will be the best primary carer, who should have the child living with them.

6.1.1 Concerns over gender

The family court system is sometimes accused of being biased against fathers, since orders are more likely to be made for children to live with their mothers, than with their fathers. However, to ask whether courts are biased against fathers (or mothers) is to ask the wrong question. Courts do not decide what is fair between mothers and fathers, they only decide what is best for children. Furthermore, a closer look at the figures finds no support for the allegation.

Orders for children to live with the applicant are sought almost as often as order for contact between a child and a parent. In 2011, for example, 35,815 children were the subject of applications for residence, while the corresponding figure for contact orders was 38,405.[63] Despite this, parents are less likely to have a real disagreement about where the child should live. Many orders are sought to confirm existing arrangements, and often made to mothers who are respondents in cases where the fathers have applied for contact. Mothers are more likely to adjust their employment to be primary carers while a couple are together, they are more likely to have their children living in their household after a separation, and therefore more likely to have a 'live with' order to confirm the status quo.[64]

Where there is a genuine contest between two parties about where the child should live, the court has to decide according to s. 1(1) and s. 1(3) of the Children Act 1989 and try to predict which household will be in the child's best interests using the welfare checklist. This frequently involves weighing any risks associated with one parent (s. 1(3)(e)), or any difficulties they may have in meeting the child's needs (s. 1(3)(f)), against the risks associated with upsetting the status quo and forcing change on a child (s. 1(3)(c)), often against their wishes (s. 1(3)(a)). A number of empirical studies have found that the courts' reluctance to subject children to change is a more important factor than a parent's gender.[65] There is always a risk that changes in residence may damage children's sense of security or weaken developmentally important bonds.[66] For similar reasons, courts also prefer to keep siblings together.[67] Thus, since children are more likely to be living with their mothers before a court case starts, they are also more likely to still be living with their mothers once the case has finished.

If a father is the established primary carer, then a change of residence will not be ordered just because the applicant is the mother, or because she may be more able to meet all

---

[63] In 2011, e.g., 35,815 children were the subject of applications for residence, while the corresponding figure for contact orders was 38,405. Ministry of Justice, *Judicial and Court Statistics (Annual) 2011* (Ministry of Justice, 2012). Available at: https://www.gov.uk/government/statistics/judicial-and-court-statistics-annual, accessed 1 July 2017.

[64] McKie, L., Bowlby, S., and Gregory, S. 'Gender, Caring and Employment in Britain' (2001) 30 *Journal of Social Policy* 233, 242.

[65] Giovannini, E. 'Outcomes of Family Justice Children's Proceedings—a Review of the Evidence, Research Summary 6/11' (Ministry of Justice, 2011), 1; Eekelaar, J. and Clive, E. *Custody after Divorce* (OUP, 1977) 5; Maclean, S. *Legal Aid Case Profiling Study* (Legal Aid Board, 1998) 48; Smart, C. *et al Residence and Contact Disputes in Court: Volume 1* (University of Leeds, 2003) 18; Harding, M. and Newnham, A. 'How do County Courts share the care of children between parents? Full report' (University of Warwick, 2015) 131. Available at: http://www.nuffieldfoundation.org/share-care, accessed 1 July 2017.

[66] *Re B (Residence Order: Status Quo)* [1998] 1 FLR 368; *D v M (Minor: Custody Appeal)* [1983] Fam 33.

[67] *B v B (Residence Order: Restricting Applications)* [1997] 1 FLR 139.

the children's needs. There must be some serious shortcomings or risks in relation to the father's care to justify a move. In *Re B*, a father, with whom the 8-year-old son had been living for most of his life, appealed against an order to change residence to the mother on the grounds that the judge had been wrong 'to put speculative improvements in contact over continuity of care'. The Court of Appeal upheld the appeal. The judge had failed to fully consider the effect of moving the child and his conclusion was therefore plainly wrong.[68]

 CONTEXT 4: CHOOSING THE LEAST BAD OPTION

In the study by Harding and Newnham, children whose residence was changed by the court were more likely to move from mothers to live with fathers than vice versa. Such moves were relatively rare, but there were 16 cases (out of 174) where children changed from having their settled home with their mum to living with their dad, and only one case where the move went in the opposite direction.[69] The fathers in these cases had often applied for their children to come and live with them because social services had deemed the mothers to be unable to continue to care for the children because of poor mental health, a chaotic lifestyle, or a new violent or otherwise dangerous partner.[70] Once the children were settled and doing well with their fathers, they were left living in that household even if some mothers improved their circumstances, demonstrating again that s. 1(3)(c) of the welfare checklist, the risks associated with forcing change on a child, is often the factor that carries most weight in the welfare balancing exercise. This happened, for example,[71] where both parents were former heroin addicts and the mother had fallen back into addiction at the beginning of the case, but was clean again before the case finished. Despite being clean once more, the status quo of the child living with the father had been established and was not subsequently altered in favour of the mother.

In some cases, both parents were struggling and the court clearly had to choose the 'least bad' option rather than the 'best'. In one case,[72] the mother had serious mental health issues, and the father applied for a change of residence. He said she was unable to keep their 18-month-old son safe, since she had, for example, let him play with a knife and a lighter. During the case, the toddler went for an overnight contact visit with his dad, but was found wandering alone on a busy London street at 7am. The police found the father in his flat so drunk that he had not noticed the child's absence. A permanent move was now ruled out, particularly as the mother had been accepting some help from children's services, was coping better, and presented much less of a risk to the child than the father.

6.1.2 A natural parent presumption?

The fact that courts are reluctant to move children away from a parent's home has sometimes been expressed as a presumption in favour of natural parents.[73] Judges are clearly right not to move children away from their settled homes in the hope that someone else may do a better job of raising them. All parents have strengths and weaknesses, and a

---

[68] [1998] 1 FLR 368.

[69] Harding, M. and Newnham, A. *How do County Courts share the care of children between parents? Full report* (University of Warwick, 2015) 74. Available at: http://www.nuffieldfoundation.org/share-care, accessed 1 July 2017.

[70] Harding, M. and Newnham, A. 'Section 8 Orders on the Public-Private Law Divide' (2017) 39 *Journal of Social Welfare and Family Law* 83–101, 88–9.   [71] Anonymised in the report as C40.

[72] Anonymised in the report as D11.

[73] *Re KD (A Minor) (Ward: Termination of Access)* [1988] 1 All ER 577.

different approach could be seen as harmful social engineering. Furthermore, the fact that a party in a case is a genetic and/or gestational parent can be a significant factor when considering what is in the child's best interests.[74] However, this does not equate to a legal presumption in favour of a natural parent.[75] In *Re B*, a dispute between a father and the maternal grandparents with whom the 4-year-old had lived since his birth, the Supreme Court criticised the judge's over-emphasis on the father–child link. It was stressed that a '[t]ransfer of [the child's] residence would involve a great deal more than a change of address. Many of the familiar aspects of his life which anchor his stability and sense of security would be changed.'[76]

In *Re B* the court was not deciding whether to remove a child from his or her parents, but whether the long-term benefits of living with a biological parent would be so great that they outweighed the risks and shorter-term problems associated with a move away from his settled home. In that case, as in the case in Key Case 1 following, the answer was no.

 Key Case 1: *Re E-R (A Child)* **[2015] EWCA Civ 405**

This was an appeal against an order for a 5-year-old to live with his father. The judge had cited a 'broad natural parent presumption' as a reason for moving the child. When the mother was diagnosed with terminal cancer, she named a friend, anonymised in the case as H, as testamentary guardian. After the mother's death, H had become the child's primary carer. The father asked for the child to come and live with him, although there had been no contact between him and his child for a while.

The Court of Appeal held that the judge had misunderstood and misapplied the law when he elevated the link between children and natural parents above the paramountcy principle. The child, who had already suffered enough sadness and upheaval, was more likely to thrive if left where she was already settled. The Court of Appeal made it clear that there is neither a legal presumption in favour of parents, nor a legal presumption against change, but that the latter is a factor that should be given considerable weight in the welfare balancing exercise.

In some cases, courts will also move children away from a parent's home to live with a non-parent, because of the risks associated with their current home. Although on paper there is a strict divide between private law s. 8 applications and public law proceedings under Parts III and IV of the Children Act 1989, Bainham has argued that private law cases with public law elements are an increasingly common phenomenon in the courts.[77] Harding and Newnham found that, in the courts they visited, residence orders were regularly used as an alternative to public law remedies where the parents were no longer able to provide good care and grandparents or other relatives took over, often at the suggestion of social services.[78] Yet, these public/private hybrid cases are an under-researched area.[79]

---

[74] *Re G (Children) (Residence: Same-Sex Partner)* [2006] UKHL 43; [2006] 2 FLR 629.

[75] [2006] UKHL 43; [2006] 2 FLR 629.   [76] [2009] UKSC 5; [2010] 1 FLR 551, at [42].

[77] Bainham, A. 'Private and Public Children Law: An Under Explored Relationship' (2013) 25 *Child and Family Law Quarterly* 138, 139.

[78] Harding, M. and Newnham, A. 'How do County Courts share the care of children between parents? Full report' (University of Warwick, 2015) 121. Available at: http://www.nuffieldfoundation.org/share-care, accessed 1 July 2017.

[79] Wall, N. 'The Courts and Child Protection—The Challenge of Hybrid Cases' (1997) 9 *Child and Family Law Quarterly* 345; Bainham, A. 'Private and Public Children Law: An Under Explored Relationship' (2013) 25 *Child and Family Law Quarterly* 138.

DEBATE 2: IS THE COURT THE BEST PLACE FOR PRIVATE CHILD LAW
DISPUTES?

The debate is not just whether these cases should be at court, but whether they are heard by the right court. Should these type of hybrid cases be heard as public child law cases (see Chapter 11)? Using a private law solution to what was initially a public law child protection case has a number of advantages, but also disadvantages which make it difficult to really help these problem families and resolve the cases through private child law.

Diversion to private law minimises formal state intervention into the family, consistent with the ideal of s. 1(5) of the Children Act 1989. Since the preference in public law is now for children to be fostered by a relative wherever possible,[80] the private law route can achieve the same outcome at less cost to the family justice system and local authorities, and without exposing children, parents, and relatives to the stress and stigma of care proceedings. A further advantage to local authorities is that if a child is moved under a private law s. 8 order, the local authority does not have to bear the considerable costs of long-term substitute care, or the responsibility for contact between the child and the parent.

From the point of view of the relative who takes over as primary carer, this is a drawback. Research has shown that relatives are often unaware of this disadvantage when they seek a s. 8 order for the child to come and live with them.[81]

This use of private law orders also raise questions. Are kinship carers left to their own devices to raise children who often have difficult backgrounds, while also managing contact with their problematic parents? Do they receive the practical, financial, or emotional support they need in order to give the children their best chance of a secure and stable future? What about the parents, many of whom lead chaotic lives and battle with addiction or mental ill health, do they receive the assistance and advice they need? Or do they sometimes give consent to the s. 8 order being made because they feel there is no real alternative; if they do not give consent, will their children will be taken into care?[82]

There are no easy answers to these questions, particularly without more research, but it is important to think about these cases when we wonder why it can sometimes be so difficult to resolve some private child law disputes.

Views on where it is best for children to live have changed with societal attitudes. For example, in *Re G* in 2006 Thorpe LJ observed that judicial attitudes to lesbian parents had changed over the last few decades. Where once lesbian mothers would only keep their children with them so long as they were not 'militant lesbians',[83] sexual orientation is now seen as irrelevant. A parent's faith is not relevant, unless the religion involves practices that present a risk of harm to the child. Courts should not 'pass any judgment on the beliefs of parents where they are socially acceptable and consistent with decent and respectable life.'[84] A parent's disability or limited financial means are irrelevant unless they put the child at risk of harm in some way that is serious enough to outweigh the harms associated with a transfer of residence.

---

[80] Children Act 1989, s. 22C brought in by the Children and Young Persons Act 2008.

[81] Hunt, J. and Waterhouse, S. *Understanding Family and Friends Care: the relationship between need, support and legal status—Carers' experiences* (Family Rights Group/Oxford University Centre for Family Law and Policy, 2012) and Selwyn, J. et al *The Poor Relations? Children and Informal Kinship Carers Speak Out* (Buttle, 2013).

[82] Harding, M. and Newnham, A. 'Section 8 Orders on the Public-Private Law Divide' (2017) 39 *Journal of Social Welfare and Family Law* 83, 88–9.

[83] *B v B (Minors) (Custody, Care and Control)* [1991] 1 FLR 402 (Callam J).

[84] *Re T (Minors) (Custody: Religious Upbringing)* (1975) 2 FLR 239.

6.2 A 'live with' order for two adults who live together: joint residence

An order can be made for a child to live with two adults, for example an aunt and uncle who have taken over care because of a mother's illness. A 'live with' order brings certain ancillary benefits, including parental responsibility for the applicant for as long as the order is in force.[85] Orders for a child to 'live with' two adults are sometimes made for this reason, to recognise and protect a parent's new partner and their role in the child's life, giving him or her the authority to obtain information about the child or make decisions about healthcare, education and other important matters.[86] This was particularly useful for same-sex couples and step-parents, prior to the enactment of civil partnerships,[87] the ability to be recognised as the second parent of a child born through assisted conception,[88] and the possibility for step-parents to acquire free-standing parental responsibility through a parental responsibility agreement or a court order.[89]

6.3 Shared residence

A 'live with' order can be made to two adults even though they do not live in the same household. This type of child arrangements order was previously known as a shared residence order, and that is the term you will see in most of the case law, and which we will use in this chapter. However, from the child's perspective the arrangement is more accurately described as 'alternating residence'. There is no firm definition of shared residence; an arrangement could often be described as either contact or shared residence, depending on which label the judge or magistrates feel is in the child's best interest.

Prior to the Children Act 1989, courts regarded it as 'prima facie wrong' to deprive a child of the security of a fixed home.[90] The preference was, and still is, for an arrangement where the child lives most of the time with one parent and has overnight contact with the other, typically every other weekend and half of the school holidays. Although the Children Act 1989 expressly allowed it,[91] the shared residence order was seen as 'an order which would rarely be made and would depend upon exceptional circumstances' since it risked subjecting the child to 'stress and confusion'.[92] Judicial attitudes have softened, and shared residence is becoming more popular. However, it is still comparatively rare. It has been estimated that between 9% and 12% of separated couples' children split their time more or less equally between two households.[93]

There is no formal definition of shared residence, neither in the Children Act 1989, nor in the case law. It seems tolerably clear that there should be direct overnight contact, but unlike some jurisdictions, there is no requirement that a certain percentage of the child's time must be spent in each household. The distinction between shared residence and an order for contact is essentially a question of degree, particularly as contact will now more often than not involve quite generous staying contact. Studies have found overnight contact to be the most common order made.[94] The two questions should be considered

---

[85] Children Act 1989 s. 12(2).

[86] See, e.g., *A v B and C (Lesbian Co-Parents: Role of Father)* [2012] EWCA Civ 285; [2012] 2 FLR 607.

[87] Civil Partnership Act 2004.   [88] Human Fertilisation and Embryology Act 2008, ss. 42–45.

[89] Children Act 1989 s. 4A.   [90] *Riley v Riley* [1986] 2 FLR 429, at 431 (May LJ).

[91] Children Act 1989 s. 11(4) omitted by the Children and Families Act 2014, Sch 2 para 6(2).

[92] *Re H* [1994] 1 FLR 717, at 722 (Purchas LJ).

[93] Peacey, V. and Hunt, J. *Problematic Contact after Separation and Divorce? A National Survey of Parents* (One Parent Families/Gingerbread, 2008) 19.

[94] Harding, M. and Newnham, A. 'How do County Courts share the care of children between parents? Full report' (University of Warwick, 2015) 84. Available at: http://www.nuffieldfoundation.org/share-care, accessed 1 July 2017.

separately: a judge should first consider how to divide the child's time and then how to label the arrangement.[95] An order can contain detailed schedules, but courts may also leave the parties to agree: 'the object of the exercise should be to maintain flexible and practical arrangements whenever possible'.[96]

 Key Case 2: D v D (Children) (Shared Residence Orders) [2001] 1 FLR 495

After the parents' marriage broke down, their three children spent substantial amounts of time with each parent, but there was also a high degree of animosity between the parents, and frequent legal proceedings to settle the disputes around contact schedules, holidays, healthcare, and education. The applicant father argued that he was being treated 'as a second-class parent' and had cited this as a main source of his grievances. The first instance judge had found that the mother was using the sole residence order as a 'weapon' in the 'war' with the father, but also that the father often acted in a way that was calculated to wind her up.

The Court of Appeal cited two reasons for upholding the shared residence order. They made it clear that shared residence orders are not exceptional or special; the ordinary s. 1(3) welfare checklist should be without any additional hurdles or unnecessary 'gloss'. In this case, the order would benefit the children by reflecting the practical reality that they were spending 46% of their time with their father. Secondly, the Court recognised that a shared residence order 'removes any impression that one parent is good and responsible whereas the other parent is not'. It was felt that the additional symbolic benefits this would bring to the father would allow him to 'go away and make contact work' so that the parties could break their pattern of escalating every disagreement by taking it to court.

This second aspect of the case was a complete reversal of cause and effect: good cooperation between parents was now seen as something that could be achieved by a shared residence order, rather than a prerequisite.

In the decade that followed this case, the use of the shared residence order was extended to cases of very high and long running conflict, in the hope that its symbolic message about the parents being 'equal in the eyes of the law' would leave the parents with nothing left to fight over.[97] The need for the order to reflect children's practical reality became less important than the sending of a clear message to primary carers that they could not marginalise the other parent.[98] This new use of shared residence was also a response to the fact that the concept of sharing 'parental responsibility' was regarded by parents as worth very little in practice. Non-resident fathers saw the shared residence order as necessary to recognise the parents' equal value and importance, presumably in the hope that this would de-escalate the fighting over anything related to the children.[99]

While this new use of the shared residence order had been championed by some members of the Court of Appeal (in particular Wall LJ and Wilson LJ as he then was), a more pragmatic scepticism developed alongside this. In *T v T*, Black LJ expressed concern that this new view of shared residence as a necessary symbol of equality had led

---

[95] *Re K* [2008] EWCA Civ 526; [2008] 2 FLR 380.

[96] *A v A* [2004] EWHC 142; [2001] 1 FLR 1195, at [118].

[97] *A v A* [2004] EWHC 142; [2001] 1 FLR 1195, at [124].

[98] *Re F* [2003] EWCA Civ 592; [2003] 2 FLR 397; *Re W* [2009] EWCA Civ 370; [2009] 2 FLR 436.

[99] Reece, H. 'The Degradation of Parental Responsibility' in R. Probert, S. Gilmore, and J. Herring (eds), *Responsible Parents and Parental Responsibility* (Hart Publishing, 2009) 94; Harris, P. and George, R. 'Parental Responsibility and Shared Residence Orders: Parliamentary Intentions and Judicial Interpretations' (2010) 22 *Child and Family Law Quarterly* 151.

to shared residence becoming a 'battleground' for adults.[100] In *Re R*, Hughes LJ endorsed the first instance judge's observation that where the hostility between parents was severe and long-standing, shared residence could be a recipe for disaster.[101]

In their study of cases from 2011, Harding and Newnham found evidence of both approaches, as well as uncertainty about what exactly a shared residence order was for, and how it should be used. The order remained comparatively rare, but what was clear was that the divorce of the formal order from practical arrangements was widely accepted: the order was only made in 19 of 174 cases, and in 12 of those 19 cases the unequal time split meant that one parent was clearly the primary carer.[102]

If there is no clear consensus on shared residence, then some very useful advice was provided by Baroness Hale in *Holmes-Moorhouse*. She reminded courts to focus on who would be caring for children, in a practical sense, rather than making aspirational statements of what would be for the best in some ideal world. She also asserted that children's wishes and feelings 'ought to be particularly important in shared residence cases, because it is the children who will have to divide their time between two homes and it is all too easy for the parents' wishes and feelings to predominate'.[103]

❓ DEBATE 3: WHAT IS SHARED PARENTING AND WHEN IS IT GOOD FOR CHILDREN?

Shared parenting is not a legal term; it can mean anything from an equal sharing of time between the parents, to comparatively marginal involvement such as contact every other Saturday afternoon, or even indirect contact via cards on birthdays and major holidays. The campaign group 'Families Need Fathers', for example, define shared parenting broadly, as: children [being] brought up with the love and guidance of both parents, to help them to be happier and more successful throughout their life.[104] This vagueness makes it difficult to understand and evaluate claims that our family justice system is letting children down because it is not doing enough to promote shared parenting. These types of claims are regularly made. In March 2017, a Conservative MP and former barrister, Suella Fernandez, introduced a Private Members' Bill to strengthen the non-resident parent's position.[105] To achieve this, she called for a more robust enforcement of contact, including a suggested 'three strikes and you're out' rule for transferring residence away from a parent who frustrates contact (provided it is safe for the child). She proposed a shared parenting presumption written in terms of meaningful contact, complaining that the recent parental involvement presumption had been watered down too far in its passage through Parliament (see 4.3). She also included proposals to make family courts more open and to encourage mediation, for example by imposing financial penalties on parents who draw out the court case.

Her Bill was unlikely ever to make it through Parliament, but kept the demands for a stronger presumption in the public eye and was praised, for example, by the campaign group

---

[100] *T v T (Shared and Joint Residence Orders)* [2010] EWCA Civ 1366; [2011] 1 FCR 267.

[101] *Re R* [2012] EWCA Civ 1326, at [9] (Hughes LJ).

[102] Newnham, A. and Harding, M. 'Sharing as caring? Contact and Residence Disputes between Parents' (2016) 28 *Child and Family Law Quarterly*, 175, 181–2; Smart, C. *et al Residence and Contact Disputes in Court: Volume 1* (University of Leeds, 2003).

[103] *Holmes-Moorhouse v Richmond-Upon-Thames London Borough Council* [2009] UKHL 7, at [36].

[104] Families Need Fathers, *What We Believe*. Available at: https://fnf.org.uk/component/phocadownload/file/120-briefing-doc-final. Accessed 1 July 2017.

[105] Suella Fernandez introduced The Family Justice Bill, Hansard HC vol 624, cols 147–8 (28 March 2017).

'Fathers4Justice'. The group's controversial founder, Matt O'Connor, hoped this was the first political step towards shared parenting being adopted as the legal norm.[106]

Any presumption like this is at odds with the paramountcy principle, and reform has been resisted on that ground, for example, by the Family Justice Review.[107] Arguments for reform are therefore usually based on the idea that shared parenting is best for children, so that any new rule is compatible with the paramountcy principle. If we are to use shared parenting as a preferred option or a starting point for all separated families, then we first have to be clear on what it means, and when it is good for children.

Is it about time?

In order for parents to be involved with and have influence over their children, they must spend enough time together to develop 'a significant relationship', but pro-shared parenting campaigners concede that 50/50 may not be the best solution for all children and all families.[108] As we have seen, our courts do not insist on an equal division of children's time before they make an order that children live with both parents, at different times and in different houses. The draftsmen behind the Children Act 1989 thought such arrangements would remain rare, because of the practical and logistical difficulties, and the potentially unsettling impact on children.[109] Interviews with young adults who grew up with alternating residence suggest children must feel that the practical and emotional sacrifices they make are worth it, in the long run, and this is measured in good, close relationships with both parents. Children who feel trapped in rigid schedules where parents insist on a precisely equal split, and feel unable to raise objections for fear of sparking another row or return to court, unsurprisingly did not feel the sacrifices they had made had been worth it in the long run.[110] Larger research studies show that it is quality time with a parent that benefits children—time on its own is not enough.[111] However, of course a parent needs time for relationships to be maintained. It is also likely that in many families, time is seen as a proxy measurement for things like closeness and importance.

Is it about status?

We have seen that the Court of Appeal in the 2000's promoted shared residence orders as a way of creating an equal playing field. Residence and contact orders were replaced with child arrangements orders for similar reasons, to remove perceptions that mothers who were granted residence orders had 'won' while fathers who had contact had somehow 'lost' the battle. However, we also know that there are a minority of parents who want to abuse their equal status to coerce, control, or undermine the other parent. In Australia, a law reform that encouraged shared parenting was amended after a few years, partly because perpetrators of domestic abuse were using the new law to continue to exercise power of their former partners, and their children, in a way that was really harmful to those

---

[106] Fathers 4 Justice, 'Latest News: March 29th, 2017: Tory MP calls for strict enforcement of child arrangement orders'. Available at: http://www.fathers-4-justice.org/2017/03/tory-mp-calls-for-strict-enforcement-child-arrangement-orders/, accessed 1 July 2017.

[107] Ministry of Justice, *Family Justice Review Final Report* (Ministry of Justice, 2011) para 4.27. Available at: https://www.gov.uk/government/publications/family-justice-review-final-report, accessed 18 July 2017.

[108] Families Need Fathers, *What We Believe.* Available at: https://fnf.org.uk/component/phocadownload/file/120-briefing-doc-final, accessed 1 July 2017.

[109] The Law Commission, *Review of Child Law: Guardianship,* (Law Com No. 172 1988) para 4.12.

[110] Smart, A. and Neale, B. *Family Fragments?* (Polity Press, 1999); Fortin, J., Hunt, J., and Scanlan, L. *Taking a Longer View of Contact: The perspectives of young adults who experienced parental separation in their youth* (Sussex Law School, 2012); Statistiska Centralbyrån, *Olika familjer lever på olika sätt—om barns boende och försörjning efter en separation* (Statistiska Centralbyrån, 2014).

[111] Fortin, J., Hunt, J., and Scanlan, L. *Taking a Longer View of Contact: The perspectives of young adults who experienced parental separation in their youth* (Sussex Law School, 2012).

children.[112] Equal status should be seen more as a means to an end, and that end point should be improved cooperation between the parents.

Is it about parents getting on better?

In *D v D*[113] (Key Case 2) the Court of Appeal clearly hoped that shared residence would give the parents a level playing field that they could use to resolve their disputes rather than take every row to court. Proponents of shared parenting sometimes cite studies from a number of jurisdictions, which show that children whose parents share 'custody' or 'residence' do better in areas such as educational achievement and mental health. However, this is a classic case of confusing correlation and cause. Parents who choose these types of arrangements often do so because they are already getting on tolerably well. Later studies found that parents who go into alternating residence against one parent's wishes or because they were strongly encouraged to do so by a court, are no better at cooperating than any other separated parents. These arrangements are likely to break down, often with children going back to living mainly with their mothers. Where they do last, there is no evidence that they can reduce conflict. In fact, studies have suggested the opposite, leaving children trapped as pawns in the middle of a battle between the parents; and one thing that is shown by research into separating parenting is that exposure to conflict creates a real risk of harm.[114] Courts should be more aware of this evidence when considering s. 1(3)(e), the risks of harm posed to the child, in the welfare checklist when considering any proposed arrangements.

Is it about the quality of relationships?

This seems like basic common sense; it is also backed up by the research. 'The overwhelming weight of evidence is that it is the quality of relationships, not the quantity, that counts.'[115] It is more difficult to say, however, how exactly family law can be used to encourage good quality relationships. Yes, a certain amount of more relaxed, free-flowing time is necessary for bonds to be maintained. However, where parents are rigid or unreasonable about time, it can become the main focus instead of the child. If both parents are closely involved in their children's everyday reality of school and after-school activities there is less of a risk that relationships deteriorate into strained, artificial time where neither party knows quite what to say to the other. On the other hand, this kind of close involvement is practically, financially, and emotionally demanding. Furthermore, the closer the involvement of both parents, the more difficult it is to coordinate all activities, and the greater the risks that rows will blow up about whose turn it is wash the football kit or whose fault it is when homework is not completed on time. It is clearly better for children if parents are flexible, respect each other, and can communicate in a civilised way. But, as we have seen there is no evidence to suggest formal orders can be used to achieve this. If we want to encourage shared parenting after separation, as a society, we need to start much earlier. We must also be more willing to see caring for children as a public concern that needs to be supported with taxpayers' money through paid parental leave, flexible working, and subsidised childcare. The availability of these kind of parent-friendly entitlements, together with a clear political focus on gender equality, are probably the main reasons why over a third of all Swedish children of separated parents alternate residence, usually on a week-about basis.[116]

---

[112] See, e.g., Trinder, L. 'Shared Residence: A Review of Recent Research Evidence' (2010) 22 *Child and Family Law Quarterly* 475.

[113] [2001] 1 FLR 495.

[114] Gilmore, S. 'Contact/Shared Residence and Child Well-Being: Research Evidence and its Implications for Legal Decision-Making' (2006) 20 *International Journal of Law, Policy and the Family* 344, 350–1.

[115] Hunt, J. Masson, J., and Trinder, L. 'Shared Parenting: The Law, the Evidence and Guidance from Families Need Fathers' [2009] *Family Law,* 831, 834.

[116] Statistiska Centralbyrån, *Olika familjer lever på olika sätt—om barns boende och försörjning efter en separation* (Statistiska Centralbyrån, 2014); Newnham, N. 'Shared Residence: Lessons from Sweden' (2011) 23 *Child and Family Law Quarterly* 251.

7. Child arrangements orders for contact

The Children Act 1989, s. 8(1) states that: In this Act 'child arrangements order' means an order regulating arrangements relating to … with whom a child is to … spend time or otherwise have contact, and … when a child is to … spend time or otherwise have contact with any person'.

In principle, under the Children Act 1989, it is the child who has a right to contact with a parent or other adult, and not vice versa. In practice, it is usually parents and other adults who come to court asking for orders. Courts also have no powers to order contact with an adult who does not want to spend time with a child.

A court making a decision on an application for contact has to decide whether the contact that has been asked for will be in the child's best interests under s. 1(1) of the Children Act 1989. Since s. 1(2A) of the Children Act 1989 came into force in 2014, courts now start with a presumption that involvement by an applicant parent will be in the child's best interests. This is only a presumption, and presumptions can be rebutted on the facts, as is made clear in the new s. 1(6) of the Children Act 1989. The new s. 1(2B) of the Children Act 1989 also makes it clear that the presumption does not mean the applicant always has to get precisely the kind of contact they have asked for. Judges and magistrates continue to use the s. 1(3) welfare checklist to weigh the perceived benefits of contact against any risks in that particular case. Contact can include overnight staying contact, or take place during the day. It can be supervised by relatives, or by staff in a contact centre, and it can also be indirect contact through phone calls, emails, Skype, or letters and cards. Regular overnight contact is now the most common outcome in cases, and seen as the norm.[117]

While most children probably benefit from seeing both parents, there is no conclusive research evidence to support the idea that contact is always good for children, or that regular contact is necessary for children to grow into healthy adults.[118]

This next section will first look at how a court makes a decision about contact, linking this to the factors in the welfare checklist. It will then give an overview of the enforcement of contact orders.

7.1 Contact and children's needs and characteristics

In the decades since the Children Act 1989, contact with a non-resident parent has been seen as a very important in helping children develop into healthy adults. Contact can also meet wider needs, for example the need for contact with wider kin, and an awareness of both cultures for children with parents from different ethnic or religious backgrounds. Sometimes, a child's other needs and characteristics can put limits on contact; a child on the autism spectrum may for example, have a greater need for contact to follow a set pattern.

7.2 Contact and the wishes of the child

Under s. 1(3)(a) a court hearing a contact application must take into account 'the ascertainable wishes and feelings of the child concerned (considered in the light of his age and understanding)'. A court gets information about what children want from their parents,

---

[117] Hunt, J. and Macleod, A. *Outcomes of Applications to Court for Contact Orders after Parental Separation or Divorce* (Ministry of Justice, 2008) 121; Newnham, A. and Harding, M. 'Sharing as Caring? Contact and Residence Disputes between Parents' (2016) 28 *Child and Family Law Quarterly* 175, 187.

[118] Barnett, A. 'The Welfare of the Child Re-Visited: In Whose Best Interests? Part I' [2009] *Family Law* 50; Gilmore, S. 'The Assumption that Contact is Beneficial: Challenging the 'Secure Foundation' [2008] *Family Law* 1226.

and in around half of cases also from s. 7 reports written by Cafcass or the local authority children's services. It is important to look at the last part of s. 1(3)(a), which refers to the child's age and understanding, and the complexity of the decision to be made, in determining how much weight is accorded to what a child wants from contact arrangements.

Contact between a 9-year-old boy and his father had dwindled and finally stopped in *Re W (Contact: Joining Child as Party)*, while the animosity between the parents had not reduced in the three years since their separation. The boy had written a letter expressing his strong objections to contact. The Court of Appeal held that the judge had been wrong to 'close the door' on contact, and asked Cafcass to explore ways to reintroduce contact. Lady Butler-Sloss stated: 'At the end of the day this father is the only biological father this child will ever have. The child has a right to a relationship with his father even if he does not want it. The child's welfare demands that efforts should be made to make it possible that it can be.'[119]

One important question to consider, particularly by Cafcass if they are talking to a child, is whether the child's objections to contact are genuinely held, or whether they are the result of the resident parent's negative influence. Parental alienation syndrome has been defined as deliberate and systematic denigration of the non-resident parent by the resident parent, until the child has vehement objections to contact but cannot link these to any reasons why they would fear or dislike their non-resident parent. Drastic measures are said to be necessary to reverse the damage of parental alienation syndrome; transfer of residence to the other parent even if there has been prior contact for years, isolation from the alienating parent, and deprogramming to undo the damage done by that parent's poisonous lies. In this jurisdiction, parental alienation syndrome is not recognised as a diagnosable psychiatric disorder,[120] and such drastic responses are not deemed necessary. However, children's wishes carry considerably less weight if they are an expression of a parent's implacable hostility. Considerable efforts will be made by courts, Cafcass, other agencies including National Youth Advocacy Service, and even court appointed experts, to change children's minds and persuade them to see a parent if the court is convinced contact is in their best interests.[121] Nevertheless, where both a resident parent and a child are implacably hostile, courts do struggle to get contact going.[122]

The courts have recognised that older children's views carry considerable weight, because their views are more likely to have been arrived at for good reasons and through mature reasoning; and also because forcing an antagonistic person into contact is more likely to damage than to strengthen that relationship. In *Re S*, three children aged 16, 14, and 12 had strong objections to contact with their father, which related to his relationships with other women both before and after the marriage and the ways the children had found out about these other women. Tyrer J acknowledged that the children were not really children, but should be 'treated as young adults with minds of their own, minds that they are capable of making up for themselves and opinions that are to be taken at face value without being criticised.' Furthermore, as teenagers, they were likely to react to any use of the force of the law to order them to have contact with the kind of 'sullen resentment' that teenagers excel in and which means making orders and demanding obedience 'is invariably counter-productive'. Tyrer J, like many other judges in similar cases,

---

[119] *Re W (Contact: Joining Child as Party)* [2001] EWCA Civ 1830; [2003] 1 FLR 681, at [16] (Lady Butler-Sloss P).

[120] See, e.g, *Re LVMH (Contact: Domestic Violence)* [2000] 2 FLR 334, at [35] and Eaton, D. Jarmain, S., and Lustigman, L. 'Parental Alienation: Surely the Time has Come to Effect Change?' [2016] *Family Law* 581.

[121] Newnham, A. and Harding, M. 'Sharing as Caring? Contact and Residence Disputes between Parents' (2016) 28 *Child and Family Law Quarterly* 175, 192–3.

[122] See, e.g., *Re A (Intractable Contact Dispute: Human Rights Violations)* [2013] EWCA Civ 1104.

preferred 'to try persuasion, to give respect to their views, to acknowledge what they are saying, to listen to them and to try and provide opportunities for negotiation.'[123]

7.3 **Risks of harm**

Since only 10% of separating parents resort to legal action, it is usually the most complex or bitter disputes that end up in front of judges and magistrates. This means that in most cases, the general and specific benefits of contact in this case, must be weighed against risks of harm that have been identified by the other parent, by Cafcass, social workers, or other professionals that have been involved with the family.

7.3.1 **Domestic violence**

When the Children Act 1989 first came into force, domestic violence was seen as an issue between the adults and therefore irrelevant to the child welfare question. There was also a reluctance to let allegations about what had happened in the past distract the court from proposals for future contact. This meant that mothers who raised objections to contact were seen as the problem (rather than the risks they were alleging arising from the abusive partner's behaviour, see Chapter 7).

In *Re O* a clear warning was issued to stubborn, unreasonable, and uncooperative parents that the courts would not allow them to frustrate contact.[124] This warning was often repeated in subsequent cases to minimise or ignore resident parent's objections to contact. The label 'implacable hostility', which was initially used to describe resident parents whose objections had no reasonable foundation, was subsequently used to describe any mother who objected to or sought to limit contact. This prompted Hale J (as she then was) to criticise this indiscriminate use of the label.[125] An influential study drew attention to the risks of not taking domestic violence seriously,[126] and a committee chaired by Wall LJ in 2001 concluded that there needed to be greater awareness of the effect of domestic violence on children, both short term and long term, as witnesses as well as victims.[127] Four different cases were then listed jointly for the Court of Appeal, with the aim of producing clear guidelines for decisions on contact where the parents' relationship had been violent prior to separation.

 Key Case 3: *Re L, V, M, H* **(Contact: Domestic Violence) [2000] 2 FLR 334**

In each case a father's application for direct contact had been refused by a judge, against a background of domestic violence between the parents, and the father had appealed. In *Re L*, the mother said the father had been violent to her when she was pregnant. She described an incident when the baby was only four weeks old and she was breastfeeding him, when the father lost his temper, swore at her, threatened to cut her long hair off, and then cut off her pubic hair, leaving her feeling shaken, scared, and degraded. The district judge who heard the case said the father had a cruel streak, which suggested a significant psychological problem. In *Re V*, the child had witnessed a serious incident when the father attacked the mother in the kitchen with a knife and caused an injury to her finger which bled profusely. The father was

---

[123] *Re S (Contact: Children's Views)* [2002] EWHC 540 (Fam); [2002] 1 FLR 1156, at 1170 (Tyrer J).

[124] *Re O (Contact: Imposition of Contact)* [1995] 2 FLR 124, at 129–30.

[125] *Re D* [1997] 2 FLR 48 (Hale J).

[126] Hester, M. and Radford, R. *Domestic Violence and Child Contact Arrangements in England and Denmark* (The Policy Press, 1996).

[127] Children Act Sub-Committee, *A Report to the Lord Chancellor on the Question of Parental Contact in Cases where there is Domestic Violence* (TSO, 2001).

convicted of the criminal offence of causing grievous bodily harm and had not seen the boy for five years. Even though his mother and step-father had tried to convince him, the boy flatly refused any kind of contact. In *Re M*, the child was born after the parents' marriage had ended because of the father's violent behaviour. After five years of boring regular visits to a contact centre, the child stopped contact after an argument between his parents at the centre. The parents in *Re H* were both Muslims who had entered into an arranged marriage, and the father had very strict standards for the mother's conduct. She said he had enforced these standards though regular and extreme, threats of violence: he once threatened to cut her up with an electric saw and on another occasion said he would cut her up into little pieces and put her down the lavatory. The mother fled to a refugee. She had now been raising the children in a non-traditional and non-religious environment for five years, but the father refused to accept and adapt to these changes. There was, therefore, not only a risk of that he could abduct the children, but also a real likelihood that he would now, as in the past, resort to threats and intimidating behaviour to correct what he felt were serious flaws in the way the mother was bringing up their children. The result was described as a clash of cultures in which the children would be likely to suffer. In all four cases, the fathers' appeals against the refusal of contact with their children were dismissed.

The Court had the benefit of a joint expert report prepared by two child psychiatrists. The psychiatrists identified a number of risks associated with making a direct contact order. An escalation of 'the climate of conflict' could undermine a child's general stability and emotional well-being, or leave the child with conflicting loyalties. Children can be very frightened, often by witnessing abuse or denigration of their mothers. Court-ordered contact could do more harm than good where the relationship with a parent was based on manipulation or bullying, or where the contact parent was unreliable or paid little attention to the child once the battle for contact with the mother had been won. Further risks included the negative impact on a child when his objections to contact were overruled, and the stress to both children and resident parents when court cases are dragged out, or a dispute is repeatedly brought back to court by a father as a means of exerting control over his former partner.

The Court of Appeal did not say that domestic violence was a bar to contact, nor that it creates a presumption against contact. The Court did, however, stress that domestic violence is an important factor in the welfare balancing exercise and the role of s. 1(3)(e) of the Children Act 1989 in assessing any risk of harm posed to the child. Where an allegation of domestic violence is made, the court has to consider whether there is evidence to back them up, and whether the risks associated with contact can be eliminated or minimised so that contact can still, overall, be in the child's best interests.

Butler-Sloss P: In conclusion, on the general issues, a court hearing a contact application in which allegations of domestic violence are raised should consider the conduct of both parties towards each other and towards the children, the effect on the children, and on the residential parent and the motivation of the parent seeking contact. Is it a desire to promote the best interests of the child or a means to continue violence and/or intimidation or harassment of the other parent? In cases of serious domestic violence, the ability of the offending parent to recognise his or her past conduct, to be aware of the need for change, and to make genuine efforts to do so, will be likely to be an important consideration.

On an application for interim contact, when the allegations of domestic violence have not yet been adjudicated upon, the court should give particular consideration to the likely risk of harm to the child, whether physical or emotional, if contact is granted or refused. The court should ensure, as far as it can, that any risk of harm to the child is minimised and that the safety of the child and the residential parent is secured before, during and after any such contact.

Have things improved so much that the courts' handling of domestic violence is no longer a problem? Unfortunately the answer is no. In 2006, research found that the guidelines from *Re LVMH* were ignored more often than they were adhered to. This was particularly true where the parents had reached a compromise which was contained in a draft consent order, that is, an order where the judge has had no input but merely gives legal force to what the parents have already agreed (see Chapter 15).[128] That is very worrying, since coercion and control are central elements of domestic violence and there is a real risk that mothers are so frightened of their former partners that their consent to the contact arrangements is not genuine.

In 2009, Practice Direction 12J was issued.[129] It requires courts to pay proper attention to allegations of domestic violence. Courts must decide early on in the case whether a fact-finding hearing should be held. Before these hearings, the party making allegations of domestic violence draws up a list of incidents, and the other party has a chance to respond to that list, before a hearing is held where a judge decides if the allegations have been proven on a balance of probabilities. The findings can then be used to assess risks of making different types of child arrangements orders, and to order a perpetrator to a domestic violence-related activity, designed to help him understand how his behaviour has impacted negatively on his former partner and their children, and to change that behaviour. Where a fact-finding has not been held, courts must still consider the safety of the child in light of the alleged domestic violence and to take action to safeguard the child from the risks posed.

In Harding and Newnham's sample from five county courts, allegations of domestic abuse were made in 86 of the 174 cases that were disputes between two parents (49%). These figures are consistent with research by Hunt and McLeod that found 'serious welfare issues' in 54% of their cases, and included domestic violence in that definition.[130] This may seem a shockingly high number, but we must remember that only an estimated one in ten separating couples apply to the family court for help with arrangements for their children, that not all of these domestic abuse allegations will have been true, and that the study adopted the government-endorsed broad definition of domestic violence.[131] Nevertheless, the study found most of these allegations to have some basis in facts, and we are right to be shocked that domestic abuse is such a common problem in families where children are harmed by exposure to violent and controlling behaviour. Fact finding hearings, which were recommended in both *Re LVMH* and Practice Direction 12J, were only scheduled in 16 of these 86 cases, and were actually held in only 8 cases (less than 10% of cases with domestic abuse allegations).[132]

Research by Barnett has found that, despite *Re LVMH* and Practice Direction 12J, legal professionals are so focused on the perceived benefits of contact, generally, that it is only in the very worst cases that the risks associated with domestic violence are taken as seriously as they should be.[133] In legal communications created by solicitors, barristers, and judges

---

[128] Craig, J. 'Everybody's Business: Applications for Contact Orders by Consent' [2007] *Family Law* 26.

[129] Practice Direction: Residence and Contact Orders: Domestic Violence and Harm [2009] 2 FLR 1400.

[130] Hunt, J. and Macleod, A. *Outcomes of Applications to Court for Contact Orders after Parental Separation or Divorce* (Ministry of Justice, 2008) 9.

[131] https://www.gov.uk/government/publications/new-government-domestic-violence-and-abuse-definition/circular-0032013-new-government-domestic-violence-and-abuse-definition, accessed 18 July 2017.

[132] Harding, M. and Newnham, A. 'How do County Courts share the care of children between parents? Full report' (University of Warwick, 2015). Available at: http://www.nuffieldfoundation.org/share-care, accessed 1 July 2017.

[133] Barnett, A. 'Contact at All Costs? Domestic Violence and Children's Welfare' (2014) 26 *Child and Family Law Quarterly* 439, 443.

women's concerns about continued contact with violent fathers are still downplayed, trivialised, or even erased.[134] Barnett has warned that to really tackle this issue:

> we need to acknowledge properly that 'the family' is not always a safe haven but a place where abuse can occur. In order to do so, we need to recognise that domestic violence is morally reprehensible and a 'significant failure in parenting', and that women's desires for safety, wellbeing and autonomy are morally legitimate. Until we are able to do so, many children may be put at risk by a prescriptive application of the presumption of parental involvement, courts will continue to clash with 'implacably hostile mothers', and contact between children and violent fathers will continue to be seen as not only feasible but as positively desirable.[135]

Two senior judges, Cobb J and Munby P, have argued for amendments to be made to Practice Direction 12J to protect victims of domestic violence within the family justice system, and improve judicial awareness of these issues.[136]

Where the child's need for contact with a parent is seen by professionals as this crucial, it can lead them to ask the wrong question: how much contact is safe? Rather than, as required by the statute: is any, and if so, what kind of contact, in this child's best interests? The same approach can be seen in relation to other child-welfare related risks.

7.3.2 Child-welfare related or safeguarding risks

A court deciding on contact often has to consider other child-welfare related risks, such as substance abuse within the family, or abuse of the child by a parent or relative. These can be raised by a parent or a relative who is a party in the case, by the local authority if they have already been involved with the family, or by Cafcass as part of their enquiries.

Research indicates that concerns that are serious enough to potentially be a reason against a parent having their children live with them or spend time with them are raised in half of cases.[137] This may seem a lot, but we have to remember that the most complicated or hostile disputes are likely to be among the estimated 10% of parents' disputes that get to a family court. If drug or alcohol addiction is alleged, the court can order drug testing. Section 7 welfare reports requested from Cafcass or the local authority children's services are the most common way for courts to investigate these kind of concerns, and they were ordered in half of the cases in Harding and Newnham's research. In one quite complex but by no means exceptional case,[138] the child had moved to live with his father. The Section 7 report concluded that the mother would not be able to adequately meet the child's needs or keep the 3-year-old safe. Social workers had been involved with the mother since the child's birth, due to her long-term substance misuse and mental health issues, but the most pressing concern was her drunken and volatile friends who put the little boy at risk

---

[134] Barnett, A. 'Contact at all Costs? Domestic Violence and Children's Welfare' (2014) 26 *Child and Family Law Quarterly* 439, 461.

[135] Barnett, A. 'Contact at All Costs? Domestic Violence and Children's Welfare' (2014) 26 *Child and Family Law Quarterly* 439, 462.

[136] Cobb, J. *Review of Practice Direction 12J FPR 2010—Child Arrangement and Contact Orders: Domestic Violence and Harm* (Court and Tribunals Judiciary, 2016). Available at: https://www.judiciary.gov.uk/publications/review-of-practice-direction-12j-fpr-2010-child-arrangement-and-contact-orders-domestic-violence-and-harm/, accessed 14 August 2017; Interview with Sir James Munby, president of the family division, in *The Guardian* on 30 December 2016. Available at: https://www.theguardian.com/society/2016/dec/30/family-courts-sir-james-munby-domestic-abuse-victims, accessed 14 August 2017.

[137] Hunt, J. and Macleod, A. *Outcomes of Applications to Court for Contact Orders after Parental Separation or Divorce* (Ministry of Justice, 2008) 9; Harding, M. and Newnham, A. 'How do County Courts share the care of children between parents? Full report' (University of Warwick, 2015) 26. Available at: http://www.nuffield-foundation.org/share-care, accessed 1 July 2017.   [138] Anonymised in the research as E23.

of witnessing or actually suffering violence. However, rather than seeing this as a binary choice between contact or no contact, the court approached the question in a more pragmatic way, and focused on how contact could be made safe enough while still maintaining the parent–child relationship. An order was made for weekly overnight contact which had to take place at the maternal grandmother's house, and be supervised by her.[139]

Another important point needs to be made. Worry is an inescapable and significant part of parenthood. Some of you who read this will have parents who worry about things that are unlikely to happen. Those worries are nevertheless genuinely held and are borne out of love for their child and a desire to protect him or her as far as possible. Where a parent is genuinely, if a bit unreasonably, worrying about something, this can take up so much time and emotional energy that it has a bad impact on their parenting, and therefore has a negative impact on the child. Experienced family court judges and magistrates are aware that these kind of genuine worries cannot be dismissed. Even where a court disagrees with a parent's view of the risks, it must take into account that forcing that parent to accept or facilitate contact may leave him/her so anxious, frightened, depressed, or distracted that he or she is less able to give the child the practical and emotional support needed. '[T] he mother's hostility to contact can of itself be of importance, occasionally of determinative importance, provided, as always, that what is measured is its effect upon the child'.[140] Pragmatic solutions are often sought. For example, where a mother resisted overnight contact because she worried that the father's large dogs would see their little girl as an intruder and attack her, contact went ahead after the father had given an undertaking to the court that his dogs would be locked away in a newly built kennel.[141]

7.3.3 Contact and risks

In relation to both domestic violence and welfare-related concerns, there is one further important factor that may determine the outcome in a contact case. That is the applicant's attitude, and in particular their ability to recognise their problems, take responsibility for the harm they may have caused their children in the past, and show a genuine desire to change. For example, in *Re P*, the father, who was serving a prison sentence for murder and had a long-standing involvement in criminal underworld activity, would have to change before direct contact could happen, and '[p]art of any change that may take place in the father would have to include a process whereby he accepts that by his own actions he has damaged his children'.[142] Where a case ends without an order for contact, it is often because that parent refuses to acknowledge their problems, or disengages from the legal process, no longer answering letters or coming to hearings.[143]

There is, as many studies has found, an overwhelming consensus in favour of contact among legal professionals, a consensus that may have been strengthened by the new presumption in favour of parental involvement in s. 1(2A) of the Children Act 1989. Orders for no contact between a child and a parent are extremely rare, and the risks posed to the child's welfare have to be very serious indeed before such a decision is made, and this point is often made in reported cases. In *Q v Q*, the father had two convictions for sexual offences with children, and a recent risk assessment concluded that he posed a risk to his son. Unsupervised contact was out of the question and it was unlikely that contact would

---

[139] Harding, M. and Newnham, A. 'How do County Courts share the care of children between parents? Full report' (University of Warwick, 2015). Available at: http://www.nuffieldfoundation.org/share-care, accessed 1 July 2017.

[140] *Re P (Contact Discretion)* [1998] 2 FLR 696.

[141] Harding, M. and Newnham, A. 'How do County Courts share the care of children between parents? Full report' (University of Warwick, 2015). Available at: http://www.nuffieldfoundation.org/share-care, accessed 1 July 2017).

[142] *Re P (Contact Discretion)* [1998] 2 FLR 696, at 701.

[143] Newnham, A. and Harding, M. 'Sharing as Caring? Contact and Residence Disputes Between Parents' (2016) 28 *Child and Family Law Quarterly* 175, 192–3.

offer any positive benefit to the boy. Nevertheless, the court expressly endorsed the current pro-contact stance: 'Almost always there should be some contact between child and parent. It would only be in a rare and exceptional case that the court would agree that there should be none.'[144]

Where direct contact cannot happen, either because a parent presents a danger, or because children are so vehemently opposed to it that forcing them to have contact would be harmful, courts usually make an order for indirect contact via letters and cards to 'keep the door open'. It is made clear to problematic parents that they are welcome to reapply at a later date if their circumstances change.[145]

As mentioned in relation to domestic violence there is a real danger that when courts reframe their question as 'how much contact is safe?' they are actually departing from the test in the Children Act 1989, which is; 'is any, and if so, what kind of contact, in this child's best interests?' Contact can be safe enough without being rewarding, for example where the child feels the time spent together is boring or that the parent is not genuinely interested in them but has asked for contact with some ulterior motive, such as for immigration purposes or to win a conflict with the other parent.

7.4 **Enforcement of contact**

A number of studies have shown that courts are keen to promote and facilitate contact. Hunt and Macleod, for example, found that few cases would end with no contact, and that when they did, it was rarely the outcome because a formal order had been made to that effect, but more often because cases were dismissed, withdrawn, or effectively abandoned by applicant parents.[146] Yet, there is still a widespread perception that the family justice system is not doing enough and is letting parents down.[147] Enforcement problems are a large part of the answer.[148] In a small study of members and supporters of the campaign group 'Families Need Fathers', half of those who said contact was not happening had a contact order, which the other parent was not complying with.[149] This was a small and self-selecting study, so cannot provide reliable evidence, but it indicates that this is a real problem that causes dissatisfaction with the system.

A parent who persistently and deliberately blocks contact is in contempt of court and can be committed to prison. However, courts know that '[i]t will hardly endear the father to the child who is already reluctant to see him to be told that the father is responsible for the mother going to prison'.[150]

New measures to help the courts deal with parents who refuse to facilitate and repeatedly cancel contact out of malice, stubbornness, or a misguided belief that they are right were introduced into the Children Act 1989 in 2006 and are contained in ss. 11 to 11P. Activity

---

[144] *Q v Q (Contact: Undertakings) (No. 3)* [2016] EWFC 5; [2017] 1 FLR 438.

[145] Newnham, A. and Harding, M. 'Sharing as Caring? Contact and Residence Disputes Between Parents' (2016) 28 *Child and Family Law Quarterly* 175, 192–3.

[146] Hunt, J. and Macleod, A. *Outcomes of Applications to Court for Contact Orders after Parental Separation or Divorce* (Ministry of Justice, 2008) 55.

[147] Fathers 4 Justice, 'Latest News: March 29th, 2017: Tory MP calls for strict enforcement of child arrangement orders'. Available at: http://www.fathers-4-justice.org/2017/03/tory-mp-calls-strict-enforcement-child-arrangement-orders/, accessed 1 July 2017.

[148] See also *Re A (Intractable Contact Dispute: Human Rights Violations)* [2013] EWCA Civ 1104; [2014] 1 FLR 1185.

[149] Families Need Fathers, 'Press Release: FNF Survey of Christmas Parenting Time 2016' (21/12/2016). Available at: https://fnf.org.uk/news-events-2/press-releases/103-press-releases-2016-archive/410-press-release-so-many-children-can-t-see-their-dads-at-christmas, accessed 1 July 2017.

[150] *Re S (Contact: Promoting Relationship with Absent Parent)* [2004] EWCA Civ 18; [2004] 1 FLR 1279, at [28] (Butler-Sloss P).

Directions can be made as part of a child arrangements order, for example telling the parents to attend a Separated Parents' Information Programme designed to reduce hostility.[151] A warning notice on the bottom of the order warns parents of the consequences of not complying with the order, and Cafcass can also be asked to monitor compliance. If the court is satisfied beyond reasonable doubt that a person has failed to comply with a child arrangements order, and had no reasonable excuse, the court can make an enforcement order that imposes an unpaid work requirement, a kind of community service. If the person the child was supposed to be having contact with has suffered financial losses, for example travel expenses, then the person in breach can be ordered to pay compensation.

Any order made against the parent with whom the child is living can also have an adverse effect on the child. Any fine a parent is ordered to pay, for example, reduces the income available to spend on food, clothes, and other household expenses.

Where a parent consistently refuses to allow or promote contact, and lets his or her own negative views of the other parent influence the child, a court may decide that the best way to deal with the situation is to make a 'live with' order for the other parent. This is not used as a way of punishing the recalcitrant parent, but because the child's long-term welfare demands they should not be denied a good relationship with the previously non-resident parent.[152] Sometimes, the order to move the child is made, but then suspended, in the hope that this will convince the recalcitrant parent to facilitate contact.[153]

A study of the enforcement of contact led by Trinder found that most cases did not fit the stereotype of implacably hostile mothers deliberately flouting contact orders, but were more complex, sometimes involving real safety concerns or children who point-blank refused to see a parent. The study concluded:

> Adequate punitive sanctions are in place, are mostly used when needed and can secure compliance. Policy attention should now focus on developing more effective measures to support safe contact across the full range of enforcement cases, particularly high conflict cases where both parents need more help to work together to implement an order.[154]

 ### Debate 4: Should the Courts do More to Promote Contact with Fathers?

No-one would dispute that most fathers make a positive contribution to their children's lives, and there is research evidence to support that statement.[155] There are also studies from other countries that show a link, for children living with single mothers, between high father involvement and better outcomes, both in terms of how well these young people do in life,

---

[151] Cafcass, 'Separated Parents Information Programme (SPIP)'. Available at: https://www.cafcass.gov.uk/grown-ups/separated-parents-information-programme-(spip).aspx, accessed 14 August 2017; Smith, L. and Trinder, L. 'Mind the Gap: Parent Education Programmes and the Family Justice System' (2012) 24 *Child and Family Law Quarterly* 428.

[152] *Re W (Residence: Leave to Appeal)* [2010] EWCA Civ 1280, *Re A* [2007] EWCA Civ 899.

[153] *Re M (Contact)* [2012] EWHC 1948 (Fam); [2013] 1 FLR 1403; *Re J & K (Children)* [2014] EWHC 330 (Fam); [2015] 1 FLR 86.

[154] Trinder, L. *et al* 'Enforcing contact: problem-solving or punishment?' (University of Exeter, 2013). Available at: http://www.nuffieldfoundation.org/enforcing-contact-orders-cases-courts-and-consequences, accessed 1 July 2017.

[155] Oxford Centre for Family Law and Policy, 'Caring for children after parental separation: would legislation for shared parenting time help children? Briefing Paper No. 7' (2011) 1. Available at: http://www.nuffield-foundation.org/shared-parenting-0, accessed 19 July 2017.

and how they feel about themselves.[156] Children growing up in single parent households are more likely to experience poverty, with a cumulative negative effect on education, health, and life chances more generally. These types of arguments are used to argue against divorce,[157] and are used by judges to stress the need to keep fathers involved.[158] They are employed to great effect by campaign groups such as 'Fathers 4 Justice', whose founder Matt O'Connor is a marketing consultant, to warn that court-endorsed fatherlessness has 'been mirrored by an explosion in anti-social behaviour, gang crime, and young offending'.[159] The group 'Families need Fathers' use more measured language, but also interpret research selectively, in order to claim that having both parents involved benefits children in a variety of ways.[160]

However, Gilmore has shown that the available research does not support the jump from the observation 'that most children benefit from ongoing contact' to a legal assumption or presumption that 'contact will be beneficial' as a starting point for each child and each case.[161] First, there are many reasons why a parent loses touch with a child, and in some of those cases it may be better for the child for there to be no contact, for example if a parent is struggling with addiction, or has moved on to a new family and has no time or emotional energy left to devote to their first child. Secondly, a child's development is influenced by so many internal and external factors (personality, poverty, the quality of parenting to name a few), that there is no reliable research evidence to back up the assertion that all families (or all children) need fathers.

Despite this, studies have also concluded that our family courts are not biased against fathers, but rather have operated with a strong focus on encouraging and facilitating contact between fathers and the children since the implementation of the Children Act 1989. Courts have even acknowledged that sometimes this promotion of contact has gone too far and has led to risks not being properly identified.[162]

It is true that there are some cases, like *Re A,* where blameless fathers are let down by the family justice system, which through delay, inaction, and caution has allowed an implacably hostile mother to frustrate contact.[163] This is a debate that has been on-going for a long time, but is still current. Suella Fernandez, a Conservative MP, introduced a Private Members' Bill into Parliament in 2017 in an attempt to strengthen fathers' legal position.[164] Have the courts and legislators, as 'Fathers 4 Justice' claim, deliberately demoted fathers to second-class parents and cashpoints?[165] Or are courts weak and unwilling to use their powers?

Unfortunately, neither of these simplistic questions catch the complexity of contact disputes.

---

[156] See, e.g., Amato, P. 'The Consequences of Divorce for Adults and Children' (2000) 62 *Journal of Marriage and the Family* 1269; Breivik, K. and Olweus, D. 'Adolescents' Adjustment in Four Post-Divorce Family Structures' (2006) 44 *Journal of Divorce and Remarriage* 99.

[157] Sir Edward Leigh's response to Richard Bacon's introduction of the No Fault Divorce Bill, House of Commons Hansard HC Deb vol 600, col 192 (13 October 2015). Available at: https://hansard.parliament.uk/Commons/2015-10-13/debates/15101362000001/NoFaultDivorce, accessed 1 July 2017.

[158] *Re A* [2008] EWCA Civ 867, at [35] (Adam J as quoted by Sir Mark Potter).

[159] Fathers 4 Justice, 'Frequently Asked Questions'. Available at: http://www.fathers-4-justice.org/about-f4j/campaign-faqs/, accessed 1 July 2017.

[160] Families Need Fathers, 'Shared Parenting Research'. Available at: https://fnf.org.uk/publications/shared-parenting-research#faqnoanchor, accessed 1 July 2017.

[161] Gilmore, S. 'The Assumption That Contact is Beneficial: Challenging the 'Secure Foundation' [2008] *Family Law* 1226, 1227.

[162] See, e.g., *Re LVMH (Contact: Domestic Violence)* [2000] 2 FLR 334, at 367–9 (Thorpe LJ).

[163] *Re A (Intractable Contact Dispute: Human Rights Violations)* [2013] EWCA Civ 1104; [2014] 1 FLR 1185.

[164] Suella Fernandez introducing The Family Justice Bill, Hansard HC vol 624, cols 147–8 (28 March 2017).

[165] Fathers 4 Justice, 'Campaign on Child Support'. Available at: http://www.fathers-4-justice.org/our-campaign/our-campaigns/, accessed 1 July 2017.

It is important to recognise the difference between a court being in favour of a particular outcome, and a court being able to ensure that it happens, and in the case of contact, happens regularly and without complications through changing circumstances and as the child grows up. Baroness Hale has observed that 'Making contact happen and, even more importantly, making contact work is one of the most difficult and contentious challenges in the whole of family law'.[166]

Contact is difficult, not because judges do not believe in the benefits of contact, but for other reasons. First, only 10% of cases come to court, but they are the most complex ones, where there are often risks associated with violence, addiction, mental illness, and unreliability that outweigh the general benefits of contact. Secondly, contact is difficult because if two parents are inflexible and angry with each other then every contact handover, every holiday, and every birthday is an opportunity for conflicts and a risk that contact will be derailed. In an enforcement case where a boy refused to see his mother and the father refused to make him go, Sedley LJ made this final observation:

> This last point brings me to something which I venture to say less as a judge than as a parent. The critical attitude which [the son] has acquired or developed towards his mother is not one of simple hostility. He wants her to be the mother he remembers when he was little. There is a real pathos about this in a boy, still only ten or eleven years old, who has had and is still having to live through an acrimonious family rift and realignment. If instead of seeking to restore relations with his mother by letting her see him for a few hours at a time the courts were to abandon the blunt instrument of coercion and were to let time take its course, it seems to me much more likely that [he] will in his own time find his own way back to the affectionate relationship with his mother which both of them wish for. It may not happen, of course; but if we continue down the present road [of litigation] it will certainly not happen. The law does its best in the absence of other means, and modern legislation has done what it can to make the law's own means practical and fair; but the law is not omnicompetent, perhaps most of all when, equipped only with its received or inherent powers, it is called on to intervene in the subtle and unpredictable business of child care and human relations.[167]

The quote is an excellent example of judicial recognition of the limits of the law in the area. The law is a very heavy-handed tool, and it does not have the power to mend broken relationships between people, either by prohibiting something or dictating that something must be done. Often the best outcomes in cases are achieved by judges who realise the limitations of the law and work within them to slowly encourage change, increase trust, and reduce bitterness.

8. Prohibited steps orders and specific issue orders

These are two very useful orders that allow a court to resolve one particular dispute or stalemate between the parents without having to make long-term changes to contact or residence or in any way affect the parents' on-going rights and responsibilities. Therefore, they are very consistent with the non-intervention principle (see 4.5) even though they do allow courts to decide some of the finer details of the child's upbringing.

---

[166] *Re G (Children)* [2006] UKHL 43, [2006] 2 FLR 629, at [41].

[167] *Re L-W (Children) (Enforcement and Committal: Contact)* [2010] EWCA Civ 1253; [2011] 1 FLR 1095, at [124].

A court decides whether or not to make prohibited steps and specific issue orders by focusing on the paramountcy of the child's welfare as required by s. 1(1) and weighing the relevant factors in the s. 1(3) checklist against each other.

The first thing to note is that a prohibited steps order or specific issue order can only be used to regulate aspects of parental responsibility. So an order can be made to prevent a parent with whom the child lives from moving away with the child to another part of the country, but an order cannot be made to prevent a parent from moving without the child.

In a further restriction, which was part of the aim of having a clear boundary between public and private child law, s. 9(5) of the Children Act 1980 stipulates that prohibited steps orders and specific issue orders cannot be used to achieve something which could also be achieved with a child arrangements order. This is to prevent local authorities (who cannot apply for child arrangement orders, see 5.3.1.) from using prohibited steps orders or specific issue orders to avoid having to fulfil the more demanding requirements for public law orders (see Chapter 11). In *Re C*, for example, where the local authority wanted to prevent the mother from naming her newborn twins Preacher and Cyanide, they were prohibited from seeking a specific issue order and instead applied under the High Court's inherent jurisdiction under s.100 of the Children Act 1989.[168] You may be relieved to know that the Court approved of the local authority's plan to let the twins' older half-siblings choose names, since Cyanide, in particular, went 'beyond the unusual, bizarre, extreme or plain foolish', and was likely to cause the girl significant harm in the future.

Only in exceptional circumstances will an order be made for a child who is aged 16 to 18; for example due to the child's disabilities.

8.1 Prohibited steps orders

The Children Act 1989, s. 8(1) states that: … 'a prohibited steps order' means an order that no step which could be taken by a parent in meeting his parental responsibility for a child, and which is of a kind specified in the order, shall be taken by any person without the consent of the court'.

Orders can be used to tell a parent not to let the child come into contact with a third party who presents a risk (e.g. a new partner who has convictions for sexual or violent offences) or forbid certain medical treatment including circumcision for religious reasons. The words 'any person' in s. 8(1) mean that prohibited steps orders can be used to regulate adults who are not parents, and do not have parental responsibility, if they interact with the child in a way that falls within the description of parental responsibility.[169]

In urgent situations, the worried parent can obtain an order *ex parte*, that is, without notice given to the other parent,[170] and this can be very useful if the worry is that a parent will abduct the child. Interim orders are often made to protect the status quo until a court has had the time to hear both parents' arguments and decide whether a move will be in a child's best interests.[171]

A prohibited steps order can also be used together with a 'live with' child arrangements order and/or a non-molestation order under s. 42 of the Family Law Act 1996 in cases with a background of domestic violence where threatened or actual abductions,

---

[168] *Re C (Children: Power to Choose Forenames)* [2016] EWCA Civ 374; [2017] 1 FLR 487.

[169] *Re M (A Child) (Prohibited Steps Order: Appeal)* [2002] All ER (D) 401 (Nov); *Re H (Prohibited Steps Order)* [1995] 1 FLR 638.

[170] Family Proceedings Rules, Practice Direction 18A, para 5.1. Available at: https://www.justice.gov.uk/courts/procedure-rules/family/practice_directions/pd_part_18a, accessed 18 July 2017.

[171] *Re C (Internal Relocation)* [2015] EWCA Civ 1305; [2017] 1 FLR 103.

and late returns of children after scheduled contact are used by fathers to terrorise, coerce, and control mothers (see Chapter 7). Such a framework of protective orders can allow mothers to facilitate contact with a father whom their children genuinely love, without having to live in a state of fear so serious and constant that the children are likely to pick up on it.[172]

In *Re L and B*,[173] the parents' relationship broke down when the mother took their two sons, now aged 4 and 6, and moved across the country. The mother was granted a prohibited steps order to stop the father from taking the children out of the UK. The Court had made findings that the father had been physically and emotionally abusive and that he had threatened to take the children to Algeria (his country of origin) on a permanent basis. Since that country is not a signatory to the Hague Convention on the Civil Aspects of International Child Abduction 1980 (see Chapter 14), it would be very difficult to secure the children's return to England. The magnitude of the consequences for these young children if abduction or retention were to occur would be catastrophic. Once contact had been agreed and was progressing well, the father applied to have this order discharged. Applying the paramountcy principle and the welfare checklist, the court concluded that the potential risks associated with a trip abroad far outweighed the benefits associated with a visit to Algeria to meet wider kin. The prohibited steps order should remain in place.

8.2 **Specific issue orders**

The Children Act 1989, s. 8(1) states that: ... 'a specific issue order' means an order giving directions for the purpose of determining a specific question which has arisen, or which may arise, in connection with any aspect of parental responsibility for a child'.

Again, a court will decide what is in the child's long-term best interests, using the factors in the s. 1(3) checklist wherever relevant and often relying on expert evidence about medical matters, education, religion, and other important matters.

In *Re L and B*,[174] the father had also applied for a specific issue order to have the two boys circumcised in accordance with the teaching of his Muslim faith. On that issue, Roberts J stated:

> [45] In relation to the specific issue of circumcision and its consequences for these children, my starting point is their welfare which is paramount. All the factors set out in s 1(3) of the 1989 Act must be considered again in the context of this discrete application.

> [143] Taking all these matters into account, my conclusion is that it would be better for the children that the court make no order at this stage in relation to circumcision than to make the order which the father seeks. I am not dismissing his application on the basis that they must develop into adulthood as uncircumcised Muslim males. I am simply deferring that decision to the point where each of the boys themselves will make their individual choices once they have the maturity and insight to appreciate the consequences and longer-term effects of the decisions which they reach.

---

[172] Harding, M. and Newnham, A. 'How do County Courts share the care of children between parents? Full report' (University of Warwick, 2015) 28–9. Available at: http://www.nuffieldfoundation.org/share-care, accessed 1 July 2017.

[173] *Re L and B (Children: Specific Issues: Temporary Leave to Remove from the Jurisdiction: Circumcision)* [2016] EWHC 849 (Fam); [2017] 1 FLR 1316.

[174] *Re L and B (Children: Specific Issues: Temporary Leave to Remove from the Jurisdiction: Circumcision)* [2016] EWHC 849 (Fam); [2017] 1 FLR 1316.

Similar conclusions regarding circumcision have been reached in other cases,[175] but there has also been a reported case where circumcision was allowed, because it would be in that child's best interests given his circumstances.

The applicant mother in *Re S*,[176] wanted a specific issue order to change her 3-year-old son's name and allow his circumcision. The little boy was the product of a comparatively short marriage between a young Muslim woman, who had previously led a sheltered life, and a young Sikh man. When they eloped to Gretna Green to get married, the historic mistrust and antagonism between these two communities meant the mother's family suffered considerable shame and disgrace. The marriage broke down in acrimonious circumstances, where the father behaved badly and probably lost focus on what was best for their son, and the mother was reconciled to her parents. In the court order, contact with the father would be limited to twice-yearly visits at a contact centre. It was held that the change of names from Sikh names was, in these unusual circumstances, in the child's best interests. In order for the little boy and his mother to be able to integrate back into their local East London Muslim community, the boy must be known on a day-to-day basis by a Muslim name. The Court also accepted that he should eventually be circumcised. This, too, was in the boy's best interests, as there were otherwise risks he could be seen as 'odd' or 'different' by his peers and this could adversely affect his self-esteem.

Specific issue orders are also commonly used to settle disputes about education, medical treatment, and travel.

In *Re N*,[177] the Court was asked to decide, among other things, which school the 4-year-old boy should attend, whether the father should be allowed to take the boy abroad on holiday, the child's involvement in religious practices, and consent to medical treatment, specifically blood transfusions. The parents had managed to agree on the choice of school between the application and the hearing. The Court decided that there were no welfare reasons against the father taking the child on holiday abroad, and made the order. The most difficult question, which meant the case had to be transferred to an experienced judge in the High Court, was how much the parents should be allowed to involve their son in their two different religions. The father went to his local Church of England church most Sundays. The mother was a Jehovah's Witness, and the father said that since the separation her beliefs and practices had become 'overwhelming and extreme'. Bellamy J made it very clear that the court's task was not to evaluate which religion was 'better', but to respect both, and to set a reasonable level of exposure to both religions that would enable the child to choose his faith (or no faith) for himself when he grew up. In the meantime, where what the mother believed, said, and did was likely to have a negative impact on her son (e.g. by excluding him from many social activities with his peers or involving him in door-to-door ministry or religious meetings), the court could use the paramountcy principle in s. 1(1) and the welfare checklist in s. 1(3) of the Children Act 1989 to restrict the mother's freedom to manifest her religion in way that was permitted under Article 9 ECHR. In relation to the question of medical treatment, the courts have consistently favoured authorising blood transfusions for children of Jehovah's Witnesses where the parents refuse to give consent because of their religious beliefs. The order, therefore, stipulated that the father should be notified of any medical emergency, and that his consent would be enough to let doctors go ahead with treatment.

---

[175] *Re S (Specific Issue Order: Religion: Circumcision)* [2004] EWHC 1282 (Fam); *Re J (Specific Issue Orders: Child's Religious Upbringing and Circumcision)* [2000] 1 FLR 571.

[176] *Re S (Change of Names: Cultural Factors)* [2001] 2 FLR 1005.

[177] *Re N (A Child) (Religion: Jehovah's Witness)* [2011] EWHC 3737 (Fam); [2012] 2 FLR 917.

9. Further questions: surnames and international relocation

Where a child arrangements order has been made that states with whom a child should live, that is, an order as to residence, the Children Act 1989 includes two additional provisions that limit the parents' ability to unilaterally exercise parental responsibility. Under s. 13(1), the child's surname cannot be changed, and the child cannot be taken out of the United Kingdom for more than a month without either the written consent of every person who has parental responsibility for the child or the leave of the court.

9.1 Change of a child's surname

Where names are concerned, the courts have insisted on the agreement of all holders of parental responsibility, whether or not a residence (or now a 'live with') order is in force. In *Dawson v Wearmouth*[178] the Court reasoned that to hold the opposite could lead to absurd situations where two parents in a dispute would regularly and unilaterally change their child's surname, causing a lot of confusion. It is less clear whether the consent of a sufficiently mature or *Gillick* competent (see Chapter 10)[179] child is necessary before a name can be changed. That question was left unanswered in *Re P C*.[180]

In the reported cases, courts have been very reluctant to change a child's name in the face of a father's objections. Surnames are said to be a permanent and important reminder of the link between fathers and their children (even in cases where everyone accepts that there will be no direct contact). Therefore, keeping their father's surname is regarded as being in a child's long-term best interests (even where older children want to change their surnames). This old-fashioned and patriarchal view of surnames has been criticised by academics,[181] and by some judges, with Hale LJ (as she then was) remarking that women, who have traditionally changed surnames upon marriage, are more likely to 'depend on more substantial things' to feel close to their children.[182]

However, a recent case shows a more pragmatic and child-focused approach. In *Re W*,[183] the mother appealed against an order for the baby boy to carry her ex-partner's first name as his middle name. She claimed the father had pressured her into promising this just hours after the birth, and described it as part of a wider pattern of controlling behaviour. At the time of the appeal the father had refused to take up opportunities for supervised contact because he disagreed with the Court's findings. The mother's appeal argued that since the father had effectively walked out on his child, to leave the little boy with his father's middle name would be nothing but a painful reminder of what could have been. The Court of Appeal allowed the appeal, stating that 'matters have moved on and this court must have regard to the realities. The welfare equation is not the same'.

9.2 Relocation

Relocation to a new country can be a great experience and even a bit of an adventure for a child, but also creates risks. As we have seen, the welfare checklist mentions change as something that can have negative consequences in s. 1(3)(c). Under s. 13(1) of the Children

---

[178] *Dawson v Wearmouth* [1999] 2 AC 308; [1999] 2 All ER 353.
[179] *Gillick v West Norfolk and Wisbech Area Health Authority* [1986] AC 112; [1986] 1 FLR 224.
[180] *Re P C (Change of Surname)* [1997] 2 FLR 730; [1997] 3 FCR 310.
[181] Herring, J. 'The Shaming of Naming' in R. Probert, S. Gilmore, and J. Herring (eds) *Responsible Parents and Parental Responsibility*, (Hart Publishing, 2009) 105, 111.
[182] *Re R* [2001] EWCA Civ 1344; [2001] 2 FLR 1358, at [13] (Hale LJ).
[183] *Re W (Children) (Change of Name)* [2013] EWCA Civ 1488; [2014] 3 FCR 175.

Act 1989, where a 'live with' order is in force, a parent cannot travel to another jurisdiction with the children for more than a month without the agreement of everyone who has parental responsibility, or otherwise without an application to the court. In cases where there is no 'live with' child arrangements order, the other parent can still try to prevent a move by applying for a prohibited steps order under s. 8 of the Children Act 1989. In both instances, the court will decide whether the move would be in the child's best interests. A parent is always free to move away on their own; it is only moving with the child that is an exercise of parental responsibility that can be regulated by the court, either using a s. 8 order or under s. 13(1). In the case law, there has been no clear difference in the way the courts have decided cases where a 'live with' order is, or is not, in place.[184]

If an order is sought to allow a move, the court has to decide whether or not relocation would be in the child's best interests. In the controversial case of *Payne v Payne* the Court of Appeal set out a checklist of factors. Thorpe LJ summarised how a court should approach the application in four points. Firstly, is the mother's application motivated by a genuine desire to move and backed up by realistic practical proposals? Secondly, is the father's opposition genuine, or he have some ulterior motive? Would the parent-child relationship be so badly damaged by a move that this loss to the child would not be outweighed by closer ties with extended family in the mother's homeland? Thirdly, if the proposal is refused, what would be the negative impact on the mother, her new husband (if there is one) and eventually on the child?

> Finally, Thorpe LJ added that '[t]he outcome of the second and third appraisals must then be brought into an overriding review of the child's welfare as the paramount consideration'.[185]

Despite the mention of a wider welfare-based review in the last of the four points, these points were interpreted in later cases as laying down a rule that primary caregivers (who are predominantly mothers) should be allowed to relocate as long as the application was genuine (in the sense that the ulterior motive was not to marginalise the father) and realistic (so that sensible plans had been made for accommodation, education, healthcare etc). It was suggested that a refusal could impact so badly on the mother and her new husband (where there was one) that the subsequent unhappiness would seriously adversely affect the child. This approach was criticised by both academics and practitioners.[186] Advocates tried to distinguish *Payne* by arguing that its guidance should not be applied where the children alternated residence and therefore lived with both parents. This was accepted in *K v K*; in cases of genuine (i.e. not symbolic) shared residence the full s. 1(3) welfare checklist should be used rather than the *Payne* guidance.[187]

Finally, *Re F (A Child) (International Relocation Cases)* [2015] EWCA Civ 882 completed the courts' move away from *Payne*. In this case, the German mother had applied to relocate to Germany with the 12-year-old daughter, who had been living with her since the parents' relationship broke down a few years earlier. The father alleged that the mother was over-protective and uncooperative, while Cafcass had been less than impressed with the mother's willingness to help make contact happen. At first instance, the judge focused almost exclusively on the initial questions from *Payne* and allowed the move. There would be six weeks' contact each year, in school holidays. The father's appeal was allowed, with the Court of Appeal making it clear that *Payne* had

---

[184] Bainham, A. 'Camberley to Carlisle: where are we now on internal relocation?' [2016] *Family Law* 458, 459.   [185] *Payne v Payne* [2001] EWCA CIV 166; [2001] 1 FLR 1052, at [40].

[186] Devereux, D. and George, R. 'When will the Supreme Court put us out of our Payne?' [2014] *Family Law* 1586.   [187] *K v K (Relocation: Shared Care Arrangement)* [2011] EWCA Civ 793; [2012] 2 FLR 880.

been widely misunderstood, including by the first instance judge in this case. *Payne* had not laid down any rule other than the paramountcy principle contained in s. 1(1) of the Children Act 1989.

This is a better reading of the case. The initial questions about whether the plans are genuine and realistic are designed to weed out hopeless applications rather than decide the matter. To pick an extreme example, what if a mother said she wanted to go to Hollywood to become a famous actress and was hoping to house share with some of the movie stars who live locally? Such a vague and unrealistic application could clearly be refused without further ado. Similarly, if a father who only had intermittent contact when it suited him wanted to block a move predominantly to spite the mother, that is a very strong indicator that the court should say yes. The Court of Appeal in *Payne* did also make it clear that the child's welfare is paramount, and that the impact on the child of a loss of contact with the other parent is also important, so that it is significant whether the proposals include opportunities for continued contact with the parent who will be left behind.

According to *Re F*, the s. 1(3) checklist should be carefully applied to all cases, regardless of whether there is one primary carer or alternating residence. This makes good sense. Ryder J endorsed the minority view of Black LJ in *K v K* and agreed with Munby LJ in *Re F*[188] that 'The last thing that this very difficult area of family law requires is … an ever-more detailed classification of supposedly different types of relocation case' (at [26]). He also warned that 'Selective or partial legal citation from *Payne v Payne* … without any wider legal analysis is likely to be regarded as an error of law' (at [27]). The father's appeal against the order allowing the mother to move to Germany was allowed. The case was sent back to the first instance court for a rehearing since the judge had failed to carry out a full welfare analysis and had instead allowed herself to be constrained by the four-point guidance from *Payne*.

To reach a decision about relocation, a court must undertake a 'holistic analysis'. The questions from *Payne* regarding the reasonableness of the plans, and both parents' motivations for making or refusing the application remain relevant, but judges must also carefully consider the child's wishes and feelings as well as the potential advantages and risks associated both with the move (particularly the impact on the relationship with the other parent) and with making the child, her parent, and other members of the household remain in this jurisdiction.

The same approach was confirmed for internal relocation cases in *Re C (Internal Relocation)*[189] where the mother wanted to move from London to Cumbria with her 10-year-old daughter. Section 13(1)(c) applies only to international relocation. A parent who wants to block a move within the UK has to apply for a prohibited steps order, while a parent who wants to be able to move without fear that the court will later force a return can, as the mother did in *Re C*, apply for a specific issue order. It had previously been thought that a primary carer should be allowed to move within the UK with their children other than in truly exceptional cases.[190] In *Re C* it was held that this exceptionality principle was contrary to s. 1(1) of the Children Act 1989, which stipulates that the child's best interest is the first and only consideration. The Court of Appeal also found that the judge at first instance had gone beyond any narrow understanding of *Payne* to look at wider welfare factors, such as the child's clear wishes to move, the mother's extended family near Cumbria, and their desire for a rural lifestyle. Since the judge had applied the law correctly, the appeal was dismissed.

Bainham has observed that although both *Re F* on international relocation and *Re C* on relocation within the jurisdiction 'contain a great deal of technical legal argument they

---

[188] *Re F (Relocation)* [2012] EWCA Civ 1364; [2013] 1 FLR 645.   [189] [2015] EWCA Civ 1305.
[190] *Re E (Residence: Imposition of Conditions)* [1997] 2 FLR 638, at [23] (Butler-Sloss P).

come down to endorsing a broad welfare-based evaluation of the pros and cons of a move, judged from the child's position and not that of the parent'.[191]

10. Family proceedings under the High Court's inherent jurisdiction

Historically, the family courts' inherent jurisdiction developed from the monarch's role as *parens patriae* or father/mother of the nation. The Crown has a duty to look after all its subjects, and the inherent jurisdiction gives the court power to look after those who cannot look after themselves, particularly children. This chapter gives only a brief introduction to the topic. This inherent jurisdiction remains effective, and is sometimes invaluable in situations where the Children Act 1989 and other statutory regimes cannot be used. Under the inherent jurisdiction, the court makes decisions according to what will be in the child's best interests. In *A v A (Children: Habitual Residence)*[192] the inherent jurisdiction was invoked to order that a baby boy, who had been born while the mother was being held in Pakistan against her will, should be sent to join his mother, who had since escaped to the UK.

10.1 Wardship

A child can also be made a ward of court, although this is very rare. Wardship is more long term; it lets the court step in and make all the decisions that would otherwise be made by those with parental responsibility. In *T v S (Wardship)*[193] the parents were constantly at loggerheads about every decision, but both failed to see how harmful their combative stances were to the child. Wardship allowed the court to make decisions, as and when necessary, and thus remove most of the parents' opportunities for conflict. In *A Local Authority v M*,[194] wardship was used to secure the speedy return to the UK of four children, three of whom had health issues. Their mother had had attempted to travel to Syria to join ISIS, but was stopped in Turkey.

The use of wardship and the inherent jurisdiction has decreased as the volume of both public child law and private child law legislation has increased.; another limiting factor is the need to maintain reciprocal understanding and cooperation with other jurisdictions, which would be undermined if our judges were too ready to use the inherent jurisdiction to ignore or go against decisions taken in other countries' courts (see Chapter 14). However, the inherent jurisdiction remains important for a small number of cases where children (or adults) could otherwise be left without a remedy or in perilous circumstances.

SUMMARY

1. Is the court the best place for private child law disputes?
   - Only around 10% of separating parents end up in court. In a minority of cases this is because of hostile parents, but more often it is because their cases are complex, with allegations of domestic violence, neglect, and child abuse, or because relatives are having to step in where parents are failing to provide adequate care.

---

[191] Bainham, B. 'Camberley to Carlisle: where are we now on internal relocation?' [2016] *Family Law* 458.
[192] [2013] UKSC 60; [2014] AC 1.   [193] [2011] EWHC 1608 (Fam); [2012] 1 FLR 230.
[194] [2016] EWHC 1599 (Fam); [2017] 1 1389.

- Under s. 1(1) of the Children Act 1989, the court's only consideration should be what will be best for the child. The courts use the other provisions in s.1 to help them work out what that is. In reality, courts are usually trying to find the least bad option for a child. It should not be surprising that all these families' problems cannot be resolved with the limited resources of private child law.
- The restrictions on who can apply for orders are helpful in protecting children and their families from the stress of unnecessary litigation, but sometimes it can be difficult for children's views and wishes to be heard.
- Allegations about risks which need to be investigated are often made. It is in those children's best interests that the risks are investigated by the family courts.
- Specific issue orders are used to decide one important question where the holders of parental responsibility cannot agree: for example whether a child should have a particular operation, or where the child should go to school.
- Courts decide the cases according to what they think will be best for the child in the long term. Courts often rely on some expert evidence from Cafcass, doctors, or specialist in education or a particular religion.

2. What is shared parenting and when is it good for children?
   - There is no clear definition of shared parenting, and courts have used both the old shared residence order and the new 'live with' child arrangements order for symbolic purposes in a bid to reduce parental conflict. There is no empirical evidence that this actually works. While parents and children obviously need to spend time together, the quality of time is more important than quantity. Instead, if high conflict parents are coerced into shared residence, such arrangements are likely to either break down or to trap children in the middle of the conflict. Successful shared parenting requires mutual respect, trust, and good communication. The courts have no powers that can force parents to get on well.

3. Should the courts do more to promote contact with fathers?
   - There is now a parental involvement presumption in s. 1(2A) but courts have been very pro-contact since the Children Act 1989 first came in.
   - Where there are allegations of domestic violence these should now be fully investigated, but in practice there is still not enough attention being given to domestic violence and its harmful effects on children.
   - Courts rely on Cafcass and sometimes the local authority to investigate safeguarding or child welfare risks. Contact will usually go ahead as long as it is safe.
   - It is important to recognise the difference between a court being in favour of a particular outcome, and a court being able to ensure that it happens, and in the case of contact, happens regularly and without complications through changing circumstances and as the child grows up.
   - Enforcement of contact is very difficult, because contact is an on-going process, which can be disrupted by inflexible parents or changing circumstances.

Further Reading

BARNETT, A. 'Contact at all Costs? Domestic Violence and Children's Welfare' (2014) 26 *Child and Family Law Quarterly* 439

- This article is an excellent critique of how the family justice system has not yet got it right when balancing the risks of domestic violence against the benefits of contact.

HARDING, M. and NEWNHAM, A. (2015). 'How do County Courts share the care of children between parents?' (University of Warwick, 2015). Available at: http://www.nuffieldfoundation.org/share-care, accessed 27 September 2017.

- An accessible report of primary research with a lot of examples from real (anonymised) cases that give unique insight into how courts decide Section 8 cases. Chapter 5 of the full report is particularly interesting in terms of shared parenting, there is also a summary seport of the whole project.

KAGANAS, F. 'A Presumption That "Involvement" of Both Parents is Best: Deciphering Law's Messages' (2013) 25 *Child and Family Law Quarterly* 270, 283

- This article is a good introduction to a more theoretical and critical approach to family law. It also highlights the interaction between family law and policy/politics.

OXFLAP, 'Caring for children after parental separation: would legislation for shared parenting time help children?' Briefing Paper No. 7. Available at: http://www.nuffieldfoundation.org/sites/default/files/files/Would%20legislation%20for%20shared%20parenting%20time%20help%20children)OXLAP%20FPB%207.pdf, accessed 11 October 2017.

- An excellent overview of recent research on shared parenting with a lot of useful sources for further reading.

PIPER, C. 'Investing in a Child's Future: Too Risky?' (2010) 22 *Child and Family Law Quarterly* 1

- A thought provoking piece that invites reflection on how we should decide what is in a child's best interest, whilst pointing out some real problems with the courts' current approach.

PIPER, C. and KAGANAS, F. 'Re L (A Child) (Contact: Domestic Violence)' (Commentary and Judgment) in R. HUNTER, C. MCGLYNN, and E. RACKLEY, *Feminist Judgments: From Theory to Practice* (Hart Publishing, 2010)

- This piece invites you to think about how family law could be different, and how family violence could be more visible in cases about children.

SMART, C. and MAY, V. 'Why Can't They Agree? The Underlying Complexity of Contact and Residence Disputes' (2004) 26 *Journal of Social Welfare and Family Law* 347

- An accessible account of research that answers the title question and shows how parents' disputes are wider than the points argued in court.

SMART, C. 'Equal Shares: Rights for Fathers or Recognition for Children?' (2004) 24 *Critical Social Policy* 484

- This study by a sociologist looks at shared parenting through the voices of children who are actually living in two households and links those findings to family law.

10

The Medical Treatment of Children

Dianne Scullion

LEARNING OBJECTIVES

After reading this chapter you will be able to:

- Appreciate the challenges in the legal regulation of the medical treatment of children and understand when a doctor can legally treat a child;

- Comprehend the complex issue of consent, who can give consent to a child's medical treatment, and in what circumstances;

- Recognise the role of the courts within the context of disputes concerning medical treatment of children.

DEBATES

After reading this chapter you should be equipped to discuss your opinion on the following central debates:

1. What is the role of consent and *Gillick* competence in promoting the child's autonomy in decision-making?

2. Should a more honest approach to *Gillick* competence be taken?

3. Are there alternatives to the court's intervention in making medical decisions concerning children?

1. Introduction

Decisions concerning the medical treatment of children are not always (and usually seldom) decisions made by children themselves. Often parents, doctors, and/or the court make such decisions on behalf of the child. There has been a wealth of case law that has had to consider, not only disputes regarding a child's medical treatment between parents and the medical profession, but also considering the important question of when the child themselves can make these decisions. At the heart of the issue is consent. This is crucial in order for a doctor to be able to treat a patient without being guilty of a criminal offence or being exposed to civil liability. Adult decision-makers often focus on issues of child autonomy, maturity, and intelligence deciding whether children are capable of making decisions concerned with their own medical treatment. There is, on the one hand, the wish to respect a child's wishes and feelings and recognise their autonomy in making decisions, whilst on the other a wish to protect the child from possible harm. A refusal of treatment may mean the child will suffer harm, and in some cases potentially die without the treatment proposed. This is the very reason why, in some circumstances, it is found that the need to protect the child outweighs the wish to respect the child's autonomy. This tension, discussed in this chapter, reveals some of the difficult concepts the courts have had to consider.

The main focus within this context is consent. The chapter will discuss who can consent to or refuse medical treatment for a child, as well as considering in what circumstances the child themselves can make this decision. This involves discussion of *Gillick* competence, which refers to circumstances where a child is viewed as having the required maturity and understanding to make these decisions. It is also necessary to examine the role that parents play in the decision-making process.

It will then explore cases where parents and doctors disagree on the treatment proposed and consider how these disputes are resolved. In order to demonstrate the perceived importance of these issues and the social concern it raises around parents' rights in relation to their children, the chapter will draw on some of the highly publicised cases in the media as well as case law as examples of disputes between doctors and parents. The chapter will analyse the various factors involved and the role that the court plays in resolving disputes.

The chapter will conclude by considering an alternative route to settle disputes concerning the medical treatment of children and will examine the role that mediation can take in this context. It will be considered whether this has the potential to avoid extreme situations, such as that seen with Ashya King's parents removing him from the hospital and fleeing the country to avoid the treatment proposed by the doctors and receive alternative treatment abroad.[1]

2. Consent to the medical treatment of children

When discussing consent in a medical context it is not just a matter of agreeing and saying yes to a particular treatment, it is important that 'informed consent' is obtained by the doctor. This means that the individual must understand the nature of the treatment proposed, the risks and benefits involved, and the range of options for treatment that may be available. Doctors have a responsibility to ensure that these issues are discussed with the patient prior to any treatment proceeding.[2]

2.1 Who may give consent to medical treatment of a child?

In order for a doctor to provide any medical treatment to a child, it is necessary that s/he has consent to do so. Consent to treatment can be provided by:

- a child over the age of 16;
- a *Gillick* competent child under the age of 16;
- a person who has parental responsibility for the child;
- or alternatively the court may provide authority for the treatment to proceed (when either the child or a holder of parental responsibility does not consent).

---

[1] Eleftheriou-Smith, L. 'Ashya King: "Cruel NHS has not given us the treatment we need", says father of five-year-old with brain tumour who fled to Spain' *The Independent*, 31 August 2014. Available at: http://www.independent.co.uk/news/uk/home-news/ashya-king-parents-of-missing-five-year-old-arrested-9701940.html, accessed 10 May 2017.

[2] *Montgomery v Lanarkshire Health Board* [2015] UKSC 11.

The exception to the need to obtain consent or authority is where there is a medical emergency. A child who is taken to hospital and needs emergency medical treatment may not be accompanied by anyone holding parental responsibility over the child, and the child may not be able to consent for themselves. The doctors in this situation need to be able to proceed with treatment of the child despite not having explicit authority and consent. In order to recognise this need, the law provides a defence of necessity[3] to doctors who treat children in these circumstances. This prevents doctors having criminal charges brought against them, or a claim made in the civil court for compensation.

Securing informed consent ensures that any medical treatment to children is lawfully administered. As stated, this consent may be provided by the child themselves, if they are competent to consent, or alternatively by those with parental responsibility (usually parents, see Chapter 8). This will always be the case for very young children where the child cannot articulate consent, or understand the implications of medical treatment. Even for older children, there are limits placed on a child's competence to consent to treatment on their own behalf. This is often referred to a child being 'Gillick' competent.

3. Consent by the child to their own medical treatment

Where the child themselves want to make their own decision about proposed medical treatment, the law makes a distinction between children who have reached the age of 16 and those under this age. Under statutory provision, a child who has reached the age of 16 may consent to treatment providing they are competent to do so.

3.1. Consent to medical treatment by a child over 16

Where the child has reached the age of 16, the right to consent to '… surgical, medical or dental treatment … ' is contained within statute.

 Key Legislation 1 : Family Law Reform Act 1969, s. 8

8 Consent by persons over 16 to surgical, medical and dental treatment

(1) The consent of a minor who has attained the age of sixteen years to any surgical, medical or dental treatment which, in the absence of consent, would constitute a trespass to his person, shall be as effective as it would be if he were of full age; and where a minor has by virtue of this section given an effective consent to any treatment it shall not be necessary to obtain any consent for it from his parent or guardian.

(2) In this section, 'surgical, medical or dental treatment' includes any procedure undertaken for the purposes of diagnosis, and this section applies to any procedure (including, in particular, the administration of an anesthetic) which is ancillary to any treatment as it applies to that treatment.

This section therefore provides that a child who has reached the age of 16 has the legal right to consent to treatment, regardless of any parental opinion. Children of this age are presumed to have sufficient capacity to decide on their own medical treatment and this would only be overruled in circumstances where there was significant evidence to suggest the child lacks capacity. This means that even if a 16-year-old child's parent(s) withhold

---

[3] *Re F (Mental Patient Sterilisation)* [1990] 2 AC 1.

their consent to particular medical treatment, the child themselves is presumed to have the capacity and legal right to consent. This consent will override any refusal by their parent(s) and the doctor can rely on the child's consent alone in order to proceed with treatment.[4]

3.2 *Gillick* **competence and the consent of children under 16**

Children under the age of 16 do not fall within the scope of s. 8 of the Family Law Reform Act 1969. It would appear that they do not therefore have competence to consent to medical treatment, and their parents may decide on their behalf what treatment they receive. For young children, this may be entirely suitable, as only an adult may be able to understand the medical risks and comprehend the need for treatment underpinning informed consent. For older children and young adults under the age of 16 however, they may have a good understanding of the need for and risks of medical treatment, particularly if they have experience of living with a health condition. Children may also wish to seek medical treatment on their own behalf in some form, without consulting a parent, for example contraceptive medication. In these circumstances, the law has been more flexible in determining whether a child can be deemed 'competent' to take such decisions on their own behalf, instead of relying on, or even informing, a parent.

The term '*Gillick* Competence' derived from the case of *Gillick v W Norfolk and Wishbech AHA*[5] and it determines when a child is deemed competent to consent to their own medical treatment.

Key Case 1: *Gillick v W Norfolk and Wishbech AHA* **[1985] 3 All ER 402; [1986] 1 FLR 229; [1986] AC 112 HL**

The case involved Mrs Gillick who was the mother to five girls under the age of 16. When the Department of Health and Social Security produced guidance for family planning services, including particular provision for contraceptive advice and treatment for young people, Mrs Gillick sought assurances from her local area health authority that no contraceptive advice or treatment would be provided to any of her daughters without her knowledge and consent. This assurance was not provided and Mrs Gillick sought a declaration from the courts that the guidance was unlawful and affected parental rights and duties.

The provision contained within the guidance relating to the contraceptive advice and treatment for young people was aimed at providing contraceptive healthcare and clinics for all ages, including children under 16. This did not mean that doctors would treat any child under the age of 16 and provide advice or treatment without any attempt to involve the child's parents. The health authority aimed to maintain confidentiality between doctor and patient, even for those under the age of 16. It sought to avoid the situation where those under 16 would not seek medical advice and in not doing so, place themselves at risk of pregnancy or sexually transmitted diseases. If the Court made the declaration sought by Mrs Gillick, the doctor would potentially be obliged to inform the parent of any child under 16 of the fact that the child had sought contraceptive advice in order to obtain parental consent to the treatment. This would breach confidentiality between the child patient and the doctor, and potentially undermine a child's willingness to seek suitable contraceptive advice.

The Court held that the guidance was not unlawful and refused to issue the declaration Mrs Gillick sought.

---

[4] General Medical Council, '*0–18 all years: guidance for doctors*' (2007) 14, para 31. Available at: http://www.gmc-uk.org/0_18_years___English_1015.pdf_48903188.pdf, accessed 21 July 2017.

[5] [1985] 3 All ER 402; [1986] 1 FLR 229; [1986] AC 112 HL.

In relation to the doctor, the Court laid down clear circumstances where the doctor would be permitted to proceed to provide contraceptive advice and treatment, even where there is no parental consent or knowledge of the proposed treatment. The doctor must be satisfied:

(1) That the girl (although under 16 years of age) will understand his advice
(2) That he cannot persuade her to inform her parents or allow him to inform the parent that she is seeking contraceptive advice
(3) That she is very likely to begin or to continue having sexual intercourse with or without contraceptive treatment
(4) That unless she receives contraceptive advice or treatment her physical or mental health or both are likely to suffer
(5) That her best interests require him to give her contraceptive advice, treatment or both without parental consent.[6]

The Court made important points for doctors regarding the advice and treatment of children under the age of 16. The Court recognised the importance of parental rights over their children, however, it also stated that parental rights were dwindling and the extent and duration of them were not determined by a particular fixed age of the child.[7] Lord Denning MR commented (obiter) in *Hewer v Bryant*[8]

… that the legal right of a parent to the custody of a child ends at the 18th birthday: and even up till then, it is a dwindling right which the courts will hesitate to enforce against the wishes of the child, and the more so the older he is. It starts with a right of control and ends with little more than advice.

In *Gillick* itself, Lord Scarman found that:

… parental right or power of control of the person and property of his child exists primarily to enable the parent to discharge his duty of maintenance, protection, and education until he reaches such an age as to be able to look after himself and make his own decisions.[9]

Rather than focusing on a set age where a child would be presumed to be competent, the court in *Gillick* recognised the difficulties associated with such an approach. A child's age does not automatically correspond with a child's capacity, maturity, and understanding and not all children of a particular age will assume capacity at the exact same time. For example, you may have a 15-year-old who is mature for their age, who fully understands the implications of proposed medical treatment and is capable of making an informed decision, whilst on the other hand, another 15-year-old faced with a similar medical decision may lack the emotional and intellectual abilities required to reach an informed decision. Instead of focusing on age alone, the Court held that the level of intelligence and understanding of the particular child were the important factors, coupled with the judgement of the doctor, who may be better placed than the parents in some instances to decide what was best for the welfare of the particular child concerned.[10]

The importance of this case extends beyond contraceptive advice and treatment. The assessment of whether a child is deemed '*Gillick* competent' will arise in many different medical situations and, if the treating doctor deems the child competent it is possible that the child will be able to consent to medical treatment on their own behalf.

---

[6] [1986] AC 112 HL, at [174] (Lord Fraser).   [7] [1986] AC 112 HL, at [172] (Lord Fraser).
[8] [1970] 1 QB 357, 369.   [9] [1986] AC 112, at 185.   [10] [1986] AC 112 HL, at [172] (Lord Fraser).

The idea of a child being 'Gillick competent' also extends beyond the medical sphere to many decisions involving children more generally (see Chapter 13). For example, private family law proceedings have involved discussion of Gillick competence when deciding whom a child should live with following separation of the parents[11] and in circumstances where the court considered whether to order DNA testing on a 15-year-old child in order to prove paternity.[12] The overall aim of the court in circumstances such as these is not for the child to make the ultimate decision and be able to consent (as in the medical cases discussed). Instead, establishing whether the child is deemed Gillick competent allows the court to determine the weight that should be given to the wishes and feelings of the child when the court is reaching their final decision on the matter involved. The context and consequences of these decisions can determine the level of intelligence and understanding required for the child to be considered competent. The more serious the potential outcome, the higher level of understanding is required. As the Court stated in Mr L v Mrs P:

> It is important to remember that competence is an issue-based question and that a person may be competent to decide some issues, all issues or no issues and likewise may be incompetent in the same way.[13]

Unlike children aged 16 or 17 who have the statutory right to make the ultimate decision to consent to treatment, those under 16 years old do not have such a straightforward right. The medical professional has to determine whether a child under 16 is Gillick competent to consent to the medical treatment. This is not just a matter of being able to consent to *any* treatment, but to the *particular* medical treatment proposed.

Where the court is involved, the court would take into account the wishes and feelings of the child and the older the child the more weight would be given to their wishes and feelings, however the ultimate decision would lie with the court who would decide what they deem to be in the child's best interests. The court would also be involved in situations where they find the child is not Gillick competent and no consent can be obtained from the parents. The child may still have wishes and feelings about the proposed treatment and the court will still consider these, but the difference is that the court will not give as much weight to these wishes and feelings when determining their ultimate decision. This concept is reflected in the welfare checklist contained in s. 1(3) of the Children Act 1989 which requires the court to have regard to 'the ascertainable wishes and feelings of the child concerned (considered in the light of his age and understanding)'[14] when making decisions relating to the child.

Clearly, there is a difference between a child being able to consent to treatment when having reached the age of 16, a child under this age being found competent to consent to a particular treatment, and a child having their wishes and feelings considered as part of the decision made by the court. The former is a statutory right, the latter two will be dependent on the child's competence, coupled with their ability to make their wishes and feelings clear. Even then, this is only one factor to be balanced against others and the ultimate decision, when considering all the circumstances, will always be made by the court with the child's welfare as the paramount consideration.[15] This is in stark contrast with the position for adults. For an adult, being competent means that they have the right to make autonomous decisions relating to any proposed medical treatment regardless of the risks involved and regardless of medical opinion.

---

[11] *Re K (Children)* [2014] EWCA Civ 1195, at [44].   [12] *Mr L v Mrs P* [2011] EWHC 3399 (Fam), at [19].

[13] *Mr L v Mrs P* [2011] EWHC 3399 (Fam), at [19].   [14] Children Act 1989, s. 1(3)(a).

[15] Children Act 1989, s. 1(1).

In 2004, the Department of Health published updated guidance on the provision of advice and treatment of those under the age of 16 within the context of contraception advice and treatment.[16] The legality of this guidance was challenged in the case of *R (On the Application of Axon v Secretary of State for Health (Family Planning Association intervening).*[17] The mother of two girls, aged 12 and 15, did not want her daughters to be provided with advice or contraceptive treatment, or alternatively information on, or access to, abortion. This was due to the mother's personal experience, guilt, and grief following an abortion she went through 20 years earlier. She wanted to be informed before any such advice or treatment was provided to her daughters. She argued that the 2004 guidelines were unlawful, that doctors were not obliged to maintain confidentiality when advising or treating a child under the age of 16 in relation to contraception or abortion, and that doctors were not actually permitted to provide this advice or treatment without parents' knowledge. The Court rejected these arguments and the 2004 guidance was found to be lawful, in that it followed the guidance laid down in *Gillick*. Whilst allowing doctors to advise or treat children without parents' knowledge violated parents' Article 8(1) European Convention on Human Rights (ECHR) right to respect for their private and family life, the rights of the child to privacy and medical treatment under Article 8 also had to be protected and took priority over the parents' rights. It has previously been established that where parents' rights and children's rights under Article 8 are in question, the child's rights are the primary consideration.[18]

3.3 The level of understanding required for a child to be found competent to consent to medical treatment

As discussed, *Gillick* competence is based on the maturity, intelligence, and understanding of the individual child, but this still leaves the question of what exactly this requires of a child in relation to medical treatment.

Lord Donaldson in *Re R (A Minor) (Wardship: Consent to Medical Treatment)*[19] suggested that that the child needed to have:

> not merely an ability to understand the nature of the proposed treatment … but a full understanding and appreciation of the consequences both of the treatment in terms of intended and possible side effects and, equally important, the anticipated consequences of a failure to treat.[20]

Children are required to reach a high level of understanding before they would be considered competent in relation to medical decisions. As Lord Donaldson stated, it is not enough to understand just the nature of the proposed treatment, although without a doubt this is crucial, but also the intended and possible side effects. This requires doctors to discuss the treatment, risks, and benefits with the child in order for them to assess the child's competence in this context. However, doctors in some circumstances may withhold information where they feel it would be harmful to a child and their welfare for them to disclose particular information. This in itself could undermine any assessment of capacity and remove the possibility of the children themselves being able to make the decision to consent.

---

[16] Department of Health 'Best Practice Guidance for Doctors and Other Health Professionals on the Provision of Advice and Treatment to Young People Under 16 on Contraception, Sexual and Reproductive Health' (gateway reference No. 3382, 2014). Available at: https://www.bashh.org/documents/1993.pdf, accessed 12 May 2017.

[17] [2006] 1 FCR 175.

[18] *Yousef v Netherlands* [2003] 1 FLR 210, at [73]. [19] [1992] Fam 11.

[20] At [26] (Lord Donaldson.

A child's understanding of the possible consequences of not receiving treatment have been the consideration of the courts. In *Re L* (*Medical Treatment: Gillick Competence*) [21] the court was concerned with a 14-year-old girl's refusal of a blood transfusion due to her religious beliefs as a Jehovah's Witness and whether she was *Gillick* competent and therefore able to withhold her consent to treatment. She was found to have a high level of maturity, but also found to be a child who had limited life experience[22] and the Court ultimately found that she was not competent, as she did not fully appreciate the 'horrible death' she would experience without treatment.[23] The Court ordered that the blood transfusion should be administered despite L's refusal.

Interestingly in this case, the reason why the 14-year-old girl had been found to not understand the nature of her death was due to the fact that her doctors had thought it would cause her undue stress if they were to have told her and had therefore withheld this information from her. This raises the question of how a child can be found to lack competence when the information that would have potentially made the difference in this decision was purposely withheld from her.

CONTEXT 1: THE DIFFICULTIES FACING THE MEDICAL PROFESSION IN THEIR DECISION-MAKING

The General Medical Council have produced guidance for doctors who are treating children. This explicitly states that doctors should only keep information from children or young people if it would '... cause them serious harm (and not just upset them or make them more likely to want to refuse treatment)'[24] In addition, doctors must decide:

> ... whether a young person is able to understand the nature, purpose and possible consequences of investigations or treatments proposed, as well as the consequences of not having treatment. Only if they are able to understand, retain, use and weigh this information, and communicate their decision to others can they consent to that investigation or treatment. [That means that] ... doctors must make sure that all relevant information has been provided and thoroughly discussed before deciding whether or not a child or young person has the capacity to consent.[25]

The responsibility given to doctors when treating children and young people is one not to be taken lightly. Providing treatment to a young person, without their parent's knowledge must always require the doctor to make a judgement of the child's capacity to make this decision themselves and to weigh it against the risks of refusing to provide treatment. This is not always an easy choice to make and does at times result in harm to the child, despite the intentions of the medical profession.

There has been criticism of the use of *Gillick* competence because, if a child is determined by a medical practitioner to be competent and able to consent to particular treatment, it allows a child to be treated even when their parents or holders of parental responsibility

---

[21] [1998] 2 FLR 810.   [22] [1998] 2 FLR 810, at [813].

[23] [1998] 2 FLR 810, at [811] 'Gangrene would supervene and there would be a very distressing period for some time, not only for the patient but also for all those who were attending her.'

[24] General Medical Council, '*0–18 all years: guidance for doctors*' (2007) 10, para 20. Available at: http://www.gmc-uk.org/0_18_years___English_1015.pdf_48903188.pdf, accessed 21 July 2017.

[25] General Medical Council, '*0–18 all years: guidance for doctors*' (2007) 11, para 24. Available at: http://www.gmc-uk.org/0_18_years___English_1015.pdf_48903188.pdf, accessed 21 July 2017.

are not informed. Parents do not want to be excluded from what they perceive as important medical decisions about their minor child. This criticism is illustrated by the case of Britney Mazzoncini who unfortunately died after committing suicide a few weeks after being prescribed a course of powerful anti-anxiety drugs without her mother's knowledge or consent.[26] In Scotland, where Britney lived, legislation has incorporated the concept of *Gillick* competence into the law.[27] Britney had reportedly gone to her General Practitioner (GP) telling them that she was having suicidal thoughts and extremely bad panic attacks. Britney was 16 at the time of her visit to her GP and in response to Britney's symptoms, her GP gave her a prescription for 86 anti-anxiety pills and told her to return in four weeks. Following Britney's death, her mother launched an online petition, which was supported by her local MP urging for the law to be changed in order to avoid similar future incidents. On the petition, Mrs McKenzie wrote: 'This was the first I knew of my daughter's prescription and consultation with her GP, despite the fact she expressed to her GP that she had mental health concerns. I was not made aware of this until after my daughter's death.' The family lodged a complaint about the GP with the General Medical Council, but the GP was cleared of any wrongdoing. Britney's mother intends to appeal and continue her campaign for the law around children's competence to consent to medical treatment, without information being provided to parents, or subject to parental consent, to be changed.[28]

4. Refusal of treatment

Up to this point, the discussion has focused on children's ability to consent to their own medical treatment. Although it may be assumed that if a child has the capacity and is found to be competent to consent to treatment, they would also have the corresponding right to refuse treatment, this is not necessarily the case and the law deals with a child's refusal of treatment differently from that of consent. Section 8 of the Family Law Reform Act 1969 only gives a child who has reached the age of 16 the right to consent to treatment; (see 3.1) it does not provide the statutory right to refuse. The same applies to those under the age of 16 who are *Gillick* competent.

4.1 The child refuses

Following *Gillick* it was initially thought that a child did have a right to refuse as well as consent to proposed treatment. Eekelaar and Dingwell, in commenting on *Gillick* stated: 'as a result of this decision it seems that, provided the 'maturity test' is satisfied, parents can neither compel nor prevent medical treatment'.[29] This view did not last following subsequent cases such as *Re R*[30] and *Re W*.[31] *Re R*[32] was the first case to consider the concept of the '*Gillick* competent' child since *Gillick* itself was decided.

---

[26] Stewart, K. 'Tragic teenager's mother calls for parent consent on prescriptions', *The Scotsman*, 11 November 2016. Available at http://www.scotsman.com/news/tragic-teenager-s-mother-calls-for-parent-consent-on-prescriptions-1-4285683, accessed 15 July 2007.

[27] Age of Legal Capacity (Scotland) Act 1991, s. 2.

[28] Boyle, J. 'Mum calls for change to law after a trainee GP is cleared over her daughter's suicide', *Sunday Post*, 2 April 2017. Available at: https://www.sundaypost.com/fp/mum-calls-change-law-trainee-gp-cleared-daughters-suicide/, accessed 15 July 2017.

[29] Eekelaar, J. and Dingwell, R. *The Reform of Child Care Law: A Practical Guide to the Children Act 1989* (1st edn, Routledge, 1990) 24.

[31] [1992] 3 WLR 758.   [32] [1992] Fam 11.   [30] [1992] Fam 11.

Key Case 2: *Re R (A Minor) (Wardship: Consent to Medical Treatment)* [1992] Fam 11

In *Re R*, a 15-year-old girl, in local authority care, was suffering from a mental illness, which caused violent and suicidal behaviour during psychotic episodes. During her lucid periods, she clearly stated that she wanted to refuse any proposed drug therapy. Her doctors provided evidence suggesting that without the treatment she would return to a psychotic state. The local authority subsequently applied to the court for permission for the medical treatment to be given in order to prevent psychosis, even without R's consent. As the girl was in local authority care, this required the court to exercise its jurisdiction in wardship.

Wardship jurisdiction is part of the court's inherent jurisdiction, which requires the court to ensure that a child who is the subject of proceedings is protected and taken care of properly. The court may make any order or determine any issue in respect of a child unless limited by case law or statute, or unless the issues can be resolved under the Children Act 1989. Wardship is different to inherent jurisdiction in respect of: (a) custody of a child who is a ward of court is vested in the court; and (b) although day-to-day care and control of the child is given to an individual or to a local authority, no important step can be taken in the child's life without the court's consent.[33]

Initially, the Court in *Re R* stated that when exercising its wardship jurisdiction it could not override the decision of a 'competent' minor to refuse treatment, but that in this case R's mental condition meant that she could not achieve that competence. Permission was granted for treatment to be administered as this was deemed to be in the best interests of R. On appeal, Lord Donaldson confirmed that, due to the fluctuating nature of R's illness, she was not competent and treatment could be administered when necessary.

However, in addition to the question of this particular child's competence, the Official Solicitor had asked the Court to give guidance on the extent of the court's powers in situations such as this.[34] Lord Donaldson stated that in exercising its wardship jurisdiction, the Court was entitled to override a minor's refusal of treatment, irrespective of their competence stating that:

> In many cases of wardship the parents or other guardians will be left to make decisions for the child, subject only to standing instructions to refer reserved matters to the court, e.g. the taking of a serious step in the upbringing or medical treatment of a child, and to the court's right and, in appropriate cases, duty to override the decision of the parents or other guardians. If it can override such consents, as it undoubtedly can, I see no reason whatsoever why it should not be able, and in an appropriate case willing, to override decisions by 'Gillick competent' children who are its wards or in respect of whom applications are made ... [35]

Again, it can be seen that a child's ability to refuse treatment is limited and can be overridden by the court where it is felt to be in their best interests to do so, despite the child's wishes.[36]

Had R been an adult and not a ward of court, the decision may have been decided differently. As a competent adult R could have refused the treatment and in this situation the decision of R would have to be respected. Competent adults have the right to consent to, or refuse, any treatment, regardless of medical opinion and regardless of the potential consequences of not receiving the treatment. The exception to this is if R, as an adult, was found

[33] The Family Procedure Rules 2010 and Practice Direction 12D—Inherent Jurisdiction (including wardship) Proceedings, paras 1.1 and 1.3.
[34] [1992] Fam 11, at [17].
[35] [1992] Fam 11, at [25].   [36] [1992] Fam 11, at [26].

to lack capacity under the Mental Capacity Act 2005. In these circumstances, the court would be involved and medical decisions made on the basis of the patient's best interests. In *Re B (Adult: Refusal of Medical Treatment)*[37] Butler-Sloss P stated:

> … unless it is an exceptional case, the judicial approach to mental capacity must be largely dependent upon the assessments of the medical profession whose task it is on a regular basis to assess the competence of the patient to consent or refuse the medical/surgical treatment.[38]

There has been much debate on whether a child can ever refuse treatment, and the question of whether s. 8 of the Family Law Reform Act 1969 gave a child the right to not only consent to medical treatment, but also refuse once they reached the age of 16. This was the issue the Court had to consider in *Re W*.

 Key Case 3: *Re W (A Minor) (Medical Treatment: Court's Jurisdiction)* **[1993] Fam 64**

W suffered with anorexia nervosa and her condition was deteriorating. W had reached the age of 16, and wished to refuse medical treatment for her condition. Under s. 8 of the Family Law Reform Act 1969, she was competent to consent to medical treatment. However, the Court had to consider whether the right contained within s. 8 of the Family Law Reform Act 1969 also encompassed the right of the child to refuse treatment. The Court also had to consider whether, if she was competent to refuse treatment, and treatment was refused by W, whether the Court could override such refusal and grant consent to the treatment.

The Court was clear that under s.8 of the Family Law Reform Act 1969 it is presumed that any child who has reached the age of 16 has the capacity and the right to consent to medical treatment. However, this does not extend to a statutory right to refuse medical treatment and, although a court will take into account the wishes and feelings of the child in its decision, any refusal by the child can be overridden by consent provided by the court based on the child's best interests.

Even when a child reaches the age of 16 and has a statutory right under s 8 of the Family Law Reform Act 1969 (see 3.1) to consent to their medical treatment, this statutory right does not extend to a right to refuse treatment. Where the child refuses treatment, the courts can use their inherent jurisdiction and override a child's wishes if the court finds it to be in the best interests of the child to do so. Effectively, *Re W (A Minor) (Medical Treatment: Court Jurisdiction)*[39] provides what Lord Donaldson described as a 'flak jacket' for doctors to provide doctors with protection from prosecution.[40] Providing they have consent from someone authorised to provide consent, or from the court, then that is all that is required, even if the child themselves refuses treatment.

Re W (A Minor) (Medical Treatment: Court's Jurisdiction) was considered in *An NHS Foundation Trust Hospital v P*[41] where a 17-year-old was admitted to hospital after having taken an overdose of paracetamol. She refused treatment which needed to take place within eight hours to avoid liver failure and death. She had been found to have capacity to make decisions about her medical treatment and care by the consultant psychiatrist. Due to her refusal, the only option left to the hospital was to make an application to the court for permission to treat her for the overdose. The hospital also asked for permission to

---

[37] [2002] EWHC 429 (Fam).   [38] [2002] EWHC 429 (Fam), at [89].   [39] [1993] Fam 64.
[40] [1993] Fam 64, at [78].   [41] [2014] EWHC 1650 (Fam).

restrain or sedate her if necessary in order to carry out the required treatment. In making the orders, the Court considered *Re W (A Minor) (Medical Treatment: Court Jurisdiction)*[42] and *Re P (Medical Treatment: Best Interests)*,[43] to support the premise that where a child under 18 (although *Gillick* competent) refuses treatment, the court may exercise its inherent jurisdiction and override the child's wishes if it is in their best interests and consent to her treatment. Therefore, even when a child over the age of 16 is found competent and has a statutory right to consent to the medical treatment, this does not prevent the court from overriding their refusal of that treatment. This means that *Gillick* competence is still a consideration for children aged 16 or 17 when they wish to refuse the treatment proposed, despite the fact that *Gillick* itself concerned those under the age of 16.

4.2 The child refuses treatment but the parents consent

If a child does not, or cannot, consent to treatment, the doctor can treat the child if the parents, or those holding parental responsibility, consent on the child's behalf, as long as it is promoting the welfare of the child. It is not necessary for both parents to consent to the treatment, providing that the doctors have consent of at least one of them, this is sufficient. This was the situation dealt with in *Re K, W and H (Minors) (Medical Treatment)*.[44] The question raised in this case was whether a *Gillick* competent child's refusal of treatment affected the parent's capacity to consent on a child's behalf. Following advice provided by a health authority committee, the hospital applied for a Children Act 1989, s. 8 specific issue order to ensure that no doctor would be open to prosecution for treatment of a child following the child's refusal of such treatment. The Court clearly stated that in each of the three children's cases, there was parental consent for the treatment and that was sufficient to enable it to go ahead. There was no need to apply for a s. 8 specific issue order, as this was inappropriate. The refusal by the child did not affect the consent provided by the parent, which in effect overruled the child's refusal to consent, irrespective of the child's competence to make the decision.

Similarly, in *Re M (Medical Treatment: Consent)*[45] a 15-year-old girl's mother had consented to the heart transplant operation, although the girl herself refused. When an application was made to the court, they authorised the operation. Johnson J found that, although M was a mature and intelligent girl, events had occurred very quickly for M over a very short period of time and she was unable to fully comprehend or come to terms with what was happening to her. On the one hand, she did not want someone else's heart and to have to take medication for the rest of her life, but on the other, she was clear in stating that she did not want to die. The Court found that as the doctors were acting in the child's best interests and the mother had provided the required consent then, despite the risk that she may resent the treatment being carried out against her wishes, her certain death if the operation did not take place outweighed her refusal to consent to treatment. Lord Donaldson stated in *Re W*:

> No minor of whatever age has power by refusing consent to treatment to override a consent to treatment by someone who has parental responsibility for the minor.[46]

Even when a child has reached the age of 16 and has consented to the proposed treatment, it may still be appropriate for the court to consent to the treatment on the child's behalf. This may seem unnecessary, given that the 16-year-old has already consented. However, in some circumstances where it is felt that this consent may be subsequently withdrawn it may be appropriate for the court to also provide consent. In doing so, it ensures that treatment can continue, even if the child's consent is withdrawn. The court may also attach

---

[42] [1993] Fam 64. [43] [2003] EWHC 2327 (Fam). [44] (1993) 4 Med LR 200.
[45] [1999] 2 FLR 1097. [46] [1993] Fam 64, at [84].

to the order the right of the medical professionals treating the child to use force to fa-cilitate the treatment, if this became necessary. This was seen in *Re C (Detention: Medical Treatment)*,[47] where the girl had earlier left the clinic four times over a one-month period and was described as disturbed, aggressive, and sometimes suicidal. The only way that the clinic's director and psychiatrist would readmit her to the clinic for the treatment that she needed was if they had a court order which gave permission to treat her and also restrain her if necessary in order to do so. It was felt that even though she had eventually consented to the treatment, she could easily and would be likely to withdraw consent and leave the clinic again. Even though she was 16 and had consented, this did not prevent the court using inherent jurisdiction to secure the child's welfare by ensuring that the treatment could take place and she could be detained in order to carry it out.

❓ DEBATE 1: WHAT IS THE ROLE OF *GILLICK* COMPETENCE IN PROMOTING THE CHILD'S AUTONOMY IN DECISION-MAKING?

The facts of *Gillick*[48] were not directly concerned with a child's refusal of treatment, but instead concentrated on their access to, and ability to, consent to treatment. Following the decisions in *Re R*[49] and *Re W*[50] distinctions that were drawn between consent and refusal have been subject to some debate. The Court in these cases refused to accept that a *Gillick* competent child could have the right to refuse treatment. In *Re R* this applied to those children under 16 years old whilst *Re W* concerned those aged 16 or 17.

Lord Donaldson's reasoning in *Re R* and *Re W* was heavily criticised. Fortin was critical of the 'implicit authorisation of the use of physical force' that may be required to administer the treatment against the wishes of a mature child, without the explicit consideration of the practical details and what this would, in reality, mean for the child being forced to have the treatment.[51] Huxtable was also extremely critical of the Court's decision observing that, although not directly part of the final binding decision, there were clear indications in *Gillick* that a refusal of treatment by a competent minor should be decisive when determining if the treatment should proceed or not.[52] He was critical of the introduction of what he viewed as distinctions drawn solely on status, in this case age, and noted that medical law approached issues on the basis of competence, not status, ' ... at least in theory'.[53] He went on to say:

> The conventional attention to competence is prompted by the law's respect for the autonomy ... but competent minors are denied the right to refuse. The inconsistent adherence to the principle of self-determination is obvious, and, without the right to refuse, the right to consent seems devoid of any real import.[54]

Bridgeman was also critical of *Re W* claiming that although 'logically there is no difference between an ability to consent to treatment and an ability to refuse treatment, an illogical distinction has been entrenched into the law'.[55] This view is, at first sight, somewhat supported by the words of Balcombe LJ in *Re W* when he stated ' ... in logic there can be no difference

---

[47] [1997] 2 FLR 180.   [48] [1985] 3 All ER 402.   [49] [1992] Fam, 11.   [50] [1992] 3 WLR 758.
[51] Fortin, J. 'Children's rights and the Use of Physical Force' (2001) 13 *Child and Family Law Quarterly* 243, 261.
[52] Huxtable, R. '*Re M (Medical Treatment: Consent)*—Time to remove the "flak jacket"?' (2000) 12 *Child and Family Law Quarterly* 83, 84.
[53] Huxtable, R. '*Re M (Medical Treatment: Consent)*—Time to remove the "flak jacket"?' (2000) 12 *Child and Family Law Quarterly* 83, 84.
[54] Huxtable, R. '*Re M (Medical Treatment: Consent)* Time to remove the "flak jacket"?' (2000) 12 *Child and Family Law Quarterly* 83, 84.   [55] Bridgeman, J. 'Old Enough to Know Best?' (1993) 13 *Legal Studies* 69, 80.

between an ability to consent to treatment and an ability to refuse treatment'.[56] However, he went on to say that:

> ... there must come a point at which the court, while not disregarding the child's wishes, can override them in the child's own best interests, objectively considered. Clearly such a point will have come if the child is seeking to refuse treatment in circumstances which will in all probability lead to the death of the child or to severe permanent injury.[57]

This is not a settled and accepted view and there is no clear consensus on this issue. There remains tension between a child's right to consent to treatment and the restrictions placed on a child who wishes to refuse treatment.

It has been argued by Gilmore and Herring that: 'The distinction drawn between the weight attached to refusal of treatment and consent to treatment is not ... as illogical as some commentators have suggested.'[58] They argue that it makes a difference whether a child is refusing a particular treatment or all treatment generally. In order for the child to be competent and able to refuse a particular treatment proposed, it is suggested that all that is required is '... merely an understanding of that which is proposed by way of treatment'. By contrast, the refusal of all treatment requires a conscious decision to accept the consequences of failing to undergo treatment.[59] However, this viewpoint has been described as 'unworkable' in clinical practice.[60] Additionally, whereas Gilmore and Herring state that the need to understand relates purely to the treatment, Cave and Walbank argue that there are circumstances where a minor will lack the competence to consent unless (s)he understands the implications of refusal. This includes not only those implications that relate to the treatment itself, but also the 'deeper, emotional understanding' that is more dependent on the particular context. [61]

There is however some support for the decision in *Re W*, and the Court's decision to override the child's wishes and feelings. For example, there is a view that the approach taken in this case protects the child against 'wrong-headed parents and against itself with the final safeguard ... of giving the court the last word in cases of dispute'.[62] It has been argued that *Re W* correctly takes the approach that the child's best interests must be at the heart of any decision made about a child's medical treatment, particularly where there is a risk of death or permanent damage to the child in the future.

Given that a child's best interests are at the heart of any decisions concerning medical treatment, the different approaches taken to the child's ability to make these decisions is something that has led to this level of debate. On the one hand, a child is deemed competent to consent to a particular treatment, whilst on the other they are found to lack the capacity to refuse. As Davidson and Schweppe stated:

> We cannot ignore the influence of Gillick nor the Convention on the Rights of the Child nor the recent children's rights constitutional amendment in terms of giving children

---

[56] [1992] 3 WLR 758, at [88].   [57] [1992] 3 WLR 758, at [88].

[58] Gilmore, S. and J Herring, J. '"No" is the Hardest Word: Consent and Children's Autonomy' (2011) 23 *Child and Family Law Quarterly* 3, 22.

[59] Gilmore, S. and J Herring, J. '"No" is the Hardest Word: Consent and Children's Autonomy' (2011) 23 *Child and Family Law Quarterly* 3, 25.

[60] Cave, W. and Wallbank, J. 'Minors' Capacity to Refuse Treatment: A Reply to Gilmore and Herring' (2012) 20 *Medical Law Review* 423–449, 448.

[61] Cave, R. and Wallbank, J. 'Minors' Capacity to Refuse Treatment: A Reply to Gilmore and Herring' (2012) 20 *Medical Law Review* 423, 430.

[62] Lowe, N. and Juss, S. 'Medical Treatment—Pragmatism and the Search for Principle' (1993) 56 *Modern Law Review* 865, 872.

more rights and acknowledging that they are advancing in their decision-making capabilities and maturity. It is important that those advances in terms of children's rights are not just 'tick box' exercises, which they are in danger of being if we do not allow children to refuse as well as consent to treatment.[63]

This difference in approach could potentially be explained by the fact that when consenting to treatment, a child would be agreeing to treatment proposed and recommended by a doctor, whilst refusal is going against such qualified medical opinion. At this point, the question of whether the treatment is in the child's best interest is crucial and issues of whether the child is competent and fully understands all the implications is brought into play.

4.3 An explanation for the differences in approaches to a children's competence

Medical professionals make complex decisions every day in terms of proposed treatment, and in doing so, use their knowledge and skills to weigh up the risks and benefits involved. No medical treatment, however minor, can be guaranteed to be completely risk free, so this balancing exercise is crucial in order for both doctors and patients to be able to make informed decisions. Doctors have to negotiate their way through the complexities of the legal framework and ensure that they are following General Medical Council guidance. For example, in relation to treating children, there is not only a need to be aware of when a child has capacity,[64] but also doctors have an overall responsibility to ensure that they are protecting and safeguarding children.[65] Although the guidance itself is not legally enforceable, the General Medical Council clearly state that where there are serious or persistent failures to follow the guidance, doctors' registration will be put at risk. Therefore, when making decisions concerning the treatment of children, doctors need to be aware of both their legal and ethical obligations.

Where the court is involved, the court must take the medical evidence of risks and benefits of any proposed treatment into account, but must also consider the ultimate potential consequences for the individual child. For example, the court will be particularly focused on what harm the child may experience if the treatment proceeds or not. This is important, not only for the immediate future, but also for child's more long-term future. The likely consequences can greatly influence the courts' approach and the weight given to a child's wishes and feelings.

It is useful to consider the case of *Re JS (Disposal of Body)*[66] as this case, when compared with cases such as *Re R*[67] and *Re W*,[68] may help to explain why the courts will not always respect a child's view of their medical treatment and may use their inherent jurisdiction to override a child's refusal. This case concerned a 14-year-old girl (JS) who despite previous treatment for cancer was terminally ill. She had researched cryogenics extensively on the internet and wished for her body to be frozen and stored in the hope that future medical

---

[63] Davidson, H. and Schweppe, J. 'Time for Legislative Clarity on Consent to Medical Treatment: Children, Young people and the "Mature Minor"' (2015) 21 *Medico-Legal Journal of Ireland* 65.

[64] General Medical Council Guidance, '*0–18 years: guidance for all doctors*' (2007). Available at: http://www.gmc-uk.org/static/documents/content/0_18_years.pdf, accessed 23 July 2017.

[65] General Medical Council Guidance, '*Protecting children and young people: the responsibilities of all doctors*' (2012). Available at: http://www.gmc-uk.org/Protecting_children_and_young_people___English_1015.pdf_48978248.pdf, accessed 23 July 2017.

[66] *Re JS (Disposal of Body)* [2016] EWHC 2859 (Fam).   [67] [1992] Fam 11.   [68] [1992] 3 WLR 758.

developments would enable her to be cured and resuscitated, even if that was far into the future. In order for this to take place and for her body to be stored in America (the only place apart from Russia to offer this facility) she needed consent from both of her parents. She had not seen her father for eight years and did not wish to have contact with him, or for him to know the details of her condition. Her father refused consent. She applied to the court for permission for her mother, on her own, to be able to make the decisions as to what would happen to her body when she died. Her mother supported JS in the decision she was making.

Once the questions of legality and practicality of the proposal to seek cryogenic freezing were satisfied, the focus then turned to the key issue of consent. The fact was that, as a child, JS could not make a will and in doing so appoint her mother as her executor which would involve her mother arranging for the disposal of her body upon her death. In his judgment, Jackson J aimed to remove this disadvantage due to her age, but no more than that.[69] Any order provided was not made to endorse or reject cryogenics or to stipulate how her body should be disposed of; instead, it was to settle the dispute between JS's parents about who could make the arrangements for after her death, whatever the nature of those eventual arrangements.[70]

In relation to JS's competence, the Court found that she had the capacity to bring the case to the Court. She was found to be 'a bright, intelligent young person … able to articulate strongly held views' and was found to have 'pursued her investigations with determination, even though a number of people … tried to dissuade her, and that she had not been coerced or steered by her family or anyone else'.[71] Jackson J stated that: 'The making of a specific issue order is governed by the welfare principle. In this case the predominant features are JS's wishes and feelings and her acute emotional needs.'[72] The case was 'not about whether JS's wishes are sensible or not'. He continued by stating: 'We are all entitled to our feelings and beliefs about our own life and death, and none of us has the right to tell anyone else—least of all a young person in JS's position—what they must think'.[73]

In this case, great weight was put on the wishes and feelings of JS. Statements of her intelligence and capacity, and also the decision to exclude consideration of whether her choice was in fact 'sensible or not' sits awkwardly aside cases such as *Re R* and *Re W* when considering the level of respect shown for the children's wishes in those cases.

The case of JS demonstrates that there are differences in the way a child's wishes and feelings and their capacity are considered in cases involving children where lack of treatment could possibly result in the child's death, and cases such as JS where death was inevitable, regardless of the Court's decision. All three cases involved medical treatment, but have approached capacity, wishes, and feelings of the child in determining what they want regarding their own life and death in different ways. Where there is a possibility of death, as in *Re R*[74] because she was showing suicidal behavior, and *Re W*,[75] where the girl's condition was deteriorating rapidly as a result of her anorexia nervosa, the courts have been less willing to respect the wishes and feelings of the child to the same extent as they were in *Re JS*. In *Re W*, Lord Donaldson stated that the child's wishes and feelings at this stage 'were completely outweighed by the threat of irreparable damage to her health and risk to her life'.[76] Clearly the determining factor here is that the Court did not want to make a

---

[69] [2016] EWHC 2859 (Fam), at 25.   [70] [2016] EWHC 2859 (Fam), at [33] and [37].
[71] [2016] EWHC 2859 (Fam), at [9].   [72] [2016] EWHC 2859 (Fam), at [46].
[73] [2016] EWHC 2859 (Fam), at [31].   [74] [1992] Fam 11.   [75] [1993] Fam 64.
[76] [1992] 3 WLR 758, at [768].

declaration which, although it would completely respect the competent child's wishes and feelings, may result in the child's death.

There is no shame in wanting to protect children from harm and there are understandable and valid arguments that minors are still developing physically, emotionally, and intellectually and that affects their capacity to make such decisions.[77] However, rather than explicitly dealing with *Gillick* competence and acknowledging the obvious limitations in determining when a child may be found to be competent, in relation to making life-changing medical decisions, the courts are manipulating the concept and instead finding either that children lack the capacity to make the decision,[78] or that even when a child is competent, then the court is acting in the child's best interests and overriding the child's own wishes and feelings in refusing treatment.[79]

In these circumstances, the child's best interests and welfare under Article 3 of the United Nations Convention on the Rights of the Child 1990 (UNCRC), are being prioritised over a child's right to be heard and have their opinion taken into account under Article 12 UNCRC (see Chapter 13). This approach adopts the perspective of the doctors and courts rather than of the children themselves who wish for their decisions to be respected. Both best interests and the child's right to be heard are protected by the UNCRC, but in situations such as refusal of medical treatment by a child there is potential for tension between these rights.[80] On the one hand the child's autonomy and their right for their wishes and feelings to be heard and respected is regarded as important in order to recognise children as right holders, capable of making their views known. Whilst on the other, the child's best interests under Article 3 UNCRC is often used within medical decisions by doctors, parents, and the court to justify why the child requires a more paternalistic, protection-focused decision to be taken. The UN Committee on the Rights of the Child has found no tension between these Articles, which they view as being able to work together,[81] however, in practice this may not always be the case. As Fortin states: 'Children's rights should not be lost somewhere in the middle, between parental, medical and judicial paternalism.'[82]

This paternalistic approach is understandable, as you cannot undo death,[83] whereas a child you could argue, once they reach adulthood can make a later decision for themselves where their capacity will be presumed. This will avoid the courts having to deal with potential criticism for 'letting a child die' and will preserve the appearance that they are acting in the most appropriate way for the benefit of the child. Clearly, the more serious the potential outcome, then the higher level of competence is required by the court before the child may make their own decision.[84] Disputes about treatment, short of life-saving treatment, are more likely to result in the court giving greater weight to the child's wishes and feelings about the proposed treatment.

---

[77] Mann, L. *et al* 'Adolescent Decision-Making: The Development of Competence' (1989) 12 Journal of Adolescence 265–78, 265.

[78] *Re E (A Minor) (Wardship: Medical Treatment)* [1993] 1 FLR 386.

[79] *Re W (A Minor) (Medical Treatment: Court Jurisdiction)* [1992] 3 WLR 758, [81].

[80] Freeman, M. 'Laws, Conventions and Rights' (1993) 7 *Children and Society* 37, 45.

[81] Committee on the Rights of the Child (2013) *The right of the child to have his or her best interests taken as a primary consideration* (art. 3, para 1), General comment No. 14, CRC/C/GC/14.

[82] Fortin, J. '*Children's Rights and the Developing Law*' (3rd edn, Cambridge University Press, 2009) 402.

[83] Lowe, N. and Juss, S. 'Medical Treatment—Pragmatism and the Search for Principle' (1993) 56 *Modern Law Review* 865, 871.

[84] [1992] 3 WLR 758, at [88] and Stavrinides, Z. 'Adolescent Patients' Consent and Refusal to Medical Treatment: an Ethical Quandary in English Law' (2012) 8 *Humanicus* 1, 14.

? DEBATE 2: SHOULD A MORE HONEST APPROACH TO *GILLICK* COMPETENCE BE TAKEN?

The repercussions of the case law subsequent to *Gillick* and the restrictions on the ability of a child to refuse medical treatment have brought what was generally felt as huge strides in advancements of respect of children's autonomy,[85] established in *Gillick,* into question.

The earlier discussion raises the question of whether a child will ever be found to be competent and a refusal of treatment respected which goes against doctors' views, or can a child only be competent when they are agreeing with the medical opinion on the best way forward for their treatment? Alternatively, if the court is making the decision based on what they believe to be the in the best interests of the child, is it only possible for a child to be acting in their own best interests when they are in agreement with the court's, and normally the medical practitioners', preferred treatment option?

If the court is willing to override a competent child's decision to refuse treatment, as Sir Stephen Brown P stated in *Re L*,[86] then is *Gillick* competence not merely a pretense, to suggest that children's autonomy, intelligence, and maturity is being respected in the decisions children make about issues that directly affect them. In fact, it could be argued that this respect is only accorded to the child when the child's decision is consistent with the doctors' opinion and ultimately with the court's judgment on their welfare.

Should there not be a more honest approach to *Gillick* competence and a child's right to make their own medical decisions? Arguably, it would be a more consistent position for the law to acknowledge the limitations of *Gillick* competence and admit the validity of the dominant focus on protection of children in need of medical treatment, and the priority accorded to the protection of their welfare. The fact that the courts are reluctant to respect a child's refusal to treatment, which often involve life-threatening situations, is understandable, but some honesty in relation to this would be welcome. *Gillick* competence could be applied and a child's decision (consent or refusal) respected where there are medical decisions to be made that affect the child, but not decisions of such significance as to whether the child will live or die.

This suggestion, to acknowledge and accept the limitations of *Gillick* competence, goes against arguments in favour of children's autonomy in decision-making and the suggestion that *Gillick* competent minors' decisions should be respected, despite the outcome.[87] However, to argue that *Gillick* competence respects children's rights is flawed, given the way that the courts are implementing the principle and the limits applied to its use. As Brazier states: '… adolescent autonomy is little more than a myth, for no young person under 18 has the right to refuse treatment'.[88]

Given the way that *Gillick* competence is used by the courts with adolescents being denied the right to refuse treatment even when found to be competent, they should at least be open, honest, and explicit about '… owning up to the fact that until the age of 18 the courts will remain the final arbitrators when it comes to determining the long-term interests of minors'[89] and should explicitly acknowledge that *Gillick* competence is firmly confined to circumstances where the child agrees and consents to treatment proposed by the medical profession.

[85] Freeman, M. 'Taking Children's Rights Seriously' (1987–8) 4 Children and Society 299, 311.

[86] [1998] 2 FLR 810.

[87] Heywood, R. 'Mature Teenagers and Medical Intervention Revisited: A Right to Consent, A Wrong to Refuse' (2008) 37 *Common Law World Review* 191, 201.

[88] Brazier, M. and Cave, E. 'Medicine, Patients and the Law' (4th edn, Penguin, 2007) 404.

[89] Grubb, A. *Medical Law*, (3rd edn, Butterworths, 2000) 989.

5. Disputes between doctors and parents over the treatment of children

Before any medical treatment can be provided to a child, as stated earlier, a doctor (except in cases of emergency) must obtain consent. This consent is usually sought from those with parental responsibility[90] for the child, generally parents, who are therefore legally permitted to consent to treatment. It is not necessary for everyone with parental responsibility to consent to the treatment; doctors may proceed with treatment once they have obtained consent from one person with parental responsibility.[91] If the other parent objects to the treatment, the onus is on them to apply to the court for a prohibited steps order under s. 8(1) of the Children Act 1989 to prevent the doctors proceeding with the treatment.

In a great many situations, there will be no issues raised concerning the treatment of children. Most often, a child is taken to see a doctor, the doctor will discuss treatment with parent(s), who then consent, and the child is treated. However, the situation is more complex where the holders of parental responsibility (usually parents) refuse to give their consent to the medical treatment proposed for their child.

5.1 Parents refuse to consent to medical treatment

When parents or those with parental responsibility have all withheld consent to the treatment proposed by the child's doctors, the medical team may apply to the court for permission to treat the child, despite the parental refusal. Parents are, in such cases, often acting in, what they believe to be, the best interests of their child. However, if the medical view differs and regards the child's best interests as requiring the administration of treatment, then the only option for doctors is to apply to the court for permission to proceed despite parental refusal. In theory, this would apply to any proposed treatment no matter how minor, however in practice these disputes only tend to arise in circumstances where doctors feel that without the treatment the child will suffer significant harm. To not treat the child or at least seek guidance from the court may be viewed as negligent and a failure by the medical profession to do their duty to safeguard the welfare of their minor patient. Many of the cases that have come before the courts have involved blood transfusions, where due to religious grounds the parents refuse to consent to the treatment.

This was the case in *Re R (A Minor) (Blood Transfusion)*[92] where parents of a 10-month-old girl refused consent to blood transfusions which doctors believed would prolong the child's life. The parents refused consent to treatment due to their religious belief as Jehovah's Witnesses. The local authority applied for a specific issue order under s. 8 of the Children Act 1989, seeking permission for the medical professionals to administer the blood transfusions to the child, despite the parents' refusal. The parents argued that if such an order was granted, the doctors should be required to consult with them first on each occasion before any transfusion, as the treatment was expected to be an ongoing issue for a number of years. The parents wanted the opportunity to suggest and discuss alternative treatments that would not involve blood products, given rapidly developing medical advancement. The Court gave permission for the blood transfusion to take place at this time, but also

---

[90] Children Act 1989, s. 3.

[91] Children Act 1989, s. 2(7). 'Where more than one person has parental responsibility for a child, each of them may act alone and without the other (or others) in meeting that responsibility'.

[92] [1993] 2 FCR 544.

acknowledged the parents' concerns by restricting treatment of their child without them being consulted to situations where:

> In any imminently life-threatening situation, when it is the professional opinion of those medically responsible for the said child, that she is in need of the administration of blood products, she shall be given such blood products without the consent of her parents.[93]

Ultimately, the court retains the right to override a parent's refusal to the proposed treatment of their child and any decision made by the court focuses on the child's best interests.

There are some cases where both the parents and the *Gillick* competent child refuse to give consent to treatment proposed by the medical profession. This was the situation in the case of *Re P (Medical Treatment: Best Interests)*[94] which concerned a boy aged 16 years and 10 months. Due to both his and his parents' religious beliefs as Jehovah's Witnesses they refused the blood transfusion that doctors said he needed. As he was over the age of 16, he had a statutory right to consent to medical treatment under s. 8(1) of the Family Law Reform Act 1969; however, this right did not extend to the refusal of treatment (see 3.1).

The parents argued that the immediate medical necessity for a blood transfusion had passed and therefore there was no need for the order at this time. However, the Court took the view that it was beneficial to consider the decision with the parties present at the hearing. This was preferable to a hearing via a telephone, in the middle of the night where an immediate need for treatment arose and an urgent application to the court is made, as is often the case. The Court made its decision based on possible future need for a blood transfusion in an 'immediately life threatening' situation and 'when it is the professional opinion of those medically responsible ... that he is in need of the administration of blood and/or blood products', and importantly, 'that there is no reasonable practical alternative'.[95] Despite Johnson J's admitted reluctance to make the order and in doing so override the adolescent's wishes and feelings, he took into account the words of Balcombe LJ in *Re W*:[96]

> As children approach the age of majority they are increasingly able to take their own decisions concerning their medical treatment ... It will normally be in the best interests of a child of sufficient age and understanding to make an informed decision that the court should respect its integrity as a human being and not lightly override its decision on such a personal matter as medical treatment. All the more so if that treatment is invasive.[97]

Johnson J went on to make the order to provide that blood transfusions could be administered in the circumstances of an immediately life threating situation. The statement of Nolan LJ in *Re W*, to which he also referred, influenced his thinking:

> In general terms the present state of the law is that an individual who has reached the age of eighteen is free to do with his life what he wishes, but it is the duty of the court to ensure so far as it can that children survive to attain that age.[98]

In the case of *Re E (A Minor) (Wardship: Medical Treatment)*[99] a very similar issue arose regarding permission for a blood transfusion despite the refusal of treatment by both the parents and child on the basis of their religious beliefs as Jehovah's Witnesses. The boy concerned was nearly 16 years old and needed a blood transfusion as part of his

---

[93] [1993] 2 FLR 757, at [761].   [94] [2003] EWHC 2327 (Fam).   [95] [2003] EWHC 2327 (Fam), at [6].
[96] [1992] 3 WLR 758, at [776].   [97] Re W [1992] 3 WLR 758, at [776].
[98] Re W [1992] 3 WLR 758, at [781].   [99] [1993] 1 FLR 386.

treatment for leukaemia. His condition was critical and he was made a ward of court. The local authority applied to the court for permission for treatment of the boy, despite the objections of both the child and his parents. The parents argued that as their son was nearly 16, his consent to any treatment would be required under s. 8 of the Family Law Reform Act 1969. Besides that, they argued that their son was *Gillick* competent and therefore the court would be wrong to use the jurisdiction of wardship to override his decision. The Court found that s. 8 of the Family Law Reform Act 1969 did not apply as he had not reached the age of 16 (see 3.1) and that he was not competent to make such a medical decision as he did not fully understand the effect of refusing a blood transfusion. Therefore, the Court had to make a decision based on the boy's best interests and ordered the treatment, despite the parents' objections. When the boy reached the age of 18 and required another blood transfusion, he exercised his right to refuse and he subsequently died. Clearly, nothing had changed in relation to his beliefs in this time and he may have felt that his competent, well thought out decision regarding the earlier transfusion was unjustifiably overruled.

5.2 **The limit on parental rights to refuse treatment on behalf of their child**

In *Gillick* Lord Scarman stated that:

> … as a matter of law the parental right to determine whether or not their minor child below the age of 16 will have medical treatment terminates if and when the child achieves a sufficient understanding and intelligence to enable him or her to understand fully what is proposed.[100]

As stated earlier, a child who has reached the age of 16 has a statutory right to consent to medical treatment.[101] This right will override any refusal by a parent or those with parental responsibility to provide or withhold consent to the treatment. For example, if the parents do not wish their child to receive vaccinations, after 16 the child is entitled to consent to the treatment, even if their parents still withhold their consent. Equally, taking into account Lord Scarman's words in *Gillick*, where a child under 16 is found to be competent and consents to treatment proposed by the medical profession, this too would override parents' refusal. Note that the discussion is focused on when parents can no longer override a child's consent to treatment, but this still leaves parents with the ability to override a refusal by their child, potentially until the child reaches the age of 18 and adulthood.

 Context 2: The Impact of the Seriousness of Treatment on the Approach Taken

The seriousness of the treatment proposed will make a difference to when treatment will proceed and whether the court needs to be involved. Minor procedures such as a routine (but not compulsory) childhood vaccination or treatment for common ailments with antibiotics are dealt with differently than the more invasive or major procedures that doctors may propose as being in the best interests of the child. Table 10.1 illustrates the different approaches dependent on who consents or refuses such treatment.

---

[100] [1986] AC 112; [1986] 1 FLR 224, at 253.
[101] Family Law Reform Act 1969, s. 8.

Table 10.1 Approaches to consent or refusal of treatment

Doctor proposes procedure[*]	
Child (over 16) consents	Treatment proceeds—even if parents refuse
Child (under 16) who is *Gillick* competent consents	Treatment proceeds—even if parents refuse
Parent(s) consent	Treatment proceeds
Child (of any age) refuses but parent(s) consent	Treatment proceeds
Child (of any age) refuses and parent(s) refuse	Court rules whether treatment is in the child's best interests or not.
Parents refuse (minor procedure)	Refusal is likely to be respected
Parents refuse (major procedure)	Court rules whether treatment is in the child's best interests or not.

[*] There may be some exceptions to this general approach if the specific circumstances involved require it.

6. Withholding treatment

So far, we have considered situations where there is a perceived need for invasive treatment, but there are also circumstances where the courts are asked to give permission for treatment to be withheld. The issue here does not usually involve the child's competence as the child is either often too young or not in a position to be deemed competent to make decisions over their care. Very often such circumstances will arise where a child is receiving treatment for a severe critical or chronic illness and doctors do not want to carry out invasive resuscitation should the need arise.

Again, in these circumstances, any decisions made must be in the individual child's best interests. In *Re B (Medical Treatment)*[102] a child, aged 22 months, in local authority care, suffered both severe physical and mental disabilities and was not expected to reach the age of 5. Her condition was deteriorating rapidly and it was felt by the doctors treating her that it would not be in her best interests to carry out invasive resuscitation should it become necessary to keep her alive for a short period. The child's mother, who was herself still a child, was in agreement with whatever course of treatment the doctors decided upon. Despite the child being in local authority care (see Chapter 11), the medical team sought a declaration from the court that their proposed actions were permitted. The Court confirmed that this was the correct approach since, although the local authority held parental responsibility over the child, it would be unlikely to extend to a decision such as this and even if it did extend to this decision, the court should be involved in any circumstances such as these. The Court gave permission for the doctors to withhold intrusive resuscitation where there was a 'deteriorating illness' or if she became 'severely unwell' which persisted 'despite less intrusive treatment'.[103] Ultimately, the Court's aim in making this order was that the child's care and treatment should be provided 'in such a way as to cause her the least distress and pain, and retain the greatest dignity'.[104] Just as where invasive treatment is in dispute, the court's focus is to make any decision in the best interests of the child concerned.

---

[102] [2008] EWHC 1996 (Fam); [2009] 1 FLR 1264. [103] [2009] 1 FLR 1264, at 1266.
[104] [2009] 1 FLR 1264, at 1266.

6.1 Parental objection to the withdrawal of treatment

There are situations that involve doctors viewing withholding treatment to be in the best interests of the child concerned, whilst the parents do not agree with this view. In a highly publicised and prolonged legal battle, this was the situation of Charlie Gard and his parents.

 Key Case 4: *Gard and others v United Kingdom* **App. No. 39793/17 [2017] ECHR 39793/17; [2017] All ER (D) 165 (Jun)**

8-month-old Charlie Gard was suffering a progressive condition and his parents raised £1.2 million for Charlie to undergo pioneering treatment in America. Charlie's condition caused progressive muscle weakness and doctors at Great Ormond Street Hospital said that there was no cure for his condition and he should be allowed to die with dignity. Charlie's parents disagreed and wanted to take Charlie to America where they had agreement from a hospital there to carry out the treatment. Although it had never been attempted on a human being with Charlie's condition, his parents wanted to give him a chance to access the treatment. Doctors at Great Ormond Street Hospital took the view that there was no treatment that could undo the brain damage that he had already suffered, or change the fact that he was both deaf and blind and his quality of life would not be improved. Additionally, doctors believed Charlie was in pain and the proposed journey to America for this unproven treatment would only serve to prolong his suffering.

Charlie's parents clearly objected to the proposed withdrawal of treatment and when the hospital turned to the court seeking an order that permitted them to withdraw artificial ventilation and provide only palliative care, they requested the court to require the hospital to continue treatment. In the High Court, Francis J initially adjourned proceedings to allow time for Charlie's parents to gather evidence to present to the Court about treatment that may be available for Charlie in America.[105] In hearing the case, the Court had to decide what was in Charlie's best interests. After hearing the evidence that there was unlikely to be any benefit to Charlie of the treatment in America, it was determined that Charlie's life support was to be withdrawn and palliative care provided as this was felt to be in Charlie's best interests in order to let him die with dignity.[106] Charlie's parents appealed this decision to the Court of Appeal[107] but were unsuccessful and Francis J's judgment was upheld. They made a further application for permission to appeal to the Supreme Court, but this was declined as there had been no error in law, the right test had been applied and the factual findings could not be challenged on appeal.[108] This left Charlie's parents with only one legal option remaining and that was to take their case to the European Court of Human Rights (ECtHR), which they did.[109] The ECtHR declared that that there had been no violations of their rights under Articles 2, 5, 6, and 8 ECHR and their complaints were inadmissible.[110] Charlie's parents had exhausted every legal avenue available to them and

---

[105] *Great Ormond Street Hospital v Yates and Others* [2017] EWHC 972 (Fam).

[106] [2017] EWHC 972 (Fam), at [88].

[107] *Yates and Anor v Great Ormond Street Hospital For Children NHS Foundation Trust and Anor* [2017] EWCA Civ 410; [2017] All ER (D) 20 (Jun).

[108] *In the matter of Charlie Gard* UKSC 2017/0094; [2017] EWCA Civ 410. See https://www.supremecourt.uk/news/permission-to-appeal-hearing-in-the-matter-of-charlie-gard.html, accessed 29 September 2017.

[109] *Gard and others v United Kingdom* App. No. 39793/17 [2017] ECHR 39793/17; [2017] All ER (D) 165 (Jun).

[110] See the full judgment for discussion of each Article and the claim of violations, *Gard and others v United Kingdom* App. No. 39793/17 [2017] ECHR 39793/17; [2017] All ER (D) 165 (Jun).

had tried to stop the withdrawal of treatment, but were then faced with the inevitable death of their son once artificial ventilation was withdrawn. In one last plea to the Court, they requested that Charlie could be taken home so that they could spend the last hours with him in a non-clinical setting. Although taking Charlie home was not an option that the Court felt they could approve, the Court did say that he could be moved to a hospice. Charlie died shortly after being moved from the hospital to the hospice.[111]

In cases such as Charlie's, both doctors and parents strongly believe that they are acting in the best interests of the child. These diametrically opposed views as to the best way forward result in the court being involved and as was seen in Charlie's case, this can sometimes lead to a long and protracted legal battle.

7. Where does the responsibility lie for decisions about a child's medical treatment?

There are competing responsibilities and rights involved when discussing medical treatment of children. Firstly, there is parental responsibility and doctors' medical judgements, but also the court has a role to play in determining the child's best interests, separate of the medical assessment. Each party wants what is best for the child and is concerned with the welfare of the child. Each of these parties have a role to play when disputes arise, but the extent of their role is dependent on the circumstances.

There are situations where the court cannot make the decision about a child's medical treatment because they do not have the jurisdiction to do so. *LA v SB, AB & MB*[112] is an interesting case in that it demonstrates the limits of the courts' involvement in medical decisions concerning treatment of children. In this case, the local authority had initially applied for care orders for MB who was a 6-year-old boy suffering from a rare but progressive brain disease, as well as for his siblings. The local authority subsequently applied to the Court for a care order for MB along with the setting aside of applications for his siblings as original welfare concerns were no longer affecting them.

In MB's case, his doctor had raised concerns about the lack of cooperation from the parents in relation to the options for his treatment, and particularly the doctor's view that he needed to undergo surgery. Given that the local authority informed the Court that they did not intend to actually use a care order to remove MB from his home,[113] the judge found that this was the wrong process to decide whether permission for surgery should be granted by the Court. The hospital were invited either to intervene in the proceedings or to issue proceedings so that the decision concerning the proposed surgery could be made on the correct basis.

Consequently, the local authority withdrew their original application for a care order. Instead, they asked the Court either to use its inherent jurisdiction under s.100 of the Children Act 1989, or to allow the local authority to apply for a Children Act 1989, s. 8 specific issue order regarding the decision over consent to surgery. However, once the Court was informed that the hospital would not be intervening or issuing proceedings, the Court refused to make a decision regarding the surgery. They stated that only if the local

---

[111] *The Guardian* 'Timeline: Charlie Gard and his parents' legal battle to save him', The Guardian, 28 July 2017. Available at: https://www.theguardian.com/uk-news/2017/jul/24/timeline-charlie-gard-and-his-parents-legal-battle-to-save-him, accessed 31 July 2017.
[112] [2010] EWHC 1744 (Fam).   [113] [2010] EWHC 1744 (Fam), at [14].

authority was intending to continue the application for a care order with a care plan in place in relation to the surgery could they hear the case, otherwise there was no valid case before them and they did not have jurisdiction. The request made by the local authority for the Court to use its inherent jurisdiction was not open in these circumstances and the decision was for the parents or, those with parental responsibility, to decide in consultation with the medical professionals.

This case demonstrates very clear lines of responsibility. The responsibility for decisions made concerning the medical treatment and children should, first and foremost, be for the doctors and parents. Only when an application is made to the court under the appropriate jurisdiction, can the court be involved.[114] An application for a care order, without a care plan in place for the treatment and with no intention to remove the child from their parents' care, is not such an order. A local authority cannot ask the court to use their inherent jurisdiction under s. 100 of the Children Act 1989 in these circumstances and it is for the medical profession to apply to the court if the need arises when treatment is believed to be in the child's best interests and parental consent cannot be obtained.

7.1 Extreme steps taken by parents

Where parents are opposed to the treatment proposed by the medical profession, this has at times led to a situation where parents take extreme action to do what they believe to be in the best interests of their child despite medical opinions. There have been a series of high profile cases reported in the media where parents have clearly disagreed with the approach taken by the medical profession in the treatment of their child's illness. One such case concerned Ashya King.

Ashya was a 5-year-old boy who was diagnosed with a medulloblastoma, a type of brain tumour, which was successfully removed by surgeons in August 2014. Following the successful surgery, doctors proposed a course of chemotherapy and radiotherapy in order to prevent the tumour returning. Ashya's parents did not have as much confidence in this treatment due to the potential side effects and preferred non-invasive proton beam therapy as an alternative, which had fewer side effects. This treatment was not available via the National Health Service (NHS) in the UK, but doctors could refer patients to other countries, although in this case a referral had been refused on the basis that it was not the most effective treatment for the child.

Given that doctors were still insisting that the chemotherapy and radiotherapy was the best treatment, the parents removed their seriously ill child from Southampton General Hospital against medical advice and 'fled' taking Ashya abroad with the aim of getting the proton beam therapy for him where it was available. A huge Europe-wide media campaign was launched in order for the child and his parents to be found. Ashya was made a ward of court[115] and an arrest warrant was issued against the parents. They were found and held in prison in Spain for over 24 hours, until subsequently released when the arrest warrant was dropped due to the UK prosecutors stating that the risk to Ashya's life was 'not as great or immediate as … originally thought.'[116]

Ashya eventually received the proton beam therapy in a hospital in Prague and was declared cancer-free in March 2015. The authority for the treatment was obtained from the English High Court[117] in 2014. Once Baker J was satisfied that arrangements could be made for Ashya to be transferred from Spain to Prague for treatment and that the costs of this

---

[114] See Sch 1 of the Family Court (Composition and Distribution of Business) Rules 2014 (SI 2014/840).
[115] *In the Matter of Ashya King*, PO14P00645, Sir Gavyn Arthur J, 29 August 2014.
[116] See http://www.bbc.co.uk/news/uk-england-32013634, accessed 29 September 2017.
[117] *Re Ashya King* [2014] EWHC 2964 (Fam).

were available[118] then he declared that this could take place. He stressed that it was Ashya's welfare which was the Court's paramount consideration under s.1 of the Children Act 1989, along with his rights under the ECHR, particularly Article 2, his right to life and Article 8 right to respect for his private and family life. In addition to this, Baker J stated that:

> … it is a fundamental principle of family law in this jurisdiction that responsibility for making decisions about a child rest with his parents. In most cases, the parents are the best people to make decisions about a child and the State—whether it be the court, or any other public authority—has no business interfering with the exercise of parental responsibility unless the child is suffering or is likely to suffer significant harm as a result of the care given to the child not being what it would be reasonable to expect a parent to give.[119]

Baker J considered that the situation had changed considerably from when Ashya's parents first removed him from the hospital. The medical team, although it could not recommend or provide the treatment at the hospital, was not opposed to it.[120] Permission was therefore granted for the proposed treatment to take place and it was declared that when Ashya arrived at the hospital in Prague, he would no longer be a ward of court.[121]

In January 2016, media news headlines of 'So Ashya's parents were RIGHT'[122] appeared following the publication of a study that stated that the proton beam therapy Asyha had undergone caused fewer side effects in child cancer patients than conventional radiotherapy.[123] The research said that proton beam radiotherapy 'resulted in acceptable toxicity and had similar survival outcomes to those noted with conventional radiotherapy … '.

Given the adversarial nature of the dispute and the ultimate outcome, the dispute was clearly about what doctors thought was the best treatment for Ashya and what the parents thought was the best treatment for their child, having conducted their own research. A situation such as this may have been ideal for mediation so that both doctors and the parents could have put their views and concerns about both options forward. This arguably would have allowed the parties to seek agreement on the form the treatment would take and avoided the situation where Ashya's parents felt that they were not being listened to and resorted to 'fleeing' with their son abroad. Obviously, there are no guarantees that mediation would have worked in reaching a resolution, but it would certainly have let all parties have their voices heard at the very least.

Ashya's case is not an isolated one. The mother of 7-year-old Neon Roberts disagreed with doctors' recommendation that he should have radiotherapy following the removal of a tumour, as she feared it would cause long-term harm to her son. Doctors believed that unless he received this treatment, Neon would die within three months. Proceedings were issued to obtain the court's consent, but by the time the Court ruled that the treatment should proceed, Neon and his mother had disappeared and could not be located for four days. Bodey J said 'I am worried that her judgment has gone awry as to the extent of the seriousness of the threat which N currently faces'.[124] Neon's mother sought out alternative treatments she hoped would avoid or reduce the long-term side effects of post-operative treatment for brain cancer. However, she failed to produce any evidence at all of the effectiveness of the alternative treatments[125] and

---

[118] The NHS ultimately agreed to pay for the treatment.   [119] [2014] EWHC 2964 (Fam), at 31.

[120] [2014] EWHC 2964 (Fam), at 20.   [121] [2014] EWHC 2964 (Fam), at 35.

[122] Gianluca Mezzofiore, 'So Ashya's parents were RIGHT: Proton beam cancer therapy that forced family to go on the run to Spain because they couldn't get it on the NHS is as good as chemotherapy—and has fewer side effects', *Daily Mail,* 30 January 2016. Available at: http://www.dailymail.co.uk/news/article-3424058/ So-Ashya-s-parents-RIGHT-Proton-beam-cancer-therapy-forced-family-run-Spain-couldn-t-NHS-good-chemotherapy-fewer-effects.html, accessed 15 July 2017.

[123] Yock, T. *et al* 'Long-term toxic effects of proton radiotherapy for paediatric medulloblastoma: a phase 2 single-arm study' (2016) 17 *Lancet Oncology Journal* 287.

[124] *An NHS Trust v SR* [2012] EWHC 3842 (Fam), at [22].   [125] [2012] EWHC 3842 (Fam), at [24].

the Court ultimately ordered the treatment recommended by the doctors to proceed and even placed Neon in his father's care in order to ensure that the treatment took place.

Despite both Ashya's and Neon's parents both resisting recommended treatment and disappearing with their children there is clearly a distinct difference between Ashya's case and Neon's. In the former, Ashya's parents had researched and found an alternative treatment that they truly believed was the better option for him, whereas Neon's mother, despite believing there was an alternative was unable, when given the opportunity, to provide any evidence of such an alternative.[126]

7.2 A move away from 'doctors know best'

Instances such as these do bring into question whether doctors are always best placed to know which treatment is best for children. At one time, the attitudes towards doctors and the culture was one where it was thought that 'doctor knows best', with patients readily accepting doctors' recommendations for treatment without question.[127] Now more parents do question doctors' reasoning and given the vast amount of easily accessible information on the internet are often prepared to extensively research their child's condition and look for possible alternatives to the treatment proposed by the medical profession where they feel that the prospects of success or the potential side effects are too severe. As Anderson stated:

> Patient expectations have changed. Patients are more internet savvy, better able to negotiate the healthcare system and almost certainly more sceptical of the doctor in front of them. The rise in patient as consumers and the well worn mantra of 'no decision about me, without me' have changed patient perceptions on the healthcare system with more vocal and more 'empowered' patients… [128]

In a shift away from the 'doctor knows best' culture, the Royal College of Surgeons has released new guidelines[129] that say that clinicians should take patients through every possible option—even if they believe some will have disadvantages.[130] This guidance was as a direct result of the case of *Montgomery v Lanarkshire Health Board* [131] in which the Court explicitly stated that: '… patients are now widely regarded as persons holding rights, rather than as the passive recipients of the care of the medical profession.'[132]

The Royal College of Surgeons' guidelines advise the medical profession:

> This resolute move away from the more paternalistic traditional model of consent and towards a patient-centred perspective requires a change in attitude from surgeons in discussions about consent, as they are no longer the sole arbiter of determining what risks are material to their patients.[133]

---

[126] [2012] EWHC 3842 (Fam), at [24].

[127] Bodkin, H. and Donnelly, L. 'The end of doctor knows best as medics are told to let patients make their own decision about treatment', *The Telegraph*, 27 October 2016. Available at: http://www.telegraph.co.uk/news/2016/10/26/the-end-of-doctor-knows-best-as-medics-are-told-to-let-patients/, accessed 15 July 2017.

[128] Anderson, F. 'The doctor still knows best' *Health Service Journal*, 15 October 2013. Available at: https://www.hsj.co.uk/comment/the-doctor-still-knows-best/5064259.article, accessed 20 July 2017.

[129] Royal College of Surgeons, 'Consent: Supported Decision-Making, A Guide to Good Practice' (RCS Professional and Clinical Standards, November 2016). Available at: https://www.rcseng.ac.uk/library-and-publications/college-publications/docs/consent-good-practice-guide/, accessed 17 July 2017.

[130] Bodkin, H. and L Donnelly, L. 'The end of doctor knows best as medics are told to let patients make their own decision about treatment', *The Telegraph*, 27 October 2016. Available at: http://www.telegraph.co.uk/news/2016/10/26/the-end-of-doctor-knows-best-as-medics-are-told-to-let-patients/, accessed 15 July 2017.

[131] [2015] UKSC 11.   [132] [2015] UKSC 11, at [75].

[133] Royal College of Surgeons, 'Consent: Supported Decision-Making, A Guide to Good Practice' (RCS Professional and Clinical Standards, November 2016) 3. Available at: https://www.rcseng.ac.uk/library-and-publications/college-publications/docs/consent-good-practice-guide/, accessed 17 July 2017.

If courts are unable to demonstrate understanding of their experiences, parents may not be persuaded that court proceedings have, or will, represent their child's best interests. As a consequence, they may ignore the order of the court and, as in the various ways the parents did in the cases noted here, may feel that they have no option but to take matters into their own hands.

7.3 Parents want to provide every chance for their child

It is understandable that parents with extremely ill children want to give their child every chance of survival and recovery, but there is a point where medical opinions need to be listened to and abided by. The court has to balance the evidence of treatment proposed by the medical profession against the parents' objections and evidence of the efficacy of proposed alternative treatments. This is undoubtedly a difficult task, but ultimately once the court is involved they have to come to a decision based on securing the child's best interests. For example, it was seen in *Re SL (Permission to Vaccinate)*[134] that the alleged risks of vaccination were outweighed by the benefits of immunisation by a clear margin.

Mediating situations such as these has the potential of avoiding a 'winner/loser' outcome and instead possibly allows both parties to feel that a true compromise, understanding, and agreement has been reached. In these circumstances, the child's treatment (whatever that may be) will be able to proceed with all parties supporting this, which has to be more beneficial than one party feeling that they have been aggrieved and forced into this situation.

Even where the court has ruled that further treatment cannot be ordered due to medical opinion, parents may themselves attempt to raise the funds to provide what they perceive their child is being denied. This was the case with Jaymee Bowen, who was 10 years old and suffering from leukaemia. The proposed treatment consisted of first an additional course of chemotherapy with a 10–20% chance of success and if successful and remission achieved then it would be followed by a second bone marrow transplant which also had the same odds of success. Her father had applied to the court to ask for them to order Cambridge Health Authority to fund the additional treatment.[135] The authority had refused because the treatment, which was viewed as experimental, would not be in the best interests of Jaymee. When the Court refused to grant this order, Jaymee's father applied to the Court asking them to end the order that was protecting her anonymity so he could raise the money required for treatment by publicising Jaymee's situation. The Court agreed to do this and an anonymous benefactor provided the money required.[136] Jaymee lived a year longer than doctors had expected her to, but ultimately died a painful death.

One of the main issues Jaymee's father had in relation to the health authority was the lack of communication between them. He wanted to discuss the alternative options for treatment with the doctors and health authority and wanted to 'sit down and thrash out the differences between them.' However, he claimed that all communications with the NHS managers were by fax and phone.[137] This lack of communication and explanation was something that was criticised in a report about Jaymee's case.[138] This lends greater support for the use of mediation in circumstances such as these, which ultimately may have avoided the adversarial proceedings through the court.

---

[134] [2017] EWHC 125 (Fam).   [135] *R v Cambridge Health Authority, ex parte B* [1995] 2 All ER 129.

[136] Bridgeman, J. 'Contested care: when disputes over child cancer treatment reach the courts', *The Conversation*, 18 August 2016. Available at: http://theconversation.com/contested-care-when-disputes-over-child-cancer-treatment-reach-the-courts-63004, accessed 21 July 2017.

[137] Lawrence, J. *The Independent*, 13 May 1998. Available at: http://www.independent.co.uk/life-style/child-b-the-truth-about-her-last-days-1159951.html, accessed 20 July 2017.

[138] Ham, C. 'Tragic Choices in Health Care: Lessons From the Child B Case' (1999) 319 *British Medical Journal* 1258.

8. Are courts the only or best option?

Given that some parents may feel that the courts are not best placed to make decisions regarding their child's medical treatment, mediation may, in some cases, result in parents feeling that they have had a full opportunity for their views and concerns to be heard. [139]

Given that disputes that arise between parents and doctors may involve the courts in an adversarial setting where the ultimate decision is made, not by the parents or doctors but by judges, it may be possible in some circumstances to use alternative methods to deal with such disputes. It is not suggested that the courts are obsolete in circumstances such as these, but instead that there may be alternative processes avoiding the need for court involvement on some occasions. Each party involved—parents, doctors, and the court— are focusing on what they believe to the best option for the child and think that they are acting in the child's best interests. The problem is that each party may come to different views over what form those best interests take. When an application is made to the court under the inherent jurisdiction to resolve disputes between parents and doctors over a child's medical treatment, the process does not always lead to the parents feeling that their views about their own child, who they would claim to know better than anyone else, have been taken seriously enough. The court process may leave parents feeling they have few choices and without a voice.[140]

The use of alternative dispute resolution is becoming more valued and in some cases is actually strongly encouraged. There is a requirement for certain family disputes to be taken to alternative dispute resolution before any application can be made to a court or tribunal. In employment disputes and claims to employment tribunals, there is a requirement that parties initially try to resolve the issues by the use of alternative dispute resolution and only if this fails can an application be made to a tribunal to hear the case if a resolution has not been possible.[141] Disputes between parents about arrangements for their children upon separation must be dealt with initially with through a Mediation Information and Assessment Meeting, attended by both parents, to consider possible alternatives to the court such as mediation (see Chapter 15).[142]

Mediation provides a forum for disputes to be dealt with outside the adversarial court setting. In the Civil Procedure Rules, alternative dispute resolution is described as a 'collective description of methods of resolving disputes otherwise than through the normal trial process'[143] whilst the Family Procedure Rules defined alternative dispute resolution as meaning '… methods of resolving a dispute, including mediation, other than through the

---

[139] The suggestion of the use of mediation as a means to avoid these extreme situations and to assist in both the medical professionals and parents both feeling that their voice has been heard and avoiding the need for court involvement was discussed in a paper presented by Scullion, D., Choong K., and McAndry, E., 'Mediating the Conflicting Attitudes of Doctors and Parents to the Treatment of Child Cancer Patients' paper presented at Changing Attitudes to Cancer Conference, 22 April 2015, University of Central Lancashire. Available at: https://mix.office.com/watch/187xk2f7i3npm, accessed 29 September 2017.

[140] Stanbury, G. 'The Shape of New Justice?' (2016) 166 *New Law Journal* 7725, 17–18, 18.

[141] ACAS Conciliation involves an independent ACAS conciliator who discusses the issues with both parties in order to help them reach a better understanding of each other's position and underlying interests. Without taking sides, the conciliator tries to encourage the parties in a dispute to come to an agreement between themselves. See http://www.acas.org.uk/media/pdf/o/g/Conciliation-Explained-Acas.pdf, accessed 11 July 2017.

[142] Employment Tribunals Act 1996, s. 18A (as amended by s. 7 of the Enterprise and Regulatory Reform Act 2013). With effect from April 2014, employment disputes have to go to ACAS for mandatory pre-claim conciliation before issuing a claim form for most types of claim.

[143] Civil Procedure Rules, glossary. Available at: https://www.justice.gov.uk/courts/procedure-rules/civil#pagetop, accessed 11 July 2017.

normal court process'. Mediation is a process that involves the voluntary participation by the parties to enable a resolution to be reached. Given that mediation is voluntary, there has been some discussion as to the courts' role and power to order mediation. In *Halsey v Milton Keynes General NHS Trust*[144] the Court acknowledged that, despite the possible benefits of alternative dispute resolution to resolving the dispute, they did not have the power to order the parties to take part in the process. However, Dyson LJ also stated that:

> Parties sometimes need to be encouraged by the court to embark on an Alternative Dispute Resolution. The need for such encouragement should diminish in time if the virtue of ADR in suitable cases is demonstrated even more convincingly than it has been thus far. The value and importance of ADR have been established within a remarkably short time. All members of the legal profession who conduct litigation should now routinely consider with their clients whether their disputes are suitable for ADR. But we reiterate that the court's role is to encourage, not to compel. The form of encouragement may be robust.[145]

The way the courts have 'encouraged' parties to take part in alternative dispute resolution is to penalise parties financially by reducing the amount of costs awarded, even when successful in their case, where they have unreasonably refused to undertake mediation prior to the case being brought to court.[146] In *Christian v The Commission of Police for the Metropolis*[147] the Court found that the defendant had failed to give a full and reasonable response, as required by the Pre-Action Protocol, as to why they were not engaging in alternative dispute resolution.[148] They had also ignored several attempts to bring the matter to alternative dispute resolution, which may have been successful in the circumstances and therefore should have been attempted. Although this case was not one which concerned medical decisions, it does demonstrate the courts' approach to mediation as a means of potentially avoiding the need for court involvement.

Overall, the benefit of engaging with alternative dispute resolution, and particularly in mediation, is that the parties themselves are able to discuss their particular concerns, raise questions, and seek answers to questions they have. Although this is something that you would hope would take place as a normal routine procedure, there may be occasions where the mediation process can help to bring this about more effectively. Where parents feel that there is an imbalance of power between themselves and the medical profession, mediation provides a forum for their concerns, thoughts, and feelings to be aired in a balanced and impartial setting. Mediation is about the parties being able to come to an agreement themselves, that both parties can accept. The role of the mediator is merely to facilitate these discussions, not to make any judgements or determine the ultimate decision or outcome.[149] This has the potential to diffuse tensions and clarify any misunderstandings that may exist between the medical professionals and the parents of a sick child, providing circumstances for a reasoned and fully considered outcome. If after mediation no agreement has been reached, it still allows the parties to turn to the court for the ultimate decision to be made as to the best interests of the child within this context.

---

[144] [2004] EWCA Civ 576; [2004] 1 WLR 3002.   [145] [2004] EWCA Civ 576, Dyson LJ.

[146] *Christian v The Commission of Police for the Metropolis* [2015] EWHC 371 (QB). In this case the successful party only received two thirds of their costs, the other third was withheld as a sanction for the party unreasonably refusing to mediate.

[147] [2015] EWHC 371 (QB).

[148] Practice Direction—Pre-Action Conduct and Protocols, para 11. Available at: https://www.justice.gov.uk/courts/procedure-rules/civil/rules/pd_pre-action_conduct, accessed 15 July 2017.

[149] National Family Mediation. Available at: http://www.nfm.org.uk/index.php/family-mediation/principles-of-mediation, accessed 15 July 2017.

**DEBATE 3: ARE THERE ALTERNATIVES TO THE COURT'S
INTERVENTION IN MAKING MEDICAL DECISIONS
CONCERNING CHILDREN?**

Given the preceding discussion, there are many reasons why the adversarial nature of these disputes are damaging for the parties involved, particularly the parents who are resisting the treatment proposed by the medical profession. This form of dispute could potentially benefit from mediation and result in better solutions, which ultimately would help to avoid the 'entrenchment and further escalation of already strongly held opinions'.[150]

In order for mediation to have a chance of success, it is crucial that the mediator is truly an independent person. In her comments on the case of Charlotte Wyatt,[151] concerning whether Charlotte should continue to receive artificial ventilation, Brazier has argued that, 'The judge is in a sense undertaking in part the role of mediator. Some of what he is asked to do resembles the function more usually accorded to that of hospital or clinical ethics committees. Yet as a mediator he cannot command total confidence because ultimately he decides.'[152]

Hospitals maintain ethics committees to help clinicians take medical decisions that impact on individuals or have wider ethical implications. There is no doubt that members of such committees would be extremely useful in terms of pooling expertise and providing a less formal process and setting when compared with courts.[153] However, they would arguably not be suitable to mediate disputes of the nature discussed in this chapter. Parents would not view members of the committees as impartial or independent. This would undermine the whole idea of the mediation and would hinder, if not make impossible, any agreement between the parties.[154] As Meller and Barclay commented on Charlotte Wyatt's case, all that was left following the long and highly adversarial battle through the court was 'an embittered and fragmented family, a child in foster care and six-figure costs for the hospital trust ... With no real closure to this tragic case.'[155] This requires complete impartiality from a mediator who has an understanding of medical law and particularly the role and importance of consent to treatment. General Medical Council guidance, concerning consent and patients and doctors making decisions together, explicitly suggests mediation as one of the ways that should be considered where disputes arise.[156]

As Meller and Barclay succinctly stated:

> ... alternative dispute resolution, if delivered in a truly independent manner by an expert mediator, might be able to provide a better solution than the externally imposed judgment of the court.[157]

---

[150] Meller, S. and Barclay, S. 'Mediation: An Approach to Intractable Disputes Between Parents and Paediatricians' (2011) 96 *Archives of Disease in Childhood* 619, 619.

[151] *Re Wyatt (A Child) (Medical Treatment: Parent's Consent)* [2004] EWHC 2247; [2005] All ER (D) 294; [2005] EWHC 693 (Fam).

[152] Brazier, M. 'An Intractable Dispute: When Parents and Professionals Disagree' (2005) 13 *Medical Law Review* 412, 417.

[153] Huxtable, R. 'The Best of Both Worlds? Combining Courts and Clinical Ethics Committees' (2013) 1 *Journal of Professional Negligence* 25, 37.

[154] S Meller and S Barclay, 'Mediation: An approach to intractable disputes between parents and paediatricians' (2011) 96 (7) Archives of Disease in Childhood 619 at 619.

[155] Meller, S. and Barclay, S. 'Mediation: An Approach to Intractable Disputes Between Parents and Paediatricians' (2011) 96 *Archives of Disease in Childhood* 619, 620.

[156] General Medical Council, (2008) 'Consent: patients and doctors making decisions together' (2008) 32, para 77. Available at http://www.gmc-uk.org/Consent___English_1015.pdf_48903482.pdf, accessed 29 September 2017.

[157] Meller, S. and Barclay, S. 'Mediation: An Approach to Intractable Disputes Between Parents and Paediatricians' (2011) 96 *Archives of Disease in Childhood* 619, 621.

There has been judicial support and, in fact, encouragement for the use of mediation in cases where there are disputes concerning the appropriate treatment of children. In the case of Charlie Gard, Francis J stated 'It is my clear view that mediation should be attempted in all cases such as this one even if all that it does is achieve a greater understanding by the parties of each other's positions.'[158] There is evidence that mediation within this context does have its benefits for both parties. Aside from the financial benefits, with mediation costing less than the court process, it facilitates parties' ability to address '… the real causes of the dispute as well as reducing the alienation of the parties and restoring relationships between them'.[159]

SUMMARY

1. What is the role of consent and *Gillick* competence in promoting the child's autonomy in decision-making?
   - Children over 16 years of age have a statutory right to consent to treatment under s. 8 of the Family Law Reform Act 1969.
   - *Gillick* competence paved the way for children's autonomy to be recognised within the sphere of the provision of medical treatment and children's competence under the age of 16 to consent to medical treatment.

2. Should a more honest approach to *Gillick* competence be taken?
   - There is evidence that the reluctance of the courts to recognise a child's autonomy and respect their wishes and feelings is most evident where there is a refusal of treatment where the ultimate outcome may be significant harm or potentially death.
   - Despite the decision in *Gillick*, the limits placed on the implementation and assessment of a child's competence has greatly limited children's ability to make decisions about their own medical treatment, particularly in relation to refusing treatment.
   - Both parents and the courts can override a child's refusal of medical treatment.
   - A parent cannot override a competent child's consent to medical treatment, however the court can if it is thought to be in the child's best interests.

3. Are there alternatives to the court's intervention in making medical decisions concerning children?
   - At times parents disagree with doctors over the best way forward and the most appropriate treatment for their child.
   - Disputes arise most often where parents do not want their child to undergo a particular treatment, for example a blood transfusion, due to the religious beliefs of both parent(s) and child. The court in these circumstances have no option but to make a decision based on what is believed to be in the best interests of the child, taking into consideration the medical opinion, the views of the parents, and the outcome for the child.

---

[158] *Great Ormond Street Hospital v Yates and Gard* [2017] EWHC 1909 (Fam), at [20].

[159] Meller, S. and Barclay, S. 'Mediation: An Approach to Intractable Disputes Between Parents and Paediatricians' (2011) 96 *Archives of Disease in Childhood* 619, 620.

- There has been a move away from a culture where 'doctor knows best'. The availability of a vast amount of information on the internet has allowed individuals to research the medical condition their child is suffering from and look for all possible avenues for treatment, even those not freely available in the UK.
- Mediation could provide an alternative, less adversarial process and setting when compared with the courts. Mediation could provide a forum where both parties are able to fully discuss and explain their views and try to reach an acceptable agreement for both parties.
- This form of mediation would require specialist independent mediators who are knowledgeable in medical ethics and law and must be truly independent from both hospital and parents.

Further Reading

ALLEN, M.T. 'A New Way to Settle Old Disputes: Mediation and Healthcare' (2005) 73 *Medico-Legal Journal* 93
- Shows that there is a spectrum of useful processes available for the resolution of medical disputes. Also considers the blame culture, how this can be managed in practice through mediation and whether the mediation process might offer a channel to moderate issues of blame more subtly than that offered by the traditional court approach.

BRIDGEMAN, J. 'Old Enough to Know Best?' (1993) 13 *Legal Studies* 69
- Discusses whether there are any circumstances in which a teenager may effectively withhold their consent to medical treatment where the decision is actually respected and the treatment prevented. Argues that it is necessary to stop and re-assess the relationship between the generations, looking to what young people want for themselves rather than finding ways to achieve what others—parents, doctors, local authorities, the judiciary—desire in an attempt to satisfy their own need to act.

CAVE E, 'Goodbye Gillick? Identifying and Resolving Problems With the Concept of Child Competence.' (2014) 34 *Legal Studies* 103–22
- Assesses the viability of the test of a child's competence to consent to medical treatment as set out by the House of Lords in *Gillick v West Norfolk and Wisbech AHA*. Highlights potential deficiencies with the concept of *Gillick* competence. Looks at arguments that provisions of the Mental Capacity Act 2005 could be applied instead to minors, possibly in conjunction with a new common law test for child incapacity.

GILMORE, S. and HERRING, J. '"No" is the Hardest Word: Consent and Children's Autonomy' (2011) 23 *Child and Family Law Quarterly* 3–25
- Defends the view expressed by the Court of Appeal in *Re R (A Minor) (Wardship: Consent to Treatment)* and *Re W (A Minor) (Medical Treatment: Court's Jurisdiction)*, in relation to *Gillick* competence in cases where a child refuses to give consent to medical treatment, that there could be concurrent powers to consent in parent and child.

PEARCE, J. 'Consent to Treatment During Childhood, The Assessment of Competence and Avoidance of Conflict' (1994) 165 *British Journal of Psychiatry* 713
- Discusses the decisions in *Re R* and *Re W* and the idea of assessing the competence of a child. Draws distinctions between competence for giving consent and that required for refusal. Argues that a more stringent test should be applied when assessing a child's ability to refuse consent than when assessing competence to consent.

11

Public Law Protection

Penelope Russell

LEARNING OBJECTIVES

After reading this chapter you will be able to:

- Appreciate the difficulties facing the court and safeguarding agencies in the public law protection of children;
- Identify the rules which enable intervention into family life and the range of orders available to the court;
- Provide a critical analysis of the statutory framework and case law development in public law protection.

DEBATES

After reading this chapter you should be equipped to discuss your opinion on the following central debates:

1. Given the threat of compulsory state intervention, can a partnership between parents and safeguarding agencies ever be truly voluntary?

2. What balance should be struck between protecting children from harm and avoiding unwarranted interference in family life?

3. In care proceedings, to what extent should the court allow parents to present their case, given the disadvantages that delay may bring for a child?

4. Is the standard of proof in care proceedings set at the right level?

1. Introduction

Public law protection of children challenges one of the fundamental principles of England and Wales: that children are best brought up by their parents. Unlimited state intervention in the family is not permitted and the courts have to strike a balance between maintaining stability for children within their family, and protecting them from harm. This is a difficult balancing act for the court as the picture is complex. Removal from the family may enable a child to avoid further abuse at the hands of their parents, yet they may face an uncertain future in the care system, enduring multiple changes of carer if adoption is not possible.

Statistics show that 68% of looked after children in England had one placement during the year, 21% had two placements, and 10% had three or more placements.[1] Outcomes for children in the care system are poor. Care leavers are over-represented in prison[2]: they are six times more likely to be cautioned or convicted of an offence than other children.[3] Children in care underachieve at school: in 2015 14% of children in care in England achieved five or more A*–C GCSEs or equivalent, including English and mathematics, compared to 53% of children in the general population.[4] Some children even suffer abuse in the care system.[5] On the other hand, returning the child to their parents runs the risk of further abuse and eventual final removal, with the NSPCC reporting that around half of those returned home then suffer further abuse or neglect.[6]

The approach of public law protection is that children should remain with their families unless that is not in their best interests. Removal of a child from their family is a violation of the child's and the child's parents' rights to respect for a private and family life under Article 8 of the European Convention on Human Rights and Fundamental Freedoms 1950 (ECHR) (see further Chapter 13) unless the intervention can be shown to be proportionate to the aims pursued.[7] Thus the state, in the form of the local authority, should exhaust all options before removal of the child from their family and obtain court sanction of steps to remove a child forcibly. In addition there must be procedural fairness for the parents: otherwise there would be a potential breach of Article 6 ECHR (the right to a fair and timely hearing) if parents are not fully involved in the decision-making process.

The legal framework provided by the Children Act 1989 tries to strike a balance between intervention and non-intervention.[8] There have been notable failures of the system: of both intervening too readily, for example the Cleveland child abuse scandal in the 1980s where more than 100 children were removed from their parents on suspicion of sexual abuse based on the evidence of only two paediatricians using subsequently discredited methods, and more recently of not intervening soon enough including horrific abuse suffered by Victoria Climbie in 2001 and Peter Connolly in 2007 amongst many others. A number of reviews have been undertaken into child safeguarding and they all emphasise better interagency working. For example the Cleveland Report[9] in 1987 recommended improved communication between professionals. The Laming Report[10] in 2003, following the death of Victoria Climbie, criticised social workers in that case for poor coordination, limited sharing of information, and a lack of accountability. The latest review[11] in 2009, following the death of Peter Connolly, suggested changes

---

[1] Department for Education Statistical First Release SFR 41/2016 (DfE, 2016).

[2] Lord Laming 'In Care, Out of Trouble' (Prison Reform Trust, 2016) 5.

[3] Lord Laming 'In Care, Out of Trouble' (Prison Reform Trust, 2016) 26.

[4] Lord Laming 'In Care, Out of Trouble' (Prison Reform Trust, 2016) 26.

[5] Department of Health 'Lost in Care: Report of the Tribunal of Enquiry into the Abuse of Children in Care in the former County Council areas of Gwynedd and Clwyd since 1974' (Department of Health, 2000); Biehal, N. et al 'Keeping Children Safe: Allegations Concerning the Abuse or Neglect of Children in Care' (NSPCC, 2014).

[6] NSPCC, 'Returning Home from Care' (NSPCC, 2012).

[7] *Kutzner v Germany* [2003] 1 FCR 249.

[8] Unless stated otherwise, all references to statutory provisions in this chapter are to the Children Act 1989.

[9] Butler-Sloss, E. 'Report of the Inquiry into Child Abuse in Cleveland 1987' (Cm 412, 1988).

[10] Lord Laming 'Report of the Victoria Climbie Inquiry' (HMSO, 2003).

[11] Lord Laming 'The Protection of Children in England: A Progress Report' (HMSO, 2009).

to the recruitment and training of social workers but also put the onus on working in partnership: partnership between parents, the local authority, and all other safeguarding agencies including schools, housing authorities, National Health Service organisations, police, and voluntary agencies.

Working in partnership is now required by the Children Act 2004: under s. 10 all agencies must work together to protect children. Families can access services through local multi-agency support teams comprising representatives from a range of safeguarding agencies, with the aim that services are coordinated across the area and tailored to each family's needs. A troubled family may be involved with a number of organisations: the local authority children's social work team, the police pursuing neighbour complaints of antisocial behaviour, and the environmental health team investigating living conditions at the family home, as well as the school, GP, health visitor, and voluntary agencies such as mental health and alcohol dependency charities. These agencies (and others) are required to share information with each other about the family so that all can be alert to the risks posed to the children and take prompt emergency action if needed.

In this chapter we consider the statutory duties of the local authority towards children as well as emergency action to protect a child. What has to be proven to obtain a care order and the evidential difficulties connected with this are examined, in particular the difficulties posed for the courts where harm is caused to a child by an unknown perpetrator. The chapter ends by exploring the options available to the court at the welfare assessment once the threshold criteria have been met.

2. Local authority duties

Part III of the Children Act 1989 sets out duties of the local authority to provide support for children and their families in their area. There are three duties of the local authority that are considered here: the general duty to children in need, the duty to provide accommodation, and the duty to carry out an investigation.

2.1 Duty to children in need

The local authority has a general duty to safeguard and promote the welfare of children in need and to promote the upbringing of such children by their families by providing services.[12] 'Children in need' are defined widely within the Children Act 1989.

 Key Legislation 1: s. 17(10)

A child shall be taken to be in need if:

(a) he is unlikely to achieve or maintain, or to have the opportunity of achieving or maintaining, a reasonable standard of health or development without the provision of services by a local authority;

(b) His health or development is likely to be significantly impaired, or further impaired, without the provision for him of such services; or

(c) He is disabled.

---

[12] Section 17(1) of the Children Act 1989.

The definition in s. 17(10) includes children who may suffer detriment in the future as well as those currently disadvantaged. The definition of 'child in need' refers to the child's health or development which is also defined widely: 'health' means physical or mental health and 'development' means physical, intellectual, emotional, social, or behavioural development.[13] A child is 'disabled' within the statutory definition if he is blind, deaf, or dumb or suffers from mental disorder of any kind or is substantially and permanently handicapped by illness, injury, or congenital deformity or such other disability.[14]

As the aim of s. 17 is to promote the upbringing of a child by their family, support can be provided to the child's family members as well as to the child himself.[15] The support can include advice, guidance, and counselling; occupational, social, cultural, or recreational activities; home help and assistance with travel and holiday expenses.[16] It can be given in kind or in cash[17] so, by way of example, it could include the provision of cash to pay bills, a washing machine for the family, or a place at a family centre. Services can be provided to the child and his family by a range of agencies. These may include the local children's services authority, the local housing authority, or the local National Health Service trust.[18]

The s. 17 duty has been watered down by successive court judgments. For example, it was held in the High Court case of *R v London Borough of Barnet, ex parte B*[19] that the local authority has discretion about how to meet the duty and can take into account budgetary restraints when deciding on the services to be provided to children in need and their families. In this case, the parents challenged by way of judicial review the local authority's decision to close their child's nursery but their application was dismissed by the Court.

In addition an individual child does not have an enforceable right to services under s. 17. In the conjoined appeals of *R (G) v Barnet London Borough Council; R (W) v Lambeth London Borough Council; R (A) v Lambeth London Borough Council*[20] the Supreme Court considered the nature of the s. 17 duty. By a majority, the Court held that s. 17 imposes a general duty towards children in the local authority's area, not a specific duty to each individual child in need. Lord Nicholls said: 'The so-called "general duty" in s.17(1) is owed to all the children who are in need within their area and not to each child in need individually ... A child in need within the meaning of s.17(10) is eligible for the provision of those services but he has no absolute right to them.'[21]

Although a parent cannot challenge the local authority's use of their discretion in meeting their s. 17 duty, a parent can challenge the process of assessment of their child's needs: for example whether the information gathered by the local authority was sufficient. Ryder LJ sitting in the Court of Appeal in the case of *R (C) v Southwark London Borough Council*[22] set out the requirements: a local authority must be able to demonstrate that the assessment of the child complied with their own local assessment protocol and with the requirements set out in the common assessment framework as prescribed by the Secretary of State.[23] He said: 'The section 17 scheme involves an exercise of social work judgement based on the analysis of information derived from an assessment that is applicable to a heterogeneous group of those in need.'[24] Nevertheless, the family's appeal against a refusal of judicial review was dismissed because the local authority was held to have not followed a flawed policy or practice fettering its discretion.

---

[13] Section 17(11).   [14] Section 17(11).   [15] Section 17(3).   [16] Schedule 2, para 8.
[17] Section 17(6).   [18] Section 27(3).   [19] [1994] 1 FLR 592.   [20] [2003] UKHL 57.
[21] [2003] UKHL 57, at [85].   [22] [2016] EWCA Civ 707.
[23] HM Government 'Working Together to Safeguard Children' (HMSO, 2015).
[24] [2016] EWCA Civ 707, at [22].

2.2 **Duty to provide accommodation**

One route for a child to enter the care system is under s. 20 of the Children Act 1989. By virtue of this provision the local authority can provide accommodation for a child and this includes both respite care as well as more long-term accommodation. It most commonly occurs where the relationship between parent and child has broken down and they cannot continue to live together.[25]

The local authority has a duty to provide accommodation to a child in need if one of the conditions within s. 20(1) are met namely that there is no person who has parental responsibility for the child or that the child is lost or abandoned or that the person who has been caring for the child is prevented from providing the child with suitable accommodation or care.

In addition, under s. 20(4), the local authority has a discretionary power to provide accommodation to a child if it would safeguard or promote the child's welfare, even where the child is not a child in need and where there is a person with parental responsibility for him who is able to provide accommodation.

 Context 1: Accommodation Under s. 20

In the year ending 31 March 2016, 19,400 children in England started to be accommodated under s. 20 of the Children Act 1989. This represents 61% of all the children who started to be looked after by the local authority in that period.[26] This means that the majority of children who enter local authority care do so under s. 20 without court scrutiny. However, the position is different when considering a snapshot of looked after children at any one time: as at 31 March 2016, 18,730 children were being accommodated under s. 20 compared to 45,440 children being looked after under care orders.[27] This is because accommodation under s. 20 tends to be of shorter duration. Nevertheless s. 20 accommodation agreements remain of significance as they constitute the entry route into care for more than three fifths of children entering care and the legal status of over a quarter of children already in the care system.

A child being accommodated under s. 20 would be removed from the care of the resident parent and placed with a (non-resident) parent or person with parental responsibility unless this would not be consistent with his welfare or reasonably practicable[28] or with a relative, friend, or other person connected with them.[29] Alternatively, a child might be placed with foster parents or in a care home. A placement should be within the child's local area so that there is no disruption to their schooling and they are able to live with siblings[30] and maintain contact with parents.[31] The local authority should consider the child's wishes, having regard to their age and understanding, in determining the place of accommodation[32] and also before taking any decisions about the child.[33]

Unlike s. 17, the local authority does have an enforceable duty to individual children to provide accommodation. This is illustrated by *R (G) v Southwark London Borough Council*[34]

---

[25] *Practice Guidance for the use of s.20 provision in the Children Act 1989 in England and Wales and the equivalent s.76 of the Social Services and well-being (Wales) Act 2014 in Wales* 2014 (ADCS, Cafcass, and ADSS Cymru) para 10.

[26] Department for Education Statistical First Release SFR 41/2016 (DfE, 2016).

[27] Department for Education Statistical First Release SFR 41/2016 (DfE, 2016).

[28] Section 22C(3) and (4).   [29] Section 22C(6).   [30] Section 22C(8).   [31] Section 34.

[32] Section 20(6).   [33] Section 22(4).   [34] [2009] UKHL 26.

where the House of Lords allowed the appeal of a homeless sofa-surfing 17-year-old that he should have been accommodated by the local authority under s. 20, not simply provided with help under s. 17 by being referred to the local housing department. It was held that the local authority was not allowed to avoid its duty to accommodate under s. 20 by giving the provision of accommodation a different label. Baroness Hale, who gave the lead judgment, said that applying the provision 'involves an evaluative judgement on some matters but not a discretion'.[35] There is an enforceable duty to an individual child under s. 20.

The provision of accommodation under s. 20 is deemed to be a voluntary arrangement, taken in partnership with the child and their parents. The local authority does not acquire parental responsibility when providing such accommodation. Hedley J sitting in the High Court case of *Coventry City Council v C*[36] said: 'The emphasis in Part III is on partnership and it involves no compulsory curtailment of parental responsibility'.[37] Any person with parental responsibility can remove the child at any time without notice[38] and the duty to provide accommodation does not arise if a person with parental responsibility objects and is able to accommodate the child themselves.[39] There are two exceptions. The first exception is where the child is aged 16 or over and the child agrees to being accommodated by the local authority.[40] The second exception is where there is a child arrangements order specifying with whom the child is to live and that person consents to the local authority accommodation.[41]

Accommodation under s. 20 may therefore not be appropriate where the child is suffering or is likely to suffer significant harm and the cooperation of the parents cannot be guaranteed: the commencement of care proceedings would be needed instead to ensure the child's protection. In fact, the local authority is obliged by the pre-proceedings Public Law Outline[42] to give a warning to parents if care proceedings are envisaged. Such a warning may enable the local authority to avoid the risk and expense of care proceedings but challenges the voluntary nature of a s. 20 arrangement.

In the case of *N (Children) (Adoption: Jurisdiction)*[43] the President of the Family Division, Sir James Munby, commented on the use of s. 20 arrangements. In that case, the children were accommodated in May 2013 but care proceedings were not commenced until eight months later, in January 2014. Munby P. said: '. . . section 20 may, in an appropriate case, have a proper role to play as a short term measure . . . but the use of section 20 as a prelude to care proceedings for a period as long as here is wholly unacceptable'.[44] He reviewed recent case law concerning s. 20 arrangements which highlighted a number of problems, including a failure to obtain informed consent from parents at the outset, a reluctance to return the child to the parents immediately upon a withdrawal of parental consent, and arrangements that were allowed to go on for far too long. Munby P. said that the misuse of s. 20 arrangements by local authorities 'will no longer be tolerated' and 'must stop'.[45] He set out requirements for good practice which include any s. 20 arrangement being set out in writing and signed by the parents.[46]

---

[35] [2009] UKHL 26 at [31].   [36] [2012] EWHC 2190 (Fam).
[37] [2012] EWHC 2190 (Fam), at [25].   [38] Section 20(8).   [39] Section 20(7).
[40] Section 20(11).   [41] Section 20(9).
[42] Department for Education 'Court orders and pre-proceedings for local authorities' (DfE, 2014) Annex A: Pre-proceedings flow chart; Practice Direction 12A Public Law Outline 2014.
[43] [2015] EWCA Civ 1112.   [44] [2015] EWCA Civ 1112, at [157].
[45] [2015] EWCA Civ 1112, at [171].   [46] [2015] EWCA Civ 1112, at [170].

❓ Debate 1: Given the Threat of Compulsory State Intervention, can a Partnership Between Parents and Safeguarding Agencies Ever be Truly Voluntary?

One debate concerns the appropriate use of s. 20 accommodation agreements. They are entered into against a backdrop of possible state intervention which causes commentators to question the voluntary nature of these arrangements. This is a particularly pressing issue because of the prevalence of accommodation agreements: the majority of children who enter local authority care do so by agreement with the parents under s. 20.[47]

For some families, arrangements to accommodate a child can provide a welcome respite at a time of acute pressure such as parental illness or bereavement. However, the voluntary nature of s. 20 arrangements means that they are not subject to court scrutiny so can offer the local authority a convenient way of bypassing legal safeguards for parents. Undoubtedly, there is the potential for misuse: parents can feel pressured into consenting to accommodation even in circumstances where the local authority would struggle to meet the threshold criteria for a care order. This is a particular concern where the parents lack legal advice.

The President of the Family Division has recently criticised the practice of some local authorities of entering into s. 20 agreements without first having obtained consent from the parents.[48] Munby P has said: 'The misuse and abuse of section 20 in this context is not just a matter of bad practice. It is wrong; it is a denial of the fundamental rights of both the parents and the child; it will no longer be tolerated; and it must stop. Judges will and must be alert to the problem and pro-active in putting an end to it'.[49] However, a requirement for genuine consent is problematic, taking into account the coercive environment of child safeguarding, in which lack of parental cooperation can be used to justify removal of the child. In reality, many parents may find it difficult to object to accommodation under s. 20.

The threat of public law proceedings can be seen as undermining any agreement entered into by parents. Such arrangements have the potential to be oppressive if parents feel that signing is their only option because the alternative (enforced removal of their child) would be worse. For example, agreements for s. 20 placement are common at the early stages of care proceedings. This is because parents wish to avoid a court finding that the threshold for an interim care order is met and prefer to retain some semblance of control over what happens to their child, even if illusory.

Arguably s. 20 arrangements are most appropriate when triggered by the parent suffering a temporary, short-term difficulty. The President of the Family Division has criticised the long-term use of s. 20 agreements (such as where the child had been in a s. 20 placement for two years[50]) because prolonged use deprives the child of court planning for their welfare and legal restrictions on delay. However, Judith Masson has argued that in some circumstances the child's interests may be served by delaying the commencement of care proceedings: a voluntary arrangement can be right for the child if the accommodation is envisaged as temporary only or if the child is in safe care and the immediate commencement of care proceedings would be oppressive because of the vulnerability of the parent at that particular time.[51]

The availability of s. 20 arrangements can benefit parents needing respite care for the child by enabling them to avoid compulsory intervention and, for some parents, s. 20 can

---

[47] Department for Education Statistical First Release SFR 41/2016 (DfE, 2016).
[48] *N (Children) (Adoption: Jurisdiction)* [2015] EWCA Civ 1112.   [49] [2015] EWCA Civ 1112 at [171].
[50] *Re P (A child: Use of Section 20)* [2014] EWFC 775.
[51] Masson, J. 'Questioning the use of s.20' *Family Law Week* (2015) 46. Available at: http://www.familylawweek. co.uk/site.aspx?i=ed151621, accessed 29 September 2017.

offer a legitimate alternative to court imposed controls. Judith Masson has argued that the prevalence of such agreements could be viewed as a consequence of the success of working partnerships for planning between parents and safeguarding agencies, rather than a result of coercive action.[52] Nevertheless, can s.20 accommodation arrangements ever be considered truly voluntary and, if not, what is their appropriate use?

It is important to note that voluntary accommodation of a child under s. 20 is entirely different from compulsory accommodation pursuant to a care order. Under s. 20, the powers of the local authority are limited as they are not allowed to remove a child forcibly. In the High Court case of *R (G) v Nottingham City Council* [53] Munby J returned a newborn baby to his mother because no court order had been made authorising the removal of the child. This was despite the fact that the mother had a history of alcohol, drug abuse, and self-harming. If the local authority wish to remove the child without the consent of the parents, a court order authorising that step is required. In addition, the local authority is not able to move a child to different accommodation without the agreement of the parents under s. 20. In the High Court case of *R v Tameside MBC, ex parte J* [54] it was held that a severely disabled 13-year-old girl could not be moved from a residential home into foster care because her parents did not agree with the move and the local authority had not obtained court approval.

Although the powers of the local authority are more limited under a s. 20 arrangement, the status of a voluntarily accommodated child (if accommodated for a continuous period of more than 24 hours[55]) is the same when being accommodated by virtue of a care order. They are both a 'looked after' child under s. 22. This brings benefits to a child because the local authority has additional duties to safeguard and promote the child's welfare.[56] In the High Court case of *R (A) v Coventry City Council*[57] it was held that this includes a duty to maintain the child 'in other respects apart from the provision of accommodation' such as financial support and payment of an allowance for carers. The local authority also has a duty to advise, assist, and befriend a looked after child once they have ceased to accommodate him.[58] This can have long-term practical benefits, particularly for an older child.

2.3 Duty to carry out an investigation

There are two ways that the duty to carry out an investigation may arise: either circumstances may trigger the need for an investigation (s. 47) or the local authority may be directed by the court to carry out an investigation (s. 37).

2.3.1 Section 47 investigation

The local authority has a duty to make enquiries about a child's welfare where the child lives in their area and there is reasonable cause to suspect that the child is suffering or is likely to suffer significant harm.[59] The enquiries are to enable the local authority to decide whether any action is needed to safeguard or promote the child's welfare.[60]

For example, a referral may be made to the local authority's children's social care team by a teacher, GP, police officer, health visitor, family member, or concerned member of

---

[52] Masson, J. 'Questioning the use of s.20' *Family Law Week* (2015) 48. Available at: http://www.familylawweek. co.uk/site.aspx?i=ed151621, accessed 29 September 2017.

[53] [2008] EWHC 152 (Admin).   [54] [2000] 1 FLR 942.   [55] Section 22(2).

[56] Section 22(3).   [57] [2009] EWHC 34 (Admin).   [58] Schedule 2, para 19A.

[59] Section 47(1).   [60] Section 47(1).

the public.[61] There is a low threshold to trigger a s. 47 investigation, as reasonable cause for a suspicion is all that is needed, not proof to the civil standard on the balance of probabilities, that abuse had occurred. In *R (S) v Swindon Borough Council*[62] the High Court refused an application by an alleged perpetrator for judicial review against the local authority's decision to investigate allegations of sexual abuse, even though the alleged perpetrator had been acquitted in criminal proceedings. Scott Baker J said: 'In my judgment the need to establish facts on the balance of probability has no place in the exercise by a local authority of its various protective responsibilities under the Children Act.'[63] The investigation is to gather information to enable the local authority to decide whether the child is a child in need and/or at risk of significant harm.[64]

2.3.2 Section 37 investigation

Under s. 37 of the Children Act 1989 the local authority has a duty to carry out an investigation of a child's circumstances if directed to do so by the court in existing private law family proceedings. For example in contact proceedings the father may make allegations that the mother is an alcoholic and neglecting the child which would need to be investigated by the local authority.

The purpose of the investigation is for the local authority to decide whether to apply for a care or supervision order or to provide services or assistance to the child or their family.[65] If the local authority decides not to apply for a care or supervision order, it must inform the court within eight weeks of its reasons and give details of any other proposed action.[66]

When the court directs a s. 37 investigation, the court also has the power to make an interim care order or interim supervision order, of its own motion.[67]

2.3.3 The enquiries

Statutory guidance sets out the steps to be taken by a local authority to carry out enquiries. They should be organised and coordinated by a social worker and should involve liaison with everyone who comes into contact with the child[68] including medical staff, schools, and carers as well as the police. They should also involve speaking to the child without the parents being present[69] and possibly carrying out a medical or psychiatric assessment on the child. The focus of the enquiries are the needs of the child and the capacity of the parents to meet those needs, taking into account the wider cultural, ethnic, and religious contexts.[70]

2.3.4 Child assessment order

Nothing within s. 37 or s. 47 gives power to the local authority to enter premises to gain access to a child and so, if access to the child is refused, the local authority must apply to the court for an order unless they are satisfied that the child's welfare can be satisfactorily safeguarded without their doing so.[71]

The local authority may apply for a child assessment order under s. 43 of the Children Act 1989 on the basis that the local authority needs but is being denied access to the child.

---

[61] HM Government, 'Working Together to Safeguard Children' (HMSO, 2015) 16, para 19.
[62] *R (S) v Swindon Borough Council* [2001] EWHC (Admin) 334.
[63] [2001] EWHC (Admin) 334, at [34].
[64] HM Government, 'Working Together to Safeguard Children' (HMSO, 2015) 19, para 29.
[65] Secton 37(2).   [66] Section 37(3) and (4).   [67] Section 38(1).
[68] HM Government, 'Working Together to Safeguard Children' (HMSO, 2015) 9, para 16.
[69] HM Government, 'Working Together to Safeguard Children' (HMSO, 2015) 23, para 41.
[70] HM Government, 'Working Together to Safeguard Children' (HMSO, 2015) 23, para 42.
[71] Section 47(6).

The purpose of the order is to speak to the child or to carry out an assessment on them in order to facilitate an investigation into their welfare.

To make a child assessment order, the court must be satisfied that the local authority has reasonable cause to suspect that the child is suffering or is likely to suffer significant harm, that an assessment of the child's health or development, or of the way in which the child has been treated, is necessary and that, unless an order is made, it is unlikely that an assessment will take place.[72] The threshold for the granting of a child assessment order is low, being reasonable cause for suspicion, so the powers of the court are correspondingly limited. The order must specify the date by which the assessment is to begin and can last no more than seven days from that date.[73]

A child assessment order will require the parents to produce the child for assessment,[74] although a child with sufficient understanding to make an informed decision can refuse to submit.[75] The order will set out directions to enable an assessment to take place.[76]

A child assessment order does not constitute emergency action. Indeed, an application for a child assessment order has to be made on full notice to the parents of the child.[77] Where a child is at immediate risk, the court should make an emergency protection order instead.[78] In fact, child assessment orders are relatively rare: in 2015 only 73 children in England and Wales were involved in proceedings for a child assessment order.[79]

2.4 Child protection conference

A child protection conference is convened when the local authority has carried out an investigation and formed the view that the child may be at risk of significant harm. This should be within 15 days of the s. 47 investigation being started.[80] The conference should be attended by representatives from all agencies connected with the child's life including the child's school or nursery, medical practitioner, children's services, and the police. The purpose of the conference is to share information about the child and to plan what should happen to safeguard and promote the child's welfare.

There are a range of options available for discussion at a case conference. Firstly, it may be decided that the child is a child in need which would result in the provision of services under Part III. Alternatively, the local authority may suggest that they accommodate the child voluntarily under s. 20 or it may be decided that formal care proceedings (and the acquisition of parental responsibility by the local authority) are needed to protect the child. The child may be recorded as being at risk of significant harm under one or more categories: physical, emotional, or sexual abuse, or neglect. Neglect can include a failure to provide food, clothing, and shelter as well as unresponsiveness to the child's emotional needs.[81] Neglect is the most common category: 46% of children in England who were the subject of a child protection plan at 31 March 2016 had neglect as their initial category of abuse.[82] Emotional abuse was the second most common initial category, at 35%.[83]

There are a number of procedural safeguards for parents. First, they should be invited to attend the case conference. In *Re M (Care: Challenging Decisions by Local Authority)*[84] the High Court quashed a decision made at a case conference because the mother and father

---

[72] Section 43.   [73] Section 43(5).   [74] Section 43(6).   [75] Section 43(8).
[76] Section 43(6).   [77] Section 43(11).   [78] Section 43(4).
[79] Ministry of Justice, *Family Court Statistics Quarterly: April to June 2016.*
[80] HM Government, 'Working Together to Safeguard Children' (HMSO, 2015) Flow Chart 4.
[81] HM Government, 'Working Together to Safeguard Children' (HMSO, 2015) 93.
[82] Department for Education Statistical First Release SFR 52/2016 (DfE, 2016).
[83] Department for Education Statistical First Release SFR 52/2016 (DfE, 2016).   [84] [2001] 2 FLR 1300.

had not been invited to the meeting. In addition, parents should be given disclosure of relevant documents, such as minutes of meetings and attendance notes. Munby J sitting in the High Court in *Re G (Care: Challenge to Local Authority's Decision)*[85] held that the parents in this case had been seriously prejudiced by the local authority's failure to supply copies of records of all meetings, particularly as the local authority only told the parents that they were considering making significant changes to the care plan (including taking the children into care) two days after the relevant meeting had taken place. Parents should also be allowed to bring a solicitor to the case conference unless it would lead to confrontation. The High Court held in *R v Cornwall County Council, ex p LH*[86] that it was unlawful for a local authority to impose a blanket ban on the attendance of solicitors at case conferences.

The child may also attend if they are of sufficient age and understanding.[87] If they do not attend, the child's social worker or advocate should communicate the child's views and wishes at the conference.[88]

2.5 Child protection plan

At the child protection conference, it may be decided to make the child subject to an outline protection plan if the child is considered to be at risk of significant harm. The aim of the protection plan is to ensure that the child is safe from harm, to prevent the child suffering further harm, to promote the child's health and development, and to support the family and wider family members to safeguard and promote the welfare of the child, provided it is in the best interests of the child.[89] The plan sets out steps that are agreed to be taken which may include the commencement of care proceedings. A date is usually set for review in three months' time. Further reviews take place at intervals of six months[90] unless it is decided at a child protection review that the child should no longer be the subject of a child protection plan as they are no longer at risk of significant harm.

3. Emergency action

Emergency action can be taken by the local authority under an emergency protection order or action can be taken by the police. The need for emergency action may be triggered by concerns for the child's immediate safety[91] and could include, for example, substantiated allegations of sexual abuse by a person living with the child.

3.1 Emergency protection order

If it is considered that emergency action is needed, the local authority can apply for an emergency protection order. An order can be obtained relatively quickly (on the same day) because the application can be made without giving notice of proceedings to the parents. In fact, this may be necessary to avoid alerting the parents and putting

---

[85] [2003] EWHC 551.   [86] *R v Cornwall County Council, ex parte LH* [2000] 1 FLR 236.

[87] Department for Education 'Court orders and pre-proceedings for local authorities' (DfE, 2014) ch 2. para 20.

[88] Department for Education 'Court orders and pre-proceedings for local authorities' DfE, 2014) ch 2, para 20.

[89] HM Government, 'Working Together to Safeguard Children' (HMSO, 2015) 45.

[90] HM Government, 'Working Together to Safeguard Children' (HMSO, 2015) 46.

[91] HM Government, 'Working Together to Safeguard Children' (HMSO, 2015) 30.

the child under further risk. The order is draconian in nature because, as set out in s. 44(4) of the Children Act 1989, the order authorises the removal of a child from his parents and authorises the local authority to enter specified premises and search for the child.[92]

Although in most cases the applicant is the local authority, in theory any person can apply for an emergency protection order.[93] There are three possible grounds for such an order, depending on the identity of the applicant.

- The first ground is available to anyone: that *the court* is satisfied that there is reasonable cause to believe that the child is likely to suffer significant harm if he is not removed from his current accommodation.[94]

- The second ground is only available to the local authority: that *the applicant* has reasonable cause to believe that access to the child is required as a matter of urgency and their enquiries are being frustrated by access to the child being unreasonably refused.[95]

- The third ground is available to the local authority or the NSPCC: that *the applicant* has reasonable cause to suspect that the child is suffering or is likely to suffer significant harm and the applicant has reasonable cause to believe that access to the child is required as a matter of urgency and their enquiries are being frustrated by access to the child being unreasonably refused.[96]

When considering an application for an emergency protection order, the court's paramount consideration is the welfare of the child.[97] Any interference with the parents' Article 8 rights under the ECHR must be justifiable by being shown to be necessary in accordance with the law.[98] The court must be satisfied that the local authority isn't erring too heavily on the side of caution for fear of the consequences. In *X Local Authority v B (Emergency Protection Orders)*[99] Munby J sitting in the High Court set out 14 points of guidance to provide procedural safeguards for parents and their rights under Article 8. These safeguards include the requirement that, if applying without giving notice to the parents, the local authority must make out a compelling case for applying without notice and must subsequently provide proper information to the parents about what happened at the hearing in their absence, if requested.[100] The local authority may be seeking an emergency protection order because they have concerns about the child but have been unable to carry out s. 47 investigations as the parents have denied access. Munby J said that in such circumstances:

> If the real purpose of the local authority's application is to enable it to have the child assessed then consideration should be given to whether that objective cannot equally effectively, and more proportionately, be achieved by an application for, or by the making of, a child assessment order. Any order must provide for the least interventionist solution consistent with the preservation of the child's immediate safety.[101]

If a child being investigated is safe from immediate danger, the appropriate order would be a child assessment order instead.[102]

---

[92] Department for Education, 'Court orders and pre-proceedings for local authorities' (DfE, 2014), ch 4, para 25.

[93] Section 44(1).   [94] Section 44(1)(a).   [95] Section 44(1)(b).   [96] Section 44(1)(c).

[97] Section 1(1).   [98] *Haase v Germany* [2004] Fam Law 500.   [99] [2004] EWHC 2015.

[100] [2004] EWHC 2015, at [57].   [101] [2004] EWHC 2015, at [49].

[102] Department for Education 'Court orders and pre-proceedings for local authorities' (DfE, 2014) ch 4, para 16.

Key Case 1: *Re X (A Child)* [2006] EWHC 510

This case concerned a nine-year-old girl who had been in foster care for 14 months, following the grant of an emergency protection order and then a succession of interim care orders. At the final hearing of care proceedings, McFarlane J sitting in the High Court was very critical of the local authority's actions and refused their application for a final care order. He made the girl a ward of court so that she could be returned to her parents' care.

The Judge approved the 14 point guidance set out in the earlier case of *X Local Authority v B*[103] and commented that there were multiple failings at the initial hearing of the emergency protection order before lay magistrates. The hearing had taken place without notice to the parents yet no statement of the magistrates' reasons for granting the order was prepared or disclosed to the parents. At the hearing the magistrates lacked any written materials and were totally reliant on the oral submissions of the social worker, who was the team manager with only broad knowledge of the case. The judge commented that every element of her evidence was 'misleading or incomplete or wrong' which led the magistrates to reach a totally erroneous view.

The local authority had applied for the emergency protection order on the basis that the mother suffered from a mental health condition called Munchausen's Syndrome by Proxy and was fabricating symptoms in the child to attract attention to herself. This was because the mother had taken the girl to hospital, asking that the girl be seen by a doctor for stomach pain even though the triage nurse had assessed her and considered that there was no problem. However, by the time of the final hearing, the local authority had dropped their concerns of fictitious illness and was relying solely on alleged emotional abuse.

MacFarlane J said that the guidance in the earlier case of *X Local Authority v B*[104] should be required reading for all magistrates at hearings of an emergency protection order. He also suggested an additional procedural safeguard: that all without notice hearings for an emergency protection order should be tape recorded and that parents should always be given full disclosure of all materials, whether they ask for them or not.

An emergency protection order is short-term only as the next step by the local authority would be to seek an interim care order. An emergency protection order can be made for up to eight days[105] but the court may specify a shorter duration: the minimum period necessary to protect the child.[106] The court may extend the order for up to seven days on the application of the local authority provided the court has reasonable cause to believe that the child is likely to suffer significant harm if the order is not extended.[107] Only one extension is possible.[108]

The applicant acquires parental responsibility for the child[109] but the parental responsibility is only for the duration of the order and is limited to doing what is necessary to safeguard or promote the welfare of the child.[110] The exercise of parental responsibility only comprises day to day decision-making, not major long-term decisions.

Concerns about the draconian nature of emergency protection orders are exacerbated by the fact that there is no right of appeal against the making of an emergency protection order and parents can only apply to discharge the order in limited circumstances, such as where they did not receive notice of the application.[111] However, the local authority should return the child once it appears to the applicant that it is safe for the child to be returned.[112]

---

[103] [2004] EWHC 2015.   [104] [2004] EWHC 2015.   [105] Section 45(1).

[106] [2004] EWHC 2015, at [57].   [107] Section 45(5).   [108] Section 45(6).

[109] Section 44(4)(c).   [110] Section 44(5).   [111] Sections 45(10) and (11).

[112] Section 44(10).

3.2 **Police protection**

The police have the power to take a child into police protection under s. 46 of the Children Act 1989 if the constable has reasonable cause to believe that the child would otherwise be likely to suffer significant harm. This is at the discretion of the police officer and no court order is necessary. For example, a police officer may place a child in police protection if they find a toddler living in squalid conditions with no one caring for him. However, the police have no power under s. 46 to enter and search property.[113]

The police can remove a child immediately, without the delay of applying for a court order, but the child can only remain in police protection for no more than 72 hours.[114] As soon as reasonably practicable after taking the child into police protection,[115] the designated officer must notify the local authority so that they can provide accommodation[116] and the parents so that contact can be arranged.[117] A full hearing to which all parties are invited should take place within two days, when the court will consider making an emergency protection order.[118] The police do not acquire parental responsibility for the child but they are required to do what is reasonable in all the circumstances to safeguard and promote the child's welfare.[119]

Police protection should only be used in exceptional circumstances where there is insufficient time to apply for an emergency protection order or for reasons relating to the immediate safety of the child.[120] If a court order is already in force, such as an emergency protection order, a police officer should not take a child into police protection unless there are compelling reasons to do so. In *X v Liverpool City Council*[121] the Court of Appeal held that the removal of the child by the police had been unlawful because there was an emergency protection order in force and the police officer had failed to ask himself whether there were compelling reasons why he should effect the removal, rather than waiting for the local authority to execute the court order. LJ Dyson said that it is preferable that a child is removed by a social worker who is known to them rather than a police officer who may be a stranger.[122]

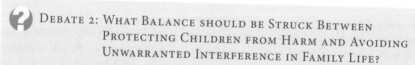

DEBATE 2: WHAT BALANCE SHOULD BE STRUCK BETWEEN PROTECTING CHILDREN FROM HARM AND AVOIDING UNWARRANTED INTERFERENCE IN FAMILY LIFE?

One debate is whether police powers should be used when emergency action is needed to remove a child from their family. Government guidance on child protection discourages the removal of children by means of police protection, stating:

> If it is necessary to remove a child from their home, a local authority must, wherever possible and unless a child's safety is otherwise at immediate risk, apply for an Emergency Protection Order (EPO). Police powers to remove a child in an emergency should be used only in exceptional circumstances where there is insufficient time to seek an EPO or for reasons relating to the immediate safety of the child.[123]

---

[113] Home Office Circular 017/2008, para 19.   [114] Section 46(6).   [115] Section 46(3)(a).
[116] Section 46(3)(f).   [117] Section 46(10).   [118] *A v East Sussex County Council* [2010] EWCA Civ 743
[119] Section 46(9)(b).
[120] Department for Education, 'Court orders and pre-proceedings for local authorities' (DfE, 2014) ch 4, para 30.
[121] [2005] EWCA Civ 1173.   [122] [2005] EWCA Civ 1173, at [39].
[123] HM Government, 'Working Together to Safeguard Children' (HMSO, 2015) Flow Chart 1.

Judith Masson has carried out research which found a use of police protection in excess of that envisaged by legislators.[124] The research found that removal of the child by the police is often the first step in protective action, instead of court approved removal under an emergency protection order and, although there are no national statistics, it is thought that the use of police powers is widespread.[125] Judith Masson writes: 'Where parents do not accept the offer of s.20 accommodation with relatives or foster carers or some other voluntary protective arrangement for their children, police protection appears to be the primary route for compulsory emergency intervention.'[126]

Some local authorities have an arrangement with their local police force that the police will use their s. 46 powers whenever removal is to be effected out of normal working hours, because of staffing issues in emergency duty social work teams and the closure of out of hours court services. On such occasions, the local authority contacts the police to make the necessary arrangements and, once removed, the child is taken to the police station where they stay until a social worker arrives. When the court opens, the local authority files an application for an emergency protection order and arranges service of the application on the parents.

Another reason for the use of police powers is to minimise delay. Removal of the child by the police is quicker than waiting for the outcome of a court application, particularly since the guidance in *X Local Authority v B (Emergency Protection Orders)*[127] requires that applications for emergency protection orders are made on notice to the parents unless there are compelling reasons to do otherwise. There is often a correlation between the use of police powers and local authority without notice applications for emergency protection orders as a first step: in some areas, magistrates are perceived to be less willing to grant applications without notice to parents and in these areas the use of police protection powers is greater.[128] The local authority may also prefer to use police powers as removal is not at the discretion at the court: there is no obligation to present legal arguments to justify a without notice application.

Concerns about the routine use of s. 46 police protection powers to effect removal of children include lack of accountability, as police protection is not subject to judicial controls. Dyson LJ said: 'The removal of children, usually from their families, is a very serious matter. It is therefore not at all surprising that Parliament decided that the court should play an important part in the process. This is a valuable safeguard.'[129] Once the child has been removed, the local authority is less likely to be refused an application for an emergency protection order, so the use of police protection can strengthen and consolidate the local authority's position.

It could be argued that, for the parents, removal by the police poses no procedural disadvantage because the alternative would be under an emergency protection order obtained without notice, the making of which would have taken place without their knowledge anyway. However, for the child, removal by a police offer to a police station may be more traumatic than removal by a social worker. Judith Masson has found that most removals are

---

[124] Masson, J. 'Emergency Protection: The Impact of Court Control on Safeguarding Children' [2010] *Family Law* 1088.

[125] Masson, J. 'Emergency Intervention to Protect Children: Using and Avoiding Legal Controls' (2005) 17 *Child and Family Law Quarterly* 75, at 78.

[126] Masson, J. 'Emergency Protection: The Impact of Court Control on Safeguarding Children [2010] *Family Law* 1088, 1091.

[127] [2004] EWHC 2015.

[128] Masson, J. 'Emergency Intervention to Protect Children: Using and Avoiding Legal Controls' (2005) 17 *Child and Family Law Quarterly* 75.

[129] *X v Liverpool City Council* [2005] EWCA Civ 1173, at [36].

effected by ordinary officers on general policing duties, with very little experience of child protection.[130] Arguably, the process of removal would be better for a child's welfare if planned and effected by a social worker known to them and did not involve a stay at the police station at which there are likely to be limited facilities for children.

Police protection plays a key role in the emergency removal of children from their families but is free from judicial scrutiny. Is this the best way for the state to effect the removal of children from their families? What should be the role of the police in emergency child protection?

4. Starting care proceedings

It might be decided at a child protection conference that care proceedings should be started. This would be in order to seek a care order or supervision order over the child. However, this is very much a last resort, only when all efforts to work in voluntary partnership with the parents have failed. Care proceedings are usually commenced where the parents have multiple vulnerability factors such as mental health problems, drug/alcohol problems, chaotic lifestyles, domestic violence, and housing problems.[131]

 CONTEXT 2: RISING NUMBERS OF CARE CASES

21,591 children in England and Wales were involved in care proceedings in 2015.[132] This number has increased substantially over the years. Over the last ten years, care cases have more than doubled: from 6,786 in 2006 to an estimated 14,713 in 2016.[133] The President of the Family Division, Sir James Munby, recently referred to a 'looming crisis' caused by the 'seemingly relentless rise in the number of new care cases'.[134] In his 'View from the President's Chambers' he argued that the increase is being caused by a change in local authority behaviour—that local authorities are becoming more adept at identifying and dealing with child abuse and/or local authority thresholds for intervention have lowered. The President supported this contention with the fact that there are very wide variations between the numbers of applications made by different authorities.

4.1 Who can apply for a care or supervision order?

An application for a care order or supervision order can only be made by a local authority or the NSPCC as an authorised person.[135] In practice, applications are made by the local authority legal department on the instruction of a social worker, having followed the pre-proceedings checklist set out in the Public Law Outline.[136] The court cannot require the local authority to commence care proceedings and the court cannot make a care order or supervision order unless the local authority applies for one.[137] If the court perceives that a child is in need of protection, it would instead make a direction under s. 37 of the Children Act 1989 that the local authority investigates the child's circumstances.

---

[130] Masson, J. 'Emergency Intervention to Protect Children: Using and Avoiding Legal Controls' (2005) 17 *Child and Family Law Quarterly* 75, 78.

[131] Brophy, J. 'Research Review: Child care proceedings under the Children Act 1989', DCA Research Series 5/06 (2006) ii; Ministry of Justice 'Care Profiling Study' (2008) 20.

[132] Ministry of Justice, *Family Court Statistics Quarterly: April to June 2016.*

[133] Cafcass, 'Care application demand—latest figures for September 2016'.

[134] Sir James Munby 'View from the President's Chambers' 2016.

[135] Section 31(1); section 31(9).   [136] Practice Direction 12A Public Law Outline 2014.

[137] *Nottinghamshire County Council v P* [1993] 2 FLR 134.

4.2 **The child**

An order can only be made in respect of a child who is habitually resident in England and Wales[138] and under 17 years of age.[139] No order can be made in respect of a married child aged 16[140] or over a foetus.[141]

4.3 **Who is a party**

A party to the proceedings is entitled to read all documents filed in the case and to attend and make representations at all court hearings. Every person with parental responsibility is automatically a party to the proceedings.[142] This would include the mother. Other people can apply for the court's permission to be joined as a party. For example, if a father does not have parental responsibility, he can apply to be joined to the proceedings and his application should be granted unless there is some justifiable reason otherwise. To refuse permission might breach the father's right to family life under Article 8 of the European Convention.[143] In *Re K (Care Proceedings: Joinder of Father)*[144] Holman J sitting in the High Court allowed a father's appeal against the making of a care order over his son as the father had not been allowed to participate in proceedings and present his views to the court. The magistrates had wrongly refused permission for him to be joined as a party. In *Re P (Care Proceedings: Father's Application to be joined as Party)*[145] Connell J sitting in the High Court said that a justifiable reason to refuse permission to a father would include the care proceedings being at an advanced stage at the time of the father's application. In this case the father was present at the first two hearings but was uncommunicative throughout the proceedings until applying to be joined as a party at a final directions hearing.

Other interested people, such as grandparents, can apply for permission to be joined as a party but their application would be unlikely to be granted if they are not able to put forward a point of view independent and separate of existing parties to the proceedings.[146] In *Re W (A Child) (Care Proceedings: Leave to Apply)*[147] the High Court dismissed an appeal by an aunt against a refusal to allow her to be a party to the proceedings. This was because she wanted to make submissions about contact but her views were the same as the grandmother who was already a party. In fact, she was going to appear as a witness for the grandmother so her views would still be heard.

The child is automatically a party to the proceedings[148] although they do not attend court hearings. Instead a court appointed guardian attends all hearings on their behalf (see 6.1). The child has separate legal representation from the other parties because of the potential for conflicts of interest.

5. **Interim hearing**

Once care proceedings are issued, the court gives a date for an interim hearing to take place.[149] At the interim hearing there are a number of different orders that can be made by the court. The orders are all to do with where the child should stay while evidence is assembled, pending a final hearing.

---

[138] *Lewisham London Borough Council v D* [2008] 2 FLR 1449.   [139] Section 31(3).
[140] Section 31(3).   [141] *Re F (In Utero)* [1988] Fam 122.
[142] Family Procedure Rules 2010 r. 12.3(1).   [143] *McMichael v UK* (1995) 20 EHRR 205.
[144] [1999] 2 FLR 408.   [145] [2001] 1 FLR 781.   [146] [2004] EWHC 3342 (Fam).
[147] [2004] EWHC 3342 (Fam).   [148] Family Procedure Rules 2010, r. 12.3(1).
[149] Practice Direction 12A Public Law Outline 2014.

5.1 **Child to be removed from the parents in the interim**

If the court agrees that the local authority should have the power to remove the child from the parents, the court may make an interim care order.[150] The purpose of an interim care order is to provide arrangements to protect the child before the final hearing. The order gives parental responsibility to the local authority which they share with the parents, although the local authority has the power to determine the extent to which parents are allowed to meet such responsibilities.[151]

The requirements for making an interim care order are lower than for making a final care order. The local authority simply has to prove on the balance of probabilities that there are *reasonable grounds to believe that* the threshold criteria set out in s. 31(2) of the Children Act 1989 for a final order are met.[152]

As the threshold for the grant of an interim care order is lower, evidence considered at an interim hearing is more limited than that considered at a final hearing. An interim hearing is not a trial run for the final hearing and issues are limited to ones that cannot await trial.[153] Thorpe LJ sitting in the Court of Appeal in *Re H (A Child) (Interim Care Order)*[154] said:

> Above all it seems to me important to recognise the purpose and bounds of an interim hearing. There can be no doubt that a full and profound trial of the local authority's concerns is absolutely essential. But the interim hearing could not be allowed to usurp or substitute for that trial. It had to be properly confined to control the immediate interim before the court could find room for the essential trial.[155]

In that case the Court of Appeal allowed the parent's appeal against the making of an interim care order over their son because the judge had made a premature determination of the case based on longer-term evidence about the risk of emotional abuse instead of considering just the next four months.

The courts have applied additional considerations to the statutory grounds. In *F1 v M1*[156] it was held that removal from parents is only justifiable where the court is satisfied that it is necessary in the interests of the child. In that case Cobb J sitting in the High Court held that it was not necessary to remove a child at an interim hearing because of exposure to the mother's mental illness and negativity. In *Re B (Children) (Interim Care Order)*[157] the Court of Appeal held that the continued removal of the child from the parents must be proportionate to the risk of harm posed to the child if returned to the parents' care. In that case, the children were removed from the mother's care temporarily to establish whether she would be able to care for the children and protect them from her former partner who had been violent towards her and the children. It was held by the court that the requirements for removal are not so high as to require imminent risk of serious harm. Instead, separation from parents is only to be ordered if the child's safety demands immediate separation, as established in *Re L-A (Children)*.[158]

A relatively recent example of an interim care order being confirmed on appeal is provided in *Re T (Children) (Interim Care Order: Removal of Children Where No Immediate Emergency)*.[159] The Court of Appeal upheld the making of such an order, removing two young children from the care of their grandparents so that they could be assessed in a

---

[150] Section 38(1).   [151] Section 33(3).   [152] Section 38(2).
[153] *Re F (Children) (Care Proceedings: Interim Care Order)* [2010] EWCA Civ 826.
[154] [2002 [EWCA Civ 1932.   [155] *Re H (A Child) (Interim Care Order)* [2002] EWCA Civ 1932, at [38].
[156] [2013] EWHC 4150 (Fam), at [59].   [157] [2010] EWCA Civ 324.
[158] [2009] EWCA Civ 822.   [159] [2015] EWCA Civ 453.

special foster home pending a final hearing. This was despite the fact that the Court had not ruled out the grandparents as potential long-term carers. The trial judge had considered that the children's safety required their immediate removal because there were concerns that the grandparents could not cope with the children's deteriorating behaviour. McFarlane LJ said 'the children's safety in emotional terms did indeed require separation at this stage'.[160]

Before an interim care order is made, the court has to consider the local authority's arrangements for contact between the child and his parents.[161] The local authority should, if possible, place the child with a relative or, if that is not appropriate, in accommodation near to the child's home.[162] An interim care order is temporary and subject to continuous review. It has to be renewed at regular intervals so that the court has ongoing scrutiny into the local authority's actions. The order can be made for any period at the court's discretion as it sees fit.[163]

DEBATE 3: WHAT BALANCE SHOULD BE STRUCK BETWEEN PROTECTING CHILDREN FROM HARM AND AVOIDING UNWARRANTED INTERFERENCE IN FAMILY LIFE?

One debate is whether the legal threshold for granting an interim care order is set at the right level: is the threshold sufficiently robust to trigger protection for children when needed but not so low as to authorise unnecessary separation from parents?

The statutory test only requires the local authority to establish reasonable grounds for believing that the circumstances in s. 31(2) exist, namely that the child is suffering or is likely to suffer significant harm attributable to lack of reasonable parental care or the child being beyond parental control.[164] In other words, the local authority does not have to prove the existence of these elements, only that there are reasonable grounds for believing that they exist.

The argument that the interim threshold is low is supported by the additional considerations applied by the courts to the statutory wording: an interim care order can only be made if necessary for the child's immediate safety.[165] While reducing the risk of unnecessary and traumatic separation from parents, the judicial raising of the bar has caused some commentators to argue that some children may have to endure intolerable treatment with parents while waiting for the final hearing, in cases of chronic neglect for example.[166] On the other hand, even taking into account the additional judicial requirements, the threshold may still be too low in the perception of parents.

In *Re G (Minors) (Interim Care Order)*[167] interim care orders were described as an impartial step favouring neither side preserving the status quo and not giving the local authority any advantage in the eyes of the court. However, this is debatable. It has been argued that what is decided in the interim period can have long-lasting consequences for the rest of the child's life. Andrew Bainham writes: 'There is a case for saying that the single most important battle is fought out at the interim stage. In particular, there is a widely held view that once a child has been separated from a parent there is a strong likelihood that

---

[160] [2015] EWCA Civ 453, at [39].　　[161] Section 34.　　[162] Section 22C(8).

[163] Section 38(4) as amended by the Children and Families Act 2014; Explanatory Notes to the Act.

[164] Section 38(2).　　[165] *Re L-A (Children)* [2009] EWCA Civ 822.

[166] Howe, D. 'Removal of Children at the Interim hearing: Is the Bar Now set too High?' [2009] *Family Law* 321.

[167] [1993] 2 FLR 839.

they will remain separated'.[168] Although an interim care order has to be renewed at regular intervals,[169] renewals are a mere formality so the initial making of an interim care order will determine the child's living arrangements for the rest of the proceedings (potentially 26 weeks[170]), thus establishing a new status quo which could influence the outcome for the child at the final hearing.

The risks for parents of a low threshold are exacerbated by the fact that it can be particularly difficult to mount an effective legal challenge to the local authority's case at an interim hearing. This is because the courts limit the evidence that can be presented, requiring that an interim hearing should not be a trial run for the final hearing.[171] In addition, with the imposition of the reduced time limit for proceedings of 26 weeks, there is less opportunity for parents to obtain evidence to challenge the local authority's case.

As the interim period is so crucial, what balance should be struck between protecting children from harm and avoiding unwarranted interference in family life?

5.2 Child to stay in home and the suspected abuser to be excluded in the interim

When making an interim care order, the court can enable the child to continue living at home by including an exclusion requirement within the court order. For example the court may require a suspected abuser to leave the home and exclude them from a defined area around the home.[172] A power of arrest can be attached to the exclusion requirement.[173] However, imposing an exclusion requirement is only possible if the conditions set out in s. 38A(2) of the Children Act 1989 are met. One of the conditions is that the parent remaining in the home must consent to the exclusion requirement, obliging the parent to choose between their child and their partner.

An exclusion requirement can only be part of an interim care order[174] and is not a long-term measure. It cannot last longer than the interim care order and may be for a shorter duration.[175] The requirement ceases to have effect if the local authority subsequently removes the child from the home to other accommodation for a continuous period of more than 24 hours.[176]

5.3 Child to remain with parents in the interim

If the court considers that it is safe for the child to remain living with their parents pending the final hearing, the court may make an interim supervision order.[177] The local authority would appoint a supervisor to advise, assist, and befriend the child.[178] The supervisor would also ensure that any directions within the supervision order, such as attending medical assessments,[179] are complied with.[180] To make such an order, the court must be satisfied that there are reasonable grounds for believing that the threshold criteria set out in s. 31(2) of the Children Act 1989 are met.[181]

---

[168] Bainham, A. 'Interim Care Orders: Is the Bar set too Low?' [2011] *Family Law* 374, 376.
[169] Section 38(4).
[170] Section 32(1)(a).   [171] *Re F (Children) (Care Proceedings: Interim Care Order)* [2010] EWCA Civ 826.
[172] Section 38A(3).   [173] Section 38A(5); Practice Direction 12K.   [174] Section 38A(1)(a).
[175] Section 38A(4).   [176] Section 38A(10).   [177] Section 38(1).   [178] Section 35(1)(a).
[179] Section 38(6).   [180] Section 35(1)(b).   [181] Section 38(2).

5.4 Child to stay with relatives in the interim

If the court considers that the child should stay with a relative, the court may make an interim child arrangements order[182] that the child lives with the named adult. The purpose of the interim child arrangements order is to give parental responsibility to the relative for the duration of the order.[183] At the same time as making the child arrangements order, the court must also make an interim supervision order unless satisfied that the child's welfare will be satisfactorily safeguarded without it.[184]

When considering making an interim child arrangements order, the court's paramount consideration is the welfare of the child.[185] The court must also be satisfied that a court order is needed.[186] Given that parental responsibility would be needed by the relative, satisfaction of this requirement would not pose a difficulty for the court.

6. Investigations

Once an interim hearing has taken place, evidence is gathered pending the final hearing.

6.1 Court appointed guardian

A guardian is appointed to safeguard the child's interests in the proceedings.[187] The court will make a direction to this effect, unless satisfied that it is not necessary.[188] The guardian is usually a trained social worker employed by the Children and Family Court Advisory and Support Service (Cafcaas) which is an independent public body established to promote the interests of children in court proceedings.

The guardian attends all court hearings to make representations on behalf of the child. They carry out their own enquiries which include meeting the child and finding out their views. The guardian has the right to examine local authority records relating to the child[189] and these records become admissible in evidence.[190] In *Re R (A Child) (Care Proceedings: Disclosure)*[191] the Court of Appeal held that this entitled the guardian to read the full version (as opposed to the executive summary) of a report about the death of the child's sibling, written by the local authority's Area Child Protection Committee.

When the guardian has finished their enquiries, they file a written report in the proceedings, making recommendations as to what should happen in the best interests of the child. The guardian is independent and does not have to agree with the proposals of the parents or the local authority, or with the child's wishes.

The guardian also appoints a solicitor for the child, unless the court has already appointed one.[192] The guardian gives instructions to the solicitor: if the child's instructions conflict with those of the guardian, the solicitor must follow the child's instructions if the solicitor considers that the child has sufficient understanding.[193] The guardian would then seek the court's permission to have separate legal representation.

6.2 Section 38(6) assessments

An interim care order or interim supervision order, unlike a final care order, can include directions for the examination or assessment of the child under s. 38(6) of the Children

---

[182] Section 8; section 11(3).
[183] Section 12(2).   [184] Section 38(3).   [185] Section 1(1).
[186] Section 1(5).   [187] Section 41(2)(b).   [188] Section 41(1); Family Procedure Rules 2010, r. 12.6.
[189] Section 42(1)(a).   [190] Section 42(2).   [191] [2000] 2 FLR 751.
[192] Family Procedure Rules 2010, r. 6.2.   [193] Family Procedure Rules 2010, r. 16.29.

Act 1989. For example, the court may direct that the parents and child should stay at a residential unit over a period of weeks so that an assessment of their parenting capabilities can take place. Such a direction can only be made if the court is of the opinion that the examination or assessment is necessary to assist the court to resolve the proceedings justly.[194] Within s. 38(7B) there is a list of matters to which the court must have regard and they include the likely impact on the child's welfare, the issues the assessment would assist the court with, other available evidence, the impact on the duration of the proceedings, and the cost involved.

Cost is a difficulty, particularly for residential assessments as they can be very expensive and funding is often an issue. The Legal Services Commission can no longer be required to contribute to the cost of a residential assessment (following amendments to the Funding Code[195]) and the local authority may object to a residential assessment being directed by the court because of the cost involved.

The House of Lords considered whether there should be a residential assessment in *Re C (A Minor) (Interim Care Order: Residential Assessment)*.[196] The Court allowed the parents' appeal and held that 'assessment' in s. 38(6) was to be given a broad construction and could include assessment of the relationship between the parents and child, where it would provide relevant evidence to enable the court to decide whether a full care order should be granted. In this case the court directed that the parents and child should stay at a residential assessment unit to determine whether the child could eventually be returned to his parents' care, after having suffered serious non-accidental injuries which the parents were not able to explain.

In *Re W (A Child)*[197] the Court of Appeal again considered an appeal against a refusal to make a direction for a lengthy residential assessment. The Court of Appeal held that there was nothing wrong in the trial judge's approach when refusing the assessment: he was concerned that assessing the mother when she was in good health might give a falsely positive picture. Wilson LJ said 'the basic principle is well established, namely that, if the court considers that an assessment is necessary for the proper determination of the application for a care order, it should ordinarily exercise its discretion to direct that it should take place.'[198] However, he went on to refer to the issue of cost and said that, while he found it logically difficult to understand how cost can be a relevant factor in the exercise of discretion, 'the particularly difficult financial situation of local authorities today certainly militates in favour of a rigorous approach by a judge to a contention that an assessment, particularly a residential assessment, is necessary'.[199]

Nevertheless, in *Local Authority v M (Funding of Residential Assessments)*, Bodey J sitting in the High Court still made a s. 38(6) direction for a seven-week residential assessment even though the local authority had submitted that it could not afford to pay for it. He made the direction because the local authority itself had positively regarded the intended residential assessment as the way forward.[200]

In *Re G (A Child) (Interim Care Order: Residential Assessment)*,[201] the House of Lords restricted the power of the court to direct a residential assessments under s. 38(6). The Court held that, to come within s. 38(6) the assessment must be 'of the child'. This may include an assessment of the child's relationship with her parents, the risks the parents may present, and ways in which those risks may be avoided or managed. Nevertheless, the purpose of the provision is to enable the court to obtain the information needed to make a

---

[194] Section 38(7A) as inserted by the Children and Families Act 2014.
[195] Access to Justice Act 1999, s. 8.   [196] [1996] 4 All ER 871.
[197] [2011] EWCA Civ 661.   [198] *Re W (A Child)* [2011] EWCA Civ 661, at [6].
[199] [2011] EWCA Civ 661, at [6].   [200] [2008] EWHC 162 (Fam), at [22].   [201] [2005] UKHL 68.

decision about the future of the child; any services provided to the family must be ancillary to that information-gathering. The House of Lords held that the trial judge was entitled to conclude that s. 38(6) would not cover assessment of the parents over many months as inpatients at a hospital aimed at bringing about long-term change.

In *Re L (A Child)*,[202] the Court of Appeal allowed the appeal of parents against the refusal of the trial judge to order a residential assessment and held that the final hearing of the proceedings should be fair and the court should have before it all the relevant evidence necessary for a decision.[203] Wall LJ went on to say that: 'if the professional evidence in the instant case was unanimous that a s.38(6) assessment would serve no purpose, it would be unlikely that the judge could have been criticised for refusing to order one. But that is patently not the case.'[204] In this case, the residential assessment had been recommended by a clinical psychologist and it was manifestly in the child's interests to see whether the parents would be able to care for him.

In *TL v Hammersmith and Fulham London Borough Council*[205] the Court of Appeal held that the trial judge had been entitled to come to the conclusion that a residential assessment would be pointless and, in refusing to order a residential assessment, there was no breach of Articles 6 or 8 under the European Convention.[206] The mother suffered from personality disorders as well as depression and a residential assessment would not provide evidence of how the mother would function in a community placement.

6.3 **Expert evidence**

The local authority may wish to instruct an expert such as a psychiatrist, psychologist, or paediatrician, for example, to prove that the parents' actions are causing emotional harm to the child or that physical injuries sustained by the child were non-accidental. Expert evidence obtained without the permission of the court is inadmissible in the proceedings.[207] Therefore a party seeking to rely on expert evidence must obtain the permission of the court. The court will only give permission if the expert opinion is considered to be necessary to assist the court to resolve the proceedings justly.[208] The matters to which the court must have regard are listed within s. 13(7) of the Children Act 1989 and they include the likely impact on the child's welfare, the issues it would assist the court with, other available evidence, the impact on the duration of the proceedings, and the cost involved.

Once an expert's report is obtained, legal professional privilege does not apply and the report must be disclosed to all parties and the court, even if adverse to the instructing party. In *Re L (A Minor) (Police Investigation: Privilege)*[209] the House of Lords considered whether a report commissioned by the parents' solicitor about the parents' drug use should be disclosed to the police. It was held that legal professional privilege does not attach to experts' reports in care proceedings because of the duty of the court to consider the welfare of the child. In this case the parents were drug addicts and the child had been admitted to hospital after drinking the parents' methadone. The mother had claimed that it was an accident but her solicitor instructed a chemical pathologist to prepare a report which cast doubt on the mother's explanation. The House of Lords held that the report should be disclosed to the police.

A parent may wish to challenge the local authority's submission that injuries were non-accidental by the instruction of a second expert. In the case of *Re W v Oldham Metropolitan*

---

[202] [2007] EWCA Civ 213.   [203] *Re L (A Child)* [2007] EWCA Civ 213, at [85].
[204] [2007] EWCA Civ 213, at [88].   [205] [2011] EWCA Civ 812.
[206] [2011] EWCA Civ 812, at [54] and [58].   [207] Children and Families Act 2014, s. 13(2).
[208] Children and Families Act 2014, s. 13(6).   [209] [1996] 1 FLR 731.

Borough Council[210] the Court of Appeal held that a second opinion should normally only be permitted where the question to be addressed goes to an issue of critical importance. In that case the Court of Appeal held that the parents were entitled to a second opinion because the critical issue was the cause of their son's brain injury.

6.4 **Time limit on proceedings**

The final report of the Family Justice Review published in 2011 was critical of delays in care proceedings[211] and subsequently legislation imposed a 26-week time limit on the duration of care proceedings.[212] The court can grant an extension beyond the 26 weeks but only for eight weeks at a time[213] and only if it is considered necessary to enable the court to resolve the proceedings justly.[214] The court must have regard to the impact of the extension on the welfare of the child and on the duration and conduct of proceedings.[215] Extensions are not to be granted routinely and are to be seen as requiring special justification.[216]

 CONTEXT 3: DURATION OF CARE PROCEEDINGS

The current average duration of care proceedings in England and Wales is 27 weeks and has remained consistent for the last 12 months; 60% of cases are disposed of within less than 26 weeks.[217] This can be contrasted with an average duration of 61 weeks in county courts five years previously at the time of the Family Justice Review.[218] At that time, delay was caused by exhaustive processes to ensure fairness to parents involving multiple reports from expert witnesses. The Review expressed concerns that delay can harm the child's long-term prospects for stability and also prolong uncertainty and anxiety for the child. The President of the Family Division, Sir James Munby, has recently expressed concern that the court's ability to comply with the strict time limit of 26 weeks may be being put at risk by the increasing numbers of care applications. In his 'View from the President's Chambers', he asked for shorter court documents and more stringent scrutiny of applications for permission to file expert evidence.[219]

In *Re S (A Child) (Interim Care Order: Residential Assessment)*[220] the President of the Family Division, Sir James Munby, gave guidance on the meaning of 'necessary' in the context of seeking an extension for a residential assessment. Munby P. said that courts must consider whether there is solid evidence that first the parent is committed to making the necessary changes, secondly the parent would be able to maintain that commitment, and thirdly the parent would be able to make changes within the child's timescale.[221] In that case, he refused an application for an extension because the mother had not satisfied him on these issues. She wanted an extension so that there could be a residential assessment of herself and her baby. However, Munby P. considered that there was no evidence to believe that the mother would be able to maintain any changes or to make changes in the child's timescale. The mother had mental health problems, a low IQ, and a history of drug use and prostitution.

[210] [2005] EWCA Civ 1247.   [211] Norgrove, D. 'Family Justice Review: Final Report' (2011) para 3.5.
[212] Section 32(1)(a) as amended by the Children and Families Act 2014.   [213] Section 32(8).
[214] Section 32(5).   [215] Section 32(6).   [216] Section 32(7).
[217] *Ministry of Justice, Family Court Statistics Quarterly: April to June 2016.*
[218] Norgrove, D. 'Family Justice Review: Final Report' (2011) para 3.2.
[219] Sir James Munby 'View from the President's Chambers' 2016.   [220] [2014] 2 FLR 575.
[221] [2014] 2 FLR 575, at [38].

> **?** DEBATE 4: IN CARE PROCEEDINGS, TO WHAT EXTENT SHOULD
> THE COURT ALLOW PARENTS TO PRESENT THEIR CASE,
> GIVEN THE DISADVANTAGES THAT DELAY MAY BRING
> FOR A CHILD?
>
> One debate concerns the imposition of a reduced 26-week time limit for the conduct of care proceedings under s. 32(1)(a): whether the rigidity of a fixed deadline (of any length) can be compatible with child welfare. Natasha Watson warns of the risks of an 'artificial lawyer-centric deadline' 'prioritising any outcome over the right outcome'.[222] Families subject to care proceedings often have multiple vulnerability factors and complex needs.[223] Can it be in the interests of the child to apply a blanket time limit to all cases, regardless of their circumstances?
>
> In addition it is not known whether 26 weeks is a sufficiently long period of time to secure the right outcome for a child. Given that the reduced deadline was only introduced in 2014, empirical data about children's progress is not yet available and the long-term consequences of the shorter time limit may not be known for years.
>
> Nevertheless, even without longitudinal data, it is generally acknowledged that delay can reduce a child's prospects for adoption, by causing the child to be older when permanency plans are drawn up. In addition delay prolongs the duration of anxiety for parents and children while the outcome of proceedings is awaited and, if the child stays with parents while proceedings are ongoing, delay can maximise the child's exposure to defective parenting. Indeed, the undesirability of delay is enshrined in statute, namely s. 1(2) of the Children Act 1989 which states that delay is likely to prejudice the welfare of the child.
>
> On the other hand, delay in some circumstances can be used constructively, giving parents additional time to work through their difficulties and enabling the child to maintain stability with their birth family. Although a great deal of work is now carried out pre-proceedings in accordance with the Public Law Outline,[224] (including the collation of experts reports, exploration of options for the child, and identification of support or treatment for the family), the imposition of a shorter time limit on proceedings necessarily reduces the opportunity for parents to obtain evidence to challenge the local authority case, for example by demonstrating capability. In addition, the reduced time limit is now combined with court documents being shorter in length and fewer in number, as well as scrutiny of the care plan being limited to the permanence provisions.[225] This all serves to restrict parents' access to justice and reduce the opportunity for the child to maintain stability with their parents.
>
> Is the imposition of a fixed 26-week time limit compatible with parental rights and the best outcomes for children?

7. Evidential issues

At the final hearing, the judge considers the evidence at a fact finding hearing to determine whether the threshold for the making of a final supervision or care order is met.

---

[222] Watson, N. 'Achieving Justice in no More Than 26 Weeks: The Role of the Local Authority' [2014] *Fam Law* 829, 832.

[223] Brophy, J. 'Research Review: Child care proceedings under the Children Act 1989', DCA Research Series 5/06 (2006) ii; Ministry of Justice 'Care Profiling Study' (2008) 20.

[224] Department for Education, 'Court orders and pre-proceedings for local authorities' (DfE, 2014) Annex A: Pre-proceedings Flow Chart; Practice Direction 12A Public Law Outline 2014.

[225] Section 31(3A).

7.1 Hearsay evidence

The evidence available in care proceedings can pose challenges for the court when trying to make a finding of fact. Evidence may be contradictory or absent. For example, often the only witness to abuse is the child who may be frightened into silence or too young to say anything. Parents may keep the child out of school or delay seeking medical treatment so that the abuse is not detected. Even if there are any physical signs, they can be difficult to interpret and there are often disputes between experts over the medical evidence, particularly if the court gives permission for a party to obtain a second opinion.

For these reasons, the rules about the admissibility of evidence are relaxed in care proceedings. For example, hearsay is permitted as evidence in care proceedings.[226] This means that the court can admit in evidence anything said by a teacher or foster carer to the guardian provided they are quoted in the guardian's report. However, the President of the Family Division, Sir James Munby, recently warned in *Re A (Application for Care Placement Orders: Local Authority Failings)*[227] that hearsay evidence may be less compelling and amount to a 'tottering edifice built on inadequate foundations'.[228] Munby P. said 'hearsay evidence is, of course, admissible in family proceedings. But . . . a local authority which is unwilling or unable to produce the witnesses who can speak of such matters first hand, may find itself in great, or indeed insuperable, difficulties if a parent not merely puts the matter in issue but goes into the witness box to deny it'.[229] To be able to discharge the burden of proof, the local authority should call witnesses who can give evidence first hand.

The relaxed rules of evidence also mean that the child does not have to give live, direct evidence in court. Instead, a pre-recorded video can be shown of an earlier interview with the child. The Supreme Court in *Re W (Children) (Abuse: Oral Evidence)*[230] held that courts must strike a balance between the advantages live evidence would bring to the determination of the truth against the damage it might do to the welfare of the child. Lady Hale (who gave the lead judgment) actually acknowledged that 'striking that balance in care proceedings may well mean that the child should not be called to give evidence in the great majority of cases, but that is a result and not a presumption or even a starting point'.[231]

In the recent Court of Appeal case of *Re E (A Child) (Family Proceedings: Evidence)*[232] McFarlane LJ said that, despite the decision in *Re W (Children) (Family Proceedings: Evidence)*[233] the approach of care courts has not changed 'with the previous presumption against children giving evidence remaining intact. That state of affairs is plainly contrary to the binding decision of the Supreme Court which was that such a presumption is contrary to Article 6 of the European Convention on Human Rights'.[234] McFarlane LJ said that courts should engage with the factors set out in *Re W (Children) (Family Proceedings: Evidence)*[235] together with factors relevant to the particular child, before coming to a reasoned conclusion.[236]

Subsequent guidelines set out factors for the court to consider when deciding whether the child should be called to give live evidence. These include the nature of the allegations and whether or not the child is willing to give live evidence.[237] However, these guidelines

---

[226] Section 96(3); Children (Admissibility of Hearsay Evidence) Order 1993 (SI 1993/621).
[227] [2015] EWFC 11.   [228] [2015] EWFC 11, at [11].   [229] [2015] EWFC 11, at [9].
[230] [2010] UKSC 12.   [231] *Re W (Children) (Family Proceedings: Evidence)* [2010] UKSC 12, at [22].
[232] [2016] EWCA Civ 473.   [233] [2010] UKSC 12.
[234] *Re E (A Child) (Family Proceedings: Evidence)* [2016] EWCA Civ 473, at [56].
[235] [2010] UKSC 12.
[236] *Re E (A Child) (Family Proceedings: Evidence)* [2016] EWCA Civ 473, at [57].
[237] *Guidelines in Relation to Children Giving Evidence in Family Proceeding* [2012] *Fam Law* 79.

are shortly to be replaced following the recommendations of the Vulnerable Witnesses and Children Working Group that practice from the criminal courts should be adopted in order to facilitate the giving of direct oral evidence by children so that they can feel listened to and heard.[238] This would include the use of special measures such as a live link to prevent the child seeing other parties. As a result, greater numbers of children may end up giving live evidence in court.

7.2 **Standard of proof**

The standard of proof is very important because it sets the benchmark for the certainty of evidence needed to authorise state intervention in family life: if set too high, children may suffer unacceptable treatment at home but, if set too low, children may suffer unnecessary harm by being removed from their parents.

 Key Case 2: Re H and R (Child Sexual Abuse: Standard of Proof) [1996] AC 563

This case concerned four sisters in a family. The eldest girl, aged 13, alleged that her step-father had sexually abused her over a period of years. The three younger sisters made no allegations. The step-father was tried on four counts of rape but acquitted by a jury after only a very short retirement. The local authority sought care orders over the three sisters, simply on the basis of the eldest girl's allegations.

The trial judge at the final care hearing was not impressed with the evidence of the mother and step-father but he found that the standard of proof was not met. He did have doubts: he was not satisfied that the girl's complaints were untrue and he thought that there was a real possibility that they were in fact true.

On the appeal of the local authority, the House of Lords considered the standard of proof to be applied in care proceedings. All Law Lords agreed that the requisite standard of proof is the ordinary civil standard, namely balance of probabilities; the majority considered that the judge's doubts could not form a proper basis for concluding that there was likely significant harm. Lord Nicholls said: 'a conclusion that the child is suffering or likely to suffer significant harm must be based on facts, not just suspicion'.[239] The local authority's appeal was dismissed.

The standard of proof in care proceedings is the balance of probabilities, that is, that the alleged facts are more probable than not[240] However, there has been controversy over whether there should be a gloss on the standard of proof for more serious allegations, that is, that there should be a heightened standard of proof where the allegations are more serious. The majority of the House of Lords in *Re H and R (Child Sexual Abuse: Standard of Proof)*[241] agreed with Lord Nicholls that stronger evidence is required to prove more serious allegations: 'the inherent probability or improbability of an event is itself a matter to be taken into account when weighing the probabilities'.[242] However, Lord Lloyd pointed out in his dissenting speech that it would be a bizarre result if the more serious the injury, the more difficult it became for the local authority to prove it.[243]

The issue of a gloss on the standard of proof was reconsidered by the House of Lords in *Re B (Children)(Sexual Abuse: Standard of Proof)*.[244] The House of Lords held that the

---

[238] Final Report of the Vulnerable Witnesses and Children Group (2015) para 35.
[239] *Re H and R (Child Sexual Abuse: Standard of Proof)* [1996] AC 563, at [592].
[240] [1996] AC 563.   [241] [1996] AC 563.   [242] [1996] AC 563, at [586].
[243] [1996] AC 563, at [577].   [244] [2008] UKHL 35.

standard of proof is to be applied without gloss or elaboration. There is no heightened standard of proof where the allegations are serious. Baroness Hale gave the lead judgment and said that the standard of proof is 'the simple balance of probabilities, neither more nor less. Neither the seriousness of the allegation nor the seriousness of the consequences should make any difference to the standard of proof to be applied in determining the facts'.[245] The standard of proof is the ordinary civil standard.

7.3 Comparison with the criminal standard of proof

The standard of proof in care proceedings is lower than the standard of proof in criminal proceedings. The care proceedings standard of proof is the balance of probabilities; the criminal standard of proof is beyond a reasonable doubt. This different standard of proof can permit a situation where a child can be removed from a parent in care proceedings even if the parent has been acquitted in a criminal trial.

In the conjoined cases *Re U (A Child) (Serious Injury: Standard of Proof); Re B (A Child) (Serious Injury: Standard of Proof)*[246] Dame Butler-Sloss sitting in the Court of Appeal used the opportunity to set out some of the reasons for the difference in the standard of proof. She said that the relaxed rules of evidence in care proceedings mean that more material is available to care courts than would be admitted in a criminal trial.[247] In addition, care proceedings allow a consideration of a wider range of choices to enable the protection of a child so 'a false positive in care proceedings may not be as dire as the consequence of the conviction of an innocent in criminal proceedings'.[248]

 Debate 5: Is the Standard of Proof in Care Proceedings Set at the Right Level?

The wrongful convictions of Sally Clark and Angela Cannings prompted debate about potential miscarriages of justice in care proceedings, including the risks of over-reliance on medical evidence and the standard of proof to be applied in care cases. Sally Clark served three years in prison for the murder of her two baby sons, Christopher and Harry, but the conviction was subsequently quashed by the Court of Appeal in 2003.[249] Her appeal was allowed because the Home Office had not disclosed evidence at the original trial that Harry had died from a bacterial infection. Similarly, Angela Cannings was wrongly convicted of the murder of her two baby sons, Jason and Matthew, and served 18 months in prison before her conviction was quashed in 2003.[250] Her appeal was allowed because medical research had moved on and it was now generally accepted that there could be a natural cause for multiple infant deaths in one family. Both cases concerned cot death where the only evidence against the mother was the repetition of occurrence. One expert, Sir Roy Meadow, had attracted attention because he had given evidence at Sally Clark's trial that the chance of two cot deaths in an affluent family was one in 73 million, a statistic which is now widely discredited. The Court of Appeal subsequently stated that 'in cases where reputable experts disagree on the causes of death and there is no other cogent evidence, prosecutions should not go ahead'.[251]

This controversy in the criminal courts had implications for the care courts as similar expert evidence is used, yet the requisite standard of proof is lower than the criminal standard.

---

[245] [2008] UKHL 35, at [70].   [246] [2004] EWCA Civ 567.   [247] [2004] EWCA Civ 567, at [22].
[248] [2004] EWCA Civ 567, at [27].
[249] *R v Clark (Sally) (Appeal against Conviction) (No. 2)* [2003] EWCA Crim 1020.
[250] *R v Cannings (Angela)* [2004] EWCA Crim 1.   [251] [2004] EWCA Crim 1 at [178].

Munby J said in in *Re Webster; Norfolk County Council v Webster and others (Nos 1 and 2)*: 'We cannot afford to proceed on the blinkered assumption that there have been no miscarriages of justice in the family justice system. This is something that has to be addressed with honesty and candour if the family justice system is not to suffer further loss of public confidence.'[252] The government subsequently ordered a review of all care cases where children had been removed from parents on the basis of disputed medical evidence alone. This resulted in the overturning of a number of care orders, suggested to be in the double figures.[253]

These miscarriages of justice have caused commentators to question whether the standard of proof in care proceedings is set at the right level. Lauren Devine and Stephen Parker argue: 'The lower standard of proof leaves parents particularly vulnerable, especially if the focus is not on whether specific acts or omissions have occurred but on a broad "picture" painted at a time when parents are not legally represented'.[254] In care courts, the evidence of the local authority is only required to satisfy the balance of probabilities for the threshold for intervention in family life to be crossed. However, as abuse often happens behind closed doors, the evidence before the court may be limited and contradictory. Because of the evidential difficulties inherent in care cases and the risk of miscarriages of justice, should the courts apply a higher standard of proof than the ordinary civil standard of balance of probabilities?

8. Final hearing: two stage test

At the final hearing, the court considers the issues in two stages:

1. Meeting the threshold criteria under s. 31(2) of the Children Act 1989;

2. If the threshold criteria is met, assessing the welfare of the child to determine what should happen in the best interests of the child.

The first stage is the threshold criteria. In this stage, the court must be satisfied that, on the balance of probabilities, all parts of the threshold criteria in s. 31(2) of the Children Act 1989 are met. If they are not all met, the court cannot intervene. In the recent case of *Re B (A Child) (Care Proceedings: Appeal)*[255] the Supreme Court gave lengthy guidance on the nature of the court's evaluation. The decision whether all parts of the threshold are crossed is a value judgement[256] which must be made on the basis of established facts.[257] The welfare principle is not relevant and the family's rights under Article 8 ECHR have no part to play in deciding whether the threshold is crossed.[258]

The second stage is the welfare assessment. This takes place only if all parts of the threshold criteria have been met. The court will decide what order to make, using the principles in the Children Act 1989, with the child's welfare being the paramount consideration,[259] and taking into account the family's Convention rights.[260] The order could be a care order, a supervision order, a Children Act 1989, s. 8 order or no order at all. Even if the threshold criteria are met, there is no obligation on the court to make a care order: in the House of Lords case of *Lancashire County Council v B (A Child) (Care Orders: Significant Harm)*

---

[252] [2006] EWHC 2733 (Fam), at [103].

[253] Dyer, C. 'So what happened to all the feared miscarriages of justice?' *The Guardian*, 9 January 2006.

[254] Devine, L. and Parker, S. 'Public Law Family Cases in the context of Miscarriages of Justice'[2015] *Argument and Critique* 12.

[255] [2013] UKSC 33.   [256] [2013] UKSC 33, at [44].   [257] [2013] UKSC 33, at [199].

[258] [2013] UKSC 33, at [62].   [259] Section 1(1).

[260] *Re B (A Child) (Care Proceedings: Appeal)* [2013] UKSC 33, at [62].

Lord Clyde said that 'the section merely opens the way to the possibility that an order may be made'.[261] The court may decide to make no order at all if this would be better for the welfare of the child in accordance with the non-intervention principle.[262]

8.1. **Final hearing: threshold criteria**

The first stage for the court in care proceedings is to establish whether all parts of the threshold criteria set out in s. 31(2) of the Children Act 1989 are met.

 Key Legislation 2: s. 31(2)

A court may only make a care order or supervision order if it is satisfied—

(a)   that the child concerned is suffering, or is likely to suffer, significant harm; and

(b)   that the harm, or likelihood of harm, is attributable to—

    (i)   the care given to the child, or likely to be given to him if the order were not made, not being what it would be reasonable to expect a parent to give to him; or

    (ii)   the child's being beyond parental control.

8.2 **'Child concerned is suffering'**

The first part of the threshold criteria is that the court must be satisfied, on the balance of probabilities, that the child either is suffering or is likely to suffer significant harm. One issue for the courts has been the meaning of 'is suffering'. This part of the threshold criteria is expressed in the present tense but, by the time of the hearing, the child may no longer be suffering harm. For example, the child may have been removed from the abusive situation by earlier local authority intervention. The courts have had to decide whether this part of the threshold criteria can be met even if, at the date of the hearing, the child is no longer suffering harm.

 Key Case 3: *Re M (A Minor) (Care Order: Threshold Conditions)* [1994] 2 AC 424

This case concerned a little boy whose mother had been brutally stabbed to death by his father when he was 4 months old. The murder took place in the family home in front of him and his three half-siblings.

By the time of the appeal hearing before the House of Lords, the boy had spent the past seven months living with his brothers and sisters, cared for by his mother's cousin. The local authority accepted that he was well settled there and those arrangements should continue.

The issue before the court was whether a care order could or should be made. The Court of Appeal had held that the court had no jurisdiction to make a care order because the 'is suffering' requirement in the threshold criteria was not met as the little boy was no longer suffering harm.

The House of Lords unanimously held that the court did have jurisdiction to make a care order even though, by the date of the hearing, the boy was a boisterous, happy and healthy child. Lord Nolan said:

---

[261] *Lancashire County Council v A (A Child) (Care Orders: Significant Harm)* [2000] 2 AC 147.
[262] Section 1(5).

> Parliament cannot have intended that temporary measures taken to protect the child from immediate harm should prevent the court from regarding the child as one who is suffering . . . The focal point of the inquiry must be the situation which resulted in the temporary measures being taken, and which has led to the application for a care or supervision order.[263]

The relevant date for assessing the harm that the child 'is suffering' is the date on which the local authority initiated protective arrangements for the child.[264] This could include the local authority voluntarily accommodating the child,[265] obtaining an emergency protection order, obtaining an interim care order, or commencing proceedings for a care order. However, for this to apply, the protective arrangements must have been continuously in place from the time of the intervention to the date of assessment by the court.[266] Therefore, even if the child is no longer suffering harm at the date of the hearing, the court is not precluded from finding that this part of the threshold is crossed. A balance is struck between allowing the court intervention for the better protection of the child and enabling parents to move on with their lives once the protective arrangements are no longer in place.

Although the relevant date of the harm is the date that protective arrangements were first put in place, the court can take into account information that was not known at that time. In *Re G (Children) (Care Order: Evidence)*,[267] the Court of Appeal held that the local authority can rely on information acquired after the date that the local authority first intervened. Lady Hale said that later information may throw light on the facts known at the relevant date and gave the following examples: 'further medical evidence on the interpretation of X-rays and scans, further complaints by the children, or confessions by the parents'.[268] These types of later information can show what the situation was at the relevant date and so can be relied upon at the hearing.

In addition, the Court of Appeal held that later events can also be relied upon at the hearing but only if they are capable of illustrating the position at the time the local authority first intervened.[269] Lady Hale said, whereas later acts of violence may be admissible,[270] the local authority would not be able to rely on other later events such as the parent's collapse brought on by the stress and strain of the proceedings because that would 'introduce a completely different risk which did not exist at the relevant date'.[271]

The admissibility of later events means that the local authority can commence proceedings on one basis, yet satisfy the threshold criteria on a different basis. In *Re L (Children) (Care Proceedings: Threshold Criteria)*[272] Wall LJ sitting in the Court of Appeal said that 'as a matter of law, it is open to a local authority to advance a case on the satisfaction of the threshold criteria which is different from the basis upon which it instituted the proceeding',[273] provided that the new basis existed at the date of the date the proceedings were started and the parents are given good notice of the new grounds.[274] In this case the local authority had started the proceedings on the basis that the children had been whipped but, on realising that evidence was lacking, then sought to rely on other allegations that the father was aggressive, that he had failed to protect the daughter from a sexual assault,

---

[263] *Re M (A Minor) (Care Order: Threshold Conditions)* [1994] 2 AC 424, at [441].
[264] [1994] 2 AC 424.   [265] *Southwark London Borough Council v B* [1998] 2 FLR 1095.
[266] *Re M (A Minor) (Care Order: Threshold Conditions)* [1994] 2 AC 424, at [434].
[267] [2001] EWCA Civ 968.   [268] [2001] EWCA Civ 968, at [22].   [269] [2001] EWCA Civ 968.
[270] [2001] EWCA Civ 968, at [15].   [271] [2001] EWCA Civ 968, at [14].
[272] [2006] EWCA Civ 1282.   [273] [2006] EWCA Civ 1282, at [42].
[274] [2006] EWCA Civ 1282, at [42].

and that the children were at risk of emotional harm because of the parents' severe learning difficulties. In fact, although allowed to introduce a different basis, the local authority's evidence did not satisfy the court and the parents' appeal was allowed.

In *Re A (Children) (Split Hearings: Practice)*[275] the Court of Appeal approved the making of a final care order on the basis of the mother's personality disorder even though this was diagnosed after the proceedings had been started and represented a totally different basis from the event which caused the local authority to start the proceedings, namely the child suffering a fractured skull. The personality disorder existed before the date of the local authority's intervention, even if it was not diagnosed until after the proceedings were started.

8.3 'Likely to suffer'

The first part of the threshold criteria sets out two possibilities: both harm that has already been caused to the child and any harm that is likely to happen in the future. This means that the local authority can take action to protect a child at risk of significant harm, even if it has not yet occurred, for example if a known abuser is planning to move in with the child or one of the child's siblings has made allegations of abuse.

One issue for the courts has been the meaning of 'likely'.

Key Case 4: *Re R (A Child) (Care Order: Threshold Criteria)* [2009] EWCA Civ 942

This case concerned two girls: one a baby and the other a toddler. The mother had led a chaotic lifestyle, exposing the toddler to drug taking and violence. The toddler was taken into interim care and the baby was too, at birth. The local authority was seeking a care order over both children with a view to adoption.

The mother conceded that the threshold was crossed for the toddler but not for the baby. The mother had reformed her lifestyle after the birth of the baby and had not taken drugs for 20 months. Supervised contact with the children had gone very well.

At first instance, the recorder found the threshold crossed for the toddler but not for the baby and ordered the placement of both children with their mother. On appeal, the Court found the threshold crossed with respect to both children and made a care order. Wilson LJ gave the lead judgement. He said that the recorder had equated the word 'likely' with probability. This approach was incorrect; it needed to be a real possibility or one that could not sensibly be ignored. This was clearly demonstrated on the evidence in this case. As the threshold was crossed, the Court was able to make an interim care order over both children.

The meaning of 'likely' is 'real possibility'.[276] Lord Nicholls sitting in an earlier Supreme Court case of *Re H and R (Child Sexual Abuse: Standard of Proof)* gave the following guidance: 'likely is being used in the sense of a real possibility, a possibility that cannot sensibly be ignored having regard to the nature and gravity of the feared harm in the particular case'.[277]

This is a low threshold. In *Re B (A Child) (Care Proceedings: Appeal)* Lady Hale sitting in the Supreme Court said: 'The reason for adopting comparatively low threshold of likelihood is clear: some harm is so catastrophic that even a relatively small degree of likelihood should be sufficient to justify the state in intervening to protect the child before it happens,

---

[275] [2006] EWCA Civ 714.   [276] [2009] EWCA Civ 942.
[277] *Re H and R (Child Sexual Abuse: Standard of Proof)* [1996] AC 563, at [585].

for example from death or serious injury or sexual abuse'.[278] It therefore appears that the required level of possibility varies according to the degree of seriousness. If the feared harm is that the child may be killed, a lower level of possibility will satisfy the court than that required if the feared harm is that the child may miss school.[279] The test of likelihood is flexible.

To assess likelihood, the court must firstly make a finding of actual facts on the balance of probabilities that the disputed event did occur,[280] that is, that the child was abused by a known, identifiable abuser. It is only once that finding of fact is made that the court can go on to consider whether significant harm is likely to the child or to another child. If the primary facts are not proven on a balance of probabilities, the court cannot take those facts into account to conclude that significant harm is likely.[281] The court's approach causes difficulties in cases where the child is an 'unharmed sibling' in an 'unknown perpetrator' case: where it is not known which of the carers caused the harm, the court cannot make a finding of fact and so there is no likelihood of harm to an unharmed sibling in the future.[282] This is discussed in section 9.4.

8.4 'Significant harm'

The threshold test requires a finding of significant harm: either actual significant harm that has already happened to the child or a risk of significant harm that is likely in the future.

 Key Legislation 3: s. 31(9)

'harm' means ill-treatment or the impairment of health or development including, for example, impairment suffered from seeing or hearing the ill-treatment of another;
'development' means physical, intellectual, emotional, social or behavioural development;
'health' means physical or mental health; and
'ill-treatment' includes sexual abuse and forms of ill-treatment which are not physical.

A definition of 'harm' is set out in the Children Act 1989 but Lady Hale also provided the following additional guidance in *Re B (A Child) (Care Proceedings: Appeal)*:

> Ill-treatment will generally involve some active conduct, whether physical or sexual abuse, bullying or other forms of active emotional abuse. Impairment may also be the result of active conduct towards the child, but it could also be the result of neglecting the child's needs, for food, for warmth, for shelter, for love, for education, for health care[283]

The statutory definition also includes impairment suffered from seeing or hearing the ill treatment of another, so a child witnessing domestic violence may be harmed, even if they are not physically harmed. This is therefore a broad definition of harm.

For the threshold to be met, the harm must be significant. In each case, the court must carry out an assessment as to whether the seriousness of the alleged harm is sufficient to justify a determination that the threshold is met, authorising state intervention in family life.

---

[278] *Re B (A Child)* [2013] UKSC 33, at [188].
[279] *Re S-B (Children) (Care Proceedings: Standard of Proof)* [2009] UKSC 17, at [9].
[280] [2009] UKSC 17, at [49].   [281] *Re H and R (Child Sexual Abuse: Standard of Proof)* [1996] AC 563.
[282] *Re J (Children) (Care Proceedings: Threshold Criteria)* [2013] UKSC 9.
[283] *Re B (A Child) (Care Proceedings: Appeal)* [2013] UKSC 333, at [192].

Key Case 5: *Re MA (Children) (Care Threshold)* [2009] EWCA Civ 853; [2009] EWCA Civ 853

This case concerned three siblings aged 3 years, 1 year, and 4 months. It was an appeal against the lower court's refusal to make a finding of significant harm.

The local authority had commenced care proceedings after finding out that their parents had abused a young niece when she came to live with them. The trial judge made a finding that the niece had suffered significant harm because the parents had subjected her to 'shocking' abuse including physical beatings. It was agreed by all parties that the threshold was crossed for the niece and that she should never be returned to the parents' care.

However, the position over the natural children was less straightforward. The children appeared to be well nourished, well cared for with close attachments to the parents and had suffered no apparent harm as a result of exposure to the mistreatment of the niece. The local authority's case was partly based on their exposure to the ill-treatment of the niece but there were also allegations of physical abuse to the eldest child including slapping, kicking, and pushing.

The majority in the Court of Appeal dismissed the local authority's appeal and held that the judge was entitled to decline to find significant harm. Hallett LJ said: 'Slaps and even kicks vary enormously in their seriousness . . . What M alleged, therefore, was not necessarily indicative of abuse. It will all depend on the circumstances.'[284]

Although the treatment of the niece was shocking, it was held that the natural children were not likely to suffer similar harm as there had been good evidence before the trial judge that the parents had treated their own biological children differently from the niece.

The Court of Appeal considered the threshold not to be crossed: any harm must be significant enough to justify the intervention of the state. Ward LJ said:

> Society must be willing to tolerate very diverse standards of parenting, including the eccentric, the barely adequate and the inconsistent. It follows too that children will inevitably have both very different experiences of parenting and very unequal consequences flowing from it . . . These are the consequences of our human fallibility and it is not the provenance of the state to spare children all the consequences of defective parenting. In any event, it simply could not be done.[285]

There is no statutory definition of the meaning of 'significant' and judicial guidance is mixed about whether a dictionary definition should be used. Historically the courts have applied the ordinary dictionary definition meaning of 'considerable, noteworthy or important' initially suggested by Booth J sitting the High Court case of *Humberside County Council v B*.[286] However, more recently, the majority in the Supreme Court case of *Re B (A Child) (Care Proceedings: Appeal)*[287] tried to avoid using a definition. Lord Wilson said: 'In my view this court should avoid attempting to explain the word 'significant'. It would be a gloss; attention might then turn to the meaning of the gloss and, albeit with the best of intentions, the courts might find in due course that they had travelled far from the word itself.'[288] The court should consider the facts specific to each case when determining whether the harm is significant or not.

---

[284] *Re MA (Children) (Care Threshold)* [2009] EWCA Civ 853, at [39].
[285] [2009] EWCA Civ 853, at [49].   [286] [1993] 1 FLR 257.   [287] [2013] UKSC 33.
[288] *Re B (A Child) (Care Proceedings: Appeal)* [2013] UKSC 33, at [26].

8.5 **Similar child**

When considering whether harm is significant, the court can compare the child's health or development with that of a similar child under s. 31(10).

Key Legislation 4: s. 31(10)

> Where the question of whether harm suffered by a child is significant turns on the child's health or development, his health or development shall be compared with that which could reasonably be expected of a similar child.

This test has caused difficulties because one of the issues for the court is who can be deemed to be a similar child. It is generally accepted that the child should be compared with a child of the same gender and age, and, where the child has health issues, the child should be compared with a child suffering similar issues. It has been suggested that the child should be compared with a similar child from the same cultural, social, or religious background. In *Re K*[289] the High Court found the threshold not met because, although the 15-year-old girl had married a much older man, the family had recently arrived in this country from Iraq where cultural expectations are different. However, in the High Court case of *Re O (A Minor) (Care Proceedings: Education)*,[290] it was held that, in relation to a child who is truanting from school, the comparison should be made with a child of similar intellectual and social development who is going to school, rather than a child who is truanting from school.

DEBATE 6: WHAT BALANCE SHOULD BE STRUCK BETWEEN PROTECTING CHILDREN FROM HARM AND AVOIDING UNWARRANTED INTERFERENCE IN FAMILY LIFE?

One debate concerns the application of the similar child comparator as required by s. 31(10) which states: 'Where the question of whether harm suffered by a child is significant turns on the child's health or development, his health or development shall be compared with that which could reasonably be expected of a similar child.'

Although accepted by the courts that a child should be compared with one of the same gender and age, controversy surrounds the issue of whether additional characteristics may be factored into any comparison. For example, it could be argued that a child should be compared with another from the same socio-economic background. A child's failure to thrive could be caused by the family's income rather than deficits in parental care and such a comparison would enable the court to make allowances for factors external to the parents' capabilities. Otherwise, the court would risk removing children with low birth weight and subsequent under-development simply because they are living in families constrained by poverty. However, taking into account the characteristics of similarly deprived children means that the court would apply a higher threshold for intervention to children living in areas of high unemployment and deprivation than those living in affluent areas. Such an approach could permit neglect not tolerated for other children living within the same jurisdiction.

Another issue is whether under s. 31(10) the child should be compared with another from the same cultural or religious background. Julia Brophy has carried out research which

---

[289] [2005] EWHC 2956 (Fam).   [290] [1992] 1 WLR 912.

identified differences in parenting practice between ethnic groups.[291] For example, some African, South-Asian, and Afro-Caribbean parents in her study said that their approach to physical punishment differed from that of white parents. It could be argued that, when evaluating impairments in health caused by physical chastisement, comparison should be made with children from the same ethnic or religious background; if the culture of the family is ignored in any similar child comparison, the values of Western European parenting would be imposed on all families, whereas the courts acknowledge that family diversity should be respected. For example, Hedley J writes: 'The essential issues of family life—culture, religion, discipline, working parents and childcare, parental separation and lifestyles generally, however profound their impact on the child, remain a matter for parental responsibility'.[292] However, taking into account cultural differences would allow the background of the family to affect the level of protection afforded to the child. For some commentators, this would be unacceptable. Heather Keating argues: 'Cultural relativism has no place in child protection cases: all children, whatever their ethnic origin, have an equal right to protection under the high threshold for statutory intervention'.[293]

Should the type and level of harm required to trigger state intervention differ according to the socio-economic and cultural background of the family?

8.6 Attributable to a lack of reasonable parental care or the child being beyond parental control

The final part of the threshold criteria requires that the harm, or likelihood of harm, must be attributable: either to a lack of reasonable parental care or to the child being beyond parental control.[294]

8.6.1 Attributable to lack of reasonable parental care

If the local authority is alleging this part of the criteria, the court must consider whether the care given to the child is not what it would be reasonable to expect a parent to give to him.[295] The care can include causing harm to the child. In addition the care can include failing to protect the child from harm. In *A (A Child) v Leeds City Council*[296] the Court of Appeal allowed the local authority to remove a 3-year-old child from her aunt's care because the aunt had little appreciation of what constituted risks and failed to cooperate with professionals.

Again, there must be a causal link between the harm and the parents. In the High Court case of *Islington London Borough Council v Al Alas*[297] the local authority was not able to prove on a balance of probabilities that the child's injuries were the result of inflicted deliberate harm by the parents so the threshold was not met. In criminal proceedings it had been established that the child's sibling had died as a result of Vitamin D deficiency.

Any harm must be proven by the local authority to be non-accidental. Otherwise, the causal connection between the harm and parents is not established. In *Re L (A Child) (Care Proceedings: Responsibility for Child's Injury)*[298] the Court of Appeal held that the local authority had not proven on the balance of probabilities that the parents had caused

---

[291] Brophy, J. 'Child Maltreatment in Diverse Households: Challenges to Law, Theory and Practice' (2008) 35 *Journal of Law and Society* 75, 83.

[292] Hedley, M. 'Family Life and Child Protection: Cleveland, Baby P et al' (2014) 26 *Child and Family Law Quarterly* 7, 8.

[293] Keating, H. 'Re MA: The Significance of Harm' (2011) 23 *Child and Family Law Quarterly* 115, 124.

[294] Section 31(2)(b).   [295] Section 31(2)(b)(i).   [296] [2011] EWCA Civ 1365.

[297] [2012] EWHC 865 (Fam).   [298] [2006] EWCA Civ 49.

their baby's fractured skull because the local authority had not demonstrated on the evidence that the injury was non-accidental. Wall LJ said: 'a child may receive serious accidental injuries whilst in the care of his or her parents, even where those parents are both conscientious and competent.'[299] However, the threshold could be met by the parents' subsequent actions if they included a failure to call an ambulance. Wall LJ continued: 'The failure to call the ambulance could legitimately constitute a proper basis for the proposition that BL was likely to suffer significant harm due to the parent's failure to ensure that he received immediate treatment.'[300]

A parent's character or behaviour (e.g. a criminal record) will only satisfy this part of the threshold if it can be shown to affect the care of the child. In *Hertfordshire County Council v H*[301] it was held that the mother's mental health problems were not sufficient in the absence of non-accidental injury to meet the threshold. Parker J sitting in the High Court said: 'I am satisfied that the mother's mental health problems cannot prove what is otherwise unprovable. The most it can do it set the scene to provide an explanation.'[302] Similarly, learning difficulties do not automatically meet the threshold. In *Re L (Children) (Care Proceedings: Threshold Criteria)*[303] Wall LJ sitting in the Court of Appeal said:

> The family courts do not remove children from their parents into care because the parents are not intelligent enough to care for them or have low intelligence quotas. Children are only removed into care (1) if they are suffering or likely to suffer significant harm in the care of their parents; and (2) if it is in their interests that a care order is made. Anything else is social engineering and wholly impermissible.[304]

The Supreme Court made it clear in *Lancashire County Council v B (A Child) (Care Orders: Significant Harm)*[305] that the reasonable parent test is an objective one. For example Lord Nicholls said: 'To be within section 31(2)(b)(i) the care given or likely to be given must fall below an objectively acceptable level. That level is the care a reasonable parent would provide for the child concerned.' The care given by a parent with mental health problems or learning difficulties would be compared with that given by a reasonable parent and any deficiencies in care would not automatically meet the threshold.

Hughes LJ gave an explanation for the objective test in the Court of Appeal case of *Re D (A Child) (Care Order: Evidence)*:[306]

> For the avoidance of doubt, the test under s.31(2) is and has to be an objective one. If it were otherwise, and the "care which it is reasonable to expect a parent to give" were to be judged by the standards of the parent with the characteristics of the particular parent in question, the protection afforded to children would be very limited indeed, if not illusory.[307]

Providing the necessary causative link is established, the parents do not have to be badly intentioned or their conduct blameworthy. The issue is simply whether their care meets the objective standard set by a reasonable hypothetical parent.

The objective standard is tolerant of different styles of parenting. In *Re B (A Child) (Care Proceedings: Appeal)*[308] Lady Hale said:

> We are all frail human beings, with our fair share of unattractive character traits, which sometimes manifest themselves in bad behaviours which may be copied by our children.

---

[299] *Re L (A Child) (Care Proceedings: Responsibility for Child's Injury)* [2006] EWCA Civ 49, at [51].
[300] [2006] EWCA Civ 49, at [55].   [301] [2013] EWHC 4049 (Fam).
[302] [2013] EWHC 4049 (Fam), at [15].   [303] [2006] EWCA Civ 1282.
[304] [2006] EWCA Civ 1282, at [49].   [305] [2000] 2 AC 147.   [306] [2010] EWCA Civ 1000.
[307] [2010] EWCA Civ 1000, at [35].   [308] [2013] UKSC 33.

But the State does not and cannot take away the children of all the people who commit crimes, who abuse alcohol or drugs, who suffer from physical or mental illnesses or disabilities, or who espouse antisocial political or religious beliefs.[309]

In the recent case of *Re A (Application for Care Placement Order: Local Authority Failings)*[310] the President of the Family Division, Sir James Munby, held that the threshold was not met simply because the father was immature, lacked insight, and enjoyed drinking alcohol and smoking cannabis. He said 'I can accept that the father may not be the best of parents, he may be a less than suitable role model, but that is not enough to justify a care order let alone adoption. We must guard against the risk of social engineering.'[311]

8.6.2 Attributable to the child being beyond parental control

The local authority may allege this part of the criteria if for example the child is beyond parental control[312] because the child is a drug addict or keeps running away. There must be a causal connection between harm and the parents, even if the causal connection is only slight. In the High Court case of *Re P (Permission to Withdraw Care Proceedings)*[313] the threshold was not met because, even though the child was suffering from mental health problems and was out of control, her adoptive parents were not culpable in any way. The child's behaviour was caused by her early abusive childhood before adoption.

9. Shared care and unknown perpetrators

It is very difficult for the court in unknown perpetrator cases, where it is proven that the child has suffered a non-accidental injury but the perpetrator of the abuse cannot be identified on the facts, perhaps because the care of the child is shared and the available evidence cannot establish when the child suffered the injury.

9.1 Meeting the threshold criteria under Children Act 1989, s. 31(2)

The issue for the court is still whether the threshold criterion is met: whether the harm can be said to be attributable to parental care even if the harm may have been caused by a third party. This is important, given the fact that the care of children is often shared between adults. If the threshold criteria are not met in cases of unknown perpetrators, a significant number of children would remain unprotected.

 Key Case 6: *Lancashire County Council v A (A Child) (Care Orders: Significant Harm)* [2000] 2 AC 147

This case concerned a 7-month-old baby girl who had suffered serious injury due to violent shaking. The perpetrator of the harm was not known: her mother, her father, or her childminder. The childminder had a baby boy of about the same age who had suffered no injury. The local authority brought care proceedings over both children, arguing that the baby girl had suffered significant harm and the baby boy was likely to suffer significant harm.

The trial judge dismissed the care order applications. This was because he could not make a clear finding of fact as to who caused the injuries. He held that the threshold criteria were not

---

[309] [2013] UKSC 33, at [143].   [310] [2015] EWFC 11.   [311] [2015] EWFC 11, at [96].
[312] Section 31(2)(b)(ii).   [313] [2016] EWFC B2.

met for either child. The local authority appealed. The Court of Appeal allowed the appeal in respect of the baby girl, but dismissed it in respect of the childminder's baby boy. The parents of the baby girl appealed to the House of Lords. No appeal was taken in relation to the childminder's baby boy.

The House of Lords dismissed the parents' appeal and upheld the Court of Appeal decision that the threshold for the baby girl was crossed. They unanimously held that the attributable condition was met even where there is no more than a possibility that a parent was responsible for inflicting the injuries.

The words in the threshold criteria 'care given to the child' can mean given by any carer of the child so it is not necessary for the court to make a finding that the deficient care was provided by a parent for the threshold to be crossed. Lord Nicholls gave the lead judgement. He said: 'The phrase "care given to the child" is apt to embrace not merely the care given by the parents or other primary carers; it is apt to embrace the care given by any of the carers.'[314]

Where a non-carer causes harm, the threshold is not met unless there is a causal connection between the harm and the parents. Lord Clyde specifically excluded 'harm which is not attributable to the care given to the child, for example, harm which has come about through some unforeseeable event against which no one could have taken any precaution'.[315]

The causal connection need not be strong and does not require fault. Lord Nicholls said that the connection 'need not be that of a sole or dominant or direct cause and effect: a contributory causal connection suffices'.[316] The attributable requirement can therefore be satisfied by a failure to protect the child and can be unintentional.

The attributable part of the threshold criteria can still be met even where the perpetrator of the harm cannot be identified.[317] Where the care of the child is shared, it is sufficient for the court to be satisfied that the deficit was attributable to any of the carers. This may mean that a child is removed from their parents unnecessarily but that concern is outweighed by the need to protect the child from further harm. However, if the harm is caused by someone other than a primary carer (e.g. by a stranger in the park), it would not be deemed to be attributable to parental care unless it would have been reasonable to expect a parent to have prevented it.

The precise meaning of the word 'carer' can cause difficulties. The term clearly covers people who have day-to-day care of the child such as childminders.[318] Lady Hale sitting in the Supreme Court case of *Re S-B (Children) (Care Proceedings: Standard of Proof)*[319] has suggested that 'carer' would exclude teaching and health professionals.[320] She said: 'If the harm has been caused by someone outside the home or family, for example at school or in hospital or by a stranger, then it is not attributable to the parental care unless it would have been reasonable to expect a parent to have prevented it'.[321] It is unclear whether a babysitter or home tutor would come within the remit of 'carer'.

9.2 Pool of possible perpetrators

The approach of the courts in unknown perpetrator cases is to identify a pool of possible perpetrators. If the court cannot identify the perpetrator on a balance of probabilities,[322]

---

[314] *Lancashire County Council v A (A Child) (Care Orders: Significant Harm)* [2000] 2 AC 147, at [166].
[315] [2000] 2 AC 147, at [168].   [316] [2000] 2 AC 147, at [162].   [317] [2000] 2 AC 147.
[318] [2000] 2 AC 147.   [319] [2009] UKSC 19.   [320] [2009] UKSC 19, at [21].
[321] [2009] UKSC 19, at [40].   [322] [2009] UKSC 19, at [34].

all must be treated as suspect. The court would then use the list of possible perpetrators in any subsequent welfare assessment. In *Re S-B (Children) (Care Proceedings: Standard of Proof)*[323] Lady Hale said that it is important to identify the pool of possible perpetrators because 'it will help to identify the real risks to the child and the steps needed to protect him. It will help the professionals in working with the family. And it will be of value to the child in the long run'.[324]

This approach makes the welfare assessment more difficult when the judge has to assess what to do in the best interests of the child.[325] If the perpetrator remains unknown, assessing risk and deciding what protective measures to put in place becomes much harder. Therefore, in the Court of Appeal case of *Re D (Children) (Non-Accidental Injury)*[326] Wall LJ who was giving the lead judgment commented that: 'if the perpetrator can be identified on the balance of probabilities, it is the judge's duty to do so, although the court should not strain to make a finding of fact if the evidence is not available'.[327] In this case the evidence was not available for the court to be able to exclude either the mother or the father as perpetrator.

9.3 Test for inclusion in the pool of possible perpetrators

The test for inclusion in the pool of possible perpetrators was considered by the Court of Appeal in *North Yorkshire County Council v SA*.[328] This case set out the correct approach as to how to decide whether or not to include someone in the list of possible perpetrators. In this case, there were four possible perpetrators of the harm caused to the child: the mother, the father, the grandmother, and the night nanny. The trial judge had applied a 'no possibility' test: the court could only exclude a person if there was no possibility that the person had injured the child. On this basis, he had included all four people in the pool of possible perpetrators. Dame Butler-Sloss said that the 'no possibility' test was 'patently too wide and might encompass anyone who had even a fleeting contact with the child in circumstances in which there was the opportunity to cause injuries'.[329] She preferred a test of likelihood and real possibility: the court can include someone in the pool if there is likelihood or a real possibility that they were a perpetrator of the injuries.[330] On that basis, the parents were included in the pool of possible perpetrators, but not the grandmother or night nanny.

In summary, the court will include a person in the pool of possible perpetrators if there is a likelihood or real possibility that they caused the harm. Thorpe LJ said that, when deciding whether to include a person in the pool, courts should carry out 'a review of all relevant facts and circumstances including opportunity'.[331]

9.4 Unknown perpetrators and unharmed siblings

Another difficult situation for the courts is how to treat an unharmed sibling in unknown perpetrator cases. When a child has suffered a non-accidental injury but the identity of the perpetrator cannot be established and the parents have gone on to live separately, the courts have had to decide whether the threshold is crossed for any other child living in the household who has not been injured (an 'unharmed sibling').

---

[323] [2009] UKSC 19.
[324] *Re S-B (Children) (Care Proceedings: Standard of Proof)* [2009] UKSC 17 at [40].
[325] Section 1(1).   [326] [2009] EWCA Civ 472.   [327] [2009] EWCA Civ 472 at [12].
[328] [2003] EWCA Civ 839.   [329] [2003] EWCA Civ 839 at [25].
[330] [2003] EWCA Civ 839 at [26].   [331] [2003] EWCA Civ 839 at [44].

Key Case 7: *Re J (Children) (Care Proceedings: Threshold Criteria)* [2013] UKSC 9

This case concerned three children living with a woman who had been in a pool of possible perpetrators. The woman's first child had died seven years previously of non-accidental injuries. At that time, the woman was living with a former partner and it was not established on the evidence who had caused the fatal injuries to her first child. Subsequently the woman went on to live with a new partner and have a child with him. He had two children by a previous relationship who also lived with them.

The issue for the Supreme Court was whether the woman's inclusion in a pool of possible perpetrators in earlier proceedings involving a different child and a different relationship could meet the threshold for a subsequent unharmed child in later proceedings. The Court unanimously held that it could not: the threshold was not crossed for the unharmed siblings.

Lady Hale commented on the rarity of the case before them. The local authority had deliberately presented a one point case for the sake of legal precedent and had not relied on other available arguments such as the mother's deception of the authorities.

The Supreme Court held that being in a pool of possible perpetrators will not automatically meet the threshold for an unharmed sibling as 'a real possibility that something has happened in the past is not enough to predict that it will happen in the future'.[332] However, the majority considered that it may be relevant when combined with other facts such as colluding to deceive the authorities and delaying medical assistance for the harmed child.

The threshold is not crossed for an unharmed sibling if the court cannot say which parent was the perpetrator and they are now living separately.[333] Previously Lady Hale had said *Re S-B (Children) (Care Proceedings: Standard of Proof)*:[334] 'a prediction of future harm has to be based upon findings of actual fact made on the balance of probabilities'.[335] In this case the Supreme Court allowed the mother's appeal against the making of care orders and remitted the case for rehearing: only one of the children had been harmed, the parents had subsequently separated, both boys were now living with their mother, and it was not known which of the parents had caused the harm.

Being in a pool of possible perpetrators for injury to another child is not by itself sufficient for a finding of likely significant harm in future proceedings in relation to other children. More evidence is needed besides being in a pool of possible perpetrators for the threshold to be met. However, being in a pool of possible perpetrators can be relevant when coupled with other facts or circumstances. Lord Hope in *Re J (Children) (Care Proceedings: Threshold Criteria)*[336] said 'it may have a bearing on the weight of evidence when looked at as a whole, including an assessment of the balance of probabilities'.[337] The court can take into account the parent's actions at the time of the original injury in order to assess the parents' capabilities and the likelihood of harm to an unharmed sibling. The actions may include delay in seeking medical attention or concealment of the child's injuries from the authorities.[338] The court can also take into account the parent's current circumstances such as having separated from the other parent.[339]

---

[332] *Re J* [2013] UKSC 9 at [49].   [333] [2013] UKSC 9.   [334] [2009] UKSC 17.
[335] [2009] UKSC 17, at [49].   [336] [2013] UKSC 9.   [337] [2013] UKSC 9, at [87].
[338] [2013] UKSC 9, at [52].   [339] [2013] UKSC 9, at [53].

10. Final hearing: welfare assessment

If all parts of the threshold criteria are met, the court moves onto the welfare assessment and decides what order to make. The court acquires jurisdiction to make a care order or supervision order under Part IV of the Children Act 1989. However, there is no obligation on the court to make such an order as the court may feel it more appropriate to make a private law Children Act 1989, s. 8 order (see Chapter 9) or no order at all.

10.1 Principles

When deciding what order to make, the court applies a number of principles set out in the Children Act 1989. The paramount consideration of the court is the welfare of the child under s. 1(1).

 Key Legislation 5: s. 1(1)

When a court determines any question with respect to—
   (a) the upbringing of a child; or
   (b) the administration of a child's property or the application of any income arising from it,the child's welfare shall be the court's paramount consideration.

The court also takes into account the no delay principle: that any delay in determining the question is likely to prejudice the welfare of the child.[340] This means that the court will try to make a final order if at all possible, instead of prolonging the proceedings by adjourning the hearing and making an interim order.

   Even if the court is prepared to make an order, the court must also consider whether it is actually necessary. This is because of the non-intervention principle: the court will not make an order unless it considers that doing so would be better for the child than making no order at all.[341]

10.2 Welfare checklist

When considering the welfare of the child, the court must take into account the factors in the welfare checklist set out in s. 1(3) of the Children Act 1989.

 Key Legislation 6: s. 1(3)

A court shall have regard in particular to—
   (a) the ascertainable wishes and feelings of the child concerned (considered in the light of his age and understanding);
   (b) his physical, emotional and educational needs;
   (c) the likely effect on him of any change in his circumstances;
   (d) his age, sex, background and any characteristics of his which the court considers relevant;
   (e) any harm which he has suffered or is at risk of suffering;

---

[340] Section 1(2).   [341] Section 1(5).

> (f) how capable each of his parents, and any other person in relation to whom the court considers the question to be relevant, is of meeting his needs;
>
> (g) the range of powers available to the court under this Act in the proceedings in question.

Within s. 1(3)(e) of the welfare checklist the court must take into account 'any harm which the child has suffered or is at risk of suffering'. An issue for the courts has been whether harm that is not proven can be taken into account. This might occur, for example, where the threshold criteria are satisfied on the basis of emotional harm but there are allegations of sexual abuse not proven on a balance of probabilities. In *Re O and N (Children) (Non-Accidental Injury: Burden of Proof); Re B (A Child) (Non-Accidental Injury: Compelling Medical Evidence),*[342] Lord Nicholls in the House of Lords said that such unproven allegations should not be taken into account: in the welfare assessment 'the court should proceed on the footing that the unproven allegations are no more than that' because of the risk of 'depriving the child and the family of the protection intended to be afforded by the threshold criteria'.[343] His view accorded with the judgment of an earlier Court of Appeal case, *Re M & R (Minors) (Child Abuse: Expert Evidence).*[344] In this case, the court upheld the trial judge's decision that allegations of sexual abuse should not be taken into account in the welfare assessment because the evidence available on this point had not proved the abuse as a fact on the balance of probabilities and did not satisfy the threshold criteria. Butler-Sloss LJ held that conclusions must be based on facts, not on suspicion or doubts.

Thus the House of Lords held that the welfare checklist factor s. 1(3)(e) should be interpreted in the same way as s. 31(2)(a) of the threshold criteria.[345] However, it could be argued that this decision is incorrect and, if there is an identified risk of harm, it should perhaps be considered in the welfare assessment, even if it has not been proven as a fact at the threshold stage. The factor in the welfare checklist at s. 1(3)(e) uses the phrase 'risk of any harm', not 'likely significant harm'. This could be regarded as much broader phrasing than the threshold criteria.

Within s. 1(3)(g) of the welfare checklist the court must have regard to the range of powers available to the court and therefore must be able to consider all of the orders available. This means that, even if the threshold criteria are satisfied, the court must still consider whether to make a private law s. 8 order. Although theoretically the court can make a private law order even if the threshold criteria are not satisfied, the court must first decide whether the public law threshold criteria are met so that the full range of orders is available to the court, both in public law and in private law.

10.3 **Available options**

If the threshold criteria are met, the court has a great deal of choice as a number of options are available to the court in the welfare assessment. For example, the court has the power to make a care order under s. 33 or a supervision order under s. 35. This is not limited by

---

[342] [2003] UKHL 18.

[343] *Re O and N (Children) (Non-Accidental Injury: Burden of Proof); Re B (A Child)(Non-Accidental Injury: Compelling Medical Evidence)* [2003] UKHL 18, at [38].

[344] [1996] 2 FLR 195.

[345] *Re O and N (Children) (Non-Accidental Injury: Burden of Proof); Re B (A Child)(Non-Accidental Injury: Compelling Medical Evidence)* [2003] UKHL 18.

what the parties are seeking: the court has the power to make a care order even if the local authority has only applied for a supervision order and vice versa.[346] However, in the High Court case of *Oxfordshire County Council v L (Care or Supervision Order)*[347] it was held that there should be cogent reasons to impose an order more draconian than that sought by the local authority.

The court also has the power to make a child arrangements order or other s. 8 order, regardless of whether the threshold criteria are met. For example, the court may make a child arrangements order for a parent to have contact with the child at the same time as making a care order. Alternatively, the court may decline to make a care or supervision order, despite having the power to do so, and may instead choose to make a child arrangements order: for example, that the child lives with a relative or that the child lives with the parents on condition that they stay at a residential unit for a period of time. The court may make a specific issue order or prohibited steps order instead of a care or supervision order: for example, a specific issue order authorising medical treatment on the child in the absence of the parents' consent. The court can make a s. 8 order of its own motion, even if there is no application for such an order before the court.

There are restrictions on the powers of the court. The court cannot make both a care order and a supervision order. A care order can only be accompanied by a s. 8 child arrangements order, but not a specific issue order or prohibited steps order.[348] A child arrangements order cannot be made in favour of the local authority.[349] The court cannot make a specific issue order requiring the local authority to provide services to a child under Part III of the Children Act 1989.[350]

If the court decides to make a child arrangements order that the child lives with a parent or other family member, the court must also make an interim supervision order unless satisfied that the child's welfare will be satisfactorily safeguarded without an interim order being made.[351] In *DH (A minor) (Child Abuse)*[352] the High Court ordered that the child should live with his father and have contact with his mother, supervised by the local authority. Wall J achieved this by making a supervision order and considered that it was appropriate to make such an order because there was an element of child protection involved, as the mother was suffering from a mental health condition called Munchausen's Syndrome by Proxy and had previously harmed the child to attract attention to herself.

10.4 Care order or supervision order?

Although the threshold criteria are the same for a care order or a supervision order, the orders are different: a care order is defined within the Children Act 1989 as an order 'placing the child . . . in the care of a designated local authority'[353] whereas a supervision order is defined as an order putting the child 'under the supervision of a designated local authority'.[354] A care order allows much more intervention in family life than a supervision order.

A care order allows the local authority to remove the child immediately (although a care order can be made even if the child is to remain living with the parents[355]). A supervision order allows the child to remain with their parents and, if the local authority subsequently wants to remove the child, they would have to start fresh care proceedings. A care order lasts until the child reaches the age of 18 unless brought to an end earlier;[356] a supervision

---

[346] Section 31(5).   [347] [1998] 1 FLR 70.   [348] Section 9(1).   [349] Section 9(2).
[350] *Re J (A Minor) (Specific Issue Order: Leave to Apply)* [1995] 1 FLR 669.   [351] Section 38(3).
[352] [1994] 1 FLR 679.   [353] Section 31(1)(a).   [354] Section 31(1)(b).
[355] *Re T (A Minor) (Care or Supervision Order)* [1994] 1 FLR 103.   [356] Section 91(12).

order only lasts for up to one year,[357] although it can be renewed for no more than three years in total.[358]

In the case of *Re D (Care or Supervision Order)*[359] Judge Tyrer ,sitting in the High Court, reviewed the authorities and set out the questions the court should ask if the balance between a care order and supervision order is equal. These include whether:

- the stronger order is needed to protect the child;
- the risks could be met by a supervision order;
- there is a need for the speed of action that a care order would give the local authority;
- the parent could protect the child without sharing parental responsibility;
- parental cooperation could only be obtained through the more draconian order;
- the child's needs could be met without sharing parental responsibility and;
- there have been improvements seen by objective observers during the current proceedings.

10.5 **Effects of a care order**

 Key Legislation 7: s. 33(1)

Where a care order is made with respect to a child it shall be the duty of the local authority designated by the order to receive the child into their care and to keep him in their care while the order remains in force.

A care order gives parental responsibility to the local authority[360] and they control what happens to the child. The local authority holds parental responsibility jointly with any other holder[361] but the local authority can determine the extent to which others can meet their parental responsibility[362] if satisfied that to do so is necessary to safeguard or promote the child's welfare.[363] Before making any decision, the local authority should take into account the wishes and feelings of the child and parents.[364] The local authority has a general duty to safeguard and promote the child's welfare[365] and to promote contact between the child and their parents.[366]

Most other court orders are incompatible with a care order. A care order automatically discharges any s. 8 order[367] and discharges any supervision order already in force.[368] The court cannot impose any conditions on a care order. For example, the court cannot make a care order on condition that certain contact takes place.[369] Instead, the court should use its powers under s. 34 to make an order for contact.

There are limitations on the local authority's powers. While a care order is in force, no person may cause the child to be known by a new surname without the written consent of every person with parental responsibility or the leave of the court.[370] Also, while a care order is in force, no person may remove the child from the United Kingdom without the written consent of every person with parental responsibility or the leave of the court.[371] However the local authority can arrange for the child to leave the United Kingdom for a period of less than one month.[372]

---

[357] Schedule 3, para 6(1).   [358] Schedule 3, para 6(4).   [359] [2000] Fam Law 600.
[360] Section 33(3)(a).   [361] Section 2(6).   [362] Section 33(3)(b).   [363] Section 33(4).
[364] Section 22(4) and section 22(5).   [365] Section 22(3)(a).   [366] Section 34.
[367] Section 91(2).   [368] Section 91(3).
[369] *Re T (A Minor) (Care Order: Conditions)* [1994] 2 FLR 423.   [370] Section 33(7)(a).
[371] Section 33(7)(b).   [372] Section 33(8).

10.6 **Effects of a supervision order**

 Key Legislation 8: s. 35(1)

While a supervision order is in force it shall be the duty of the supervisor—

(a) to advise, assist and befriend the supervised child;

(b) to take such steps as are reasonably necessary to give effect to the order; and

(c) where (i) the order is not wholly complied with; or(ii) the supervisor considers that the order may no longer be necessary, to consider whether or not to apply to the court for its variation or discharge.

A supervision order puts the child under the supervision of a local authority.[373] The local authority appoints a supervisor who advises, assists, and befriends the child. The supervisor does not acquire parental responsibility for the child and their powers depend on the terms of the order.

Schedule 3 lists the directions that a court can attach to any supervision order. These include requiring the child to comply with the supervisor's requests that he lives at a specified place, attends specified appointments, or participates in specified activities.[374] Regarding medical or psychiatric examination or treatment, the supervisor does not have the power to require this:[375] the court must make provision for this in the supervision order,[376] by specifying the place of the examination or treatment.[377]

Benefits of a supervision order include 'their capacity to promote parental self-esteem'[378] as well as bringing about entitlement to local authority resources. However, there are concerns that supervision orders lack teeth and are unenforceable. A supervision order relies on the cooperation of the parents as the directions within a supervision order cannot be enforced either by the supervisor or the court. The supervisor monitors compliance with the requirements of the court and, if they are not complied with, the supervisor can only seek a variation or discharge of the order.[379] Fresh proceedings would have to be started to seek an emergency protection order or care order if needed.

A supervision order lasts for up to one year[380] but it can be extended to a maximum total of three years.[381] An application to extend a supervision order does not require the threshold criteria to be met; instead the local authority has to justify to the court that the welfare of the child requires the supervision order to continue.[382] The application to extend can be made after the term of the order has expired. In *A Local Authority v D*[383] the High Court granted an extension of a supervision order even though the application was issued after the order had already expired.

10.7 **Human rights**

The impact of human rights on the conduct of care proceedings has been most apparent in the welfare assessment. The courts have consistently recognised that making a care

---

[373] Section 31(1)(b).   [374] Schedule 3 para (2)(1).
[375] Schedule 3 para 2(3).   [376] Schedule 3 para 4(1).   [377] Schedule 3 para 4(2).
[378] Harwin, J. *et al* 'Spotlight on supervision orders: what do we know and what do we need to know?' [2016] *Family Law* 365.
[379] Section 35(1)(c).   [380] Schedule 3, para 6(1).   [381] Schedule 3, para 6(4).
[382] *Re A (A Minor) (Supervision Order: Extension)* [1995] 1 FLR 335.   [383] [2016] EWHC 1438 (Fam).

order is a breach of the child's and the child's parents' rights to respect for family life under Article 8 ECHR unless the intervention is shown to be proportionate to the aims pursued.[384]

In *Re B (A Child) (Care Proceedings: Appeal)*[385] the Supreme Court held that all Convention rights must be taken into account when the court is deciding whether or not to make a care order. Lord Wilson said that any interference with Article 8 rights is lawful only if it is in accordance with the law and is also necessary for the protection of the child.[386]

The Court of Appeal considered an appeal by the parents against the removal of their children in *Re W (Children: Removal into Care)*.[387] Thorpe LJ said that the local authority must have 'due regard to the parents' Convention rights and the Convention rights of the children. At first sight [removal] was manifestly a breach of those rights and accordingly was only lawful if it could be justified on both the heads of legitimacy and proportionality'.[388] The appeal by the parents was dismissed because the judge's conclusion that the removal of the children had been legitimate and proportionate was clearly reasoned and within his discretion.

In the welfare assessment, the court should adopt the least interventionist approach. In *Re C and B (Children) (Care Order: Future Harm)*[389] the Court of Appeal discharged care orders over two very young children because they were not proportionate to the concerns expressed for the children. The concerns related to the risk of harm to the children's intellectual and emotional development. Hale LJ said: 'one comes back to the principle of proportionality. The principle has to be that the local authority works to support, and eventually to reunite, the family, unless the risks are so high that the child's welfare requires alternative family care.'[390]

This was repeated in the Court of Appeal case of *Re T (A Child) (Care Proceedings: Appropriate Order)*.[391] Sir Mark Potter said that human rights considerations require that the court should favour the making of a supervision order where that was consistent with the child's welfare, in preference to a more intrusive care order. He said: 'the necessity to consider proportionality means that in any case where there is a fine balance to be struck as to which order is appropriate, the reasoning behind the order made should be clearly spelt out in the judgement as a matter of detailed analysis rather than overall impression'.[392] In that case the Court of Appeal allowed the local authority's appeal against the making of a care order and made a supervision order instead as all parties agreed that the child should be returned to the parents under a phased rehabilitation plan. This was despite the fact that the parents still denied the findings of an earlier non-accidental injury.

In the High Court case of *Re C (A Child) (Care Order or Supervision Order)*[393] Sumner J. made a supervision order and allowed the child to continue to live with his mother where the risk to the child was low. The boy had been seriously injured by his father but the parents were now living separately. The judge found that in the circumstances the risk to the child from the mother allowing another violent man into her household was low and a supervision order represented a proportionate response.

Again, in *Re O (A Child) (Supervision Order: Future Harm)*[394] the Court of Appeal upheld the making of a supervision order because it was considered that this represented a

---

[384] *Kutzner v Germany* [2003] 1 FCR 249.   [385] [2013] UKSC 33.

[386] *Re B (A Child) (Care Proceedings: Appeal)* [2013] UKSC 33 at [32].

[387] [2005] EWCA Civ 642.   [388] [2005] EWCA Civ 642, at [17].   [389] [2001] 1 FLR 611.

[390] *Re C and B (Children) (Care Order: Future Harm)* [2001] 1 FLR 611, at [31].

[391] [2009] EWCA Civ 121.

[392] *Re T (A Child) (Care Proceedings: Appropriate Order)* [2009] EWCA Civ 121, at [33].

[393] [2001] 2 FLR 466.   [394] [2001] EWCA Civ 16.

proportionate response. The mother had a history of mental illness but the risk of harm to the child was at the lower end of the spectrum as it was envisaged that any deterioration in the mother's mental health would be slow. Lady Hale said: 'Proportionality, therefore, is the key. It will be the duty of everyone to ensure that, in those cases where a supervision order is proportionate as a response to the risk presented, a supervision order can be made to work.'[395]

More recently, in *Re B (Children) (No. 3)*[396] the President of the Family Division, Sir James Munby, held that care orders were simply not necessary and would represent a disproportionate response where the two children were to be cared for by their father who had shown unwavering commitment and was deemed to be trustworthy. The mother was suffering from mental illness but Munby P. considered that their best interests required a framework of supervision and s. 8 orders for the children to live with the father and spend time with the mother.

 Key Case 8: *Re G (A Child)(Care Proceedings: Welfare Evaluation)* [2013] EWCA Civ 965

This case concerned a 9-year-old boy with severe autism. His mother had abandoned him twice because she could not cope. The local authority had started care proceedings and the trial judge had granted a final care order, ordering that the boy should stay in long-term foster care. The mother appealed, arguing that the boy should live with her under a supervision order and the trial judge had not really considered this option.

The Court of Appeal granted the mother's appeal and ordered a fresh rehearing. This was because the Court of Appeal held that the trial judge had used the wrong approach. Instead of considering and discounting each option one by one (a linear approach), the Court should have taken a global, holistic view of all the options, comparing all of the options with each other to determine which was the least interventionist in order to promote the welfare of the child. McFarlane LJ said: 'The judicial exercise should not be a linear process whereby each option, other than the most draconian, is looked at in isolation and then rejected because of internal deficits that may be identified, with the result that, at the end of the line, the only option left standing is the most draconian and that is therefore chosen'.[397]

10.8 Court's consideration of the care plan

In the welfare assessment, the court considers the care plan that the local authority has prepared for the child.[398] A care plan sets out the local authority's proposals for the child if a care order is made. The content of the care plan is prescribed by regulations[399] and include the proposed placement and contact arrangements, with details of the child's needs. For example, the local authority may propose in the care plan that the child should stay in foster care but have contact with their parents.

Under s. 31(3A), the court is only required to consider the permanence provisions although the court is at liberty to consider other parts of the care plan if it chooses to do so. Permanence provisions are defined as the long-term plan for the upbringing of the child including any proposals that they live with a parent, relative, friend, or foster carer or are adopted.[400]

---

[395] *Re O (A Child) (Supervision Order: Future Harm)* [2001] EWCA Civ 16, at [28]. [396] [2015] EWFC 27.
[397] *Re G (A Child) (Care Proceedings: Welfare Evaluation)* [2013] EWCA Civ 965, at [49].
[398] Section 31A(1).
[399] Local Authority Circular LAC (99) 'Care Plans and Care Proceedings under the Children Act 1989'.
[400] Section 31(3B).

If the permanence provisions are unclear, a final care order should not be made. In the Court of Appeal case of *Plymouth City Council v G*[401] Black LJ said:

> There was still a live issue as to whether long term fostering or adoption would be right for the children and, on the facts of this case, the difference between those two types of placement was a potentially fundamental difference . . . Matters had not yet reached the stage, therefore, when the court should have made a full care order.[402]

In that case there was insufficient evidence before the Court as to whether adoption was better for the children than long-term fostering so the Court of Appeal dismissed the care orders and adjourned the proceedings for the filing of expert evidence made by the lower court.

However, where the permanence provisions are clear but the court disagrees with them, the court cannot force the local authority to change them. In *Re L (Care Proceedings: Human Rights Claims)*[403] Munby J sitting in the High Court said: 'It is elementary that the only power of the court under Part IV is either to approve or refuse to approve the care plan put forward by the local authority. The court cannot dictate to the local authority what the care plan is to say.'[404] The court can adjourn the proceedings and ask the local authority to reconsider its care plan more than once. In the High Court case of *Re K (Care Proceedings: Care Plan)*[405] Munby J said that 'the court is not obliged to retreat at the first rebuff. In an appropriate case the court can properly require the local authority to reconsider its care plan more than once.'[406] Wall LJ sitting in the Court of Appeal said in *Re S (Children) and W (A Child):*[407]

> Not only does the court have the duty rigorously to scrutinise the care plan and to refuse to make a care order if it does not think the plan in the child's best interests; the court also has the right to invite the local authority to reconsider the care plan if the court comes to the conclusion that the plan—or any change in the plan—involves a course of action which the court believes is contrary to the interests of the child.'[408]

However, the court must be careful when making interim care orders. In *Re J (Minors) (Care: Care Plan)*[409] the guardian sought interim care orders until the local authority's care plan was clarified but Wall J sitting in the High Court made final care orders. The Court held that interim orders should only be used with caution and should not be used 'as a means of exercising the now defunct supervisory role of the court'.[410]

10.9 **Court's consideration of contact with family members**

In the welfare assessment, the court must also consider the proposed arrangements for contact between the child and other family members.[411] This could include direct face-to-face contact but also indirect contact by telephone, letter, text, or skype. The court can make an order about contact at the same time as making a care order or later.[412] The order for contact can also be made even if no application has been made by a party for contact as long as the court is making a care order at the same time.[413]

There are two types of orders available to the court: an order setting out what contact should be allowed[414] and an order authorising a local authority to refuse contact.[415] There

---

[401] [2010] EWCA Civ 1271.   [402] *Plymouth City Council v G* [2010] EWCA Civ 1271, at [54].
[403] [2003] EWHC 665 (Fam).
[404] *Re L (Care Proceedings: Human Rights Claims)* [2003] EWHC 665 (Fam) at [11].
[405] [2007] EWHC 393 (Fam).   [406] [2007] EWHC 393 (Fam) at [18].
[407] *Re S (Children) and W (A Child)* [2007] EWCA Civ 232.   [408] [2007] EWCA Civ 232, at [30].
[409] [1994] 1 FLR 253.   [410] *Re J (Minors) (Care: Care Plan)* [1994] 1 FLR 253.
[411] Section 34(11).   [412] Section 34(10).   [413] Section 34(5).
[414] Section 34(3).   [415] Section 34(4).

is no power to stop the local authority allowing contact to take place.[416] In *Re W (A Child) (Parental Contact: Prohibition)*[417] the Court of Appeal held that the court could not order the local authority to prohibit contact which the local authority considered beneficial, even if the guardian disagreed. In that case a final care order had been made and the guardian wanted to stop staying contact taking place between the child and her mother. The Court of Appeal dismissed the guardian's appeal. The obligation under s. 34 is a positive one requiring local authorities to promote contact.

Although theoretically the court can refuse to make a care order if it is not satisfied with the local authority's proposals for contact, it was held in *Re K (Care Proceedings: Care Plan)*[418] that a court should not do this. This is because the court has the power to determine the issue itself and to make an order as to what contact there should be. Munby J said: 'In the final analysis it is for the court, exercising its powers under section 34, to determine questions of contact, whatever the care plan may or may not have to say on the subject'.[419]

10.10 Power to order ongoing review

When carrying out the welfare assessment, the court may be tempted to make an order enabling ongoing review by the court of the arrangements for the child. However, there are limitations on the powers of the court to do this. In the High Court case of *Re B (A Minor) (Care Order: Review)*[420] it was held that a direction that a care order would be subject to review by the court in six months' time was ultra vires. The court cannot timetable a review after a final care order is made. Similarly, in *Kent County Council v C*[421] the High Court held that, once a care order is made, responsibility for the child is firmly with the local authority and the court cannot retain a power of review over the care order by including directions. Therefore, with the exception of the arrangements for contact, the court has no jurisdiction to review the implementation of the care plan once a final care order is made.

SUMMARY

1. Given the threat of compulsory state intervention, can a partnership between parents and safeguarding agencies ever be truly voluntary?

    • Safeguarding agencies work in partnership with parents and the local authority has a duty to support families and children in their area. This duty has been watered down by successive court judgments and the s. 17 duty to a child in need has been held to be a general duty, not a duty enforceable by an individual child.

    • Although the provision of accommodation under s. 20 is deemed to be a voluntary arrangement, taken in partnership with parents, concerns have been expressed about parents' ability to give informed consent. This is particularly important because the majority of children who enter local authority care do so by agreement with the parents under s. 20.

---

[416] *Re W (A Child) (Parental Contact: Prohibition)* [2000] 1 FLR 502.   [417] [2000] 1 FLR 502.
[418] [2007] EWHC 393 (Fam).   [419] *Re K (Care Proceedings: Care Plan)* [2007] EWHC 393 (Fam) at [26].
[420] [1993] 1 FLR 421.   [421] [1993] 1 FLR 308.

2. What balance should be struck between protecting children from harm and avoiding unwarranted interference in family life?

- The approach of public law protection is that children should remain with their families so compulsory intervention in family life requires court sanction. However, taking a child into police protection is used more often than court approved removal under an emergency protection order.

- For the court to be able to make a final care order, all parts of the threshold criteria under s. 31(2) must be satisfied.

- When considering whether harm is significant, the court can compare the child's health or development with that of a similar child under s. 31(10). Comparing children raises issues of identifying an appropriate comparator. It is controversial whether a child should be compared with a child from a similar socio-economic or cultural background.

- The courts' interpretation of the threshold criteria relating to unknown perpetrators has been controversial, particularly as they mean that unharmed siblings may remain unprotected simply because the perpetrator of harm cannot be identified on a balance of probabilities.

- Once the threshold criteria are met, the court moves onto the welfare assessment where it has a wide choice of options: the court has the power to make a care order, supervision order, private law s. 8 order, or no order at all. The court should make the least intrusive order where that is compatible with the interests of the child.

3. In care proceedings, to what extent should the court allow parents to present their case, given the disadvantages that delay may bring for a child?

- Parents (those with parental responsibility) are automatically a party to care proceedings and are entitled to read all papers filed at court and to attend and make representations at all hearings.

- Parents may seek a direction under s. 38(6) that they and the child undergo a residential assessment funded by the local authority. Such a direction can only be made if the court considers that it is necessary to resolve the proceedings justly, taking into account (amongst other matters) the impact on the duration of the proceedings and the cost involved.

- There is a fixed 26-week time limit on the duration of care proceedings. This can improve the child's chances of adoption but can limit the parents' opportunity to obtain evidence of their parenting capabilities.

4. Is the standard of proof in care proceedings set at the right level?

- The standard of proof in care proceedings is the balance of probabilities. This is lower than the standard of proof in criminal proceedings which is beyond a reasonable doubt.

- There have been a series of miscarriages of justice caused by deficiencies in medical evidence given at trial. Similar medical evidence is used in care proceedings and this has caused some commentators to question the standard of proof used in care proceedings.

Further Reading

DOUGHTY, J. 'Care Proceedings—Is There a Better Way?' (2014) 26 *Child and Family Law Quarterly* 113

- Julie Doughty gives an interesting overview of the state's approach to public law protection including alternative dispute resolution methods.

FOX-HARDING, L. 'The Children Act 1989 in Context: Four Perspectives in Child Care Law and Policy' (1991) *Journal of Social Welfare and Family Law* 179 and 285

- This article explores different perspectives of child care law enabling a critical analysis of the public law provisions of the Children Act 1989.

GILLESPIE, A. 'Establishing a Third Order in Care Proceedings' (2014) 28 *Child and Family Law Quarterly* 239

- Andrew Gillespie makes a thought provoking argument for a different approach in public law proceedings.

NORGROVE, D. (Chair) *Family Justice Review: Final Report* 2011, 91–129

- This section of the Family Justice Review considers the effectiveness of state protection of children and sets the context for the subsequent reform.

TIMMS, J. and THOBURN, J. 'Your Shout! Looked After Children's Perspectives on the Children Act 1989' (2006) 28 *Journal of Social Welfare and Family Law* 153

- This article provides a helpful reminder of the child's voice in child protection proceedings.

12

Adoption

Julie Doughty

LEARNING OBJECTIVES

After reading this chapter you will be able to:

- Explain the legal process of adoption of children, and special guardianship, in England and Wales;
- Discuss the potential benefits to a child's welfare of being adopted, compared with other legal options for secure family life;
- Analyse the human rights implications of adoption for children and adult parties.

DEBATES

After reading this chapter, you should be equipped to discuss your opinion on the following central debates:

1. How should legal obligations to provide continued support to the child be balanced with the privacy and autonomy of family life?

2. How can an order that a child be adopted, without her birth parents' consent, be justified?

3. How should decisions be made between adoption and other types of placement?

1. Introduction

When an adoption order is made by a court in England and Wales, the legal connection between a child and her birth family is completely and permanently ended and she is transferred in to a new family.

Historically, adoption carried a moral stigma, being associated with illegitimacy and infertility. It was normally kept as a family secret, or at least hardly discussed. In recent decades, adoption has become far more open in the sense that the situation is not kept hidden, but it is still closed, in that it is unusual for children to retain contact or any sort of direct relationship with their birth family. Changes in society during the second half of the twentieth century created a new model of adoption, reflected in the legislative framework of the Adoption and Children Act 2002, but there are ongoing complex questions about what the purpose of adoption should be.

The idea that a court order can overcome biological and social relationships in this way can seem artificial, imposing a fictitious narrative that might be difficult to sustain throughout a lifetime. Adoption can leave birth parents bereft, and create confusion about identity for children, especially as they reach their teenage years. Law and policy on the adoption of children in England and Wales are controversial and generate some strong emotional responses. On the one hand, there is strong evidence that adoption provides the best opportunity for a young child to grow up in a stable environment and recover from psychological damage they have suffered through abuse or neglect. On the other hand, the idea of a transplant of a child from one family to another can be criticised as social engineering and a denial of biological and social reality. Some argue that the state should be investing more in keeping families together and preventing abuse and neglect, rather than removing children.

This chapter will explain the law of adoption in the context of the themes set out above.[1] You will be able to relate this topic to others covered elsewhere in this book on parentage and parenthood (Chapter 8); Children Act 1989 orders in private law (Chapter 9); and public law child protection (Chapter 12). Adoption law relates mainly to public law, because most adoptions are of children from care. However, it is also relevant in private law because a child arrangements order (with residence) or a special guardianship order might be an alternative put forward to adoption.

Apart from some situations that arise through assisted reproductive technology (Chapter 8), almost the only way a biological parent who has parental responsibility can lose that status is if their child is adopted. If a child is taken into local authority care, or has ceased all contact with a non-residential parent, and even if she is abandoned, the parent will still retain some level of parental responsibility. It is only an adoption order that will end this legal relationship but, even more extremely, adoption will end the legal status of being a parent.

Adoption against the wishes of the child's birth parents (sometimes referred to as natural parents) is particularly controversial and troubling. Some parents vigorously defend court applications by explicitly withholding their consent to adoption and defending or contesting points in the court proceedings. But it is not only the birth parents we can read about in court judgments who have to adjust to losing their child. In other cases, birth parents may lose hope of keeping their child at an early stage of proceedings, but be just as traumatised and grief-stricken.

Recent court judgments have suggested that an adoption order against the wishes of the birth parents is a very extreme type of order, one that calls for very careful consideration of the human rights of the birth parents as well as the child.[2] Although adoption legislation was completely reformed in 2002, and encompasses principles of human rights law and the Children Act 1989, some critics claim that England and Wales practise what they call 'forced adoption', an oppressive denial of birth parents' rights.

This controversy is exacerbated by the comparatively high rate of adoption of children from care in England and Wales, compared to other European and Commonwealth countries. This has led to some political debate, especially where children born in or brought into the UK by families in Eastern Europe have been adopted here, rather than returned to their parents' jurisdiction. This chapter will examine this problem and will also, briefly, outline the law relating to intercountry adoption.

Adoption legislation was comprehensively reformed by the Adoption and Children Act 2002, in recognition of the changes in adoption since previous legislation made in 1976. The rationale and operation of the Act will be explained, including its provisions

---

[1] Statistics in this chapter are taken from annual returns by the Department for Education and the Welsh Government, and can found on their websites.

[2] *Re B (A Child) (Care order)* [2013] UKSC 33 and subsequent cases, discussed in section 6.

for ongoing post-adoption support that is needed by some families. Adopted young people growing up can struggle with establishing a secure identity. In recent years, conflicting views were expressed about how successful adoption really was, and what the rate of breakdown might be. Large-scale government funded studies reported in 2015 that the disruption rates were low, but that many families had struggled against significant challenges in order to stay together.[3]

This chapter concludes with an explanation of special guardianship in the context of alternatives to adoption. Adoption is only one form of permanence[4] for children who cannot be brought up by their own parents and should be seen in the wider context of the role of law and policy in meeting the needs of children in care. Statistically, adoption is not going to be the outcome for many children who enter the care system, but it is seen as the best outcome for some and continues to raise important legal questions.

2. History of adoption law

It is now recognised that adoption offers what is known as 'reparative parenting'[5] and the best opportunity for particular groups of children to grow up in a stable and secure environment. However, it is only relatively recently that adoption has been perceived in this child-centred way. Adoption law and practice developed as a largely private matter, whereby a charitable society made confidential arrangements for healthy new babies to be placed with married couples and everyone expected secrecy to be maintained. These arrangements may have suited unmarried mothers and infertile married couples, but the needs of individual children were secondary. As family relationships have increasingly diversified from this traditional nuclear model, so the reasons for adoption have changed and the numbers of adoptions have declined.

2.1 Early history

Adoption legislation was passed during the nineteenth century in some states of the USA, Australia, and New Zealand, but it was not until the early 1920s that recommendations were made to the British government for legal recognition of informal, precarious arrangements that were being made in respect of some children abandoned by their parents. The Adoption Act 1926 created the legal status of adoption as a permanent and irrevocable transfer of parentage. At first, succession rights were not affected, but this was amended by the Adoption of Children Act 1949, so that adopted children would lose rights to any property of their birth family but acquire rights to that of their new family.[6] Adoption was further regulated by the Adoption Act 1976 but was omitted from the otherwise comprehensive review and consultation process that resulted in the Children Act 1989.

---

[3] Selwyn, J., Wijedasa, D., and Meakings, S. *Beyond the adoption order: challenges, interventions and adoption disruption* (Department for Education/University of Bristol, 2014); Selwyn, J. and Meakings, S. *Beyond the adoption order (Wales): Discord and disruption in adoptive families* (Welsh Government, 2015).

[4] 'Permanence' is defined in government guidance as ensuring that children in care have a secure, stable, and loving family to support them through childhood and beyond and to give them a sense of security, continuity, commitment, identity, and belonging (Department for Education *Children Act 1989 Guidance Volume 2* (DfE, 2105) 22.

[5] To try to repair psychological damage caused by abuse and neglect in early childhood, see Luckock, B. and Hart, A. 'Adoptive Family Life and Adoption Support: Policy Ambivalence and the Development of Effective Services' (2005) 10 *Child and Family Social Work* 125.

[6] The history of adoption as a legal order and developments until the 1990s are discussed in Lowe, N.V. 'English Adoption Law: Past, Present and Future' in S. Katz, J. Eekelaar, and M. Maclean (eds) *Cross Currents: Family Law and Policy in the US and England* (OUP, 2000).

Following the Adoption Act 1926, the numbers of children adopted in England and Wales gradually rose to about 24,000 per year in the late 1960s, when numbers began to decline to about 4,000 per year in the late 1990s. In 1968, 76% of adoptions were of babies and 91% were of illegitimate children.[7] Subsequent decades saw changing social attitudes toward single parents, alongside advances in medical technology that could address infertility in couples. Fewer healthy babies became available, and sought, for adoption. The demographic picture was no longer one of babies born to unmarried mothers who could not keep them for economic and social reasons, and an answer for married couples with fertility problems. By the 1990s, the numbers of children who were available for adoption had dwindled. Adoption was no longer a means to resolve the shame of unwed mothers and infertile couples, but became a child-centred route to permanence for children in state care.

2.2 Legislative reform

Attempts at modernising the legislation, still comprised in the Adoption Act 1976, were made until 2000, when the Prime Minister, Tony Blair, commissioned a report by his Performance and Innovation Unit (PIU).[8] It is thought that this was partly in response to emerging scandals about abuse in large children's homes.[9] The PIU identified three ways in which looked-after children were being failed: decisions were not being taken early enough or sufficiently focused on permanence; once plans were made they were not followed through quickly to meet the child's timescale; and more support was needed for adoptive families.[10] By the end of the year a government white paper had been issued.[11] Its aims included legislative reform to align with the Children Act 1989 and giving rights and facilities for post-adoption support.

Adoption came to be seen as a way of securing permanence for children who would otherwise be growing up in state care, either because they had disabilities and needs that their parents could not meet or because of child protection concerns. This development has been neatly described by Lowe as a shift from a 'gift or donation model' to a 'contract or services' model. The former was a brief relationship between the birth parents, an agency, and adopters, whereas the new model entailed a longer-term relationship for the local authority which had duties and obligations toward the birth parents, the child, and the adopters.[12] This new model was recognised in policy development that led to comprehensive legislative reform by the Adoption and Children Act 2002, fully implemented by December 2005.

The 2002 Act aimed to meet these evolving needs and to remedy problems that had arisen under the previous legal framework. Section 1 sets out the considerations applying to decisions made both by a court and by an adoption agency about the adoption of a child. Although these principles are modelled on those of s. 1 of the Children Act 1989, they apply equally to an adoption agency as to a court, because an adoption is both a judicial and an administrative process. The legislative framework is set out below in 4.

2.3 Early legislation on birth parents' consent

When drafting the Adoption and Children Act 2002, particular attention was paid to reforming the law on dispensing with birth parents' consent because previously the law had become confused. The Adoption Act 1976, s. 16(2) had listed grounds on which a parent's consent

---

[7] Bridge, C. and Swindells, H. *Adoption: The Modern Law* [2003] *Family Law* 30.

[8] *Prime Minister's Review: Adoption: issued for consultation, a Performance and Innovation Unit Report*, July 2000.   [9] Cullen, D. 'Adoption—A '(Fairly) New Approach' (2005) 17 *Child and Family Law Quarterly* 475.

[10] *Prime Minister's Review: Adoption: issued for consultation, a Performance and Innovation Unit Report*, July 2000.   [11] Department of Health, *Adoption—a new approach* (Cm 5017, 2000).

[12] Lowe, N. V. 'The Changing Face of Adoption—The Gift/Donation Model Versus the Contract/Services Model' (1997) 9 *Child and Family Law Quarterly* 371.

could be dispensed with, the most commonly used being that the parent was 'withholding their consent unreasonably'. This was explained by Lord Hailsham in *Re W (An Infant)*:

> the test is unreasonableness and not anything else. It is not culpability. It is not indifference. It is not failure to discharge parental duties. It is reasonableness, and reasonableness in the context of the totality of the circumstances. But, although welfare *per se* is not the test, the fact that a reasonable parent does pay regard to the welfare of his child must enter into the question of reasonableness as a relevant factor.[13]

Nevertheless, applying this test was problematic, in that it envisaged a hypothetical reasonable parent who would agree to part with their child on the grounds of the child's welfare.[14] The new test for the court, introduced by s. 52(1)(b), is that 'the welfare of the child requires the consent to be dispensed with'.[15] This is discussed in detail in 5.

2.4 Reforms of process

Other notable reforms made by the 2002 Act were to separate the placement and adoption order stages of court proceedings; widen the pool of potential adopters; and place duties on local authorities to assess and provide adoption support services.

The restrictions on who was eligible to be approved as adopters were relaxed to include unmarried and same-sex couples (see 4.4.4) Provisions were made for other types of orders to achieve better outcomes for permanence where adoption was not appropriate. These were the new status of special guardianship, and power to extend residence orders to age 18.[16]

This thorough overhaul of the law followed consultation and lengthy Parliamentary debate, and was found still fit for purpose by a Parliamentary committee in 2012.[17] The Children and Families Act 2014 added stronger provision for post-adoption support.[18]

Before explaining the legislation, we will look at what we know about the children who are being adopted, their characteristics, and their new families.

3. Adopted children and their families

 CONTEXT 1: THE NUMBER OF CHILDREN ADOPTED

At the end of March 2016, 70,440 children were in care in England and 5,662 in Wales. About three quarters of them were living with local authority foster carers. During that year, 31,710 children in England left care (more than half of whom were aged 10 or over), under the following arrangements:

- Returned home: 33%
- Adopted: 15%
- Young people aged 16 and older who moved into independent living: 13%
- Special guardianship orders: 12%
- Child arrangements orders: 4%
- Other arrangements: 21%

---

[13] [1971] AC 682, at 699.

[14] Cooke, E. 'Dispensing with Parental Consent to Adoption—A Choice of Welfare Tests' (1997) 9 *Child and Family Law Quarterly* 259.   [15] Adoption and Children Act 2002, s. 52(1)(b).

[16] Adoption and Children Act 2002, s. 114 amended Children Act 1989, s. 12 which had restricted the effect of residence orders to children aged 16 and under.

[17] HL Select Committee, *Adoption: pre-legislative scrutiny* HL Paper 127 (2013).

[18] Now s. 4A of the Adoption and Children Act 2002.

In 2015–16, 4,690 children in care were adopted in England and 340 in Wales.

These figures indicate that most children leave care by returning home or growing up, and that only a relatively small number of children in care are likely to be adopted.

3.1 Profile of adopted children

Most children who are adopted in England and Wales have been taken into care because of abuse or neglect and some will have experienced a number of moves between foster carers or attempted rehabilitation with parents. Such experiences will have adverse effects on their psychological development. Children who have suffered maltreatment with their birth families will carry risks of developmental problems and difficulties in forming healthy psychological attachments to their new carers. They are likely to be subject to genetic vulnerability and pre-birth experiences of drug and alcohol dependence or exposure to domestic violence. Most will have had more than one foster placement before their adoptive placement. These factors combine to create complex needs which can manifest in disruption in the teenage years. The disruption research showed that in some cases this can become very extreme, with children violently attacking their adoptive parents.[19]

At the end of 2015-16, the average age of an adopted child was 3 years and 5 months. Only 5% of the children were aged less than 1 year old when the adoption order was made; about three quarters were aged between 1 and 4. There is a clear tension between allowing birth parents time to demonstrate that they can safely parent their child, and the pressure on the courts to reduce delay. As care proceedings become shorter, and the 26 weeks' timescale introduced by the Children and Families Act 2014 becomes embedded, we may expect to see a lower average age of children at adoption (see 6.4 in Chapter 11 on child protection). Consequently, the needs of adopted children may become less severe but, currently, their profile is still one of disadvantage.[20]

3.2 Post-adoption support

Despite the duties placed by the 2002 Act on local authorities to assess needs and provide post-adoption support services to adoptive families, the types of services offered are discretionary and have been sporadic over the country.[21]

> ❓ DEBATE 1: HOW SHOULD LEGAL OBLIGATIONS TO PROVIDE
> CONTINUED SUPPORT TO THE CHILD BE BALANCED WITH
> THE PRIVACY AND AUTONOMY OF FAMILY LIFE?

The traditional 'gift/donation' model of adoption normalised the adoptive family in the private sphere. Even when more children began to be adopted from care rather than removed as new babies, this model allowed the state to withdraw and leave all the responsibility for

[19] Selwyn, J., Wijedasa, D., and Meakings, S. *Beyond the adoption order: challenges, interventions and adoption disruption* (Department for Education/University of Bristol, 2014); Selwyn, J. and Meakings, S. *Beyond the adoption order (Wales): Discord and disruption in adoptive families.* (Welsh Government, 2015).

[20] Anthony, R. *et al* 'Factors Affecting Adoption in Wales: Predictors of Variation in Time Between entry to Care and Adoptive Placement' (2016) 67 *Children and Youth Services Review* 184.

[21] Holmes, L. McDermid, C., and Lushey, C. *Post adoption support: a rapid responses survey of local authorities in England* (Loughborough University, 2013); Ottaway, H. Holland, S., and Maxwell, N. *The provision and experience of adoption support services in Wales* (Cardiff University/Welsh Government, 2014).

bringing up the child to the adopters. There was a distinct contrast between attitudes toward children who remained in foster or residential care and received support and those who had a new 'forever family', who did not.

However, there is an underlying conflict between the concept of adoption as reconstituting a stable family and the reality of adopting a child with ongoing support needs.

An important aspect of the 'contract/services' model of adoption is that adoptive families often need support to help their child recover from the effects of abuse and neglect, or because the children might have disabilities.[22] The adoptive family should no longer be abandoned by services in a vague and optimistic hope that 'love will be enough' and children will adjust, unaided, to a stable family life.

Luckock used the case of adoption support as an example of a tension at the heart of family policy, between legitimating family status by supporting parental authority, discretion and autonomy on the one hand, and, on the other, targeting interventions to ensure specific child well-being outcomes with increased accountability for and surveillance of parenting behaviour.[23]

Prior to the 2002 Act, availability of services for adoptive families was very limited. An advantage to the state of the traditional gift/donation model was that after the order, a socially reconstituted family was like any other, in not expecting or requiring additional assistance to function; adoption might be seen as a cost-cutting option.

Some parents were reluctant to seek help as they felt this was stigmatising; others who did ask met with responses that their parenting skills were lacking. However, having 'rescued' children from an abusive home environment, it made little sense for the state to figuratively walk away from continuing problems.

Harris-Short expressed doubts that applying a rights-based discourse to the question of adoption support indicated that families could expect a huge improvement in services from the Act. She argued that there was little evidence that adopted children had more complex needs than others and that there were inherent weaknesses in the Act because a duty to assess needs, if requested, was not accompanied by a duty to provide services to meet those needs. She did not envisage, therefore, that the positive obligation on the state under Article 8 of the European Convention on Human Rights (ECHR) to promote respect for family life would be enforced any more effectively for these vulnerable children than they are for those in any other family.[24] The recent research has, however, identified particular needs for therapeutic services, which are the focus of the new support provision.

The government in England, which has pursued a policy of promoting adoption as a preferable alternative to fostering since 2012, introduced an adoption support fund to provide a range of therapeutic treatment for families who need help for their child in respect of socialisation, school, behaviour, and other problems. This fund will amount to

[22] Data is not collected on the number of children with disabilities who are adopted but it is estimated at between 10 and 25% of all children adopted. (See Grant, M. and Thomas, C. 'Adoption of disabled children' (CoramBAAF 2013)). Of the sample of 374 children in the Wales Adoption Study, 22 (6%) had serious and enduring health disabilities while 67 (18%) had developmental delays. Some of the children in this latter group will have caught up with their peers. Anthony, R. *et al* 'Factors Affecting Adoption in Wales: Predictors of Variation in Time Between Entry to Care and Adoptive Placement' (2016) 67 *Children and Youth Services Review* 184.

[23] Luckock, B. 'Adoption Support and the Negotiation of Ambivalence in Family Policy and Children's Services' (2008) 35 *Journal of Law and Society* 3.

[24] Harris-Short, S. 'Making and Breaking Family Life: Adoption, the State and Human rights' (2008) 35 *Journal of Law and Society* 28.

£28 million in 2017–18 and has recently been extended to children who leave care under special guardianship orders.[25]

4. Adoption under the Adoption and Children Act 2002

The law of adoption in England and Wales is found entirely in statute and its interpretation. There was no recognition of adoption at common law.

4.1 The effect of an adoption order

Section 67 Adoption and Children Act 2002 states that an adopted person is to be treated in law as if born as the child of the adopters, from the date of the adoption. Under s. 46, the order operates to extinguish the parental responsibility of any other person who held this before the date of the order. Adoption by a British citizen will usually confer British citizenship on the child, under s. 1(5) of the British Nationality Act 1981. The child's name can be changed with effect from the date of the order, as part of the adoption application.[26]

The law explored in this chapter, for the most part, relates to adoptions by adults who did not have a pre-existing relationship with the child. However, it should be noted that an adoption order can also be applied for by a step-parent who has married the child's parent, thereby transferring parentage from one birth parent to the new partner. This was quite a common situation before the 2002 Act, but step-parent adoptions have declined because s. 112 inserted a new s. 4A in the Children Act 1989, 'Acquisition of parental responsibility by step parents'. This is a more straightforward process under which the step-parent may apply for shared parental responsibility, securing a legal relationship with the child without her losing that with her other birth parent. Clearly, this is a more satisfactory arrangement for most families than cutting one of the birth parents out of the child's life.

It is also possible for someone who is biologically related, namely a member of the child's extended family, to adopt. This is unusual, as explained in 4.4.4 and Chapter 8 on parenthood.

4.2 Principles of the legislation

One of the aims of the Adoption and Children Act 2002 was to align adoption law with the principles of the Children Act 1989, and make the child's welfare central to all decision-making. This is reflected in s .1.

 Key Legislation 1: Adoption and Children Act 2002, s. 1

Considerations applying to the exercise of powers

(1) This section applies whenever a court or adoption agency is coming to a decision relating to the adoption of a child.

(2) The paramount consideration of the court or adoption agency must be the child's welfare, throughout his life.

(3) The court or adoption agency must at all times bear in mind that, in general, any delay in coming to the decision is likely to prejudice the child's welfare.

---

[25] Department for Education, *An Action Plan for Adoption* (DfE, 2012); Department for Education, *Adoption: a vision for change* (DfE, 2016). Special guardianship is covered in section 11 below.

[26] Adoption and Children Act 2002, s. 77.

(4) The court or adoption agency must have regard to the following matters (among others)—

   (a) the child's ascertainable wishes and feelings regarding the decision (considered in the light of the child's age and understanding),

   (b) the child's particular needs,

   (c) the likely effect on the child (throughout his life) of having ceased to be a member of the original family and become an adopted person,

   (d) the child's age, sex, background and any of the child's characteristics which the court or agency considers relevant,

   (e) any harm (within the meaning of the Children Act 1989) which the child has suffered or is at risk of suffering,

   (f) the relationship which the child has with relatives, with any person who is a prospective adopter with whom the child is placed and with any other person in relation to whom the court or agency considers the relationship to be relevant, including—

      (i) the likelihood of any such relationship continuing and the value to the child of its doing so,

      (ii) the ability and willingness of any of the child's relatives, or of any such person, to provide the child with a secure environment in which the child can develop, and otherwise to meet the child's needs,

      (iii) the wishes and feelings of any of the child's relatives, or of any such person, regarding the child.

(5) In placing a child for adoption, an adoption agency in Wales must give due consideration to the child's religious persuasion, racial origin and cultural and linguistic background. [This subsection has been repealed in England. See section 8].

(6) In coming to a decision relating to the adoption of a child, a court or adoption agency must always consider the whole range of powers available to it in the child's case (whether under this Act or the Children Act 1989); and the court must not make any order under this Act unless it considers that making the order would be better for the child than not doing so.

Section 1(4) lists the factors that the court takes into account when considering applications relating to placement and adoption under the 2002 Act. Applications relating to the care proceedings, and to any alternative placement sought, such as special guardianship, will be based on the checklist in the 1989 Act.

The wording echoes s. 1 of the Children Act 1989, but with special emphasis on the long-term effects of an adoption decision by adding the words 'throughout his life' to s. 1(2). There is a similar checklist to s. 1(3) in the 1989 Act, but s. 1(4)(c) and (f) of the 2002 Act differ from the earlier Act. Section (1)(4)(c) adds that the court and agency must have regard to the effect on the child of this particular type of order with this phrase: 'the likely effect on the child throughout his life of having ceased to be a member of the original family and become an adopted person'. Section 1(4)(f) requires the court and agency to have regard to the child's current and future relationships with their relatives and any person that the court consider relevant. (This could be, e.g, a family friend or a foster carer.) This subsection includes the likely continuation and value of these relationships and the ability and willingness of any of these people as potential safe carers, and their wishes and feelings.

Recent legislation amended s. 1(4)(f) to add 'a prospective adopter with whom the child is placed' as a person whose relationship with the child may be relevant. The court might formerly have also considered an adoptive applicant under the generic 'any person' description, but the position of adopters with whom a child has been placed is now specifically strengthened. This amendment was made in response to cases where questions arose about removing a child after placement, despite having bonded with the adoptive applicant.[27]

Following the principles set out in s. 1, ss. 2–17 of the Act provide for adoption services, and ss. 18–65 set out the details of how a placement and an adoption are effected. This operates through a combination of adoption agency processes, local authority responsibilities, and court proceedings.

4.3 Adoption agencies

Private adoption is unlawful in English law unlike, for example, the USA. This means that step-parent adoptions, intercountry adoption, or any other private arrangement can only proceed subject to appropriate reports to the court. An adoption by people unconnected to the child can only proceed where the placement is made by an adoption agency.[28]

'Adoption agency' is the generic term for local authorities and registered adoption societies (voluntary organisations such as children's charities) which are authorised by the Act to provide adoption services. Local authorities, however, have additional responsibilities where the child is subject to care proceedings. The local authority will be making administrative decisions about whether adoption is the right plan for the child, but only a court can formalise those decisions.

4.4 Placement and adoption process

There are two routes to an adoption, one where birth parents voluntarily decide to ask for their child to be adopted, and the other where the local authority applies for a placement order during care proceedings.[29]

 CONTEXT 2: NUMBER OF CHILDREN VOLUNTARILY GIVEN UP FOR ADOPTION

Although precise figures on this particular point are not kept, government statistics indicate that only about 10% of adopted children are placed voluntarily with their parents' consent, with 90% being subject to court orders.[30] As discussed in the introductory sections, giving up a child for adoption is now relatively rare.

There is a two-stage process in court proceedings, with the aim of separating the decision about an adoption plan from the subsequent adoption order. At the first stage, the local authority will apply for a placement order (either with or without birth parents' consent) and at the second stage, when the child is living with the adopters, the local authority will support them in applying for an adoption order.

---

[27] The new phrase was inserted by s. 9 of the Children and Social Work Act 2017, passed in April 2017. Cases where this problem had arisen included *Re RA (Baby Relinquished for Adoption)* [2016] EWFC 47; *Re W Re W (A Child) (Adoption: Grandparents' Competing Claim)* [2016] EWCA Civ 793, discussed at 4.4.1 and 6.2 respectively.

[28] Section 92 but note that an adoption by a step-parent or relative will require a social work report on the child's welfare for the court, under s. 44(5) and (6).   [29] Adoption and Children Act 2002 s. 19; s. 21.

[30] Fenton-Glynn, C. *Adoption without consent Update* (European Parliament, 2016).

4.4.1 Placing a child for adoption with birth parents' consent

This section explains the process when parents agree to their child being placed for adoption.

 Key Legislation 2: Adoption and Children Act 2002, ss. 19 and 20

19 Placing children with parental consent

(1) Where an adoption agency is satisfied that each parent or guardian of a child has consented to the child—

    (a) being placed for adoption with prospective adopters identified in the consent, or

    (b) being placed for adoption with any prospective adopters who may be chosen by the agency,and has not withdrawn the consent, the agency is authorised to place the child for adoption accordingly.

(2) Consent to a child being placed for adoption with prospective adopters identified in the consent may be combined with consent to the child subsequently being placed for adoption with any prospective adopters who may be chosen by the agency in circumstances where the child is removed from or returned by the identified prospective adopters.

20 Advance consent to adoption

(1) A parent or guardian of a child who consents to the child being placed for adoption by an adoption agency under section 19 may, at the same or any subsequent time, consent to the making of a future adoption order.

(2) Consent under this section—

    (a) where the parent or guardian has consented to the child being placed for adoption with prospective adopters identified in the consent, may be consent to adoption by them, or

    (b) may be consent to adoption by any prospective adopters who may be chosen by the agency.

(3) A person may withdraw any consent given under this section.

(4) A person who gives consent under this section may, at the same or any subsequent time, by notice given to the adoption agency—

    (a) state that he does not wish to be informed of any application for an adoption order, or

    (b) withdraw such a statement.

(5) A notice under subsection (4) has effect from the time when it is received by the adoption agency but has no effect if the person concerned has withdrawn his consent.

(6) This section is subject to section 52 (parental etc. consent).

Under s. 19, an agency may place a child for adoption where it is satisfied that each parent or guardian has given their consent.[31] Where a birth mother voluntarily relinquishes her baby for adoption, her formal consent is valid only if given more than after six weeks after the baby is born.[32] This provision is intended to avoid risks of her giving less than fully informed consent while perhaps recovering from a difficult birth.

After the first six weeks, mothers would still be required to demonstrate full understanding (see 5.1), so there should be a safeguard against any risk of giving up a child

---

[31] The meaning of a 'parent' and 'consent' under the Adoption and Children Act 2002 are explained at 5.1–5.2.   [32] Adoption and Children Act 2002, s. 52(3).

because of a relatively short-term problem such as post-natal depression. Under s. 20, the parents may also give advance notice that they agree to an adoption order being made and that they do not wish to be informed of future proceedings. If these consents are not withdrawn, the placement and the adoption can proceed without the birth parents being further involved.

 Key Case 1: *Re JL (Babies Relinquished for Adoption)* [2016] EWHC 440 (Fam)

In these linked cases, the parents were from eastern Europe, having come to the UK seeking work. The mothers had concealed their pregnancies from their respective employers. In the High Court, Baker J applied the human rights principles recently developed in adoption judgments where parents had opposed, not sought, adoption orders (see 6.1–6.2)

JL's mother and father were Estonian nationals. JL's mother had said she could not look after the baby; he was voluntarily accommodated under s. 20 of the Children Act 1989 in foster care from birth. The mother did not want JL placed with a family member but wanted him to be adopted in the UK, and the father (although he did not have parental responsibility) agreed. The mother signed advance consent to adoption under s. 19 of the Adoption and Children Act 2002. The local authority made enquiries in Estonia, but found no family member who wanted to care for JL. They applied for a placement order under s. 20 of the 2002 Act. The Estonian government authorities confirmed that they agreed that JL be adopted in the UK and said they wished to play no further part in proceedings. AO's parents were Hungarian and her parents were in a similar position to JL's and, additionally, said they did not want the baby to have information about her origins and history. However, the Hungarian authorities believed that AO should be placed in Hungary.

Amongst the jurisdictional issues that arose, the Court also considered what factors to take into account when making decisions about relinquished babies, the possible outcomes, and the procedures to be followed. These were reviewed in the light of important judgments since 2013 on the proportionality of an adoption order where there were other options.

Baker J explained that where parents have relinquished their baby and expressed a wish that she be adopted outside the natural family, the degree of interference with family life rights is less than where the parent–child relationship is severed against the parents' wishes. The fact that the parents had taken this decision was an important consideration when determining whether the interference is necessary and proportionate. Court approval of adoption in such cases does not depend on the local authority or court reaching the conclusion that nothing else will do, but the parents' wishes, although important, are not decisive and must be evaluated within the s. 1(4) welfare checklist, so a thorough analysis of the realistic options for the child is still required. He also confirmed that where parents have given a valid consent to placement for adoption (unconditionally and with full understanding of what is involved), this is sufficient authority for the local authority to place the child for adoption. There was no need to apply for placement orders.

Parents who give advance consent have the right to change their minds, but their consent cannot be withdrawn after the child has been placed for adoption. In *Re RA (Baby Relinquished for Adoption)*, parents who were Latvian nationals had abandoned their baby in hospital. The baby was therefore looked after by a local authority, who placed him with foster carers who subsequently applied to adopt him.[33] The placement for adoption was made with the birth parents' consent. However, late in the adoption proceedings, the parents changed their minds and applied for leave to oppose the adoption (see 4.4.7). Cobb

---

[33] [2016] EWFC 47.

J, sitting in the Family Court, concluded that the parents did not meet the requirements for leave, partly because the child, now 14 months old, had been living with the adoptive applicants since a few days after birth and it would not be in his welfare for an application to oppose the adoption to go ahead.[34]

4.4.2 Applying for a placement order

Unlike a voluntary placement under s. 19, only a local authority, not a voluntary adoption agency, is able to arrange an adoption by applying for a placement order. This application will normally be heard by the Family Court, unless the care proceedings have been transferred to the High Court Family Division.

During care proceedings, local authorities must submit a care plan to the court, which will set out details of their proposals for the child's future when the care order is made (see further Chapter 11).[35] A senior officer of the local authority who is the designated 'adoption decision maker' will have concluded on the basis of social work reports that the child should be placed for adoption, before such a plan is submitted to court.[36] Once this decision has been made, the local authority must apply for a placement order if the parents do not consent to adoption.[37] Even where the parents do agree, the local authority may apply for a placement order for added certainty if, unlike the case of *Re JL* discussed earlier, there is a possibility that parents might withdraw consent.

Key Legislation 3: Adoption and Children Act, s. 21

21 Placement orders
 (1) A placement order is an order made by the court authorising a local authority to place a child for adoption with any prospective adopters who may be chosen by the authority.
 (2) The court may not make a placement order in respect of a child unless—
  (a) the child is subject to a care order,
  (b) the court is satisfied that the conditions in section 31(2) of the 1989 Act (conditions for making a care order) are met, or
  (c) the child has no parent or guardian.
 (3) The court may only make a placement order if, in the case of each parent or guardian of the child, the court is satisfied—
  (a) that the parent or guardian has consented to the child being placed for adoption with any prospective adopters who may be chosen by the local authority and has not withdrawn the consent, or
  (b) that the parent's or guardian's consent should be dispensed with.This subsection is subject to section 52 (parental etc. consent).
 (4) A placement order continues in force until—
  (a) it is revoked under section 24,
  (b) an adoption order is made in respect of the child, or
  (c) the child marries, forms a civil partnership or attains the age of 18 years.

Under s. 21, the court may make a placement order only if the child is already subject to a care order; or the threshold criteria for a care order are met under s. 31(2) of the Children

---

[34] The baby had been placed with the adopters under a fostering for adoption placement; see 4.4.4.
[35] Children Act 1989, s. 31A.
[36] Department for Education, *Statutory Guidance on Adoption* (DfE, 2014) 26–8.
[37] Adoption and Children Act 2002, s. 22.

Act 1989; or the child has no parent or guardian. Secondly, the court must be satisfied that the parents have given consent to placement, or that their consent should be dispensed with.

Although s. 21(4)(c) states that a placement order can last until the child has grown up, this is very unlikely to happen. If a successful adoptive placement is not made in a reasonable time, the care planning and review process will ensure that the plan is amended to another type of placement, to suit the child's needs.[38] In these cases, the local authorities themselves will need to apply to court for the placement orders to be revoked. During the year 2014-15, for example, 3,310 children were placed for adoption in England, but 950 children subject to placement orders had those adoption decisions reversed.

In accordance with the 'no delay' principle,[39] an application for a placement order is usually timed to be made on the same date as the care order. This means that the court is considering the respective welfare checklists in both the Children Act 1989 and the Adoption and Children Act 2002. A freestanding application for a placement order can be made after the order, but this is unusual. The legislation provides for a placement order to be made either with named adopters having been put forward, or on the basis that the local authority is now in a position to find suitable adopters.[40] The latter is the most common situation because until the placement order is actually made, the local authority cannot be confident that its adoption plan will be approved by the court. In these circumstances, it would be unwise to begin work with linking and matching a child with potential adopters. Making a placement order does not guarantee that suitable adopters will be found; but it does authorise the local authority to start to look for them.

4.4.3 Effects of a placement order

When a placement order is made, parental responsibility continues to be shared between the birth parent and the local authority, just as it was under the care order.[41]

As noted at 4.4.2, the existence of a placement order does not in itself ensure that the child will be adopted. Some children are known to be hard to place: this includes sibling groups; children with disabilities; and those who are more than 4 years old. There are certain characteristics associated with longer periods in care before a placement is made, notably a child who appears to be developmentally delayed or who is exhibiting signs of behavioural problems.[42] Some potential adopters feel they may struggle to parent a child who has a history of trauma, and an agency may have to go to considerable lengths to find adopters who can meet specific needs. There is a range of services that can help agencies address delays and problems in making a link between a child after a placement order and an approved adopter who may then be matched with them. These include the National Adoption Registers of England and of Wales.[43]

While a placement order is in force, s. 34 of the Children Act 1989 no longer applies to contact arrangements, but instead, contact can be applied for under s. 26 of the Adoption and Children Act 1989.

If the birth parents do not want their child to be adopted, there is provision under s. 24 whereby they can try to stop the process at this point. However, they will first have to obtain the leave (permission) of the court to apply to revoke the placement order and, if successful, go on to make that application. Once the child has been placed with adopters, the placement order cannot be revoked.[44]

---

[38] Department for Education, *Children Act 1989 Guidance and Regulations: Volume 2: Care Planning, Placement and Case Review* (DfE, 2010).

[39] Children Act 1989, s. 1(2) and Adoption and Children Act 2002, s. 1(3).

[40] Adoption and Children Act 2002, ss. 21(1) and 21(3)(a).   [41] Adoption and Children Act 2002, s. 25.

[42] Anthony, R. *et al* 'Factors Affecting Adoption in Wales: Predictors of Variation in Time Between Entry to Care and Adoptive Placement' (2016) 67 *Children and Youth Services Review* 184.

[43] Adoption and Children Act 2002, ss. 125–131.   [44] Adoption and Children Act 2002, s. 24(2)(b).

Key Legislation 4: Adoption and Children Act 2002, s. 24

24 Revoking placement orders

(1) The court may revoke a placement order on the application of any person.

(2) But an application may not be made by a person other than the child or the local authority authorised by the order to place the child for adoption unless—

   (a) the court has given leave to apply, and

   (b) the child is not placed for adoption by the authority.

(3) The court cannot give leave under subsection (2)(a) unless satisfied that there has been a change in circumstances since the order was made.

(4) If the court determines, on an application for an adoption order, not to make the order, it may revoke any placement order in respect of the child.

(5) Where—

   (a) an application for the revocation of a placement order has been made and has not been disposed of, and

   (b) the child is not placed for adoption by the authority,the child may not without the court's leave be placed for adoption under the order.

Under s. 24(5), an ongoing application to revoke will have the effect of stopping the local authority from placing a child with adopters until the issues about revocation have been determined by the court. This does not apply at the earlier stage of seeking leave, but it is not good practice for a local authority to place a child if they are aware that leave to revoke is being sought.[45] The test to be applied by the court to the first stage in whether or not to grant leave is the same as laid down by Wall LJ in *Re P (Adoption: Leave Provisions)*[46] discussed at 4.4.7 below. This is whether a change of circumstances is such to justify the issues being reviewed. The second stage is the exercise of the court's discretion in considering all the circumstances, including the prospects of success and the child's welfare.

4.4.4 Eligibility to adopt

People who wish to adopt have to undertake rigorous assessment and training by an adoption agency before they are approved. This is a separate process to that through which a child becomes subject to a placement order.

An adoption order may be made to a couple or to a single person. At least one of the adopters must be aged 21 or over, and be domiciled and habitually resident in the UK for at least one year.[47] Before the 2002 Act, an adoption order could be made only to one adopter or to a married couple. This meant that if an unmarried couple wanted to adopt, the only option they had was for one of them to adopt and then enter into a parental responsibility agreement with their partner. The reforms under the 2002 Act provided an opportunity to widen the available pool of potential adopters and remove discriminatory provisions by extending adoption to a greater range of applicants. The Act made provision for applications to be made by one person or by couples who were in an enduring family relationship. This meant that unmarried and same-sex couples in long-term relationships were eligible to adopt. Subsequently, these provisions have come to include couples in civil partnerships and married same-sex couples. Section 144(4) defines 'a couple' as (a) a married couple, or (b) two people (whether of different sexes or the same sex) living as partners in an enduring family relationship.

---

[45] *Re F (Placement order)* [2008] EWCA Civ 439.   [46] [2007] EWCA Civ 616.

[47] Adoption and Children Act 2002, s. 49(2).

Step-parent adoptions are now unusual, because making a parental responsibility agreement under s. 4A of the Children Act 1989 is simpler. An adoption application can be made by a birth parent's spouse or civil partner under s. 51(2) of the Adoption and Children Act 2002. The child must have lived with the applicant for at least six months before the application is made.

Adoption by relatives, such as grandparents, is also possible, although this has not been encouraged by the courts because it is seen as potentially confusing the family's relationships. Special guardianship is generally more appropriate, but there may be exceptional circumstances where adoption by grandparents is in the child's best interests.[48] In a non-agency arrangement like this, the child will have to have lived with the relative for at least three of the previous five years before the application.

Finally, if a child's foster carers decide that they would like to adopt the child, they may make an application, but because this placement has not been arranged by an adoption agency, they must give the local authority at least three months' notice of their intention to adopt. The child must have been living with them for a year (or less, with leave of the court). Foster carers and adopters have traditionally been recruited through different systems, with the former acquiring no parental responsibility, acting as agents of the local authority and being paid modest financial allowances.

Generally, these extended periods of residence and notice for non-agency placements are intended to discourage adoption in these circumstances, where other options might be more suitable for the child.

There is an exception for foster carers who are recruited under a relatively new scheme known as 'fostering for adoption' where a baby, for whom adoption may soon be the plan, lives with foster carers who are also approved adopters. This was introduced by the Children and Families Act 2014, s. 2, which amends s. 22C of the Children Act 1989 to add subsection (9A), placing an extra duty on a local authority in England, when arranging accommodation for a child under s. 20 of the 1989 Act, if they are satisfied that adoption will be the plan but are not yet authorised to place under s. 19 or s. 21 of the Adoption and Children Act 2002. In this situation, the local authority may place the child with foster carers who are also approved adopters. The aim is to reduce the number of times a child has to move in and out of different foster homes before they are living with their adopters. It is as yet uncertain how popular this option will be, especially as there is only a very small number of children for whom it might be suitable and, arguably, an even smaller number of adults who could cope with the unpredictability of whether the child will eventually be available for adoption. A fostering for adoption placement was made, for example, in the case of *Re RA (Baby Relinquished for Adoption)*.[49] A similar scheme known as 'foster to adopt' was introduced in Wales in 2016 by s. 81(10) and (11) of the Social Services and Well-being (Wales) Act 2014.

4.4.5 Placing a child with adopters

By clearly separating the processes of placement and adoption orders, Parliament intended to ensure that issues relating to the removal of the child from their birth parents were resolved before the child went to live with their new family. Prior to the 2002 Act, a process known as freeing for adoption was often used, but practice was inconsistent. There were reported cases of long delays in finding adopters, or never finding any, and of foster placements where parties were confused about the legal status of the child.[50] Under the current law, the child will only be in an adoptive placement once the local

---

[48] *Re S (A Child) (Adoption Order or Special Guardianship Order)* [2007] Civ 90.
[49] [2016] EWFC 47. See 4.4.1.
[50] Bridge, C. and Swindells, H. *Adoption: The Modern Law* [2003] *Family Law* 160.

authority has been given authorisation for such a placement either by the parents under s. 19 or by the court under s. 21.

If the matching and linking process and introduction meetings between the child and the potential adopters are successful, the local authority will then arrange for the child to be moved (from foster care) to live with the potential adopters. From this point, the placement order cannot be revoked (see 4.4.3). The child must live with the applicants for at least ten weeks before they can lodge their application to court to adopt.[51] During the period between placement and adoption, the child continues to be looked after by the local authority, with parental responsibility now shared three ways between the birth parents, local authority, and adoptive applicants. However, contact with the birth family will be being phased out. Visits to the child and adopters by the social workers who were responsible for the child's case and who worked with the adopters, respectively, will continue. On some occasions, the placement does not work as everyone had hoped, and the child may have to be returned shortly after the placement, for the local authority to review its plans. If the adopters and the agencies all feel that the relationships are going well, the next stage is for the adopters to make an application for an adoption order. Unless any serious legal problems emerge, adopters will not have any legal representation, and will be making the application to court themselves, with advice from the social workers.[52]

4.4.6 Moving a child after placement

Once a child has been placed with adopters, there are restrictions on their being moved again, under ss. 30–41. If the child was placed with consent, only the agency can remove her. If the parent changes their mind and withdraws consent between placement and adoption, the agency must either return the child or apply for a placement order within 14 days.[53] If either the agency or the prospective adopters decide that the placement is failing before an adoption order has been made, and give notice that the child should be returned to the care of the local authority, she must be returned within seven days of that notification and the birth parents must be informed that the placement has ended.

4.4.7 Opposing an adoption order

Usually adopters will apply for the order shortly after the ten weeks has expired, unless they are uncertain about matters which need some clarification or testing out, such as whether the child's support needs will continue to be met. The 2002 Act was designed to resolve any legal issues regarding the parents' agreement before the child is placed but, even after placement for adoption, the legislation requires that birth parents' consent to the adoption order must be obtained, or dispensed with.

The case of *Re P* (Key Case 2) explains the legal process by which a birth parent may apply to oppose an adoption order, even after the child has been placed with prospective adopters under a placement order, under s. 47. This section is intended to provide a birth parent with a meaningful and real remedy, and the mere fact that a child is living with adopters should not rule out any possibility of granting leave to oppose.[54] However, in making a decision about leave to oppose, the court looks carefully at how likely the parent is to succeed in having the original welfare decision overturned.

---

[51] s.42.2 Adoption and Children Act 2002, s. 42.2.

[52] Doughty, J. Meakings, S., and Shelton, K. 'The Legal and Administrative Processes in Adoption: Views and Experiences of Newly Formed Adoptive Families' (forthcoming) *Journal of Social Welfare and Family Law*.

[53] Adoption and Children Act 2002, ss. 30–33.   [54] *Re B-S (Children)* [2013] EWCA Civ 1146, at 74–5.

Key Case 2: *Re P (Adoption: Leave Provisions)* [2007] EWCA Civ 616

This was the first case heard by the Court of Appeal on s. 47. The child had been removed under an emergency protection order when she was 1 month old and had remained in foster care under care orders for nearly a year when a placement order was made. This was unsuccessfully opposed by the parents. The child was placed with adopters a month later and they applied for an adoption order when she had been with them for four months and was 15 months old. By this point, the parents' circumstances had changed from the time of the original intervention. They argued that their substance abuse and violence issues had been resolved and that their relationship was now stable. This was evidenced by the fact that they were safely caring for a younger sibling, and that the local authority was satisfied that no proceedings in respect of the younger child were necessary. In this way, their circumstances had clearly changed but they were unsuccessful in their application for leave to oppose the adoption order, and appealed.

Wall LJ confirmed, first, that s. 1 of the 2002 Act applied to a decision to be made under s. 47 about granting leave to oppose an order, and so the child's welfare was the paramount consideration. He then stated that an application for leave to oppose an application for an adoption order comprised a two-stage test: the change in circumstances and the welfare of the child. The change in circumstances does not have to be significant, but needs to be of a nature and degree sufficient to open the door to a consideration of whether leave to apply should be given. Moving on to the exercise of judicial discretion, the judge had been bound to give considerable weight to the fact that, for the year between the date of the care order and the date of the hearing of the application, the plan for the child had been adoption, which had been implemented, and was working. By the time the application for leave was heard, the mother was pregnant with the parents' third child. The judge was, accordingly, bound to take into account the fact that, if the adoption application was, in some way, refused and the child returned to her parents' care, they would be caring for three children under the age of 3.

Taking the child's welfare as its paramount consideration, the Court's clear view was that the parents would have no realistic prospect of succeeding in their opposition to the proposed adoption application. The child's needs remained the same: a secure and permanent placement in which she could form and maintain proper attachments to her carers. In the context of the parents as carers, there was 'simply no or minimal evidence that they are capable within this child's timescale of providing her with the secure environment in which she can develop and otherwise of meeting her needs'.[55]

Unless there is any possibility of an appeal, a birth parent who is unable to persuade the court to give him or her leave under s. 47 to oppose the adoption order will permanently lose their child and, unlike other types of placement, probably also lose all contact. The *Re P* test appears very high.

 DEBATE 2: HOW CAN AN ORDER THAT A CHILD BE ADOPTED,
             WITHOUT HER BIRTH PARENTS' CONSENT, BE JUSTIFIED?

Notice of the application for the adoption order must be served on the birth parents, who may give their consent to the application going ahead. If they do not, the court will consider whether their consent should be dispensed with. Birth parents, understandably, may feel they cannot sign a document which gives up their child, but at the same time they may not actively contest the application. In such a situation, the court will consider the evidence pro-

---

[55] [2013] EWCA Civ 1146, at [50].

vided by the officer from the Children and Family Court Advisory and Support Service (Cafcaas) who has visited the birth parents to ensure that they have been given full information but, if they do not participate in the proceedings, their consent is likely to be dispensed with because the evidence points to the conclusion that the child's welfare requires this. Where adoption is the plan, further delay is to be avoided, under s. 1(3).

On the other hand, some birth parents will want to make a legal challenge to the adoption going ahead. At this point, they do have another opportunity to try to stop the adoption because they may apply for leave to oppose the order being made, under s. 47. If parents do not apply for leave, or are unsuccessful in their application, the court may make an adoption order, dispensing with their consent, if that is what the child's welfare requires. This is a controversial issue that has received considerable judicial attention in recent years and is explored further as a key debate when we discuss statute and more recent cases about consent.

4.4.8 Post-adoption contact

Any contact arrangements made while the placement order was in force, under s. 26 of the Adoption and Children Act 2002, will cease on the making of an adoption order.

Until 2014, the only way that post-adoption contact could be secured through a court order was by a member of the birth family making an application for an order under s. 8 of the Children Act 1989. However, courts were reluctant to impose such orders on adopters prior to the 2002 Act, because this would create potential friction and future litigation.[56] Section 46(6) of the 2002 Act indicated a possible change of approach by directing the court, before making an adoption order, to consider whether there should be arrangements for allowing any person contact with the child and for any existing or proposed arrangements, obtaining any views of the parties to the proceedings. However, the Court of Appeal stated that the imposition of contact orders in adoption proceedings would continue to be extremely unusual. Attempting to formalise contact arrangements was still seen as likely to generate tensions and risks of recourse to future legal proceedings.[57]

Now, under s. 51A, inserted by the Children and Families Act 2014, birth parents and relatives may apply for post-adoption contact as part of the adoption proceedings, rather than have to make a Children Act 1989, s. 8 application. The leave of the court is required before an application can be made.[58] It still appears that contact orders will be unusual, and that indirect or 'letterbox' contact is the norm, where direct contact might unsettle the child.[59] The 2014 Act also introduced s. 51A(2)(b), whereby the court can expressly prohibit future contact with any named person. The rationale for this provision is that, during proceedings, some members of birth families or their supporters can be seen as potentially seeking out and threatening the adoptive family. Sloan argues that, overall, the effect of s. 51A is to strengthen a presumption against post-adoption contact with birth families.[60] However, the High Court has held that a birth parent's Article 8 rights cease on the making of an adoption order, and the provisions for post-adoption contact under s. 51A are compatible with the Convention. The local authority running a post-adoption letterbox service in *Re A (A Child) (Adoption: Human Rights)* was obliged under Article 8 to respect correspondence between the mother and the adopted child and adopters, but it

---

[56] *Re C (A Minor) (Adoption Order: Conditions)* [1998] 2 FLR 159.

[57] *Re R (A Child) (Adoption Orders: Contact)* [2005] EWCA Civ 1128. Letterbox contact is an exchange of information between the adopters and the birth family, such as annual letters, via the local authority.

[58] Adoption and Children Act 2002, s. 51A(4).

[59] *Re A (A Child) (Adoption: Human Rights)* [2015] EWHC 2609 (Fam).

[60] Sloan, B. 'Post-Adoption Contact Reform: Compounding the State-Ordered Termination of Parenthood?' (2014) 73 *Cambridge Law Journal* 378.

was able to edit the communications to ensure that the service did not become a means of persuasion or pressure on the new family.[61]

In *Re W*, discussed at 6.2, the judge in the High Court rehearing endorsed the agreement that the adopters and the paternal extended family had been able to reach regarding future contact, so that orders were unnecessary.

There are, however, facilities for people affected by adoption to try to make contact in later life. An adult adopted person may seek out their birth records and add their details to the Adoption Contact Register if they want to find members of their birth family. The Register can also be used by birth relatives to register that they do or do not want to be contacted. Links can therefore be made where both parties want this.[62]

5. Birth parents' consent to placement and adoption

The court's ability to override a parent's wishes and make an adoption order is a controversial aspect of adoption law, which has featured in a number of cases already mentioned. Compatibility of the law with human rights principles will be considered later. First, the legal provisions regarding consent contained in the Act will be explained.

5.1 Definition of consent

'Consent' has the same meaning under the Act, whether the parent is agreeing to an adoptive placement or to an adoption order.

 Key Legislation 5: Adoption and Children Act 2002, s. 52(5)

> Consent means consent given freely and unconditionally and with full understanding of what is involved; but a person may consent to an adoption without knowing the identity of the person in whose favour the order will be made.

The proviso about not knowing who will adopt is in place for two reasons. Linking and matching to adopters will not have started when the birth parents are being asked to give consent to a placement under s. 19 or an order under s. 21. Secondly, the adopters may be advised by the adoption agency to make their adoption application under a serial number, which anonymises them in the court documents.

The court will ensure that s. 52 is complied with by appointing an officer from Cafcass, who is independent of the agencies, to witness the written consent.[63] If the birth parent lacks the mental capacity to fully understand the nature of the proceedings, the Official Solicitor may be appointed by the court to represent her interests (see 5.5).

5.2 Whose consent is required?

In this chapter, the term 'birth parents' is used generically to refer to the persons whose consent must be sought. In many cases, this will be only the birth mother. A parent is

---

[61] *Re A (A Child) (Adoption: Human Rights)* EWHC 2609 (Fam).

[62] The registers are maintained by the General Register Office under ss. 77–81 of the Adoption and Children Act 2002.   [63] Adoption and Children Act 2002, s. 102.

defined by s. 52(6) as one with parental responsibility. Therefore, the following people have the right to consent:

- the birth mother;
- the birth father, if he has parental responsibility;
- an adoptive parent, if the child was subject to a previous adoption;
- a guardian (including a special guardian).

As noted earlier, the birth mother's consent to adoption is valid only when given later than six weeks after birth (see 4.4.1). If a baby has been relinquished under s. 19, the local authority can place the baby in a fostering for adoption placement from birth, but the mother's consent will only be effective regarding the placement stage. Consent to adoption cannot be given before the baby is six weeks old.

5.3 Birth fathers who do not have parental responsibility

Although a father who does not hold parental responsibility (see Chapter 8) is not required to consent, a question arises about his rights under Article 8 and whether he should be notified of the pending court applications.

Where the identity of the father is known to the agency and the agency believes it is appropriate to notify him, the adoption regulations require them to ascertain so far as possible whether he wishes to apply for parental responsibility or child arrangements order for contact with a child in care.[64] There may be good reasons, such as the mother being at risk of domestic violence, for the court agreeing that father should not be notified.[65] The starting point when looking for an alternative carer is extended maternal and paternal family, but there is no duty to make enquiries about the wider birth family if this will not further the child's interests; such enquiries must genuinely further the prospect of finding a long-term carer without delay. Where a mother refuses to identify the father, the court will normally expect the agency to have made some enquiries but if the mother continues to refuse, the court will not try to force her to do so.[66] If the agency is in doubt about how extensive an effort they should make to ascertain a father's identity and notify him of the adoption plan, it may ask the court for directions. Alternatively, the court may of its own motion make a direction that the father be notified.

Since the introduction of the public law outline pre-proceedings process in care cases (as explained in Chapter 11), there is of course pressure on local authorities to assess potential family carers as early as possible, and avoid situations where viable carers come forward at a late stage. It is therefore becoming less likely that fathers will be marginalised and not actively sought out by social workers before the care proceedings begin. Although the local authority will be expected to assess alternative family carers, they are not obliged to do so if the mother is adamant she does not want her family to be informed.[67] In situations where pregnancies have been concealed from fathers and/or extended family, the court will take into account the fact that there is no existing family relationship with the father or relative in question, in the context of Article 8 ECHR.

5.4 The views of the child

The consultation process that preceded the 2002 Act involved a recommendation that the consent of the child should be sought if she was aged over 12 but this was not brought forward into the legislation. Section 1(4)(a) provides that the court and agencies must have

---

[64] Adoption Regulations 14(3) and (4); ss. 8 and 34 of the Children Act 1989.   [65] *Re M* [2001] 1 FLR 745.
[66] *Re C (A Child)* [2007] EWCA Civ 1206.   [67] *Z CC v R* [2001] 1 FLR 365.

regard to the child's ascertainable wishes and feelings regarding the decision (considered in the light of the child's age and understanding). These wishes and feelings would be ascertained by a Cafcass officer, appointed by the court to represent the child.[68] Most children are adopted as infants, so Cafcass will be focusing on other factors in the s. 1(4) checklist.

 CONTEXT 3: THE AGE THAT CHILDREN ARE ADOPTED

In 2015–16:

- 5% of children adopted during the year were under one year old;
- 72% were aged between one and four years old;
- 22% were aged between five and nine years old;
- 1% were aged between 10 and 15 years old.

Children who are old enough to make their wishes and feelings known should be being consulted about placement options throughout the care planning process, in accordance with statutory guidance and Article 12 of the United Nations Convention on the Rights of the Child (UNCRC).[69]

5.5 Dispensing with consent

It is widely believed that the law of England and Wales is unusual in allowing a court order that can sever a child's relationship with their birth parents, in the face of their opposition. For example, Lady Hale commented in 2006 that: 'The United Kingdom is unusual amongst members of the Council of Europe in permitting the total severance of family ties without parental consent.'[70]

However, Fenton-Glynn's review of the law across the European Union concludes that, although adoption without consent appears more common in England than in other European countries, in fact every one of these countries does have a legal mechanism for permitting adoption without consent. She categorises these mechanisms in three groups: abandonment or lack of interest in the child; parental misconduct or deprivation of parental rights; and where consent is unjustifiably withheld or because adoption is in the child's best interests.[71] It is therefore arguably through policy, not law, that the UK has gained a reputation for 'forced adoption'.[72]

 DEBATE 2: HOW CAN AN ORDER THAT A CHILD BE ADOPTED, WITHOUT HER BIRTH PARENTS' CONSENT, BE JUSTIFIED?

Adoption culminates in extreme interference with the rights of the birth family and the child to respect for their private and family life under Article 8 ECHR and, after placement, also engages the Article 8 rights of the adoptive applicants. These respective rights, and the wel-

---

[68] Adoption and Children Act 2002, s. 102(3).

[69] Department for Education, *Children Act 1989 Guidance and Regulations: Volume 2: Care Planning, Placement and Case Review* (DfE, 2010).

[70] *Down Lisburn Health and Social Services Trust v H* [2006] UKHL 36, at [34]. See also 7.1.

[71] Fenton-Glynn, C. *Adoption without consent* (European Parliament, 2015); *Adoption without consent Update* (European Parliament, 2016).

[72] Fenton-Glynn, C. *Adoption without consent* (European Parliament, 2015); *Adoption without consent Update* (European Parliament, 2016) concluded that the lack of comparative data made it impossible to estimate the frequency with which children were taken into care and placed for adoption in different EU states.

fare principle, will comprise competing interests and will have to be balanced by the agency and the court. Removing the birth parents' parental rights, against their will, can only be justified where there is compelling evidence that child's best interests require this. The debate about non-consensual (often labelled as 'forced') adoption overlaps with Debate 3 on decisions to be made about the options for placement.

The term 'forced adoption' is most commonly associated with historical events in Australia where the government issued an official apology to thousands of parents, adopted people, and their families about the way in which babies had been removed at birth between 1950 and 1975.[73] Other well-documented instances of forced adoption have occurred in Spain and in Ireland.[74] Deception and corruption played a part in some of these tragic histories; this has created a legacy of mistrust of the whole concept of adoption. It is essential for the student of family law to disentangle this narrative and take an objective approach when evaluating the current law.

As you can see from this chapter, there is a lengthy and multi-agency process involved in an adoption. Care (and placement) proceedings are one of the rare occasions where legal aid is still universally provided for birth parents. An adoption can only be arranged by an adoption agency (usually a local authority) which is subject to strict regulation and inspection. There should therefore be minimal risk of an adoption in this country being made without due process.

Nevertheless, the irrevocability of adoption orders (see section 9) combined with policy objectives to increase the numbers of those orders, inevitably creates complexity in balancing the legal rights and interests of all involved. These are followed up in 6 below on human rights. First, the statutory provisions on dispensing with consent are explained.

Placement orders and adoption orders can be made where the birth parents have already given their free and unconditional consent, as described in 4.4.1. If consent is not obtained, the court will be asked by the local authority to dispense with this, on one of three grounds.

 Key Legislation 6: Adoption and Children Act 2002, s. 52

s. 52 Parental etc. consent

(1) The court cannot dispense with the consent of any parent or guardian of a child to the child being placed for adoption or to the making of an adoption order in respect of the child unless the court is satisfied that—

　(a) the parent or guardian cannot be found or lacks capacity (within the meaning of the Mental Capacity Act 2005) to give consent, or

　(b) the welfare of the child requires the consent to be dispensed with

---

If parents cannot be found, the local authority will need to show that all reasonable steps have been taken to find them.[75] This would include making enquiries through the Department of Work and Pensions and other appropriate agencies.

Under s. 2 of the Mental Capacity Act 2005 'a person lacks capacity in relation to a matter if at the material time he is unable to make a decision for himself in relation to the matter because of an impairment of, or a disturbance in the functioning of, the mind or brain'.

---

[73] Australian Government Attorney General's Department, *National Apology for Forced Adoptions* (2013).

[74] See, e.g., Vinyes, R. *et al Los Niños perdidos del Franquismo* (Debolsillo, 2003); Sixsmith, M. *The Lost Child of Philomena Lee* (Pan, 2010).　　　　[75] *Re F (An Infant)* [1970] 1 QB 385 CA.

Whether or not the parent had capacity to instruct a solicitor in care proceedings will be relevant here, but there will need to be a new cognitive assessment of their understanding of the meaning and consequences of agreeing to placement and adoption orders. If they do not have capacity, they will be represented by a litigation friend in the proceedings, usually the Official Solicitor. Guidance on the roles and responsibilities of the parent's lawyer; the local authority and the Official Solicitor is given in *Re P (A Child) (Care and Placement Order Proceedings: Mental Capacity of Parent).*[76]

The test under s. 52(1)(b), is whether the child's welfare 'requires' consent to be dispensed with. 'Requires' has been interpreted by the courts as necessary because of an overriding requirement for adoption for the child's welfare, as we will discuss in the next section.

6. Adoption and human rights

Consultation and debate leading to the 2002 Act featured attention to the Article 8 interests of children and birth parents in the context of the recent implementation of the Human Rights Act 1998.[77] The Act was examined by the European Court of Human Rights (ECtHR) in *YC v the United Kingdom.*[78] This concerned the adoption of an 11-year-old boy who had been in care for about three years. His mother argued that decisions in the domestic courts to make care and placement orders had not taken all relevant factors into account and were in breach of her Article 8 rights. The ECtHR identified two considerations in establishing a child's best interests: first, that his ties with his family are maintained except in cases 'where the family has proved particular unfit' and, second, ensuring his development in a safe and secure environment. It is clear that 'family ties may only be severed in very exceptional circumstances' and everything must be done to preserve and rebuild the family, where possible. However 'where the maintenance of family ties would harm the child's health and development, a parent is not entitled under article 8 to insist that such ties be maintained'.[79] The ECtHR concluded in this case that the local authority and courts had complied with the Convention and come to a proportionate decision about adoption.

By way of contrast, in another ECtHR case, *Soares de Melo v Portugal*, the Court held that there was a violation of a mother's Article 8 rights where her poverty had been the main reason for the Portuguese court's decision that her children should be taken into care with a view to adoption, that she and her husband should be deprived of all parental responsibility and denied all contact with the children. The unanimous judgment was that such an order had not been appropriate to the legitimate aim pursued or necessary in a democratic society, bearing in mind the absence of any violent conduct, the existence of strong emotional ties amongst the family, and the failure of the state to address the mother's material deprivation, having to raise a large number of children with almost no assistance.[80]

6.1 Proportionality and adoption decision-making

In *YC* discussed earlier, the ECtHR had found English law on adoption compliant with Article 8, and the test for dispensing with consent seemed settled after challenges brought

---

[76] [2008] EWCA Civ 462.
[77] Bridge, C. and Swindells, H. *Adoption: The Modern Law* [2002] *Family Law* 107.
[78] (2012) 55 EHRR 33.   [79] (2012) 55 EHRR 33, at [134].
[80] App. No. 72850/14, 16 February 2016.

by parents seeking revocation of a placement order or opposing an adoption.[81] However, the scene changed in 2013.

 Key Case 3: *Re B (A Child) (Care order)* [2013] UKSC 33

The importance of this judgment lies in it being the first time that a case about adoption without consent was examined by the Supreme Court (or formerly as the House of Lords) since the Human Rights Act 1998.[82] As noted by both Rix LJ in the Court of Appeal and Lady Hale in the Supreme Court, the case raised troubling questions about the power of the state to permanently remove a child from her parents solely on the ground of risk of future significant emotional harm. The facts were unusual. Although there was compelling evidence of the risks posed by the parents' psychological and criminal histories and their complete inability to tell the truth to anyone in authority, there was no evidence of either of them directly harming a child. They had maintained a positive record of supervised contact with their daughter since birth, for three years in foster care, while they fought every stage of the case.

The Supreme Court justices agreed that Article 8 required a high degree of justification in making an order with adoption as the plan. This principle was expressed in strong terms:

Lord Wilson agreed that the judge had correctly reflected both domestic law and the proportionality requirement of the ECHR when he concluded that adoption was 'the only viable option' for the child's future care [48]. Lord Neuberger said that a care order with an adoption plan should be a last resort and made only if the judge is satisfied it is necessary to do so to protect the interests of the child. This was clear in the 1989 Act itself but put beyond doubt by Article 8 and consistent with the UNCRC [76]–[77]. He added that 'Adoption of a child against her parents' wishes should only be contemplated as a last resort—when all else fails'. [104]. Lady Hale described the decision before the court as one on '. . . the proportionality of planning the most drastic interference possible, which is a closed adoption, in a case where the threshold had not been crossed in the most extreme way . . . ' [197]. She said:

> The test for severing the relationship between parent and child is very strict: only in exceptional circumstances and where motivated by overriding requirement pertaining to the child's welfare, in short, where nothing else will do. In many cases, and particularly where the feared harm has not yet materialised and may never do so, it will be necessary to explore and attempt alternative solutions ([198] Lady Hale).

Despite the unusual facts and the concerns expressed by the judges at Court of Appeal and Supreme Court level, they all agreed that the judge in the High Court had arrived at the right decision, except Lady Hale, whose dissenting opinion was based on her view that more work might be done to engage the cooperation of the parents.

Re B was subsequently referred to as 'a very clear wake-up call' about concerns that insufficient attention was being paid to evidence and analysis about all the options for placement and permanence in the lower courts.[83] These concerns were forcefully addressed by the Court of Appeal some three months after the *Re B* judgment, in the case of *Re B-S*.

---

[81] *Re P (Adoption: Leave Provisions)* [2007] EWCA Civ 616 discussed at 4.4.7.
[82] See Case comment: Doughty, J. '*Re B (A Child)(Care order)* [2013] UKSC 33; (2013) 35 *Journal of Social Welfare and Family Law* 491.   [83] *Re G* [2013] EWCA Civ 965, at [43] (McFarlane LJ).

Key Case 4: *Re B-S (Children)* [2013] EWCA Civ 1146

This was an appeal by a mother of two children against an order in the county court refusing leave under s. 47(5) of the Adoption and Children Act 2002 to oppose the making of adoption orders. The mother's appeal was dismissed. Although the mother's circumstances had changed sufficiently to satisfy the first stage of the test, the Court of Appeal held that the judge had been correct in refusing leave because it was entirely improbable that the mother would have succeeded in persuading a court that it was in the children's welfare to oppose the order, at the second stage of the test.

Sir James Munby, President of the Family Division, took the opportunity to address wider concerns about adoption without consent, following the *Re B* judgment. He itemised three important points emphasised by Lord Neuberger in *Re B*:

- 'Although the child's interests are paramount, a court must never lose sight of the fact that those interests include being brought up by the natural family, unless the overriding requirement of the child's welfare makes that impossible' [26].
- 'The court must consider all the available options before coming to a decision' [27].
- 'The court's assessment of a parent's ability to provide good enough care for a child must take into account the assistance and support that the local authorities would offer' [28].

The President said that the Court of Appeal had concerns that centred on 'recurrent inadequacy of the analysis and reasoning' in local authority and Cafcass evidence as well as in 'too many judgments' in the lower courts. He noted that these flaws had been criticised in four other Court of Appeal cases that year.[84] Aiming to draw the threads together and spell out what was demanded by good practice, the legislation, and the European Convention of Human Rights, he identified the following two elements as essential.

1. There must be proper evidence from the local authority and from the children's Cafcass guardian which addresses all the options which are realistically possible and which contains an analysis of the arguments for and against each option. This requires analysis of the pros and cons and a fully reasoned recommendation, presented in a way that was described as a 'balance sheet' approach.
2. There must be an adequately reasoned judgment by the judge, avoiding a 'linear analysis' but applying instead a 'global holistic evaluation' of the available options. These terms were originally used by McFarlane LJ in *Re G (A Child)*,[85] which he subsequently explained in *Re F (A Child) (International Relocation Cases)* to mean taking all the welfare factors into account to arrive at a balanced decision, rather than approach each factor and each option separately, so as to arrive at a conclusion with only one type of order left standing.[86]

6.2 The *Re B-S* effect

Following the publication of the *Re B-S* judgment in September 2013, both the number of adoption decisions being made internally by local authorities and the number of placement orders being made by courts began to fall. By March 2016, these numbers had almost halved in England. Although there is no definitive research on the reasons for this, it seems

---

[84] Namely, *Re V (Children)* [2013] EWCA Civ 913; *Re S, K and the London Borough of Brent* [2103] EWCA Civ 926; *Re P (A Child)* [2013] EWCA Civ 963; and *Re G (A Child)* [2013] EWCA Civ 965.

[85] [2013] EWCA Civ 965 and Chapter 11 on child protection.

[86] *Re F (A Child) (International Relocation Cases)* [2015] EWCA Civ 882.

likely that agencies became less confident that courts would agree with adoption plans and were therefore making fewer applications for placement orders.[87]

In an effort to reassure local authorities, a body set up by the government in England to take a lead in adoption policy, The National Adoption Leadership Board, issued a document it described as a 'mythbuster' about what had and had not changed in the expectations of the courts regarding adoption practice.[88] This was closely followed by a judgment *Re R (A Child)* where Munby P clarified that *Re B-S* was not intended to change the law.[89] The case was, he said, focused on practice and the realistic options, so that the court is confident and clear which options would have a real prospect of being chosen if a full welfare evaluation of all the pros and cons were undertaken. He observed:

> There appears to be an impression in some quarters that an adoption application now has to surmount a much higher hurdle or even that adoption is over … a thing of the past. There is a feeling that "adoption is a last resort" and "nothing else will do" have become slogans too often taken to extremes. There is concern that the fact that ours is one of the few countries in Europe which permits adoption notwithstanding parental objection is adding to the uncertainly as to whether adoption can still be put forward as the right and best outcome for a child [41].

The President also pointed out that the National Adoption Leadership Board document was written as guidance for local authorities, and had not been endorsed by the judiciary.[90]

The contrast between the messages from the flow of post-*Re B-S* judgments and from government guidance continued as a source of some confusion.[91] A rise in the numbers of children being placed with family members under special guardianship orders added to the impression that courts were more reluctant to make adoption orders after the proportionality analysis in *Re B* (see 11.3).

 Key Case 5: *Re W (A Child) (Adoption: Grandparents' Competing Claim)* [2016] EWCA Civ 793

As noted by the President in *Re R*, it appeared that the phrase 'nothing else will do', applied to adoption decisions, was becoming a slogan for preferring other types of order. In 2016, the problems of over-simplification of the *Re B* judgment were addressed by the Court of Appeal in *Re W*, where members of the paternal family had already been caring for a child under a special guardianship order when they became aware that he had a half-sibling who had been placed for adoption. When the second baby was born, the father had not informed the local authority about his extended family. On discovering this, the paternal grandparents applied for leave to oppose the adoption of the second child outside the birth family. The welfare decision here was finely balanced between either continuing a stable placement, where the child had been placed at six months old and had lived for 18 months (at the date of the Court of Appeal hearing), but would lose his legal relationship with his birth family, or moving him to an untried placement, where his half-sibling was already being well cared for.

At first instance, Bodey J refused the adopters' application and made a special guardianship order in favour of the grandparents. The adopters appealed.

---

[87] Research in Practice, *Impact of the family justice reforms Phase 3: exploring variation across 21 local authorities* (Department for Education, 2016).

[88] National Adoption Leadership Board, *Impact of Court Judgments on Adoption: What the judgments do and do not say* (2014).   [89] [2014] EWCA Civ 1625.

[90] [2014] EWCA Civ 1625, at [70].

[91] Doughty, J. 'Myths and Misunderstanding in Adoption Law and Policy' (2014) 27 *Child and Family Law Quarterly* 331.

In the Court of Appeal, McFarlane LJ was critical of repeated references in the evidence before the Court to the child's 'right' to be brought up by his birth family, which had erroneously been treated as a presumption. As he put it, in lay terms:

the existence of a viable home with the grandparents should make that option 'a runner' but should not automatically make it 'a winner' in the absence of full consideration of any other factor that is relevant to her welfare; the error of the ISW [independent social worker] and the Guardian appears to have been to hold that 'if a family placement is a "runner", then it has to be regarded as a "winner"' [70].

The Court of Appeal overturned the High Court decision that the child should be removed from the adopters, and remitted the case to the High Court, where Cobb J decided in favour of the adoption, but noted that post-adoption contact had been agreed between the adopters and the paternal family so that the siblings could remain in touch (see 4.4.8).

Speaking extra-judicially shortly afterwards, McFarlane LJ reviewed the post *Re B* cases and acknowledged that some practitioners had found them 'less than helpful'. He described *Re B* as a reconnection to the core principles and described 'nothing else will do' as a 'firmly worded illustration of the impact of ECHR Art 8 and the requirement that a highly interventionist order such as adoption will only be justified if it is necessary and proportionate'.[92]

7. Globalisation and international aspects of adoption

In this section, we consider, first, the position of children whose parents are not settled in the UK coming into care and being adopted here, and, second, intercountry adoption.

7.1 Children of foreign nationals being adopted in England and Wales

At present, a parent who is a national of any country in the European Union and has lived in the UK for five years will acquire a permanent right to reside, or settle, in the UK and their children born here would be British citizens.[93] If they have lived in the UK for less than five years, or they are from outside the EU and have not acquired leave to remain, their children will not acquire British citizenship, although currently any EU citizens are able to exercise rights of freedom of movement in and out of the UK. Following the result of the UK referendum in June 2016 to leave the EU, the position regarding freedom of movement is uncertain. In future, it may be that a child born in the UK to EU citizens, and taken into care by an English or Welsh local authority, would not have British citizenship status before being adopted.

Child protection cases with an international element are the subject of Chapter 14 in this book. The following cases are featured in this chapter because they raise questions about variations in adoption law and policy between jurisdictions.

In *Re CB*, the mother of the child being adopted was a Latvian national living in London and complained of systemic failure to inform the Republic of Latvia of the proceedings.[94] She argued a change in circumstances in support of her application under s. 47(5) to oppose an adoption order being made. One of the changes was that the Latvian government

[92] McFarlane, A. 'Nothing Else Will Do'. Keynote address at FLBA National Conference, 22 October 2016, 19
[93] Directive 2004/38/EC of the European Parliament and of the Council, 29 April 2004.
[94] [2015] EWCA Civ 888.

had intervened in the proceedings. She also argued that the UK was out of step with the rest of Europe in that it caused or permitted too many children to be adopted. This was rejected by the Court of Appeal.

Nevertheless, there have been a series of cases featuring an underlying theme of unhappiness with English adoption law being applied to children of parents from other European states where adoption may be less common.[95] This perception was addressed by the President of the Family Division with an eye to an international audience in a detailed judgment in 2015, *Re N*.[96]

Key Case 6: *Re N (Children) (Adoption: Jurisdiction)* [2015] EWCA Civ 1112; [2016] UKSC 15

This case concerned two sisters born to Hungarian parents in England (and found by the court to be habitually resident in the UK). The parents were unable to care for them and the local authority plan was for the children to be adopted. The issue was whether the care proceedings should be transferred to Hungary. In the Court of Appeal, Munby P took the opportunity to acknowledge the 'concerns voiced in many parts of Europe about the law and practice in England and Wales in relation to what is sometimes referred to as "forced adoption" but which I prefer, and I think more accurately, to refer to as non-consensual adoption'. [8]

The President made the following points in response to those wider concerns:

1. Non-consensual adoption is not new and has been possible for as long as adoption had been regulated in England and Wales. It has become more common than in previous years because social changes means that a typical adoption now is of a child from care whose parents' consent is being dispensed with under s.52(1)(b).

2. The courts have consistently interpreted the word 'requires' in s.52(1)(b) in accordance with the ECHR.

3. There is no suggestion that domestic adoption law in England and Wales is incompatible with the ECHR.

4. Because non-consensual adoption is allowed by parliament, local authorities and courts must follow the law and not shy away from making an adoption decision or order when this is in the child's best interests.

With regard to the case in front of them, the Court of Appeal decided that the proceedings should be transferred to Hungary. However, on appeal to the Supreme Court, a different view was taken on the jurisdictional issue, partly because there was a range of options available in England, including that preferred by the local authority, whereas there were no identified potential carers in Hungary.[97]

7.2 **Intercountry adoption**

The legal framework relating to applications for adoption of children from abroad, and that relating to children in England and Wales who are moving abroad to be adopted is known as intercountry adoption. These procedures are greatly simplified if they are made under the Hague Convention Protection of Children and Co-operation in respect of Intercountry Adoptions 1993. More than 70 countries, including the UK, are party to this Convention, the purpose of which is to ensure that arrangements are made in the best

---

[95] Fenton-Glynn, C. and Lamont, R. 'Cross Border Care and Adoption Proceedings in the European Union' (2015) 38 *Journal of Social Welfare and Family Law* 94.

[96] Fenton-Glynn, C. 'Foreign Element Adoption: Re N' [2015] *Family Law* 1433.

[97] *Re N (Children)* [2016] UKSC 15. See case comment Doughty, J. 'The Best Interests of Children and the Mutual Trust Principle That Goes Both Ways' (2016) 38 *Journal of Social Welfare and Family Law* 333.

interests of children, that there is cooperation between states and that a Convention adoption is recognised in all Member States.

7.2.1 Children adopted in England and Wales from overseas

There are three types of adoption orders made in other jurisdictions which are automatically recognised in England and Wales. These are:

- Orders made elsewhere in the UK;[98]
- 'Overseas adoptions' as defined in Adoption (Designation of Overseas Adoptions) Order 1973 and (from 2014) the Adoption (Recognition of Overseas Adoptions) Order 2013. These include many Commonwealth countries, the USA, and China;
- 1993 Hague Convention orders.

Any adoption order made in another state which does not come within these three categories is not treated as a valid adoption in England and Wales and an application will need to be made here. It will be preferable to ensure that consent is validly obtained in the country of origin if that is where the placement was originally made. This will need to accord with legal processes in England and Wales in the sense that the court here will want evidence that the birth parents were as fully informed and involved as possible.

There are regulations on bringing a child into the UK for the purposes of adoption, breach of which may be a criminal offence. Furthermore, there are special restrictions on bringing in a child from certain countries, currently Cambodia, Guatemala, Nepal, and Haiti, because of the high risk of trafficking.[99]

7.2.2 Children in England and Wales adopted abroad

A child who is habitually resident in the UK may not be removed abroad for the purpose of adoption unless the adopters have been granted parental responsibility under s. 84 of the Adoption and Children Act 2002. The child must have lived with the applicants for at least ten weeks preceding the s. 84 application. Therefore where adopters normally live abroad, they will need to reside in the UK for several weeks before the child can be moved.

8. Differences in law and policy between England and Wales

England and Wales share the same jurisdiction and the court system is therefore the same across both countries, but there are differences in the law relating to local authorities and adoption agencies because these come within devolved powers to the Welsh Government.[100] This means that although practitioners in the family justice system are largely following the same laws and policies in Wales as in England, the Welsh Government is able to take a different approach to the delivery of children's services and adoption services. There are separate sets of regulations and statutory guidance for each country.

Although the reasons for a less zealous approach to adoption than England have not been made explicit, they may result from different political relationships between government and local authorities in Wales, where policies on education, health, and social care are increasingly diverging from those in England.

The policies to promote adoption in England since 2012 do not all apply in Wales, where a National Adoption Service focuses on improving the timeliness and quality of adoption services rather than on trying to increase the numbers of children who are adopted.[101] The Adoption and Children Act 2002, as originally drafted, applied in Wales but some

---

[98] Adoption and Children Act 2002, s. 66.
[99] Special Restrictions from Abroad Orders 2008.
[100] Government of Wales Act 2006.
[101] Social Services and Well-being (Wales) Act 2014, s. 170.

amendments by the Children and Families Act 2014 apply only in England. These include the repeal of s. 1(5) in England only, leaving a duty on Welsh adoption agencies to give due consideration to the child's religious persuasion, racial origin, and cultural and linguistic background (and courts to appreciate that this difference in agency decision-making exists) (see 4.2). There are some differences in approach between fostering for adoption introduced by s. 2 of the Children and Families Act 2014 and fostering for adoption under s. 81(10) of the Social Services and Well-being (Wales) Act 2014 (see 4.4.4).

9. The irrevocability of an adoption order

An adoption order made by a court in England and Wales is irreversible, once the time limit (21 days) for an appeal has passed. The very few exceptions to this are discussed in this section.

 Key Case 7: *Webster v Norfolk County Council* [2009] EWCA Civ 59

The parents applied for permission to appeal out of time against adoption orders made three years earlier of their three oldest children. This was because all the children had been taken into care after one of them (aged 2 at the time of his hospital admission) suffered several unexplained fractures, but some doubts had subsequently arisen about the medical evidence in the care proceedings, which had been the basis of the local authority intervention. Dismissing the parents' application, Wall LJ said:

> In my judgment, however, the public policy considerations relating to adoption, and the authorities on the point – which are binding on this court –simply make it impossible for this court to set aside the adoption orders even if, as Mr and Mrs Webster argue, they have suffered a serious injustice.

> This is a case in which the court has to go back to first principles. Adoption is a statutory process. The law relating to it is very clear. The scope for the exercise of judicial discretion is severely curtailed. Once orders for adoption have been lawfully and properly made, it is only in highly exceptional and very particular circumstances that the court will permit them to be set aside [148]–[149].

The public policy considerations in Wall LJ's mind would have included the undermining of the permanence of adoption if old judgments could be revisited, perhaps when subsequent advances in medical science might lead to a different result.

There are very few reported cases where the court considered applications, out of time, to set aside an adoption order. Exceptionally, some irregularity in process may bring the order into question.

In 1991, a father was granted leave to appeal out of time against the adoption of his children by their step-father with the mother, because he had given his consent without knowing that his ex-wife was terminally ill. After her death, the children returned to live with their father. The Court here decided that his consent had not been valid, and the orders were set aside.[102] In 1995, a 35-year-old man discovered that his birth father was of Muslim origin although he had been adopted and brought up as Jewish. He encountered suspicion when he wanted to settle in Israel and applied to set his own adoption aside. The

---

[102] *(Re M (Minors) (Adoption)* [1991] 1 FLR 458 CA.

Court of Appeal did not agree, saying that it had no power to do this, in the absence of any procedural irregularity or mistake.[103] In another case, an orphan from Bosnia was adopted in England by foster carers, although she still had close relatives who were alive and wanted to care for her. The proceedings here were found to be flawed, as the judge had not made any direction to try to trace any relevant family or services in Bosnia. The adoption order was set aside as it had been made in breach of natural justice, because a party who should have been heard had not been notified.[104]

More recently, in *Re W (A Child) (Revocation) (Inherent Jurisdiction)*, the local authority asked the High Court to use its inherent jurisdiction (see Chapter 9) to set aside an adoption order that had been made nine years ago, because the arrangements had disrupted.[105] Bodey J refused, explaining that:

> It is far less likely than likely that a revocation order would ultimately come to be made and the 'process' would stir up all the sorts of potential problems at the human level which I have tried to envisage. In short, it is a Pandora's box and the court should in my view only go there if it seems proportionate, necessary and reasonably likely to be ultimately successful. I do not think that the application fulfils those pre-requisites [12].

He added that the child was doing very well in a foster placement and that, if everything is well explained to her by the social worker in child-appropriate language, it may well be that the whole issue would naturally resolve once the litigation process was withdrawn from her life.

However, in *PK v K*[106] a 14-year-old girl herself wanted to reverse an adoption that was based on a private agreement, having been abused by the relatives who adopted her when she was four, and subsequently returning to live with her mother. The adopters took no part in these proceedings. The judge, Pauffley J, pointed out that all adults in the case were fully informed, the girl was happily settled with her mother, and there would be emotionally harmful consequences for PK if she were to remain the adopted child of Mr and Mrs K. She said, 'The only advantage of a refusal of the application to revoke the adoption order would be the public policy considerations in upholding a validly made adoption order. I am in no doubt. The right course is to allow both applications in these highly exceptional and very particular circumstances and for the reasons given.' [26]–[28].

So it can be seen from this brief review of the cases where attempts were made to undo adoption orders, that the court will be looking closely at the individual child's welfare in balancing any policy factors.

10. Alternative placements to adoption

 DEBATE 3: HOW SHOULD DECISIONS BE MADE BETWEEN ADOPTION AND OTHER TYPES OF PLACEMENT?

Before moving on to discuss special guardianship in more detail, we will review the alternative types of placement that the court may consider to ensure permanence for the child.

As we have seen in the discussions in 6.1 about which type of permanence plan and court order is proportionate in the context of Article 8, all the realistic options must be fully

---

[103] *(Re B (Adoption: Jurisdiction to Set Aside)* [1995] EWCA Civ 48.
[104] *(Re K (Adoption and Wardship)* [1997] 2 FLR 221, CA.   [105] [2013] EWHC 1957 (Fam).
[106] [2015] EWHC 2316 (Fam).

assessed when making decisions about which will best meet the child's welfare needs. Only then will the court be able to evaluate the plan, but this is not an easy task in the context of what may be available to support different types of placement.

At the care proceedings stage, the court will consider s.1 of the Children Act 1989, but if a placement order is also being applied for, the court and the agency must also consider the child's welfare under s.1 of the Adoption and Children Act 2002. This includes the effect on him or her, throughout his or her life, of becoming an adopted person.

10.1 **Placement options**

On making a care order, if the child cannot be placed with birth parents, the options are placement with extended family either as foster carers, under a child arrangements order, or a special guardianship order; placement in a residential home (e.g. a specialist educational or health establishment); or, most commonly, a foster placement. Some foster placements are long term, with contact with the birth family terminated. The question therefore arises as to when adoption is a more proportionate response than long-term fostering.

10.2 **Comparing adoption to long-term fostering**

The advantages to a child of fostering are that the local authority retains shared parental responsibility and therefore continues with a planning and support role, which includes promoting contact between the child and their birth family.[107] The disadvantages are the insecurity that can arise if social workers and carers change and the child has to get used to new people, and move around different households and schools. Although local authorities have a corporate parenting role that means, in principle, they have oversight of the child's needs and development, systems cannot in themselves guarantee that a child will experience a continuous pattern of care and support. Regulations in England allow for long-term foster placement to be agreed, where the carers will continue to act as foster carers until the child is 18.[108] However, fostering will always harbour risks of the local authority changing its plans or the birth parents making applications for contact or discharging the care order, that are not in the child's best interests.

In *Re V (long-term fostering or adoption)*,[109] Black LJ set out a non-exhaustive list of the differences between adoption and long term fostering:

- Adoption makes the child a permanent member of the family, which will feel different to being fostered
- Adoption is not open to challenge by the birth family and the law relating to contact arrangements is different
- The local authority will not routinely remain as having a part in the child's life.

As Pauffley J put it in *Re LRP (Care Proceedings: Placement Order)*, 'a long term foster child does not have the same and enduring sense of belonging within a family as does a child who has been adopted'. She described a plan for long-term foster care for a baby as an 'extraordinarily precarious legal framework'.[110]

---

[107] Children Act 1989, s. 34.
[108] Care Planning, Placement and Case Review (England) Regulations 2010 (SI 959/2010), reg 2(1).
[109] [2013] EWCA Civ 913.   [110] [2013] EWHC 3974 (Fam).

11. Special guardianship

The concept of special guardianship orders as one of the range of options that a court may consider when making decisions about a child's welfare crosses the boundary between private and public law and is an example of the flexibility of the Children Act.

A special guardian differs from a testamentary guardian who has been appointed under a will, because the former can be appointed only by a court and the order takes effect during a parent's lifetime.

11.1 Purpose of special guardianship

Special guardianship was introduced as an alternative type of placement for children by s. 115 of the Adoption and Children Act 2002.[111] This provision inserted a new set of sections, 14A—G in Part II of the Children Act 1989, the part of the Act that relates to child arrangements orders and other matters seen as private law (see Chapter 9). However, most special guardianship orders are made as a result of public law proceedings.

The white paper that informed the drafting of the Adoption and Children Act 2002 gave examples of the sort of situation where a special guardianship order might better meet a child's needs than adoption or a residence order.[112] These indicate the reasoning behind introducing the new type of order that could provide stability and permanence for a child who needed the benefits of a stronger order than residence but where adoption was not a likely or desired outcome.

- Older children who do not wish to be legally separated from their birth families.
- Children being cared for on a permanent basis by members of their wider birth family.
- Children in some minority ethnic communities, who have religious and cultural difficulties with adoption as it is set out in law.
- Unaccompanied asylum-seeking children who need secure, permanent homes, but have strong attachments to their families abroad.

Key Legislation 7: Adoption and Children Act 2002, s. 14C, Special guardianship orders: effect

(1) The effect of a special guardianship order is that while the order remains in force—
  (a) a special guardian appointed by the order has parental responsibility for the child in respect of whom it is made; and
  (b) subject to any other order in force with respect to the child under this Act, a special guardian is entitled to exercise parental responsibility to the exclusion of any other person with parental responsibility for the child (apart from another special guardian).
(2) Subsection (1) does not affect—
  (a) the operation of any enactment or rule of law which requires the consent of more than one person with parental responsibility in a matter affecting the child; or

---

[111] The judgment in *Re S (A Child) (Adoption Order or Special Guardianship Order)* [2007] EWCA Civ 90 has a useful addendum setting out in detail the legal differences between an adoption order and a special guardianship order.   [112] Department of Health *Adoption—a new approach* (Cm 5017, 2000).

> (b) any rights which a parent of the child has in relation to the child's adoption or placement for adoption.
> (3) While a special guardianship order is in force with respect to a child, no person may—
>   (a) cause the child to be known by a new surname; or
>   (b) remove him from the United Kingdom,without either the written consent of every person who has parental responsibility for the child or the leave of the court.
> (4) Subsection (3)(b) does not prevent the removal of a child, for a period of less than three months, by a special guardian of his.

This means that the special guardian is the carer who is expected and required to carry out the powers and duties that come with the status of parental responsibility. In contrast to adoption, therefore, the legal relationship between the child and parents is not severed, but the special guardian can make day-to-day decisions about the child's upbringing without consulting with the parents or the local authority. In this way, the special guardian exercises parental responsibility exclusively, not sharing it as an adult who holds a child arrangements order would have to do.

Another difference to adoption is that the special guardianship order is effective only until a child turns 18, when parental responsibility ceases in any event, while an adoptive parent would still be a parent, albeit of an adult. This is reflected in the fact that the court will consider the Children Act 1989 welfare checklist here, whereas in adoption, the checklist includes the effect of the decision on the child throughout their lifetime, in s. 1(4)(c) of the Adoption and Children Act 2002.

Making a special guardianship order has the effect of terminating any existing care order or interim care order in respect of the child. This ends any parental responsibility that was held by the local authority, although support may continue (see 10.2).

11.2 Applying for a special guardianship order

The legislation created a rigorous process, in accordance with the obligations that a special guardianship order confers.

Under section 14A(5), an application for an order may be made only by:

- a testamentary guardian;
- an individual with whom the child lives under a child arrangements order;
- an individual with whom the child has lived for three of the five years preceding the application;
- an individual who has the agreement of everyone holding parental responsibility; or
- a foster carer or a relative with whom the child has lived for at least a year preceding the application.

Any applicant outside these groups will need to apply first for leave from the court. An applicant must be aged 18 or over under s. 14A(2)(a) and may be a single person or a couple.[113] They are required to give three months' notice of their intention to apply for leave to the local authority, whether or not the child is in care. This is to enable the local

---

[113] Adoption and Children Act 2002, s. 14A(2).

authority to prepare a written report in the statutory form, assessing the child's needs and whether these might be met by the applicants. Special guardianship is a very serious order for a court to make if a child is subject to a care application, because the applicant will need to show the court that he or she can safeguard and protect the child from whatever risks the child faces that are attributable to their parents, without the local authority sharing parental responsibility.

Although the parents' parental responsibility is restricted, it is not extinguished, as it is by an adoption order. However, an application by a parent for variation or discharge of the order would first require the leave of the court. There are some limitations on the special guardian, and serious decisions that require the agreement of all holders of PR, such as immunisation or circumcision, would still require agreement by parents.

11.3 Meeting a child's needs under special guardianship

It should be borne in mind that this order is being applied for because a child cannot safely be cared for by their parents and that, where it is being considered by a local authority or a court, it will be one option that forms part of the global holistic evaluation required. There are a number of features that will require specific attention in decision-making.

It can be seen that special guardianship is not designed to cut parents out of their child's life. This is emphasised by s. 14B(1)(a) requiring the court to consider whether to make a child arrangements order regarding contact, to run alongside the special guardianship order and the obligation on the local authority to make recommendations about contact in its report. Even where contact is not ordered or agreed, the parent is entitled to make an application under s. 8 of the Children Act 1989. This is one type of application that a parent can make without first getting leave. Therefore, the guardian will need to be in a position to manage any contact arrangements that are in place. Where the guardian is a relative, for example grandparents, this adds new complexity to family dynamics which can be difficult to adjust to. A grandparent will not necessarily find it easy to prioritise the grandchild's needs over their own son or daughter, nor to always recognise risks posed through contact. Research with kinship carers indicates that managing contact is one of the most challenging aspects.[114]

In recent years, special guardianship orders have increasingly been made for young children and even to carers they were not living with. This led to concerns that one aspect of the *Re B-S* effect was greater use of special guardianship where adoption might better meet the child's needs. There were also indications that not all special guardians were getting the support they needed.[115]

Although the local authority does not have the same continuing duties to a child under special guardianship that it would to a looked-after child (see Chapter 11), the child is likely to have ongoing needs for care and support. This was recognised by s. 14F requiring local authorities to make support services available. This can include financial assistance. The processes for assessment and planning to meet these needs are set out in regulations and guidance. A problem is that a foster carer who becomes a special guardian will lose foster allowances and instead be means tested before receiving any special guardianship allowance. Like all aspects of support services for children, restrictions on public spending and local authority budgets imposed by central government since 2010 mean that the level of demand for support cannot be met in every case.

---

[114] Hunt, J., Waterhouse, S., and Lutman, E. *Keeping them in the family* (BAAF, 2008).
[115] Department for Education *Special guardianship review: report on findings* (DfE, 2015).

The changing nature of special guardianship as a more common permanent option has been recognised by new regulations and guidance in England in 2016, including extending the benefits of the adoption support fund to guardians.[116]

SUMMARY

1. How should legal obligations to provide continued support to the child be balanced with the privacy and autonomy of family life?
   - Adoption had traditionally been a private family arrangement to normalise the social problems of unmarried mothers and childless couples. As this model changed to one of permanence for children in care, legal reforms were introduced to address continuing needs that children may have. The Adoption and Children Act 2002 gave adoptive families a right to be assessed for post-adoption support. As awareness of the problems facing many families has increased, and with policies which encourage more and quicker adoption, provision of post-adoption support services is now being made more generally available and can extend to special guardians. Aiming for the right balance between normalising the adoptive family and recognising the obligations of the state toward children who have suffered abuse and neglect is part of the welfare decision-making duties of the court and the adoption agencies.
   - This debate includes the extent to which the state should try to regulate post-adoption contact. Adoptive families are now encouraged to be open with their children about the adoption, and to help them make sense of their identity as an adopted child. Indirect contact arrangements with birth parents are common and siblings being placed together or having some direct contact is preferred practice. However, face-to-face contact between adopted children and their birth parents is rare, making most adoption 'closed'. This may become unsustainable if the internet and social media are replacing the regulated access to records in later life.
   - Although special guardianship does not exclude birth parents in the same way, contact can be difficult to manage. Special guardians can also struggle financially, and need support.

2. How can an order that a child be adopted, without her birth parents' consent, be justified?
   - The legislation offers a number of opportunities for birth parents to challenge an adoption plan, but more recent policies designed to speed up court proceedings have raised concerns about giving parents sufficient time to prove that they can improve their parenting skills and environment to meet their child's needs.
   - The welfare requirement that can override parental opposition to adoption has been subjected to intense scrutiny by the courts, especially since the Supreme Court judgment in *Re B* in 2013, and has been found to be compliant with the ECHR. However, there are still many reported cases where

---

[116] Special Guardianship (Amendment) Regulations 2016 (SI 111/2016).

complex facts and relationships pose difficulties in coming to timely decisions. Recent judgments and legislative reform have attempted to clarify the
evaluation of respective rights of children and adult parties, but the ideological and practical dilemmas of closed adoption against parents' wishes are not
going to be easily resolved.

3. How should decisions be made between adoption and other types of placement?
   - Adoption has been shown to offer the best chance for babies and young
     children to overcome early adverse childhood experiences and grow up in a
     stable placement.
   - However, the draconian nature of an adoption order means that agencies
     and courts constantly need to pay close attention to balancing the interests
     of the child in retaining links with their birth family with their best option for
     secure permanence. While outcomes for looked-after children in fostering
     and residential placements continue to be poor, adoption or special guardi-
     anship may appear to be more stable, but courts require all realistic options
     to be rigorously assessed.

Further Reading

LOWE, N.V. 'Will Adoption Do? Reflections on the Law and Practice in Public Law Adoptions in
England and Wales' in J Eekelaar (ed) *Family Law in Britain and America in the New Century
-Essays in Honour of Sanford N Katz* (Brill/Nijhoff, 2016) 161–76
   - This book chapter provides a helpful overview of developments since Lowe's earlier
     work cited in this chapter.
MEAKINGS, S. *et al* 'The support needs of newly formed adoptive families: findings from the
Wales Adoption Study' (forthcoming) *Adoption & Fostering*
   - An article on adopters' support needs in the early stages of an adoptive placement,
     which will contribute to long-term stability.
PALACIOS, J. and BRODZINSKY, D. 'Adoption Research: Trends, Topics and Outcomes (2010) 34
International Journal of Behavioural Development 270
   - Reviews the research on the benefits and outcomes of adoption of children in care.
SELWYN. J. and MASSON, J. 'Adoption, Special Guardianship and Residence Orders: A Compari-
son of Disruption Rates' [2014] *Family Law* 1709
   - Reviews research on the durability of adoption compared with other types of
     placement.

13

Human Rights, Children's Rights, and Family Law

Helen Stalford and Seamus Byrne

LEARNING OBJECTIVES

After reading this chapter you will be able to:

- Understand the basic normative, legal, and theoretical framework at international, European and domestic (England and Wales) level relating to children's rights in the context of family law;
- Determine the nature and scope of children's rights in a number of substantive contexts;
- Engage on a profoundly critical level with children's rights norms, theories, and practices in the context of family life;
- Appreciate the legal, institutional, economic, and procedural resources children need to exercise their rights;
- Conduct an informed debate on discrete children's rights questions, including the nature and scope of children's best interests, and the balance between parental responsibility and the autonomous status of children;
- Suggest and support proposals for further development and reform.

DEBATES

After reading this chapter you should be equipped to discuss your opinion on the following central debates:

1. Should children be allowed to make decisions about their own lives, particularly in matters concerning their family life?
2. Should parents have a right to use corporal punishment on their own children?

1. Introduction

It should be understood from the outset that this chapter is primarily concerned with exploring children's rights in the context of family law and family life. In that sense, it should be distinguished from work that is concerned with presenting child law (law pertaining to children) in a broader sense. In approaching this topic from a *children's rights* perspective, we aim to look at family law through the lens of the human rights of children (some, but not all of which has been codified in domestic law), and the associated theoretical, doctrinal, and empirical scholarship.[1] The importance of adopting an explicitly children's rights-based perspective is emphasised by Michael Freeman, who stated:

> The language of 'rights' can make visible what has for too long been suppressed. It can lead to different and new stories being heard in public ... [2]

Adopting a children's rights framework from the outset promotes children's status as valid, active human beings (as opposed to adults-in-the-making) [3] with an equal claim to entitlement as adults. A rights-based approach goes beyond articulating what children's legal entitlement is; it identifies what children's rights *should* be, how those rights can be balanced against the rights of others, and what needs to be achieved to transform rights written down on paper to rights realised in practice.

The broader literature identifies essentially three features of a children's rights-based perspective which can be applied equally to the study of family law. It involves:

1. **Recognition that *all* children have human rights which are enshrined in international and domestic law that have to be upheld in procedural and substantive terms.**

   Children hold rights by virtue of their status as a family member but while their rights and interests may be dependent on or facilitated by the actions of their family (particularly their parents), they are not synonymous with them. This is especially important when it comes to children in the context of family law because it takes more effort and attention to separate out the distinct interests of children from those of other family members. Whilst some children's rights apply equally to adults (such as the right to respect for private and family life), they have to be interpreted and applied in a manner that responds to children's specific interests and needs. Other rights are exclusive to children and need to be explicitly recognised and implemented in accordance with clear principles and processes (such as rights related to adoption, or the right to know and be cared for by one's parents).

2. **Recognition that as states and state authorities are duty bearers under international law, they have an obligation to support those working directly with children to ensure that their rights can be properly fulfilled.**

   Effort and public resources have to be invested in building capacities among adults working with children. This includes ensuring that adult professionals in the justice system receive appropriate training and education as to what obligations they have in regard to children's rights and that appropriate procedural adjustments are made

---

[1] For further discussion of the difference between children's rights, child law, and children's rights law, see Vandenhole, W. 'Children's rights from a legal perspective' in Vandenhole, W. *et al* (eds) *Routledge International Handbook of Children's Rights Studies* (Abingdon, 2015).

[2] Freeman, M. 'Why It Remains Important to Take Children's Rights Seriously' (2007) 15 *International Journal of Children's Rights* 5, 6–7.

[3] James, A. and Prout, A. (eds), *Constructing and Reconstructing Childhood: Contemporary Issues in the New Sociology of Childhood* (Routledge, 1997).

to enable children to express those rights in practice. Exploring children's family-related rights in isolation from the resource, capacity, and procedural constraints associated with the family justice system is neither helpful not realistic.

3. **Regard for children as active rights-holders and agents shaping their own lives rather than as passive objects of protection.**

   This requires providing children with the support and opportunities to actively enforce their rights and to bring others to account when violations occur. But this does not mean that children act in isolation from others. Quite the contrary; an important aspect of a children's rights-based approach is acknowledgement of and support for the role that others, particularly their parents, siblings, wider family, and community play in facilitating the fulfilment of children's rights. This means involving family and community members in identifying problems and/or risks, and in brokering solutions that are enduring and conducive to children's well-being in the longer term.[4]

Each of these components will be explored in more depth in Debates 1 and 2. To begin with, it is important to present a brief overview of the international children's rights framework underpinning this area, including the UN Convention on the Rights of the Child and the European Convention on Human Rights in section 2. The chapter then points to some of the cultural, legal, and practical obstacles to the protection of children's rights in the context of family law in section 3.

2. International sources of children's family-related rights

2.1 The UN Convention on the Rights of the Child

No academic treatment of children's family-related rights is complete without reference to the framework of the UN Convention on the Rights of the Child 1989 (UNCRC). The UNCRC was ratified by the UK in 1991 and presents a detailed catalogue of children's civil, political, economic, social, and cultural rights, as well as the corresponding duties of states to uphold those rights. As such, it is universally acknowledged as the 'fulcrum' upon which all children's rights activities are developed and measured.[5] The interpretation and application of these provisions are underpinned by four 'general principles':

- Article 2 UNCRC: all children should have equal enjoyment of their rights;
- Article 3 UNCRC: the best interests of the child be a primary consideration in all matters concerning the child;
- Article 6 UNCRC: all children have a right to life, survival and development;
- Article 12 UNCRC: all children have a right to express their views and to participate in decisions that affect them in accordance with their age and capacity.[6]

The UNCRC contains a number of provisions in support of children's family life: Article 16 protects children against any arbitrary or unlawful interference with his or her privacy, family, home, or correspondence; Article 9 protects them from being separated from

---

[4] Collins, T. and Paré, M. 'A Child Rights-Based Approach to Anti-Violence Efforts in Schools' (2016) 24 *International Journal of Children's Rights* 764, 775; Herring, J. 'Forging a Relational Approach: Best Interests or Human Rights?' (2013) 13 *Medical Law International* 32; and Herring, J. *Caring and the Law* (Hart Publishing, 2013).

[5] Freeman, M. 'Why It Remains Important to Take Children's Rights Seriously' (2007) 15 *International Journal of Children's Rights* 5, 55.

[6] Kilkelly, U. 'Operationalising Children's Rights: Lessons from Research' (2006) 1 *Journal of Children's Services* 36, 40.

their parents against their will unless it is in their best interests; and Article 19 protects them from all forms of violence, including that inflicted by parents. Equally, the UNCRC promotes the primary responsibility of parents for the upbringing and welfare of their children (Article 18 and 27), and children's relationship with their family, and particularly with their parents, is upheld as fundamental for their growth (Preamble and Article 8(1)).

Insofar as the UNCRC has been ratified by the UK, the UK is legally bound to 'respect and ensure the rights set forth in [the Convention] to each child within their jurisdiction'[7] and to take 'all appropriate legislative, administrative and other measures for the implementation of the rights recognized in the Convention'.[8] Critically, however, as an international treaty, the UNCRC is not of itself directly enforceable in the UK in the absence of implementing domestic legislation and there are no sanctions imposed on UK authorities for failure to comply with the obligations set out in the instrument.[9] Rather, the approach of the UNCRC is more constructive: it sets out a series of benchmarks by which national provision for the promotion and protection of children's rights can be amended and monitored. State compliance with the Convention is monitored at five year intervals by the UN Committee on the Rights of the Child.[10] In June 2011 the UN Human Rights Council adopted an Optional Protocol on a communications procedure for children's rights (not ratified as yet by the UK) which took effect in 2012 and which enables individuals within the states that have ratified the protocol to submit complaints to the UN Committee on the Rights of the Child in respect of alleged violations of their UNCRC rights by state bodies.[11]

2.2 Alternative international sources of children's rights: the European Convention on Human Rights and Fundamental Freedoms 1950

Many have argued that its lack of legal force renders the UNCRC ineffective in enforcing children's rights in the UK.[12] It is arguably more useful, therefore, to allude to an alternative international source of children's rights that has been incorporated into domestic UK law, notably the European Convention on Human Rights and Fundamental Freedoms 1950 (ECHR). The ECHR has been described as 'a beacon of European democracy and public order',[13] containing a comprehensive checklist of civil and political rights, all of which have been interpreted teleologically (with the purpose of the document in mind) through the extensive jurisprudence of the European Court of Human Rights (ECtHR).[14] The ECHR is more accessible and potent in the UK since

---

[7] Article 2 UNCRC.   [8] Article 4 UNCRC.

[9] The extent to which the UNCRC gives rise to justiciable rights at the domestic level depends very much on the constitutional order of the state concerned. See further Alston, P. and Tobin, J. *Laying the Foundations for Children's Rights* (UNICEF Innocenti Research Centre, 2005); Lundy, L., Kilkelly, U., and Byrne, 'Incorporation of the United Nations Convention on the Rights of the Child in Law: A Comparative Review' (2013) 21 *International Journal of Children's Rights* 442. For an analysis of the ways in which the UNCRC has informed judicial decision-making in family law cases in England and Wales, see Gilmore, S. 'Use of the UNCRC in Family Law Cases in England and Wales' (2017) 25 *International Journal of Children's Rights* 500.

[10] For further details of this procedure and an archive of monitoring reports, see http://www.ohchr.org/EN/HRBodies/CRC/Pages/CRCIndex.aspx, accessed 10 October 2017.

[11] Official Records of the General Assembly, Sixty-sixth Session, Supplement No. 53 (A/66/53) ch I. See further Buck, T. and Wabwile, M. (2013) 'The Potential and Promise of Communications Procedures under the Third Protocol to the Convention on the Rights of the Child', (2013) 2 *International Human Rights Law Review* 205.

[12] 'Interrogating the Concentration on the UNCRC Instead of the ECHR in the Development of Children's Rights in England?' (2007) 21 *Children and Society* 147.

[13] *Loizidou v Turkey (Preliminary Objections)* App. No. 15318/89) [1995] Series A Vol 310, 27, at [75].

[14] Dubout, E. 'Interprétation Téléologique et Politique Jurisprudentielle de la Cour Européenne des Droits de L'homme' (2008) 19 *Revue Trimetrielle des Droits de L'Homme*, 383; Kaczorowska, A. *Public International Law* (4th edn, Routledge, 2010).

its incorporation into domestic law by virtue of the Human Rights Act 1998.[15] This is important in the context of family law because it requires that all public authorities (including local authorities) act in a way that is compatible with the rights contained in the ECHR unless this conflicts with their obligations under other domestic legislation.[16] Moreover, all legislation is to be interpreted in a manner that is consistent with the rights set out in the ECHR.[17] If it is not possible to interpret domestic legislation in accordance with the ECHR, the legislation can be enforced as it stands but the courts can issue a declaration of incompatibility requiring Parliament to amend or affirm the offending legislation.[18]

Notwithstanding the fact that the text of the ECHR barely refers to children,[19] it has been applied to numerous cases involving children of all ages and backgrounds, particularly in the context of their family life.[20] Key provisions for children include:

- Article 3 ECHR: protects individuals against torture or inhuman or degrading treatment;[21]
- Article 6 ECHR: the right to a fair trial, including in matters of family justice;[22]
- Article 8 ECHR: affords everyone a right to respect for private and family life, home and correspondence.

We will consider how each of these provisions are applied in specific children's rights contexts later in this chapter, suffice to say that an important feature of them (specifically Articles 3 and 8 ECHR) is that they entail positive as well as negative obligations. In other words, contracting states do not meet their obligation to secure the rights enshrined in these Articles simply by refraining from interferences; they can also be obliged to actively deploy certain measures with a view to ensuring that children's rights in the context of their family life are effective and practicable. Measures states have to take to meet their positive obligations may include, (but are not limited to): passing legislation in order to ensure the enjoyment of rights guaranteed in the ECHR; conducting effective investigations in cases of alleged violations of children's rights (such as abuse or neglect); or ensuring that the

[15] For an analysis of some of the challenges and potential contradictions arising from this, see Fortin, J. 'Accommodating Children's Rights in a Post Human Rights Act Era' (2006) 69 *Modern Law Review* 299.

[16] Human Rights Act 1998, s. 6.   [17] Human Rights Act 1998, s. 3.

[18] See also Herring, J. 'Who decides on Human Rights?' (2009) *Law Quarterly Review* 125, 1; For much more detailed analysis of impact of human rights on domestic family law, see Choudhry, S. and Herring, J. *European Human Rights and Family Law* (Hart Publishing, 2010); and Harris-Short, S. 'Family Law and the Human Rights Act 1998: Judicial Restraint or Revolution?' (2005) 17 *Child and Family Law Quarterly* 329.

[19] Article 2 Protocol 1 recognises a universal right to education and supports this with the guarantee that children should have a right to be educated in accordance with their parents' (rather than their own) religious and cultural beliefs; Article 5(1)(d) sets out the circumstances in which lawful detention of a minor is justifiable; and Article 6(1) restricts public access to trials in the interests of juveniles. Of course, generic provisions such as Article 1 which guarantees the Convention rights and freedoms to 'everyone', and Article 14 which prohibits discrimination on various grounds including age, extend the scope of the instrument to a range of groups not expressly mentioned in the remaining provisions. See Kilkelly, U. 'The Impact of the Convention on the Case-Law of the European Court of Human Rights' in D. Fottrell, (ed) *Revisiting Children's Rights: Ten Years of the UN Convention on the Rights of the Child* (Kluwer, 2000) 87.

[20] See, for instance, the body of case law relating to the application of Article 8 which provides a right to respect for private and family life, discussed at length in Opromolla, A. 'Children's Rights under Articles 3 and 8 of the European Convention: Recent Case Law' (2001) 26 *European Law Review, Human Rights Supplement* 46.   [21] See, e.g., *Z and Others v UK* App. No. 29392/95) [2001] 2 FLR 612.

[22] See, e.g., *Sahin v Germany* App. No. 30943/96) [2003] 2 FLR 671.

material, institutional, and procedural mechanisms are in place to enable these rights to be met in practice.

The ECtHR has demonstrated a growing willingness to interpret the ECHR dynamically to ensure adequate protection for children in a range of contexts.[23] This ingenuity has been manifested in the ECtHR's deference to relevant provisions of the UNCRC to achieve a more child-focused interpretation of otherwise age-neutral provisions.[24] For example, Article 7 UNCRC acknowledges the child's right to know and be cared for by his/her parents, and was referred to by the ECtHR in support of a father's challenge to his son's adoption which had occurred without his knowledge.[25] In *Sahin v Germany*[26] and *Sommerfield v Germany*,[27] both concerning applications for child contact, the ECtHR referred to Article 12 UNCRC in determining both the extent to which the child should be allowed to participate in proceedings and the weight that should be attached to the views expressed by the child. Equally, in the context of juvenile justice and the involvement of children in criminal proceedings, the ECtHR has referred to Article 40(3) UNCRC,[28] which requires States Parties to promote the establishment of laws, procedures, authorities, and institutions specifically applicable to children who are alleged accused or recognised as having infringed the penal law, to inform its interpretation of Article 6 ECHR concerning the right to a fair trial.[29]

2.3 Other sources of children's rights

Other international (Council of Europe) sources of children's rights in the context of family life should be noted too, although these are more obscure or specific to particular types of cases than the framework described earlier. The European Convention on Social and Economic Rights, for instance, regulates state compliance with their obligations to secure social and economic rights from birth relating to housing, health, education, employment, legal and social protection, free movement of persons, and non-discrimination.[30] For example, Articles 11 and 16 relating to the right to health and the right of the family to social, legal, and economic protection respectively apply equally to children. Specific child-focused

---

[23] All ECtHR cases relevant to children are accessible through the specialised Council of Europe Database, Theseus, Available at: https://www.coe.int/en/web/children/case-law, accessed 1 October 2017.

[24] For an analysis of the extent to which the UNCRC has informed the ECtHR, see Kilkelly, U. 'The Best of Both Worlds for Children's Rights: Interpreting the European Convention on Human Rights in the Light of the UN Convention on the Rights of the Child' (2001) 23 *Human Rights Quarterly* 308; and Kilkelly, U. 'Effective Protection of Children's Rights in Family Cases: An International Approach' (2002) 12 *Transnational Law and Contemporary Problems* 336.   [25] *Keegan v Ireland* App. No. 16969/90 [1994] ECHR Series A 290.

[26] *Sahin v Germany* App. No. 30943/96) [2001] not yet published.

[27] *Sommerfield v Germany* App. No. 31871/96) ECHR 2003-VIII 341.

[28] See further Kilkelly, U. 'The CRC in Litigation under the ECHR' in T. Liefaard and J. Doek (eds) *Litigating the Rights of the Child: The UN Convention on the Rights of the Child in Domestic and International Jurisprudence* (Springer, 2015).

[29] *Nortier v the Netherlands* App. No. 13924/88 [1994] 17 EHRR 273. For further examples, see *Pini and Bertani, Manera and Altripaldi v Romania* App. Nos 78028/01 and 78030/01, Reports of Judgments and Decisions 2004-V, at para 157; *Havelka and Others v Czech Republic* App. No. 23499/04 [2007] not yet published; *Saviny v Ukraine* App. No. 39948/06) [2008] not yet published; *EP v Italy* App. No. 31127/96) [1999] not yet published; *KA v Finland* App. No. 27751/95 [2003] not yet published; and *Haase v Germany* App. No. 11057/02, Reports of Judgments and Decisions 2004-III. See further Kilkelly, U. 'The CRC in Litigation under the ECHR' in T. Liefaard and J. Doek (eds), *Litigating the Rights of the Child: The UN Convention on the Rights of the Child in Domestic and International Jurisprudence* (Springer, 2015).

[30] For further discussion of this instrument and other broader human rights instruments of relevance to children in the context of family proceedings, see Vandenhole W. 'Children's Rights from a Legal Perspective: Children's Rights Law' in Vandenhole, W. *et al* (eds) *Routledge International Handbook of Children's Rights Studies* (Routledge, 2015) 27–42.

provisions are contained in Article 7 (the right of children and young persons to protection) and Article 17 (right of children and young persons to social, legal and economic protection). Other lesser known 'soft law' instruments and guidance, such as the European Convention on the Exercise of Children's Rights,[31] the European Convention on Contact concerning Children 2003,[32] and the Council of Europe Guidelines on Child Friendly Justice[33] promote the rights of the children in family proceedings before judicial authorities.

Of relevance also are European Union sources such as the EU Charter of Fundamental Rights of the European Union[34] and EU secondary legislation, which govern aspects of family law and children's rights that fall within EU competence. Issues include the recognition and enforcement of cross-border orders relating to child maintenance,[35] child contact and care arrangements, and parental child abduction[36] (see Chapter 14). The UK's decision to exit from the European Union places the future regulation of these areas in flux and creates some uncertainty for children implicated in cross-national family proceedings within the EU. There is a strong possibility that the UK will resort to the regulatory framework that governs such issues between non-EU Member States, notably that of the Hague Conference on Private International Law.[37] However, one of the most important features of *EU*-level regulation in this area has been the existence of an explicit, underpinning constitutional obligation, by virtue of Article 24 EU Charter of Fundamental Rights, to ensure that children's rights are protected in the course of such proceedings.[38] This obligation is rather more implicit under the Hague conference regime.

Notwithstanding the existence of a comprehensive international children's rights framework, it is in the context of family life and family relationships that children continue to experience some of the most routine and extreme violations of their rights.

 CONTEXT 1: THE FAMILY JUSTICE REVIEW

The impact of more practical and structural obstacles to children's ability to enforce their rights have been brought to the fore in England and Wales by a series of recent reforms introduced since 2011 in response to the findings of the Family Justice Review (see Chapter 15).[39] The review was driven by a need to achieve more effective organisational structures, including better managed courts, a reduction in delays, and more specialised judges. Such

---

[31] European Treaty Series No.160.   [32] European Treaty Series No.192.

[33] Council of Europe, *Guidelines on Child-Friendly Justice* (Council of Europe, 2010).

[34] 2010/C 83/02, [2010] OJ C 83/389.

[35] Council Regulation (EC) No. 4/2009 of 18 December 2008 on jurisdiction, applicable law, recognition and enforcement of decisions and cooperation in matters relating to maintenance obligations, [2009] OJ L7, 1–79.

[36] Council Regulation (EC) No. 2201/2003 of 27 November 2003 concerning jurisdiction and the recognition and enforcement of judgments in matrimonial matters and the matters of parental responsibility, repealing Regulation (EC) No 1347/2000, [2003] OJ L338, 1–29.

[37] Notably, the Hague Convention of 25 October 1980 on the Civil Aspects of International Child Abduction and the Hague Convention of 19 October 1996 on Jurisdiction, Applicable Law, Recognition, Enforcement and Co-operation in Respect of Parental Responsibility and Measures for the Protection of Children.

[38] Article 24 incorporates key family-related provisions of the UNCRC, notably children's right to such protection and care as is necessary for their well-being; their right to express their views freely and for such views to be taken into account in accordance with their age and maturity; a restatement that the child's best interests must be a primary consideration in all decisions affecting the child; and a child's right to maintain regular, direct contact with both parents, unless that is contrary to his or her interests.

[39] Ministry of Justice *Family Justice Review—Final Report* (2011). Available at: https://www.gov.uk/government/uploads/system/uploads/attachment_data/file/217343/family-justice-review-final-report.pdf, accessed 24 July 2017. For a critical review of how the reforms have impacted on children, see Holt, K. and Kelly, N. 'What has Happened Since the Family Justice Review: A Brighter Future for Whom?' [2015] *Family Law* 807.

reforms, it was claimed, are instrumental to safeguarding the welfare of the child, a paramount consideration in both private and public family proceedings.

Some of the reforms introduced as a result of the review are certainly conducive to the enforcement of children's rights. For instance, the introduction of the single Family Court[40] to deal with all family cases in a particular area should facilitate a more consistent, coordinated response to cases involving children. The review also highlighted the importance of ensuring that children are given an opportunity to be heard in relation to matters that affect them, and encouraged the resolution of private family disputes through out-of-court mediation which, it is claimed, lends itself to less acrimonious and more mutually empowering approaches to dispute resolution.[41]

However, as thoughtful and well-intentioned as this review may have been, it has operated within the constraints of government spending cuts and welfare reform which affect families (particularly lone parent families with young children) more dramatically than almost any other sector of society. A particular casualty of this process has been the almost complete decimation of legal aid by virtue of The Legal Aid, Sentencing and Punishment of Offenders Act (LASPO) 2012. Private family law, as well as many other areas of law affecting children and families (such as immigration, welfare benefits, employment, and some aspects of criminal justice) now no longer qualify for legal aid funding. There are some exceptions to this in the context of family law proceedings, including: applications for protective orders relating to domestic violence; cases involving allegations of child abuse where the proceedings are aimed at protecting the child, forced marriage; or where a child is party to proceedings[42] or other 'exceptional cases' determined on a case-by-case basis. As far as the latter is concerned, there is a right under LASPO, s.10 to civil legal aid for any out-of-scope matter where an exceptional case determination ('ECD') has been made by the Director of Legal Aid Casework. An ECD must be made where not to provide legal aid would breach either the individual's ECHR rights (within the meaning of the Human Rights Act 1998) or any rights of the individual to the provision of legal services that are enforceable EU rights (s. 10(3) (a)). It is worth noting that exceptional funding has been granted in only a small number of family cases.[43]

A fundamental challenge in family proceedings relates to achieving an appropriate balance between the imperative to protect and uphold children's independent interests and rights, on the one hand, whilst preserving the privacy and sanctity of the family on the other.[44] The former may require varying degrees of monitoring and intervention if the child's rights and welfare are deemed to be at risk; the latter requires maintaining a degree of privacy and autonomy to enable family members, particularly parents, to decide what is best for their children, unfettered by intrusive interference by state authorities. Article 8(2) ECHR assists us in achieving this balance. It provides that the public authorities

---

[40] Crime and Courts Act 2013, s. 17(3).

[41] But for a critique of the presumed benefits of mediation, see Hunter, R. 'Inducing Demand for Family Mediation—Before and After LASPO' (2017) 29 *Journal of Social Welfare and Family Law*, Special Issue; and Maclean, M. and Eekelaar, J. *Lawyers and Mediators: The Brave New World of Services for Separated Families*, (Hart Publishing, 2016).   [42] LASPO 2012, Sch 1.

[43] See further Emerson, D. and Platt, J. 'Legal Aid, Sentencing and Punishment of Offenders Act 2012: LASPO Reviewed' [2014] *Family Law* 515; and more generally, see Mant, J. and Wallbank, J. 'The Post LASPO Landscape: Challenges for Family Law' (2017) 39 *Journal of Social Welfare and Family Law* 149.

[44] For a more detailed discussion of the different approaches to regulating family life, see Herring, J. *Family Law* (8th edn, Pearson Education Ltd, 2017) ch 1; and Fink, H. and Carbone, J. 'Between Private Ordering and Public Fiat: A New Paradigm for Family Law Decision-Making' (2003) 5 *Journal of Law and Family Studies* 1.

can justify an alleged breach of the right to respect for private and family life by demonstrating that it is: (i) in accordance with the law; (ii) necessary to protect national security, public safety, or the economic well-being of the country; (iii) for the prevention of disorder or crime; (iv) for the protection of health or morals; or (v) for the protection of the rights and freedoms of others (including children within the family). In justifying their action, the public authorities must also demonstrate that their interference is proportionate and necessary to achieve one of these aims. In practice, these present quite high thresholds: there has to be at least a risk of significant abuse of children's rights before state authorities will interfere with parents' decisions and actions. This reinforces a tendency, albeit erroneous in legal, moral, and human rights terms, to treat children as the property of their parents. This is particularly apparent in private family proceedings.

3. A children's rights-based approach to private family proceedings

 DEBATE 1: SHOULD CHILDREN BE ALLOWED TO MAKE DECISIONS ABOUT THEIR OWN LIVES, PARTICULARLY IN MATTERS CONCERNING THEIR FAMILY LIFE?

The challenges of accommodating children's independent rights and wishes alongside those of their parents and wider family are brought into sharp focus in disputes about children's care following their parents' relationship breakdown. This debate requires deep engagement with the notion and parameters of children's autonomy, the weight we are willing to attach to children's expressed wishes, and feelings concerning their ongoing contact with and care from their parents, and the extent to which concerns around children's welfare or 'best interests' can justify overruling children's agency. As such, this debate demands some consideration of how we reconcile seemingly clashing rights and agendas and a more critical look at who should have the final say in decisions that may well change the course of a child's life forever. Why do we presume that adults (particularly parents) know what is best for their children?; why do we presume that children lack the capacity, experience and insight to determine what is in their own best interests, just because they are younger?; is it realistic or ethical to expect children to shoulder the burden of making decisions about such delicate, sometimes emotionally complex issues at such a tender stage in their lives?

Whilst it is universally acknowledged that the family is central to children's development, it is only in the past 20 years or so that research has specifically explored children's individual perceptions and experiences of family life. There has been a marked increase, particularly since the mid-1990s, of qualitative research exploring the impact of parental separation, divorce, and family restructuring on children. This work has challenged presumptions that parental separation of itself has an inevitable negative economic, social, and psychological impact on children, and exposed an impressive array of coping and negotiation strategies employed by children. It has also revealed the important, supportive role children play in relation to their parents and siblings in such circumstances.[45] That said, we know that children's exposure to *conflict* between their parents is contrary to children's well-being. In

---

[45] Butler, I. *et al Divorcing Children: Children's Experience of Their Parents' Divorce* (Jessica Kingsley, 2003) 103–3; Douglas, G.F. and Murch, M.A. 'Taking Account of Children's Needs in Divorce: A Study of Family Solicitors' Responses to New Policy and Practice Initiatives' (2002) 14 *Child and Family Law Quarterly* 57; Neale, B. 'Dialogues with Children: Children, Divorce and Citizenship' (2002) 9 *Childhood* 455.

particular, protracted, acrimonious negotiations around where the child should live and how much contact they should have with their parents following parental separation can be harmful to children in the short, medium, and longer-term.[46] This highlights the importance of putting in place well-supported processes to minimise trauma and uncertainty for children implicated in such issues. The extent to which such support is available to children implicated in family proceedings in England and Wales is highly debatable.

For instance, the Family Justice Review (outlined in Context 1) has prompted a move away from in-court settlement of such disputes to out of-court mediation and alternative dispute resolution, at least in the first instance. The courts only step in where parents are unable to resolve such issues amicably and fairly. Cuts to legal aid in private family law matters, however, have made it increasingly difficult for lower income families, and certainly children, to obtain the legal advice and representation that they might need should matters have to go to court.[47] Indeed, most commentators perceive the shrinking of legal aid as a rather more cynical exercise in austerity rather than a bid to promote more efficient, autonomous decision-making:

> In reality, costs to the public purse have simply been passed onto the individual and the not-for-profit advice sector. Such cases are taking up more time and causing more aggression and distress in court, not less. Rather than prompting individuals to pursue less litigious alternatives to dispute resolution, these cuts have triggered an unprecedented and worrying trend in self-representation before the courts, creating longer delays than ever and significantly disempowering those without the skills or knowledge to represent themselves effectively. Those without the possibility (notably children and the poor) or will to represent themselves are denied access to justice altogether.[48]

Notwithstanding the practical challenges of pursuing children's rights in practice, a number of principles and provisions should inform decisions around children's care, residence, and contact following parental separation. First of all, normative tools developed at international level (discussed in 2) assist practitioners in accommodating and regulating the complex dynamics of children's family life following parental separation and divorce. The Preamble of the UNCRC endorses the status of the family as 'the fundamental group of society and the natural environment for the growth and well-being of all its members and particularly children' and recognises 'that the child, for the full and harmonious development of his or her personality, should grow up in a family environment, in an atmosphere of happiness, love and understanding'. Such aspirations are certainly not confined to 'intact' nuclear families; Articles 5, 7, 8, 9, 16, and 20 UNCRC all uphold children's rights to care, contact, and development in various family contexts.

There are two particular challenges confronting a children's rights-based approach to determining care, residence, and contact. The first relates to who should have the determinate say in what arrangements are best for a child—should the child's wishes and feelings count? And what weight should they bear if they do count? The second relates to the extent

---

[46] Lucas, N., Nicholson, J., and Erbas, B. 'Child Mental Health After Parental Separation: The Impact of Resident/Non-Resident Parenting, Parent Mental Health, Conflict and Socioeconomics' (2013) 19 *Journal of Family Studies* 53; and Friesen, M. *et al* 'Exposure to Parental Separation in Childhood and Later Parenting Quality as an Adult: Evidence From a 30-Year Longitudinal Study' (2017) 58 *Journal of Child Psychology and Psychiatry* 30.

[47] For further evidence of this, see 'Access Denied? LASPO Four Years On: A Law Society Review' (The Law Society of England and Wales, 2017). For an analysis of the extent to which children are involved in out-of-court family dispute settlement, see Ewing, J. *et al* 'Children's Voices: Centre-Stage or Sidelined in out-of-Court Dispute Resolution in England and Wales' (2015) 27 *Child and Family Law Quarterly* 43.

[48] Stalford, H. and Hollingsworth, K. (2017 forthcoming) 'Judging Children's Rights: Tendencies, Tensions, Constraints and Opportunities' in H. Stalford, K. Hollingsworth, and S. Gilmore (eds) *Rewriting Children's Rights Judgments: From Academic Vision to New Practice* (Hart Publishing, 2017).

to which children's interests in such cases should be prioritised over the interests of other family members implicated in the same dispute.

3.1 Reconciling welfare and autonomy

Two of the four general principles of the UNCRC (see 2.1), the best interests principle under Article 3 and children's right to have a say in decisions that affect them under Article 12, are cornerstones of private family law and practice. The former dictates that achieving the best possible outcome for the child (rather than for the parents or other adults) is *a primary* consideration when it comes to deciding on matters of care, residence, and contact. The latter tells us that the child who is capable of forming his or her own views on such issues not only has a right to express those views freely in all family proceedings, but that those views should be given 'due weight in accordance with the age and maturity of the child'.

Adult decision-makers have a risky tendency to consider these principles as mutually exclusive and competing: best interests, it is presumed, requires a paternalistic assessment based on the accepted wisdom that adults instinctively and experientially know what is best for children. Enabling a child to have a say in decisions that affect him or her, on the other hand, is seen as undermining children's welfare because children are routinely perceived as lacking the experience and insight to know what is good for them and as being prone to impulsive, short-sighted decisions. The law, research,[49] and guidance[50] tells us otherwise, however. In particular, the UN Committee on the Rights of the Child asserts that:

> There is no tension between articles 3 and 12, only a complementary role of the two general principles: one establishes the objective of achieving the best interests of the child and the other provides the methodology for reaching the goal of hearing either the child or the children. In fact, there can be no correct application of article 3 if the components of article 12 are not respected.[51]

In other words, actively involving children in decisions about issues that are central to their lives, such as where they will live and how much contact they will have with each parent, is the most effective way of identifying what is in their best interests. If applied in a balanced and sensitive way, these children's rights principles should serve to accommodate children's vulnerabilities and agency simultaneously.[52]

3.2 Reconciling children's rights with the rights of other family members

It is important to remember that adherence to children's rights is not concerned with isolating children's interests in a self-serving individualistic way. Rather, fulfilment of

---

[49] For a theoretical consideration of how these two notions can be reconciled, see Archard, D. and Skivenes, M. 'Balancing a Child's Best Interests and a Child's Views' (2009) 17 *International Journal of Children's Rights* 1; and for more empirically-grounded insights, see Tisdall, K. and Morrison, F. 'Children's Participation in Court Proceedings when Parents Divorce or Separate: Legal Constructions and Lived Experiences' (2012) 14 *Law and Childhood Studies: Current Legal Issues* 156. The latest research underpinning children's autonomy in best interests proceedings, including family proceedings, is also presented in detail in Aoife Daly's thought-provoking book, *Children, Autonomy and the Courts: Beyond the Right to be Heard* (Brill Nijhoff, 2017).

[50] UN Committee on the Rights of the Child, General Comment No. 12 on the right of the child to be heard, CRC/C/GC/12 (2009) para 74; and UN Committee on the Rights of the Child, General Comment No. 14 on the right of the child to have his or her best interests taken as a primary consideration, CRC/C/GC/14 (2013) art. 3, para. 1, 43–45;

[51] UN Committee on the Rights of the Child, General Comment No. 12 on the right of the child to be heard, CRC/C/GC/12 (2009) para 74.

[52] See further the findings of longitudinal research by Kaltenborn, K-F. 'Children's and Young People's Experiences in Various Residential Arrangements: A Longitudinal Study to Evaluate Criteria for Custody and Residence Decision Making' (2001) 31 *British Journal of Social Work* 81, 110. These finding point to a strong correlation between positive long-term outcomes for children's welfare and adherence to children's wishes.

children's rights is best achieved when the child's relationships with those around him or her are acknowledged, nurtured, and protected by the law. This can be challenging in practice insofar as parents and other adults responsible for the care of the child may have views and interests that compete with those of the child.

As discussed earlier in this chapter (at 2) judicial interpretations of certain ECHR provisions (notably Articles 6 ECHR and 8 ECHR) have advanced our understanding of how children's rights can be reconciled with parents' and other family members' rights in such circumstances.[53] When interpreting Article 8 ECHR, the right to respect for private and family life, for instance, the correct approach where the wishes of the parents and the children purportedly clash is, as Jonathan Herring notes, to look at whether the wishes of each individual engages their Article 8 right. If it does, then the court will need to consider whether an infringement of that right is justified:

> So, a parent may have a right under Article 8(1) to have contact with a child, but under Article 8(2) it may be permissible to interfere with that right if necessary in the interests of the child or the resident parent.[54]

Where the rights appear to be evenly matched (for instance, if a child deemed to be of sufficient maturity does not want to live with a parent and yet the parent wants to the child to live with him or her at least some of the time), the child's wishes may prevail unless there are compelling reasons to force the child to adhere to the wishes of the parent.[55]

With these concerns in mind, let us consider how this international guidance plays out in private family law decision-making in England and Wales.

3.3 Children's rights under family law in England and Wales

Both public (care) and private (divorce, 'contact' and 'residence'[56] maintenance) proceedings are governed by the Children Act 1989, the most important source of child law in England and Wales.

The central principle underpinning Children Act proceedings is the welfare principle, set out in s. 1(1) of the Children Act 1989:

 Key Legislation 1: Children Act 1989, s. 1(1), welfare principle

1. When a court determines any question with respect to—

    (a) the upbringing of a child; or

    (b) the administration of a child's property or the application of any income arising from it,

    the child's welfare shall be the court's paramount consideration.

---

[53] See further Opromolla, A. 'Children's Rights under Articles 3 and 8 of the European Convention: Recent Case Law' (2001) 26 *European Law Review, Human Rights Supplement* 46; and Harris-Short, S. 'Family Law and the Human Rights Act 1998: Judicial Restraint or Revolution?' (2005) 17 *Child and Family Law Quarterly* 329. See, more broadly, Kilkelly, U. *The Child and the European Convention on Human Rights* (Ashgate, 1998), and more recently the Council of Europe programme, *Building A Europe For And With Children*, including a database of child-specific case law. Available at: https://www.coe.int/en/web/children/case-law, accessed 10 October 2017.

[54] Herring, J. *Family Law* (8th edn, Pearson Education Ltd, 2017) 469.

[55] *Hendriks v Netherlands* (1982) 5 D&R 225; *Scott v UK* [2000] 2 FCR 560; *Yousef v The Netherlands* [2000] 2 FLR 118; and *Neulinger and Schuruk v Switzerland*; *Haase v Germany* [2004] 2 FCR 1 and *Chepelev v Russian* [2007] 2 FCR 649. See further Eekelaar, J. 'The Role of the Best Interests Principle in Decisions Affecting Children and Decisions about Children' (2015) 23 *International Journal of Children's Rights* 3.

[56] These terms are used as a shorthand. The Children and Families Act 2014 replaced these with the term 'child arrangement orders' to signify a shift away from the notion that children's care is to be bartered over by parents rather than shared and negotiated on an ongoing basis for the good of children.

The welfare principle had been explained by Lord MacDermott in the 1970 case of *J v C* [1970] AC 668 as:

> a process whereby when all the relevant facts, relationships, claims and wishes of parents, risks, choices and other circumstances are taken into account and weighted, the course to be followed will be that which is most in the interests of the child's welfare as that term is now to be understood. This is the first consideration because it is of first importance and the paramount consideration because it rules upon or determines the course to be followed.

In practice, the term 'welfare' is often used synonymously with the international children's rights term, 'best interests', discussed earlier. Judges increasingly frame their deliberations as to what living and care arrangements are in the child's welfare under s. 1(1) of the Children Act 1989 by reference to the term 'best interests', and are required to consider a range of factors, including the child's expressed wishes and feelings, as part of such deliberations.[57]

Key Legislation 2: Children Act 1989, s. 1(3), welfare checklist

In an attempt to help refine the conditions and criteria for determining the welfare of the child, the Children Act 1989 introduced a statutory checklist under s. 1(3). As discussed in Chapter 9, this requires the court to have regard to:

   (a) the ascertainable wishes and feelings of the child concerned (considered in the light of his age and understanding);

   (b) his physical, emotional and educational needs;

   (c) the likely effect on him of any change in his circumstances;

   (d) his age, sex, background and any characteristics of his which the court considers relevant;

   (e) any harm which he has suffered or is at risk of suffering;

   (f) how capable each of his parents, and any other person in relation to whom the court considers the question to be relevant, is of meeting his needs;

   (g) the range of powers available to the court under this Act in the proceedings in question.

Matters of residence and contact are regulated through what are now referred to as child arrangements orders under s. 8(1) of the Children Act 1989.[58] This must be read in conjunction with s. 1(2)(A) of the Children Act 1989[59] which introduces a presumption that, unless the contrary is shown, involvement of each parent in the life of the child concerned will further the child's welfare.

In England and Wales, the court must examine the likely outcomes for the child from every angle, with the aim of choosing the care option that appears best for the child in the

---

[57] A similar checklist of factors is applied to adoption by virtue of the Adoption and Children Act 2002, s. 1(4).   [58] As amended by s. 12 of the Children and Families Act 2014.
[59] As amended by s. 11 of the Children and Families Act 2014.

short, medium, and longer term.[60] In a case concerning public care proceedings, the Court of Appeal in England and Wales explained that:

> The judicial exercise should not be a linear process whereby each option, other than the most draconian, is looked at in isolation and then rejected ... the judicial task is to undertake a global, holistic evaluation of each of the options available for the child's future upbringing before deciding which of those options best meets the duty to afford paramount consideration to the child's welfare.[61]

It is important to note that no premium is attached to any of the factors in the list (including the ascertainable wishes and feelings of the child), neither is the list to be regarded as exhaustive.[62] On paper at least, they are all given equal value and weight along with any other factors that the court thinks are appropriate. In practice, the judge has significant discretion to give more weight to one of the factors over the others. Suffice to say, that the judge has a responsibility to treat each child as an individual and consider each case on its own facts. He or she may elicit expert advice to facilitate that adjudication,[63] or may even ask to speak to the child directly (usually in private).[64] This interview should be solely aimed at determining what outcome would best promote the child's welfare.[65] But it is only in rare cases that children in private family cases will be separately represented by his or her own counsel. This is because it is assumed that the child's specific interests and needs can be effectively addressed in proceedings involving the parents because child's welfare is always 'paramount' in the proceedings. It is also no doubt because the resources and time implications of securing separate representation for the child are outweighed by the desire to expedite decision-making and avoid placing the interests of the child in hostile competition with the interests of the other family members.

3.4 How much weight should be attached to the ascertainable wishes and feelings of the child in family proceedings?

It was acknowledged as far back as 1970, in *Krishnan v Sutton London Borough Council*[66] and in *Hewer v Bryant*[67] that parental rights 'dwindle' as the child approaches the age of majority but at least 'survive' until then. But while these cases acknowledged that children's wishes *could* be different to and perhaps even override those of their parents, they were decidedly vague on the conditions required to achieve this. It was not until the landmark case of *Gillick v West Norfolk and Wisbech Area Health Authority*,[68] that the courts provided a clearer and, to some, quite a radical articulation of how children's wishes could prevail. Whilst the facts are specific to the medical treatment of children, the 'Gillick competence' test arising from the decision is now the defining feature of a range of legal decisions involving children, including in the private family

---

[60] See further Eekelaar, J. 'The Role of the Best Interests Principle in Decisions Affecting Children and Decisions about Children' (2015) 23 *International Journal of Children's Rights* 2, 7. Eekelaar's analysis confirms earlier criticism that judges are not always rigorous or transparent in their consideration of the various factors under the welfare checklist, particularly the views and wishes of the child. This is discussed further in Stalford, H. Hollingsworth, K. and Gilmore, S. (eds) *Rewriting Children's Rights Judgments: From Academic Vision to New Practice* (Hart Publishing, 2017).   [61] *Re G* [2013] EWCA Civ 965, at [49] and [50] (MacFarlane LJ).
[62] Baroness Hale in *Re G (Children)(Residence: Same-Sex Partner)* [2006] UKHL 43, at [40].
[63] Children Act 1989, s. 7(1).
[64] *Re A (Fact-Finding Hearing: Judge Meeting with Child)* [2012] EWCA Civ 185. Jackson J in this case went as far as addressing his judgment directly to the 14-year-old child concerned in the form of a letter.
[65] *Re KP (A Child)* [2014] EWCA Civ 554.   [66] [1970] Ch 181.
[67] [1970] 1 QB 357, at 369 (Lord Denning).
[68] [1984] AC 778.

law arena (see further Chapter 10 on decisions in relation to the medical treatment of children).

 Key Case 1: *Gillick v West Norfolk and Wisbech Area Health Authority* **[1986] 1 AC 112**

In 1980, the then Department of Health and Social Security issued a Circular to the effect that, although it would be 'most unusual', a doctor could, in exceptional circumstances, lawfully give contraceptive advice to a *girl* under 16 years of age without prior parental consultation or consent. In doing so, he would be required to act in good faith to protect her against the harmful effects of sexual intercourse.

Victoria Gillick was a Roman Catholic mother of five girls under the age of 16. (Interestingly, the fact that Mrs Gillick also had five sons did not feature in the discussions around this case). As discussed in Chapter 10, she objected to this advice and sought assurances from her own area health authority that no minor daughter of hers would receive such advice or treatment without her permission. The health authority refused to give such assurances, at which point Mrs Gillick applied for a declaration that the advice in the Circular was unlawful. Victoria Gillick lost at first instance, won unanimously in the Court of Appeal, and eventually lost to a 3.2 majority in the House of Lords.

The first contention raised by Mrs Gillick was that a girl under 16 years old could never provide a valid consent on her own behalf primarily because she is deemed to lack capacity by virtue of being under the age of sexual consent. The House of Lords concluded that a child under 16 does not lack capacity by virtue of age alone, but rather acquires capacity when he or she demonstrates a sufficient understanding and intelligence to be capable of making up his or her own mind on the matter at issue. This approach endorses an individualistic assessment of the child's level of maturity and intellectual ability.

That said, the House of Lords envisaged that a high level of understanding would be required before the child's consent alone would suffice, extending beyond the purely medical implications of receiving the medical treatment in question. Referring specifically to contraception Lord Scarman noted:

> It is not enough that she should understand the nature of the advice which she is being given: she must have sufficient maturity to understand what is involved. There are moral and family questions, especially her relationship with her parents, long-term problems associated with the emotional impact of pregnancy and its termination and there are risks to health of sexual intercourse at her age, risks which contraception might diminish but cannot eliminate (189, [C]).

The second contention raised in the case was whether parents retained any authority, notwithstanding the child's perceived competence, to override the wishes or consent of the child. Again, the House of Lords ruled that parental power over their children is not absolute and reminded us that parents only have rights vis-à-vis their children insofar as they are used to carry out their parental responsibilities. Children are not the property of their parents; parents exercise rights for the benefit of the child, not for the benefit of the parent:

> the parental right yields to the child's right to make his own decisions when he reaches a sufficient understanding and intelligence to be capable of making up his own mind on the matter requiring decision (186, [D] Lord Scarman).

Thus, while the majority opinion in *Gillick* recognised the importance of parents' participation in children's decision-making, they were willing to afford priority to the wishes of a competent adolescent where their views clashed, provided that the child's wishes, if acted upon, were deemed to be in the child's best interests.

The decision has been applied in a family law context, signalling a shift away from arbitrary age-based assessments of capacity towards a more nuanced, individualised assessment of the child's understanding and maturity. But that is not to say that a *Gillick* capacity-based test is unproblematic. As Aoife Daly notes:

> capacity is not a straightforward concept and it is inaccurate to view it as a moderator of paternalism in best interest proceedings ... judges essentially have absolute discretion to override children's wishes.[69]

While Daly acknowledges the importance of a legal framework that prevents children from making disastrous (life-changing, perhaps even life-threatening) decisions, she goes on to illustrate how, in practice, courts do *not* generally seek to establish whether children have reached a level of mental capacity in the legal sense. Other commentators have argued that judges tend to evaluate whether children have sufficient capacity to make autonomous choices from a normative standpoint—based on what they (the judges) believe is 'right' or 'wrong' for children to do or not to do, rather than from empirical investigations about children's actual degrees of capacity or autonomy.[70]

Indeed, there is an abundance of academic research highlighting how easily opaque and poorly evidenced 'best interests' arguments can trump the wishes of mature and well-informed children.[71]

3.5 Why is it so important to give children a say in decisions that affect them?

An extensive body of research has emerged over the last 20 years serving to illustrate how a routine failure to confer with children when it comes to decisions about where and with whom they live can exacerbate the trauma, confusion, and isolation commonly associated with relationship breakdown. This research almost unanimously advocates honest and open dialogue with children from the outset with a view to allaying any misconceptions they may have about their role in events, enabling them to express their views on how post-separation living and contact arrangements should work, and providing both parents and children with the opportunity to draw on each other's emotional support in a more

---

[69] Daly, A. *Children, Autonomy and the Courts: Beyond the Right to be Heard* (Brill Nijhoff, 2017) ch 1.

[70] Hansen, K. 'Children's Participation and Agency When They Don't "do the Right Thing" (2016) 23 *Childhood* 471.

[71] There has been a considerable amount of academic commentary critiquing the limitations of the *Gillick* decision in the context of children who refuse medical treatment contrary to the advice of their parents and medical practitioners. Freeman, M. 'Rethinking Gillick' (2005) 13 *Journal of Child Rights* 201; Cave, C. 'Goodbye Gillick? Identifying and Resolving Problems with the Concept of Child Competence' (2014) 31 *Legal Studies* 123; Gilmore, S. and Herring, J. '"No" is the Hardest Word: Consent and Children's Autonomy' (2011) 23 *Child and Family Law Quarterly* 3; Cave, E. and Wallbank, J. 'Minors' Capacity to Refuse treatment: A reply to Gilmore and Herring' (2012) 20 *Medical Law Review* 423; Gilmore, S. and Herring, J. 'Children's Refusal of Treatment: The Debate Continues' [2012] *Family law* 973; Perera, A. 'Can I Decide Please? The State of Children's Consent in the UK' (2008) 15 *European Journal of Health Law* 411.

reciprocal way.[72] Moreover, there is also general consensus, mined through empirical work involving children and young people, that children want to be given a say in decisions that affect their lives and that facilitating such participation reveals richer, unique insights and yields more enduring, fairer decisions.[73] This intelligence has permeated judicial thinking at the highest level. Over a decade ago, Baroness Hale noted in *Re D (A Child) (Abduction: Rights of custody)*[74] that:

> there is now a growing understanding of the importance of listening to the children in- volved in children's cases. It is the child, more than anyone else, who will have to live with what the court decides. Those who do listen to children understand that they often have a point of view which is quite distinct from that of the person looking after them. They are quite capable of being moral actors in their own right. Just as the adults may have to do what the court decides whether they like it or not, so may the child. But that is no more a reason for failing to hear what the child has to say than it is for refusing to hear the parents' views.

Despite such developments, the reality is that perspectives on children's participation are largely driven by notions of children's inherent vulnerability and immaturity. Parents' per- spectives are often tainted by their own conflicted emotions towards each other or by an overwhelming sense of responsibility to shield them from any further trauma associated with their own relationship breakdown (particularly in relation to very young children or in cases of domestic abuse). Such perspectives are all the more influential now that contact and residence disputes are increasingly resolved out of course, through parent-led mediation.

Where such disputes do get to court, some judges are more aware of the need to give proper consideration to children's views. In *Re B (Minors) (Change of Surname)*,[75] for ex- ample, it was held that it would be exceptional for a court to make orders contrary to the wishes of a teenager. Similarly, in *Re R (A Child) (Residence Order: Treatment of Child's Wishes)*,[76] the Court of Appeal was critical of the court at first instance for failing to con- sider the views of a 10-year-old child.

But hearing and considering the views of children is one thing; attaching due weight to them, as required by Article 12 UNCRC, is quite another. It is to this issue that the last section of this debate turns.

3.6 Involving children meaningfully in family decision-making: attaching due weight

Providing a platform for children to express their views on care and residence arrange- ments gives the child a sense of being valued and makes it easier for them to understand and live with the decision ultimately made. But there is a risk that the 'right to be heard'

---

[72] For examples, see Maclean, M. (ed) *Parenting after Partnering: Containing Conflict after Separation*, Onati International Series in Law and Society (Hart Publishing, 2007); Trinder, L. 'Maternal Gatekeeping and Gate- Opening in PostDivorce Families: Strategies, Contexts and Consequences (2008) 29 *Journal of Family Issues* 1298; Smart, C., Neale, B., and Wade, A. *The Changing Experience of Childhood: Families and Divorce.* (Polity Press, 2001). On the value of, and approaches to, child participation in a range of other contexts, see Percy- Smith, B. and Thomas, N. (eds) *A Handbook of Children and Young People's Participation: Perspectives from Theory and Practice* (Routledge, 2010).

[73] Presented in Stalford, H. Hollingsworth, K. and Gilmore, S. (eds) *Rewriting Children's Rights Judgments: From Academic Vision to New Practice* (Hart Publishing, 2017). But for the counterview that supports a reso- lutely paternalistic stance, see Goldstein, J., Freud, A., and Solnit, A.J. *Beyond the Best Interests of the Child* (The Free Press, 1973); and Goldstein, J., Freud, A., and Solnit, A. J. *Before the Best Interests of the Child* (The Free Press, 1979).

[74] [2006] UKHL 51, at [57].

[75] [1996] 1 FLR 791.   [76] [2009] 2 FCR 572.

remains largely superficial and tokenistic rather than genuinely informative to the outcome. The Committee on the Rights of the Child, in its General Comment No. 12 on the right of children to be heard, notes:

> Article 12 stipulates that simply listening to the child is insufficient; the views of the child have to be seriously considered when the child is capable of forming her or his own views (para 28).

We know something about children's experiences and expectations of 'being heard'—they want more than a good process in which they are seen to be heard; they want what they say to actually influence the outcome.[77] And yet research, commentary and legal guidance on children's participation in decision-making says remarkably little about the extent to which children's views actually do influence outcomes in court. Defensive slogans such as 'voice, not choice' are commonly used to assuage the fears of those who protest against allowing children an inappropriate and reckless level of influence over family decision-making. Rather, it captures the ideal of enabling the child's views to be properly presented to the decision-making body.[78] Adults are generally very comfortable with this idea, and judges are increasingly willing to meet children in person to ascertain their personal experiences and perspectives, but to actually allow children to determine what decisions should be made is seen as radical and reckless, even in relation to the most competent, mature children.

Moreover, the idea that giving children greater visibility in the family justice *process* is enough to fulfil the Article 12 UNCRC obligations is particularly apparent when it comes to younger children who 'currently appear to have little voice or influence.' [79] Notwithstanding the efforts in *Gillick* to separate determinations of children's autonomy from a generic age-based presumption, there is overwhelming evidence that age remains a determining factor in assessing how much weight to attach to a child's views in family cases. In short, the older the child is, the more 'weight' their views are likely to have. That said, there is significant inconsistency on this point, with welfare often trumping the views of even the most capacitous child. Thus, in *Re S. (Contact: Intractable Dispute)*[80] an appeal court held that the trial judge was wrong to make the implementation of a contact order (now child arrangements orders, see Chapter 9) contingent on the wishes of children aged 12 and 13. The appeal judge was firmly of the view that 'children of his age have to have their lives regulated by adult judgment'.[81]

One persuasive justification for failing to attach any weight to the views of children is a presumption that children have limited life experience and future vision to be able to predict with any accuracy the impact of a potential outcome on their medium to long-term

---

[77] Children's Hearings Scotland, *Children and Young People's Views and Experiences of Children's Hearings— A Summary* (Children's Hearings Scotland, 2014) 15; EU Agency for Fundamental Rights 'Child-friendly justice: Perspectives and experiences of children involved in judicial proceedings as victims, witnesses or parties in nine EU Member States' (EU: Luxembourg, 2017) 69; and Timms, J. Bailey, S., and Thoburn, J. 'Children's Views of Decisions Made by the Court: Policy and Practice Issues arising from the Your Shout Too! Survey' (2008) 14 *Child Care in Practice* 257; and Douglas, G. *et al Research into the Operation of Rule 9.5 of the Family Proceedings Rules, 1991* (Department for Constitutional Affairs, 2006). These studies are discussed in more depth in Daly, A. *Children, Autonomy and the Courts: Beyond the Right to be Heard* (Brill Nijhoff, 2017) ch 5.

[78] Douglas, G. *The Separate Representation of Children—In Whose Best Interests?* in Thorpe, Rt Hon Lord Justice (ed) *Durable Solutions: The Collected Papers of the 2005 Dartington Hall Conference* (Bristol: Family Law, 2006) 13–22.

[79] May, V. and Smart, C. 'Silence in Court? Hearing Children in Residence and Contact Disputes' (2004) 16 *Child and Family Law Quarterly* 305, 315. See also Winter, K. 'The Perspectives of Young Children in Care about Their Circumstances and Implications for Social Work Practice' (2010) 15 *Child and Family Social Work* 186.   [80] [2010] 2 FLR 1517.

[81] [2010] 2 FLR 1517, at [7] cited in Daly, A. *Children, Autonomy and the Courts: Beyond the Right to be Heard* (Brill Nijhoff, 2017) ch 5.

interests; they simply react to their feelings in the here and now. This argument was put forward in *M. v B*,[82] a cross-national dispute involving two children, aged 12 and 10, who had been living with their father in England, but who were forced to have contact and, subsequently, reside with their mother in France. One might respond to this by interrogating what, exactly, makes the courts or other adults are any better placed to make such long-term predictions. Do they have specific intelligence at their disposal to which the child is not privy? Have they simply had enough experience of life and of family breakdown to predict with a greater degree of certainty patterns in human behaviour? In some cases, of course, they do, but in other cases, parents may struggle to disentangle their own negative feelings towards the other parent from their assessment of what is in their children's best interests.

A further common justification for failing to attach weight to the expressed preferences of children, even those judged to be old enough and competent, is that they have been unduly influenced by a parent such that the views expressed are not really their own. In *M v B*,[83] according to the expert report on the children's wishes and feelings, the father referred to their mother as 'evil' and had told the children that France, their mother's country of residence, was racist (note that the children were mixed race). Such concerns also featured in the decision in *Puxty v Moore*[84] when the Court of Appeal refused to uphold a 9-year-old child's stated wishes to live with her mother on the basis that the mother had allegedly bribed her with a new pony. Similarly, in *Re M (Intractable Contact Dispute: Court's Positive Duty*,[85] the Court would not support a 15- and 13-year-old's opposition to contact with their mother when it transpired that they had been heavily influenced by their father's ill-feeling towards the mother. Such decisions may well be robust in some respects, but they also paint a somewhat oversimplified picture of the dynamics of parent–child relationships and are dismissive of the ability and readiness of children to exercise agency. To suggest that children should not be influenced by their parents' views is absurd: the law paints it as a key function and, indeed, a right of parents to influence their children's thinking in matters of religious upbringing and education.[86] Why, then, would parents naturally not seek to influence their children regarding where they should live and whether they should have contact with a parent, and why should the child not take those views on as her own, at least to a degree?

Of course, the courts have to be alert to situations in which the child forms an opinion on the basis of only partial 'facts', conveyed by only one parent, which deliberately and unfairly vilifies the other parent or indulges the parents' own selfish needs, as in the case of *M v B*.[87] Equally, the courts want to avoid situations in which the child is unable to express her own (differing) views for fear of reprisals from the parent/s or, more likely, for fear of hurting the parents that they love. But concerns of parental influence should be treated with some caution; rather than aspiring to an artificial expression of independent thought, courts should point to ways of disentangling the wishes of the various parties and interrogating further the views of the child, if necessary through appropriate expert intervention and assessment. The child friendly judgment of Peter Jackson in *Re A (Fact-Finding Hearing: Judge Meeting with Child)*[88] is an excellent illustration of how to achieve this balancing act in a sensitive, honest, and rigorous way.

---

[82] [2016] EWHC 1657.   [83] [2016] EWHC 1657.   [84] [2005] EWCA Civ 1386.

[85] [2006] 1 FLR 627.

[86] Article 2 Protocol 1 ECHR states that 'No person shall be denied the right to education. In the exercise of any functions which it assumes in relation to education and to teaching, the State shall respect the right of parents to ensure such education and teaching in conformity with their own religious and philosophical convictions.'   [87] [2016] EWHC 1657.

[88] *Re A (Fact-Finding Hearing: Judge Meeting with Child)* [2012] EWCA Civ 185.

In summary, upholding children's rights in the context of private family disputes, whilst relatively straight forward and robust on paper, presents particular challenges in practice. This is not least because of the difficulties of balancing the child's independent needs and rights from the interests and rights of other family members, particularly their parents. Of course, the extent to which children can and should be empowered to assert their own views, and the extent to which those views should have a persuasive impact on the outcome, depends on the specific circumstances of the case, the experiences and insights of the child, and the perceived current and future interests of the child. But a children's rights-based approach adopts children's participation as the default position: children should be engaged in such decisions in a meaningful way if they want to be. The onus should not be on them to prove their capacity to have a say, but rather the onus should be on adult decision-makers to develop their own capacities to engage children effectively, to build trust and to elicit and deliberate on children's views in a transparent and respectful way.

4. Corporal punishment

The historical and legal underpinnings of corporal punishment reflect the age-old intersection between the rights of parents and the rights of children. Despite its ingrained social, historical, and philosophical foundations, corporal punishment as a method of discipline raises a number of profound and competing claims. Is it inconsistent with established children's rights standards? Does it undermine the best interest's principle? Does it amount to unacceptable physical violence towards children or is it entirely compatible with the rights of parents to discipline their children in a reasonable and appropriate manner? Associated with such issues are the overarching sensitivities which invariably attach to the privacy of the family and the longstanding deference accorded to not only the role of parents as carers, guardians, custodians, and protectors of children[89] but also the role of the family unit of itself. Although corporal punishment has been abolished in many countries across the globe, it still enjoys legitimacy in a number of jurisdictions including the UK, Canada, Australia, and the USA.

However, the prevalence and acceptability of corporal punishment as a lawful and appropriate means of discipline has been brought into sharp dispute with the ascendancy of human rights law generally and the articulation of children's rights specifically. Universal endorsement of rights-based values and standards such as human dignity,[90] autonomy, and freedom from torture, inhuman, and degrading treatment (see 4.2) as proven and immovable cornerstones of many political, social, and constitutional arrangements has directly challenged the sustainability and legality of corporal punishment as a means of discipline. Such values have since become entrenched in the constitutional and legal landscapes of many countries, generating some profound soul-searching as to the scope and extent of the rights of parents to discipline their children by using corporal punishment.[91]

This debate demands some difficult, perhaps quite personal, soul-searching as to why we continue to protect parents' ability to physically punish children in the home. In considering this issue, most of us tend to reflect on and perhaps endorse our parents' approach to our own childhood discipline: 'it never did me any harm' is a popular mantra. But how do those who use such justifications know how different (better?) their lives might

---

[89] For more on parental responsibilities, see Children Act 1989, s. 3.

[90] e.g., the Preamble to the Universal Declaration of Human Rights (1945) recognises the 'inherent dignity ... of all members of the human family'.

[91] For more, see Nolan, A. 'Litigating the Child's Right to a Life Free from Violence: Seeking the Prohibition of Parental Physical Punishment of Children Through the Courts' (2012) 14 *Law and Childhood Studies* 530.

have turned out if they never experienced the alternative? Do the so-called disciplinary objectives of corporal punishment serve children's protective interests so well that they outweigh any calls for a ban, or are there equally effective alternatives?

4.1. **Historical antecedents**

Traditionally, the common law viewed children as objects or *chattels* of their parents, particularly their father. As such, parental authority reigned supreme and children were considered as both secondary and subordinate to their parents. This was particularly evident in the fields of discipline and punishment, best exemplified by the ancient Roman laws which accorded the father the powers of life or death over his children. McGillivray argues that the use of corporal punishment 'has been viewed as both necessary and virtuous since Roman times'[92] with its legitimacy anchored within the inviolability of the private sphere of family life and the '[P]aternal powers of private justice'.[93] Although such excessive dictums have gradually subsided to a more moderate conception of familial authority,[94] the primacy of the parental role when it comes to disciplining children nonetheless endures.

Proponents of corporal punishment also drew on religious texts. Biblical maxims such as 'Thou shalt beat him with the rod, and deliver his soul from hell'[95] have been interpreted by some as affirming violence against children for the greater good of their eternal soul. Similarly, in Blackstone's historical *Commentaries on the Laws of England,* parental authorisation regarding corporal punishment was regarded as an inseparable and related function that stemmed from the parental duties of maintenance, protection, and education. According to Blackstone, the parent 'may lawfully correct his child, being under age, in a reasonable manner; for this is for the benefit of his education'.[96]

Central to all justifications for corporal punishment was its developmental (character-building!) function. Underpinning the acceptance of corporal punishment was the notion that it was fundamental to correcting and rectifying the innate and intrinsic wrongs and sins of the individual, a sentiment best exemplified in the judgment of Cockburn LJ in the nineteenth-century case of *R v Hopley* wherein he stated;

> By the law of England, a parent or a schoolmaster (who for this purpose represents the parent and has the parental authority delegated to him), may for the purpose of correcting what is evil in the child inflict moderate and reasonable corporal punishment.[97]

Thus, as a method of discipline and control, corporal punishment has been used for generations and in a variety of settings, including in the home, in the classroom, and also as a means of formal criminal retribution. Similarly, the power to use corporal punishment has been automatically bestowed on parents but, historically, was also extended to others who exercised control or authority over children and young people, including those acting in loco parentis (in the place of the parent). Currently however, the right to administer corporal punishment to children and young people is solely the preserve of parents. This will be explained in further detail later.

---

[92] McGillivray, A. "'He'll learn it on his body": Disciplining Childhood in Canadian Law', in Freeman, M. (ed) *Children's Rights: Progress and Perspectives* (Martinus Nijhoff, 2011).

[93] McGillivray, A. "'He'll learn it on his body": Disciplining Childhood in Canadian Law', in Freeman, M. (ed) *Children's Rights: Progress and Perspectives* (Martinus Nijhoff, 2011) 319.

[94] See *Gillick v West Norfolk and Wisbech AHA* [1986] 1 AC 112 where Lord Scarman at [183] stated that a father's power over his child was 'rightly remaindered to the history books'.

[95] Book of Proverbs 23:14, Old Testament.

[96] Blackstone, W. *Commentaries on the Laws of England,* Book One, Chapter Sixteen, Of Parent and Child, 1765.   [97] *R v Hopley* [1860] 175 ER 1024, at [206].

Sweden's abolition of corporal punishment in 1979, the first country to take the lead on this issue, was prompted by the recognition 'that children are full human beings with inherent rights to physical integrity and dignity'.[98] More recently however, following a successful constitutional referendum on children's rights in Ireland in 2012, Article 42A of the Irish Constitution as inserted thereafter states that: 'The State recognises and affirms the natural and imprescriptible rights of all children and shall, as far as practicable, by its laws protect and vindicate those rights'.[99] Such constitutional protections, in laying the foundations for a more clear and robust commitment to children's rights was soon followed by legislation prohibiting corporal punishment in all spheres including the home. The enactment of the Children First Act 2015 in Ireland abolished the common law defence of 'reasonable chastisement'[100] by amending the Non-Fatal Offences Against the Person Act 1997[101] thereby resulting in the complete eradication of all forms of corporal punishment and any potential defences arising therefrom.

4.2 International sources

At the international level, the legal regulation of corporal punishment has habitually been contained in the general prohibitions against violence and torture. These prohibitions find expression in a number of international covenants including the International Covenant on Civil and Political Rights (ICCPR)[102] and the Convention Against Torture and Other Cruel, Inhuman and Degrading Treatment and Punishment (CAT).[103] However, from a children's rights perspective, the strongest defence against corporal punishment is contained in Article 19 UNCRC which asserts;

> States Parties shall take all appropriate legislative, administrative, social and educational measures to protect the child from all forms of physical or mental violence, injury or abuse, neglect or negligent treatment, maltreatment or exploitation, including sexual abuse, while in the care of parent(s), legal guardian(s) or any other person who has the care of the child.

Moreover, Article 37 UNCRC also prohibits the infliction of torture, inhuman or degrading treatment, or punishment to children in comparable terms to that enunciated in the preceding international covenants. In their elaboration of the duties expected of States Parties pursuant to Article 19 UNCRC, the Committee on the Rights of the Child, the monitoring body of the UNCRC, in recognition of the 'widely accepted and practised forms of violence against children'[104] issued a General Comment in 2008 which set out the key responsibilities of Contracting Parties, including the UK, regarding the regulation of corporal punishment. In defining it as 'any punishment in which physical force is used and intended to cause some degree of pain or discomfort, however light'[105] the Committee on the Rights of the Child specify a wide array of circumstances which fall within the parameters of corporal punishment. From 'smacking' and striking children with hand-held objects to the forcible ingestion of foreign materials, the Committee set out an extensive catalogue of practices which contravene Article 19 UNCRC. In their rejection of both faith-based and common law justifications for corporal punishment the Committee on the

---

[98] For more, see Durrant, J.E. 'Legal Reform and Attitudes Toward Physical Punishment in Sweden', in Freeman, M. *Children's Rights: Progress and Perspectives* (Martinus Nijhoff, 2011).

[99] Article 42A(1) Bunreacht na hEireann.

[100] Children First Act 2015, s. 28.

[101] Non-Fatal offences Against the Person Act 1997, s. 24A(1) now states that 'The common law defence of reasonable chastisement is abolished'.   [102] Article 7 ICCPR.

[103] Article 17 CAT.   [104] General Comment No. 8, para 1.   [105] General Comment No. 8, para 11.

Rights of the Child enunciated key measures for States to adopt and implement to comply with their Article 19 UNCRC obligations.

 CONTEXT 3: UNCRC, GENERAL COMMENT NO. 8, 2006

KEY POINTS

- The Committee recommends that States Parties remove any provisions, either in common law or statute, which authorise any degree of violence towards children. This extends to the family, school, or any other setting, including the working environment, in which children are present.
- The Committee states that the law regarding corporal punishment must operate in the best interests of the child. This may require specific sectoral reform in the laws governing education, juvenile justice, alternative care, and family life.
- The Committee recognise that the prohibition on corporal punishment requires more than legal regulation and necessitates the awareness-raising of children's rights. This includes the enactment of educational and other measures which promote non-violent forms of parenting and the instillation of appropriate educational polices in the delivery of health, welfare, and general children's services.
- The Committee states that Contracting Parties are under a continuous obligation to monitor the progress made in the elimination of corporal punishment.

4.3 Regional sources

The regional development of human rights law regarding corporal punishment, much like their international counterparts, has also been cultivated along the prohibitions against violence, torture, and inhuman treatment.[106] However, unlike international treaties, the normative content and correlative duties of which are unenforceable within the existent legal and constitutional framework of the UK,[107] regional human rights mechanisms have provided more fertile ground from which to challenge corporal punishment on human rights grounds. This is one context in which the ECHR has provided the necessary scaffolding to support claims arising out of the physical punishment of children. In particular, Article 3 ECHR, a non-derogable right which protects against torture, inhumane, and degrading treatment, has provided frequent refuge to those challenging the legality of corporal punishment. However, for a claim to succeed under Article 3 ECHR, the facts must establish a minimum level of severity or degradation, sufficient to contravene the prohibition contained therein. This elemental standard has been consistently applied by the ECtHR[108] and has established itself as the threshold upon which an Article 3 claim will be adjudicated. In the case of *R (Limbuela) v Secretary of State for the Home Department*[109] Lord Bingham, in the context of a matter concerning the domestic provision of asylum support, reiterated the core tenets of an Article 3 claim by stating; 'As in all Article 3 cases, the treatment, to be proscribed, must achieve a minimum standard

---

[106] For example, see Article 5 African Charter of Human and Peoples Rights and Article 5 American Convention on Human Rights.

[107] In particular, see judgment of Lord Alymerton in *Rayner (Mincing Lane) Ltd v Department of Trade and Industry* (1990) 2 AC 418.

[108] See *Ireland v UK* [1979] 2 EHRR 25; *Keenan v United Kingdom* [2001] 33 EHRR 913; *JC v United Kingdom* [2003] 36 EHRR 14.   [109] [2007] 1 All ER 951.

of severity'.[110] The minimum level of severity required to render corporal punishment a violation of Article 3 ECHR has been considered by the ECtHR.

Key Case 2: *Tryer v UK* App. No. 5856/72, 25 April 1978

Anthony Tyrer, a 16-year-old boy, submitted a claim to the European Commission of Human Rights in 1972, claiming that his rights had been breached by a judicial birching order made against him by a court in the Isle of Man. The order provided that he was to receive three strokes from a birch rod. Tryer had pleaded guilty before the local juvenile court to unlawful assault occasioning actual bodily harm to a senior pupil at his school. The claim was subsequently referred to the ECtHR. The Court ruled that judicial birching amounted to degrading punishment in breach of Article 3 ECHR. In particular, the Court stated;

> the Court finds that the applicant was subjected to a punishment in which the element of humiliation attained the level inherent in the notion of 'degrading punishment' ... The indignity of having the punishment administered over the bare posterior aggravated to some extent the degrading character of the applicant's punishment but it was not the only or determining factor.[111]

Tryer demonstrates that the ECtHR will consider the totality of the circumstances in support of a claim alleging a breach of Article 3 ECHR. In this regard, the Court reflects not only on the nature of the punishment inflicted, but its duration and effect on the claimant. It is upon the conclusion of their determination of such factors that the Court will objectively determine whether a claim falls within the purview of Article 3 ECHR.

Key Case 3: *Costello-Roberts v United Kingdom* App. No. 13134/87, 25 March 1993

A seven-year-old boy was subjected to corporal punishment by the headmaster of the private boarding school which he attended. The punishment was in line with the school's disciplinary code and involved being 'slippered' three times over the clothes with a rubber-soled shoe three days after the boy was notified that he was to face corporal punishment for his actions. The boy and his mother challenged the legality of the proposed corporal punishment alleging that the boy had suffered degrading treatment and unjustified interference with his right to respect for his private life. It was further alleged that he had no effective remedy under UK law in respect of his complaints.

The Court found that the particular corporal punishment administered was not degrading and that neither the boy's nor his mother's rights had been violated. In differentiating the case from the previous *Tryer* case, the Court noted that the applicant had adduced no evidence of any long-terms effects of the punishment and, while accepting that such effects were not a prerequisite for establishing a claim under Article 3 ECHR, the Court further noted that the nature of the punishment in question did not attain the minimum level of severity to engage Article 3 ECHR.

While these cases exemplify the legal responsibility assumed by public authorities in discharging their obligations in the area of corporal punishment, Article 3 ECHR also entails specific positive obligations which are of equal importance. Positive obligations denote the activities and actions required of states, beyond the mere abstention from a

---

[110] [2007] 1 All ER 951.   [111] *Tryer v UK* App. No. 5856/72, 25 April 1978, at [35].

particular practice, to comply with the requirements of a particular human rights obligation in question. Although Article 3 ECHR gives rise to the automatic requirement that
states, either directly or through their agents, desist or refrain from engaging in practices which amount to torture, inhuman, or degrading treatment, the European Court's
jurisprudence has assisted in the development of various positive obligations which fall
within and under the ambit of Article 3 ECHR. For example, in *M.C. v Bulgaria* the Court
held that 'States have a positive obligation inherent in Articles 3 and 8 of the Convention
to enact criminal-law provisions effectively punishing rape and to apply them in practice through effective investigation and prosecution.'[112] Such obligations have also been
enunciated in the area of corporal punishment and specifically as to whether domestic
legislation provides the necessary protective safeguards against excessive abuse. This matter directly arose in the case of *A v United Kingdom,* where the adequacy of the defence of
reasonable chastisement against a charge of assault causing actual bodily harm was called
into question.

 **Key Case 4: *A. v United Kingdom* App. No. 25599/94, 23
September 1998**

The applicant was a nine-year-old boy who was beaten with a cane by his step-father. He was
subsequently examined by a paediatrician who found multiple bruises consistent with a beating from a garden cane, applied with considerable force on more than one occasion. The step-
father was subsequently charged with assault occasioning actual bodily harm and tried before
a jury. He claimed the defence of reasonable punishment and was acquitted by the jury. The
applicant claimed that the UK had failed to protect him from ill-treatment by his step-father.
The step-father had been previously cautioned by the police for hitting the applicant.

The ECtHR held that the beating of the applicant by his step-father constituted 'inhuman or
degrading punishment' in breach of Article 3 ECHR and that the UK domestic legislation, which
retained the defence of reasonable chastisement, failed to provide adequate protection to the
applicant against such treatment. In citing the earlier case of *Costello-Roberts*, the Court highlighted that any assessment of whether conduct complained of amounts to an infringement of
Article 3 ECHR was 'relative' in nature and dependant on a variety of circumstances including '
... the nature and context of the treatment, its duration, its physical and mental effects, and in
some instances, the sex, age and state of health of the victim'.[113]

Of significance in the *A v United Kingdom* case was the articulation by the Court of the need
for states to 'take measures designed to ensure that individuals within their jurisdiction are
not subjected to torture or inhuman or degrading treatment', thereby signifying the positive
obligations expected of Contracting Parties.

The test developed in these cases indicates that a minimum level of severity must be attained in order to activate an Article 3 ECHR claim in the context of corporal punishment.
The 'minimum level of severity' test is not exclusive to corporal punishment but rather
applies to any allegation which falls under Article 3 ECHR. This test has also been applied
in domestic case law including *R v H (Assault of a Child: Reasonable Chastisement)*[114] and
XA v YA[115] which demonstrate that, when considering the reasonableness or otherwise of
the physical punishment of the child, the Court will consider the nature of the defendant's

---

[112] App. No. 39272/98, 4 December 2003.
[113] *A. v United Kingdom* (App. No. 25599/94), 23 September 1998, at [20].
[114] [2001] 3 FCR 144.   [115] [2010] EWHC 1983 (QB).

behaviour, the duration of the punishment, its physical and mental consequences in relation to the child, the age and personal characteristics of the child, and the reasons given by the defendant for administering such punishment. Furthermore, reasonableness of the force used during the chastisement will be judged by the prevailing standards of the time. Thus, the domestic approach to corporal punishment, in reflecting ECHR jurisprudence, is one which seeks to strike the requisite and appropriate balance between force which is 'reasonable' and that which is excessive, with such a deductive task influenced by the subjective nature of the effects of corporal punishment on the individual concerned. Such legal navigation, and the difficulties invariably attached to it, is the inescapable by-product of a legal system wherein corporal punishment is still permitted (albeit in the home).

4.4 Corporal punishment and domestic legislation

While many countries across the globe have outlawed corporal punishment in all spheres, both public and private; the United Kingdom, while having abolished corporal punishment in schools[116] still permit it to apply in the home, although an outright ban on corporal punishment is due to be introduced in Scotland. Extending to all devolved regions within the UK, corporal punishment is still permissible in the home provided the behaviour complained of is either demonstrably 'reasonable' or 'justifiable'. The current law in the United Kingdom has developed largely in response to the ruling in *A v United Kingdom* which highlighted the then pre-existing legislative deficiencies which failed to protect children and young people from inhuman and degrading treatment.

In England and Wales corporal punishment is permitted by virtue of s. 58 of the Children Act 2004 which provides for the defence of 'reasonable punishment'. Although s. 58 is silent on what constitutes behaviour which amounts to 'reasonable punishment', certain identifiable offences are excluded from the defence. These are outlined in s. 58(2) of the Act and include, *inter alia,* wounding or causing grievous bodily harm contrary to ss. 18 and 20 of the Offences Against the Persons Act 1861, assault occasioning actual bodily harm contrary to s. 47 of the Offences Against the Persons Act, and cruelty to a person under 16 years contrary to s. 1 of the Children and Young Persons Act 1933. Further guidance has been provided by the Crown Prosecution Service for England and Wales in the form of the Charging Standard which states that injuries should be more than 'transient and trifling'.[117]

In Scotland, corporal punishment is permitted under s. 51 of the Criminal Justice (Scotland) Act 2003 which provides for the defence of 'justifiable assault'. Following an extensive consultation process[118] it was subsequently decided to permit corporal punishment within certain constrained parameters. Unlike s. 58 of its English and Welsh counterpart, the Scottish legislation goes slightly further in scope and guidance and expressly prohibits behaviour such as blows to the head, shaking, or the use of an implement from the ambit of the defence. [119] Moreover, s. 51 also expressly outlines the factors previously articulated in the preceding case law to which the courts in Scotland must have regard to when considering the defence of justifiable assault. This includes: the nature and reasons of the corporal punishment in question; its duration, frequency, effects on the child; the age of the child; and the child's personal characteristics.[120] However, in 2017, the Scottish

---

[116] Corporal Punishment was abolished in state-supported education in 1986 by virtue of Education (No. 2) Act 1986. This was extended to private schools in England and Wales in 1998, in Scotland in 2000, and in Northern Ireland in 2003.

[117] Crown Prosecution Service for England and Wales. Available at: http://www.cps.gov.uk/legal/l_to_o/ offences_against_the_person/#correction, accessed 27 May 2017.

[118] *The Physical Punishment of Children in Scotland (A Consultation)* (Scottish Executive, 2000).

[119] Criminal Justice (Scotland) Act 2003, s. 51(3).

[120] Criminal Justice (Scotland) Act 2001, s. 51(1)(a)–(e).

government has supported a Private Members Bill in the Scottish Parliament proposing an outright ban on corporal punishment.

Lastly, in Northern Ireland, corporal punishment is permissible pursuant to Article 2 of the Law Reform (Miscellaneous Provisions) (Northern Ireland) Order 2006 which provides for the defence of 'reasonable punishment'. However, punishment which amounts to either grievous bodily harm, aggravated assault, assault occasioning actual bodily harm, common assault, or cruelty to a person under 16 are excluded from the reach of Act's defence.

The direct incorporation of the ECHR into UK domestic law by virtue of the Human Rights Act 1998 also provided a platform on which to challenge the corporal punishment defence on human rights grounds. While the majority of corporal punishment cases have, to date, centred on the alleged incompatibility of the chastisement in question with the child's right to be free from torture, inhuman, and degrading treatment, the case of *R (on the application of Williamson) v Secretary of State for Education and Employment*[121] was unique in that it involved a direct challenge on human rights grounds against the statutory prohibition on corporal punishment in schools.

 Key Case 5: *R (on the application of Williamson) v Secretary of State for Education and Employment* [2005] UKHL 15

The applicants were the parents, teachers, and head teachers of children at four independent schools. They alleged that the statutory ban on corporal punishment, and in particular s. 548 of the Education Act 1996, which outlawed the practice in schools, was inapplicable where parents, pursuant to their common law right to discipline their children, delegated this power to the teacher. They further argued that the statutory ban on corporal punishment was incompatible with their Convention rights under the Human Rights Act 1998 and, in particular, their rights to freedom of religion, to educate their children in conformity with their religious convictions, and to respect for their private and family life under the ECHR and its First Protocol. Central to the applicants' claim was that 'loving corporal punishment' was an integral aspect of their faith and consequently, their religious liberty permitted them to delegate to the school the ability and power to train and educate their children, using corporal punishment where necessary, in accordance with their religious convictions.

The House of Lords held that while parents are entitled to hold the religious conviction that mild corporal punishment is necessary for the upbringing of their children, the right to freedom of religion is not unqualified or absolute and the law banning corporal punishment in schools respects children's rights and freedoms by protecting them from the deliberate and potentially harmful infliction of physical violence. In dismissing the applicants' case, the House of Lords stated that the government is entitled to weigh and balance these different rights as it sees fit, and its decision to ban corporal punishment in all schools is in the best interests of children.

In upholding the legality of the statutory ban on corporal punishment in schools, the *Williamson* case highlighted in clear and unmistakeable terms the intersection of parental rights with broader social policy considerations pertaining to children's rights. In his judgment, Lord Nicholls of Birkenhead stated that although the ban on corporal punishment did constitute an interference with parental religious rights, such an interference was permissible as it pursued a legitimate aim by protecting children and promoting their well-being, stating that 'Parliament was entitled to take this course because this issue is

---

[121] [2005] UKHL 15.

one of broad social policy'.[122] Moreover, in her judgment, Lady Hale of Richmond, after examining the relevant international human rights standards regarding corporal punishment, outlined that the child's rights to brought up without institutional violence should be respected 'whether or not his parents and teachers believe otherwise'.[123]

Comparably, in Northern Ireland, a challenge to the legality of the general parental defence of reasonable punishment was launched by the Northern Irish Children's Commissioner in 2007. In the case of *In the Matter of an Application for Judicial Review by the Northern Ireland Commissioner for Children and Young People of Decisions Made by Peter Hain the Secretary of State and David Hanson the Minister of State*[124] the Belfast High Court, upheld the legality of the defence on a number of grounds. First, in drawing on similar Canadian jurisprudence and in highlighting the functional importance of the family unit, the Court held that 'the family should not be subjected to the incursion of criminal law enforcement for every trivial slap and that extending the law to all disciplinary force would have potentially a negative impact upon families and hinder parental efforts to nurture children'.[125] Secondly, the Court held that the textual and legal configuration of the defence of 'reasonable punishment' was not 'imprecise or vague'[126] and was not inconsistent with the prohibition contained in Article 3 ECHR. The Court proceeded to state that the minimum degree of severity test encased in Article 3 ECHR 'will be judged according to the facts of each case and the nature and context of the punishment meted out'.[127]

 DEBATE 2: SHOULD PARENTS HAVE A RIGHT TO USE CORPORAL PUNISHMENT ON THEIR OWN CHILDREN?

The domestic provisions, as outlined earlier, which permit corporal punishment in the home, are largely the state's legislative responses to the ruling in *A v United Kingdom*.[128] Such provisions exist within ostensibly flexible parameters, where the legality of the punishment in question is subject to a well-established fact-specific and fact-dependant exercise. Therefore, the validity of the punishment will be broadly determined by the nature, context, and duration of the practice in association with its resultant effects on the child. In essence, the domestic framework attempts to strike an appropriate balance along two clear fracture lines. The first is an effort to accommodate the rights of parents with those of children. While retaining the parental right to administer corporal punishment, albeit in qualified circumstances, the government have clearly affirmed the primacy of parental rights regarding the administration of disciplinary measures. For example, a 2007 Departmental Review of s. 58 of the Children Act 2004 reveals a governmental unwillingness to deviate from the current legislative position.

> we do not believe that the state should intervene in family life unnecessarily –unless there are clear reasons to intervene, parents should be able to bring up their children as they see fit.[129]

However, despite the current position, the devolved administration in Wales has signified a clear commitment to end the current defence of reasonable punishment. In their programme for government, *Taking Wales Forward 2016–2021*, one of the stated aims of the Welsh gov-

[122] [2005] UKHL 15, at [51].   [123] [2005] UKHL 15, at [86].   [124] [2007] NIQB 115.
[125] [2007] NIQB 115, at [50].   [126] [2007] NIQB 115, at [67].   [127] [2007] NIQB 115.
[128] App. No. 25599/94, 23 September 1998.
[129] Department of Children, Schools and Families, *Review of Section 58 of the Children Act 2004* (2007) para 55.

ernment is to seek 'cross party support for legislation to end the defence of "Reasonable Punishment"'.[130] Similarly, in Scotland, the recent launch of a consultation process by the Scottish Green Party regarding the introduction of an equal protection Bill which will ultimately, if passed, abolish the defence of justifiable assault, also signifies existent discontent with the current framework.[131] Although the law in both devolved regions continues to endorse the permissibility of corporal punishment in the home, future legislative enactments will determine the continued existence of the defence in UK law.

The second balancing exercise which UK law regarding corporal punishment attempts to achieve is to curtail the level of violence permissible while exacting corporal punishment. To this end, the legislative provisions, in concert with current judicial pronouncements, demarcate a legal dividing line between acceptable and unacceptable punishment. Central to this demarcation is the autonomy afforded to parents to administer reasonable chastisement or punishment within the regulatory scope of the available provisions. As outlined by Gillen J in *In the Matter of an Application for Judicial Review by the Northern Ireland Commissioner for Children and Young People of Decisions Made by Peter Hain the Secretary of State and David Hanson the Minister of State:*[132]

> Not only has the chastisement to be reasonable, but it has to be actual chastisement and not merely loss of temper, acts of frustration or irrational outbursts by a parent unconnected with reasonable punishment within the confines of the offence of assault.[133]

Such legislative defences have been the subject of much international scrutiny and condemnation. Although Parliament has asserted the compatibility of the current framework with the UK's current ECHR obligations,[134] it's incongruity with Article 19 UNCRC has been noted. In particular, the Joint Committee on Human Rights state that;

> we do not consider that there is any room for discretion as to the means of implementing Article 19 CRC as interpreted by the Committee on the Rights of the Child: it requires the reasonable chastisement defence to be abolished altogether.[135]

Various international monitoring bodies have also criticised such provisions as being totally inconsistent with the UK's wider international human rights obligations. Specifically, the Committee on the Rights of the Child, in its Concluding Observations on the UK's performance under the UNCRC, have urged the UK to prohibit 'as a matter of priority' corporal punishment in the home, including the abolition of the defences currently available.[136] Similar views have also been echoed by the Committee on Economic, Social and Cultural Rights[137] and the Committee Against Torture,[138] all of which further undermine, or seriously destabilise the ongoing legitimacy of the defences available currently in the UK.

---

[130] *Taking Wales Forward 2016–2021*, 9.

[131] See   http://www.parliament.scot/S5MembersBills/John_Finnie_Final_Consultation_Document_pdf. pdf, accessed 27 May 2017.   [132] [2007] NIQB 115.   [133] [2007] NIQB 115, at [47].

[134] See Joint Committee on Human Rights, 19th Report (2004). In particular the Committee note 'no present incompatibility' between the defence of corporal punishment and ECHR obligations (para 143).

[135] Joint Committee on Human Rights, 19th Report (2004) para 156.

[136] Committee on the Rights of the Child Concluding Observations on the Fifth Periodic Report of the United Kingdom of Great Britain and Northern Ireland, CRC/C/GBC/CO/5 (2016) para 41.

[137] See Committee on Economic, Social and Cultural Rights Concluding Observations on Fourth/Fifth Report, E/C.12/GBR/CO/5 (2009) para 24.

[138] See Committee Against Torture Concluding Observations on Fifth Report, CAT/C/GBR/CO/5 (2013) para 29.

These contentions cast serious doubts over the permissibility of corporal punishment as an acceptable and appropriate from of discipline. First among them is the extent to which the practice is consistent with the rights of parents to family and private life,[139] or whether a proposed ban would impact such parental rights. As demonstrated in the *Williamson* case wherein parental religious rights came under the judicial lens, the qualified nature of human rights in and of themselves, aside from the prohibition against torture, inhuman, and degrading treatment, came into sharp focus. Therefore, the non-absolute nature of rights provides a legal pliability whereby competing rights may co-exist. Although this may result in the diminution in the enjoyment of a certain right in question (in the *Williamson* case this involved the religious rights of parents) the balance which human rights law strives to achieve is such that everyone's rights, children and parent alike, are equally upheld and vindicated.

Further to this pursuit, in all actions concerning children, Article 3 UNCRC states that the best interests of the child shall be a primary consideration in the determination of the dispute in question. Described by Stalford as the 'normative axis around which decisions relating to children revolve',[140] the best interest's principle occupies a central position within the adjudicative function of decision-making bodies where children's rights issues are involved. Therefore, despite the intentions and wishes of parents such parental objectives do not automatically occupy an impervious sphere of influence. Rather, they will be considered against and where appropriate, give way to what is ultimately in the best interests of the child. Since the enactment of the Children Act 1989 and the subsequent centralisation of the paramountcy of the 'welfare'[141] principle, children's rights are now a more visible and potent source of authority. Indeed, Fortin contends that it 'gave official approval to the change of emphasis emerging through case law and legislation that parents were no longer seen as having 'rights' over children, in the proprietorial sense, but instead were deemed to owe 'responsibilities' to them'.[142]

Although corporal punishment is secured within the confines of statutes across the UK pressures from outside and within, coupled with a greater appreciation of children's rights, are such that the future of such permissible punishment is insecure. With concerted movements towards the total abolition of corporal punishment afoot both domestically and regionally, particularly at European level,[143] the currency of corporal punishment as a method of discipline and correction is fast losing appeal. This has also been supported through well-organised campaigns which encourage not only positive parenting[144] but also a fundamental re-orientation of the manner in which the interface of parenting and discipline is both governed and dispensed.[145] Underpinning such approaches such

---

[139] See Article 8 ECHR.

[140] Stalford, H. (2017) 'The Broader Relevance of Features of Children's Rights Law: The "Best Interests Of The Child" Principle, in E. Brems, E. Desmet, and W. Vandenhole *Childrens Rights Law in the Global Human Rights Landscape* (Routledge Press, 2017) 37.

[141] Children Act 1989, s. 1.

[142] Fortin, J. *Children's Rights and the Developing Law*, (2nd edn, Cambridge University Press, 2005) 275.

[143] See, e.g., Council of Europe, Commissioner for Human Rights, 'Children and Corporal Punishment: 'The Right Not to be Hit, Also a Children's Right'", (CommDH/IssuePaper 2006, updated 2008). Available at: https://rm.coe.int/16806da87b, accessed 14 July 2017. See also, Position Paper by the Council of Europe Commissioner for Human Rights 'Commissioner for Human Rights Position Paper on Children's Rights, (CommDH/PositionPaper, 2010). Available at: https://rm.coe.int/16806db89e, accessed 14 July 2017.

[144] See, e.g., The Council of Europe recommendation on policies to promote positive parenting, Rec(2006)19 (Adopted by the Committee of Ministers on 13 December 2006 at the 983rd meeting of the Ministers deputies). Available at: https://search.coe.int/cm/Pages/result_details.aspx?ObjectID=09000016805d6dda, accessed 14 July 2017.

[145] See, e.g., Council of Europe, *Raise your Hand Against Smacking*. Details available at: https://www.coe.int/en/web/children/corporal-punishment, accessed 1 October 2017.

as the *Raise your Hand Against Smacking*[146] campaign is the overarching appreciation of children's rights and the espousal of non-violent methods of child-rearing and conflict-resolution in concert with appropriate educational and awareness raising arrangements.

Further underpinning the movement to abolish corporal punishment is the appreciation also of the inherently imbalanced nature of the legal protections currently afforded to children and young people as victims of such punishment in countries where such practices are permitted. These lesser protections were outlined by the Council of Europe in their 2010 Commission Paper on Human Rights which stated:

> That children, uniquely, should have less protection under the criminal law from assault is additionally discriminatory and completely unacceptable, given the obvious particular vulnerability of children.

In view of the mobilisation against corporal punishment and the increasing protection of children against violence of all descriptions,[147] the current domestic framework which permits corporal punishment stands in stark contrast to both not only accepted human rights standards generally but also the specific articulation of children's rights specifically. In that regard, a number of obvious and indeed uncomfortable questions arise. Why are children and young people permitted to be disciplined in a manner which objectively allows violent means? And why are such methods deemed acceptable as either 'reasonable' or 'justifiable' when they would fall within the purview of criminal law if inflicted on an adult to adult basis? Such questions therefore invigorate a discussion on what potential legal reform could and should look like. First, in view of the movements and commitments underway in both Scotland and Wales, such measures should be reflected on a nationwide basis to avoid regional privileges and disparities in the treatment of children and young people. Therefore, corporal punishment should be abolished in all parts of the UK to avoid any potential protective legislative imbalances. Secondly, the practical ramifications of such a ban ought to be considered and in particular whether it would result in the prosecution of parents for disciplining their children as they see fit. In view of the introduction of the ban in many countries across the globe, including more socially conservative countries such as Ireland, no evidence of familial destabilisation or dislocation has emerged. Rather, a statutory ban on corporal punishment in addition to appropriate rights-based training, awareness raising, and the multi-sectoral encouragement of non-violent child rearing methods could yield both positive and beneficial results for both child and adult alike. Such a ban would also accord children and young people the same basic (and indeed elemental) legislative protections that adults currently enjoy against violence.

To conclude, since the ratification of the UNCRC by the UK government in 1991, the provisions therein have had a sweeping impact on UK law and policy.[148] From the establishment of children's commissioners in all devolved regions[149] to the specific enactment

---

[146] Council of Europe, *Raise Your Hand Against Smacking*. Details available at: https://www.coe.int/en/web/children/corporal-punishment, accessed 1 October 2017.

[147] See, e.g., Council of Europe Convention on the Protection of Children Against Sexual Exploitation and Sexual Abuse (2007) (Also known as the Lanzarote Convention).

[148] e.g., in March 2015, the Department of Education issued new guidance, *Working Together to Safeguard Children*, with the purpose outlining the duties of those working with children in England.

[149] In England the Office of Children's Commissioner was set up pursuant to Part 1 of the Children Act 2004. In Scotland, the office was established under the Commissioner for Children and Young People (Scotland) Act 2003 while in Wales the office was established through Part V of the Care Standards Act 2000 and the Children's Commissioner for Wales Act 2001. In Northern Ireland, the office was established under The Commissioner for Children and Young People (Northern Ireland) Order 2003.

of regional measures[150] designed to enhance the operative impact of the UNCRC at government level, children's rights now occupy a more prominent position within and against the legal and political landscape of the UK. Such rights, including the rights to participate and be heard and freedom from torture, inhuman, and degrading treatment have been most influential in further rendering children more visible as individual rights-holding actors in their own right. While the footrace has at times been slow, many hurdles have however been overcome. Some nonetheless persist and it is likely that the issue of corporal punishment is one which will dominate legal, social, and political thought until such time that children are afforded legislative protection comparable to adults.

SUMMARY

1. Should children be allowed to make decisions about their own lives, particularly in matters concerning their family life?
   * The international children's rights framework makes it clear that children have a right to express their views in decisions that affect them and that such views should be given due weight in the light of their age and capacity.
   * Such rights should be balanced against the need to protect children from the trauma and complexity associated with decision-making around care arrangements, particularly in the context of court proceedings;
   * But the desire to protect children should not be used as a smokescreen for arbitrary, adult-focused decisions. There is now an abundance of evidence attesting to the unique insights that children can bring to bear on such decisions, and to the positive outcomes associated with a genuinely participatory process.

2. Should parents have a right to use corporal punishment on their own children?
   * International children's rights expressly prohibits the use of physical force against children, and the UN Committee on the Rights of the Child has repeatedly called upon the UK government to introduce legislation to prohibit corporal punishment in the home.
   * Article 3 ECHR has provided a successful remedy against corporal punishment in certain circumstances, but has stopped short of endorsing an outright ban.
   * The UK remains somewhat remarkable as one of a minority of European states that have yet to remove all defences to corporal punishment. It remains to be seen whether the devolved nations, particularly Wales, will act on its proposals to initiate such a ban in the coming years.

---

[150] See, e.g. Rights of Children and Young Persons (Wales) Measure 2011 and Children and Young People (Scotland) Act 2014, both of which pursuant to s. 1 respectively mandate both devolved administrations in furtherance of their functions to have due regard for the rights of the child under the UNCRC.

Further Reading

DALY, A. *Children, Autonomy and the Courts: Beyond the Right to be Heard* (Brill Nijhoff, 2017)
- This provides a detailed, comparative review of the arguments and associated case law relating to best interests assessments in medical and family cases. The author presents thought-provoking proposals that there should be a presumption in favour of respecting children's wishes in such cases, save where it is likely to cause them significant harm.

EWING J. *et al* 'Children's Voices: Centre-Stage or Sidelined in Out-of-Court Dispute Resolution in England and Wales?' (2015) 27 *Child and Family Law Quarterly* 43
- This provides a useful insight into how children's rights are respected in out-of-court proceedings, particularly mediation proceedings. This is particularly important given the increasing reliance on mediation to resolve private family disputes.

FREEMAN. M. and SAUNDERS, B.J. 'Can We Conquer Child Abuse if we don't Outlaw Physical Chastisement of Children' (2014) 22 *International Journal of Children's Rights* 681
- This offers a critical overview of the current regulatory response to corporal punishment.

GILMORE, S. 'Use of the UNCRC in Family Law Cases in England and Wales' (2017) 25 *International Journal of Children's Rights* 500
- This offers an updated review of how the courts use different provisions of the UNCRC to support family decision-making involving children.

NAYLOR, B. and SAUNDERS, B.J. 'Parental Discipline, Criminal Laws, and Responsive Regulation' in Freeman. M. (ed) (2012) 14 *Law and Childhood Studies: Current Legal Issues* 529
- This offers a critical discussion of the pros and cons of using the criminal law to sanction parents who physically discipline their children.

STALFORD, H., HOLLINGSWORTH, K., and GILMORE, S. (eds) *Rewriting Children's Rights Judgments: From Academic Vision to New Practice* (Hart Publishing, 2017)
- This presents a collection of judgments from various jurisdictions that have been re-written by children's rights experts with a view to exploring how a children's rights perspective can be brought to bear more effectively on judicial decision-making. Each judgment is accompanied by an explanatory commentary and the collection includes two detailed introductory chapters on a children's rights-based approach to judging.

TURNER, S.M. (2004) 'Justifying Corporal Punishment of Children loses its appeal' (2004) 11 *International Journal of Children's Rights* 219
- This article confronts the main arguments in favour of retaining parents' right to physically chastise their children.

14

International Family Law

Ruth Lamont

LEARNING OBJECTIVES

After reading this chapter you will be able to:

- Appreciate the impact of family migration and the international dimensions of family life, and the need for English family law to respond to the links individuals may have to countries other than England;

- Identify the rules for recognition of marriage, and the English court jurisdiction over divorce, parental responsibility, and the law governing international child abduction;

- Provide a critical analysis of the impact of different concepts and rules relating to the family on the development of international family law.

DEBATES

After reading this chapter you should be equipped to discuss your opinion on the following central debates:

1. Which country's courts and family law should govern family relationships where members of a family have links to a country other than England?

2. How can the law help families to manage relationships when family members live in different countries?

3. What should happen when different legal systems recognise different types of family relationship?

1. Introduction

Family life is increasingly international and spread across different countries. People travel from their home country to work, study, and live abroad and in doing so may meet and form relationships abroad. It is increasingly easy to create and maintain relationships with people in other countries across a globalised world using ever-developing means of communication. This global phenomenon has led to a rise in the number of relationships where the parties do not originate from the same country, or both partners are from the same country but living together in a foreign country. This has meant that the adult partners in a relationship, and their children, may have connections to more than one country. For English family lawyers, international families may have connections with more than one legal system. For family members themselves, their international connections may mean that their personal relationships will fall to be regulated under a legal system that is different to that of the country from which they originate.

This chapter explores when the English court will recognise family relationships created in other countries and take decisions regulating relationships with a foreign dimension. In this chapter, the central aspects of international family law, the law relating to foreign marriage, divorce and children, including international child abduction, will be considered to examine how English law responds to these concerns. The increasingly international nature of family life affects a range of other family relationships regulated through law. For example, an agreement between English parents and a surrogate mother abroad to give birth to their child in another country before the child is brought to the UK may give rise to difficult questions relating to the validity of the agreement and the status of the child.[1] After the end of the parental relationship, one parent may seek to relocate abroad, taking the children with them and significantly affecting the nature of the relationship with the other parent (see section 6 and Chapter 9). Refugee children may migrate between countries, or a child may be forcibly trafficked into the UK, affecting their legal status and placing the child in need of protection (see 5.1). English law must be able to respond to the issues raised by these situations and identify when it is appropriate to take decisions and regulate the relationships of individuals in a cross-national situation.

When family members have created their relationship abroad, and subsequently travelled to England, we have to know whether English law will accept their status as family members and regulate that relationship. It has to be clear which country's courts have the power, or *'jurisdiction'* to resolve any legal disputes between the parties.

Even if a case is heard in the English courts, it is possible for a foreign law to be applied to the facts of a case in certain circumstances. Identifying which law will govern the outcome of a dispute is known as a *'choice of law'* rule, for determining the relevant law that will govern the substantive outcome of the dispute.

If a foreign law governs the dispute, the English courts will take evidence on the state of the foreign law and apply that to resolve the dispute, but normally in family law, English law is applied. The issues of jurisdiction and choice of law are decided by the court before the substantive elements of the litigation are heard, for example the division of assets on divorce or the arrangements for the children.

In this chapter we will explore the circumstances in which English law will recognise a marriage celebrated abroad as a binding valid marriage in England, and when the spouses can petition for divorce in England. In relation to children, we will identify when the English court can act to protect the welfare of a child, and the legal remedies available where one parent moves a child to another country, without the other parent's permission.

2. International families and English law

2.1 Sources of international family law

English family law has developed its own common law and statutory rules to regulate relationships created in another country when the family members migrated to England. In some contexts, such as the recognition of foreign marriages, these rules remain in place.

---

[1] For example, *Re L (Children)* [2015] EWFC 90. See Chapter 8.

However, English family law on international relationships has been changed enormously by the impact of international conventions, and measures adopted by the EU, binding Member States, including the UK.

Agreements, in the form of international treaties, with other countries about international family law rules enable decisions to be taken on the same basis across different legal systems. These types of international agreement encourage the acceptance of decisions taken in other countries by English law and *vice versa*. This helps individuals who have been involved in international family litigation because they are more likely to have the decisions made by one legal system accepted by other legal systems if they subsequently migrate abroad. The aim of coordinating the law between different countries is to make the law much more certain for individuals and courts to apply predictably and cheaply. The coordination of international family law between different countries has changed English law affecting international families. The Hague Conference on Private International Law provides a forum for the development and conclusion of international agreements and the UK is a signatory to a number of treaties developed by the Conference.

The UK is bound, along with over 90 other countries,[2] by The Hague Convention on the Civil Aspects of International Child Abduction 1980. All the signatories operate the international convention in their national law, applying the same rules in the national court. This encourages cooperation between countries when a parent has abducted a child. On 1 November 2012, the Hague Convention on Jurisdiction, Applicable Law, Recognition and Enforcement and Cooperation in Respect of Parental Responsibility and Measures for the Protection of Children 1996 entered into force in the UK. This Convention governs jurisdiction over decisions in relation to children, and the enforcement of judgments in another country. It binds countries other than EU Member States, including the USA, and these measures are likely to form the basis of the rules relating to children in international families if the EU Brussels II Revised Regulation (BIIR) no longer binds the UK following Brexit.

The EU has been engaged in regulating international family law since the Treaty of Amsterdam in 1999. The EU has accepted that its policy of encouraging migration of European citizens between the Member States had also created more international families and affected the number of international divorces, and children involved in cross-border proceedings.[3] It has adopted a series of measures, but the key measure affecting English law is known as BIIR (or Brussels II *bis*).[4] This Regulation binds all EU Member States, except for Denmark. The provisions of BIIR replaced the English common law on jurisdiction over divorce proceedings and parental responsibility disputes. The English courts make decisions on cases governed by this Regulation, and can currently refer cases as preliminary references providing guidance on interpretation of its provisions to the Court of Justice of the European Union.[5] Proposals to revise and update BIIR are now being developed and considered by the EU.[6] The Regulation was due for review in 2015 and the Commission has taken the opportunity to revise and update some of the rules in the light of practice since 2005.

---

[2] Hague Convention on the Civil Aspects of International Child Abduction 1980 Status Table.

[3] Commission Working Document 'Mutual Recognition on Decisions of Parental Responsibility' COM(2001) 166 final.

[4] Regulation 2201/2003 concerning jurisdiction and the recognition and enforcement of judgments in matrimonial matters and the matters of parental responsibility, repealing Regulation 1347/2000 [2003] OJ L338.

[5] Article 267, Treaty on the Functioning of the European Union [2012] OJ C326/1.

[6] Proposal for a Council Regulation on jurisdiction, the recognition and enforcement of decisions in matrimonial matters and the matters of parental responsibility, and on international child abduction (recast) COM(2016) 411/2.

> ### 👤 Context 1: Brexit Vote
>
> The UK referendum in June 2016 resulted in a vote to leave the EU. Before the UK referendum vote, the UK government had concluded that cooperation between EU Member States in relation to international family law was helpful and that BIIR had led to valuable developments in the law.[7] The underlying basis of BIIR is that each Member State should trust that the family law of other Member States protects individuals' human rights and encourages close cooperation.
>
> The position of the UK as a Member State will change as a result of the UK referendum vote but the legal effects of exiting the EU on fields such as family law have yet to become fully clear. It is likely that the legal framework provided by BIIR will not bind the UK. The impact of withdrawal from the EU on areas of law where close cooperation is desirable, such as family law, may be highly problematic, particularly where there are close family ties and migration links with other countries, such as Ireland.

Despite the existence of international agreements and the current role for EU law in regulating aspects of cross-border family disputes, English law rules still apply in a number of circumstances. English private international family law rules are traditionally based upon the exercise of discretion by the English court to hear and decide cases.

2.2 Migration and the connections of international families

The quality and nature of the international connections developed by family members who travel to different countries may vary extensively. For example, a French husband and his French wife are legally married in France, but migrate to England to work for the next ten years and subsequently seek to divorce in England. Although both spouses are French, their married life has been conducted in England and their social connections are most recently in England. On the other hand, if an English couple choose to celebrate their marriage on holiday on a beach in Barbados and immediately return home to England, their connection to a foreign country is transient. The marriage will not have been conducted according to the English law on marriage, even though they are closely connected to England. These international links also affect children. Where a child's parents have separated and live in two different countries, their child may spend significant amounts of time in each country to maintain contact with both parents. A child living in Russia could also spend significant periods of time in England being educated at boarding school. The extent of the connection to a particular country can determine whether that legal system should govern the outcome of any family disputes.

For family lawyers, families that have international connections give rise to legal concerns in accepting the legal status in England of formalised family relationships created abroad. We need to know which law will govern individual family relationships and whether English law will accept those relationships as legally valid. National family law varies extensively between different countries, informed by different religious, cultural, and social backgrounds.[8] The national characteristics and approach to family law is bound into the web of social life of any country. This means that some forms of relationships,

---

[7] Review of the Balance of Competences between the United Kingdom and the European Union: Civil Judicial Cooperation February 2014.

[8] Antokolskaia, M. 'Harmonisation of Family Law in Europe: A Historical Perspective' in Antokolskaia, M. (ed) *Convergence and Divergence of Family Law in Europe* (Intersentia, 2007) 11.

which are acceptable in some countries, may not be acceptable in others. For example, from March 2014 same-sex marriage has been permitted in England and a valid same-sex marriage concluded abroad will now be accepted as legally valid in England.[9] However, prior to the passage of the Marriage (Same Sex Couples) Act 2013, a same-sex marriage celebrated abroad would only be accepted in English law as creating a civil partnership.[10] Whilst English law has to respect the family law of other countries, it is not obliged to accept as having legal status the family relationships concluded abroad. English law creates rules to identify when it will recognise a legally formalised family relationship created by a foreign legal system.

Families with international connections also give rise to the ongoing issue of identifying which national court should take decisions about the future of the family when disputes arise. In the circumstances where the spouses in a marriage have connection to different countries, if they seek a divorce, a country has to be identified that is closely connected to the parties and their marriage to grant the divorce. An appropriate court, in a country expected by the spouses to have jurisdiction, should decide on the divorce petition and the consequences of the divorce in relation to division of assets and contact with children of the relationship. Where a child has connections to two different countries, the courts of one country should make decisions affecting the child's welfare and resolving any legal disputes between the child's parents about the care and responsibility for the child. Identifying the most appropriate court to take these decisions can be a very important because different countries may adopt different approaches aimed at securing a child's welfare. If one court issues a judgment potentially affecting family life in another country, that judgment has to be accepted as valid in the other country, or recognised, to be fully effective. For the purposes of English law, it has to be identified when the English court is the most appropriate place to hear a case and has jurisdiction to take decisions over family life. The English court should only take decisions over individual's family life when the family has connections to England.

> ### ❓ DEBATE 1: WHICH COUNTRY'S COURTS AND FAMILY LAW SHOULD GOVERN FAMILY RELATIONSHIPS WHERE MEMBERS OF A FAMILY HAVE LINKS TO A COUNTRY OTHER THAN ENGLAND?
>
> Identifying which law should govern family relationships is important and potentially contentious. Different legal systems recognise different rights and responsibilities arising from family relationships and have highly variable rules for granting family status, such as divorce. Individuals may therefore want to ensure that one particular law governs the litigation to access the 'best' potential legal outcome from their perspective. This is known as forum shopping and countries normally have to guard against accepting cases with limited connection to the country. The English courts have traditionally been very accepting of foreign cases and the English High Court is a centre of family law litigation. Whilst this may be desirable to ensure the court protects people within the jurisdiction, it can mean that cases with limited connection to England are still litigated, potentially inappropriately, with evidence and resources more easily available abroad.
>
> Identifying a connection between a person and a country enables a lawyer to determine whether the English courts should take decisions over a family. When a family has migrated to another country, they may have links to both countries. Connecting a person to a country will be straightforward when they have lived in the same country all their life and

---

[9] Marriage (Same Sex Couples) Act 2013. s. 13.   [10] *Wilkinson v Kitzinger* [2007] 1 FLR 295.

their connections are clearly with one country. Where a person has recently moved from one country to another, for example to work, it may not be clear to which country they are most closely connected, or if they work for a long period of time in one country, returning to their family for short periods of time. This may be even more difficult when a person has lived a peripatetic lifestyle, travelling from place to place with no clear home.[11] The English courts have been criticised in the past for making 'exorbitant' claims of jurisdiction through generous interpretation of connecting factors and hearing cases where the parties had little connection to the country. This may be desirable, for example to protect a child at risk, but may infringe the rights of the court more closely connected to the dispute.

There are different ways in which to identify a connection between a person and a country. These are known as 'connecting factors'.

- A connecting factor should reflect the reality of an individual's links to a particular country so that the law governing their personal relationships is the law they would expect to have knowledge of to enable their compliance with their legal obligations and fulfil their expectations.
- Connecting factors can work by considering the legal and long-term connections between an individual and a country. These are relatively stable and will not change over time but will not necessarily reflect the most recent migrations of individuals. Modern rules tend to look at the recent connections between an individual and a country to reflect the increasing migration patterns of individuals and their new connections but identifying where a person is most closely connected is more difficult depending on assessment of the factual circumstances of the individual.
- In English family law, two main connecting factors are used to identify a link between a person and a country: domicile and habitual residence. In other civil law countries, nationality is also used as a connecting factor. Domicile and nationality consider legal and long-term connections to a country. Habitual residence considers the factual connections between a person and a country. These connecting factors are interpreted and applied to the facts to determine whether the English court has jurisdiction.

2.2.1 Domicile

Domicile is the traditional English connecting factor and refers to a person's permanent home. You only ever have one domicile at a time so even if you spend time in two different countries, only one of them will be your domicile and govern your family legal status. There are three different ways of determining your 'domicile' depending on your circumstances.

The first way of determining domicile is through *domicile of origin*. Domicile of origin is determined at birth. If the child is legitimate, that is, born within marriage, the child's domicile of origin is the same domicile of the father at the time of birth. The domicile of the father at that moment in time has to be determined to identify the child's domicile of origin. If the child is illegitimate, that is, born outside of marriage, the child's domicile of origin is the same of the mother at the time of birth. A domicile of origin remains in abeyance throughout life unless you lose your domicile of choice, when the domicile of origin revives to fill the gap in your domicile of choice.[12]

---

[11] Lamont, R. 'Habitual Residence and Brussels II*bis*: Developing Concepts for European Private International Family Law' (2007) 3 *Journal of Private International Family Law* 261.

[12] *Udny v Udny* (1869) LR 1 Sc&Div 441.

The second way of determining domicile is to identify the *domicile of choice* of an adult. Your domicile of choice is your permanent home. To demonstrate domicile of choice, there must have been a period of residence and it must be possible to demonstrate that a person intends to make that place their permanent home. Most adults will have a domicile of choice. The emphasis on where you intend to make your permanent home can mean that an individual may have limited physical connection in a country but it may still be their domicile. In *Ramsay v Liverpool Royal Infirmary*[13] George Bowie had a Scottish domicile of origin and had moved to Liverpool in England for the last 36 years of his life. He did not return to Scotland in this time and declared an intention not to return there. When he died, if he was domiciled in Scotland, his will was valid, but it was not valid if he was domiciled in England. The House of Lords decided that he was still domiciled in Scotland at his death. Despite having lived in England for such a long period before he died there, the Court concluded that he had not formed the requisite intention to reside permanently in England. Whilst this is an extreme case, it demonstrates how important demonstrating a positive intention to be permanently resident in a country is to determining a domicile of choice. A period of residence alone will not be sufficient. Even a long period of residence may not mean a country is your permanent home.

When an individual leaves their current domicile of choice and no longer intends to reside there permanently, their domicile there is lost.[14] To establish a new domicile of choice in the new place of residence, there must be an intention to reside there permanently. If there is no such intention, then there may be no domicile of choice and the individual's domicile of origin revives. For example, if Mark migrates from England to Italy to work and intends to spend the rest of his life there he will acquire a domicile of choice in Italy. If he then decides to leave on a world tour with no idea of having a permanent home, his domicile of origin will revive, even if he does not live in the country of his domicile of origin, until he decides to settle somewhere, with an intention to permanently reside, and then acquires a new domicile of choice. The rule reviving the domicile of origin where the domicile of choice has been lost without establishing a new one has been criticised because it means that your domicile could be in a place where you have no factual connections. If your domicile of origin is somewhere you have never been, or have only a limited connection with and are not currently living, it is not suitable to govern your family relationships. The Law Commission recommended the removal of the use of the domicile of origin on this basis.[15]

The third way of determining domicile applies to those who cannot have an intention to reside somewhere, such as children, whose parents will decide where they live. Children have a *domicile of dependency* which makes their domicile exactly the same as the domicile of one of their parents until they reach the age of 16.[16] Under s. 4(4) of the Domicile and Matrimonial Proceedings Act 1973, if the child is legitimate, born inside marriage, then the child's domicile depends upon the domicile of their father. If the child is illegitimate (born outside of marriage) then child's domicile depends on their mother's domicile. If the mother and father are living apart, even if they are still married, under s. 4(2) of the Domicile and Matrimonial Proceedings Act 1973, a child having a home with the mother will have the same domicile as the mother. As the parent's domicile changes, the child's domicile automatically changes until they reach the age of 16 and may form a domicile of choice for themselves.

The emphasis on intention has meant that the rules on domicile do not properly respond to changing circumstances of individuals. The rules surrounding attribution of the

---

[13] [1930] AC 588.   [14] *Re Flynn (No. 1)* [1968] 1 WLR 103.
[15] Law Commission, *The Law of Domicile* (Law Com Working Paper No. 88, 1985).
[16] Domicile and Matrimonial Proceedings Act 1973, s. 3(1).

domicile of origin at birth, and the revival of the domicile of origin, which may bear no relationship to the place an individual is currently located, are problematic. In 1987, the Law Commission proposed reforms to the rules on domicile to simplify the rules for the attribution of domicile to children but the government refused to adopt the proposals.

2.2.2 Habitual residence

Habitual residence is a connecting factor that seeks to reflect the evolving factual connections between an individual and a country as they migrate. As a factual concept, the emphasis has been upon the level of integration of the individual into a country, identifying the 'centre of their interests'.[17] If an individual has been in a country for a significant period of time, normally more than three months, then they will be deemed to be integrated and habitually resident.

The difficulty with establishing habitual residence occurs when there is only a very short period of residence in a country, making it difficult to classify the residence as 'habitual'. In these circumstances, the focus of litigation has been over determining the intention of the individual to remain in that country for the foreseeable future. The court will look at the factual circumstances of the migration very closely to determine whether an individual is committed to living in the country and making their residence 'habitual'. If the individual can demonstrate a settled intention to remain in the country, then they will be habitually resident.

 Key Case 1: *Marinos v Marinos* **[2007] EWHC 2047 (Fam)**

The husband was a Greek national and the wife was British. They met and married in London before moving to Greece for a trial period of a year with their children, who were sent to local Greek schools. The wife argued that the relocation was subject to termination at any time. The wife subsequently returned to England after four years in Greece and issued in a divorce petition in the English court the day after her return, arguing that she was 'habitually resident' in England for the purpose of assuming jurisdiction (see section 3).

The English Court held that she could be habitually resident in England, even though she had only been resident for one day before raising the divorce petition because she was making a ' ... planned, purposeful and permanent relocation from one country to another.'[18] In the circumstances, her settled intention to remain in England meant that she was habitually resident. The decision in this case encourages consideration of the intentions of the wife rather than on her factual connections to the country, making it much easier to establish 'habitual' residence after a short period of residence.

In the same way as adults, identifying the habitual residence of a child requires a factual assessment of the level of their integration into their country and environment. In very young children and infants, this will be heavily influenced by the circumstances and habitual residence of the parents, but the court will consider a range of personal circumstances including schooling, language skills, medical registrations, and family situation.[19] For infant children, the primary site of care of the child is normally the determining factor.[20] The Supreme Court considered how the habitual residence of a child is to be identified

---

[17] Lamont, R. 'Case Comment: Case C-523/07 *A*' (2010) 47 *Common Market Law Review* 235.

[18] [2007] EWHC 2047 (Fam), at [89].   [19] Case C-523/07 *A* EU:C:2009:39.

[20] Case C-497/10 PPU *Mercredi v Chaffe* [2010] ECR. I-14309.

in *A v A*.[21] A child must have an actual presence in the country before s/he can be deemed habitually resident. The focus should be on the situation of the child, and the parent's intention will only be one factor in this assessment. The opinions and perception of an adolescent child regarding their residence and the centre of their interests may be taken into account. It is not clear why only the views of an adolescent child are relevant,[22] however, the approach the Supreme Court has taken is focused on the links the child has to a country, rather than the intentions of their parents. This represents a desirable development in the law because it is more likely to reflect the child's factual connections to a country.[23]

The connecting factors of domicile and habitual residence are used to link both adults and children to a country to determine which courts and law should govern their personal relationships in a variety of different legal contexts.

3. Adults: recognition of marriages concluded abroad

3.1 Validity of a foreign marriage

If a marriage is celebrated in a country other than England, it will have been conducted according to different marriage rites and procedure, and under a different governing law. For example, if a marriage is celebrated in Thailand under Thai law and according to Thai marriage rites, it will create a binding legal marriage in Thailand. From the English perspective, if the spouses travel to England it has to be clear whether those two individuals can be accepted as having the equivalent status of being 'married' in English law. The marriage must be 'recognised' in English law as a valid marriage. This is important for the spouses because, if the marriage is not recognised in England, they will not legally hold the status of married and have access to tax and succession benefits.

In these circumstances, there are two different countries affected by the marriage. The Thai authorities have an interest in ensuring that the law on how to conclude a valid marriage is adhered to in their country. However, when the couple travel to England, the English authorities must ensure that the relationships they accept in law as constituting a 'marriage' concluded abroad, matches the English conception of what constitutes a valid marriage (see Chapter 2). If English law accepted marriages concluded abroad that did not comply with the English concept of marriage, it would be possible to travel abroad to avoid the English requirements for a valid marriage, for example, by marrying a child under 16.[24] English law has developed to accommodate both countries interests in governing the recognition of the relationship as a marriage where it is celebrated abroad. Some forms of marriage have historically not been accepted by English law, even if they have been validly concluded in another country. This has been the case for same-sex marriages and polygamous marriages, where the husband has more than one wife, but English law has adapted to address these forms of marriage.

In 2007, the Office for National Statistics found that the number of UK residents marrying abroad was rising, but 90% of those marriages were to another UK resident. Most marriages abroad were within the 25 to 34 years old age group and from mid-2001–7 there were approximately 300,000 marriages of UK residents abroad.[25]

---

[21] *A v A and another (Children: Habitual Residence)* [2013] UKSC 60. See also *Re L (A Child) (Custody: Habitual Residence)* [2013] UKSC 75; *Re LC* [2014] UKSC 1.

[22] Gilmore, S, and Herring, J. 'Listening to Children … Whatever' (2014) 130 *Law Quarterly Review* 531.

[23] Schuz, R. 'Habitual Residence of the Child Revisited: A Trilogy of Cases in the UK Supreme Court' (2014) 26 *Child and Family Law Quarterly* 342.

[24] The marriage would be void under s. 11(a) of the Matrimonial Causes Act 1973.

[25] 'Report: Marriages abroad 2002–2007' Population Trends 133 (2009). Available at: https://www.statistics. gov.uk/statbase/product.asp?vlnk=6303, accessed 1 October 2017.

3.2 **Recognition of a marriage celebrated abroad in English law**

The law on the recognition of a valid foreign marriage is divided into two elements: formal validity and essential validity.

- Formal validity refers to the procedure governing the celebration of the marriage.
- Essential validity refers to the capacity of the parties to contract a valid marriage.

The foreign marriage must be both formally and essentially valid before the English court will recognise it as a marriage in England. When a couple marry abroad and subsequently move to England, they will have to prove the marriage was both formally and essentially valid at the time of the marriage. The rules governing formal and essential validity of the marriage depend upon which law governs each element on the facts of the case. The relevant governing law is identified using a choice of law rule. Different choice of law rules are used to establish the law governing formal validity and essential validity.

3.2.1 **Formal validity**

When a marriage is celebrated, there are a series of formal requirements that must be complied with for the marriage to be valid.[26] These factors include the requirements for a civil or religious ceremony; how many witnesses are required to the ceremony; when, where and by whom the ceremony must be conducted; and whether parental consent is required before the marriage can be celebrated.[27] The law governing these practical elements for celebrating the marriage is the law of the country where the marriage is celebrated. So, if an English couple decide to have the ceremony of marriage conducted in Australia, the ceremony should comply with the local form of marriage celebration.

 Key Case 2: *McCabe v McCabe* [1994] 1 FLR 410

A marriage was concluded in Ghana under a local customary form of law. The marriage was not publicised beforehand and the spouses were not present and were married by proxy. The husband provided £100 and a bottle of gin before the ceremony, which took place at the home of the wife's father in front of family members.

The Court of Appeal in England concluded that the marriage was validly celebrated under the local customary law of Ghana and accepted the foreign ceremony as creating a formally valid marriage in England. The Ghanian form of marriage was not the same as English law and if the marriage had been celebrated in this form in England, it would not have been valid. However, it was a valid form of marriage under Ghanaian law, the law of the place of celebration of the marriage, and this was sufficient for the marriage to be deemed formally valid.

Requiring the spouses to comply with the local form of marriage is practical. If the marriage is not celebrated in England, it is not possible to comply with the English procedure of marriage. It is normally only possible to comply with the local form of marriage rites. This rule accommodates the interest of the law of the country in regulating the behaviour of people on its territory. Individuals seeking to marry would be expected to comply with the local rules on the celebration of marriage.

This rule does not apply if there is some impossibility in complying with the local form of celebration, or the country where the marriage is celebrated is under belligerent

---

[26] In England and Wales, these are governed by the Marriage Act 1949.

[27] *Ogden v Ogden* [1908] P. 46.

occupation and the marriage is conducted under the occupying forces' national law, or marriages falling under the scope of the Foreign Marriage Act 1892, including marriage of members of HM Forces serving abroad and marriages conducted in British consulates.

3.2.2 Essential validity

Essential validity refers to the capacity of the spouses to be married. Capacity refers to the personal status of each party to meet the conditions to marry, such as reaching the right age, the nature of their family relationship with their putative spouse, or their sex. The requirements of capacity to marry may vary between different national laws, so it is necessary to identify which law determines whether a person had capacity to contract a valid marriage. The place where the marriage is celebrated may only be a transient location for the parties. For example, if an English couple decide to marry in Jamaica on holiday, they will be in Jamaica for a short period of time and will have no substantial connection with the country. The parties to the marriage would not expect Jamaican law to govern the substance of the marriage because their primary connection is with England. The law governing the essential validity of the marriage has to have a connection to the individual seeking to marry and reflect their expectations regarding the marital relationship.

There are two alternative rules that are used to determine the law governing the essential validity of a marriage:

- dual domicile rule;
- intended matrimonial home rule.

The rule normally applied to determine the essential validity of a foreign marriage is the *dual domicile rule*. The court will consider where each of the parties to the marriage was domiciled (see section 2.2.1) at the time of the marriage, because this is the law of the country to which they are closely connected. The English court will assess whether, according to the law of their domicile, each party had the capacity to marry. If they did have capacity under their domiciliary law, the marriage will be accepted as valid. So, if the husband was domiciled in Romania, and the wife was domiciled in Italy at the time of the marriage, they would both have to have capacity under the law of their domicile, either Romanian law or Italian law, to be recognised as married. This rule is criticised because it provides for the consideration of two different laws on marriage, making it more likely the marriage will be deemed invalid, but it does recognise the interest of the country to which an individual is connected in their personal relationships.

The alternative *intended matrimonial home rule* instead considers where the spouses planned to live as a matrimonial couple after the marriage ceremony and uses the law of that country to determine whether they had capacity to marry. The rule links the marriage to a country, rather than looking at the individual connections of the spouses. This rule tends to be used rarely where the marriage has no connection to England to ensure a marriage, that would otherwise be deemed invalid under the dual domicile rule, is recognised.[28] If the spouses are mobile during the period of the marriage, it can be difficult to establish which country should be identified as the matrimonial home for the purposes of the rule. A Law Commission Working Paper in 1985 concluded that the dual domicile rule was to be preferred over the intended matrimonial home rule because of its uncertainties of determining the single matrimonial home when the spouses have migrated and the fact that the parties would normally consider their own domiciliary law in determining their capacity to marry.[29]

---

[28] *Radwan v Radwan (No. 2)* [1973] Fam 35.

[29] Law Commission, *Choice of Law Rules on Marriage* (Law Com. No. 165, 1987), (Law Com Working Paper No. 89, 1985).

An exception to the use of the dual domicile rule occurs where one spouse is domiciled in England at the time of the marriage and the marriage is celebrated in England. In these circumstances, the marriage is so closely connected with England that only English law will be used to determine the essential validity of the marriage.[30] The domiciliary law of the other spouse will not be considered.

If one of the spouses at the time of the marriage is under the age of 16, the marriage will not be recognised as valid in English law, even if the child under 16 had capacity to marry under the law of their domicile.[31] The age of consent to sexual intercourse and marriage in English law is 16.[32] This rule protects children from marriage abroad. The rule establishes that marriage to children under 16 is not accepted in English law and will not be recognised, even if the foreign law governing the child's personal relationships would permit the marriage. There are few countries that permit the marriage of a child under 16 years old, but for example, in Malaysia, in some circumstances, child marriage may be judicially sanctioned.

The rules on essential validity require the court to consider the content of foreign law on capacity to marry. The law in different countries on marriage will vary in terms of which family relationships fall within the prohibited degrees of relationship, whether they permit marriage by proxy, the impact of consent on the validity of the marriage, and whether sexual consummation of the marriage is necessary. The English court will normally recognise a marriage where the parties have capacity under the law of their domicile. However, in exceptional circumstances, the English court may refuse to recognise a marriage as valid on the grounds that it offends public policy. This means that, even though the marriage is valid under laws identified under the dual domicile rule, there is an aspect to the marriage that fundamentally offends the English concept of marriage and it will not be recognised by the English court as valid.

 Key Case 3: *Westminster CC v C and others* [2009] Fam 11

IC was a 25-year-old man domiciled in England suffering from a severe disability of mental function that meant his mental age was around 8 years old. IC went through a ceremony of marriage to a woman, NK, domiciled in Bangladesh over telephone. This marriage was valid under the law of Bangladesh and NK had capacity to marry under the law of her domicile. The local authority in England sought to have the marriage annulled on the grounds that IC did not have the capacity to consent to marriage under English law.

The Court of Appeal concluded that the English local authority could not petition for annulment of the marriage due to a lack of capacity to consent to marriage under s. 12(1)(c) of the Matrimonial Causes Act 1973. Section 12(1)(c) is a ground for making a marriage voidable, not void, and a petition on this basis may only be issued by one of the parties to the marriage.[33] The marriage is valid until a petition of nullity is successful and the petition to annul a voidable marriage had not been brought by one of the spouses. The marriage was valid and would be recognised in English law if the dual domicile rule was applied as both spouses had capacity under the law of their domicile. However, the English court was not obliged to recognise a marriage that did not conform to the English conception of marriage and recognition could be refused for offending public policy:

Not every marriage valid according to the law of some friendly foreign state is entitled to recognition in this jurisdiction. In the present case it is common ground that IC lacks the

---

[30] *Sottomayer v De Barros (No. 2)* (1879) 5 PD 94.   [31] *Pugh v Pugh* [1951] 2 All ER 680.

[32] Matrimonial Causes Act 1973, s. 11(a).   [33] Matrimonial Causes Act 1973, s. 13.

capacity to marry in English law. Even having regard to the relaxations that have permitted marriage to be celebrated in a variety of places and by a variety of celebrants, it is simply inconceivable that IC could be lawfully married in this jurisdiction ... I would propose a declaration that the marriage between IC and NK, valid according to the law of Bangladesh, is not recognised as a valid marriage in this jurisdiction (22, Thorpe, LJ).

3.3 Recognising different types of marriage

 DEBATE 2: WHAT SHOULD HAPPEN WHEN DIFFERENT LEGAL SYSTEMS RECOGNISE DIFFERENT TYPES OF FAMILY RELATIONSHIP?

Marriage does not bear the same meaning in different societies and cultures. How far the English legal system should accept other types of family relationship recognised by other cultures can be thought provoking and insightful about the English concept of relationships such as marriage. The English courts have been protective of its legal conception of family life, refusing to accept marriages validly concluded under foreign law because they were different to English rules on marriage. The English courts have been resistant to accepting forms of marriage not accepted by English law. This can cause problems for individuals, because if the English court does not accept forms of marriage from other cultures, individuals who thought they were married will not hold this status in England. However, this approach protects the English concept of 'marriage' which is regarded as a core to English family law.[34]

In *Hyde v Hyde and Woodmansee*[35] in 1865 the English Court was asked to consider whether a marriage concluded in the Mormon faith, which at the time permitted a man to take more than one wife, was recognised in English law. In judgment, Lord Penzance stated that:

> I conceive that marriage, as understood in Christendom, may for this purpose be defined as the voluntary union for life of one man and one woman, to the exclusion of all others.[36]

Since this statement was made, English society has changed significantly and the concept of marriage has evolved in English law: marriage is no longer necessarily for life as divorce is easier to obtain, and a marriage may be celebrated between same-sex partners after the adoption of the Marriage (Same Sex Partners) Act 2013. Marriage should still be voluntary and between two people. Yet, the question of the extent to which English law should accept and recognise marriage forms adopted by other cultures still remains in modern law. The acceptance of other forms of marriage to English law has been particularly tested in two different contexts: same-sex marriage and polygamous marriages.

3.3.1 Same-sex marriages

Before the Civil Partnership Act 2004, same-sex couples had no way of legally regularising their relationship in English law. A marriage between same-sex partners was void under s. 11(c) of the Matrimonial Causes Act 1973. Valid same-sex marriages concluded abroad would not be recognised as a valid marriage in England.

---

[34] Auchmuty, R. 'What's So Special About Marriage? The Impact of *Wilkinson v Kitzinger*' (2008) 40 *Child and Family Law Quarterly* 425.   [35] (1865–69) L.R. 1 P&D 130.

[36] (1865–69) L.R. 1 P&D 130, at 133.

⬤ CONTEXT 2: SAME-SEX MARRIAGE GLOBALLY

The Pew Research Centre on Religion and Public Life surveyed attitudes to same-sex marriage and the countries that permitted same-sex couples to contract a valid marriage around the world.[37] The Netherlands has permitted same-sex marriage since 2000, Belgium since 2003, and Canada since 2005. There are currently 24 countries that permit same-sex marriage. The majority of countries worldwide still do not permit same-sex marriage. In many countries there is still active prejudice towards homosexuality for a variety of historical social and religious reasons. 76 countries punish homosexuality as a criminal offence, and homosexual activity is subject to the death penalty in seven countries. The great diversity in cultural acceptability of homosexuality globally means that a same-sex marriage validly concluded in England may not be recognised in other countries and may in fact provide notice of behaviour deemed illegal in a foreign country.

Following the entry into force of the Civil Partnerships Act 2004, a registered partnership or a marriage concluded by a same-sex couple abroad was recognised as a civil partnership in English law.[38] The recognition of a same-sex marriage as a civil partnership was subject to challenge by a Canadian couple in *Wilkinson v Kitzinger*.[39] The lesbian couple had contracted a valid same-sex marriage in Canada and, on migrating to live in England, wished to have their marriage recognised, rather than having it recognised as a civil partnership. They alleged that the failure to recognise the marriage breached their Article 8 of the European Convention on Human Rights (ECHR) right to respect for their private and family life and their Article 14 ECHR right not to be discriminated against in relation to Article 8. The English court rejected these arguments, stating that the recognition of a foreign same-sex marriage as a civil partnership had been explicitly provided for by the legislature within the scheme of the Civil Partnership Act 2004 and fell within the margin of appreciation that signatories to the ECHR have in regulating family life.

The position of the litigants in *Wilkinson v Kitzinger* has been changed by the adoption of the Marriage (Same Sex Couples) Act 2013. A valid same-sex marriage celebrated in another country will be now recognised in England as a valid marriage,[40] subject to the same rules and obligations as a same-sex marriage concluded in England.

However, if a valid registered or civil partnership has been concluded under the law of another country, it will still be recognised as a civil partnership in England and Wales.[41] Section 216 of the Civil Partnership Act 2004 restricts the recognition of a civil partnership concluded abroad to same-sex partners because, in England, civil partnerships are only open to same-sex couples.[42] This means that some valid registered partnerships concluded between opposite-sex couples abroad will not be recognised in England and Wales under the Civil Partnership Act 2004 because the civil partnership status is not available to opposite-sex couples.[43] In other countries there exist legal statuses, other than marriage, such as the France PACS arrangement,[44] available to opposite-sex couples. These validly concluded legal statuses would not be recognised as a civil partnership under the Civil

---

[37] Pew Research Centre, 'Gay Marriage Around the World' (2015).

[38] Civil Partnership Act 2004, s. 215.   [39] [2007] 1 FLR 295.

[40] Marriage (Same Sex Couples) Act 2013, Sch 2, para 5.   [41] Civil Partnership Act 2004, s. 215.

[42] *Steinfeld v Secretary of State for Education* [2016] EWHC 128 (Admin).

[43] On the position between England and Scotland, see Norrie, K. 'Now the Dust has Settled: The Marriage and Civil Partnership (Scotland) Act 2014' (2014) 2 *Juridical Review* 135.

[44] Gaffney-Rhys, R. 'Same-sex Marriage but not Mixed-Sex Partnerships: Should the Civil Partnership Act 2004 be extended to opposite sex couples?' (2014) 26 *Child and Family Law Quarterly* 173.

Partnership Act 2004, but it is not yet clear if they would be recognised as equivalent to English marriage.[45]

The development of the law in this context demonstrates that the English court will not accept marriages celebrated abroad that do not accord with the English notion of marriage. However, as society and perceptions of the family evolve, the acceptability of new formalised relationships to English law also changes.

3.3.2 Polygamous marriages

Some countries permit polygamous marriages, where a husband may take more than one wife, a practice also known as polygamy. Few countries permit wives to take more than one husband, known as polyandry. *Hyde v Hyde and Woodmansee*[46] established that polygamous marriages were not a form of marriage acceptable to English law and would not be recognised if concluded abroad. In English family law, if a husband goes through a ceremony of marriage with more than one wife, the second marriage is void under s. 11(b) of the Matrimonial Causes Act 1973 and he is liable for the criminal offence of bigamy.[47] The historical resistance to polygamy as a form of marriage was strong in English law, but it caused significant difficulties for some communities who migrated to the UK from Asia, and there has been increased flexibility in the rules.

In recognising a marriage concluded abroad, the first question we have to consider is the form of the marriage. If the marriage is polygamous in form, the circumstances in which the marriage will be recognised in England requires further consideration. If the law of the place of celebration of the marriage permits polygamy as a form of valid marriage, the form of the marriage is polygamous.[48] If a country permits both polygamous and monogamous marriage forms, the type of ceremony adopted by the parties will determine its form. Even if a husband has contracted a marriage to only one wife, if the marriage was celebrated in a country permitting polygamy as a valid form of marriage, the marriage is polygamous in form. The marriage to a first wife is termed 'potentially polygamous' because the law governing the form of the marriage contemplates future marriages to additional wives. If a husband subsequently contracts a marriage to a second wife, the marriage is then 'actually polygamous'.

Following *Hyde v Hyde*,[49] the English court refused to recognise potentially polygamous marriages in English law, even if the husband had never taken a second wife. A person domiciled in England at the time of the marriage did not have capacity to contract a valid polygamous marriage and any marriage celebrated in a country adopting that form of marriage would not be recognised. This rule caused significant difficulties where members of British Asian communities married in a country permitting polygamy because their domicile meant that the marriage was not recognised in England, even if they never intended to take a second wife.

The English courts made attempts to mitigate the effects of this rule by applying the intended matrimonial home rule when the parties did not live in England.[50] In *Hussain v Hussain*[51] the Court held that if neither party to the marriage had capacity to take a second spouse under the law of their domicile, then the marriage could be recognised in English law. This meant that husbands domiciled in England but married abroad under a law permitting polygamy would have a valid marriage when they returned to England because they could not marry again under English law. However, wives domiciled in England

---

[45] Norrie, K. 'Recognition of Foreign Relationships under the Civil Partnership Act 2004' (2006) 2 *Journal of Private International Law* 137.   [46] (1865–69) L.R. 1 P&D 130.

[47] Offences Against the Person Act 1861, s. 57.   [48] *Lee v Lau* [1967] P. 14.

[49] (1865–69) L.R. 1 P&D 130.   [50] *Radwan v Radwan (No. 2)* [1973] Fam 35.

[51] [1983] Fam 26.

but married abroad under a law permitting polygamy would not have a valid marriage because, assuming their husband was domiciled in a country permitting polygamy, they would have capacity to take a second wife. This made the rule sexist in its application.

Eventually, Parliament intervened with statutory provision in 1995.

 Key Legislation 1: Private International Law (Miscellaneous Provisions) Act 1995, s. 5(1)

A marriage entered into outside England and Wales between persons neither of whom is already married is not void under English law on the ground that it was entered into under a law which permits polygamy and that either party is domiciled in England and Wales.

This section applies only to potentially polygamous marriages where the marriage was concluded under a law where the form of marriage was polygamous, but the husband has only one wife. In these circumstances, the marriage is recognised as valid in England, even if the spouses were domiciled in England. It does not apply to actually polygamous marriages, which will not be recognised in England if either party was domiciled in England at the time of the marriage under s. 11(d) of the Matrimonial Causes Act 1973. Restricting the scope of s. 5(1) to potentially polygamous marriages only keeps the form of English marriage between two spouses, but it can cause hardship where a second wife goes through a ceremony of marriage that will not be recognised as valid in England.[52]

The situation is different for marriages where the spouses were not domiciled in England. This would be the case for a marriage in Pakistan celebrated between Muslims domiciled in the country. If all spouses had capacity to contract a valid polygamous marriage under the law of their domicile at the time of the marriage, and they married in a country that permits polygamy, then the first and second marriages would both be valid. In these circumstances, English law will recognise the marriage as valid, including the second wife, even though it is actually polygamous.[53] Under s. 47 of the Matrimonial Causes Act 1973, the English court may grant matrimonial relief on both actually and potentially polygamous marriages. This rule reflects the fact that the parties, at the time of contracting the marriage, had no connection to English law and could not be expected to comply with the requirement of only one spouse. Once the parties have an English domicile however, they are prevented from contracting subsequent valid marriages.

 DEBATE 3: WHAT SHOULD HAPPEN WHEN DIFFERENT LEGAL SYSTEMS RECOGNISE DIFFERENT TYPES OF FAMILY RELATIONSHIP?

The English court has historically been resistant to the acceptance of polygamous marriage. English law will not accept religious marriages to an English second wife, and as a consequence second wives do not receive the protection of the law. This has arguably placed second wives in communities where the practice is acceptable in a vulnerable legal position as their marriage is not recognised by English law and may be regulated by religious means

---

[52] Walsh, K. 'Polygamous Marriages and Potentially Polygamous Marriages in Irish Law: A critical reappraisal' (2013) 36 *Dublin University Law Journal* 249, 251.

[53] *Mohamed v Knott* [1969] 1 QB 1.

only, not through the English civil law on divorce.[54] The reforms of s. 5(1) of the Private International Law (Miscellaneous Provisions) Act 1995 means that a potentially polygamous marriage contracted by an English domiciliary will be recognised, but there is no suggestion that an actually polygamous marriage will ever be recognised as valid. This prevents a person domiciled in England travelling abroad to avoid the restrictions in s. 11(d) of the Matrimonial Causes Act 1973 making a marriage void. Despite different cultural practices, English law has remained strongly supportive of the Christian tradition that marriage is exclusive between two spouses but, in adopting this approach, potentially exposes some religious second marriages to a lack of protection from the law.

4. Adults: cross-national divorce

It has been suggested that marital partners who have migrated or originate from different countries are more likely to divorce.[55] The laws relating to divorce vary greatly between countries depending on the religious and cultural history of the country. Some countries, such as China and Sweden, allow divorce when the spouses demand, without any demonstration of fault. English law, under s. 1 of the Matrimonial Causes Act 1973, permits divorce but the petitioner normally has to demonstrate fault for the divorce to be granted (see Chapter 3). Other countries, such as Ireland, limit access to divorce by requiring long separation periods before the divorce petition may be issued. Following a national referendum, Malta permitted divorce only in 2011. When spouses have links to different countries, identifying which court has jurisdiction to determine the divorce petition and the consequences of the divorce is important. Differences in national law, both in the ease of obtaining the divorce, and in the consequences of the divorce in dividing assets and arrangements for any children of the marriage, will have a significant impact on the spouses going forward after the end of the marriage. Family lawyers advising a client with links to more than one country will consider these factors carefully in deciding where to issue a divorce petition.

 CONTEXT 3: LONDON: DIVORCE CAPITAL OF THE WORLD?

The division of assets on divorce in England and Wales is governed by the Matrimonial Causes Act 1973. Following *Miller v Miller/McFarlane v McFarlane*[56] the court aims to achieve a fair outcome between the spouses, based on meeting the parties' needs, compensating for any economic disadvantage arising from the marriage, and sharing the assets (see Chapter 4 for more detail). The discretion the court has to adjust the financial assets between the parties makes the English jurisdiction a very desirable destination for economically weaker spouses, normally the wife, divorcing a rich spouse. The economically weaker spouses, if they have a connection to England, will attempt to issue proceedings in the English court and establish that court has jurisdiction over the divorce to access the discretion of the English court over the division of the assets. The richer spouse will normally try and issue proceedings in an

[54] Ahmed, F. and Calderwood Norton, J. 'Religious Tribunals, Religious Freedom, and Concern for Vulnerable Women' (2012) 24 *Child and Family Law Quarterly* 364.

[55] Morano-Foadi, S. 'Problems and Challenges in Researching Bi-National Migrant Families within the European Union' (2007) 21 *International Journal of Law, Policy and the Family* 1.   [56] [2006] 2 AC 618.

alternative jurisdiction. The attraction of divorcing in England has led to the suggestion that England is the divorce capital of the world.[57]

This has led to disputes over the jurisdiction of the English court in a number of very high profile divorce cases with limited connection to England.[58] The parties will expend a lot of money litigating over where the divorce should be heard, before the substantive issues of division of assets are considered. An exorbitant use of the English jurisdiction over divorce can mean that cases are heard in a country where the spouses have no true links and would not have expected to have the divorce heard. In these circumstances, the interpretation of the connecting factors, linking the parties to the jurisdiction, is highly important to ensure there is an appropriate connection between the English court and the divorce proceedings.

4.1 Jurisdiction over divorce petitions

4.1.1 Brussels II revised and residual jurisdiction in English law

For a divorce petition to be heard in England, the English court must have jurisdiction over the case. One or both spouses must have a connection to England before the English court may assume jurisdiction. Under s. 5(2) of the Domicile and Matrimonial Proceedings Act 1973 the English court has jurisdiction only if it has jurisdiction under BIIR,[59] or, if no EU Member State has jurisdiction under BIIR and one of the parties to the marriage is domiciled in England at the date of issuing proceedings.[60] The primary grounds of jurisdiction are now under Article 3 BIIR.[61] Residual jurisdiction under Articles 6 and 7 BIIR only arises where the respondent is not habitually resident in a Member State, is not a national of a Member State, is not domiciled in the UK or Ireland, but the applicant is domiciled in England.

 Key Legislation 2: Article 3 BIIR

In matters relating to divorce, jurisdiction shall lie with the courts of the Member State in whose territory:

- The spouses are habitually resident, or
- The spouses were last habitually resident, insofar as one of them still resides there, or
- The respondent is habitually resident, or
- In the event of a joint application, either of the spouses is habitually resident, or
- The applicant is habitually resident if he or she resided there for at least a year immediately before the application was made, or

---

[57] Thorpe, M. 'London—The Divorce Capital of the World' [2009] *Family Law* 21.

[58] *Tan Sri Dr Khoo Peng v Pauline Siew Phin Chai* [2015] EWCA Civ 1312.

[59] Article 1(1) BIIR states that the Regulation also covers petitions for nullity and legal separation.

[60] See *A v L* [2009] EWHC 1448 (Fam).

[61] No changes to these grounds are proposed by the Commission in its reforms to BIIR. European Commission 'Proposal for a Council Regulation on jurisdiction, the recognition and enforcement of decisions in matrimonial matters and the matters of parental responsibility, and on international child abduction (recast)' COM(2016) 411/2.

- The applicant is habitually resident if he or she resided there for at least six months immediately before the application was made and is either a national of the Member State in question, or, in the case of the United Kingdom and Ireland, has his or her 'domicile' there, or
- Of the nationality of both spouses, or in the case of the United Kingdom and Ireland, of the 'domicile' of both spouses.

Article 3 provides seven alternative grounds of jurisdiction without any hierarchy. No one ground has precedence over any other. If the connecting factors are proved, for example, that both spouses are habitually resident in England at the time of issuance of the divorce petition, then the English court has jurisdiction over their divorce. The key connecting factor used in Article 3 BIIR is habitual residence (see section 2.2.2),[62] used in all the grounds except for the final one based on joint nationality or domicile. Domicile bears its traditional meaning under English law, so most adults will have a domicile of choice (see section 2.2.1). The respondent to the divorce petition is protected by the grounds in requiring the applicant to petition in the respondent's habitual residence, unless there is a joint application, or the applicant has resided in their habitual residence for a significant period.

4.1.2 Principle of *lis pendens*

The seven alternative grounds listed in Article 3 BIIR potentially give the applicant for a divorce a choice regarding the jurisdiction in which they issue a petition depending on the connections of the parties to different countries. For example, a marital couple, both of whom are of German nationality, emigrate to London to live and work. The marriage breaks down and the husband takes a job in France where he has lived for a year. If the husband petitions for divorce, several courts may have jurisdiction over the application. As the couple are both of German nationality, the petition could be issued in the German courts under ground 7 of Article 3, the joint nationality of both parties. The last common habitual residence of the couple is England, where they lived and worked, and the wife still lives there, so the husband could issue proceedings in England under ground 2 of Article 3. Finally, if he is habitually resident in France and has been resident there for a year, the husband could issue proceedings in France under ground 5 of Article 3.

In Case C-168/08 *Hadadi*[63] the Court of Justice of the European Union clarified that where several grounds of jurisdiction under Article 3 potentially apply, it is for the applicant to choose where to issue divorce proceedings. This means that the applicant for a divorce has significant control over which jurisdiction they choose for their divorce. Given the differences in national laws on divorce, a well advised applicant will most likely attempt to issue proceedings in the most beneficial jurisdiction for their legal and financial interests after the divorce, a practice known as forum shopping.[64] This element of choice can lead to a competition between spouses over where the divorce should be heard. Where proceedings for divorce are issued in the courts of two different countries, there has to be a way of resolving which court has the authority to grant the divorce. In BIIR this is resolved by the principle of *lis pendens* under Article 19 BIIR.

---

[62] *Marinos v Marinos* [2007] EWHC 2047 (Fam).   [63] EU:C:2009:474, at [53].

[64] Shuilleabhain, M.N. 'Ten Years of European Family Law: Retrospective Reflections from a Common Law Perspective' (2010) 59 *International and Comparative Law Quarterly* 1021, 1031.

Key Legislation 3: Article 19 BIIR, *lis pendens*

Article 19 states:

Where proceedings relating to divorce ... between the same parties are brought before the courts of different Member States, the court second siesed shall of its own motion stay proceedings until such time as the jurisdiction of the court first seised is established.

Article 19 governs the situation where proceedings are issued for a divorce in two different jurisdictions, for example, if the wife issues a petition for divorce in England, and the husband issues a petition for divorce in France. In these circumstances, the court first seised, where proceedings were issued first in time, takes priority. The court second seised is expected to halt proceedings and wait for the first in time court to either accept jurisdiction under Article 3 BIIR, hear and grant the divorce, or decline jurisdiction if none of the grounds under Article 3 BIIR are made out. If the wife issued proceedings first in England, the English court would be first seised and would take priority in hearing the divorce petition.

Article 19 governs the priority between courts when a court has been seised of proceedings. There needs to be existing proceedings for a divorce court to remain seised, so if an application is required to revive proceedings, the court is not seised.[65] To identify which court was seised first in time, it is necessary to establish when a court is seised of proceedings. Article 16 BIIR establishes that a court is 'seised' of proceedings when the documents instituting proceedings are lodged at the court, or if service is required before lodging the petition, at the time when it is received by the authority responsible for service. The relevant time is the moment when the document instituting proceedings is lodged at the court, even if that document is not sufficient to institute proceedings under national law.[66]

The principle of *lis pendens* applies only when the two courts seised of proceedings are in EU Member States.[67] When the English court has been seised of a divorce petition, but the other spouse has issued proceedings in a non-EU Member State court, in Australia for example, the English court has refused to apply the principle of *lis pendens*.[68] Instead, the English law principle of *forum non conveniens* is applied.[69] Under this principle, the English court exercises its discretion to stay proceedings in favour of a more appropriate forum.[70] If a party claims there is a more appropriate forum to resolve the dispute than the English court, the English court will stay proceedings if the other forum has a real and substantial connection to the dispute.[71] To establish a real and substantial connection, factors such as connections of the parties, convenience of proceedings, and expense will be considered. If there is another forum which is more appropriate for the proceedings, a stay of the English proceedings will normally be granted unless justice requires a hearing in England. This principle gives the English court discretion to examine practical factors in relation to the divorce litigation and stay proceedings where the proceedings are more closely connected to a different country, even if the English proceedings were issued first in time.

---

[65] *C v S (Divorce: Jurisdiction)* [2010] EWHC 2676 (Fam).

[66] Case C-173/16 *MH v MH* EU:C:2016:542.

[67] Domicile and Matrimonial Proceedings Act 1973, Sch 1, para 9.

[68] *JKN v JCN* [2010] EWHC 843 (Fam). The alternative jurisdiction was New York.

[69] *AB v CB (Divorce and Maintenance: Discretion to Stay)* [2013] EWCA Civ 1255. The alternative jurisdiction was India. See Amos, T, and Brooks, D. 'Divorce Proceedings, *Forum Conveniens* and Stays: England Still Open for Business in the Wider World' (2014) 36 *Journal of Social Welfare and Family Law* 76.

[70] *Spiliada Maritime Corporation v Cansulex Ltd* [1987] AC 460.

[71] *The Abidin Daver* [1984] AC 198, 415.

DEBATE 4: WHICH COUNTRY'S COURTS AND FAMILY LAW SHOULD
GOVERN FAMILY RELATIONSHIPS WHERE MEMBERS OF
A FAMILY HAVE LINKS TO A COUNTRY OTHER THAN
ENGLAND?

The connections international couples develop to different countries as they migrate means
that, if their marriage breaks down they may be able to issue a petition for divorce in more
than one jurisdiction. Article 3 BIIR facilitates this opportunity by providing several alternative grounds of jurisdiction. Spouses will attempt to issue proceedings in the jurisdiction
most advantageous to their financial and personal interests after the divorce, leading to com-
petitions over jurisdiction. The principle of *lis pendens* under Article 19 encourages parties to
issue proceedings quickly to be first in time and ensure they litigate in their chosen jurisdiction. The use of *lis pendens* potentially encourages spouses to issue a divorce petition, rather
than try to resolve their differences with their spouse. This does not always ensure that the
case is heard in the country with the closest connection to the marriage, but instead in the
country where proceedings are issued first in time.[72]

The *lis pendens* rule provides certainty in application; once proceedings have been issued
and a court is seised it is clear that the court first seised takes priority. However, this certainty
may not mean that the country with the closest connection to the divorce hears proceedings,
instead encouraging the parties to seek the court likely to grant them the most advantageous
arrangements after the divorce. The alternative approach would be to enable the parties to dispute over which court is best placed to hear a divorce petition, potentially making proceedings
lengthy and more expensive, but more considered. Arguably Article 19 does not encourage the
parties to consider their marital dispute carefully, potentially pushing them towards the divorce
court, rather than seeking to reconcile their differences and maintain the marriage, which is
normally regarded as desirable. However, the law draws a certain, bright line rule of priority in
adopting *lis pendens*, despite its practical consequences in causing a rush to jurisdiction.

4.2 Choice of law on divorce

Once the English court has jurisdiction over the divorce, English law will be applied to the
divorce petition and the associated proceedings for ancillary financial relief.[73] The English
court applies the law of the forum,[74] English law, to all divorce petitions because it would
be unacceptable to public policy to apply foreign law on a field as socially and culturally
defined as divorce.

4.3 Jurisdiction over ancillary relief for foreign divorces

If the spouses have divorced abroad,[75] the English court can assume jurisdiction over
the financial consequences of the divorce under s.15 of the Matrimonial and Family

---

[72] Bradley, C. 'The *Lis Pendens* Rules under Brussels II: Certainty over Flexibility?' [2015] 3 *International
Family Law* 197.

[73] In civil law jurisdictions in the EU, it is possible to apply a foreign law to the granting and consequents
of divorce under Regulation 1250/2010 implementing enhanced cooperation in the area of the law applicable
to divorce and legal separation [2010] OJ L343/10. The UK opted out of this Regulation and it does not bind
the English courts.

[74] Matrimonial Causes Act 1973, s. 46(2) repealed by s. 17(2) and Sch 6 of the Domicile and Matrimonial
Proceedings Act 1973 without affecting the principle that the law of the forum will be applied to divorce proceedings in England.

[75] On validity of the marriage prior to the divorce, see *Shagroon v Sharbatly* [2012] EWCA Civ 1507.

Proceedings Act 1984. The English court can assume jurisdiction if either spouse was domiciled, or habitually resident for a year, in England on the date of application for leave or on the date the divorce took effect in the foreign jurisdiction, or if either party had a beneficial interest in a property in England that acted as the matrimonial home. To obtain the leave of the English court, the applicant is required to demonstrate 'substantial ground' for the application.[76] This statutory provision is designed to protect individuals from the consequences of a divorce granted in another country that fails to make adequate financial provision for one spouse. The court may only assume jurisdiction if England is an appropriate jurisdiction,[77] having regard to all the circumstances of the case and the welfare of any children.[78] The primary concern is the welfare of any children, and if the English court assumes jurisdiction, it will provide for the reasonable needs of the applicant spouse.[79] The provisions of the Matrimonial and Family Proceedings Act 1984 should not be used to enable a spouse with a connection to England to adjust the division of assets made in a foreign court in their favour, but if the connections with England are very strong, the court may make an order in accordance with the principles of domestic law under Part II of the Matrimonial Causes Act 1973 (see Chapter 4).

5. Children: cross-national family arrangements

A child may develop international family links either as their parents migrate to a different country and they migrate with them, or in circumstances where their parents live in different countries to another and the child spends time with both parents. When the parents have separated, the questions regarding who is to care for the child and what arrangements can be made for effective contact and access for the parents (see Chapter 9) to the child take on an additional cross-national dimension. Identifying who has legal responsibilities in relation to the child, who the child lives with, and how contact is arranged with a parent in another country become more complex because a judgment governing these arrangements is issued in one country but will have effects in another country. We need to know when the English court has jurisdiction over any parental responsibility dispute, and whether a judgment issued in another country regarding the arrangements for the care of a child will be effective in England. Where a judgment on parental responsibility arrangements is issued abroad, the English court will be asked to recognise the judgment as having legal effect, and to enforce the judgment, ensuring compliance with its terms. Judgements are still referred to as 'parental responsibility', 'custody', or 'access' judgments in the international context.

 DEBATE 5: HOW CAN THE LAW HELP FAMILIES TO MANAGE RELATIONSHIPS WHEN FAMILY MEMBERS LIVE IN DIFFERENT COUNTRIES?

The challenge for family lawyers is that countries adopt different approaches to family arrangements to care for children after the parents' relationship has dissolved. The best interests of the child under Article 8 ECHR, and Article 3 of the UN Convention of the Rights of the Child 1990 (UNCRC) should be a primary consideration in decision-making in relation

---

[76] Matrimonial and Family Proceedings Act 1984, s. 13.
[77] Matrimonial and Family Proceedings Act 1984, s. 16.
[78] Matrimonial and Family Proceedings Act 1984, s. 18.
[79] *Agbaje v Akinnoye-Agbaje* [2010] UKSC 13.

to the child. In the EU, this obligation is reinforced by Article 24(2) Charter of Fundamental Rights of the European Union.[80] The court making the decision should hear from the child if the child is of an appropriate age and maturity.[81] The arrangements for hearing a child in court proceedings vary greatly between different countries, as does the age at which children are normally heard in proceedings (see Chapter 9).

The decisions over the arrangements for a child where the parents live in different countries should be taken in their best interests by the courts of a country that has a connection to the child so that evidence may be taken about the issues affecting their welfare, including education, medical history, and potential arrangements for care. The circumstances of the child will change over time as the child ages and their needs adjust. However, where the parents of a child live in different countries, or have different social, cultural, and religious backgrounds, they may have very different expectations about the arrangements suitable for the care of their child. The concept of the child's best interests and hearing the child in proceedings may vary depending on the culture and legal system adjudicating on matters relating the child. Whilst the standards of decision-making are the same, the reasoning of different national courts may vary.

The links to different countries may mean that parents attempt to adjust legal arrangements in a different legal jurisdiction, or move a child abroad away from the other parent, to access decisions of another legal system. The English court has to respect the connections a child may have to a foreign country, but where a child is at risk of harm, or has closer links to England must act in the child's best interests to protect them.[82]

5.1 Jurisdiction over children

Determining whether the court has jurisdiction over the child should link the child to the place where the dispute is to be heard to facilitate hearing the child and the availability of relevant, up-to-date evidence about the child's welfare. Under s. 2(1) of the Family Law Act 1996, the English court should not make an order over a child unless it has jurisdiction under BIIR, or the Hague Convention on Jurisdiction, Applicable Law, Recognition, Enforcement and Cooperation in Respect of Parental Responsibility and Measures for the Protection of Children 1996. If the English court does not have jurisdiction under either of these measures, under s. 2(3) of the Family Law Act 1996, if the child is present in England and the court considers the exercise of its powers necessary for the child's protection, it may assume jurisdiction.

If the child is habitually resident in an EU Member State, then the rules of jurisdiction under BIIR will apply. If the child is habitually resident in a country outside the EU that is bound by the Hague Convention 1996 then the provisions of the Convention will apply. If the provisions of BIIR or the Hague Convention 1996 do not apply, then s. 2(3) of the Family Law Act 1996 will apply.

5.1.1 Jurisdictional provisions of BIIR

BIIR applies to decisions relating to parental responsibility, including care proceedings under public law including placing the child in institutional care or foster care.[83] Article 1(3) BIIR states that it does not apply to establishing the status of parent, adoption, decisions over the naming of a child, succession, or maintenance obligations. (For cross-national

---

[80] [2010] OJ C83/396.   [81] Article 24(1) EU Charter; Article 12 UNCRC.

[82] McGlynn, C.M.S. *Families and the European Union: Law, Politics and Pluralism* (Cambridge University Press, 2006).   [83] Case C-435/06 C [2007] ECR I-10141.

maintenance obligations, see Chapter 6). BIIR therefore applies to jurisdiction over both private and public law disputes under the Children Act 1989. The aim of the Regulation is to provide uniform grounds of jurisdiction across the EU so that judgments issued by EU Member States will be recognised in all the other states as easily as possible with minimum legal formalities.

 Key Legislation 4: Article 8 BIIR

Article 8 states:

> The courts of a member State shall have jurisdiction in matters of parental responsibility over a child who is habitually resident in that Member State at the time the court is seised.

Article 8 is the general ground of jurisdiction, and the court with jurisdiction is the place where there child is habitually resident.[84] If the child is habitually resident in England when the proceedings are issued, the English court will have jurisdiction over proceedings (see 2.2.2 on interpretation of habitual residence). The child's habitual residence is regarded as the country with which the child has the closest connection and the most appropriate jurisdiction to hear any dispute as they should be resident and information about their welfare will be available. All the other grounds of jurisdiction in BIIR are exceptions to this primary rule.

The general ground of jurisdiction is made subject to a number of exceptions under the terms of BIIR when it may be more suitable and appropriate to hear a case in a different jurisdiction. Where more than one court is seised of the same issue of parental responsibility, the principle of *lis pendens* applies, so the court first seised takes priority.[85]

Article 9 BIIR permits the retention of jurisdiction by the country of the child's former habitual residence after the child has migrated to another country only for the purpose of amending rights of access for three months after the child's habitual residence has changed.

Article 12(1) grants jurisdiction over parental responsibility to the court of a Member State exercising jurisdiction under Article 3 BIIR for the purpose of divorce proceedings. One of the spouses must have parental responsibility over the child, the assumption of jurisdiction must be in the 'superior interests of the child',[86] and the parties must expressly accept jurisdiction in the same court over the parental responsibility dispute.[87] This is a sensible ground of jurisdiction, enabling the court hearing a divorce petition to also assume jurisdiction over future arrangements in relation to the affected children. Under Article 12(2) BIIR, jurisdiction under Article 12(1) ceases when the divorce proceedings are concluded, or if parental responsibility proceedings are yet to conclude, when judgment has been delivered.

Alternatively, under Article 12(3) BIIR a court, other than those of the child's habitual residence, has a 'substantial connection' with that Member State either, if a holder of parental responsibility is habitually resident in that Member State, or the child is a national of that State, can have jurisdiction over the child. So, if the child is habitually resident in England but is a national of the Czech Republic, proceedings could be issued in the Czech Republic under Article 12(3) BIIR.[88] The jurisdiction of the alternative court must

---

[84] Case C-523/07 *A* [2009] ECR I-02805.   [85] Article 19(2) BIIR.

[86] This phrase is equivalent to 'the best interests of the child', *VC v GC* [2012] EWHC 1246.

[87] *Bush v Bush* [2008] EWCA Civ 865.

[88] Article 12(3) is an independent ground of jurisdiction over a parental responsibility dispute; no other extant proceedings are required in the alternative country, Case C-656/13 *L v M* EU:C:2014:2364.

be accepted by all parties to the proceedings and be in the best interests of the child. Even if the holders of parental responsibility mutually agree to the assumption of juris-diction under Article 12(3), a review in each case must be conducted of whether pro-rogation of jurisdiction is in the child's best interests.[89] Once judgment has been issued under proceedings issued under Article 12(3) BIIR, jurisdiction ceases and the court of the child's habitual residence may assume jurisdiction under Article 8 BIIR over subse-quent proceedings.[90]

Where the child's habitual residence cannot be established, for example if they are a refugee, then jurisdiction may be assumed under Article 13 BIIR on the basis of the child's presence. This is a catch all provision to ensure that a child present in the EU falls within the protective scope of BIIR. For a child present in the jurisdiction, but not habitually resident, and in need of emergency protection, the country where the child is currently present may adopt provisional, protective measures over the child under Article 20 BIIR. Article 20 enables the English court to adopt temporary protective orders over a child such as an emergency protection order or in some circumstances an interim care order under the Children Act 1989 (see Chapter 11). For example, if a child is on holiday in another Member State and their parents are killed in a car accident, provisional protective measures may be adopted to arrange for the temporary care of the child until they return to their habitual residence and longer-term arrangements may be made. Article 20 is an exception to the general rule that decisions over a child should be made by the courts of the child's habitual residence and the requirements should be strictly interpreted.[91] There is risk that Member States will use Article 20 to assert their own jurisdiction over a child and avoid the normal jurisdictional provisions of BIIR. The need to adopt measures over the child must be urgent and the measures adopted must have only a temporary effect to protect the child until the habitual residence court has the opportunity to assume jurisdic-tion over the child.[92]

Even if jurisdiction is assumed under Article 8 on the basis of the child's habitual resi-dence, it is possible under Article 15 BIIR for the English court to transfer jurisdiction to another Member State court better placed to hear the case. The transfer must be to a country with which the child has a particular connection, such as their former habitual residence or the country of their nationality,[93] and the transfer must be in the best interests of the child. An application for a transfer may be initiated by the parties or by the court[94] and the country to which the case is to be transferred must consider that assumption of jurisdiction is in the best interests of the child.[95] All elements of Article 15 must be made out before the English court can authorise transfer of jurisdiction to another jurisdiction.[96] There must be a substantial connection between the child and alternative jurisdiction, as defined by the Regulation. The alternative court must be 'better placed' to hear the case. This requires consideration of factual issues, such as location of evidence, language of the case, and availability of parties as witnesses. Consideration of whether the transfer is in the best interests is a separate issue taking into account all circumstances affecting the child, including an assessment of the longer-term welfare outcomes for the child of transferring the case to another country.[97]

[89] Case C-436/14 E EU:C:2014:2246, at [47].

[90] Re S (A Child) Jurisdiction: Brussels II Revised: Prorogation) [2013] EWHC 647 (Fam); Case C-436/14 E EU:C:2014:2246.

[91] Case C-523/07 A [2009] 2 ECR I-2805.

[92] Case C-403/09 PPU Deticek [2009] ECR I-12193.   [93] Article 15(3) BIIR.

[94] Article 15(1) BIIR.   [95] Article 15(5) BIIR.   [96] AB v JLB [2008] EWHC 2965 (Fam).

[97] Re J (Children) (Brussels II Revised: Article 15) [2016] UKSC 15. See also AG Opinion C-428/15 Child and Family Agency EU:C:2016:458.

CONTEXT 4: CHILD PROTECTION AND THE TRANSFER OF PROCEEDINGS

Article 15 BIIR has assumed importance in the practice relating to child protection where a child is a national of another Member State of the EU and is identified as at risk of harm in England under s 31(2) of the Children Act 1989.[98] If the child is habitually resident in England under Article 8 BIIR, the English court may adopt orders under Children Act 1989 to protect the child[99] in England. This has caused considerable political controversy when parents from other EU Member States have had their children removed for their protection, and eventually adopted in England.[100] The question of whether jurisdiction over the care proceedings should be transferred to the country of the child's nationality under Article 15 BIIR should always be considered in care proceedings involving a foreign national child.[101] However, there have been practical difficulties in the process for transferring jurisdiction to the foreign court,[102] and concerns expressed over the differences in law and practice in relation to child protection in the different Member States of the EU. In English care proceedings, the English court has been increasingly willing to transfer jurisdiction over a child national to another Member State to respect the interest of the other country in protecting their nationals, but this should only occur when transfer is in the child's best interests.[103]

In *Bristol CC v HA*[104] the child, HA, was an 8-year-old Lithuanian boy who had travelled to the UK with his mother. There was evidence that the mother had been trafficked into the UK and was suffering from alcoholism, affecting her ability to care for HA who was suffering neglect. HA was made subject to an interim care order for his protection and was living with foster carers in England. The English court ordered that the Lithuanian court was better placed to hear the care proceedings and sought transfer jurisdiction over the case to Lithuania in HA's best interests. The Lithuanian court failed to assume jurisdiction over HA's case and did not accept the transfer. HA had now been living in England with foster carers for two years. His first foster placement had broken down as he began to act out behaviours associated with the abuse he had experienced. The local authority applied again to the English court for a care order over HA. Given the change in HA's circumstances, the English court was now better placed to take decisions over HA in his best interests and would assume jurisdiction over the decision relating to a care order. This case demonstrates how difficult cooperation between two countries and legal systems can be, even when a child is deemed to be at risk. The cases have caused significant political controversy. Where a child is at risk, the English court is obliged to act for the child's protection, but if the child is a foreign national, other countries have expressed concern regarding the English courts' intervention.[105]

[98] Lamont, R. 'Care Proceedings with a European Dimension under Brussels IIa: Jurisdiction, Mutual Trust and the Best Interests of the Child' (2016) 28 *Child and Family Law Quarterly* 67.

[99] Adoption proceedings fall outside the scope of BIIR, see *CG (A Child)* [2015] EWCA Civ 888.

[100] Bowcott, O. 'Lithuanian MPs petition Lords Speaker over child custody case', *The Guardian* 12 May 2015. Available at: http://www.theguardian.com/society/2015/may/12/lithuanian-mps-lords-speaker-child-custody-case, accessed 2 October 2017.

[101] *In Re E (A Child) (Care Proceedings: European Dimension) Practice Note* [2014] EWHC 6 (Fam).

[102] *Re HA (A Child) (Brussels IIA Art. 15)* [2015] EWHC 1310 (Fam).

[103] *Re J (Children) (Brussels II Revised: Article 15)* [2016] UKSC 15.

[104] [2014] EWHC 1022 (Fam); [2015] EWHC 1310 (Fam).

[105] Lamont, R. and McGlynn, C. 'Cross-Border Care and Adoption Proceedings in the European Union' (2016) 38 *Journal of Social Welfare and Family Law* 94.

5.1.2 The Hague Convention on Jurisdiction, Applicable law, Recognition, Enforcement and Cooperation in Respect of Parental Responsibility and Measures for the Protection of Children 1996

The Hague Convention 1996 is designed to ensure that a court will have jurisdiction over a child in any circumstance to ensure their protection. Jurisdiction is normally assumed under Article 5 of the 1996 Convention, based on the habitual residence of the child as this is the place with which the child has the closest factual connection.

In defined circumstances, jurisdiction may be assumed on alternative grounds.[106] Under Article 10, the courts of a contracting state holding jurisdiction over divorce proceedings may also assume jurisdiction over an associated parental responsibility dispute. One of the child's parents must be habitually resident in that state and hold parental responsibility over the child, all holders of parental responsibility must agree to the court assuming jurisdiction, and the assumption of jurisdiction must be in the best interests of the child.

A case may be transferred to a more appropriate jurisdiction where the alternative court is better placed to assess the best interests of the child under Article 8 Hague Convention 1996. The alternative jurisdiction must have a substantial connection to the child, or the child must be a national of the country, or hold property within the jurisdiction. The alternative court must consider whether transfer is in the child's best interests before assuming jurisdiction over the case.

In all cases of urgency, measures may be adopted in relation to a child who is present in the territory, but not habitually resident, under Article 11 Hague Convention 1996. The concept of 'urgency' is not defined, nor is the scope of the measures adopted. Jurisdiction under Article 11 lasts until the court in the country where the child is habitually resident assumes jurisdiction over the child. The UK Supreme Court in *Re J (A Child)*[107] stated that Article 11 requires urgency, presence of the child in the territory, and circumstances making measures of protection necessary. The court assuming jurisdiction under Article 11 should not make decisions that properly belong to the jurisdiction of the child's habitual residence.

The Hague Convention 1996 has only recently been ratified by the UK and new signatories to the Convention are expected to develop the law and practice under its provisions.[108] If the UK is no longer bound by the provisions of BIIR following withdrawal from the European Union, all Member States of the EU are also signatories of the 1996 Convention,[109] and the Convention is then likely to assume much greater importance in English practice.

5.2 Choice of law

The English court traditionally applies English domestic law to the resolution of disputes over children. This is confirmed by Article 15(1) Hague Convention 1996 which states that

---

[106] Where the child's habitual residence cannot be determined, or the child is a refugee, jurisdiction may be assumed over the child on the basis of presence under Article 6 Hague Convention 1996. Where there a child has been abducted (see section6), Article 7 provides for the continuance of jurisdiction of the child's habitual residence prior to the wrongful removal or retention.

[107] [2015] UKSC 70, at [33].

[108] Scarano, N. 'Protection of Children and the 1996 Hague Convention' (2016) 38 *Journal of Social Welfare and Family Law* 205.

[109] Council Decision 2003/93 authorising the Member States, in the interest of the Community, to sign the 1996 Hague Convention on jurisdiction, applicable law, recognition, enforcement and cooperation in respect of parental responsibility and measures for the protection of children [2003] OJ L48.

contracting states will apply their own law to disputes.[110] This enables the English court to apply provisions with which it is familiar and considerations that may be highly contextual to national law.

5.3 Recognition of foreign judgments on parental responsibility

Recognising a judgment originating from a legal system other than England means that the English court accepts that it is a legal judgment having legal effects and consequences. Enforcement is the process of giving effect to the legal judgment. If a judgment over parental responsibility made in France is recognised and enforced in England, the English court will ensure that the requirements of the judgment are complied with in England.

Deciding whether a foreign judgment will be recognised in England depends upon the country from which the judgment originated. The first question we have to ask is which country issued the judgment. If the judgment was delivered in an EU Member State covered by BIIR, it will be recognised under that Regulation. If the judgment originates from a country that is bound by the Hague Convention 1996, the judgment will be recognised under the Convention. If the judgment originates from any country not bound by these arrangements, the judgment will be recognised under the traditional English common law rules.

5.3.1 Recognition of foreign judgments under BIIR

The aim of BIIR was to make the recognition of judgments on the family as simple as possible between EU Member States so that EU citizens could be confident that a judgment relating to their children would be effective to govern their family arrangements in more than one country as they migrated. Under Article 21 BIIR, a judgment given in one Member State shall be recognised in the other Member States without any special procedure being required.

There are limited defences to the recognition of a parental responsibility judgment under Article 23 BIIR. Article 23(e) and (f) address the situation where there are irreconcilable judgments and Article 23(d) covers the circumstances where a holder of parental responsibility over the child was not given the opportunity to be heard in proceedings. If a judgment was given in default of appearance in court because the person served was not issued with documents in time, then recognition of the judgment may be refused in England under Article 23(c) BIIR.[111]

Under Article 23(a), if recognition is manifestly contrary to public policy, taking account of the best interests of the child, then it may be refused. It is a high hurdle to establish this defence; recognition of the judgment must be manifestly contrary to public policy and it will only be successful in exceptional circumstances.[112] The Court of Justice of the European Union in Case C-455/15 *P*[113] has made it clear that there must be a manifest breach of the best interests of the child in the judgment, an essential rule of law of the Member State, or a fundamental right. The Court stated that:

> Recourse to the public policy rule in Article 23(a) should only come into consideration where, taking into account the best interests of the child, recognition of the judgment given in another Member State would be at variance to an unacceptable degree with the legal order of the State where recognition is sought, in that it would infringe a fundamental principle.

---

[110] This is extended to cover decisions following the assumption of jurisdiction under BIIR by the Parental Responsibility and Measures for the Protection of Children (International Obligations) Regulations 2010 (SI 2010/1898).

[111] *MD v CT (Parental Responsibility Order: Recognition and Enforcement of Foreign Judgment)* [2014] EWHC 871 (Fam).

[112] *Re L (A Child)* [2012] EWCA Civ 1157.   [113] EU:C:2015:763, at [39].

The final defence to recognition of a foreign judgment in England under BIIR is that, except in urgent cases, it was given without the child having been given an opportunity to be heard, in violation of the fundamental principles of procedure in the recognising state under Article 23(b) BIIR.

 Key Case 4: *Re D (A Child) (Recognition and Enforcement of a Romanian Order* [2016] EWCA Civ 12

The child, D, was 9 years old and had lived with his mother in England since birth. Both parents were Romanian in origin and the father still lived in Romania. The father brought custody proceedings in the Romanian courts and was awarded custody of D. He sought to have the judgment awarding him custody recognised in England. D was aged 7 at the time of proceedings, but was not heard in the Romanian court proceedings.

The English Court of Appeal[114] decided that under Article 23(b) BIIR the judgment would not be recognised because D had not been given the opportunity to be heard in the Romanian proceedings in violation of a fundamental rule of procedure. The mother had also not been served with documents in time to prepare a defence to the Romanian proceedings under Article 23(c) BIIR.

> A principle that is of universal application consistent with our international obligations under Article 12 of the United Nations Convention on the Rights of the Child is on its face a fundamental principle. In every case, the court is required to ensure that the child is given the opportunity to be heard. This means asking the questions, whether and if so how is the child to be heard. Furthermore, the provisions of Article 24 of the Charter of Fundamental Rights are directly applicable with the consequence that the court is required to ask the question I have identified ([41] Ryder LJ).

Whilst the threshold to refusal of recognition of a foreign judgment under BIIR is high, the importance of the fundamental principle that a child of appropriate age and maturity should be heard in proceedings meant that recognition of a judgment delivered in breach of this procedure would be refused in England. The Romanian custody judgment was therefore not recognised in England.

In the overwhelming majority of cases, judgments on parental responsibility issued in one Member State will be recognised in another Member State. The English court cannot refuse the recognition of a judgment under BIIR on the basis that the judgment would not be the same under English law,[115] and the judgment cannot be reviewed as to its substance.[116]

5.3.2 Recognition of foreign judgments under the Hague Convention 1996

Article 23(1) Hague Convention 1996 states: 'The measures taken by the authorities of a Contracting State shall be recognised by operation of law in all other Contracting States.' A judgment on parental responsibility in relation to a child emanating from a state bound by the 1996 Convention should be recognised in England.

Defences to the recognition of a judgment under the Convention are listed under Article 23(2) Hague Convention 1996. Recognition of a judgment may be refused if the court issuing judgment did not have jurisdiction to do so under the terms of the 1996

---

[114] Leave to appeal to the UK Supreme Court has been refused, see *Re D (A Child) (Supreme Court: Jurisdiction)* [2016] UKSC 34.　　　　　　　　　　　　　　　　　　　　　　　　[115] Article 25 BIIR.

[116] Article 26 BIIR.

Convention. It may also be refused if there are irreconcilable judgments, or a holder of parental responsibility was not given an opportunity to be heard in proceedings. If recognition of the judgment is manifestly contrary to public policy, taking account of the best interests of the child, it may be refused. There is, as yet, little authority on the interpretation of Article 23(b), but the phrasing of the public policy defence to recognition means that it is likely to be strictly interpreted by the English courts. Article 23 also provides a defence to recognition of a judgment where the child was not given an opportunity to be heard in violation of the fundamental rules of procedure of England. This was successfully cited in defence of recognition of a Russian judgment in *G v G*.[117]

5.3.3 Recognition of foreign judgments under the English common law rules

Under the English common law, the English court can make any order it regards as necessary to secure the child's welfare under s. 1(1) of the Children Act 1989. This has meant that, despite the existence of a foreign custody order, the English court can review the content of the foreign order and is not obligated to recognise it.[118] Decisions over children are never final orders because they may need to be varied as the circumstances of the child change over time. However, in practice, if the foreign judgment is recent and the circumstances of the child have not greatly changed, the decision of the foreign court will carry weight with the English court and it is unlikely to adjust the judgment.[119]

6. Children: international parental child abduction

Ease of travel and migration has created a situation where many families will have links to other countries. When the relationship between a child's parents breaks down, one parent may wish to move with the child to another country, either to return to their home country, or migrating in a new relationship, or simply to make a new start. It is possible to seek permission from the other parent, or the English court, to allow the child to relocate with the parent (see Chapter 9).[120] However, the ease of migration has encouraged the movement of children to manipulate connections to a jurisdiction and parenting arrangements. If one parent moves a child to another country without the permission of the other parent, this may constitute international child abduction. If a mother removes their child from England to Spain without the permission of the father, he may not know where his child is, and the relationship between the father and child is interrupted and will be significantly undermined by the mother.

This behaviour poses considerable difficulties because, through the unilateral actions of one parent, the child is living in a different legal jurisdiction and is potentially subject to different rules on contact and access. There have been significant efforts by the Hague Conference on Private International Law and the EU to provide a civil remedy to international child abduction to help to return children to the country from which they were taken, and to encourage cooperation between countries to ensure the effectiveness of the legal framework. England is frequently a destination for parents who have taken their children to another country, and children are also removed from this jurisdiction to other countries and parents seek their child's return back to the UK.[121] Child abduction is also a criminal offence under s.1 of the Child Abduction Act 1984 but it is rarely prosecuted.

---

[117] [2014] EWHC 4182 (Fam).   [118] *J v C* [1970] AC 668.   [119] *McKee v McKee* [1951] AC 352.

[120] Children Act 1989, s. 13.

[121] Hague Conference, 'A Statistical Analysis of applications made in 2008 under the Hague Convention on the Civil Aspects of International Child Abduction: Global Report 2008'. Available at: https://www.hcch.net/en/publications-and-studies/details4/?pid=6224&dtid=57, accessed 2 October 2017.

The Hague Convention on the Civil Aspects of International Child Abduction 1980 (the Hague Convention 1980) provides an international Convention with a civil remedy of return where a child has been abducted to another country. It binds the UK and all other EU Member States, and many other states globally, including Ireland, USA, Canada, South Africa, Australia, New Zealand, and Japan.[122] The EU has adopted the Hague Convention 1980 and the remedy of return, but amended its procedure of operation in BIIR. The BIIR rules only apply to abductions between EU Member States, for example between Germany and France. The Hague Convention 1980 applies when the abduction occurs between two signatory states outside the EU, for example between Canada and Australia.

> **?** DEBATE 6: HOW CAN THE LAW HELP FAMILIES TO MANAGE
> RELATIONSHIPS WHEN FAMILY MEMBERS LIVE IN
> DIFFERENT COUNTRIES?
>
> When a parent moves a child to another country without the permission of the other parent there may be many different motivations, but the return remedy operates in the same way irrespective of the reasons behind the abduction. The Hague Abduction Convention 1980 is designed as an almost automatic system for returning the child to their habitual residence so that decisions may be taken in that jurisdiction.
>
> It was originally expected that most abductors would be fathers seeking to change the custody arrangements in relation to their children by taking them to another jurisdiction. Despite this assumption, of the majority of abductions globally, 67% are carried out by mothers, most of whom are the primary carer of the child.[123] In some cases, the mother has migrated to another country with the child's father, and when the relationship has broken down, she has attempted to return to her home with her child to her wider family without seeking permission. In other cases, women have left for another country alleging that the father of the child is violent towards her and, in some cases towards the children.[124]
>
> The Hague Abduction Convention 1980 assumed that simplifying the process of returning the child to their familiar, home country is the best solution to child abduction as the left behind parent would not lose contact with their child. However, since primary carer mothers now carry out the majority of abductions, the legitimacy of this assumption may be questioned. This has been more problematic in cases where the left behind parent is alleged to have been violent towards the mother and child. The return remedy can mean that both the mother and child are exposed to the risk of further violence on the child's return.[125] Despite these concerns, the return remedy has been regarded as effective to resolve disputes to ensure that the courts with the closest connection to the child should hear any custody dispute after the child's return. This potentially places some children at risk of harm, but realistic alternatives to the Convention remedy have not been seriously considered. The balance between return and the exceptions, where return may be refused, are therefore very important to the operation of the Convention. The interpretation of the exceptions to return is strict in the interests of ensuring automatic return of the child, but this risks returning children in circumstances where their welfare may be affected.

---

[122] Hague Convention 1980 Status Table.

[123] Lowe, N. and Horosova, K. 'Operation of the 1980 Hague Abduction Convention: A Global View' (2007) 41 *Family Law Quarterly* 59, 76.

[124] Weiner, M. 'International Child Abduction and the Escape from Domestic Violence' (2000) 69 *Fordham Law Review* 593.

[125] Keating, H. and Reddaway, A. 'Child Abduction: Would protecting vulnerable children drive a coach and four through the principles of the Hague Convention?' (1997) 5 *International Journal of Children's Rights* 77.

It is notable that the decision to return a child after an abduction is not made in the child's best interests. Decisions in relation to children are normally made with their best interests as a primary consideration, but returning a child is designed as a rapid summary process and the child's best interests will be considered in any subsequent custody hearing. This has been criticised as failing to respond to the circumstances of individual children, but makes the return remedy much quicker and more efficient to adjudicate. The benefits of the return of the child are deemed to be in the best interests of the child in the majority of cases.

6.1 The Hague Convention on the Civil Aspects of International Child Abduction 1980

The Hague Convention 1980 aims to ' … protect children internationally from the harmful effects of their wrongful removal or retention and to establish procedures to ensure their prompt return to the state of their habitual residence …'. It does not directly regulate the jurisdiction of the courts of the countries involved in the dispute. It assumes the country from which the child was removed has jurisdiction and provides a civil remedy to return the child to that country so that any custody dispute then takes place in the place to which the child is most closely connected. The aim of the Convention is to resolve cases quickly by returning the child before they have chance to settle in the jurisdiction to which they were abducted.

6.1.1 Defining an abduction and convention framework

 Key Legislation 5: Article 3 Hague Abduction Convention 1980

A *removal* or *retention* of a child is viewed to be wrongful where it is *in breach of rights of custody* attributed to a person, an institution or any other body, either jointly or alone, under the law of the State in which *the child was habitually resident* immediately before the removal or retention and at the time of the removal or retention those rights were actually exercised …

The child must have been wrongfully *removed* or *retained* from their habitual residence. Removal and retention are alternative concepts: a child is either removed or retained. A removal occurs where the child is moved across an international border. A retention occurs where the child was initially moved for a holiday or a period of access with one parent, and is then kept in the other country without permission, so the initial move was lawful but becomes unlawful.[126]

For the removal or retention to be wrongful, it must be *in breach of rights of custody*. Rights of custody may arise by operation of law, or by reason of a judicial or administrative decision, or by agreement. They may be held by a court, so a child who has been made a ward of court may still be unlawfully removed or retained abroad. In *Re K (Abduction: Inchoate Rights)*[127] the Supreme Court recently extended the scope to include 'inchoate' custody rights, which have not been formally awarded, but would have been legally awarded to the left behind parent if they had sought formal legal status for their rights before the abduction. Inchoate rights arise where an individual without formal legal rights to the child is undertaking the responsibility of primary care of the child because the person holding formal legal rights has either abandoned the child,

---

126 *Re H (Abduction: Custody Rights)* [1991] 2 AC 476.   127 [2014] UKSC 29.

or delegated responsibility for the child. If formal arrangements had been sought, it must be highly likely that rights of custody would have been awarded to that individual.[128]

Rights of custody are defined in Article 5 Hague Convention 1980 as including the right to determine the place of the child's residence. This is a minimal definition of custody rights. In *Re V-B (Abduction: Custody Rights)*[129] the right to be consulted regarding a move between countries was held not to be a right of custody within Article 5. The right must encompass the possibility of refusing permission for the move.

Finally, the child must have been unlawfully removed or retained from their *habitual residence*. The child's habitual residence is the place at the centre of their interests prior to the abduction, having regard to all the circumstances, including schooling, family arrangements, language skills, and nationality (see 2.2.2).[130] This means that when children migrate to a new country, there is potentially a period of time before they establish a new habitual residence when they may fall outside the scope of the Convention.[131] The Convention does not apply to foetuses, so when a pregnant mother unlawfully removed the elder children from Canada to England, even once she gave birth in England, the youngest child could not be made subject to a return application.[132]

The Hague Convention 1980 establishes a framework whereby the left behind parent can use resources in their home country, and the country to which the child has been abducted, to try and ensure the child's return. Each signatory state is required to establish a 'central authority' under Article 6 Hague Convention 1980. The central authority, once notified of an abduction, has responsibility to try and find the child, to exchange information about the child, initiate proceedings, and try to arrange for the voluntary return of the child. Central authorities in different countries have working relationships to ensure cooperation across borders to try and facilitate the rapid return of children between different jurisdictions. They can provide extensive assistance to those involved in a wrongful removal or retention, helping parents who would otherwise have little knowledge of the legal framework or of how to institute proceedings in a foreign country.

Under Article 10 Hague Convention 1980, the central authority should take all appropriate measures for the voluntary return of the child. This is regarded as desirable because it avoids court proceedings and a judicial order, but in England it is more usual for the child to be returned by judicial order.[133] The courts of the country to which the child was removed or retained may also request information regarding the legal arrangements affecting the child and whether the removal or retention was unlawfully in breach of custody rights under their national law under Article 15 Hague Convention 1980.[134]

---

[128] *Re K (Abduction: Inchoate Rights)* [2014] UKSC 29, at [56].   [129] [1999] 2 FLR 192.

[130] Case C-523/07 *A* [2009] ECR I-02805; Case C-497/10 PPU *Mercredi v Chaffe* [2010] ECR I-14309.

[131] *Re S (A Child) (Habitual Residence and Child's Objections: Brazil)* [2015] EWCA Civ 2.

[132] *Re G (Abduction: Withdrawal of Proceedings, Acquiescence, Habitual Residence)* [2007] EWHC 2807 (Fam).

[133] Armstrong, S. 'Is the Jurisdiction of England and Wales Correctly Applying the 1980 Hague Convention on the Civil Aspects of International Child Abduction?' (2002) 51 *International and Comparative Law Quarterly* 427.

[134] *Re D (Abduction: Rights of Custody)* [2006] UKHL 51.

Key Legislation 6: Article 12 Hague Convention 1980

Article 12 Hague Convention 1980 states:

> The judicial or administrative authority, even where proceedings have been commenced after the expiration of the period of one year ... shall also order the return of the child, unless it is demonstrated that the child is now settled in its new environment.

If the child has been unlawfully removed or retained under Article 3 Hague Convention 1980, the left behind parent may make an application for the return of the child in the courts of the country to which the child was taken. Under Article 12, if less than a year has expired from the date of the application, the return of the child will be ordered. The return order operates only over the child, not the parent who has removed or retained the child.

The application is usually dealt with in a summary hearing aimed at establishing whether the child has been abducted within the scope of Article 3, considering any claims that an exception to returning the child is established under Article 13 (see 6.1.2), and issuing an order for return under Article 12. It is not a full welfare hearing and the best interests of the child are not considered in detail during the application.

Despite the fact that the welfare of the individual child is not the focus of an application, the European Court of Human Rights has held that the Hague Convention 1980 return remedy is compliant with Article 8 ECHR, the right to respect for private and family life. In *Maumousseau v France*[135] it was argued that the enforcement of the order to return the child to the USA from France would breach both the child's and the abductor mother's Article 8 rights. The European Court of Human Rights rejected the application stating that: 'The Court is entirely in agreement with the philosophy underlying the Hague Convention.'[136] However, in *Neulinger v Switzerland*[137] the mother had removed the child from Israel to Switzerland to avoid the orthodox religious education of the child. The Swiss courts had ordered the return of a child to Israel, but the European Court of Human Rights upheld an application by the mother and child arguing that enforcement of the order for return would breach their Article 8 right to respect for their private and family life. The Court suggested that an individualised assessment of the child's circumstances would have revealed the impact that return would have on his right to respect for his private and family life and the application for the return of the child should have been refused. The Swiss court should have conducted: ' ... an in-depth examination of the entire family situation and of a whole series of factors, in particular of a factual, emotional, psychological, material and medical nature, ... with a constant concern for determining what the best solution would be for the abducted child ... '[138]

The decision in *Neulinger* appeared to undermine the overall approach of the Hague Convention 1980 in requiring a full welfare assessment, rather than assessing only whether the criteria of the 1980 Convention were met, and returning the child for substantive disputes to be resolved in the child's habitual residence.[139] The UK Supreme Court in *Re E (Children) (Abduction: Custody Appeal)*[140] clarified the effect of the decision of *Neulinger* on applications in the English court for the return of children under the 1980 Convention.

---

[135] App. No. 39388/05 (2010) 51 EHRR 35.   [136] App. No. 39388/05 (2010) 51 EHRR 35, at [69].
[137] App. No. 41615/07 (2012) 54 EHRR 31.   [138] App. No. 41615/07 (2012) 54 EHRR 31, at [139].
[139] Walker, L. 'The Impact of the Hague Abduction Convention on the rights of the family in the case law of the European Court of Human Rights and the UN Human Rights Committee: The Danger of *Neulinger*' (2010) 6 *Journal of Private International Law* 649.   [140] [2011] UKSC 27.

The UK Supreme Court stated that the contextual assessment of circumstances related to the delay in the enforcement of the return order in *Neulinger*, making return particularly disruptive for that particular child, but that the underlying principles of the 1980 Convention were not affected. The European Court of Human Rights has since retreated from the formulation in *Neulinger*, stating in *X v Latvia*[141] that the overall philosophy of the Hague Convention 1980 is to ensure the best interests of the child and to deter abduction. The court should assess the safeguards for the child on return, and considered it opportune to '… clarify that its finding in the Neulinger judgment does not in itself set out any principle for the application of the Hague Convention by the domestic court.'[142] Unless one of the exceptions to return is established, the court hearing the return application will normally return the child to their habitual residence under Article 12 and the UK Supreme Court argues that return is normally in the best interests of the child.[143]

6.1.2 Exceptions to return of the child

The exceptions to the return of the child are designed to account for the individual circumstances of the child, preventing the return of the child when it is not appropriate. In England, the interpretation of the exceptions has been strict and they are not easy to establish. The burden is on the abducting parent to demonstrate that an exception to return applies to the child. Even if the conditions of the exception to return are made out, the court retains a discretion to return the child in any case.[144] The expected outcome is the return of the child and, reflecting that aim, judges refused to return the child in only 15% of cases globally in 2011.[145]

Under Article 12(2) Hague Convention 1980, if the child has been resident in the country in which they were wrongfully removed or retained for a year prior to the application for return being issued, and the child has settled in their new environment, the court may refuse the return of the child. The lapse of a year means that this exception is rarely used. It acknowledges that a long lapse in time after the abduction may mean that the child's circumstances have changed to the extent that it is not appropriate to return them to their former habitual residence as this would cause further disruption to the child. This provision could encourage parents to abduct and hide the child in the destination country to prevent the left behind parent knowing where the child is located for the purpose of issuing return proceedings. The English court has held that in these circumstances, the child cannot be deemed to have 'settled' into their new environment.[146] For the child to be deemed to have settled in their new environment, the court is in effect considering whether the child is now more closely connected to the country to which they were abducted.[147] The court will consider whether the child is playing an active part in their new society, and has integrated into new social networks, or whether they have retained cultural and family links in the country from which they were removed.[148]

Article 13(a) states that where the person seeking the return of a child from another country consented or acquiesced in the removal or retention of the child, return may be refused. For consent to be proved, the abductor must demonstrate on the facts that there was clear and unequivocal consent and it must be operative at the time of the removal or

---

[141] App. No. 27853/09 (2014) 59 EHRR 3.   [142] App. No. 27853/09 (2014) 59 EHRR 3, at [105].

[143] *Re E (Children) (Abduction: Custody Appeal)* [2011] UKSC 27.

[144] Article 18 Hague Convention 1980. See *Re M and another (Children)* [2007] UKHL 55

[145] Hague Conference, 'A Statistical Analysis of applications made in 2008 under the Hague Convention on the Civil Aspects of International Child Abduction: Global Report 2008'. Available at: https://www.hcch.net/en/publications-and-studies/details4/?pid=6224&dtid=57, accessed 2 October 2017.

[146] *Cannon v Cannon* [2004] EWCA Civ 1330.

[147] Beaumont, P. and McEleavy, P. *The Hague Convention on International Child Abduction* (Hart Publishing, 1999) 207.   [148] *Re M and another (children)* [2007] UKHL 55.

retention.[149] Valid consent cannot be obtained by deceit.[150] To prove acquiescence, the court will consider the subjective intention of the person seeking the return of the child at the time of the removal or retention from their actions and communications but acquiescence must be unequivocally demonstrated on the facts.[151] Delaying issuing return proceedings to negotiate with the abducting parent, or attempting reconciliation, does not constitute acquiescence to the original abduction as seeking the voluntary return of the child is to be encouraged.[152]

The most controversial exception to return is Article 13(b) Hague Convention 1980. If there is a grave risk that a child will exposed to physical or psychological harm or otherwise placed in an intolerable situation on return, then return may be refused. This exception to return has caused the most difficulty in interpretation and application in part because assessing the risk posed to the child in a summary hearing in a different country can be challenging without full evidence. The standard applied to Article 13(b) by the English courts has been high and the risk to the child must be clearly demonstrated on the facts, although there is no requirement of exceptionality or gloss on the text of the Convention.[153] The risk to the child must be substantial and more severe than the inevitable disruption and anxiety associated with an unwanted return to the child's habitual residence.[154] It has been suggested that Article 13(b) should only succeed where there is imminent danger to the child posed by war or famine,[155] but this is regarded as too strict an interpretation because the exception is intended to account for the welfare of the individual child in the circumstances. However, a broad interpretation undermines the aim of the Convention in returning children who not at 'grave' risk of harm. The risk must be posed to the child, not to the child's carer, so women who allege that they will exposed to violence on returning with their child, have failed in this claim unless they can demonstrate that the risk is also posed to the child.[156] Significant evidence of a risk of harm is normally required, as occurred in *Re D (Children) (Art. 13(b): Non-return)*[157] where the left behind parent had a history of violence towards his partner, including a shooting incident, resulting in a refusal to return the child.

Under Article 13(2), if a child of appropriate age and maturity objects to returning, the court may refuse the return of the child. In England, the court will now hear the opinions of a child of appropriate age and maturity as an aspect of the return application.[158] This gives the child the opportunity to be heard in proceedings and the chance for any objections raised to return by the child to be heard. The English courts are aware of the risk that the abductor has influenced the child's views of return.[159] Article 13(2) does not specify the nature or quality of the objections to the return that will be required before the court may refuse the return of the child. There is no fixed age at which the child's views will be taken into account by the court, although the more mature the opinions of the child, the more likely they are to weigh with the court. The objection must be to returning to the

---

[149] *Re PJ (Abduction: Habitual Residence: Consent)* [2009] EWCA Civ 588.

[150] *Re M (A Minor) (Abduction: Consent or Acquiescence)* [1999] 1 FLR 171.

[151] *Re H and others (Minors) (Abduction: Acquiescence)* [1998] AC 72.

[152] *Re W (Abduction: Acquiescence: Children's Objections)* [2010] EWHC 332 (Fam).

[153] *Re E (Children) (Abduction: Custody Appeal)* [2011] UKSC 27, at [31].

[154] *Re C (Abduction: Grave Risk of Psychological Harm)* [1999] 1 FLR 1145, 1154.

[155] Silberman, L. 'The Hague Abduction Convention Turns Twenty: Gender Politics and Other Issues' (2000) 33 *New York University Journal of International Law and Politics* 221.

[156] *Re W (A Child) (Abduction: Conditions for Return)* [2004] EWCA Civ 1366; *MR v HS* [2015] EWHC 234 (Fam). See Bruch, C. 'The Unmet Needs of Domestic Violence Victims and the Children in Hague Child Abduction Convention Cases' (2004) 38 *Family Law Quarterly* 529.

[157] [2006] EWCA Civ 146.

[158] *Re D (Abduction: Rights of Custody)* [2006] UKHL 51.

[159] *Re J (Children) (Abduction: Child's Objections to Return)* [2004] EWCA Civ 428.

child's habitual residence prior to the abduction,[160] and the court retains a discretion to order the child's return, even if they object.[161]

Article 20 Hague Convention 1980 allows the return of the child to be refused if this would conflict with the fundamental freedoms and human rights principles of the state requested to return the child. The Child Abduction and Custody Act 1985 did not originally incorporate Article 20 into English law. In *Re D (A Child) (Abduction: Foreign Custody Rights)*[162] the House of Lords made it clear that since the enactment of the Human Rights Act 1998, Article 20 is part of English law and will have domestic effect, although it has not been used in the English courts and is restrictive in scope.

6.2 Abduction between EU Member States: BIIR

The Hague Convention 1980 is regarded as a highly successful global Convention so it was controversial when the EU made proposals to change the law on child abduction between EU Member States. In BIIR, the EU has adopted the fundamental basis of the Hague Convention 1980 which remains in force in all EU Member States. It has sought to ensure that a child would be returned to the country of their habitual residence prior to the abduction under Article 12(1) Hague Convention 1980 by restricting the scope of the exceptions to return under the Convention, and making available a full custody hearing if return is initially refused.[163] This has led to a complicated legal framework whereby the Hague Convention 1980 remains the legal basis for return, but the Regulation changes how it operates in abductions between EU Member States.[164]

When a child has been wrongfully removed or retained between two EU Member States,[165] in addition to the Hague Convention 1980, Article 11 BIIR will also apply to proceedings. Under Article 11(2) BIIR a child of appropriate age and maturity must be given an opportunity to be heard in the return proceedings. There is a six-week time limit once the court is seised of a return application on issuing a return order, but this has been held to be unrealistic and unenforceable.[166] If the exception to return based on the existence of a grave risk of harm to the child under Article 13(b) is raised, the court cannot refuse to return the child if arrangements have been made to secure the protection of the child on return.[167] This is intended to ensure the return of the child even if there is a risk, and can provide more protection for individuals at risk from the left behind parent,[168] but the nature of the protection may be difficult to demonstrate in summary return hearings. If the court is not satisfied that protection arrangements can be provided to mitigate the risk of harm to the child, it may still refuse return.[169]

The most controversial aspect of the BIIR reforms was Article 11(6)–(8). These provisions apply when the return of the child has been refused under Article 13 Hague Convention 1980. In these circumstances, holders of parental responsibility have the right to issue parental responsibility proceedings in the court of the child's habitual residence prior to the abduction. This means that the court of the child's habitual residence retains control over issues relating to the custody of the child, and ultimately, over whether the

---

[160] *Re M (Republic of Ireland) (Child's Objections)* [2015] EWCA Civ 26.

[161] *Re M (A Minor) (Abduction: Consent or Acquiescence)* [1999] 1 FLR 171.   [162] [2006] UKHL 51.

[163] McEleavy, P. 'The New Child Abduction Regime in the European Union: Symbiotic Relationship or Forced Partnership?' (2005) 1 *Journal of Private International Law* 5.

[164] Article 10 BIIR governs jurisdiction over parental responsibility proceedings when a child has been wrongfully removed or retained.   [165] As defined by Article 2(11) BIIR.

[166] *Vigreux v Michel and Michel* [2006] EWCA Civ 630.   [167] Article 11(4) BIIR.

[168] Lamont, R. 'Beating Domestic Violence? Assessing the EU's Contribution to Tackling Violence Against Women' (2013) 50 *Common Market Law Review* 1787.

[169] *Klentzeris v Klentzeris* [2007] EWCA Civ 533.

child is returned to their habitual residence. For example, if a child was unlawfully re-moved from England to Italy by her mother, and the Italian courts reject an application for the child's return for England on the basis of Article 13, for example because the child objects to returning under Article 13(2), the English court may retain jurisdiction over the child. The left behind parent may seek to issue English proceedings under the Children Act 1989 to arrange contact and access to the child in the future, and the order of the English court may entail the return of the child to England, despite the Italian courts initial refusal to do so.

These hearings normally take place with the child remaining in the state to which they have been removed and retained, developing social and family links in that country.[170] The hearing in the child's habitual residence is a full welfare hearing under the Children Act 1989, rather than a return application, that may entail the return of the child if it is in their best interests, even though return was initially refused.[171] If the custody judgment issued in the child's habitual residence entails the return of the child, and it is certified by that court as having heard from the child and the parties in proceedings,[172] the judgment is subject to automatic recognition and enforcement in the country to which the child was abducted. This means that there are no defences to the recognition of the custody judg-ment entailing the return of the child.

 Key Case 5: Case C-491/10 PPU *Aguirre Zarraga v Pelz* [2010] ECR I-14247

The mother unlawfully removed the child from Spain to Germany. The father made an applica-tion to the German courts for the return of the child to Spain which was refused by the German courts under Article 3(2) Hague Convention 1980 on the ground that the child objected to return to Spain. The father subsequently made a full custody application in the Spanish courts under Article 11(6)–(8) BIIR. The child was not heard in these proceedings despite being given the opportunity to do so. The Spanish court awarded custody to the father and required the return of the child from Germany to Spain. This judgment was subject to automatic recogni-tion and enforcement in Germany. The German courts refused to enforce the judgment on the ground that the child had not been heard in the Spanish proceedings.

The Court of Justice of the European Union held that the courts of the child's habitual resi-dence, in this case the Spanish courts, retained jurisdiction over decisions relating to the child and it was for that court to determine whether the child had been given an opportunity to be heard in proceedings. There was no possibility of opposing the enforcement of the judgment in the German courts entailing the return of the child to Spain.

The Court of Justice has been strict in enforcing the return of the child if the court of the child's habitual residence has ordered return in a custody judgment under Article 11 BIIR, even if the circumstances of the child have significantly evolved since the time of the child's original removal.[173] This leaves children who have settled in a new country and a long time has expired since their original removal potentially facing the upheaval of returning to their habitual residence. However, despite the requirements of BIIR, the evidence is that Arts 11(6)–(8) in the majority of cases do not result in the child's return, even if it is ordered by the state of the child's habitual residence.[174]

---

[170] *AF v A* [2011] EWHC 1315 (Fam).

[171] *M v T (Abduction: Brussels II Revised Article 11(7))* [2010] EWHC 1479 (Fam).

[172] Article 42(2) BIIR.

[173] C-211/10 *Povse* [2010] ECR I-06673; *Povse v Austria* App. No. 3890/11 [2014] 1 FLR 944.

[174] Beaumont, P., Walker, L., and Holliday, J. 'Not Heard and Not Returned: The Reality of Article 11(8) Proceedings' [2015] *International Family Law* 124.

SUMMARY

1. Which court should govern family relationships where members of a family have links to a country other than England?
   - When families migrate to different countries, they have links to different legal systems affecting their family status. This affects which court can have jurisdiction over their family disputes, such as divorce and parental responsibility.
   - Connecting factors aim to link a person to a country to identify the courts and law they would expect to govern their family relationships. Habitual residence is the most common connecting factor, identifying a factual connection between a person and a jurisdiction.
   - Individuals will seek to issue proceedings in a particular country in order to gain the best possible outcome from the litigation. This has been an issue in divorce proceedings where petitioning the English court may give economically weaker spouses an advantage.
   - When a child is unlawfully removed or retained from their habitual residence, this constitutes child abduction and it is normally expected that the child will be returned to that country for any litigation over custody of the child. Parents cannot unilaterally change which court has jurisdiction over a child without the permission of the other parent, or of the court.

2. How can the law help families to manage relationships when family members live in different countries?
   - Cooperation between different countries over the content of their family law in relation to jurisdiction and the recognition of legal judgments helps to ensure that legal family status is the same in different countries, making individual status more certain and making it easier for migrating families.
   - In parental responsibility disputes, judgments from other countries will normally be recognised as valid in England so that arrangements for the care of children where parents live in different countries will be carried out.
   - In cases of parental child abduction, the child will normally be returned to the country from which they were removed or retained, to protect the child's relationship with the left behind parent.

3. What should happen when different legal systems recognise different types of family relationship?
   - The social, cultural, and religious background of the country heavily informs the family law of different countries. English law will only recognise and accept family relationships that are in accordance with its own core notions of family life.
   - For a marriage to be recognised as valid in England and Wales, it must be both formally valid under the law of the place of celebration of the marriage, and essentially valid under the law of the spouses' domicile prior to the marriage. This protects the interest of both countries law in governing the marriage.
   - English law will not recognise actually polygamous marriages contracted by a person domiciled in England prior to the marriage because polygamous marriage is not acceptable to the English conception of marriage.

Further Reading

BEAUMONT, P. *et al* 'Child Abduction: Recent Jurisprudence of the European Court of Human Rights' (2015) 64 *International and Comparative Law Quarterly* 39
- Provides a summary and critique of the European Court of Human Rights' case law on child abduction and the operation of the Hague Convention 1980.

HODSON, D. 'What is Jurisdiction for Divorce in the EU? The Contradictory Law and Practice around Europe' [2014] *International Family Law* 170 (Sept)
- Highlights the difficulties of using Article 3 BIIR on jurisdiction over divorce in practice and different interpretations of the available grounds.

LAMONT, R. and McGLYNN, C. 'Cross-Border Public Care and Adoption Proceedings in the European Union' (2016) 38 *Journal of Social Welfare and Family Law* 94
- Considers the controversies and problems of international cooperation in care proceedings over foreign national children living in England.

MENNE, M. 'International Family Law: Some Current Practical Issues Arising from Cross-Border Children Cases' [2016] *International Family Law* 175

NASH, E. 'Recognition under the 1996 Hague Convention' [2015] *International Family Law* 264

PROBERT, R. 'Hanging on the Telephone: *City of Westminster v IC*' (2008) 20 *Child and Family Law Quarterly* 395
- Addresses the controversies of recognition of different forms of marriage and the use of public policy in refusing to recognise a marriage in England.

SCHUZ, R. *The Hague Abduction Convention: A Critical Analysis* (Hart Publishing, 2014)
- Provides an overall assessment of the operation of the Hague Abduction Convention 1980 and its application in a global context.

STALFORD, H. *Children and the European Union: Rights, Welfare and Accountability* (Hart Publishing, 2012)
- Considers the position of children in international family law and the protection of children's rights in cross-national legal proceedings in the EU.

15

Family Law in Practice

George Patrick Nicholls

LEARNING OBJECTIVES

After reading this chapter you will be able to:

- Appreciate the challenges of practising family law, the identified crisis in the family justice system, and the reforms subsequently enacted, including the creation of the single Family Court;

- Understand what the Family Procedure Rules and the Family Law Protocol are, and what is required to comply with them;

- Know about legal aid, what is now available and who and what type of cases are eligible for it, and understand the legal aid statutory charge;

- Recognise the increase in the numbers of litigants in person and McKenzie Friends, and the consequences of this;

- Understand the different types of non court dispute resolution, particularly mediation.

DEBATES

After reading this chapter you should be equipped to discuss your opinion on the following central debates:

1. When, and how, should the Legal Aid Agency statutory charge apply?

2. Should the reduction in legal aid imposed by the Legal Aid, Sentencing and Punishment of Offenders Act 2012 be repealed and funding be provided to make legal aid available to more people?

3. Should paid McKenzie Friends be permitted by law and how should they be regulated?

4. Has the government succeeded in achieving its aims by promoting mediation of family disputes?

1. Introduction

Whilst the other chapters in this book focus on substantive claims in family law, this chapter is concerned with how families use and access the legal system, and the recent changes in family justice. The procedural aspects of family law claims, and the funding of litigation has seen extensive changes in recent years that have heavily influenced the use of the courts by families and the development of the law. This chapter identifies the source of the legal procedures, and explains the underlying policies and rules which must be followed for persons to obtain what orders the family law courts can make.

In family law a distinction is made between what are termed 'private' and 'public' family law cases. Private Law cases are those involving individual family members wishing to resolve matters between themselves. Public Law cases usually concern action taken by the local authority (i.e. the state) against a family member. This may be for example to take a child into the care of the local authority for its own safety because there may be allegations of abuse. The difference between private and public family law cases is analogous to the distinction often applied to civil and criminal cases. That is civil cases are analogous to private family law cases in that they relate to individuals or private entities having issues between themselves. Whereas criminal cases are analogous to public law cases in so far as they concern the state or local authority prosecuting or pursuing a case against an alleged wrongdoer.

The rules governing how family law cases are processed to obtain court orders are often technical and complex. Therefore, in practice, to achieve the order a person is seeking, they often need to instruct a solicitor to advise them of their options and to represent them, both in discussions with the other family member, or in litigation before the court. This representation has to be paid for, and one of the most controversial issues in modern family law is how private family law cases are funded, since legal aid was severely limited by the Legal Aid, Sentencing and Punishment of Offenders Act 2012 (LASPO). These policy developments have also encouraged families to seek to resolve disputes without attending court hearings, through alternative dispute resolution methods, such as mediation. This chapter will explore the nature and influence of these developments on family law litigation.

In certain family law cases, such as those relating to the division of assets following divorce, even if the parties have agreed matters it is still necessary to obtain a court order ratifying any such agreement, as otherwise any party can make a claim for a share of the other's assets. In contrast the ethos of the law relating to children is that there is a presumption a court order will not be made. (A court shall not make an order 'unless it considers that doing so would be better for the child than making no order at all.')[1] In other words the parties are encouraged and expected to resolve matters themselves. If this is not achieved it is possible to make an application for the court to determine the case.

However, before going to court modern family law and practice requires the parties to do certain things. These requirements are set out in the Family Law Protocol. These rules require the parties to try to resolve matters between themselves before going to court which should be a last resort. Even if the parties have to go to court the Family Law Protocol requires them to try to narrow the issues and cooperate with each other with a view to resolving matters amicably. If the parties fail to resolve matters between

---

[1] Children Act 1989, s. 1(5).

themselves and wish to pursue an action in court then they must follow a certain set of procedural rules. These are called the Family Procedure Rules 2010 which require any action be commenced by issuing a petition or application in a particular format. The nature and role of the Family Law Protocol and the Family Procedure Rules will be further explained in this chapter.

This chapter also examines the consequences that the cuts to legal aid have had on the family justice system. The cuts in legal aid have resulted in many more persons acting for themselves before the court as 'litigants in person'. This has resulted in significant delays which some argue have put the family justice system in crisis and pitched the judiciary against their political counterparts. A leading barrister has expressed the view that a hearing at court which may last half an hour if the parties are represented by lawyers, may take a day if they are not represented.[2] District Judge Glover estimates cases take twice as long where the parties are unrepresented.[3] Another very important issue is the role of representation of parties where there are allegations of domestic violence.

Even if a party is granted legal aid the effect of the Legal Aid Agency statutory charge must be considered. Essentially this means if a party is granted legal aid, and as a result 'recovers' or 'preserves' property then they may have to re-pay their legal costs from what has been recovered or preserved. The effects of this charge may be quite unexpected and must be properly understood by lawyers and their clients.

Another consequence of the cuts to legal aid is the rise in the number of what are called 'McKenzie Friends' in court. Traditionally these are not qualified lawyers, but persons who assist litigants in preparing their case. This chapter examines some of the implications of this development and considers the desirability of accepting McKenzie Friends in court.

These are all incredibly important socio-legal issues, particularly as regards to access to justice. Arguably there is in place a good system of family law. Many orders are available on a range of issues concerning the family, as described in the other chapters in this book. But how and to what extent are they effective in terms of persons being able to access them, who should fund cases, and what processes should persons have to go through, such as attending a mediation information meeting before having the right to issue court proceedings?

2. The crisis in the family justice system

During the first part of the twenty-first century, the family law system in England and Wales was in crisis. Consequently, the Ministry of Justice commissioned a report undertaken by The Family Justice Review Panel. It published its Executive Summary and Recommendations Final Report in 2011[4] entitled 'The Norgrove Report'. This highlighted very severe problems in the family justice system. One of the most significant issues was the unacceptable length of time that cases were taking to be processed and decided.

---

[2] Maclean, M. Eekelaar, J., and Bastard, B. (eds) *Delivering Family Justice in the 21st Century* (Hart Publishing, 2015) 252.

[3] See https://www.lawgazette.co.uk/news/litigants-in-person-numbers-soar/62602.article, accessed 10 October 2017.

[4] Ministry of Justice, The Department of Education and the Welsh Government. *Family Justice Review Final Report* (November 2011).

CONTEXT 1: THE TIME TAKEN FOR CASES TO BE DECIDED

The Norgrove Report contained examples of public law child protection care and supervision cases taking an average of 56 weeks, 61 weeks in care centres. This, it stated, had a very damaging effect, particularly on children:

> The life chances of already damaged children are further undermined by the very system that is supposed to protect them. And in private law, an average of 32 weeks allows conflict to become further entrenched and temporary arrangements for the care of children to become the default.[5]

The Norgrove Report also identified other concerns. These were that the costs of dealing with cases in the system were too high for both the tax payer and individuals. The parties to the process, including children, were often confused. The structure of the system was unnecessarily complicated, and there was no overall accountability. Those operating in the system did not trust each other. There was a lack of shared objectives, morale was low, and those working in parts of the system did not have the levels of skills and commitment commensurate with their roles. Finally, the information technology available was inadequate.

The Norgrove Report reinforced a principle long established in English Family Law, that the welfare of children is the paramount consideration.[6] The Report also made various recommendations for how these concerns could be addressed. The government issued a response and, over the ensuing years, legislation has been enacted.

3. The Family Procedure Rules and Practice Directions

Whilst any party can act for themselves, many instruct solicitors. If a solicitor is instructed they will usually try to agree as much as possible with their opponent, certainly endeavour to narrow the issues. If a matter goes to court the solicitor will usually prepare the paperwork to issue the case at court, and if the matter does not settle eventually there will be a court hearing to decide the case. There may be several pre-hearings in court where solicitors and or barristers may represent their clients. Throughout the process solicitors, barristers and litigants in person are required to follow the procedural rules as set out in the Family Procedure Rules and the Family Law Protocol.

The procedure of dealing with family law cases is now governed by the Family Procedure Rules 2010 which came into force in 2011,[7] the same year as the Norgrove Report. The Family Procedure Rules state that its goals are twofold, to make the system simple and to make it accessible to all. To achieve this, the forms to make applications and petitions to courts were simplified. This was complemented by the Crime and Courts Act 2013, which established a single Family Court.

The Family Procedure Rules are largely based on the principles of the Civil Procedure Rules. The Courts Act 2003 set out the objectives that the Family Procedure Rules should be enacted to ensure that:

(a) The family justice system is accessible to all, fair and efficient and

(b) The rules are both simple and simply expressed.[8]

---

[6] *J v C* [1970] AC 668.

[5] Ministry of Justice, The Department of Education and the Welsh Government. *Family Justice Review Final Report* (November 2011), 5.   [7] On 6 April 2011. Family Procedure Rules 2010; SI 2010/2955.

[8] Courts Act 2003, s. 75(5).

The idea was to create a uniform and comprehensive set of laws prescribing how family law cases are processed. These apply to all levels of family courts. The forms required to process family law cases were simplified and the rules contained in what are termed Practice Directions.

The interrelationship between the rules and Practice Directions is crucial to an understanding of the current family law landscape. Practice Directions are much more important than they were in the old system. They also have other specific functions:

> As well as having much closer links to individual parts of the rules, practice directions have other roles. They tell parties and their representatives what the court will expect of them, both in respect of documents to be filed in court for a particular purpose, and as to behaviour in complying with directions and co-operating with other parties to their claims. They also tell parties what they can expect of the court.[9]

The Family Procedure Rules set out the principle. The associated Practice Direction sets out how the requirement of the rule is to be achieved, how it operates in practice, and the sanction for non-compliance.

4. The Family Law Protocol

An inherent characteristic of modern litigation and the Family Procedure Rules is that persons are encouraged, and in certain circumstances compelled, to try to resolve any issues at an early stage and before issuing court proceedings. It is hoped that this will minimise the emotional and other damage to them, save costs, and avoid the necessity of having to go to court. This again underpins the current commitment to resolving matters by any means of non court dispute resolution (see section 8). To foster this approach, the Civil Procedure Rules (the Family Procedure Rule's counterpart in civil law) introduced different types of what are termed pre-action protocols. These are procedures to follow before court proceedings are issued. They require the parties to set out a summary of their case and provide details of the documentation they intend to rely upon, in the hope that this will lead to an early settlement, before (and to avoid) any court proceedings.

Family Law has its own specific protocol.[10] It is different and much more far reaching than those protocols contained in the Civil Procedure Rules, as these are generally applicable only until court proceedings are issued (hence they are called pre-action protocols). The Family Law Protocol published by the Law Society endures after proceedings have been issued, throughout the whole process until a case is concluded. This Protocol makes specific reference to the overriding objective as defined in the Family Procedure Rules which states the rules are a: 'New procedural code with the overriding objective of enabling the court to deal with cases justly having regard to any welfare issues involved.'[11] It has been 'heralded as the authoritative set of best practice guidelines'[12] on how to conduct family law cases.

The Protocol states that:

> it endorses and should be read in conjunction with the Resolution Code of Practice. Resolution is an organisation of family lawyers committed to cooperate and deal amicably with all those involved in dealing with family disputes. Resolution's code commits

---

[9] A Court User's Guide to the Civil Justice Reforms published by The Court Service, 2013.

[10] The Law Society, *Family Law Protocol* (4th edn, The Law Society, 2015). First published in 2001.

[11] Family Procedure Rules 2010, r. 1.1 (1).

[12] Roe, T. 'Key Source of Family Guidance' (2016) *Law Society Gazette* 28.

to resolving disputes in a non-confrontational and constructive way to preserve people's dignity and to encourage settlements.'[13]

In the Family Law Protocol, there is a whole chapter dedicated to non court dispute resolution. There then follows a series of chapters dedicated to how each type of family law case should be processed. These encompass all areas of family law including divorce, children, division of property, and domestic violence.

The Protocol emphasises the importance of following it and specifies there are significant serious implications of not doing so. First, the scope of the Protocol clearly states one of its main purposes: 'This chapter details with those overarching matters family lawyers must consider in order to promote their clients' best interests.'[14] The use of the word 'must' is noteworthy and the implication is that a failure to follow the Protocol is tantamount to a lawyer not acting in their clients' best interests, a potentially serious matter in several regards. The Protocol state that all solicitors must comply with the mandatory principles as set out in the Solicitors Regulation Authorities (SRA) Code of Conduct.[15] The SRA Code requires solicitors to provide information to clients regarding their needs and circumstances including information to make informed decisions about the services they require, how these will be provided, and their cost. Failure to comply with these provisions may result in a solicitor being guilty of unprofessional conduct and be subject to disciplinary action by the SRA.

The Protocol also contains a warning of a different kind. If a party refuses to follow it, they may be held liable for the other party's costs, or have some, or all of their own costs disallowed. If a solicitor is complicit in a failure to follow the Protocol, the courts are empowered to order that solicitor to pay any party's costs in a case. A judge has a discretion to decide who pays the parties' legal costs. In family law cases the general rule is that each party pays their own legal costs. However, if a party has acted unreasonably or flagrantly breached the Family Law Protocol, the Family Procedure Rules, or not complied with a Practice Direction, a judge may punish them for this by ordering them to pay some of another party's costs. The Protocol cautions: 'Practitioners should not underestimate these rules and should make sure they are clear about all aspects relating to costs when advising a client.'[16]

 Key Case 1: *Laporte v Commissioner of Police* **[2015] EWHC 371**

The claimants lost their case for damages for assault and battery, false imprisonment and malicious prosecution and a violation of their rights under Articles 10 and 11 of the European Convention on Human Rights and Fundamental Freedoms 1950 (ECHR). The significance of the case is on the question of costs and failure to engage properly in non court dispute resolution. The claimants had offered to engage in non court dispute resolution, but the defendants persistently refused to do so. As a result of this Turner J reduced the defendants' costs by one third, despite the fact they had won the case, and would thus ordinarily have expected to receive an order that all their costs be paid by the claimants.

Turner J referred to the decision of Lord Dyson in *Halsey v Milton Keynes General NHS Trust*[17] where he stated whether a party has acted unreasonably in a refusal to engage in non court

---

[13] See http://www.resolution.org.uk, accessed 20 June 2017.

[14] The Law Society, *Family Law Protocol* (4th edn, The Law Society, 2015), para 1.1.1, 1.

[15] Solicitors Regulation Authority, *SRA Code of Conduct* 2011 (version 18, SRA, 2016). Available at: http://www.sra.org.uk, accessed 19 May 2017.

[16] The Law Society, *Family Law Protocol* (4th edn, The Law Society, 2015), para 11.3.21, 147.

[17] [2014] 1 WLR 3002.

> dispute resolution depended on the circumstances of each case. Lord Dyson ruled this should be examined in the light of the following matters; the nature of the dispute; the merits of the case; and whether other settlement methods had been attempted. The court could consider whether the cost of mediation would be disproportionately high, delay, and whether the mediation had a reasonable prospect of success. Turner J found that, on the evidence before him in *Laporte*, he was satisfied that alternative dispute resolution had a reasonable prospect of success.

The Protocol requirement that the parties must cooperate and do their best to try to resolve matters is a continuing obligation throughout the procedure, both before and after the issue of court proceedings, until a case is concluded. Further, the parties should be in a position to demonstrate that they have cooperated and tried to resolve matters amicably. Otherwise, if they have not taken such steps, they may not be able to recover their legal costs or they may be ordered to pay the other party's costs.

The Protocol stresses the importance of the first meeting with the client. It is often at this meeting that crucial decisions are made, as to what a client is seeking, whether it is achievable, how much it will cost, and how it will be funded. It is a template of how a client's case is to be dealt with from start to finish. The Protocol specifically prescribes that a solicitor should consider and, if appropriate, deal with, each of the following matters:[18]

- agree the method of communication with the client;
- consider counselling;
- consider if any emergency action is needed as regards safeguarding the client, children or any family assets;
- consider reconciliation;
- consider whether the relationship is at an end and have available details of referral agencies, including providing information about local support, guidance services, and parenting apart, who can assist and consider the different forms of non court dispute resolution available.[19]

In the Protocol, the child's welfare is the paramount consideration of the court and professionals involved in the case. The parties are encouraged to try to separate their interests from those of the children and parental responsibility.

The Protocol specifically requires solicitors to make enquires about any incidents of domestic abuse, the need to screen for it and to make a risk assessment, and if necessary to consider what civil and criminal remedies may be appropriate (see Chapter 7). Solicitors are required to consider if there are any jurisdictional issues because of international family links including, in Europe, the impact of what is known as Brussels II Revised[20] (see Chapter 14).

The Protocol is concerned to safeguard those lacking capacity to take decisions, for example a person suffering with dementia. It spells out that solicitors cannot be retained by a client incapable of giving instructions.[21] The Protocol prescribes how solicitors should communicate with a solicitor acting for an opposing party, a litigant in person, or in dealing with a McKenzie Friend. The Protocol states that maintaining professional and co-operative communications will help clients to achieve their objectives. It emphasises that

---

[18] The Law Society, *Family Law Protocol* (4th edn, The Law Society, 2015), para 1.6, 2–3.

[19] The Law Society, *Family Law Protocol* (4th edn, The Law Society, 2015), para 1.6. 6, 4.

[20] Council Regulation (EC) 2201/2003. Concerning jurisdiction and the recognition and enforcement of judgments in matrimonial matters and the matters of parental responsibility [2003] OJ L338/1.

[21] Solicitors Regulation Authority, *SRA Code of Conduct* 2011 (version 18, SRA, 2016), ch 1.7, 4–5. Available at: http://www.sra.org.uk, accessed 19 May 2017.

setting the right tone at the outset is essential: 'Patience, courtesy, good humour and an effort to understand why the person is not instructing a lawyer will get you off on the right foot. Communicate clearly and try to avoid any technical language or legal jargon.'[22] The Protocol refers to many professional guides for good practice.[23] As a continuation of this non-confrontational approach the Protocol states that solicitors should notify their opponents of any intention to commence court proceedings 'at least seven days in advance unless there is good reason not to do so'.[24] A failure to comply with this is considered to be bad practice as it may result in greater difficulty in reaching agreement. The courts are likely to disapprove of this and it may result in costs sanctions being imposed against an offending party, or their solicitor.

5. The single Family Court

In April 2014, in line with the ethos of the Family Procedure Rules, came the streamlining and unification of all Family Courts into the single Family Court.[25] The jurisdiction of England and Wales is divided into geographical areas each comprising several courts presided over by a Designated Family Judge. Depending on the type of matter, proceedings are issued in either the County Court or Magistrates' Court. There is now one point of entry for the application or petition. Upon receipt of an application or petition all cases are allocated, depending on the type of matter, by what are termed gatekeepers to the level of Judge specified in a prescribed Schedule.[26] This includes Lay Justices (Magistrates), District Judges, Circuit Judges, and High Court Judges. Generally, Lay Justices are empowered to deal with applications for periodical payments and cases relating to children in both the public and private sphere. District Judges deal with divorce, applications relating to the finances during and following divorce, and private children law. Circuit Judges and High Court Judges deal with other types of more complex and serious cases.

In practice this has not made a significant difference, save it may have caused some delay in the courts dealing with cases, while they are transferred from a designated central court to a Family Court which has jurisdiction where the applicant resides. However, many Family Courts have been closed and applicants are therefore having to attend the designated central court in any event.

6. Legal aid and funding

Legal aid is the provision of legal services to a person for which they do not have to pay the full cost, although they may have to make some financial contribution towards legal costs. It also encompasses legislation permitting remission of court fees if certain financial criteria are met. Some solicitors and barristers undertake work pro-bono or at discounted

[22] The Law Society, *Family Law Protocol* (4th edn, The Law Society, 2015), para 1.10.3, 6.

[23] The Law Society, *Family Law Protocol* (4th edn, The Law Society, 2015), para 1.10.4 refers to the guide issued by the Law Society, Bar Council, and CILEx, regarding litigants in person: Litigants in person: guidelines for lawyers (2015); the Resolution Guide to Good Practice on Working with Litigants in Person (2017), available at http://www.resolution.org.uk; The President of the Family Division's Practice Guidance: McKenzie Friends (Civil and Family Courts) (2010) (see Appendix A of the Protocol).

[24] The Law Society, *Family Law Protocol* (4th edn, The Law Society, 2015), para 1.9.1, 6.

[25] The Crime and Courts Act 2013 which inserted section 31A in to the Matrimonial and Family Proceedings Act 1984.

[26] Family Court (Composition and Distribution of Business Rules) 2014, Sch 1, as amended in 2015 (SI 2015/1421).

rates, and both of these fall within the definition of legal aid. Citizens Advice Bureaux, university law centres, and other similar organisations provide very helpful legal advice free of charge. This chapter is primarily concerned with legal aid financed by the state, because they are the biggest provider of it. This is now more commonly known as public funding.

Legal aid was historically provided in two forms: first, legal advice and assistance and secondly representation for court proceedings. However public funding is now available for a third category, that is to pay for, or towards, the costs of mediation. This demonstrates how much the legislature is hoping mediation will help to resolve cases and thereby avoid the need to go to court, and thus cut expenditure.

Historically, in England and Wales there was a comprehensive scheme of legal advice and assistance. This provided advice and assistance on almost any question of English law. There were just a very few exceptions. It was known for many years as the Green Form Scheme. It allowed for an amount of initial advice and help from a solicitor, to include writing letters and preparing documentation. This type of legal advice and assistance is of extreme value in any jurisdiction. It can provide accurate, timely advice, and lead to early resolution of potential disputes and support for persons engaged in legal proceedings. It is relatively inexpensive compared to legal aid for court proceedings. In 1972, Lord Hailsham described the aims and benefits of the advice provided as intended to: 'Radically improve the service to the public by helping to resolve different personal and social questions in their early stages, which of course is precisely when recourse to litigation can most helpfully be avoided.'[27] The reference to resolving matters at an early stage is notable as this is the ethos of the current Family Law Protocol.

6.1 The rise and fall of legal aid

The Legal Aid Act 1949 had created the most comprehensive legal aid system in Europe. By the early 1950s, it was estimated that over 80% of the population of England and Wales were eligible for some form of legal aid.[28] This was likely to secure a very high level of access to justice.

 CONTEXT 2: THE INCREASE IN THE COST OF LEGAL AID

Increasing costs meant that it was not possible to sustain comprehensive coverage. In 1980, legal aid expenditure was £266 million.[29] By 1990, it had risen almost threefold to £682 million. In 1998, it rose to £1.56 billion.[30] The then Lord Chancellor, Lord Irvine of Lairg, described legal aid as a 'Leviathan with a ferocious appetite'.[31]

Consequently, cuts to legal aid expenditure were perhaps inevitable. This is not a new phenomenon. As long ago as 1998 cuts to aid were being described as: 'After 50 years, most of the legal aid scheme is to be demolished.'[32] For decades, successive governments have expressed a determination to curb the spiralling costs of the legal aid budget. The methods

---

[27] Hansard HL col 503 (23 June 1972).

[28] Jacob, QC, I H. 'Access to Justice in England' in M. Cappelletti and B. Garth (eds), *Access to Justice—A World Survey*, Book 1 (Giuffre-Sijthoff, 1978). 445.

[29] Lane, J. and Hillyard, S. *International Directory of Legal Aid* (The International Bar Association Educational Trust and Sweet and Maxwell Limited, 1981).

[30] 'The Legal Aid System—An Overview' a statement by The Lord Chancellor's Department: http://roof.ccta.gov.uk/lcd/laid/leg-aid.htm.

[31] Lord Chancellor, Lord Irvine of Lairg, Speech to the Solicitors Annual Conference at Cardiff, October 1997.

[32] Mackay, QC, C. 'Conditional Fee Agreements—The Way ahead'. (1998) *Quantum 2*.

adopted to achieve this are generally twofold. First, certain types of work are removed from the legal aid scheme. Second, the financial criteria, the so called 'means test', which applicants have to satisfy to obtain legal aid are curtailed, resulting in fewer people being eligible. For example, in 1979, 70% of households were eligible for legal advice and assistance. Due to financial levels being adjusted, the number of households eligible for legal advice and assistance in 1990 was reduced to 40% and by 1993 just 21%.[33] It was estimated that between 1979 and 1989, 14 million people became ineligible for legal aid.[34] In a report to the Lord Chancellor in September 1997, Sir Peter Middleton GCB explained the arguable unfairness of this method of cutting legal aid costs: 'The only way to reduce future spending that is likely to prove reasonably effective is to cut eligibility or scope. This is crude and unsatisfactory because it excludes whole classes of people or cases without regard to circumstances.'[35]

Despite the fact that the intention of these cuts was to exclude millions from the legal aid scheme, remarkably, expenditure continued to rise. Successive Lord Chancellors expressed concern that they were paying more and getting less. For example, in 1997, the income from legal aid going to the legal profession had risen by 20% a year on average but there were about 13,500 fewer acts of help.[36]

There are various providers of legal aid. Historically the largest provider was the state paying solicitors and barristers operating in private practice. As part of a wider package of legal reforms, on 1 April 2000 the Community Legal Services Commission began to administer legal aid. This was a government funded body, independent of the courts. At the time, the principal change was administrative re-organisation in that the new body, the Community Legal Services Commission, replaced the Legal Aid Board.

These reforms were specifically designed to extend the providers of legal services under the legal aid scheme. They abolished the lawyers' monopoly to provide legal aid. It was no longer just solicitors and barristers who were empowered to provide legal services paid for by the state. Citizens Advice Bureaux, law Centres, and local councils were able to, and were actively encouraged to, undertake legal aid work and be remunerated accordingly. This new focus was very much based upon the stated aims of specialisation, efficiency, and competition. It was perceived by the Coalition government that legal advice centres, and the like, were in a particularly good position to choose amongst the different methods of dispute resolution and different types of legal assistance, which were available to those eligible.

Further, there was an aspect of cost saving. This was based on the presumption that lawyers in private practice undertaking legal aid work would be expected to have an element of profit included in their remuneration. Thus, if legal aid work could instead be provided by specialist, non-profit making state-sponsored law centres, this would inevitably achieve savings to the legal aid budget, as the profit element payable to lawyers would be saved. In 1997 the idea of law centres delivering legal aid was also popular in Parliament: 'Over 100 MPs, have called for a network of Law Centres to be established nationwide and we hope

[33] Klijn, A, and Huls, F: 'The International Legal Aid Scene: A Concise Comparison' Paper presented to the International Conference on Legal Aid at The Hague 13th–16th (1994), 6.

[34] Murphy, M. 'Legal Action' October 1989.

[35] Middleton, P. 'Review of civil justice and legal aid: Report to the Lord Chancellor', (1997).

[36] Hoon, G. A speech to the Legal Action Group's conference entitled 'Justice–addressing the balance'. Available at: http://roof.ccta.gov.uk/lcd/speeches/1997/lag.htm.

the Lord Chancellor will ensure that everyone in the country has access to a Legal Advice Centre in their neighbourhood.'[37] It is notable that Parliament's intention was that 'everyone in the country' should have access to legal advice. Specific sums were to be allocated to geographical areas dependent upon the perceived needs for legal services. These sums were shared amongst the providers of legal aid. Thus, for the first time, this represented a finite budget. It replaced the old demand led system, which had resulted in expenditure being, in effect, limitless.

Another feature of the reforms introduced in 2000 was that, in order to provide legal services, an organisation must have obtained a legal aid franchise. This required the provider to have in place a quality management standard. It was part of the perceived cost saving exercise and drive for efficiency. Functions known as 'devolved powers' were delegated to the franchisee so that the functions of granting legal aid to individuals and determining eligibility, hitherto undertaken by the legal aid authorities, were delegated to these firms. The notion was that because these organisations had achieved a quality mark they could be entrusted to determine whether legal aid should be granted or refused. This was designed to cut, control, and monitor costs by transferring, at least in part, some of the costs of administering legal aid from the public purse to the provider.

There had been considerable opposition to the franchising of legal services from the legal profession. However, the Chief Executive of the Legal Services Commission at the time, Steven Orchard, had repeatedly stressed that it was not going away. In 'Mr Franchise' [38] he set out the views for and against franchising at the time when plans were first made to introduce it, and when opposition was at its height.

A consequence of the requirement to hold a legal aid franchise was that the number of providers of legal aid reduced considerably. Estimates suggested that, in about 1999, some 6,000 firms of solicitors ceased to provide legally aided services.[39] This represented over a half of the total firms of solicitors who were previously providing legal aid. This was likely to significantly impair access to civil justice. The Solicitors' Sole Practioners' Group stated that the franchising requirements meant that many sole practitioners were not able to undertake legal aid work.[40] This meant that some communities, particularly in remote rural areas who were (and are) almost entirely dependent on sole practitioners for the provision of legal services, may be denied the financial means to obtain any access to justice. Ironically this was contrary to what Parliament had intended.

There occurred another major overhaul of the legal aid system with the enactment of the Legal Aid, Sentencing and Punishment of Offenders Act 2012 (LASPO) which came into force on 1 April 2013. This created the Legal Aid Agency (replacing the Community Legal Services Commission) which now administers what public funding is available. The enactment of LASPO resulted in even greater cuts to the availability of legal aid in family law cases. The Justice Gap describes the effect of the cuts as: 'By far the most severe retreat into the legal aid scheme since it was introduced in 1949.'[41]

---

[37] Grogan, A. 'Legal Aid under attack-insurance companies win at the expense of the poor', *Northwest Legal News*, 17 November 1997.   [38] Evlynne, G. 'Mr Franchise' (1994) 91 *Law Society Gazette* 6.

[39] Rose, N. '6,000 offices to drop legal aid provision' (1999) 96 *Law Society Gazette* 1.

[40] In an interview with the late Paul Boucher, then Chairman of the Sole Practitioners Group in October 1999.

[41] Taylor-Ward, S. 'Who Carries the Cost? Three Years After the LASPO Legal Aid Cuts' *The Justice Gap*. Available at: http://thejusticegap.com/2016/04/carries-cost-three-years-laspo-legal-aid-cuts/, accessed 10 October 2017.

CONTEXT 3: ELIGIBILITY FOR LEGAL AID.

A major method of cutting legal aid expenditure pursuant to LASPO has been by removing it for most types of family law case unless there is evidence of domestic violence. The Ministry of Justice describe how this has been achieved:

> For many areas of civil law, the implementation of LASPO Act led to a reduction of workload. Areas affected including family—legal aid is now only available for private family law cases (such as contact or divorce) if there is evidence of domestic violence or child abuse and child abduction cases. Legal aid remains available for public family law cases such as adoption.[42]

The cuts have excluded what is estimated to be 650,000 persons from the legal aid scheme who before LASPO entered into force, would have been eligible.[43] In a report published in 2014,[44] the Ministry of Justice provided information for the 12 months from April 2013 to March 2014 stating that:

> The volumes of new matters started for legal help have fallen by over 80 per cent between 2009-10 and 2013-14. The number of certificates granted for civil representation has fallen by 30 per cent between 2010-11 and 2013-14. In 2013-14 there were large decreases across the civil legal aid area, driven by changes to the scope of legal aid as set out in the Legal Aid, Sentencing and Punishment of Offenders Act 2012 (LASPO).

Further, it reported that since 2007–08 the number of franchised civil providers of legal aid has nearly halved.

Amnesty International investigated and published a report in 2016 stating the upshot of the changes 'is a two-tier justice system open to those who can afford it, but increasingly closed to the poorest, most vulnerable and most in need of its protection'.[45] In their report, Amnesty International stated that the cuts to legal aid were much more dramatic than anticipated. They cite that in 2012 legal aid was granted in 925,000 cases. In the year following the coming into force of LASPO, this was reduced to 497,000, a 'drop of 46%'.[46] Nimrod Ben-Cnaan, head of policy and profile at the Law Centres Network, reviewed the Ministry of Justice's quarterly legal aid statistics for January to March 2015 and concluded: 'The official statistics show a continuing decline in the uptake of civil legal aid workload year on year across most areas of civil legal aid.'[47]

Another consequence of the legal aid cuts created by LASPO is the closure of law and contact centres. Law centres provide legal advice and assistance on a range of issues. Contact centres are safe environments where parents not residing with their children can have contact, particularly if it is to be supervised contact. The Law Society recognised:

> Contact centres could be a valuable way of ensuring that children retain contact with both parents during hostile relationship breakdowns. But without early legal advice,

---

[42] Ministry of Justice and Legal Aid Agency, 'User guide to legal aid statistics, England and Wales' (2016).

[43] Legal Action Group, 'Legal aid cuts; misleading statistics from the Ministry Of Justice', *The Guardian*, 18 March 2011.

[44] Ministry of Justice and Legal Aid Agency, 'Legal aid statistics in England and Wales 2013–14' (2014).

[45] Amnesty International 'United Kingdom: The Impact of Cuts That Hurt: The Impact of Legal Aid Cuts in England on Access to Justice' (October 2016).

[46] Amnesty International 'United Kingdom: Cuts That Hurt: The Impact of Legal Aid Cuts in England on Access to Justice' (October 2016).

[47] 'Legal aid figures: the vital statistics of access to justice are failing' (Law Centre Network, 2015).

parents often do not know that such places even, exist, let alone how they could help the family.[48]

The cuts imposed by LASPO could amount to a breach of the EHCR and the Human Rights Act 1998 (HRA). A cross party Parliamentary report by the Joint Committee on Human Rights has criticised the legal aid provisions in LASPO and stated that they will lead to breaches of Articles 12, the right of the child to be heard in proceedings and Article 3, that the child's best interests are a primary consideration in proceedings of the UN Convention on the Rights of the Child 1990. On 12 March 2015, the Parliamentary cross party Justice Select Committee found that:

> The Government achieved its aim of substantially reducing the civil legal aid budget but the Justice Committee's report concludes that it had failed to target legal aid to those who need it most and had not discouraged unnecessary litigation at public expense and could not show it was delivering better overall value for money for the taxpayer.

In conclusion, LASPO has resulted in the virtual removal of legal aid for most types of family law matters and for most people. Thus, at the present time, only a very small percentage of the population in England is eligible for legal aid and it is only available for a very limited category of cases.

6.2 Categories of legal advice and assistance

What legal aid is still available now is set out in The Civil Legal Aid (Merits Criteria) Regulations 2013 and is as follows.[49]

6.2.1 Legal help

Legal help is a form of legal advice and assistance, which includes taking instructions and giving advice on the law, advising persons of their options, and identifying other organisations which may be able to help. It covers applying for other types of legal aid which are available. It includes solicitors writing letters and e-mails, and making and receiving telephone calls on behalf of clients in trying to resolve their legal issues. It can be very useful in identifying and advising a person of the realistic options that the law offers.

To be eligible, a person must be able to demonstrate there are reasonable prospects of success for their case.[50] There is also a means test. [51] If a person is in receipt of certain social security benefits, they are automatically entitled to legal help. Otherwise, a person's income and capital is calculated and must be below certain amounts for them to be eligible. These financial criteria are likely to change periodically.

6.2.2 Family help (lower)

Family help (lower) is essentially an extension of the legal help scheme described earlier. It does not generally cover work relating to court proceedings but there is an exception. If a case has settled, it covers obtaining a court order to reflect the terms of settlement. To be eligible, a person must satisfy the same prospects of success merits test as for legal help.

There are further criteria. A reasonable private paying individual test must be satisfied. This test requires the potential benefit to be gained from the provision of legal aid

---

[48] Fouzder, M. 'Contact Centres Forced to Close by Legal Aid Cuts' (2016) *Law Society Gazette*. Available at: https://www.lawgazette.co.uk/law/contact-centre-forced-to-close-by-legal-aid-cuts/5056436.article, accessed 10 October 2017.   [49] SI 2013/104.

[50] The Civil Legal Aid (Merits Criteria) Regulations 2013 (SI 2013/104) para 5.

[51] Civil Legal Aid (Financial Resources and Payment for Services) Regulations 2013. Statutory Instrument 2013/480 as amended by the Civil Legal Aid (Merits Criteria) (Amendment) Regulations 2016 (SI 2016/781).

to justify the likely costs, such that a reasonable private paying person would commence or continue the proceedings having regard to the prospects of success and all the other circumstances in the case.[52]

Legal help and family help are both described as controlled work because they can only be provided by solicitors who have a specialist quality mark and a legal aid franchise. Some lawyers argue that there is little point or justification for having two tiers of legal advice and assistance, in legal help and family help (lower). It would be simpler and more economical to administer such advice and assistance under just one scheme, as used to be the case.

6.2.3 Funding court proceedings

There are also two categories of legal aid for what are essentially contested court proceedings. These are called family help (higher) and legal representation. Both are categorised as work licensed by the Legal Aid Agency.

6.2.4 Family help (higher)

Family help (higher) covers legal representation to issue court proceedings and work up to, but not including, a final hearing. To be eligible a person must satisfy both the good prospects of success and reasonable private paying individual tests described earlier. They must also satisfy a further proportionality test requiring that the likely benefits of the proceedings to the individual, and others, justify the likely costs, having regard to the prospects of success and all the other circumstances of the case.[53] Further, the individual must show they have exhausted all reasonable alternatives to issuing court proceedings.[54]

6.2.5 Legal representation

This is available to cover preparation and representation at a final contested court hearing. Unsurprisingly, the good prospects of success and reasonable private paying individual tests both apply. An individual is also required to show that reasonable attempts have been made to settle the case. This again reinforces the policy of encouraging the parties to resolve matters amicably without court proceedings.[55]

6.2.6 Family Advocacy Scheme

The Family Advocacy Scheme permits the payment of specified fees in relation to specific matters. These are for advocacy at court hearings; advocates' meetings, (although this only applies to public law proceedings such as care proceedings over a child), and to fund conferences with barristers and for their opinions.

6.2.7 Emergency funding

In appropriate cases, it is possible to apply for emergency legal aid, for example, if it is believed a child is being abducted to another country (see Chapter 14). The applicant must satisfy the criteria for the type of legal funding they are seeking as set out earlier.

6.2.8 Exceptional funding

Legal aid is available in what are described as 'exceptional circumstances'.[56] This is designed to cover circumstances where a failure to provide legal aid would amount to a breach of a person's rights under the Human Rights Act 1998.

---

[52] The Civil Legal Aid (Merits Criteria) Regulations 2013 (SI 2013/104) para 7.
[53] The Civil Legal Aid (Merits Criteria) Regulations 2013 (SI 2013/104) para 8.
[54] The Civil Legal Aid (Merits Criteria) Regulations 2013 (SI 2013/104) para 36(1).
[55] The Civil Legal Aid (Merits Criteria) Regulations 2013 (SI 2013/104) para 39 (d).   [56] LASPO 2012, s. 10.

The legality of exceptional funding was challenged in *IS (A Protected Party, By His Litigation Friend the Official Solicitor) v The Director of Legal Aid Casework and the Lord Chancellor.* The claimant was a protected party acting by the Official Solicitor. In the Administrative Court, Collins J allowed his application for judicial review and granted declarations that:

> (1) the Exceptional Case Funding Scheme as operated is unlawful as giving rise to an unacceptable risk that an individual will not be able to obtain legal aid where failure to provide it would be a breach of that individual's rights under the European Convention of Human Rights (to the extent applied by the Human Rights Act 1998) or under directly enforceable EU law (2) the Civil Legal Aid (Merits Criteria) Regulations 2013 (the Merits Regulations) and (3) the Exceptional Case Funding Guidance (Non-Inquests) (the Guidance) are unlawful.[57]

However, the Court of Appeal reversed this decision finding that these regulations were in fact lawful.[58]

Collins J's decision had led to the highest number of applications for exceptional funding for nearly three years. However, following the Court of Appeal judgment the Legal Aid Agency introduced new regulations restricting legal aid eligibility in respect of cases with poor or borderline prospects.[59] This is likely to cause a sharp fall in applications for exceptional funding.

6.3 The types of case covered by legal aid

Table 15.1 illustrates what legal funding is now available for a particular type of case.

Table 15.1 Availability of legal aid for different types of cases

Type of case	What legal aid is available?
Getting divorced	Not available for court proceedings but advice and assistance may be obtained
Resolving financial matters relating to real property, lump sums, shares any other assets, periodical payments, pension sharing	Not available unless evidence of domestic violence
Matters relating to children—private law and public law	Not available unless evidence of domestic violence or child abuse or a child is a party to the proceedings or child abduction cases
Matters relating to children—public law	Available concerning the protection of children
Domestic violence	Available to a person claiming they have been subject to domestic violence
Forced marriage cases	Available to a person claiming they have been subject to a forced marriage.

---

[57] [2015] EWHC Admin 1965.   [58] [2016] 2 FLR 392.
[59] The Civil Legal Aid (Merits Criteria) (Amendment) Regulations 2016 (SI 2016/781).

6.4 **The domestic violence criteria**

To obtain legal aid for certain types of case, a party must provide evidence of domestic violence or forced marriage (which in itself may be considered a form of domestic violence, see Chapter 7). For these purposes domestic violence is defined as: 'any incident, or pattern of incidents, of controlling, coercive or threatening behaviour, violence or abuse (whether psychological, physical, sexual, financial or emotional) between individuals who are associated with each other'.[60] To satisfy this criteria, the applicant must supply evidence in one of the forms set out in Key Legislation 1. Many applicants are not able to supply the forms of evidence prescribed. However, unless this hurdle is satisfied, legal funding will not be available. As this criteria needs to be satisfied to get legal funding, these regulations are very important.

 Key Legislation 1: The Civil Legal Aid (Procedure) Regulations 2012, Reg. 33

This requires evidence to be submitted for an application for Public Funding being:

33. –

(1) An application for civil legal services described in paragraph 12 of Part 1 of Schedule 1 to the Act must include evidence of the domestic violence or the risk of domestic violence.

(2) For the purpose of paragraph (1), the evidence of domestic violence or risk of domestic violence must be provided in one or more of the following forms—

   (a) a relevant unspent conviction for a domestic violence offence;

   (b) a relevant police caution for a domestic violence offence given within the twenty four month period immediately preceding the date of the application for civil legal services;

   (c) evidence of relevant criminal proceedings for a domestic violence offence which have not concluded;

   (d) a relevant protective injunction which is in force or which was granted within the twenty four month period immediately preceding the date of the application for civil legal services;

   (e) an undertaking given in England and Wales under section 46 or 63E of the Family Law Act 1996;

   (f) a letter from the person appointed to chair a multi-agency risk assessment conference confirming that—

      (i) A was referred to the conference as a high risk victim of domestic violence; and

      (ii) the conference has, within the twenty four month period immediately preceding the date of the application for civil legal services, put in place a plan to protect A from a risk of harm by B;

   (g) a copy of a finding of fact, made in proceedings in the United Kingdom within the twenty four month period immediately preceding the date of the application for civil legal services, that there has been domestic violence by B giving rise to a risk of harm to A;

   (h) a letter or report from a health professional;

   (i) a letter from a social services department in England or Wales (or its equivalent in Scotland or Northern Ireland) confirming that, within the twenty four

---

[60] LASPO, Sch 1, para 2(9).

> month period immediately preceding the date of the application, A was
> assessed as being, or at risk of being, a victim of domestic violence by B;
>
> (j) a letter or report from a domestic violence support organisation in the
>   United Kingdom.

These regulations demonstrate that legal aid is now primarily only available if there has
been domestic violence and, crucially, that proof can be obtained of the violence in one
of the forms defined in the regulations. It is accepted that persons should have funding to
protect themselves and their children from domestic violence. But why a person who can
show some evidence of domestic violence should be eligible for public funding for other
matters such as to deal with matrimonial property or children's issues, in the circumstances that others who have not apparently suffered domestic violence, and thus cannot
obtain legal aid for the very same type of case some say is unfair and discriminatory.

 CONTEXT 4: EVIDENCING DOMESTIC VIOLENCE

There is evidence to suggest that even those suffering domestic violence are unable to obtain
legal aid, because they are not able to get the required evidence. Emma Scott, Director of the
charity 'Rights of Women' informed the Law Society:

> Our research has consistently shown that nearly half of women affected by domestic
> violence do not have the required forms of evidence to apply for family law legal aid
> and that more than half of those women tell us that they take no legal action as a
> result. This leaves them at risk of further violence and even death. We continue this
> legal action on behalf of those women in order to hold the government to account on
> their promise to make family law legal aid available to victims of domestic violence.[61]

It further finds that notwithstanding amendments made in April 2014, about 40% of women
are still unable to access advice and representation to participitate in family law proceedings.

This research also found that 37% of women responding to the survey who had been subject to domestic violence were not able to produce the written evidence to enable them to get
legal aid. A further barrier to women accessing justice was that 71% of those surveyed found
it difficult to find a legal aid solicitor in their area. The study concluded:

> Despite amendments to the prescribed evidence, these findings demonstrate that the
> legal aid regulations continue to act as a dangerous barrier for women. Too many
> women at risk of violence are still unable to access legal advice and representation on
> family law remedies that could afford them safety and justice.

Rights of Women, Women's Aid Federation of England, and Welsh Women's Aid have again
petitioned the UK government to urgently review the legal aid regulations so that women can
get legal aid and effectively exercise their rights and get protection from domestic violence
which is what the legislation enacted intended to achieve.

6.5 The statutory charge

The Legal Aid Agency statutory charge has been a characteristic of legal aid schemes in
England and Wales for decades. The legislation governing it is currently embodied in

---

[61] Scott, E. 'Harsh evidence tests leave 4 per cent of domestic violence victims at risk' (2016). Available
at: http://www.lawsociety.org.uk/news/stories/harsh-evidence-tests-leave-40-per-cent-of-domestic-violence-
victims-at-risk/#sthash.rl8AZyxM.dpuf, accessed 21 June 2017.

LASPO.[62] This states that if a person recovers or preserves money or property from a case for which they have legal funding, the statutory charge may apply. This means that the person with legal funding has to repay any legal costs paid out by the Legal Aid Agency, from any monies or property recovered or preserved as a result of the outcome of the case. They apply to all costs which may be incurred by the person covered by their legal aid certificate. These include solicitors' and barristers' costs, VAT, and disbursements (costs paid to third parties such as court fees or the costs of an expert such as an accountant or surveyor/valuer) and can amount to a significant cost. Thus, at the outset, it is very important that a client is fully advised about these charging provisions, and failure to do so may result in a lawyer being subject to a claim for professional negligence and misconduct.

Further, the legislation empowers regulations to be made to determine whether a legally aided person has to make a contribution towards their costs.[63] These sums may be by way of a lump sum or a periodical payment, out of capital or income. They allow interest to be charged. There are powers enabling sums paid out for such costs to be recovered, as a civil debt through the High or County Court against any legally funded persons owing such money.

 Key Case 2: *Hanlon v The Law Society* [1981] AC 124

In this case the wife received legal aid to issue court proceedings for a divorce, to make an application for title to the former matrimonial home, or a share in it, periodical payments, other financial claims under the Matrimonial Causes Act 1973, and for what was then termed custody and access.[64]

In considering how the statutory charge applied in the Court of Appeal, Lord Denning MR found it applied to the whole of the former matrimonial home, Sir John Arnold held that the wife had only recovered half of the former matrimonial home, and Donaldson LJ found no property had been recovered or preserved.[65] However, on appeal the House of Lords unanimously ruled that the statutory charge attached to all the costs covered by the legal aid certificate. Thus, it applied not just to the costs in the dispute regarding financial matters but also to the divorce costs and those relating to the dispute regarding the children. The House of Lords specifically ruled on what encompassed the meaning of 'recovered' or 'preserved' and defined this as follows:

> if its ownership or transfer had been in issue in the proceedings as a matter of fact rather than of theoretical risk; that on the facts of the present case the ownership of the whole house had been in issue between the parties; and that, accordingly, the house was property recovered by the wife in respect of the husband's interest and preserved to her in respect of her own and was subject to the charge in favour of the legal aid fund.[66]

In *Hanlon* the former matrimonial home had been in the husband's sole name. The wife applied to court and was awarded title to the former matrimonial home in its entirety. The House of Lords found that there was nothing in the statutory regulations which prevented the Law Society postponing the enforcement of the statutory charge. For example, in *Hanlon* postponement of the charge would have allowed the wife to live in the property and not have to pay back the costs to the legal aid fund until the former matrimonial home was sold. In practice this is commonplace.

---

[62] LAPSO 2012, s. 23.   [63] LAPSO 2012, s. 23.   [64] Childrens Act 1989.

[65] [1980] 1 All ER 763.   [66] [1979] AC 124, at 126.

In a subsequent case, *Curling v Law Society*,[67] the Court of Appeal adjudged that the statutory charge applies even if a party just preserves what they already own. This is what the Legal Aid Agency now term as if 'the client unlocks their interest in property'.[68] In this case, when they divorced, the husband and wife had already agreed that the wife was entitled to a half share of the former matrimonial home and that the husband would buy out the wife for a sum equivalent to half of the value of the house. The wife wanted an immediate sale, whereas the husband sought to postpone it. The entitlement was not at issue, only the point in time when the sale would occur, yet the statutory charge applied. Neil J explained:

> It is true that the sum of £15,000 merely represented her agreed share of the proceeds of sale (or indeed perhaps rather less than her full share), but the fact that a party to legal proceedings recovers in the proceedings that to which he or she in law is already entitled cannot by itself prevent the attachment of the statutory charge. The question is where the party's right to recover the property has been in issue in the proceedings and for this purpose I can see no reason to limit the relevant issue to that of ownership alone. [69]

In *Manley v The Law Society*[70] a legally aided applicant settled a case on the basis that the defendant paid £40,000 to be held on trust to pay the applicant's creditors. Lord Denning held that the statutory charge applied and explained his reasoning very clearly, sending out a clear message to lawyers and legally funded persons alike:

> The court should always look for the truth of the transaction. It should not let itself be deceived by the stratagems of lawyers, or accountants. To my mind, once we pull aside the curtain of words, and the supposed rights, the truth is that this £40,000 was to be used to pay off David Manley's debts at his request. It is, therefore, the subject of the statutory charge in favour of the legal aid fund.

 DEBATE 1: WHEN, AND HOW, SHOULD THE LEGAL AID AGENCY STATUTORY CHARGE APPLY?

It is difficult to understand why there were such differing views (and doubts) in the Court of Appeal in *Hanlon v The Law Society*[71] as to whether the statutory charge applied. The former matrimonial home was in the husband's sole name; the wife applied to court and was awarded title to the property in its entirety. There should not be any doubt that she recovered the former matrimonial home as the Court awarded her title to the property.

The facts of the *Curling* case present a much stronger case to argue that the statutory charge should *not* apply. In this case, the former matrimonial home was in the joint names of the parties. They had already agreed they were each entitled to half of it. However, the Court of Appeal found there had been an issue in the proceedings, and thus the statutory charge applied. The fact that the husband wanted to postpone the sale, whereas the wife wanted an immediate sale, was an issue to be determined in these proceedings for the purpose of exertion of the statutory charge, even though the only issue was the timing of the sale of the former matrimonial home, not who should get what shares in it.

The effects of the decision in the *Curling* case may be regarded as both harsh and disproportionate, in that a disagreement about a minor issue may trigger the repayment of all a legally aided persons costs covered by a legal aid certificate even if they relate to separate matters. For example, the statutory charge in these circumstances would attach to not just the

---

[67] [1985] 1 All ER 705.   [68] Legal Aid Agency 'The Statutory Charge Manual' (April 2014) 12.
[69] [1985] 1 ALL ER 705, 711 b-d.   [70] [1981] 1 All ER 401.   [71] [1981] AC 124.

costs of the proceedings where property was recovered or preserved, but to all proceedings which the legal aid certificate covered, such as those costs incurred relating to the children (as was in fact the case in *Hanlon*). It may lead lawyers to carefully advise their clients from the outset, about whether or not there are issues for determination, and if so, if they are in fact worth litigating about or whether a client may be better off if they settled.

The Legal Aid Agency are taking steps to actively enforce the statutory charge. In 2014 they published the 'Statutory Charge Manual'. In this manual they review the *Curling* case and interpret the justification offered in *Curling* permitting the exertion of the statutory charge as 'the client unlock(ing) their interest in property'.[72] But is this interpretation correct? Does it not seek to apply the exertion of the statutory charge to cases which the court in *Curling* would not have contemplated being covered by it? Unlocking an interest in property is neither recovering nor preserving it. Rather it is merely liquidating it.

It is arguable that the concept of the statutory charge is fair, certainly as regards it applying where assets are 'recovered'. However, it is suggested that the criteria of applying it to property which is just 'preserved' may in certain cases be unjust. If a person just preserves what they were lawfully entitled to own, why should they have to pay the costs of doing this?

The statutory charge is important both now and in the future. In view of the cuts in government spending across the board, the recoupment of the statutory charge is a potential significant source of revenue for the public purse. Some legally aided persons have owed, and still owe, the Legal Aid Agency monies pursuant to the statutory charge and have done so for decades.

The statutory charge could be extended as the basis for a separate type of legal aid to provide funding where it does not now exist. For example there are disputes regarding property where there is no domestic violence in the relationship. In these circumstances it is not currently possible to get legal aid because there is no domestic violence. If an applicant could show ultimately that the Legal Aid Agency will be repaid by the operation of the statutory charge, then financing the claim would be a de facto loan to which interest is charged. In practice, some solicitors operate a similar type of scheme in so far as if they act for a client who cannot afford to pay fees at the outset, but is likely to recover a significant share in the equity of the former matrimonial home they are prepared to wait until it is sold to get paid.

The interest rate applicable to the statutory charge is 8% per annum. Some see this as unfair in the current economic climate, where the Bank of England base interest rate is just one half of 1%. Although this rate of interest is the same as that awarded by statute on judgments,[73] because of low base rates judges often award lower rates. However former Parliamentary Under-Secretary of State at the Ministry of Justice Jonathan Djanogly suggests that the present interest rate of 8% per annum on monies owed in respect of the statutory charge, is justified to encourage monies owing to be repaid, he says:

> The rate of 8% simple interest is designed to encourage those who can raise private funds to repay their statutory charge, either through extending their mortgage, or lending from a reputable bank, to do so. Money recovered helps to keep legal aid on a sustainable footing, which reduces demand on the taxpayer.[74]

Yet the high interest rate could be regarded as a penalty for failing to make an early repayment of the statutory charge.

---

[72] Legal Aid Agency 'The Statutory Charge Manual' (April 2014) 12.   [73] County Courts Act 1984, s. 69.
[74] House of Commons Briefing Paper 'Paying the Statutory Charge: Legal Aid in England and Wales' No. 06537, December 2015.

The Legal Aid Agency are now actively pursuing the enforcement of statutory charges. In a briefing paper 'Paying the statutory charge: legal aid in England and Wales' Garton Grimwood explains:

> Since 2000, the Legal Services Commission and more recently the Legal Aid Agency have been trying to recoup the money owed to the public purse via the statutory charge. In recent years, the Legal Aid Agency has been asking about the financial circumstances of people against whom a statutory charge has been registered, to ascertain whether they are now in a position to pay, whether by paying the debt in full or by setting up a standing order to pay in instalments.[75]

Concerns have been expressed in Parliament about enforcement by constituents. However, others argue that the extent of the last recession was not anticipated and desperate measures have been needed in all areas of government monetary policy.

The obvious benefit of the statutory charge is that if the Legal Aid Agency ultimately recover the costs paid out, with interest, then it is more in the nature of a loan than a payment of costs which is never recovered. It is a useful charge for funding the legal aid system and is proportionate in that it responds to the benefits obtained from accessing legal aid in the first place. However, to be effective it does depend on it being implemented.

6.5.1 Exceptions to the statutory charge

The Civil Legal Aid (Statutory charge) Regulations 2013 set out the exceptions whereby some property recovered or preserved by a legally funded person is exempt from the statutory charge. It does not apply to cases of legal help where only the family home is recovered or preserved. It does not apply in respect of cases regarding periodical payments and pension sharing or to interim payments.[76] Further, if a legally aided party can show the enforcement of the statutory charge would cause 'grave hardship or distress' or would be 'unreasonably difficult because of the nature of the property' it can be waived.[77]

6.6. Is legal aid a human right?

There is legislation giving persons the right to a fair trial. There may be circumstances where this cannot be achieved unless the person has legal aid to get advice and representation from a lawyer. The question thus arises whether the right to legal aid is a human right?

 Key Legislation 2: Article 6 ECHR[78]

Article 6 provides, *inter alia*, for the right to a fair trial, which it described as follows:

> In the determination of his civil rights and obligations or of any criminal charge against him, everyone is entitled to a fair and public hearing within a reasonable time by an independent and impartial tribunal established by law.

This wording is adopted in the Human Rights Act 1998, which came in to force on 2 October 2000.

---

[75] Briefing Paper No. 0653717 (House of Commons Library, 2017).
[76] SI 2013/503, para 5—full exemption; and para 6—partial exemption.   [77] SI 2013/503, para 8.
[78] Effective from 3 September 1953.

The question that therefore arises is, can a person have a fair trial without legal aid? In 1979 the case of *Airey v Ireland* came before the European Court of Human Rights.[79] The Court ruled in Mrs Airey's favour determining that she would not be able to represent herself to seek an order for judicial separation from her violent husband without legal aid from the state to secure legal representation. This was because of the law, the complex procedures of the High Court in Ireland, the emotional aspects of marital disputes, and the fact that her husband may be represented. As she could not afford to pay a solicitor, and could not represent herself, the Court ruled the lack of legal aid violated her right of access to a court to have her civil rights and obligations determined in violation of Article 6 ECHR. The court stated remedies must be effective not illusory. The Court also found Article 8 ECHR, the right to respect for private and family life was breached, as she was not able to get an order for judicial separation.

 Key Case 3: *P, C, and S v UK* (2002) 35 EHRR 31: App. No. 56547/00

In this later case, the European Court of Human Rights found both Articles 6 and 8 ECHR had been breached. The case concerned a child who had been taken into care to be adopted. The Court found Article 6 had been breached because the applicant needed legal aid due to the complexity of the care proceedings, the nature of the issues at stake in the proceedings, and the emotional nature of the dispute. The Court stated: 'There is the importance of ensuring the appearance of the fair administration of justice and a party in civil proceedings must be able to participate effectively, inter alia, by being able to put forward the matters in support of his or her claims.' and 'The seriousness of what is at stake for the applicant will be of relevance to assessing the adequacy and fairness of the procedures.'[80]

The English courts have expressed concerns about parties not having legal aid. In 2013 the judge in *Kinderis v Kineriene*[81] granted an adjournment to allow a party with no knowledge of the law and limited understanding of the English language to appeal against a refusal of legal aid. The judge suggested that continuing the proceedings in the circumstances could be a breach of Article 6 ECHR. In *Re L (Application Hearing: Legal Representation)*[82] the Court of Appeal determined that a person with a mental disorder was a vulnerable litigant and entitled to legal aid.

It is likely there will be further challenges regarding access to legal aid and whether the requirements of LASPO and the associated regulations are in compliance with Article 6 ECHR (and possibly other rights, such as the right to respect for private and family life under Article 8). The test laid down by the European Court of Human Rights in *P,C,S v UK* would seem wide enough to encompass many more cases than the *Kinderis* and *Re L* cases decided in the English courts. The test in the cases decided by the European Court of Human Rights in *P,C,S v UK* was that a litigant should be able to 'participate effectively' and 'put forward the matters in support of his or her claims'.[83] This may apply to a very significant number of litigants in family law proceedings. However, the cases decided in the English courts seemingly adopt a much more restrictive test and only apply to extreme circumstances.

It is arguable that the way the Family Procedure Rules require courts to deal with family law matters and ensure the parties are on an equal footing can remove the need for many litigants to have access to legal aid. In practice some perceive that judges are becoming

---

[79] App. No. 6289/73 [1979] 2 EHRR 305. [80] (2002) 35 EHRR 31, at [91].
[81] [2013] EWHC 4139 (fam). [82] [2013] EWCA Civ 267. [83] (2002) 35 EHRR 31, at [91].

more inquisitorial in nature, thereby ensuring justice is achieved so the parties do not need legal aid, if mediation has failed.

 Debate 2: Should the Reduction in Legal Aid Imposed LASPO 2012 be Repealed and Funding be Provided to Make Legal Aid Available to More People?

There has been a lot of publicity about the effect of the cuts to legal aid funding following LASPO in 2012. However, for the last 25 years successive political parties have made cuts to the legal aid budget. A central issue is funding. Harris states:

> Over the last three decades the lord Chancellor and his civil servants have become increasingly vulnerable to pressure from the treasury and from elsewhere in the executive branch of the government to contain or reduce the expenditure on such services.[84]

On the one hand, it is argued legal aid is needed to secure access to justice for certain individuals, but there is not an infinite budget. A balance has to be struck between providing legal aid and what is available to pay for this by way of taxation. The Chair of the House of Commons Justice Select Committee, Sir Alan Beith MP, explains the dilemma and some of the effects of the cuts following LASPO:

> The urgency of the financial situation in which this country found itself in 2010 meant that the MoJ was faced with difficult decisions: making £2 billion of savings from a budget of £9.8 billion was clearly a very challenging target and it was successfully achieved.But this has limited access to justice for some of those who need legal aid the most and, in some instances, has failed to prevent cases becoming more serious and creating further claims on the legal aid budget.[85]

There are other issues which have consistently arisen during the last three decades about legal aid. It is not just the cost, but how efficiently it has been expended in the provision of legal aid services since, during this time, spending on legal aid has increased but at the same time the number of those eligible has reduced.

Despite LASPO it has been stated the desired budget cuts have not been achieved in any event. The Ministry of Justice estimated that these cuts would deliver savings of £220 million per year by 2018–19.[86] Cookson suggests the cuts have achieved 42% of what was anticipated that the government would save and that the effect of these cuts is 'insubstantial'.[87]

Others have widened the debate by asserting cutting legal aid expenditure is not the only aim and purpose of LASPO, but rather this enactment was also motivated by ideological concerns. The notion is that the state should not fund the resolution of legal disputes between

---

[84] Harris, P.G. 'Casualties of Friendly Fire: Counter Productive Campaigning on Public Funded Legal Services'. in M. Maclean, J. Eekelaar, and B. Bastard (eds) *Delivering Family Justice in the 21st Century* (Hart Publishing, 2015) 265–6.

[85] House of Commons Justice Select Committee, 'Impact of Changes to Civil Legal Aid Under the Legal Aid, Sentencing and Punishment of Offenders Act 2012', March 2015. Available at: https://www.parliament. uk/business/committees/committees-a-z/commons-select/justice-committee/news/lapso-report/, accessed 10 October 2017.

[86] Ministry Of Justice, 'Transforming legal aid: delivering a more credible and efficient system'. (September 2013).

[87] Cookson, G. 'Unintended Consequences: The Cost of the Government's Legal Aid Reforms'. A Report for the Law Society of England & Wales (King's College, 2011) 75.

individuals. Such objections to utilising state funds for legal aid in this way are termed neo-liberal. As Trinder summarises:

> The reforms also reflect a particular neoliberal ideology towards the state's role in relation to families, emphasising individual responsibility rather than state intervention.[88]

Sommerlad goes further in stating the focus of the legislation on resolving matters privately, for example through mediation:

> is fundamental to the reforms' symbolic work of eroding the very idea of state responsibility for private justice, and increasing a new moral compass or truth criteria for society, work which is clearly infused with both neoliberal and neo-conservative rationalities.[89]

Sommerlad argues that the government's intention is in fact to demolish a major part of the civil justice system:

> The disintegration of the private law justice system should be viewed as the ultimate goal, in other words the aim is to further the crisis to a point where it becomes common sense that, first as a matter of practical economics, the system is too far gone and too expensive to save, and secondly, that in any event, the state and justice system has no business intervening in people's lives.[90]

In contrast Harris argues that there are those in government who believe in the principles of legal aid, and they have been, and are doing their best in a difficult situation. He also gives a cautionary tale about pressure groups trying to oppose the cuts actually making matters worse and what he terms as scoring 'own goals':

> The examples given above seek to demonstrate the need on the part of interest groups to be careful not to hinder or undermine those within the government machine who, in the face of heavy pressure, may nonetheless be doing the best they can to protect and promote publicly funded services.[91]

In January 2017, Sir Oliver Heald announced LASPO will be reviewed. He stated:

> We will look at how the act has been affected by litigation, the various reviews of legal aid done by bodies such as the National Audit Office and others. This will lead to an initial discussion as to the extent to which changes to legal aid met their objectives, which is the test for the post-legislative memorandum. Then we will begin work on the full post-implementation review.[92]

The outcome of this review is awaited, and although many express the view there should be more funding for legal aid, the question will always be who should receive legal aid and how is it going to be paid for?

---

[88] Trinder, L, 'Taking responsibility? Legal Aid reforms and Litigants in Person in England' in M. Maclean, J. Eekelaar, and B. Bastard (eds) *Delivering Family Justice in the 21st Century* (Hart Publishing, 2015) 223.

[89] Sommerlad, H. 'Access to Justice in Hard Times and the Deconstruction of Democratic Citizenship' in M. Maclean, J. Eekelaar, and B. Bastard (eds) *Delivering Family Justice in the 21st Century* (Hart Publishing, 2015) 246.

[90] Sommerlad, H. 'Access to Justice in Hard Times and the Deconstruction of Democratic Citizenship' in M. Maclean, J. Eekelaar, and B. Bastard (eds) *Delivering Family Justice in the 21st Century* (Hart Publishing, 2015) 264

[91] Harris, PG 'Casualties of Friendly Fire: Counter Productive Cmpaigning on Public Funded Legal Services' in M. Maclean, J. Eekelaar, and B. Bastard (eds) *Delivering Family Justice in the 21st Century* (Hart Publishing, 2015) 265–6.

[92] Fouzder, M. 'At Last: MoJ Announces Timetable for LASPO Review', 18 January 2017. Available at: https://www.lawgazette.co.uk/law/at-last-moj-announces-timetable-for-laspo-review/5059442.article, accessed 10 October 2017.

7. Litigants in person and McKenzie Friends

One of the consequences of the cuts to legal aid is that it has led to more litigants acting for themselves, commonly known as 'litigants in person'.

 CONTEXT 5: THE INCREASE IN LITIGANTS IN PERSON

The National Audit Office found after the implementation of LASPO in 2013 that there was a 30% increase in cases where one or both parties were litigants in person.[93] By September 2016, government statistics showed that the proportion of family court cases with neither side represented was 34%,[94] the highest since LASPO came into force.

Trinder argues that it is difficult to predict accurately the effect of the increase in litigants in person on the family justice system without a 'Systematic analysis of the reforms'[95] and adequate research, which she says the government promised. Trinder highlights the effect of litigants in person in other jurisdictions, in particular in Canada[96] and Australia.[97]

Hunter suggests ways in which the position of litigants in person may be improved.[98] These are, *inter alia*, providing better information; the provision of more economical or free legal advice through such organisations as law centres and duty solicitor schemes, perhaps on the basis of fixed fees. She also advocates a move from the current adversarial system to a more inquisitorial system, which many have advocated. However as a consequence of the fact that judges participate more in an inquisitorial system, this can mean cases take longer and cause even more delays.

Another consequence of LASPO is the increase in the number of persons accessing online Web based services to deal with family legal issues, such as divorce. However Maclean cautions that 'We are seeing increased interest in low-cost internet access to as yet largely unregulated information services' at the same time as being directed to mediation. This she describes as 'These two new developments, it is suggested, do not so much fill the gap left by the impact of reduced public and private spending on legal advice but circle around it, like a bagel with a hole in the middle'.[99]

It is suggested that the increase in litigants in person in this jurisdiction has inevitably led to cases taking much longer. It has also been suggested that such litigants may also be deterred from pursuing a case or just give up.[100] It has also led inevitably to an increase in the use of McKenzie Friends.

---

[93] National Audit Office, *Implementing Reform to Civil Legal Aid* (HC 784 Session, 2014–15) 4.

[94] Hyde, J. 'Judges: Cuts are a False Economy' (2015) 112 *Law Society Gazette* 4.

[95] Trinder, L, 'Taking responsibility? Legal Aid reforms and Litigants in Person in England' in M. Maclean, J. Eekelaar, and B. Bastard (eds) *Delivering Family Justice in the 21st Century* (Hart Publishing, 2015) 225.

[96] Dewar, J, Smith, B., and Banks, C. *Litigants in Person in the Family Court of Australia* (Family Court of Australia, 2000).

[97] Macfarlane, *The National Self-represented Litigants Project* (University of Windsor, 2013).

[98] Hunter, R. 'Access to Justice after LASPO' [2014] *Family Law* 640.

[99] Maclean, M, 'New Ways to seek Legal Information and Advice on family Matters in England and wales: From Professional Legal services to Google and Private Ordering' in M. Maclean, J. Eekelaar, and B. Bastard (eds) *Delivering Family Justice in the 21st Century* (Hart Publishing, 2015) 323–4; and see Maclean, M, 'The Changing Professional Landscape' [2014] *Family law* 177.

[100] MacLean, M. and Eekelaar J. 'Legal Representation in Family Matters and the Reform of Legal Aid: A Research Note on Current practice' (2012) 24 *Child and Family Law Quarterly* 223.

> **Key Case 4: *McKenzie v McKenzie* [1970] 3 All ER 1034**
>
> The name 'McKenzie Friends' is derived from the case of *McKenzie v McKenzie*.[101] McKenzie presented a petition for divorce and had legal aid that was subsequently withdrawn. He was then assisted by Ian Hanger, an Australian barrister, who had no right of audience in England. Mr Hangar had hoped to sit with McKenzie and offer help and assistance. However, the trial judge ordered Mr Hangar not to take any active part in the case, except to advise McKenzie during adjournments and to sit in the public gallery. McKenzie appealed. The Court of Appeal ruled that the trial judge's intervention had deprived McKenzie of the assistance to which he was entitled and ordered a retrial.

Although the name is taken from this case, the concept of a McKenzie Friend is not new. It can be traced back to almost 150 years ago, when the then Lord Chief Justice, Lord Tenterden stated in *Collier v Hicks*:[102]

> Any person, whether he be a professional man or not, may attend as a friend of either party, may take notes, may quietly make suggestions, and give advice: but no one can demand to take part in the proceedings, contrary to the regulations of the Court as settled by the discretion of the justices.

In a report in 2014, The Legal Services Consumer Panel classified McKenzie Friends as someone in one of the following four categories;

- The family member or friend who gives one-off assistance
- Volunteer McKenzie Friends attached to an institution/charity
- Fee-charging McKenzie Friends offering the conventional limited service understood by this role
- Fee-charging McKenzie Friends offering a wider range of services including general legal advice and speaking on behalf of clients in court.[103]

7.1 The role of a McKenzie Friend

Such has been the concern about the role of McKenzie Friends in the family courts that the Lord Chief Justice commissioned a Working Group led by Asplin J (The Asplin Report)[104] to suggest possible reform of the law relating to them. This group published its findings in February 2016. It sets out three possible ways in which McKenzie Friends may assist.

7.1.1 The right to reasonable assistance

The first way in which a McKenzie Friend may assist a litigant is through the right to give reasonable assistance. Lord Donaldson MR explained this in *R Leicester City Justices, ex parte Barrow* as: 'every litigant has the right to arm himself with such assistance as he thinks appropriate, subject to the right of the court to intervene'.[105] The Asplin Report finds there is no precise definition of what constitutes 'reasonable assistance'. However, the report does refer to a Practice Direction in 2010 issued by the Master of the Rolls and The President of the Family Division[106] and usefully suggests that it includes: the provision of

---

[101] [1970] 3 All ER 1034.   [102] (1831) 2 B & Ad 663, at 669.
[103] Legal Services Consumer Panel, 'Fee-charging McKenzie Friends' (April 2014).
[104] The Lord Chief Justice of England and Wales, 'Reforming the court's approach to McKenzie Friends. A Consultation' (February 2016).   [105] [1991] 2 QB 260, at 289.
[106] Practice Guidance (McKenzie Friends: Civil and Family Courts) [2010] 4 All ER 272.

moral support; note taking; helping to prepare and sitting next to the litigant in person in court; and quietly giving advice as to what questions to ask and what submissions to make.

7.1.2 The right to exercise rights of audience

The second suggested role of a McKenzie Friend is a right of audience to represent a litigant in court, which clearly goes much further than just providing reasonable assistance. The Legal Services Act 2007 governs who is authorised to conduct litigation and have a right of audience before the English courts. It allows practising lawyers to act for litigants, a category of what are described as 'exempt persons',[107] and, crucially, those whom the court allows to act. Thus the legislation does not provide a specific right of audience to a McKenzie friend. However judges have the inherent power to allow McKenzie friends to represent litigants. An individual can of course always represent themselves in respect of their own case in both conducting litigation and appearing before any court.

7.1.3 The right to conduct litigation

Thirdly, McKenzie Friends have a right to issue proceedings, and to pursue and defend them on behalf of a litigant. These are also regulated activities pursuant to Legal Services Act 2007. Again, only practising lawyers, certain exempt persons, and those authorised by the court can undertake these functions lawfully. It is important to be aware that the court has an absolute discretion as to what latitude to allow a McKenzie Friend. To act without the permission of the court is a criminal offence.

7.2 McKenzie Friend or foe?

Historically, a McKenzie Friend was usually unpaid and it is the development of the paid McKenzie Friend that has caused the most concern. There is a Society of Professional McKenzie Friends,[108] whose members must have what is termed professional indemnity insurance. This is insurance which solicitors and barristers are required by their professional governing bodies to take out if they are in practice, to cover claims against them for negligence. However, there are McKenzie Friends who are not members of this organisation. Thus not all McKenzie Friends are professionally regulated and may not be insured. The significance of this is that if they are negligent, the litigant in person may in effect have no redress against them, because they have not the means to pay any damages.

There are additional concerns about McKenzie Friends. In 2015, a paid McKenzie Friend was banned indefinitely from court for abusing and threatening behaviour. In 2016, two persons were convicted of perverting the course of justice whilst acting in their capacity as McKenzie Friends by allegedly submitting false evidence in court.[109] The Law Society[110] and the Bar Council[111] both have concerns and have published guides for solicitors and barristers on how to deal with cases in the circumstances that they are acting against a litigant in person, who may or may not have a McKenzie Friend.

The future of paid McKenzie Friends in family cases is unclear. The Asplin Report in 2016 made various recommendations. First, it concludes that the use of the name 'McKenzie Friend' is an 'accident of history' and confusing. They recommend that this name should

---

[107] Legal Services Act 2007, s. 19 and Sch 3.   [108] The Society of Professional McKenzie Friends Ltd.

[109] Walters, M. 'McKenzie friend jailed for "deceit in family court"', 17 October 2016. Available at: https://www.lawgazette.co.uk/law/mckenzie-friend-jailed-for-deceit-in-family-court/5058352.article, accessed 10 October 2017.

[110] The Law Society, 'Litigants in person: guidelines for lawyers and a selection of relevant cases' (June 2015).

[111] The Bar Council, 'litigants in person: guidelines for lawyers' (June 2015).

be limited to covering only those offering reasonable assistance and not those permitted a right of audience by the court. The earlier Hickinbottom Report on litigants in person had also made this recommendation in 2003.[112] The Asplin Report suggests they may be called lay supporters, lay representatives, or lay litigators thus providing a clear distinction between the various roles of the McKenzie Friend.

The second finding of the Asplin Report is that updating the 2010 Practice Direction is not in itself enough to achieve the necessary reform. The Report recommends the codification of the courts' approach by providing a clear set of rules.[113] Thirdly, the Report recommended that any litigant in person and McKenzie Friend should supply standard information to the court in a specified format, which states, *inter alia*, that the McKenzie Friend has no interest in the outcome of the case. They would also have to give information about themselves in a curriculum vitae or written statement acknowledging that they understand they owe a duty to the court of confidentiality and that they understand and agree to be bound by a code of conduct to be produced to regulate litigants in person.

Finally, The Asplin Report recommends that there should be a ban on representatives receiving remuneration. It states that this is justified on the basis that it is in the public interest, and that it was the clear intention of Parliament, in the enactment of the Legal Services Act 2007, which specifically did not include McKenzie Friends as those entitled to charge for litigation services. Does this mark the end of the McKenzie friend as we know it? Parpworth expresses the view that the Asplin Report:

> Proposals do not mark the end of the McKenzie friend per se. Rather, they suggest that the demise of the professional or paid McKenzie Friend may not be very far away, and that the name will pass into history to be replaced by something which better reflects the nature of the recast role.[114]

 DEBATE 3: SHOULD PAID MCKENZIE FRIENDS BE PERMITTED BY LAW AND HOW SHOULD THEY BE REGULATED?

It is highly likely that legislation will now be enacted to clarify and govern how McKenzie Friends operate. This is highlighted by the Lord Chief Justice, Lord Thomas's open criticisms of paid McKenzie Friends. In his annual press conference in late 2016[115] he stated: 'I have seen them give legal advice that is simply wrong, they are preying on vulnerable people and that is why I am very, very cautious about payment to non-lawyers who try and assist vulnerable people.'

It has been suggested that there needs to be more regulation of professional McKenzie Friends. A report for the Ministry of Justice analysed samples of cases where McKenzie Friends had been utilised. The authors state they: 'Do not advocate more widespread use of paid McKenzie Friends acting as quasi-legal advisors without qualification, regulation or insurance.'[116] Yet, the Legal Services Board's position is that there is not enough evidence that McKenzie Friends are harming consumers of legal services. The Solicitors' Regulation

---

[112] The Judicial Working Group on Litigants in Person: Report (led by Hickinbottom, J) (Judiciary of England and Wales, 2013).

[113] A draft set of codified rules are appended to their report.

[114] Parpworth, N. 'McKenzie Fri-End', (2016) 166 *New Law Journal* 20.

[115] Lord Chief Justice, Lord Thomas, annual press conference, 30 November 2016 at The Royal Courts of Justice.

[116] Trinder, L et al 'Litigants in person in private family law cases', Ministry of Justice Analytical Series 2014, 117.

Authority suggests that a blanket ban may mean that litigants in person may not get access to support, even when there are no quality issues.[117]

Both the Law Society and the Bar Council want the imposition of a ban on remuneration for McKenzie Friends. A former President of the Law Society, Jonathan Smithers[118] makes the point that McKenzie Friends are not necessarily less expensive than solicitors, but are not regulated to the same extent as solicitors, or held to the same professional standards. He warns that solicitors have: 'Witnessed the damage done by unscrupulous' [119] McKenzie Friends. The Chair of Research on behalf of the Bar Council states their position is that: 'We believe that families and the wider public are in some cases paying for McKenzie Friends without realising these individuals are unregulated and often unqualified and uninsured.'[120] Andrew Langdon QC, Chairman of the Bar Association, has identified: 'The risks of McKenzie Friends being able to seek payment for representing their clients in court, despite being unqualified and offering no disciplinary process and no requirement to have insurance, are considerable and so vulnerable clients have little protection.'[121]

In response, the Chair of the Society of Professional McKenzie Friends states that a ban on remuneration is not in the interests of the consumer: 'nor of the administration of justice. It is protectionism, pure and simple'. He argues if the proposals in the Asplin Report are implemented this would exclude Citizen Advice Bureaux and other agencies being paid. He concludes, 'This tells the consumer that they must pay whatever charges solicitors and barristers require of them or receive no legal help at all—no alternative is permitted.'[122] It may well be that the costs of a McKenzie Friend could be capped or based on rates published by the courts, and subject to assessment, as is the case in respect of solicitors' costs and barristers' fees. The London solicitor Jeffrey Gordon, who represented McKenzie in the 1970 landmark case, does not believe McKenzie Friends should be paid for their services. However, nor does he believe they should be subject to a code of conduct.[123]

The controversy about McKenzie Friends highlights the metamorphosis that the family legal system is going through as a consequence of the significant cuts to legal aid. These cuts have left many unable to afford to pay solicitors and barristers. Many are vulnerable; are they to be left unrepresented? Or is some form of regulated McKenzie Friend something which will help those disenfranchised from legal aid?

---

[117] Hilbourne, N. 'Legal Services Board and Solicitors Regulation Authority oppose ban on professional McKenzie Friends'. Available at: http://legalfutures.co.uk/latest-news/lsb-and-sra-oppose-ban-professional-mckenzie, accessed 20 June 2017.

[118] Law Society 'McKenzie Friends are not Legal Professionals', 9 June 2016, Available at: http://www.law-society.org.uk/news/press-releases/mckenzie-friends-are-not-legal-professionals-and-should-not-be-able-to-recover-fees-says-the-law-society/, accessed 10 October 2017.

[119] Walters, M. 'McKenzie friend jailed for "deceit in family court"', 17 October 2016. Available at: https://www.lawgazette.co.uk/law/mckenzie-friend-jailed-for-deceit-in-family-court/5058352.article, accessed 10 October 2017.

[120] The Bar Council, referring to Smith, L, Hitchings, E., and Sefton., M. 'A Study of Fee-Charging McKenzie Friends and their work in Private Family Law Cases'. Available at: http://www.barcouncil.org.uk/media/573001/executive_summary.pdf, accessed 10 October 2017.

[121] See https://www.graysinn.org.uk/news/news-update-the-bar-council (9th June 2017), accessed 21 June 2017.

[122] Smith, C., 'Judiciary proposes ban on fee-charging McKenzie Friends'. 25 February 2016, *Law Society Gazette*. Available at: https://www.lawgazette.co.uk/practice/judiciary-proposes-ban-on-fee-charging-mckenzie-friends/5053851.article, accessed 10 October 2017.

[123] Walters, M. 'McKenzie Friend Pioneer says no to Charges', 22 May 2017, *Law Society Gazette*. Available at: https://www.lawgazette.co.uk/news/mckenzie-friend-pioneer-says-no-to-charges/5061220.article, accessed 10 October 2017.

This goes to the very heart of the structure of the legal system as it is, and inevitably raises the issue of whether rights of audience should be extended to bring the solicitors' and barristers' monopoly to an end. Should another tier of a paralegal type of McKenzie Friend be allowed to represent litigants?

Andrew Langdon QC, Chairman of the Bar Association, has suggested that: There is a broader issue here—that many people seeking justice, who may have been denied legal aid following years of cuts, have no choice but to turn to a McKenzie Friend, paid or otherwise, at their time of need, for legal advice and support.'[124] In cases where solicitors and barristers are not appearing due to funding, should a legal consumer not be given a cheaper, more affordable option of a McKenzie Friend providing that they are properly regulated and insured?

8. Non court dispute resolution

A very important tool of the family law legal landscape, to avoid court proceedings and to encourage settlement, is the usage of non court dispute resolution (formerly known as alternative dispute resolution).[125] Part 3 of the Family Procedure Rules is dedicated to non court dispute resolution.

Rule 3.2 imposes a specific duty on the court to consider, at *every stage* of proceedings, whether non court dispute resolution is appropriate. There are provisions to permit the court to adjourn proceedings to allow the parties to obtain information about non court dispute resolution.[126]

8.1 Forms of non court dispute resolution

Non court dispute resolution takes many forms. The most obvious and basic form of non court dispute resolution is voluntarily negotiation. This can be between the parties directly or between their lawyers. Often joint settlement meetings are held to try and resolve matters between the parties and their lawyers. These are usually stated to be without prejudice, meaning that everything said is confidential and not to be disclosed in court. This is the most common way cases are settled.

A slightly more formal procedure of non court dispute resolution is called 'early neutral evaluation'. This involves a neutral third party, with expertise of the subject matter of the dispute, providing an evaluation of the merits and likely outcome of the case. It is hoped this will then lead to the parties settling the case. A similar, but more binding procedure, is expert determination. It is similar to early neutral evaluation, save the parties are bound by the expert's decision.

8.2 Arbitration

Another form of non court dispute resolution is arbitration.

While arbitration has long been used in commercial disputes, its use as a method to deal with family law cases is evolving. It is only suitable to settle financial matters, not issues

---

[124] Walters, M. 'Nip rogue McKenzies in the bud', 12 June 2017, *Law Society Gazette.* Available at: https://www.lawgazette.co.uk/news/nip-rogue-mckenzies-in-the-bud-bar/5061484.article, accessed 10 October 2017.

[125] As referred to in The Family Procedure Rules which refers to alternative dispute resolution (ADR) but it is now known as Non Court Dispute Resolution (NCDR), and is referred to as such in this text.

[126] Family Procedure Rules, para 3.3.

relating to children. Arbitration is the closest forum to the traditional method of resolving disputes through the courts at a trial. It is governed by statute[127] and procedures which have evolved over many years. It is essentially a method of contracting out of the state system and purchasing a private forum within which to adjudicate upon a dispute. In both arbitration and the court systems fees are payable.

The parties will have to agree the identity of an arbitrator who must be a member of the Institute of Family Law Arbitrators.[128] All such arbitrators are qualified solicitors or barristers who have successfully completed an accredited arbitration course. The role of arbitrators is similar to that of judges, to hear and determine the case in accordance with the law. Arbitration may be perceived to be less formal than proceeding in a courtroom. However, it can be more expensive than processing a case through the courts. This is because the parties will have to pay the arbitrator's fees and possibly a fee for the venue. Whilst in court cases there are fees, a judge does not have to be paid directly by the parties, nor is there a specific charge for the venue. However, in recent times arbitration is often used because it can determine cases much more quickly than the current court system in which there can be significant delays.

Once an arbitrator has made an award, to be effective and binding it will have to be encompassed in a court order, by consent. This procedure has been accepted by the courts.[129] It illustrates the flexibility of the judiciary and the desire and willingness that cases be resolved otherwise than at court. It also saves the court time and money.

In *S v S* the President of the Family Division provided guidance when parties seek a consent order from the court in these circumstances: 'The judge will not need to play the detective unless something leaps off the page to indicate that something has gone so seriously wrong in the arbitral process as fundamentally to vitiate the arbitral award.'[130]

8.3 Collaborative law

Collaborative family law is another option for resolving issues and disputes without going to court. The hallmark of collaborative law is that it is non-contentious. Unlike arbitration, it can be used to resolve both financial disputes and issues relating to the children on divorce. However, it is not appropriate if there has been domestic violence in the relationship between the parties. It is a requirement that the parties have lawyers to represent them, so inevitably it is going to come at some cost.

At the outset, the lawyers representing the parties seek to ensure this process is suitable for all concerned. The parties sign an agreement and commit to trying to resolve the matter amicably. Crucially, the process requires the parties to undertake with each other not to issue court proceedings to resolve matters. A typical collaborative law agreement would require the parties to agree not to discuss past events, and to avoid threats and inflammatory language. A paramount concern in the usage of collaborative law is promoting the best interests of the children. The methodology of collaborative law is the usage of face-to-face meetings between the parties to reach agreement. In addition, psychologists or counselors can participate to support the parties in reaching an agreement. If an agreement is reached then it is only binding if the court makes a consent order.[131]

---

[127] Arbitration Act 1996.   [128] See http://ifla.org.uk/, accessed 3 October 2017.
[129] *S v S* [2014] EWHC 7 (Fam).   [130] [2014] EWHC 7 (Fam), at [21].
[131] Matrimonial Causes Act 1973, s. 33A.

8.4 **Mediation**

Mediation is an important form of non court dispute resolution in family law. It has a recognised role in several statutes: the Access to Justice Act 1999; the Legal Aid Sentencing and Punishment of Offenders Act 2012; and the Children and Families Act 2014. It is much favoured by the Judiciary. Sir James Munby, President of the Family Division has stated:

> Mediation is an established and valued part of the dispute resolution process of which the Family Court also forms a part. It is important for judges to be aware of the advantages that mediation can bring to resolving disputes between separated parents and to bear these in mind when cases come before them which may benefit from mediation. I would also encourage judges to become familiar with the mediation services which are available in their areas.[132]

8.4.1 **Regulation of family mediators**

Family mediators are regulated and governed by six member organisations, all of which are members of the Family Mediation Council and many family mediators are also qualified lawyers. The Family Mediation Council provides a Code of Practice for Family Mediators[133] and sets minimum standards for the practice requirements of family mediation.

Family mediation is characterised by the following principles:

- voluntary;
- confidential, (except where there are concerns of risk of harm to a child or vulnerable adult);
- impartial;
- all participants accepting the mediator has no vested interest in the outcome.
- any decisions are made by the parties, not the mediator.

8.4.2 **The Mediation process**

Mediation is characterised by informality. It is most definitely not an adjudication process. The experienced mediator encourages the parties to arrive at their own solution through negotiation. The role of the mediator has been explained as: 'To facilitate agreement, by the parties in dispute, through preparation, shuttle diplomacy and facilitated face-to-face meetings.'[134] The move to mediation represents a shift from the adversarial battleground of the courtroom. The essence of mediation is coaching the parties to arrive at a solution together, to which they themselves have contributed and been a part of. It has been suggested that parties to mediation can often settle cases at mediation by their own efforts to 'initiate exits from their arguments'. [135]

Once all parties have agreed to try mediation, then a qualified mediator will have to be chosen. There are several methods of identifying a mediator. Local law societies usually have

---

[132] Family Mediation Council and Family Justice Council, 'Family Mediation in England and Wales: A guide for judges, magistrates and legal advisors' 1, Forward by Sir James Munby. Available at: https://www.judiciary.gov.uk/related-offices-and-bodies/advisory-bodies/fjc/guidance/mediation-guide-for-judges-magistrates-and-legal-advisors/, accessed 10 October 2017.

[133] Available at: https://www.familymediationcouncil.org.uk/wp-content/uploads/2016/09/FMC-Code-of-Practice-September-2016-2.pdf, accessed 3 October 2017.

[134] Baxter, K. 'Game of give and take' (2016) 113 *Law Society Gazette* 16.

[135] Greatbatch, D and Dingwall, R, 'Argumentative Talk in Divorce Mediation Sessions'. (1997) 62 *American Sociological Review* 151, 151.

a panel and can nominate a mediator if asked. There are several organisations that have pan-els of mediators. It is necessary to decide where any mediation will take place. It may be at one of the parties' lawyer's place of business or rooms may be booked at a hotel or at the me-diator's offices. There is usually one room for each party and their representatives plus one additional room large enough for all the parties to congregate in. The procedure is flexible.

Traditionally, the mediator will start the process of mediation by calling all parties into one room to outline the process. Each party, through any legal representatives if they have one, will then be given the opportunity to present an opening statement. If they have a legal representative a party need not say anything when all the parties meet together. A media-tor will often begin the session by asking the parties to consider what they want to achieve. Further, mediators often set out the various scenarios concerning the outcome if the matter does not settle through mediation and goes to court for a final hearing. The mediator may do this by asking what the parties' costs are to date and spell out what the costs may be if the matter does not settle and proceeds. The mediator may set out the parties' best and worst case scenarios as regards legal costs and anything else they may lose or be ordered to pay. The parties then usually go into their own room with their legal representatives. The media-tor visits the respective parties and their legal representatives to try to facilitate a settlement. The mediator may call the parties to all meet again during the course of the mediation.

Crucially, neither party is given legal advice by the mediator. The mediator may stress the importance of both parties taking legal advice to complement the mediation that takes place. This ensures that all parties understand the legal consequences of the agreement they reach. The process can last a full day but can be shorter or longer than this. Although mediation can be expensive, if it leads to a settlement it can potentially save a lot of legal costs. Mediator's costs greatly vary. Traditionally a mediator's costs for a full day could be £1,500 to £2,000 plus VAT and the parties' costs including preparation and representation could be a similar amount. (These are the total mediators costs, the parties usually paying an equal share. Any lawyers fees are in addition to these costs.)

8.4.3 The importance of mediation in family law

The Children and Families Act 2014 enacted provisions requiring a party, before issuing certain court proceedings, to attend an initial Mediation Information Assessment Meeting (MIAM).[136] This does not require the parties to attend mediation. Rather, it requires them to attend a meeting with a suitably qualified person to explain the option of mediation to them. In obliging the parties to attend this meeting, the government hoped that both par-ties would then agree to attend mediation, rather than pursuing court proceedings. There are exceptions to having to attend this meeting where safety is a concern, primarily those relating to domestic violence. The following are the types of case where a certificate *must* be obtained that a party has attended a MIAM *before* court proceedings can be issued.

 Key Legislation 3: Children and Families Act 2014, s. 10(1)

The Act requires attendance at a MIAM before the types of proceedings as set out in Family Procedure Rules Practice Direction 3A Family Mediation Information and Assessment Meetings, paras 12 and 13.

  12. Private law proceedings relating to children

   (1) The private law proceedings relating to children are proceedings for the follow-ing orders:

---

[136] Children and families Act 2014, s. 10.

(a) a child arrangements order and other orders with respect to a child or children under section 8 of the Children Act 1989;

(b) a parental responsibility order or an order terminating parental responsibility;

(c) an order appointing a child's guardian or an order terminating the appointment;

(d) an order giving permission to change a child's surname or remove a child from the United Kingdom;

(e) a special guardianship order; and

(f) an order varying or discharging such an order.

13. Proceedings for a financial remedy

(1) The proceedings for a financial remedy for the following orders:

(a) the following financial orders –

(i) an order for maintenance pending suit;

(ii) an order for maintenance pending outcome of proceedings;

(iii) an order for periodical payments or lump sum provision;

(iv) an order for periodical payments or lump sum provision;

(v) a property adjustment order;

(vi) a variation order;

(vii) a pension sharing order; or

(viii) a pension compensation sharing order;

(b) an order for financial provision for children (under Schedule 1 to the Children Act 1989)

However, mediations following a MIAM have taken a different form from the traditional mediation described earlier in 8.4.2. They are generally shorter in duration and less expensive. One reason is that, although legal aid is available the amount is a small fraction of what a mediator may charge if it is not funded by legal aid. Generally, lawyers representing the parties are not present at this form of mediation. The parties will be invited to attend a MIAM, presided over by a mediator who will discuss the case and decide whether or not it is suitable for mediation. The mediator may see both parties separately and subsequently together. The parties both have the opportunity to state what they want from the outcome of the mediation. If an agreement is made, it can be embodied in a consent order. If not, either party can issue proceedings providing they have attended a MIAM. If a party wishes to issue proceedings in a case relating to financial matters in divorce proceedings or a private law children application they must comply with Practice Direction 3 by confirming attendance at the MIAM or that an exception to a MIAM attendance applies.

8.4.4 Advantages and disadvantages of mediation

There is no doubt that the government is committed to mediation as a way of resolving family disputes. Their view is that adults should be able to resolve matters between themselves without expending monies on court proceedings, that it is cost effective and more likely to result in a better outcome. If parties are willing to be realistic and cooperative, then mediation can provide a less confrontational and cheaper way of resolving matters and it is in the best interests of the children.

As Lord Faulks QC stated:

In its consultation paper 'Solving Disputes in the County Courts', published in February 2012, the government said that it wanted: 'to deliver a [justice] system that prevents the unnecessary escalation of disputes before cases reach the court room'.

And

But the success of mediation and other dispute resolution methods in keeping unnecessary litigation out of the courts is a key cornerstone of an effective and cost effective justice system.[137]

The Ministry of Justice advance six reasons why mediation is beneficial.[138]

1. **It allows the parties more control to govern how matters will be resolved and gives them more of an input.** The notion is that, in court, a judge makes the decision whereas, at mediation, the parties make the decision. Judges often state it is better if the parties both agree themselves the outcome of a case, rather than a judge having to decide the case and determine who is right and wrong. However, there are concerns that, although the parties may decide the outcome, inevitably one party will be stronger than the other and may manipulate or coerce the other party to make an agreement which is not fair. Diduck argues the notion of an autonomous 'system of dispute resolution that includes mediation, arbitration and provision of information hubs' has evolved and 'autonomy has become more than simply one aspect of justice to be considered alongside, for example, fairness, equality, and the rule of law, it is becoming the very essence of family justice'.[139] This has to be guarded against; mediation is not appropriate for all cases.

In financial cases following divorce there is some protection from the courts. If parties do settle a case regarding the financial matters following divorce, until the court embody the terms of such an agreement into an order, commonly called a 'consent order', it is not binding. This is because in family law cases regarding financial matters, irrespective of any agreement, the parties may make, any party can apply to court for a share of the others assets or any joint assets until a court order is made.[140] In other words the jurisdiction of the court cannot be ousted by the parties.[141] If the parties do settle, they can then apply to court for an order stating the terms of it and making provisions that neither of them can claim against the other. In these circumstances all parties are required to submit the order and a summary of their financial position to the court. This will then be considered by a judge without the need at this stage for the parties to attend. The courts will not make the order unless it is fair. It is highly recommended that this is done in every case. Otherwise, at some point in the future, a spouse, or former spouse, may be able to apply to court for a share of a spouse, or former spouse's assets, despite any agreement they may have made between themselves (see Chapter 4). If the court does not consider the order to be fair, they will refuse to make it and fix a date for a hearing which all parties should attend with their lawyers.

However, there is no such protection in cases concerning children. Indeed, the presumption is that no court order should be made and the parties should make their own arrangements. There is an argument that if the parties settle a matter through mediation or otherwise, it may not be the fairest result. In other words, it may be said a judge may be more qualified than the parties to determine what outcome the law requires as fair.

2. **Mediation is less stressful with less conflict, less upsetting for children, and can lay foundations for all parties to get on better in the future**. However, this is not necessarily the case. Parties may feel very stressed attending family mediation. They may feel better protected in a courtroom with judges and court staff, including security, present.

---

[137] Lord Faulks QC, Keynote speech at the Civil Mediation Conference, 22 May 2014.

[138] Ministry of Justice. 'Family mediation: Sorting out family disputes without going through court'. Available at: https://www.familymediationcouncil.org.uk/wp-content/uploads/2014/12/family_mediation_leaflet_web_eng.pdf, accessed 10 October 2017.

[139] Diduck, A. 'Autonomy and Family Justice' (2016) 28 *Child and Family Law Quarterly* 133.

[140] Matrimonial Causes Act 1973, s. 33A.   [141] Matrimonial Causes Act 1973, s. 34(1).

3. **Mediation improves communication and helps parties resolve their future.** This may be true if it succeeds, but that is no guarantee.

4. **Agreements made at mediation can be reviewed and changed if both parties agree.** The Ministry of Justice give an example of children getting older and thereby having different needs. But equally, following a court order the parties can, by consent, change any such arrangements and, in practice, frequently do so. For example, if the parties mutually agree to change contact arrangements between parents and children following a court order, they can do this.

5. **Mediation is better for children, as when parents cooperate this helps to continue important family relations.** This is only if it succeeds. Many agree the importance of involving children, at the appropriate stage, in trying to resolve matters concerning them. In 2014 the government announced an intention that all children over 10 would be given an opportunity to give their views in both public and private family law proceedings.[142] However Ewing and others argue that to ensure children's voices are heard effectively there will have to be much better training for those involved in the processes, including mediators and solicitors.[143]

6. **It 'is quicker, cheaper and provides a better way to sort out disagreements than long drawn-out court battles-helping you to get on with the rest of your life as quickly as possible'.** These reasons are advanced by the Ministry of Justice as the main advantages of mediation. If mediation succeeds, it may be very much cheaper than court proceedings and much quicker. However, if it fails, it can be an unnecessary expense, as if the parties then go to court they will also incur the costs of proceedings as well as the mediation fees. Also it can be expensive if it is not publicly funded, particularly if solicitors and barristers are involved.

 DEBATE 4: HAS THE GOVERNMENT SUCCEEDED IN ACHIEVING ITS AIMS BY PROMOTING MEDIATION OF FAMILY DISPUTES?

The government's aim was that cases would be settled by mediation, which would avoid the need for legal aid for court proceedings and justifies the limits placed on the availability of legal aid.

Despite the emphasis placed on mediation of family disputes by the creation of the MIAM by the Children and Families Act 2014, mediation of family disputes has fallen. The statistics show that during 2013, family mediation referrals fell by a national average of approximately 30%. This is despite legal aid having been available to fund it. The number of couples attending MIAMs fell by about 50% on average between 2012 and 2013.[144] Thus it would appear from these statistics that mediation has not succeeded as much as the government had hoped. The legal aid budget allocated for mediation has a surplus, somewhat ironically in view of the budget cuts. Beck and Connie conclude that the government's goals of divorce mediation may have been over optimistic.[145]

[142] The Rt Hon Simon Hughes MP, Minister of State for Justice and Civil Liberties, speech at the Family Justice People's Board's 'Voice of the Child' Conference, 24 July 2014.

[143] Ewing, J. *et al* 'Children's voices: Centre-stage or side-lined in out-of-court dispute resolution in England and Wales (2015) 27 *Child and Family Law Quarterly* 43.

[144] Baski, C. 'Referrals to family mediation plummet', 30 September 2013, *Law Society Gazette*. Available at: https://www.lawgazette.co.uk/practice/referrals-to-family-mediation-plummet/5037894.article, accessed 10 October 2017.

[145] Beck, C.J.A. and Sales, B.D. 'A Critical Reappraisal of Divorce Mediation and Policy' (2000) 6 *Psychology, Public Policy and Law* 989.

Why is mediation not working as well, or being used as much as the government expected? One of the reasons suggested is that parties are not aware of it because they are not getting legal advice about it as an option. The National Family Mediation expresses the view:

The government had intended that greater numbers of people would try mediation before making an application to court but the failure to publicise services has had the opposite effect and people are heading straight to the court because they do not know what else to do . . . What the government didn't see was that lawyers acted as gatekeepers for both mediation and the courts. Now the public is left with few options other than to apply to court, and now more frequently as a litigant in person.[146]

But is this argument sustainable? As the law requires most persons to attend a MIAM, it must surely be the case that, after attending a MIAM, a party is aware of the option of mediation. It has been further suggested by Resolution that, in fact, MIAM have failed to effectively to 'channel people into mediation'.[147] It is difficult to see how this can be done, especially if the parties do not want to mediate.

In practice, it would seem many persons simply just do not want to exercise the mediation option, often believing it will not lead to a resolution. Walker suggests the mediation process has become confusing because of different approaches to divorce mediation. She advocates: 'The search for greater clarity may well lessen the current gap between the rhetoric of mediation and the reality of mediation practice.'[148]

However, mediation does work in many cases. Research has shown as many as 67% of parties receiving publicly funded mediation settled their cases and did not have to go to court.[149] But mediation is not an adequate and suitable substitute for a comprehensive legal aid system because it is simply not appropriate for all cases. It is necessary to retain the family courts, as Ridley-Duff and Bennett assert: 'Sometimes mediation succeeded when all other approaches had failed. Nevertheless, family mediation research shows the reverse is also true: mediation cannot address all (perceived) conflicts of interest and that recourse to courts is still needed as an option.'[150] A detailed study based on the results of a three-year Economic and Social Research Council project concluded: 'Our research suggests that one size does not fit all when it comes to family dispute resolution, and that the absolute policy preference for mediation is not justified.'[151] There will always be parties who cannot settle and need a court to decide their case.

Mediation is not usually a viable option where there have been instances of domestic violence. This is why the government enacted an exemption allowing persons not to participate in the pre-mediation process if there has been evidence of domestic violence.

---

[146] A press release on 8 October 2013 cited in Somers, A. 'Family Mediation—Boom or Bust' 22 November 2014 *Family Law Week*. Available at: http://www.familylawweek.co.uk/site.aspx?i=ed136933, accessed 10 October 2017.

[147] Smith, C. 'Rise in divorce cases signal mediation failure'. (2017) *Law Society Gazette*. Available at: https://www.lawgazette.co.uk/law/rise-in-divorce-cases-signals-mediation-failure/5050631.article, accessed 3 October 2017.

[148] Walker, J. 'Mediation in divorce: does the process match the rhetoric?' in Messmer, M. (ed). *Restorative Justice on Trial: Pitfalls and Potential of Victim-Offender Mediation* (Springer 2012) 475.

[149] Quartermain, S, 'Sustainability of mediation and legal representation in private family law cases. Analysis of legal aid datasets', Ministry of Justice Research Series 8/11 (November, 2011) 2.

[150] Ridley-Duff, R.J and Bennett, A.J. 'Mediation: developing a theoretical framework for understanding alternative dispute resolution' in *British Academy of Management* (Sheffield, 14–16 September 2010). Available at: http://shura.shu.ac.uk, accessed 3 October 2017.

[151] Hunter, R, *et al* 'Paths to justice in Divorce cases in England and Wales' in M. Maclean, J. Eekelaar, and B. Bastard (eds) *Delivering Family Justice in the 21st Century* (Hart Publishing, 2015) 161

In conclusion, while the simplification and streamlining of court procedures, introduced by the Family Procedure Rules 2010 have improved matters, the government have not succeeded in their objective of, in effect, replacing legal aid with mediation. Courts will always be needed to determine those cases which cannot settle. It is a fundamental human right for a party to have the right for a court to decide their case. Additionally it is the function of the courts to interpret laws made by Parliament and implement them.

SUMMARY

1. When, and how, should the Legal Aid Agency statutory charge apply?
   - The Legal Aid Agency statutory charge applies if a legally aided person recovers or preserves money or property from a case for which they had legal aid funding.
   - The legislation governing it is currently embodied in LASPO.
   - It is vital legally aided persons are made fully aware of the implications of the statutory charge at the outset, as crucial decisions may be made as to whether it is more financially beneficial to fight or settle a case.
   - Whether the statutory charge applies is governed by case law. Leading cases are *Hanlon v The Law Society* and *Curling v the Law Society*.
   - In 2014 The Legal Aid Agency published a helpful guide to the law in this field entitled the 'Statutory Charge Manual'.
   - The statutory charge is important both now and in the future. In view of the cuts in government spending across the board, the recoupment of the statutory charge is a potential significant source of revenue for the public purse.

2. Should the reduction in legal aid imposed by the Legal Aid, Sentencing and Punishment of Offenders Act 2012 be repealed and funding be provided to make legal aid available to more people?
   - The Legal Aid Act 1949 had created one of the most extensive legal aid schemes in the world.
   - For the last 25 years successive political parties have made cuts to the legal aid budget. The central issue is funding. On the one hand it is argued legal aid is needed to secure access to justice for certain individuals, but there is not an infinite budget. A balance has to be struck between providing legal aid and what is available to pay for this by way of taxation.
   - An important issue is that spending on legal aid has increased but at the same time the number of those eligible has reduced.
   - Despite LASPO it has been stated the desired budget cuts have not been achieved.
   - The cuts following LASPO have had significant consequences reducing those eligible for legal aid by circa 650,000. This has excluded many from being able to obtain legal advice and representation
   - This has had serious repercussions, not just on individual access to justice but more broadly on the administration of justice itself.

- Leading Judges have stated LASPO is damaging our family justice system and that it is once again in crisis
- LASPO is currently being reviewed by the government. The outcome of this review is awaited

3. Should paid McKenzie Friends be permitted by law and how should they be regulated?
- Cuts to legal aid following LASPO have directly caused a significant increase in the number of litigants in person and McKenzie Friends.
- There has been Practice Guidance from the Master of the Rolls in 2010, A Judicial Working Party in 2013 (Hickinbottom Report), and a Working Party Consultation commissioned by the Lord Chief Justice in 2016 (Asplin Report) to examine how to deal with McKenzie Friends.
- Leading judges and lawyers have expressed concerns about McKenzie Friends for giving bad advice and overcharging for their services.
- The issues are should McKenzie Friends be allowed to charge for their services, should they be regulated and if so how, and should they be compelled to take out professional indemnity insurance?
- It has been argued many people seeking justice, who have not been able to get legal aid because of costs have had no option but to employ a McKenzie Friend.
- It is likely there will be some legislation about regulating McKenzie Friends in terms of whether they should be able to charge fees and whether they should be regulated, and if so how.

4. Has the government succeeded in achieving its aims by promoting mediation of family disputes?
- The government's aim was that cases should be settled by mediation, which would avoid the need for legal aid for court proceedings and justifies the limits placed on the availability of legal aid.
- The Children and Families Act 2014 enacted provisions requiring a party, before issuing certain court proceedings to attend an initial Mediation Information Assessment Meeting (MIAM). This requires them to attend a meeting with a suitably qualified person to explain the option of mediation
- There are exceptions to having to attend this meeting where safety is a concern, primarily those relating to domestic violence.
- Despite the emphasis placed on mediation of family disputes by the creation of the MIAM the number of mediations in respect of family disputes has fallen.
- In practice, it would seem many persons simply just do not want to exercise the mediation option, often believing it will not lead to a resolution.
- However, mediation does work in many cases.
- Mediation is not an adequate and suitable substitute for a comprehensive legal aid system because it is simply not appropriate for all cases.
- Mediation cannot address all (perceived) conflicts of interest and that recourse to courts is still needed as an option
- Further mediation is not usually a viable option where there have been instances of domestic violence.
- The government have not succeeded in their objective, of in effect, replacing legal aid with mediation. Courts will always be needed to determine those cases which cannot settle or are not appropriate for mediation.

Further Reading

AMNESTY INTERNATIONAL 'United Kingdom: Cuts That Hurt: The Impact of Legal Aid Cuts in England on Access to Justice' (October 2016)
- This provides examples of how harsh the effects of LASPO have been.

COBB, S. 'Legal Aid Reform: Its Impact on Family Law' (2013) 35 *Journal of Social Welfare and Family Law* 3
- This identifies the scope of legal aid in family law and discusses problems arising from increasing numbers of litigants in person, and the limitations on exceptional case funding.

COOKSON, G. 'Unintended Consequences: The Cost of the Governments's Legal Aid Reforms'. A Report for the Law society of England & Wales (King's College, 2011)
- This highlights many of the shortcomings of the government's reasoning behind LASPO.

GARTON GRIMWOOD, G. 'Paying the statutory charge: legal aid in England and Wales', Briefing Paper No. 06537 (House of Commons Library, 2015)
- This explains the current LAA Policy of collecting in the statutory charge

HEENAN, A. and HEENAN, S. 'Norgrove and After: An Overview of the Family Justice Review and the Government's Response' (2012) 34 *Journal of Social Welfare and Family Law* 381
- This discusses the Norgrove Review of family law and the government's response to the recommendations on family courts, and management of public and private law disputes.

THE LAW SOCIETY, *Family Law Protocol* (4th edn, Law Society Publishing, 2015)
- This contains the text of the Family Law Protocol which Solicitors must follow. It also contains an excellent account of how family law cases are processed and identifies and explains key statutes and cases.

LEGAL AID AGENCY, 'The statutory Charge Manual' (April 2014)
- This provides a detailed account of the Legal Aid Agencies statutory charge and how it operates. It provides a good commentary on the case law spanning back several decades.

THE LORD CHIEF JUSTICE OF ENGLAND AND WALES. 'Reforming the Court's Approach to McKenzie Friends. A Consultation' (February 2016)
- This Report is chaired by Asplin J and sets out the history of, and current issues with, McKenzie Friends.

PARKER, S. 'Family Procedure Rules 2010 A guide to the New Law' (The Law Society, 2011)
- This contains the text of the Family Procedure Rules and a commentary upon them

PARKINSON, L. 'Expanding the Model without Breaking the Mould: Developing Practice and Theory in Family Mediation' [2016] *Family Law* 110
- Explores different ways in which family mediation can work, the flexibility of the process, and ways to include all family members in the process, including children.

Resolution Code of Practice. Available at: http://www.resolution.org.uk, accessed 3 October 2017
- Resolution is an organisation of family lawyers committed to cooperating and dealing amicably with all those involved in dealing with family disputes. Resolution's code commits to resolving disputes in this way. This is a useful guide of how to deal with cases in practice.

RIDLEY-DUFF, R.J. and BENNETT, A.J. 'Mediation: developing a theoretical framework for understanding alternative dispute resolution' in *British Academy of Management*, (Sheffield, 14–16 September, 2010). Available at: http://shura.shu.ac.uk, accessed 3 October 2017

• This provides a thorough analysis about many aspects of mediation.

SOLICITORS REGULATION AUTHORITY, sra *Code of Conduct 2011* (version 18, SRA, 2016) chapter 1. Available at: http://www.sra.org.uk, accessed 3 October 2017

• This chapter sets out the fundamental duties and responsibilities solicitors have to their clients in practice.

Index